PHILIP'

STR____AS

Devon

Barnstaple, Exeter, Exmouth, Paignton, Plymouth, Torquay

www.philips-maps.co.uk
First published in 2003 by Philip's
a division of Octopus Publishing Group Ltd
www.octopusbooks.co.uk
Endeavour House 189 Shaftesbury Avenue
London WC2H 8JY
An Hachette UK Company
www.hachette.co.uk

Third edition 2011
First impression 2011
DEVCA

ISBN 978-1-84907-129-1 (pocket)

© Philip's 2011

OS Ordnance Survey®

This product includes mapping data licensed from
Ordnance Survey® with the permission of the
Controller of Her Majesty's Stationery Office.
© Crown copyright 2011. All rights reserved.
Licence number 100011710.

Speed camera data provided by
PocketGPSWorld.com Ltd

Post Office is a trade mark of Post Office Ltd in the
UK and other countries.

Printed in China

Contents

II	Mobile safety cameras
III	**Key to map symbols**
IV	**Key to map pages**
VI	**Route planning**
X	Major administrative and Postcode boundaries

1	**Street maps** at 1⅓ inches to 1 mile
150	**Street maps** at 2⅔ inches to 1 mile
261	**Street maps of Exeter and Plymouth** at 5⅓ inches to 1 mile

| 264 | **Index** of towns, villages, streets, hospitals, industrial estates, railway stations, schools, shopping centres, universities and places of interest |

Digital Data

The exceptionally high-quality mapping found in this atlas is available as digital data in TIFF format, which is easily convertible to other bitmapped (raster) image formats.

The index is also available in digital form as a standard database table. It contains all the details found in the printed index together with the National Grid reference for the map square in which each entry is named.

For further information and to discuss your requirements, please contact
philips@mapsinternational.co.uk

Mobile safety cameras

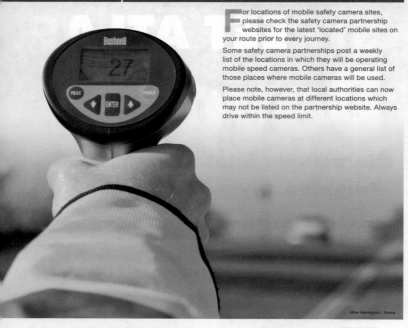

For locations of mobile safety camera sites, please check the safety camera partnership websites for the latest 'located' mobile sites on your route prior to every journey.

Some safety camera partnerships post a weekly list of the locations in which they will be operating mobile speed cameras. Others have a general list of those places where mobile cameras will be used.

Please note, however, that local authorities can now place mobile cameras at different locations which may not be listed on the partnership website. Always drive within the speed limit.

Mike Harrington / Alamy

Useful websites

Devon and Cornwall Safety Camera Partnership
www.dcsafetycameras.org

Dorset Safety Camera Partnership
www.dorsetsafetycameras.org.uk

Safecam
www.safecam.org.uk

Somerset Road Safety Partnership
www.roadsafetysomerset.org.uk

Further information
www.dvla.gov.uk
www.thinkroadsafety.gov.uk
www.dft.gov.uk
www.road-safe.org

Key to map symbols

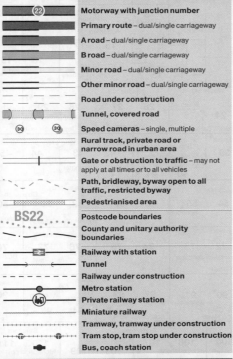

(22)	Motorway with junction number
	Primary route – dual/single carriageway
	A road – dual/single carriageway
	B road – dual/single carriageway
	Minor road – dual/single carriageway
	Other minor road – dual/single carriageway
	Road under construction
	Tunnel, covered road
(3o) (3o)	Speed cameras – single, multiple
	Rural track, private road or narrow road in urban area
	Gate or obstruction to traffic – may not apply at all times or to all vehicles
	Path, bridleway, byway open to all traffic, restricted byway
	Pedestrianised area
BS22	Postcode boundaries
	County and unitary authority boundaries
	Railway with station
	Tunnel
	Railway under construction
	Metro station
	Private railway station
	Miniature railway
	Tramway, tramway under construction
	Tram stop, tram stop under construction
	Bus, coach station

◆	Ambulance station
◆	Coastguard station
◆	Fire station
◆	Police station
✚	Accident and Emergency entrance to hospital
H	Hospital
+	Place of worship
i	Information centre – open all year
🛒	Shopping centre
P	Parking
P&R	Park and Ride
PO	Post Office
Ⓧ	Camping site
🚐	Caravan site
▶	Golf course
✕	Picnic site
Church	Non-Roman antiquity
ROMAN FORT	Roman antiquity
Univ	Important buildings, schools, colleges, universities and hospitals
	Built-up area
	Woods
River Medway	Water name
	River, weir
	Stream
	Canal, lock, tunnel
	Water
	Tidal water
	Adjoining page indicators
263 / 58 / 87	The small numbers around the edges of the maps identify the 1-kilometre National Grid lines
	The dark grey border on the inside edge of some pages indicates that the mapping does not continue onto the adjacent page

Abbreviations

Acad	Academy	Meml	Memorial
Allot Gdns	Allotments	Mon	Monument
Cemy	Cemetery	Mus	Museum
C Ctr	Civic centre	Obsy	Observatory
CH	Club house	Pal	Royal palace
Coll	College	PH	Public house
Crem	Crematorium	Recn Gd	Recreation ground
Ent	Enterprise	Resr	Reservoir
Ex H	Exhibition hall	Ret Pk	Retail park
Ind Est	Industrial Estate	Sch	School
IRB Sta	Inshore rescue boat station	Sh Ctr	Shopping centre
Inst	Institute	TH	Town hall / house
Ct	Law court	Trad Est	Trading estate
L Ctr	Leisure centre	Univ	University
LC	Level crossing	W Twr	Water tower
Liby	Library	Wks	Works
Mkt	Market	YH	Youth hostel

Enlarged maps only

	Railway or bus station building
	Place of interest
	Parkland

The map scale on the pages numbered in green is 1⅓ inches to 1 mile
2.1 cm to 1 km • 1:47 620

The map scale on the pages numbered in blue is 2⅔ inches to 1 mile
4.2 cm to 1 km • 1:23 810

The map scale on the pages numbered in red is 5⅓ inches to 1 mile
8.4 cm to 1 km • 1:11 900

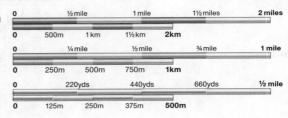

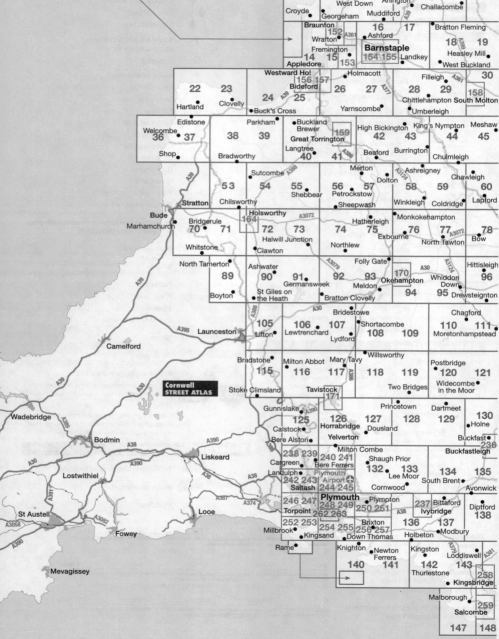

Lundy

| 1 | 2 | 3 | Woody Bay | Lynton |
Ilfracombe | Berrynarbor | | | 151 |
| 150 | | Combe Martin | | 5 |
Woolacombe | Lee | | Parracombe | Furzehill |
| 7 | 8 | 9 | Arlington | 11 | 12 |
Croyde | West Down | Muddiford | Challacombe |
Georgeham | | | |
Braunton | 152 | 16 | 17 | Bratton Fleming |
Wrafton | Ashford | | 18 | 19 |
Fremington | Barnstaple | Heasley Mill |
Appledore | 14 | 15 | 153 | 154 155 | Landkey | West Buckland |
Westward Ho! | Holmacott | Filleigh | 30 |
156 157 | 26 | 27 | 28 | 29 | 158 |
Bideford | 25 | | Chittlehampton South Molton |
Buck's Cross | Yarnscombe | Umberleigh |
| 22 | 23 | 24 | Buckland Brewer | High Bickington | King's Nympton | Meshaw |
Hartland | Clovelly | 159 | 42 | 43 | 44 | 45 |
Edistone | Parkham | Great Torrington | Beaford | Burrington | Chulmleigh |
Welcombe | 38 | 39 | Langtree | 41 | |
| 36 | 37 | Bradworthy | 40 | | |
Shop | Merton | Ashreigney | Chawleigh |
| 53 | 54 | 55 | 56 | 57 | 58 | 59 | 60 |
Stratton | Shebbear | Petrockstow | Winkleigh | Coldridge | Lapford |
Chilsworthy | Sheepwash | |
Bude | Holsworthy | Hatherleigh | Monkokehampton |
Marhamchurch | 70 | 71 | 164 | 72 | 73 | 74 | 75 | 76 | 77 | 78 |
Bridgerule | Halwill Junction | Northlew | Exbourne | North Tawton | Bow |
Whitstone | Clawton | |
North Tamerton | Ashwater | Folly Gate | Hittisleigh |
| 89 | 90 | 91 | 92 | 93 | 170 | 96 |
Boyton | Germansweek | Meldon | Okehampton | Whiddon Down | Drewsteignton |
St Giles on the Heath | Bratton Clovelly | 94 | 95 |
Bridestowe | Chagford |
| 105 | 106 | 107 | Shortacombe | 110 | 111 |
Launceston | Lifton | Lewtrenchard | 108 | 109 | Moretonhampstead |
Lydford | |
Camelford | Bradstone | Milton Abbot | Mary Tavy | Willsworthy | Postbridge |
| 115 | 116 | 117 | 118 | 119 | 120 | 121 |
Stoke Climsland | Tavistock | Two Bridges | Widecombe in the Moor |
Cornwall STREET ATLAS | 171 | |
Princetown | Dartmeet |
Gunnislake | 125 | 126 | 127 | 128 | 129 | 130 |
Calstock | Horrabridge | Dousland | Holne |
Wadebridge | Bere Alston | Yelverton | Buckfast | 236 |
Milton Combe | Buckfastleigh |
238 239 | 240 241 | Shaugh Prior |
Cargreen | Bere Ferrers | 132 | 133 | 134 | 135 |
Bodmin | Landulph | Plymouth Airport | Lee Moor | South Brent | Avonwick |
Liskeard | 242 243 | 244 245 | Cornwood |
Saltash | |
Lostwithiel | 246 247 | Plymouth | Plympton | 237 | Bittaford | Diptford |
Torpoint | 248 249 | 250 251 | Ivybridge | 138 |
252 253 | 262 263 | Brixton | 136 | 137 |
St Austell | Looe | Millbrook | 254 255 | 256 257 | Down Thomas | Holbeton | Modbury |
Fowey | Kingsand | |
Rame | Knighton | Kingston | Loddiswell |
Mevagissey | 140 | 141 | 142 | 143 | 258 |
Newton Ferrers | Thurlestone | Kingsbridge |
Malborough | 259 |
Salcombe |
| 147 | 148 |

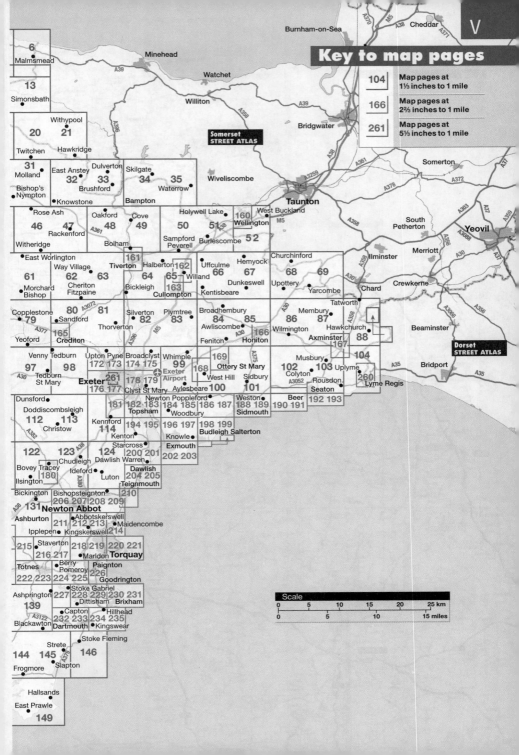

V

Key to map pages

104	Map pages at 1⅓ inches to 1 mile
166	Map pages at 2⅔ inches to 1 mile
261	Map pages at 5⅓ inches to 1 mile

Burnham-on-Sea
Cheddar

Minehead
Watchet
Williton

6 Malmsmead
13 Simonsbath

Somerset STREET ATLAS

Bridgwater

Somerton

20 Withypool **21**
Twitchen Hawkridge

Taunton

Yeovil

31 Molland
East Anstey **32** Dulverton **33** Skilgate **34** **35** Waterrow
Brushford
Bishop's Nympton
Knowstone
Bampton
Wiveliscombe

West Buckland
160 Wellington

South Petherton

Merriott

46 Rose Ash **47** Oakford **48** Cove **49** **50** Holywell Lake **51** **52**
Rackenford
Witheridge Bolham
Sampford Peverell Burlescombe

Ilminster

Chard Crewkerne

61 East Worlington **62** Way Village **63** Tiverton **64** Halberton **162** **66** Uffculme Hemyock **67** Churchinford **68** **69**
Morchard Bishop Cheriton Fitzpaine Bickleigh **65** Willand
161 Cullompton **163** Kentisbeare Dunkeswell Upottery Yarcombe
Tatworth

79 Copplestone **80** **81** **82** Silverton Plymtree **83** Broadhembury **84** **85** **86** Membury **87** **88**
Sandford Thorverton Awliscombe Wilmington Hawkchurch
165 Crediton Feniton **166** Honiton Axminster Beaminster
Yeoford **167**

Dorset STREET ATLAS

97 Venny Tedburn **98** Upton Pyne **172** **173** Broadclyst **174** **175** Whimple **99** **169** Ottery St Mary **102** Musbury **103** **104**
Tedburn St Mary **261** Exeter **178** **179** **168** West Hill Sidbury Colyton Uplyme Bridport
176 **177** Clyst St Mary **100** **101** Rousdon **260** Lyme Regis
Aylesbeare Seaton

Dunsford **181** Newton Poppleford **186** **187** Weston **188** **189** Beer **192** **193**
Doddiscombsleigh **182** **183** **184** **185** Woodbury Sidmouth **190** **191**
112 **113** Kennford Topsham
Christow **114** **194** **195** **196** **197** **198** **199**
Kenton Knowle Budleigh Salterton
122 **123** Starcross **124** **200** **201** Exmouth
Bovey Tracey Chudleigh Dawlish Warren **202** **203**
180 Ideford Luton Dawlish
Ilsington **204** **205**
Bickington Teignmouth
131 Bishopsteignton **210**
206 **207** **208** **209**
Newton Abbot
Ashburton **211** **212** **213** Abbotskerswell Maidencombe
Ipplepen Kingskerswell **214**
215 Staverton **218** **219** **220** **221**
216 **217** Marldon Torquay
Totnes Berry Pomeroy Paignton
222 **223** **224** **225** **226** Goodrington
Stoke Gabriel
139 **227** **228** **229** **230** **231** Brixham
Capton Dittisham Hillhead
232 **233** **234** **235**
Blackawton Dartmouth Kingswear
Strete Stoke Fleming
144 **145** **146**
Frogmore Slapton

Hallsands
East Prawle
149

Scale				
0	5	10	15	20 25 km
0	5		10	15 miles

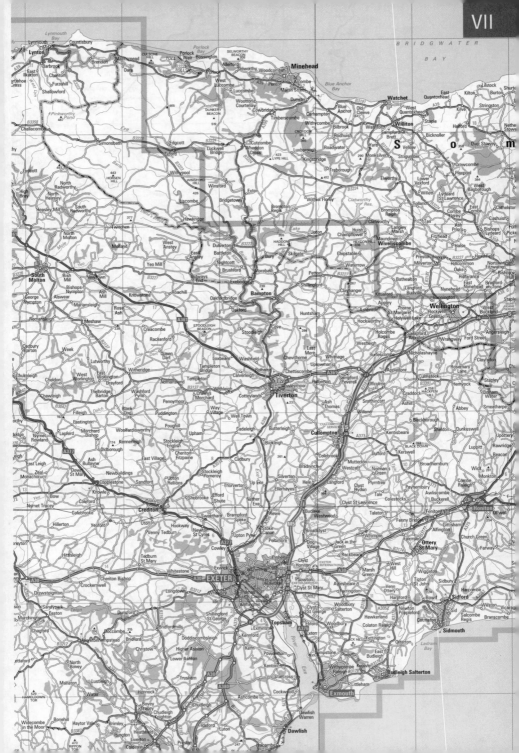

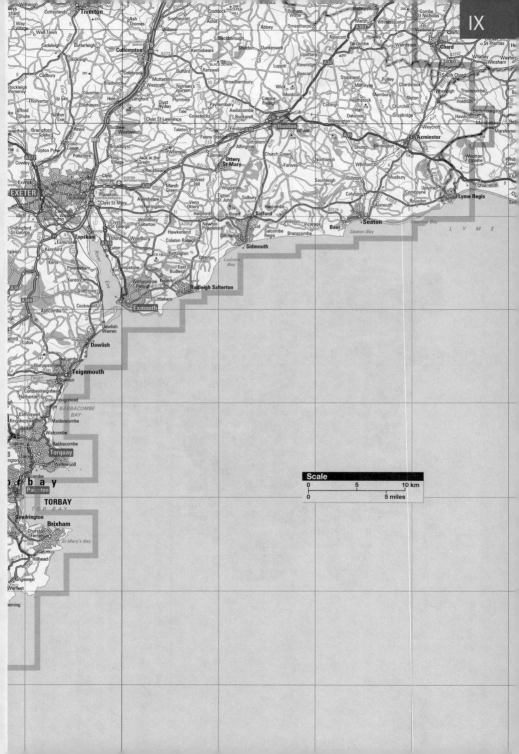

X

Major administrative and Postcode boundaries

County and unitary authority boundaries
District boundaries
Postcode boundaries
Area covered by this atlas

Scale

| 0 | 5 | 10 | 15 | 20 | 25 | 30 km |
| 0 | 5 | 10 | 15 | 20 miles |

SS ST

Somerset

Lynton
Ilfracombe
EX34
EX35
Woolacombe
Simonsbath
Croyde
EX33
EX31
TA24
Braunton
EX32
Barnstaple
North Devon
EX36
Dulverton
TA4
Bideford
EX31
South Molton
TA22
Hartland
Clovelly
Umberleigh
EX37
Bampton
TA21
Wellington
EX39
Great Torrington
Chulmleigh
Witheridge
EX16
TA3 TA20
EX38
Tiverton
Mid Devon
EX15
Dolton
EX18
Dunkeswell
TA20
Torridge
EX19
Lapford
Willand
EX14
EX22
Black Torrington
EX17
Silverton
East Devon
Axminster
EX23
Holsworthy
Hatherleigh
Bow
Devon
Honiton
Colyton
DT6
SS
SX
EX21
Crediton
Ottery St Mary
EX24
SY
EX20
EX1
EX13
PL15
Okehampton
Exeter
EX5
EX10
EX12
Seaton
Lyme Regis
West Devon
Chagford
EX2
EX3
Topsham
Sidmouth
DT7
PL16
Lydford
EX6
EX8
EX9
Lifton
Teignbridge
Exmouth
Milton Abbot
PL19
Bovey Tracey
Budleigh Salterton
PL17
Tavistock
EX7
Dawlish
PL18
PL20
Newton Abbot
TQ14
Teignmouth
Yelverton
Ashburton
TQ12
TQ2
PL12
TQ11
Torquay
City of Plymouth
PL5
PL6
Buckfastleigh
TQ10
TQ1
Saltash
PL7
South Brent
Totnes
TQ3
Paignton
PL11
Plymouth
PL21
TQ9
Torbay
Brixham
PL10
PL9
PL8
Ivybridge
TQ4
South Hams
Dartmouth
PL1
Wembury
TQ6
PL2
PL3
Kingsbridge
Slapton
PL4
Salcombe
TQ7
TQ8

Cornwall

SX SY

2

1

8

51

7

50

6

49

150

5

48

Ferry P
Lundy (summer only)

ILFRACOMBE

The Outfalls

Brandy Cove
Point

4

Flat Point

Torrs
Park

Shag Point

47

Bull
Point

Pensport
Rock

Lee Bay

South West Coast Path

Langleigh

3

Tarka Trail

LOWER
GREYSTONE

Lee

Whitestone
Farm

Mast

Higher
Slade

Hotel

PH

Lincombe

Higher
Warcombe

8 Pludd

Lower
Slade

46

NORTH
MORTE
RD

Easewell

Damage
Barton

Borough Valley

Windcutter
Hill

Lower
Campscott

DIBBON'S LA

Slade
Resrs

Mullacott

2

Mortehoe

Shaftsboro
Farm

Middle
Campscott

A361

EX34

150

45

Higher
Campscott

Holiday
Park
PH

WARCOMBE LA

Borough
Cross

Borough
Farm

Bickenbridge

Little Shelfin
Farm

B3343

A3123

1

SEYMOUR BGLWS 1
SEYMOUR VILLAS 2

SANDY LA

Pool
Farm

LEE
CROSS

B3343

MULLACOTT
CROSS

Mullacott Cross
Ind Est

44

46   **A**   47   **B**   48   **C**   49   **D**   50   **E**   51   **F**

7   **8**   **2**

For full street detail of the
highlighted area see page 150.

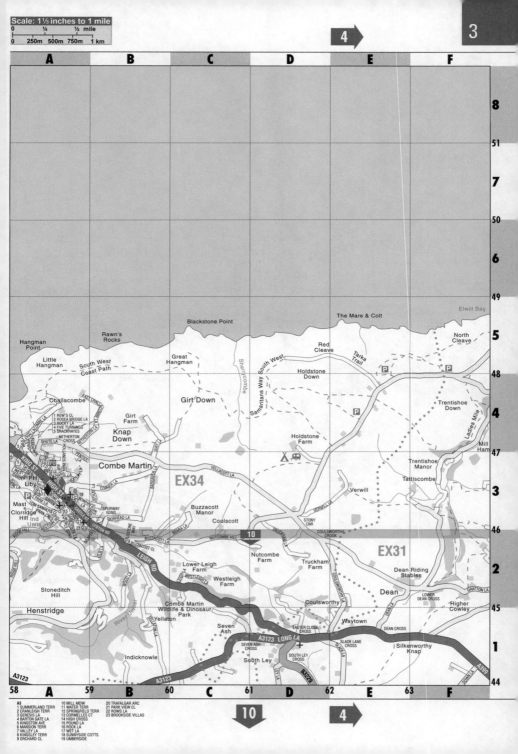

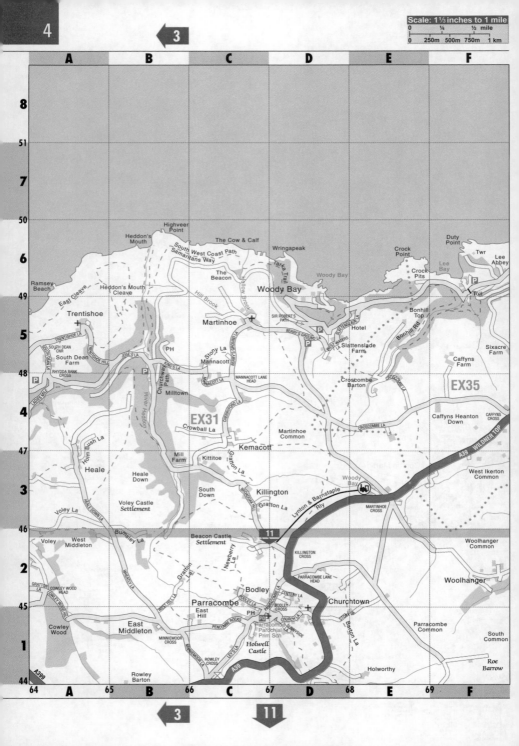

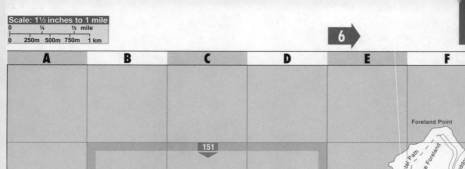

5

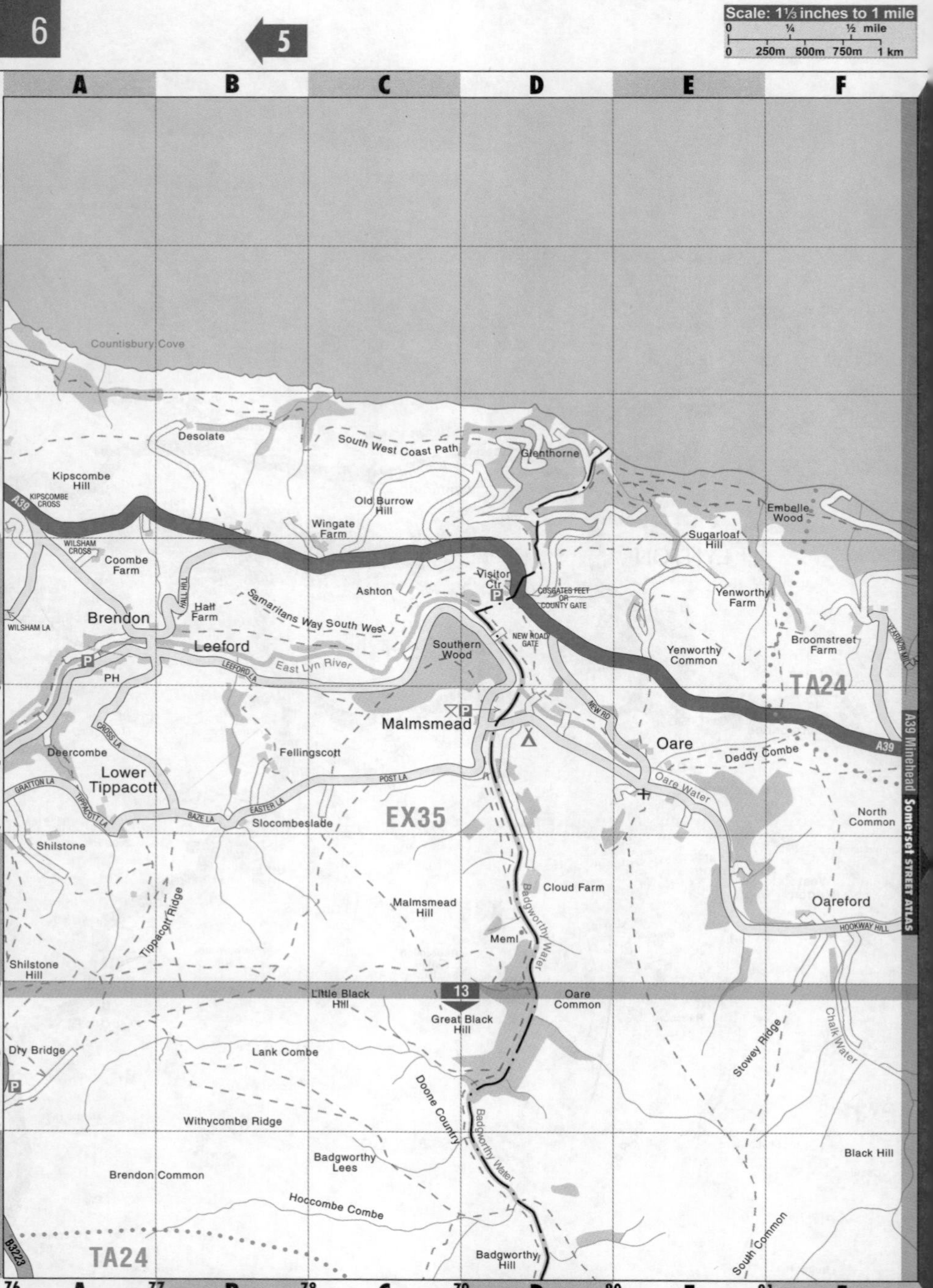

Scale: 1½ inches to 1 mile

0   ¼   ½ mile
0   250m 500m 750m 1 km

A   B   C   D   E   F

8

51

7

Countisbury Cove

50

6

Desolate

South West Coast Path

Glenthorne

Kipscombe Hill

KIPSCOMBE CROSS

Old Burrow Hill

Wingate Farm

Emballe Wood

A39

49

WILSHAM CROSS

Coombe Farm

Ashton

Visitor Ctr
P

CROSS GATES FEET OR COUNTY GATE

Sugarloaf Hill

Yenworthy Farm

Broomstreet Farm

5

WILSHAM LA

Brendon

HILL HILL

Half Farm

Samaritans Way South West

Southern Wood

NEW ROAD GATE

Yenworthy Common

TA24

Leeford

LEEFORD LA

East Lyn River

Malmsmead
P

Oare

NEW RD

A39 Minehead   Somerset STREET ATLAS

48

P

PH

CROSS LA

Fellingscott

Oare Water

Deddy Combe

A39

4

Deercombe

Lower Tippacott

GRATTON LA

TIPPACOTT LA

BALE LA

POST LA

Slocombeslade

EASTER LA

EX35

Meml

Oareford

North Common

47

Shilstone

Tippacott Ridge

Malmsmead Hill

Badgworthy Water

Cloud Farm

HOOKWAY HILL

3

Shilstone Hill

46

Little Black Hill

13

Great Black Hill

Oare Common

Stowey Ridge

Chalk Water

2

Dry Bridge

P

Lank Combe

Doone Country

Badgworthy Water

45

Withycombe Ridge

Badgworthy Lees

Black Hill

1

Brendon Common

Hoccombe Combe

South Common

B3223

44

TA24

Badgworthy Hill

76   A   77   B   78   C   79   D   80   E   81   F

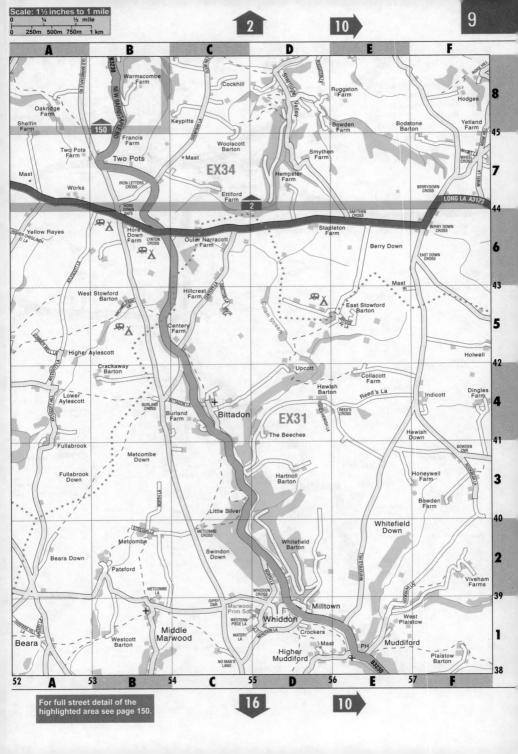

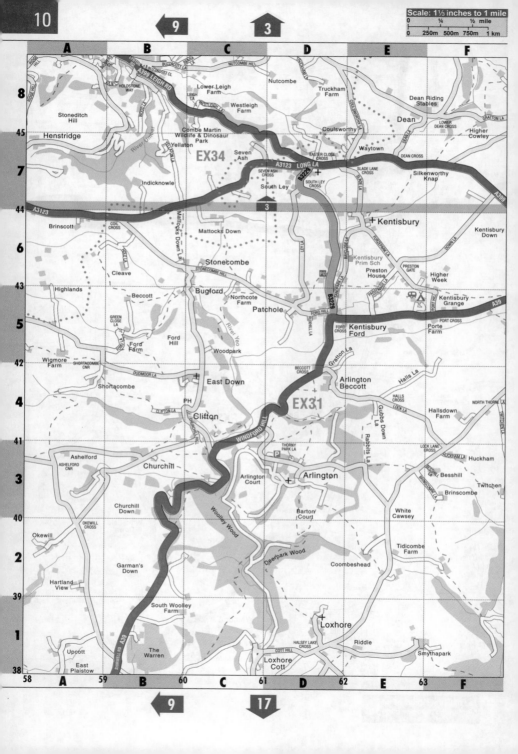

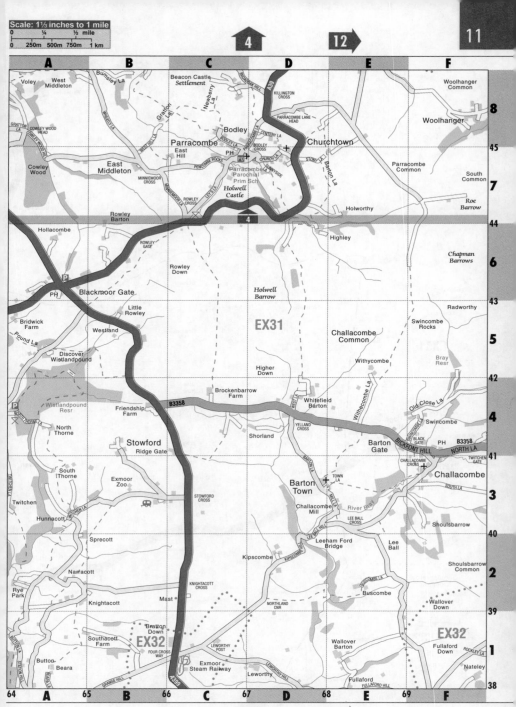

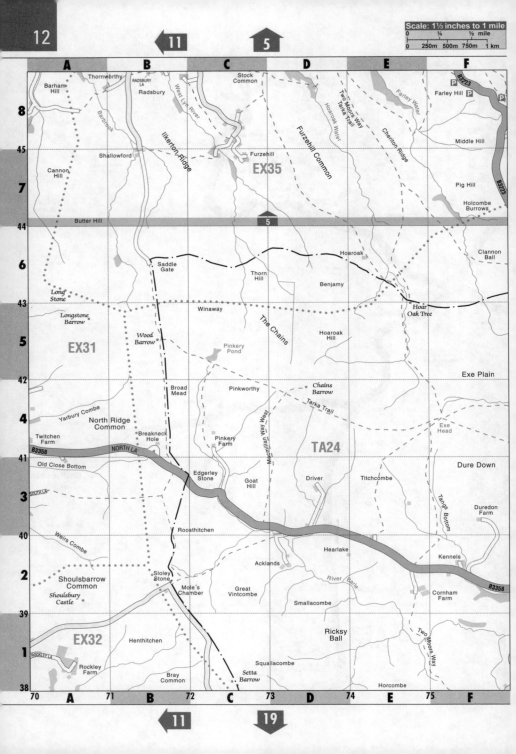

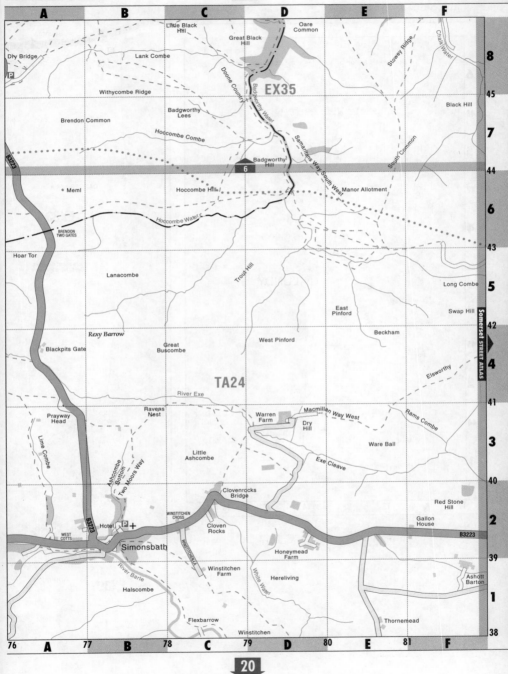

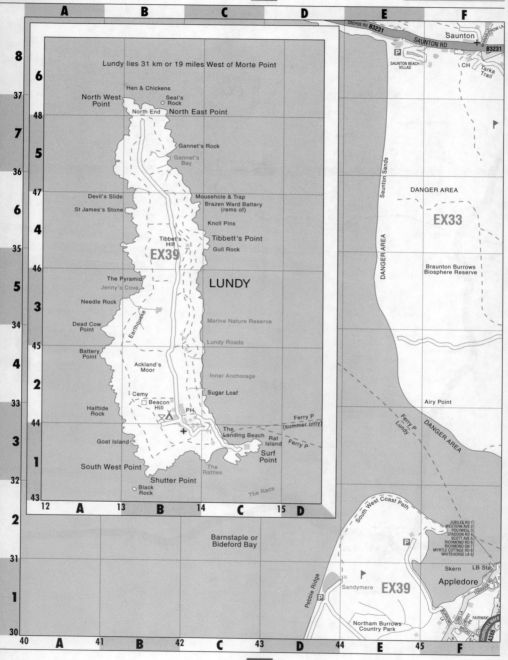

Scale: 1½ inches to 1 mile

0   ¼   ½   mile
0   250m 500m 750m 1 km

Lundy lies 31 km or 19 miles West of Morte Point

Hen & Chickens

North West Point

Seal's Rock

North End

North East Point

Gannet's Rock

Gannet's Bay

Devil's Slide

St James's Stone

Mousehole & Trap

Brazen Ward Battery (rems of)

Knoll Pins

Tibbet's Hill

Tibbett's Point

EX39

Gull Rock

The Pyramid

Jenny's Cove

LUNDY

Needle Rock

Dead Cow Point

Earthquake

Marine Nature Reserve

Battery Point

Lundy Roads

Ackland's Moor

Inner Anchorage

Cemy

Sugar Loaf

Halftide Rock

Beacon Hill

PH

Ferry P (summer only)

Goat Island

The Landing Beach

Rat Island

Ferry P

Ferry P Lundy

Airy Point

DANGER AREA

South West Point

The Rattles

Surf Point

Shutter Point

Black Rock

The Race

Saunton Sands

CROYDE RD **B3231**

SAUNTON RD

Saunton

B3231

CH

Tarka Trail

SAUNTON BEACH VILLAS

DANGER AREA

EX33

DANGER AREA

Braunton Burrows Biosphere Reserve

Barnstaple or Bideford Bay

South West Coast Path

JUBILEE RD 1
WESTERN AVE 3
POLYWEEL 3
STADDON RD 4
SCOTT AVE 5
RICHMOND RD 6
RICHMOND DN 7
MYRTLE COTTAGE 8
WHITEHORSE LA 9

Pebble Ridge

Sandymere

EX39

Skern

LB Sta

Appledore

Northam Burrows Country Park

A386

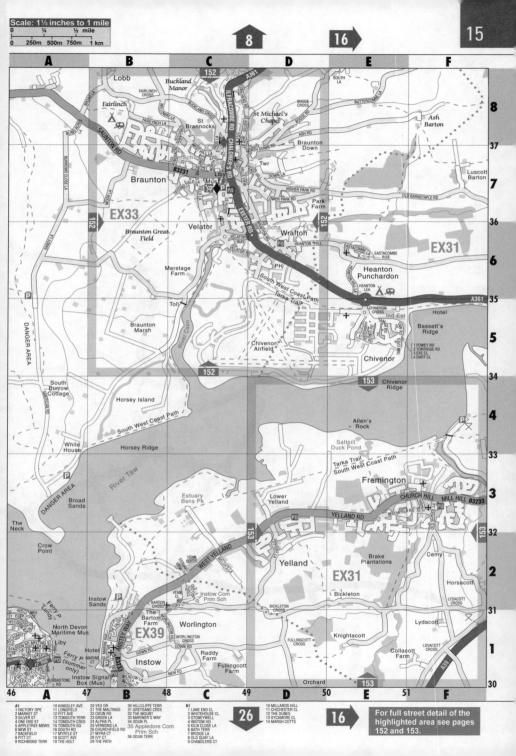

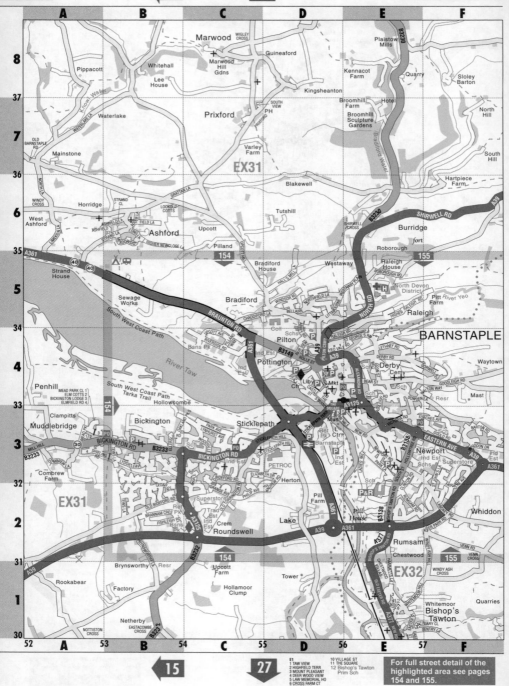

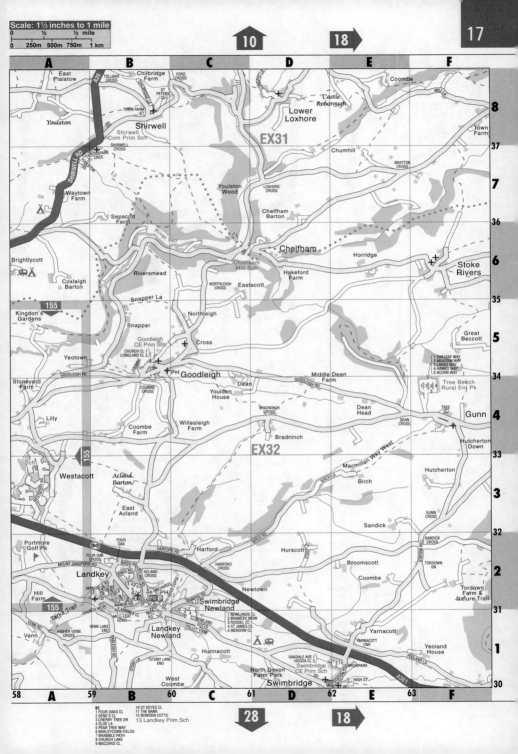

17 11

Scale: 1⅓ inches to 1 mile

0   ¼   ½ mile
0   250m 500m 750m 1 km

A B C D E F

8

Fullaford
Ovis
FULLAFORD HILL
FIVE CROSS WAY
NATSLEY LA

SENTRY CROSS
Grange
Hill and East
HOMER RD

EX31
Gratton

Bratton Fleming
1 MEADOW CL
2 CHURCH CL
3 BUTTONHILL CROSS
4 THREE WAYS
5 BEARA CROSS
6 SOUTH VIEW
7 GRANGE CL
8 Bratton Fleming Com Prim Sch

LITTLE BRAY CROSS

Berry Hill

37

EX31

Haxton

Haxton Down

BENTON RD

Fernham

Stock Down

Wort Wood

MUXWORTHY LA

Hall
Lydcott

7

Down Farm

DITCH END CROSS
MOCKHAM DOWN GATE

BENTON CROSS

Benton

Stock Farm

36

Birch

Stoke Beara

Mockham Down

Mockham Barton

Little Bray

CROSS GATE
WHITEFIELD LA

6

Orswell

Barnacott Farm

Lane

BROOMHILL VILLAS

Brayford Prim Sch

HOLEWATER HILL

Hall

35

THORNPARK CROSS

Knackershole

Brayfordshill

Brayford

Braytown Cotts

BRAYTOWN LA
BRATTON LA

High Bray

5

Yarde

KIMBLAND CROSS

Stoodleigh Down

Tossell's Barton

Higher Shutscombe

Yarrer Bray

YARDE CROSS

Slade Farm

34

STONE CROSS

Stoodleigh Barton

Whitsford

WISTFORD CROSS

Welcombe
WELCOMBE CROSS

Weir

Macmillan Way West

4

GOODLEIGH RD

Stone

Furze

The Old Rectory

CHARLES CROSS

33

Accott

GOODWELLS HEAD
UPCOTT CROSS

Stoodleigh

UPCOTT LA

Upcott Farm

Middlecott

Walland

HUDLEY MILL HILL

WALLAND CROSS

Hudley Hill

Charles

Grass Park

Newtown Bridge

POPHAM LA

3

MIDDLECOTT HILL

Sandypark

ORNSTONE CROSS

A399

32

Taddiport

STOODLEIGH CROSS
ELWELL CROSS

Elwell

Middlehill

West Buckland Sch

EAST BUCKLAND CROSS

East Buckland

Charles Bottom

Tarka Trail

EX36

2

WEST BUCKLAND CROSS
PATH FIELD CL

West Buckland

PO

Macmillan Way West

MILL LA

Blackwell

31

Bushton

Gubbs Farm

PARSONAGE LANE CROSS

Indiscombe

Huxtable Farm

Westacott

LION'S RUMP

Rapscott

RAPSCOTT CROSS

1

The Barton

Crossbury

Brayley Barton

LITCHATON CROSS

COTELAND LANE END

RAPSCOTT HILL

Litchaton Farm

LITCHATON HILL
EMBERCOMBE CROSS

Illers Leary

30

64 A 65 B 66 C 67 D 68 E 69 F

17 29

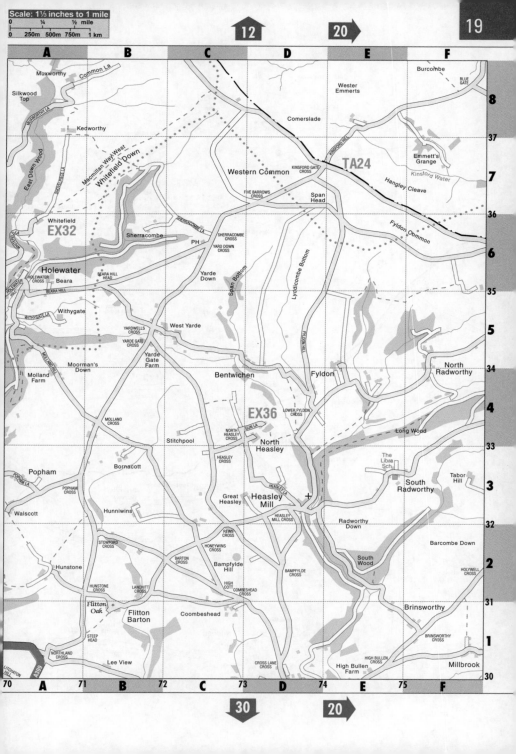

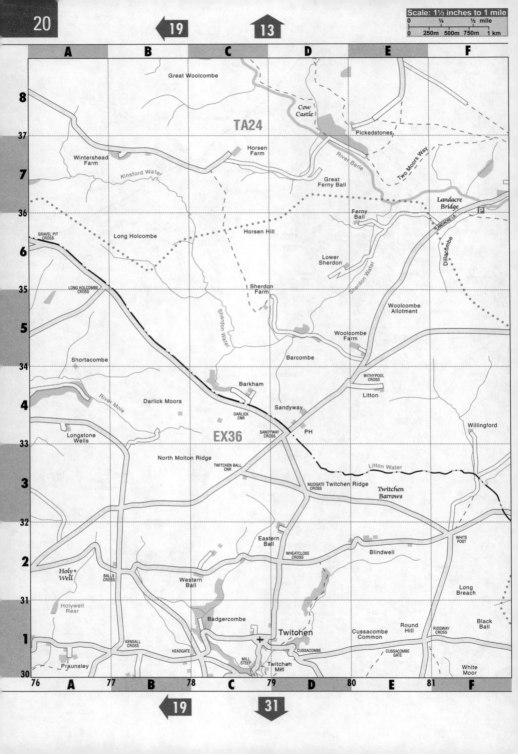

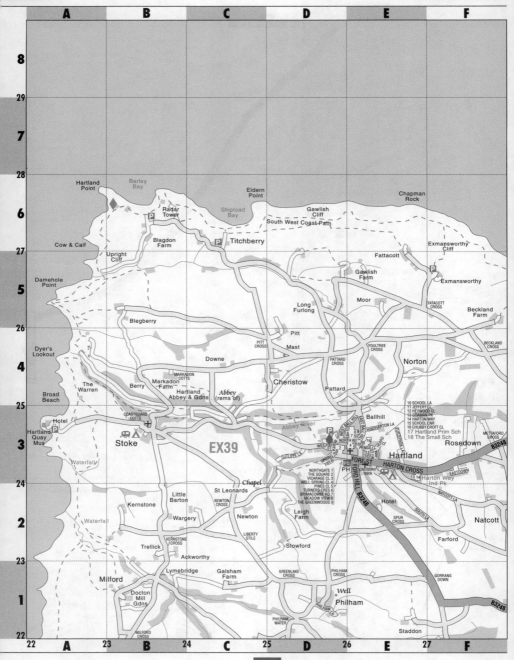

A   B   C   D   E   F

8
29
7
28
6
27
5
26
4
25
3
24
2
23
1
22

Hartland
Point

Barley
Bay

Radar
Tower

Eldern
Point

Shipload
Bay

Chapman
Rock

Gawlish
Cliff

South West Coast Path

Blagdon
Farm

Titchberry

Exmansworthy
Cliff

Cow & Calf

Upright
Cliff

Fattacott

Exmansworthy

Damehole
Point

Gawlish
Farm

FATACOTT
CROSS

Moor

Beckland
Farm

Long
Furlong

Blegberry

Pitt

BECKLAND
CROSS

Dyer's
Lookout

PITT
CROSS

Mast

YOULTREE
CROSS

Downe

Markadon
COTTS

Markadon
Farm

Cheristow

Pattard

Norton

Berry

PATTARD
CROSS

The
Warren

Hartland
Abbey & Gdns

Abbey
(rems of)

Broad
Beach

Hotel

COASTGUARD
COTTS

Ballhill

10 SCHOOL LA
11 JEFFERY CL
12 HEYWOOD CL
13 GOAMAN WAY
14 HARTON WAY
15 SCHOOL CNR
16 CHUBBY CROFT CL
17 Hartland Prim Sch
18 The Small Sch

Hartland
Quay
Mus

Abbey River

METTAFORD
CROSS

Stoke

EX39

Hartland

Rosedown

B3248

Waterfall

FOREST

HARTON CROSS

PH

GREGORY
TERR

Harton Way
Ind Pk

EASTDOWN

Chapel

St Leonards

NORTHGATE 1
THE SQUARE 2
VICARAGE CL 3
WELL SPRING CL 4
PINES CL 5
TURNERS CRES 6
BRIMACOMBE RD 7
MEADOW VIEW 8
THE GREENWOODS 9

Little
Barton

NEWTON
CROSS

Kernstone

Wargery

Newton

Leigh
Farm

Hotel

SPUR
CROSS

Natcott

LIBERTY
STILE

NATCOTT LA

Waterfall

KERNSTONE
CROSS

Trellick

Stowford

Farford

Ackworthy

GORRANS
DOWN

Lymebridge

Galsham
Farm

GREENLAKE
CROSS

PHILHAM
CROSS

B3248

Milford

Docton
Mill
Gdns

Well
Philham

PHILHAM
WATER

Staddon

MILFORD
CROSS

22   A   23   B   24   C   25   D   26   E   27   F

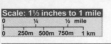

Scale: 1⅓ inches to 1 mile

0   ¼   ½ mile
0   250m   500m   750m   1 km

A   B   C   D   E   F

8

29

7

28

6

27

5

26

Beckland Bay   Windbury Point

Blackchurch Rock

Mouth Mill

Brownsham

Snaxland

Wood Rock

South West Coast Path

Gallant Rock

4

Highdown Cottage   Yapham Farm

Clovelly Court Gdns

HIGHDOWN CROSS

YAPHAM CROSS

25

Hescott Farm   Velly

Mettaford Farm   Chapel

LIGHTHOUSE CROSS

Hugglepit

UNDERDOWN

B3237

Visitor Centre

Clovelly Prim Sch

PO

PH

LB Sta

Clovelly

Bight a Doubleyou

3

WRINKLEBERRY

Sierra   Wrinkleberry

WINDCUTTER

Highford Farm

TURNPIKE CT

BURSCOTT

STOOP

Higher Clovelly

THE HOBBY RD

The Hobby

Lower Bight of Fernham

24

Holloford Farm

EX39

B3248

Clovelly Dykes

B3237

Eastacott

WOOLFARDISWORTHY CROSS

Hobby Lodge

2

Warmleigh Farm

CLOVELLY CROSS

ATLANTIC HIGHWAY

Burnstone

A39

23

Mast

Wr Twr

DOWNLAND CROSS

BAXWORTHY CROSS

Milky Way Adventure Pk

Slade Farm

1

B3248

STITTWORTHY CROSS

Thornery

A39

Burford

Highworthy

Kennerland Farm

22

28   A   29   B   30   C   31   D   32   E   33   F

Scale: 1⅓ inches to 1 mile
0   ¼   ½ mile
0   250m 500m 750m 1 km

A   B   C   D   E   F

8
29
7
28
6
27
5
26
4
25
3
24
2
23
1
22

Babbacombe Mouth
Babbacombe Cliff

Higher Rowden

Portledge

Chiddlecombe

Gauter Point

Castle

Peppercombe

Gilscott

South West Coast Path

Sloo

Northway

Horns Cross

Holiday Village

Buck's Mills

Hoops PH

PH

ATLANTIC HIGHWAY

Holwell

EX39

ACRE CL

A39

DOTHERIDGE LA

Buck's Cross

Cemy

Watershute

Waytown

Goldworthy

Bitworthy

Walland

Limebury

Broad Parkham

Foxdown Manor

Newhaven

BREWERS HILL

PARKHAM CROSS

A39

34   A   35   B   36   C   37   D   38   E   39   F

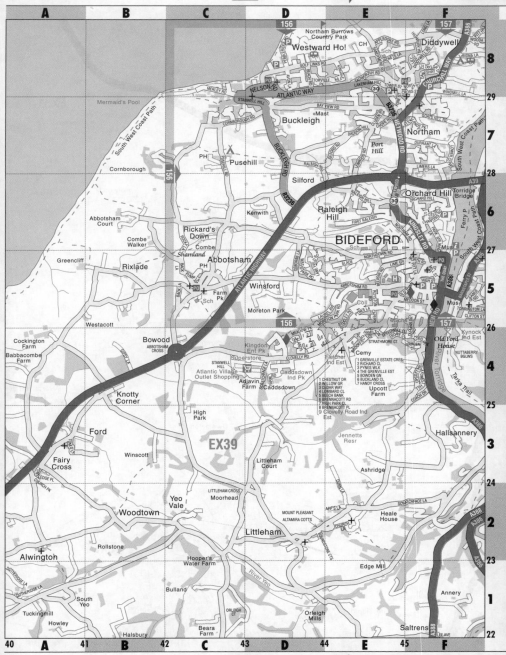

For full street detail of the highlighted area see pages 156 and 157.

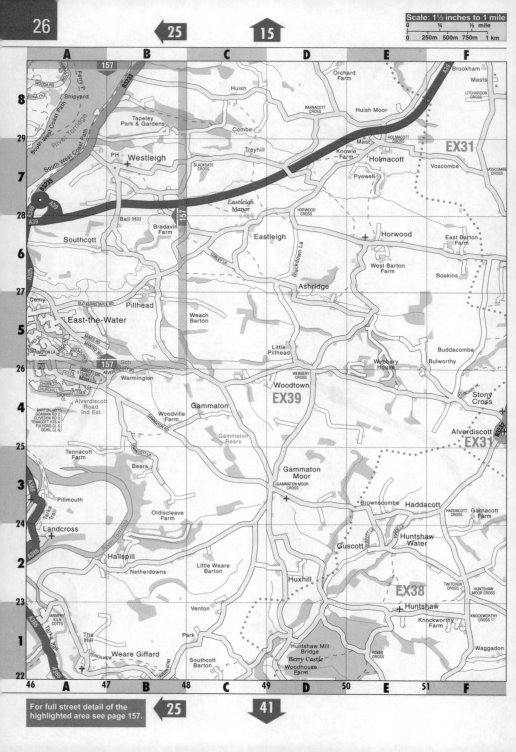

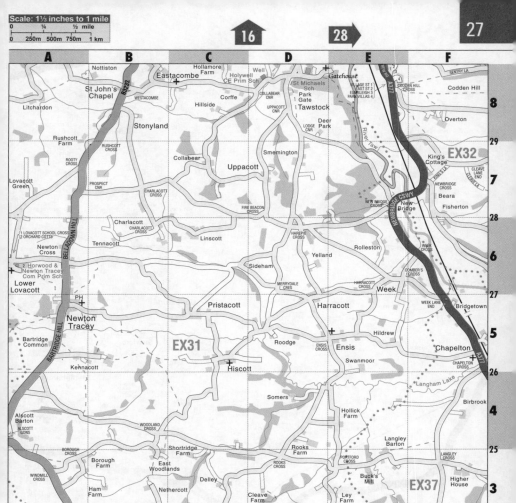

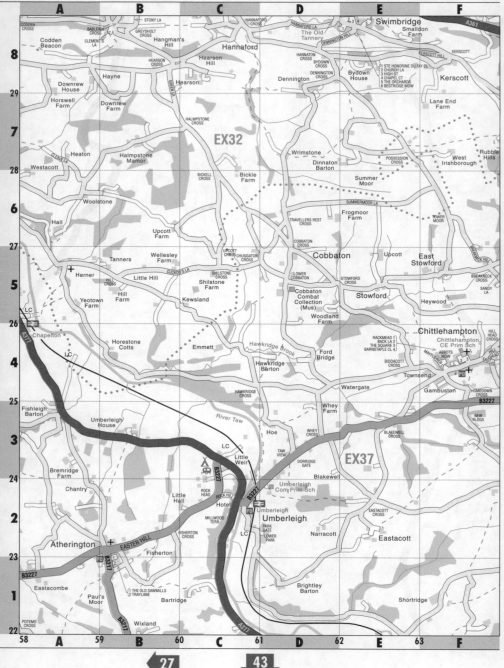

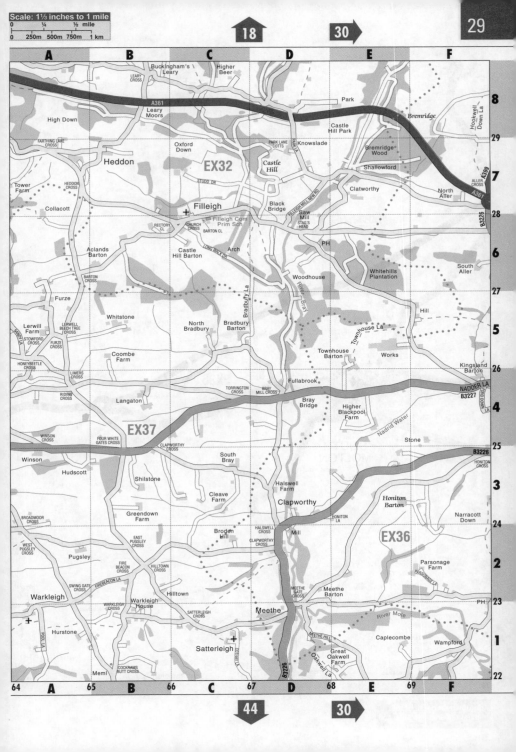

29
19

Scale: 1⅓ inches to 1 mile

0 | ¼ | ½ mile
0 | 250m | 500m | 750m | 1 km

A   B   C   D   E   F

8

Nadrid Farm
NADRID CROSS
LITCHATON CROSS
Nadrid East Cross
Stonybridge Cross
Stony Bridge
Stonybridge Hill
Portgate Cross
West Park
Oakford Cl
Oakford V
Oakford La
North Molton Prim Sch
Higher East St
Benole Lane Cross
Pitt
Pitt La

29

Wheatlands Farm
North Lee Farm
Lee Cross
North Molton
PH
PO
1 THE SQUARE
2 JUBILEE GDNS
3 NORTH MOLTON CROSS
Benole La
Upcott
Ley Cross

7

Coombe Farm
North Cockerham
South Lee Cross
South Leigh
Holdridge
Sannacott Farm
Higher Ley

Snurridge
South Cockerham
West Ford
Limeslake Farm
Burwell

28

Hacche Barton
158
Burcombe Farm
East Marsh
Drewstone
Whitechapel Manor

6

B3226
Hache Moor
Marsh Hall
MARSH LA
River Mole
Bicknor Farm
MARSH LA
Drewstone Cross
Whitechapel Moors

27

Pathfields Bssn Pk
Park House
Johnstone Moors
Rawstone Moors
Whitechapel Moors

5

Mast
Honey Farm
Sch
B3226
GUNSWELL LA
Mole Bridge
CLEAR COMM LA
Rawstone
Garliford Farm
GARLIFORD LA

26

158
B3227
NADDER LA
WEST ST
Mus
EAST ST
BROAD ST
158
EX36
Johnstone
BRIDGE CROSS

4

Ford Down
Cemy
South Molton Com Coll
MILL ST
ALSWEAR NEW RD
VENFORD VILLAS
Gorton Hill
PH
Johnstone
B3227
BISHMILL GATE
SILCOMBE HILL
Waterhouse Farm

25

B3226
Furzebray
LIMER'S LANE CROSS
LIMER'S LA
Great Hele Barton
GREAT HELE LA
River Yeo
Bish Mill
SILCOMBE CROSS
Bridge La

3

Thorne Farm
Narracott Farm
Grilstone
Slough House
Hall Park
SLOUGH LA

24

158
CHEYNEY CROSS
Blastridge Hill
RADLEY CROSS
Crosse Farm
Barton
Bishop's Nympton Prim Sch
SPIRE LAKE CL 1
JOEYS FIELD 2
PARSONAGE HILL 3
GLEBELAND VILLAS 4
MEADOW VIEW 5
ANGEL HILL CROSS 6
SPIRELAKE 7

2

Broomhouse Farm
HILLSIDE
CHEVAL LA
Ley
Great Frenchstone
FRENCHSTONE CROSS
Westwood
Eastwood
Park
WEST ST
1 GEORGE NYMPTON CROSS
2 THE ROW

23

George Nympton
Culverhill Farm
Trayne Farm
Radley La
Radley
Moorhouse
MOORHOUSE LA

1

Mill Farm
Garramarsh
Crooked Oak
Pitt Farm
Hilltown
BISHOP'S NYMPTON CROSS

22

Woodhouse
Alswear
B3137
CROOKED OAKS
MOORY HOUSE LA
PH
Mariansleigh
1 CHURCH GATE
2 MARIANSLEIGH CROSS
3 TOWNLIVING CROSS

70   A   71   B   72   C   73   D   74   E   75   F

For full street detail of the highlighted area see page 158.

29
45

SOUTH MOLTON

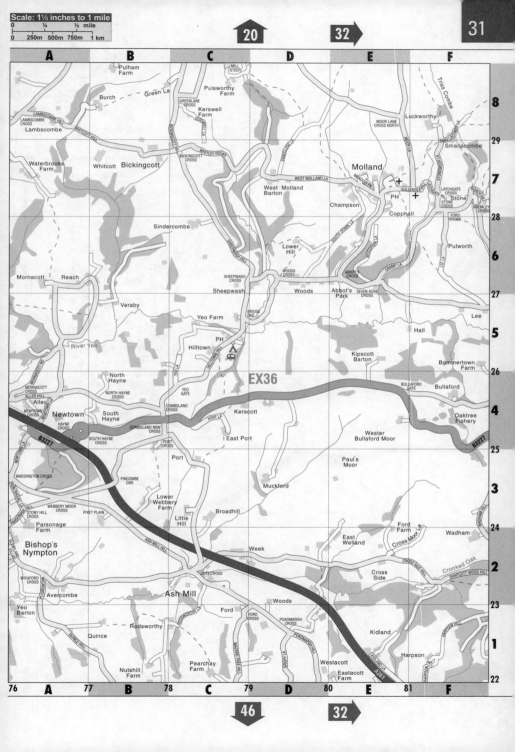

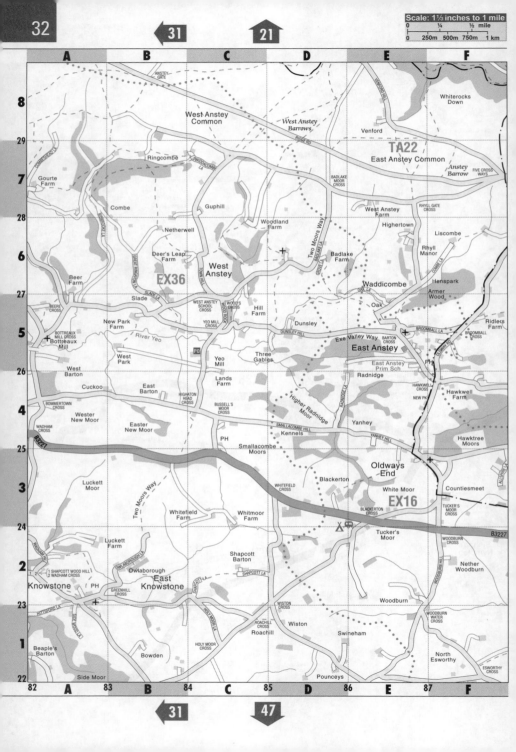

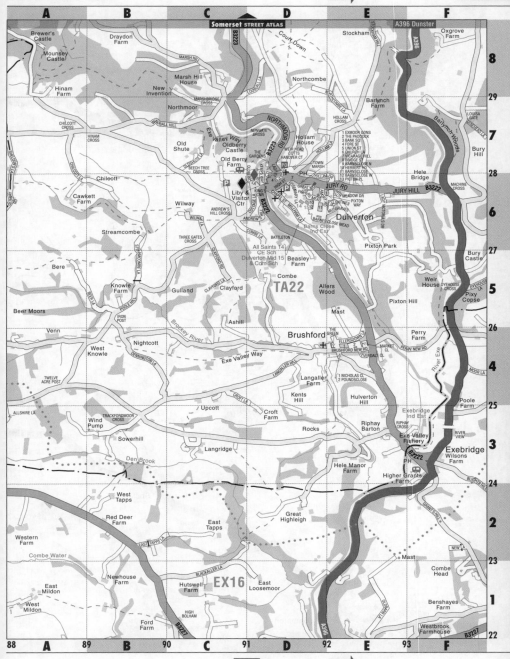

Scale: 1⅓ inches to 1 mile

Somerset STREET ATLAS

A396 Dunster

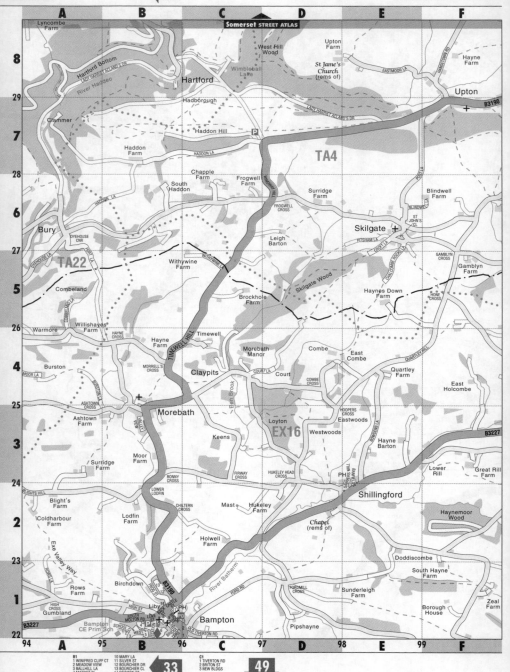

Somerset STREET ATLAS

B1
1 WINIFRED CLIFF CT
2 MEADOW VIEW
3 BALLHILL LA
4 MARKET CL
5 LORDS MEADOW LA
6 BARNHAY
7 CHURCH TERR
8 NEWTON SQ
9 FORE ST
10 MARY LA
11 SILVER ST
12 BOURCHIER DR
13 BOURCHIER CL
14 NEWTON CT

C1
1 TIVERTON RD
2 BRITON ST
3 NEW BLDGS

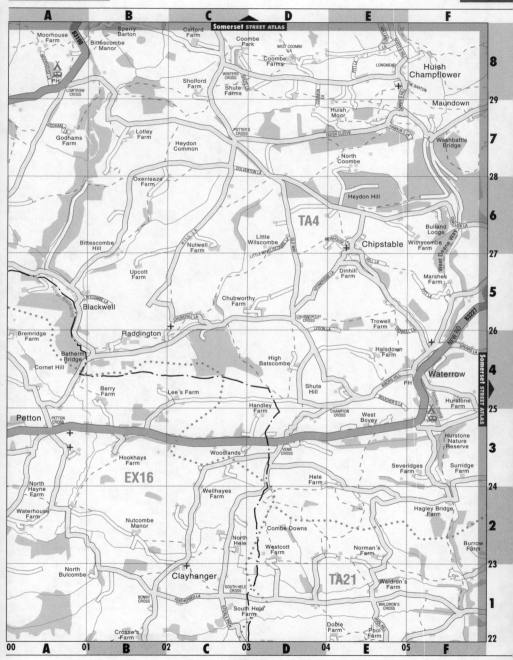

Mast

Nabor
Point

Embury
Beacon

Embury
Beach

EX39

Knaps
Head

The
Hermitage

Welcombe Mouth

P

Marsland Mouth

Gull
Rock

Marsland
Cliff

Marsland
Manor

Cornakey Cliff

Yeol Mouth

South West Coast Path

Cornakey
Farm

Cory

EX23

Henna
Cliff

Westcott
Farm

Hawker's
Hut

Well

Morwenstow

Vicarage
Cliff

P

Lucky Hole

Crosstown PH

Higher
Sharpnose Point

The Tidna

CROSSWATER

Tonacombe

WOODVILLE
CROSS

STANBURY
CROSS

WOODVILLE
RD

Cornwall STREET ATLAS

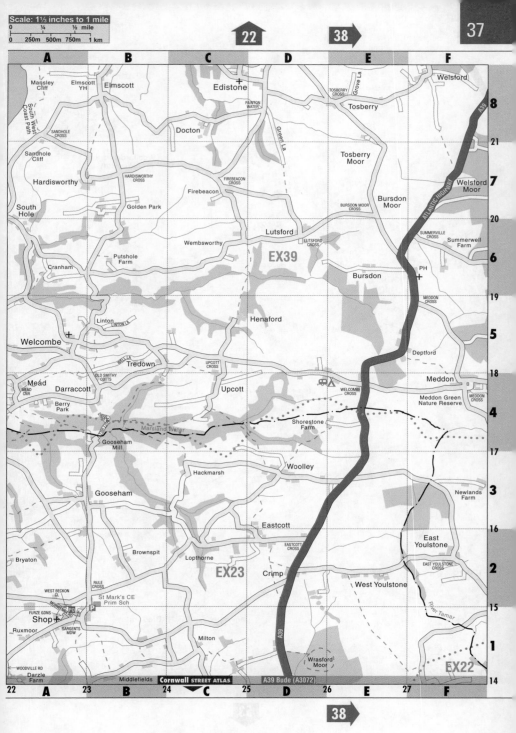

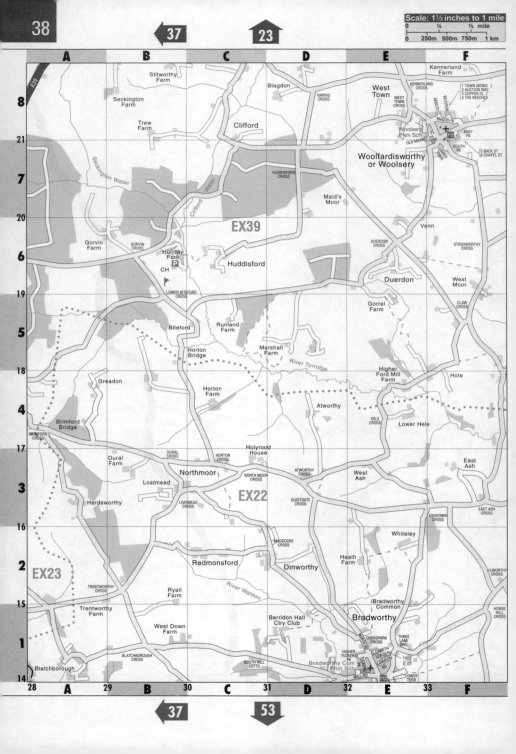

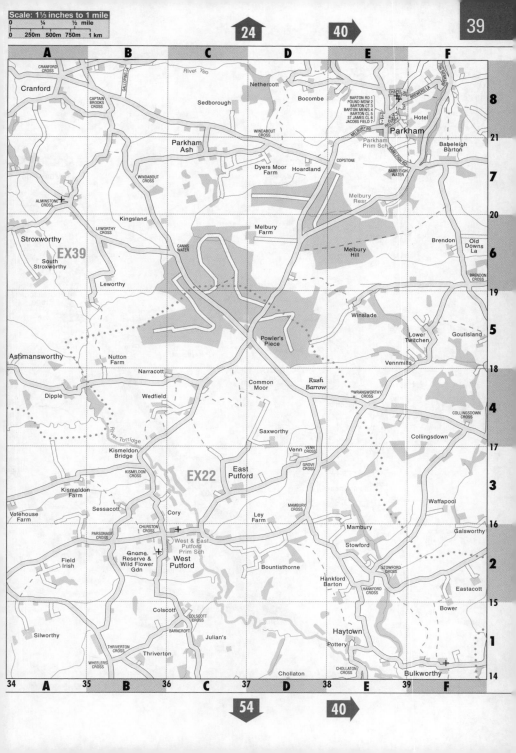

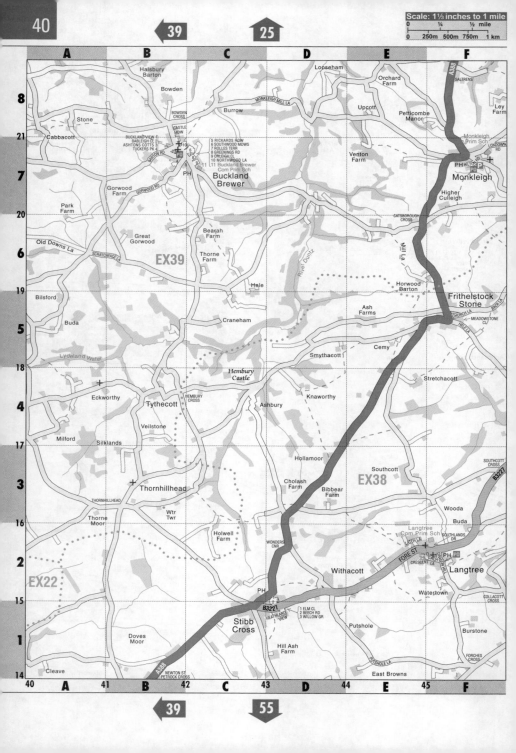

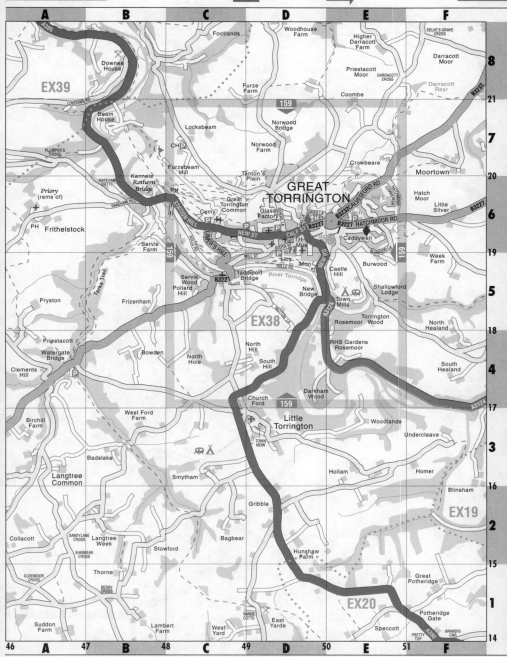

A B C D E F

8
21
7
20
6
19
5
18
4
17
3
16
2
15
1
14

EX39

A386

Downes House

Beam House

LOXDOWN RD

Footlands

Woodhouse Farm

Higher Darracott Farm

DELVE'S GRAVE CROSS

Darracott Moor

Priestacott Moor

DARRACOTT CROSS

Darracott Resr

B3232

Coombe

159

Locksbeam

Norwood Bridge

Norwood Farm

Crowbeare

Moortown

CHP

Furzebeam Hill

Tanton's Plain

PLUMPER'S CROSS

Kennels Rotherm Bridge

PH

RAKEHAM COTTS

Great Torrington Common

Hatch Moor

Little Silver

B3227

Priory (rems of)

RAKEHAM HILL

Cemy

Great Torrington

Glassic Factory

GREAT TORRINGTON

CALVESFORD RD

Ind Est

B3232

Sch

Hatch Moor

B3227

HATCHMOOR RD

PH Frithelstock

STATION HILL

LIMER'S HILL

NEW ST

Mus

JURIES LA

B3227

CALF ST

SOUTH ST

Sch

Caddywell

Servis Farm

159

MILL ST

Lib

Mon

ROLLE RD

Burwood

BURWOOD LA

Week Farm

Servis Wood Pollard Hill

B3221

Taddiport Bridge

River Torridge

New Bridge

Castle Hill

Town Mills

Shallowford Lodge

Torrington Wood

North Healand

Pryston

Tarka Trail

Frizenham

EX38

MOTHA LA

A3124

Rosemoor

RHS Gardens Rosemoor

South Healand

Priestacott

Watergate Bridge

Bowden

North Hole

North Hill

South Hill

Darkham Wood

Woodlands

Undercleave

A3124

Clements Hill

Birchill Farm

West Ford Farm

Church Ford

159

Little Torrington

Homer

Blinsham

Badslake

TOWN MDW

Hollam

EX19

Langtree Common

Smytham

Gribble

Collacott

SANDYLANE CROSS

Langtree Week

SHEBBEAR CROSS

Stowford

Bagbear

Hunshaw Farm

Great Potheridge

CUDEMOOR CROSS

Thorne

BERRY CROSS

EX20

Potheridge Gate

Suddon Farm

Lambert Farm

West Yard

YARDE COTTS

East Yarde

Speccott

PRETTY TOP

BRANDIS CNR

A386

46 A 47 B 48 C 49 D 50 E 51 F

For full street detail of the highlighted area see page 159.

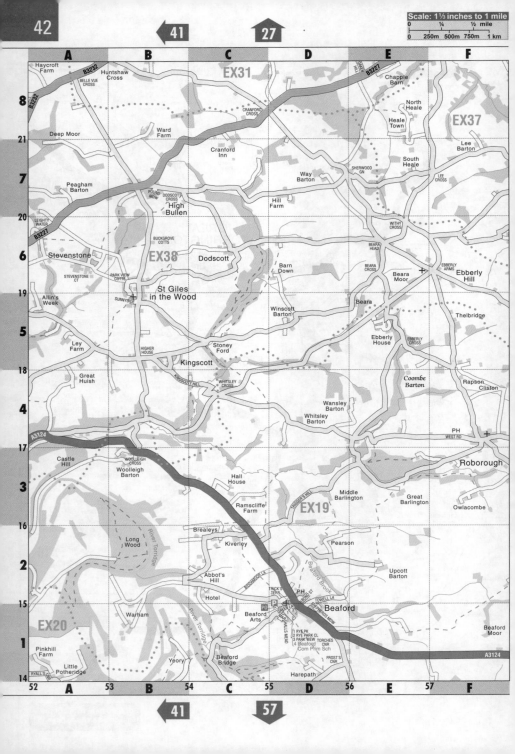

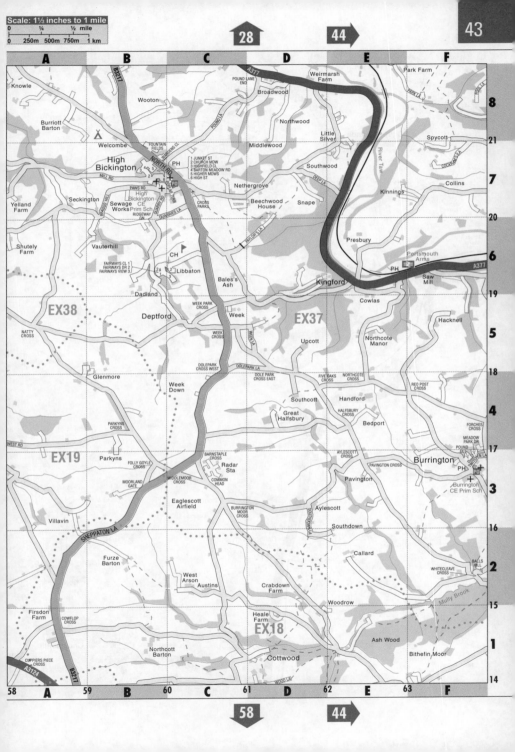

Scale: 1⅓ inches to 1 mile

0   ¼   ½ mile
0   250m   500m   750m   1 km

A   B   C   D   E   F

8
Haynetown
Edington   Newlands
NEWLAND CROSS
POOL LA
HAYNE TOWN CROSS
Watertown
Bias Wood
B3226
SAMPSON CROSS
Sampson Barton
Stone
RED GATE
JOSE'S CROSS

21
Chittlehamholt
Arshaton Wood
PH
YEOTOWN CROSS
Hele
SLETCHCOTT CROSS
Sletchcott
Down Farm
River Mole

7
ENTRANCE CROSS
Highbullen
Hele Wood
HELE CROSS
Colley Lake
Collacott Farm
Whitmore

20
Manor House
Lenton
Huxford Farm
HUXFORD LA
Whitmore
Smitha

6
Abbot's Marsh
A377
EX37
Snydles Farm
Kingsnympton Park
PH
King's Nympton
BEARA CROSS

19
Braggamarsh
Bouchland Farm
Park Wood
Wooda
King's Nympton Prim Sch
NYMET VILLAS
BRANDY WELLS
Beara
SHORELAND CROSS

5
Weir
HILL HEAD CROSS
Hill Head
Spilla La
GREAT LIGHTLEIGH
Great Lightleigh
LIGHTLEIGH CROSS
Waddington

18
Head Wood
River Taw
Head Barton
Junction Bridge Pool CROSS
Hill Head
Spittle Farm
Coombe
COOMBE LA

4
Hill
Barnpool
NEWNHAM CROSS
Newnham Barton
SPITTLE CROSS
Cutland House
Cadbury Barton
Bunson
FORCHES CROSS
POOL LA

17
TWO GATE CROSS
Catham
King's Hill
Fortescue Cross
B3226
CUTLAND CROSS
Twitchen

3
Hayne Barton
Bircham
Churchland
Kings Nympton
HIGHER ELSTONE CROSS
PYNE MEADOW CROSS
TOLL BAR CROSS
Dobbs Moor Farm
DOBBSMOOR CROSS
BALLS CNR
ELSTONE CROSS
STATION RD
Elstone
ORANGE MOOR CROSS

16
Cleave
Golland
GOLLAND LA
MILL MOOR CROSS
Colleton Mills
Lakehead
EX18
Beacon
Winswood
Mully Brook

2
MILL LA
HANSFORD CROSS
Hansford Barton
FORD CROSS
Thurle
Parsonage Farm
PARSONAGE CROSS

15
HANSFORD CROSS
BORNE CROSS
BONDS CROSS
The Community Coll Chulmleigh
CHARREYMORE CROSS

1
Borne
COLLETON GATE
Colleton Manor
Back Hill Ind Est
FOUR CROSSWAYS
MALLINGBROOK CROSS
Chulmleigh Prim Sch
LANGLEY
Chulmleigh
Hook Farm
LEIGH RD
B3096
A377
DARTRIDGE LA
Ladywell La
CRICKET CL
PARK MILL LA
Lodge La

14
64   A   65   B   66   C   67   D   68   E   69   F

E1
1 LAND PK
2 DARTMOOR VIEW
3 FOUR WAYS DR
4 THREE CROSSWAYS
5 BEACON RISE
6 LANGLEY GDNS
7 ROYAL CHARTER PK
8 WINDY CROSS
9 EGYPT LA
10 CHULMLEIGH HILL
11 FORE ST
12 THE SQUARE
13 ROCK HILL
14 NEW ST
15 CHURCH CL

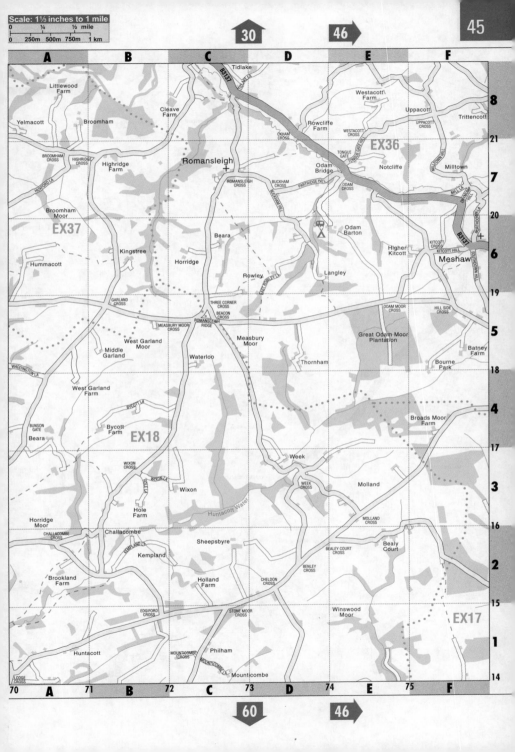

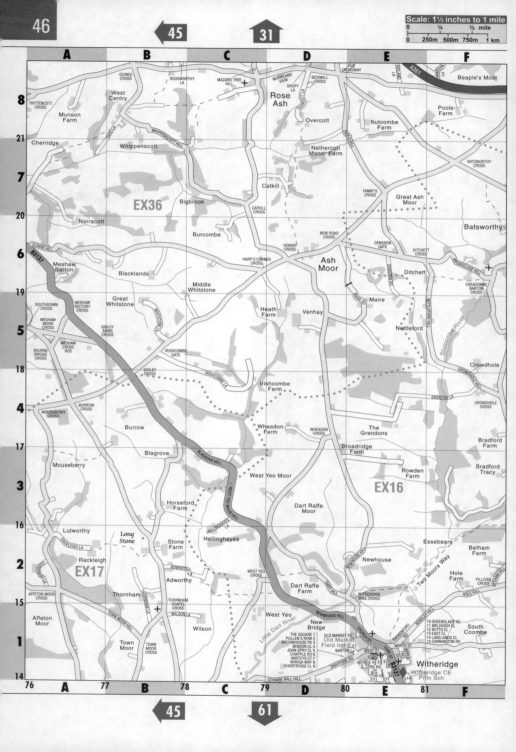

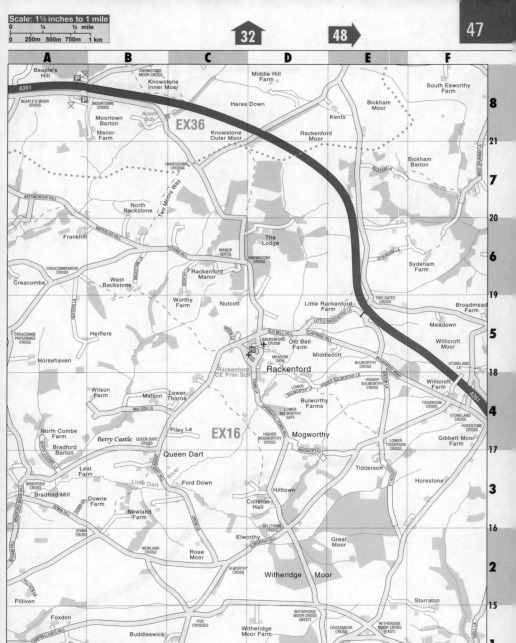

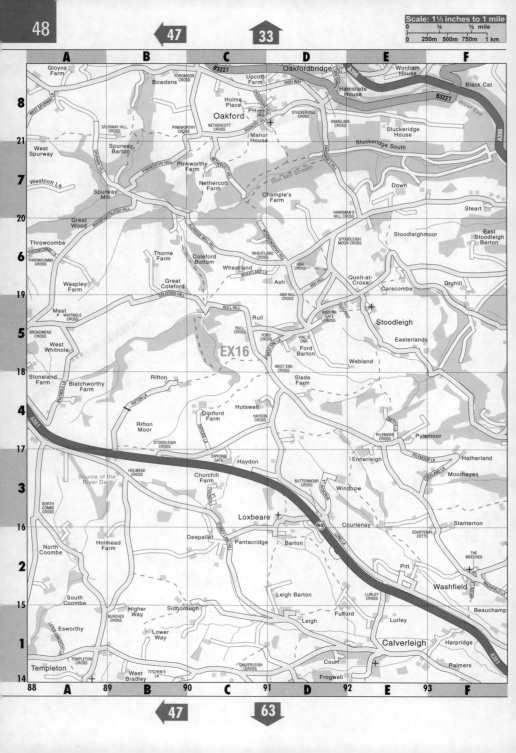

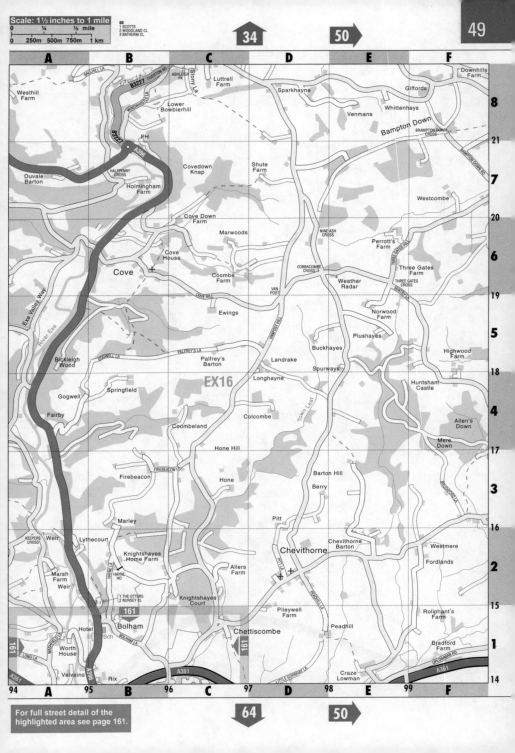

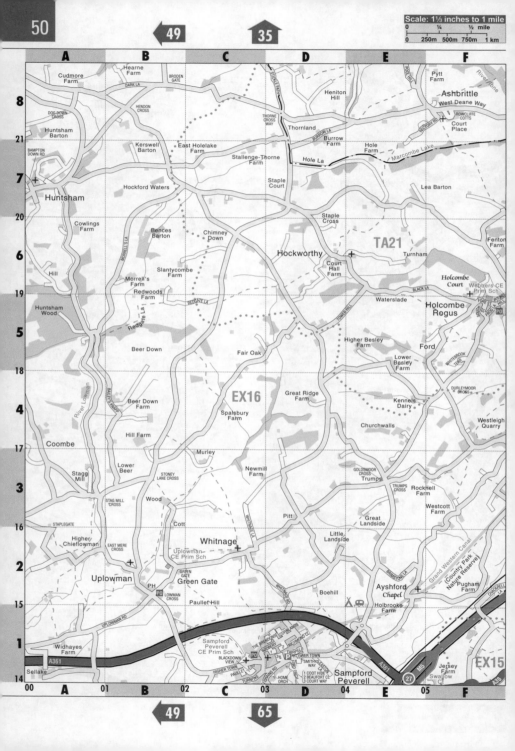

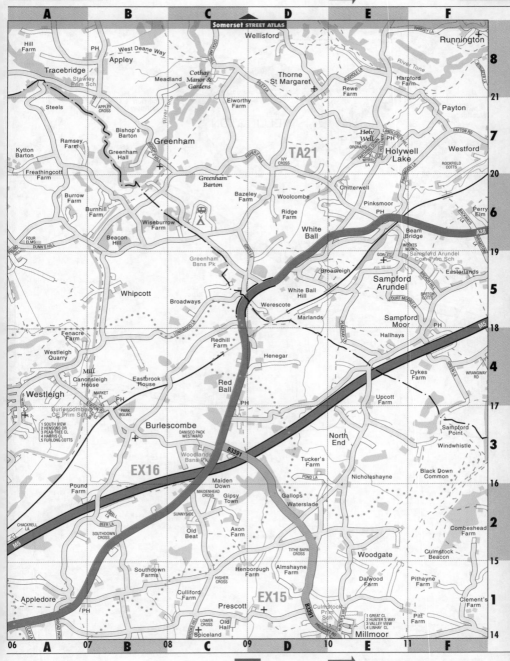

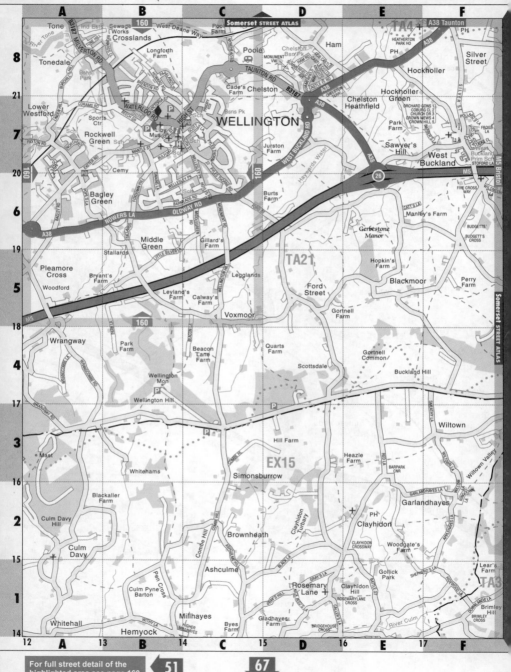

Somerset STREET ATLAS

TA4   A38 Taunton

8

Tone Ind Est

Sewage Works

West Deane Way

Poole

160

HEATHERTON PARK HO

PH

Silver Street

Crosslands

Longforth Farm

Poole

Chelston Bsns Pk

Ham

PH

A38

Hockholler

Tonedale

MONUMENT VW

Cade's Farm Chelston

Chelston Bsns Pk

21

Lower Westford

WATERLOO RD

HIGH ST

B3187

Chelston Heathfield

Hockholler Green

ORCHARD GDNS 1
COBURG CL 2
CHURCH DR 3
CROWN MEWS 4
CROWN HILL 5

7

Sports Ctr

Rockwell Green

Sch

Liby Mus

A38

Park Farm

Sawyer's Hill

West Buckland Prim Sch

FROGS

PAYTON RD

Cemy

WEST BUCKLAND RD

WELLINGTON

Jurston Farm

West Buckland

M5 Bristol

20

160

Haywards Water

26

Five Cross Way

WELLINGTON

Bagley Green

NOWERS LA

OLDWAY RD

Burts Farm

Manley's Farm

BUDGETTS CROSS

6

A38

Middle Green

Gillard's Farm

Gerbestone Manor

CATT'S LA

BUDGETT'S CROSS

19

Stallards

LITTLE SILVER LA

TA21

Hopkin's Farm

Perry Farm

5

Pleamore Cross

Bryant's Farm

Legglands

Ford Street

Blackmoor

Woodford

Leyland's Farm

Calway's Farm

Gortnell Farm

18

M5

160

Voxmoor

Park Farm

Beacon Lane Farm

Quarts Farm

Gortnell Common

4

Wrangway

Scottsdale

Buckland Hill

17

Wellington Mon

Wellington Hill

P

P

Wiltown

3

Mast

Hill Farm

BARPARK CNR

RED LA

Wiltown Valley

Whitehams

EX15

Heazle Farm

Simonsburrow

GARLANDHAYES LA

16

Blackaller Farm

Clayhidon Turbary

PH

Garlandhayes

2

Culm Davy Hill

COMBE HILL

Brownheath

Clayhidon

CLAYHIDON CROSSWAY

Woodgate's Farm

15

Culm Davy

Pen Cross

Ashculme

BLACK LA

Gollick Park

Clayhidon Hill

SHEPHERD'S LA

Lear's Farm

TA3

1

Culm Pyne Barton

GRAY'S LA

Rosemary Lane

ROSEMARYLANE CROSS

Brimley Hill

BRIMLEY CROSS

Milhayes

Byes Farm

Gladhayes Farm

River Culm

14

Whitehall

Hemyock

HIGHER MILHAYES

BRIDGEHOUSE CROSS

12   13   14   15   16   17

A   B   C   D   E   F

51

67

For full street detail of the highlighted area see page 160.

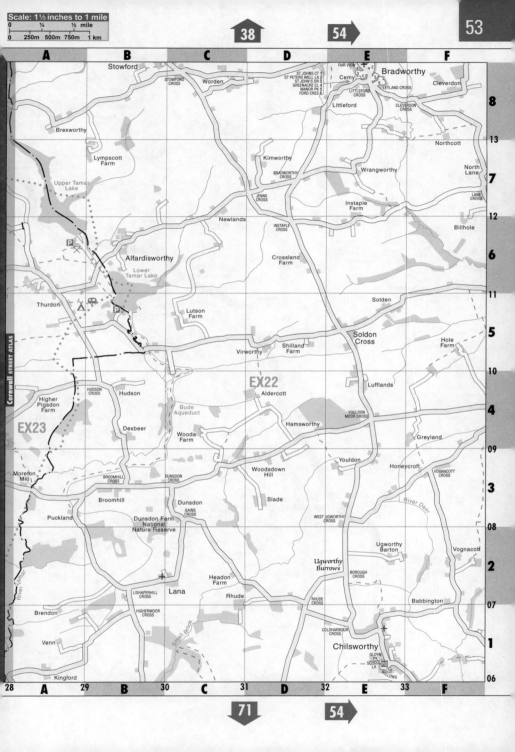

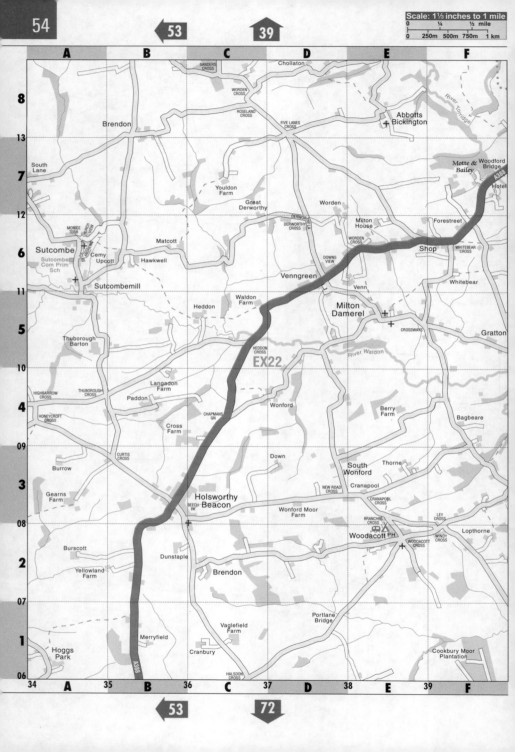

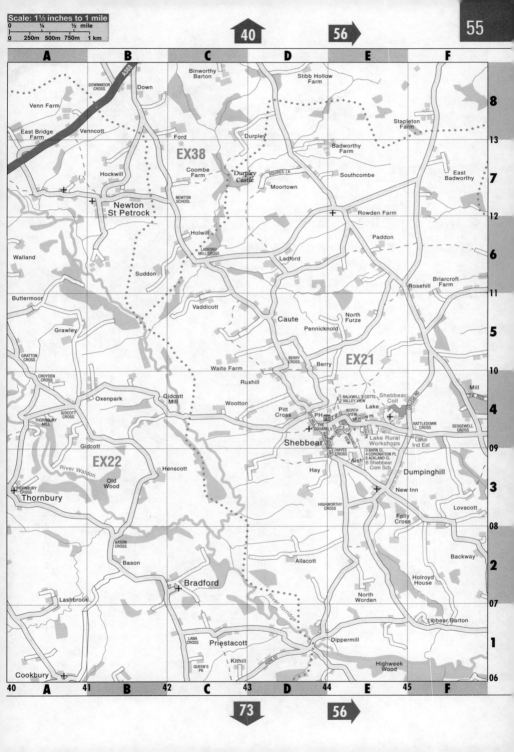

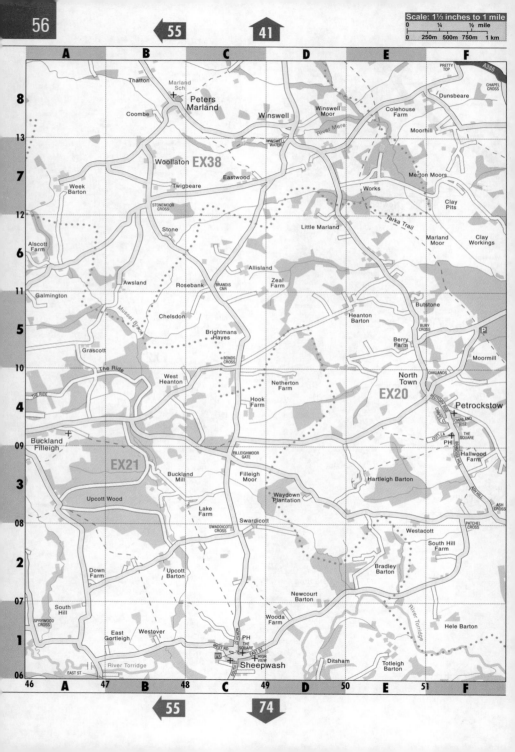

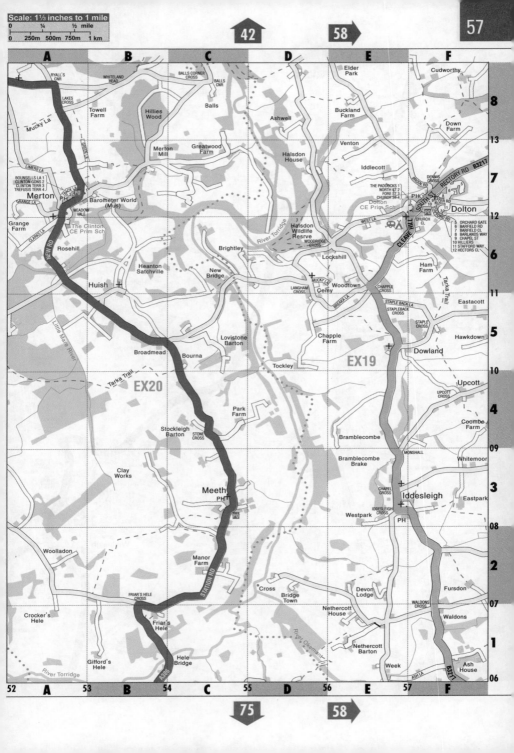

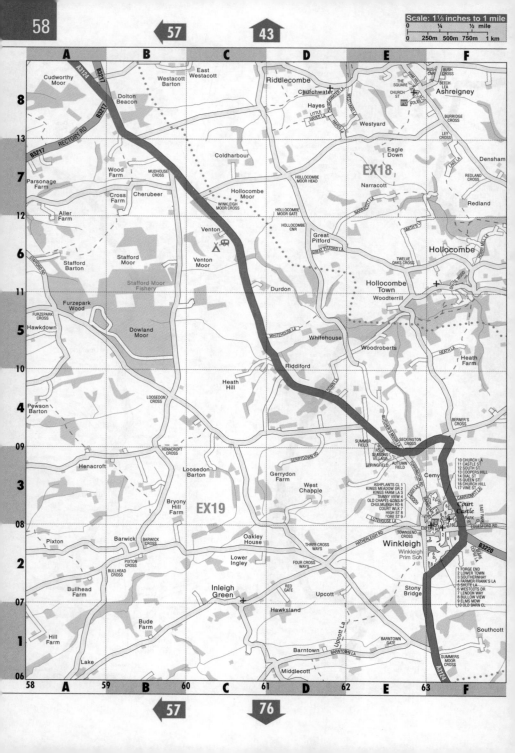

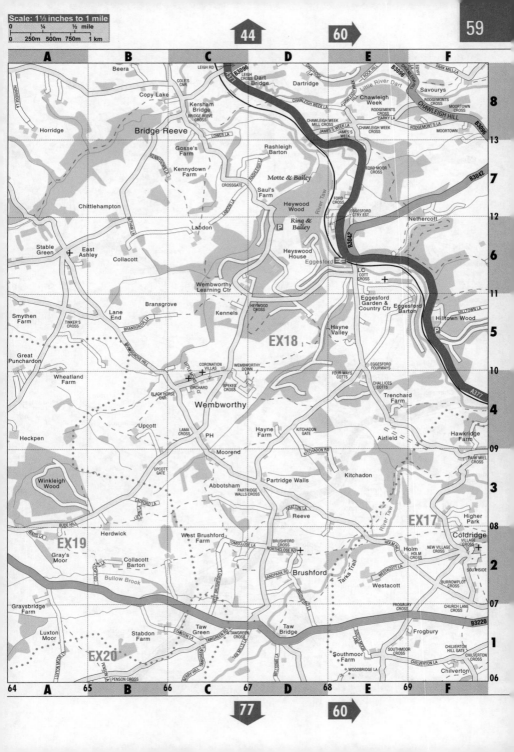

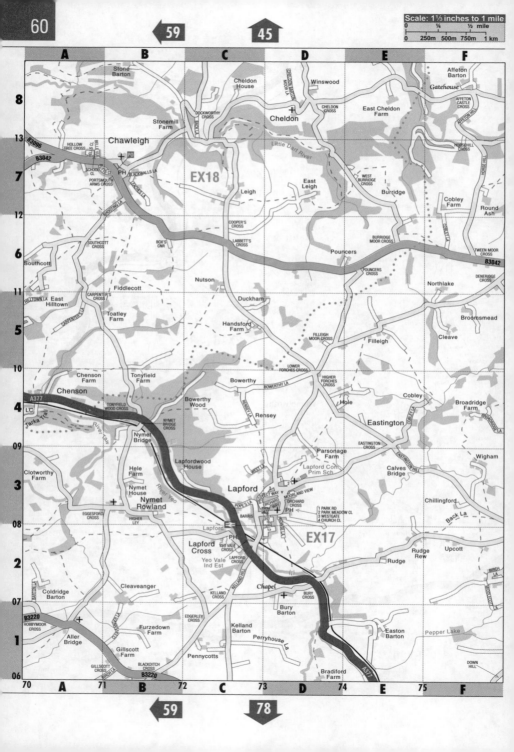

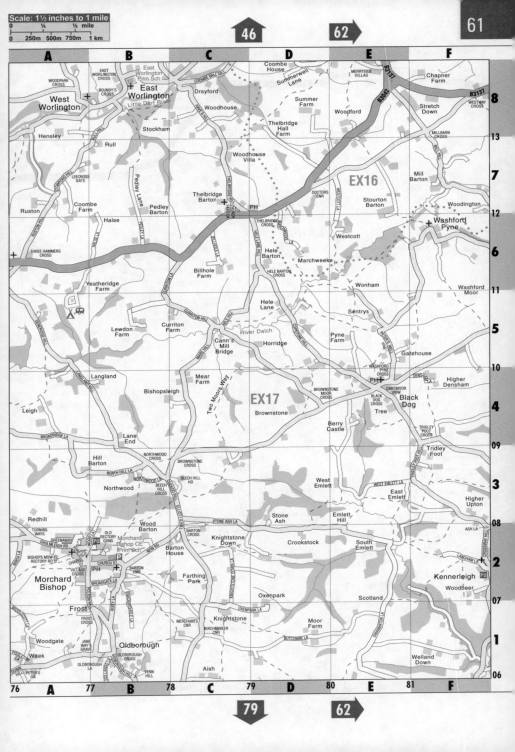

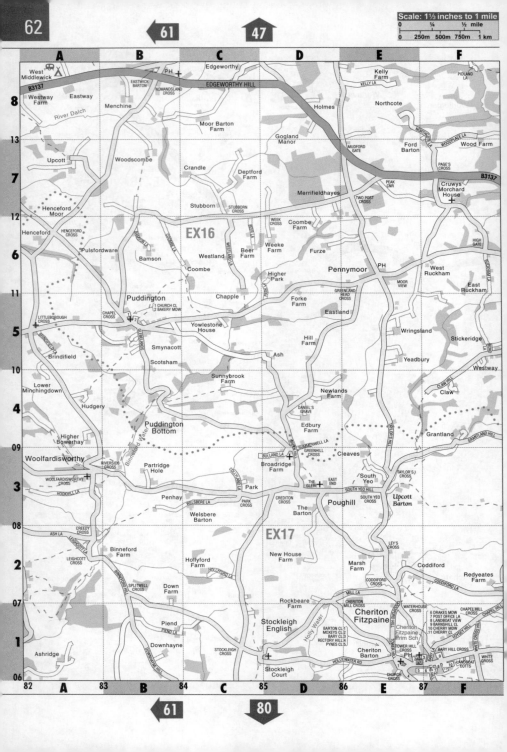

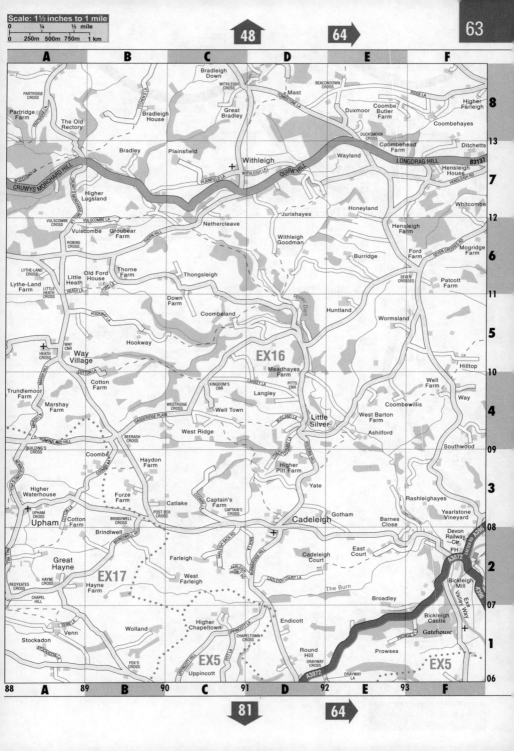

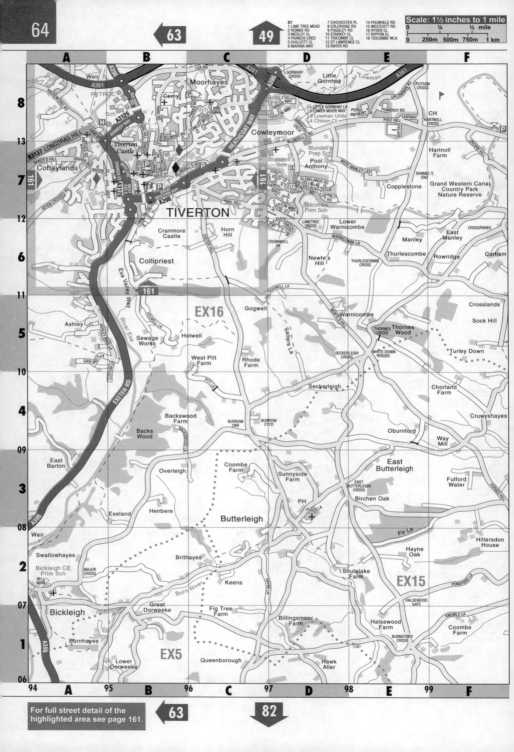

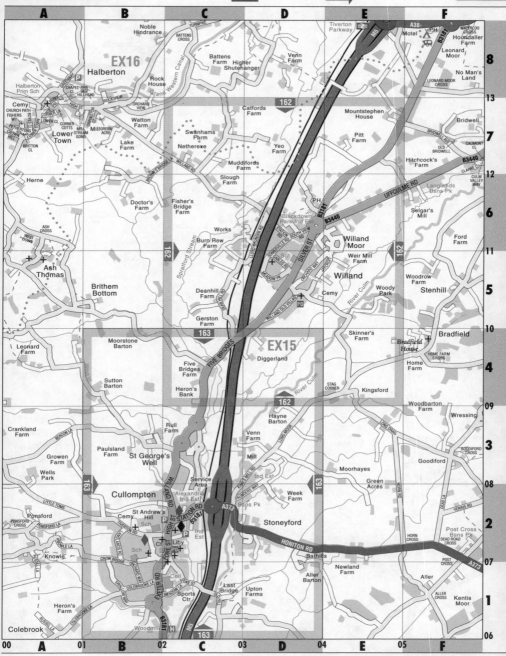

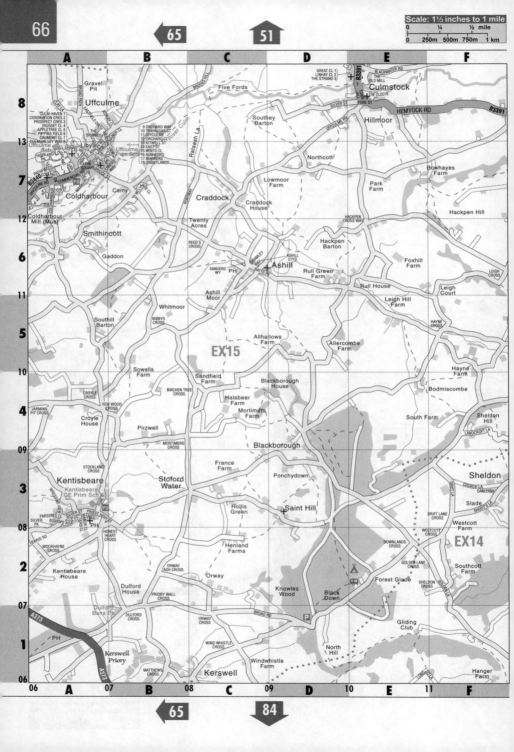

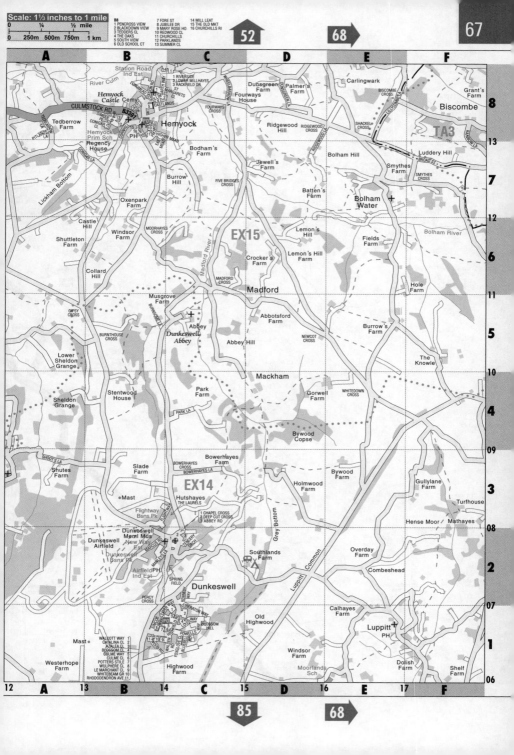

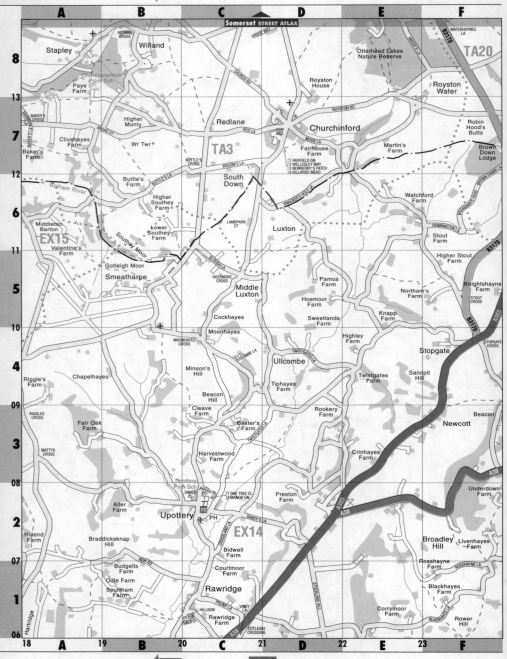

Scale: 1⅓ inches to 1 mile

0 ¼ ½ mile
0 250m 500m 750m 1 km

Somerset STREET ATLAS

TA20

8

Stapley
Willand

Churchstanton
Prim Sch
ACOMBE CROSS

13

Paye Farm
Otterhead Lakes
Nature Reserve

Royston
House

Royston
Water

Higher
Munty

Redlane
Churchinford

Robin
Hood's
Butts

7

Clivehayes
Farm

Wr Twr

RED LA

TA3

Fairhouse
Farm

Martin's
Farm

Brown
Down
Lodge

Baker's
Farm

BUTTLE'S
CROSS

1 FAIRFIELD GN
2 WELLESLEY WAY
3 NEWBERRY'S PATCH
4 GILLARDS MEAD

12

Bolham River

Buttle's
Farm

South
Down

KNACKER'S HOLE LA

Watchford
Farm

6

Middleton
Barton

Higher
Southey
Farm

LAMBPARK
CT

Luxton

EX15

Valentine's
Farm

Lower
Southey
Farm

Stout
Farm

11

Gotleigh Moor

Southey Moor

Higher Stout
Farm

Smeatharpe

HOLEMORE
CROSS

Middle
Luxton

Pamos
Farm

Northam's
Farm

Knightshayne
Farm

5

Cockhayes

Hoemoor
Farm

Knapp
Farm

STOUT
CROSS

10

Moonhayes

Sweetlands
Farm

MOONHAYES
CROSS

ULLCOMBE LA

Highley
Farm

Stopgate

STOPGATE
CROSS

4

Riggle's
Farm

Chapelhayes

Minson's
Hill

Ullcombe

TWISTGATES LA

Twistgates
Farm

Sandpit
Hill

Beacon

Newcott

09

RIGGLES
CROSS

Fair Oak
Farm

Beacon
Hill

Tiphayes
Farm

Rookery
Farm

3

Cleave
Farm

Baxter's
Farm

TWISTGATE LA

Crinhayes
Farm

A30

MATTYS
CROSS

Harvestwood
Farm

Underdown
Farm

08

Aller
Farm

Upottery
Prim Sch

PIPERS PL

1 OAK TREE CL
2 MANOR GN

Preston
Farm

DANES
CL

A303

2

Hillend
Farm

Upottery

PH

EX14

Broadley
Hill

Livenhayes
Farm

Braddicksknap
Hill

Bidwell
Farm

SANDY'S LA

Rosshayne
Farm

ROSSHAYNE LA

07

Budgells
Farm

NEW RD

Courtmoor
Farm

Blackhayes
Farm

Odle Farm

POUND LA

STOCKLAND HILL

1

Spurtham
Farm

Rawridge

Corrymoor
Farm

Rower
Hill

Hartridge

HILLSIDE

VINEY LA

OTTER
VALE CL

Rawridge
Farm

COTLEIGH
CROSSING

BLACKWELL LA

06

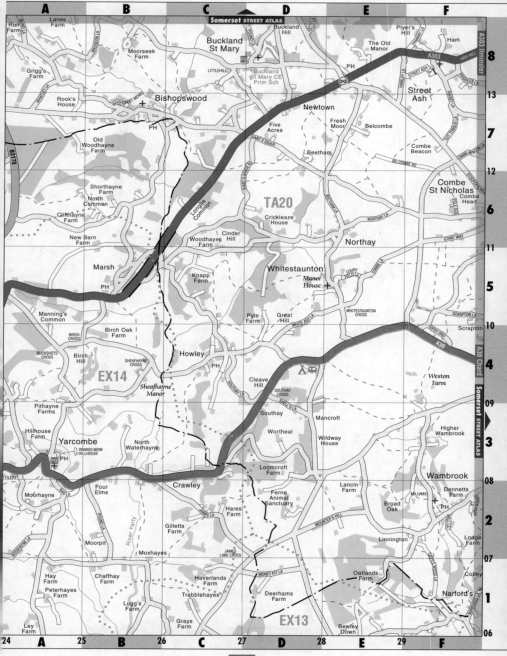

Scale: 1⅓ inches to 1 mile

¼   ½ mile

0   250m 500m 750m 1 km

Somerset STREET ATLAS

A   B   C   D   E   F

Lanes Farm
Ruil Farm
Moorseek Farm
Grigg's Farm
Rook's House
Bishopswood
Old Woodhayne Farm
Shorthayne Farm
North Common
Clifthayne Farm
New Barn Farm
Marsh
Manning's Common
Birch Oak Farm
BIRCH CROSS
BUCKSHOTS CROSS
Birch Hill
SHEAFHAYNE CROSS
EX14
Sheafhayne Manor
Pithayne Farms
Hillhouse Farm
Yarcombe
1 DRAKES MDW 2 HILLHOUSE
North Waterhayne
Tilery
Moorhayne
Four Elms
Crawley
Gilletts Farm
Moxhayes
Moorpit
Hay Farm
Peterhayes Farm
Chaffhay Farm
Trebblehayes
Lugg's Farm
Grays Farm
Ley Farm

Buckland St Mary
Buckland Hill
LITTLEHILL
Buckland St Mary CE Prim Sch
Newtown
Five Acres
GIANT'S GRAVE
Longlive Common
Woodhayes Farm
Cinder Hill
Crickleaze House
TA20
Knapp Farm
Howley
PH
Cleave Hill
Pyle Farm
Great Hill
WHITE ASH LA
SOUTHAY LA
SOUTHAY CROSS
Southay
Wortheal
Loomcroft Farm
Ferne Animal Sanctuary
Hares Farm
JAMES LA
MOUNTER'S HILL
JAMES LANE CROSS
MONEY PIT LA
Haverlands Farm
Deerhams Farm
Bewley Down
EX13

Plyer's Hill
The Old Manor
Ham
PH
A303
50
Street Ash
Fresh Moor
Belcombe
Beetham
Combe Beacon
BELCOMBE RD
Combe St Nicholas
Combe Head
Northay
NORTHAY LA
STANT WAY
Whitestaunton
Manor House
COURT FIELD LA
COMBE LA
WHITESTAUNTON CROSS
SCRAPTON LA
Scrapton
GIPSY LANE
A30
Weston Farm
Mancroft
Wildway House
Higher Wambrook
Wambrook
Lancin Farm
MILLWAY
Broad Oak
PH
Dennetts Farm
Linnington
Lodge Farm
Oatlands Farm
Cotley
Narford's

A303 Ilminster
HAM HILL
A303
STREET ASH
PICKLES LA
Somerset STREET ATLAS
A30 Chard

8
13
7
12
6
11
5
10
4
09
3
08
2
07
1
06

A   B   C   D   E   F

24   25   26   27   28   29

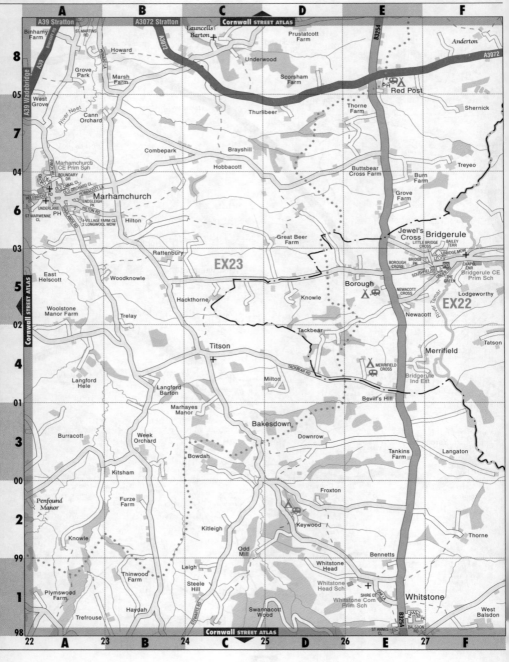

Scale: 1½ inches to 1 mile

0   ¼   ½   mile
0 250m 500m 750m 1 km

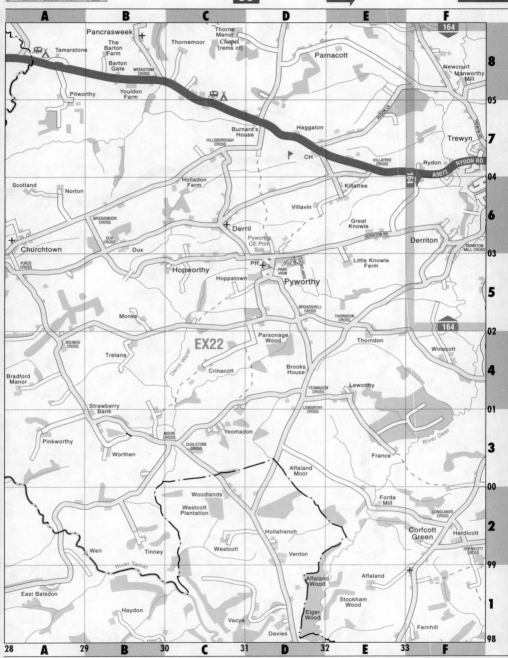

Scale: 1⅓ inches to 1 mile

0   ¼   ½ mile
0   250m   500m   750m   1 km

53

72

8

Pancrasweek

Tamarstone

The Barton Farm

Barton Gate

WEEKSTONE CROSS

Thornemoor

Thorne Manor *Chapel* (rems of)

Parnacott

Newcourt

Manworthy Mill

164

Pitworthy

Youldon Farm

05

Burnard's House

Haggaton

RYDOLLA

Trewyn

7

HILLSBOROUGH CROSS

CH

KILLATREE CROSS

Rydon

A3072

RYDON RD

164

04

Scotland

Norton

Holladon Farm

Killatree

Villavin

Great Knowle

DERRITON RD

Derriton

6

BRIDGEMOOR CROSS

Derril

Pyworthy CE Prim Sch

DERRITON MILL CROSS

DUX CROSS

Churchtown

Dux

Little Knowle Farm

03

FURZE CROSS

Hopworthy

Hoppatown

PH

PARK VIEW

Pyworthy

5

Monks

BROADSHELL CROSS

THORNDON CROSS

164

02

BOUNDS CROSS

Trelana

EX22

Parsonage Wood

Thorndon

Winscott

4

Bradford Manor

Crinacott

Derril Water

Brooks House

YEOMADON CROSS

Leworthy

Strawberry Bank

LEWORTHY CROSS

River Deer

01

Pinkworthy

MOOR CROSS

Yeomadon

France

3

Worthen

DUALSTONE CROSS

Affaland Moor

00

Woodlands

Westcott Plantation

Forda Mill

LONGLANDS CROSS

Corfcott Green

Herdicott

2

Weir

Tinney

Westcott

Hollafrench

Venton

HERDICOTT CROSS

River Tamar

99

East Balsdon

Haydon

Affaland Wood

Affaland

Stockham Wood

1

Vacye

Elger Wood

Fernhill

Davies

98

28   A   29   B   30   C   31   D   32   E   33   F

89

72

For full street detail of the highlighted area see page 164.

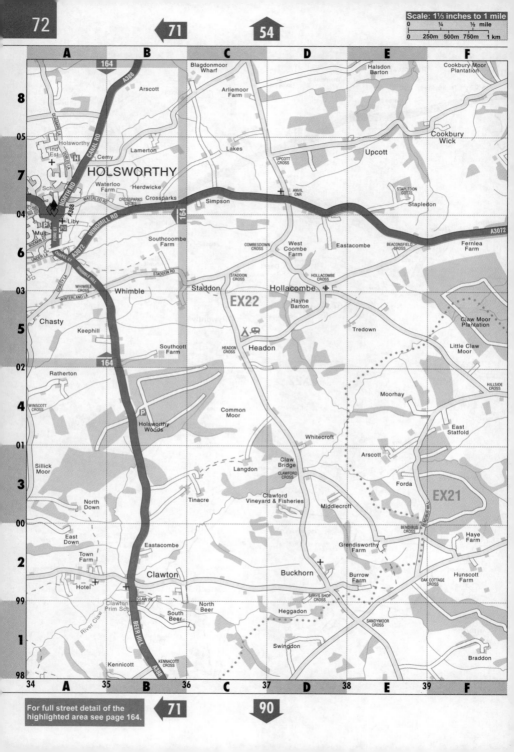

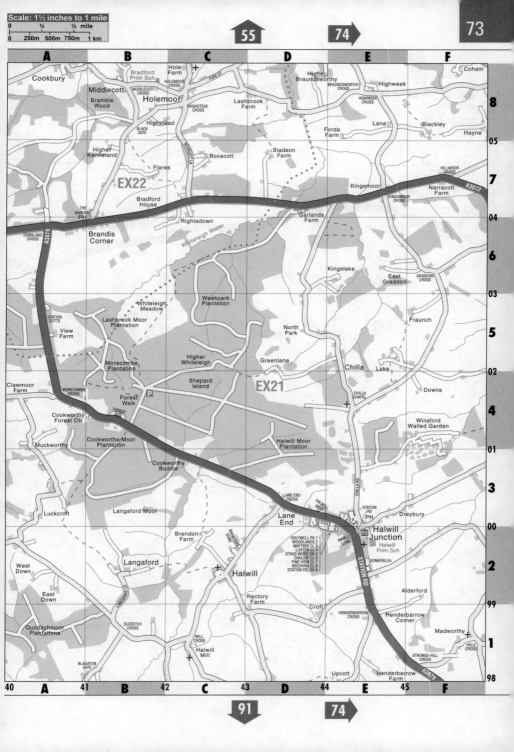

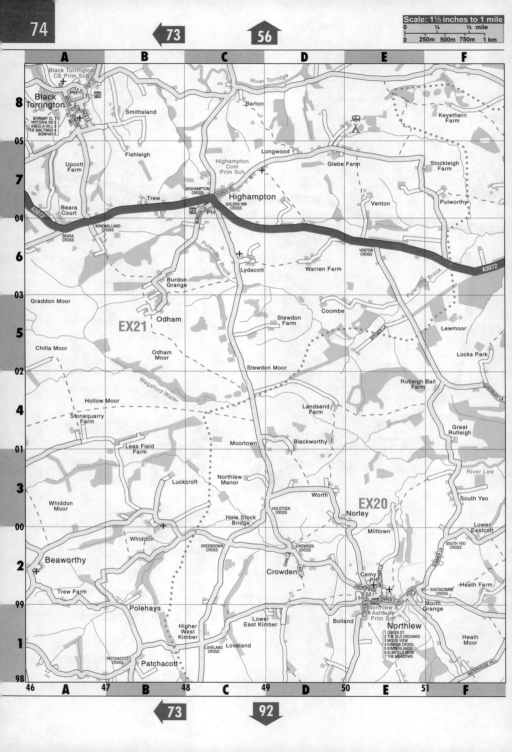

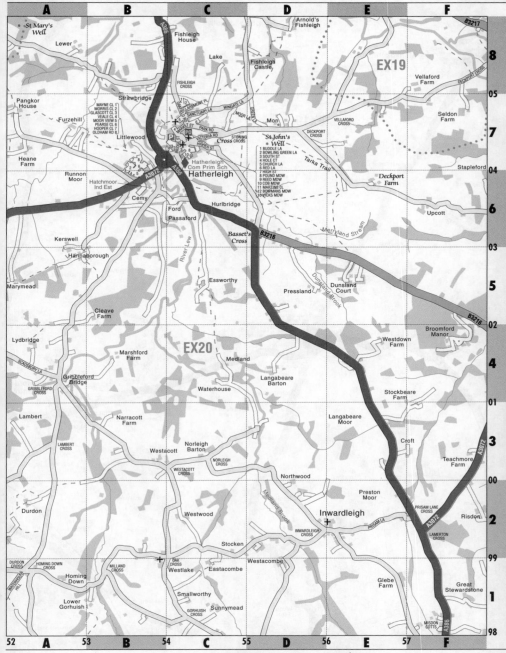

A   B   C   D   E   F

St Mary's Well
Lewer
Pangkor House
Furzehill
Heane Farm
Strawbridge
Littlewood
Fishleigh House
Lake
Arnold's Fishleigh
Fishleigh Castle
EX19
Vellaford Farm
Seldon Farm
FISHLEIGH CROSS
Mon
St John's Well
Cross CROSS
VELLAFORD CROSS
DECKPORT CROSS
Stapleford
Hatherleigh Com Prim Sch
Hatherleigh
Deckport Farm
Upcott
Runnon Moor
Hatchmoor Ind Est
Cemy
Ford
Passaford
Hurlbridge
Basset's Cross
Merryland Stream
Tarka Trail
Kerswell
Hannaborough
Marymead
Essworthy
Pressland
Dunsland Court
Broomford Manor
B3216
Cleave Farm
Lydbridge
Marshford Farm
Gribbleford Bridge
EX20
Medland
Waterhouse
Langabeare Barton
Westdown Farm
Stockbeare Farm
Lambert
Narracott Farm
Westacott
Norleigh Barton
Langabeare Moor
Croft
Teachmore Farm
LAMBERT CROSS
NORLEIGH CROSS
Northwood
Durdon
Westwood
Stocken
Inwardleigh
Preston Moor
Prisam Lane Cross
Risdon
DURDON CROSS
HOMING DOWN CROSS
Homing Down
MILLAND CROSS
OAK CROSS
Westlake
Eastacombe
Westacombe
INWARDLEIGH CROSS
LAMERTON CROSS
Lower Gorhuish
Smallworthy
GORHUISH CROSS
Sunnymead
Glebe Farm
Great Stewardstone
MISDON COTTS

St John's Well
1 BUDDLE LA
2 BOWLING GREEN LA
3 SOUTH ST
4 HOLE CT
5 CHURCH LA
6 RED LA
7 HIGH ST
8 POUND MDW
9 REED MDW
10 COB MDW
11 MARTINS CL
12 BOWMANS MDW
13 ROCKS MDW

MAYNE CL 1
MORRIS CL 2
GLASCOTT CL 3
VEALE CL 4
MOOR VIEW 5
PEARSE CL 6
HOOPER CL 7
OLDHAM RD 8

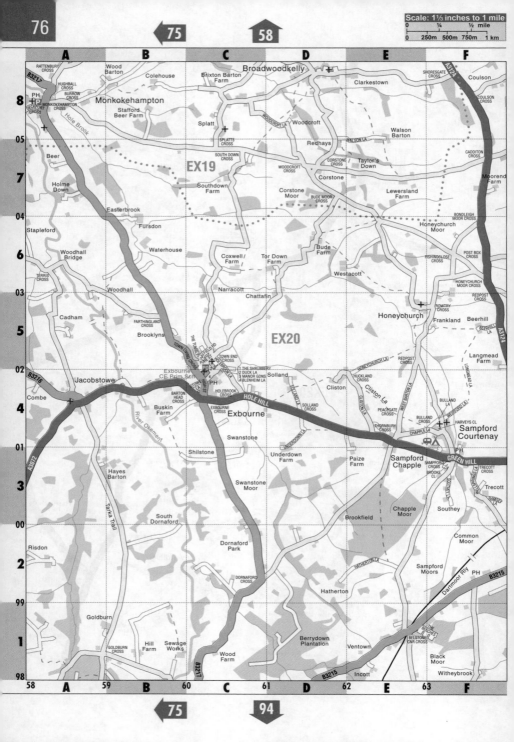

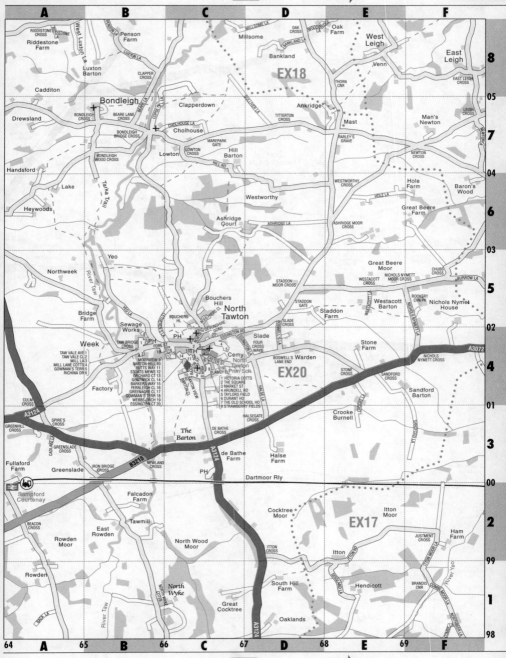

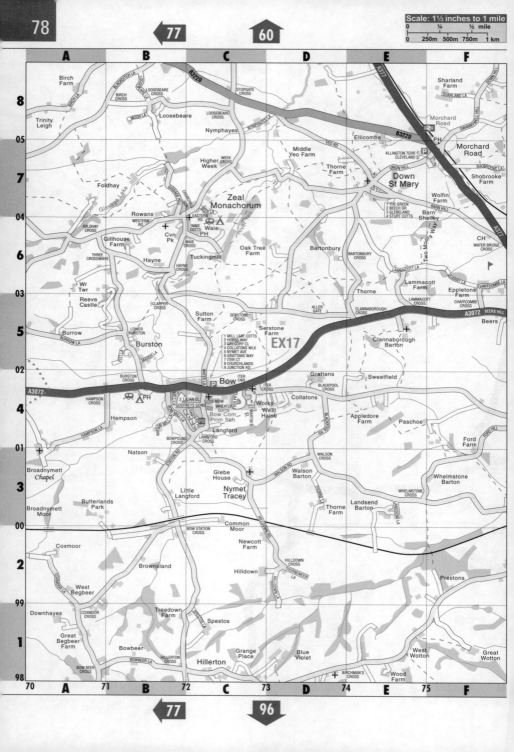

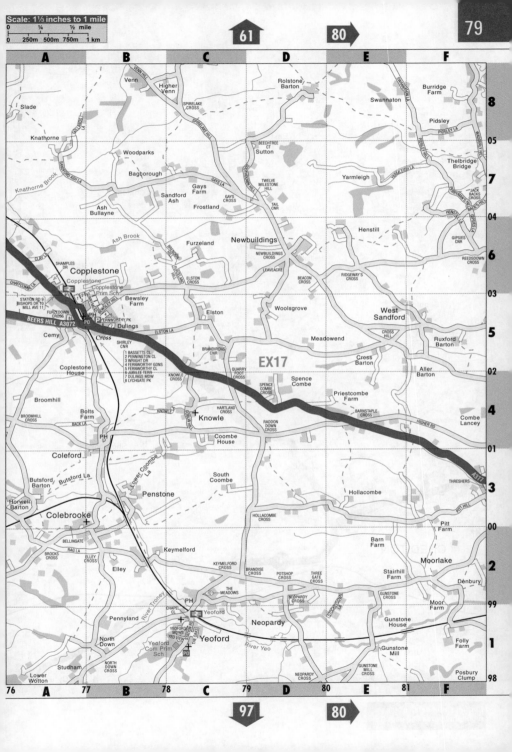

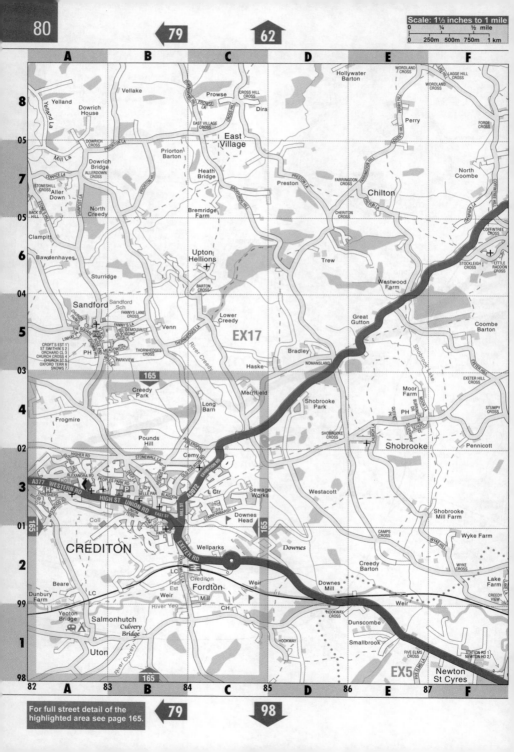

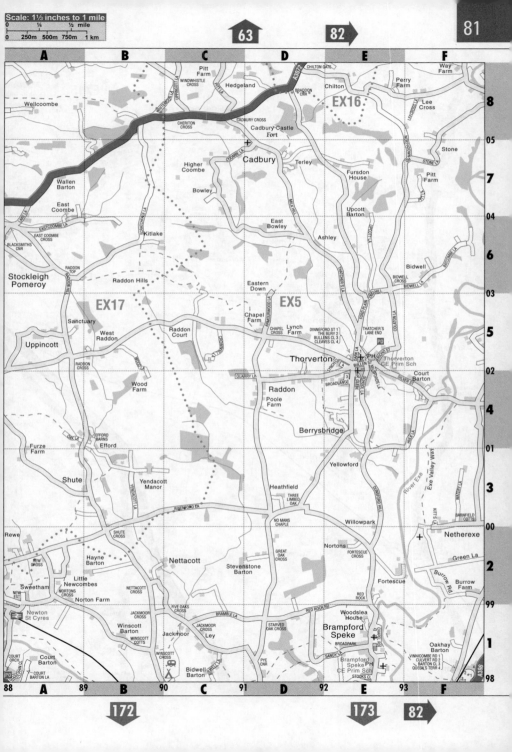

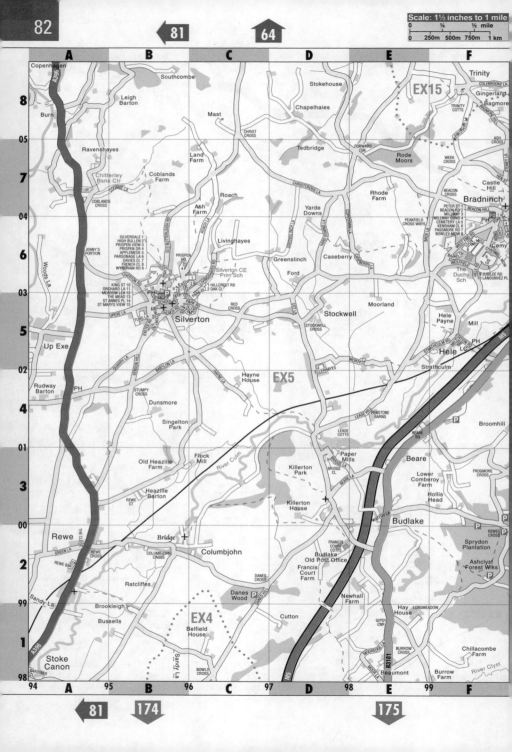

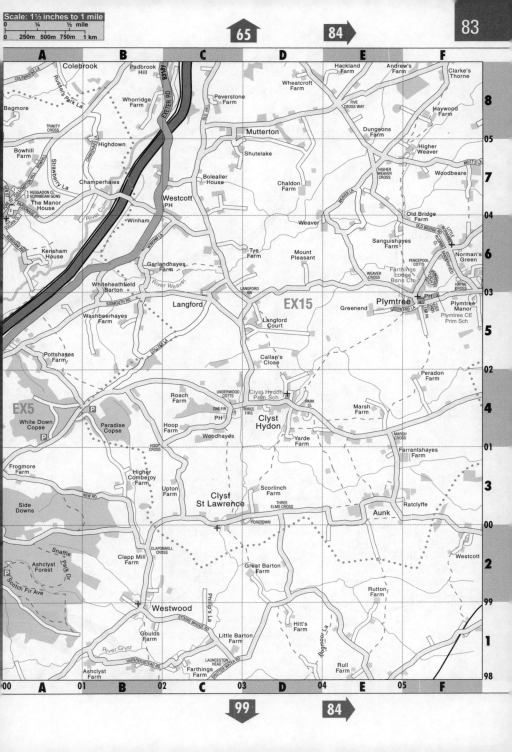

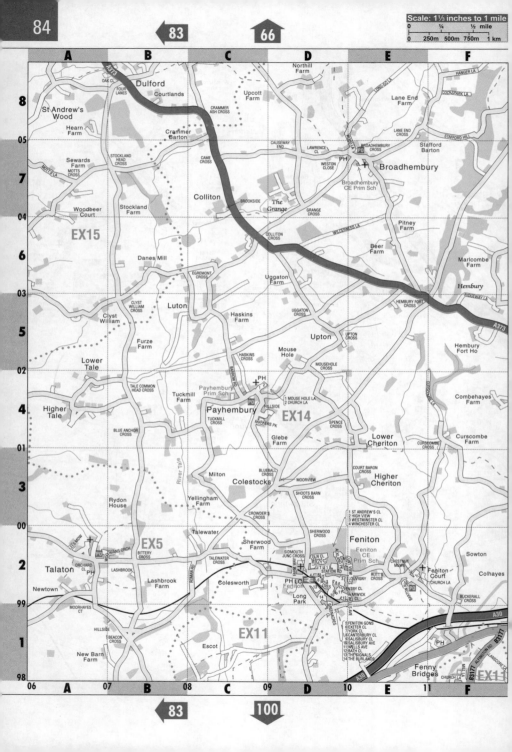

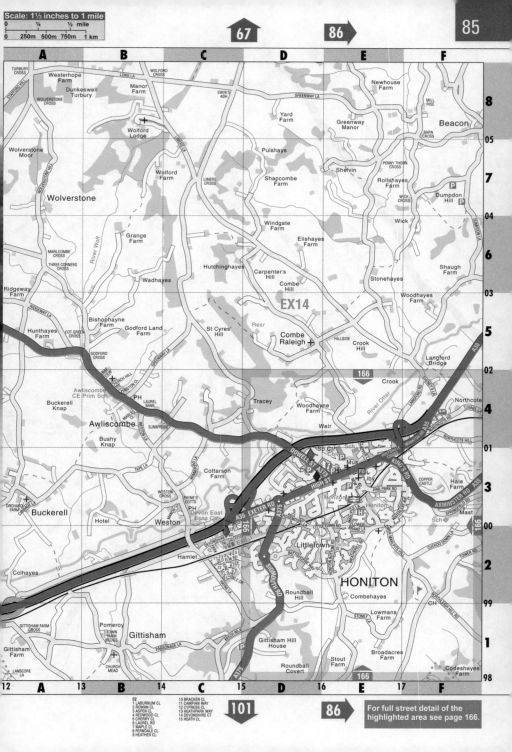

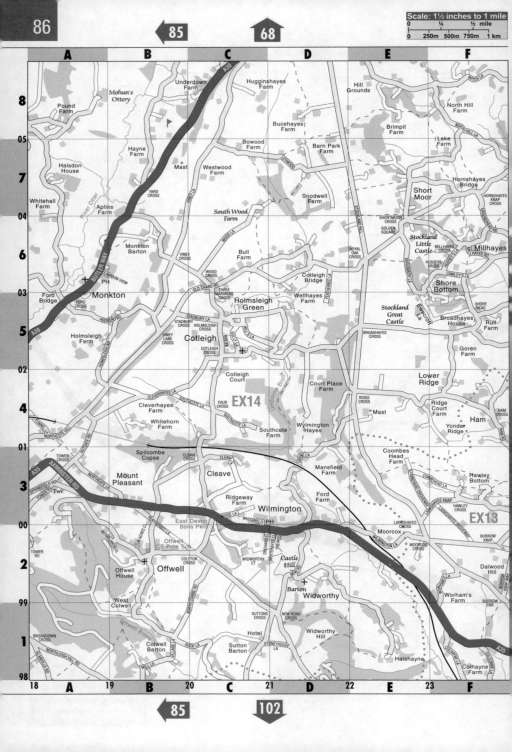

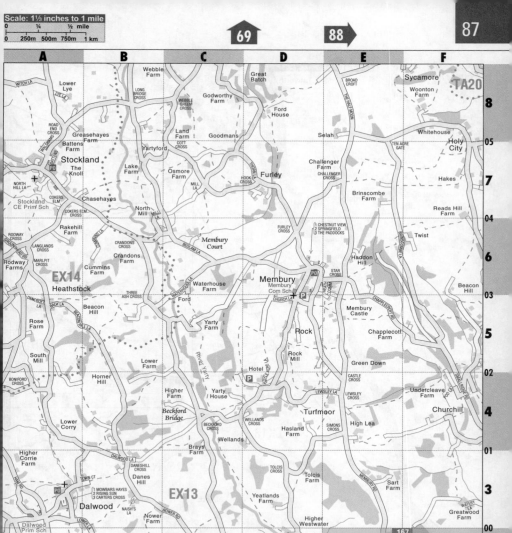

TA20

A   B   C   D   E   F

Witch La
Lower Lye
Lower Lye La

Webble Farm
Long Bridge Cross
Webble Greeny Cross

Great Batch
Broad Croft

Sycamore
Woonton Farm

8

Road End Cross
Battens Farm
Greasehayes Farm
Godworthy Farm
Land Farm
Cott Cross
Goodmans

Ford House

Selah

Whitehouse

Holy City

05

Stockland
The Knoll
Lake Farm
Yartyford
Osmore Farm
Mill La
Hook La Cross
Furley

Challenger Farm
Challenger Cross

Hakes

7

North Hill La
Stockland CE Prim Sch
Cokers Elm
Chasehayes
Cokers Elm Cross
North Mill

Brinscombe Farm

Reads Hill Farm

04

Rodway Cross
Langlands Cross
Rakehill Farm
Crandons Cross
Membury Court

Furley Cross

Chestnut View
Springfield
The Paddocks

Twist

6

Marlpit Cross
Rodway Farms
Cummins Farm
Crandons Farm
Three Ash Cross
Beeam La

Haddon Hill
Star Cross

EX14
Heathstock
Waterhouse Farm
Membury
Membury Corn Sch
Church La

Membury Castle

Beacon Hill

03

Denchop La
Sack La
Beacon Hill
Waterhouse La
Ford

Rock

Memborough Castle

Chapplecott Road

5

Rose Farm
Beacon Hill La
Yarty Farm
Rock Mill

Chapplecott Farm

South Mill
Lower Farm
Green Down

02

Boniford Cross
Boniford Cross Rd
Horner Hill
River Yarty
Avishays La

Castle Cross

Undercleave Farm

Churchill

Lower Corry
Higher House
Yarty House
Beckford Bridge
Beckford Cross
Wellands Cross

Turfmoor
Lewsley La
Lewsley Cross

4

01

Higher Corrie Farm
Dalwood La
Brays Farm
Wellands
Hasland Farm
Simons Cross
High Lea

Sart Farm

3

Town Ct
Daneshill Cross
Danes Hill
Mowbars Hayes
Rising Sun
Carters Cross
Dalwood
Naish's La

EX13

Tolcis Cross
Tolcis Farm

Watery La
Greatwood Farm

Dalwood Prim Sch
Nower Farm
Nower Rd

Yeatlands Farm

00

Lea
Woodhayes
Dulcis Cross
Higher Westwater

167

Mast Cloakham

2

Burrow Farm Gdns
Sunnylands Cross
Marsh Farm
Dulcis Farm
Woodhouse Farm

Uphay Farm

Loughwood Farm
Corry Brook
Studhayes Farm

Lower Westwater Dairy Farm

99

Andrewshayes Farm
Studhayes Cross
Fordhayes Farm
Coryton

AXMINSTER

1

Hill Crest
Gapemouth Cnr
Balfour Terr
Salisbury Terr
The Crescent
Whitehayes Cross
Coryton
Roman Rd
Whitehayes
Newtons Orch
Lynhayes
Silver St
Silver Lea
The Orchard
Whitford Rd
Brookside Cl
Whitehayes Cl

Hunthay Farm

Libr
Mus

Taunton Cross
Bakeins Mead
Shute Rd
Ashes Rd
Springhead La
Well Mead
The Street
Gammons Hill
A35
B3261
Axminster

98

24   A   25   B   26   C   27   D   28   E   29   F

103

88

For full street detail of the highlighted area see page 167.

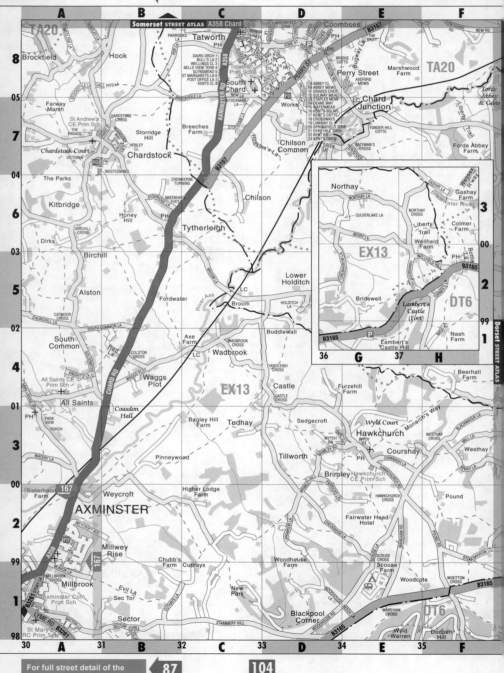

Scale: 1½ inches to 1 mile

Somerset STREET ATLAS A358 Chard

For full street detail of the highlighted area see page 167.

87

104

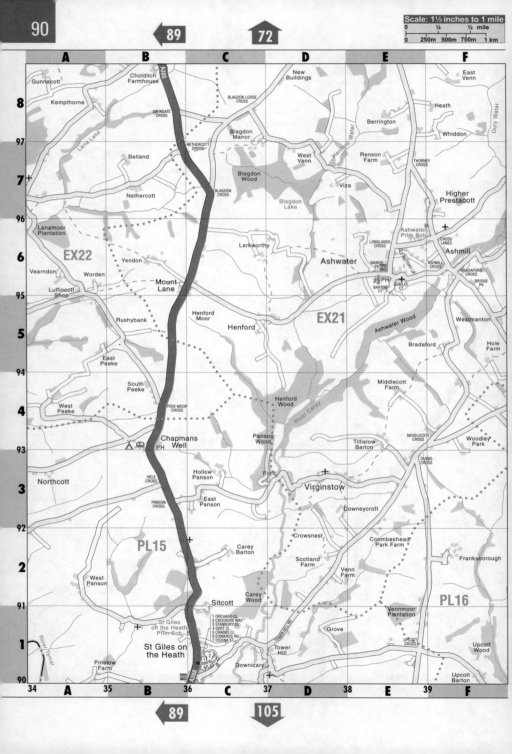

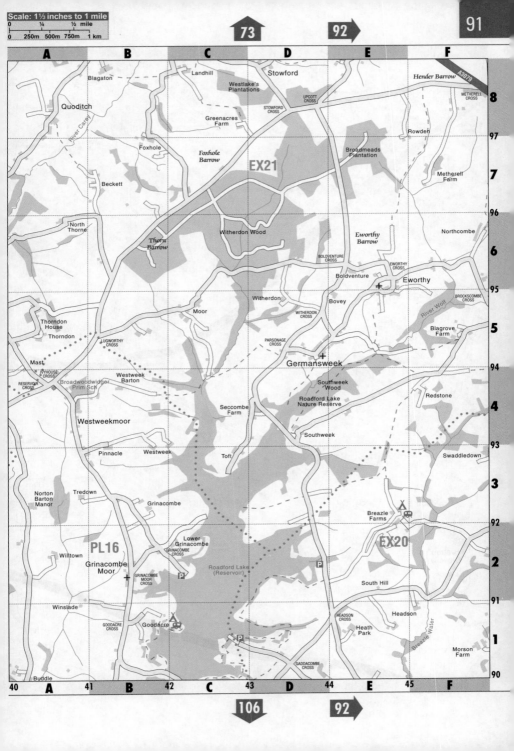

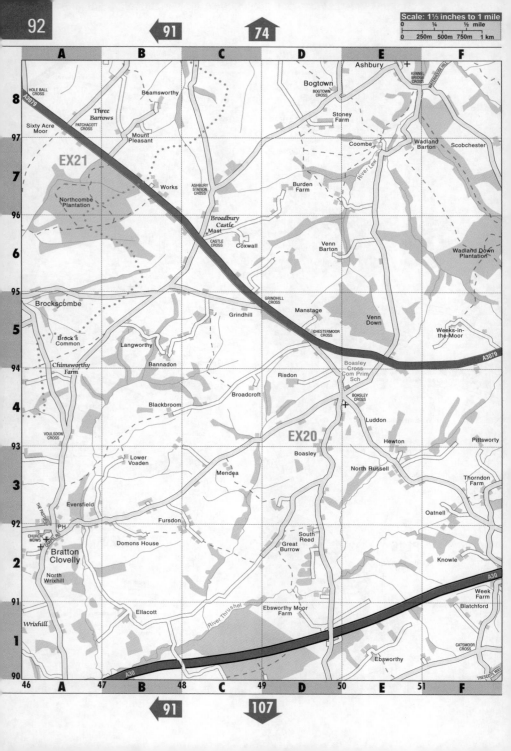

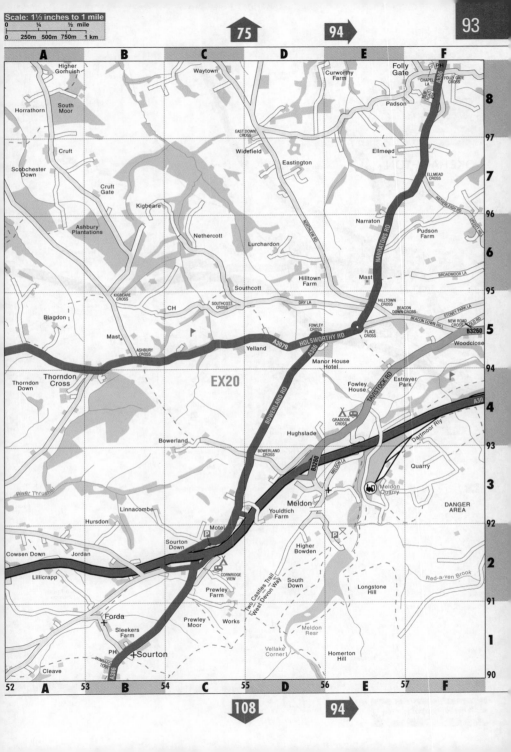

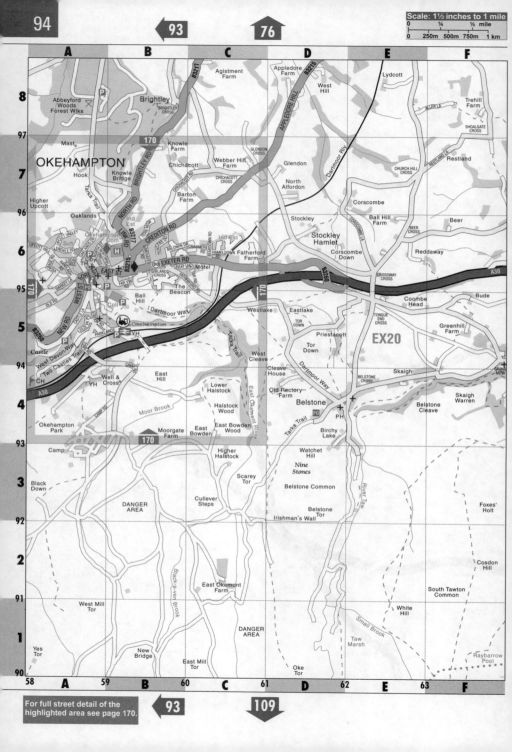

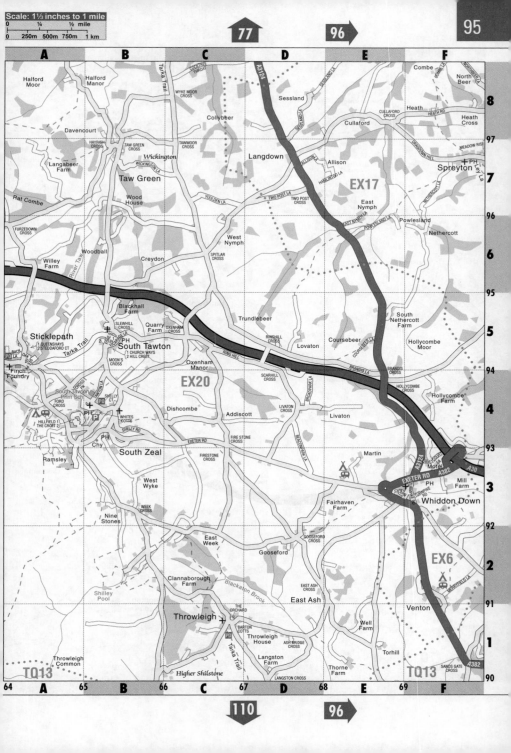

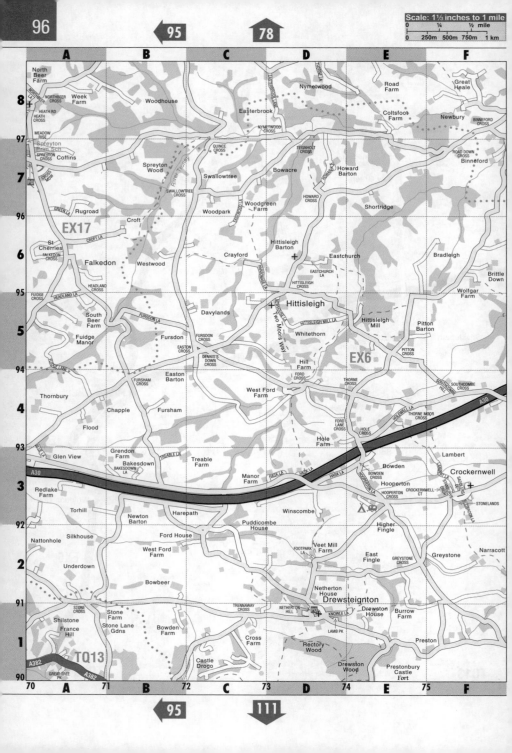

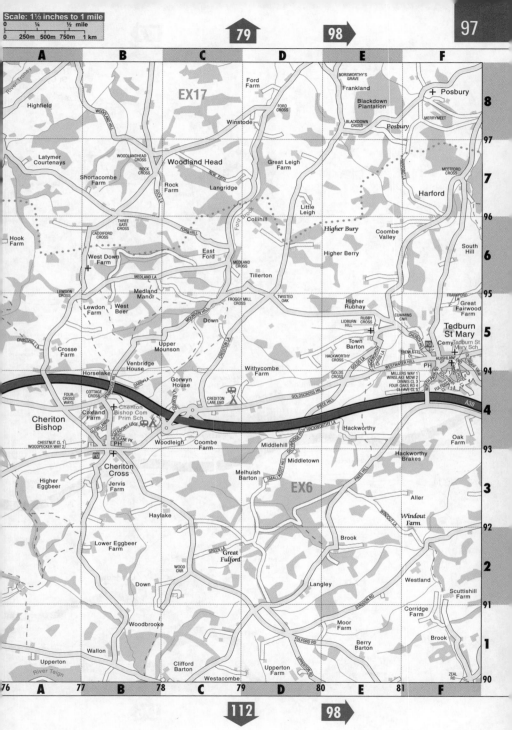

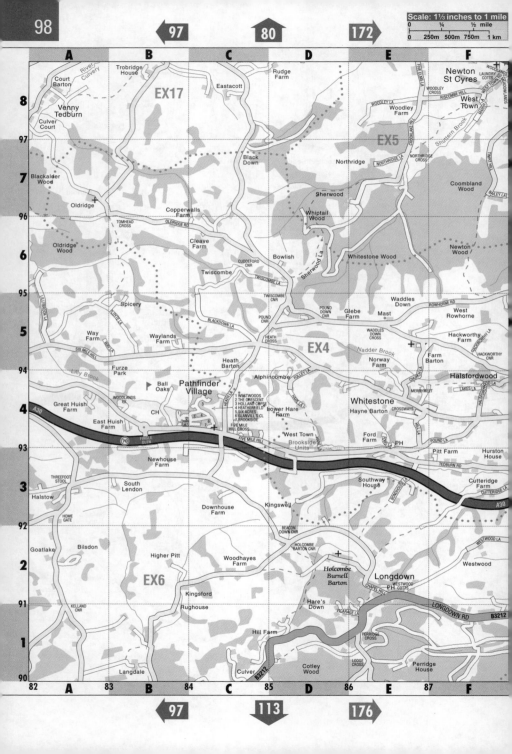

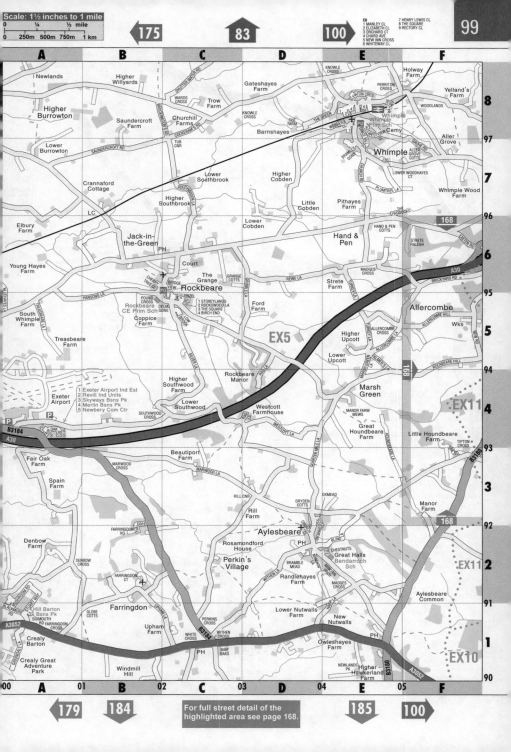

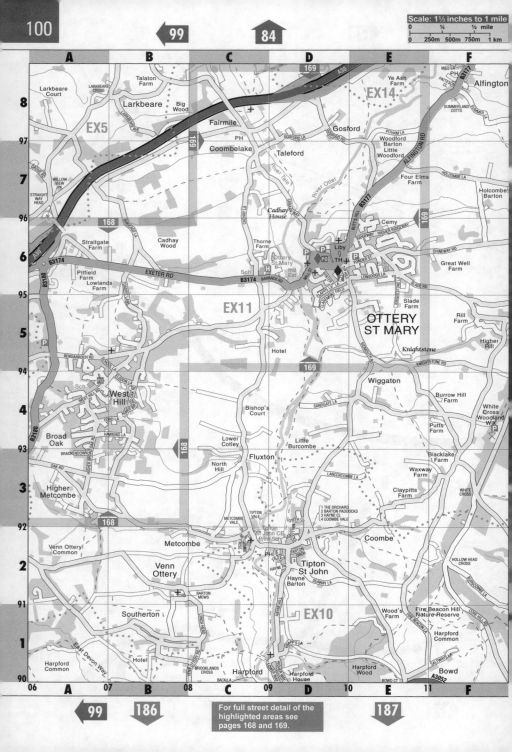

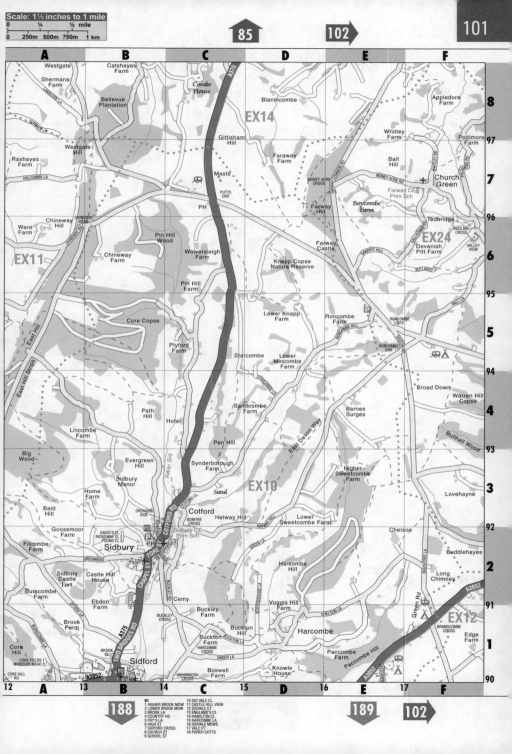

Scale: 1½ inches to 1 mile
0 ¼ ½ mile
0 250m 500m 750m 1 km

8

Glanville Farm
EX14
Townshayne Common
Slade
Home Bush
EX14
Watchcombe
OFFWELL TURN
NORTHLEIGH RD
Smallicombe Farm
Cookshayes Farm
Stockers Farm
Sutton Thorn
EX13
Summerdown
BUCKNOLE CROSS
Umborne

97

PAINTER'S CROSS
NORTHLEIGH CROSS
Blamphayne Farm
BLAMPHAYNE CROSS
EASY BRIDGE CROSS

7

Bucknole Farm
COMBE LA
Tricombe
ROCKERHAYNE CROSS
Parehayne Hill
Parehayne Farm
Logshayne Farm
LILYLAKE CROSS

96

Chilcombe
CHILCOMBE CROSS
Northleigh
BUCKHOUSE LA
Rockerhayne
Yardbury Farm
Netherton Barton
HILLSIDE
Ball Hill
FARWOOD CROSS
Carswells Moor
Downhayne Farm
THREE SYCAMORES CROSS
Tritchayne
GATE CROSS

6

Farway
COLYTON RD
WOODBRIDGE LA
Farwood Barton
Road Pitt Farm
Hamberhayne Farm
HAMBERHAYNE CROSS
Barritshayes
RED CROSS
Gittshayne Farm

95

Goldacre Farm
Woodbridge
SUDDON'S CROSS
SUDDON'S LA
PURLBRIDGE CROSS
NORTHLEIGH RD
COLEMAN'S CROSS
East Devon Way
Streathayne House
Hooperhayne
GITTSHAYNE CROSS
Widcombe Barton Farm
Holnest Farm
HORNSHAYNE RD
BLACKACRE RD
Knowle Hill
Bonehayne
River Coly

5

Widcombe Wood
Hornshayne Farm
STUBBING CROSS
Moorplash Farm
BONEHAYNE AND PURLBRIDGE RD
RATSHOLE GATE

94

Whitmoor
Blackley Down
EX24
Glebe House
Scruel Barton
Great Pen
Wadden
HEATHAYNE CROSS
Heathayne
Ox Hill
GUERNSEY CNR
RIDGWAY LA

4

Higher Wiscombe
Eppitts
Southleigh
HILLSIDE
Morganhayes
MORGANHAYES CROSS
JOBB'S LA
Ridgeway
Wiscombe Park
WHITE GATE
Bolshayne Farm
SALTER'S LA

93

Southleigh Hills
Weekhayne
Morganhayes Covert
Colyton Hill
Whitwell Farm

3

Blackbury Castle Settlement
SOUTHLEIGH HILL CROSS
Stockham
GREEN
Pratt's Hill
Holyford
Little Farm
Holyford Woods Nature Reserve

92

Radish Plantation
BURNBREACH CNR
Bovey Down
Ashdown Farm
Seaton Down
EX12

2

SEATON RD
Borcombe Farm
PH
A3052
GATCOMBE ASH
Hotel
HAREPATH HILL
A3052
Meml
190
Stafford Cross
Gatcombe Farm
Seaton Down Hill
SEATON DOWN RD
191

91

Elverway Farm
Hangman's Stone
B3174
191
Couchill Farm
HOLLYHEAD RD

1

190
Bovey House
HOLLYHEAD RD
B3174
HOLYHEAD CROSS
B3174

90

Rockenhayne
WOODHEAD CROSS
SELLER'S WOOD HILL
Woodhead
BOVEY LA

18 A 19 B 20 C 21 D 22 E 23 F

For full street detail of the highlighted area see pages 190 and 191.

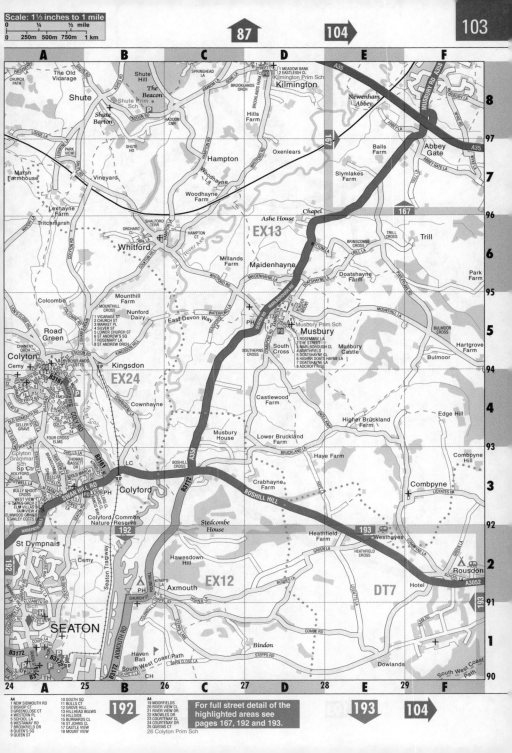

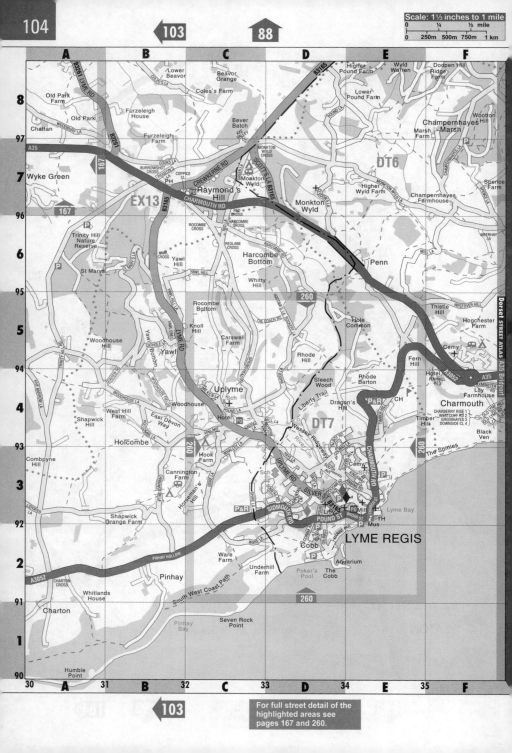

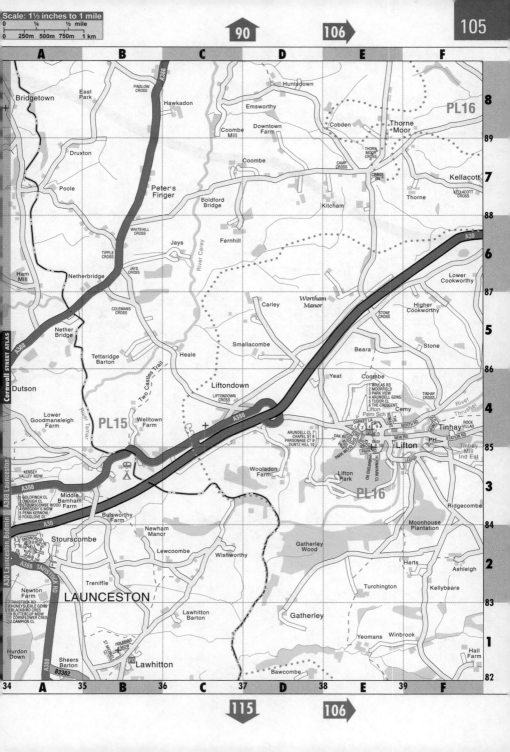

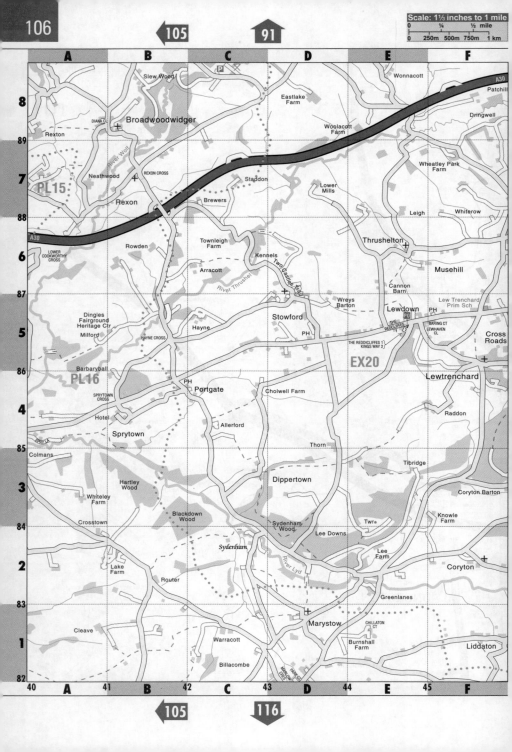

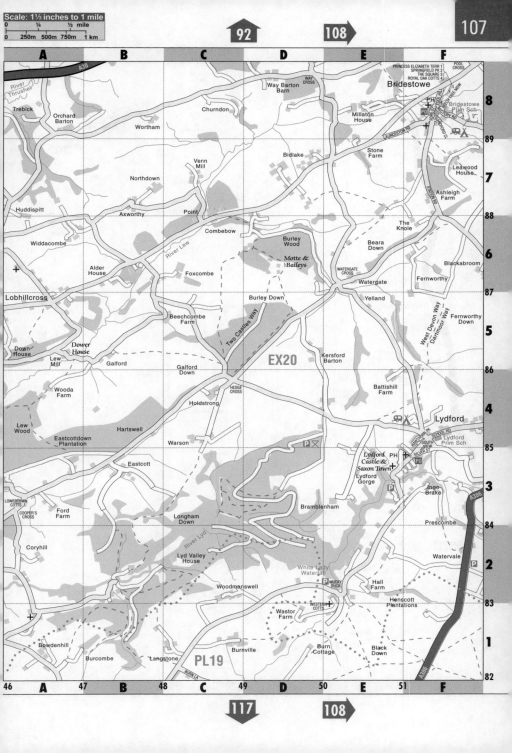

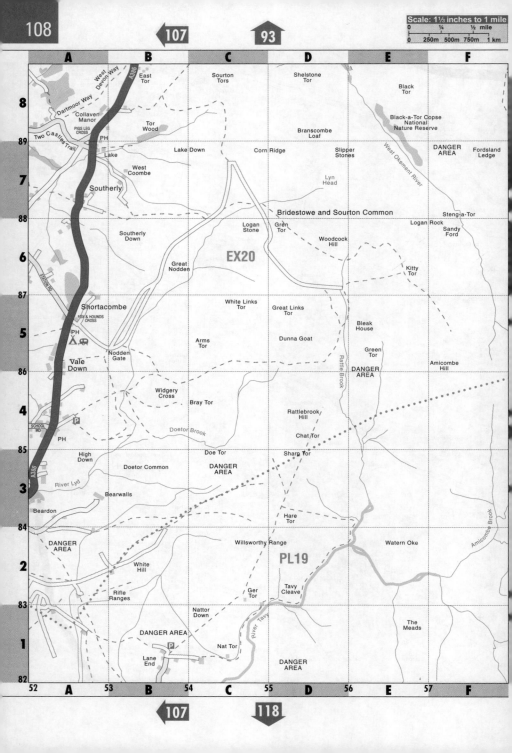

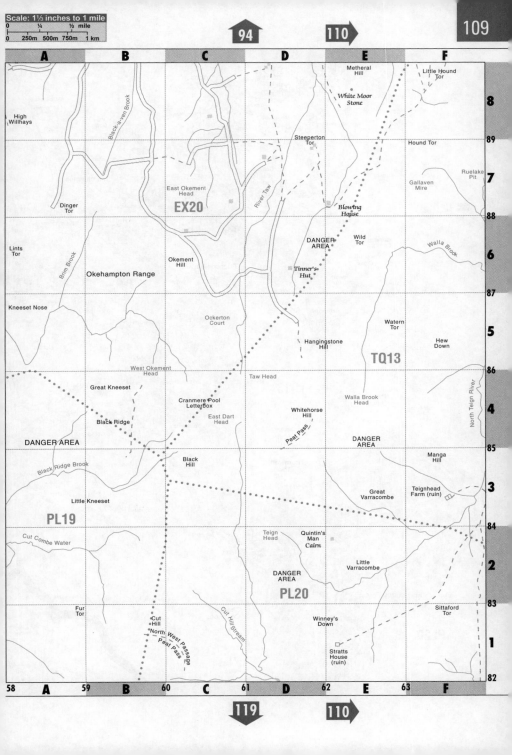

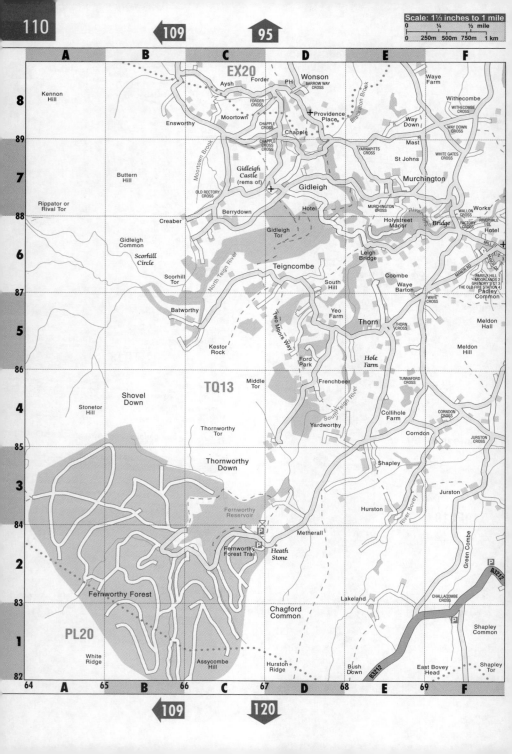

Scale: 1⅓ inches to 1 mile

0   ¼   ½ mile
0 250m 500m 750m 1 km

A B C D E F

Kennon
Hill

EX20

Aysh Forder PH Wonson
BARROW WAY
CROSS

Waye
Farm

Withecombe
WITHECOMBE
CROSS

FORDER
CROSS
Moortown
Ensworthy

Providence
Place

Way
Down

WAY DOWN
CROSS

CHAPPLE
CROSS
Chapple

Mast

CHAPPLE
CROSS CROSS

YARNAPITTS
CROSS

St Johns

WHITE GATES
CROSS

Buttern
Hill

Gidleigh
Castle
(rems of)

Gidleigh

Murchington

Rippator or
Rival Tor

OLD RECTORY
CROSS

Berrydown

Hotel

MURCHINGTON
CROSS

WALLON
CROSS

Works

RIVERVALE

Creaber

Gidleigh
Tor

Holystreet
Manor

Bridge
FACTORY
CROSS

Hotel

MILL LP

Gidleigh
Common

Scorhill
Circle

Teigncombe

Leigh
Bridge

MANOR RD

MANOR RD

PARELY HILL 1
MOORLANDS 2
GRENORY 3 CT 3
THE OLD FIRE STATION 4

Scorhill
Tor

South
Hill

Coombe

Waye
Barton

Padley
Common

Batworthy

Yeo
Farm

Thorn
THORN
CROSS

WAYE
CROSS

Meldon
Hall

TQ13

Kestor
Rock

Two Moors Way

Ford
Park

Hole
Farm

Frenchbeer

Meldon
Hill

Shovel
Down

Middle
Tor

TUNNAFORD
CROSS

Stonetor
Hill

Collihole
Farm

CORNDON
CROSS

Thornworthy
Tor

Yardworthy

Corndon

JURSTON
CROSS

Thornworthy
Down

Shapley

Jurston

Fernworthy
Reservoir

Hurston

Green Combe

P

Fernworthy
Forest Trail

P

Metherall

Heath
Stone

P
B3212

Fernworthy Forest

PL20

Lakeland

CHALLACOMBE
CROSS

P

Shapley
Common

White
Ridge

Assycombe
Hill

Hurston
Ridge

Bush
Down

B3212

East Bovey
Head

Shapley
Tor

Chagford
Common

River Bovey

South Teign River

North Teign River

Moortown Brook

Bracanton Brook

River

64 A 65 B 66 C 67 D 68 E 69 F

109 95

109 120

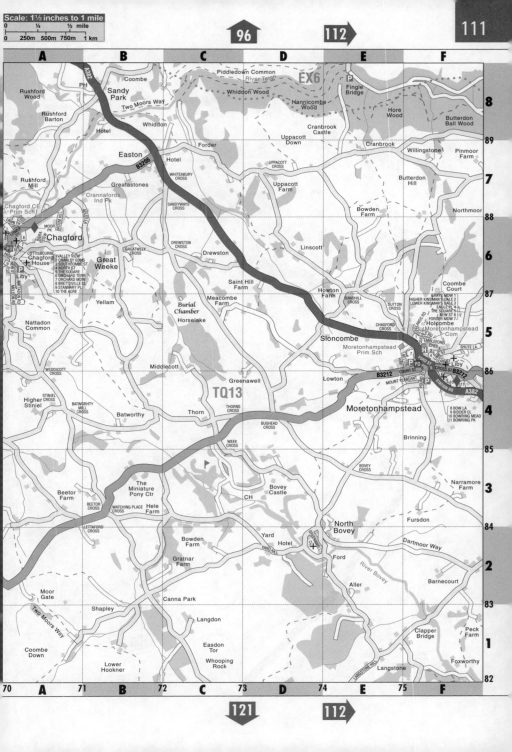

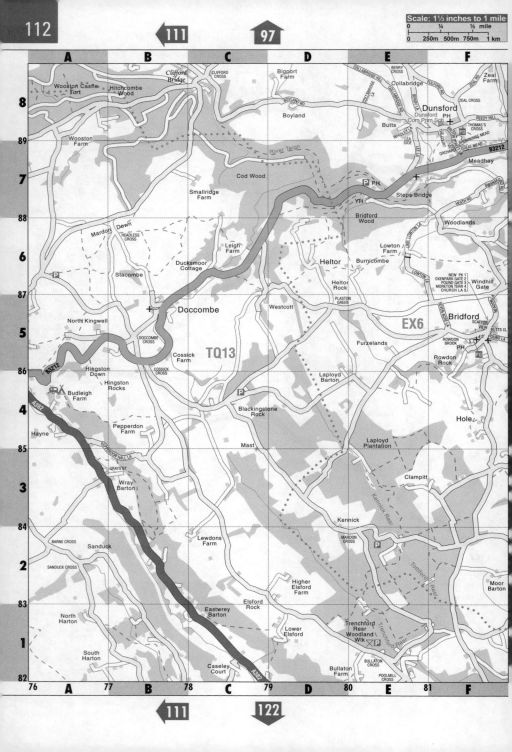

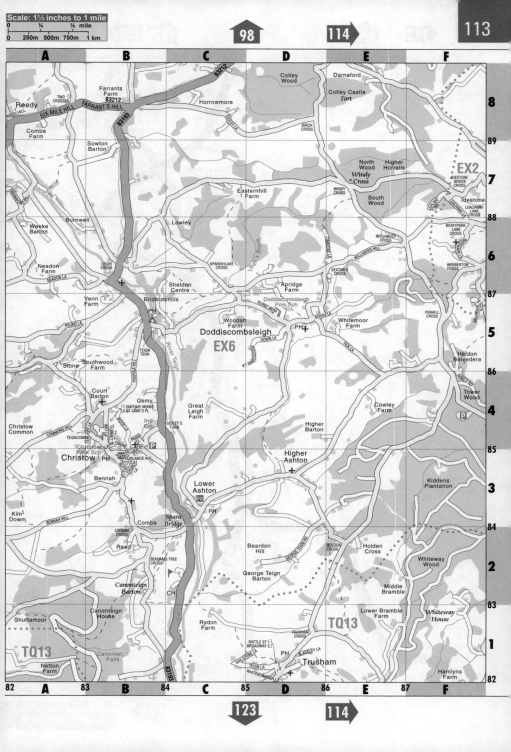

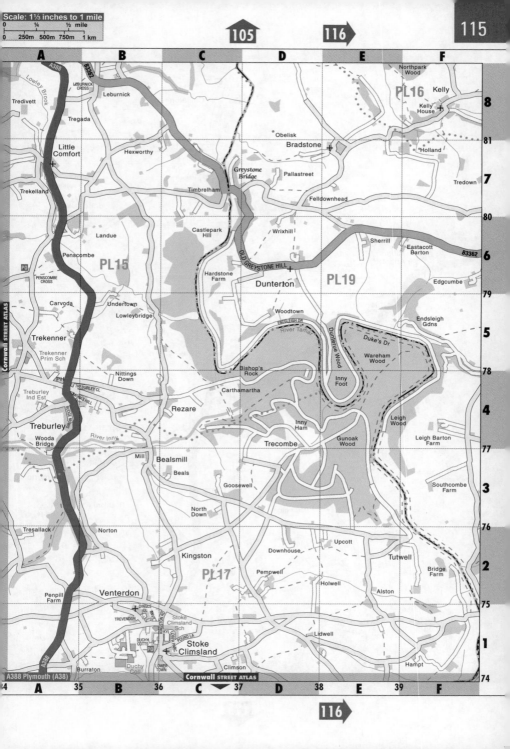

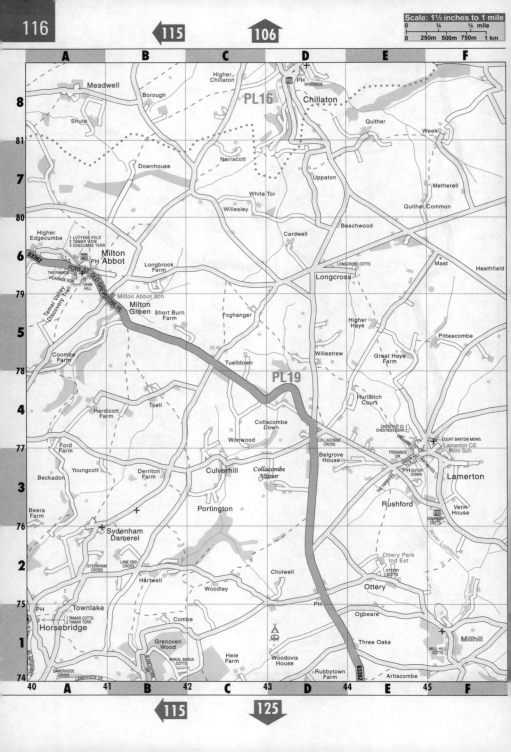

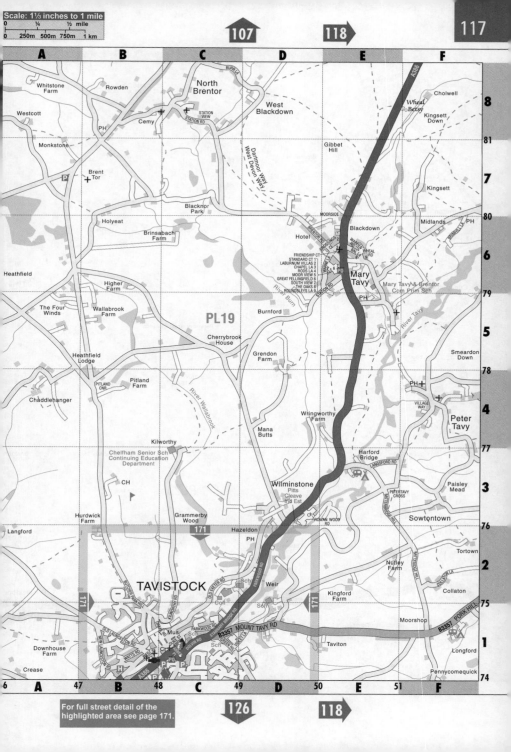

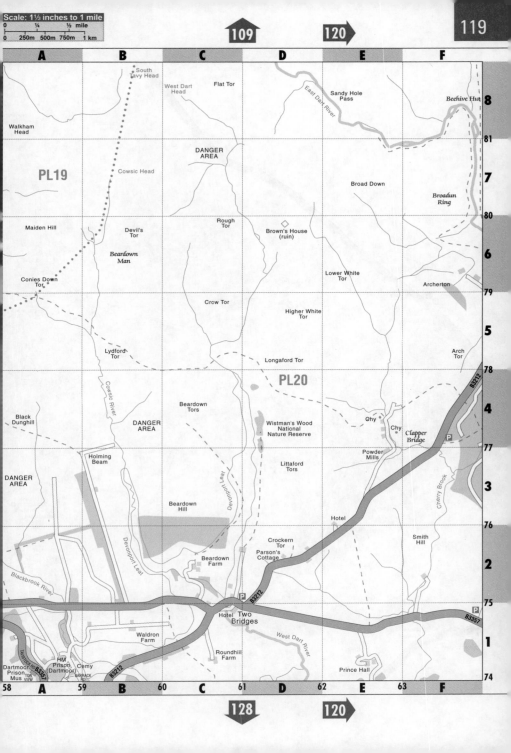

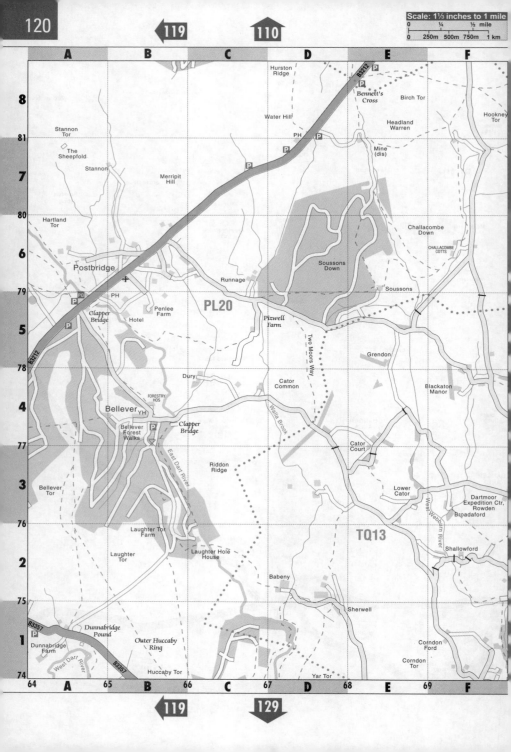

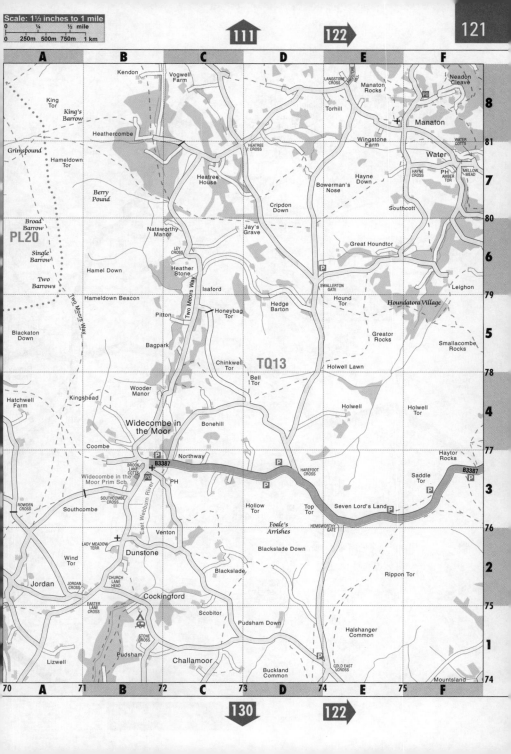

Scale: 1⅓ inches to 1 mile

0   ¼   ½ mile
0 250m 500m 750m 1 km

←121

↓131 For full street detail of the
highlighted area see page 180.

F1
1 LASKEYS HEATH
2 TAYLORS NEWTAKE
3 LEAT MDW
4 ROWELLS MEAD
5 BEAUMONT CL
6 DIVETT DR
7 MUNRO MEAD
8 POMEROY PL
9 FLOWERS MDW
10 KITTERSLEY DR
11 CHAPEL LA
12 BEANHAY CL
13 BENLEARS ACRE
14 BICKFORDS GN
15 SUMMERLANDS CL
16 SUMMERHILL RD
17 SUMMERHILL CRES
18 SUMMERHILL CL
19 BENEDICTS CL

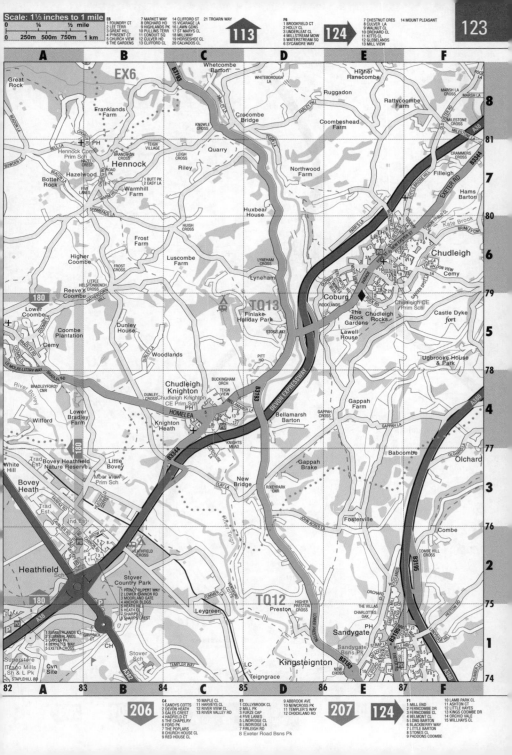

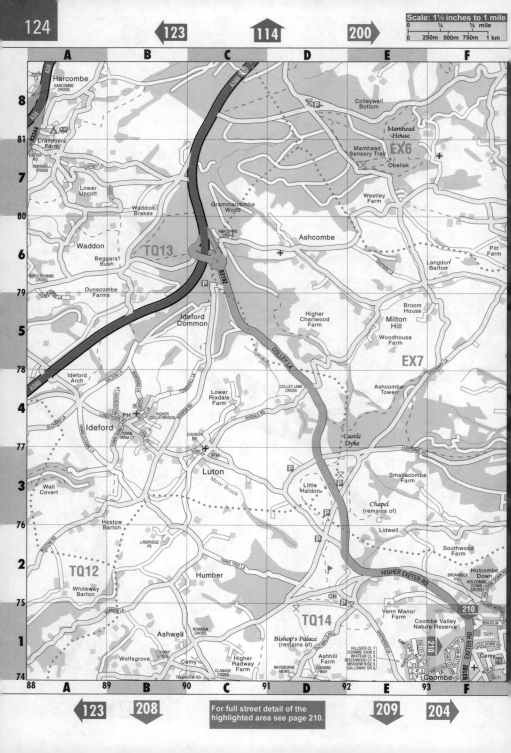

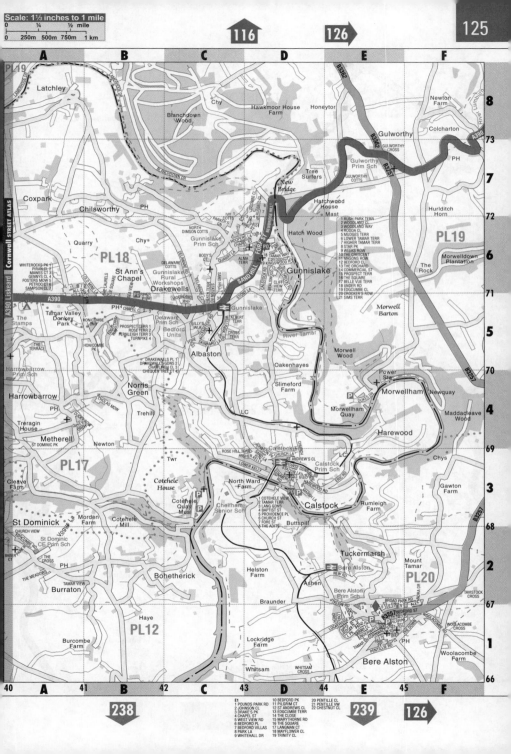

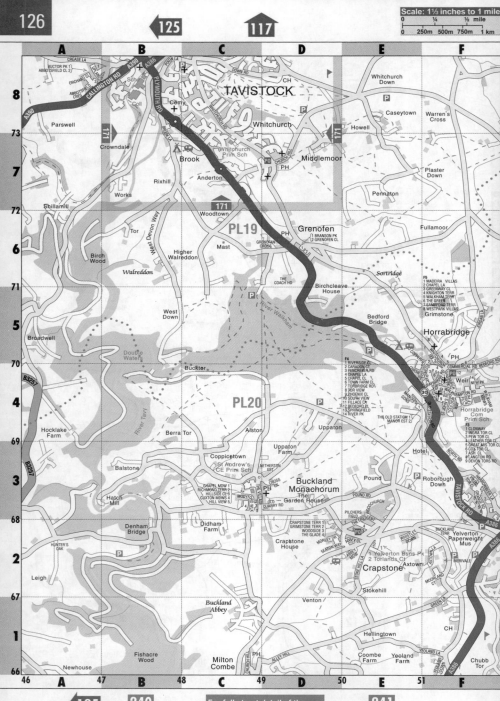

Scale: 1⅓ inches to 1 mile
0   ¼   ½ mile
0 250m 500m 750m 1 km

TAVISTOCK

PL19

PL20

For full street detail of the highlighted area see page 171.

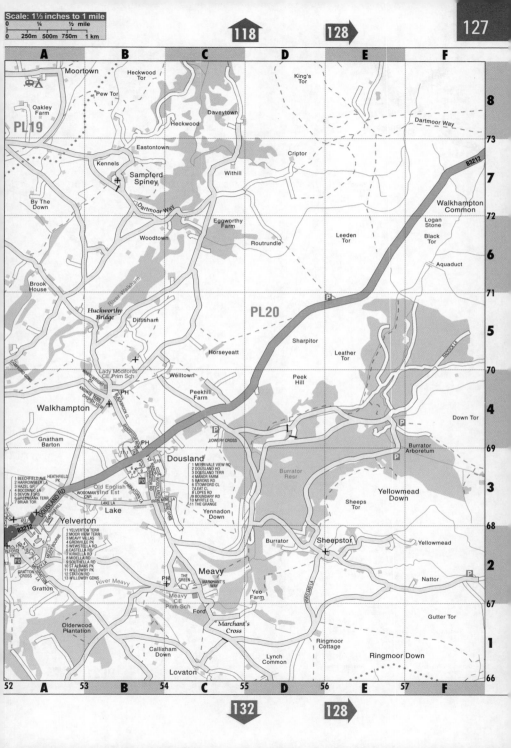

PL19

PL20

Moortown
Heckwood Tor
Pew Tor
Oakley Farm
Daveytown
Heckwood
King's Tor
Dartmoor Way
Eastontown
Criptor
Kennels
Sampford Spiney
Withill
Dartmoor Way
By The Down
Eggworthy Farm
Walkhampton Common
Logan Stone
Woodtown
Routrundle
Leeden Tor
Black Tor
Brook House
Aquaduct
Huckworthy Bridge
Dittisham
Sharpitor
Leather Tor
Horseyeatt
Lady Modfords CE Prim Sch
Welltown
Peek Hill
Down Tor
Walkhampton
Peekhill Farm
Gnatham Barton
Jowery Cross
Burrator Arboretum
Dousland
1 MERIVALE VIEW RD
2 DOUSLAND HO
3 DOUSLAND TERR
4 MANOR FARM
5 BARONS RD
6 STOWFORD CL
7 LEAT CL
8 LOPES RD
9 BOUNDARY RD
10 MYRTLE CL
11 THE GRANGE
Burrator Resr
Yellowmead Down
Old English
Woodman's Ind Est
Lake
Yennadon Down
Sheeps Tor
1 BEECHFIELD AVE
2 HARROWBEER LA
3 HAZEL GR
4 BOCONNIC LA
5 DEVON TORS
6 GREENBANK TERR
7 BRIAR TOR
Yelverton
1 YELVERTON TERR
2 MOOR VIEW TERR
3 MEAVY VILLAS
4 GRENVILLE PK
5 WELWSTELLA RD
6 EASTELLA RD
7 KIRKELLA RD
8 KASTELLA RD
9 SOUTHELLA RD
10 ST ALBANS PK
11 WILLOWBY PK
12 STATION RD
13 WILLOWBY GDNS
Burrator
Sheepstor
Yellowmead
B3212
Gratton Cross
Gratton
River Meavy
THE GREEN
Meavy
Marchant's Way
Yeo Farm
Nattor
Meavy CE Prim Sch
Ford
Olderwood Plantation
Marchant's Cross
Callisham Down
Lynch Common
Ringmoor Cottage
Gutter Tor
Ringmoor Down
Lovaton

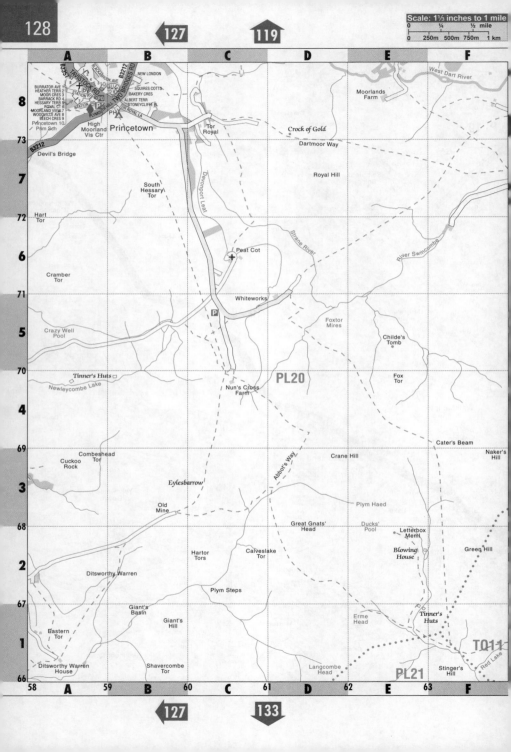

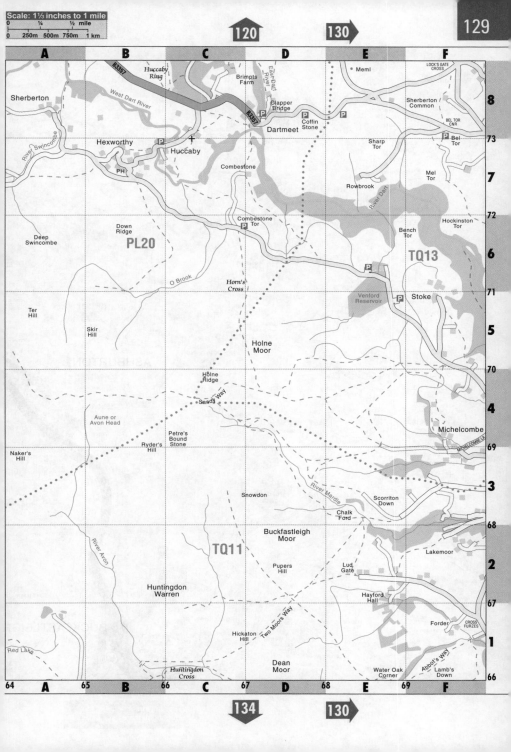

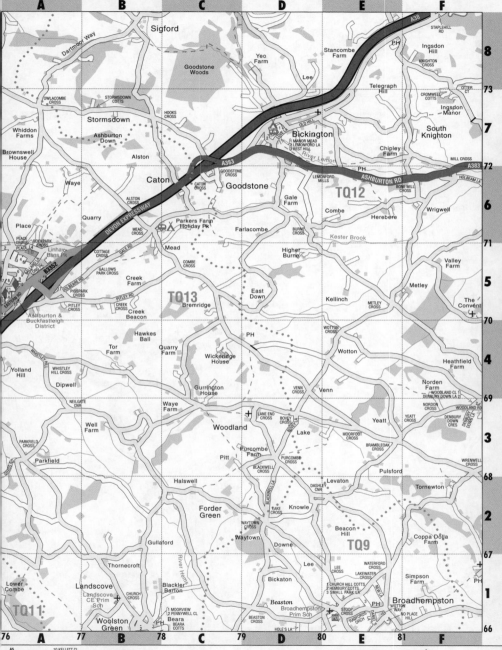

122
206
215
216
211

Scale: 1½ inches to 1 mile

0 ¼ ½ mile
0 250m 500m 750m 1 km

A B C D E F

8 73 7 72 6 71 5 70 4 69 3 68 2 67 1 66

A5
1 LONGSTONE CROSS
2 REW RD
3 ROBOROUGH GDNS
4 ROCK PK
5 BALLAND PK
6 BEVERLEY GDNS
7 ROBOROUGH LA
8 HIGHER ROBOROUGH
9 EMMETTS PK
10 KELLETT CL
11 MINERS CL
12 COOKS CL
13 HOME PK
14 DOLBEARE RD
15 JORDAN MDW
16 EAST END TERR
17 HOSPITAL LA
18 South Dartmoor
Com Coll

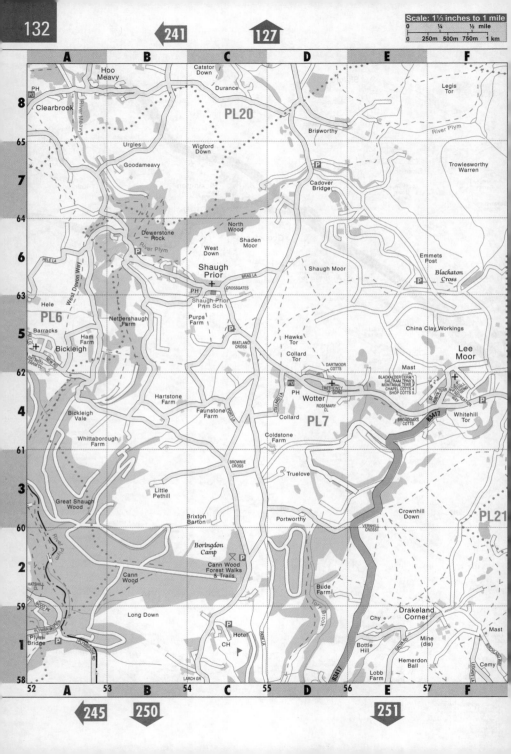

Scale: 1⅓ inches to 1 mile
0   ¼   ½   mile
0   250m   500m   750m   1 km

128
134

PL20

Hentor
Warren

Hen
Tor

Shavercombe
Head

Langcombe
Hill

Willings Walls
Warren

PL7

Yealm
Head

Lee
Moor

Broadall
Gulf

Stall
Moor

River Erme

Shell
Top

Penn
Moor

Penn
Beacon

High-House
Waste

Dendles
Waste

Broadall Lane

Cholwichtown
Farm

Rook
Tor

Dendles Wood National
Nature Reserve

PL21

Tolchmoor
Gate

Newpark
Waste

Watercombe

New
Waste

Quick
Bridge

Piall River

Rook

Yeo
Cotts

Hele
Cross

Yadsworthy
Farm

China Clay
Workings

Piall
Bridge

Heathfield
Cross

Rook La.

Tor

Wisdom
Farm

Rook
Lane End

Vicarage Hill

Blachford

Headon
Down

Delamore
House

Cornwood CE
Prim Sch

Hall
Cross

Hall
Farm

CHAPPLE PK 1
BACK LA 2
CHAPPEL LA 3
THE SQUARE 4
LONGFIELD CL 5

Green Lane

Hillcrest La.

PH

P.O.

PH

Cornwood

CROSSWAYS 1
NEWTOWN 2
CHURCH PK 3
CHURCHTOWN CL 4

Havelock
Terr

Delamore Rd

The Lane

Bridge Mill

Lutton

Harford

Tucker's Hill Head

Tucker's Wy

Dartmoor
Zoological Park

Yondertown

PL7

Corntown
Cross

Moor
Cross

Hangen
Down

Broomhill

River Erme

1 BIRCHLAND RD
2 BIRCHLAND WAY
3 BLACKLANDS CROSS

Slade

Whingreen

Combeshead
Cross

Hotel

Nats La.

Uppaton

136
134

A   B   C   D   E   F

8
65
7
64
6
63
5
62
4
61
3
60
2
59
1
58

58   A   59   B   60   C   61   D   62   E   63   F   58

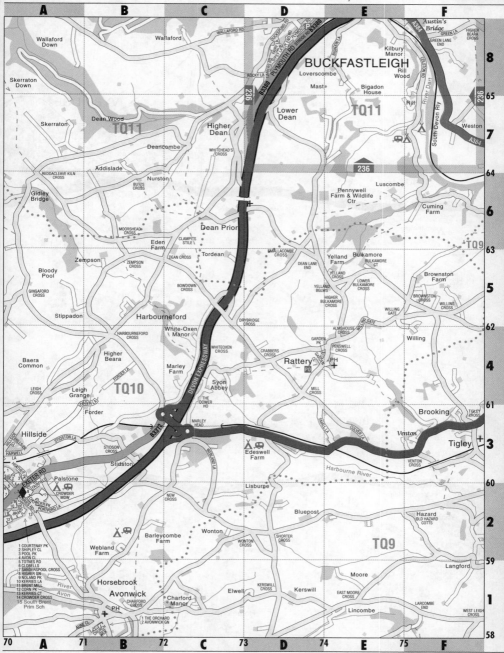

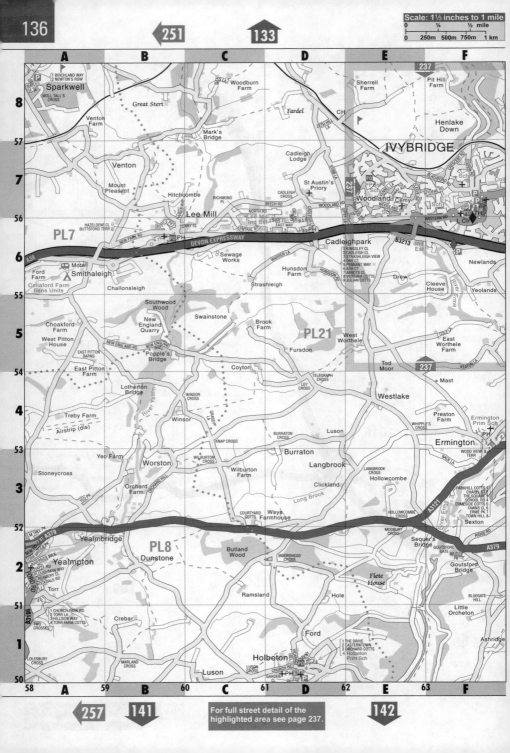

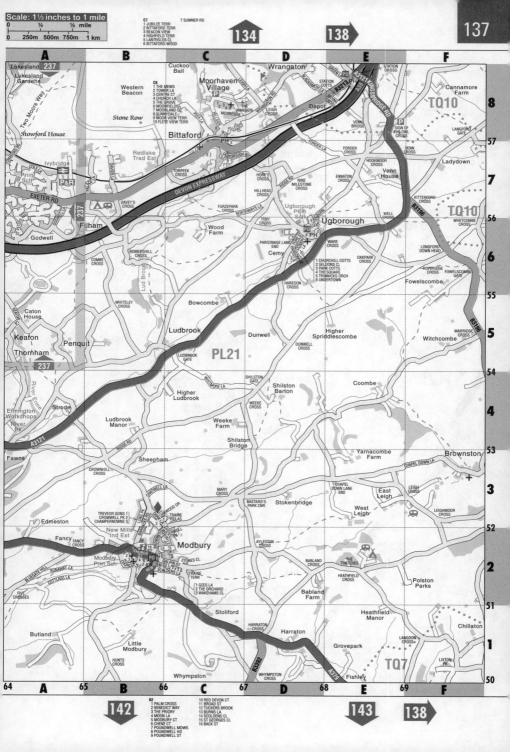

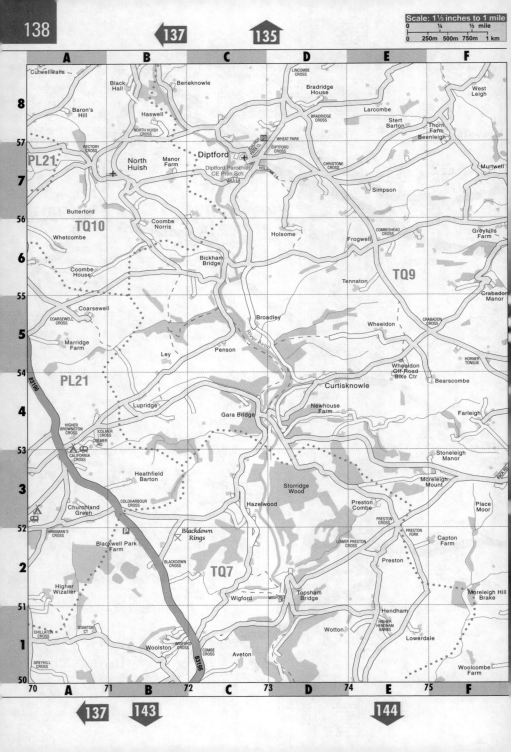

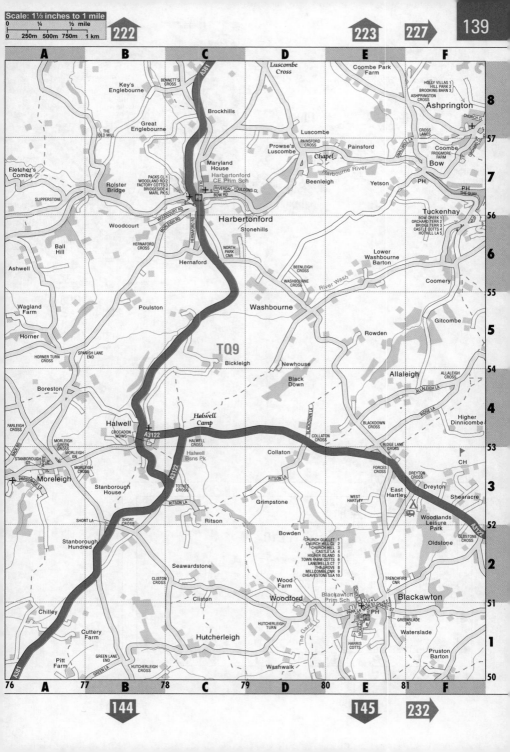

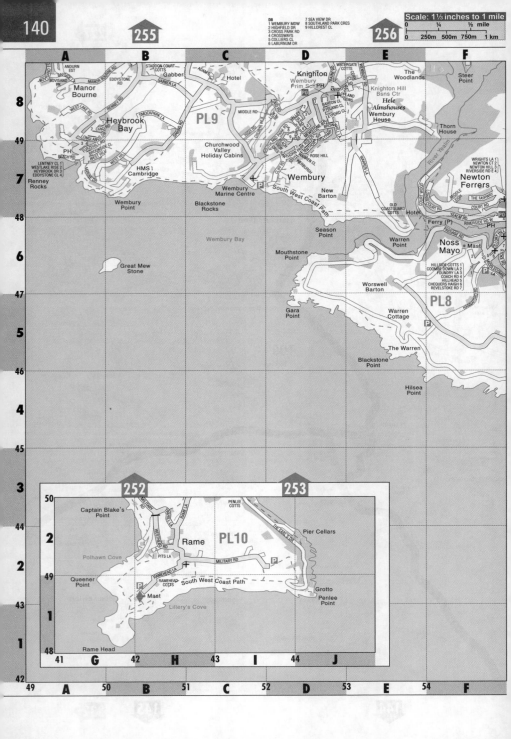

255 256

Scale: 1⅓ inches to 1 mile

D8
1 WEMBURY MDW
2 HIGHFIELD DR
3 CROSS PARK RD
4 CROSSWAYS
5 COLLIERS CL
6 LABURNUM DR
7 SEA VIEW DR
8 SOUTHLAND PARK CRES
9 HILLCREST CL

Manor
Bourne

ANDURN
EST

BOVISAND
PK

Heybrook
Bay

HMS
Cambridge

PH
BEACH RD

LENTNEY CL 1
WESTLAKE RISE 2
HEYBROOK DR 3
EDDYSTONE CL 4

Renney
Rocks

Wembury
Point

Blackstone
Rocks

Wembury Bay

Great Mew
Stone

PL9

Gabber

Hotel

STADDON COURT
COTTS

GABBER LA

Churchwood
Valley
Holiday Cabins

Wembury
Marine Centre

Knighton

Wembury
Prim Sch PH

Rose Hill

Wembury

South West Coast Path

New
Barton

Season
Point

Mouthstone
Point

Gara
Point

Worswell
Barton

Warren
Point

Warren
Cottage

The Warren

Blackstone
Point

Hilsea
Point

The
Woodlands

Steer
Point

Knighton Hill
Bsns Ctr

Hele
Almshouses
Wembury
House

Thorn
House

River Yealm

Newton
Ferrers

Ferry (P)

RIVERSIDE RD W

PH

Noss
Mayo

Mast

HILLSIDE COTTS 1
COOMBE DOWN LA 2
FOUNDRY LA 3
COACH RD 4
HILLHEAD 5
CHEQUERS HAIGH 6
REVELSTOKE RD 7

PL8

P

OLD
COASTGUARD
COTTS

Hotel

252 253

PL10

Captain Blake's
Point

Polhawn Cove

Queener
Point

Rame

Pier Cellars

PENLEE
COTTS

MILITARY RD

South West Coast Path

Grotto

Penlee
Point

Mast

Lillery's Cove

Rame Head

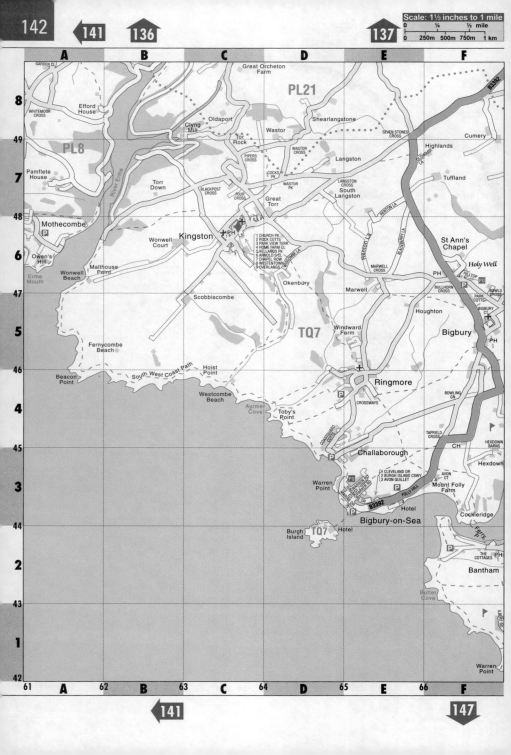

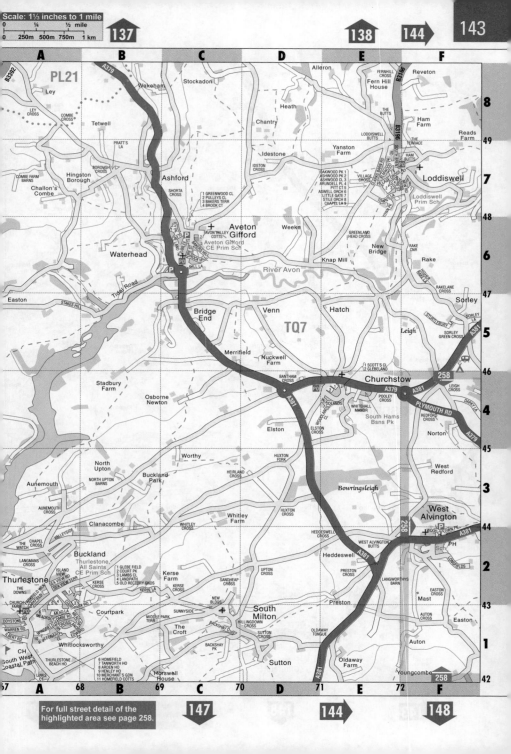

Scale: 1⅓ inches to 1 mile

0   ¼   ½ mile
0 250m 500m 750m 1 km

137

138   144

143

A   **B**   **C**   **D**   **E**   **F**

PL21

8

Ley

Wakeham

Stockadon

Alleron

FERNHILL CROSS

Reveton

Fern Hill House

49

LEY CROSS

COMBE CROSS

Tetwell

Heath

THE BUTTS

Ham Farm

Chantry

Reads Farm

Hingston Borough

BOROUGH CROSS

Ashford

LODDISWELL BUTTS

THE TERRACE

7

COMBE FARM BARNS

Challon's Combe

PRATT'S LA

SHORTA CROSS

Idestone

IDSTON CROSS

Yanston Farm

HAM BUTTS

Loddiswell

OAKWOOD PK 1
ASHWOOD PK 2
ASHWOOD CL 3
ARUNDEL PL 4
PITT CT 5
ASWELL ORCH 6
LITTLE GATE 7
STILE ORCH 8
CHAPEL LA 9

VILLAGE CROSS

Loddiswell Prim Sch

1 GREENWOOD CL
2 PULLEYS CL
3 BAKERS TERR
4 BROOK CT

48

Aveton Gifford

Weeke

GREENLAND HEAD CROSS

New Bridge

Waterhead

Aveton Gifford CE Prim Sch

RAKE CNR

Rake

6

Tidder Road

MILL LA

Knap Mill

RAKELANE CROSS

River Avon

47

Easton

STAKES HILL

Bridge End

Venn

Hatch

SORLEY LA

Sorley

SORLEY GREEN CROSS

5

Merrifield

TQ7

Leigh

Nuckwell Farm

BANTHAM CROSS

1 SCOTT'S CL
2 GLEBELAND

Churchstow

258

LEIGH CROSS

46

Stadbury Farm

POOLEY CROSS

A379

A381

PLYMOUTH RD

Osborne Newton

WOODLANDS

COLANDS

WHITEHALL MANOR

South Hams Bsns Pk

REDFORD CROSS

4

Elston

ELSTON CROSS

Norton

A379

45

Worthy

Huxton Fork

West Redford

North Upton

Buckland Park

HEIRLAND CROSS

3

Aunemouth

NORTH UPTON BARNS

Whitley Farm

HUXTON CROSS

Bowringsleigh

AUNEMOUTH CROSS

Clanacombe

WHITLEY CROSS

West Alvington

HEDDESWELL CROSS

258

44

VALLEYSIDE

THE WATCH

CHAPEL CROSS

Buckland

Kerse Farm

WEST ALVINGTON BUTTS

2

LANGMANS CROSS

ISLAND VIEW

Thurlestone All Saints CE Prim Sch

1 GLEBE FIELD
2 COURT PK
3 LAMBS CL
4 LANDPATH
5 OLD RECTORY GDNS

UPTON CROSS

Heddeswell

PRESTON CROSS

LANGWORTHYS BARN

Thurlestone

SEA VIEW TERR

KERSE CROSS

SANDHEAP CROSS

Preston

Mast

EASTON CROSS

THE DOWNS

KERSE LA

CHURCHFIELD VW

Courtpark

Sunnyside

NEW BLDGS

AUTON CROSS

Easton

43

CHURCHFIELD FARM

MIDDLE FARM TERR

HILLINGDOWN CROSS

South Milton

DDYSTONE RD

WINGFIELD COMBE RD

The Croft

BACKSHAY CL

SUTTON CROSS

Auton

1

WARREN RD

Whitlocksworthy

BACKSHAY PK

Sutton

OLDAWAY TONGUE

South West Coastal Path

LINKS CT

THURLESTONE BEACH HO

Horswell House

6 HOMEFIELD
7 TANWORTH HO
8 ARDEN HO
9 HENLEY HO
10 MERCHANTS GDN
11 HOMEFIELD COTTS

Oldaway Farm

Youngcombe

258

42

A   **B**   **C**   **D**   **E**   **F**

67   68   69   70   71   72

147

144

148

For full street detail of the highlighted area see page 258.

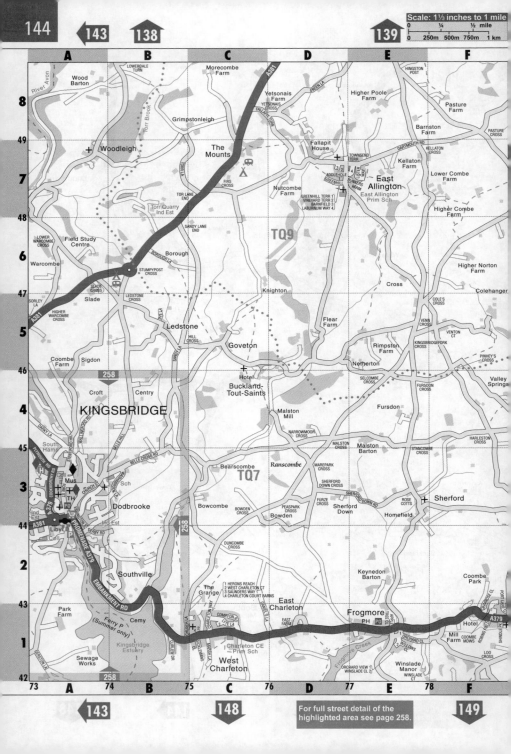

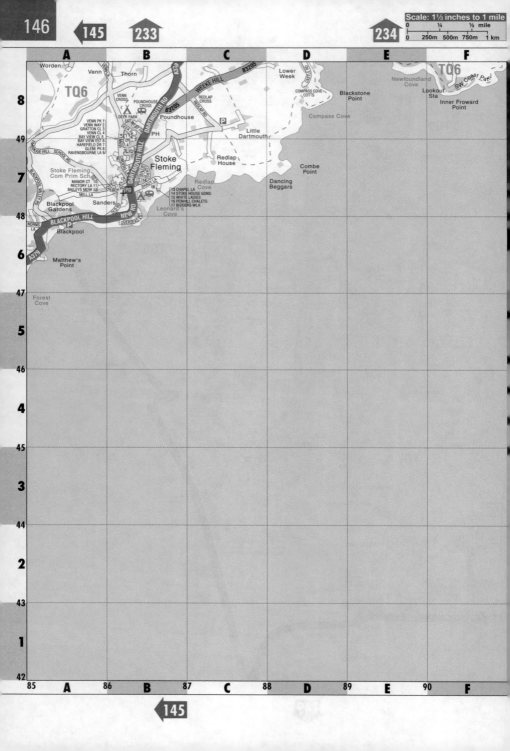

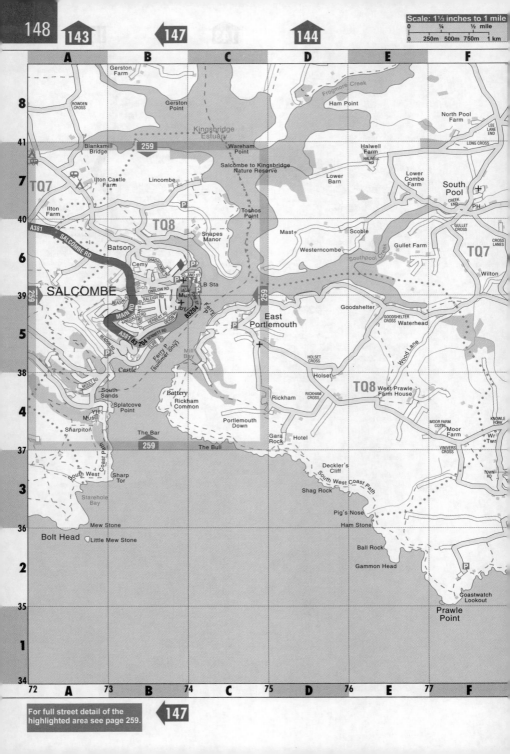

Scale: 1⅓ inches to 1 mile

0 ¼ ½ mile
0 250m 500m 750m 1 km

Molescombe

MARBER CROSS

RIDGE CROSS

DURLESTONE CROSS

EASTPARK

Kernborough

Cotmore

BEESON POOL

Widdicombe House

Mast

Hotel

SUNNYDALE

Burial Gd

FORD CROSS

Moyson

BEESON CROSS

Beeson

Dunstone

HUCKHAM BARN CROSS

DUNSTONE CROSS

Huccombe

THE COUNCIL HOUSES

Beesands

PH

Ford

COUSIN'S CROSS

Kellaton

Batton Farm

KELLATON CROSS

Higher Middlecombe Farm

South West Coast Path

Tinsey Head

TQ7

HILL PK

Muckwell

Chivelstone

NEW HOUSES

CHIVELSTONE CROSS

THE MALTINGS

South Allington

BICKERTON TOP

FORDWORTHY

Bickerton

Hotel

Greenstraight

Hallsands

LANNACOMBE GN

HOLLOWCOMBE HEAD

HIGHER BOROUGH

Down Farm

Masts

Start Farm

Nestley Point

Lower Borough

Woodcombe Farm

OWN RD

GHER PK

Lannacombe Beach

The Narrows

Start Point

Raven's Cove

East Prawle

PH

Maelcombe House

Lannacombe Bay

SEAVIEW

Langerstone Point

41

7

40

6

39

5

38

4

37

3

36

2

35

1

34

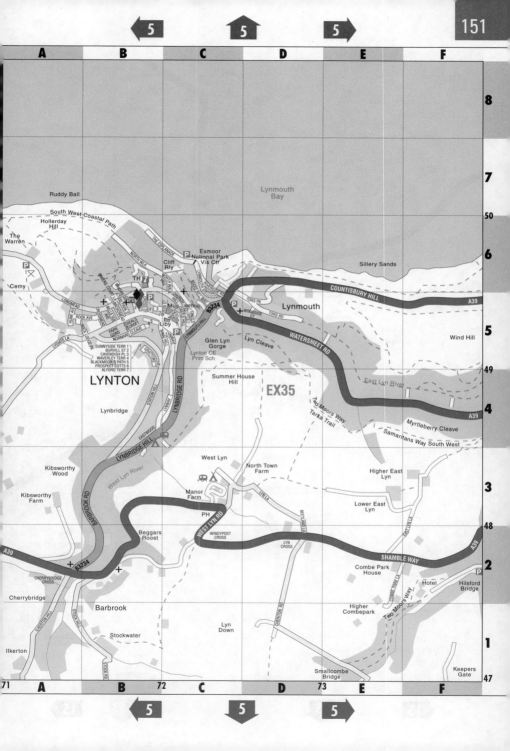

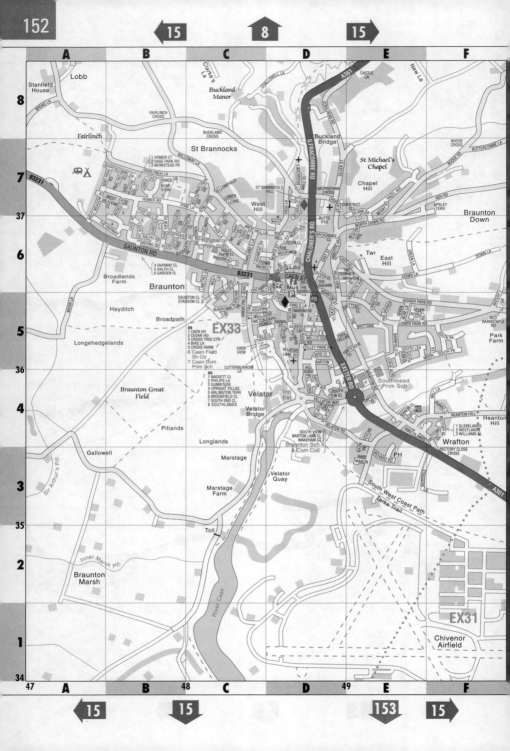

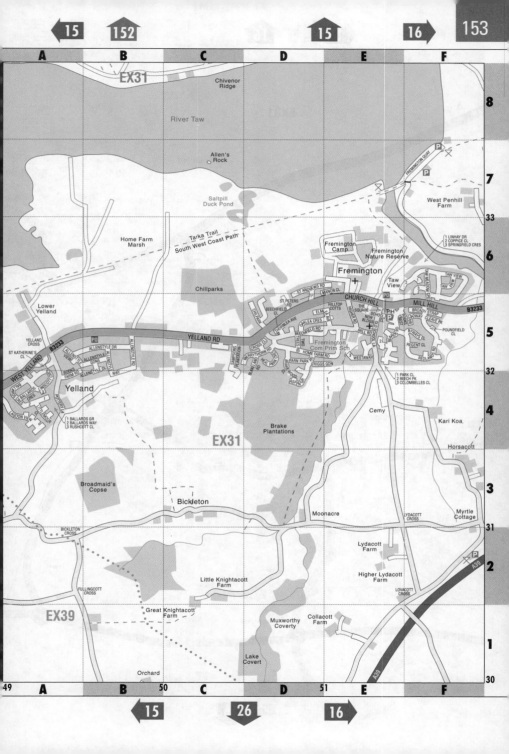

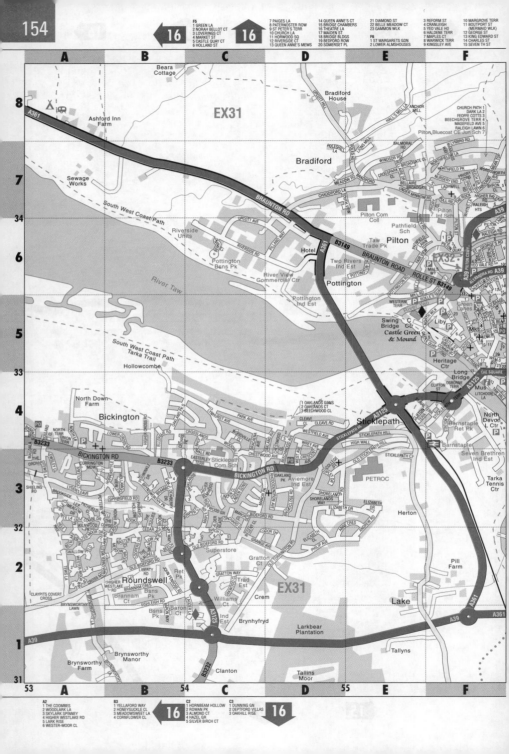

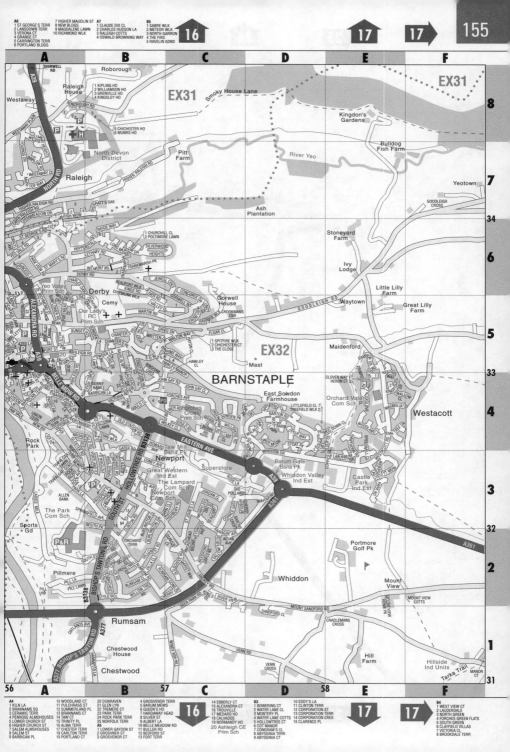

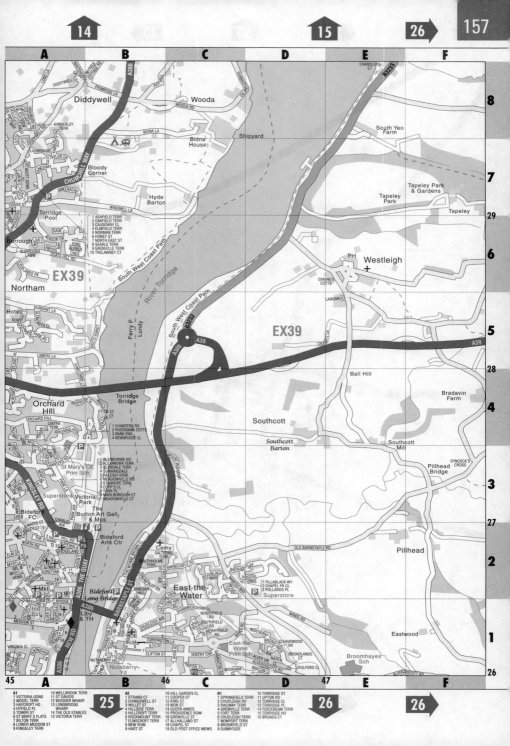

Diddywell

Wooda

WOODA RD

Shipyard

South Yeo Farm

Bidna House

CHANDLERS CT

B3233

Bloody Corner

Hyde Barton

WINDMILL LA

Tapeley Park & Gardens

Tapeley Park

Tapeley

8

7

29

6

1 ASHFIELD TERR
2 OAKFIELD TERR
3 CAUSEWAY CL
4 ELMFIELD TERR
5 NORMAN TERR
6 HONEY ST
7 NORTH EAST ST
8 SEARLE TERR
9 GRENVILLE TERR
10 TRELAWNEY CT

Torridge Pool

PH

Westleigh

Burrough

BURROUGH LAWN

KING ALFRED CRES

OXMAN'S COTTS

EX39

Northam

Hotel

South West Coast Path

River Torridge

LANGMEAD

EX39

Ferry P Lundy

South West Coast Path

B3233

A386 A39

Ball Hill

Bradavin Farm

5

28

4

Orchard Hill

Torridge Bridge

1 CHANTERS RD
2 RIVERBANK COTTS
3 BANK END
4 NEWBRIDGE CL

Southcott

Southcott Barton

Southcott Mill

Pillhead Bridge

SYNCOCK'S CROSS

1 OLENBURNIE HO
2 ALEXANDRA TERR
3 GLENDALE TERR
4 SUNNINGDALE
5 RALEIGH VIEW
6 MEADOWVILLE RD
7 STANHOPE TERR
8 COPP'S CL
9 YORK PL
10 MARLBOROUGH CT
11 MEADOWVILLE CT

St Mary's CE Prim Sch

Superstore

Victoria Park

The Burton Art Gall & Mus

Bideford FC

Bideford Arts Ctr

3

27

2

1

26

KINGSLEY RD

THE QUAY

Cemy

SALTERNS TERR

SOUTHOLME TERR

Bideford Long Bridge

NEW RD

A386

Liby & TH

East-the-Water

OLD BARNSTAPLE RD

ROGERS CRES

1 FILLABLACK WY
2 CHAPEL PK CL
3 POLLARDS PL

Superstore

Pillhead

Eastwood

NORTHFIELD RD

SOUTHFIELD RD

MERRYFIELD RD

MINES RD

East-the-Water Prim Sch

CLEAVEWOOD DR

BROADLANDS CT

Broomhayes Sch

TORRINGTON LA

CLIFTON ST

SENTRY CRE

WICKHAM

BRAYTON

FULFORD RD

BRECON CL

ALVER DR

Virginia Cl

NUTABERRY HILL

Nutaberry Yd

Mkt

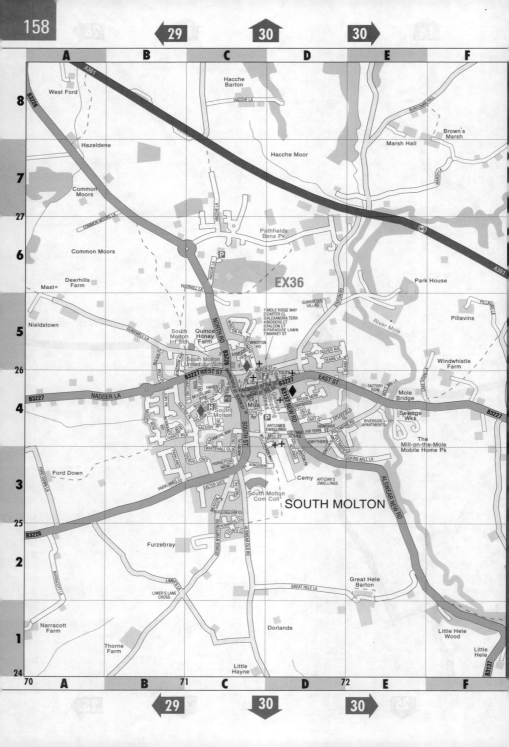

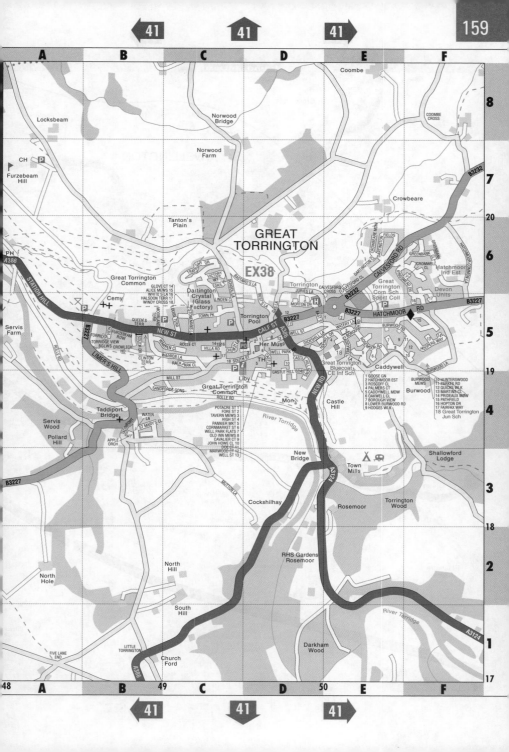

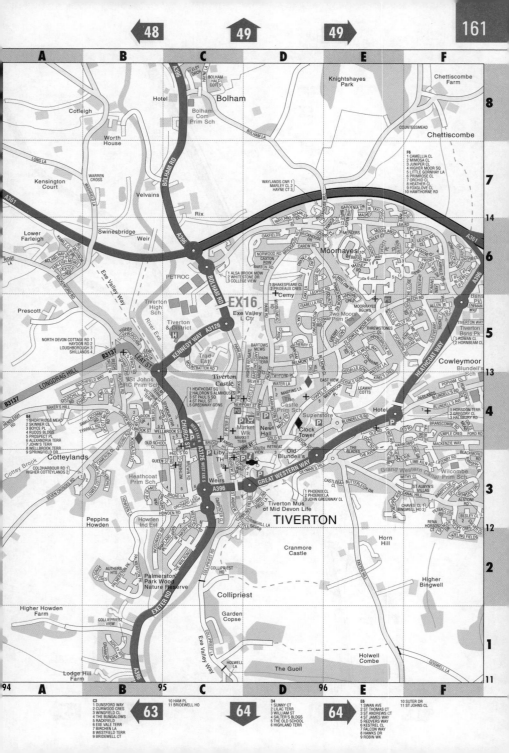

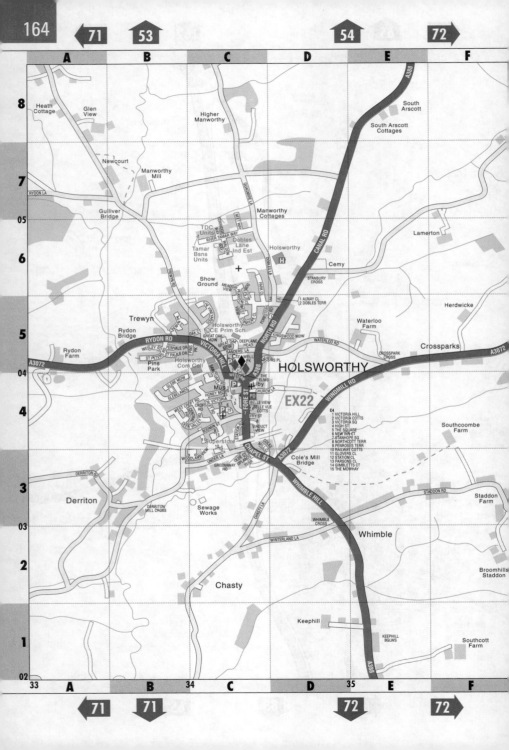

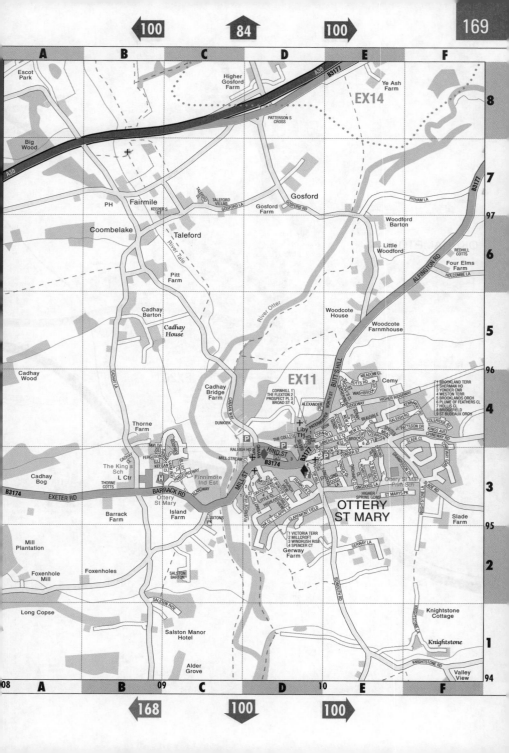

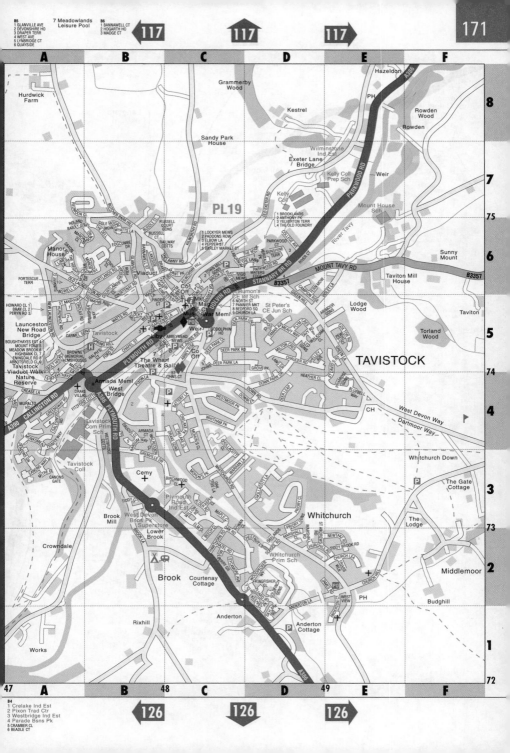

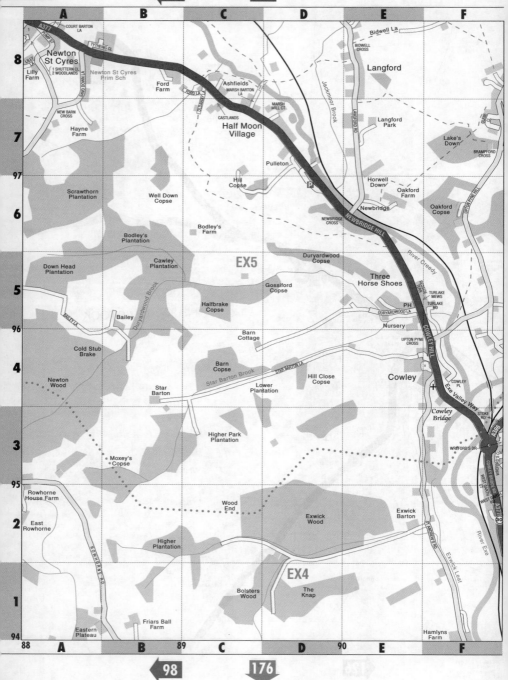

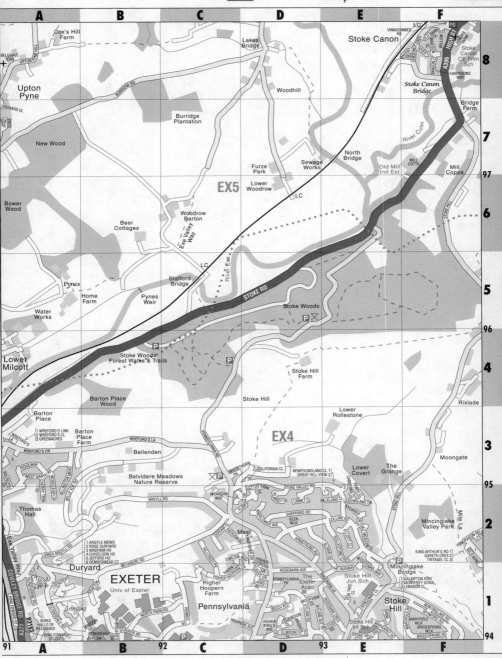

A B C D E F

8

Broadclyst Moor

Martinsfields

River Clyst

Little Burrow Farm

Haymans Farm

Burrow

FORCHES HEAD

BURROW RD

Broadclyst Com Prim Sch

QUEEN'S SQ
PH
SCHOOL LA
CHURCH CL

Clyston Mill

BURROW CROSS

7

Marker's Cottage

TOWN HILL
HELLINGS GDNS
SMALL LA
TREE RD

Lake Farm

New Inn (PH)

Loxbrook Farm

WILTSHIER CL
CHURCH CL
SUNNYFIELD

Broadclyst

Rec Gd

MAJOR

97

Caravan Site

Crabhayes

6

Wr Twr

WILLOW GDNS
MOORHEAD
POUNDS CL
MAPLE
BROAD VIEW
WOODLANDS
CEDAR CL TERR

Heath

1 WOODLAND MEWS
2 OAKTREE CL
3 SYCAMORE CU
4 GREEN TREE LA
5 WOODBURY VIEW

Southern Lake

EX4

Old Lodge

River Clyst

Jarvishayes

ELM CLOSE
ORCHARD GDNS
ACLAND RD

SANDERS CL
ORCHARD GDNS

Dog Village

Windmill (dis)

Paynes Farm

Liby

OLD CHAPEL RD
TOWER RD

Clyst Vale Com Coll

Sp Ctr

SANDY LA

Hellings Parks

5

Heathfield Farm

Beggars Bush

96

Highfield

Kerswell House

Brockhill Lodge

EX5

CHURCH LA

4

Withy Bridge

Kerswell Barton

Brockhill

Wishford Farm

HELLINGS PARKS LA

WESTCLYST

30

West Clyst Farm

STATION RD

Lodge Trad Est

RAILWAY TERR

Blue Hayes

BURCHES LA

3

Hungry Fox Est
PH

95

Pinncourt Farm

MOSSHAYNE LA

EX1

Mosshayne

ALEXANDRA TERR

CLYST RD

COTTERELL CL

SILVERSMART CL

Shermoor Farm

Clystlands

Works

2

Works

Coach Bridge

1

LANGATON LD

Hayes Farm

MILL LA

Exeter Airport

94

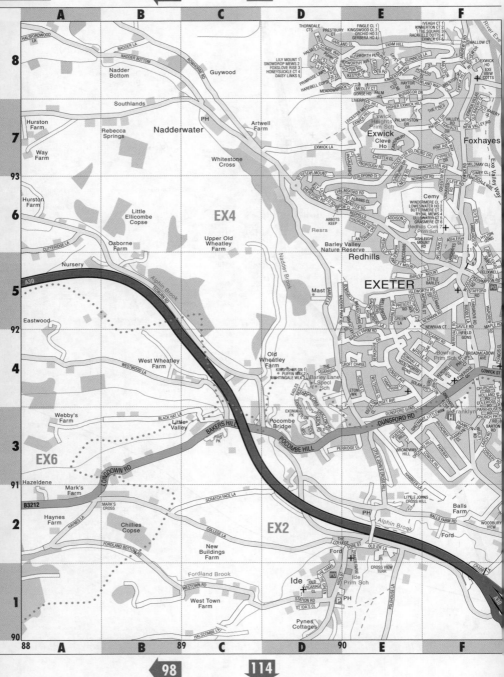

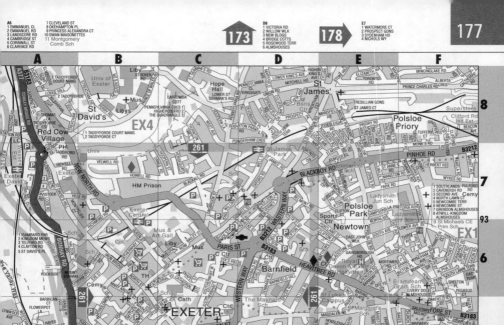

C8
1 MARK TWAIN HO
2 FLAYES ALMSHOUSES
3 PEEL ROW
4 ROYSTON CT
5 THE SEASONS
6 WILLOWBROOK AVE

7 MARGARET CT

D5
1 NELSON WAY
2 WELLINGTON CL
3 THE SQUARE
4 ALEXANDER WLK
5 DRAKE AVE
6 MONTGOMERY RD

7 CROMWELL TERR
8 3RD AVE
9 MARLBOROUGH DR
10 BADGER CL
11 RINGSWELL PK

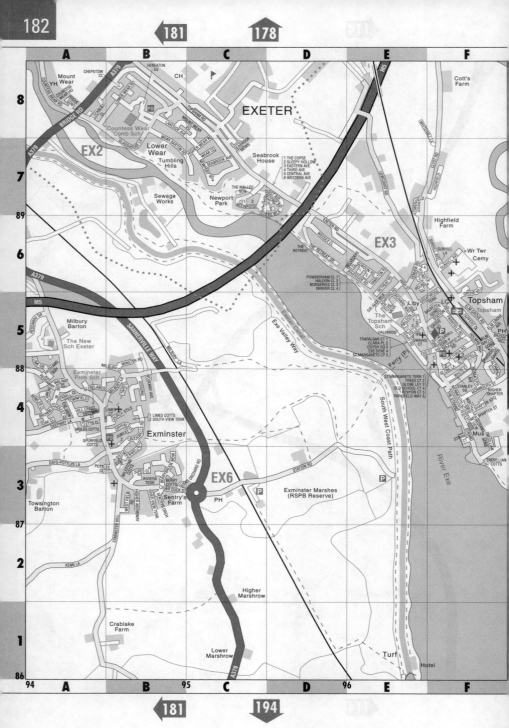

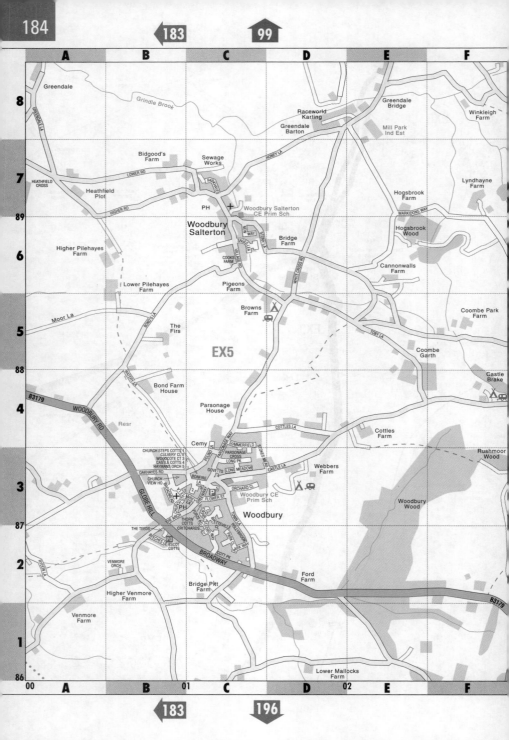

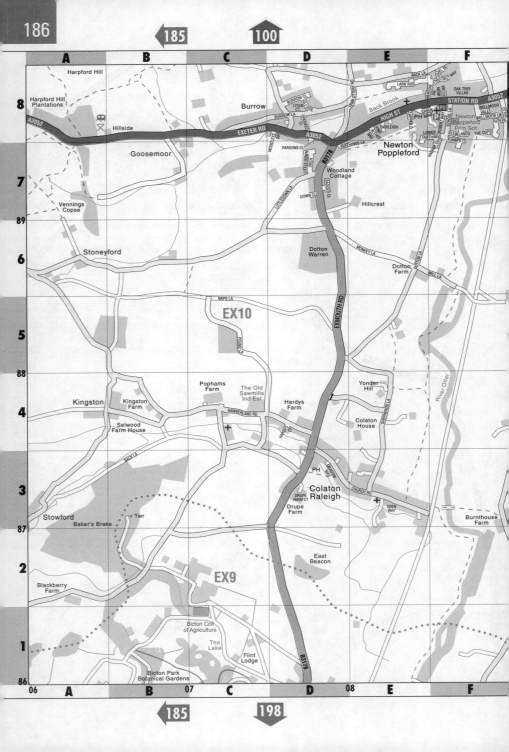

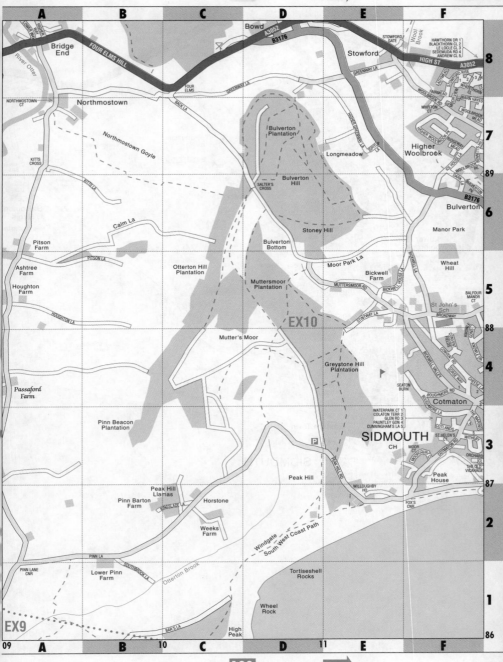

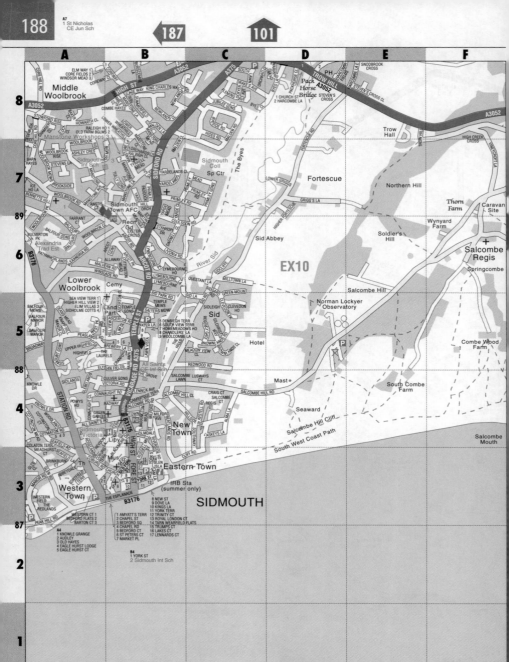

187
101

SIDMOUTH

EX10

A4
1 KNOWLE GRANGE
2 AUDLEY
3 OLD HAYES
4 EAGLE HURST LODGE
5 EAGLE HURST CT

B4
1 YORK ST
2 Sidmouth Inf Sch

A3
1 WESTERN CT 1
2 BEDFORD FLATS 2
3 BARTON ST

B3
1 AMYATT'S TERR
2 CHAPEL ST
3 BEDFORD SQ
4 CHAPEL RD
5 BEDFORD CT
6 ST PETERS CT
7 MARKET PL

8 NEW ST
9 DOVE LA
10 KINGS LA
11 YORK TERR
12 TRINITY CT
13 ROYAL LONDON CT
14 TARN WEARFIELD FLATS
15 TRUMPS CT
16 LAKES CT
17 LENNARDS CT

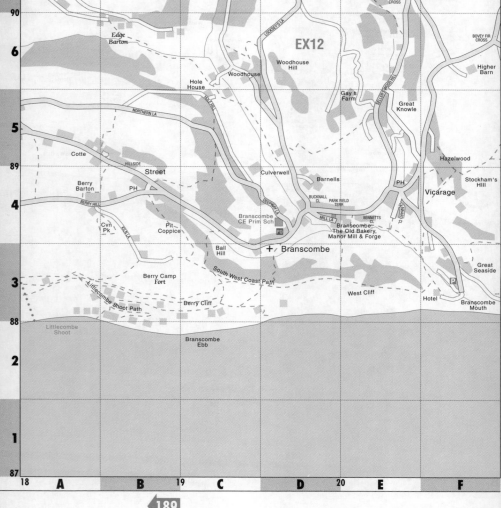

A   B   C   D   E   F

8

EX24

B3172
ROMAN WAY
HONZA
O-CHESTER DR
VENBOROUGH CL
CONSTANTINE CL
RUSSELL WAY

Couchill Farm
UPPER CHURSTON RISE
SEATON DOWN CL
AUBURTHE CL
SEATON DOWN HILL
CHURSTON RISE
STOWFORD HTS
SEATON DOWN DRI
ALBION WAY
WESTGATES
TRAVERS-L
NACK-RK
HOLLYHEAD RD
8

GATCOMBE LA

HOLLYHEAD CROSS

7

SEATON DOWN
M-JN
SEATON DOWN DRI
HARDINGTON RD
BILTON CL
MARLPIT CL
BOVEY LA

DURLEY RD
MARLPIT CL

90

STOWART LONG LA
HIGHFIELD TERR 1
MARMORA TERR 2
GORDON TERR 3
ROSE COTTS 4
PIONEER COTTS 5
WEST VIEW 6
THE SQUARE 7
BARNARDS FARM 8
BERRY HILL 9
ALLEYN CT
HIGHDEN LA
WESTSITTS

PAIZEN LA
SANDS CT

Beer
YH

EX12
PEAZEN FLATS
RATTENBURY COTTS
B3174 JOHN BARTON HILL
BERRY LA
Mast
CLAPPS
LA
B3174
HIGHCLIFFE CL
HIGHCLIFFE CT
OLD BEER RD
SEAFORTH LODGE

QUARRY COTTS
QUARRY LA

Pecorama
Pleasure Gdns
ASH HILL CT
Beer CE
Prim Sch
SHORT FURLONG
CAUSEWAY
NEW RD
COMMON
BEER
PRIOS
THE
GLEN
BEER RD
6

Beer Quarry
Caves
Beer Heights
Light Rly
UNDERLEYS
TOWNSEND
LONG HILL
8
Seaton Hole

Cemy
PIPPINS
Beer
Marine House
at Beer
5

MARE LA
WEST UNDERLEYS
PARK RD
LANEHEAD RD
HIGHER-MEAD
Beer
Roads

Friar's Park
Farm
SOUTHDOWN RD
SOUTHDOWN RD
COXES LA
SEA VIEW
TERR
89

South Down
Farm
COMMON HILL
LITTLE LA
4

Mast

South Down
Common
Arratt's
Hill
The Hall

East Cliff
Hookend Cliff
Under Hookend
South West Coast Path
3

Hookend Beach
88

Sherborne Rocks
Beer Head
2

1

87

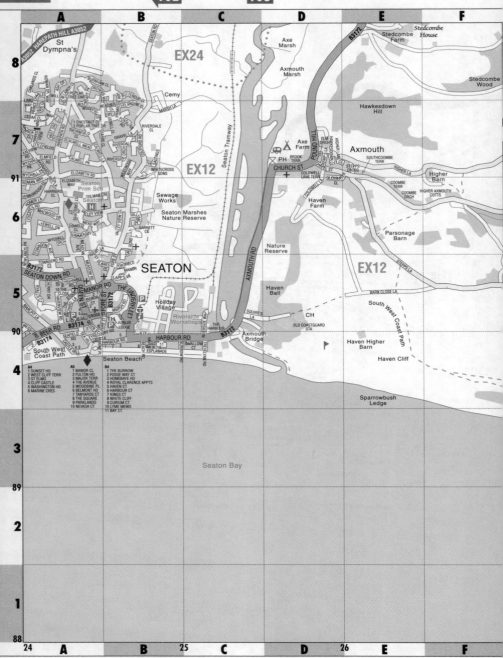

A   B   C   D   E   F

St Dympna's

EX24

Axe Marsh

Stedcombe Farm

Stedcombe House

Axmouth Marsh

Hawkesdown Hill

Stedcombe Wood

Cemy

Riverdale Cl

Seaton Tramway

EX12

Whitecross Gdns

Sewage Works

Seaton Marshes Nature Reserve

Axe Farm

PH

CHURCH ST

POUND HILL

ELM ORCHS

Axmouth

SOUTHCOMBE TERR

BROOK TERR

COLDWELL LANE TERR

STEPPS CROSS

GLENVL CL

Higher Barn

HIGHER AXMOUTH COTTS

COOMBE TERR

COOMBE ORCH

Haven Farm

Parsonage Barn

Nature Reserve

SEATON

AXMOUTH RD

EX12

STEPPS LA

Haven Ball

Seaton Down Rd

BEER RD

B3174

QUEEN ST

FORE ST

B3172

THE UNDERFLEET

Holiday Village

Riverside Workshops

Library

B3174

JUBILEE LODGE

BARN CLOSE LA

South West Coast Path

SQUIRE'S LA

Haven Higher Barn

Haven Cliff

HARBOUR RD

THE HARBOUR

B3172

Axmouth Bridge

ESPLANADE

SWALLOW CL

Old Coastguard Sta

CH

South West Coast Path

Seaton Beach

Sparrowbush Ledge

A4
1 SUNSET HO
2 WEST CLIFF TERR
3 ST ELMO
4 CLIFF CASTLE
5 WASHINGTON HO
6 MARINE CRES

A5
1 MANOR CL
2 FULTON HO
3 MAJOR TERR
4 THE AVENUE
5 WOODBINE PL
6 BELMONT HO
7 TANYARDS CT
8 THE SQUARE
9 PARKLANDS
10 NEVADA CT

B4
1 THE BURROW
2 FOSSE WAY CT
3 HOMEBAYE HO
4 ROYAL CLARENCE APPTS
5 HAVEN CT
6 HARBOUR CT
7 KINGS CT
8 WHITE CLIFF
9 CURIUM CT
10 LYME MEWS
11 BAY CT

Seaton Bay

8

7

91

6

5

90

4

3

89

2

1

88

A   B   C   D   E   F

Stedcombe
Wood

A3052
BOSHILL HILL

Heathfield
Farm

EX13

HEATHFIELD
CROSS

GREEN LA

COMBPINE LA

GREEN LA

Green Lane
Farm

8

Rousdon

Pit
Orchard

BUSHES LA

Hotel

PEEK
MEAD
SCHOOL LA

A3052

7

THE
GABLES

SPRINGHEAD
CROSS

Chadstone

91

LEGGETTS LA

DT7

FARM RD

6

THE
BOTHY

EX12

COMBE RD

OLD HOME FARM N
HOME   HOME FARM S
FARM

Bindon

STABLE
CTYD

THE
GARDENS

WEST
LODGE

STEPPS RD

Dowlands

5

90

Axmouth to Lyme Regis
Undercliffs National
Nature Reserve

4

South West Coast Path

Dowlands Cliffs and Landslips

Culverhole
Point

3

89

2

1

88

7   A   B   28   C   D   29   E   F

	A	B	C	D	E	F

8

Red Hill

Blackheath Farm

The Decoy

LC

7

Blackheath Cottage

Powderham New Plantation

Exwell Barton

Exe Valley Way

South West Coast Path

Exwell Hill

85

Mellands

Powderham Arch

Round House

6

Willsworthy Farm

Gos Hayes

Kenton Bridge

White House

Discombes

River Kenn

Sampsons

Rose Cottage

Powderham

Mill Farm

Powderham Old Plantation

5

Chiverstone Farm

EX6

Mills

Belvedere

84

Clumpit Wood

SWING GATE

CLUMPIT LA

The Old House

CHIVERSTONE LA

Powderham Park (Deer Park)
P

4

CHIVERSTONE RD

High House

Powderham Castle

River Kenn

Ringsdon Clump

EXETER HILL

BRIDGE RD

PENHAYES CL.

3

TORRINGTON PL.1
EAST TOWN LA.2
VICTORIA CL.3
CHURCHILL CL.4

HIGH ST

FORE ST

Kenton Prim Sch

ST ANNES

SUNNYBANK

KENTON HILL

SOUTHTOWN

CASTLE GATE

PARK VIEW

Kenton

Ford Farm CT

83

Kenton Vineyard

Cemy

Warboro House

Helwell Barton

MARSH RD

RIDGE WAY

A379

2

Witcombe

Church Brake

BUTTS LA

1

Black Forest Lodge

Wood Brake

Warboro Plantation

82

94	A	B	95	C	D	E	96	F

A   B   C   D   E   F

8

Lympstone
Commando

PORTER'S LA

STONY LA

PH

7

Training
Centre

Lower
Nutwell

Lower
Withhayes

A376

EXMOUTH RD

Home
Farm

Gulliford
Farm

85

Nutwell
Court

MUTWLL RD

EX8

Nutwell Park

GULLIFORD
COTTS

HAREFIELD RD

6

Belvedere

MEETING LA

EDINBURGH
CRES

CHURCHILL
CT

LIBELLAND

Thorn
Farm

River Exe

JACKSON
MDW

MUN COTT

Lympstone

ORCHARD
CL

OLGA TERR 1
BAKERS COTTS 2
WEST VIEW TERR 3
MEADOW VIEW 4

Powderham
House

CHURCH RD

Powderham
Pool

Darling's
Rock

MANOR
HO

Lympstone
Village

GREENHILL

Lympstone CE
Prim Sch

BIRCH RD

GRANGE CL

5

HAREFIELD COTTS 1
BRIDGE COTTS 2
CHAPEL RD 3
BROOKFIELD COTTS 4

PH

CHURCH RD

ENGMEADOW RD

JUPITER LA
HALL
FIELD

A376

PH

84

P

UNDERHILL

LONGBROOK LA

Sowden
Edge

HIGHCLIFFE CT

UNDERHILL CRES

CLAY LA

DAWLISH
PARK TERR

COURT LANES LA

4

HIGHCLIFFE
CT

SOWDEN LA

Sowden
Farm

EX6

Exe Valley Way

East Devon Way

Courtlands

LONGMEADOW

3

83

West
Lodge

Painter's
Wood

Exmouth
Nature Reserve

2

Stile Farm

Staplake
Mount

Lower
Halsdown
Farm

THE STRAND

STAPLAKE
RISE

A379

1

Starcross

COURTENAY
CL

A   98   B   C   99   D   E   F   82

South West Coast Path

197
186

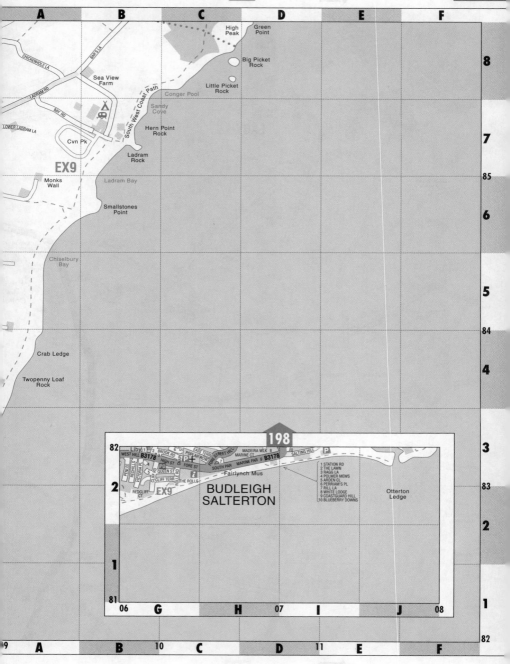

A B C D E F

187

8

Green
Point

High
Peak

Big Picket
Rock

Sea View
Farm

Little Picket
Rock

Conger Pool

7

Sandy
Cove

Hern Point
Rock

Cvn Pk

EX9

Ladram
Rock

85

Monks
Wall

Ladram Bay

Smallstones
Point

6

Chiselbury
Bay

5

84

Crab Ledge

4

Twopenny Loaf
Rock

198

3

Liby
WEST HILL
B3178
High St

EAST TERR
FORE ST
POR AIR ROW
SOUTH PAR

MADEIRA WLK
MARINE CT
MARINE PAR
B3178

SALTING HILL

P

83

2

QUEEN ST
THE ROLLE

Fairlynch Mus

1 STATION RD
2 THE LAWN
3 RAGG LA
4 POLMER MEWS
5 ARDEN CL
6 PERRIAM'S PL
7 RILL LA
8 WHITE LODGE
9 COASTGUARD HILL
10 BLUEBERRY DOWNS

Otterton
Ledge

REDCLIFF
CT
EX9

BUDLEIGH
SALTERTON

2

1

81

06 G H 07 I J 08

1

82

Quentance Farm

Knowle Hill Plantations

West Down

EX9

Littleham Brook

CASTLE LA

CASTLE COTTS

Woodlands Farm

West Down Beacon

South West Coast Path

EX8

ST MARGARET'S VIEW

REXTER CL

WEST DOWN LA

World of Country Life

The Floors

Crowden Point

ORCHARD CL

West Down Farm

CEDARS

DORE LA

MEADOW VIEW

WEST DOWN VIEW

Holiday Park

Littleham Cove

DANGER AREA

Otter Cove

DANGER AREA

Sandy Bay

DANGER AREA

Straight Point Rifle Range

Straight Point

B3178 WEST HILL

GREENWAY LA

WEST HILL CT

WEST HILL GDNS

CH

SHERBROOK CL

SHERBROOK HILL

VANES RD

ROPERS HILL

NORTHVIEW RD

MERTON HILL

BELVIDERE

WESTERCLYNE TERR

EX7

South West Coast Path

WARREN RD

Langstone Rock

PINE WOOD DR

PO

THE
ROCKSTONE

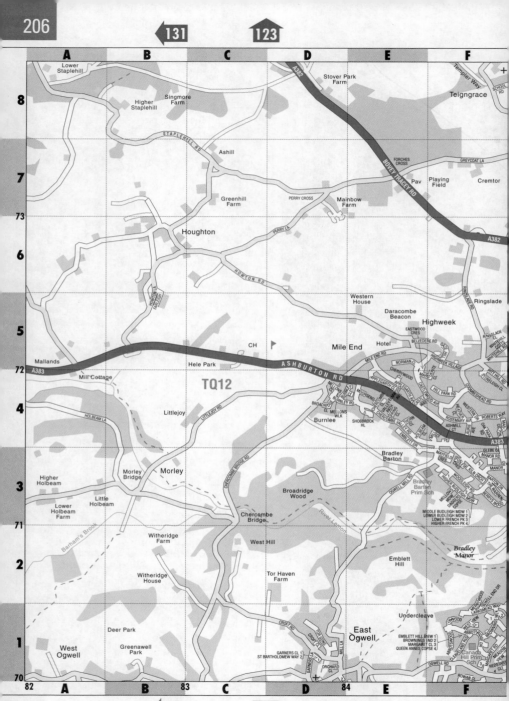

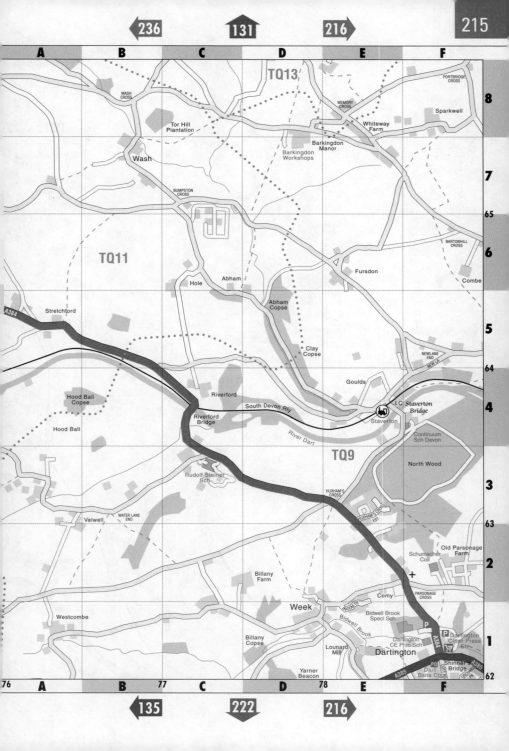

217
212

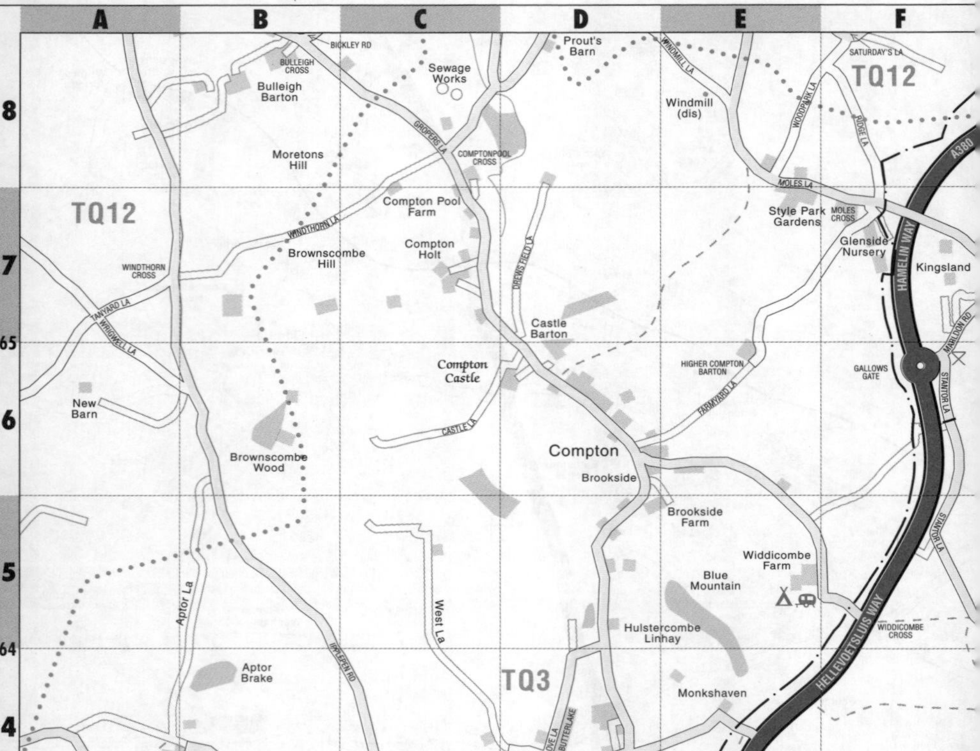
A
B
C
D
E
F
8
7
65
6
5
64
4
3
63
2
1
62
85
86
87
BICKLEY RD
BULLEIGH CROSS
Bulleigh Barton
Sewage Works
Prout's Barn
WINDMILL LA
Windmill (dis)
SATURDAY'S LA
TQ12
WOODPARK LA
RIDGE LA
A380
GROPERS LA
Moretons Hill
COMPTONPOOL CROSS
MOLES LA
Style Park Gardens
MOLES CROSS
TQ12
Compton Pool Farm
WINDTHORN LA
Compton Holt
Brownscombe Hill
Glenside Nursery
HAMELIN WAY
Kingsland
WINDTHORN CROSS
DREWS FIELD LA
TANYARD LA
WRIGWELL LA
Castle Barton
MARLDON RD
Compton Castle
HIGHER COMPTON BARTON
GALLOWS GATE
New Barn
STANTOR LA
CASTLE LA
FARMYARD LA
Compton
Brownscombe Wood
Brookside
Brookside Farm
STANTOR LA
Widdicombe Farm
Blue Mountain
Aptor La
West La.
Hulstercombe Linhay
WIDDICOMBE CROSS
HELLEVOETSLUIS WAY
IPPLEPEN RD
Aptor Brake
TQ3
Monkshaven
LOVE LA
BUTTERLAKE
PH
P
Stanton Linhay
Aptor
MARLDON LA
Neller Copse
CHURCH HILL
LOVE LANE CL
MEADOW PK
Hopper Wood
VILLAGE RD
PARKFIELD CL
Butterball Copse
Marldon Tor
Marldon
KILN CROSS
POTTERY MEWS
PEMBROKE PK
LOVENTOR LA
Strainytor Copse
MILLMANS RD
NETHER MDW
KILN RD
PETERS CRES
VICARAGE HILL
MARLDON GR
Marldon CE Prim Sch
OCCOMBE CROSS
COCKINGTON RD
Burrow Orchard
BELFIELD WAY
BELFIELD RISE
BELFIELD CL
BELFIELD AVE
Masts
SMALLWELL LA
FARTHING CROSS
FURZEGOOD
MARLDON CROSS HILL
Occombe House
FIVE LANES
PRESTON DOWN RD
WT Sta
Hazelwood
MOORVIEW END
WEST VIEW RD
FIVE LANES RD
TQ9
Hazel Wood
PO
MARLDON CROSS
MOORVIEW
BAMPTON CL
Culvertor Wood
FARTHING LA
MARLDON WAY
VICARAGE RD
Round Down Wood
CHURSCOMBE PK
POPLARS DR
SINGMORE RD
WESTERLAND GN
CHURSCOMBE RD
PH
WESTERLAND LA
LEADER LA
Churscombe
Occombe Valley Woods Nature Reserve
CHURSCOMBE GN
GENTIAN CL
HAYHURST PK
1 OAK END CT
2 WEEKABOROUGH DR
3 LOVENTOR CRES
4 BROWNSCOMBE CL
GREEN PARK WLK
LONGMEAD WLK
GREEN PARK RD
GREAT TOR CL
SHARPTOR CL
MANATON TOR RD
Wildwoods Farm
MIDDLE WESTERLAND CROSS
B3060
A380
LONGMEAD RD
WINDMILL LA
Oakend
Westerland
Windmill Hill
DOLPHIN COURT RD
TOTNES RD
KING'S ASH RD
MARLDON RD
Oak End Wood
FOREST RIDGE RD
DOLPHIN CRES
JAMES AVE
DIXON CL
DUNSTONE CL
DUNSTONE RISE
BADGER CL
SOUTHFIELD AVE
DOLPHIN CRES
The Old Farm House
Wildwoods Plantation
DUNSTONE CT
B3060
MARINERS WAY
ANTHEA RD
Mast
DUNSTONE PARK RD
BLAKEY DOWN LA

217
225

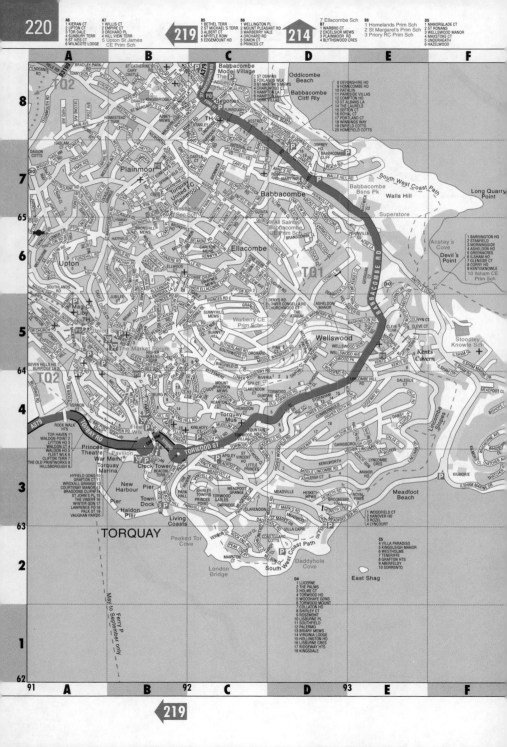

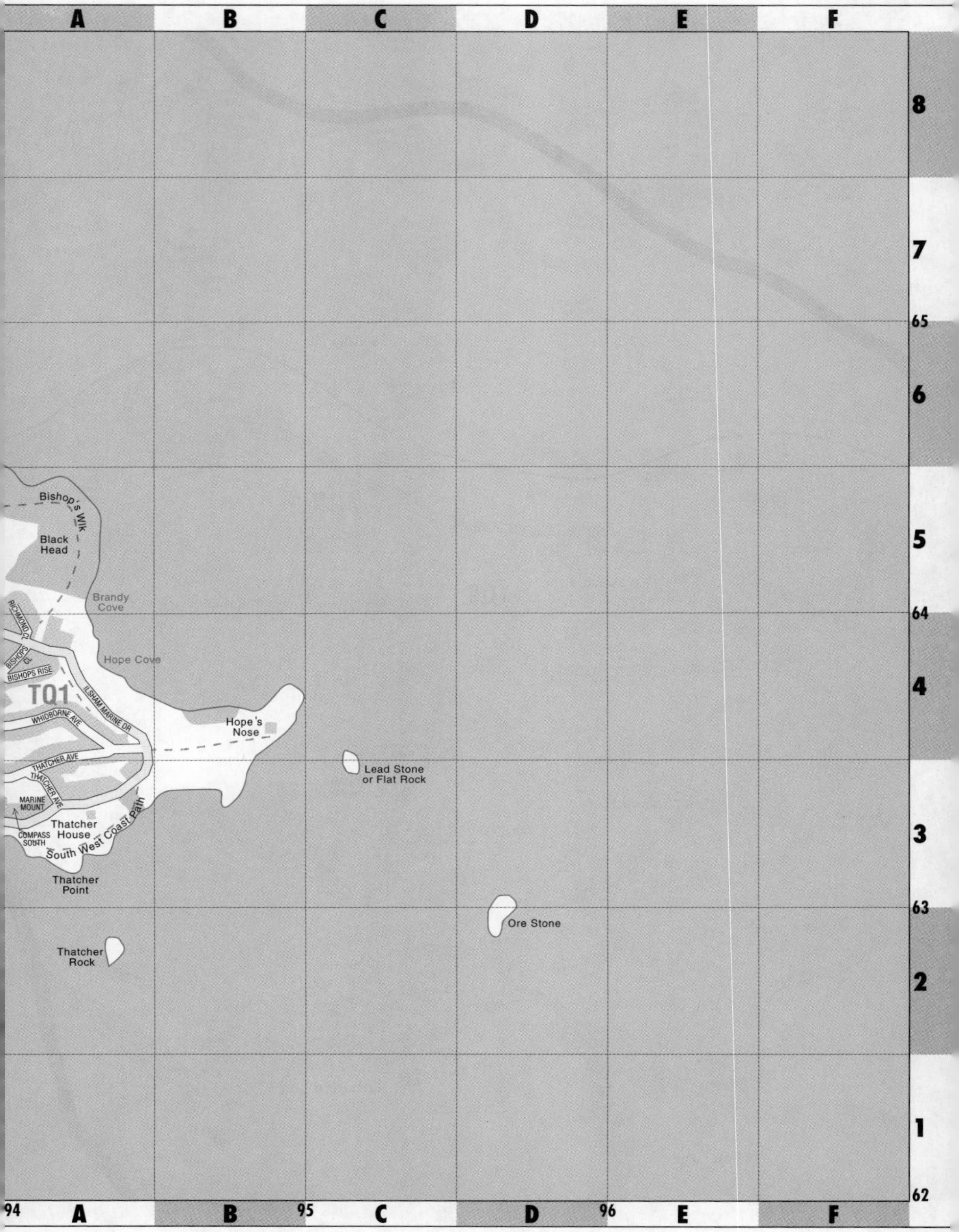
A
B
C
D
E
F
8
7
65
6
5
64
4
3
63
2
1
62
94
95
96
Bishop's Wlk
Black Head
Brandy Cove
RICHMOND CT
BISHOPS CL
BISHOPS RISE
Hope Cove
TQ1
ILSHAM MARINE DR
WHIDBORNE AVE
Hope's Nose
THATCHER AVE
THATCHER AVE
MARINE MOUNT
Lead Stone or Flat Rock
Thatcher House
COMPASS SOUTH
South West Coast Path
Thatcher Point
Ore Stone
Thatcher Rock

135 215

	A	B	C	D	E	F

Beacon Copse
Yarner Farm
LOWNARD CROSS
Cedar Units
A385

Higher Allerton
DUN CROSS
Webbers Yard Est
Droridge
Cott
PH
BARRACKS HILL
8

Lower Allerton
Beacon Park
REDLAKE CROSS
YARDE S. GRAVE
CROSSING CROSS

Bidwell Brook
South Downs
Peek Plantation
HUNTERS MOON
Copland
7

Penny's Grove
Brook House
61

A385
Whiteley Farm
Malt Mill Lake
6

Lower Ashridge
Dorsley Park Cottages
JACKMANS CL
BROOK VIEW
WINSLAND
FOLLATON GATE
SHORTS WAY
PLYMOUTH RD
QUARRY CL

Ashridge House
Follaton Farm

Dorsley Barton
Follaton House (Council Offices)
5

Fork Cross
Blakemore
TQ9
60

BLAKEMORE CROSS
4

Higher Cholwell
CHOLWELL CROSS
LANES LA

Sandwell Old Manor
COPPERTHORN CROSS
Tristford House
Lower Cholwell
3

Belsford
59

Harbourne River
MILL CROSS
GILL'S CROSS
PEAK CROSS
A381

2

VICARAGE HALL
Trisford Farm
ST CLEMENT'S TERR
PENDARVES
CHURCH CT
PH
MEADOW CL
FORDBARN CROSS

Leigh Hill
EAST LEIGH CROSS
WESLEY PL
PRESTON BARNS
Harberton
DUNDRIDGE CT
LANBRIDGE CROSS
1

East Leigh
Dundridge Hall
58

76	A	B	77	C	D	78	E	F

135 139

A   B   C   D   E   F

8

VINEYARD HILL
A385
Bidwell Brook
PH
Puddaven
CLAY LA
LABURNHAM GR
SAWLE LA
PUDDAVINE TERR
Water Works
South Devon Rly
A381
Wood Cottage
Coombe Park

7

61

ASHBURTON RD
Longcause Cross
LONGCAUSE
King Edward VI Com Coll
Ct
Totnes Littlehempston
Swallowfields
RIVERSIDE
DARTMOUTH RD
FOLLATON RD
Ind Est
THE BOURTONS
Marlands Farm Sewage Works
Snipe Island
Lower Bourton
Bourton

6

Broomborough House Farm
COPLAND MDWS
MALT MILL
ARGYLE TERR
ST JOHN'S TERR
CASTLE CT
COPLAND LA
A381
STATION RD
Totnes Pavilion
REDWORTH TERR
Totnes
PARKLANDS
Alpha Ctr
Broad Marsh
TOTNES
THE PADDOCKS
THE STABLES
JUBILEE RD
BLACKPOST CROSS
BRIDGETOWN HILL
A385

5

Cemy
FURLONG CT
PLYMOUTH RD
SMITHFIELDS
BROOMBOROUGH RD
KELLOCK DR
JELLICOE VILLAS 1
BROOMBOROUGH CT 2
WESTERN VILLAS 1
ORCHARD WAY 2
CISTERN ST 3
WESTERN BY-PASS
PAIGE ADAMS RD
LOWER COLLAPARK
Totnes Castle
ALPHA TERR
SPARROW RD
ROTHERFOLD
THE GR
BELL
20
HIGH ST
SOUTH ST
THE LAMB
ROTHERFOLD
MAUDLIN RD
PRIORY AV
PRIORY DR
MANOR RD
THE MANOR
MILL TAIL
MILL RD
Totnes Com
Superstore
VICTORIA ST
ST KATHERINE'S WAY
CHAPEL
WESTON LA
SOMERSET PL
FIELDS
Bridgetown
FURZE GDNS
ELM WLK
RUSH WAY
HOPE WLK
BLACKPOST LA
Elizabeth Ct
Library
Mus
21
6
TICKLEMORE ST
WESTWARD CL
ORCHARD TERR
MOAT
PH
Totnes St John's CE Prim Sch
OATHFIELD
BECTONFIELDS
Christina Par
CHRISTIAN PK
LANGDON LA
WESTERN LA

60

Harper's Hill
Windmill Down
TRISTFORD CROSS
GREEN LA
FISHCHOWTER'S LA
CHERRY CROSS
THE MOUNT
THE ORCHARD
DART VILLAS
FAIRSEAT CL
TOTNES DOWN HILL
E5
1 STAFFORD CT
2 HILLBROOK RISE
3 COLDHARBOUR
4 VARIAN CT

4

GERSTON CROSS
Gerston
BOWDEN PILLARS
Baltic Wharf Bsns Pk
River Dart
Ferry P (summer only)

3

59

TQ9

Higher Bowden
Bowden House

2

Little Bowden

1

58

Stancombe
Sharpham Barton House
Linhay Plantation

9   A   80   B   C   D   81   E   F

C5
1 HEATH CT
2 MOUNT VIEW TERR
3 GROVE CL
4 VICTORIA CT
5 ST KATHERINE'S MEWS
6 BANK LA
7 THE CARRIONS
8 SUNNYMEAD TERR
9 SHAFTSBURY PL
10 ALBERT PL
11 EIFFEL PL
12 GARFIELD PL
13 GILLS NURSERY
14 ATHERTON LA
15 TIMES MEWS
16 GROVE MEWS
17 MOORASHES
18 BLUEBALL HL

19 The Grove Prim Sch
20 Totnes Costume Mus
21 King Edward VI Com Coll

C6
1 ALEXANDRA TERR
2 NORTH ST
3 PRIORY CT
4 QUEEN'S TERR
5 ANTRIM TERR
6 GLENARM TERR
7 PRIORY TERR
8 NORTH CASTLE MEWS

D5
1 THROGMORTON HO
2 TAUNTON CT
3 REEVES CL
4 WINDEATT SQ
5 THE MALTHOUSE
6 APPLE WHARF
7 THE CHAPEL
8 WATERSIDE HO
9 SEYMOUR CT
10 ELIZABETHAN HO
11 STEAMER QUAY WHARF
12 TOLLIT GDN
13 BROAD OAK CRES
14 BARING COTTS
15 DEVON PL
16 DEVON TERR
17 SOMERSET CT
18 MEADOW BROOK

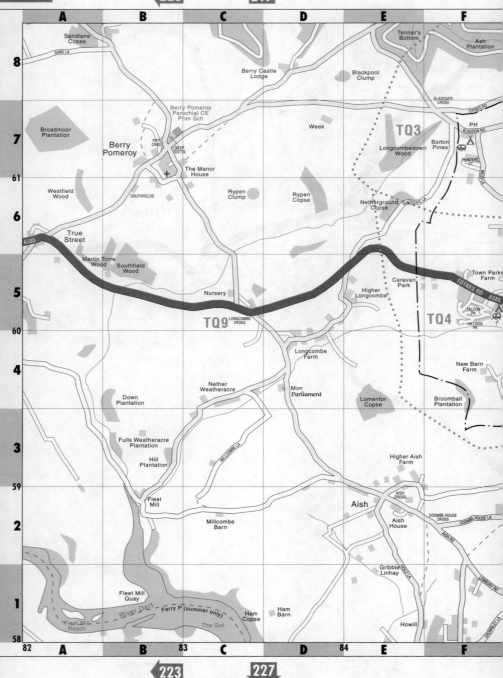

Lower Gribble Plantation

Avenue Cottage Gdn

Sharpham Vineyard & Cheese Dairy

Sharpham House

Sharpham Point

Ham Barn

Sharpham Reach

Cottage Plantation

Long Plantation

TQ9

Stockern Plantation

Cemy

Ham Reach

Sharpham Wood

Ferry P (summer only)

Ashprington Point

Duncannon Reach

Duncannon House

TQ9

Duncannon Copse

Stoke Gabriel

Stoke Gabriel Prim Sch

Rowes Farm

THE BARNHAY

PH

Langham Wood Point

Langham Wood Barn

Stoke Point

Duncannon Copse

Woods House

Mill Point

River Dart

Bow Creek

Kirkham Copse

White Rock

Long Stream

Will's Copse

Efford's Close Copse

Great Wood

New Linhay

Whitestone Farm

Corkscrew Hill

TQ9

Cornworthy

CORNWORTHY CROSS

ABBEY RD

ABBEY CROSS

JASPERS COTTS

PRIORY VIEW

PH

Cornworthy Court

Court Prior

WATER LA

WILLOW LA

LANE END POOL

LONGLAND CROSS

Sprat Lane End

Sprat La

East Cornworthy

FURZEHILL CROSS

BUTTS CROSS

Higher Broadgates

Longlands Farm

WOODLAND LA

Broadgates

FURZE CROSS

Southills Barn

Poor Bridge

Hotel

Kerswell

Lower Tideford Farm

Barberry Farm

Barberry Water Bridge

TQ6

Broadridge

TIDEFORD CROSS

Higher Tideford

Kingston

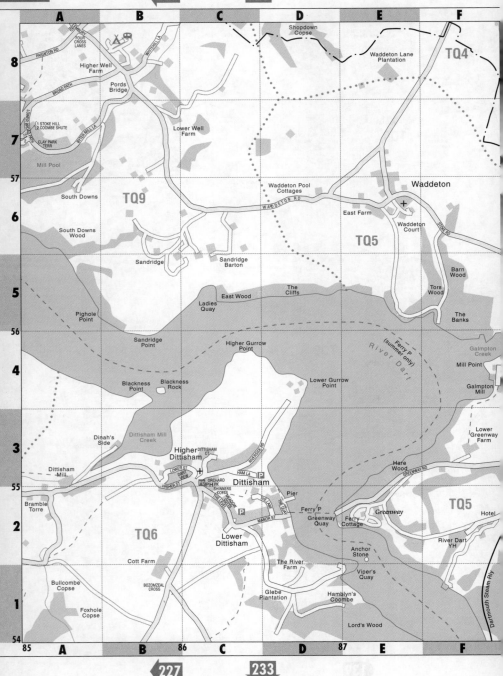

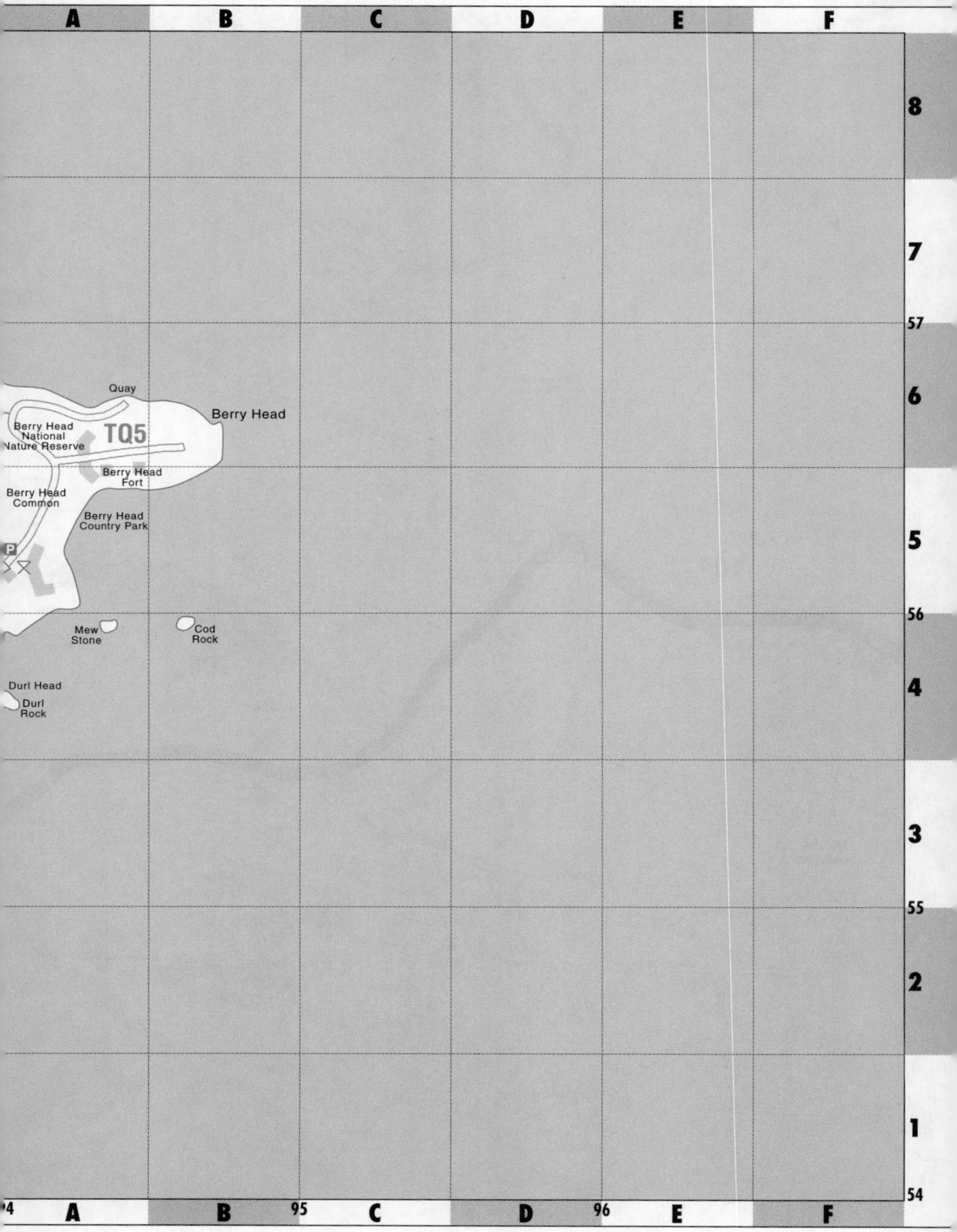
A
B
C
D
E
F
8
7
57
6
5
56
4
3
55
2
1
54
Quay
Berry Head
Berry Head
National
Nature Reserve
TQ5
Berry Head
Fort
Berry Head
Common
Berry Head
Country Park
P
Mew
Stone
Cod
Rock
Durl Head
Durl
Rock
94
95
96

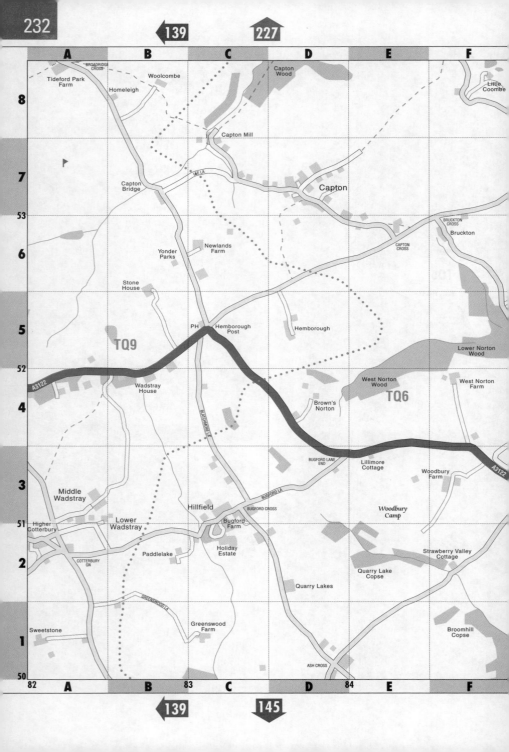

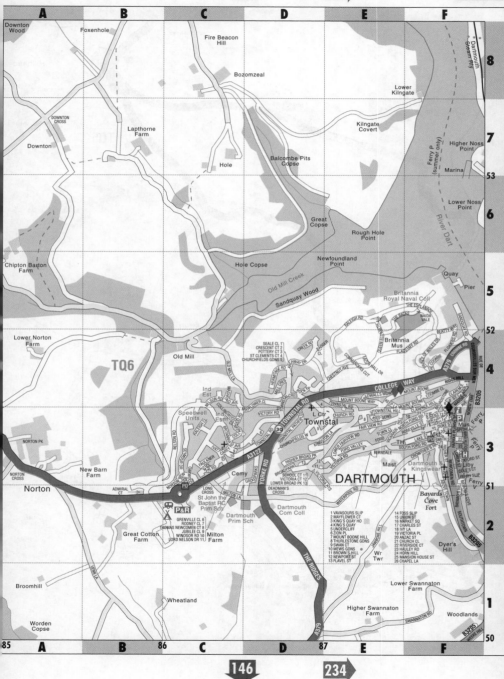

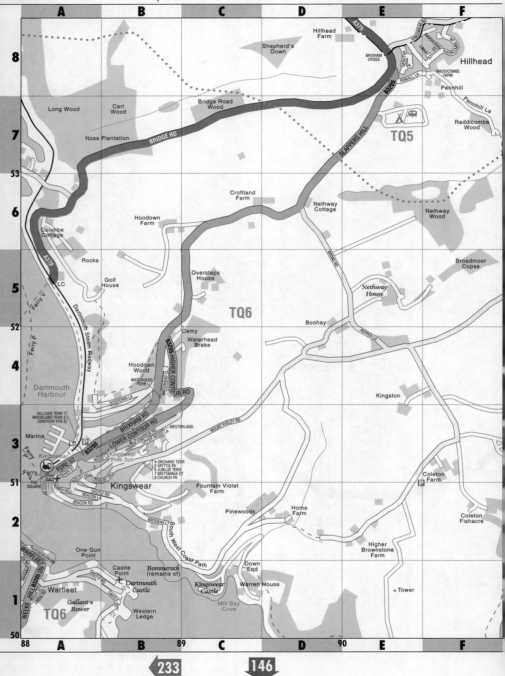

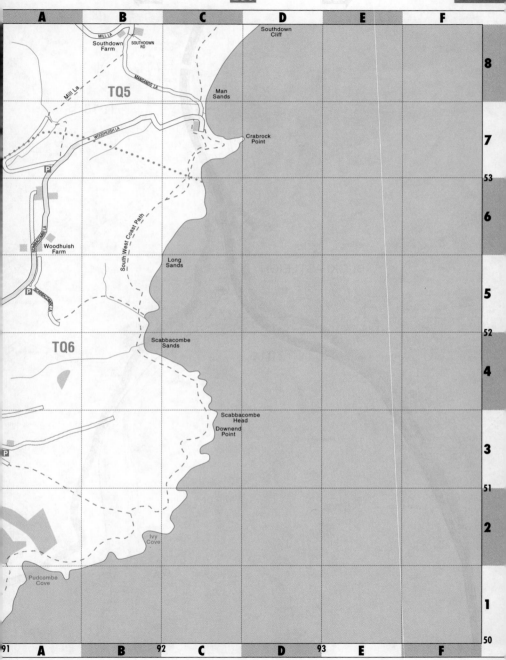

A B C D E F

8

SOUTHDOWN
Cliff

Southdown
Farm

SOUTHDOWN
RD

MILL LA

MANSANDS LA

Mill La

TQ5

Man
Sands

7

WOODHUISH LA

Crabrock
Point

53

P

South West Coast Path

6

Woodhuish
Farm

SCABBACOMBE LA

Long
Sands

5

P

SCABBACOMBE LA

52

TQ6

Scabbacombe
Sands

4

Scabbacombe
Head

Downend
Point

3

P

51

2

Ivy
Cove

Pudcombe
Cove

1

50

91 A B 92 C D 93 E F

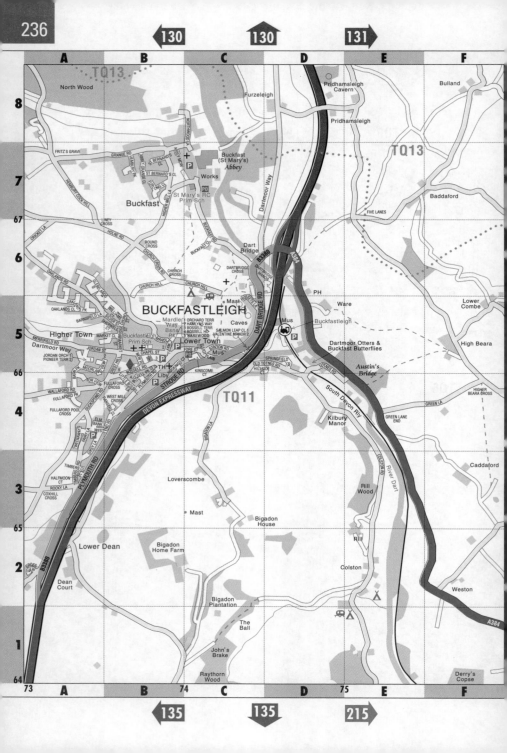

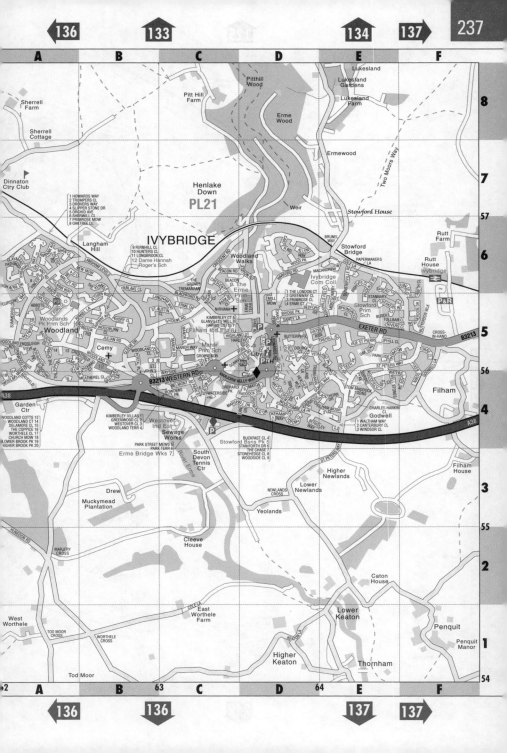

125

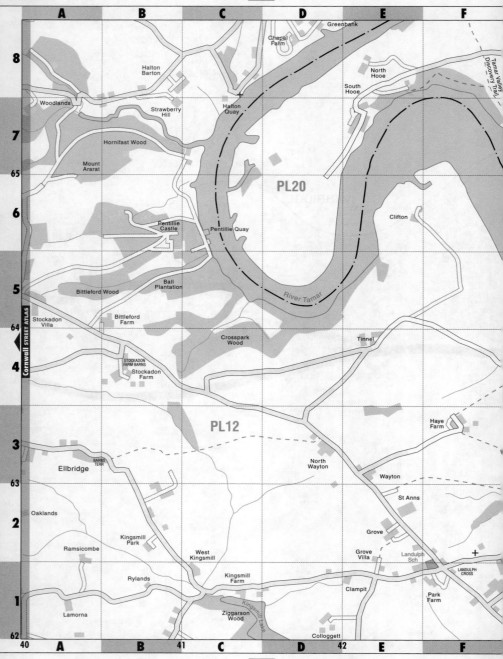

PL20

PL12

Greenbank
Chapel Farm
Halton Barton
North Hooe
South Hooe
Woodlands
Strawberry Hill
Hatton Quay
Hornifast Wood
Mount Ararat
Clifton
Pentillie Castle
Pentillie Quay
River Tamar
Bittleford Wood
Ball Plantation
Bittleford Farm
Stockadon Villa
Crosspark Wood
Tinnel
STOCKADON FARM BARNS
Stockadon Farm
Haye Farm
North Wayton
Wayton
Ellbridge
BARNE TERR
St Anns
Oaklands
Grove
Kingsmill Park
Grove Villa
Landulph Sch
Ramsicombe
West Kingsmill
LANDULPH CROSS
Rylands
Kingsmill Farm
Clampit
Park Farm
Lamorna
Ziggarson Wood
Kingsmill Lake
Colloggett

Tamar Valley Discovery Trail

Cornwall STREET ATLAS

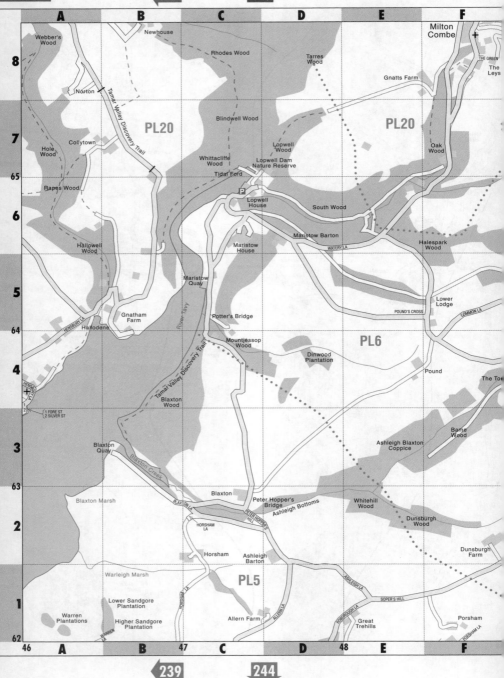

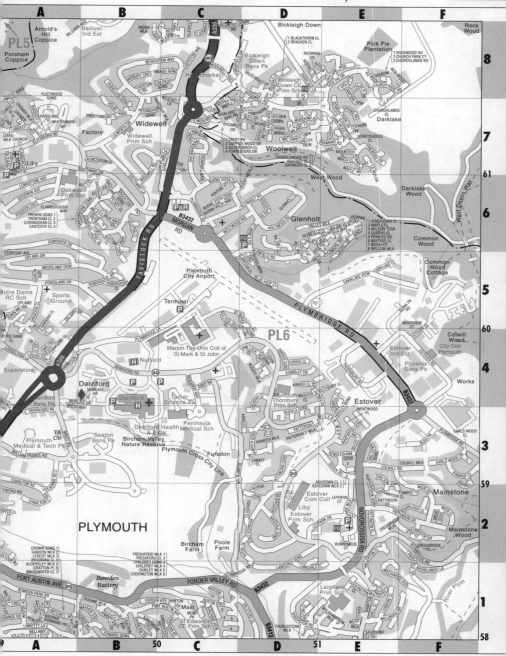

C7
1 BRAMBLE WLK
2 BOWRYS WLK
3 BRISMAR WLK
4 MOORFIELD WLK
5 BEAUDYN WLK
6 BEESTON WLK

245

250

249

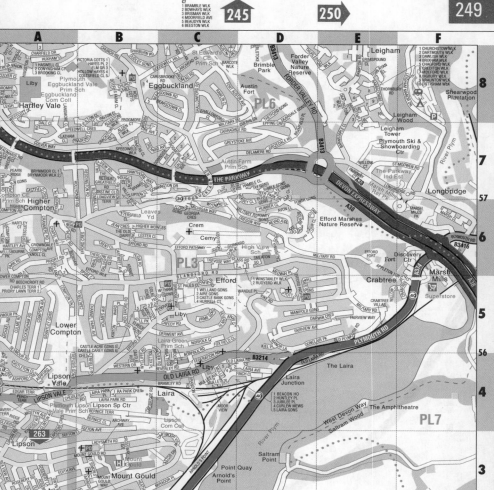

For full street detail of the
highlighted area see page 263.

255

250

A B C D E F

8

Ford
Vanderbands
St John's Lake

ST JOHNS LA
GODSPORT LA

JACK LA
+ CHURCH LA
PH
St John
Vanderbands
Farm
Sango
Island

7

Penhale Lake

St John's
Down
Mendennick
Penhale

53
B3247
Mendennick
Hill
PL11

Insworke
EDGCUMBE CRES

6

Works
Millbrook
Bsns Pk
Sewage
Wks

Millbrook
Bsns Pk

MANOR
GDNS

Cornwall STREET ATLAS

TRELUSIS
TERR
POTTERY
EST

1 HEANTON TERR
2 CLINTON TERR

Millbrook
CE Prim Sch

5

New Barn
Millbrook
Resr

Blindwell

MOUNT
PLEASANT

RICHARDS TERR 1
THE PARADE 2
WEST QUAY 3
PH

52

Withnoe
Barton
Higher Hounster
Farm
ST ANDREW ST
WEST ST
Millbrook
Anderton

Withnoe
P
WEST ST
Cemy

4

Tregonhawke
Farm
Dadbrook
Sollack

Tregonhawke
Treninnow
Grove

Mon
MILITARY RD
Treninnow
Plantation
Fourlanesend
Com Prim Sch

3

Treninnow
The Hats
B3247

51

Whitsand Bay
PL10
Wiggle

2

South West Coast Path
Wringford
Farm
Wringford
Down

1

Wiggle Cliff
P
Knatterbury
Forder

50
40 A B 41 C D 42 E F

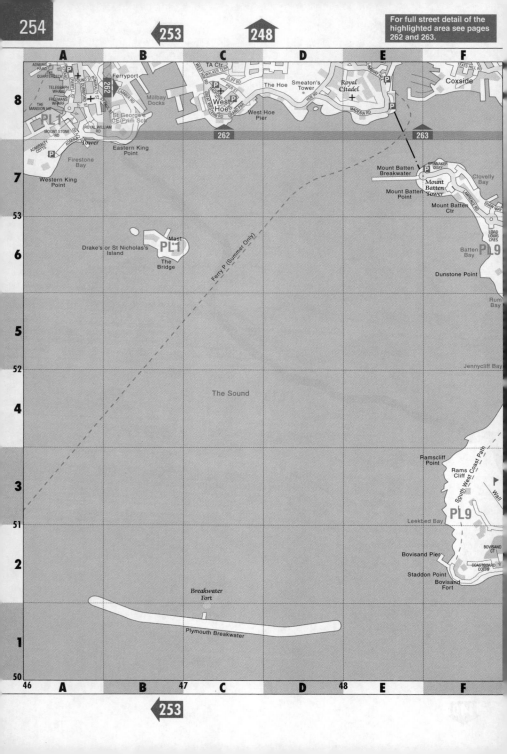

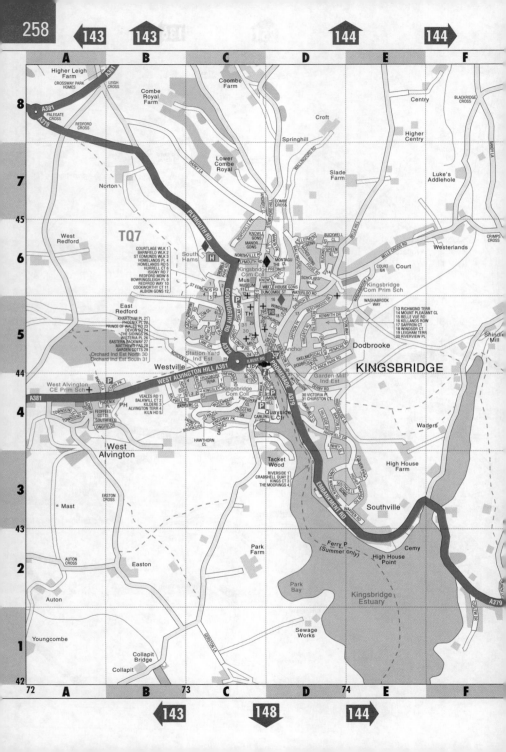

A   B   C   D   E   F

Higher Leigh Farm
CROSSWAY PARK HOMES
LEIGH CROSS

8 A381 PALEGATE CROSS
REDFORD CROSS

Combe Royal Farm

Coombe Farm

Centry

BLACKRIDGE CROSS

Croft

Springhill

Higher Centry

Luke's Addlehole

7 Norton

45

West Redford

TQ7

Lower Combe Royal

Slade Farm

COMBE CROSS

Westerlands

CRIMPS CROSS

6 South Hams

COURTLAGE WLK 1
BARNFIELD WLK 2
ST EDMUNDS WLK 3
HOMELANDS PL 4
HOMELANDS RD 5
HURRELL CT 6
ISIGNY RD 7
REDFORD MDW 8
BOWRINGSLEIGH PL 9
REDFORD WAY 10
COOKWORTHY CT 11
ALBION GDNS 12

KNOWLE GDNS
MANOR GDNS
NORTHVILLE RD
PLYMOUTH RD
MONTAGU CL

Kingsbridge Com Coll
Mus
MUSEUM

WELLE HOUSE GDNS
DUNCOMBE ST
WATERLOO RD

KINGS GN
SCHOLARS WLK

COURT GN
Court

Kingsbridge Com Prim Sch

WASHABROOK WAY

13 RICHMOND TERR
14 MOUNT PLEASANT CL
15 BELLE VUE RD
16 KELLANDS ROW
17 SAFFRON CT
18 WINDSOR CT
19 LEIGHAM TERR
20 RIVERVIEW PL

5 East Redford

KHARTOUM PL 21
PHOENIX PL 22
PRINCE OF WALES RD 23
DEVON SQ 24
THE SIDINGS 25
WISTERIA PL 26
EASTERN BACKWAY 27
MATTHEWS PAS 28
GARDEN COTTS 29
Orchard Ind Est North 30
Orchard Ind Est South 31

Station Yard Ind Est

Westville

Anchor

Dodbrooke

Shindle Mill

KINGSBRIDGE

44 West Alvington CE Prim Sch

WEST ALVINGTON HILL A381

Lib

Kingsbridge Com Coll

Quayside L Ctr

Garden Mill Ind Est

Waders

A381

VEALES RD 1
BALKWILL CT 2
KILDERE 3
ALVINGTON TERR 4
KILN HO 5

PHOENIX
PH

FEOFFEES COTTS
SOUTHFIELD
LONGFIELDS

TOWNSEND RD

4 West Alvington

HAWTHORN CL

30 VICTORIA PL
31 CHURSTON CT

High House Farm

Tacket Wood

RIVERSIDE 1
CRABSHELL QUAY 2
KINGS CT 3
THE MOORINGS 4

Southville

3 EASTON CROSS

Mast

43

Park Farm

Cemy

High House Point

2 AUTON CROSS

Easton

Ferry P (Summer only)

Auton

Park Bay

Kingsbridge Estuary

A379

1 Youngcombe

Collapit Bridge

Collapit

Sewage Works

42

72 A   73 B   C   D 74 E   F

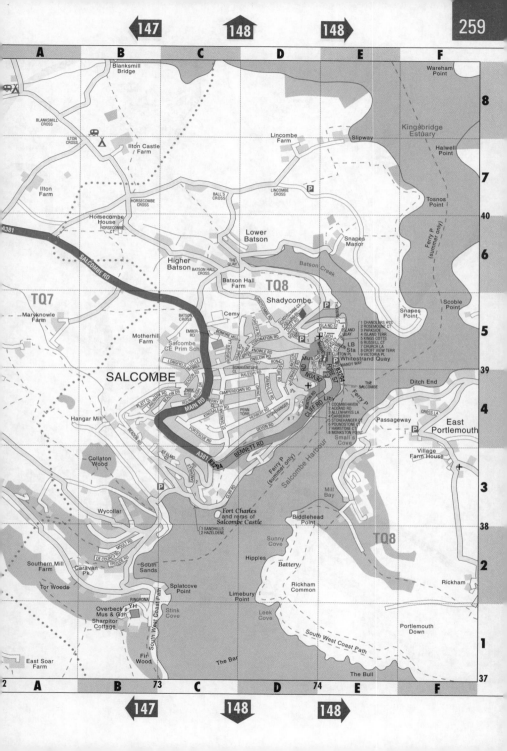

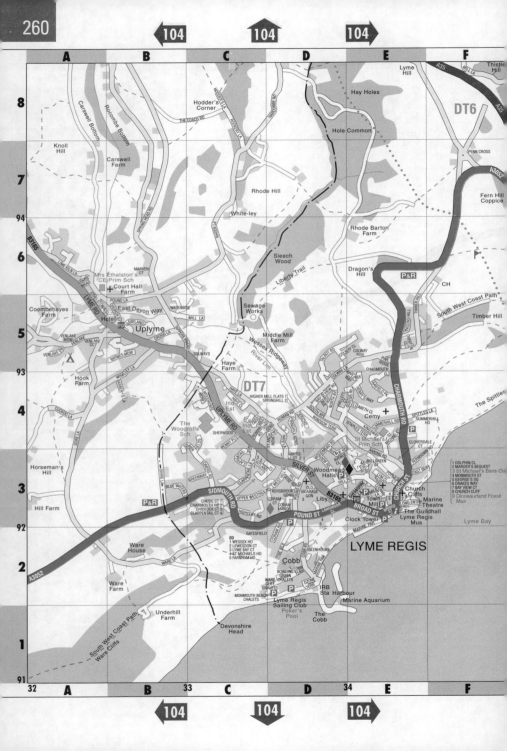

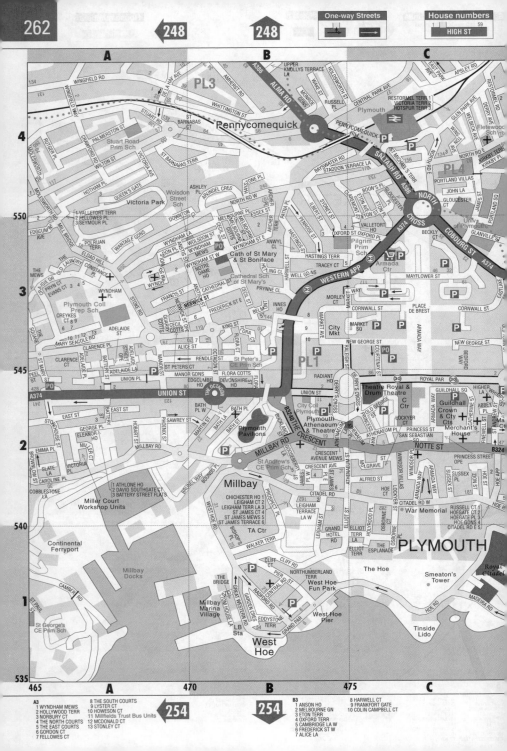

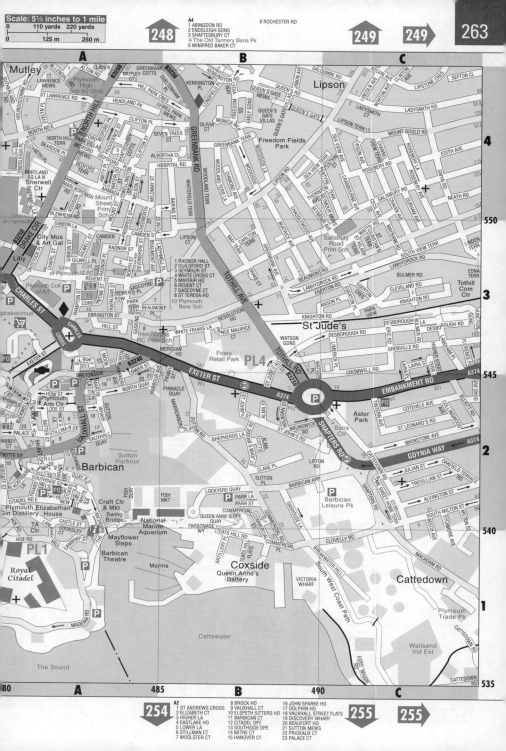

Index

Place name May be abbreviated on the map

Location number Present when a number indicates the place's position in a crowded area of mapping

Locality, town or village Shown when more than one place has the same name

Postcode district District for the indexed place

Page and grid square Page number and grid reference for the standard mapping

➤ **Church Rd** **6** Beckenham BR2.........**53** C6

Cities, towns and villages are listed in CAPITAL LETTERS

Public and commercial buildings are highlighted in magenta   **Places of interest** are highlighted in blue with a star ★

Abbreviations used in the index

Acad	**Academy**	Comm	**Common**	Gd	**Ground**	L	**Leisure**	Prom	**Promenade**
App	**Approach**	Cott	**Cottage**	Gdn	**Garden**	La	**Lane**	Rd	**Road**
Arc	**Arcade**	Cres	**Crescent**	Gn	**Green**	Liby	**Library**	Recn	**Recreation**
Ave	**Avenue**	Cswy	**Causeway**	Gr	**Grove**	Mdw	**Meadow**	Ret	**Retail**
Bglw	**Bungalow**	Ct	**Court**	H	**Hall**	Meml	**Memorial**	Sh	**Shopping**
Bldg	**Building**	Ctr	**Centre**	Ho	**House**	Mkt	**Market**	Sq	**Square**
Bsns, Bus	**Business**	Ctry	**Country**	Hospl	**Hospital**	Mus	**Museum**	St	**Street**
Bvd	**Boulevard**	Cty	**County**	HQ	**Headquarters**	Orch	**Orchard**	Sta	**Station**
Cath	**Cathedral**	Dr	**Drive**	Hts	**Heights**	Pal	**Palace**	Terr	**Terrace**
Cir	**Circus**	Dro	**Drove**	Ind	**Industrial**	Par	**Parade**	TH	**Town Hall**
Cl	**Close**	Ed	**Education**	Inst	**Institute**	Pas	**Passage**	Univ	**University**
Cnr	**Corner**	Emb	**Embankment**	Int	**International**	Pk	**Park**	Wk, Wlk	**Walk**
Coll	**College**	Est	**Estate**	Intc	**Interchange**	Pl	**Place**	Wr	**Water**
Com	**Community**	Ex	**Exhibition**	Junc	**Junction**	Prec	**Precinct**	Yd	**Yard**

Index of towns, villages, streets, hospitals, industrial estates, railway stations, schools, shopping centres, universities and places of interest

3rd – Ald

3rd Ave **8** EX2 .....**178** D5

A

Abbeville Cl EX2 ....**177** E3
Abbey Cl
  Axminster EX13.........**167** C4
  Bovey Tracey TQ13.....**180** C7
  Crapstone PL20.........**126** E2
  Paignton TQ3...........**225** E5
  Tatworth TA20 ....**88** D8
  Teignmouth TQ14.......**210** C7
Abbey Cross TQ9........**227** A4
Abbey Ct
  Exeter EX2.............**178** F5
  Plymouth PL1...........**263** A2
Abbeydale EX10.........**188** A3
Abbeyfield Ho **7** TQ14 .**210** C5
Abbeyford Ct EX20......**170** C5
ABBEY GATE...........**167** C2
Abbey Gate La EX13....**167** C2
Abbey Grange Cl TQ11 .**236** B7
Abbey La EX13..........**167** B3
Abbey Mdw
  Buckfast TQ11.........**236** B7
  Yelverton PL20........**126** E2
Abbeymead Mews PL19 .**171** C5
Abbey Mews
  Tatworth TA20 ....**88** D8
  Torquay TQ1...........**220** B8
Abbey Pl
  Plymouth PL1..........**262** C2
  Tavistock PL19........**171** C5
Abbey Rd
  Barnstaple EX31......**154** E6
  Bovey Tracey TQ13....**180** D7
  Cornworthy TQ9.......**227** A4
  Dunkeswell EX14......**67** C2
  Exeter EX4............**177** F7
  Torquay TQ2...........**220** A5
Abbey Rise
  Okehampton EX20......**170** D6
  Tavistock PL19.......**171** C5
Abbey Sch The TQ1 ....**220** C8
Abbot Rd PL21.........**237** A6
ABBOTSBURY...........**207** B4
Abbotsbury Rd TQ12 ..**207** B4
Abbotsbury Sch TQ12 .**207** D2
Abbotsbury Way PL2 ..**247** F8

Abbots Cl
  Lee Mill PL21.........**136** D6
  Woolfardisworthy EX39...**38** F8
Abbotscourt La PL11 ..**246** A2
Abbot's Cross EX36....**31** E6
Abbots Ct PL21.........**237** A5
Abbots Dr EX39........**26** A4
Abbotsfield Cl PL19 ..**126** A8
Abbotsfield Cres PL19..**126** A8
ABBOTSHAM............**156** A2
Abbotsham Cross EX39..**25** C4
Abbotsham Rd EX39....**156** E2
Abbotshill Pk TQ12....**212** A6
Abbots Keep EX4 ......**176** D6
ABBOTSKERSWELL......**212** B6
Abbotskerswell Cross
  TQ12 ....**212** A7
Abbotskerswell Prim Sch
  TQ12 ....**212** B6
Abbots Mdw EX37......**28** F4
Abbot's Rd EX4........**177** E8
Abbotsridge Dr TQ12..**206** F1
Abbotswood
  East Ogwell TQ12.....**206** F1
  Kingsteignton TQ12...**207** F8
ABBOTS BICKINGTON ..**54** E8
Abbotts Hill EX33.....**152** D6
Abbotts Pk PL21.......**133** C2
Abbotts Rd PL3........**248** E6
Abbrook Ave **9** TQ12 .**123** E1
Aberdeen Ave PL5.....**244** D3
Aberfeldy **3** TQ1.....**220** C5
Abingdon Rd **1** PL4..**263** A4
Abney Cres PL6........**245** B6
Above Down TQ7......**147** D7
Above Town TQ6.......**233** F2
Abscott La PL9........**255** C5
Abyssinia Ct EX32....**155** B3
Abyssinia Terr **8** EX32..**155** B3
Acacia Cl
  Bideford EX39........**156** L1
  Kingsteignton TQ12...**207** F6
Acacia Mews EX6......**181** B1
Ackland Ct EX2........**55** E4
Ackland Pk EX4.......**84** D2
Acklington Pl PL5.....**243** E4
Acland Cross EX32....**17** B2
Acland Rd
  Broadclyst EX5......**175** C6
  Exeter EX4...........**261** C4
  Ivybridge PL21.......**237** A6

Acland Rd continued
  Landkey EX32 ....**17** B2
  Salcombe TQ8 ....**259** D4
Aclands EX36..........**158** D3
Acland Terr EX4 ....**261** C4
Acland Way EX16......**161** A6
Acombe Cross TA3.....**68** B8
Acorn Sch EX36........**47** B8
Acorn Way EX32 ....**17** F4
Acre Cl EX39...........**24** E2
Acre Cotts
  Plymouth PL1........**247** F3
  Wellington TA21......**160** E6
Acre La TQ1...........**220** E6
Acre Pl PL1...........**247** F3
Acre Rd EX39..........**24** E2
Acre The TQ13.........**111** A6
Adams Cl
  Plymouth PL5........**243** F1
  Torpoint PL11........**246** F3
Adams Cres PL11......**246** E3
Adam's La PL9........**140** C8
Adcroft Rise EX13....**103** D5
Adder La EX31.........**16** B6
Addington Ct EX4.....**261** B4
Addiscombe La EX6...**113** D5
Addison Cl EX4........**176** E6
Addison Rd
  Newton Abbot TQ12..**207** E1
  Paignton TQ4.........**226** A5
  Plymouth PL4.........**263** A4
Addlehole TQ9.........**144** D7
Adelaide Ct
  Exeter EX2...........**261** A1
  Exmouth EX8.........**202** A5
Adelaide La PL1.......**262** A2
Adela Rd PL11.........**247** A3
Adelphi La TQ4........**226** C5
Adelphi Mans TQ4....**226** C5
Adelphi Rd TQ4.......**226** C5
Adit La PL21..........**242** E3
Adits The PL18........**125** D3
Adley La TQ13.........**111** B7
Admiral Ct TQ6.......**233** B2
Admirals Ct
  2 Exmouth EX8....**202** A6

Admirals Ct continued
  5 Northam EX39.....**156** F7
Admiral's Hard PL1 ....**254** A8
Admiral Swimming Ctr
  TQ5..................**230** D4
Admirals Wlk
  Exmouth EX8..........**196** D2
  Teignmouth TQ14.....**210** A8
Admiralty Cotts PL1....**254** A7
Admiralty Rd
  Plymouth, Millbay PL1..**254** A8
  Plymouth, St Budeaux PL5 **243** C2
Admiralty St
  Plymouth, Keyham PL2 ..**247** E6
  Plymouth, Millbay PL1..**254** A8
Adrian Cl EX39.........**157** A4
Adworthy La EX17......**46** B2
Affeton Castle Cross EX17 **60** F8
Affeton Hill EX17.......**60** F8
Affeton Moor Cross EX17. **46** A2
AFTON................**217** E2
Agaton Rd PL5.........**243** E3
Aidan Ave EX32.........**155** C2
Ailescombe Dr TQ3....**225** F6
Ailescombe Rd TQ3....**225** F6
Ainslie Terr PL2.......**247** E7
Aire Gdns PL3.........**249** B5
Airfield Ind Est EX14 ..**67** B2
AISH
  Paignton **224** E2
  South Brent **134** F3
Aish Cross TQ9........**224** E2
Aish La TQ10...........**134** E3
Aish Lane End TQ10....**134** F2
Aish Pk EX21..........**55** E4
Aish Rd
  Paignton TQ4.........**225** B2
  Stoke Gabriel TQ9....**224** F2
Alamein Ct PL12.......**242** E2
Alamein Rd PL12.......**242** D2
Alandale Cl PL14......**210** C6
Alandale Rd TQ14.....**210** C6
Alansway EX11.........**169** C3
A-La Ronde★ EX8 ....**196** A4
Alba Ct EX1...........**178** E7
Albany Cl EX38........**196** E2
Albany Rd TQ3.........**226** B7
Albany Rd TQ3.........**219** A1
Albany St
  10 Newton Abbot TQ12..**207** C3
  Plymouth PL1.........**247** E2
ALBASTON.............**125** C5
Albemarle Villas PL1..**247** F3

Alberta Cres EX4......**177** F8
Alberta Ct **14** TQ14...**210** C5
Albert Cl **11** EX17....**165** C5
Albert Cotts TQ12.....**208** E3
Albert Ct
  7 Ilfracombe EX34 ..**150** C6
  3 Torquay TQ1......**220** B5
Albertha Cl PL4........**263** B4
Albert La **9** EX32.....**155** A5
Albert Pl
  Exmouth EX8.........**202** A6
  10 Totnes TQ9......**223** C5
Albert Rd
  Crediton EX17........**165** C5
  Plymouth PL2.........**247** F3
  Saltash PL12.........**243** A2
  Torquay TQ1..........**220** B5
Albert St
  18 Dawlish EX7.....**204** D6
  Exeter EX1...........**261** C4
Albert Terr
  Bovey Tracey TQ13....**180** C7
  Gunnislake PL18......**125** C5
  4 Newton Abbot TQ12..**207** C3
  Princetown PL20......**128** B8
Albert Villas PL1......**247** E4
Albion Cl EX12.........**191** F8
Albion Ct
  Brixham TQ5.........**230** C3
  6 Exmouth EX8....**202** A7
Albion Dr PL21........**247** B3
Albion Dr PL2.........**248** B7
Albion Gdns TQ7......**258** C6
Albion Hill
  Exmouth EX8.........**202** B7
  Newton Abbot TQ12..**207** C3
Albion Pl
  Exeter EX1...........**261** C4
  Exmouth EX8.........**202** A7
Albion Rd PL11.......**247** B3
Albion St
  Exeter EX4...........**177** A5
  Exmouth EX8.........**202** A7
  Teignmouth TQ14.....**210** A3
Albion Terr **8** EX5....**202** A7
Alcester Cl PL2........**247** E4
Alcester St PL2........**247** F4
Aldborough Ct EX8....**202** B8
Aldens Bsns Ct EX2....**181** B8
Aldens Rd EX2.........**181** B8
Alden Wlk PL6.........**249** B7
Alder Cl
  Newton Abbot TQ12..**212** F8

Alder Cl continued
Teignmouth TQ14 . . . . . . 210 B7
Alder Glade EX31 . . . . . 154 C3
Alderney Rd PL6 . . . . . . 244 F7
Alder Rd PL19 . . . . 171 C3
Aldersley Wlk PL6 . . . . . 245 A1
Alderson Dr EX2 . . . . . . 178 D5
Alders Way TQ4 . . . . . . 225 D3
Aldridge Mill Hill EX16 . . 48 C6
Aldrin Rd EX4 . . . . 173 E2
Alexander Ct EX17 . . . . . 165 D4
Alexander Pl EX1 . . . . . . 169 D4
Alexander Rd 22 EX7 . . . 204 D6
Alexander Way 4 EX2 . . 178 D5
Alexandra Cl
Crediton EX17 . . . . . . 165 A6
Plymouth PL9 . . . . 255 B8
Alexandra Ct 15 EX32 . . 155 A5
Alexandra Dr PL20 . . . . . 125 F1
Alexandra Ho TQ12 . . . . 207 E2
Alexandra La TQ1 . . . . . 220 B6
Alexandra Mews EX6 . . . 201 B8
Alexandra Pl
Cornworthy TQ9 . . . . . 227 B4
5 Plymouth PL4 . . . . . 248 E4
Alexandra Rd
Axminster EX13 . . . . . 167 C5
Barnstaple EX32 . . . . . 155 A5
Crediton EX17 . . . . . . 165 B6
1 Newton Abbot TQ12 . 207 C2
Plymouth, Crownhill PL6 . 244 F2
Plymouth, Ford PL2 . . . 247 F5
Plymouth, Mutley PL4 . . 248 F4
Torquay TQ1 . . . . 220 B6
Wellington TA21 . . . . . 160 D6
Alexandra Sq PL12 . . . . 243 A2
Alexandra Terr
Bideford EX39 . . . . . . 157 A3
Clyst Honiton EX5 . . . . 175 E3
Exeter EX4 . . . . 177 E7
Exmouth EX8 . . . . 201 F6
Newton Abbot TQ12 . . 207 C2
Plymouth PL2 . . . . 247 F5
South Molton EX36 . . . 158 C5
1 Teignmouth TQ14 . . . 210 B4
1 Totnes TQ9 . . . . . . 223 C6
Alexandria Ind Est EX15 . 163 A6
Alexandria Rd EX10 . . . . 188 B8
Alexandria Terr 6 EX16 . 161 B4
Alexandria Trad Est
EX10 . . . . 188 A8
ALFARDISWORTHY 53 B6
ALFINGTON 100 F8
Alfington Rd
Alfington EX11 . . . . . . 84 F1
Ottery St Mary EX11 . . 169 F6
Alford Cl EX1 . . . . 178 C7
Alford Cres EX1 . . . . . . 178 B7
Alfred Pl PL2 . . . . 247 F5
Alfred Rd PL2 . . . . 247 F5
Alfred St PL1 . . . . 262 C2
Alfriston Rd TQ3 . . . . . 225 D7
Alger Wlk PL6 . . . . 244 E6
Alice La PL1 . . . . 262 B3
Alice Mews EX38 . . . . . 159 C5
Alice St PL1 . . . . 262 A3
Aklsom Rd TQ3 . . . . . . 219 A1
ALLALEIGH 139 F1
Allaleigh Cross TQ9 . . . 139 F4
Allaleigh La TQ9 . . . . . 139 F4
Allaway EX10 . . . . 188 B6
Allen Bank EX32 . . . . . 155 A3
Allenby Rd PL2 . . . . . . 248 A6
Allen Cl EX16 . . . . 161 F5
Allendale Rd PL4 . . . . . 263 A4
Allenhayes La TQ8 . . . . 259 D4
Allenhayes Rd TQ8 . . . . 259 D4
Allens Rd PL21 . . . . . . 237 D6
Allenstyle Cl EX31 . . . . 153 B5
Allenstyle Dr EX31 . . . . 153 B5
Allenstyle Gdns EX31 . . 153 B5
Allenstyle Rd EX31 . . . . 153 B5
Allenstyle View EX31 . . 153 B5
Allenstyle Way EX31 . . . 153 B5
Aller Brake Rd TQ12 . . . 212 F8
Aller Brook Nature Reserve*
TQ12 . . . . 207 E4
Aller Cl TQ12 . . . . 213 A6
ALLERCOMBE 168 A6
Allercombe Cross EX5 . . 99 E5
Allercombe Hill EX5 . . . 168 A6
Allercombe La EX5 . . . . 99 E5
Aller Cotts TQ12 . . . . . 212 F7
Aller Cross
Chillington TQ7 . . . . . 145 A1
Kentisbeare EX15 . . . . 65 F1
Kingskerswell TQ12 . . . 212 E6
South Molton EX36 . . . 29 F7
Allerdown Cross EX17 . . 80 A7
Aller Gate EX17 . . . . . . 78 D5
Aller Grove Cotts EX5 . . 99 F7
Aller Hill
Bishops Nympton EX36 . 31 A4
Dawlish EX7 . . . . 204 B5
Aller La EX20 . . . . 94 F8
Allern La PL5 . . . . 240 D1
Aller Park Rd TQ12 . . . . 212 F8
Aller Rd
Dolton EX19 . . . . 57 F7
Kingskerswell TQ12 . . . 212 E6
Allerton Wlk PL6 . . . . . 249 B7
Aller Vale Bldgs TQ12 . . 212 F6
Allervale Cl EX14 . . . . . 178 B4
Alley Hill PL20 . . . . . . 126 D1
Alleyn Ct EX12 . . . . . . 191 F7
Alleyn Gdns PL3 . . . . . 248 E8

Allhalland St 17 EX39 . . 157 A2
Allhallows Ct
Exeter EX4 . . . . 261 A2
1 Honiton EX14 . . . . . 166 C6
Allhallows Mus* EX14 . . 166 C6
All Hallows Rd TQ3 . . . . 219 C2
Allington Mead EX4 . . . 173 A3
Allington Terr EX17 . . . . 78 F7
Allison La EX17 . . . . . . 95 D7
Allotment Gdns TQ7 . . . 258 D6
ALL SAINTS 88 A4
All Saints Babbacombe CE
Prim Sch TQ1 . . . . . . 220 D6
EX10 . . . . 188 B4
All Saints CE Inf Sch
EX13 . . . . 88 A4
All Saints CE Sch TA22 . 33 D6
All Saints Ct EX9 . . . . . 198 B6
All Saints Ct EX14 . . . . 166 A5
Allshire La EX16 . . . . . 32 F3
Alma Cotts PL4 . . . . . . 263 B2
Alma La EX10 . . . . 188 C4
Alma Rd
Brixham TQ5 . . . . 230 C5
Plymouth PL3 . . . . . . 248 C4
St PL4 . . . . 263 B2
Alma Terr
16 Barnstaple EX32 . . . 155 A4
Gunnislake PL18 . . . . . 125 D6
Almeria Ct PL7 . . . . . . 250 D4
Alminstone Cross EX39 . . 39 A7
Almond Cl 3 EX31 . . . . 154 C2
Almond Dr PL7 . . . . . . 251 B6
Almshouse Cross TQ10 . . 135 E4
Almshouses 6 EX4 . . . . 177 D8
Almshouses The 7
TQ13 . . . . 180 D8
Alpha Ctr TQ9 . . . . 223 C6
Alpha Pl 24 EX39 . . . . . 15 A1
Alpha St EX1 . . . . 177 F6
Alpha Terr TQ9 . . . . . . 223 B6
Alphin Brook Ct EX2 . . . 177 C1
Alphin Brook Rd EX2 . . . 177 C1
ALPHINGTON 181 B7
Alphington Comb Sch
EX2 . . . . 177 B1
Alphington St EX2 . . . . 261 A1
Alphington Road Ret Pk
EX2 . . . . 261 A1
Alpine Rd TQ1 . . . . . . 220 B5
Alsa Brook Mdw EX16 . . 161 C6
Alscott Gdns EX31 . . . . 27 A4
ALSTON 88 A5
Alston Cross
Ashburton TQ13 . . . . . 131 B6
Slapton TQ7 . . . . 145 B5
Alstone Rd EX16 . . . . . 161 F3
Alston La TQ5 . . . . 229 D4
Alston Terr EX8 . . . . . . 201 F6
ALSWEAR 30 C1
Alswear New Rd
Alswear EX36 . . . . . . 30 C1
South Molton EX36 . . . 158 E3
Alswear Old Rd EX36 . . 158 C2
Altamira EX33 . . . . 182 F5
Altamira Cotts EX39 . . . 25 D2
Alta Vista Cl TQ14 . . . . 210 D7
Alta Vista Rd TQ14 . . . . 210 D7
Alton Pl PL4 . . . . 248 E4
Alton Rd PL4 . . . . 263 A4
ALVERDISCOTT 26 F4
Alverdiscott Rd EX39 . . 26 A4
Alverdiscott Road Ind Est
EX39 . . . . 26 A4
Alwyns Cl 3 TQ14 . . . . 210 C5
Alwyns Ct 6 TQ14 . . . . 210 C5
Amados Dr PL9 . . . . . . 255 B6
Amados Cl PL7 . . . . . . 250 B4
Amados Dr PL7 . . . . . . 250 C4
Amados Rise PL7 . . . . . 250 C4
Ambassador Dr EX1 . . . 178 E7
Ambassador Ho TQ4 . . . 226 C5
Amberley Cl TQ13 . . . . 130 E5
Amber Torr TQ13 . . . . . 121 F7
American Rd EX33 . . . . 15 A4
Amersham Ct EX2 . . . . 178 A4
Amherst Rd PL3 . . . . . . 262 B4
Amity Pl PL4 . . . . 263 A4
Amory Pl EX36 . . . . . . 158 C4
Amory Rd
Dulverton TA22 . . . . . 33 D6
Tiverton EX16 . . . . . . 161 C2
Amyas Way EX39 . . . . . 157 A6
Amyatt's Terr EX10 . . . . 188 B3
Anchorage Cl TQ5 . . . . 230 E5
Anchorage The TQ4 . . . 226 C5
Anchor Bldgs TQ12 . . . 123 B2
Anchor Cotts TQ7 . . . . 147 B7
Anchor Mill EX31 . . . . . 154 E8
Anchor Sh Ctr TQ7 . . . . 258 D5
Ander's La TA3 . . . . . . 68 E8
ANDERTON 252 F4
Anderton Ct PL19 . . . . 171 C2
Anderton Ct PL19 . . . . 171 D2
Anderton Rise PL10 . . . 252 F4

Andor Ave TQ12 . . . . . 207 D7
Andrew Allan Rd TA21 . . 160 B4
Andrew Cl EX10 . . . . . . 187 F8
Andrew Rd EX31 . . . . . 154 E3
Andrewshayes La EX13 . 87 A1
Andrew's Hill TA22 . . . . 33 D6
Andrew's Hill Cross TA22 . 33 C6
Andurn Cl PL9 . . . . . . 256 B6
Andurn Est PL9 . . . . . . 140 A8
Angel Hill EX16 . . . . . . 161 C4
Angelhill Cross EX36 . . . 30 F2
Angel Mews 2 EX14 . . . 166 C6
Angel The 4 EX14 . . . . 166 C6
Anne Cl EX4 . . . . 173 E1
Anne Cres EX31 . . . . . 154 E3
Annery Kiln Cotts EX39 . . 26 A1
Anning Rd DT7 . . . . . . 260 E4
Ann's Pl PL3 . . . . 248 A4
Anson Ho 9 PL1 . . . . . 262 B3
Anson Pl
Plymouth, Devonport
PL2 . . . . 247 F4
Plymouth, St Jude's PL4 . 263 C3
Anson Rd EX8 . . . . 196 C2
Anstey Cres EX16 . . . . 161 F3
Anstey Gate TA22 . . . . 32 B8
Anstey's Cove Rd TQ1 . . 220 E6
Ansteys Ct TQ1 . . . . . . 220 E5
Anstey's Cove Rd TQ1 . . 46 E1
Anstey Way EX39 . . . . . 15 B1
Anstis Ct EX10 . . . . . . 188 A7
Anstis St PL1 . . . . 262 A3
Anthea Rd TQ3 . . . . . . 218 F1
Anthony Rd EX1 . . . . . 177 F6
Antonine Cres EX4 . . . . 176 E6
Antony Gdns PL2 . . . . . 248 C8
Antony House* PL11 . . 246 D5
Antony Rd PL11 . . . . . . 247 B3
Antony Woodland Gdn*
PL11 . . . . 246 D6
Antrim Terr 5 TQ9 . . . . 223 C6
Anvil Cnr EX22 . . . . . . 72 D7
Anvil Ct PL17 . . . . 115 B1
Anwyl Cl PL1 . . . . 262 B3
Anzac Ave PL5 . . . . . . 244 A4
Anzac St TQ6 . . . . 233 F3
Applebee Way DT7 . . . . 260 E4
Appleby Wlk PL5 . . . . . 244 D4
Apple Cl EX18 . . . . . . 196 B3
APPLEDORE
Bideford 14 F1
Uffculme 51 A1
Appledore Cl EX15 . . . . 163 B3
Appledore Com Prim Sch 55
EX39 . . . . 15 A1
Appledore Hill EX20 . . . 170 F8
Appledore Rd EX39 . . . 156 F8
Apple Dr EX15 . . . . . . 162 D4
Apple Farm Grange EX2 . 178 E3
Applegarth Ave TQ12 . . 206 E4
Applegarth Cl TQ12 . . . 206 E4
Applehayes EX6 . . . . . 52 F2
Applehayes La EX15 . . . 52 F2
Apple La EX2 . . . . 178 E4
Apple Orch EX38 . . . . . 159 B4
Appleton Tor Cl PL3 . . . 249 F5
Appletree Cl
Barnstaple EX32 . . . . 155 D4
Uffculme EX15 . . . . . 66 A7
Apple Tree Cl
Frogmore TQ7 . . . . . . 144 E1
Witheridge EX16 . . . . 46 E1
Appletree Mews 5 EX15 . 15 A1
Apple Wharf 6 TQ9 . . . 223 D5
APPLEY 51 B8
Appley Cross TA21 . . . . 51 B7
App's La EX39 . . . . 25 E2
April Cl EX8 . . . . 196 B3
Apsley Ho TQ1 . . . . . . 220 C3
Apsley Rd PL4 . . . . 248 D4
Apsley Terr
1 Ilfracombe EX34 . . . 150 C5
Apsley Villas 4 EX34 . . 150 C5
Apters Hill 1 TQ5 . . . . 230 C5
Arbour Cl EX34 . . . . . . 150 B3
Arbour The PL6 . . . . . . 244 E5
Arcade Ho EX14 . . . . . 166 C6
Arcade The EX20 . . . . . 170 B5
Arcadia Rd PL9 . . . . . . 256 D6
Arcadia Rd PL9 . . . . . . 256 C6
Arch Cotts TQ12 . . . . . 207 D7
Archer Pl PL1 . . . . 262 B4
Archers Ct EX15 . . . . . 163 B3
Archers La EX3 & PL8 . . 141 A7
Archer Terr PL1 . . . . . . 262 B3
Archery Cl TQ7 . . . . . . 258 C7
Arches The EX2 . . . . . . 177 A4
Archibald Rd EX1 . . . . 261 C3
Archipark EX32 . . . . . . 17 E1
Arch St 6 TQ14 . . . . . . 210 A3
Arch The EX5 . . . . 184 B3
Archway Ave PL4 . . . . . 249 B3
Archway Dr TQ6 . . . . . 233 D4
Arcot Gdns EX10 . . . . . 188 B6
Arcot Pk EX10 . . . . . . 188 B6
Arcot Rd EX10 . . . . . . 188 B6
Arden Cl EX9 . . . . 199 B2
Arden Dr TQ2 . . . . 219 D6
Arden Ho TQ7 . . . . 143 A1
Ardennes Cl EX16 . . . . 161 E5
Ardenney Ct EX8 . . . . . 202 C5
Ardwyn TA21 . . . . 160 D4
Arena Pk EX4 . . . . 174 B1
Argent Ct EX16 . . . . . . 161 D4
Argus Cl EX14 . . . . . . 166 E6
Argyle Mews EX4 . . . . . 173 A1

Argyle Terr TQ9 . . . . . . 223 B6
Argyll Rd EX4 . . . . 173 B2
Arimoor Gdns PL19 . . . 171 C5
Ark Royal Cl PL5 . . . . . 247 D8
Arkwright Gdns PL5 . . . 243 F2
Arley Cl PL6 . . . . 245 B6
ARLINGCOTT BECCOTT . 10 C4
ARLINGTON 10 D3
Arlington Court* EX31 . . 10 D3
Arlington Pl EX34 . . . . . 8 A6
Arlington Rd
Plymouth PL4 . . . . . . 248 F4
Woolacombe EX34 . . . 7 F6
Arlington Terr 5 EX33 . . 152 D5
Armada Cl EX12 . . . . . 192 A7
Armada Ct PL19 . . . . . 171 B4
Armada Dr TQ14 . . . . . 210 A8
Armada Rd PL12 . . . . . 253 A1
Armada (Sh) Ctr PL1 . . 262 C3
Armada St PL4 . . . . . . 263 A4
Armada Way
Plymouth PL1 . . . . . . 262 C2
Westward Ho! EX39 . . 156 B6
Armourwood La EX5 . . . 81 D5
Armstrong Ave EX4 . . . 173 D2
Armytage Rd EX9 . . . . . 198 A2
Arnison Cl PL9 . . . . . . 255 F5
Arnold Cres EX16 . . . . 161 B2
Arnold's Ct TQ7 . . . . . . 142 C6
Arnold's Point PL4 . . . . 249 C3
Arnside Cl PL6 . . . . . . 245 D3
Arran Cl TQ2 . . . . 213 E2
Arscott Gdns PL9 . . . . 255 C5
Arscott La PL9 . . . . . . 255 D5
Arthington TQ1 . . . . . . 219 F7
Art Ho 17 EX1 . . . . . . 261 A2
Arthurs Cl EX38 . . . . . 196 D2
Arthurs Lea EX39 . . . . 156 B2
Arthur Terr PL11 . . . . . 247 B2
Artillery Ct EX2 . . . . . . 177 E3
Artillery Pl PL4 . . . . . . 263 B1
Artizan's Dwellings
EX36 . . . . 158 D4
Arun Cl PL3 . . . . 249 C5
Arundel Cl EX2 . . . . . . 181 B8
Arundel Cres PL1 . . . . . 262 B4
Arundel Cl PL16 . . . . . 105 E4
Arundell Cl PL16 . . . . . 105 E4
Arundell Gdns PL16 . . . 105 E4
Arundell Rd EX39 . . . . 77 C4
Arundells Cnr 3 EX17 . . 165 D5
Arundel Terr PL2 . . . . . 247 F4
Ascension Way TQ2 . . . 213 F2
Ascerton Cl EX10 . . . . 188 B5
Ascerton Rd EX10 . . . . 188 B5
ASH 145 E8
Ashacre Cross TQ10 . . . 214 B6
Ash Bridge Cross EX20 . 95 D1
ASHBRITTLE 50 F8
Ashburn Parc PL12 . . . . 242 B3
Ashburn Cl TQ13 . . . . . 130 F4
Ashburn Gdns TQ13 . . . 130 F4
Ashburnham Rd PL5 . . . 244 A3
Ashburn Wlk TQ4 . . . . . 229 B8
ASHBURTON 130 E5
Ashburton & Buckfastleigh
District Hospl TQ13 . . 131 A5
Ashburton Cl TQ13 . . . . 180 C5
Ashburton Mus* TQ13 . 130 F4
Ashburton Prim Sch
TQ13 . . . . 130 F4
Ashburton Rd
Bovey Tracey TQ13 . . . 180 C5
Newton Abbot TQ12 . . 206 D4
Totnes TQ9 . . . . 223 B7
ASHBURY 92 E8
Ashbury Cross EX20 . . . 93 B5
Ashbury Station Cross
EX20 . . . . 92 C7
Ash Cl 7 EX20 . . . . . . 126 F3
Ashclyst View EX5 . . . . 175 D6
ASHCOMBE 204 C7
Ashcombe Cl PL7 . . . . . 250 C7
Ashcombe Cross EX7 . . 124 C6
Ashcombe Hill PL8 . . . . 257 F2
Ashcombe Rd EX7 . . . . 204 B8
Ash Cross
Bradninch EX5 . . . . . . 82 F7
Dartmouth TQ6 . . . . . 232 F8
Halberton EX16 . . . . . 65 A6
Oakford EX16 . . . . . . 48 D6
Petrockstow EX20 . . . 56 F3
Ash Ct
Crediton EX17 . . . . . . 165 C6
Lee Mill PL21 . . . . . . 136 D6
Shillingford St George EX2 . 114 D8
ASHCULME 52 C1
Ashculme Hill EX15 . . . 52 C2
Ashdown Cl PL6 . . . . . 245 E3
Ashdown Cross EX22 . . 38 F3
Ashdown Wlk PL6 . . . . 245 E3
Ashelford Cl PL7 . . . . . 251 C5
Asheldon Ho TQ1 . . . . 220 D5
Asheldon Manor TQ1 . . 220 D5
Asheldon Rd TQ1 . . . . 220 D5
Ashelford Dr EX31 . . . . 10 A3
Ashery Dr PL9 . . . . . . 255 C6
Ashes Rd
Dalwood EX13 . . . . . . 87 B1
Shute EX13 . . . . 103 B8
Ash Farm Cl EX14 . . . . 174 F1
Ashfield Cl
Ashburton EX31 . . . . . 16 B6
Exmouth EX8 . . . . . . 196 E1
Ashfield Rd TQ2 . . . . . 219 E5
Ashfield Terr EX39 . . . . 157 A7

ASHFORD
Aveton Gifford 143 C7
Barnstaple 16 B6
Ashford Cl PL3 . . . . . . 249 A4
Ashford Cres PL3 . . . . 249 A4
Ashford Hill PL4 . . . . . 249 A4
Ashford Rd
Plymouth PL4 . . . . . . 248 F4
Topsham EX3 . . . . . . 182 E5
Wellington TA21 . . . . 160 D4
Ash Gr
Exmouth EX8 . . . . . . 196 B2
Ivybridge PL21 . . . . . 237 E5
Plymouth PL2 . . . . . . 247 F7
Seaton EX12 . . . . . . 192 A8
Ashgrove Rd TQ13 . . . . 180 C4
Ash Hill
Oakford EX16 . . . . . . 48 D6
Petrockstow EX20 . . . 56 F3
Ash Hill Cross EX16 . . . 48 D6
Ash Hill Ct EX12 . . . . . 191 C5
Ash Hill Rd TQ1 . . . . . 220 A6
ASHILL 66 D6
Ashill Cl TA14 . . . . . . 209 A8
Ashill Ctyd EX15 . . . . . 66 C6
Ash La
Iddesleigh EX19 . . . . . 57 F1
Withypool TA24 . . . . . 21 F6
Woolfardisworthy EX17 . 62 A2
Ashlake Rd EX6 . . . . . . 113 F7
Ash Leigh EX2 . . . . . . 181 A8
Ashleigh CE Prim Sch 20
EX2 . . . . 155 A5
Ashleigh Cl
Exeter EX4 . . . . 176 F6
Plymouth PL5 . . . . . . 244 C7
Ashleigh Cres EX32 . . . 155 B4
Ashleigh Dr TQ14 . . . . 210 B7
Ashleigh La PL5 . . . . . 240 D1
Ashleigh Mount TQ14 . . 210 B7
Ashleigh Mount Rd EX4 . 176 F6
Ashleigh Pk
Bampton EX16 . . . . . 49 C8
Teignmouth TQ14 . . . . 210 B7
Ashleigh Rd
Barnstaple EX32 . . . . 155 A5
Exmouth EX8 . . . . . . 202 C7
Honiton EX14 . . . . . . 166 B6
Kingsbridge TQ7 . . . . 258 B4
Ashleigh Rise TQ14 . . . 210 B7
Ashleigh Way
Bideford EX39 . . . . . . 156 F1
13 Ilfracombe EX34 . . 150 B5
Ashley Back La EX16 . . 64 A5
Ashley Brake EX11 . . . 168 D4
Ashley Cl EX15 . . . . . . 66 A8
Ashley Cres EX10 . . . . 188 A7
Ashley Ho 2 EX8 . . . . 202 B6
Ashley Pl PL1 . . . . 262 B4
Ashley Priors La TQ1 . . 214 C4
Ashley Rd
Uffculme EX20 . . . . . 170 C5
Uffculme EX15 . . . . . 66 A7
Ashley Rise TQ14 . . . . 161 B1
Ashley Terr
19 Ilfracombe EX34 . . 150 B5
Ashley Way EX7 . . . . . 204 F7
ASHMANSWORTHY . . . 39 A5
Ashmead Gr EX33 . . . . 152 C6
ASHMILL 90 F6
ASH MILL 31 C2
Ashmill Cross EX21 . . . 90 F6
Ashmill Ct TQ12 . . . . . 206 F4
Ash Mill Hill EX36 . . . . 31 B2
Ashmore Cl EX2 . . . . . 261 A1
Ashplants Cl EX16 . . . . 58 F3
Ash Plants Cl EX19 . . . 156 D2
ASHPRINGTON 139 F8
Ashprington Cross TQ9 . 139 F8
Ash Rd
Braunton EX33 . . . . . 152 F7
Kingsteignton TQ12 . . 207 E6
ASHREIGNEY 58 F8
ASHRIDGE 26 D6
Ashridge Gdns
Kingsteignton TQ12 . . 207 F6
Plymouth PL5 . . . . . . 244 B2
Ashridge La EX20 . . . . 77 D6
Ashridge Moor Cross
EX20 . . . . 77 E6
ASH THOMAS 65 A5
Ashton Bsns Ctr EX2 . . 177 B2
Ashton Cl PL6 . . . . 245 C6
Ashton Cres EX33 . . . . 152 C5
Ashton Ct 12 TQ12 . . . 207 B3
Ashton Ind Units EX2 . . 177 B2
Ashton Rd EX2 . . . . . . 177 B2
Ashtons Cotts EX39 . . . 40 B7
Ashton Terr TQ1 . . . . . 220 B5
Ashton Way PL12 . . . . 242 D3
Ashtown Cross EX16 . . 34 A3
Ashtree Cl PL9 . . . . . . 256 C8
Ash Units EX17 . . . . . . 165 F5
Ash Vale PL16 . . . . . . 105 E4
ASHWATER 90 D6
Ashwater Prim Sch EX21 . 90 F6
Ash Way TQ12 . . . . . . 207 D6
Ashway EX36 . . . . 124 B1
Ashwell La TQ13 . . . . . 122 E6
Ashwood 5 TQ10 . . . . 134 F3

Ashwood Cl
Loddiswell TQ7 . . . 143 E7
Plymouth PL7 . . . 251 B5
Ashwood Ct TQ12 . . . 207 E2
Ashwood Park Rd PL7 . . . 251 C6
Ashwood Pk TQ7 . . . 143 E7
Ashwood Rd EX2 . . . 177 B3
Aspen Cl
Exeter EX2 . . . 178 C4
3 Honiton EX14 . . . 85 C2
Tavistock PL19 . . . 171 C3
Aspen Dr TQ12 . . . 212 F8
Aspen Gdns PL7 . . . 251 B5
Aspen Gr EX31 . . . 153 D4
Aspen Way
Paignton TQ4 . . . 225 D3
Tiverton EX16 . . . 161 E7
Astley Corte EX20 . . . 170 A5
Astor Dr PL4 . . . 249 C3
Aswell Orch TQ7 . . . 143 F7
Athelstan Cl EX13 . . . 167 D4
Athelstan Rd EX1 . . . 261 C3
Athenaeum La PL1 . . . 262 B2
Athenaeum Pl PL1 . . . 262 C2
Athenaeum St PL1 . . . 262 B2
ATHERINGTON . . . 28 A2
Atherton La 14 TQ9 . . . 223 C5
Atherton Pl PL2 . . . 247 E4
Atherton Way EX16 . . . 64 D7
Athlone Ho PL1 . . . 262 A2
Atkinson Cl EX4 . . . 174 A1
Atlantic Highway EX39 . . . 156 E4
Atlantic Village Outlet Shopping EX39 . . . 25 D4
Atlantic Way EX39 . . . 156 D7
Attwyll Ave EX2 . . . 178 A5
Atway Cl 3 TQ13 . . . 180 C8
Atwill-Kingdom Almshouses EX1 . . . 177 E6
Atwill's Almshouses EX4 . . . 261 A4
Atworthy Cross EX22 . . . 38 D3
Auckland Rd 3 PL2 . . . 248 A5
Auction Way EX39 . . . 38 F8
Audley 2 EX10 . . . 188 A4
Audley Ave TQ2 . . . 219 F8
Audley Rise TQ12 . . . 208 A1
Augusta Ct 16 EX1 . . . 261 A2
Augustine Cl EX12 . . . 191 F8
Aunay Cl EX22 . . . 164 D5
Aune Cl TQ10 . . . 135 B1
Aunemouth Cross TQ7 . . . 143 A3
AUNK . . . 83 E3
Ausewell Cross TQ13 . . . 130 D7
Austen Cl EX4 . . . 178 C8
Austin Ave PL2 . . . 248 A6
Austin Cres PL6 . . . 245 C1
Austin Farm Prim Sch PL6 . . . 249 C7
Authers Hts EX16 . . . 161 B2
Auton Cross TQ7 . . . 258 A2
Autumn Field EX19 . . . 58 E3
Avalon Cl EX4 . . . 174 A2
Aveland Rd TQ1 . . . 220 C7
Avent Wlk PL7 . . . 250 F7
Avenue Cl DT7 . . . 260 D3
Avenue Cottage Gdn★ TQ9 . . . 227 A8
Avenue Ho EX17 . . . 165 C6
Avenue Mezidon-Canon EX14 . . . 166 D5
Avenue Rd
Bovey Tracey TQ13 . . . 180 C6
Ilfracombe EX34 . . . 150 B6
Kingskerswell TQ12 . . . 213 A5
Lyme Regis DT7 . . . 260 D3
Torquay TQ2 . . . 219 F5
Avenue Terr TQ5 . . . 229 E5
Avenue The
Exton EX3 . . . 183 C1
Newton Abbot TQ12 . . . 207 D4
4 Seaton EX12 . . . 192 A5
Tiverton EX16 . . . 161 E3
Avery Ct EX8 . . . 196 D2
Avery Hill TQ12 . . . 207 E8
Avery Way PL12 . . . 242 C5
AVETON GIFFORD . . . 143 C6
Aveton Gifford CE Prim Sch TQ7 . . . 143 C6
Aviemore Ind Est EX31 . . . 154 D3
Avoca Ave TQ1 . . . 219 F6
Avocet Dr EX3 . . . 183 C2
Avocet Rd EX2 . . . 178 F6
Avon Cl
Plymouth PL3 . . . 249 D6
South Brent TQ10 . . . 135 A2
Avon Ct TQ7 . . . 142 F3
Avondale Ho 10 TQ10 . . . 134 F2
Avondale Rd
Exeter EX2 . . . 178 A5
Exmouth EX8 . . . 202 D8
Avondale Wlk 11 TQ10 . . . 134 F2
Avon Dam★ TQ11 . . . 134 D8
Avon La EX39 . . . 156 D7
Avon Quillet TQ7 . . . 142 E3
Avon Rd
Bideford EX39 . . . 157 C1
Torquay TQ2 . . . 219 B7
Avon Valley Cotts TQ7 . . . 143 C6
AVONWICK . . . 135 B1
Avonwick TQ1 . . . 220 C7
Avonwick Gn TQ10 . . . 135 B1
Avranches Ave EX17 . . . 165 A6
AWLISCOMBE . . . 85 B4
Awliscombe CE Prim Sch EX14 . . . 85 B4
Axe Cl PL3 . . . 249 D6
Axeford TA20 . . . 88 E8
Axeford Mdws TA20 . . . 88 E8
Axe Valley Cl EX13 . . . 104 C7
Axe Valley Com Coll The EX13 . . . 167 D6
Axe Valley Sports Ctr EX13 . . . 167 E6
Axeview Rd EX12 . . . 192 A7
AXMINSTER . . . 167 C6
Axminster Com Prim Sch EX13 . . . 167 E6
Axminster Hospl EX13 . . . 167 D6
Axminster Mus★ EX13 . . . 167 D5
Axminster Rd
Charmouth DT6 . . . 104 F4
Honiton EX14 . . . 166 F5
Musbury EX13 . . . 103 D5
Offwell EX14 . . . 86 A3
Tatworth TA20 . . . 88 C7
Axminster Sta EX13 . . . 167 C5
AXMOUTH . . . 192 E7
Axmouth Rd EX12 . . . 192 C5
Axmouth to Lyme Regis National Nature Reserve★ DT7 . . . 193 D4
Axtown La PL20 . . . 126 F2
Aycliffe Gdns PL7 . . . 251 A3
AYLESBEARE . . . 99 D2
Aylesbury Cres PL5 . . . 244 B5
Aylescott Cross EX37 . . . 43 E3
Aylescott Hill EX34 . . . 9 A4
Aylescott La EX34 . . . 9 A4
Ayleston Cross PL21 . . . 137 D2
Ayleston Pk PL21 . . . 137 C2
Aylwin Cl PL7 . . . 250 E6
Ayres Cl EX39 . . . 157 C1
Ayreville Rd PL2 . . . 248 B7
Aysha Gdns EX39 . . . 156 D8
AYSHFORD . . . 50 E2
Ayshford EX15 . . . 66 A7
Azalea Cl EX14 . . . 67 C1
Azes La EX32 . . . 155 A5

B

BABBACOMBE . . . 220 D7
Babbacombe Bsns Pk TQ1 . . . 220 E7
Babbacombe Cl PL6 . . . 249 E8
Babbacombe Cliff TQ1 . . . 220 D7
Babbacombe Cliff Rly★ TQ1 . . . 220 D8
Babbacombe Downs Rd TQ1 . . . 220 D8
Babbacombe Model Village★ TQ1 . . . 220 C8
Babbacombe Rd TQ1 . . . 220 E6
Babbage Rd TQ9 . . . 223 D6
Babbages EX31 . . . 154 A4
Babblebrook Mews EX1 . . . 178 F8
Babeleigh Rd EX39 . . . 39 E7
Babeleigh Water EX39 . . . 39 E7
Baber Ct PL12 . . . 125 A2
Babis Farm Cl PL12 . . . 242 F1
Babis Farm Ct PL12 . . . 242 F1
Babis Farm Mews PL12 . . . 242 F2
Babis Farm Row PL12 . . . 242 F1
Babis Farm Way PL12 . . . 242 F2
Babis La PL12 . . . 242 F1
Babland Cross PL21 . . . 137 D2
Bableigh Cl EX39 . . . 40 B7
Bableigh Cross EX32 . . . 28 B8
Bableigh Rd EX32 . . . 17 B1
Babylon La EX5 . . . 82 B5
Backfield 7 EX39 . . . 15 A1
Back Hill PL12 . . . 242 D2
Back Hill Ind Est EX18 . . . 44 E1
Back La
Abbotsham EX39 . . . 156 A1
Bickleigh EX16 . . . 63 D2
Black Torrington EX21 . . . 74 A8
Bradninch EX5 . . . 82 E6
Chawleigh EX18 . . . 60 C8
Chittlehampton EX37 . . . 28 F4
Chulmleigh EX18 . . . 44 E1
Colaton Raleigh EX10 . . . 186 B3
Copplestone EX17 . . . 79 A4
Ermington PL21 . . . 136 F3
Frithelstock Stone EX38 . . . 40 F5
Lutton PL21 . . . 133 B2
Merton EX20 . . . 57 A7
Newton Poppleford EX10 . . . 186 E8
North Molton EX36 . . . 30 D8
Okehampton/North Tawton EX20 . . . 77 A1
Plymouth PL7 . . . 250 E4
Sandford EX17 . . . 80 A5
Sidmouth EX10 . . . 187 C7
Sticklepath EX20 . . . 95 A5
Stockland EX14 . . . 87 A5
Back Rd
Calstock PL18 . . . 125 D3
Moreleigh TQ9 . . . 139 A3
Newton Abbot TQ12 . . . 207 B3
Backshay Cl TQ7 . . . 143 C1
Backshay Pk TQ7 . . . 143 C1
Back's Hill
Crediton EX17 . . . 79 F7
Sandford EX17 . . . 80 A7
Back St
Bampton EX16 . . . 34 B1
16 Modbury PL21 . . . 137 B2
Woolfardisworthy EX39 . . . 38 F8
Backs The TQ6 . . . 233 E5
Backstone La EX16 . . . 47 B6
Backswood La EX16 . . . 64 B4
Backways La TA21 . . . 51 F6
Backwells Mead EX24 . . . 102 B6
Badgaver La EX34 . . . 3 B3
Badger Cl
Dartmouth TQ6 . . . 233 D4
10 Exeter EX2 . . . 178 D5
Honiton EX14 . . . 166 E7
Newton Poppleford EX10 . . . 186 D7
Paignton TQ3 . . . 218 F1
Badgers Cl
Ivybridge PL21 . . . 237 A5
Kingsbridge TQ7 . . . 258 C4
Kingsteignton TQ12 . . . 207 D8
Badgers Gn TQ7 . . . 258 C4
Badgers Holt EX20 . . . 170 A5
Badger's Way TQ13 . . . 180 D7
Badgers Wlk PL12 . . . 242 D4
Badger View PL9 . . . 255 E5
Bad Homburg Way EX2 . . . 181 D8
Badlake Cl EX7 . . . 204 C7
Badlake Hill EX7 . . . 204 C7
Badlake La EX36 . . . 32 D6
Badlake Moor Cross TA22 . . . 32 D7
Badon Cl EX4 . . . 174 A2
BADWORTHY . . . 134 D4
BAGLEY GREEN . . . 160 A3
Bagley Rd TA21 . . . 160 A3
Bagmore Hill EX5 . . . 82 F8
Bagshot Ave EX2 . . . 177 D3
Bailey La EX5 . . . 98 F7
Bailey's Knapp EX16 . . . 50 B4
Baileys Mdw TQ6 . . . 146 B7
Bailey St EX4 . . . 261 B3
Bailey Terr EX22 . . . 70 F5
Bainbridge Ave PL3 . . . 248 F7
Bainbridge Ct PL7 . . . 250 E7
Baker Cl EX10 . . . 188 A8
Bakers Cl PL7 . . . 251 C5
Bakers Cotts EX8 . . . 195 F5
Bakers Court La EX35 . . . 151 B5
Baker's Cross TA3 . . . 68 A7
Bakers Ct EX35 . . . 151 B5
Bakers Hill
Aveton Gifford TQ7 . . . 143 C6
Brixham TQ5 . . . 230 C3
Exeter EX2 . . . 176 C3
Baker's Hill
Newton Abbot TQ12 . . . 207 B3
Tiverton EX16 . . . 161 A4
Baker's La
Churchinford TA3 . . . 68 A7
Wellington TA21 . . . 160 E6
Bakers Mead EX13 . . . 87 A1
Baker's Pk TQ13 . . . 130 A4
Bakers Pl PL1 . . . 247 F1
Baker St EX2 . . . 177 F5
Bakers Terr TQ7 . . . 143 C6
Bakers View TQ12 . . . 207 A3
Bakery La EX8 . . . 202 A7
Bakery Mdw EX16 . . . 62 B5
Bakery Way EX32 . . . 17 B2
BAKESDOWN . . . 70 C3
Bakesdown La EX6 . . . 96 B3
Bala Brook Cl TQ5 . . . 229 F2
Baldwin Ct EX20 . . . 170 D6
Baldwin Dr EX20 . . . 170 D6
Balfour Cl EX14 . . . 166 E5
Balfour Gdns EX10 . . . 188 A6
Balfour Manor EX10 . . . 188 A5
Balfour Manor Ct EX10 . . . 187 F5
Balfour Mews EX10 . . . 188 A5
Balfours EX10 . . . 188 A6
Balfour Terr
Kilmington EX13 . . . 87 C1
Plymouth PL2 . . . 247 E4
Balkwill Ct TQ7 . . . 258 C4
Balkwill Rd TQ7 . . . 258 B4
Balkwill's Cotts EX21 . . . 55 E4
Bal La PL19 . . . 117 E6
Balland La TQ13 . . . 131 A5
Balland Pk 5 TQ13 . . . 131 A5
Ballards Cres EX31 . . . 153 A4
Ballards Gr EX31 . . . 153 A4
Ballards Way EX31 . . . 153 A4
Balleroy Cl EX21 . . . 55 E4
Ball Hill EX17 . . . 63 A2
Ballhill La EX16 . . . 49 B8
Ball La EX24 . . . 101 F5
Ball Mdw EX20 . . . 170 D5
Balls Cnr EX37 . . . 44 A3
Balls Corner EX20 . . . 57 C8
Balls Corner Cross EX20 . . . 57 C8
Balls Cross EX36 . . . 20 B2
Ball's Cross TQ8 . . . 259 C7
Balls Farm Rd EX2 . . . 176 F2
Balls Hill EX37 . . . 44 A2
Balmoral Ave PL2 . . . 247 F5
Balmoral Cl TQ12 . . . 207 E2
Balmoral Cres EX20 . . . 170 D5
Balmoral Gdns EX3 . . . 182 F5
Balmoral Ho EX31 . . . 154 E7
Balmoral La 7 TQ10 . . . 134 F3
Balmoral Terr 12 EX34 . . . 150 B5
Balsdon Rd EX22 . . . 70 E1
Baltic Wharf Bsns Pk TQ9 . . . 223 D4
Bampflyde Way PL6 . . . 244 D6
Bampfylde Cl
Poltimore EX4 . . . 174 F6
Tiverton EX16 . . . 161 F3
Bampfylde Cross EX36 . . . 19 D2
Bampfylde Rd TQ2 . . . 219 F5
Bampfylde St EX1, EX4 . . . 261 C3
BAMPTON . . . 34 C1
Bampton CE Prim Sch EX16 . . . 34 B1
Bampton Cl TQ3 . . . 218 D2
Bampton Down Rd EX16 . . . 49 F7
Bampton Rd PL6 . . . 245 E1
Bampton St EX16 . . . 161 D4
Bamson La EX16 . . . 62 B6
Banbury Pk TQ2 . . . 219 C8
Banfield Way EX14 . . . 166 B4
Bank End EX39 . . . 157 B4
Bank La
11 Brixham TQ5 . . . 230 C5
6 Totnes TQ9 . . . 223 C5
Bankland La EX20 . . . 77 D8
Banksia Cl EX16 . . . 161 E7
Bankside EX8 . . . 196 C3
Bank Sq TA22 . . . 33 D6
Bank St
Newton Abbot TQ12 . . . 207 B3
12 Teignmouth TQ14 . . . 210 C4
Bank The 11 EX32 . . . 17 B2
Bannawell Ct 1 PL19 . . . 171 B6
Bannawell St PL19 . . . 171 B6
Banner Ct 4 TQ3 . . . 226 A6
BANTHAM . . . 142 F2
Bantham Cross TQ7 . . . 143 D4
Baptist Chapel Ct EX17 . . . 165 C5
Baptist St PL17 . . . 125 D3
Bapton Cl EX8 . . . 196 B2
Bapton La EX8 . . . 196 B1
Barber's La
Uplyme DT7 . . . 260 B4
West Buckland TA21 . . . 52 F7
BARBICAN . . . 263 A2
Barbican App PL4 . . . 263 B2
Barbican Cl EX32 . . . 155 A4
Barbican Ct
Exeter EX4 . . . 177 A5
11 Plymouth PL4 . . . 263 A2
Barbican La EX32 . . . 155 B4
Barbican L Pk PL4 . . . 263 C2
Barbican Pl 9 EX32 . . . 155 A4
Barbican Rd
Barnstaple EX32 . . . 155 A4
Plymouth PL7 . . . 250 E4
Barbican Stps EX4 . . . 261 A2
Barbican Terr EX32 . . . 155 A4
Barbican The PL1 . . . 263 A2
Barbican Theatre★ PL1 . . . 263 A1
BARBROOK . . . 151 B1
Barbrook Rd EX35 . . . 151 B3
Barbury Cres PL6 . . . 245 B8
Barchington Ave TQ2 . . . 213 F3
Barcombe Hts TQ3 . . . 226 B8
Barcombe La TQ3 . . . 226 B8
Barcombe Mews TQ3 . . . 226 B8
Barcombe Rd TQ3 . . . 226 A8
Barcote Wlk PL6 . . . 249 C8
Bardsey Cl PL6 . . . 245 A7
Barewell Cl TQ1 . . . 220 B8
Barewell Rd TQ1 . . . 220 B8
Barfield Cl EX19 . . . 57 F7
Barfield Rd EX19 . . . 57 F7
Baring Cotts 14 TQ9 . . . 223 D5
Baring Cres EX1 . . . 177 E6
Baring Ct
Exeter EX2 . . . 261 B1
Lewtrenchard EX20 . . . 106 F5
Baring Flats EX1 . . . 177 E6
Baring St PL4 . . . 263 B4
Baring Terr EX1 . . . 261 B1
Barker's Hill PL12 . . . 242 C1
Barkers Way EX20 . . . 77 C4
Barkingdon Workshops TQ9 . . . 215 D7
Barlands Way EX19 . . . 57 F7
Barle Cl EX2 . . . 178 D4
Barle Ct EX16 . . . 161 E7
Barley Cl EX15 . . . 163 B2
Barleycorn Fields 6 EX32 . . . 17 B2
Barley Farm Rd EX4 . . . 176 E4
Barley La EX4 . . . 176 D5
Barley Lane Specl Sch EX4 . . . 176 D4
Barley Market St PL19 . . . 171 C6
Barley Mount EX4 . . . 176 F5
Barley Valley Nature Reserve★ EX4 . . . 176 D6
Barley Wlk EX6 . . . 201 A8
Barline EX12 . . . 191 D5
Barlow Gdns PL2 . . . 248 B7
Barlow Rd EX31 . . . 155 A7
Barnacott Cross EX39 . . . 26 D8
Barnardo Rd EX2 . . . 261 C1
Barnards Farm EX12 . . . 191 D5
Barnards Hill La EX12 . . . 192 A7
Barn Cl
Barnstaple EX32 . . . 155 C3
Ivybridge PL21 . . . 237 A6
Plymouth PL7 . . . 251 D4
Shebbear EX21 . . . 55 E4
Whiddon Down EX20 . . . 95 F3
Barn Close La EX12 . . . 192 E5
Barncroft EX22 . . . 39 C1
Barn Cross EX14 . . . 85 F8
Barn Ct TQ5 . . . 229 E4
Barndale Cres PL6 . . . 245 B6
BARNE BARTON . . . 247 C8
Barne Cl PL5 . . . 247 C8
Barne Cross TQ13 . . . 112 A2
Barne La PL5 . . . 243 D1
Barne Rd PL5 . . . 247 C8
Barnes Cl
Honiton EX14 . . . 166 B4
Willand EX15 . . . 162 C5
Barnes Close Mead TA22 . . . 33 D6
Barnes Mdw DT7 . . . 260 B5
BARNFIELD . . . 261 C3
Barnfield
Crediton EX17 . . . 165 C5
East Allington TQ9 . . . 144 D7
Barnfield Ave EX8 . . . 202 D7
Barnfield Cl
Braunton EX33 . . . 152 E5
Crediton EX17 . . . 165 C5
Galmpton TQ5 . . . 229 C5
Barnfield Cotts EX5 . . . 81 F3
Barnfield Cres EX1 . . . 261 B3
Barnfield Dr PL7 . . . 251 C5
Barnfield Hill EX1 . . . 261 C3
Barnfield Rd
Brixham TQ5 . . . 230 D3
Exeter EX1 . . . 261 B3
Paignton TQ3 . . . 226 A7
Torquay TQ2 . . . 219 D2
Barnfield Terr TQ12 . . . 212 B6
Barnfield Theatre★ EX1 . . . 261 B3
Barnfield Wlk TQ7 . . . 258 C6
Barnhay 6 EX16 . . . 34 B1
Barn Hayes EX10 . . . 187 F7
Barnhay The TQ9 . . . 227 F7
Barn Hill EX17 . . . 78 F7
Barnhill Rd TQ12 . . . 213 A4
Barningham Gdns PL6 . . . 245 B6
Barn La EX9 . . . 197 F2
Barn Meads Rd TA21 . . . 160 E4
Barn Owl Cl TQ2 . . . 213 D3
Barnpark Cl TQ14 . . . 210 C6
Barn Park Cl TQ12 . . . 211 E2
Barn Park Gdns EX21 . . . 73 C2
Barnpark Rd TQ14 . . . 210 C5
Barn Park Rd
Fremington EX31 . . . 153 D5
Plymouth PL3 . . . 248 D6
Barnpark Terr TQ14 . . . 210 C6
Barn Pk
Ashwater EX21 . . . 90 E6
Buckfastleigh TQ11 . . . 236 A5
Coldeast TQ12 . . . 122 F1
Crediton EX17 . . . 165 C5
Saltash PL12 . . . 242 F3
Stoke Gabriel TQ9 . . . 227 F8
Wrafton EX33 . . . 152 E3
Barn Rd TQ4 . . . 226 C2
Barns Cl
Bradninch EX5 . . . 82 F6
Kingsteignton TQ12 . . . 207 E6
Barnsclose TA22 . . . 33 D6
Barns Close Ind Est TA22 . . . 33 D6
Barnsclose N TA22 . . . 33 D6
Barnsclose W TA22 . . . 33 D6
Barnsey Gdns TQ13 . . . 130 F5
Barnsfield La TQ11 . . . 236 A5
Barnshill Cl EX17 . . . 62 F1
Barnsley Cl 1 TQ14 . . . 210 C5
Barnsley Dr TQ14 . . . 210 C6
Barns Rd EX9 . . . 198 B1
BARNSTAPLE . . . 155 C4
Barnstaple Cl
Chittlehampton EX37 . . . 28 F4
Plymouth PL6 . . . 249 E7
Barnstaple Cross
Burrington EX37 . . . 43 C3
Crediton EX17 . . . 79 E4
Barnstaple Heritage Ctr★ EX31 . . . 154 F5
Barnstaple Ret Pk EX31 . . . 154 F4
Barnstaple St
Bideford EX39 . . . 157 B2
South Molton EX36 . . . 158 C4
Winkleigh EX19 . . . 58 F3
Barnstaple Sta EX31 . . . 154 F4
Barns Terr PL12 . . . 238 A3
Barnstone Ct EX2 . . . 181 A8
Barntown Gate EX19 . . . 58 E1
Barntown La EX19 . . . 58 D1
Barnwood Cl PL9 . . . 255 E5
Barometer World (Mus)★ EX20 . . . 57 A7
Baron Ct EX31 . . . 154 B1
Barons Pyke PL21 . . . 237 E4
Barons Rd PL20 . . . 127 B3
Baron Way EX31 . . . 154 B1
Barossa Rd PL11 . . . 247 B3
Barpark Cnr EX15 . . . 52 E3
Barrack La EX2 . . . 181 A6
Barrack Pl PL1 . . . 248 A1
Barrack Rd
Exeter EX2 . . . 177 E4
Ottery St Mary EX11 . . . 169 C3
Princetown PL20 . . . 128 B8
Yelverton PL20 . . . 119 A1
Barracks Hill TQ9 . . . 223 A7
Barracks Rd PL21 . . . 137 B3
Barrack St PL1 . . . 247 E2
Barradon Cl TQ2 . . . 214 A4
Barrington Ct TQ4 . . . 226 C5
Barrington Ho TQ1 . . . 220 E5
Barrington Mead EX10 . . . 188 B4
Barrington Rd TQ1 . . . 220 E5
Barrington St EX16 . . . 161 D4
Barris EX17 . . . 60 C3
Barrowdale Cl EX8 . . . 196 C3
Barrow Down PL12 . . . 242 B3
Barrow Rd EX14 . . . 84 C4
Barrow Way Cross EX20 . . . 110 D8
Bar's La EX9, EX10 . . . 199 B8
Bartholomew Rd PL2 . . . 248 B5
Bartholomew Street E EX4 . . . 261 A3
Bartholomew Street W EX4 . . . 261 A2
Bartholomew Terr EX4 . . . 261 A2
BARTON . . . 213 F3
Barton Ave
Braunton EX33 . . . 152 D4
Paignton TQ3 . . . 225 F7
Plymouth PL2 . . . 247 E5
Bartonbury Cross EX17 . . . 78 E6

Barton Cl
Cheriton Fitzpaine EX17 .... 62 E1
Exton EX3............... 183 C1
Filleigh EX32 .... 29 C6
Georgeham EX33......... 8 B4
Kingsbridge TQ7 .... 258 D4
North Tawton EX20 .... 77 C4
Okehampton EX20....... 170 C5
Paignton TQ3 .... 225 F7
Parkham EX39 .... 39 E8
Plymouth PL7............ 251 C5
Stoke Canon EX5......... 81 F1
Wembury PL9 .... 140 D8
Barton Cnr EX17 .... 61 B2
Barton Cotts EX20 .... 95 C1
Barton Cres
Dawlish EX7............. 204 C6
Paignton TQ3 .... 225 F7
Barton Cross
East Anstey EX16......... 32 E5
Filleigh EX32 .... 29 A6
Heasley Mill EX36 .... 19 C2
Instow EX39 .... 15 B2
Morchard Bishop EX17 ... 61 C2
Poltimore EX5 .... 174 B8
Sandford EX17........... 80 C6
Torquay TQ2............ 213 F4
Barton Ct
Ashwater EX21 .... 90 E6
Exeter EX1.............. 178 C1
Parkham EX39 .... 39 E8
Sidmouth EX10 .... 188 A3
Barton Dr
Newton Abbot TQ12..... 206 F3
Paignton TQ3 .... 225 F7
BARTON GATE 11 E4
Barton Gate La EX34... 3 A3
Barton Head Cross EX20.. 76 C4
Barton Hill
Berrynarbor EX34 .... 2 E4
Daccombe TQ1, TQ12... 214 A6
Dawlish EX7............. 204 D6
North Tawton EX20 .... 77 C4
Bartonhill Cross TQ12.. 215 F6
Barton Hill Rd TQ2 ..... 213 F6
Barton Hill Way TQ2 ... 213 F2
Barton Ho PL20 .... 126 A4
Barton La
Barton Town EX31 .... 11 D3
Berrynarbor EX34 .... 2 E4
Braunton EX33.......... 152 D5
Brayford EX32 .... 18 F4
Dawlish EX7............. 204 D6
Lapford EX17............. 60 A2
Shillingford Abbot EX4... 114 C7
Staverton TQ9 .... 216 A5
Witheridge EX16......... 46 E1
Barton Lane Cl EX3 .... 152 D4
Barton Meadow Rd EX37.. 43 B7
Barton Mews
Exton EX3............... 183 C1
Millbrook PL10.......... 252 F6
Parkham EX39 .... 39 E8
Venn Ottery EX11 .... 100 B2
Barton Orch EX10 ...... 100 D2
Barton Paddocks EX11.. 100 D2
Barton Prim Sch TQ2... 213 F2
Barton Rd
Barnstaple EX32 .... 155 D4
Buckland Brewer EX39... 40 B7
Exeter EX2.............. 176 F4
Okehampton EX20....... 170 C5
Paignton TQ3 .... 225 F7
Parkham EX39 .... 39 E8
Plymouth PL9............ 255 B6
Tiverton EX16 .... 161 D6
Torquay TQ2............ 219 E7
West Down EX34 .... 8 F5
Woolacombe EX34 .... 7 F6
Barton Rise EX14 .... 84 E2
Barton Road Ind Units
TQ2.................... 219 E8
Barton St EX20.......... 77 C4
Barton Steep EX35 ...... 5 E4
Barton Terr EX7 .... 204 D6
Barton Tors EX39 .... 157 C1
Barton View EX20 .... 77 C4
Barton Villas EX7 .... 204 C6
Bartows Cswy EX16..... 161 D5
Bartows Mews EX16.... 161 D5
Bartridge Hill EX31..... 27 A5
Barum Arc EX32 .... 155 A5
Barum Cl TQ3 .... 226 C7
Barum Gate Bsns Pk
EX32................... 155 D3
Barum Mews EX32 ..... 155 A5
Barwick Cross EX19..... 58 B2
Bary Cl EX17............ 62 F1
Bary Hill Cross EX17 ... 62 F1
Bary La EX17........... 62 F1
Bascombe Cl TQ5 ...... 229 D6
Bascombe Rd TQ5 ...... 229 D6
Basinghall Cl PL9 ...... 255 E5
Basket Ope PL4 .... 263 A2
Bason Cross EX22 ...... 55 B2
Bassett Cl 1 EX33 ..... 152 D5
Bassetts Cl
Copplestone EX17 .... 79 A5
Dunsford EX6 .... 156 F8
Bassetts Farm Prim Sch
EX8.................... 196 E1
Bassetts Gdns EX8 ..... 196 D2
Bastard's La EX14 ...... 84 E2
Bastard's Park Cnr PL21 137 D3
Batavia Dr EX2.......... 178 D1

Batcombe La EX5 .... 81 F6
Bate Cl EX2............. 177 A1
Bateman's Cross EX13.... 88 E7
Bath Cl EX14............. 84 D2
Bath Ct EX39........... 156 C7
Batherm Cl 3 EX16 ...... 49 B8
Bathern Rd EX2.......... 178 D4
Bath Hotel Rd EX39 ..... 156 C7
Bath La
Plymouth PL1............ 262 B2
Torquay TQ2............ 219 F5
Bath Meadow Dr TA22.... 33 E4
Bath Pl
Ilfracombe EX34 .... 150 B6
Plymouth PL1............ 262 B2
Bath Place W PL1 .... 262 B2
Bath Rd EX8 .... 202 A6
Bath St PL1............. 262 B2
Bath Terr
6 Instow EX39.......... 15 B1
12 Teignmouth TQ14 ..... 210 C4
Batson Cross TQ8 ...... 259 C5
Batson Gdns TQ4 ...... 226 B4
Batson Hall Cross TQ8 .. 259 C5
BATSWORTHY 46 F6
Batsworthy Cross EX16.. 46 F7
Batsworthy Hill EX16.... 47 A7
Battens EX14 .... 87 A7
Battens Cross EX16 ..... 65 C8
Batterbridge Hill PL19.. 117 E3
Batteridge Hill PL19.... 117 F2
Battershall Cl PL9....... 255 F5
Battery La PL4 .... 263 A2
Battersway Rd TQ4...... 225 E4
Battery La PL19......... 171 C4
Battery St PL1 .... 262 A2
Battery Street Flats PL1. 262 A2
BATTISBOROUGH
CROSS 141 E7
Battisford Pk PL7 .... 251 E3
Battishorne Way EX14... 166 H4
Battledown Cross EX21... 55 F4
Battleford La TQ9 .... 217 C5
Battle Rd TQ12.......... 180 F2
Battle St EX15 .... 52 D6
Battleton TA22.......... 33 D6
Batt's La EX11.......... 169 D3
Batts Pk EX15 .... 66 C6
Batworthy Mill Cross
TQ13.................. 111 A4
Bavent Cl EX5........... 173 F8
Bate Cl EX2............ 172 C8
Baxworthy Cross EX39... 23 A1
Bayard's Cove TQ6 ...... 233 F3
Bayards Cove Fort TQ6 233 F3
Bayard's Hill TQ6 .... 233 F3
Bayclose La EX31....... 10 D6
Baydon Cl PL6.......... 245 C1
Bay Fort Mans TQ1..... 220 A4
Bayly's Rd PL9.......... 255 B7
Baymount Rd TQ3....... 226 A7
Baynes Ct TA21......... 160 E7
Bay Rd EX9............. 199 A7
Bayside La PL9 .... 140 A8
Bayswater Rd PL1...... 262 B4
Baythorpe Lodge TQ2... 219 E2
Baytor Ind Est TQ4 ..... 225 E3
Baytree Cl PL6.......... 245 D6
Baytree Gdns PL2....... 248 A7
Bay Trees EX6 .... 114 D4
Bay View TQ4.......... 219 D1
Bay View Cl TQ6 .... 146 B7
Bay View Ct
Lyme Regis DT7......... 260 E3
Northam EX39 .... 156 F6
Bay View Dr TQ14....... 210 C6
Bay View Est TQ6 ...... 146 B7
Bay View Rd
Lyme Regis DT7......... 260 D4
Northam EX39 .... 156 E6
Woolacombe EX34 .... 7 F6
Baze La EX35 .... 6 B4
Bazley Sq EX1 .... 178 E8
Beach Rd
Croyde EX33 .... 7 D2
Dawlish Warren EX7 ..... 201 B2
Heybrook Bay PL9....... 140 A7
Ilfracombe EX34 .... 150 F6
Paignton TQ4 .... 226 C6
Seaton EX12 .... 192 B4
Westward Ho! EX39...... 156 D7
Woolacombe EX34 .... 8 A6
Beach St 12 EX7 .... 204 E6
Beach View Cres EX7 .... 140 D7
Beach Wlk TQ4 .... 226 C2
BEACON.................. 85 F8
Beacon Ave EX4 .... 178 A8
Beacon Castle EX34 .... 150 A6
Beacon CE Prim Sch The 20
EX8................... 202 A6
Beacon Cl PL21 .... 237 C6
Beacon Cotts TQ13...... 130 C8
Beacon Cross
Bradninch EX5 .... 82 F7
Copplestone EX17 .... 79 D6
North Tawton EX20 .... 77 A2
Romansleigh EX36........ 45 C5
Talaton EX5 .... 84 B1
Beacon Down Ave PL2 .. 248 B7
Beacon Down Cnr EX6 .. 98 D2
Beacondown Cross EX16.. 63 D8
Beacon Down Cross EX20 93 E5
Beacon Down Hill EX20 .. 93 F5
Beaconfield Rd PL2 ..... 248 B7
Beacon Heath EX4 ...... 174 C1
BEACON HILL 174 C3

Beacon Hill
Bradninch EX5 .... 82 F7
12 Plymouth EX8 .... 202 A6
Torquay TQ1............ 220 B3
Beacon Hill La EX14..... 87 A5
Beacon Ho PL3 .... 249 D4
Beacon Hts EX33....... 152 E6
Beacon La
Cullompton EX15......... 65 A3
Exeter EX4.............. 178 A8
Hennock TQ13 .... 123 A7
Kingswear TQ6.......... 234 A2
Wellington TA21......... 52 C4
Beaconpark La EX20 .... 95 D3
Beacon Park Rd PL2 .... 248 B7
Beacon Pk PL15......... 89 D2
Beacon Pl EX8........ 202 A6
Beacon Quay TQ1 ...... 220 B3
Beacon Rd
Bradninch EX5 .... 82 F7
Ivybridge PL21.......... 237 C6
Kingswear TQ6.......... 234 A2
Beacon Rise 5 EX8 ..... 44 E1
Beaconsfield Cross EX22.. 72 E6
Beacon Terr
4 South Brent TQ10.... 134 F2
Torquay TQ1............ 220 B3
Beacon The EX8 .... 202 A6
Beacon View
3 Bittaford PL21 .... 137 C7
Dartington TQ9 .... 222 F8
8 South Brent TQ10.... 134 F2
Beadle Cl 6 PL19 ...... 171 B4
Beadon Dr TQ8 .... 259 C4
Beadon La TQ13 .... 123 A8
Beadon Rd TQ8 .... 259 B4
BEAFORD 42 D1
Beaford Arts TQ12...... 42 D1
Beaford Com Prim Sch
EX19................... 42 D1
Bealey Court Cross EX18.. 45 E2
BEALSMILL 115 C3
Bealswood Cl PL18 ..... 125 D6
Bealswood Rd PL18 .... 125 D6
Beanhay Cl TQ12........ 122 F1
Beans Mdw EX20........ 170 A5
Beaple's Moor Cross
EX36.................... 47 A8
BEARA.................... 9 A1
Beara Cotts TQ13 ...... 131 C1
Beara Cross
Bratton Fleming EX31 .... 18 A8
Highampton EX21 .... 74 A6
King's Nympton EX37 .... 44 F6
Roborough EX38 .... 42 E6
Beara Down Cross EX5... 8 F1
Beara Head EX38 .... 4 A2
Beara Hill Head EX36... 19 B6
Beara La
Bratton Fleming EX31 .... 18 A8
Combe Martin EX34...... 3 C3
Beardown Rd EX20...... 170 C5
Beards Rd EX31......... 153 E5
BEARE 82 E3
Beare Bridge Rd EX20... 170 C6
Beare Cl PL9............ 255 B5
Beare Copse La EX19.... 58 F2
Beare La
Beare EX5 .... 82 E3
Bondleigh EX20 .... 77 B7
Beare Lane Cross EX20... 77 B7
Beare Sq EX5 .... 82 E3
Bearne's La 4 TQ12 ... 207 B3
Bearne's Prim Sch 10
TQ12.................. 207 C3
Bearsdown Cl PL6....... 249 C8
Bearsdown Rd PL6...... 249 C8
Bears Farm Cotts EX20.. 170 B7
Bears La EX9 .... 197 E3
Bear St
Barnstaple EX32 .... 155 A5
Braunton EX33.......... 152 C7
Wellington TA21......... 160 C6
Beatrice Ave
Plymouth, Keyham PL2... 247 E5
Plymouth, St Jude's PL4.. 263 B3
Saltash PL12............ 242 E2
Beatrice Gdns PL12 ..... 242 E1
Beattie Rd PL5.......... 243 D3
Beatty Cl PL6........... 245 A4
Beatty Way TQ6......... 233 F4
Beauchamp Cres PL2 ... 248 C7
Beauchamp Rd PL2 .... 248 C7
Beaudyn Wlk 5 PL6 .... 249 C7
Beaufort Cl EX16 .... 50 D1
Beaufort Ho PL2........ 247 E4
Beaufort Hts EX32...... 155 B6
Beaufort Rd EX2 .... 261 A1
Beaufort Wlk EX33...... 155 B6
Beauly Cl PL7........... 251 A5
Beaumaris Gdns PL3.... 248 F8
Beaumaris Rd PL3 ...... 248 F7
Beaumont Cl EX16 ..... 263 A3
Beaumont Cl
5 Coldeast TQ12 .... 122 F1
Torquay TQ2............ 219 D6
Beaumont Pl PL4 .... 263 A3
Beaumont Rd
Newton Abbot TQ12..... 207 C3
Plymouth PL4............ 263 B3
Beaumont St PL2........ 248 A5
Beaumont Terr PL12 .... 242 F4
Beauvale Cl EX11 .... 169 E4
Beavers Brook Cl TQ3... 219 B2

Beavor La EX13 .... 167 F6
BEAWORTHY 74 A2
Beaworthy CE Prim Sch.. 74 A3
Beccott Cross EX31 ..... 10 D4
Becket Rd TQ13......... 180 E7
Beckfield Pl PL7 .... 251 A5
Beckford Cl EX7......... 204 D6
Beckford Cross EX13.... 87 C4
Beckham Pl PL3 .... 249 A6
Becklake Cl EX31 .... 154 A2
Beckland Cross EX39.... 22 F4
Beckly Ct PL1........... 262 C3
Bede Gdns PL5......... 244 C1
Bedford Cl PL18 .... 125 C6
Bedford Ct EX10 .... 188 B3
Bedford Flats EX10...... 188 A3
Bedford Gr PL21 .... 237 D5
Bedford Mews PL4...... 263 A4
Bedford Park Villas PL4. 263 A4
Bedford Pk
10 Bere Alston PL20.... 125 C1
Plymouth PL4............ 263 A4
Bedford Pl
6 Bere Alston PL20.... 125 C1
12 Horrabridge PL20... 126 F4
Bedford Rd
Horrabridge PL20 .... 126 F4
Plymouth PL9............ 255 E8
Torquay TQ1............ 220 B4
Bedford Row 19 EX31... 154 F5
Bedford Sq
Sidmouth EX10 .... 188 B3
Tavistock PL19 .... 171 C5
Bedford St
12 Barnstaple EX32 .... 155 A5
Bere Alston PL20......... 125 C1
Plymouth PL2............ 247 F5
Bedford Terr PL4 .... 263 A4
Bedford Units PL18 .... 125 C5
Bedford Villas 7 PL20.. 125 C1
Bedford Way PL1 .... 262 C3
Bedlam La EX9......... 197 F2
Bedland's La EX9 .... 197 F2
Beech Ave
Exeter EX4.............. 173 D1
Plymouth PL4............ 263 C2
Beech Bank EX39 .... 25 D4
Beech Cl
Barnstaple EX31 .... 154 B2
Broadclyst EX5 .... 175 D6
Honiton EX14 .... 166 A4
Tavistock PL19 .... 171 C2
Torpoint PL11 .... 247 A3
Totnes TQ9 .... 222 F6
Willand EX15 .... 162 D4
Beech Cres PL20........ 128 A8
Beech Croft EX15 ...... 163 C5
Beechcroft Rd
Plymouth, Lower Compton
PL3................... 249 A6
Plymouth, North Prospect
PL2................... 248 B7
Beech Ct
Plymouth PL6............ 245 D5
2 Wellington TA21 ..... 160 D6
Beech Dr
Down St Mary EX17...... 78 E7
Ipplepen TQ12 .... 211 E2
Beeches The
Okehampton EX20....... 76 E1
Woolfardisworthy EX39... 38 F8
Beechfield Ave
Torquay TQ2............ 213 F2
Yelverton PL20.......... 127 A3
Beechfield Cl EX31...... 153 D5
Beechfield Gr PL3....... 248 E6
Beechfield Pl TQ2....... 213 F2
Beechfield Rd EX31 ..... 153 D5
Beech Gr
Barnstaple EX31 .... 154 F7
Braunton EX33.......... 152 C7
Wellington TA21......... 160 C6
Beech Grove Prim Sch
TA21.................. 160 C6
Beechgrove Terr EX31... 154 F7
Beech Hill EX21......... 160 F5
Beech Hill Ho EX17 ..... 61 D3
Beech Hill Rd EX17 ..... 61 C3
Beeching Cl EX21....... 73 E3
Beech La EX13.......... 88 E1
Beech Lea EX18.......... 58 F8
Beech Pk
Crediton EX17 .... 165 D6
Fremington EX31 .... 153 E5
Holsworthy Beacon EX22.. 54 C3
West Hill EX11........... 168 D4
Beech Rd
Lee Mill PL21 .... 136 C7
Stibb Cross EX38.......... 40 D1
Beech Tree Cross EX21... 33 C7
Beechtree Cl EX17 ...... 79 D7
Beech Tree Dr EX16..... 161 B5
Beechtree La EX10, EX12.. 101 F2
Beech Trees La TQ12.... 211 C3
Beechway EX2.......... 202 A8
Beech Wlk EX14 .... 85 C1
Beechwood Ave
Barnstaple EX31 .... 154 D4
Bovey Tracey TQ13...... 180 C4
Newton Abbot TQ12..... 207 E1
Plymouth PL4............ 248 D4
Beechwood Cl EX31 ..... 153 D5
Beechwood Cross PL7 ... 251 F7
Beechwood Ct TQ14..... 124 E1

Beechwood Dr TQ7 ..... 258 D5
Beechwood Prim Sch
PL6.................... 244 E6
Beechwood Rd TQ13 .... 123 E6
Beechwood Rise PL6.... 245 E1
Beechwood Terr PL4.... 248 D4
Beechwood Way PL7.... 251 D5
Beeley Orch EX16....... 161 C8
Beenleigh Cross TQ9 ... 139 D6
BEER 191 E5
Beerash Cross EX16 ..... 63 B4
Beer CE Prim Sch EX12 . 191 C5
Beer Cross EX20 .... 94 E6
Beere Cross EX36 .... 32 A5
Beer Heights Light Rly
EX12.................. 191 C5
Beer Hill
Clawton EX22 .... 72 B1
Seaton EX12 .... 191 E6
Beerhill La EX20 .... 76 F5
Beer La
Burlescombe EX16........ 51 B2
Dulverton TA22........... 33 B5
Puddington EX16 .... 62 C6
Zeal Monachorum EX17... 78 C7
Beer Quarry Caves
EX12.................. 191 A5
Beer Rd EX12 .... 191 E6
Beers Cotts EX6 .... 181 B2
Beers Hill EX17 .... 79 A5
BEESANDS 149 E7
Beesands TQ7.......... 149 E7
BESON 149 D7
Beeson Cross TQ7 ...... 149 D7
Beeson Pool TQ7 .... 149 C8
Beeston Wlk 6 PL6..... 249 C7
Beetham La TA20......... 69 E6
Beetland La EX35........ 151 D2
Beetor Cross TQ13 ...... 111 B3
Beggar's Bush TQ10..... 134 F2
Beggars La EX14......... 166 A5
Behind Hayes EX9....... 198 E7
Bekhams Tree Cross
EX6................... 113 B2
Belair Rd PL2 .... 248 C7
Belcombe Dro TA20 ..... 69 E7
Belfield Ave PL3......... 218 D3
Belfield Cl TQ3 .... 218 D3
Belfield Rd TQ3 .... 225 E7
Belfield Rise TQ3 .... 218 D3
Belfield Way TQ3 .... 218 D3
Belgrave Ct EX9 .... 203 F8
Belgrave La PL4 .... 248 F4
Belgrave Mews 5 TQ2.. 219 F5
Belgrave Rd
Exeter EX1.............. 261 C3
Newton Abbot TQ12..... 207 F1
Plymouth PL4............ 248 F4
Torquay TQ2............ 219 F5
Belgrave Terr
6 Teignmouth TQ14..... 210 C5
Upton Pyne EX5......... 173 A8
Belhaven Hill EX31...... 27 A6
Bellaire EX33 .... 152 C7
Bellaire Dr EX31........ 154 E7
Bellamarsh La TQ13..... 123 C4
Bellamy Cl PL6 .... 245 A1
Bella Vista Rd TQ5...... 230 C6
Bell Cl PL7 .... 250 F6
Bellever Cl EX4......... 261 A3
Belle Acre Cl PL3 .... 248 F6
Belle Ave EX17.......... 165 B5
Belle Cross Rd TQ7 ..... 258 E6
Belle Ct EX17........... 165 B5
Belle Hill TQ7.......... 258 E6
Belle Isle Dr EX2 .... 261 C1
Belle Meadow Ct 22
EX32.................. 154 F5
Belle Meadow Rd 10
EX32.................. 155 A5
Belle Parade EX17....... 165 D5
BELLEVER 120 B4
Belliver Dr PL20 .... 128 B8
Belliver Tor Dr TQ5 ..... 229 F2
Belliver View EX22...... 164 C4
Belle View Terr TA20 ..... 88 C8
Belle Vue
Axminster EX13 .... 167 D6
Chawleigh EX18.......... 60 A7
Belle Vue Ave
Lynton EX35............. 151 B5
Plymouth PL9............ 255 B5
Belle Vue Cl EX16 ...... 114 E4
Belle Vue Cross EX38 ... 42 A8
Belle Vue Dr PL9........ 255 B5
Belle Vue Rd
Exeter EX4.............. 173 A2
Exmouth EX8 .... 202 A8
Kingsbridge TQ7 .... 258 C5
Paignton TQ3 .... 226 C5
Saltash PL12............ 242 F2
Torquay TQ2............ 219 E5
Belle Vue Rise PL9 ...... 255 B5
Bellevue Sq PL1 .... 247 B2
Belle Vue Terr
Bideford EX39 .... 156 F2
Cullompton EX15........ 163 C4
Gunnislake PL18 .... 125 D6
Kenford EX6............ 114 D4

Belliver Way PL6 . . . . 241 B1
Bell La
  Hennock TQ13 . . . . 123 A7
  Paignton TQ3 . . . . 225 B7
Bell Mdw EX16 . . . . 64 A2
Bellrock Cl TQ2 . . . . 214 B3
Bells Cl EX18 . . . . 60 A7
Bell St EX9 . . . . 198 F7
Belmont EX32 . . . . 155 A5
Belmont Ave
  Combe Martin EX34 . . . . . . 2 F4
  Ilfracombe EX34 . . . . 150 A5
Belmont Cl
  4 Kingsteignton TQ12 . . . 123 F1
  Tiverton EX16 . . . . 161 D5
Belmont Ct 8 PL3 . . . . 248 A4
Belmont Ho
  Exeter EX4 . . . . 261 C4
  6 Seaton EX12 . . . . 192 A5
Belmont Pl PL3 . . . . 248 A4
Belmont Rd
  Barnstaple EX32 . . . . 155 B6
  Brixham TQ5 . . . . 230 C4
  Exeter EX1 . . . . 261 C4
  Ilfracombe EX34 . . . . . . 150 A5
  Ivybridge PL21 . . . . 237 C4
  Tiverton EX16 . . . . 161 D5
  Torquay TQ1 . . . . 220 C6
Belmont St PL1 . . . . 262 B3
Belmont Terr
  Exmouth EX8 . . . . 196 C1
  1 South Brent TQ10 . . . 134 F3
  Totnes TQ9 . . . . 223 C6
BELSFORD 222 B3
BELSTONE 94 D4
Belstone Cl PL5 . . . . 244 A3
Belstone Cnr Cross EX20 . . 76 E1
Belstone Cross EX20 . . . . . 94 E4
Bel Tor Cnr TQ13 . . . . . . 129 F8
Beltor Cross TQ12 . . . . . . 211 D1
Belvedere Cl EX3 . . . . 182 E6
Belvedere Ct
  5 Dawlish EX7 . . . . 204 E6
  3 Wellington TA21 . . . . 160 D6
Belvedere Pk EX22 . . . . . . 113 F5
Belvedere Rd
  Exmouth EX8 . . . . 202 A7
  Ilfracombe EX34 . . . . . . 150 B6
  Newton Abbot TQ12 . . . . . 206 E5
  Plymouth PL4 . . . . 249 B2
Belvidere Meadows Nature
  Reserve★ EX4 . . . . 173 B3
Belvidere Rd EX4 . . . . 173 B2
Belvoir Rd EX39 . . . . 156 F2
Benbow St PL2 . . . . 247 F4
Bench Tor Cl TQ2 . . . . . . 219 A5
Bendarroch Rd EX11 . . . . 168 D5
Bendarroch Sch EX11 . . . . 99 E2
Bendibus Cross EX22 . . . . 72 E2
Bendibus Hill EX21 . . . . . . 72 E3
Bendle La EX36 . . . . 30 E8
Bendle Lane Cross EX36 . . . 30 E8
Bendley Hill EX16 . . . . 46 E1
Benedict Cl TQ14 . . . . 210 C7
Benedicts Cl 图 TQ12 . . . . 122 F1
Benedicts Rd TQ12 . . . . . . 122 F1
Benedict Way 2 PL21 . . . . 137 B2
Ben Jonson Cl TQ2 . . . . . 219 D6
Benlears Acre 图 TQ12 . . . 122 F1
Benley Cross EX18 . . . . . . 45 D2
BENNACOTT 89 B3
Bennah Hill EX6 . . . . 113 A3
Bennets La PL21 . . . . 242 F3
Bennett Cl EX2 . . . . 181 B8
Bennett Rd TQ8 . . . . 259 D3
Bennetts Cl EX12 . . . . 190 E4
Bennett's Cross TQ9 . . . . . 139 C8
Bennetts Hill EX10 . . . . . . 187 F7
Bennett Sq EX4 . . . . 178 A8
Bennett St PL1 . . . . 247 E1
Benning Ct EX31 . . . . 154 C6
Bens Cl TQ7 . . . . 147 D7
Benson Cl EX16 . . . . 46 E1
Benson Dr EX39 . . . . 157 A6
BENTON 18 B7
Benton Cross EX30 . . . . . . 18 B7
Benton La EX31 . . . . 18 B7
Benton Rd EX32 . . . . 18 B8
BENTWICHEN 19 C4
Ben Venue Cl TQ1 . . . . . . 220 C5
Berachah Rd TQ1 . . . . 220 C5
BERE ALSTON 125 E1
Bere Alston Prim Sch
  PL20 . . . . 125 E1
Bere Alston Sta PL20 . . . . 125 E2
Berea Rd TQ1 . . . . 220 C6
BERE FERRERS 239 E3
Bere Ferrers Sta PL20 . . . 239 E3
Bere Hill EX7 . . . . 204 E8
Beresford Dr PL2 . . . . 248 A4
Berkeley Ave TQ2 . . . . . . 213 C1
Berkeley Pl 6 EX34 . . . . . 150 B5
Berkeley Rise TQ2 . . . . . . 213 C1
Berkeley Way PL21 . . . . . . 237 D4
Berkshire Dr
  Exeter EX4 . . . . 176 E4
  Plymouth PL2 . . . . 247 F5
Bernadette Cl EX4 . . . . . . 174 C1
Berner's Cross EX19 . . . . . 58 F4
Bernice Cl PL4 . . . . 249 B4
Bernice Terr PL4 . . . . 249 B4
Berrian Rd TQ12 . . . . 123 A1
Berrow Park Rd PL3 . . . . . 248 E6
Berry Ave TQ3 . . . . 225 F6
Berryball Cl EX20 . . . . . . 170 C6

Berrybrook Mdw EX6 . . . 182 B3
Berry Cl
  Abbotskerswell TQ12 . . . . 212 B6
  Exmouth EX8 . . . . 202 E8
  Salcombe TQ8 . . . . 259 C4
Berry Cotts EX6 . . . . 182 B3
Berry Cross
  Dunsford EX6 . . . . 112 E8
  Langtree EX38 . . . . 41 B1
  Shebbear EX21 . . . . 55 D5
Berrydown Cross EX34 . . . 2 F1
Berry Down Cross EX34 . . . 9 F6
Berry Dr TQ3 . . . . 226 A6
Berry Head Country Pk★
  TQ5 . . . . 231 A6
Berry Head Gdns PL6 . . . . 244 E1
Berry Head National Nature
  Reserve★ TQ5 . . . . 231 A6
Berry Head Rd TQ5 . . . . . 230 E6
Berry Hill
  Beer EX12 . . . . 191 D5
  Bishopsteignton TQ14 . . . 208 F8
  Branscombe EX12 . . . . . 190 A4
  North Tawton EX20 . . . . . 59 C1
Berry La
  Axminster EX13 . . . . 88 F3
  Beer EX12 . . . . 191 D6
  Combe Martin EX34 . . . . . 2 F4
  Dunsford EX6 . . . . 112 E8
  Kingsteignton TQ12 . . . . 207 E6
Berry Mdw TQ12 . . . . 207 E6
BERRYNARBOR 2 E3
Berrynarbor Pk EX34 . . . . 2 E3
Berrynarbor Prim Sch
  EX34 . . . . 2 E3
Berry Park Rd PL9 . . . . . . 255 E6
Berry Park Rd PL9 . . . . . . 255 E7
Berry Pk PL12 . . . . 242 D4
Berry's Ground La EX31 . . . 4 C5
Berry Sq TQ4 . . . . 226 C6
Berrys Wood TQ12 . . . . . 206 F3
Berthon Rd PL5 . . . . 247 C8
Berwick Ave PL5 . . . . 244 E3
Besigheim Pl 图 TQ12 . . . 207 B3
Besigheim Way TQ12 . . . . 207 F4
Besley Cl EX16 . . . . 161 F3
Besley Ct EX2 . . . . 177 B3
Besshill La EX31 . . . . 10 F3
Bestridge Mdw EX32 . . . . 28 E8
Best's La EX30 . . . . 159 D5
Betham La EX18 . . . . 46 F2
Betham La EX18 . . . . 59 B6
Bethelcombe Cross
  TQ12 . . . . 122 C1
Bethel Cross TQ12 . . . . . 122 C1
Bethel Terr 图 TQ1 . . . . . 220 B5
Betjeman Wlk PL5 . . . . . 244 C3
Betjemen Dr EX8 . . . . . . 196 C3
Betony Rise EX2 . . . . 178 C3
Betton Way TQ13 . . . . . . 111 F5
Bettys Mead EX4 . . . . . . 178 A8
Beuvron Cl EX39 . . . . 38 F8
Bevan Rd EX32 . . . . 155 A5
Beverley Cl EX2 . . . . 178 B8
Beverley Gdns 图 TQ13 . . 131 A5
Beverley Rd PL3 . . . . 249 C4
Beverley Rise TQ5 . . . . . . 230 B4
Beverley Way TQ4 . . . . . . 207 A2
Beverston Way PL6 . . . . . 245 B8
Bevil Cl EX39 . . . . 157 A1
Beweys Pk PL2 . . . . 242 C2
Bewhay Gdns TQ9 . . . . . . 222 F8
Bewsley Hill EX17 . . . . 79 B5
Bexley La 图 TQ2 . . . . . . 219 F5
Beyrout Pl 6 PL1 . . . . . . 247 F3
Bhutan Cl EX14 . . . . 146 D6
Bias La 4 EX32 . . . . 152 D6
Bibors Hill EX14 . . . . 35 E4
Bicclescombe Ct EX34 . . . 150 B4
Bicclescombe Gdns
  EX34 . . . . 150 B4
Bicclescombe Park Rd
  EX34 . . . . 150 B4
Bickell Cross EX32 . . . . . . 28 C6
Bickern Rd PL11 . . . . 247 B3
BICKERTON 149 D5
Bickerton Top TQ7 . . . . . 149 C5
Bickfont Hill EX31 . . . . . . 11 F4
Bickford La 图 TQ14 . . . . 210 C4
Bickfords Gn 14 TQ12 . . . 122 F1
BICKHAM
  . . . . 241 A7
  . . . . 241 A7
Bickham La EX16 . . . . 47 E2
Bickham Park Rd PL3 . . . . 248 D7
Bickham Rd PL5 . . . . 243 D2
BICKINGCOTT 31 B7
Bickingcott Cross EX36 . . . 31 C7
Bickingcott Hill EX36 . . . . 31 C8
BICKINGTON
  Ashburton 131 D7
  Barnstaple 154 B4
Bickington Lodge EX31 . . . 16 A3
Bickington Rd EX31 . . . . . 154 C3
BICKLEIGH
  Plymouth 132 A5
  Tiverton 64 A1
Bickleigh Castle★ EX16 . . 63 F1

Bickleigh CE Prim Sch
  EX16 . . . . 64 A2
Bickleigh Cl
  Exeter EX4 . . . . 174 D2
  Plymouth PL6 . . . . 245 A1
Bickleigh Down Bsns Pk
  PL6 . . . . 245 D8
Bickleigh Down CE Prim Sch
  PL6 . . . . 245 D7
Bickleigh Down Rd PL6 . . . 241 D1
Bickleigh Mill★ EX16 . . . . 63 F2
Bickley Mill Cross TQ12 . . 212 C1
Bickley Rd TQ12 . . . . 212 C1
BICKLETON 153 C3
Bickleton Cross EX31 . . . 153 A2
Bickley House La EX10 . . . 187 E5
Bickwell La EX10 . . . . 187 F5
Bickwell Valley EX10 . . . . 187 F4
Bickwill Cross EX36 . . . . . 46 D8
Bicton Cl PL6 . . . . 245 D1
Bicton Coll of Agriculture
  EX9 . . . . 186 C1
Bicton Park Botanical Gdns★
  EX9 . . . . 198 C8
Bicton Pl
  Exeter EX1 . . . . 177 F6
  Exmouth EX8 . . . . 202 A6
Bicton St
  Barnstaple EX32 . . . . 155 A5
  Exmouth EX8 . . . . 202 A6
Bicton Villas EX8 . . . . . . 202 B6
Bidbrooke La EX36 . . . . . . 32 A6
Biddacott Cross EX37 . . . . 28 E4
Biddamoor La EX19 . . . . . 42 C2
Bidder Cl TQ13 . . . . 111 F4
Bidder Rd TQ12 . . . . 146 B7
Bidders Cl EX36 . . . . 158 C4
Bidders Wlk TQ6 . . . . 146 B7
Biddiblack Way EX36 . . . . 157 C2
Biddick Dr PL2 . . . . 247 F6
Biddington Way EX14 . . . 166 A4
Biddiecombe Cross
  TQ13 . . . . 124 A6
Biddypark La EX2 . . . . . . 113 F6
Biddypark Lane Cross
  EX2 . . . . 113 F6
BIDEFORD 156 E3
Bideford Arts Ctr★ EX39 157 A2
Bideford Coll EX39 . . . . . . 156 E1
Starcross EX6 . . . . 201 B8
Torquay TQ1 . . . . 221 A4
Bideford Com Hospl
  EX39 . . . . 156 F2
Bideford Wlk PL6 . . . . . . 249 E8
Bidmead Cl EX8 . . . . 202 E7
Bidna La EX39 . . . . 157 B8
Bidwell Brook Dr TQ4 . . . 226 C1
Bidwell Brook Specl Sch
  TQ9 . . . . 215 F1
Bidwell Cross
  Langford EX5 . . . . 172 E8
  Thorverton EX5 . . . . 81 E6
Bidwell La
  Brampford Speke EX5 . . . 81 C1
  Thorverton EX5 . . . . 81 F6
Bidwell Wlk TQ4 . . . . . . 226 B1
Biera View TQ13 . . . . . . 111 A6
Bigadon La TQ11 . . . . . . 236 C4
BIGBURY 142 F5
Bigbury Ct TQ7 . . . . 142 F5
BIGBURY-ON-SEA 142 E3
Bigbury Way TQ4 . . . . . . 214 B2
Bigbury Wlk PL6 . . . . . . 249 F8
Biggin Hill PL5 . . . . 243 F4
BIG Sheep (Farm Pk) The★
  EX39 . . . . 156 B1
Bilbie Cl EX15 . . . . 163 B3
Bilbury St PL4 . . . . 263 A3
BILLACOMBE 255 F8
Billacombe Rd PL9 . . . . . . 255 E7
Billacombe Villas PL9 . . . 255 E8
Bill Douglas Centre for the
  History of Cinema &
  Popular Culture (Mus)★
  EX4 . . . . 177 B8
Billhole La EX17 . . . . 61 C6
Billings Cl PL6 . . . . 244 D6
Billington Cl PL6 . . . . 249 B7
Bilton Terr 图 EX32 . . . . 155 A4
Bilton Rd TQ12 . . . . 211 D1
Bilver Cross TQ12 . . . . . . 217 C8
Bimbom La EX13 . . . . . . 103 C8
Bindon Rd EX4 . . . . 174 E2
Binford Cl EX1 . . . . 178 B6
Bingfield Cl TQ1 . . . . 220 C5
Bingham Cres EX32 . . . . . 155 B4
Bingwell Ho EX16 . . . . . . 161 F3
Binhamy Rd EX23 . . . . 70 A8
Binkham Hill PL20 . . . . . . 127 A3
Binnamore Cross TQ10 . . 134 E4
Binneford Cross EX17 . . . . 96 F8
Binneford Hill EX17 . . . . . . 62 B2
Birchan Valley Nature
  Reserve★ PL6 . . . . 245 C1
Bircham View PL6 . . . . . 245 C1
Birchanger Cross TQ13 . . 122 B2
Birch Cl PL6 . . . . 245 E7
Birch Cross
  Doddiscombsleigh EX6 . . 113 D8
  Yarcombe EX14 . . . . 69 A4
  Zeal Monachorum EX17 . . 78 B8
Birchen End EX5 . . . . 99 C5
Birchen La
  Highampton EX20, EX21 . . 74 E5
  7 Tiverton EX16 . . . . . 161 C3
Birches Tree Cross EX15 . . 66 C4
Birchfield Ave PL2 . . . . . 248 B6

Birch Gr EX11 . . . . 168 D3
BIRCHILL 88 A5
Birchill Cross EX13 . . . . . . 88 A6
Birch La
  Barnstaple EX31 . . . . . . 154 C2
  Landkey EX32 . . . . 17 D3
  Morchard Bishop EX17 . . . 61 A2
  Zeal Monachorum EX17 . . . 78 A8
Birchland Rd PL7 . . . . . . 133 A1
Birchland Way PL7 . . . . . 136 A8
Birchlea TQ13 . . . . 180 C4
Birchman's Cross EX17 . . . 78 E1
Birch Pond Rd PL9 . . . . . 255 D7
Birch Rd
  Landkey EX32 . . . . 17 B2
  Lympstone EX8 . . . . 195 F5
  Newton Abbot TQ12 . . . . 207 F1
  Wellington TA21 . . . . . . 160 E5
Birch Wlk TQ2 . . . . 219 C8
Birchwood Cl
  Tavistock PL19 . . . . 171 C3
  Totnes TQ9 . . . . 223 B5
Birchwood Gdns PL7 . . . . 251 A7
Birchwood Rd EX8 . . . . . 196 D2
Birchy Barton Hill EX1 . . . 178 B6
Birdcage La EX11 . . . . . . 168 E8
Birdcage Wlk EX34 . . . . . . 2 D1
Birdswell La EX34 . . . . 2 D1
Birkbeck Cl PL7 . . . . 250 E7
Birkdale Cl PL12 . . . . 242 C2
Birkett Cl EX2 . . . . 178 C4
Birks Halls of Residence
  EX4 . . . . 173 A1
BISCOMBE 67 F8
Biscombe Cross TA3 . . . . . 67 E8
Biscombe Gdns PL12 . . . . 243 A2
BISH MILL 30 E4
Bishmill Gate EX36 . . . . . . 30 E4
Bishop Cornish CE Prim Sch
  PL12 . . . . 242 F1
Bishop Cl 图 EX24 . . . . . 103 A4
Bishop Dunstan Sch The
  TQ12 . . . . 207 B2
Bishop Pasterfield Ho 图
  EX2 . . . . 261 B2
Bishops Ave TQ14 . . . . . 208 F8
Bishops Cl
  Ivybridge PL21 . . . . 237 E6
  Saltash PL12 . . . . 242 E3
Bishop's Clyst EX5 . . . . . 179 A3
Bishops Court Ind Est
  EX2 . . . . 178 E4
Bishop's Court La EX5 . . . 179 C4
Bishops Ct
  Bishopsteignton TQ14 . . . 208 F8
  Bishop Dr EX17 . . . . 79 A6
  Bishop's Hill TA21 . . . . . . 51 B7
  Bishops Mdw EX17 . . . . . . 61 A2
  Bishop Mead 图 TQ10 . . 134 F3
  BISHOPS NYMPTON 31 A2
  Bishop's Nympton Cross
    EX36 . . . . 30 F1
  Bishops Nympton Prim Sch
    EX36 . . . . 30 F2
Bishop's Pi
  Paignton TQ3 . . . . 226 B6
  Plymouth PL1 . . . . 262 B1
Bishops Rise
  Kentisbeare EX15 . . . . . . 66 A3
  Torquay TQ1 . . . . 221 A4
BISHOP'S TAWTON 16 F1
Bishop's Tawton Prim Sch 图
  EX32 . . . . 16 E1
Bishop's Tawton Rd
  Barnstaple EX32 . . . . . . 155 B2
  Bishop's Tawton EX32 . . . 16 E1
BISHOPSTEIGNTON 208 E7
Bishopsteignton Mus of
  Rural Life★ TQ9 . . . . . 209 A8
Bishopsteignton Prim Sch
  TQ14 . . . . 208 F8
Bishopsteignton Rd
  TQ14 . . . . 209 D6
BISHOPSWOOD 67 C7
Bishop Westall Ho 图
  EX2 . . . . 261 B2
Bishop Westall Rd EX2 . . . 178 A2
Bishop Wilfrid Rd TQ14 . . 209 D8
Bishop's Wood Nature
  Reserve★ EX17 . . . . . . 61 C6
Bitmey La TQ12 . . . . 212 C5
BITTADON 9 C4
Bittadon La EX31 . . . . 9 C4
Bittaford Rd PL21 . . . . . . 137 C8
Bittaford Wood 6 PL21 . . 137 C7
Bittam's La TQ9 . . . . 217 B4
Bittern Ind Units EX2 . . . . 181 C1
Bittern Rd EX2 . . . . 178 E6
Bittery Cross EX5 . . . . 84 B2
Bitton Ave TQ14 . . . . 210 B5
Bitton Ct TQ14 . . . . 210 A5
Bitton Park Rd 图 TQ14 . . 210 A5
Bitton St TQ14 . . . . 210 A4
Blachford Rd PL21 . . . . . . 237 C5
Blackaborook Ave PL20 . . 128 A8
Blackacre Rd EX24 . . . . . 102 C6
Blackadder Terr PL7 . . . . 132 F4
Blakall La EX16 . . . . 33 C1
Blakall Rd EX4 . . . . 261 B4
Black-a-Tor Copse National
  Nature Reserve★ EX20 . . 108 E8
BLACKAWTON 139 F2
Blackawton Prim Sch
  TQ9 . . . . 139 E2
Blackball La TQ5 . . . . . . 230 C6

Blackberry Cl PL9 . . . . . . 255 E8
Blackberry Ct TA21 . . . . . 160 D4
Blackberry La
  Bigbury TQ7 . . . . 142 E6
  Plymouth PL9 . . . . 255 E8
Blackberry Way 6 TQ12 . . 123 F1
Blackbird Cres PL15 . . . . 105 A2
BLACKBOROUGH 66 D4
Blackboy Rd EX1 . . . . . . 177 E7
Blackbrook Ave TQ4 . . . . 226 B1
Blackbrook Cl PL20 . . . . . 127 B4
Blackbrook Wlk TQ4 . . . . 226 B1
Blackditch Cross EX17 . . . 66 E1
Black Dog 61 E4
Black Dog Cross EX17 . . . . 61 E4
Blackdown Bsns Pk
  TA21 . . . . 160 E6
Blackdown Cross
  Cornworthy TQ9 . . . . . . 139 E4
  Loddiswell TQ7 . . . . 138 B2
  Tedburn St Mary EX17 . . . 97 E8
Blackdown La
  Halwell TQ9 . . . . 139 D4
  Tedburn St Mary EX4 . . . . 98 C5
Blackdown Pk EX15 . . . . 162 C5
Blackdown Rd TA21 . . . . 160 B4
Blackdown View
  2 Hemyock EX15 . . . . . 67 B8
  Sampford Peverell EX16 . . 50 C1
Blackenway La TQ12 . . . . 213 B7
Blackerton Cross EX16 . . . 32 E3
Blackett Cl PL21 . . . . 237 E4
Blackeven Cl PL6 . . . . . . 241 D1
Blackeven Hill PL6 . . . . . 241 E1
Blackfriars La PL1 . . . . . . 263 A2
Black Gate
  Challacombe EX31 . . . . . . 11 F4
  Holemoor EX22 . . . . 73 C5
Blackgate Cross EX39 . . . . 26 C7
Blackhall Gdns PL6 . . . . . 244 D6
Black Hat La EX6 . . . . . . 176 B3
Blackhaven Cl TQ4 . . . . . 229 B8
Blackhayes La EX14 . . . . . 68 F1
BLACKHORSE 179 B7
Black Horse Cnr EX18 . . . . 59 C4
Blackhorse La EX5 . . . . . 179 B8
Black La
  Hemyock EX15 . . . . 52 D2
  Holcombe Rogus TA21 . . . . 50 E6
Blackler's Land Cross
  TQ9 . . . . 216 B5
Black La TQ13 . . . . 113 D1
Black Lion Ct 图 EX14 . . . 166 C6
BLACKMORE 52 E5
BLACKMOOR GATE 11 A6
Blackmoor Rd TA21 . . . . 160 F4
Blackmoor's Path EX35 . . 151 B5
Blackmore Cres PL6 . . . . 244 D6
Blackmore Ct EX36 . . . . . 196 C1
Blackmore Dr EX10 . . . . . 188 B4
Blackmore Mews EX2 . . . 178 C4
Blackmore Rd
  Exeter EX5 . . . . 99 A1
  Tiverton EX16 . . . . 161 F3
Blackmore Theatre★
  EX8 . . . . 202 A6
BLACKPOOL 122 F1
Blackpool CE Prim Sch
  TQ12 . . . . 122 F1
BLACKPOOL CORNER 88 C1
Blackpool Cross EX7 . . . . 204 D4
Blackpool Gdns★ TQ6 . . . 146 A7
Blackpool Hill TQ6 . . . . . 146 A6
Blackpool Rd EX7 . . . . . . 78 D4
Blackpool Valley Rd TQ6 . 146 A7
Blackpost Cross
  Kingston TQ7 . . . . 142 C7
  Totnes, Littlehempston
    TQ9 . . . . 217 A2
  Totnes TQ9 . . . . 223 F6
Blackpost La TQ9 . . . . . . 223 F5
Blackridge Cross TQ7 . . . 258 F8
Blacksmith La TQ10 . . . . 137 D8
Blacksmiths Cnr EX17 . . . 81 A6
Blackstone Cl PL20 . . . . . 256 B6
Blackstone Cross TQ12 . . 211 D1
Blackstone Rd TQ12 . . . . 211 D1
Blackswan Pl 图 EX7 . . . . 204 D6
Blackthorn Ave EX16 . . . 161 F6
Blackthorn Cl
  Honiton EX14 . . . . 166 C4
  Plymouth, Honicknowle
    PL5 . . . . 244 B3
  Plymouth, Woolwell PL6 . . 245 D8
  Sidmouth EX10 . . . . 187 F8
Blackthorn Cres EX1 . . . . 178 C6
Blackthorn Way TQ4 . . . . 225 D4
BLACK TORRINGTON 74 A8
Black Torrington CE Prim
  Sch EX21 . . . . 74 A8
Blackwalls La EX18 . . . . . . 60 B7
Blackwater La EX13 . . . . . 88 F3
Blackwater Rd EX15 . . . . . 66 E8
BLACKWELL 35 B5
Blackwell Cross
  Broadhempston TQ13 . . . 131 D3
  Strete TQ6 . . . . 145 E7
Blackwell La TQ13 . . . . . 131 D2
Bladder La PL5 . . . . 244 E2
Bladon Cl TQ12 . . . . 206 E3
Bladon Ct EX21 . . . . 73 B1
Blagdon EX17 . . . . 165 D5
Blagdon Cl EX17 . . . . . . 165 D5
Blagdon Cross
  Ashwater EX21 . . . . 90 C7
  Paignton TQ3 . . . . 225 D2

Blagdon Lodge Cross
EX21. . . . . .90 C8
Blagdon Rd TQ3 . . . . .225 B6
Blagdon Rise EX17 . . . . . .165 D6
Blagrove Hill EX17 . . . . .46 C3
Blairgowrie Rd PL5 . . . . . .243 C2
Blair Rd PL21. . . . . .237 D5
Blake Cl TQ1. . . . . .220 B8
Blake Gdns PL5. . . . . .244 C3
Blakeland Rd EX31. . . . . . .153 D5
BLAKEMORE. 222 B5
Blakemore Cross TQ9 . . . .222 A4
Blakes Hill Rd EX32 . . . . . .17 B2
Blakewell Cross EX37 . . . . .28 E3
Blakewell Hill EX32 . . . . . .18 E2
Blakey Down La TQ3 . . . . .218 F1
Blamphayne Cross EX24 . .30 D7
Blanchard Pl 2 PL7. . . . . .250 E7
Blanchdown Dr PL18. . . . .125 C7
Blandford Rd PL3 . . . . . . .249 C6
Blangy Cl EX20. . . . . .77 C4
Blanksmill Cross TQ7 . . . .259 A8
Blatchborough Cross
EX22. . . . . .38 B1
Blatchcombe Dr TQ3. . . . .225 F7
Blatchcombe Rd TQ3. . . . .226 A7
Blatchfords Ct EX20. . . . . .170 B5
Blatchmore La TQ6 . . . . . .232 C4
Blaxton La PL5. . . . . .240 C2
Blenheim Cl
Newton Abbot TQ12. . . . . .207 A5
Torquay TQ1. . . . . .220 E4
Willand EX15 . . . . .162 D5
Blenheim Ct EX21. . . . . . . .177 C1
Blenheim Ct EX15. . . . . . . .162 D5
Blenheim Dr EX15. . . . . . . .162 D4
Blenheim La EX20. . . . . .76 C4
Blenheim Rd
Exeter EX2. . . . . .177 B2
Plymouth PL4. . . . . .263 A4
Blenheim Terr TQ13. . . . . .180 C7
Bligh Cl TQ12. . . . . .210 A8
Blights Hill EX16, TA22. . . .33 F3
Blind Acres La EX33. . . . . . .15 A8
Blind La
Aylesbeare EX5. . . . . .99 E2
Buckland St Mary TA20 . . . .69 A8
Huxham EX5. . . . . .174 B8
BLINDWELL. 252 E5
Blindwell Ave TQ12. . . . . . .207 F7
Blindwell Farm Cotts
TQ12. . . . . .207 E7
Blindwell Hill PL10. . . . . . .252 E5
Blindwell La TA4. . . . . .34 E6
Blindwylle Rd TQ2 . . . . . . .219 E5
Blogishay La TQ13 . . . . . . .130 F4
Bloomball Cl PL3. . . . . .249 B6
Blossom Cl EX14. . . . . .67 C1
Blossom Hill EX14. . . . . . . .67 C1
Blue Anchor Cross EX14. . .84 D3
Blueball Cross EX14. . . . . . .84 D3
Blueball Hill 1 TQ9 . . . . .223 C5
Blue Bell TQ9 . . . . .223 C5
Bluebell Ave EX16. . . . . . . .161 F6
Bluebell Cl
Saltash PL12 . . . . .242 D4
Seaton EX12 . . . . .192 B7
Bluebell Rd EX14. . . . . .67 C1
Bluebell Way
Launceston PL15. . . . . .105 A2
Tavistock PL19. . . . . .171 E4
Blueberry Downs EX9 . . . .199 C2
Blue Cedar Cl EX8 . . . . . . .202 B6
Blue Gate TA24 . . . . .19 F8
Bluegate Hill PL21 . . . . . . .137 A2
Bluehayes La
Clyst Honiton EX5 . . . . . . .175 F3
Rockbeare EX5. . . . . .99 A5
Blue Haze Cl PL6. . . . . .245 D5
Blue La EX17. . . . . .96 A3
Blueridge Rd TQ13. . . . . . .180 C4
Bluett Rd TQ11. . . . . .160 D4
Blue Waters Dr
Lyme Regis DT7. . . . . .260 B3
Paignton TQ4 . . . . .229 C8
Blue Waters Ind Est
TQ13. . . . . .180 C5
Blundell's Ave EX16. . . . . .161 F4
Blundells Prep Sch EX16. 64 D8
Blundell's Rd
Tiverton, Cowleymoor
EX15. . . . . .64 D8
Tiverton EX15 . . . . .161 E4
Blundell's Sch EX16. . . . . .64 D7
Blunt's La PL6. . . . . .245 C3
Blyth Ct EX39 . . . . .156 B6
Blythswood Cres 4 TQ1. .220 B7
Boarden Barn EX8 . . . . . . .202 B6
Boasley Cross EX20 . . . . . . .92 E4
Boasley Cross Com Prim Sch
EX20. . . . . .92 E4
Bockland Cl EX15. . . . . . . .163 A3
Boconnic La PL20. . . . . . . .127 A3
BODLEY. 4 C2
Bodley Cl EX1 . . . . .178 B7
Bodley Cross EX31. . . . . . . .4 D1
Bodley La EX31 . . . . .4 C2
Bodmin Rd PL5. . . . . .244 D3
Bodmin St EX22. . . . . .164 C4
Body Hayes Cl TQ9. . . . . . .227 F7
Body's Ct PL18. . . . . .125 C6
BOGTOWN. 92 D8
Bogtown Cross EX20. . . . . .92 D8
BOHETHERICK. 125 B5
BOLBERRY 147 D6
Bolberry Cross TQ7 . . . . . .147 E6
Boldventure PL8. . . . . .257 F3
Boldventure Cross EX21. . .91 E6

BOLHAM. 161 C8
Bolham Halt Cotts EX16 . .161 C8
Bolham La EX16 . . . . .161 D8
Bolham Prim Com Sch
EX16. . . . . .161 C8
Bolham Rd EX16 . . . . .161 C7
BOLHAM WATER. 67 E7
Bolt House Cl PL19. . . . . . .171 A5
Bolton Ct 8 TQ5. . . . . .230 C4
Bolton St TQ5. . . . . .230 C4
Bommertown Cross EX36. .32 A4
Bonair Ct TQ5. . . . . .230 C3
Bonaventure Cl TQ8. . . . . .259 D5
Bonaventure Rd TQ8. . . . .259 D5
Bondhouse La EX6. . . . . . . .98 E3
Bond La EX16. . . . . .62 F5
BONDLEIGH 77 B7
Bondleigh Bridge Cross
EX20. . . . . .77 B7
Bondleigh Cross EX20. . . . .77 B7
Bondleigh Moor Cross
EX20. . . . . .76 F6
Bondleigh Wood Cross
EX20. . . . . .77 B7
Bonds Cross
Chulmleigh EX18 . . . . .44 E1
Petrockstow EX20 . . . . .56 C5
Bond's La EX5. . . . . .184 B5
Bonds Mdw TQ13 . . . . . . .180 C8
Bone St
Beaford EX19. . . . . .42 D2
Cornwood PL21. . . . . .133 C2
Plymouth PL6. . . . . .244 E6
Bonehayne and Purlbridge
Rd EX24 . . . . .102 E5
Bone Mill Cross TQ12. . . .131 F6
Bonfire Cross EX10 . . . . . .101 C3
Bonfire Hill
Black Torrington EX21. . . . .74 A8
Salcombe TQ8 . . . . .259 C5
Bonfire La EX5. . . . . .184 C3
Bonhay Cl EX6. . . . . .201 B8
Bonhay Rd
Exeter EX4. . . . . .177 A6
Starcross EX6. . . . . .201 B8
Boniford Cross EX14 . . . . . .87 A4
Bonners Cswy EX13. . . . . .167 F1
Bonners Dr EX13. . . . . .167 F6
Bonners Glen EX13. . . . . . .167 F6
Bonnicott La EX33 . . . . .7 D1
Bonnington Gr EX1 . . . . . .177 F6
Bonny Cross
Clayhanger EX16 . . . . .35 B1
Morebath EX16 . . . . .34 B3
Bonville Cl EX1 . . . . .178 B7
Bonville Cres EX16. . . . . . . .64 D7
Bonville Rd PL6. . . . . .244 E6
Boobery EX16. . . . . .50 D1
Boode Cross EX33. . . . . . . .152 F7
Boode Rd EX33. . . . . .152 F7
Booklands EX32. . . . . .18 B2
Boon's Pl PL1. . . . . .262 C4
Booth Way EX8 . . . . .196 B2
Borden Gate EX16. . . . . . . .50 B8
Border Rd EX14. . . . . .201 A6
Boringdon Ave PL5 . . . . . .247 D8
Boringdon Cl PL7. . . . . . . .250 D7
Boringdon Hill PL7. . . . . . .250 D7
Boringdon Mdl Bsns Ctr
PL7. . . . . .250 F6
Boringdon Pk PL21. . . . . . .237 A5
Boringdon Prim Sch
PL7. . . . . .250 D7
Boringdon Rd
Plymouth, Plympton PL7. .250 D6
Plymouth, Turnchapel PL9. 255 A7
Boringdon Terr
Plymouth, Plympton PL7. .250 D6
Plymouth, Turnchapel PL9. 255 A7
Boringdon Villas PL7. . . . .250 D6
BORNE. 44 B1
Borne Cross EX37. . . . . . . .44 B2
BOROUGH. 70 E5
Borough Cl TQ4. . . . . .225 E3
Borough Cross
Aveton Gifford TQ7 . . . . . .143 B7
Bridgerule EX22. . . . . .70 E5
Chilsworthy EX22. . . . . .53 E2
Newton Tracey EX31. . . . . .27 A3
Woolacombe EX34. . . . . . . .1 B1
Borough Ct PL11. . . . . .246 E4
Borough La TQ9 . . . . .144 B6
Borough Park Rd
Paignton TQ4 . . . . .225 E5
Torquay TQ9. . . . . .223 C6
Borough Pk PL11 . . . . .246 E4
Borough Rd
Combe Martin EX34. . . . . . .2 F4
Great Torrington EX38. . . .159 C5
Paignton TQ4 . . . . .225 E4
Torquay TQ1. . . . . .214 B1
Borough The PL8 . . . . .257 F4
Borough View EX38. . . . . .159 E5
Borrowdale Cl PL6. . . . . . .244 D5
Boscastle Gdns PL2. . . . . .248 C8
Boscawen Pl
Plymouth PL2. . . . . .247 E4
10 Teignmouth TQ14. . . .210 B5
Boscundle Row PL12. . . . .243 A2
Boshill Hill
Axmouth DT7. . . . . .193 C8
Colyford DT7. . . . . .103 D3
Bossell Ho TQ11 . . . . .236 B4
Bossell Pk TQ11 . . . . .236 B4
Bossell Rd TQ11 . . . . .236 B5
Bossell Terr TQ11 . . . . . . .236 B5
Bosuns Point TQ4. . . . . . . .226 C4
Boswell Cl PL5. . . . . .244 B2

Boswell's La EX20. . . . . . . .77 D4
Boswell's Lane End EX20. .77 D4
Boswell Way EX12 . . . . . . .191 F8
Bothy The DT7. . . . . .193 E6
Bottle Bridge Hill TQ13. . .123 F7
Bottle Pk PL21. . . . . .136 B6
Bottom La EX13. . . . . .103 D6
Bottompark La TQ2 . . . . . .213 F3
Bottoms La EX33. . . . . .8 B2
Bottom's La TQ12. . . . . . . .213 E4
Bottreaux Mill Cross
EX36. . . . . .32 A5
BOTUSFLEMING. 242 B7
Boucher Rd EX9 . . . . .198 B1
Bouchers Hill EX20. . . . . . .77 C5
Boucher's La TA4. . . . . .35 E4
Boucher Way EX9. . . . . . . .198 B1
Bouchiers Cl EX20 . . . . . . .77 C5
Boughmore La EX10. . . . . .187 F3
Boughmore Rd EX10 . . . . .187 F4
Boughthayes Est PL19. . . .171 A5
Boulden Cl PL7. . . . . .251 C5
Boulter Cl PL6. . . . . .241 C1
Boundary Cl TQ12. . . . . . . .212 F5
Boundary Dr EX23 . . . . . . .70 A6
Boundary Pk
Bideford EX39 . . . . .26 F4
Seaton EX12 . . . . .192 A8
Boundary Rd
Dousland PL20. . . . . .127 B3
Torquay TQ1. . . . . .219 D5
Bounds Cross EX22 . . . . . . .71 A4
Bounds Pl PL1. . . . . .262 B2
Boundstone Cross EX39 . .25 D2
Bound The PL10 . . . . .253 A1
Boundy's Cross EX17. . . . . .61 B8
Bounsells La EX20 . . . . .57 A7
Bourchier Cl 13 EX16. . . . .34 B1
Bourchier Dr 12 EX16. . . . .34 B1
Bourne Bridge Cross
EX36. . . . . .46 A5
Bourne Cl PL3 . . . . .249 D6
Bourne La EX16. . . . . .229 F2
Bourne Rd TQ12 . . . . .213 A5
Bourn Rise EX4 . . . . .174 D2
Bourton La TQ9 . . . . .223 E6
Bourton Rd TQ9 . . . . .223 E6
Bourtons The TQ9 . . . . . . .223 D7
Boutport St (Mermaid Wlk)
13 EX31. . . . . .154 F6
Boutport St EX31 . . . . .154 F5
Bovacott La EX22 . . . . .73 C7
Bovemoor's La EX2 . . . . . .178 A4
Bove Park Rd TQ2. . . . . . . .214 A4
Bovet St TA21. . . . . .160 C6
Bovey Cross
Broadhempston TQ13 . . . .131 D3
Moretonhampstead TQ13. 111 E3
Bovey Fir Cross EX12. . . . .190 F4
BOVEY HEATH. 180 E4
Bovey Heathfield Nature
Reserve ★ TQ12 . . . . .123 A3
Bovey La
Beer EX12. . . . . .191 B7
Broadhempston TQ13. . . . .131 D3
BOVEY TRACEY 180 C7
Bovey Tracey Heritage Ctr ★
TQ13. . . . . .180 C7
Bovey Tracey Hospl
TQ13. . . . . .180 D8
Bovey Tracey Prim Sch
TQ13. . . . . .180 C8
Bovey Tracey Rd TQ12. . . .190 F5
Boville La PL9 . . . . .256 C7
Bovisand Cl PL9 . . . . .254 F2
Bovisand Est PL9 . . . . .140 A8
Bovisand La
Down Thomas PL9 . . . . . . .255 B2
Staddiscombe PL9. . . . . . . .255 D3
Bovisand Pk
Down Thomas PL9 . . . . . . .255 A1
Heybrook Bay PL9 . . . . . . .140 A8
Bovisand Rd PL9. . . . . .255 C3
BOW
Ashprington. 139 F7
Blackawton 145 B8
Copplestone. 58 C4
Bow Beer Cross EX17 . . . . .78 A1
Bowbeer La EX17. . . . . .78 B1
Bowbridge Cross TQ9. . . .145 B8
Bow Com Prim Sch EX17 .78 C4
Bow Creek TQ9 . . . . .139 F6
Bow Cross
Bishops Tawton TQ9. . . . . .145 B8
Staverton TQ9 . . . . .216 C7
Bowd Cl EX10. . . . . .100 E1
Bowd Ct EX10. . . . . .100 E1
BOWDEN. 145 F8
Bowden Cnr EX31. . . . . . . .9 F3
Bowden Cotts 12 EX32. . .17 B2
Bowden Cross
Buckland Brewer EX39 . . . .40 B8
Drewsteignton EX6 . . . . . . .96 E3
Kingsbridge TQ7 . . . . .144 F4
Bowden Farmhouse PL8. .257 F4
Bowden Gn EX39. . . . . .25 E4
Bowden Hill
Ashburton TQ13. . . . . .130 F4
Crediton EX17. . . . . .165 D5
Newton Abbot TQ12. . . . . .207 C2
Yealmpton PL8. . . . . .257 F4
Bowden Hill Terr 1
EX17. . . . . .165 D5
Bowden La TQ13. . . . . .123 A1
Bowden Park Rd PL6. . . . .245 E1
Bowden Pillars TQ9 . . . . . .223 B3
Bowden Rd TQ12. . . . . .211 E2

Bowdens Cl TQ13 . . . . .180 C7
Bowdens La
Ideford TQ13. . . . . .124 B4
Shillingford EX16. . . . . .34 E3
Bowdens Pk PL21 . . . . .237 C4
Bowdown Cross TQ10 . . . .135 C5
Bowe Ct EX1. . . . . .177 E7
Bowerhayes Cross EX14. . .67 C3
Bowerhayes La EX14 . . . . .67 C3
Bowering Ct 1 EX32 . . . . .155 B3
Bowerland Ave TQ2 . . . . . .213 F4
Bowerland Cross EX20 . . . .93 D3
Bowerland Rd EX20 . . . . . .93 D4
Bowers Park Dr PL6. . . . . .245 E7
Bowers Rd PL2 . . . . .248 B5
Bowerthy La EX17. . . . . . . .60 C4
Bowhay EX21 . . . . .74 A8
Bowhay Ct EX21. . . . . .74 A8
Bowhay La
Combe Martin EX34. . . . . . .3 A3
Exeter EX4. . . . . .176 E4
Bowhays Wlk 2 PL6. . . . . .249 C7
Bowhill EX5. . . . . .83 A7
Bowhill Prim Sch EX4. . . .176 F4
Bow La TQ13. . . . . .111 F4
Bowland Cl TQ4. . . . . .226 A2
Bowley Mdw EX5. . . . . .82 F6
Bowling Gn TQ7 . . . . .142 F4
Bowling Green Chalets
DT7 . . . . .260 D2
Bowling Green La
Combe Martin EX34. . . . . . .3 A3
Hatherleigh EX20. . . . . .75 B7
Bowling Green Rd EX13 . .183 A4
Bowls Cross
Bigbury TQ7 . . . . .142 F5
Exeter EX4. . . . . .82 C1
Bowmans Mdw EX20 . . . . .75 C7
Bow Mill La EX17 . . . . .78 B4
Bowmans Wlk
Barnstaple EX31. . . . . .154 B3
1 Plymouth PL6. . . . . .249 C7
Bramdean Gram Sch
EX4. .177 F6
Bramfield Pl PL6. . . . . .249 D7
Bramley Ave EX15 . . . . . . .178 C6
Bramley Cl
Kenton EX6. . . . . .194 E3
Tiverton EX16 . . . . .161 D7
Wellington TA21. . . . . .160 F7
Willand EX15 . . . . .162 D4
Bramley Gdns EX5 . . . . . . .99 E7
Bramley Mdw EX32 . . . . . .17 C2
Bramley Rd PL3. . . . . .249 C4
Bramley Way EX15. . . . . . .66 C5
Brampford Cross EX5 . . . .172 F7
BRAMPFORD SPEKE 81 E1
Brampford Speke CE Prim
Sch EX5. . . . . .81 E1
Brampton Down Cross
EX16. . . . . .49 F8
Branches Cross EX22. . . . . .54 E3
Brancker Rd PL2. . . . . .248 C6
Brand Cl EX14 . . . . .166 C4
Brandirons Cross EX17 . . .79 C5
Brandis Cnr
Little Torrington EX20 . . . . .41 F1
North Tawton EX17 . . . . . . .77 F1
Petrockstow EX20 . . . . .56 C6
Rackenford EX16 . . . . .47 F1
BRANDIS CORNER 73 B6
Brandis Cross EX20 . . . . . . .95 E4
Brandise Cross EX17 . . . . . .79 C2
Brandise Hill EX20 . . . . . . .56 F3
Brandis La EX20. . . . . .95 E4
Brandize Pk EX20 . . . . .170 B3
Brandon Rd PL3. . . . . .249 C4
Brand Rd EX14. . . . . .166 C4
Brandreth Rd 3 PL3. . . . .248 F6
Brandy Wells EX37 . . . . . . .44 E6
Branksome St TQ3. . . . . . .219 C2
Brannam Cres EX31 . . . . . .154 B2
Brannams Ct 1 EX32. . . .155 A4
Brannams Sq 2 EX32. . . .155 A4
BRANSCOMBE 190 D3
Branscombe CE Prim Sch
EX12. . . . . .190 D3
Branscombe Cl
Colyford EX24 . . . . .103 A3
Exeter EX4. . . . . .176 E5
Torquay TQ1. . . . . .220 D6
Branscombe Cross EX10. .101 F1
Branscombe Gdns PL5 . . .244 A3
Branscombe La EX7. . . . . .200 C3
Branscombe Rd EX39 . . . . .26 B7
Branscombe: The Old Bakery,
Manor Mill & Forge ★
EX22. . . . . .190 D4
Bransgrove Hill EX18. . . . .59 B5
Bransgrove La EX18. . . . . .59 B5
Branson Ct 3 PL7 . . . . . . .251 C5
Branson Pk PL19. . . . . .126 D6
Brantwood Cl TQ4 . . . . . . .226 A4
Brantwood Cres TQ4. . . . .226 A3
Brantwood Dr TQ4. . . . . . .226 A3
BRATTON CLOVELLY 92 A2
Bratton Cross EX31 . . . . . .17 E7
BRATTON FLEMING. 18 A8
Bratton Fleming Com Prim
Sch EX31. . . . . .18 A8
Braundsworthy Cross
EX21. . . . . .73 E8
BRAUNTON. 152 B6
Braunton Burrows Biosphere
Reserve ★ EX33. . . . . .15 F5

Bowdens Cl TQ13 . . . . .180 C7

Bradworthy Com Prim Sch
EX22. . . . . .38 E1
Bradworthy Cross EX22 . .53 D7
Brady Cl EX17. . . . . .80 B5
Braemar Ct PL7. . . . . .251 C4
Braeside Mews TQ4 . . . . .226 C4
Braeside Rd
Paignton TQ4 . . . . .214 A4
Torquay TQ2. . . . . .214 A4
Braggs Hill PL15 . . . . .89 E3
Braggs' Hill EX37 . . . . .43 B7
Brag La PL7 . . . . .132 C6
Brahms Way EX32. . . . . . .155 C5
Brakefield TQ10 . . . . .135 A2
Brake Ho TQ12. . . . . .207 E2
Brake La PL10 . . . . .252 B5
Brake Rd PL5. . . . . .244 E2
Brakeridge Cl TQ5 . . . . . .229 C6
Brake Wood Cl EX31 . . . .153 D5
Bramble Cl
Budleigh Salterton EX9 . . .198 C1
Dartington TQ9 . . . . .222 F8
Plymouth PL3. . . . . .249 B7
Sidmouth EX10. . . . . .188 B8
Torquay TQ2. . . . . .219 D5
Bramble Hill Ind Est
EX14. . . . . .166 B6
Bramble La
Brampford Speke EX5. . . . .81 C1
Crediton EX17. . . . . .165 E6
Honiton EX14. . . . . .166 B5
Bramble Mead EX5. . . . . . .99 D2
Brambleoak Cross TQ12 . .131 E3
Bramble Path 7 EX32. . . .17 B2
Brambles The TA21 . . . . . .160 D4
Bramble Wlk
Barnstaple EX31. . . . . .154 B3
1 Plymouth PL6. . . . . .249 C7

Braunton & District Mus★
EX33 ....152 D6
Braunton Rd EX31....154 D7
Braunton Sch & Com Coll
EX33 ....152 E4
Braunton Wlk PL6 ....249 E8
Bray Cl
Burlescombe EX16........51 B3
Tavistock PL19.......171 A5
BRAYFORD 18 E5
Brayford Cl PL5.......244 B3
Brayford Prim Sch EX32.. 18 F5
BRAYFORDSHILL 18 E5
Brayhams Terr EX20 ..170 C6
Bray Hill EX32 ....18 F3
Brayley Hill EX32.......18 E1
Bray Mill Cross EX37 ..29 D4
Brays Cl EX17.........165 C5
Braytown Cotts EX32 ..18 F5
Breach Hill TA21........51 F5
Breaka La EX19.........57 E5
Breakneck Cross EX37 ..28 F5
Breakneck Hill
Chittlehampton EX37...28 F5
Teignmouth TQ14.....124 F2
Breakwater Ct TQ5....230 E6
Breakwater Hill PL4...263 C1
Breakwater Ind Est PL9.255 C8
Breakwater Rd PL9 ...255 C8
Brean Down Cl PL3 ...248 E6
Brean Down Rd PL3...248 E7
Brecon Cl
Bideford EX39........157 D1
Paignton TQ4.........225 D4
Plymouth PL3.........249 A7
Breech Cotts TA21.....51 F5
Bremley Cross EX36....31 F7
BRENDON
Bradworthy 54 B8
Holsworthy Beacon 54 C2
Lynton 6 A5
Brendon Cross EX39 ..39 F6
Brendon Hill EX17 ....79 C6
Brendons Ave TQ2....219 C3
Brendons The EX16....50 D1
Brendon Two Gates TA24.13 A6
Brennacott Pl EX39 ..25 D4
Brennacott Rd EX39 ..25 D4
Brent Cl EX5..........184 C3
Brentford Ave PL5 ....244 B5
Brent Hill PL8.........136 D1
Brent Knoll Rd 1 PL3..248 E6
Brent Mill TQ10.......135 A2
Brent Mill Ind Est TQ10.134 F2
Brenton Rd EX4.......114 C5
Brentor Cl EX4........176 F8
Brentor Rd
Mary Tavy PL19 ....117 D6
Plymouth PL4.........249 B2
Brent Rd 1 TQ3 .....226 B6
Brent Tor★ PL19......117 B7
Brest Rd PL6..........245 A3
Brest Way PL6.........245 A3
Breton Way EX8 ......196 E1
Bretteville Cl
Chagford TQ13........111 A6
Woodbury EX5........184 C3
Brett Wlk PL7.........250 F7
Brewer Rd EX32.......155 C4
Brewers Ct EX1........261 A1
Brewers Hill EX39......39 F8
Brewers La EX39.......39 F8
Brewery La
12 Brixham TQ5......230 C5
Exeter EX2...........177 F5
Sidmouth EX10........188 B5
Brewin Rd EX16.......161 C3
Briansway PL12........242 D2
Briar Cl
Exmouth EX8..........202 D8
Honiton EX14.........166 C3
Briar Cres EX2........177 F2
Briardale Rd PL2......247 F6
Briarleigh Cl PL6......245 F2
Briar Rd PL3..........248 F7
Briarside Rd PL6......245 A4
Briar Tor PL20........127 A3
Briary La TQ1.........220 B5
Briary Mews 13 TQ1...220 D4
Brick Cross EX9.......198 C7
Brickfields Sp Ctr PL1...247 H7
Brickhouse Dr EX16...161 D6
Brickhouse Hill EX16..161 D6
Brickyard La EX6.......201 A8
Brickyard Rd EX5......168 A7
Bridespring Rd EX4....173 F1
Bridespring Wlk EX4...173 F1
BRIDESTOWE 107 F8
Bridestowe Prim Sch
EX20................107 F8
Bridewell Ct 9 EX16..161 C3
Bridewell Ho 10 EX16..161 C3
BRIDFORD 112 F5
Bridford Rd EX2.......177 C2
BRIDGE BALL 5 E3
Bridge Bldgs 11 EX31..154 F5
Bridge Chambers 15
EX31................154 F5
Bridge Cl EX15........82 D3
Bridge Cotts
Chard Junction TA20 ..88 D8
East Budleigh EX9....198 B5
4 Exeter EX4.........177 D8

Bridge Cotts continued
Lympstone EX8........195 D5
Bridge Croft TQ13.....130 F5
Bridge Cross
Bishops Nympton EX36..30 F4
Fortescue Cross EX37...44 B4
Bridge Ct EX4.........261 A3
BRIDGE END
Aveton Gifford.......143 C5
Newton Poppleford....187 A8
Bridge End EX31.......31 C5
Bridgefield EX11......169 E4
Bridge Hill EX33.......182 F5
Bridgehill Garth EX32..182 F5
Bridge Ho 1 TQ12...207 C3
Bridgehouse Cross EX15..52 D1
Bridge La
Budlake EX5..........82 D3
7 Instow EX39.......15 B1
Bridgeland St EX39 ...157 A2
Bridge Mill La PL21 ...133 C2
Bridgemoor Cross EX22..71 B6
Bridgend Hill PL8 ....141 A7
Bridge Park La EX31 ...9 E5
Bridge Pk
Ashwater EX21.......90 F6
Bridgerule EX22.......70 F5
Ermington PL21.......136 F2
Ivybridge PL21.......237 D5
Bridge Plats Way EX39..156 E2
Bridge Rd
Budleigh Salterton EX9..198 B2
Churston Ferrers TQ5..229 D5
Exeter EX2, EX6......182 A8
Exmouth EX8.........202 A8
Kingswear TQ5, TQ6..234 B7
Teignmouth TQ14.....202 E1
Torquay TQ2.........219 F5
Totnes TQ9..........222 F6
BRIDGE-REEVE 59 B8
Bridge Reeve Cross EX18..59 C8
Bridge Ret Pk TQ2....219 E8
BRIDGERULE 70 F6
Bridgerule CE Prim Sch
EX22................70 E1
Bridgerule Ind Est EX22..70 E1
Bridgeside TQ9.......139 C7
Bridge St
Bideford EX39........157 A1
Buckfastleigh TQ11...236 B5
Dulverton TA22.......33 D6
Hatherleigh EX20.....75 C7
Ipplepen TQ12.......211 D2
Kingsbridge TQ7......258 D5
Lyme Regis DT7......260 E3
Sidbury EX10........101 B2
Tiverton EX16.......161 C4
Uffculme EX15.......66 A7
Bridges The PL12......242 E1
Bridge Terr
Ashprington TQ9 .....139 F6
Bampton EX16........34 B1
Bridge The PL11......262 B1
BRIDGETOWN
Launceston 105 A8
Totnes 223 F5
Bridgetown TQ9.......223 D5
Bridgetown Ct TQ9...223 D5
Bridgetown Hill TQ9..223 D5
Bridge View EX5.......99 C6
Bridgewater Gdns TQ9..223 E5
Bridgwater Cl PL6.....245 B1
Bridle Cl
Paignton TQ4.........229 B8
Plymouth PL7.........251 B7
Bridle Path The TQ9 ..223 C5
Bridle Way PL12.......242 D4
Bridwell Ave EX15.....65 F7
Bridwell Cl PL5.......247 E8
Bridwell Lane N PL5...247 E8
Bridwell Rd PL5.......247 E8
BRIGHTLEY 94 B8
Brightley Cross EX20..94 B8
Brightley Rd EX20....170 C8
Bright View EX20.....170 A4
Brimacombe Rd EX39..22 E3
Brim Brook Ct TQ2...219 B8
Brimford Cross EX39..38 A4
Brimhay TQ9.........222 F8
Brimhay Bglws TQ9...222 F8
Brim Hill TQ1........214 C5
Brimhill Cl PL7.......251 B3
Brimhill La PL19......117 F6
Brimlands TQ5.......230 B4
Brimlands Ct TQ5.....230 B4
BRIMLEY 88 D3
Brimland Gdns PL9...256 A8
Brimland La PL9......255 F8
Brimley Bsns Pk TQ13..180 C5
Brimley Cnr TQ13.....123 F6
Brimley Cross
Bovey Tracey TQ13....180 B5
Hemyock TA3.........52 F1
Brimley Ct TQ13......180 B5
Brimley Gdns TQ13...180 C5
Brimley Grange TQ13..180 C5
Brimley Halt TQ13....180 C5
Brimley Hill TQ13.....88 D2
Brimley La TQ13......180 A5
Brimley Pk TQ13......180 C5
Brimley Rd
Axminster EX13.......88 D3
Bovey Tracey TQ13....180 B5
Brimley Vale TQ13....180 C6
Brimpenny Rd EX8....196 C1
Brimstone La
Rockwell Green TA21..160 A2
Sampford Arundel TA21..51 F6

Brimstone La continued
Sampford Peverell EX16..50 E2
Brindifield La EX17.....62 A5
Brindiwell Cross EX17...63 B3
Brindiwell Hill EX17....63 B2
Brinkburn Ct EX10 ....188 A3
Brinscombe Cross EX13..103 E6
Brinscombe La
Arlington EX31........10 F3
Membury EX13........87 E6
BRINSWORTHY 19 F1
Brinsworthy Cross EX36..19 F1
Briseham Ct TQ5.....230 D3
Brisham Rd TQ5......230 D3
Brismar Wlk 3 PL6...249 C7
Britannia Ave TQ6....233 C3
Britannia Mus★ TQ6...233 E4
Britannia Pl EX2......249 B2
Britannia Row 5 EX34..150 C6
Britannia Royal Naval Coll
TQ6.................233 F5
Britannia Way EX39...156 E7
Britannia Wharf EX39..156 B7
BRITHEM BOTTOM 65 B5
Britcheston Cl PL9....256 A5
Briton St 2 EX16......34 C1
Briton Streetlane EX6..112 F7
Brittannia Ct TQ6.....234 B3
Brittany Rd EX8.......196 C4
Britten Dr
Barnstaple EX32......155 B5
Exeter EX2...........178 B5
Britton Cl EX16........65 A7
Brittons Cl EX33......152 E5
Brittons The EX33....152 E5
Briwere Rd TQ1......219 F2
BRIXHAM 230 E3
Brixham CE Prim Sch
TQ5.................230 D4
Brixham Coll TQ5.....230 D4
Brixham Cross TQ5...234 E8
Brixham Enterprise Est
TQ5.................230 D4
Brixham Heritage Mus★
TQ5.................230 C5
Brixham Hospl TQ5...230 C3
Brixham Rd
Kingswear TQ6.......234 B3
Paignton TQ4........225 E3
Brixham Theatre★ TQ5..230 C5
Brixham Wlk PL6......249 E8
BRIXINGTON 196 D1
Brixington Dr PL6.....249 E8
Brixington La EX8.....196 C2
Brixington Prim Sch
EX8.................196 C2
BRIXTON 256 F4
257 A5
Brixton Lodge Gdns PL8..256 F5
Broadacre Dr TQ5....230 D5
Broad Cl
Crediton EX17........165 A6
North Molton EX36....30 E8
Broadclose Rd EX31..154 D3
BROADCLYST 175 C5
Broadclyst Com Prim Sch
EX5.................175 C7
Broadclyst Sports Ctr
EX5.................175 D5
Broad Croft EX13......87 E8
Broaddown Cross EX4..86 A1
Broadfield Rd EX32...155 B4
Broadfields Rd EX2...178 C5
Broadgate
Barnstaple EX31......154 E7
Exeter EX1...........261 A3
Broadgate Cl
Barnstaple EX31......154 D6
Braunton EX33........152 D6
Broadgate Cres TQ12..212 F4
Broadgate Rd TQ12...213 A4
Broadhayes Cross EX14..84 D6
BROADHEMBURY 84 E7
Broadhembury CE Prim Sch
EX14................84 E7
BROADHEMPSTON ...131 F1
Broadhempston Prim Sch
TQ9.................131 E1
Broad La
Appledore EX39.......14 F1
Braunton EX33........152 A8
Hawkridge TA22.......21 D1
Tiverton EX16........161 C3
Broadland Gdns PL9...256 A8
Broadland La PL9......255 F8
BROADLANDS 207 A4
Broadlands
Bideford EX39........157 D1
Northam EX39........156 F8
Teignmouth TQ14.....210 A3
Thorverton EX5........81 E4
Broadlands Ct
Newton Abbot TQ12...207 A3
Ottery St Mary EX11..169 A4
Broadleaf Cl EX5......175 C6
Broadley Ct PL6.......241 B2
Broadley Dr TQ2......219 C3
Broadley Ind Pk PL6...241 B2
Broadley Park Rd PL6..241 B2

Broadmead
Exmouth EX8.........196 D2
Woodbury EX5........184 B3
Broadmead Bglws EX32..155 C2
Broadmead Cross EX16..48 A5
Broadmead Ct TQ12...207 D2
Broadmead Gdns EX35..151 B5
Broadmeadow Ave EX4..176 F4
Broadmeadow Ind Est
TQ14................209 D7
Broadmeadow La TQ14..209 D7
Broadmeadow Sports Ctr
TQ14................209 D7
Broadmeadow View
TQ14................209 D7
Broadmoor Cross EX37..29 A2
Broadmoor La EX20...170 A5
BROAD OAK 168 D3
Broad Oak Cres 1 TQ9..223 D5
Broadoak Hill EX31.....4 C3
Broadoaks Cotts PL7..132 E4
Broadpark
Paignton TQ3........226 A7
Torquay TQ2.........219 D2
Broad Park Ave EX34..150 A5
Broad Park Cl EX33.....7 E2
Broad Park Cres EX34..150 A4
Broadpark La EX20....95 D4
Broadpark Rd
Paignton TQ3........226 A7
Torquay TQ2.........219 D2
Broad Park Rd
Bere Alston PL20......125 C2
Exmouth EX8.........196 C1
Plymouth PL3.........248 D6
Broadparks Ave EX4...174 E2
Broadparks Cl EX4....174 E2
Broad Path
Stoke Gabriel TQ9....228 A8
Uffculme EX15........66 A8
Broad Pk PL9.........255 C7
Broad Rd
Kerswell EX15........66 A8
Kingswear TQ6.......234 D5
Broad Reach TQ4.....229 C7
Broadridge Cl TQ12...206 D4
Broadridge Cross TQ9..232 A8
Broadridge La EX17....61 A4
BROADSANDS 229 C7
Broadsands Bend TQ4..229 C8
Broadsands Ct TQ4...229 C7
Broadsands TQ4......229 B7
Broadsands Park Rd
TQ4.................229 C8
Broads Cl 10 EX39....157 B1
Broadshell Cross EX22..71 D5
Broad St
Black Torrington EX21..74 A8
Churchinford TA3......68 A7
Ilfracombe EX34......150 C6
Lifton PL16..........105 E4
Lyme Regis DT7......260 E3
Ottery St Mary EX11..169 D5
South Molton EX36....158 C4
Broadstone TQ6......233 F4
Broadstone Park Rd
TQ2.................219 D3
Broad View
Broadclyst EX5.......175 C6
Dartington TQ9......222 F8
Broadway
Exeter EX2...........176 F3
Fremington EX31......153 F5
Sidmouth EX10.......187 F5
Trusham TQ13........113 D1
Woodbury EX5........184 C2
Broadway Ave TQ12...207 D2
Broadway Hill EX2....176 E3
Broadway La EX33......7 D3
Broadway Rd TQ12....207 D2
Broadways Head EX14,
TA20................68 F6
Broadway The
Exmouth EX8.........202 E8
Plymouth PL9.........255 E7
Broad Wlk PL12.......242 B2
BROADWOODKELLY ...76 D8
BROADWOODWIDGER..106 B8
Broadwoodwidger Prim Sch
PL16................91 A4
Broady Strap EX31....153 F5
BROCKFIELD 88 A8
Brock Ho 8 PL4.....263 A2
Brockhole La
Plymouth PL7.........250 E8
Tatworth EX13, TA20..88 B7
Brockhurst Pk TQ3...218 D2
Brockington's Rd EX5..99 C8
Brockmans Rd PL3....249 C4
BROCKSCOMBE 92 A5
Brockscombe Cross EX17..91 F5
Brocks Cross EX17....79 A2
Brocks La PL10.......252 F5
Brockton Gdns PL6...245 B6
Brockton Gdns PL6...245 A6
Brodick Cl EX4........173 D1
Bromley Ho 6 PL2...248 A4
Bromley Pl 5 PL2....248 A4
Bronescombe Ave TQ14..209 A8
Bronshill Ho TQ1.....220 B6
Bronshill Mews TQ1...220 B6
Bronshill Rd TQ1.....220 B6
Bronte Pl PL5.........244 D1

BROOK.................171 B2
Brook Cl
Bovey Tracey TQ13....180 C7
Exeter EX1...........178 B8
Holcombe EX7........210 E8
Plymouth PL7.........251 A3
Sidford EX10.........101 B1
Brook Ct
Aveton Gifford TQ7 ..143 C6
Barnstaple EX31......154 B3
Brookdale EX11......169 E4
Brookdale Cl EX34....150 A5
Brookdale Ct TQ5....230 B4
Brookdale Pk
Brixham TQ5.........230 B4
Exeter EX2...........178 A2
Brookdale Terr
8 Barnstaple EX32...155 B4
10 Dawlish EX7......204 E6
Brookdown Terr PL12..242 E3
Brookdown Villas PL12..242 E3
Brooke Ave EX2.......177 F3
Brooke Cl
Saltash PL12.........243 A2
Sampford Courtenay EX20..76 F3
Brookedor TQ12......207 E2
Brookedor Gdns TQ12..212 F5
Brooke Rd EX16.......46 E1
Brookesby Hall TQ1...220 D3
Brookfield EX39.......25 E4
Brookfield Cl
8 Braunton EX33....152 D5
Kingsteignton TQ12...207 E7
Paignton TQ4........226 C8
Plymouth PL7.........251 B5
Brookfield Cotts EX8..195 D5
Brookfield Ct
7 Colyton EX24.......103 A4
Teignmouth TQ14.....210 C7
Brookfield Gdns EX2..177 B1
Brookfield Ho TQ3....226 C8
Brookfield Pl EX34....150 B5
Brookfield Rd EX7.....247 F1
Brookfields Cl PL21...247 F1
Brookfield St 8 EX39..157 B1
Brook Green Ctr for Learning
PL5.................244 B4
Brook Green Terr EX4..261 C4
Brook Haven Cl TQ12..212 F5
Brookhayes Cl EX8....202 B8
Brookhill TQ6.........234 B2
Brook Ho PL7.........204 C6
BROOKING 135 F3
Brooking Barn TQ9...139 F8
Brooking Cl PL6.......249 A8
Brookingfield Cl PL7..250 C5
Brooking Way PL12...242 C4
Brook La
Calverleigh EX16......48 F2
Shaldon TQ14.........209 D5
3 Sidford EX10.......101 B1
Virginstow PL16......171 B2
Brooklands
24 Dawlish EX7......204 D6
Tavistock PL19.......171 D6
Totnes TQ9..........223 D5
Brooklands Cross EX10..100 C1
Brooklands Ct EX16...244 B3
Brooklands Farm Cl
EX13................103 D8
Brooklands La TQ2...219 D4
Brooklands Orch
Kilmington EX13......103 D8
Ottery St Mary EX11..169 E4
Brooklands Rd
Exmouth EX8.........196 D1
Rockwell Green TA21..160 B5
Brookland Terr EX11...169 E3
Brook Lane Cotts TQ13..121 B3
Brookleigh Ave EX1...178 B5
Brooklyn Pk EX8......196 C1
Brook Mdw
Exmouth EX8.........196 C1
Newton Poppleford EX10..186 F8
South Molton EX36....158 D4
Brook Orch TQ12......212 F4
Brook Rd
Budleigh Salterton EX9..199 G2
Cullompton EX15......163 B2
Dolton EX19..........57 F7
Ipplepen TQ12.......211 D2
Ivybridge PL21.......237 D5
Brooks Hill EX15......66 C8
Brookside
Barnstaple EX31......154 A3
Broadhembury EX14....84 C7
Kingsbridge TQ7......258 C4
Pathfinder Village EX6..98 A4
Sidmouth EX10.......188 A3
Brookside Cl
Heybrook Bay PL9....140 A7
Kilmington EX13......87 C1
Teignmouth TQ14.....210 A5
Brookside Cres EX4...174 B2
Brookside Ind Units EX4..174 D1
Brookside Units EX4...98 C3
Brookside Villas 22 EX34..3 A3
Brooks Pl TA21.......160 E6
Brook St
Bampton EX16........34 B1
Dawlish EX7.........204 D6
Ottery St Mary EX11..169 E4
Slapton TQ7.........145 C3
Tavistock PL19.......171 C6
Brook Terr EX12......192 D7
Brook The PL12.......242 E4

Brookvale Orch TQ14 . . . 209 D4
Brook View TQ9 . . . 222 F6
Brookway EX1 . . . 178 C7
Brook Way TQ12 . . . 123 F1
Brookwood Cl 4 TQ10 . . 134 F3
Brookwood Rd PL9 . . . 256 D7
Broomball Cross TA22 . . . 32 F5
Broomball La EX16 . . . 32 E5
Broomborough Ct TQ9 . . 223 B5
Broomborough Dr TQ9 . . 223 A5
Broom Cl
Dawlish EX7 . . . 204 F8
Exeter EX2 . . . 178 A5
Broome Cl EX13 . . . 167 E6
Broomfield Dr PL9 . . . 255 C5
Broomham Cross EX37 . . 45 A7
Broomhayes Sch EX39 . . 157 E1
BROOMHILL . . . 133 F1
Broom Hill
Chagford TQ13 . . . 111 A6
Saltash PL12 . . . 242 D2
Broomhill Cross
Chilsworthy EX22 . . . 53 B3
Copplestone EX17 . . . 79 A4
Broomhill Rd EX16 . . . 161 B4
Broomhill Sculpture Gdns★
EX31 . . . 16 E7
Broomhill Villas EX32 . . . 18 E5
Broomhill Way TQ2 . . . 213 E1
Broomhouse La EX36 . . . 30 A2
Broomhouse Pk EX16 . . . 46 E1
Broom La EX13 . . . 88 C5
Broom Pk
Dartington TQ9 . . . 215 E1
Plymouth PL9 . . . 255 D5
Torquay TQ2 . . . 213 F3
Broom's La TA3 . . . 68 C7
Broughton Cl PL3 . . . 248 F7
Brow Hill TQ12 . . . 123 B2
Brown Down La TA20 . . . 68 F7
Browne Memorial
Almshouses PL19 . . . 171 A5
BROWNHEATH . . . 52 C2
Brownhill La PL9 . . . 140 D8
Brownhills Rd TQ12 . . . 207 A3
Brownie Cross PL7 . . . 132 C3
Browning Cl EX2 . . . 178 A4
Browning Rd PL2 . . . 248 A5
Brownings End TQ12 . . . 206 F1
Brownings Mead EX6 . . . 112 F7
Brownings Wlk TQ12 . . . 206 F1
Brownlands Cl EX10 . . . 188 C5
Brownlands Rd EX10 . . . 188 C5
Brownlees EX6 . . . 182 A4
Brownlow St PL1 . . . 262 A2
Brown's Bridge La EX15 . . 65 B7
Browns Bridge Rd TQ2 . . 213 D2
Brownscombe Cl TQ3 . . 218 D2
Brown's Ct EX6 . . . 114 C4
Brown's Hill TQ6 . . . 233 F3
Brown's Hill Head EX37 . . 27 F2
BROWNSTON . . . 137 F3
Brownston Cross TQ10 . . 135 F5
Brownstone Cross EX17 . . 61 C3
Brownstone Moor Cross
EX17 . . . 61 D4
Brownston St PL21 . . . 137 B2
Broxfords Hill EX17 . . . 80 C7
Broxton Dr PL9 . . . 249 E1
Bruckland La EX12, EX13 103 D3
Bruckton Cross TQ6 . . . 232 F6
Brunel Ave
Plymouth PL2 . . . 247 F5
Torquay TQ2 . . . 214 B4
Brunel Cl
Exeter EX4 . . . 177 A7
Teignmouth TQ14 . . . 210 C6
Brunel Ct 16 EX7 . . . 204 E6
Brunel Lodge Hospl
TQ12 . . . 207 A1
Brunel Mews TQ2 . . . 219 F4
Brunel Prim Sch PL12 . . 242 E2
Brunel Rd
Newton Abbot TQ12 . . . 207 D3
Paignton TQ4 . . . 229 D6
Saltash PL12 . . . 242 C4
Starcross EX6 . . . 201 A8
Brunel Terr 3 PL2 . . . 247 F5
Brunel Way
Ivybridge PL21 . . . 237 E6
Plymouth PL1 . . . 262 A2
Brunenburg Way EX13 . . 167 D4
Brunswick Ho 2 TQ12 . . 207 B4
Brunswick Pl
Dawlish EX7 . . . 204 E6
10 Plymouth PL2 . . . 247 F4
Brunswick Rd PL4 . . . 263 B2
Brunswick Sq 4 TQ1 . . . 219 F6
Brunswick St
Exeter EX4 . . . 177 A5
Teignmouth TQ14 . . . 210 C4
Brunswick Terr TQ1 . . . 219 F6
BRUSHFORD
Bondleigh . . . 59 D2
Dulverton . . . 33 D4
Brushford La
Chevithorne EX16 . . . 49 F3
Chulmleigh EX18 . . . 59 D2
Brushford New Rd TA22 . . 33 E4
Brynmoor Cl PL3 . . . 249 A7
Brynmoor Pk PL3 . . . 249 A6
Brynmoor Wlk PL3 . . . 249 A6
Brynsworthy La EX31 . . . 154 A1
Brynsworthy Lawn EX31 . 154 A2
Brynsworthy Pk EX31 . . 154 B3
Buchanan Cl EX14 . . . 166 B4
Buckerall Cross EX14 . . . 84 F2
BUCKERELL . . . 85 A3
Buckerell Ave EX2 . . . 177 E3
Buckeridge Ave TQ14 . . 210 B6
Buckeridge Rd TQ14 . . . 210 B6
Buckeridge Twrs 2
TQ14 . . . 210 B6
BUCKFAST . . . 236 B7
Buckfast Cl
Buckfast TQ11 . . . 236 C6
Ivybridge PL21 . . . 237 D4
Plymouth PL2 . . . 248 A8
BUCKFASTLEIGH . . . 236 C5
Buckfastleigh Prim Sch
TQ11 . . . 236 B5
Buckfastleigh Sta★
TQ11 . . . 236 D5
Buckfast Rd TQ11 . . . 236 C6
Buckfast (St Mary's) Abbey★
TQ11 . . . 236 C7
Buckgrove Cotts EX38 . . . 42 B6
Buckham Cross EX36 . . . 45 D7
Buckham Hill EX36 . . . 45 D7
BUCKHORN . . . 72 D2
Buckhouse La EX24 . . . 102 C7
Buckingham Cl
Exmouth EX8 . . . 202 E7
South Molton EX36 . . . 158 C3
Buckingham Orch TQ13 . 123 C4
Buckingham Pl PL5 . . . 243 E2
Buckingham Rd EX2 . . . 178 D3
BUCKLAND
Newton Abbot . . . 207 E3
Thurlestone . . . 143 B2
Buckland Abbey★ PL20 . . 126 C1
Buckland Brake TQ12 . . 207 E2
BUCKLAND BREWER . . . 40 C7
Buckland Brewer Com Prim
Sch EX39 . . . 40 C7
Buckland Cl
Bideford EX39 . . . 25 E4
Plymouth PL7 . . . 250 D7
Buckland Cross
Braunton EX33 . . . 152 C8
Slapton TQ7 . . . 145 C6
BUCKLAND FILLEIGH . . . 56 A4
Buckland Hall TQ13 . . . 130 D7
BUCKLAND IN THE
MOOR . . . 130 C8
BUCKLAND
MONACHORUM . . . 126 D3
Buckland Rd
Georgeham EX33 . . . 8 B3
Newton Abbot TQ12 . . . 207 F4
BUCKLAND ST MARY . . . 69 C8
Buckland St Mary CE Prim
Sch TA20 . . . 69 D8
Buckland St PL1 . . . 262 B2
Buckland Terr PL20 . . . 126 F2
BUCKLAND-TOUT-
SAINTS . . . 144 C4
Buckland View
Buckland Brewer EX39 . . . 40 B7
Newton Abbot TQ12 . . . 207 D4
Buckland Wlk EX6 . . . 181 F5
BUCKLEIGH . . . 156 D6
Buckleigh Cross EX39 . . 156 C6
Buckleigh Grange EX39 . 156 C6
Buckleigh Rd EX39 . . . 156 C5
Buckley Cross EX10 . . . 101 C1
Buckley Rd EX10 . . . 101 C2
Buckley St TQ8 . . . 259 E5
Bucknall Cl EX12 . . . 190 D4
Bucknill Cl EX6 . . . 182 A4
Bucknole Cross EX14 . . . 102 A8
Bucknole Hill Rd EX24 . . 102 A7
Bucks Cl TQ13 . . . 180 D7
BUCK'S CROSS . . . 24 A1
Buckshots Cross EX14 . . . 69 A4
BUCK'S MILLS . . . 24 B2
Buckton La EX10 . . . 101 C1
Buckwell TA21 . . . 160 E6
Buckwell Cl TQ7 . . . 258 D6
Buckwell Rd TQ7 . . . 258 D6
Buckwell St PL1, PL4 . . . 263 A2
Buctor Pk PL19 . . . 126 A8
Budbrook La EX6 . . . 96 F3
Buddle Cl
Ivybridge PL21 . . . 237 E5
Plymouth PL9 . . . 256 A5
Tavistock PL19 . . . 171 B6
Buddle La
Exeter EX4 . . . 176 F5
Hatherleigh EX20 . . . 75 C7
Bude Hill EX19 . . . 59 A3
Bude Moor Cross EX19 . . 76 D7
Bude St
Appledore EX39 . . . 15 A1
Exeter EX4 . . . 261 B3
Budge Mdws PL15 . . . 115 A4
Budgetts TA21 . . . 52 F6
Budgett's Cross TA21 . . . 52 F6
BUDLAKE . . . 82 E3
Budlake Cross EX24 . . . 101 F6
Budlake Old Post Office★
EX5 . . . 82 D2
Budlake Rd EX2 . . . 177 C1
Budlake Units EX2 . . . 177 C1
Budleigh Cl
Plymouth PL9 . . . 255 F5
Torquay TQ1 . . . 220 D6
Budleigh Hill EX9 . . . 198 B5
BUDLEIGH SALTERTON . . 198 A2
Budleigh Salterton Hospl
EX9 . . . 198 B1
Budshead Gn PL5 . . . 244 C4
Budshead Rd PL5 . . . 244 C4
Budshead Way PL5 . . . 244 E2
Budshead Wood Nature
Reserve★ PL5 . . . 244 A4
Buena Vista Cl PL6 . . . 245 D6
Buena Vista Dr PL6 . . . 245 C6
Buena Vista Gdns PL6 . . 245 C6
Buena Vista Way PL6 . . . 245 C6
BUGFORD . . . 10 C5
Bugford Cross TQ6 . . . 232 C3
Bugford La TQ6 . . . 232 D3
Bugford Lane End TQ6 . . 232 D3
Bughead Cross TQ13 . . . 111 D4
Bughole La TA21 . . . 51 E8
Building's Cross EX17 . . . 63 A4
Bulford TA21 . . . 160 D5
Bulford La TA21 . . . 160 D5
Bulgis Pk EX36 . . . 158 B5
Bulkamore Ct TQ10 . . . 135 E5
BULKWORTHY . . . 39 F1
Bullaford Gate EX36 . . . 31 E4
Bulland Cross EX20 . . . 76 E4
Bulland La
Poughill EX17 . . . 62 D3
Sampford Courtenay EX20 . 76 F4
Bullands Cl 4 TQ13 . . . 180 C8
Bullaton Cross TQ13 . . . 112 E1
Bull Ct EX31 . . . 154 F5
Bulleid Cl PL2 . . . 247 F7
Bulleigh Cross TQ12 . . . 218 B8
Bulleigh Elms Cross
TQ12 . . . 212 A1
Bullens Cl EX5 . . . 81 E4
Bullen St EX5 . . . 81 E5
Buller Cl
Plymouth PL7 . . . 250 F4
Torpoint PL11 . . . 247 A3
Buller Ct EX2 . . . 177 A4
Buller Pk PL12 . . . 242 D3
Buller Rd
11 Barnstaple EX32 . . . 155 A5
Crediton EX17 . . . 165 B6
Exeter EX4 . . . 177 A5
Newton Abbot TQ12 . . . 207 D2
Torpoint PL11 . . . 247 B3
Bullfinch Cl EX15 . . . 163 A2
Bullhead Cross EX19 . . . 58 B2
Bull Hill
Barnstaple EX31 . . . 154 F7
Bideford EX39 . . . 157 A1
Bullhorn Cross TQ7 . . . 142 F6
Bull Meadow Rd EX2 . . . 261 B2
Bullow View EX19 . . . 58 F2
Bull Ring TQ13 . . . 130 F4
Bulls Ct 11 EX24 . . . 103 A4
Bull's La TA20 . . . 88 C8
Bully Shoot Cross EX24 . . 103 A3
Bulmer Rd PL4 . . . 263 C3
Bulmoor Cross EX13 . . . 103 F5
Bulteel Gdns PL6 . . . 244 E7
BULVERTON . . . 187 F6
Bulverton Pk EX10 . . . 187 F6
Bulworthy Cross EX16 . . . 47 E5
Bulworthy Knap EX16 . . . 47 E5
Bumpston Cross TQ11 . . 215 C7
Bungalows The
Axminster EX13 . . . 167 C4
Dawlish Warren EX7 . . . 201 B2
4 Tiverton EX16 . . . 161 C3
Bunkers Farm TQ9 . . . 144 E7
Bun La 8 TQ14 . . . 210 B4
Bunneford Cross EX15 . . . 64 E1
Bunn Rd EX8 . . . 196 D4
Bunson Gate EX18 . . . 45 A4
Bunting Cl
Newton Abbot TQ12 . . . 207 A1
Teignmouth TQ14 . . . 210 A5
Buntings The EX6 . . . 181 F4
Bunts La EX12 . . . 191 F7
Bunyan Cl PL5 . . . 244 C2
Burch Cl EX8 . . . 196 E2
Burches Cross EX16 . . . 48 A1
Burch Gdns EX7 . . . 200 E1
Burchills Cl TA21 . . . 160 A6
Burchill's Hill TA21 . . . 160 B7
Burcombe Hill EX36 . . . 158 E8
Burdon La EX21 . . . 74 C7
BURFORD . . . 23 C1
Burgage TA21 . . . 160 D6
Burgh Island Cswy TQ7 . . 142 E3
Burgmanns Hill EX8 . . . 195 D5
Burke Rd TQ9 . . . 223 D6
Burland Cross EX31 . . . 9 B4
Burland La EX33 . . . 8 F1
Burlands The EX14 . . . 84 D2
Burleigh La
Malborough TQ7 . . . 147 E7
Plymouth PL3 . . . 248 D7
Burleigh Lane End TQ7 . . 147 E8
Burleigh Manor PL3 . . . 248 D7
Burleigh Park Rd PL3 . . . 248 D6
Burleigh Rd TQ2 . . . 219 C7
BURLESCOMBE . . . 51 B3
Burlescombe CE Prim Sch
EX16 . . . 51 B3
BURLESTONE . . . 145 D7
Burlington Cl EX32 . . . 155 B3
Burlington Gr EX32 . . . 155 B2
Burnard Cl PL6 . . . 244 E7
Burnards Cl 15 EX24 . . . 103 A4
Burnards Field Rd EX24 . 103 A4
Burnbreach Cnr EX24 . . . 102 B2
Burnbridge Hill EX16 . . . 63 D2
Burne Cross TQ12 . . . 131 D6
Burnet Cl EX2 . . . 178 C3
Burnett Cl PL12 . . . 242 D2
Burnett Rd PL6 . . . 248 F8
Burnham Cl EX12 . . . 192 A8
Burnham Ct TQ12 . . . 207 E7
Burnham Park Rd PL3 . . 248 D6
Burniston Cl PL7 . . . 251 A3
Burnistone Cl PL7 . . . 251 A3
Burn La
Lydford PL19 . . . 107 C1
North Brentor PL19 . . . 117 C8
Burnley Cl TQ12 . . . 206 D4
Burnley Rd TQ12 . . . 206 D4
Burn River Rise TQ2 . . . 219 B8
Burns Ave
Exeter EX2 . . . 177 F3
Plymouth PL5 . . . 244 C2
Burns Ct EX7 . . . 204 E5
Burnside EX8 . . . 196 B1
Burnside Rd EX34 . . . 150 A3
Burns La 13 PL21 . . . 137 B2
Burnsome La EX14, EX15 . . 67 B5
Burnthouse Cross EX14 . . 67 B5
Burnthouse Hill TQ12 . . . 212 E1
Burnthouse La EX2 . . . 177 F3
Burnt Mdw EX6 . . . 113 D5
BURRATON
Ermington . . . 136 D3
Saltash . . . 242 D4
St Dominick . . . 125 A2
BURRATON COOMBE . . . 242 C2
Burraton Cross PL21 . . . 136 D4
Burraton Prim Sch PL12 . 242 C3
Burraton Rd PL12 . . . 242 C4
Burrator Arboretum★
PL20 . . . 127 E3
Burrator Ave PL20 . . . 128 A8
Burrator Dr EX4 . . . 176 E8
Burrator Rd PL20 . . . 127 B3
BURRIDGE . . . 16 E6
Burridge Ave TQ2 . . . 219 D5
Burridge Cross EX18 . . . 58 F8
Burridge La TQ2 . . . 220 A5
Burridge Moor Cross
EX18 . . . 60 E6
Burridge Rd
Torquay TQ2 . . . 219 D5
Upton Pyne EX5 . . . 173 B8
BURRINGTON . . . 43 F3
Burrington CE Prim Sch
EX37 . . . 43 F3
Burrington Dr EX17 . . . 80 E4
Burrington Ind Est PL5 . . 244 A1
Burrington Moor Cross
EX37 . . . 43 C3
Burrington Rd PL5 . . . 244 A1
Burrington Way PL5 . . . 244 B1
Burrough Lawn EX39 . . . 157 A6
Burrough Rd EX39 . . . 157 A6
Burrough Way TA21 . . . 160 D4
BURROW
Broadclyst . . . 175 E8
Newton Poppleford . . . 186 C8
Burrow Cl EX10 . . . 186 D8
Burrow Cnr
Butterleigh EX16 . . . 64 C4
Dalwood EX13 . . . 86 F2
Burrow Cross
Budlake EX5 . . . 82 E1
Burrow EX5 . . . 175 E7
Meshaw EX17 . . . 46 A4
Monkokehampton EX19 . . . 76 A8
Burrow Ctyd EX16 . . . 64 C4
Burrowe The 2 EX17 . . . 165 C5
Burrow Farm Gdns★
EX13 . . . 87 A2
Burrow Hill PL9 . . . 255 E6
Burrow Knap EX13 . . . 87 A2
Burrow Knap Way EX13 . . 86 F2
Burrow La
Ashbrittle TA21 . . . 50 D8
Bow EX17 . . . 78 A5
Newton Poppleford EX10 . 186 D8
Burrowplot Cross EX17 . . 59 F2
Burrow Rd
Burrow EX5 . . . 175 E8
10 Ilfracombe EX34 . . . 150 B5
Seaton EX12 . . . 192 B4
Burrows Cl EX33 . . . 152 C5
Burrows Close La EX33 . . 15 A7
Burrowshot Cross EX13 . 104 B7
Burrows La EX39 . . . 14 F1
Burrows Pk EX33 . . . 152 C5
Burrows Way EX39 . . . 156 F8
Burrow The 1 EX12 . . . 192 B4
Burscombe La EX10 . . . 101 A1
Burscott EX39 . . . 23 D3
Bursdon Moor Cross
EX39 . . . 37 E7
Bursledon Ct EX7 . . . 204 F6
BURSTON . . . 78 B5
Burston Cross EX17 . . . 78 B4
Burston La EX16 . . . 34 A4
Burton Art Gallery & Mus
The★ EX39 . . . 157 A3
Burton Cl PL6 . . . 245 B6
Burton Pl TQ5 . . . 230 C4
Burton Rd EX39 . . . 156 E1
Burton St TQ5 . . . 230 C3
Burton Villa Cl TQ5 . . . 230 C4
Burvill St EX35 . . . 151 B5
Burwell Cl PL6 . . . 245 E4
Burwell La EX36 . . . 30 F7
Burwood La EX38 . . . 159 F5
Burwood Mews EX38 . . . 159 F4
Burwood Rd EX38 . . . 159 E5
BURY . . . 34 A6
Bury Cross
Lapford EX17 . . . 60 D2
Petrockstowe EX20 . . . 56 F5
Bury Rd TQ12 . . . 207 B4
Bury The EX5 . . . 81 E5
Buscombe La EX31 . . . 11 E2
Bushayes Cnr EX3 . . . 183 C6
Bush Cnr EX18 . . . 58 F8
Bush Cross EX18 . . . 58 F8
Bushell Rd TQ12 . . . 207 A4
Bushes La EX12, DT7 . . . 193 B7
Bushmead Ave TQ12 . . . 213 A5
Bush Pk PL6 . . . 245 F3
Busland La EX16 . . . 63 D4
Bussell's Moor Cross
EX36 . . . 32 C4
Butcher Park Hill PL19 . . 171 B7
Butcher's Moor La EX19 . . 58 E4
Butchers Row EX31 . . . 154 F5
Butcombe La EX17 . . . 61 D1
Bute Rd PL4 . . . 249 A4
Butlakes La EX24 . . . 101 F6
Butland Ave TQ3 . . . 219 C1
Butland Rd TQ12 . . . 207 D8
Butlands Ind Est TQ12 . . . 211 F2
Butler Cl
Plymouth PL6 . . . 245 B6
Tiverton EX16 . . . 161 E3
Butler Way EX14 . . . 86 A6
Buttercombe Cl TQ12 . . . 211 F8
Buttercombe La
Braunton EX33 . . . 15 E8
Knowle EX31, EX34 . . . 8 F1
West Down EX34 . . . 8 E5
Buttercup Cl EX12 . . . 192 B8
Buttercup Mdw PL15 . . . 105 A2
Butterdon Wlk PL21 . . . 237 F5
Butterdown PL12 . . . 242 B3
Butterfly La TQ12 . . . 209 C2
Butterlake TQ3 . . . 218 D3
BUTTERLEIGH . . . 64 C3
Butterleigh Dr EX16 . . . 161 E3
Buttermere Ct EX4 . . . 176 F5
Buttermoor Cross EX16 . . 48 D3
Butterpark PL21 . . . 237 D5
Buttery Cl EX14 . . . 166 C4
Buttery Rd EX14 . . . 166 C4
Buttgarden St EX39 . . . 157 A1
Buttle's Cross TA3 . . . 68 C7
Buttle's La TA3 . . . 68 B6
Buttonhill Cross EX31 . . . 18 A8
Button La EX31 . . . 11 A1
Butt Park Rd PL5 . . . 244 B3
Butt Parks EX17 . . . 165 D4
Butt Pk
Hennock TQ13 . . . 123 B7
Stokenham TQ7 . . . 145 B1
Butts Cl
Bridford EX6 . . . 112 F5
Chawleigh EX18 . . . 60 B7
Honiton EX14 . . . 166 B4
Witheridge EX16 . . . 46 E1
Butts Cross
Buckfastleigh TQ11 . . . 135 B6
Cornworthy TQ9 . . . 227 C3
Butts Ct EX2 . . . 178 A5
Buttsford Terr PL21 . . . 136 B6
Butts Hill
Kenton EX6 . . . 194 D3
Paignton TQ3 . . . 225 B8
Butt's Hill EX11 . . . 169 E4
Buttshill Cross TQ3 . . . 225 B8
Butts La
Christow EX6 . . . 113 B3
Ideford TQ13 . . . 124 B4
Kenton EX6 . . . 194 D1
Starcross EX6 . . . 200 D8
Buttsons Cl TQ7 . . . 145 B1
Butts Park Ct PL8 . . . 141 A7
Butts Path EX33 . . . 152 D6
Butts Pk PL8 . . . 141 A7
Butts Rd
Exeter EX2 . . . 178 A5
Ottery St Mary EX11 . . . 169 E4
Butts The
Colyton EX24 . . . 103 A4
Loddiswell TQ7 . . . 143 E8
Newton Ferrers PL8 . . . 141 A7
Butts Way EX20 . . . 77 C4
Buzzacott Cl EX34 . . . 3 B2
Buzzacott La EX34 . . . 3 B2
Buzzard Rd PL19 . . . 171 D2
Byard Cl PL5 . . . 243 E1
Bycott La EX18 . . . 45 B4
Bydown Cross EX32 . . . 28 D8
Bye Cross EX33 . . . 8 B3
Byes Cl EX10 . . . 188 C8
Byeside Rd EX10 . . . 188 C8
Byes La EX10 . . . 188 D8
Bygones (Mus)★ TQ1 . . . 220 C8
Byland Rd PL3 . . . 249 A6
Byron Ave PL5 . . . 244 C2
Byron Cl EX31 . . . 154 F7
Byron Rd
Exeter EX2 . . . 178 C5
Torquay TQ1 . . . 220 A8
Byron Way EX8 . . . 196 C3
Bystock Cl EX4 . . . 261 A4
Bystock Mews EX8 . . . 196 E3
Bystock Rd EX8 . . . 196 D4
Bystock Terr EX4 . . . 261 A4
Byter Mill La TQ9 . . . 228 A7
Byways Cl EX31 . . . 153 F5

C

Cabbage Hill TQ13 . . . 130 F4
Cabbage La EX14 . . . 85 A3
Cabot Cl PL12 . . . 242 E2
Cabourg Cl TQ8 . . . 259 D5
CADBURY . . . 81 D7
Cadbury Cross EX17 . . . 81 C8
Cadbury Gdns EX9 . . . 198 B6

Caddiford Cross EX17 .... 97 B6
Cadditon Cross EX20 .... 76 F7
Caddsdown Ind Pk EX39 .. 25 D4
Caddywell La EX38 ..... 159 E5
Caddywell Mdw EX38 .... 159 E5
CADELEIGH 63 D3
Cades Mead EX21 ...... 160 F7
Cadewell Cres TQ2 ..... 213 D1
Cadewell La TQ2 .... 219 C8
Cadewell Park Rd TQ2 .. 213 C1
Cadford La EX19 .... 59 B3
Cadhay Cl EX11 .... 169 B5
Cadhay House ★ EX11 .. 169 B5
Cadhay La EX11 .... 169 B4
Cadlake La EX20 .... 77 A3
Cadleigh Cl PL21 .... 136 D6
Cadleigh Court La EX16 .. 63 D2
Cadleigh Cross PL21 .... 136 D7
Cadleigh La PL21 .... 136 D6
CADLEIGHPARK 136 D6
Cadover Cl PL6 .... 245 A1
Cadway Cl EX11 .... 169 B3
Cadwell Rd TQ3 .... 226 D7
Caen Com Prim Sch 7
  EX33 .... 152 D6
Caen Field EX33 .... 152 D6
Caen Field Sh Ctr 6
  EX33 .... 152 D6
Caen Gdns EX33 .... 152 D6
Caen La 1 EX33 .... 152 D6
Caen St EX33 .... 152 D6
Caen View EX33 .... 152 C5
Caernarvon Gdns PL2 ... 248 B7
Caffyns Cross EX35 .... 5 A4
Cairn Rd EX34 .... 150 B4
Cairn Side EX34 .... 150 B3
Cake Down La EX36 .... 158 E4
Calder Cl PL3 .... 249 B6
Caldicot Gdns PL6 ...... 245 C8
Caledonia Cl 1 PL7 .... 251 B5
Calf St EX38 .... 159 D5
California Ct EX4 .... 173 A3
California Cross PL21 ... 138 A3
California Gdns PL3 .... 249 D6
Caller's La EX15 .... 52 D1
Callington Rd
  Saltash PL12 .... 242 E3
  Tavistock PL19. .... 171 A4
CALSTOCK 125 D3
Calstock Prim Sch PL18 125 D3
Calstock Rd PL18 ...... 125 D6
Calstock Sta PL18. ...... 125 D3
Calthorpe Rd EX4 ...... 177 F8
Calvados 1 EX32 ...... 155 A5
Calvados Cl 10 TQ13. ... 123 E6
Calvados Pk TQ12 ...... 207 F7
CALVERLEIGH 48 E1
Calverleigh Cross EX16. .. 48 C1
Calvesford Cl EX38 ..... 159 E5
Calvesford Cross EX38 .. 159 E5
Calvez Cl PL10 .... 252 F6
Cambercombe Terr 5
  EX34. .... 150 D5
Camber Rd PL1 .... 262 A1
Camborne Cl PL5 ...... 244 A5
Camborne Cres TQ4. ... 229 B8
Cambrian Cl TQ4 ...... 225 D5
Cambridge Gr 3 EX34 .. 150 C5
Cambridge Lane W 5
  PL1. .... 262 B3
Cambridge Rd
  Brixham TQ5 .... 230 A4
  Plymouth PL2. .... 247 E5
  Torquay TQ1 .... 214 B1
Cambridge St 4 EX4 .... 177 A4
Cambridge Terr EX10 ... 188 B4
Camden Cl PL4 .... 263 A3
Camden St
  Plymouth PL4 .... 263 A3
Came Cross EX14 .... 84 C7
Camellia Cl
  Churston Ferrers TQ5 ... 229 F5
  1 Tiverton EX16 ...... 161 F6
Camelot Cl EX4 .... 174 A1
CAMELS HEAD 247 E7
Cameron Cl EX16 ...... 161 B3
Cameron Dr PL21 ...... 237 A5
Cameron Way PL6 ...... 245 B1
Camfield Dr EX14 ...... 161 F6
Camilla Ct EX4. .... 261 B4
Camilla Terr PL2 .... 248 D7
Campbellhays Hill EX16 .. 47 A1
Campbell Rd PL9 .... 255 F7
Camp Cross PL15 ...... 105 E7
Camperdown Rd TQ8 ... 259 C4
Camperdown St PL2 .... 247 F4
Camperdown Terr PL8 .. 201 F6
Camperknowle Cl PL10. 252 F6
Campian Way 11 EX14. .. 85 C2
Campion Cl
  Launceston PL15. .... 105 A2
  7 Plymouth PL7 ...... 251 C5
  Saltash PL12 .... 242 D4
Campion Ct
  Torquay TQ1 .... 214 B1
  Willand EX15. .... 162 D5
Campion Dr EX32 ...... 155 E3
Campion Gdns EX2 ..... 178 C3
Campion Rise PL19 ..... 171 D6
Campion View PL6 ..... 245 E8
Camp Rd EX20 .... 170 C2
Camps Cross EX17 ...... 80 E2
Canaan Way EX11 ...... 169 D3

Canada Hill Prim Sch
  TQ12 .... 206 F1
Canal Cl TA21. .... 160 B8
Canal Hill EX16 .... 161 F3
Canal Rd
  Holsworthy EX22. ...... 164 D6
  Tavistock PL19. .... 171 B5
Canberra Cl EX4 .... 173 E2
Candar The EX34. ...... 150 B6
Candish Dr PL9 .... 256 D7
Candys Cotts 1 TQ13 .. 123 C4
Canefields Ave PL7 ..... 251 B3
Cane's Cotts PL8. .... 257 A5
Canhaye Cl PL7 .... 251 A3
Cann Gdns PL6 .... 244 D6
Cannington La DT7. ..... 104 B3
Cannington Rd EX16 ..... 46 E1
Cannon Rd TQ12 .... 123 B2
Cannon St PL1. .... 247 D2
Canns Water EX39 .... 39 C6
Cann Woods Nature
  Reserve ★ PL6. .... 244 C5
Cann Wood View PL6 .. 245 E7
Canons Cl TQ14. .... 208 F8
Canons Gate PL19. ...... 171 A3
Canons Way PL19 ...... 171 A3
Canonteign Falls ★ EX6. 113 B1
Canon Way EX2. .... 181 B8
Canterbury Cl
  Feniton EX14 .... 84 D2
  Ivybridge PL21 .... 237 E4
Canterbury Dr PL5 ..... 244 B4
Canterbury Rd EX4 ..... 176 E7
Canterbury Way EX8 ... 196 E4
Capel La EX8 .... 202 F8
Capern Cl EX33 .... 152 E4
Capern Rd EX39 .... 156 F1
Capper Cl EX10 .... 186 E8
Capstone Cres EX34. .... 150 C6
Capstone Ct EX34 ...... 150 D5
Capstone Pl 4 EX34 .... 150 C6
Capstone Rd EX34 ...... 150 C6
Captain Brooks Cross
  EX39. .... 39 B8
Captain's Cross EX6 ..... 63 C3
Captains Gdns PL5 ...... 244 E1
Captains Rd TQ12 ...... 207 D8
CAPTON 232 D7
Caradon Cl PL6 .... 245 A5
Caradon Terr PL12 ..... 242 E3
Caradon Terr 2 PL20 .. 126 F4
Carbeile Jnr Sch PL11. .. 247 A3
Carbeile Rd PL11 ...... 247 A2
Carberry TQ8 .... 259 D4
Carberry Ave EX8 ...... 196 A1
Carders Ct EX2 .... 261 A2
Cardiff Pl PL7. .... 251 B4
Cardigan Rd PL6 .... 245 C1
Cardinal Ave PL5 ...... 247 D8
Carehouse Cross TQ7 ... 145 B1
Careswell Ave PL2 ..... 247 F8
Carew Ave PL5. .... 244 B3
Carew Gdns
  Newton Abbot TQ12. .... 207 F3
  Plymouth PL5. .... 244 B3
  Saltash PL12 .... 242 D3
Carew Gr PL5. .... 244 B3
Carew Rd EX16 .... 161 D6
Carew Terr PL11 .... 247 B2
Carew Wharf PL11 ..... 247 B2
Carew Wharf Bsns Ctr
  PL11. .... 247 C2
Carey Ct TQ12 .... 242 E3
Carey Rd TQ6 .... 233 C3
CARGREEN 239 A2
Carhaix Way EX7. ...... 204 F8
Carisbrooke Rd PL6 .... 245 C1
CARKEEL 242 C6
Carkeel Barns PL12 .... 242 C5
Carkeel Ind Est PL12. ... 242 D5
Carlile Rd
  Brixham TQ5 .... 230 A5
  Exeter EX2. .... 178 A5
Carling Ct TQ7 .... 258 C4
Carlisle Rd PL5 .... 244 D3
Carlisle St 4 TQ12 ..... 207 C3
Carlton Cl
  Paignton TQ3 .... 219 C2
  Plymouth PL3. .... 249 B5
Carlton Ct TQ12 .... 209 B2
Carlton Dr TQ3 .... 219 C2
Carlton Hill EX8. .... 202 A5
Carlton Mews TQ1 ..... 220 C6
Carlton Rd 20 TQ14 ... 210 C4
Carlton Rd
  Exeter EX2. .... 178 A4
  Torquay TQ1 .... 220 C6
Carlton Terr
  18 Barnstaple EX32 .... 155 A4
  6 Dawlish EX7. .... 204 E6
  Plymouth, Lipson PL4 ... 263 A3
  Plymouth, Weston Mill PL5 247 E8
Carlyle Ave EX32 .... 155 A6
Carlyon Cl
  Exeter EX1. .... 178 A6
  Torpoint PL11 .... 246 F4
Carlyon Gdns EX1. ...... 178 A6
Carmarthen Rd PL4 .... 249 B2
Carmel Gdns PL19 ..... 171 A5
Carnegie N EX39. .... 156 F6
Carnegie S EX39 .... 156 F6
Carnock Rd PL2 .... 248 D8
Carnoustie Dr PL12 .... 242 C2
Carolina Gdns PL2 ..... 247 F5
Caroline Ave EX4 ...... 178 D1
Caroline Cl
  Exmouth EX8 .... 196 D1

Caroline Cl continued
  Kingskerswell TQ12 ..... 213 A3
Carousel Ct EX4 .... 177 A4
Carpenter Cl
  Exeter EX4. .... 261 A3
  Tiverton EX16 .... 161 C3
Carpenter Rd PL9 ...... 255 F8
Carpenter's Cross EX18 .. 60 A5
Carpenter's La EX18. ..... 60 A5
Carradale Rd PL6 ...... 249 C7
Carrington Terr 5 EX32. 155 A6
Carrionpit La EX19 ...... 58 F3
Carrions The 7 TQ9 ... 223 C5
Carrisbrooke Way PL12 .. 242 B2
Carr La TQ7 .... 145 C4
Carroll Rd PL5 .... 244 C2
Carrolls Way PL9 ...... 256 A5
Carron La PL6 .... 241 D1
Carswells TQ12 .... 212 F5
Carter Ave EX8 .... 202 D8
Carter Cl EX34 .... 158 C5
Carter Rd PL21 .... 237 D6
Carters Cross EX13. ..... 87 A3
Cartwright Cres TQ14 .. 209 D8
Cary Ave TQ1 .... 220 C7
Cary Castle TQ1. .... 220 B8
Cary Parade TQ2 ...... 220 B4
Cary Park Rd TQ1 ..... 220 C7
Cary Pk TQ1 .... 220 C7
Cary Rd
  Paignton TQ3 .... 219 A1
  Torquay TQ2 .... 220 A4
Casberry La EX5. .... 82 E6
Case Gdns EX12. .... 192 B6
Cassiobury Way TQ2 ... 213 E2
Castlands EX5 .... 172 C7
CASTLE 88 D4
Castle Acre Gdns PL3 .. 249 B5
Castle Bank Gdns PL3 .. 249 B5
Castle Barbican PL7. .... 250 E4
Castlebar Cl EX16. ...... 161 E3
Castle Bldgs PL12. ...... 242 D4
Castle Carey Gdns PL3 .. 249 B5
Castle Cir TQ1 .... 220 A5
Castle Circus Ct TQ1 ... 220 A5
Castle Cotts
  Exmouth EX8 .... 203 A7
  Tuckenhay TQ9 .... 139 F6
  Wellington TA21. .... 52 D8
  Woodbury EX5. .... 184 C3
Castle Cross
  Axminster EX13. .... 88 D4
  Bratton Clovelly EX20 ..... 92 C6
  Membury EX13 .... 87 E4
Castle Ct
  Saltash PL12 .... 242 C2
  Totnes TQ9 .... 223 B6
Castle Down Sch EX8 .. 202 F7
Castle Drogo ★ EX6 .... 96 C1
Castle Farm EX11 ...... 168 C4
Castle Gate EX6. .... 194 E3
Castlehayes Gdns PL7 .. 250 E4
Castle Hill
  Axminster EX13. .... 167 D6
  Berrynarbor EX34 .... 2 E3
  Ilfracombe EX34 .... 150 C6
  Lynton EX35. .... 151 C5
  Seaton EX12 .... 192 B7
Castle Hill Ave EX34 ... 150 C6
Castle Hill Gdns EX38 .. 159 D5
Castle Hill Ind Pk EX13 . 167 C6
Castle Hill View 1 EX10. 101 B1
Castle Hill Villas 14
  EX34. .... 150 C6
Castle Ho EX13 .... 167 D6
Castle Hts EX35. .... 151 C5
Castle La
  Blackawton TQ9 .... 139 E2
  Budleigh Salterton EX9 .. 197 C1
  Exmouth EX8, EX9 ..... 203 B8
  Okehampton EX20 ...... 170 A3
  Paignton TQ3 .... 219 D8
  Plymouth PL7 .... 250 E4
  Torquay TQ1. .... 220 B5
  Woodbury EX5. .... 184 C3
Castle Mdw EX39 .... 40 B8
Castlemead Cl PL12. .... 242 D3
Castlemead Dr PL12. .... 242 D3
Castle Mount EX4 ...... 261 A4
Castle Park Ind Est EX32 155 E3
Castle Park Rd EX32 ... 155 E3
Castle Pk EX15. .... 67 B8
Castle Prim Sch The
  EX16. .... 161 D4
Castle Quay EX31 ...... 154 F5
Castle Quay 5 EX31. ... 154 F5
Castle Rd
  Dartmouth TQ6 .... 234 B1
  Kingswear TQ6. .... 234 A2
  Okehampton EX20 ...... 170 B4
  Torquay TQ1. .... 220 B5
  Wellington TA21. .... 52 D8
Castle Rise
  Plymouth PL3. .... 249 B4
  Saltash PL12 .... 242 D1
Castle Rock EX34 .... 7 F7
Castle St
  Axminster EX13. .... 167 C6
  Bampton EX16. .... 34 B1
  Barnstaple EX32 .... 154 F5
  Combe Martin EX34. ..... 3 A3
  Exeter EX4. .... 261 B3
  Great Torrington EX38. 159 D5
  Northam EX39 .... 156 F6
  Plymouth PL1. .... 263 A2
  Tiverton EX16 .... 161 D4

Castle St continued
  Totnes TQ9. .... 223 C6
  Winkleigh EX19 .... 58 F3
Castle Terr 5 EX34 .... 150 C5
Castleton Cl PL3. .... 249 A4
Castleton Tor TQ1 ..... 219 F7
Castle View
  17 Colyton EX24 ...... 103 A4
  Saltash PL12 .... 242 D1
Castle Way TQ12 ...... 206 E4
Castlewood Ave TQ12 .. 206 F4
Castle Wood La TA20. ... 69 F1
Castor Cl TQ5 .... 230 D3
Castor La TQ4 .... 226 B1
Castor Rd TQ5 .... 230 C3
Catalina Cl EX14 .... 67 C1
Catalina Villas PL9. ..... 255 A6
Cater Rd EX32 .... 155 B4
Cat & Fiddle Pk EX5. ... 179 E3
Catharine Cl EX16. ..... 161 E5
Cathcart Ave PL4 ...... 249 B2
Cathedral Cl EX1. ...... 261 B3
Cathedral of St Mary's & St
  Boniface ★ PL1 ...... 262 B3
Cathedral School of St Mary
  EX4 .... 182 D7
Cathedral St PL1. ...... 262 B3
Catherine Cres EX4 .... 225 F4
Catherine St
  Exeter EX1. .... 261 B3
  Plymouth PL1. .... 262 C2
Cathole La DT7 .... 104 B5
Catkill Cross EX36 ...... 46 C7
Cat La EX34. .... 150 E5
Catmoor Cross EX13 .... 88 A5
Catnip Cl EX13 .... 167 E6
CATON 131 C6
Caton Cross TQ12. ..... 131 A6
Catrage Hill EX22. ...... 18 C2
Catsborough Cross EX39 . 40 E6
Catshole La EX39 ...... 156 F1
Catsmoor Cross EX20 .... 92 F1
Catson Gn PL8. .... 257 A5
CATTEDOWN 263 C1
Cattewater Ct PL5 ..... 243 E5
Cattewater Rd PL4 ..... 249 B1
Catt's La TA21 .... 52 E6
Caulston Cl EX18 ...... 196 A2
Caulfield Cl 7 TQ12 ... 207 C3
Caumont Cl EX15 .... 65 F7
Caunters Cl TQ12 ...... 211 D2
Causeway EX12. .... 191 D5
Causeway Cross EX39 .. 157 A7
Causeway Cl EX32 ..... 211 E2
Causeway Cross TQ12. . 211 E2
Causeway End EX14. .... 84 D7
Causeway The TQ12. ... 211 D2
Causey Gdns EX1 ...... 174 F6
Causey La EX1 .... 174 F1
CAUTE. 55 D5
Cavalier Ct EX38. ...... 159 D5
Cavalier Rd TQ12 ...... 180 F3
Cavalry Dr TQ12 .... 180 F1
Cavell Way EX20 .... 170 C6
Cavendish Cl EX7 ...... 204 C7
Cavendish Dr EX35. .... 151 B5
Cavendish Rd
  Exeter EX1. .... 177 F6
  Plymouth PL4. .... 249 B1
Cavern Rd
  11 Brixham TQ5 ...... 230 C4
  Torquay TQ1. .... 220 B5
Cavie Cres EX33 .... 152 B6
Cavie Rd EX33 .... 152 B6
Cawley Ave EX13. ...... 167 F7
Cawley's La EX14 .... 86 F6
CAWSAND 253 B1
Caxton Gdns PL5. ...... 244 C2
Caxton Row EX16. ...... 161 D6
Cayley Way PL5 .... 243 F2
Cayman Cl TQ2 .... 213 E3
Cecil Ave
  Paignton TQ3 .... 226 B8
  Plymouth PL4. .... 263 C4
Cecil Cotts PL1 .... 262 B3
Cecilia Rd TQ3 .... 219 B1
Cecil Mews TQ3 .... 226 B7
Cecil Rd
  Exeter EX2. .... 177 A4
  Paignton TQ3 .... 226 B7
  Plymouth PL1. .... 262 B3
Cedar Ave EX7. .... 201 A2
Cedar Ave PL9 .... 255 C5
Cedar Cl
  Axminster EX13. .... 167 D5
  Exmouth EX8 .... 196 D3
  Honiton EX14. .... 166 B5
  Seaton EX12 .... 192 A7
  Teignmouth TQ14 ...... 210 D7
  Torpoint PL11. .... 246 F2
Cedar Court Rd TQ1 ... 220 B7
Cedarcroft Rd PL2 ..... 248 B7
Cedar Ct
  Saltash PL12 .... 242 F2
  Wellington TA21. .... 160 C8
Cedar Dr PL11. .... 246 F2
Cedar Gdns EX13 ...... 167 D5
Cedar Gr EX31. .... 154 B2
Cedar Ho 2 EX33 ..... 152 D6
Cedar Rd
  Newton Abbot TQ12. ... 212 F8
  Paignton TQ3 .... 219 C1
  Tiverton EX16 .... 161 F5
  Torquay TQ1. .... 220 D5
Cedar Units TQ9 .... 222 F8

Cedar Way
  Bideford EX39 .... 25 D4
  Brixham TQ5 .... 230 A2
Celandine Cl EX12 ..... 192 B7
Celandine Gdns PL7. ... 251 C5
Celandine Lawns EX15 . 162 D5
Celia Cres EX4. .... 174 A2
Cembra Cl EX4. .... 166 E5
Cemetery La EX5. .... 82 F6
Cemetery Rd PL18 ..... 125 C5
Centenary Way TQ2 ... 213 C2
Centery La
  Bittadon EX31 .... 9 C5
  Parracombe EX31 .... 4 D2
Central Ave
  Exeter, Countess Wear
  EX2 .... 182 D7
Central Ave EX4. .... 174 A2
Central Ave PL9 .... 255 F8
Central Ave EX4 .... 174 B2
Central Park Ave PL4. .. 262 C4
Central Pl 16 EX16 .... 166 C6
Central Rd PL1 .... 262 B1
Central Station Chambers
  EX4 .... 261 A3
Centre Ct 3 PL21. ..... 137 C8
Centry Ct TQ5 .... 230 E4
Centry Rd TQ5 .... 230 E4
Centurion Ho 13 EX1. .. 261 A2
Century Dr EX39. ...... 156 E6
Ceramic Terr 2 EX32 .. 155 A4
Chackrell La EX16. ...... 50 F2
Chaddiford La EX31. .... 154 D7
CHADDLEWOOD 251 B6
Chaddlewood Ave PL4 .. 263 B3
Chaddlewood Cl PL7. ... 251 A4
Chaddlewood Ho PL7 .. 251 B5
Chaddlewood Prim Sch
  PL7 .... 251 A5
Chad Rd PL9. .... 140 A8
Chaffcombe Cross EX17. . 78 F5
Chaffcombe La EX17 ... 79 A6
Chaffinch Dr EX15 ..... 163 B2
CHAGFORD 111 A7
Chagford CE Prim Sch
  TQ13. .... 111 A7
Chagford Cross TQ13. .. 111 E5
Chagford Wlk PL6 ..... 249 E8
Chains Rd EX16. .... 50 D1
Chalcombe Rocks La TA4. 34 E5
Chalfield Cl TQ2 .... 213 F3
CHALLABOROUGH 142 E3
Challabrook La TQ13 ... 180 B6
CHALLACOMBE 11 A3
Challacombe Cotts PL20. 120 F6
Challacombe Cross
  Chagford TQ13. .... 110 F2
  Challacombe EX31 .... 11 B3
  Chulmleigh EX18 .... 45 A2
Challacombe Hill EX34 .... 8 A5
Challacombe Hill Rd EX34 . 7 F6
Challenger Cross EX13 .. 88 D7
Challeycroft Rd TQ5. ... 230 A1
Challgood Cl 1 PL9. .... 255 F5
Challgood Rise PL9 .... 255 F5
Challices Cotts EX18 .... 59 E4
Challick La TA4 .... 35 F6
Challock Cl PL6. .... 245 D4
Challowell La EX33. .... 152 D8
Chaloner's Rd EX33. ... 152 D6
CHAMBERCOMBE 150 D6
Chambercombe La EX34. 150 E4
Chambercombe Manor ★
  EX34. .... 150 E4
Chambercombe Park Rd
  EX34. .... 150 D5
Chambercombe Rd EX34 150 E5
Chambercombe Pk Terr
  EX34. .... 150 D5
Chambercombe Rd
  EX34. .... 150 D5
Chamberlain Rd EX2 ... 261 A1
Chamberlayne Dr PL7. .. 250 E6
Chambers Cl EX10 ..... 188 A8
Champernhayes La DT6 . 104 F7
Champernowne PL21. ... 137 B3
Champernowne Cres 7
  EX34. .... 150 D5
Champford La EX14 .... 161 C5
Champford Mews 2
  TA21. .... 160 D5
Champion Cross TA4. .... 35 E3
Chancel Cl EX4 .... 174 D1
Chancel La EX4 .... 174 D1
Chancellor's Way EX4. .. 174 A2
Chandlers Cl 2 EX11 ... 169 D3
Chandlers Hts TQ8 ..... 259 D5
Chandler's La EX10 ..... 188 B5
Chandlers Wlk EX2. .... 150 B3
Channel Park Ave PL3. .. 249 B5
Channel View
  Ilfracombe EX34 .... 150 D5
  Woolacombe EX34. .... 1 A2
Channel View Dr TQ7 .. 147 B6
Channel View Rd EX7. .. 204 C3
Channel View Terr PL4. . 263 C4
Channon Rd PL12 ...... 242 C4
Channons Cl 5 EX14. ... 166 B6
Chanter Ct EX2 .... 178 A2
Chanter's Hill EX32 .... 155 B5
Chanters Rd EX39 ..... 157 A3
Chantry Ave EX39. ..... 157 A3
Chantry Cl TQ14 .... 210 D7
Chantry Ct PL7. .... 250 E5
Chantry Hill TQ7 ...... 145 D4
Chantry Mdw EX2. ..... 181 B8

Chantry Orch EX24 ...... 103 A5
Chantry The EX20 ...... 170 C5
Chapel Cl
 Crediton EX17 .... 79 C1
 Gunnislake PL18 .... 125 B5
 Halberton EX16 .... 65 A8
 5 Horrabridge PL20 .... 126 F4
 Petrockstow EX20 .... 56 F4
Chapel Cnr EX22 .... 70 F5
Chapel Cots PL7 .... 132 F4
Chapel Cross
 Dunkeswell EX14 .... 67 C2
 Iddesleigh EX19 .... 57 E3
 Petrockstow EX20 .... 56 F8
 Puddington EX16 .... 62 B5
 Thorverton EX5 .... 81 D5
 Thurlestone TQ7 .... 143 A2
Chapel Ct
 Exeter EX2 .... 177 A4
 Stoke Gabriel TQ9 ...... 227 F8
 Swimbridge EX32 .... 28 E8
 Torquay TQ1 .... 219 F7
Chapel Down La PL21 .... 137 F3
Chapel Down Lane End
 PL21 .... 137 E3
Chapeldown Rd PL11 .... 247 A2
Chapel Downs Dr EX17 .. 165 A6
Chapel Downs Rd EX17.. 165 A6
Chapel Fields **6** TQ10 .. 134 F3
Chapel Hill
 5 Budleigh Salterton
  EX9 .... 198 A1
 Cheriton Fitzpaine EX17 .. 62 F1
 Clyst St George EX3 .... 183 C6
 15 Exmouth EX8 .... 202 A6
 Longdown EX6 .... 98 E2
 5 Newton Abbot TQ12 .. 207 B3
 Uffculme EX15 .... 66 A7
Chapel Hill Cross EX17 .. 62 F1
Chapel Ho **4** EX39 ...... 156 F7
Chapel Knap EX13, EX24 . 102 F7
Chapel La
 10 Coldeast TQ12 ...... 122 F1
 Combe Martin EX34 ...... 3 A3
 Dartmouth TQ6 .... 233 F3
 Folly Gate EX20 .... 93 F8
 4 Horrabridge PL20 .... 126 F4
 2 Horrabridge PL20 .... 126 F5
 Loddiswell TQ7 .... 143 E7
 Lutton PL21 .... 133 B2
 Malborough TQ7 .... 147 E6
 Mary Tavy PL19 .... 117 E6
 Ottery St Mary EX11 .... 169 E4
 Stoke Fleming TQ6 ...... 146 B7
 Totnes TQ9 .... 223 D5
 Yealmpton PL8 .... 257 F4
Chapel Mdw PL20 ...... 126 C3
Chapel Park Cl EX39 .... 157 C2
Chapel Rd
 Brampford Speke EX5 .... 81 C1
 Bratton Clovelly EX20 .... 92 A2
 Exeter EX2 .... 177 B1
 Lympstone EX8 .... 195 D5
 Newton Abbot TQ12 .... 207 D3
 Parkham EX39 .... 39 E8
 Saltash PL12 .... 242 B3
 Sidmouth EX10 .... 188 B3
 Yealmpton PL8 .... 136 A2
Chapel Row TQ7 .... 142 C6
Chapelry The **5** TQ13 .. 213 C4
Chapel St
 Axmouth EX12 .... 192 D7
 4 Bere Alston PL20 .... 125 E1
 18 Bideford EX39 ...... 157 A2
 Rlackawton TQ9 .... 139 E1
 Braunton EX33 .... 152 C6
 Buckfastleigh TQ11 ...... 236 B5
 Budleigh Salterton EX9 .. 199 G2
 Dolton EX19 .... 57 F7
 Dulverton TA22 .... 33 D6
 Ermington PL21 .... 136 F4
 1 Exmouth EX8 .... 202 A6
 Georgeham EX33 .... 8 A2
 Gunnislake PL18 .... 125 D6
 Holsworthy EX22 .... 164 C3
 Honiton EX14 .... 166 C6
 Lifton PL16 .... 105 E4
 Morchard Bishop EX17 .. 61 A2
 Plymouth, Mount Wise PL1 247 E2
 Plymouth PL4 .... 263 A3
 Sidbury EX10 .... 101 B2
 Sidmouth EX10 .... 188 B3
 Tavistock PL19 .... 171 B5
 19 Teignmouth TQ14 .. 210 B4
 Tiverton EX16 .... 161 D4
 Woolfardisworthy EX39.. 38 F7
Chapel The **7** TQ9 .... 223 D5
Chapel Way PL3 .... 249 A6
Chapman Ct PL12 ...... 242 B3
Chapmans Gn EX12 .... 191 C5
Chapmans Ope PL1 .... 247 D2
Chapple Cl EX5 .... 201 B8
Chapplecroft Rd EX13 .. 87 E5
Chapple Cross
 Bovey Tracey TQ13 ...... 180 B5
 Chagford TQ13 .... 110 D8
 Dolton EX19 .... 57 E6
Chapple Cross Cross
 TQ13 .... 110 D7
Chapple La EX20 .... 76 E4
Chapple Rd
 Bovey Tracey TQ13 ...... 180 A6
 Witheridge EX16 .... 46 E1
Charberry Rise DT6 .... 104 F4

Chard Ave **4** EX5 ...... 99 E8
Chard Barton PL5 ...... 244 B3
CHARD JUNCTION 88 E7
Chard Rd
 Axminster EX13 .... 88 B4
 Exeter EX1 .... 178 A6
 Plymouth PL5 .... 243 D2
Chard St
 Axminster EX13 .... 167 D6
 Chardstock EX13 .... 88 B7
CHARDSTOCK 88 B7
Chard Stock Cl EX11 .. 178 D6
Charfield Dr PL6 ...... 249 A8
Charford Cross TQ10 .. 135 B1
Charlacott Cross EX31.. 27 B6
Charlemont Rd TQ14 .. 210 B8
CHARLES 18 E3
Charles Ave EX39 ...... 157 A2
CHARLES BOTTOM 18 E2
Charles Cross
 East Buckland EX32 ...... 18 E3
 Plymouth PL4 .... 263 A3
Charles Dart Cres EX32. 155 A6
Charles Hankin Cl PL21.. 237 E4
Charles Hudson La **2**
 EX31 .... 155 A7
Charles Rd
 Honiton EX14 .... 166 C6
 Kingskerswell TQ12 .... 213 A2
Charles St
 14 Barnstaple EX32 .... 154 F6
 Dartmouth TQ6 .... 233 F3
 53 Exmouth EX8 .... 202 A7
 Plymouth PL4 .... 263 A3
 Charles Terr PL3 .... 249 A6
Charleton CE Prim Sch
 TQ7 .... 144 C1
Charleton Court Barns
 TQ7 .... 144 C1
Charleton Way TQ7 .... 144 C1
Charlotte Cl TQ1 ...... 219 F8
Charlotte Ct TQ1 ...... 214 B1
Charlotte Mews **1** EX2.. 261 B2
Charlottes Oak TQ12 .. 123 E1
Charlotte St
 Crediton EX17 .... 165 D5
 Plymouth PL2 .... 247 E4
Charlton Cres PL6 ...... 245 A2
Charlton Ho EX7 .... 204 F6
Charlton Rd PL6 ...... 245 A3
Charlton Terr PL20 .... 237 D5
Charlwood Ct TQ1 .... 220 C8
CHARMOUTH 104 F4
Charmouth Cl
 Lyme Regis DT7 .... 260 E4
 Torquay TQ1 .... 220 D6
Charmouth Ho DT7 .... 260 C3
Charmouth Rd
 Lyme Regis DT7 .... 260 E4
 Raymond's Hill EX13 .. 104 C7
Charneymore Cross EX18. 44 E1
Charnhill Cl PL9 ...... 256 A6
Charnhill Way PL9 .... 256 A6
Charnley Ave EX4 ...... 176 E5
Charter Cl EX16 .... 161 B4
CHARTON 104 A1
Charton Cross DT7 .... 104 A2
Chartwell Cl TQ3 ...... 225 E7
Chartwell Dr TQ12 .... 207 A4
Charwell Mdw EX5 ...... 82 F6
Chase The
 Honiton EX14 .... 166 D7
 Ivybridge PL21 .... 237 D4
CHASTY 164 C2
Chasty La EX22 .... 164 C3
Chatham Cl EX3 .... 202 D8
Chatsworth Gdns PL5 .. 243 F3
Chatsworth Rd TQ1 .. 220 B6
Chatto Rd TQ1 .... 220 A7
Chatto Way TQ1 ...... 220 A7
Chatwell La PL21 ...... 137 B3
Chaucer Ave EX2 ...... 177 F3
Chaucer Rd PL19 ...... 171 D5
Chaucer Rise EX8 ...... 196 C3
Chaucer Way PL5 ...... 244 C1
Chaves Cl EX16 .... 62 F4
CHAWLEIGH 60 B7
Chawleigh Cl PL18 .... 125 C5
Chawleigh Hill EX18... 59 F8
Chawleigh Week Cross
 EX18. .... 59 E8
Chawleigh Week La EX18. 59 D8
Chawleigh Week Mill Cross
 EX18. .... 59 D8
Cheavestone Lea TQ9 .. 139 E1
Checkridge La EX13 .... 88 D2
Cheddar St PL4 .... 263 A3
Cheeke St EX1 .... 261 C3
Cheese La EX10 .... 187 F4
CHEGLINCH. 8 A5
Cheglinch Cnr EX34 ...... 8 F5
Cheglinch La EX34 ...... 8 F6
CHELDON 60 D8
Cheldon Barton Moor La
 EX18. .... 60 D8
Cheldon Cross
 Chawleigh PL18 .... 60 D8
 Chulmleigh EX18 .... 45 D2
CHELFHAM 17 D6
Chelfham Mill Sch EX32.. 17 C6
Chelfham Senior Sch
 Bere Alston PL20 ...... 125 C3
 Tavistock PL19 .... 117 C3
Chelmer Cl PL7 .... 251 A5
Chelmsford Pl PL5 .... 244 C4
Chelmsford Rd EX4 .... 176 E6
Chelsea Pl **8** TQ14 .... 210 B5
Chelsea Trad Ctr EX2.. 178 E5

Chelson Gdns PL6 ...... 245 E3
Chelson La EX10 ...... 101 E1
CHELSTON
 Torquay 219 E4
 Wellington 52 D8
Chelston Bsn Pk TA21 .. 52 D8
CHELSTON HEATHFIELD.. 52 E7
Chelston Rd
 Newton Abbot TQ12... 207 B4
 Torquay TQ2 .... 219 E3
Chelston Terr TA21 .... 52 D8
Cheltenham Cl EX4 .... 176 E7
Cheltenham Pl PL4 .... 263 A4
Chelwood Gr PL7 ...... 250 F5
Chene Ct **6** PL21 ...... 137 B2
Cheney's La EX14 ...... 166 E8
CHENSON 60 A4
Chepstow Ave PL6 .... 245 C8
Chepstow Cl EX2 ...... 182 B8
Chequers Haigh PL8 .. 140 A6
Chequer Tree Ct PL18 .. 125 C5
Chercombe Bridge Rd
 TQ12 .... 206 C3
Chercombe Cl TQ12 .. 206 B4
Chercombe Valley Rd
 TQ12 .... 206 E4
CHERISTOW 22 D3
Cheriswood Ave EX8 .. 196 D1
Cheriswood Cl EX8... 196 D1
CHERITON 5 D3
CHERITON BISHOP 97 B4
Cheriton Bishop Com Prim
 Sch EX6 .... 97 B4
Cheriton Cl PL5 ...... 244 A3
Cheriton Cross 97 B3
Cheriton Cross
 Cadbury EX5 .... 81 C8
 Chilton EX17 .... 80 D7
CHERITON FITZPAINE .. 62 E1
Cheriton Fitzpaine Prim Sch
 EX17 .... 62 E1
Cheriton Hill EX35 ...... 5 D3
Cheriton Mill Cross EX17 62 E2
Cheriton Rd EX35 ...... 151 D1
Cherry Arbour EX32 .. 155 C3
CHERRYBRIDGE 5 A4
Cherrybridge Cross
 EX35. .... 5 A4
Cherry Brook Dr TQ4 .. 229 B8
Cherry Brook Sq TQ4 .. 229 B8
Cherry Brook Wlk TQ4 . 226 B1
Cherry Cl
 Cheriton Fitzpaine EX17 .. 62 F1
 Exmouth EX8 .... 196 C3
 5 Honiton EX14 ...... 85 C2
 Tiverton EX16 .... 161 D5
 Willand EX15 .... 162 D4
Cherry Cross TQ9 ...... 223 C4
Cherry Dr EX12 .... 192 A5
Cherryford La EX31 ...... 4 C4
Cherry Gdns
 Crediton EX17 .... 165 C5
 Exeter EX2 .... 178 A4
 Paignton TQ3 .... 226 A7
Cherry Gr EX32 .... 155 C2
Cherry Mdw EX17 ...... 62 F1
Cherry Park Cl TQ2 .. 219 D2
Cherry Pk
 Appledore EX39 .... 14 F1
 Plymouth PL7 .... 251 A3
Cherry Tree Cl
 Exeter EX4 .... 173 A2
 Rockbeare EX5 .... 99 B6
Cherry Tree Dr
 Brixton PL8 .... 257 A5
 3 Landkey EX32 ...... 17 B2
Cherry Tree Gdns EX16.. 161 E5
Cherry Tree La PL7 .... 251 A4
Cherry Tree Rd EX13 .. 167 E6
Cherrywood Cl TQ12 .. 206 E4
Cheshire Dr PL6 ...... 244 D6
Cheshire Rd EX8 ...... 196 E2
Chesil Ct DT7 .... 260 C3
Chesnut Cl PL12 ...... 242 D4
Chester Cl EX4 .... 176 E7
Chester Ct EX4 .... 201 F7
Chesterfield Rd PL3... 249 B4
Chestermoor Cross EX20 92 D5
Chester Pl **4** PL4 ...... 248 E4
Chester Terr **9** EX32... 155 A4
Chesterton Cl PL5 .... 244 C3
Chestnut Ave
 Cullompton EX15 ...... 163 C2
 Dartmouth TQ6 .... 233 E4
 Exeter EX2 .... 178 A3
 Plymouth PL9 .... 255 C5
 Torquay TQ2 .... 219 F4
Chestnut Cl
 22 Bere Alston PL20 .. 125 E1
 Braunton EX33 .... 152 E6
 Cheriton Bishop EX6 .... 97 B4
 Crediton EX17 .... 165 D6
 Exmouth EX8 .... 196 C3
 Leaman PL19 .... 116 E4
 Seaton EX12 .... 192 A7
 Tavistock PL19 .... 171 D2
 Torpoint PL11 .... 246 F3
 Wellington TA21 ...... 160 E5
Chestnut Cres
 7 Chudleigh TQ13 .... 123 F6
 Exeter EX4 .... 173 F8
Chestnut Ct EX2 ...... 181 B8
Chestnut Dr
 Bideford EX39 .... 25 D4
 Brixham TQ5 .... 230 A2
 Kingsteignton TQ12 .. 207 F6
 Newton Abbot TQ12... 208 A1
 Willand EX15 .... 162 C4

Chestnut Mews EX14... 84 E2
Chestnut Pk TQ7 ...... 149 D7
Chestnut Prim Sch TQ5 . 230 A2
Chestnut Rd
 Plymouth PL3. .... 248 D7
 Tiverton EX16 .... 161 F5
Chestnuts The EX5 ...... 99 D2
Chestnut Terr PL19 .. 116 E3
Chestnut View EX13... 87 D6
Chestnut Way
 Honiton EX14 .... 166 A4
 Newton Poppleford EX10 186 F8
 Chestnut Wlk EX7 ...... 204 C5
Cheston Cross TQ10 .. 134 E1
Chestwood Ave EX31 .. 154 C3
Chestwood Cl EX31 ... 154 D4
Chestwood Villas EX32.. 16 E1
Chettiscombe EX11 ... 161 F8
CHETTISCOMBE 161 F8
CHEVITHORNE 49 E2
Cheyne Beach **2** EX34 . 150 C6
Cheynegate La EX14 .. 174 C3
Cheyne Rise EX4 ...... 174 D2
Cheyney Cross EX36... 30 B2
Cheyney La TQ36. ...... 30 B2
Chibbet Hill TA24 ...... 21 B8
Chibbet Post TA24 .... 21 C8
Chichacott Cross EX20 . 170 F7
Chichacott Rd EX20 .. 170 D7
Chichester Cl
 Barnstaple EX32 ...... 155 B2
 Exmouth EX8 .... 202 C8
 Ilfracombe EX34 ...... 150 A4
 11 Stowe EX39 .... 15 B1
Chichester Cres
 Barnstaple EX32 ...... 155 B2
 Saltash PL12 .... 242 E1
Chichester Ct
 Barnstaple EX32 ...... 155 C5
 Horrabridge PL20 ...... 126 F4
 Outer Hope TQ7 ...... 147 B7
Chichester Ho
 Barnstaple EX31 ...... 155 A4
 Exeter EX2 .... 178 B5
 Plymouth PL1. .... 262 B2
Chichester Mews **3** EX31. 155 A4
Chichester Pk EX34 ...... 8 A6
Chichester Pl **7** EX16.. 64 F7
Chichester Rd **3** EX32. 155 B2
Chichester Way
 East Budleigh EX9 .... 198 B6
 Newton Abbot TQ12 .. 207 F3
 Plymouth PL9 .... 256 D8
Chideock Ct DT7. ...... 260 C3
Chilbridge La EX31 ...... 17 B8
Chilcombe Cross EX24.. 102 B7
Chilcombe La EX24 .. 102 A6
Chilcote Cl TQ1 .... 220 A7
Chilcott Cl **5** EX16 .... 64 D7
Chilcott Cross TQ22 .... 33 A7
Chilcott La TA22 .... 33 A7
Childrey Gdns PL6 .... 245 C1
Childrey Wlk PL6 ...... 245 C1
CHILLA 73 E5
Chilla Chapel EX21 .... 73 E4
Chilla Rd EX21 .... 73 E3
CHILLATON 116 D8
Chillaton Cross TQ7 .. 138 A1
Chillaton Ct PL16 .... 106 E1
CHILLINGTON 145 A2
Chill Pits La EX13 ...... 88 B8
Chilpark EX31 .... 153 D5
CHILSON 88 C6
CHILSON COMMON 88 D7
CHILSWORTHY
 Gunnislake. 125 B7
 Holsworthy 53 E1
Chiltern Cl TQ2 .... 219 D3
Chiltern Cross EX16 .. 34 B2
CHILTON 80 E7
Chilton Ave TQ14 .... 210 C6
Chilton Cl PL6 .... 249 B7
Chilton Gate EX16 ...... 81 D8
Chilton La EX17 .... 80 E7
Chilverton Hill EX17 .. 59 F1
Chilverton Hill Gate EX17. 59 F1
Chilverton La EX17 ...... 59 F1
Chineway Gdns EX11 .. 169 F3
Chineway Head EX11 .. 101 B6
Chineway Hill EX11 ... 101 A6
Chineway Rd EX11 .... 169 F4
Chingswell St **2** EX39.. 157 A2
Chinkwell Rise TQ2 .. 219 B8
Chinon Ct EX14 .... 64 D8
Chinon Pl EX16 .... 161 A6
Chinston Cl EX14 ...... 85 B4
Chipmunk Wlk EX32... 155 B6
CHIPSTABLE 35 E6
Chircombe La EX39 ...... 157 A4
Chiselbon Farm TQ5 .. 230 B2
Chiseldon Hill TQ5 .. 230 C2
Chiseldon Ho EX4 .... 173 A1
Chitterley Bsns Ctr EX5. 82 A4
Chittleburn Bsns Pk PL8 256 F6
Chittleburn Cl PL8 .. 256 E5
Chittleburn Hill PL8 .. 256 E5
CHITTLEHAMHOLT 44 B8
CHITTLEHAMPTON 28 A1
Chittlehampton CE Prim Sch
 EX37. .... 28 A1
CHIVELSTONE 149 A6
Chivelstone Cross TQ7 . 149 A6
CHIVENOR 15 E5
Chivenor Airfield EX31 . 152 F1
Chivenor Ave PL5 ...... 243 D4
Chivenor Cross EX31... 15 E5
Chiverstone La EX6 ... 194 C4

Chiverstone Rd EX6 ... 194 C4
Chockenhole La EX9 .. 199 A8
Chockland Rd **12** TQ12 . 123 E1
Cholhouse La EX20 ...... 77 C7
Chollacott Cl PL19 ... 171 C4
Chollacott La PL19 ... 171 D3
Chollaton Cross EX22 .. 39 E1
Cholwell Cross TQ9 .. 222 F4
Chopes Rd EX39 ...... 156 F6
Chopes Cl EX39 .... 26 A4
Chough Cl PL15 ...... 105 A2
Christ Cross EX5 .... 82 C8
Christcross La EX5 ...... 82 D7
Christian Mill Bsns Pk
 PL6. .... 244 E4
Christina Par TQ9 .... 223 F5
Christina Pk TQ9 ...... 223 E5
Christone Cross TQ9 .. 138 D7
CHRISTOW 113 A3
Christow Prim Sch EX6. 113 A4
Christow Rd EX2. ...... 177 B2
Chrystel Cl EX10 ...... 100 D2
Chubb Dr PL3. .... 248 A4
Chubb Rd EX39 .... 26 A4
Chubby Croft Cl EX39 .. 22 E3
Chubb Tor EX39 .... 22 E3
Chubs Cross EX20. ...... 77 F1
Chubworthy Cross TA4.. 35 D5
CHUDLEIGH 123 F6
Chudleigh Ave EX39... 157 B1
Chudleigh CE Prim Sch
 TQ13 .... 123 E6
CHUDLEIGH KNIGHTON . 123 C4
Chudleigh Knighton CE Prim
 Sch TQ13 .... 123 C4
Chudleigh Rd
 2 Bideford EX39 ...... 157 B1
 Exeter EX2 .... 181 B7
 Kingsteignton TQ12 .. 207 D8
 Plymouth PL4. .... 249 A4
Chudleigh Terr **6** EX39 157 B1
Chudley Cl EX18 ...... 44 F1
Chuggaton Cross EX37.. 28 C5
Chuley Cross TQ13 ... 130 F3
Chuley Hill TQ13 .... 130 F4
Chuley Rd TQ13 ...... 130 F4
CHULMLEIGH 44 F1
Chulmleigh Hill **10** EX18.. 44 F1
Chulmleigh Prim Sch
 EX18. .... 44 F1
Chulmleigh Rd
 Morchard Bishop EX17 .. 61 A2
 Winkleigh EX19 .... 58 F3
Church Ave EX20. ...... 170 A5
Church Cl
 Ashprington TQ9 ...... 139 F8
 Aylesbeare EX5 .... 99 C2
 Bratton Fleming EX31 .. 18 A8
 Broadclyst EX5 .... 175 C4
 13 Chulmleigh EX18 .... 44 E1
 Dartmouth TQ6 .... 233 F3
 Exmouth TQ6 .... 202 B8
 Goodleigh EX32 .... 17 B5
 Kingsbridge TQ7 ...... 258 D5
 Lapford EX17 .... 60 D3
 Plymouth PL7 .... 250 B7
 Puddington EX16 ...... 62 B5
 Totnes TQ9 .... 223 C6
 Yealmpton PL8 .... 257 F4
Church Cliff DT7 ...... 260 E3
Church Cross
 Buckfastleigh TQ11 .. 236 B6
 Cheriton Fitzpaine EX17 .. 62 E1
 Exeter EX4 .... 174 D3
 Filleigh EX32 .... 29 C6
 Sandford EX17 .... 80 A5
 Church Cross Rd TQ11. 236 B6
Church Ct
 Harberton TQ9 .... 222 D2
 Kingsteignton TQ12 .. 207 D6
 14 Newton Abbot TQ12 . 207 B3
 Plymouth PL6 .... 245 A2
Church End
 Ipplepen TQ12 .... 52 F7
 Church End Rd TQ12 .. 212 F4
 Church Farm TQ7 .... 143 A1
Churchfield Rd **20** EX39 . 15 A1
Churchfields TQ11 .... 160 D7
Churchfields Dr TQ9 .. 180 D7
Church Fields TA21 .. 160 E6
Churchfields Dr TQ13 . 180 D7
Churchfields W TQ6. .. 233 D3
Church Flats EX6 ...... 201 B8
Churchford Rd EX33 ...... 8 D1
Church Gate EX36. ...... 30 E1
CHURCH GREEN 101 F7
Church Hill
 Awliscombe EX14 ...... 85 B4
 Beer EX12 .... 191 D5
 Blackawton TQ9 ...... 139 E1
 Brendon EX35 .... 5 F4
 Buckfastleigh TQ11 ... 236 C6
 Calstock PL18 .... 125 E4
 Exeter EX4 .... 174 E2
 Freemington EX31 ...... 153 E5
 Holbeton PL8. .... 136 D1
 Honiton EX14 .... 166 D5
 Ilfracombe EX34 ...... 150 A5
 Kingswear TQ6 .... 234 A2
 Lynton EX35. .... 151 C5
 Marldon TQ3 .... 218 D4
 Milton Combe PL20 .. 126 C1
 Musbury EX13 .... 103 D5
 Otterton EX9 .... 198 D7
 Plymouth PL6. .... 245 B1
 Tavistock PL19 .... 171 E2

Church Hill continued
Tedburn St Mary EX6. . . . . . 97 F5
Winkleigh EX19 . . . . 58 F3
Church Hill Cl TQ9 . . . . . 139 E2
Church Hill Cotts TQ9 . . 131 E1
Church Hill Cross EX20 . . 94 E7
Church Hill E TQ5 . . . . 230 C5
Church Hill La EX33 . . . . . . 8 D1
Church Hill Rd PL9. . . . 255 A6
Church Hill W TQ5 . . . . 230 C5
Church Ho
Exeter EX2 . . . . 177 A4
Saltash PL12 . . . . 243 A2
Church House Cl
TQ13 . . . . 123 C4
CHURCHILL
Axminster 87 F4
Barnstaple 10 B3
Churchill EX34. . . . . 8 F4
Churchill Ave EX7. . . . . 204 D5
Churchill Cl
Barnstaple EX32 . . . . 155 B6
Kenton EX6 . . . . 194 D3
Churchill Cotts PL21 . . 137 D6
Churchill Cres EX36 . . . 158 C3
Churchill Ct
7 Brixham TQ5 . . . . 230 C4
Lympstone EX8 . . . . 195 E6
Churchill Dr
Crediton EX17 . . . . 165 B6
Newton Abbot TQ12 . . . . 210 C6
Churchill Gdns EX17 . . . . 78 C7
Churchill Hill EX31. . . . . 10 C4
Churchill La
Axminster EX13 . . . . 88 A5
Calverleigh EX16 . . . . 48 C3
Chipstable TA4 . . . . 35 C5
Churchill Rd
Bideford EX39 . . . . 26 A4
Exeter EX2 . . . . 176 F4
Exmouth EX8 . . . . 196 D2
Tavistock PL19 . . . . 171 D2
Tiverton EX16 . . . . 161 A4
Churchills EX15 . . . . 67 B8
Churchills Nature Reserve★
TQ12 . . . . 207 A5
Churchills Rise EX15 . . . 67 B8
Churchills The TQ12 . . . 207 A4
Churchill Way
Appledore EX39 . . . . 14 F1
Northam EX39 . . . . 157 A7
Plymouth PL3. . . . . 248 E6
Churchill Wlk PL12. . . . . 242 E1
CHURCHINFORD 68 D7
Church La
Alfington EX11 . . . . 84 F1
10 Barnstaple EX31. . . . 154 F5
Bideford EX39 . . . . 25 E2
8 Bittaford PL21 . . . . . 137 C8
Bridford EX6 . . . . 112 F5
Broadclyst EX5 . . . . 175 C7
Calstock PL18 . . . . 125 D3
Cargreen PL12 . . . . 239 A1
Christow EX6. . . . . 113 B3
Clyst St Mary EX5 . . . . . 179 B2
Crediton EX17 . . . . 165 D5
Dulverton TA22 . . . . 33 D6
East Budleigh EX9 . . . . . 198 B6
Exeter, Heavitree EX2 . . . 177 F5
Exeter, Pinhoe EX4. . . . . 174 D2
Feniton EX14 . . . . 84 E2
Frithelstock Stone EX38. . 40 F5
Great Torrington EX38. . . 159 C5
Hatherleigh EX20. . . . . . . 75 C7
Holsworthy EX22. . . . . . 164 C4
Kingsbridge TQ7 . . . . . . 258 F2
Langtree EX38. . . . . 40 F2
Membury EX13 . . . . 87 D5
Modbury PL21 . . . . 137 B2
Parracombe EX31 . . . . 4 D1
Salcombe TQ8 . . . . 259 E5
Sheldon EX14 . . . . 66 F3
Shobrooke EX17 . . . . 80 E4
Slapton TQ7 . . . . 145 D3
St John PL11 . . . . 252 B8
Stokeinteignhead TQ12 . . 209 B2
Swimbridge EX32. . . . . . . 28 E8
Tavistock PL19. . . . . 171 C5
Torquay TQ2 . . . . 219 F5
Whitestone EX4 . . . . 98 E4
Winkleigh EX19 . . . . 58 F3
Yealmpton PL8. . . . . 257 F4
Church Lake 8 EX32. . . . 17 B2
Churchlands EX17 . . . . . 78 C4
Churchlands Rd PL6 . . . . 245 E8
Church Lane Cross EX17. . 59 F2
Church Lane Head TQ13. 121 B2
Church Lea PL19. . . . . . . 171 E2
Church Mdw
High Bickington EX37 . . . . 43 B7
Ivybridge PL21 . . . . 237 A4
Landkey EX32 . . . . 17 B2
Church Mdws
Bratton Clovelly EX20 . . . 92 A2
Okehampton EX20 . . . . . 170 A5
Church Mead EX14. . . . . 85 B1
Church Mews TQ12 . . . . 207 E6
Church Park Cl TQ9 . . . . 138 C7
Church Park Rd PL6 . . . 245 E8
Church Park Rd
11 Newton Ferrers PL8. . 141 A7
Plymouth PL6. . . . . 245 E8
Yealmpton PL8. . . . . 136 A2
Church Parks EX17. . . . . 80 A5

Church Path
Ashburton TQ13. . . . . . . 130 F4
Barnstaple EX31 . . . . . . 154 F7
Exeter EX1. . . . . 178 A5
Halberton EX16 . . . . 65 A7
Okehampton EX20 . . . . . 170 A5
6 Paignton TQ3 . . . . . . 226 B6
Shute EX13 . . . . 102 F8
Church Path Rd EX2 . . . 176 F3
Church Pk
Bideford EX39 . . . . 25 A3
Cornwood PL21 . . . . 133 C2
Horrabridge PL20 . . . . . . 126 F4
Kingston TQ7 . . . . 142 C6
Kingswear TQ6 . . . . 234 B3
2 Newton Ferrers PL8. . 141 A7
Paignton TQ4 . . . . 225 D4
Church Pool EX34. . . . . . . 8 F5
Church Quillet TQ9 . . . . 139 E1
Church Rd
Bishopsteignton TQ14 . . . 209 A7
Brixham TQ5 . . . . 229 E5
Churchinford TA3. . . . . . . 68 C8
Colaton Raleigh EX10 . . . 186 E3
Dartmouth TQ6 . . . . 233 E3
Ermington PL21 . . . . 136 F4
Exeter, Alphington EX2 . . 177 B1
Exeter, St Thomas EX2. . . 177 A4
Exmouth EX8 . . . . 202 A7
Georgeham EX33. . . . . 8 A2
Hennock TQ13 . . . . 123 B7
Highampton EX21 . . . . . . 74 C7
Ideford TQ13. . . . . 124 B4
Ilfracombe EX34 . . . . . . 150 A5
Kenton EX6 . . . . 194 F5
Luton TQ13. . . . . 124 C4
Lympstone EX8 . . . . 195 E5
Newton Abbot TQ12 . . . . 207 C2
Plymouth, Plympton PL7 . 250 F4
Plymouth, Plymstock PL9 255 F7
Saltash PL12 . . . . 242 D2
Silverton EX5. . . . . 82 B5
Stoke Fleming TQ6. . . . . 146 B7
Torquay, Barton TQ2 . . . . 214 A3
Torquay, St Marychurch
TQ1. . . . . 220 B8
Wembury PL9 . . . . 140 D8
Whimple EX5. . . . . 99 E7
Church Row La PL5. . . . . 244 C6
Church St Mews 4 TQ3. 226 B6
Church Side EX5. . . . . . . 179 D7
Church St
Axminster EX13 . . . . 167 D5
Axmouth EX12 . . . . 192 D7
Bradninch EX5. . . . . 83 A7
Braunton EX33. . . . . 152 D7
4 Brixham TQ5. . . . . . . 230 D5
Buckfastleigh TQ11 . . . . 236 B5
Calstock PL18 . . . . 125 D3
Chulmleigh EX18 . . . . 58 E8
Colyton EX24 . . . . 103 A5
Combe Martin EX34. . . . . . 3 A3
Crediton EX17 . . . . 165 D5
Cullompton EX15 . . . . . . 163 C3
Dawlish EX7. . . . . 204 C6
Dolton EX19. . . . . 57 F7
Exeter EX2. . . . . 177 F5
Exeter EX4. . . . . 202 A6
3 Honiton EX14 . . . . . . 166 C6
Ilfracombe EX34 . . . . . . 150 B5
Kenton EX6 . . . . 194 D3
Kingsbridge TQ7 . . . . . . 258 D5
Kingsteignton TQ12 . . . . 207 E6
Lyme Regis DT7. . . . . . . 260 E3
Modbury PL21 . . . . 137 B2
Morchard Bishop EX17 . . 61 B2
Okehampton EX20 . . . . . 170 B5
Paignton TQ3. . . . . 226 B6
Plymouth PL3. . . . . 248 A4
Salcombe TQ8 . . . . 259 E5
Sandford EX17. . . . . 80 A5
Sidbury EX10 . . . . 101 C2
6 Sidford EX10 . . . . . . 101 B1
Sidmouth EX10 . . . . 188 B3
14 South Brent TQ10. . . 134 F3
South Molton EX36 . . . . 158 C4
Starcross EX6 . . . . 201 B8
Tiverton EX16 . . . . 161 C4
Torquay TQ2 . . . . 219 F5
Uplyme DT7 . . . . 260 B5
Witheridge EX16 . . . . . . 46 E1
Churchstanton Prim Sch
TA3 . . . . 68 B8
Church Steps Cotts EX5. 184 B3
Church Stile EX36. . . . . . 182 B4
Church Stile La EX5. . . . 184 B3
CHURCHSTOW 143 E4
Churchstow Wlk PL6. . . . 249 E8
Church Terr
7 Bampton EX16. . . . . . 34 B1
Exeter EX2. . . . . 177 F5
CHURCHTOWN
Bridgerule 71 A6
Parracombe. 4 D2
Churchtown Cl PL21 . . . 133 C2
Churchtown Vale PL12 . . 242 D1
Church View
Bideford EX39 . . . . 26 A1
5 Chudleigh TQ13. . . . . 123 E6
Dawlish EX7. . . . . 204 C6
Kingsteignton TQ12 . . . . 207 E6
Ottery St Mary EX11 . . . 169 D3
St Dominick PL12 . . . . . . 125 A2
Sutcombe EX22 . . . . 54 A6
Walkhampton PL20 . . . . 127 B4
Church View Ho EX5. . . . 184 B3
Churchward Rd TQ3. . . . 226 B7

Churchwater La EX18 . . . . 58 D8
Churchway TQ1. . . . . . . 220 C7
Church Way
Newton Abbot TQ12. . . . 207 E1
Plymouth PL5. . . . . 247 E8
Yealmpton PL8. . . . . 257 F4
Church Ways EX20 . . . . . 95 B5
Church Wlk
Avonwick TQ10. . . . . . . 135 B1
Stoke Gabriel TQ9 . . . . . 227 F7
Wembury PL9 . . . . 140 C8
Churchwood Ct TQ1. . . . 220 C5
Churchyard La EX17. . . . . 61 C7
CHURSCOMBE 218 E2
Churscombe Gn TQ3 . . . 218 E2
Churscombe Pk TQ3 . . . 218 D2
Churscombe Rd TQ3 . . . 218 D2
Churston Broadway TQ4. 229 B7
Churston Cl TQ5. . . . . . . 229 C5
Churston Cross
Churston Ferrers TQ5 . . . 229 E4
West Putford EX22 . . . . . 39 B2
Churston Ct TQ7 . . . . . . 258 D4
CHURSTON FERRERS . . . 229 E4
Churston Ferrers Gram Sch
TQ5. . . . . 229 C5
Churston Rd TQ5 . . . . . . 229 E5
Churston Rise EX12 . . . . 191 F8
Churston Sta★ TQ5 . . . . 229 C5
Churston Way TQ5 . . . . . 230 B4
Chute St EX1 . . . . 261 C4
Cinders La TQ9 . . . . 146 B7
Cistern La TQ9 . . . . 157 A4
Cistern St TQ9. . . . . 223 B5
Citadel Ope 12 PL1. . . . . 263 A2
Citadel Rd PL1. . . . . 262 B2
Citadel Road E PL1. . . . . 263 A2
Citadel Road W PL1. . . . 262 C2
City Arc EX4. . . . . 261 A2
City Bsns Pk PL3. . . . . . 248 A4
**City Coll Plymouth (Camels
    Head Tech Ctr)** PL5 . . 247 E8
**City Coll Plymouth (Deep
    Blue Sound)** PL1. . . . 263 A2
**City Coll Plymouth (Estover
    Tech Ctr)** PL6. . . . . . 245 F4
**City Coll Plymouth (Goschen
    Ctr)** PL2 . . . . 247 E5
**City Coll Plymouth (Kings
    Warehouse)** PL1. . . . 248 A2
**City Coll Plymouth (Learning
    Skills Ctr)** PL1. . . . . 247 F1
**City Coll Plymouth (Marine
    Trust Ctr)** PL4. . . . . 263 A2
City Ind Est EX2. . . . . . . 261 B1
Claddon La TQ1, TQ2. . . . 214 A5
Clampet La 2 TQ14 . . . . 210 A4
Clampitts Stile TQ11 . . . 135 C6
Clampitt Cl TQ12 . . . . . . 211 D1
Clampitt Rd TQ12 . . . . . 211 D2
Clampitts EX15 . . . . 163 B2
Clanage Cross TQ14 . . . . 124 C1
Clanage St TQ14 . . . . . . 208 F8
Cannaborough Cross
EX17. . . . . 78 E5
CLAPHAM 114 B6
Claponmill Cross EX5 . . . 83 B2
Clappentail Ct DT7. . . . . 260 C4
Clappentail La DT7. . . . . 260 C3
Clappentail Pk DT7 . . . . 260 C3
Clapperbrook La EX2. . . 177 B1
Clapper Cross
Bondleigh EX20 . . . . 77 B8
Zeal Monachorum EX17. . 78 B5
Clapper La EX14 . . . . . . 166 C7
Clapps La EX11 . . . . 169 D3
Clapp's La
Beer EX12 . . . . 191 D5
Seaton EX12 . . . . 192 B5
CLAPWORTHY 29 D3
Clapworthy Cross EX36 . . 29 D2
Clara Pl EX3 . . . . 182 E5
Claredale Rd EX4. . . . . . 202 B6
Clare Dr EX16 . . . . 161 F6
Claremont Ave TQ12 . . . 213 A4
Claremont Field EX11 . . 169 D3
Claremont Gr
Exeter EX2. . . . . 261 C1
Exmouth EX8 . . . . 202 B7
Claremont Pl EX20 . . . . . 75 C7
Claremont St PL1. . . . . . 262 C4
Claremont St
16 Barnstaple EX32 . . . 155 B3
Exeter EX4. . . . . 261 C4
Plymouth, Morice Town
    PL2 . . . . 247 E4
Clarence Rd
Budleigh Salterton EX9 . . 198 A2
6 Exeter EX4 . . . . 177 A5
Exmouth EX8 . . . . 202 A7
Torpoint PL11 . . . . 247 B3
Clarence St TQ6 . . . . . . 233 F4
Clarendon Cl TQ1 . . . . . 220 C3
Clarendon Ho TQ1. . . . . 220 C3
Clarendon La TQ1. . . . . . 219 F6
Clarendon La 10 PL3 . . . 247 F3
Clarendon La 11 PL3 . . . 247 F3
Clarendon Rd TQ12 . . . . 211 D2
Clare Pl PL4. . . . . 263 B2
Clare St PL21. . . . . 237 C4

Claridge The TQ3 . . . . . . 226 C8
Clarke Cl EX15. . . . . 65 F7
Clarke Ctr The EX2 . . . . 177 C2
Clarke Mead EX2 . . . . . . 178 C4
Clarks Barn Rd TQ7 . . . . 143 E7
Clarks La EX20. . . . . 57 A6
Claude Dix Cl 6 EX31 . . . 155 A7
Claw Cross EX39 . . . . 38 F5
Clawford Cross EX22 . . . . 72 D3
**Clawford Vineyard &
    Fisheries**★ EX22. . . . . 72 D3
Claw Hill EX16 . . . . 62 F4
Claw Pk EX22. . . . . 72 B2
Claw Pk EX22. . . . . 72 B2
Clawton Prim Sch EX22 . . 72 B1
Clayfield Villas 6 EX32. 155 B4
Clayford La TA22. . . . . . . 33 C5
Clayford Rd TA22. . . . . . . 33 C5
CLAYHANGER 35 C1
CLAYHIDON 52 E2
Clayhidon Crossway EX15 52 E2
Clay La
Chudleigh Knighton
    TQ13. . . . . 123 C3
Colyton EX24 . . . . 103 A4
Copplestone EX17 . . . . . . 79 A6
Dartington TQ9 . . . . 223 A8
Lympstone EX8 . . . . 195 E4
Teignmouth TQ14. . . . . . 210 B5
Uffculme EX15 . . . . 66 A8
Clayland Cross TQ4 . . . . 225 E4
Claylands Dr TQ4 . . . . . . 225 F4
Claylands Pk TQ4 . . . . . . 225 F4
Claymans Pathway PL21. 237 A6
Claypark Hill EX16 . . . . . . 47 D5
Clay Park Terr TQ9. . . . . 228 A7
CLAYPITS 34 C4
Claypits Covert Cross
EX31. . . . . 154 A2
Claytonia Cl PL6 . . . . . . 241 C1
Clayton Pl PL4. . . . . 249 B2
Clayton Rd
Exeter EX4. . . . . 177 A7
Plymouth PL4. . . . . 249 B2
CLEARBROOK 132 A8
Clearbrook Ave PL5. . . . 243 E1
Clear View PL12 . . . . . . 242 E3
CLEAVE 86 C3
Cleaveanger La EX17. . . . 60 B1
Cleave Cl
Bishop's Tawton EX32 . . . 27 F7
Burrington EX37 . . . . 44 A2
Chapelton EX32 . . . . 28 A7
Wilmington EX14. . . . . . . 86 C3
Cleaveland Rise TQ12 . . 206 F1
Cleave Lane End EX32. . . 27 F7
Cleave Pk EX31 . . . . 153 F5
Cleave Rd EX31 . . . . 154 D4
Cleaves Cl EX5. . . . . 81 E5
Cleave The PL10 . . . . . . 253 B2
Cleavewood Dr EX39 . . . 157 D1
Cleeve Dr PL21. . . . . 237 B5
Cleeve Gdns PL2. . . . . . 248 A8
Cleeve The EX15 . . . . 66 E8
Clegg Ave PL11 . . . . 246 E3
Cleland Ct TQ14 . . . . . . 208 F8
Clement Rd PL7. . . . . . . 251 B5
Clement's La EX32 . . . . . . 28 B8
Clennon Ave TQ4 . . . . . . 226 B4
Clennon Ct
5 Brixham TQ5. . . . . . . 230 C3
Torquay TQ2 . . . . 214 A2
Clennon Dr TQ4 . . . . 226 B4
Clennon Gdns TQ4 . . . . . 226 B4
Clennon Hts TQ4 . . . . . . 226 B4
Clennon La TQ4 . . . . 214 A2
Clennon Pk TQ4 . . . . 226 B4
Clennon Rise TQ4 . . . . . 226 B4
Clennon Summit TQ4 . . . 226 B4
Clennon Valley TQ4. . . . . 226 B4
Clerk Cl EX8. . . . . 196 C3
Cleve Ct TQ1 . . . . 220 E5
Clevedon Cl EX4 . . . . . . 173 D1
Clevedon Ho EX10 . . . . . 188 C5
Clevedon Park Ave PL2. . 248 B6
Clevedon Pk EX10. . . . . 188 C5
Cleveland EX17 . . . . 78 F7
Cleveland Ct
Exeter EX1. . . . . 261 C4
Paignton TQ4 . . . . 226 C6
Cleveland Dr TQ7 . . . . . . 142 E3
Cleveland Gdns EX1. . . . 261 C4
Cleveland Pl
3 Dawlish EX7. . . . . . . 204 E6
Exmouth EX8 . . . . 201 F6
Cleveland Rd
Paignton TQ4 . . . . 226 C6
Plymouth PL4. . . . . 263 C3
Torquay TQ2 . . . . 219 F6
Clevelands EX39. . . . . . . 157 A6
Cleveland St 7 EX4. . . . . 177 A5
Cleveland Terr EX39 . . . . 156 C7
Cleve Rd EX4 . . . . 176 F6
Cleverdon Cross EX22 . . . 53 F8
Cleverhayes La EX14 . . . . 86 B4
Cliff Bank Cl EX22 . . . . . . 72 C5
Cliff Bastin Cl EX2 . . . . . 178 C4
Cliff Castle 4 EX12 . . . . 192 A4
Cliff Ct PL1. . . . . 262 B1
Cliffden Cl TQ14 . . . . . . 210 C5
Cliff Ho TQ4. . . . . 226 D5

Cliff La PL10. . . . . 252 A4
Cliff Mews TQ4 . . . . 226 D5
CLIFFORD 38 C8
Clifford Ave TQ12 . . . . . 123 E1
Clifford Cl
15 Chudleigh TQ13 . . . . 123 E6
Exeter EX1. . . . . 178 B7
Kingsteignton TQ12 . . . . 207 E7
Plymouth PL5. . . . . 243 E2
Teignmouth TQ14. . . . . . 210 A3
Clifford Cross EX6 . . . . . 112 C8
Clifford Dr TQ12 . . . . . . 180 F2
Clifford Gdns EX17 . . . . 165 D5
Clifford Mews TA21 . . . . 160 E6
Clifford Rd EX4 . . . . 176 F6
Clifford Rd Ind Est EX4. . 177 F8
Clifford St
14 Chudleigh TQ13 . . . . 123 E6
Kingsteignton TQ12 . . . . 207 E7
Clifford Terr TA21 . . . . . 160 E6
Cliff Park Ave TQ4 . . . . . 226 C3
Cliff Park Ct TQ4 . . . . . . 226 C3
Cliff Park Rd TQ4 . . . . . . 226 C2
Cliff Rd
Budleigh Salterton EX9 . . 199 G2
Paignton TQ4 . . . . 226 D5
Salcombe TQ8 . . . . 259 C3
Sidmouth EX10 . . . . 188 C3
Teignmouth TQ14. . . . . . 210 D7
Torquay TQ2. . . . . 219 E2
Wembury PL9 . . . . 140 D7
Cliffside EX24 . . . . 7 F6
Cliffside Rd TQ1 . . . . 220 C8
Cliff Terr EX9 . . . . 199 G2
Cliff View Terr PL18. . . . 125 D6
CLIFTON 10 C4
Clifton Ave PL7 . . . . 250 F7
Clifton Bank 5 TQ3. . . . . 226 A6
Clifton Cl
Paignton TQ3 . . . . 225 F6
Plymouth PL7. . . . . 250 E7
Clifton Cres TQ3 . . . . . . 226 A6
Clifton Ct
Croyde EX33 . . . . 7 E3
Exeter EX1. . . . . 177 E7
3 Ilfracombe EX34 . . . . 150 B5
Clifton Gdns TQ3. . . . . . 226 A6
Clifton Gr TQ3. . . . . 226 A6
Clifton Hill EX1 . . . . 177 E7
Clifton Hill Sp Ctr EX1 . . 177 E7
Clifton Ho 11 TQ14 . . . . 210 C5
Clifton La EX31 . . . . 10 B4
Clifton Pl
Dawlish EX7. . . . . 204 C6
16 Ilfracombe EX34 . . . . 150 B5
Plymouth PL4. . . . . 263 A4
Salcombe TQ8 . . . . 259 C5
Clifton Rd
Exeter EX4. . . . . 261 C3
Paignton TQ3 . . . . 226 A6
Clifton Rise TQ3 . . . . . . 225 F6
Clifton St
Barnstaple EX31 . . . . . . 154 F4
Bideford EX39 . . . . 157 B1
Exeter EX1. . . . . 177 E6
Plymouth PL4. . . . . 263 A4
Clifton Terr
Barnstaple EX31 . . . . . . 154 E4
12 South Brent TQ10. . . 134 F3
Torquay TQ1. . . . . 220 B4
Climsland Rd TQ4. . . . . . 226 A5
Clinton Ave
Exeter EX4. . . . . 177 E8
Plymouth PL4. . . . . 249 A4
Clinton CE Prim Sch The
EX20. . . . . 57 A6
Clinton Cl EX20 . . . . 197 F2
Clinton Gdns EX20 . . . . . 57 A7
Clinton Rd EX32 . . . . . . 155 B3
Clinton Rise EX12 . . . . . 191 E6
Clinton Sq EX8. . . . . 201 F6
Clinton St EX4 . . . . 177 A5
Clinton Terr
11 Bideford EX32 . . . . . 155 B3
Budleigh Salterton EX9 . . 198 A2
Great Torrington EX38. . . 159 B5
Merton EX20 . . . . 57 A7
Millbrook PL10. . . . . 252 F6
Clipper Quay EX2 . . . . . . 261 B1
Clipper Wharf EX8 . . . . . 201 E6
Cliston Ave EX16 . . . . . . 196 E2
Cliston Cross TQ9 . . . . . 139 C2
Cliston La EX20 . . . . 76 E4
Clittaford Rd PL6 . . . . . . 244 F7
Clittaford View PL6 . . . . 244 F7
Cliveden Rd EX39 . . . . . . 26 A4
Cloake Pl PL12. . . . . 239 A2
Clobells 3 TQ10 . . . . . . 134 F3
Cloggshill Cross EX31. . . 27 B1
Cloister Rd EX4 . . . . 177 F7
Clonway 1 PL20. . . . . . . 126 F3
Close The
Barnstaple EX32 . . . . . . 155 C5
14 Bere Alston PL20. . . . 125 E1
Ilfracombe EX34 . . . . . . 150 C6
Paignton TQ9 . . . . 229 C8
Rewe EX5. . . . . 173 C6
Saltash PL12 . . . . 242 C3
Seaton EX12 . . . . 192 A5
Tiverton EX16 . . . . 161 F6
Clovelly TQ9 . . . . 7 E2
CLOVELLY 23 E8
Clovelly Apts 17 EX34 . . 150 B5
Clovelly Cl EX39 . . . . 156 E1
Clovelly Court Gdns★
EX39. . . . . 23 D4

Clovelly Cross EX39 . . . . . 23 D2
Clovelly Gardens N EX39 156 E1
Clovelly Gardens S � 156 E1
  EX39. . . . . 156 F1
Clovelly Prim Sch EX39. . 23 D3
Clovelly Rd
  Bideford EX39 . . . . 25 D4
  Plymouth PL4 . . . . 263 C1
Clovelly Rise
  Dawlish EX7. . . . . 204 D5
  Paignton TQ3 . . . . 225 E6
Clovelly Road Ind Est
  Bideford EX39 . . . . 25 D4
  Bideford EX39 . . . . 25 D4
Clovelly View PL9. . . . . . 255 A7
Clover Ave EX4 . . . . 176 E8
Cloverdale Ct DT7 . . . . . 260 E3
Clover Dr EX15 . . . . 163 B2
Clover Rise PL6. . . . . . . 245 E8
Clover Way EX32. . . . . . 155 E4
Clover Wlk PL12 . . . . . . 242 C3
Clowance Cl PL1. . . . . . 247 F1
Clowance La PL1. . . . . . 247 E1
Clowance St PL1. . . . . . 247 F1
Cluden Rd EX39. . . . . . 156 F6
Cludens Cl EX2 . . . . . . 181 B8
Clumpit La EX6 . . . . 194 A4
Clydesdale Ct EX5 . . . . 173 A1
Clydesdale Rd EX4 . . . . 173 A1
Clyde St PL2. . . . . 247 F5
Clyst Ave
  Brixham TQ5 . . . . 230 A2
Clyst Honiton EX5 . . . . . 175 E2
Clyst Halt Ave EX2 . . . . 178 E3
Clyst Heath Prim Sch
  EX2. . . . . 178 D3
CLYST HONITON 179 D8
Clyst Honiton CE Prim Sch
  EX5. . . . . 179 D7
CLYST HYDON 83 D4
Clyst Hydon Prim Sch
  EX15. . . . . 83 D4
Clyst Rd
  Exeter EX3. . . . . 178 F2
  Topsham EX3. . . . . 182 F7
CLYST ST GEORGE. . . . 183 C6
CLYST ST LAWRENCE. . . 83 C3
CLYST ST MARY. 83 C3
Clyst St Mary Prim Sch
  EX5. . . . . 179 A2
Clyst Units EX2 . . . . . . 177 D1
Clyst Vale Com Coll EX5 175 D5
Clyst Valley Rd EX5 . . . 175 A1
Clyst William Cross EX5. . 84 B5
Coach Dr EX39. . . . . 25 F4
Coach Ho The
  Grenofen PL19. . . . . . . 126 D6
  Paignton TQ3 . . . . 225 F7
Coach House Mews PL9. 256 B6
Coach Pl TQ12. . . . . . . 207 C2
Coach Rd
  Newton Abbot TQ12. . . . 207 B1
  Noss Mayo PL8 . . . . . . 140 F6
  Silverton EX5. . . . . 82 B6
Coach Rd The DT7 . . . . 260 C8
Coarsewell Cross PL21 . 138 C4
Coastguard Cotts
  Challaborough TQ7 . . . . 142 D4
  Dawlish EX7. . . . . 204 F6
  Down Thomas PL9 . . . . 254 F2
  Inner Hope TQ7 . . . . . . 147 B6
  Stoke EX39 . . . . 22 B3
  Torquay TQ1. . . . . 220 D2
Coastguard Hill EX9. . . 199 H2
Coastguard Rd EX9 . . . 198 B1
Coates Rd EX2 . . . . 178 B5
COBB 260 D2
Cobbacombe Cross EX16. 49 D6
COBBATON 28 D5
Cobbaton Combat Collection
  (Mus)* EX37 . . . . 28 D5
Cobbaton Cross EX37 . . 28 D6
Cobbett Rd PL5. . . . . . 244 B2
Cobb La PL9. . . . . 255 F6
Cobblestone La PL1. . . 248 A1
Cobb Rd DT7 . . . . 260 D2
Cobb Terr DT7 . . . . 260 D2
Cobb The* DT7. . . . . . 260 D1
Cob Castle TA21 . . . . . . 52 D8
Coblands Cross EX5. . . 82 A7
Cobley La
  Bideford EX39 . . . . 26 C6
  West Worlington EX17. . . 60 F6
Cob Mdw EX20. . . . . . . 75 C7
Cobourg St PL1. . . . . . 262 C3
COBURG 123 E5
Coburg Cl TA21 . . . . 52 F7
Coburg Pl
  Cullompton EX15. . . . . 163 C6
  Torquay TQ2. . . . . 220 B4
Coburg Rd EX10 . . . . . 188 A3
Coburg Terr
  🔶 Ilfracombe EX34 . . . 150 C6
  Sidmouth EX10 . . . . . . 188 A3
Cockeram's Rd EX5. . . . 99 C8
Cockhaven Cl TQ14 . . . 208 F7
Cockhaven Mead TQ14 . 208 F7
Cockhaven Rd TQ14. . . 208 F7
COCKINGFORD 121 B2
Cockington 219 C4
Cockington Cl PL6. . . . 245 E1
Cockington Com Prim Sch 🔢
  TQ2. . . . . 219 F5

Cockington La
  Paignton TQ3 . . . . 219 C1
  Torquay TQ2. . . . . 219 C1
Cockington Rd TQ3 . . . 219 A3
Cockington Wlk PL6 . . . 245 C1
Cockland Hill TA21. . . . . 51 C8
Cockland La EX16. . . . . . 48 F3
Cockles La 🔢 EX17. . . . 165 D5
Cockles Rise EX17 . . . . 165 D5
Cockpit Hill EX15 . . . . . 163 C3
Cockrams Butt Cross
  EX37. . . . . 29 B1
Cockram's La EX37. . . . . 43 F7
Cockspark La EX4. . . . . 84 F8
Cocks Pk TQ7. . . . . . . 142 D7
Cocktree Throat EX20 . . 95 C8
COCKWOOD 201 B5
Cockwood Prim Sch EX6 201 B6
Codden Cross EX32 . . . . 28 A8
Codden Hill Cross EX32 . . 27 E8
Coddiford Cross EX17 . . . 62 E2
Coddiford Hill EX17. . . . . 62 E1
Coddiford La EX17. . . . . 62 F2
Codrington St EX1. . . . 261 C3
Coffins La EX6. . . . . . . 181 F4
COFFINSWELL 213 B6
Coffinswell La TQ12. . . 213 A4
Coffintree Cross EX17. . . 80 F6
Coffintree Hill EX17. . . . 80 F7
COFTON. 200 F5
Cofton Hill EX6 . . . . . . 201 A5
Cofton La EX6 . . . . 200 F5
Cofton Rd EX2 . . . . 177 D1
Coil Cross EX31. . . . . . . 10 B6
Cokers Elm La EX4. . . . . 87 A7
Cokers Elm Cross EX14. . 87 A7
Colands Ct EX2 . . . . . . 181 A8
Colaton La EX5 . . . . 81 E5
COLATON RALEIGH . . . 186 D3
Colaton Terr EX10 . . . . 187 F4
Colborne Rd PL6. . . . . 245 A2
Colcombe La
  Dalwood EX13 . . . . 86 F1
  Shute EX13 . . . . 102 F8
Colcombe Rd EX24. . . . 103 A5
COLDEAST. 180 D1
Cold East Cross TQ13 . . 121 C1
COLDHARBOUR 66 A7
Coldharbour
  Bideford EX39 . . . . 157 A2
  🔢 Totnes TQ9 . . . . . . 223 E5
  Uffculme EX15. . . . . . . 66 A7
Coldharbour Cross
  Chilsworthy EX22 . . . . . 53 E1
  Loddiswell PL21. . . . . . 138 E3
Coldharbour Mill (Mus)*
  EX15. . . . . 66 A7
Coldharbour Rd EX16 . . 161 A3
Coldrenick St PL5. . . . . 243 D1
COLDRIDGE. 59 F2
Coldwell La EX12 . . . . . 192 D6
Coldwell Lane Terr
  EX12. . . . . 192 D7
COLEBROOK
  Cullompton. 65 A1
  Plymouth 250 B6
COLEBROOKE 79 A3
Colebrooke La EX15. . . . 65 A1
Colebrook La PL7. . . . . 250 E7
Colebrook Rd
  Plymouth, Plympton PL7 . 250 E6
  Plymouth, St Budeaux PL5 243 D1
COLEFORD 79 A3
Cole La
  Ivybridge, Higher Keaton
    PL21. . . . . 237 C1
  Ivybridge PL21 . . . . . . 237 E6
Coleman La EX5 . . . . . . 81 A8
Coleman Dr PL9 . . . . . . 255 F4
Coleman's Cross PL15 . . 105 B5
Coleman's Cross EX24 . . 102 D6
Cole Moore Mdw PL19 . 171 B6
Coleridge Ave PL6 . . . . 244 F2
Coleridge Barns TQ7 . . 145 A2
Coleridge Cl EX8. . . . . 196 C4
Coleridge Cl TQ2 . . . . . 214 A2
Coleridge La TQ7 . . . . . 145 A2
Coleridge Rd
  Exeter EX4. . . . . 176 F4
  Ottery St Mary EX11 . . 169 F4
  Plymouth PL4. . . . . . . 249 A4
  🔶 Tiverton EX16. . . . . . 64 D7
Cole's Cnr EX18. . . . . . . 59 C8
Coles Cotts PL9. . . . . . 255 C1
Cole's Cotts PL7 . . . . . 250 E6
Cole's Cross TQ9. . . . . 144 F5
Coles Ct EX18. . . . . . . 58 E8
Cole's Ct TQ6. . . . . 233 F3
Coleridge Way PL9 . . . . 250 B1
Cole's La TQ12. . . . . . . 212 C5
Coles Mead EX16 . . . . 161 F4
Coles Mill Cl EX22. . . . 164 C4
Coles La EX13 . . . . 104 B8
Colesworthy Cross TQ12. 212 D7
Coleton Fishacre* TQ6. . 234 F2
Colhayne La
  Dalwood EX13 . . . . 86 F1
  Shute EX13 . . . . 102 F8
Colin Campbell Ct 🔢
  PL1. . . . . 262 B3
Colin Rd TQ3 . . . . 226 C7
Collabear Cnr EX31. . . . . 27 D8
Collabridge La EX6. . . . 112 C8
Collabridge Rd EX6. . . 112 E8
Collacombe Cross PL19 . 116 D4

Collacott Cross EX38. . . . 40 F2
Collacotts La EX19 . . . . 59 B2
Collaford Cl PL7 . . . . . 251 A4
Collaford Farm Bsns Units
  PL7 . . . . 136 A6
Collapark TQ9 . . . . 223 B6
Collard La PL7. . . . . . . 132 D4
Collaton Cross
  Halwell TQ9 . . . . 139 D4
  Malborough TQ7 . . . . . 147 F6
  Yealmpton PL8. . . . . . 141 B8
Collaton Ct TQ2. . . . . . 219 C8
Collaton Ho 🔢 TQ2. . . . 220 D4
Collaton La PL19 . . . . . 117 F2
Collaton Mews TQ4 . . . 225 D4
Collaton St
  Malborough TQ7 . . . . . 147 F6
  Torquay TQ2. . . . . 219 C8
COLLATON ST MARY*. . 225 C4
Collaton St Mary CE Prim
  SchTQ3. . . . . 225 C5
Collatons Wlk EX17. . . . 78 C4
Colclt Cl EX15 . . . . 66 A7
College TQ13 . . . . 180 E8
College Ave
  Exeter EX2. . . . . 261 C2
  Plymouth PL3. . . . . . . 248 E5
  Tavistock PL19. . . . . . 171 D6
College Cl EX39. . . . . . 156 C6
College Ct
  Barnstaple EX31 . . . . . 154 D3
  🔢 Torquay TQ1. . . . . . 219 F6
College Dean Cl PL6 . . . 245 C5
College Gn
  Bideford EX39 . . . . . . 156 F2
  Plymouth PL3. . . . . 66 A7
College La
  Clyst Hydon EX5, EX15 . . 83 B5
  Ide EX2 . . . . 176 C2
  Plymouth PL4. . . . . . . 248 F4
College Park Pl PL3. . . 248 E5
College Rd
  Cullompton EX15 . . . . 163 C4
  Exeter EX1. . . . . 261 C3
  Newton Abbot TQ12. . . 207 C2
  Plymouth PL2. . . . . . . 247 E5
  Shebbear EX21 . . . . . . 55 C7
College Road Prim Sch
  PL2. . . . . 247 E5
College The
  Exeter EX2. . . . . 176 D2
  Ottery St Mary EX11 . . 169 D4
College View
  Plymouth PL3. . . . . . . 248 E4
  Tiverton EX16 . . . . . . 161 C6
College Way TQ6 . . . . . 233 E4
Colleton Cl EX8. . . . . . 202 C8
Colleton Cres EX2 . . . . 261 B2
Colleton Ct 🔢 TQ2 . . . 220 B4
Colleton Gate EX18 . . . . 44 C1
Colleton Gr EX2. . . . . . 261 B1
Colleton Hill EX2 . . . . . 261 B1
Colleton Ho EX2. . . . . . 261 B1
Colleton Mews EX2 . . . 261 B1
Colleton Row EX2. . . . . 261 B1
Colleton Way EX8 . . . . 202 C8
Collett Way TQ12 . . . . 207 E3
Colleybrook Cl 🔢 TQ12. 123 E1
Colley Cres TQ3. . . . . . 226 A6
Colley End Pk TQ3 . . . . 226 A6
Colley End Rd TQ3 . . . . 226 A6
Colley La EX7, TQ13. . . 124 A7
Colley Park Rd EX13. . . 152 D5
Colliepriest View EX16 . 161 B1
Colliers Cl 🔢 PL9 . . . . 140 D8
Collier's Mews 🔢 EX20. . 170 B6
Collin Cl PL5. . . . . 243 D1
Collingsdown Cross EX39. 39 F4
Collingwood Ave PL4 . . 263 C2
Collingwood Cl
  Dartmouth TQ6. . . . . . 233 C3
  Torquay TQ2. . . . . 220 C2
Collingwood Rd
  Dartmouth TQ6. . . . . . 233 C3
  Paignton TQ4 . . . . 226 A5
  Plymouth PL1. . . . . . . 248 A3
Collingwood Villas 🔢
  PL1. . . . . 248 A3
Collins Pk EX9 . . . . . . 198 B6
Collins Rd
  Exeter EX4. . . . . 173 C2
  Totnes TQ9. . . . . 223 B6
COLLIPRIEST 161 C2
Collipriest Ho EX16 . . . 161 C2
Collipriest La EX16 . . . 161 C1
Collipriest Rd EX16 . . . 161 C2
COLLITON 84 C7
Colme Park La EX5 . . . 151 E2
Colliton Cross EX14 . . . 84 C6
Collyland La EX17 . . . . . 62 C3
Colmer Cross PL21 . . . 138 A4
Colmer Cross EX13 . . . 103 A6
Colmer Ho PL21 . . . . . 138 A4
Colne Gdns PL3 . . . . . 249 B5
Colombelles CE EX31 . . 153 E5
Colscott Cross EX22 . . . 39 C1
Colston Cl PL6 . . . . . . 245 B6
Colston Cross EX13 . . . 88 B4
Colston Cl EX16 . . . . . . 47 E1
Coltishall Cl PL5. . . . . 243 F4
Coltness Rd PL9 . . . . . 256 B5
Coltsfield Cl PL5 . . . . . 249 B8
COLUMBJOHN 82 C2
Columbjohn Cross EX5. . 82 B2
Colvin Cl PL5. . . . . 202 D7
Colway Cl DT7 . . . . . . 260 D5

Colway Cross TQ14. . . . 124 B1
Colway La
  Chudleigh TQ13 . . . . . 123 F6
  Lyme Regis DT7. . . . . . 260 D4
Colway Rise DT7. . . . . 260 E5
Colwill Rd PL6. . . . . . . 245 E3
Colwill Wlk PL6. . . . . . 245 F3
Colwyn Ct TQ1. . . . . . . 220 E5
Colwyn Rd PL11. . . . . . 247 A3
COLYFORD 103 B3
Colyford Comm Nature
  Reserve* EX24 . . . . . . 103 B3
Colyford Rd EX12 . . . . 192 B7
Coly Rd
  Colyton EX13, EX24. . . . 103 A6
  Northleigh EX24. . . . . 102 C6
Colyton Cross EX14 . . . . 86 C2
Colyton Gram Sch EX24 103 A3
Colyton Hill EX13, EX24 . 103 B6
Colyton Prim Sch 🔢
  EX24. . . . . 103 A4
Colyton Rd
  Colyton EX13, EX24. . . . 103 A6
  Sidford EX10. . . . . 188 B8
COLYTON 103 A5
Colyton Sports Ctr EX24 103 A3
Coly Vale EX24 . . . . . . 103 A4
Combas La EX33 . . . . 7 E2
COMBE
  Brixton. 256 E5
  Buckfastleigh. 130 A2
Combe Beacon La TA20 . . 69 F7
Combe Cl EX13 . . . . . . 167 D5
Combe Cross
  Ashburton TQ13. . . . . 131 C5
  Aveton Gifford PL21. . . 143 A8
  Bridge PL21 . . . . 137 B6
  Kingsbridge TQ7 . . . . 258 D7
  Loddiswell TQ7. . . . . . 138 C1
  Shillingford EX16. . . . . 34 D4
  Strete TQ6 . . . . 145 E7
Combe Farm Barns TQ7 143 A7
COMBE FISHACRE . . . 217 E7
Combefishacre Cross
  TQ12. . . . . 217 D8
Combefishacre La TQ9,
  TQ12. . . . . 217 D8
Combe Hayes EX10. . . 188 B8
Combe Hill Cross TQ13 . 122 F2
COMBEINTEIGNHEAD . 208 E4
Combe La
  Dulverton TA22 . . . . . . 33 D6
  East Anstey TA22 . . . . 32 F6
  Galmpton TQ5 . . . . . . 229 B3
  Northleigh EX24. . . . . 102 B7
  North Tawton EX17 . . . 77 F1
  Spreyton EX17 . . . . . . 95 F8
  Torquay TQ2. . . . . . . 214 A1
  Whitestaunton TA20. . . 69 F5
Combeland La TA22 . . . . 34 A5
COMBE MARTIN 3 B3
Combe Martin Mus* EX34. . 2 F4
Combe Martin Prim Sch
  EX34. . . . . 3 B3
Combe Martin Wildlife &
  Dinosaur Pk* EX34. . . . . 3 C2
Combe Moor La EX17 . . 77 F1
COMBE PAFFORD 214 A1
Combe Pafford SchTQ2 214 B1
Combepark Cross TQ9 . 217 A1
Combe Pk EX34. . . . . . 150 D5
COMBE RALEIGH 85 D5
Combe Rd
  Axmouth EX12, DT7. . . 193 B6
  Torquay TQ2. . . . . . . 214 B2
Comber's Cross EX31 . . 27 E6
COMBE ST NICHOLAS. . 69 F6
Combesdown Cross EX22. 72 C6
Combeshead Cross
  Cornwood PL21 . . . . . 133 F1
  Diptford TQ9. . . . . . . 138 E6
  Heasley Mill EX36 . . . . 19 C2
Combeshead La
  Dunchideock EX2. . . . 114 A7
  West Anstey EX36 . . . . 32 A8
Combley Dr PL6 . . . . . 245 D4
COMBPYNE. 103 F3
Combpyne La DT7, EX13 . 193 E8
Combpyne Rd EX13 . . . 103 D5
Combrew La EX31. . . . . 16 A3
Combsland Cross EX36 . 31 B4
Combsland New Cross
  EX36. . . . . 31 B4
Comburg Cl EX14 . . . . 196 E3
Comer Park La EX5 . . . 151 E2
Comer's Cross TA24. . . . 21 E6
Comer's Gate TA24. . . . 21 E6
Comers La EX34 . . . . 3 B3
Comilla Cl EX8. . . . . . . 196 C4
Commander's Cut TQ6. . 233 E4
Commanders La PL21 . . 137 E6
Commercial Ope PL4. . 263 B2
Commercial Pl PL4. . . . 263 B1
Commercial Rd
  Barnstaple EX31 . . . . . 154 F5
  Calstock PL18 . . . . . . 125 D3
  🔶 Dawlish EX7. . . . . . . 204 E6
  Exeter EX2. . . . . 261 A2
  Horrabridge PL20 . . . . 126 F4
  Paignton TQ4 . . . . 226 B6
  Plymouth PL4. . . . . . . 263 B2
  Uffculme EX15. . . . . . . 66 A7
Commercial St
  Gunnislake PL18 . . . . . 125 D6

Commercial St continued
  Plymouth PL4. . . . . . . 263 B2
Commin's Rd EX1. . . . . 177 F7
Commodore Cl EX39 . . 156 E7
Common Head EX37 . . . 43 C3
Common Hill EX12 . . . 191 D4
Common La
  Beer EX12 . . . . 191 D5
  Huish Champflower TA4. . 35 D7
  Kingskerswell TQ12. . . 212 E2
  Milton Combe PL6 . . . . 126 C1
Commonmarsh La EX17. 165 E5
Common Moors La EX36. 158 A6
Commons Hill EX6. . . . 113 A4
Commons La TQ14 . . . . 210 A2
Common St EX39 . . . . 156 E7
Commons Old Rd TQ14 . 210 A2
Community College
  Chulmleigh The EX18 . . . 44 E1
Compass Dr PL7 . . . . . 251 A7
Compass Quay EX2 . . . 261 B1
Compass South TQ1. . . 221 A3
COMPTON. 218 D6
Compton Ave PL3. . . . . 249 A5
Compton Castle* TQ3. . 218 C6
Compton CE Prim Sch
  PL3. . . . . 249 A6
Compton Ho TQ2 . . . . 220 C7
Compton Knoll Cl PL3. . 249 A6
Compton Leigh PL3 . . . 249 A6
Compton Park Rd PL3. . 248 F5
Compton Pl TQ1. . . . . . 214 B1
Comptonpool Cross TQ3 218 C8
Compton Pl TQ1 . . . . . 144 C1
Compton Vale PL3 . . . . 249 A5
Concorde Dr EX32. . . . 155 C5
Concorde Rd EX8 . . . . 196 F1
Condor Dr TQ2 . . . . . . 213 D2
Conduit Sq 🔢 TQ13 . . 123 E6
Coney Ave EX32. . . . . . 155 B3
Coney Ct EX2 . . . . 261 A1
Coneypark La EX34. . . . . 3 A3
Congella Rd TQ1 . . . . . 220 C6
Congram's Cl 🔢 EX32. . 155 B3
Congreve Gdns PL5 . . . 244 C1
Conifer Cl EX15. . . . . . 163 C5
Conifer Mews EX2. . . . 178 D3
Conifers The
  Bovey Tracey TQ13. . . 180 C4
  Torquay TQ2. . . . . . . 214 B3
Conigar Cl EX15 . . . . . . 67 B8
Conigar La EX15 . . . . . . 67 A7
Conigar Close EX8 . . . 196 B7
Coniston Cl TQ5 . . . . . 230 A2
Coniston Gdns PL6. . . 244 F4
Coniston Rd TQ12 . . . . 211 F8
Connaught Ave PL4. . . 248 C6
Connaught La 🔢 PL4. . . 248 C4
Connabear Cross TQ12 . 213 B8
Connybeare Cross TQ12 213 B8
Connybear La TQ12 . . . 213 C7
Conqueror Dr PL5 . . . . 244 E1
Conrad Ave EX4. . . . . . 178 B8
Conrad Rd PL5. . . . . . . 244 D1
Consort Cl PL3. . . . . . 248 B7
Consort Ho PL5. . . . . . 243 B2
Constable Cl PL5. . . . . 244 D3
Constance Pl PL1 . . . . 262 A3
Constantine Cl EX12 . . 191 F8
Constantine St PL4. . . . 263 A3
Constitution Hill EX32. . 155 B4
Continuum Sch Devon
  TQ9. . . . . 215 F4
Contour Hts TQ6. . . . . 234 A3
Convent Cl
  Barnstaple EX32 . . . . 155 C2
  Saltash PL12 . . . . 242 E3
Convent Fields EX10 . . 187 F4
Convent Lodge 🔶 TQ14 210 B6
Convent Rd EX10 . . . . 187 F4
Conway Cres 🔢 TQ4 . . 226 A5
Conway Ct EX1 . . . . . . 261 C2
Conway Gdns PL2 . . . . 248 B7
Conway Ho 🔶 TQ3 . . . 226 A5
Conway Rd TQ4. . . . . . 226 A5
Conybeare Cl EX4 . . . . 178 B7
Conybeare Dr EX39 . . . 156 E6
Conyngham Ct PL6. . . . 249 A8
Cooban Ct PL6. . . . . . . 249 A8
COOKBURY 73 A8
COOKBURY WICK 72 F8
Cook Ct PL12 . . . . 242 B3
Cooke Dr TQ12 . . . . . . 211 E2
Cooks Cl
  🔢 Ashburton TQ13 . . 131 A5
  Kingsteignton TQ12 . . 207 F7
Cooks Cross EX18 . . . 158 C3
Cooks Farm EX5 . . . . . 184 C6
Cooks La TQ13 . . . . 131 C2
Cookseley Ct PL1 . . . . 263 A1
Cooks Mead DT7. . . . . 260 A6
Cookson's Rd EX6. . . . 201 A8
Cookworthy Ct TQ7 . . . 258 C5
Cookworthy Forest Ctr*
  EX21. . . . . 73 A4
Cookworthy Mus of Rural
  Life* TQ7 . . . . 258 C6
Cookworthy Rd
  Kingsbridge TQ7 . . . . 258 C5
  Plymouth PL2. . . . . . . 247 F6
COOMBE
  Tipton St John 100 E2
  Tiverton 50 A4

Coombe Ave TQ14 ...... **210** A5
Coombe Ball Hill
  East Worlington EX17 .... **61** C8
  Witheridge EX16 .... **46** D1
Coombe Cl
  Bovey Tracey TQ13........ **180** E7
  Dartmouth TQ6 .... **233** F4
  Goodleigh EX32 .... **17** B5
  Honiton EX14............ **166** C4
Coombe Cross
  Bovey Tracey TQ13........ **180** E7
  Christow EX6............ **113** B2
  Goodleigh EX32 .... **17** B4
  Great Torrington EX38.... **159** F8
Coombe Dean Sch PL9 .. **256** A6
Coombe Dean Sp Ctr
  PL9 .... **256** A6
Coombe Down La PL8 .... **140** F6
Coombe Dr PL12........ **239** A2
Coombefield La EX13.... **167** D5
Coombehaven TQ8....... **259** D4
Coombe Hill EX16....... **47** F1
Coombe House Cross
  TQ9 .... **224** F2
Coombe House La TQ9 .. **225** A2
Coombe La
  Axminster EX13.......... **167** D5
  Bickleigh EX16.......... **63** C3
  Bovey Tracey TQ13........ **180** F8
  Cadbury EX5............ **81** C7
  Cargreen PL12........... **239** A2
  Cheriton Fitzpaine EX16,
    EX17................. **63** B3
  Chulmleigh EX18 .... **44** E4
  Plymouth PL5........... **244** D7
  Puddington EX16......... **62** B6
  Silverton EX5........... **82** B7
  Teignmouth TQ14........ **210** A7
COOMBELAKE.......... **169** B6
Coombe Mdw TQ13...... **180** E7
Coombe Mdws TQ7 ..... **144** F1
Coombe Orch EX12 ..... **192** E6
Coombe Park Cl PL10 ... **253** A2
Coombe Park La PL5..... **244** A3
Coombe Park Rd TQ14 .. **210** A6
Coombe Pk
  Kingsand PL10.......... **253** A2
  Saltash PL12 .... **242** F2
Coombe Rd
  Dartmouth TQ6 .... **233** F4
  Paignton TQ3 .... **219** C1
  Saltash PL12 .... **243** A2
  Shaldon TQ14........... **209** C1
Coombesend Rd TQ12.... **207** F7
Coombesend Road E
  TQ12 .... **208** A7
Coombeshead Coll TQ12 **207** A4
Coombeshead Rd TQ12... **206** F4
Coombe Shute TQ9 ..... **227** F7
Coombe St
  Exeter EX1............. **261** B2
  Lyme Regis DT7.......... **260** E3
Coombes The [1] EX31... **154** E2
Coombe Terr EX12...... **192** E6
Coombe The
  Dartmouth TQ6 .... **233** F4
  Galmpton TQ5 .... **229** B5
Coombe Vale EX10....... **100** D2
Coombe Vale Rd TQ14 ... **210** A5
Coombe Valley Nature
  Reserve★ TQ14 .... **124** E1
Coombe View
  Plymouth PL2........... **247** F7
  Plymouth PL5........... **243** F1
Coombe Way
  Bishopsteignton TQ14 .... **209** B8
  Plymouth PL5........... **243** F1
Coopers Cross EX37..... **44** E6
Cooper's Cross
  Chawleigh EX18.......... **60** C6
  Lydford EX20........... **107** A3
Coopers Dr EX31........ **154** B2
Coopers Hill EX19....... **58** F3
Cooper St [1] EX39 ...... **157** A2
Coot Hide EX16......... **50** D1
Copland La TQ9......... **223** A6
Copland Mdws TQ9 ..... **223** B6
Copleston Rd PL6 .... **244** E5
Copley Cl TQ3 .... **225** F6
Copley Dr EX31......... **154** D3
Coppard Mdws TQ7 ..... **143** E2
Copper Beech Way PL6 .. **245** C7
Copper Castle EX14 ..... **166** B6
Copper La EX39 .... **38** F8
Copperfield Cl EX8....... **196** C2
Copperfields PL20 ...... **126** E5
Copper Pl PL1 .... **262** A3
Coppers Pk PL5......... **245** E7
Copperthorn Cross TQ9 **222** D4
Copper Tree Cross TQ9 **216** C5
Copperwood Cl TQ13.... **130** F4
Copp Hill La EX9 .... **198** A2
Coppice Cl
  Barnstaple EX32......... **155** E3
  Fremington EX31........ **153** F6
  Raymond's Hill EX13..... **104** B7
Coppice Gate EX32...... **155** C3
Coppice Gdns PL5 ...... **244** E2
Coppice La EX17........ **80** A7
Coppice The
  Dawlish EX7............ **204** D4
  Ivybridge PL21.......... **237** A4
Coppice Wood Dr PL6.... **245** C7
Coppledown Gdns EX9 .. **197** F2
COPPLESTONE **79** B6

Copplestone Dr EX4..... **173** A1
Copplestone Prim Sch
  EX17.................. **79** B5
Copplestone Rd EX9 .... **198** A1
Copplestone Sta EX17... **79** A6
Copp Path EX7.......... **204** C5
Copp's Cl EX39 .... **157** A3
Copse Cl PL7 .... **250** D4
Copse Hill La EX20 ..... **77** B7
Copse Rd PL7........... **250** D4
Copse The
  Barnstaple EX31......... **154** B3
  Chillington TQ7......... **145** A1
  Exeter EX2............. **182** C7
  Exmouth EX8........... **196** E2
  Newton Poppleford EX10 **186** F8
  Okehampton EX20 .... **170** D6
  Totnes TQ9............. **222** G6
Copsey La TQ12......... **211** B6
Copstone EX39 .... **39** E7
Copthorne Hill EX17 .... **61** D5
Copthorne Gdns PL9 .... **255** F5
Copydown La EX5........ **82** D6
Copythorne Cl TQ5...... **230** A4
Copythorne Pk TQ5 ..... **230** A4
Copythorne Rd TQ5 ..... **230** A4
Coral Ave EX39 .... **156** D7
Coram Ave DT7 .... **260** D2
Coram Ct DT7 .... **260** D3
Coram Manor DT7 ...... **260** D3
Corams La TQ21........ **160** B6
Cordery Rd EX2 .... **176** F3
Corea Terr PL1......... **248** A2
Core Fields EX10........ **188** B8
Core Hill Rd EX10....... **100** F1
Coreway EX10.......... **188** B8
Coreway Cl EX10........ **188** B8
CORFCOTT GREEN **57** A1
Corfe Ave PL3 .... **248** F8
Corfe Cl PL21.......... **237** D4
Corfe Cres TQ2 .... **213** F1
Corilhead Rd EX33...... **152** D8
Coringdean Cl PL6...... **245** B6
Coriolis Way N EX1 ..... **178** D7
Cormelles Ct [3] EX34 ... **3** A3
Cormorant Cl TQ2 ...... **213** D3
Cornacre Cl TQ2........ **219** C7
Cornacre Rd TQ2 .... **219** C7
Cornborough Rd EX39.. **156** B6
Corndon Cross TQ13 .... **110** F4
Corner Brake PL6....... **245** D7
Corner Cl TA21......... **160** D4
Corner Cotts EX16 ..... **65** A7
Corner La
  Combe Martin EX34....... **3** B3
  Halberton EX16......... **65** A7
Cornermoor Cross EX16.. **47** C1
Cornerstone Ct PL11.... **247** B3
Cornfield Cl PL7........ **251** B7
Cornfield Gn TQ2 ...... **214** B2
Cornflower Cl
  [4] Barnstaple EX31...... **154** B3
  Willand EX15........... **162** E5
Cornflower Cres PL15.... **105** A2
Cornflower Hill EX4..... **176** D8
Cornhill
  Hemyock EX15.......... **67** B8
  Ottery St Mary EX11 ..... **169** D4
  [5] Wellington TA21 ..... **160** D6
Cornlands EX16......... **50** D1
Cornmarket St EX18..... **159** D5
Corn Mill Cres EX2...... **177** A1
Corn Park Rd TQ12...... **212** A6
Corn Pk TQ10.......... **134** F2
Cornridge View EX20.... **93** C2
Cornwall Cross PL21 .... **133** C1
Cornwall Beach PL1..... **247** D2
Cornwall Coll Saltash
  PL12.................. **242** D2
Cornwall St
  Bere Alston PL20........ **125** E1
  [5] Exeter EX4.......... **177** A5
  Plymouth, Morice Town
    PL1................. **247** D2
  Plymouth PL1........... **262** C3
CORNWOOD **133** C2
Cornwood CE Prim Sch
  PL21.................. **133** C2
Cornwood Rd
  Ivybridge PL21.......... **237** A5
  Plymouth PL7........... **251** B4
CORNWORTHY **227** B4
Cornworthy Cl PL2...... **248** A7
Cornworthy Cross TQ9.. **227** A4
Coronation Ave EX7..... **204** D5
Coronation Cres EX15.... **66** A7
Coronation Pl
  Plymouth PL5........... **247** E8
  Shebbear EX21.......... **55** E4
Coronation Rd
  Bideford EX39 .... **156** F1
  Exeter EX2............. **178** A4
  Kingsbridge TQ7 .... **258** D5
  Kingsteignton TQ12 ..... **207** F7
  [1] Newton Abbot TQ12.. **207** B3
  Salcombe TQ8 .... **259** D5
  [1] Teignmouth TQ14 .... **210** A3
  Totnes TQ9............. **223** D6
Coronation St EX32...... **154** F6
Coronation Villas EX1 ... **59** C4
Corondale Rd PL2....... **248** B7
Coronet Cl EX2 .... **178** D3
Corporation Cres [14]
  EX32................. **155** B3

Corporation Rd PL2..... **248** D7
Corporation St [12] EX32.. **155** B3
Corporation Terr [13]
  EX32................. **155** B3
Corry Ho TQ1........... **220** E5
Corscombe La EX20..... **94** E6
Corsham Cl PL6......... **245** B6
Corsham Rd TQ14....... **226** A5
Corstone Cross EX19.... **76** D7
Cory Ct PL9............ **140** E8
CORYTON
  Axminster **87** D1
  Lewtrenchard **106** F2
Coryton Cl EX7 .... **204** E6
Coryton La EX13........ **87** C1
Cosdon Pl PL6.......... **244** F7
Cosgates Feet or County
  Gate EX35............. **6** D5
Cossick Cross TQ13 ..... **112** B5
Costly St PL21.......... **237** D5
Cosway Rd EX16........ **161** D5
Cotehele Ave
  Plymouth, Keyham PL2 ... **247** F5
  Plymouth, Prince Rock PL4 **263** C2
Cotehele Dr TQ3........ **225** D7
Cotehele House★ PL12.. **125** C3
Cotehele Quay Mus★
  PL12.................. **125** C3
Cotehele View PL18..... **125** D3
Coteland La EX32 ...... **18** F1
Cotland Lane End EX32.. **18** F1
Cotfield Cl EX4 .... **166** D7
Cotfield St EX2 .... **177** C3
COTFORD **101** C3
Cotford Cl EX10........ **101** C3
Cotford Rd EX10........ **101** C3
Cot Green Cross EX14... **85** B5
Cothay La EX37......... **29** C1
Cothay Manor & Gdns★
  TA21.................. **51** C8
Cot Hill PL7 .... **250** B5
Cot Hill Trad Est PL7.... **250** B6
Cot La EX5............. **82** D5
Cotlands EX10.......... **187** F3
Cotleigh Cross EX14..... **86** C5
Cotleigh Crossing EX14.. **68** C1
Cotley La EX6.......... **113** C8
Cot Manor [6] EX32..... **155** B3
COTMATON **187** F4
Cotmaton Rd EX10...... **187** F3
Cotmore Cl
  Brixham TQ5 .... **230** A2
  Chillington TQ7......... **145** A1
Cotmore Way TQ7 ...... **145** A1
Cotswold Cl TQ2........ **219** D3
COTT **222** F8
Cottage Cl EX33........ **8** D1
Cottage Cross
  Ashburton TQ13......... **131** B5
  Cheriton Bishop EX6..... **97** B4
Cottage Homes EX36.... **158** D4
Cottage La EX33 .... **8** D1
Cottage Mews PL7 ...... **250** E4
Cottages The TQ7....... **142** F2
Cott Cross
  Ash Mill EX36.......... **31** C2
  Chawleigh EX36......... **59** E6
  Dartington TQ9 .... **222** F8
  Membury EX13 .... **87** C7
Cotterbury Gn TQ9...... **232** A2
Cotterell Rd EX5........ **175** E2
Cotters Cl EX15 .... **66** A3
Cottey Brook EX16...... **161** B4
Cottey Cres EX4 .... **174** A2
COTTEYLANDS.......... **161** B5
Cottey Mdw TQ12....... **207** E6
Cottey Meadows EX16... **161** B5
Cottingham Cres EX39 .. **156** F3
Cottington Ct EX10...... **188** A4
Cottington Mead
  Sidmouth, Lower Woolbrook
    EX10............... **188** B6
  Sidmouth, Weston Town
    EX10............... **188** A4
Cottisbourne TQ13...... **111** A6
Cott La
  Croyde EX33 .... **7** E1
  Petrockstow EX20....... **56** F4
  Totnes TQ9............. **222** F8
Cottlass La PL21........ **137** A2
Cottles La EX5 .... **184** D4
Cott Mdw TQ9.......... **222** F8
Cotton Cl PL7.......... **250** F4
Cotton La
  Cheriton Fitzpaine EX17 .. **63** A3
  Tiverton EX16.......... **63** B5
Cott Pk EX5............ **184** C2
Cott Rd TQ9............ **222** F8
Cotts PL20............. **239** B7
Cottshayne La EX24..... **102** E5
COTTWOOD **43** D1
Couchill Dr EX12........ **191** F8
Couchill La EX12........ **191** F8
Couldon Rd EX10....... **188** B6
Coulson Cross EX20..... **76** F8
Coulsworthy Crook EX34 **3** D2
Coulsworthy La EX34.... **3** C5
Council Chambers [2]
  EX9 .... **198** A1
Council Hos
  Brixton PL8............ **257** B5
  Clyst St Mary EX5....... **179** A3
Council Hos The EX5 .... **179** E7
Council Houses The
  TQ7 .... **149** D7
Council La EX5 .... **175** E4
Countess Cl EX16 ...... **161** F8
Countess Pl EX16 ...... **161** E5

COUNTESS WEAR **178** B1
Countess Wear Comb Sch
  EX2................... **182** B8
Countess Wear Ho EX2.. **182** A8
Countess Wear Rd EX2.. **182** A8
Counties Cres EX6 ...... **201** B7
COUNTISBURY **5** E6
Countisbury Hill EX35... **151** E5
Country Cousins EX34... **150** B4
Country La EX10........ **101** D6
County Ho [4] EX10 ..... **101** A1
County CI EX7 .... **251** A5
Couper Mdws EX2 ...... **178** D3
Coursebeer La EX20..... **95** E5
COURSHAY **88** E3
Court Baron Cross EX14.. **84** E3
Court Barton TQ7 .... **147** D8
Court Barton Cotts
  Coffinswell TQ12 .... **213** C6
  Down Thomas PL9....... **255** C1
Court Barton Hill EX12.. **191** D6
Court Barton Mews PL19 **116** F4
Court Dr
  Cullompton EX15........ **163** C5
  Wellington TA21........ **160** D5
Courtenay EX14........ **166** A5
Courtenay Cl
  [23] Colyton EX24 ...... **103** A4
  Starcross EX6.......... **195** A1
Courtenay Cotts EX16.... **48** F2
Courtenay Dr [24] EX24.. **103** A4
Courtenay Gdns
  Exeter EX2............. **181** A8
  Newton Abbot TQ12...... **207** C2
Courtenay Manor TQ1... **220** C4
Courtenay Park Rd TQ12 **207** C2
Courtenay Pl EX10....... **135** A3
Courtenay Pl [17] TQ14.. **210** C4
Courtenay Rd
  Exeter EX2............. **177** B3
  Newton Abbot TQ12...... **207** C2
  Okehampton EX20 .... **170** C4
  Paignton TQ4 .... **226** C2
  Tavistock PL19.......... **171** B6
Courtenay St
  Newton Abbot TQ12...... **207** B3
  Plymouth PL1........... **262** C3
  Salcombe TQ8 .... **259** D5
Courtenay Terr EX6..... **201** B8
Court Farm Barns TQ12 **212** B6
Courtfield TQ9.......... **223** F5
Courtfield Cl EX11...... **168** D5
Court Field La TA20 ..... **69** E5
Courtfield Rd PL3....... **248** F5
Court Fields Com Sch
  TA21.................. **160** C5
Court Gate TQ7......... **258** E6
Court Grange TQ12...... **212** B6
Courtis Gdns EX17...... **165** D5
Court La
  Morebath EX16......... **34** D4
  Seaton EX12 .... **192** A6
Courtlage Wlk TQ7...... **258** C6
Courtland Cres PL7 ..... **250** D7
Courtland Cross TQ12... **211** A4
Courtland Rd
  Paignton TQ3 .... **226** B7
  Torquay TQ2 .... **219** B7
  Wellington TA21........ **160** D6
Courtlands Cl PL21...... **242** E1
Courtlands Cross EX8 ... **196** A3
Courtlands La EX8 ...... **195** F3
Courtlands Rd
  Newton Abbot TQ12...... **207** D2
  Tavistock PL19.......... **171** B6
Courtlands Spec Sch
  PL6 .... **244** F1
Court Moors La TA21.... **51** E5
Courtney Ho PL5........ **244** B2
Court Rd EX16.......... **161** F5
Court Orch EX5......... **81** A1
Court Park Rd TQ7 ...... **143** A1
Court Pk TQ7 .... **143** A2
Court Rd
  Abbotskerswell TQ12..... **212** B6
  Newton Ferrers PL8 ..... **140** F7
  Torpoint PL11.......... **219** C5
  Torquay TQ2 .... **219** C5
Court St TQ13.......... **111** F4
Court Terr TA21........ **160** C5
Court The
  Dunsford EX6........... **112** F8
  Plymouth PL6........... **245** C7
Court View PL8......... **256** F4
Court View EX16........ **50** D1
Court View TQ16........ **59** F3
Court Wlk EX16......... **58** F3
Court Wood Pl EX8...... **140** E2
Courtyard Cotts PL21.... **136** C3
Cousens Cl EX17........ **165** D5
Cousin's Cross TQ7...... **149** A6
COVE **49** B6
Cove Hill EX16.......... **49** C6
Cove Mdw PL11......... **247** A6
Coventry Cl EX14........ **84** D2
Coventry Farm Est TQ2 **213** B2
Coventry Rd EX4 .... **176** F6
Coverdale Pl PL5........ **244** C1
Coverdale Rd
  Exeter EX2............. **177** B3
  Paignton TQ3 .... **226** B6
Cow Down Rd TA20 ..... **88** F8
Cowdray Cl PL12........ **242** E2
Cowdray Terr PL12 ..... **242** E2
Cowdup Cross EX18..... **43** A1
Cowick Hill EX2......... **176** F3
Cowick La EX2 .... **176** F3

Cowick Rd EX2 .... **177** A4
Cowick St EX4 .... **177** A4
Cow Le EX34........... **150** B6
COWLEY **172** E4
Cowley Bridge Rd Bsns Pk
  EX4................... **173** A1
Cowley Hill EX5......... **172** F4
COWLEYMOOR **161** F5
Cowley Moor Rd EX16... **161** E5
Cowley Pl EX5.......... **172** F5
Cowley Rd PL5.......... **244** D3
Cowley Wood Head EX31 **4** A2
Cowley Wood Hill EX31.. **4** A2
Cownhayne La EX24..... **103** B4
Cowpark Terr [1] EX39.. **156** F7
Cowper Ave EX2 .... **177** F3
Coxhill Cross TQ11...... **236** A3
Coxley La EX13, EX24.... **102** F7
Coxmoor Cross EX17.... **78** A1
Coxmoor La EX17 .... **78** A2
COXPARK **125** A7
Cox Rd TA21........... **160** B6
Cox's Cl PL6............ **245** B1
COXSIDE **263** B1
Cox Mdw EX22.......... **89** F7
Cox Tor Cl PL6 .... **126** F3
Cox Tor Rd PL19........ **171** E5
Coypool Rd PL7......... **250** A6
Coysh Sq EX3 .... **182** E5
Crabadon Cross TQ9 .... **138** F5
Crabbers Cross TQ10.... **135** D4
Crabb La EX2 .... **177** A2
Crabbs Cl PL15......... **90** C1
Crabshell Quay TQ7..... **258** D4
CRABTREE **249** F5
Crabtree Cl PL3......... **249** F5
Crabtree Villas PL3 ..... **249** E5
Crackston Cl PL6 .... **245** B1
CRADDOCK **66** C7
Cradlemans Cross EX32 **155** E1
Craig Ct EX10.......... **188** C4
Craigie Dr PL1 .... **262** A3
Craigmore Ave PL2 ..... **247** F5
Cramber Cl
  Roborough PL6 .... **245** C8
  [5] Tavistock PL19 ...... **171** B4
Crammer Ash Cross EX15 **84** C8
Crammers Cross TQ13.. **123** F7
Crampit La EX39 .... **157** E5
Cramp La EX36.......... **31** E6
Cranapool Cross EX22... **54** E3
Cranbourne Ave PL4 .... **263** C4
Cranbrook Rd EX2 ...... **178** A5
Crandford Cross EX20 ... **107** F8
Crandons Cross EX14 ... **87** B6
Cranes La EX9 .... **198** B6
Cranfield PL7........... **250** C7
CRANFORD **39** A8
Cranford Cl EX10 .... **188** B5
Cranford Ave EX8....... **202** D6
Cranford Cross EX16 .... **202** C6
Cranford Cross
  Great Torrington EX38.... **42** C8
  Woolfardisworthy EX39 ... **39** A8
Cranford Ho EX8........ **202** D6
Cranford Rd TQ3........ **219** A1
Cranford View EX38..... **42** C8
Cranishaies La EX5...... **83** B7
Cranleigh [3] EX32...... **154** F6
Cranleigh Terr [2] EX34 **3** A3
Cranley Gdns TQ13..... **111** A6
Cranmere Ct EX2 .... **181** C8
Cranmere Rd
  Okehampton EX20 .... **170** C6
  Plymouth PL3........... **249** A6
Cranmore View EX16.... **161** B1
Crannafords Ind Pk
  TQ13.................. **111** B7
Crantock Terr [7] PL2... **248** A5
Craon Gdns EX20 .... **170** D6
CRAPSTONE **126** E2
Crapstone Terr PL20 .... **126** E2
Crashaw Cl PL5......... **244** D3
Craven Ave PL4 .... **263** C4
Crawford Gdns EX2 ..... **177** A3
Crawford Rd PL1........ **262** A4
CRAWLEY **69** C2
CRC Units EX1 .... **177** D7
Creacombe Barton Cross
  EX16................. **46** F6
Creacombe Cross PL8.... **141** E8
Creacombemoor Cross
  EX16................. **47** A6
Creacombe Parsonage Cross
  EX16................. **47** A5
Crealy Great Adventure Pk★
  EX5 .... **99** A1
Creamery Cl PL8........ **136** A2
Crease La PL19......... **171** A4
CREDITON **165** D4
Crediton Cross EX17 .... **62** D3
Crediton Hospl EX17 .... **165** A6
Crediton La End EX6.... **97** C4
Crediton Rd EX20 .... **170** C5
Crediton Sta EX17 ...... **165** E3
Crediton Wlk PL6 .... **249** E8
Creedy Bridge EX17 ..... **165** F7
Creedy Cross EX17...... **62** A2
Creedy Rd
  Crediton EX17.......... **165** D5
  Plymouth PL3........... **249** C6
Creedy View EX5........ **80** F2
Creek Cross TQ13....... **131** B6
Creek End TQ7......... **148** F7
Creek Rd TQ6.......... **233** D4
Creely Cl EX2........... **181** C8
Crelake Cl PL19......... **171** C4

Crelake Ind Est 1 PL19 . 171 B4
Crelake Pk PL19 . . . . 171 C4
CREMYLL. 253 E7
Cremyll Rd PL11 . . . . 247 B2
Cremyll St PL1. . . . . 254 A8
Crescent Ave
Barnstaple EX31 . . . . 154 D3
Plymouth PL1. . . . . 262 B2
Crescent Avenue Mews
PL1. . . . . 262 B2
Crescent Ct TQ6 . . . . 233 D4
Crescent Gdns PL21 . . . . . . 237 C6
Crescent Mansions Flats
EX2 . . . . 261 C2
Crescent Rd PL21 . . . . 237 C6
Crescent The
Brixham TQ5 . . . . 230 D3
Brixton PL8 . . . . 257 A5
Crapstone PL20. . . . . 126 E3
Exmouth EX8 . . . . 202 E8
Gunnislake PL18 . . . . 125 D6
Kilmington EX13 . . . . 87 C1
Langtree EX38. . . . . 40 E2
Lifton PL16. . . . . 105 E4
Pathfinder Village EX6. . . . . 98 B4
Plymouth PL1. . . . . 262 B2
Cresents Gdns PL21 . . . . . 237 C6
Cressbrook Cl PL6 . . . . 245 F2
Cressbrook Dr PL6 . . . . . . 245 F2
Cressbrook Wlk PL6 . . . . . 245 E2
Cresswell Cl TQ12. . . . . . . 213 A5
Crestfield Rise PL21. . . . . 237 A5
Crestfields TQ6 . . . . 145 E5
Crest Hill TQ11 . . . . 236 B5
Cresthill Rd PL2 . . . . 248 B7
Crestway TQ6. . . . . 145 E5
Crewkerne Rd EX13 . . . . . 104 C7
Crewkerne Turning EX13 . 88 C6
Creykes Ct PL1 . . . . 262 A3
Cricket Cl EX18 . . . . 44 F1
Cricketers Gn TQ2 . . . . . . 219 E8
Cricketers The EX13 . . . . 167 D7
Cricketfield Cl TQ13. . . . . 123 F6
Cricket Field Ct EX9. . . . . 198 A1
Cricket Field La EX9 . . . . 198 A1
Cricketfield Rd TQ1, TQ2. 219 F7
Cricket Field Rd 9
TQ12. . . . . 207 C3
Cricket La TQ11. . . . . 236 A6
Cricket Pk EX23. . . . . 70 A6
Cricklepit Mill★ EX2 . . . . . 261 A2
Cridlake EX13. . . . . 167 E5
CRIMP 37 D2
Crimps Cross TQ7. . . . . . . 258 F6
Crispin Rd TQ7 . . . . 258 C5
Critchards EX5 . . . . 184 C2
Criterion Pl 14 EX8. . . . . . 202 A6
Crocadon Mdws TQ9. . . . . 139 B4
Crockaton Cotts TQ13 . . . 130 F5
Crocken Tor Rd EX20. . . . 170 D5
CROCKERNWELL 96 F3
Crockernwell Ct EX6 . . . . . 96 F3
Crocker's Row PL18. . . . . . 125 D6
Crockers Way PL15 . . . . . . 90 C1
Crockwells Cl EX6 . . . . . . 182 B3
Crockwells Rd EX6. . . . . . . 182 B4
Croft Chase EX4 . . . . 176 E4
Croft Cl TQ12 . . . . 206 D1
Croft Cotts TQ12. . . . . 211 D2
Croft Ct TQ2 . . . . 220 A5
Croft Hill TQ2. . . . . 220 A5
Croft Ho EX22 . . . . 164 C4
Croft La
Brushford TA22 . . . . 33 C4
Skilgate TA4. . . . . 34 E6
Spreyton EX17. . . . . 96 A6
Croft Mdw TQ12 . . . . 211 D2
Croft Orch TQ12 . . . . 211 D2
Croft Pk PL6. . . . . 245 C7
Croft Rd
East Ogwell TQ12. . . . . 206 D1
Holsworthy EX22. . . . . 164 C4
Ipplepen TQ12. . . . . 211 D2
Salcombe TQ8 . . . . 259 D5
Torquay TQ2. . . . . 220 A5
Croft's Est EX17. . . . . 80 A5
Croftside 5 EX34 . . . . 150 B5
Crofts Lea EX34. . . . . 2 E3
Crofts Lea Pk EX34. . . . . . . 150 D5
Croftswood EX34 . . . . 150 D5
Croftswood Gdns EX34 . . 150 D4
Croft The EX20. . . . . 95 A4
Croft View Terr TQ8. . . . . . 259 E5
Crogg La DT7. . . . . 260 B5
Croker's Mdw TQ13 . . . . . 180 C8
Crokers Way TQ12 . . . . . . 211 D2
Cromartie Point Flats
TQ2 . . . . 219 E2
Cromartie Rd PL4. . . . . 249 B1
Cromer Cl PL6. . . . . 245 A7
Cromer Wlk PL6 . . . . 245 A7
Cromlech Ho EX38. . . . . . . 159 B5
Cromwell Cl EX38 . . . . 159 F6
Cromwell Cotts TQ12. . . . . 131 F7
Cromwell Ct EX1. . . . . 178 A5
Cromwell Gate PL6 . . . . . . 245 C7
Cromwell Pk
Modbury PL21 . . . . 137 B3
Tiverton EX16 . . . . 64 D6
Cromwell Rd PL4 . . . . 263 C3
Cromwells Mdw EX17 . . . . 165 E6
Cromwells Way TQ13. . . . . 180 C8
Cromwell Terr 7 EX2. . . . . 178 D5
Crookeder Cl PL9. . . . . 256 A5
Crooked Oaks EX36 . . . . . . 30 C1
Crooke La EX20. . . . . 77 E3
Crooklake Hill EX5. . . . . 98 E8
Crookmans Cnr EX32. . . . 155 C5
Croscombe La EX35. . . . . 4 E4
CROSS 7 F2
Cross Cl EX31. . . . . 153 D5
Crosscut Way EX14. . . . . . 166 C5
Cross Farm 5 EX33 . . . . . . 152 D6
Cross Farm Ct 6 EX32 . . . . 16 E1
Cross Furzes TQ11 . . . . . . 129 F1
Crossgate EX18 . . . . 59 C7
Cross Gate EX32 . . . . 18 F6
Crossgates PL7 . . . . 132 C6
Cross Gn PL15 . . . . 105 E7
Crossgrange Trad Est
TQ12. . . . . 180 F3
Cross Hill
Combeinteignhead TQ12 . . 208 D3
Crediton EX17 . . . . 79 E5
East Village EX17. . . . . 80 C8
Plymouth PL2. . . . . 247 E4
Cross Hill Cross EX17 . . . . 80 C8
Crosshill La EX6 . . . . 97 A5
Crossing Cross TQ9. . . . . . 222 F7
Crossingfields Dr EX8 . . . 196 A1
Crossings Cl PL19. . . . . . . 117 E6
Cross-in-Hand PL21 . . . . . 237 F5
Cross La
Berrynarbor EX34 . . . . 2 E3
Brendon EX35 . . . . 6 A4
East Portlemouth TQ8 . . . . 259 F4
Crossland La EX14 . . . . 68 C2
CROSSLANDS 160 C8
Crosslands
Barnstaple EX31 . . . . 154 C4
Thurlestone TQ7 . . . . 143 A1
Wellington TA21. . . . . 160 B8
Cross Lane Cross EX36 . . . . 19 D1
Cross Lanes
Ashprington TQ9 . . . . 139 F8
Ashwater EX21 . . . . 90 F6
South Pool TQ7 . . . . 148 F6
Crossley Cl TQ12. . . . . 207 E7
Crossley Moor Rd TQ12 . 207 E7
Cross Mdw EX17. . . . . 96 A7
Cross Mdws EX31. . . . . 154 A2
Crossmead EX35. . . . . 151 B5
Crossmoor Cross EX16 . . . 47 E1
Cross Moor La EX36. . . . . . 31 E2
Crosspark Ave TQ2. . . . . . 219 C8
Cross Park Ave PL6 . . . . . 244 F1
Crosspark Cl EX31 . . . . . . 154 F7
Crosspark Cres EX31 . . . . . 17 A7
Crosspark Cross
Bradworthy EX22. . . . . 38 E1
Holsworthy EX22. . . . . 164 E5
Crosspark Hill EX16 . . . . . . 48 C8
Cross Park Rd
Plymouth PL6. . . . . 244 F1
3 Wembury PL9. . . . . 140 D8
CROSSPARKS 164 F5
Crossparks
Dartmouth TQ6 . . . . 233 D3
Tiverton EX16 . . . . 64 F6
Cross Parks
Cullompton EX15 . . . . 163 A2
High Bickington EX37 . . . . . 43 C7
Cross Park Way PL6. . . . . 244 F1
Cross Pk
Berrynarbor EX34 . . . . 2 E3
Brixham TQ5 . . . . 230 B3
Brixton PL8 . . . . 257 B5
Buckland Monachorum
PL20 . . . . 126 D3
Combeinteignhead TQ12 . . 208 D4
Ilfracombe EX34 . . . . 150 B6
South Zeal EX20 . . . . 95 A4
Totnes TQ9. . . . . 223 E6
CROSS ROADS 106 F5
Cross Side Hill EX36. . . . . . 31 F2
Cross St
Barnstaple EX31 . . . . 154 F5
Combe Martin EX34. . . . . 2 F4
Lynton EX35. . . . . 151 B5
Moretonhampstead TQ13 . 111 F5
Northam EX39 . . . . 157 A7
Seaton EX12 . . . . 192 A5
Cross Terr PL18. . . . . 125 C5
Cross The
Kilmington EX13 . . . . 87 D1
St Dominick PL12. . . . . 125 A2
Cross Tree EX9 . . . . 198 E7
Cross Tree Ctr 3 EX33 . . 152 D6
Cross View
Buckfastleigh TQ11 . . . . . . 236 A2
Exeter EX2. . . . . 177 B1
Cross View Terr EX2 . . . . 176 E2
Crosswater EX23. . . . . 36 F1
Crossway
Paignton TQ4 . . . . 226 C2
Plymouth PL7 . . . . 250 D7
Crossway Ave PL4 . . . . . . 249 B3
Crossway Cross EX20. . . . . 94 E6
Crossway Hill EX17. . . . . . . 61 F2
Crossway Park Homes
TQ7 . . . . 258 A8
Crossways
Cornwood PL21 . . . . 133 C2
Milton Damerel EX22. . . . . . 54 E5
9 Paignton TQ4 . . . . 226 B6
Ringmore TQ7 . . . . 142 E4
Tatworth TA20 . . . . 88 D8
4 Wembury PL9. . . . . 140 D8
Whitestone EX4. . . . . 98 E4
Crossways Ct EX34. . . . . 7 F7
Crossways Sh Ctr TQ3. . . 226 B6
Crowbeare Mdw EX38. . . . 159 E6
Crowborough Rd EX33 . . . . 8 A2
Crow Bridge EX15. . . . . . . 163 B3
Crowbridge Pk EX15 . . . . 163 B2
CROWDEN. 74 D2
Crowden Cres EX16 . . . . . 161 F3
Crowden Cross EX20 . . . . . 74 D2
Crowden Rd EX20. . . . . 74 E2
Crowder Cross TQ10 . . . . 135 A2
Crowder Mdw TQ10 . . . . . 135 A2
Crowder Pk TQ10 . . . . 135 A2
Crowder's Cross EX14. . . . 84 C3
Crowdhole Cross EX16 . . . 46 F4
Crowdhole Hill EX16 . . . . . 46 F4
Crow Gn EX15 . . . . 163 B3
Crow La EX16. . . . . 47 C3
Crown and Anchor Way 5
TQ3 . . . . 226 B6
Crowndale Ave PL3 . . . . . 249 A6
Crown Gdns PL6 . . . . 245 A1
CROWNHILL 244 F2
Crown Hill
Halberton EX16 . . . . 64 F7
West Buckland TA21 . . . . . . 52 F7
Crownhill Cross PL21 . . . 137 B3
Crownhill Ct PL6. . . . . 244 F2
Crown Hill Ct TQ2. . . . . . . 219 E6
Crownhill Fort★ PL6 . . . . 244 F3
Crownhill Fort Rd PL6. . . 244 F3
Crownhill La EX5 . . . . 81 C5
Crown Hill Pk TQ2 . . . . . . 219 E6
Crownhill Rd PL5 . . . . 244 C3
Crown Hill Rise TQ2. . . . . 219 E6
Crown Hill Terr 9 EX17 . 165 C5
Crownley La TQ9. . . . . 227 F8
Crown Mews TA21 . . . . 52 F7
Crown Sq 6 TQ14 . . . . . . 210 A3
Crown Way EX2. . . . . 178 D3
Crow Pk PL3. . . . . 248 F5
Crowther's Hill TQ6. . . . . 233 F3
Crow View EX32 . . . . 155 C5
CROYDE. 7 E2
CROYDE BAY 7 D2
Croyden Cross EX22. . . . . . 55 A4
Croyde Rd EX33. . . . . 7 D1
Croyde Sands Bglws EX33 . 7 D2
Croydon Gdns PL5 . . . . . . 243 E4
Croylands Ct EX8 . . . . 202 C6
Croyle Cross EX15 . . . . 66 A4
Crozier Rd 6 PL4. . . . . 248 F4
Cruel Cross TQ3 . . . . 225 D8
Cruffen Cross EX33 . . . . 8 B1
Cruffen La EX33. . . . . 8 B1
Cruwys Morchard Hill
EX16. . . . . 63 A7
Cruwy's Morchard Mill La
EX16. . . . . 63 A7
Crystal Cl TQ4 . . . . 226 C2
Cuckoo Down La EX14 . . 166 E4
Cuckoo Hill EX17 . . . . 61 C3
Cuckoo La DT7 . . . . 260 A4
Cuckoo's La EX32 . . . . 28 B5
Cuddeford Cnr EX4 . . . . . . 98 C6
Cuddenhay La EX17 . . . . . . 46 A2
Cuddyford Cross TQ13 . . 130 F5
Cudemoor Cross EX38. . . . 41 A1
Cudhill Rd TQ5 . . . . 230 B4
CUDLIPPTOWN. 118 A6
Cudmore Pk EX16. . . . . 64 D6
Cuffe Rd PL3 . . . . 248 C4
Culbin Gn PL6 . . . . 249 D7
Culdrose Cl PL5. . . . . 243 E4
Cullaford Cross EX17. . . . . 95 E8
CULLOMPTON 163 A3
Cullompton Com Coll
EX15 . . . . 163 C2
Cullompton Hill EX5 . . . . . 83 A7
Culm Cl
Bideford EX39 . . . . 157 C2
Exeter EX2. . . . . 178 D4
Torquay TQ2. . . . . 219 B8
Culm Cross EX20. . . . . 77 A4
CULM DAVY 52 A2
Culme Cl EX14. . . . . 67 C1
Culme Rd PL3 . . . . 249 A5
Culme Way EX14. . . . . 67 C1
Culm Gr EX2. . . . . 178 D4
Culm Haven EX15 . . . . 66 A7
Culm Lea EX15. . . . . 163 E3
CULMSTOCK. 66 E8
Culmstock Prim Sch EX15 51 E1
Culmstock Rd EX15 . . . . 67 B8
Culm Valley Sports Ctr
EX15 . . . . 163 C2
Culm Valley Way EX15. . . . 65 F7
Culver Cl
Bradninch EX5. . . . . 83 A6
Plymouth PL6. . . . . 249 A8
Tiverton EX16 . . . . 161 F3
Culver Ct PL12 . . . . 242 F2
Culverdale TQ9 . . . . 223 E4
Culver Gdns EX10. . . . . 188 B4
CULVERHILL. 116 C3
Culver Ho 12 TQ13 . . . . . . 123 E6
Culver La
8 Chudleigh TQ13 . . . . . . 123 F6
Rattery TQ10 . . . . 135 E3
Culverlake La EX13. . . . . . . 88 G3
Culverland Cl EX4. . . . . 177 D8
Culverland Rd EX4 . . . . . . 177 D8
Culver Park Cl TQ7. . . . . . 258 E3
Culver Rd PL12 . . . . 242 F2
Culvert Rd EX5 . . . . 81 F1
Culver Way PL6. . . . . 249 A7
Culverwood Cl PL7. . . . . . 251 C6
Culvery Cl EX5. . . . . 184 C3
Culvery Cross EX17 . . . . . 165 C2
Culvery Gn TQ2 . . . . 219 B8
Cumber Cl
Brixham TQ5 . . . . 230 B5
Malborough TQ7 . . . . 147 F6
Cumber Dr TQ5. . . . . 230 B5
Cumberland Cl EX8 . . . . . 202 D8
Cumberland Dr EX2. . . . . . 178 D4
Cumberland Gn TQ5 . . . . 230 B5
Cumberland Rd PL1. . . . . . 247 F1
Cumberland St PL1 . . . . . . 247 E2
Cumbernauld TQ1 . . . . . . 220 D4
Cummings Cross TQ12 . . 180 C1
Cummings Ct TQ12. . . . . . 180 C1
Cummins Cnr EX6. . . . . 97 E5
Cummins La EX14. . . . . 87 B6
Cundy Cl PL7 . . . . 250 A7
Cunliffe Ave PL9 . . . . 255 A6
Cunningham Ave EX13 . . 167 F7
Cunningham Rd
Exmouth EX8 . . . . 196 D2
Plymouth PL5. . . . . 244 C8
Cunningham's La EX10. . 187 F3
Cunningham Way PL12. . 242 D3
Cuppiers Piece Cross
EX19. . . . . 43 A1
Curie Mews EX2 . . . . 177 E4
Curium Ct 9 EX12 . . . . . . 192 B4
Curledge St TQ4 . . . . 226 B5
Curledge Street Prim Sch 4
TQ4. . . . . 226 B5
Curlew Cl
Okehampton EX20 . . . . . . 170 A6
Torquay TQ2. . . . . 213 C3
Curlew Dr
Kingsbridge TQ7 . . . . 258 F1
Torquay TQ2. . . . . 213 C2
Curlew Mews PL3. . . . . . . 249 C4
Curlew Way EX4 . . . . 173 C2
Currington Mdw EX31. . . 154 A3
Curriton Hill EX17. . . . . 61 C5
Curriton La EX17. . . . . 61 B6
Curscombe Cross EX14. . . 84 F4
Curscombe La EX14. . . . . . 84 F4
Cursons Way PL21 . . . . . . 237 A5
Curtis Cross EX22 . . . . 54 B3
CURTISKNOWLE. 138 D4
Curtis St PL1 . . . . 247 E1
Curve Acre EX33 . . . . 152 E5
Curwood Cres 2 EX16 . . 161 C3
Cussacombe EX36 . . . . 20 D1
Cussacombe Gate EX36 . . 20 E1
Custance Ho 8 EX14. . . . 166 C6
Custom House Hill 4
TQ14 . . . . 210 B4
Custom House La PL1. . . . 262 B1
Custom La EX16 . . . . 64 B4
Cuthays La EX13 . . . . 88 B1
Cuthbert Cl TQ1 . . . . 214 A1
Cutland Cross EX18 . . . . . . 44 D4
Cutliffe La EX39. . . . . 22 D3
Cutterburrow La EX33. . . 152 C5
Cutteridge La EX4 . . . . . . 176 A6
Cut Tongue La TA20. . . . . . 69 F7
Cutwell Cross TQ10 . . . . . 134 E1
Cuxton Mdws PL20. . . . . . 126 C3
Cygnet Ct EX2 . . . . 261 C1
Cygnet Units EX2 . . . . 178 E5
Cypress Cl
12 Honiton EX14 . . . . 85 C2
6 Plymouth PL7 . . . . 251 C5
Torquay TQ2. . . . . 220 A5
Cypress Dr EX4 . . . . 176 F7
Cyprus Rd EX8. . . . . 202 B6
Cyprus Terr EX32 . . . . 155 B3

D

Dabby La EX6. . . . . 97 B4
Daccabridge Rd TQ12 . . . 212 F4
DACCOMBE. 213 E5
Daccombe Cross TQ12 . . 213 E5
Daccombe Hill TQ2, TQ12 213 E4
Daccombe Mill La TQ12 . 213 B4
DADBROOK. 252 E4
Daddon Hill EX39 . . . . 156 E6
Daddyhole Rd TQ1 . . . . . . 220 D3
Daggeridge Plain EX16. . . . 63 B4
Daggers Copse TQ12. . . . 206 F3
Dagmar Rd EX8. . . . . 202 A6
Dagmar St TQ14 . . . . 210 A3
Dagra La TQ12, TQ14. . . . 209 B4
Daimonds La TQ14 . . . . . 210 B5
DAINTON. 212 A2
Dainton Elms Cross
TQ12 . . . . 211 F2
Dainton Mews TQ4. . . . . . 226 B5
Dairs Orch TA20 . . . . 88 C8
Dairy Cl EX6. . . . . 182 B3
Dairy Hill TQ2 . . . . 219 C7
Dairy La PL21. . . . . 237 D5
Daison Cotts TQ1 . . . . 220 A7
Daison Cres TQ1. . . . . 220 B8
Daisy Links EX4. . . . . 176 D8
Dalbury Ct TQ12 . . . . 207 C4
Dalditch La EX9. . . . . 197 D3
Dale Ave PL6 . . . . 249 C7
Dale Gdns PL4. . . . . 248 D4
Dale Rd PL4 . . . . 248 D4
Daleside Ct TQ1 . . . . 220 E4
Daleside Rd EX4 . . . . 173 E1
Daleswood Rd PL19 . . . . . 171 A4
Dalton Gdns PL5. . . . . 243 E3
Dalverton Ct TQ5 . . . . 230 C6
DALWOOD. 87 B3
Dalwood La EX13 . . . . 87 B3
Dalwood Prim Sch EX13. . 87 A3
Dame Hannah Rogers' Sch
PL21. . . . . 237 B5
Damerel Cl PL1. . . . . 247 F2
Damson Cl EX15 . . . . 162 D4
Danby Heights Cl TQ1. . . 220 E4
Danby Terr EX8. . . . . 202 A7
Dandy La EX4. . . . . 174 D5
Dane Ct EX39. . . . . 157 A6
Daneheath Bsns Pk
TQ12. . . . . 180 F3
Danes Cl EX14 . . . . 68 C2
Danes Cross EX5. . . . . 82 C2
Daneshay EX39 . . . . 157 A7
Danes Hill EX4, EX5. . . . . . 82 C2
Daneshill Cross EX13. . . . . 87 B3
Danes Mead EX15. . . . . . . 163 C6
Danes' Rd EX4 . . . . 261 B4
Danesway EX4 . . . . 174 E2
Daniel's Grave EX16. . . . . . 62 D4
Daniel's La
Broadhempston TQ9 . . . . . 131 E1
West Charleton TQ7. . . . . . 144 C1
Danisco Pack Westward
EX16. . . . . 51 C3
Danum Dr PL7. . . . . 251 B3
Danvers Rd TQ2 . . . . 213 F2
Daphne Cl TQ1 . . . . 220 D5
D'arcy Ct TQ12. . . . . 207 C4
Dares Orch EX24. . . . . 103 A3
Darkey La
Lifton PL16. . . . . 105 E4
Okehampton EX20 . . . . . . 170 A5
Dark La
Barnstaple EX31 . . . . 154 F7
Budleigh Salterton EX9 . . . 197 F1
Hockworthy EX16 . . . . 50 B8
Modbury PL21 . . . . 137 B3
Northlew EX20. . . . . 74 D2
Sidmouth EX10 . . . . 187 F6
Thorverton EX5 . . . . 81 E5
Darklake Cl PL6. . . . . 245 E5
Darklake La PL6 . . . . 245 D8
Darklake View PL6. . . . . . 245 E5
Dark Street La PL7 . . . . . . 250 E4
Darky La
Chulmleigh EX18 . . . . 59 E8
Kingsbridge TQ7 . . . . 258 C7
Darlick Cnr EX36. . . . . 20 C4
Darnell Cl EX10 . . . . 188 B6
DARRACOTT. 37 A4
DARRACOTT 8 B2
Darracott Cross EX38 . . . . 41 E8
Darracott Hill EX39 . . . . . . 37 B4
Darran Cl TQ12 . . . . 207 F7
Darran Rd TQ12. . . . . 207 F7
Dart Ave TQ2 . . . . 219 C7
Dartbridge Cross TQ11 . . 236 C6
Dartbridge Manor TQ11 . 236 C6
Dart Bridge Rd TQ11 . . . . 236 C5
Dart Bsns Ctr TQ9. . . . . . . 215 F1
Dart Cl
Braunton EX31. . . . . 15 E5
Plymouth PL3. . . . . 249 D7
St Giles on t H PL15 . . . . . . 90 C1
Dart Hill EX16. . . . . 46 D2
DARTINGTON 215 E1
Dartington CE Prim Sch
TQ9. . . . . 215 F1
Dartington Cider Press Sh
Ctr★ TQ9. . . . . 215 F1
Dartington Cl EX38. . . . . . 159 E6
Dartington Coll of Arts
TQ9. . . . . 216 B2
Dartington Crystal (Glass
Factory)★ EX38. . . . . 159 C5
Dartington Fields EX38. . 159 E6
Dartington Hall★ TQ9 . . . 216 B2
Dartington La TQ9 . . . . . . 223 B7
Dartington Wlk
Exminster EX6. . . . . 181 F5
Plymouth PL6. . . . . 249 E8
DARTMEET 129 D8
Dartmeet★ PL20 . . . . 129 D8
Dartmeet Ave PL3. . . . . . . 249 B6
Dartmoor Cotts PL7. . . . . 132 D4
Dartmoor Ct TQ13 . . . . . . 180 C7
Dartmoor Expedition Ctr,
Rowden★ TQ13 . . . . 120 F3
Dartmoor Otters & Buckfast
Butterflies★ TQ11. . . . . . 236 D5
Dartmoor Prison Mus★
PL20 . . . . 119 A1
Dartmoor Rly★ EX20 . . . . 170 B3
Dartmoor View
2 Chulmleigh EX18 . . . . 44 E1
Plymouth PL4. . . . . 249 C3
Saltash PL12 . . . . 242 E4
Woolfardisworthy EX17. . . . 61 E4
Dartmoor Zoological Pk★
PL7. . . . . 133 A1
DARTMOUTH 233 E3
Dartmouth Castle★ TQ6 . 234 B1
Dartmouth Com Coll
TQ6. . . . . 233 D2
Dartmouth Hill TQ6 . . . . . 146 B7
Dartmouth & Kingswear
Hospl TQ6. . . . . 233 F3
Dartmouth L Ctr TQ6. . . . 233 E3
Dartmouth Mus★ TQ6 . . . 233 F3
Dartmouth Prim Sch
TQ6. . . . . 233 D2
Dartmouth Rd
East Allington TQ9 . . . . . . 144 E7
Paignton TQ4, TQ5 . . . . . . 226 C3
Stoke Fleming TQ6. . . . . . . 146 B8
Dartmouth Steam Rly★
Churston TQ5. . . . . 229 C5
Kingswear TQ6. . . . . 234 A4
Paignton TQ4 . . . . 226 C2
Dartmouth Wlk PL6 . . . . . 249 E8
Darton Gr TQ9 . . . . 227 F7
Dart Pk EX36 . . . . 158 D4

Dartridge La EX18. . . . . . . 44 D1
Dartside TQ9 . . . . 223 B7
Dart View TQ6. . . . . 228 C3
Dart View Rd TQ5 . . . . 229 B6
Dart Villas TQ9 . . . . 223 C4
Darwin Cres PL3 . . . . 249 D5
Darwin Ct **11** EX2 . . . . . . 261 B2
Dashley Cnr TQ9 . . . . 131 D2
Dashpers TQ5 . . . . 230 B3
Daucus Cl PL19 . . . . 171 B4
Davenham Cl PL6 . . . . 245 B6
Daveycourt La EX20 . . . . . . 95 F3
Davey's Cross PL21 . . . . . . 137 B7
David Cl
  Braunton EX33. . . . . 152 D5
  Plymouth PL7. . . . . 250 F6
David Rd TQ3 . . . . 226 A7
David's Cl EX10 . . . . 101 B2
David's Hill EX33. . . . . 8 A2
Davids La PL21 . . . . 137 B7
David Southgate Ct PL1 . . 262 A2
Davies Ave TQ4 . . . . 229 A8
Davies Cl EX5. . . . . 82 B6
Davis Ave TQ2 . . . . 219 D6
Davis Rd TQ6 . . . . 233 C3
Davy Cl PL11. . . . . 246 F3
Davy Rd PL6 . . . . 245 C4
Dawes Cl TQ12. . . . . 211 F8
Dawes Ct TQ4 . . . . 226 B5
Dawes La
  Millbrook PL10. . . . . 252 E5
  Plymouth PL9. . . . . 256 D7
DAWLISH. 204 F6
Dawlish Bsns Pk EX7. . . . . 200 F2
Dawlish Com Coll EX7 . . . 204 F7
Dawlish Com Hospl EX7 204 D6
Dawlish L Ctr EX7. . . . . . . 204 D6
Dawlish Mus★ EX7. . . . . . 204 D6
Dawlish Park Terr EX8 . . 195 F4
Dawlish Rd
  Exeter EX2. . . . . 181 C8
  Teignmouth TQ14 . . . . . 210 C6
Dawlish St **18** TQ14 . . . . 210 C5
Dawlish Sta EX7 . . . . 204 E6
DAWLISH WARREN 201 A1
Dawlish Warren National
  Nature Reserve★ EX7 . . 201 D3
Dawlish Warren Rd EX6. . 201 B4
Dawlish Warren Sta EX7 201 B2
Dawlish Wlk PL6. . . . . 249 E8
Dawn Cl EX1. . . . . 178 A6
Daws Ct PL12. . . . . 243 A2
Daws Mdw TQ12. . . . . 207 E6
Daws Rd PL12. . . . . 243 A2
Daymond Rd PL5 . . . . 243 D2
Days–Pottles La EX6,
  EX2. . . . . 181 D4
Dayton Cl PL6 . . . . 244 E3
Deacon Cl EX2. . . . . 181 B8
Deacon Dr PL2 . . . . 242 F1
Deacons Gn PL19 . . . . 171 A3
Deadhorse La EX13 . . . . . 103 C5
Dead La EX15. . . . . 65 F2
Deadman's Cross TQ6. . . 233 D2
Dead Road Cross EX15 . . . 65 F2
DEAN
  Combe Martin 3 E2
  Lynton 8 E5
  West Down 8 E5
Dean Cross
  Combe Martin EX31. . . . . 3 E1
  Gunn EX32. . . . . 17 E4
  Lynton EX35. . . . . 5 A5
  Plymouth PL9. . . . . 255 E7
  South Brent TQ10 . . . . . 135 C5
  West Down EX34. . . . . 8 E5
Dean Cross Rd PL9. . . . . . 255 E7
Deane Cl EX33 . . . . 8 D1
Deane La TQ12. . . . . 209 D2
Deane Rd TQ12 . . . . 209 B2
Deanes The EX16 . . . . 161 B3
Deane Way TA20. . . . . 88 D8
Dean Hill PL9. . . . . 255 E7
Dean Rd EX15. . . . . 162 B3
Dean La
  Combe Martin EX31. . . . . 3 E1
  Lynton EX35. . . . . 5 A5
  West Down EX34. . . . . 8 F5
Dean Lane End TQ10 . . . . 135 D5
Dean Park Rd PL9. . . . . . . 255 D7
DEAN PRIOR 135 C6
Dean Rd PL7. . . . . 250 D6
Dean St
  Bishopsteignton TQ14 . . 208 F8
  Northam EX39 . . . . 156 F7
Deans La EX36. . . . . 158 D5
Deans Mead EX10. . . . . . . 188 A5
Deans Pk EX36. . . . . 158 D5
Dean St
  Crediton EX17 . . . . 165 D5
  Exeter EX2. . . . . 261 B2
Dean Steep EX35. . . . . 5 A4
De Bathe Cross EX20 . . . . 77 C3
Debden Cl PL5. . . . . 243 D4
De Brionne Hts EX20 . . . . 77 C3
Deckport Cross
  Hatherleigh EX20. . . . . . . 75 D7
  Winkleigh EX19 . . . . 75 F8
De Courcy Rd TQ8 . . . . . . 259 B2
Decoy Ctry Pk★ TQ12 . . 207 C1
Decoy Ind Est TQ12 . . . . . 212 D8
Decoy Prim Sch TQ12 . . . 207 D1
Decoy Rd TQ12 . . . . 207 D1
Deeble Cl PL7 . . . . 250 E7
Deep Cut Cross EX14. . . . . 67 C2

Deep Dene Cl TQ5 . . . . . . 230 A3
Deepdene Pk EX2. . . . . . . 177 E4
Deep La
  Crediton EX17 . . . . 165 C6
  High Bickington EX37 . . . . 43 D7
  Plymouth PL7. . . . . 251 C3
Deeplane Head EX22 . . . . 164 C5
Deepway Ct EX6 . . . . 182 A4
Deepway Gdns EX6 . . . . . 181 F4
Deepway La
  Branscombe EX12 . . . . . 190 D4
  Exeter EX2. . . . . 181 D4
  Exminster EX6 . . . . 182 A4
Deepways EX9 . . . . 197 F2
Deerhill La EX36 . . . . 158 C6
Deer Leap PL19. . . . . 171 D4
Deer Park Ave TQ14. . . . . 210 A6
Deer Park Cl
  Tavistock PL19. . . . . 171 C5
  Teignmouth TQ14. . . . . . 210 A6
Deer Park Cres PL19 . . . . 171 C5
Deer Park Dr
  Plymouth PL3. . . . . 249 D7
  Teignmouth TQ14. . . . . . 210 A6
Deer Park Est TQ6 . . . . . . 146 B8
Deer Park La
  Daccombe TQ12. . . . . . . 213 E7
  Tavistock PL19. . . . . 171 C5
Deer Park Rd
  Barnstaple EX32 . . . . . . 155 C2
  Newton Abbot TQ12. . . . 207 D1
  Stoke Fleming TQ6. . . . . 146 B8
  Tavistock PL19. . . . . 171 C5
Deer Pk
  Ivybridge PL21 . . . . 237 E5
  Saltash PL12 . . . . 242 F3
Deers Leap Cl TQ13 . . . . . 219 B2
Deer Valley Rd EX22. . . . . 164 C4
Deer Wood View **4** EX32. 16 E1
Defoe Cl PL5 . . . . 244 C1
Delacombe Cl PL7 . . . . . . 250 F7
De la Hay Ave PL3. . . . . . . 262 A4
Delamere Rd PL6. . . . . . . 249 D7
Delamere Cl TQ12 . . . . . . 237 A5
De La Rue Way EX4 . . . . . 174 D1
Delaware Cotts PL18 . . . . 125 C6
Delaware Ct PL18 . . . . 125 C5
Delaware Gdns PL2 . . . . . 247 F7
Delaware Prim Sch
  PL18 . . . . 125 C6
Delaware Rd PL18 . . . . . . 125 C6
Delderfield Gdns EX8 . . . 202 C6
Delgany Dr PL6 . . . . 245 A5
Delia Gdns EX5 . . . . 99 C5
Delius Cres EX3 . . . . 178 C5
Dell The
  Plymouth PL7. . . . . 250 B6
  Tavistock PL19. . . . . 171 B6
Delve's Grave Cross EX38 41 F8
Demouville Gdns EX17 . . 80 B5
Denbigh Terr EX10. . . . . . 188 B5
Denbow Cross EX5. . . . . . . 99 A2
Den Brook Cl TQ4 . . . . . . 220 D6
DENBURY 211 B6
Denbury Cross TQ12 . . . . 211 D3
Denbury Ct EX2. . . . . 181 D8
Denbury Down Cross
  TQ12. . . . . 131 F3
Denbury Down La TQ12 . 131 F3
Denbury Prim Sch TQ12 211 A6
Denbury Rd TQ12 . . . . . . 211 E6
Denby Ho TQ4 . . . . 226 C5
Dencross La TQ14 . . . . . . 210 C4
Dencroft La EX14 . . . . 87 A5
Dendles Wood National
  Nature Reserve★ PL21 . 133 D4
Dendy Rd TQ4 . . . . 226 B6
Dene Cl EX8 . . . . 196 F1
Deneridge Cross EX17. . . 60 F6
Deneridge Hill EX17. . . . . 61 A5
Dene's Cl **2** EX32. . . . . . 17 B2
Denes Rd EX22 . . . . 17 B2
Dengie Cl PL7 . . . . 251 B5
Denham Cl PL5. . . . . 244 C2
Dening Ct EX8 . . . . 202 B8
Denise Cl EX7 . . . . 181 B8
Denmark Rd
  Exeter EX1, EX2. . . . . . . 261 C3
  Exmouth EX8 . . . . 202 D8
Denners Way EX15. . . . . . . 66 A7
Denmesdene Cl EX8 . . . . 196 B3
Dennington Cross EX22 . 28 D8
Dennington Hill EX32 . . . 28 D8
Dennington La
  Churchinford EX14. . . . . . 68 F6
  Dulverton TA22 . . . . 33 B4
Dennis Cl PL5. . . . . 247 C7
Dennis Cross EX19. . . . . . . 57 F7
Dennis's Down Cross EX6 96 C5
Dennysmead Ct EX4. . . . . 173 A1
Den Prom TQ14 . . . . 210 C4
Densdon Gate EX16 . . . . . 46 E6
Densdon Rd EX36 . . . . 46 E6
Densham La EX17 . . . . 61 F4
Den The TQ14 . . . . 210 C4
Denver Cl EX3 . . . . 182 E6
Denver Rd EX3. . . . . 182 E6
Denys Rd
  Torquay TQ1. . . . . 220 C5
  Totnes TQ9 . . . . 223 C5
DEPTFORD. 43 B5
Deptford Pl PL4. . . . . 263 A4
Deptford Villas **2** EX31 . 154 C3
DERBY 155 B6
Derby Rd
  Barnstaple EX32 . . . . . . 155 B6
  Kingsbridge TQ7 . . . . . . 258 D4

Derby Rd continued
  Plymouth PL5. . . . . 244 C4
Derick Rd EX16. . . . . 161 B5
Derncleugh Gdns EX7 . . 210 F8
Derrell Rd TQ14. . . . . 226 A4
DERRIFORD 245 B4
Derriford Health & L Ctr
  PL6. . . . . 245 B3
Derriford Hospl PL6. . . . . 245 B4
Derriford Pk PL6. . . . . 245 A3
Derriford Rd PL6. . . . . 245 B4
DERRITON 164 A3
Derriton Mill Cross EX22 164 B3
Derriton Rd EX22 . . . . 71 E6
Derry Ave PL4 . . . . 262 C4
Derry's Cross PL1. . . . . . . 262 B2
Derwent Ave PL3 . . . . 249 C5
Derwent Rd TQ1. . . . . 220 B7
Derworthy Cross EX22. . . 54 D6
Derworthy La EX22. . . . . . 54 D6
Desborough La PL4 . . . . . 263 C3
Desborough Rd PL4. . . . . 263 C3
De Tracey Pk TQ13 . . . . . 180 F7
Deveron Cl PL7 . . . . 251 A5
Devil's Cross PL5 . . . . 163 D4
Devon Cliffs Holiday Pk
  EX8 . . . . 203 B5
Devoncourt TQ5 . . . . 230 E6
Devondale Ct EX7. . . . . . . 204 F6
Devon East Bsns Ctr EX14 85 C3
Devon Expressway
  Ashburton TQ13. . . . . . . 131 B6
  Buckfastleigh TQ11 . . . . 236 B4
  Exeter EX6. . . . . 181 C3
  Lee Mill PL21. . . . . 136 C6
  Plymouth PL6. . . . . 243 C2
  Plymouth PL7. . . . . 250 C3
Devon Guild of Craftsmen
  The★ TQ13. . . . . 180 D7
Devon Heath **2** TQ13 . . 123 C4
Devon Ho TQ13 . . . . 180 E8
Devon House Dr TQ13 . . 180 E8
Devonia Cl PL7 . . . . 250 E7
Devon Pl **15** TQ9 . . . . . . 223 D5
DEVONPORT 247 D4
Devonport High Sch for Boys
  PL1 . . . . 248 A2
Devonport High Sch for Girls
  PL2. . . . . 248 C6
Devonport Hill
  Kingsand PL10. . . . . 253 A2
  Plymouth PL1. . . . . 247 F1
Devonport Leat PL6. . . . . 241 B5
Devonport Rd PL3 . . . . . . 247 F3
Devonport Sta PL1. . . . . . 247 F3
Devon Railway Ctr★ EX16 63 F2
Devon Rd
  Exeter EX4. . . . . 177 F8
  Salcombe TQ8 . . . . 259 D4
Devonshire Ct
  14 Honiton EX14. . . . . . 85 C2
  Torpoint PL11. . . . . 247 B3
Devonshire Gdns EX20 . . 77 C4
Devonshire Ho
  Plymouth PL1. . . . . 262 B2
  2 Tavistock PL19 . . . . . 171 B5
Devonshire Pl EX9. . . . . . 157 A1
Devonshire Pl EX4 . . . . . . 177 D8
Devonshire Rd EX14. . . . . 85 C2
Devonshire Rise EX16 . . . 161 E3
Den Shleigh 143 C2
Devonshire Way **4** EX14 166 A4
Devon Sq
  Kingsbridge TQ7 . . . . . . 258 C5
  Newton Abbot TQ12 . . . 207 C3
Devon Tor TQ1. . . . . 220 C7
Devon Terr
  Plymouth PL3. . . . . 248 E5
  16 Totnes TQ9 . . . . . . 223 D5
Devon Tors Rd EX22 . . . . 164 C5
Devon Tors Rd **9** PL20. . 126 F3
Devon Units
  Exeter EX2. . . . . 177 C1
  Great Torrington EX38. . . 159 F6
Devon View EX7 . . . . 201 B2
Dewberry Dr EX31 . . . . . . 154 B3
Deyman's Hill EX16 . . . . . 161 D3
Dial Ho The EX9 . . . . 198 A1
Dial St EX19 . . . . 58 F3
Diamond Ave PL4 . . . . . . 263 B4
Diamond La TQ10 . . . . . . 134 C5
Diamond Rd EX22 . . . . . . 261 A1
Diamond Cl PL9 . . . . 256 B5
Diana Cl EX8. . . . . 196 D4
Dibbon's La EX34 . . . . 1 D2
Dickens Dr EX2 . . . . 177 F3
Dickens Rd PL5 . . . . 244 B1
Dickers Terr TQ12 . . . . . . 207 E7
Dickiemoor La PL5. . . . . . 244 C2
Dickna St PL15 . . . . 90 C1
Dick's Hill EX36. . . . . 46 E8
Dickshill La EX38 . . . . 159 D5
DIDDYWELL 157 B8
Diddywell Cl EX39. . . . . . 157 A8
Diddywell Rd EX39. . . . . . 157 A8
DIDWORTHY. 134 E5
Didworthy Bglws TQ10 . . 134 E5
Dieppe Cl PL1 . . . . 247 F2
DIGBY 178 D3
Digby Dr EX2 . . . . 178 D3
Digby Gr PL5. . . . . 243 F5
Digby Gr PL5 . . . . 243 F5
Digby & Sowton Sta EX2 178 E4
Diggerland★ EX15 . . . . . . 162 C2

Diggories La **5** EX14. . . 166 B6
Dillons PL8. . . . . 141 A7
Dillybridge Hill EX6 . . . . . 97 D4
Dinan Way EX4 . . . . 196 E3
Dinan Way Trad Est EX8 . 196 F1
Dince Hill Cl EX5. . . . . 99 E7
Dingle Cl PL17 . . . . 115 B1
Dingle Rd
  Plymouth, North Prospect
    PL2 . . . . 248 A6
  Plymouth, Plympton PL7 . 250 C6
Dingles Fairground Heritage
  Ctr★ PL16. . . . . 106 A5
Dingwall Ave PL5. . . . . . . 244 E3
Dinham Cres EX4 . . . . 261 A3
Dinham Mews EX4 . . . . . . 261 A3
Dinham Rd EX4 . . . . 261 A3
Dinneford St EX5. . . . . 81 E5
Dinnis Cl EX6. . . . . 97 F6
Dinosaurland Fossil Mus★
  DT7. . . . . 260 E3
DINWORTHY 38 D2
Dipford Gate EX16 . . . . . . 48 C3
Dipford Cross EX16 . . . . . 48 C4
DIPPERTOWN 106 D3
DIPTFORD 138 C7
Diptford Cl TQ4 . . . . 225 E3
Diptford Cross TQ9 . . . . . 138 C7
Diptford Parochial CE Prim
  Sch TQ9. . . . . 138 C7
Dirty La PL12 . . . . 242 B5
Discover Wistlandpound★
  EX31. . . . . 11 A5
Discovery Wharf **19** PL4 263 A2
Distine Cl PL3 . . . . 249 B7
Ditch End Cross EX32 . . . 11 D2
Ditchett Cross PL4. . . . . . 46 E6
Dittiscombe Cross TQ9 . . 145 A6
DITTISHAM 228 C3
Dittisham Ct TQ4 . . . . 228 C3
Dittisham Wlk PL6. . . . . . 249 E8
Ditton Ct PL6. . . . . 249 A8
Divett Dr **8** TQ12 . . . . . . 122 F1
Dixon Cl TQ3 . . . . 218 E1
Dixon Pl PL2 . . . . 247 F4
Dixon Terr PL8 . . . . 257 F3
Dix's Field EX1 . . . . 261 B3
Doatshayne Cl EX13. . . . . 103 D5
Doatshayne La
  Musbury EX13 . . . . 103 D6
  Musbury, Maidenhayne
    EX13. . . . . 103 D5
Dobbin Arch TQ12. . . . . . 212 F4
Dobbsmoor Cross EX18 . . 44 F3
Dobles Cl EX22 . . . . 164 C5
Dobles Cl EX22 . . . . 164 C5
Dobles La Ind Est
  EX22. . . . . 164 C6
Dobles Terr EX22 . . . . 164 D5
Dobree Pk TA21 . . . . 160 A4
Doccombe Cross TQ13 . . 112 B5
Dockeys La TQ7. . . . . 145 D1
Dockray Cl PL6 . . . . 245 D4
Dock Rd EX8. . . . . 201 F6
Dockworthy Cross EX18 . 60 C8
Dockyard Sta PL2. . . . . . . 247 E4
Doctor Mill Gdns★ EX39 21 B6
Doctors Cnr EX16 . . . . 61 D7
Doctors Rd **3** TQ5 . . . . . 230 C3
DODBROOKE 258 E5
Dodbrooke Ct TQ7 . . . . . 258 D5
DODDISCOMBSLEIGH . . 113 C5
Doddiscombsleigh Prim Sch
  EX6. . . . . 113 C5
Doddridge Cl PL9. . . . . . . 255 F4
DODSCOTT 42 C6
Dodscott Cross EX38. . . . 42 B7
Doe Ct EX38 . . . . 159 D5
Dog Down Cross EX16. . . 50 A8
DOG VILLAGE 175 B4
Dolbeare Rd **4** TQ13 . . . 131 A5
Dolbeare Rd TQ13 . . . . . . 131 A5
Dole Park Cross East
  EX37. . . . . 43 D5
Dolepark Cross West
  EX37. . . . . 43 C5
Doddridge Cl PL9. . . . . . . 255 F4
DODSCOTT 42 C6
Dolphin Cl
  Lyme Regis DT7. . . . . . . 260 E3
  Plymouth PL9. . . . . 255 F6
Dolphin Court Rd
  Paignton TQ3 . . . . 218 F1
Dolphin Cres TQ3 . . . . . . 218 F1
Dolphin Ct
  Brixham TQ5 . . . . 230 C6
  Cullompton EX15 . . . . . . 163 C3
  13 Honiton EX14. . . . . . 166 C6
  2 Teignmouth TQ14 . . 210 C4
Dolphin Ho **4** PL4. . . . . 263 A2
Dolphin Sch The **5** EX8. 202 B6
Dolphin Sq
  Bovey Tracey TQ13. . . . . 180 C7
  Plymouth PL9. . . . . 255 F6
DOLTON. 57 F7
Dolton CE Prim Sch EX19 57 E7
Dolvin Rd PL19 . . . . 171 C5
Domehayes EX20 . . . . 170 B5
Dommett Cl EX13 . . . . 167 E7
Donkey La
  Uplowman PL21 . . . . 137 D6
Donkey Sanctuary The★
  EX10. . . . . 189 B7

Donnington Dr PL3 . . . . . 249 C7
Doomsford La EX37 . . . . . 44 B5
Doone Way EX34. . . . . . . 150 B4
Dorchester Ave PL5 . . . . . 244 D4
Dorchester Gr TQ2 . . . . . 213 F1
Dorchester Way EX8 . . . . 196 F4
Doreena Rd PL9 . . . . 256 C7
Doriam Cl EX4 . . . . 173 C2
Dormy Ave PL3 . . . . 248 F5
Dornafield Cl TQ12. . . . . . 211 D2
Dornafield Cross
  Abbotskerswell TQ12. . . 211 E5
  Ipplepen TQ12. . . . . 211 D3
Dornafield Drive E TQ12. 211 E5
Dornafield Drive W
  TQ12. . . . . 211 D2
Dornafield La TQ12. . . . . . 211 E4
Dornafield Rd TQ12 . . . . . 211 D3
Dornaford Cross EX20 . . . 76 C2
Dorridge Gate EX37. . . . . 28 D3
Dorset Ave EX14 . . . . 176 E4
Dorset Pk PL15 . . . . 89 D2
DORSLEY BARTON 222 D5
Dorsmouth Terr PL7 . . . . 250 E4
Dosson Gr TQ1 . . . . 219 E7
Dotheridge La EX39 . . . . . 25 A1
Dotton Cl EX1 . . . . 178 D6
Dotton La EX10 . . . . 186 E6
Doughy La TQ12 . . . . 211 A7
Douglas Ave
  Brixham TQ5 . . . . 230 E4
  Exmouth EX8 . . . . 202 C6
Douglas Dr PL9. . . . . 256 A6
Douglass Rd PL3 . . . . 249 C6
Douro Ct PL21 . . . . 237 D5
DOUSLAND 127 C3
Dousland Ho PL20 . . . . . . 127 B3
Dousland Rd PL20. . . . . . 127 A3
Dousland Terr PL20 . . . . . 127 A3
Dove Cl
  Cullompton EX15. . . . . . . 163 A2
  Honiton EX14. . . . . 166 B4
Dovedale Cl EX34. . . . . . . 150 E5
Dovedale Rd PL2. . . . . . . 248 A7
Dove Gdns PL3 . . . . 249 D7
Dove La EX10. . . . . 188 B3
Dovel Rd PL6. . . . . 245 E3
Dover's Hill EX17 . . . . 80 E8
Dove Way EX2 . . . . 176 D3
Dowell St EX14 . . . . 166 B6
Dower Ct TQ3 . . . . 226 C8
Dower Ho The TQ10. . . . . 135 C4
Dower Rd TQ1 . . . . 220 A7
DOWLAND 57 F5
Downash La EX13 . . . . 88 E3
Downaway La TQ12 . . . . . 213 E5
Down Cl
  Newton Poppleford
    EX10. . . . . 186 D7
Down Cl PL21. . . . . 242 C2
Down Cross EX16. . . . . 47 A2
Down End EX17. . . . . 165 F5
Downeshead La EX17 . . . 165 E5
Downfield Cl TQ5 . . . . 230 A3
Downfield Dr PL7 . . . . 250 F5
Downfield Way PL7 . . . . . 250 F5
Downgate Gdns PL2. . . . . 248 D8
Downham Gdns PL5. . . . . 244 C7
Downhayne Specl Sch
  PL9 . . . . 255 F7
Downhayne Brake Rd
  EX24. . . . . 102 E6
Downhayne Hill PL7 . . . . . 62 B1
Downhayne Rd EX24 . . . . 102 F6
Down Hill
  Morchard Bishop EX17 . . 78 F8
  Rackenford EX16. . . . . . . 47 A3
Downhorne Pk PL9 . . . . . 255 F6
Down La
  Braunton EX33. . . . . 152 E6
  Doddiscombsleigh EX6. . 113 D5
  Georgeham EX33. . . . . . . 8 A4
  Georgeham, North Buckland
    EX33. . . . . 8 B3
  Kentisbury EX31 . . . . 10 F6
  Knowle EX33 . . . . 8 F2
  Rackenford EX16. . . . . . . 47 A3
  Winkleigh EX19 . . . . 58 D4
Downland Cross EX39. . . . 23 E1
Downlands Cross EX15 . . 66 E2
Downlands La TA3. . . . . . . 52 F1
Downlea PL19. . . . . 171 D4
Downmoor Cross EX38. . . 55 B8
Down Park Dr PL19 . . . . . 171 D4
Down Rd
  Instow EX39 . . . . 15 B1
  Plymouth PL7. . . . . 251 C5
  Tavistock PL19 . . . . 171 D4
DOWN ST MARY 78 C5
Downs Ave PL6 . . . . 249 C7
Downside Cl TQ16. . . . . . 104 F4
Downs The TQ7 . . . . 143 A2
DOWNSTOW 134 F5
Downstow Cross TQ10 . . 134 F5
Downs View EX22 . . . . . . 54 D6
Down THOMAS. 255 C1
Downton Cl PL1 . . . . 262 A4
Downton Cross TQ6 . . . . 233 A7
Down View Rd TQ6. . . . . . 211 A6
Dowrich Cross EX17. . . . . 80 A7
Dracaena Ave EX31. . . . . . 17 C2
Dragon Hill EX14. . . . . 95 F7
Dragon Hill EX38. . . . . 40 F2
Dragons Hill EX13 . . . . . . 260 E5
Dragon's Mead EX13 . . . . 167 C4

Dragon's Tail TQ5...... 230 E4
Dragoon Cl TQ12..... 180 E3
Drake Ave
 5 Exeter EX2 ....178 D5
 Teignmouth TQ14......210 A8
 Torquay TQ2............219 C6
Drake Cir PL1, PL4.....263 A3
Drakecircus Sh Ctr PL1 .263 A3
Drake Cl EX39 ....156 B6
Drake Ct
 Plymouth, Ernesettle
  PL5....................243 E4
 Plymouth, St Jude's PL4 . 263 B3
Drake Dr TQ4 ....226 B2
Drakefield Dr PL12.......243 A3
Drake Gdns PL19.........171 C4
Drake La TQ13...........180 E7
DRAKELAND CORNER.... 132 E1
Drake Rd
 Bovey Tracey TQ13.......180 E7
 Cullompton EX15........163 C4
 Newton Abbot TQ12......207 F3
 Salcombe TQ8 ....259 C5
 Tavistock PL19...........171 C6
Drake's Ave
 Exmouth EX8 ....202 D8
 Sidmouth EX10 ....188 C8
Drakes Cl PL6 ....244 F4
Drakes Cres TA20 .... 88 D8
Drakes Ct TQ1 ....220 B8
Drakes Farm EX2 ....176 E2
Drakes Gdns EX8 ....202 D8
Drakes Mdw
 Cheriton Fitzpaine EX17 .. 62 F1
 Yarcombe EX14 .... 69 A3
Drakes Pk TA21.........160 D7
Drakes Pk N TA21.......160 D7
Drake's Prim Sch EX9 . 198 B6
Drake Rd EX4...........177 A4
Drake's Rd TQ4 ....225 E4
Drakes Way DT7 ....260 E3
Drake Villas PL19 ....171 A4
Drakewalls Gdns PL18...125 C5
Drakewalls Pl PL18 .....125 C5
Drake Way PL9 ....125 C5
DRAKEWELLS 125 C6
Drapers Cl EX14 .... 3 B3
Draper Terr 3 PL19.....171 B5
Drax Gdns PL6...........248 E8
Draycott Cl EX2 ....178 A4
Dray Ct 4 EX8...........202 A6
Drayford Rd EX16........ 46 E1
Drayton Rd PL5..........244 C1
Drayway Cross EX16 ..... 63 D1
Drayway La EX16.........63 E1
Drew's Cl EX6 ....201 A8
Drews Field La TQ13 ....218 D7
Drewsmead TQ13 ....122 C3
Drew St TQ5.............230 C3
DREWSTEIGNTON 96 D2
Drewston Cross TQ13 ...111 C6
Drewstone Cross EX36 ... 30 E6
Dreys Ct EX1 ....177 E6
Dreyton Cross TQ9 ......139 F3
Drift Cl EX14 .... 66 F3
Drift Lane Cross EX14 ... 66 F3
Drift The TA20 .... 88 E8
Drive The
 Bishopsteignton TQ14 ...208 E8
 Brixham TQ5 ....230 C2
 Dawlish EX7..............204 E6
 East Budleigh EX9 ......198 D8
 Exeter EX5................99 B3
 Holbeton PL8 ....136 D1
 Kingskerswell TQ12 .....213 A4
 Plymouth PL3............248 E7
Droridge TQ9...........222 F8
Droridge La TQ9.........222 E8
Drovers Way
 Ivybridge PL21 ....237 A6
 Seaton EX12 ....192 A8
Drove Way TA3 .... 68 C8
Druid Cross TQ13 ....130 E5
Drum Bridge TQ12 ......180 F1
Drummond Cl PL2 ....247 E1
Drummond Pl PL1 ....247 F3
Drum Theatre★ PL1.....262 C2
Drum Way TQ12 ....180 F2
Drunken Bridge Hill PL7 250 D4
Drupe Farm Ct EX10 ....186 D3
Drybridge Cross TQ10...135 C5
Dryburgh Cres PL2.......248 A8
Dryden Ave PL5..........244 C1
Dryden Cl EX8 ....196 C4
Dryden Cotts EX5......... 99 C2
Dryden Rd EX2..........177 F4
Dryfield EX6..............182 B4
Dry La
 Christow EX6.............113 B4
 Okehampton EX20........ 93 D5
Drymupp Hill EX36....... 45 F7
Dualstone Cross EX22 ... 71 C3
Dubbs Cross EX21....... 90 E3
Ducane Wlk PL6 ....245 B1
Duchy Ave TQ3 ....219 B2
Duchy Coll Pl PL17 .....115 B1
Duchy Cotts PL17 ....115 B1
Duchy Dr TQ3...........219 A2
Duchy Gdns TQ3.........219 A3
Duchy Rd TQ3 ....219 A3
Duchy Rd EX14 ....166 A4
Duck La TQ10........... 76 C5
Ducksmoor Cross EX16.. 63 E8
Ducks Orchard Rd EX6..182 B3
Duckspond Rd TQ11.....236 A4
Duckworth Rd EX2.......177 A4

Duckworth St 3 PL2....248 A4
Ducky Row PL17........125 A4
Dudley Gdns PL6........249 B8
Dudley Rd PL7...........250 B5
Dudley Way EX39 ....156 B6
Dudmoor La EX31........ 10 B4
DUERDON 38 E6
Duerdon Cross EX39 ..... 38 E6
Duke of Cornwall Cl EX8 196 E1
Dukes Cl
 Otterton EX9 ....198 E7
 Paignton TQ3 ....225 E6
Dukes Cres EX8.........196 E1
Dukes Dr PL19..........125 E4
Dukes Mead EX15.......163 C2
Dukes Orch EX5......... 82 F6
Dukes Rd TQ9 ....223 F5
Duke's Rd EX9 ....197 F2
Dukes Ryde The 1 PL9.. 255 F7
Duke St
 Cullompton EX15 ....163 C2
 Dartmouth TQ6 ....233 F3
 Kingsbridge TQ7 ....258 D5
 Plymouth PL1............247 E2
 South Molton EX36 ......158 C4
 Tavistock PL19 ....171 C6
Dukes Way EX13 ....167 C4
Dulcis Cross EX13........ 87 C2
DULFORD 84 B8
Dulford Bsns Pk EX15 ... 66 A1
Dulford Cross EX15 ......66 B1
Dulings Mdw EX17 ...... 79 B5
Duloe Gdns PL2..........248 C8
DULVERTON 33 E6
Dulverton La TA4 .... 35 D7
Dulverton Mid & Com Sch
 TA22..................33 D6
Dumfries Ave PL5........244 D3
Dumpdon La EX14 .... 85 F6
Dumpdon View EX14 .... 86 A6
DUMPINGHILL............ 55 F3
Duncan Ho TQ1 ....220 C4
Duncannon La TQ9 ......227 E2
Duncannon Mead TQ9...227 F7
Duncan St PL1...........247 E1
DUNCHIDEOCK............114 A6
Dunclair Pk PL3.........249 D5
Duncombe Ave PL5......244 A2
Duncombe Cross TQ7...144 C2
Duncombe St TQ7 ......258 D6
Dun Cross TQ9 ....222 C8
Dundas St 4 PL2........248 A4
Dundonald St PL2.......247 F4
Dundridge Ct TQ9.......222 E1
Dunes The 12 EX39...... 15 B1
Dune View
 Braunton EX33...........152 B7
 Westward Ho! EX39......156 D3
Dune View Rd EX33......152 B6
Dunheved Rd PL12......242 F2
DUNKESWELL.............. 67 C8
Dunkeswell Airfield EX14. 67 B2
Dunkeswell Bsns Pk EX14 67 B2
Dunkeswell C of E Prim Sch★
 EX14..................67 B2
Dunkeswell Meml Mus★
 EX14..................67 B2
Dunkirk PL11............169 C4
Dunley Cross TQ13......123 B4
Dunley La TQ13 ....123 B5
Dunmere Rd TQ1 ....220 B6
Dunmore Ct TQ14 ......210 B2
Dunmore Dr TQ14 ......210 B2
Dunnet Rd PL6..........244 D7
Dunning Ct EX14........166 B6
Dunning Gn 1 EX1......154 C3
Dunning Rd TQ14 ....210 A7
Dunning Wlk TQ14 ......210 A6
Dunn La EX39............ 25 E2
Dunns Cl EX33..........152 F4
Dunn's Hill TA21......... 51 A6
Dunraven EX32..........155 A4
Dunraven Dr PL6 ....245 A6
Dunrich Cl EX2 ....261 C2
Dunscombe La
 Chudleigh TQ13 ....124 A5
 Sidmouth EX10 ....188 A5
Dunsdon Cross EX22 .... 53 C3
Dunsdon Farm National
 Nature Reserve★ EX22 . 53 B2
DUNSFORD 112 F8
Dunsford Cl EX8 ....202 D6
Dunsford Cross
 EX6....................112 F8
Dunsford Hill EX5........ 81 E3
Dunsford Rd EX2 ....178 A4
Dunsford Way 1 EX16 ..161 C3
Dunsgreen La EX15 ...... 67 D8
Dunsland Cross EX22.... 73 A6
Dunsley Hill EX16, EX36.. 32 D5
Dunster Cl PL7...........251 C4
Dunsterville Rd PL11....237 E6
Dunster Wlk EX6.........181 F5
DUNSTONE
 Chillington.............. 145 C5
 Widecombe in the Moor . 121 B2
 Holmingham............ 136 B2
Dunstone Ave PL9 ......256 A7
Dunstone Cl
 Paignton TQ3 ....218 E1
 Plymouth PL9............255 F7
Dunstone Cross TQ7 ....149 C7
Dunstone Dr TQ3 ....218 E1
Dunstone Ho TQ9 ....255 F7
Dunstone La PL9.........256 A7
Dunstone Park Rd TQ3..218 E1
Dunstone Prim Sch PL9 256 A8

Dunstone Rd
 Plymouth, Plymstock PL9 . 255 F7
 Plymouth, St Budeaux PL5. 243 F3
Dunstone Rise TQ3......218 E1
Dunstone View PL9 ......256 A7
DUNTERTON 115 D6
Duntz Hill PL16 ....105 E4
Dunvegan Cl EX4 ....177 A8
Dunwell Cross PL21 .....137 D5
Dural Cross EX22 .... 38 B3
Durant House EX20 ...... 77 C4
Durban Rd PL3 ....248 D5
Durbin Cl EX14 ....166 D5
Durdon Cross EX20 ..... 75 A1
Dure La EX36............ 30 E8
Durham Ave PL4.........263 C4
Durham Cl
 Exeter EX1..............178 C7
 Exmouth EX8 ....196 D4
 Paignton TQ3 ....219 B1
Durham Way EX14 ......166 A4
Durleigh Rd TQ5........238 B4
Durlestone Cross TQ7...149 B8
Durleymoor Cross EX16.. 50 C4
Durley Rd EX12 ....191 F7
Durnford St PL1..........247 E1
Durnford Street Ope
 PL1....................248 A1
Durrant Cl
 Northam EX39...........157 A5
 Plymouth PL1...........247 E3
Durrant La EX39 ....157 A5
Durris Cl PL6 ....245 D4
Durris Ct PL6 ....245 D4
Dursley Way EX39.......156 E2
Durweston Cl EX31...... 3 D1
DURYARD 173 A1
Duryardwood La EX5....172 E1
DUTSON 105 A4
Dux Cross EX22......... 71 B6
Duxford Cl PL5...........247 B8
Dyehouse Cnr TA22.....34 A6
Dyehouse Cross TA22 ... 33 F5
Dyehouse La TA22 ...... 34 A5
Dyers Cl
 Braunton EX33..........152 D6
 West Buckland TA21.... 52 F7
Dyke Cl EX2 ....261 A2
Dyke Hill Terr TA20 .....88 C6
Dymond Ct (Kingdom Pl)
 PL12..................242 F2
Dymond Rd EX39........156 F1
Dynevor Cl PL3 ....248 F7

E

Eager Way EX6 ....181 F5
Eagle Cl TQ2............123 E1
Eagle Cotts EX4.........177 A5
Eagle Ct TQ2 ....219 C7
Eagle Hurst Ct 5 EX10 .188 A4
Eagle Hurst Lodge 4
 EX10..................188 A4
Eagle Rd TQ3...........111 F5
Eagle Rd PL7 ....251 C4
Eaglescott Airfield EX37 . 43 C3
Eagles Nest EX2 ....176 D4
Eagle Way EX2..........178 F5
Eaglewood Cl TQ2 ......213 C2
Ealing Cl TQ5 ....230 D3
Earl Richard's Road N
 EX2...................177 F2
Earl Richard's Road S
 EX2...................177 F2
Earl's Acre PL3 ....248 C4
Earls Ct TQ1 ....219 F6
Earl's Dr The
 Cawsand PL10 ....253 A1
 Rame PL10..............140 D7
Earls Mdw EX15.........151 F2
Earlswood Dr PL6 ......225 D7
Earls Wood Cl PL6 .....245 F3
Earls Wood Dr PL6 .....245 F3
EASTACOMBE 27 C8
Eastacombe Cross
 Barnstaple EX31 ....16 B1
 Northlew EX20 ....74 E2
Eastacombe La EX31 ...15 E6
Eastacombe Rise EX31 .15 C6
EASTACOTT 28 E2
Eastacott Cross EX37 ...28 E2
EAST ALLINGTON 144 E7
East Allington Prim Sch
 TQ9....................144 D7
EAST ANSTEY 32 E5
East Anstey Prim Sch
 EX16...................32 E5
EAST ASH 95 D2
East Ash Cross
 Bradworthy EX22........38 F3
 Whiddon Down EX20.....95 D2
East Ave EX1 ....177 E6
East Ball Hill EX39 ......22 E3
Eastbourne Terr EX39 ...156 D7
EAST BUCKLAND 18 D2
East Buckland Rd
 Budleigh Salterton EX9 .198 B3
 East Budleigh EX9 ......198 A3
Eastbury Ave PL5 ....244 A2
EAST BUTTERLEIGH 64 E3

East Butterleigh Cross
 EX15...................64 E3
East Challacombe La EX34. 3 B4
EAST CHARLETON........144 D1
Eastchurch La EX6...... 96 D6
East Cl EX16............. 46 E1
East Cliff DT7 ....260 E3
East Cliff Cl EX7 ....204 E7
East Cliff Gdns EX7 .....204 E7
East Cliff Rd EX7 ....204 E7
Eastcliff Wlk TQ14 ......210 D5
East Cliff Wlk TQ4 ......210 D7
East Coombe Cross EX17. 81 A6
Eastcoombe La EX17.... 81 A6
Eastcote Cl PL6..........245 B6
EASTCOTT 37 D2
Eastcott Cross EX23..... 37 D2
East Courts The 3 PL1. 262 A3
East Dartmoor Woods &
 Heaths National Nature
 Reserve★ TQ13 ....122 B5
East Devon Bsns Pk EX14. 86 C3
EASTDON 201 B4
Eastdown EX39 .... 22 E3
Eastdown Cross TQ9 ...145 D8
East Down Cross
 Combe Martin EX34...... 9 F6
 Okehampton EX20...... 93 D8
East Dr EX8.............196 A1
Eastella Rd PL20 ....127 A2
East End EX17 .... 62 D3
East End Terr 16 TQ13 .131 A5
Easterbrook La EX6 ..... 96 D8
Eastern Close Cross EX31.. 3 D1
Easter Ct EX31...........154 E2
Easterdown Cl PL9 ......255 F7
Easterfield La TQ1 ......214 C2
Easter Ground La EX34. 8 F5
Easter Hill EX37.......... 28 B2
Easter Hill La EX6.......201 A7
Easter Lane Cross TQ13 .121 B2
Easterley Terr EX31 .....154 C3
Eastern Ave
 Barnstaple EX32 ....155 C4
 Exeter EX2...............182 C7
Eastern Backway TQ7...258 D5
Eastern Espl TQ4........226 C6
Eastern Rd
 Ashburton TQ13..........131 A5
 Zeal Monachorum EX17.. 78 C7
EASTERN TOWN..........188 B3
Eastern Wood Rd PL7...255 A4
Easter St EX32 ....16 E1
East Farm TQ7...........144 D1
Eastfield EX11 ....168 D4
Eastfield Ave PL9........255 C6
Eastfield Cres PL3 ......249 A6
Eastfield Orch EX5...... 66 A8
East Grove Rd EX2 ......261 A2
Easthay La TA20.........88 F4
East Hill EX33...........152 E6
EAST ILKERTON........... 5 B3
EASTINGTON............. 60 E4
Eastington Cross EX17.. 60 E4
Eastington Hill EX17.... 60 E3
East John Wlk EX1......178 C6
EAST KNOWSTONE...... 32 B2
Eastlake Ho 4 PL1......263 A2
Eastlake St PL4 ....262 C3
Eastlands EX15 .... 67 B8
EASTLEIGH..............26 C6
EAST LEIGH
 Haberton 222 B1
 Zeal Monachorum 77 F8
East Leigh Cross
 Harberton TQ9..........222 B1
 Zeal Monachorum EX17. 77 F8
East Lyn La EX35........151 F2
East Meadow Rd EX33...152 B7
East Mere Cross EX16... 50 B2
EAST MIDDLETON......... 4 B1
East Moore Cross TQ9..135 E1
Eastmoor La TA4........ 34 E8
East Nymph La EX17 .... 95 E6
EAST OGWELL...........206 E1
EASTON.................111 B7
Easton Cross
 Hittisleigh EX6..........96 C5
 West Alvington TQ7 .....258 B3
Easton La EX16..........50 D1
Easton Moor Cross EX31. 27 A2
East Pafford Ave TQ2 ...214 B3
Eastpark 5 TQ7 ....149 B8
East Park Ave PL4.......262 C4
East Park Cl EX19 ...... 58 F3
East Park Rd EX32 ......155 D4
East Pitton Barns PL7 ...36 A1
East Pk EX39............ 38 F8
EAST PORTLEMOUTH 259 F4
East Prawle Cross EX37 .29 B2
EAST PRAWLE 149 A3
EAST PUTFORD 39 C3
East Ridge View EX39 ...157 B1
East Rowley La EX36 ....45 D6
East Sherford Cross PL8. 257 A8
East St
 Ashburton TQ13 ....130 C5
 Bishop's Tawton EX32 .. 16 E1
 Black Torrington EX21.... 74 A8
 Bovey Tracey TQ13......180 D8
 Braunton EX33..........152 D6
 Chittlehampton EX37..... 28 F4
 Chulmleigh EX18........ 44 E1

East St continued
 Crediton EX17...........165 D5
 Denbury TQ12...........211 A7
 Great Torrington EX38...159 D5
 Ipplepen TQ12..........211 C2
 Newton Abbot TQ12.....207 C3
 Okehampton EX20.......170 C5
 Plymouth PL1............262 A2
 Sheepwash EX21........ 56 C1
 Sidmouth EX10 ....188 B3
 South Molton EX36 .....158 D4
 Torquay TQ2............219 F6
 Uffculme EX15........... 66 A7
EAST STOWFORD........ 28 F5
East Tapps La EX16 .....33 B2
East Terr
 Budleigh Salterton EX9 .199 H2
 Exeter EX1..............178 A6
EAST-THE-WATER.......157 C2
East-the-Water Prim Sch
 EX39...................157 C1
EAST TOWN 165 E6
East Town La EX6 ....194 D3
East View Cotts 5 EX14.166 C6
East View Pl EX16.......161 E4
EAST VILLAGE 80 C8
East Village Cross EX17 . 80 C8
East Way PL11...........136 D6
Eastwick Barton EX16... 62 B8
East Wonford Hill EX2...178 B5
Eastwood EX35 ....151 B4
Eastwood Cres TQ12 ...206 E5
Eastwood Cross TQ12 ...96 C7
EAST WORLINGTON..... 61 B8
East Worlington Cross
 EX17...................61 B8
East Worlington Prim Sch
 EX17...................61 B8
East Youlstone Cross
 EX23...................37 F2
Easy Bridge Cross EX13 .102 F7
Easy La TQ13 ....123 B7
Eaton Ct TQ14 ....210 B7
Eaton Dr EX1 ....261 C3
Eaton Hall Dr TQ6......233 E4
Eaton Pl EX1............261 C3
Eaton Pl TQ4 ....226 B5
Ebberley Lawn EX32 ....155 A5
Ebberly Arms EX38......42 F5
Ebberly Cross EX19 .... 42 E5
Ebberly Ct 14 EX32....155 A5
EBBERLY HILL 42 F6
Ebdon Way TQ1.........219 F6
Ebenezer Rd TQ3 ......226 A5
EBFORD.................183 C4
Ebford La EX3...........183 D4
Ebrington Rd EX2 ....177 B3
Ebrington St
 Kingsbridge TQ7 ....258 D5
 Plymouth PL4............263 A3
Echo Cres PL5 ....244 D2
Eddy's La 10 EX32......155 B3
Eddystone Cl
 Heybrook Bay PL9 ......140 A7
 Plymouth PL3............249 C6
Eddystone Rd
 Down Thomas PL9 ......255 C1
 Thurlestone TQ7 ....143 A1
Eddystone Rise TQ7 ....147 D7
Eddystone Terr PL1 .....262 B1
Eden Cl TQ5 ....230 C3
Eden Gr TQ3............225 F7
Eden Park Prim Sch
 TQ5....................230 C3
Eden Pk TQ5............230 C3
Edenside PL3............248 F6
Edenvale Rd TQ3........225 F8
Eden Way EX10 ....186 E3
Edgar Terr PL4 ....249 A4
Egbaston Mead EX2....178 C4
Edgcumbe Ave PL1 .....262 A3
Edgcumbe Cres PL10...252 F6
Edgcumbe Ct 3 PL3 ...248 A3
Edgcumbe Dr PL19......171 B6
Edgcumbe Ho PL1 ......262 B2
Edgcumbe Park Rd PL3 .248 D6
Edgcumbe Rd
 Saltash PL12............242 C5
 St Dominick PL12.......125 A2
Edgcumbe St PL1 ....248 A1
Edgcumbe Terr
 5 Bere Alston PL20 ....125 E1
 Milton Abbot PL19.......116 A6
Edgecombe Way PL18...125 B5
Egeland Cross TQ12 ....217 D8
Edgelands La TQ12......211 C1
Edgeley Rd TQ12 ....214 A2
Edgeley Rd TQ5.........230 B5
Edgerley Cross EX17 ... 60 C1
Edgerton Park Rd EX4...177 D8
Edgeworthy Hill EX16... 62 C8
Edgiford Cross EX18.... 45 B1
EDGINSWELL............213 B1
Edginswell Cl TQ2 ......213 A2
Edginswell La TQ12, TQ2 213 A1
Edinburgh Cres EX5 ....195 E6
Edinburgh Dr EX4.......176 E6
Edinburgh Rd PL5 ......230 D3
Edinburgh St PL1.......247 E1
EDISTONE 37 C8
Edith Ave PL4...........263 C4
Edith St PL5............243 D1
Edmonton Cl EX4 ....178 A8

Edmund St EX2, EX4 .... 261 A2
Edna Terr PL4 .... 263 C3
Edward Cl TQ7 .... 143 A1
Edwards Cl PL7 .... 251 B4
Edwards Cres PL12 ...... 242 C2
Edwards Ct EX2 .... 178 D4
Edwards Dr
  Plymouth PL7 .... 251 B5
  Westward Ho! EX39 .... 156 E7
Edwards Rd PL15 .... 90 C1
Edwin Rd EX2 .... 177 B3
Effingham Cres PL3 ..... 248 D7
EFFORD 249 C5
Efford Barns EX17 ...... 81 B4
Efford Cres PL3 .... 249 B6
Efford Fort PL3 .... 249 B6
Efford La PL3 .... 249 B5
Efford Marshes Nature
  Reserve ★ PL3 .... 249 B6
Efford Pathway PL3 ..... 249 C6
Efford Rd PL3 .... 249 B6
Efford Wlk PL3 .... 249 B6
Egerton Cres PL4 .... 263 C3
Egerton Pl PL4 .... 263 C3
Egerton Rd
  Plymouth PL4 .... 263 C3
  Torquay TQ1 .... 220 C6
EGGBUCKLAND 249 C8
Eggbuckland Rd PL3 ..... 249 C7
Eggesford Ctry Est EX17.. 60 A3
Eggesford Ctry Est EX18.. 59 E6
Eggesford Fourways EX18 59 E5
Eggesford Garden & Country
  Ctr ★ EX18 .... 59 E6
Eggesford Rd EX19 ...... 58 F3
Eggesford Sta EX18 ..... 59 E6
Egg Moor La EX13 .... 88 A7
Egham Ave EX2 .... 177 D3
Egremont Cross EX14 .... 84 C6
Egremont Rd EX8 .... 202 A7
Egret Cl PL10 .... 253 A6
Egypt La [8] EX18 ...... 44 E1
Eiffel Pl [11] TQ9 ..... 223 C5
Eight Acre Cl [1] PL7 .. 251 C5
Eight Acre La TA21 ..... 160 E5
Eight Trees TQ9 .... 216 A5
Elaine Cl
  Exeter EX4 .... 174 A2
  Plymouth PL7 .... 250 B5
Elba Cl TQ4 .... 226 C1
Elberry Farm La TQ4 .... 229 D7
Elberry La TQ5 .... 229 D7
Elbow La PL10 .... 171 C6
ELBURTON 256 B6
Elburton Prim Sch PL9 .. 256 C7
Elburton Rd PL9 .... 256 B8
Eldad Hill PL1 .... 262 A3
Elderberry Way EX15 .... 162 E5
Elder Cl [3] PL7 .... 251 B5
Elder Gr EX17 .... 165 E6
Eldertree Gdns EX4 ..... 177 A7
Eldridge Ho EX13 .... 167 F7
Eleanor Ho PL1 .... 262 A2
Elford Cres PL7 .... 250 E7
Elford Pl W PL20 .... 255 C7
Elford Pk PL20 .... 127 A2
Elgar Cl
  Barnstaple EX32 ...... 155 C5
  Exeter EX2 .... 178 C5
Elgin Cres PL5 .... 244 E3
Elim Cl EX10 .... 188 B5
Elim Cl PL3 .... 248 E5
Elim Terr PL3 .... 248 E5
Elim Villas EX10 .... 188 B5
Eliot St PL5 .... 247 E8
Elizabeth Ct
  [2] Plymouth PL1 ..... 263 A2
  Torquay TQ2 .... 219 F5
  Totnes TQ9 .... 223 F5
Elizabeth Dr EX1 .... 154 D3
Elizabeth Ave
  Brixham TQ5 .... 230 A1
  Exeter EX4 .... 177 E8
Elizabeth Cl
  Barnstaple EX31 ...... 154 D2
  Ivybridge PL21 .... 237 F5
  Lyme Regis DT7 .... 260 E4
  [4] Whimple EX5 ...... 99 E8
Elizabeth Ct
  [2] Plymouth PL1 ..... 263 A2
  Torquay TQ2 .... 219 F5
  Totnes TQ9 .... 223 F5
Elizabeth Dr EX1 .... 154 D3
Elizabeth House Mus & Arts
  Gall ★ PL4 .... 263 A2
Elizabeth Lea Cl EX22 .. 38 E1
Elizabeth Pl PL4 .... 263 A4
Elizabeth Rd
  Exmouth EX8 .... 196 C2
  Seaton EX12 .... 192 A7
Elizabeth Sq [4] TQ12 .. 207 C3
Elizabeth Way EX12 ..... 192 A6
Elkins Hill TQ5 .... 230 D5
ELLACOMBE 220 C6
Ellacombe Church Rd
  TQ1 .... 220 C6
Ellacombe Rd TQ1 ...... 220 B6
Ellacombe Sch [7] TQ1 . 220 B6
Ellards Cl EX2 .... 177 C4
Ellen Tinkham Spccl Sch
  EX1 .... 178 E7
Elleraie Ho TQ14 .... 210 B3
Ellerhayes EX5 .... 82 D4
Ellersdown La TA22 ..... 33 E4
Ellerslie Rd EX31 ...... 154 B4
Ellesmere TQ1 .... 220 E5
Ellesmere Rd TQ1 ...... 220 E5

Elley Cross EX17 .... 79 B2
Elliot Cl
  Barnstaple EX32 ...... 155 C4
  Ottery St Mary EX11 .. 169 C3
Elliot Ho EX2 .... 261 B2
Elliot Plain TQ11 ...... 236 C5
Elliots Hill TQ13 ...... 130 C8
Elliot Sq PL11 .... 247 B3
Elliot St PL1 .... 262 B1
Elliott Cl
  Exeter EX4 .... 173 E2
  Saltash PL12 .... 242 D2
Elliott Ct TQ12 .... 211 C2
Elliott Terr PL1 .... 262 C1
Elliott Terrace La PL1 . 262 C1
Elliott Gr TQ5 .... 230 B4
Elliott Rd PL4 .... 263 B2
Elliotts Hill PL8 ...... 257 A4
Elliott's Hill EX17 .... 61 C3
Elliott's Store ★ PL12 . 243 A2
Elliott Way EX2 .... 178 D5
Ellwood Cl TQ1 .... 220 B6
Ellwood Rd EX16 .... 196 D2
Elm Bank TQ11 .... 236 A4
Elmbank Gdns [3] EX4 .. 226 A5
Elmbank Rd TQ4 .... 226 A5
Elmbridge Gdns EX4 .... 177 A8
Elm Cl
  Broadclyst EX5 .... 175 C6
  Stibb Cross EX38 ..... 40 D2
  Tavistock PL19 .... 171 C3
Elm Cotts
  Barnstaple EX31 ...... 16 A3
  Saltash PL12 .... 242 C3
Elm Cres PL3, PL4 ...... 249 A4
Elm Croft PL2 .... 248 B7
Elm Ct EX6 .... 201 B8
Elmdale Rd EX39 .... 157 A3
Elmdon Cl EX4 .... 173 D1
Elm Farm La EX24 ...... 103 A3
Elmfield Cres EX36 ..... 196 B2
Elmfield Mdw EX20 ...... 74 E1
Elm Gr
  Bideford EX39 .... 156 F2
  Exmouth EX8 .... 201 F6
  Plymouth, Eggbuckland
    PL6 .... 249 B8
  Plymouth, Plympton PL7. 250 E5
  Teignmouth TQ14 ...... 210 B8
Elm Grove Ave EX8 ..... 182 F5
Elm Grove Cl EX7 ...... 204 E7
Elm Grove Dr EX7 ...... 204 E7
Elm Grove Gdns EX3 .... 182 F5
Elm Grove Rd
  Dawlish EX7 .... 204 E7
  Exeter EX4 .... 261 A4
  Topsham EX3 .... 182 F5
Elmhirst Dr TQ9 .... 223 E5
Elmhurst Ct [3] TQ14 .. 210 B5
Elm La EX8 .... 202 F7
El Monte Ct [5] TQ14 .. 210 B6
Elm Orch EX12 .... 192 D7
Elmore Way EX16 .... 161 E5
Elm Pk
  Millbrook PL10 .... 253 B6
  Paignton TQ3 .... 225 F6
Elm Rd
  Brixham TQ5 .... 230 A2
  Exeter EX4 .... 202 C7
  [8] Newton Abbot TQ12. 207 C3
  Plymouth, Glenholt PL6 249 B8
  Plymouth, Mannamead PL4 248 F4
ELMSCOTT 37 B8
Elmscott Terr [7] EX39 . 157 A2
Elmside
  Budleigh Salterton EX9 198 A1
  Exeter EX4 .... 177 E7
Elmside Cl EX4 .... 162 D3
Elmside Cl EX4 .... 177 E7
Elmsleigh Cl EX4 ...... 27 E8
Elmsleigh Pk TQ4 ...... 226 B5
Elmsleigh Rd TQ4 ...... 226 B5
Elms Mdw EX19 .... 58 F2
Elms Rd TA21 .... 160 F5
Elms The
  Colyford EX24 .... 103 A3
  Holsworthy EX22 ...... 164 C4
  Plymouth PL3 .... 248 A3
Elm Terr
  Honiton EX14 .... 166 D6
  [1] Plymouth PL3 ..... 248 F5
  Tiverton EX16 .... 161 B4
Elm Tree Cl PL8 .... 257 F4
Elm Tree Pk PL8 .... 136 A2
Elm Units EX2 .... 177 B2
Elm Villas EX24 .... 103 A3
Elm Way EX10 .... 101 A1
Elm Wlk TQ9 .... 223 F5
Elmwood Ave TQ12 ...... 206 E4
Elmwood Cl PL6 .... 245 D5
Elmwood Cres EX7 ...... 204 E7
Elmwood Gdns EX14 ..... 166 B3
Elmwood Pk TQ7 .... 143 E7
Elphinstone Rd PL2 .... 248 C7
Elsdale Rd EX4 .... 226 A4
Elsdon Cl EX11 .... 168 E4
Elsdon La EX11 .... 168 E4
Elsdon Rd EX11 .... 168 E4
Elspeth Sitters Ho [10]
  PL4 .... 263 A2

Elston Cross
  Churchstow TQ7 .... 143 D4
  Copplestone EX17 ..... 79 C6
ELSTONE 44 D3
Elstone Cross EX18 ..... 44 C3
Elston La EX17 .... 79 B5
Elston Mdw EX17 .... 165 A5
Elton Rd EX4 .... 177 E8
Elvestone EX9 .... 198 B1
Elvis Rd EX8 .... 202 D7
ELWELL 18 C2
Elwell Cross EX32 ..... 18 B2
Elwell Rd PL12 .... 243 A2
Elwick Gdns PL3 .... 249 B5
Elworthy Cross EX16 ... 47 C2
Elworthy Dr TA21 ...... 160 D4
Elworthy Hill EX16 .... 47 D2
Elwyn Rd EX8 .... 202 C6
Ely Cl
  Exeter EX4 .... 176 D6
  Feniton EX14 .... 84 D2
Elysian Ct EX36 .... 158 D5
Elysian Fields EX10 ... 188 B5
Embankment La PL4 ..... 249 B2
Embankment Rd
  Kingsbridge TQ7 ...... 258 D3
  Plymouth PL4 .... 249 B2
Embankment Road Lane N
  PL4 .... 249 B2
Embercombe Cross EX32. 18 F1
Ember Rd TQ8 .... 259 C5
Embleford Cres TQ13 .. 111 F5
Emblett Dr TQ12 .... 206 E4
Emblett Hill View TQ12. 206 F1
Embridge Cross TQ6 ... 145 F7
Embridge Hill TQ6 .... 146 A1
Embury Cl TQ12 .... 213 A4
Emily Gdns PL4 .... 263 B4
Emmanuel Cl [1] EX4 .. 177 A5
Emmanuel Rd [2] EX4 .. 177 A5
Emma Pl PL1 .... 248 A1
Emma Place Ope PL1 ... 248 A1
Emmasfield EX9 .... 202 D7
Emmetts Pk [1] TQ13 .. 131 A5
EMPACOMBE 253 D6
Emperor Way EX1 ...... 178 E7
Empire Ct [2] TQ1 .... 220 A7
Empire Rd TQ1 .... 220 A7
Empsons Cl EX7 .... 204 C6
Empsons Hill EX7 ..... 204 C6
Endeavour Ct PL1 ..... 248 A3
Endfield Cl EX1 ...... 178 B6
Endsleigh Ct EX5 ..... 179 B7
Endsleigh Dr PL15, PL19. 115 D5
Endsleigh Gdns [8] PL9. 115 F5
Endsleigh Gdns [2] PL4. 263 A4
Endsleigh Park Rd PL3. 248 D6
Endsleigh Pl PL4 ..... 263 A4
Endsleigh Rd PL9 ..... 255 C7
Endsleigh View PL21 .. 237 A3
Energlc Terr EX15 .... 163 C4
Ensign Ct EX39 .... 156 E7
Ensis Cross EX31 ..... 27 D5
Entrance Cross EX37 .. 44 B7
Epping Cres PL6 ...... 249 D7
Epworth Terr [4] PL2 . 247 F5
Erica Dr TQ2 .... 213 F3
Eric Rd
  Calstock PL18 .... 125 E3
  Plymouth PL4 .... 263 C3
Erith Ave PL2 .... 248 A7
Erle Gdns PL7 .... 250 F3
Erlstoke Cl PL6 ...... 245 D1
Erme Bridge Wks PL21. 237 C4
Erme Ct PL21 .... 237 D5
Erme Dr PL21 .... 237 D5
Erme Gdns PL3 .... 249 C5
Erme Pk PL21 .... 136 F3
Erme Prim Sch The
  PL21 .... 237 D5
Erme Rd PL21 .... 237 D5
Ermeside Cotts PL21 .. 136 F4
Erme Terr PL21 .... 237 D5
ERMINGTON 136 F4
Ermington Prim Sch
  PL21 .... 136 F4
Ermington Terr PL4 ... 248 E4
Ermington Workshops
  PL21 .... 137 A4
Ernborough Ct EX2 .... 261 C2
ERNESETTLE 243 E3
Ernesettle Com Sch PL5. 243 E3
Ernesettle Cres PL5 .. 243 E3
Ernesettle Gn PL5 .... 243 E4
Ernesettle La PL5 .... 243 D4
Ernesettle Rd PL5 .... 243 E3
Ernsborough Gdns EX14. 166 B5
Ernol Fer Pk PL7 ..... 250 C5
Escot Cotts PL21 ..... 184 B2
Escot ★ EX11 .... 84 C1
Escot Pl EX38 .... 159 C6
Esmonde Gdns PL5 ..... 247 B8
Esplanade
  Exmouth EX8 .... 202 A5
  Seaton EX12 .... 192 B4
  Teignmouth TQ14 ..... 210 C4
Esplanade Rd TQ4 ..... 226 C6

Esplanade The
  Dartmouth TQ6 .... 233 F5
  Plymouth PL1 .... 262 C1
Sidmouth EX10 .... 188 B3
Woolacombe EX34 ...... 7 F7
Essa Rd PL12 .... 242 F2
Essex Cl EX4 .... 176 E4
Essex St PL1 .... 262 B4
Essington Cl EX8 ..... 196 B3
Essington Ct EX20 .... 77 C4
Essington La EX20 .... 77 D4
Essington Rd EX20 .... 77 C4
Esso Wharf Rd PL4 .... 263 C1
ESTOVER 245 E4
Estover Cl PL6 .... 245 F5
Estover Com Coll PL6 . 245 D2
Estover Ind Est PL6 .. 245 E4
Estover Prim Sch PL6 . 245 D2
Estover Rd PL6 .... 245 F4
Estuary View
  Budleigh Salterton EX9. 198 B1
  Northam EX39 .... 157 A8
  Yelland EX31 .... 15 C2
Esworthy Cross EX16 .. 32 F1
Ethelston's Cl DT7 ... 260 A5
Ethelwynne Brown Cl
  EX39 .... 157 B2
Eton Ave PL1 .... 262 C4
Eton Cl EX39 .... 156 F3
Etonhurst Cl EX2 ..... 178 D3
Eton Pl PL1 .... 262 C4
Eton St PL1 .... 262 C4
Eton Terr [3] PL1 .... 262 B3
Eton Wlk EX4 .... 176 E4
Eugene Rd TQ3 .... 226 C8
Eureka Terr
  Bovey Tracey TQ13 ... 180 D8
  [1] Honiton EX14 .... 166 C5
Europa Pk EX34 .... 8 B6
Evans Cl PL1 .... 262 A3
Evans Pl PL2 .... 248 A5
Evenlgh Cl [2] TQ5 .. 230 C3
Eveleigh Cl EX4 ..... 261 B4
Eveleighs Ct EX4 .... 261 B4
Evelyn Pl PL4 .... 263 A4
Evelyn St PL5 .... 243 D1
Evenden Ct PL11 .... 247 A3
Eventide Homes TQ5 .. 230 C2
Everest Dr EX2 ..... 192 A7
Everest Cl EX16 .... 161 E6
Everett Pl EX16 .... 161 E6
Evergreen Cl EX8 ... 196 D3
Evett Cl EX8 .... 202 E8
Evran Dr EX8 .... 196 E3
Ewings Sq EX2 ...... 261 A2
Ewin's Ash EX14 .... 85 C8
EWORTHY 91 E6
Eworthy Cross EX21 . 91 E6
EXBOURNE 76 C4
Exbourne CE Prim Sch
  EX20 .... 76 C4
Exbourne Cross EX20 . 76 C4
Excalibur Cl EX4 .... 174 A1
Excelsior Mews [2] TQ1 220 B7
Exchange St PL4 ..... 263 A2
EXEBRIDGE 33 F3
Exebridge Ind Est TA22. 33 F3
Exe Bridge Retail Ctr
  EX4 .... 261 A1
Exe Cl EX31 .... 15 E5
Execliff EX8 .... 202 A5
Exe Dene EX3 .... 182 E5
Exe Gdns PL3 .... 249 C7
Exe Hill TQ2 .... 219 B8
Exe St
  Exeter EX4 .... 261 A3
  Topsham EX3 .... 182 F5
Exe Vale Rd EX2 .... 178 C3
EXETER 261 B4
Exeter Acad The EX4. 173 D1
Exeter Airport EX5 .. 99 A4
Exeter Arprt Bsns Pk
  EX5 .... 99 A4
Exeter Arena Athletics
  Stadium EX4 .... 174 B1
Exeter Bsns Ctr EX2 . 177 C2
Exeter Cath (Church of St
  Peter) ★ EX1 ...... 261 B3
Exeter Cathedral Sch
  EX1 .... 261 B3
Exeter Central Sta EX4 261 A4
Exeter Cl
  Feniton EX14 .... 84 D2
  Plymouth PL5 .... 243 D4
Exeter Coll EX4 ..... 261 A3
Exeter Cross
  Coldeast TQ12 ...... 123 A1
  Sidmouth EX10 ...... 188 B6
Exeter Foyer EX2 ... 261 A2
Exeter Gate EX36 .. 158 C3
Exeter Hill
  Cullompton EX15 ... 163 B2
  Kenton EX6 .... 194 D3
  Shobrooke EX17 .... 80 F5
  Tiverton EX16 ..... 161 E2
Exeter Hill Cross EX17. 80 F4
Exeter Phoenix EX1 . 261 B3
Exeter
  Racecourse ★
  EX6 .... 114 C2
Exeter Rd
  Braunton EX33 ...... 152 E4
  Chudleigh TQ13 ..... 123 F7
  Crediton EX17 ...... 165 D4
  Cullompton EX15 .... 163 B2
  Dawlish EX7 .... 204 D6
  Exmouth EX8 .... 196 A3
  Exmouth EX8 .... 202 A7
  Honiton EX14 .... 166 A5
  Ivybridge PL21 ..... 237 E5

Exeter Rd continued
  Kennford EX6 .... 181 A2
  Kingsteignton TQ12 .. 207 D8
  Newton Abbot TQ12 .. 207 B5
  Newton Poppleford EX10. 186 C8
  Okehampton EX20 .... 170 D5
  Ottery St Mary EX11 . 169 A3
  Rockwell Green TA21 . 160 B5
  Silverton EX5 ...... 82 B5
  South Brent TQ10 ... 135 A3
  Teignmouth TQ14 .... 210 B6
  Tiverton EX16 ...... 64 B4
  Topsham EX2, EX3 ... 182 D6
  West Hill EX11 ..... 168 E7
  Whiddon Down EX20 .. 95 F3
  Whimple EX5 .... 168 B8
  Winkleigh EX19 ..... 58 F2
Exeter Road Bsns Pk [8]
  TQ12 .... 123 E1
Exeter Road Com Prim Sch
  EX8 .... 202 A7
Exeter Road Ind Est
  EX20 .... 170 E6
Exeter Royal Acad for Deaf
  Education EX2 ...... 261 C1
Exeter St David's Sta
  EX4 .... 177 A7
Exeter St
  North Tawton EX20 .. 77 C4
  Plymouth, Barbican PL4. 263 B2
  Plymouth, St Jude's PL4. 263 B2
  Teignmouth TQ14 .... 210 B5
Exeter's Underground
  Passage Mus ★ EX4 . 261 B3
Exeter Trad Cir EX2 . 181 C8
Exe Units EX2 .... 177 D1
Exe Vale EX2 .... 178 C3
Exe Vale Terr [6] EX16. 161 C3
Exe Valley Fishery ★ TA22. 33 F3
Exe Valley L Ctr EX16. 161 C5
Exe View EX6 .... 182 A4
Exe View Cotts EX4 .. 176 F8
Exe View Rd EX8 .... 196 C6
Exhibition Rd EX17 .. 165 E6
Exhibition Way EX17 . 178 D8
EXMINSTER 182 C4
Exminster Hill EX6 . 182 B2
Exminster Marshes (RSPB
  Reserve) ★ EX6 ... 182 A1
Exminster Prim Sch EX6 182 A4
Exmoor Cl EX16 ..... 161 E6
Exmoor Gdns TA22 ... 33 D6
Exmoor National Park Visitor
  Ctr ★ EX35 .... 151 C6
Exmoor View EX36 ... 158 C5
Exmoor Zoo ★ EX31 .. 11 B3
EXMOUTH 202 B7
Exmouth Archery Club
  EX8 .... 197 B4
Exmouth Com Coll EX8. 202 A6
Exmouth Ct
  Exmouth EX8 .... 202 B6
  Plymouth PL1 .... 247 F3
Exmouth Hospl EX8 .. 202 B7
Exmouth Model Rly ★
  EX8 .... 203 B5
  Exmouth EX8 .... 202 A7
Exmouth Mus ★ EX8 . 202 A7
Exmouth Nature Reserve★
  EX8 .... 195 E2
Exmouth Rd
  Budleigh Salterton EX9. 197 E1
  Clyst St Mary EX5 .. 179 A1
  Exton EX3 .... 183 C3
  Lympstone EX8 ...... 195 F7
  Newton Poppleford EX10. 186 D5
  Plymouth PL1 .... 247 F3
Exmouth Sports Ctr EX8. 201 F7
Exmouth Sta EX8 .... 201 F7
Exmouth Tennis & L Ctr
  EX8 .... 202 B8
Exonia Pk EX2 ...... 176 D3
Explorer Ct PL2 .... 248 B5
Explorer Wlk TQ2 ... 213 F3
EXTON 183 D2
Exton La EX3 .... 183 C3
Exton Rd EX2 .... 177 C3
Exton Sta EX3 ...... 183 C1
EXWICK 176 E7
Exwick Ct EX4 ...... 176 F8
Exwick Heights Prim Sch
  EX4 .... 176 E7
Exwick Hill EX4 .... 176 F8
Exwick Ho EX4 ...... 176 F8
Exwick La EX4 ...... 176 D7
Exwick Rd EX4 ...... 176 F7
Exwick Villas EX4 .. 176 F7
Eyewell Gdn EX12 ... 192 A6
Eymore Dr EX11 ..... 168 C3
Eyrecourt Rd EX12 .. 192 A4

F

Factory Cotts TQ9 ... 139 C7
Factory Cross TQ13 . 110 F6
Factory La TA20 ..... 88 D8
Factory Ope [1] EX39. 15 A1
Factory Row
  South Molton EX36 .. 158 E4
  Torquay TQ2 .... 220 A5
Fairacre Ave EX32 .. 155 C2
Fairby Cl EX16 ..... 161 D6
Fairfax Gdns EX2 ... 177 B2
Fairfax Pl TQ6 ..... 233 F3
Fairfax Rd
  Cullompton EX15 ... 163 C4
  Heathfield TQ12 ... 180 F3

Fairfax Terr 5 PL2 . . . . . 247 F4
Fairfax Way EX38 . . . . . 159 F5
Fairfield
Bratton Fleming EX31 . . . . . 18 A8
Ilfracombe EX34 . . . . . 150 C5
Plymouth PL7 . . . . . 250 E7
Sampford Peverell EX16 . . . 50 D1
South Brent TQ10 . . . . . 135 A2
Fairfield Ave
Exeter EX4 . . . . . 178 C8
Plymouth PL2 . . . . . 248 C7
Fairfield Cl
Axminster EX13 . . . . . 167 D5
Bovey Tracey TQ13 . . . . 180 C7
Exmouth EX8 . . . . . 202 B6
Kingsbridge TQ7 . . . . . 258 D4
Fairfield Gdns EX14 . . . . 166 C5
Fairfield Gn TA3 . . . . . 68 D7
Fairfield Pk DT7 . . . . . 260 E4
Fairfield Rd
Crediton EX17 . . . . . 165 C6
Exeter EX2 . . . . . 181 B8
Exmouth EX8 . . . . . 202 B5
Kingskerswell TQ12 . . . . 213 A3
Torquay TQ2 . . . . . 219 F8
Fairfield Terr
Exeter EX2 . . . . . 177 A4
Newton Abbot TQ12 . . . . 207 C3
Fairfield Way TQ7 . . . . 145 A1
Fairhazel Dr EX4 . . . . . 176 F7
Fairholme Rd EX34 . . . . . 7 F6
Fair Isle Cl TQ2 . . . . . 213 E2
Fairlands Ave EX6 . . . . . 113 B3
Fairlawn Ct EX10 . . . . . 188 B5
Fairlawns Pk TQ4 . . . . . 226 B2
Fairlea TQ5 . . . . . 230 C6
Fairlea Cl EX7 . . . . . 200 F1
Fairlea Cres EX39 . . . . 156 F6
Fairlea Ct EX9 . . . . . 197 E1
Fairlea Gdns EX39 . . . . 156 F6
Fairlea Rd EX7 . . . . . 200 F1
Fairleigh EX10 . . . . . 186 E8
Fairlinch Cross EX33 . . . 152 B8
Fairlynch Cl EX33 . . . . . 152 B7
Fairlynch Gr EX33 . . . . 152 C7
Fairlynch La EX33 . . . . 152 B7
Fairlynch Mus* EX9 . . . 199 H2
Fairmead EX10 . . . . . 187 F8
Fairmead Ct TQ2 . . . . . 213 F2
Fairmead Mews PL12 . . . 242 C3
Fairmead Rd PL12 . . . . 242 C2
FAIRMILE 169 A7
Fair Oak Rd EX5 . . . . . 99 A4
Fair Oaks TQ14 . . . . . 210 A6
Fairpark Cl EX2 . . . . . 261 C2
Fairpark Rd EX2 . . . . . 261 B2
Fairplace Terr EX20 . . . 170 B5
Fairseat Cl TQ9 . . . . . 223 D4
Fair View
Barnstaple EX31 . . . . . 154 E6
Bradworthy EX22 . . . . . 53 E8
Colyford EX24 . . . . . 103 A3
Fairview Ave
Clyst St Mary EX5 . . . . 179 D2
Plymouth PL3 . . . . . 249 D5
Fair View La EX24 . . . . 103 A3
Fairview Pk TQ13 . . . . 180 C5
Fairview Rd TQ12 . . . . 211 A7
Fair View
Dartmouth TQ6 . . . . . 233 E3
Honiton EX14 . . . . . 166 C5
Fairview Terr EX1 . . . . 174 F1
Fairview Way PL3 . . . . 249 E5
Fairwater Cl TQ12 . . . . 207 F7
Fairwaters TQ12 . . . . . 207 E8
Fairway
Appledore EX39 . . . . . 14 F1
Saltash PL12 . . . . . 242 C2
Tiverton EX16 . . . . . 64 E8
Fairway PL21 . . . . . 237 B5
Fairway Cl
Braunton EX33 . . . . . 152 B6
Churston Ferrers TQ5 . . . 229 D5
Fairways Cl EX37 . . . . . 43 B6
Fairways Dr EX37 . . . . . 43 A6
Fairways The EX39 . . . 156 D7
Fairways View EX37 . . . 43 C6
Fairway The
Braunton EX33 . . . . . 152 B6
Exeter EX4 . . . . . 173 E1
Newton Ferrers PL8 . . . 140 F7
FAIRY CROSS 25 A3
Fairy La TQ11 . . . . . 236 A4
Falcon Cl EX36 . . . . . 158 C4
Falcon Pk TQ4 . . . . . 224 F5
Falcon Rd EX2 . . . . . 178 E4
Falcon Units TQ12 . . . . 207 A3
Falcon Way 7 EX16 . . . 161 E6
FALKEDON 96 A6
Falkedon Cross EX17 . . 96 A6
Falkland Cl EX4 . . . . . 173 E2
Falkland Dr TQ12 . . . . 207 F8
Falkland Rd TQ2 . . . . . 219 F5
Falkland Way TQ14 . . . 210 A6
Fallapit Turn TQ9 . . . . 144 C8
Fallowfield EX12 . . . . . 214 A2
Fallowfield Cl TQ12 . . . 207 F3
Fallowfields TQ9 . . . . . 223 A5
Fallow Fields EX2 . . . . 155 C2
Falmouth Cl TQ2 . . . . . 213 B8
Fancy Cross PL21 . . . . 137 A2
Fanny's Cross EX36 . . . . 46 E7
Fanny's La EX17 . . . . . 62 B5
Fannys Lane Cross EX17 . 80 B5
Fanshawe Way PL9 . . . 255 C6
Faraday La EX16 . . . . . 177 E6
Faraday Mill Bsns Pk
PL4 . . . . . 249 B1

Faraday Rd PL4 . . . . . 249 B1
Faringdon Rd PL4 . . . . 249 B3
Farleigh TQ12 . . . . . 206 B5
Farleigh Back Rd EX16 . . 63 C2
Farleigh Cross TQ9 . . . 139 A4
Farleigh Front Rd EX16 . 63 C2
Farleigh Mdws EX16 . . 161 A6
Farley Hill TQ13 . . . . . 123 D8
Farley La EX35 . . . . . 5 E3
Farley's Grave EX20 . . . 77 E7
Farm Cl
Exeter EX2 . . . . . 178 C4
Kingskerswell TQ12 . . . 212 F6
Plymouth PL7 . . . . . 250 C7
Farmer Frank's La EX19 . 58 F7
Farm Hill EX4 . . . . . 176 E8
Farmhouse Ave EX1 . . . 178 F8
Farm House Rise EX6 . . 181 F4
Farm La
Plymouth PL5 . . . . . 244 B2
Saltash PL12 . . . . . 242 D1
Farm Rd
Bideford EX39 . . . . . 25 D4
Rousdon DT7 . . . . . 193 E6
Farm The EX5 . . . . . 99 D8
Farm Way EX14 . . . . . 84 D2
Farmyard La TQ3 . . . . 218 E6
Farnham Ho 8 DT7 . . . 260 D3
Farnham Terr 6 TQ3 . . 226 B7
Farnley Cl PL6 . . . . . 245 B6
Farpark Hill La EX31 . . . 9 A1
Farrant Ct EX10 . . . . . 188 A6
Farrant's Hill EX6 . . . . 113 B8
Farriers Cotts PL7 . . . . 250 E7
Farriers The PL19 . . . . 116 E4
FARRINGDON 99 B1
Farringdon Cross
Chilton EX17 . . . . . 80 E7
Exeter EX5 . . . . . 99 A1
Farringdon Ct EX5 . . . . 99 B2
Farringdon Hill EX17 . . . 80 E7
Farringdon Rd EX5 . . . . 99 B2
Farthing Cross TQ3 . . . 218 C3
Farthing Down TA21 . . . 51 F7
Farthing Lake EX32 . . . 29 A7
Farthingland Cross EX20 . 76 B5
Farthings La EX10 . . . . 186 E7
Farthings Lodge Bsns Ctr
EX15 . . . . . 83 F6
Farthing's Pitts TA21 . . . 160 C4
Far View Rd EX20 . . . . 170 C5
FARWAY 102 A6
Farway CE Prim Sch
EX24 . . . . . 101 F7
Farway Common Rd EX14,
EX24 . . . . . 101 E7
Farwell Rd TQ9 . . . . . 223 B6
Farwood Cross EX24 . . 102 C6
Fatacott Cross EX39 . . . 22 F5
Fatherford Rd EX20 . . . 170 D5
Faulkner Cl PL21 . . . . 233 C3
Fawns Cl PL21 . . . . . 136 F4
Fay Rd EX7 . . . . . 204 E6
Fayre View PL12 . . . . 242 B1
Fearnside Way PL12 . . . 242 C3
Featherbed La
Clayhanger EX16 . . . . 35 C1
Exmouth EX8 . . . . . 196 B2
Monkton EX14 . . . . . 86 D6
Offwell EX14 . . . . . 86 B2
Featherstone Rd EX8 . . 196 A2
Federation Rd PL3 . . . 249 C4
Fegen Rd PL5 . . . . . 243 B1
Felixwell Ct EX4 . . . . 176 F5
Fell Cl PL8 . . . . . 141 B8
Fellowes Ct 7 PL1 . . . 262 A3
Fellowes Pl PL1 . . . . 248 A2
Feltrim Ave EX2 . . . . 261 C1
FENITON 84 E2
Feniton CE Prim Sch
EX14 . . . . . 84 E2
Feniton Gdns EX14 . . . 84 D2
Feniton Sta EX14 . . . . 84 D2
Fenten Pk PL12 . . . . 242 F3
Feoffe Cotts EX31 . . . 154 F7
Feoffee Cotts TQ7 . . . 258 A4
Ferguson Cl EX11 . . . 169 B3
Fernbank Ave PL21 . . 237 A6
Fern Cl
Brixham TQ5 . . . . . 230 D4
Okehampton EX20 . . . 170 C5
Plymouth PL7 . . . . . 251 C5
Ferncombe Cl 3 TQ12 . 123 F1
Ferncombe Dr 2 TQ12 . 123 F1
Ferndale Cl TQ12 . . . . 233 E3
Ferndale Ave PL2 . . . . 247 E7
Ferndale Cl
8 Honiton EX14 . . . . 85 C2
Ilfracombe EX34 . . . . 150 D8
Ferndale Gdns EX2 . . . 177 A4
Ferndale Mews EX2 . . . 219 B7
Ferndale Rd
Exeter EX2 . . . . . 177 A4
Plymouth PL2 . . . . . 247 F7
Teignmouth TQ14 . . . 210 B6
Torquay TQ2 . . . . . 219 B7
Ferndown Cl EX39 . . . 156 E2
Ferndown Rd DT7 . . . . 260 E3
Ferne Animal Sanctuary*
TA20 . . . . . 69 D5
Fernery The 6 EX34 . . 150 D5
Fernhill Cl PL21 . . . . 237 B5
Fernhill Cross TQ7 . . . 143 E8
Fernhill Hts DT6 . . . . 104 F4
Fernicombe Rd TQ3 . . 225 E7
Fernleigh Cl EX20 . . . . 77 C4
Fernleigh Rd PL3 . . . . 248 F5

Fernleigh Terr PL18 . . . 125 B5
Fern Mdw
Okehampton EX20 . . . 170 C6
Tavistock PL19 . . . . . 171 D6
Fernpark Cl EX2 . . . . 177 E2
Fern Pk EX34 . . . . . 150 B5
Fern Rd TQ12 . . . . . 207 F1
Fern Way EX34 . . . . . 150 B4
Fernworthy Cl
Copplestone EX17 . . . . 79 B5
Torquay TQ2 . . . . . 219 A7
Fernworthy Forest Trail*
TQ13 . . . . . 110 D2
Fernworthy Gdns EX17 . 79 B5
Fernworthy Pk EX17 . . . 79 B5
Ferrers Gn TQ5 . . . . . 229 E4
Ferrers Rd PL5 . . . . . 243 E1
Ferry La PL11 . . . . . 246 D5
Ferryman's Reach TQ14 . 210 B3
Ferry Rd
Plymouth PL1 . . . . . 247 E3
Topsham EX3 . . . . . 182 E5
Ferry Slip TQ6 . . . . . 233 F3
Ferry St PL11 . . . . . 247 C3
Feversham Cl PL7 . . . . 251 B6
Field Cl
Braunton EX33 . . . . . 152 C5
Paignton TQ3 . . . . . 219 B2
Field End
Axminster EX13 . . . . 167 E5
Bideford EX39 . . . . . 156 E2
Field La
Ashford EX31 . . . . . 16 B6
Braunton EX33 . . . . . 152 C5
FILHAM 237 F4
Filham Ind Est PL21 . . . 237 F5
Filham Moor Cl PL21 . . 237 E4
Fillablack Way EX39 . . 157 C2
Fillace La PL19 . . . . . 126 F4
Fillace Pk PL20 . . . . . 126 F4
FILLEIGH 29 C7
Filleigh Com Prim Sch
EX32 . . . . . 29 C6
Filleigh Mill New Rd
EX32 . . . . . 29 D7
Filleigh Moor Cross EX17 . 60 D5
Filleighmoor Gate EX21 . 56 C2
Filmer Way EX21 . . . . 177 B3
Fincer Dr PL21 . . . . . 237 A6
Finch Cl PL3 . . . . . 249 D4
Finches Cl PL9 . . . . . 256 C7
Finch Foundary* EX20 . . 95 A5
Findon Gdns PL6 . . . . 245 D4
Finewell St PL1 . . . . . 262 C2
Fingle Bridge* TQ13 . . 111 E8
Fingle Cl EX4 . . . . . 176 E8
Fingle Glen EX6 . . . . . 98 B4
Finnigan Rd PL4 . . . . 249 B1
Finnimore Ind Est EX11 . 169 C3
Firbank Rd EX7 . . . . . 200 F1
Fir Cl
Honiton EX14 . . . . . 166 B5
Willand EX15 . . . . . 162 D5
Fircroft Rd PL2 . . . . . 248 B7
Firebeacon Cross EX39 . 37 C7
Fire Beacon Cross
Bishop's Tawton EX31 . . 27 D7
Chittlehampton EX37 . . 29 B2
Fire Beacon Hill Nature
Reserve* EX10 . . . . 100 F1
Firebeacon La
Bolham EX16 . . . . . 49 C3
Chittlehampton EX37 . . 29 B2
Fire Beacon La EX10 . . 100 E1
Fire Brigade Hos EX4 . . 261 A4
Firestone Cross EX20 . . 95 C3
Fire Stone Cross EX20 . . 95 C4
Firestone La TQ12 . . . 212 A8
Firlands TQ14 . . . . . 210 B7
Firlands Rd TQ2 . . . . . 214 A2
Firleigh Rd 6 TQ12 . . . 123 E1
Firs Cross TQ9 . . . . . 144 C7
Firs Gr EX22 . . . . . 155 E5
Firs Pk EX2 . . . . . 176 C3
First Ave
Axminster EX13 . . . . 167 F7
Dawlish EX7 . . . . . 204 D5
Exeter, Countess Wear
EX2 . . . . . 182 D7
Exeter, Heavitree EX1 . . 177 F6
Plymouth, Billacombe PL9 . 255 F8
Plymouth, Stoke PL1 . . 248 A2
Teignmouth TQ14 . . . 210 A5
Torquay TQ1 . . . . . 220 A8
First Dr TQ14 . . . . . 210 B5
Firs The
4 Barnstaple EX32 . . . 155 B5
Kennford EX6 . . . . . 114 D4
Wilmington EX14 . . . . 86 D2
First Raleigh EX39 . . . 156 E3
First Sands EX7 . . . . 158 D4
Fir Tree Cross EX36 . . . 31 E8
Firtree Rise PL21 . . . . 237 D5
Firway Cross EX16 . . . 34 C3
Fir Wlk TQ2 . . . . . 219 C8
Fisgard Way PL1 . . . . 246 D3
Fishacre Cross TQ9 . . . 216 F6
Fishacre Cross TQ12 . . 216 F6
Fishchowter's La TQ9 . . 223 C4
Fishcombe Rd TQ5 . . . 230 B6
Fisher Rd
Newton Abbot TQ12 . . 207 B3
Plymouth PL2 . . . . . 248 A5
Fishers Hill TA21 . . . . 51 D7
Fishers Mead TQ12 . . 211 D2
Fisher St TQ4 . . . . . 226 B5
Fishers Way EX16 . . . . 65 A1
Fisherton Cross EX37 . . 28 C2

Fishingclose Cross EX20 . 76 F6
Fishleigh Cross EX20 . . . 75 C8
Fishleigh Rd EX31 . . . 158 B2
Fish Mkt PL4 . . . . . 263 B2
Fish Quay PL4 . . . . . 263 A2
Fistral Cl PL11 . . . . . 246 F4
Fitzford Cotts PL19 . . . 171 B4
Fitzroy Rd
Exeter EX1 . . . . . 178 E6
Plymouth PL1 . . . . . 248 A3
Fitzroy Terr 7 PL1 . . . . 248 A3
Five Acres TQ13 . . . . 180 C4
Five Barrow La EX13 . . 104 A4
Five Barrows Cross EX36 . 19 D7
Five Bridges EX15 . . . 163 C6
Five Bridges Rd EX15 . . 67 C7
Five Cross TQ12 . . . . 122 C1
Five Crosses
Modbury PL21 . . . . . 137 A2
Rackenford EX16 . . . . 47 C1
Five Crossway EX36 . . . 46 D8
Five Cross Way
Brayford EX32 . . . . . 18 F8
Plymtree EX15 . . . . . 83 E8
West Buckland TA21 . . . 52 F6
Five Cross Ways TA22 . . 32 F7
Five Elms Cross EX5 . . . 80 E1
Five Elms La EX5 . . . . 80 E1
Five Ho TA21 . . . . . 160 B8
Five Lane End EX38 . . . 159 A1
Five Lanes
Buckfastleigh TQ13 . . . 236 E7
Dawlish EX7 . . . . . 200 A3
Hennock TQ13 . . . . . 123 B7
4 Kingsteignton TQ12 . 123 E1
Marldon TQ3 . . . . . 218 E3
Five Lanes Cross EX22 . . 54 D8
Five Lanes Rd TQ3 . . . 218 D2
Five Mile Hill EX6 . . . . 98 C4
Five Mile Hill Cross EX6 . 98 C4
Five Oaks TQ11 . . . . . 130 C2
Five Oaks Cross
Brampford Speke EX5 . . 81 C1
Burrington EX37 . . . . 43 D4
Five Turnings EX37 . . . . 3 A4
Five Wyches Cross TQ13 . 180 B7
Flagstaff Rd TQ6 . . . . 233 F4
Flamborough Rd PL6 . . 245 A7
Flamborough Way PL6 . . 245 A6
Flamsteed Cres PL5 . . . 243 E1
Flavel Pl TQ6 . . . . . 233 F3
Flavel St TQ6 . . . . . 233 F3
Flaxmeadow La EX13 . . 167 E6
Flayes Almshouses 2
EX4 . . . . . 178 C8
Fleet St
Plymouth PL2 . . . . . 247 E6
Torquay TQ1, TQ2 . . . 220 B4
Fleet Walk Sh Ctr TQ2 . . 220 B4
Fleetwood Gdns PL6 . . 245 A7
Fleming Ave EX10 . . . 188 C8
Fleming Way EX2 . . . . 177 E4
Flemons Ct 6 TQ4 . . . 226 A5
Fletcher Cl TQ2 . . . . . 219 E7
Fletcher Cres PL9 . . . . 256 B6
Fletcher Ind Est EX39 . . 25 E4
Fletcher Way PL9 . . . . 256 A6
Flete 1 PL21 . . . . . 136 E2
Flete Ave TQ12 . . . . . 207 F2
Flete Cl TQ12 . . . . . 207 F2
Flete Rd PL21 . . . . . 136 E2
Fletemoor Rd PL5 . . . . 243 E1
Flete View Terr 10 PL21 . 137 C8
Flexapark EX34 . . . . . 3 A3
Flexton The EX11 . . . . 169 D4
Flightway EX14 . . . . . 67 B3
Flightway Bsns Pk EX14 . 67 B3
FLITTON BARTON 19 B1
Floaters Rd TQ6 . . . . 233 F4
Flood's La EX15 . . . . 163 B3
Flood's Way TQ9 . . . . 227 F8
Flora Cotts PL1 . . . . . 262 B2
Flora Ct PL1 . . . . . 262 B3
Flora St PL1 . . . . . 262 B3
Florence Cotts TQ7 . . . 145 D1
Florence Pl
Newton Abbot TQ12 . . 207 D1
Plymouth PL4 . . . . . 263 C3
Florence St PL5 . . . . . 243 D1
Florida Dr EX4 . . . . . 173 D2
Florida Gdns PL3 . . . . 249 C6
Florida Rd TQ2 . . . . . 220 C6
Flowerpot La EX4 . . . . 177 A5
Flowers Mdw 8 TQ12 . . 122 F1
Flower St EX5 . . . . . 184 C3
Flow La TQ14 . . . . . 208 F7
Floyd Cl PL2 . . . . . 247 F7
Floyers-Hay Ct EX2 . . . 261 A1
Floyte La EX6 . . . . . 98 B5
Fluder Cres TQ12 . . . . 213 B3
Fluder Hill TQ12 . . . . 213 B3
Fluder La TQ12 . . . . . 213 F5
Fluder Rise TQ12 . . . . 213 B3
FLUXTON 100 C3
Foldhay Cross EX17 . . . 78 A6
Foliot Ave PL2 . . . . . 248 A6
Foliot Rd PL2 . . . . . 248 A6
Follafield Pk TQ5 . . . . 230 B2
Follaton Bglws TQ9 . . . 223 A5
Follaton Gate TQ9 . . . 222 F5
Follett Rd
Tiverton EX16 . . . . . 64 D7
Topsham EX3 . . . . . 182 E5
Folly Farm Cl EX33 . . . 152 C6
FOLLY GATE 93 E8

Folly Gate Cross EX20 . . 93 F8
Folly Goyle Cross EX19 . . 43 B3
Folly Hill TQ7 . . . . . 142 E3
Folly La
Buckland St Mary TA20 . . 69 D8
South Molton EX36 . . . 30 C4
Poulall La TQ12 . . . . 207 E8
Footland La
Daccombe TQ12 . . . . 213 F5
Ipplepen TQ12 . . . . . 217 F5
Footland Rd TQ4 . . . . 226 A4
Footpark La EX6 . . . . . 96 D2
Forbes Cl TQ12 . . . . . 180 F2
Forcefield Rd EX15 . . . 163 B2
Forces Cross TQ9 . . . . 139 E3
Forches Ave EX32 . . . 155 C4
Forches Cnr EX17 . . . . 165 C6
Forches Cross
Burrington EX37 . . . . 43 F4
Crediton EX17 . . . . . 165 C6
Langtree EX38 . . . . . 40 F1
Newton Abbot TQ12 . . 206 F7
Forches Cross Prim Sch
EX32 . . . . . 155 C4
Forches Green Flats 4
EX32 . . . . . 155 B4
Forches Head EX5 . . . 175 F8
Forches Hill TQ12 . . . 209 B2
FORD
Bideford 25 B3
Chillington 149 A7
Holbeton 136 D1
Holcombe Rogus 50 F5
Plymouth 248 A5
Ford TQ6 . . . . . 233 E3
FORDA 93 B1
Fordbarn Cross TQ9 . . 222 E2
Ford Cl PL21 . . . . . 237 A5
Ford Cres EX22 . . . . . 53 E8
Ford Cross
Ash Mill EX36 . . . . . 31 D1
Chawleigh EX18 . . . . 59 E7
Chulmleigh EX18 . . . . 44 D2
Ford TQ7 . . . . . 149 A7
Hittisleigh EX6 . . . . . 96 D4
Ilminster EX31 . . . . . 10 D5
Molland EX36 . . . . . 31 F7
Monkton EX14 . . . . . 86 A5
Oakford EX16 . . . . . 48 D5
Shirwell EX31 . . . . . 17 C8
South Zeal EX20 . . . . 95 A4
Staverton TQ9 . . . . . 216 E5
Tedburn St Mary EX17 . . 97 D8
Ford Down La EX36 . . 158 A3
Forde Abbey & Gardens*
TA20 . . . . . 88 F8
Forde Cl
Abbotskerswell TQ12 . . 212 A7
Newton Abbot TQ12 . . 207 D3
Forde Cross EX17 . . . . 80 F8
Forde Gdns TQ12 . . . 207 D1
Forde La EX38 . . . . . 26 E2
Fordens La EX7 . . . . . 204 C3
Forde Pk TQ12 . . . . . 207 D2
FORDER
Cawsand 252 F1
Saltash 242 C1
Forder Cross
Bishopsteignton TQ14 . . 208 D8
Blackawton TQ9 . . . . 145 C8
Chagford EX20 . . . . . 110 D8
Ugborough PL21 . . . . 137 E7
Forder La
Bishopsteignton TQ14 . . 208 A8
Bovey Tracey TQ13 . . . 122 E7
Cawsand PL10 . . . . . 252 F1
Dartington TQ9 . . . . 222 E8
South Brent TQ10 . . . 135 B4
Forder Mdw TQ13 . . . 111 F5
Forder Valley Nature
Reserve* PL6 . . . . . 249 D8
Forder Valley Rd PL6 . . 249 D8
Ford Farm Ct EX6 . . . 194 D3
Ford Grange EX7 . . . . 204 A7
Ford Hill
Bow EX17 . . . . . 78 F4
Bishop Dinham EX6, EX17 . 97 C6
Hartland EX39 . . . . . 22 E3
Kentisbury EX31 . . . . 10 D5
Plymouth PL2 . . . . . 248 A5
Thorverton EX5 . . . . . 81 E6
Fordishaies La EX5, EX15 . 82 F8
Ford La
Clawton Fitzpaine EX16 . 63 B6
Clifton EX31 . . . . . 10 B5
West Hill EX11 . . . . 168 E3
Whitestone EX4 . . . . . 98 E4
Fordland Bottom Rd EX2,
EX6 . . . . . 176 B2
Fordlands Cross EX16 . . 156 F5
Fordlands Cres EX39 . . 156 E5
Fordlands Rd TQ13 . . . 111 F5
Ford Lane Cross EX6 . . 96 D4
Fordmill Cross EX16 . . . 34 D1
Fordmoor Cross EX16 . . 48 C8
Ford Moor Cross EX18 . . 59 E7
Ford Orch EX16 . . . . . 50 D2
FORD PARK 248 D4
Ford Park La PL4 . . . . 248 E4
Ford Park Rd PL4 . . . . 248 D4

282 For–Gar

Ford Pk
6 Chudleigh Knighton TQ13 ... **123** C4
Plymouth PL4 ... **248** E4
Ford Plain EX5 ... **81** E5
Ford Prim Sch PL2 ... **247** F5
Ford Rd
Abbotskerswell TQ12 ... **212** B7
Bampton EX16 ... **34** C1
Tiverton EX16 ... **64** D7
Totnes TQ9 ... **223** D6
Wembury PL9 ... **140** D8
Yealmpton PL8 ... **136** A2
Ford Rise EX39 ... **25** F4
Fords Rd EX2 ... **261** A1
Ford St
Moretonhampstead TQ13 ... **111** F5
Tavistock PL19 ... **171** B5
Wellington TA21 ... **160** F4
FORD STREET ... **52** D5
FORDTON ... **165** E3
Fordton Cross EX17 ... **165** E2
Fordton Ind Est EX17 ... **165** E3
Fordton Plain EX17 ... **165** E3
Fordton Terr EX17 ... **165** D3
Ford Valley TQ6 ... **233** E3
Fordworth Cotts TQ7 ... **149** D5
Foredown La TQ12 ... **212** E4
Foredown Rd TQ12 ... **211** E2
Foreland Ho EX34 ... **150** A4
Foreland View EX34 ... **150** B4
Fore St
Aveton Gifford TQ7 ... **143** C6
9 Bampton EX16 ... **34** B1
Beer EX12 ... **191** D5
Bere Alston PL20 ... **125** E1
Bere Ferrers PL20 ... **239** F3
Bishopsteignton TQ14 ... **208** F8
Bovey Tracey TQ13 ... **180** D7
Bradninch EX5 ... **82** F6
Bridestowe EX20 ... **107** F8
Brixham TQ5 ... **230** C5
Buckfastleigh TQ11 ... **236** C5
Budleigh Salterton EX9 ... **199** G2
Calstock PL18 ... **125** D3
Cargreen PL12 ... **239** A2
Chudleigh TQ13 ... **123** E6
11 Chulmleigh EX18 ... **44** E1
Cornwood PL21 ... **133** C2
Cullompton EX15 ... **163** C3
Culmstock EX15 ... **66** E8
Dartmouth TQ6 ... **234** A3
Dolton EX19 ... **57** F7
Dulverton TA22 ... **33** D6
Exbourne EX20 ... **76** C5
Exeter EX4 ... **261** A2
Exeter, Heavitree EX1 ... **177** F5
Exmouth EX8 ... **202** A6
Great Torrington EX38 ... **159** D5
Gunnislake, Albaston PL18 **125** C5
Gunnislake PL18 ... **125** D6
Harberton TQ9 ... **222** D2
Hartland EX39 ... **22** E3
7 Hemyock EX15 ... **67** B8
Holbeton PL8 ... **136** D1
Holcombe Rogus TA21 ... **50** F5
Holemoor EX22 ... **73** C8
Holsworthy EX22 ... **164** C4
Ide EX2 ... **176** E2
Ideford TQ13 ... **124** B4
Ilfracombe EX34 ... **150** C6
Ipplepen TQ12 ... **211** D2
Ivybridge PL21 ... **237** D5
Kentisbeare EX15 ... **66** A3
Kenton EX6 ... **194** D3
Kingsand PL10 ... **253** A2
Kingsbridge TQ7 ... **258** C6
Kingskerswell TQ12 ... **213** A4
Kingsteignton TQ12 ... **207** E7
Langtree EX38 ... **40** E2
Lifton PL16 ... **105** E4
Loddiswell TQ7 ... **143** E7
Luton TQ13 ... **124** C3
Millbrook PL10 ... **252** E5
Milton Abbot PL19 ... **116** A6
Morchard Bishop EX17 ... **61** A2
Moretonhampstead TQ13 ... **111** F5
Northam EX39 ... **156** F6
North Molton EX36 ... **30** D8
North Tawton EX20 ... **77** B4
Okehampton EX20 ... **170** B5
Otterton EX9 ... **198** E7
Plymouth, Devonport PL1 ... **247** F2
Plymouth, Plympton PL7 ... **250** E4
Plymouth, Tamerton Foliot PL5 ... **244** B6
Salcombe TQ8 ... **259** E4
Saltash PL12 ... **242** F2
Seaton EX12 ... **192** B5
Shaldon TQ14 ... **210** A3
Shebbear EX22 ... **55** D1
Sidbury EX10 ... **101** B2
Sidmouth EX10 ... **188** B3
Silverton EX5 ... **82** B5
13 South Brent TQ10 ... **134** F3
South Tawton EX20 ... **95** B5
Tatworth TA20 ... **88** D8
19 Teignmouth TQ14 ... **210** B5
8 Teignmouth TQ14 ... **210** C4
Tiverton EX16 ... **161** D4
Topsham EX3 ... **182** F5
Torpoint PL11 ... **247** B3
Torquay, Barton TQ2 ... **214** A2
Totnes TQ9 ... **223** C5
Fore St *continued*
Uffculme EX15 ... **66** A7
Ugborough PL21 ... **137** D6
Wellington TA21 ... **160** D6
Winkleigh EX19 ... **58** F3
Witheridge EX16 ... **46** E1
Yealmpton PL8 ... **257** F4
Forest Ave PL2 ... **248** C7
Foresters Rd
Holsworthy EX22 ... **164** C5
Plymouth PL9 ... **255** D7
Forester's Terr TQ14 ... **210** B4
Forest Hill EX39 ... **25** F4
Forest Hos EX21 ... **73** B4
Forest Rd TQ1 ... **220** A7
Fore Street Ctr EX4 ... **261** A2
Fore Street Hill EX9 ... **199** H2
Fore Street Mews 15 EX4 ... **261** A2
Forest Ridge Rd TQ3 ... **218** F1
Forestry Hos PL20 ... **120** B4
Forest View PL6 ... **245** D7
Foretown EX15 ... **83** D3
Forge Cl EX9 ... **197** F2
Forge End EX19 ... **58** F2
Forge La
Butterleigh EX15 ... **64** D3
Saltash PL12 ... **242** C4
Forge Pl TQ13 ... **180** C7
Forges Hill EX15 ... **64** F3
Forge Way EX15 ... **163** C3
Forgeway Cl TQ2 ... **219** D4
Fork Cross TQ9 ... **222** A5
Forresters Dr PL6 ... **245** D7
Forrest Units EX2 ... **177** D1
Forster Rd TQ8 ... **259** D5
Forsythia Dr PL12 ... **242** C3
Fort Austin Ave PL6 ... **245** C1
FORTESCUE ... **188** D7
Fortescue Bglws EX34 ... **8** C6
Fortescue Cl EX33 ... **152** E5
FORTESCUE CROSS ... **44** C4
Fortescue Cross EX5 ... **81** E2
Fortescue Pl PL3 ... **249** A6
Fortescue Rd
Barnstaple EX32 ... **155** B2
Exeter EX2 ... **177** B3
Ilfracombe EX34 ... **150** B6
Paignton TQ3 ... **219** C1
Salcombe TQ8 ... **259** C4
Sidmouth EX10 ... **188** D7
Fortescue Terr PL19 ... **171** A6
Fortfield EX12 ... **192** B5
Fortfield Terr EX10 ... **188** A3
Forth Gdns PL3 ... **249** D6
Fort Hill Dr EX32 ... **155** B5
Fortmead Cl EX32 ... **155** A5
Forton Rd EX8 ... **196** C1
Fort Picklecombe PL10 ... **253** F4
Fort St EX32 ... **155** A5
Fort Terr
13 Barnstaple EX32 ... **155** A5
5 Bideford EX39 ... **157** B1
Plymouth PL6 ... **244** F3
Fort The PL10 ... **253** A1
Fortune Way TQ1 ... **220** B7
Forward Gn EX5 ... **82** E7
Fosbrooke Ct 10 PL3 ... **248** F6
Fosketh Hill EX39 ... **156** C6
Fosketh Terr EX39 ... **156** C6
FOSS ... **253** A5
Fosse Rd TQ7 ... **258** D6
Fosseway Cl EX13 ... **167** D5
Fosse Way Ct 2 EX12 ... **192** B4
Foss Slip TQ6 ... **233** F3
Foss St TQ6 ... **233** F3
Fosterlea EX15 ... **163** B3
Fosters Mdw PL18 ... **125** A6
Foulston Ave PL5 ... **247** B8
Foundary Mews PL19 ... **171** D6
Foundry Ct 1 TQ13 ... **123** E6
Foundry La PL8 ... **140** F6
Fountain Ct TQ13 ... **180** D7
Fountain Fields EX37 ... **43** B7
Fountain Hill EX9 ... **203** F8
Fountain Ho TQ1 ... **220** C4
Fountains Cres PL2 ... **248** C8
Fouracre Cl EX4 ... **174** A1
Four Acres EX39 ... **156** D2
Four Acres Cl EX14 ... **86** B2
Fouracre Way TQ12 ... **207** F8
Four Cross
Axminster EX13 ... **167** B7
Ilsington TQ12 ... **122** C2
Kingston TQ7 ... **142** C7
Wilmington EX14 ... **86** C4
Four Cross Elms EX24 ... **103** A4
Fourcross Hill EX13 ... **167** B7
Four Cross Lanes TQ9 ... **228** A8
Four Cross Way EX32 ... **11** C1
Four Crossways EX18 ... **44** E1
Four Cross Ways
Cheriton Bishop EX6 ... **97** A4
North Tawton EX20 ... **77** D4
Willand EX15 ... **162** D5
Winkleigh EX19 ... **58** D2
Four Elms
Holcombe Rogus TA21 ... **51** A6
Sidmouth EX10 ... **187** C8
Four Elms Hill EX10 ... **187** B8
Four Firs EX5 ... **185** A1
Four Lanes EX15 ... **84** B8
Fourlanesend Com Prim Sch PL10 ... **252** F3
Four Mills La EX17 ... **165** D4
Four Oak EX32 ... **17** B2
Four Oak Cross EX32 ... **17** B2
Four Oaks Cl 1 EX32 ... **17** B2
Four Oaks Rd EX6 ... **97** F4
Four Seasons Village EX19 ... **58** E3
Fourth Ave TQ14 ... **210** A6
Fourview Cl TQ5 ... **230** E5
Four Ways Cotts EX18 ... **59** E4
Fourways Cross EX15 ... **67** C8
Four Ways Dr 3 EX18 ... **44** E1
Four White Gates Cross EX37 ... **29** B4
Fowelscombe Gate PL21 **137** F6
Fowey Ave TQ2 ... **219** B8
Fowey Cl EX1 ... **177** F7
Fowey Gdns PL3 ... **249** D6
Fowey Rd EX31 ... **15** E5
Fowler Cl EX6 ... **182** A4
Fowley Cross EX20 ... **93** D5
Foxbeare Rd EX34 ... **150** E5
Fox Cl
Okehampton EX20 ... **170** D6
Rockwell Green TA21 ... **160** A6
Foxdown Hill TA21 ... **160** C4
Foxdown Ho TA21 ... **160** C4
Foxdown Terr TA21 ... **160** D4
Foxes' Cross EX38 ... **26** E1
Foxes Lair EX20 ... **170** A6
Fox Field Cl PL3 ... **249** C5
Foxglove Chase EX15 ... **162** D5
Foxglove Cl
Barnstaple EX32 ... **155** E4
Dunkeswell EX14 ... **67** C1
Launceston PL15 ... **105** A2
9 Tiverton EX16 ... **161** F6
Foxglove Rd EX12 ... **192** B7
Foxglove Rise EX4 ... **176** D8
Foxglove Way PL12 ... **242** B3
FOXHAYES ... **176** F7
Foxhayes Rd EX4 ... **176** F6
Fox Hill EX39 ... **156** F6
Foxhole Hill EX6 ... **113** B4
Foxhole La EX39 ... **156** F6
Foxhole Rd
Paignton TQ3 ... **225** F7
Torquay TQ2 ... **219** D5
Foxholes Hill EX8 ... **202** D4
Foxhollows TQ12 ... **208** A2
Fox & Hounds Cross EX20 ... **108** A5
Foxlands Wlk TQ1 ... **220** C8
Foxley Cres TQ12 ... **206** F3
Fox Rd EX4 ... **174** B2
Fox's Cnr EX10 ... **187** F2
Fox's Cross EX17 ... **63** B1
Foxtor Cl PL5 ... **244** B3
Fox Tor Cl TQ4 ... **229** B7
Foxtor Rd EX4 ... **176** E8
Foxwell La TQ12 ... **207** A4
Foxwood Gdns
Plymouth, Plymstock PL9 ... **255** F5
Plymouth, Southway PL6 ... **244** E5
Foyle Cl PL7 ... **251** A5
Frances Homes EX1 ... **261** C3
Francis Cl EX4 ... **176** F4
Francis Court Cotts EX5 ... **82** D2
Francis Cres 4 EX16 ... **64** D7
Francis Ct
3 Crediton EX17 ... **165** C5
Exeter EX2 ... **177** E5
Francis Dr EX39 ... **156** C6
Francis St PL1 ... **262** A3
Francis Way EX24 ... **103** B3
Franeth Cl TQ12 ... **207** D8
Frankford La EX6 ... **97** F5
Frankfort Gate 9 PL1 ... **262** B3
Franklea Cl EX11 ... **169** D3
Franklin St EX2 ... **261** B2
Franklyn Ave EX33 ... **152** E6
Franklyn Cl EX2 ... **176** F3
Franklyn Dr EX2 ... **176** F3
Franklyn Hospl EX2 ... **176** F3
Franklyns' PL6 ... **245** A4
Franklyns Cl PL6 ... **245** A4
Frankmarsh Pk EX32 ... **155** B6
Frankmarsh Rd EX32 ... **155** B6
Frank Webber Rd TA21 ... **160** A5
Fraser Dr TQ14 ... **210** A6
Fraser Pl PL5 ... **244** C7
Fraser Rd
Exmouth EX8 ... **196** D2
Plymouth PL5 ... **244** C7
Fraser Sq PL5 ... **244** C7
Frederick Street E PL1 ... **262** B3
Frederick Street W 6 PL1 ... **262** B3
Frederick Terr 6 EX7 ... **204** D6
Fredington Gr PL2 ... **248** B6
Free Cotts EX4 ... **261** A3
Freedom Sq PL4 ... **263** B4
Freelands Cl EX8 ... **202** D8
Freemans Wharf PL1 ... **254** A8
Freestone Rd TQ12 ... **207** D8
Fremantle Gdns 4 PL2 ... **247** F4
Fremantle Pl PL2 ... **247** F4
FREMINGTON ... **153** E6
Fremington Com Prim Sch EX31 ... **153** D5
Fremington Nature Reserve* EX31 ... **153** E6
Fremington Quay EX31 ... **153** F7
Fremington Rd EX12 ... **191** F7
French Cl EX5 ... **82** B6
French St 7 TQ14 ... **210** C4
Frenchstone Cross EX36 ... **30** B2
Frensham Ave PL6 ... **245** C7
Frensham Gdns PL6 ... **245** C7
Freshford Cl PL6 ... **245** C1
Freshford Wlk PL6 ... **245** C1
Freshwater Dr TQ4 ... **229** B8
Frewin Gdns PL6 ... **245** B6
Frewins EX9 ... **197** F2
Friars' Gate EX2 ... **261** B2
FRIARS' GREEN ... **261** A2
Friar's Hele Cross EX20 ... **57** B2
Friars' La PL1 ... **263** A2
Friars Lodge EX2 ... **261** B2
Friars Wlk PL19 ... **171** E2
Friars' Wlk EX2 ... **261** B2
Friary Pk PL4 ... **263** B3
Friary St PL4 ... **263** B3
Friendship Ct PL19 ... **117** E6
Friernhay Ct EX4 ... **261** A2
Friernhay St EX4 ... **261** A2
FRITHELSTOCK ... **41** A6
FRITHELSTOCK STONE ... **40** F5
Frith Rd PL12 ... **242** D3
FRITTISCOMBE ... **145** B2
Fritz's Grave TQ11 ... **236** A7
Frobisher App PL5 ... **244** D2
Frobisher Cl TQ14 ... **210** A8
Frobisher Dr PL12 ... **242** E2
Frobisher Gn TQ2 ... **219** C6
Frobisher La TQ8 ... **259** C5
Frobisher Rd
Exmouth EX8 ... **196** C2
Newton Abbot TQ12 ... **207** F4
Frobisher Way
Paignton TQ4 ... **226** B2
Tavistock PL19 ... **171** B5
Torpoint PL11 ... **246** D3
Frogbury Cross EX17 ... **59** F1
Froggy Mill Cross EX6 ... **97** C5
Frog La
Braunton EX33 ... **152** D7
Clyst St Mary EX5 ... **179** A3
Holcombe Rogus TA21 ... **50** F5
FROGMORE ... **144** E1
Frogmore Ave PL6 ... **249** B7
Frogmore Cross EX5 ... **82** F3
Frogmore Ct PL6 ... **249** B7
Frogmore Farm TQ9 ... **139** F7
Frogmore Rd EX9 ... **198** C6
Frogmore Terr TQ7 ... **258** C4
Frogs La TA21 ... **52** F7
Frog St
Bampton EX16 ... **34** B1
Exeter EX1, EX2 ... **261** A2
Woolacombe EX34 ... **7** F6
Frogstreet Hill EX33 ... **8** A2
Frogwell Cross TA4 ... **34** D6
Frome Cl PL7 ... **251** A4
Frontfield Cres PL6 ... **244** E5
FROST ... **61** A1
Frost Cross
Bovey Tracey TQ13 ... **123** B6
Morchard Bishop EX17 ... **61** B1
Frost's Cnr EX19 ... **42** D1
Froude Ave TQ2 ... **214** B3
Froude Rd TQ8 ... **259** B2
Fry's La 5 EX10 ... **101** B1
Fry St EX22 ... **164** C4
Fuge Cross TQ6 ... **145** E6
Fuidge Cross EX17 ... **96** A5
Fuidge La EX17 ... **96** A5
Fulda Cres EX17 ... **165** D4
Fulford Cl
Bideford EX39 ... **157** D1
Tedburn St Mary EX6 ... **97** F4
Fulford Dr EX15 ... **163** B2
Fulford Rd
Cheriton Bishop EX6 ... **97** D1
Dunsford EX6 ... **112** F8
Exeter EX1 ... **177** F7
Fulford Way EX5 ... **184** C2
Fullaford Cross TQ11 ... **236** B4
Fullaford Hill EX31 ... **18** E8
Fullaford Pk TQ11 ... **236** A4
Fullaford Pool Cross TQ11 ... **236** A4
Fullers Ct 12 EX2 ... **261** A2
Fullerton Rd PL2 ... **248** A5
Fullingcott Cross EX39 ... **153** A2
Fulton Cl TQ12 ... **211** D2
Fulton Ho 2 EX12 ... **192** A5
Furland Cl PL9 ... **255** C5
FURLEY ... **87** D7
Furley Cross EX13 ... **87** D6
Furlong Cl TQ11 ... **236** B7
Furlong Cotts EX16 ... **51** A4
Furneaux Ave PL2 ... **248** B5
Furneaux Rd PL2 ... **248** B6
Furness Cl TQ4 ... **226** A2
Furrough Cross TQ1 ... **220** C8
Furrough Ct TQ1 ... **220** C8
Fursdon Cl PL9 ... **256** C6
Fursdon Cross
East Allington TQ7 ... **144** E4
Hittisleigh EX6 ... **96** C5
Fursdon House* EX5 ... **81** E7
Fursdon La EX6, EX17 ... **96** B5
Furse Pk PL5 ... **247** C7
Fursham Cross EX6 ... **96** B4
Furzeacre Cl PL7 ... **251** A7
Furzebeam Row EX38 ... **159** B5
Furzebeam Terr 14 EX39 **157** B1
Furzebrook EX11 ... **169** E4
Furze Cap 3 TQ12 ... **123** E1
Furze Cross
Bridgerule EX22 ... **71** A5
Chittlehampton EX37 ... **29** A5
Cornworthy TQ9 ... **227** A2
Kingsbridge TQ7 ... **144** D3
Furzedown Cross
Copplestone EX17 ... **79** A5
Taw Green EX20 ... **95** A6
Furzedown Rd TQ12 ... **213** A5
Furze Gdns
Shop EX23 ... **37** A1
Totnes TQ9 ... **223** F5
Furzegood TQ3 ... **218** D3
Furzeham Ct TQ5 ... **230** B5
Furzeham Pk TQ5 ... **230** B5
Furzeham Prim Sch TQ5 **230** C5
Furzehatt Ave PL9 ... **256** A6
Furzehatt Park Rd PL9 ... **256** A6
Furzehatt Rd PL9 ... **255** F6
Furzehatt Rise PL9 ... **256** A6
Furzehatt Villas PL9 ... **255** F6
Furzehatt Way PL9 ... **256** A6
Furzehill EX10 ... **101** B2
Furzehill Cross TQ9 ... **227** B3
Furzehill Rd
Heybrook Bay PL9 ... **140** A7
Plymouth PL4 ... **248** F4
Torquay TQ1 ... **220** A6
Furze Hill Rd EX34 ... **150** B4
Furze La 2 TQ5 ... **230** D5
Furzeland Hill EX17 ... **79** C6
Furzeleigh Cross TQ13 ... **122** F6
Furzeleigh La TQ13 ... **180** D8
Furzepark Cross
Bittaford PL21 ... **137** C7
Dolton EX19 ... **58** A5
Furzepark La
Hartland EX39 ... **22** E3
Kentisbury EX31 ... **10** E6
Furze Park Rd EX31 ... **18** A8
Furze Pk EX34 ... **2** F3
Furze Rd
Totnes TQ9 ... **223** F5
Woodbury EX5 ... **184** C3
FYLDON ... **19** D4
Fyldon Hill EX36 ... **19** D5

G

Gabber La PL9 ... **140** B8
Gable Pk TQ1 ... **220** C6
Gables Lea EX15 ... **162** C4
Gables Rd EX15 ... **162** C4
Gables The
Combe Martin EX34 ... **2** F4
Exmouth EX8 ... **202** D6
Rousdon DT7 ... **193** F7
Teignmouth TQ14 ... **210** A5
Wellington TA21 ... **160** C6
Gabriel Ct 11 EX2 ... **261** A2
Gabriels Wharf EX2 ... **177** C3
Gabwell Hill TQ1, TQ12 ... **214** C7
Gabwell La TQ12 ... **214** C7
Gaddacombe Cross EX20 . **91** D1
Gainsborough Cl TQ1 ... **220** E4
Gainsborough Dr EX39 ... **156** B6
Gainsborough Ho
Exeter EX1 ... **177** E6
Tavistock PL19 ... **171** B6
Gains Cross EX22 ... **53** C3
Gala Cross PL8 ... **257** F1
Galahad Cl EX4 ... **174** A1
Galbraith Rd EX20 ... **170** F6
Gale Rd TQ13 ... **131** B5
Gales Crest 3 TQ13 ... **123** C4
Galileo Cl PL7 ... **250** E6
Gallacher Way PL12 ... **242** B3
Galleon Way EX39 ... **156** E7
Gallery Cl 4 EX14 ... **166** B6
Galloping La EX39 ... **39** B8
Gallops The PL12 ... **242** D4
Galloway Dr TQ14 ... **124** E1
Gallows Cross TQ12 ... **207** C8
Gallows Gate TQ3 ... **218** F6
Gallows Park Cross TQ13 ... **131** B5
GALMPTON
Malborough ... **147** C7
Paignton ... **229** A6
Galmpton CE Prim Sch TQ5 ... **229** B5
Galmpton Cross TQ7 ... **147** D7
Galmpton Ct TQ5 ... **229** B5
Galmpton Farm Cl TQ5 ... **229** B5
Galmpton Glade TQ5 ... **229** B5
Galmpton Rise EX4 ... **173** E1
GALMPTON WARBOROUGH ... **229** B6
Galpin St PL21 ... **137** C2
Galsworthy Cl PL5 ... **244** C2
Galsworthy Sq EX4 ... **178** C8
Galva Rd
Hemerdon PL7 ... **251** C8
Sparkwell PL7 ... **132** E1
Gamberlake EX13 ... **167** C4
Gamberlake Cross EX13 . **167** C4
Gamblyn Cross TA4 ... **34** F5
GAMMATON ... **26** C4
GAMMATON MOOR ... **26** D3
Gammaton Moor Cross EX39 ... **26** D3
Gammaton Rd EX39 ... **26** B4
Gammons Hill EX13 ... **87** D1
Gammon Walk 23 EX31 ... **154** F5
Gandy St EX4 ... **261** A3
Ganges Rd PL2 ... **248** A5
Ganna Park Rd PL3 ... **248** D6
Gapemouth Cnr EX13 ... **87** C1
Gappah Cross TQ13 ... **123** E4
Gappah La TQ13 ... **123** E4
Gara Cl PL9 ... **256** B6
Gara Lodge TQ12 ... **212** F4
Gard Cl TQ2 ... **214** A3
Garden Cl
Braunton EX33 ... **152** B6
Exeter EX2 ... **178** C4

Garden Cl continued
Holbeton PL8 . . . . 142 A8
Plymouth PL7 . . . . 251 D5
Rattery TQ10 . . . . 135 D4
Garden Cotts TQ7 . . . . 258 C5
Garden Cres PL1 . . . . 262 B1
Garden Ct EX9 . . . . 198 A1
Garden House The★
PL20 . . . . 126 D3
Gardenia Dr EX16 . . . . 161 E7
Garden La PL19 . . . . 171 B5
Garden Mill Ind Est TQ7 258 D4
Garden Park Cl PL9 . . . . . . 256 C7
Garden Pk TQ10 . . . . 135 D4
Garden Rd TQ1 . . . . 220 B6
Garden Spot La TQ13 . . . . 123 F6
Garden St PL2 . . . . 247 E4
Gardens The
  Chudleigh TQ13 . . . . 123 E6
  Dulverton TA22 . . . . 33 D7
  Holemoor EX22 . . . . 73 B7
  Rousdon DT7 . . . . 193 E5
  Wellington TA21 . . . . 160 D5
Garden Terr
  Cullompton EX15 . . . . 163 C4
  Wellington TA21 . . . . 160 B7
Garden Village PL9 . . . . . 255 F8
Gardiner Cl EX5 . . . . 82 A1
Gards La PL5 . . . . 243 E2
Gareth Cres EX4 . . . . 173 F2
Garfield Pl ☑ TQ9 . . . . 223 C5
Garfield Rd TQ4 . . . . 226 C6
Garfield Terr PL1, PL3 . . . . 248 A3
Garland Cl EX4 . . . . 176 E8
Garland Cross EX37 . . . . . . 45 B5
GARLANDHAYES 52 F2
Garlandhayes La EX15 . . . . 52 E2
Garland's La EX16 . . . . 64 A5
Garlic Rea TQ5 . . . . 230 D5
Garliford La EX36 . . . . 30 F4
Garners Cl TQ12 . . . . 206 D1
Garners La TQ12 . . . . 206 D1
Garratt Cl EX8 . . . . 196 C3
Garratt Ct EX12 . . . . 192 B6
Garrett St PL10 . . . . 253 A1
Garrick Cl PL5 . . . . 244 C2
Garrison Cl PL1 . . . . 247 E1
Garrow Cl ☑ TQ5 . . . . 230 C3
Garston Ave TQ12 . . . . 207 B4
Garston Cl PL9 . . . . 256 A8
Garth Rd TQ2 . . . . 214 A2
Gascoyne Ct PL4 . . . . 263 A3
Gascoyne Pl PL4 . . . . 263 A3
Gashay La EX13 . . . . 88 H3
Gashouse La PL4 . . . . 263 B2
Gasking St PL4 . . . . 263 A3
Gas La EX38 . . . . 159 D5
Gatcombe Ash EX12 . . . . . 102 E2
Gatcombe La
  Beer EX12 . . . . 191 C8
  Seaton EX12 . . . . 102 E2
Gate Cl EX13 . . . . 88 E3
Gate Cross EX24 . . . . 102 F6
Gatedown La
  Salcombe Regis EX10 . . . . . 101 E1
  Sidmouth EX10 . . . . 189 D8
Gate Field Rd EX39 . . . . . . 156 E2
Gatehouse Cl
  Cullompton EX15 . . . . 163 B3
  Dawlish EX7 . . . . 204 E7
Gatehouse City Prim Sch
  EX7 . . . . 204 E8
Gatehouse Hill EX7 . . . . . . 204 E7
Gatehouse Rise EX7 . . . . . . 204 E7
Gater La EX1 . . . . 261 B2
Gatesfield DT7 . . . . 260 C2
Gate Tree Cl TQ12 . . . . 207 F7
GATHERLEY 105 D1
Gattery La TQ5 . . . . 229 F1
Gavel The EX36 . . . . 158 D4
Gaverick Ct TQ12 . . . . 123 B1
Gay Cl TA21 . . . . 160 E6
Gaydon St EX1 . . . . 155 A5
Gays Cross EX17 . . . . 79 C7
Gay St TA21 . . . . 160 E6
Gaze Hill TQ12 . . . . 206 F5
Gdynia Way PL4 . . . . 263 C2
Geasons La PL7 . . . . 250 E5
Gees La PL21 . . . . 137 C2
Generals Ct EX6 . . . . 201 A7
Generals La EX6 . . . . 201 B7
Genesis La EX34 . . . . 3 A3
Geneva Cl EX2 . . . . 177 E4
Geneva Ct
  Bideford EX39 . . . . 156 F1
  Exeter EX2 . . . . 177 E4
Geneva Pl EX39 . . . . 156 F1
Gennys Cl PL18 . . . . 125 B6
Gentian Cl TQ12 . . . . 218 D2
George Ave PL7 . . . . 250 F6
George Cross PL7 . . . . 250 F5
George Downing Ho
  PL6 . . . . 245 A1
GEORGEHAM 8 B2
Georgeham CE Prim Sch
  EX33 . . . . 8 A2
Georgeham Cross EX33 . 152 D7
Georgeham Rd
  Croyde EX33 . . . . 7 F2
  Woolacombe EX34 . . . . 8 B5
George Hill EX17 . . . . 165 B6
George Hill Cross EX17 . 165 A6
George La
  Kilmington EX13 . . . . 87 C1
  Plymouth PL7 . . . . 250 F5
GEORGE NYMPTON 30 A1

George Nympton Cross
  EX36 . . . . 30 A2
George Nympton Rd
  EX36 . . . . 158 C2
George Pl PL1 . . . . 262 A2
George Rd TQ3 . . . . 219 B1
Georges Cl EX1 . . . . 178 B6
George Shopping Mews
  EX36 . . . . 158 C4
George Sq PL1 . . . . 247 F1
George's Sq DT7 . . . . 260 E3
George St
  Axminster EX13 . . . . 167 D6
  ☑ Barnstaple EX32 . . . . . . 154 F6
  Exeter EX1 . . . . 261 A2
  ☑ Exmouth EX8 . . . . 202 A7
  Honiton EX14 . . . . 166 C6
  Newton Abbot TQ12 . . . . . 207 B3
  Okehampton EX20 . . . . . . 170 B5
  Plymouth PL1 . . . . 247 F1
  ☑ Teignmouth TQ14 . . . . . 210 C4
  Wellington TA21 . . . . 160 D6
George Teign Rd EX6 . . . . 113 D2
Georgia Cres PL3 . . . . 249 C6
Georgian Ct TQ1 . . . . 220 E6
Georgian Ho The EX6 . . . . 201 B8
Gerald Dinnis Units EX2 177 D1
Geraldine Terr PL12 . . . . . . 242 C1
Gerbera Ho EX4 . . . . 176 E8
Gerbestone La TA21 . . . . . . 52 E6
GERMANSWEEK 91 D5
Gerrydown Rd EX19 . . . . . . 58 D3
Gerston Cross TQ9 . . . . . . 223 A3
Gerston La TQ7 . . . . 258 C1
Gerston Pl ☑ TQ3 . . . . 226 B6
Gerston Rd TQ4 . . . . 226 B6
Gervase Ave EX5 . . . . 261 A1
Gerway La EX11 . . . . 169 E2
Gestridge Cross TQ12 . . . . 207 D7
Gestridge Rd TQ12 . . . . . . 207 D7
Giant's Grave TA21 . . . . 69 D7
Giant's Grave Rd TA20 . . . 69 D7
Gibb Hill PL21 . . . . 133 B2
Gibbon La PL4 . . . . 263 A3
Gibbon St PL4 . . . . 263 A3
Giblands Cross EX20 . . . . . 170 D5
Giblands Pk EX20 . . . . 170 D5
Gibraltar Rd EX8 . . . . 195 E6
Gibson Cl EX8 . . . . 196 E1
Gibson Ct TQ4 . . . . 226 A1
Gibson Dr TQ4 . . . . 226 A1
Gibson Gdns TQ4 . . . . 226 A1
Gibson Rd TQ4 . . . . 226 A1
Gidcott Cross EX22 . . . . . . 55 A4
GIDLEIGH 110 A5
Gidley Arms Cross EX36 . 46 A5
Gidley Cross EX36 . . . . 46 B4
Gidleys Mdw TQ9 . . . . 222 F8
Gidley's Turn EX6 . . . . 113 C4
Gifford Pl PL3 . . . . 248 B6
Gifford Terrace Rd PL3 . . 248 E5
Gilbert Ave
  Exeter EX2 . . . . 178 C4
  Teignmouth TQ14 . . . . . . 210 A7
Gilbert Cl TQ12 . . . . 219 D6
Gilbert Ct PL7 . . . . 251 B6
Gilbert Gr ☑ EX34 . . . . . . 150 C6
Gilbert La PL12 . . . . 248 C5
Gilbert Rd TQ12 . . . . 207 E3
Gilbert Way TQ4 . . . . 226 A3
Gilchrist Way EX10 . . . . . . 188 C5
Gillard Rd TQ5 . . . . 230 F4
Gillards Cl TA21 . . . . 160 B4
Gillards Mead TA3 . . . . . . 168 B4
Gillard Way PL21 . . . . 136 D6
Gill Pk PL3 . . . . 249 B5
Gillscott Cross EX17 . . . . . 60 B1
Gill's Cross TQ9 . . . . 222 D2
Gills Nursery ☑ TQ9 . . . . 223 C5
Gilly's Wlk PL18 . . . . 125 C5
Gilpin Cl EX7 . . . . 204 F8
GILSCOTT 24 E2
Gilston Rd TQ12 . . . . 242 D4
Gilwell Ave PL4 . . . . 256 B7
Gilwell St PL4 . . . . 263 A3
Gimbletts Ct ☑ EX22 . . . . 164 C7
Gingaford Cross TQ10 . . . 135 A5
Gipsies Cnr EX17 . . . . 79 F6
Gipsies La EX17 . . . . 79 F6
Gipsy Cnr
  Bradninch EX5 . . . . 82 E1
  Whiddon EX31 . . . . 9 C1
Gipsy Cross EX14 . . . . 67 A5
Gipsy Dro TA20 . . . . 69 F4
Gipsy Hill EX14 . . . . 67 A5
Gipsy Hill Mews EX1 . . . . 178 F7
Gipsy La
  Bideford EX39 . . . . 25 B4
  Bittadon EX31 . . . . 9 F3
  Buckfastleigh TQ11 . . . . . . 236 A4
  Exeter EX1 . . . . 178 F8
  Exmouth EX8 . . . . 202 B8
  Ilfracombe EX34 . . . . 150 D5
  Sampford Arundel TA21 . . . . 51 D5
Girt La EX34 . . . . 3 B4
Gissage Hill EX17 . . . . 78 F7
Gissage View ☑ EX14 . . . . 166 B6
Gissons EX6 . . . . 182 B4
Gissons La EX6 . . . . 114 D4
GITTISHAM 85 B1
Gittisham Ct EX14 . . . . 178 D6
Gittisham Farm Cross
  EX14 . . . . 85 A1
Gittshayne Cross EX24 . 102 F5
Glade Cl PL6 . . . . 245 A4

Glades The EX16 . . . . 161 E3
Glade The PL20 . . . . 126 E2
Glade Wlk EX5 . . . . 179 E2
Gladstone Pl ☑ TQ12 . . . . 207 C3
Gladstone Rd EX1 . . . . 177 E6
Gladstone Terr
  ☑ Teignmouth TQ14 . . . . . 210 C5
  Wellington TA21 . . . . 160 E6
Glanville Ave ☑ PL19 . . . . 171 B5
Glanville Rd
  Offwell EX14 . . . . 102 A8
  Tavistock PL19 . . . . 171 B6
Glanvilles Mill PL21 . . . . . 237 D5
Glanvilles Rd PL21 . . . . . . 237 D5
Glanville St PL1 . . . . 262 C3
Glanville Terr PL12 . . . . . . 242 F3
Glanvill's Cl EX6 . . . . 98 C4
Glanvill Way EX14 . . . . 166 B4
Glascott Cl EX20 . . . . 75 B6
Glasshouse La EX2 . . . . . . 182 B7
Glastonbury Ct EX14 . . . . 174 A2
Glave Saunders Ave EX2 . 178 C4
Glazebrook Ct TQ10 . . . . . 134 E2
Glazegate Cross TQ3 . . . . 224 F7
Glazegate La TQ3, TQ4,
  TQ9 . . . . 224 E6
Glazon Way EX39 . . . . 157 A8
Glebe Ave PL12 . . . . 242 F3
Glebe Cl
  Exmouth EX8 . . . . 202 F7
  Lympstone EX8 . . . . 195 E6
  Newton Abbot TQ12 . . . . . 206 F3
  Otterton EX9 . . . . 198 E7
  Upton Pyne EX5 . . . . 172 F7
Glebe Cotts EX5 . . . . 99 B1
Glebe Ct EX39 . . . . 156 F6
Glebefield EX33 . . . . 8 A2
Glebe Field TQ7 . . . . 143 A2
Glebefields EX39 . . . . 156 F6
Glebe Hos EX39 . . . . 156 A1
Glebeland
  Churchstow TQ7 . . . . 143 E4
  Down St Mary EX17 . . . . . . 78 E7
Glebe Land TQ7 . . . . 143 C6
Glebelands
  Buckfastleigh TQ11 . . . . . 236 A6
  Cheriton Bishop EX6 . . . . . . 97 B4
  ☑ Chudleigh TQ13 . . . . . 123 F6
  Exminster EX6 . . . . 182 A4
  Holsworthy EX22 . . . . 164 B4
  Lympstone EX8 . . . . 195 E6
  Newton Poppleford EX10 . 186 F8
  Puddington EX16 . . . . 62 B5
  Sidmouth EX10 . . . . 188 A4
  Uplyme DT7 . . . . 260 B5
  Wrafton EX33 . . . . 152 E4
Glebelands Rd EX16 . . . . . . 64 D7
Glebeland Villas EX36 . . . . 31 A2
Glebeland Way TQ2 . . . . . 219 B8
Glebe Mdw EX2 . . . . 164 B4
Glebe The
  Ipplepen TQ12 . . . . 211 C2
  Poughill EX17 . . . . 62 D3
  Thorverton EX5 . . . . 81 E4
Glenann Terr ☑ TQ9 . . . . 223 C6
Glenavon Rd PL3 . . . . 248 E5
Glenburn Cl PL3 . . . . 248 E7
Glenburnie Ho EX39 . . . . 157 A3
Glenburnie Rd EX39 . . . . . 157 A3
Glencarnock Cl TQ1 . . . . . 219 E2
Glen Cl
  Clyst St Mary EX5 . . . . . . 179 E2
  Sidmouth EX10 . . . . 188 A3
Glencoe EX2 . . . . 177 E5
Glendale Rd EX20 . . . . 170 A6
Glendale Terr EX39 . . . . . . 157 A3
Glendaragh Rd ☑ TQ14 . . 210 C5
Glendon Cross EX20 . . . . . 170 F8
Glendower Rd PL3 . . . . . . 248 D5
Gleneagle Ave ☑ PL3 . . . . 248 F6
Gleneagle Rd PL3 . . . . 248 F6
Gleneagle Villas ☑ PL3 . . 248 F6
Glen Farm Cres EX14 . . . . 166 D5
Glenfield Cl PL6 . . . . 245 D6
Glenfield Rd
  Bideford EX39 . . . . 157 A4
  Plymouth PL6 . . . . 245 D5
Glenfield Way PL6 . . . . . . 245 E6
Glengarth Cl EX39 . . . . . . 157 A5
Glen Gdns EX39 . . . . 156 F4
Glenholme DT7 . . . . 260 D2
GLENHOLT 245 D6
  245 D6
Glenholt Cl PL6 . . . . 245 D6
Glenholt Rd PL6 . . . . 245 D6
Glenhurst Rd ☑ PL3 . . . . . 248 E6
Glen Isla EX10 . . . . 188 B3
Glen Lyn EX39 . . . . 156 F4
Glen Lyn Gorge★ EX35 . . 151 C5
Glen Lyn Pk TQ13 . . . . . . 180 D5
Glenmore Ave PL2 . . . . . . 247 F5
Glenmore Rd
  Brixham TQ5 . . . . 230 C4
  Exeter EX2 . . . . 178 A5
  Glenmore EX2 . . . . 251 C6
Glenorchy Ct ☑ EX8 . . . . 202 A7
Glen Park Ave PL4 . . . . . . 262 C4
Glen Park Prim Sch ☑
  PL7 . . . . 251 B5
Glen Rd
  Paignton TQ3 . . . . 226 B7
  Plymouth, Mannamead PL3 248 F5
  Plymouth, Plympton PL7 . . 251 B5
  Sidmouth EX10 . . . . 188 A3
Glenside Cl ☑ PL5 . . . . 243 E1
Glenside Ct TQ1 . . . . 220 E5
Glenside Rise PL7 . . . . 250 E6

Glen The
  Beer EX12 . . . . 191 E6
  ☑ Newton Abbot TQ12 . . . 207 F2
  Okehampton EX20 . . . . . . 170 B4
Glenthorne Cl TQ1 . . . . . . 220 D4
Glenthorne Rd EX4 . . . . . . 173 A1
Glentor Rd PL3 . . . . 248 E7
Glentorr Rd EX39 . . . . 157 A3
Glenview EX14 . . . . 166 D5
Glenwater Cl EX12 . . . . . . 192 C6
Glen Wlk EX4 . . . . 173 D2
Glenwood Rd PL3 . . . . 248 E6
Glenwood Rise EX2 . . . . . 261 C1
Globe Ct EX15 . . . . 163 C3
Globefield EX3 . . . . 182 F8
Globe Hill EX5 . . . . 184 B2
Globe La EX3 . . . . 182 F4
Globe Ley EX3 . . . . 182 F5
Gloster Rd EX32 . . . . 155 A4
Gloucester Cl
  Honiton EX14 . . . . 166 A5
  Torquay TQ2 . . . . 213 F1
Gloucester Cres EX14 . . . . 166 A5
Gloucester Ct PL1 . . . . 262 C4
Gloucester Pl PL1 . . . . 262 C4
Gloucester Rd
  Exeter EX4 . . . . 176 E7
  Exmouth EX8 . . . . 196 E3
  Newton Abbot TQ12 . . . . . 207 C3
  ☑ Teignmouth TQ14 . . . . . 210 B5
Glove Ct EX38 . . . . 159 C5
Glovers Cl ☑ EX22 . . . . . . 164 C4
Gloyn Pk EX22 . . . . 53 E1
Glynsmead TA20 . . . . 88 C8
Gnaton Cotts PL8 . . . . 141 C8
Gnome Reserve & Wild
  Flower Gdn★ EX22 . . . . . 39 B2
Goad Ave
  Plymouth PL4 . . . . 263 C2
  Torpoint PL11 . . . . 246 E3
Goad Cl PL11 . . . . 246 F3
Goaman Pk EX39 . . . . 22 E3
Goaman Rd EX39 . . . . 26 A4
Go Ape! (Haldon)★ EX6 . 114 A3
Goats Hill Rd EX39 . . . . . . 157 A6
Godborough EX39 . . . . 157 A6
Godborough View EX39 156 D2
Godding Gdns PL6 . . . . . . 244 E6
Godford Cross EX14 . . . . . . 85 B5
Godfrey Ave TQ3 . . . . 219 B2
Godfrey Cl EX11 . . . . 169 C3
Godfreys Gdns EX17 . . . . . . 78 C4
Godhams La TA4 . . . . 35 A7
Godolphin Cl EX5 . . . . 81 A1
Godolphin Ho PL19 . . . . . 171 C5
Godwell La PL21 . . . . 237 F5
Gogwell La
  Cove EX16 . . . . 49 B5
  Tiverton EX16 . . . . 161 F1
Goldburn Cross EX20 . . . . . 76 B1
Golden Bay Ct EX39 . . . . . 156 C7
Golden Cl TQ5 . . . . 230 B2
Golden Hind (Mus Ship)
  The★ TQ5 . . . . 230 D5
Golden Inn Cross EX21 . . . 74 C7
Golden Joy EX17 . . . . 165 D6
Golden Lane Cross EX14 . . 66 E2
Golden Lion Ct TQ13 . . . . 130 F4
Golden Park Ave TQ2 . . . . 213 F4
Golden Square EX14 . . . . . . 86 E6
Golden View ☑ EX17 . . . . 165 C6
Goldfinch Cl PL15 . . . . . . 105 A2
Goldfinch Gdns PL9 . . . . . 171 D2
Goldfinch Gr
  Cullompton EX15 . . . . 163 A2
  Saltash PL12 . . . . 242 D4
Golds Cross EX6 . . . . 97 F4
Golds Cross PL7 . . . . 250 D8
Golds La EX6 . . . . 97 E5
Goldsmith Gdns PL5 . . . . . 244 D3
Goldsmith La EX13 . . . . 88 A4
Goldsmith St
  Exeter EX4 . . . . 261 A3
  Stonehouse Cross EX16 . . . 50 E8
Gold St
  Ottery St Mary EX11 . . . . . 169 D4
  Tiverton EX16 . . . . 161 D4
GOLDWORTHY 24 F1
Golf Links Rd
  South Brent TQ10 . . . . . . 134 D1
  Westward Ho! EX39 . . . . . 156 D7
Golland La EX37 . . . . 44 B2
Gollands TQ5 . . . . 230 B5
Gollands Cl TQ5 . . . . 230 A5
Gollands La
  Copplestone EX17 . . . . 79 B8
  Morchard Bishop EX17 . . . . 61 B1
Golvers Hill Cl TQ12 . . . . . 207 E7
Golvers Hill Rd TQ12 . . . . 207 E7
Goodacre Cross PL16 . . . . . 91 B1
Goodeve Cl PL9 . . . . 255 E6
Goodgates Cl EX33 . . . . . . 152 C6
Goodgates Cres EX33 . . . . 152 B6
Goodgates Pk EX33 . . . . . . 152 B6
Goodgates Rd EX33 . . . . . . 152 B6
Gooding Rise EX36 . . . . . . 161 B4
GOODLEIGH 17 C5
Goodleigh CE Prim Sch
  EX32 . . . . 17 B5
Goodleigh Rd EX32 . . . . . . 155 D5
Goodridge EX7 . . . . 204 E8

GOODRINGTON 226 B2
Goodrington Rd TQ4 . . . . . 226 B1
Goodrington Sands Halt★
  TQ4 . . . . 226 C4
Goodshelter Cross TQ8 . . 148 E5
Good Shepherd Dr ☑
  EX2 . . . . 261 B2
GOODSTONE 131 C6
Goodstone Cross TQ12 . . . 131 C6
Goodstone Way TQ4 . . . . . 225 F3
Goodwells Head EX32 . . . . 18 C3
Goodwin Ave PL6 . . . . 245 A6
Goodwin Cres PL2 . . . . 248 A6
Goodwood Park Rd
  EX39 . . . . 157 A5
Gooseberry La PL1 . . . . . . 262 B2
Gooseford Cross EX20 . . . . 95 D2
Goosefoot La PL11 . . . . . . 252 C8
Goose Gn EX38 . . . . 159 E5
GOOSEHAM 37 B3
GOOSEMOOR 186 B7
Goose Moor La EX6 . . . . . . 114 B4
GOOSEWELL 2 D4
Goosewell Hill PL6 . . . . . . 249 C8
Goosewell Park Rd PL9 . . 255 F6
Goosewell Prim Sch PL9 255 F6
Goosewell Rd PL9 . . . . 255 F5
Gora La EX34 . . . . 8 A6
Gordon Ct
  ☑ Plymouth PL1 . . . . 262 A3
  Saltash PL12 . . . . 242 D2
Gordon Rd
  Exeter EX1 . . . . 177 E7
  Topsham EX3 . . . . 182 E6
Gordon's Pl EX1 . . . . 177 F5
Gordon Terr
  Beer EX12 . . . . 191 D5
  Plymouth PL4 . . . . 248 E4
Gore La
  Exmouth EX8 . . . . 202 E4
  Kilmington EX13 . . . . 103 C8
  Uplyme DT7 . . . . 260 A4
Gorfin Cl EX8 . . . . 202 E8
Gorhuish Cross EX20 . . . . . 75 C1
Gorlegg TA21 . . . . 51 F6
Gornhay Cross EX16 . . . . . 64 D8
Gornhay Orch EX16 . . . . . . 64 D8
Gorran Down EX39 . . . . . . 22 F1
Gorse Ho EX4 . . . . 176 E8
Gorse La EX8 . . . . 196 D4
Gorse Way
  Ivybridge PL21 . . . . 237 E4
  Sidmouth EX10 . . . . 187 F4
Gorsey Cl PL5 . . . . 244 E2
Gorvin Cross EX39 . . . . 38 B6
Gorway TQ14 . . . . 210 C6
Gorwell Rd EX32 . . . . 155 C5
Gorwood Rd EX39 . . . . 40 B7
Gorwyn La EX6 . . . . 97 C4
Gosceline Wlk EX14 . . . . . 166 C4
GOSFORD 169 D7
Gosford La EX11 . . . . 169 C7
Gosford Rd EX11 . . . . 169 D7
Goshawk Units EX2 . . . . . 178 F6
Goshen Rd TQ2 . . . . 219 E4
Goslings The TQ7 . . . . . . 145 B4
Goss Mdw EX17 . . . . 78 C4
Gostwick Cl EX20 . . . . 77 C4
Goswela Cl PL9 . . . . 255 F5
Goswela Gdns PL9 . . . . . . 255 F5
Gothic Rd TQ12 . . . . 207 B2
Gould Cl EX32 . . . . 155 B4
Gould Rd
  Barnstaple EX32 . . . . 155 C4
  Salcombe TQ8 . . . . 259 D5
Gourders La TQ12 . . . . 212 F2
Goutsford Gate PL21 . . . . 136 F2
Govers Mdw EX24 . . . . . . 103 A4
GOVETON 144 C5
Govetts EX5 . . . . 184 C3
Gower Ridge Rd PL9 . . . . . 255 D6
Gowman's Terr EX20 . . . . . 77 B4
Goyle Acre La EX13 . . . . . . 87 B3
Grace Parade EX2 . . . . 177 B2
Grace Road Central EX2 177 C2
Grace Road S EX2 . . . . . . 177 D1
Grace Road W EX2 . . . . . . 177 B2
Graddon Cross
  Black Torrington EX21 . . . . 73 F6
  Okehampton EX20 . . . . 93 E4
Grafton Ct TQ1 . . . . 220 B4
Grafton Hts ☑ TQ1 . . . . . 220 C5
Grafton Pl ☑ TQ12 . . . . . . 207 B3
Grafton Rd
  Exeter EX4 . . . . 173 B1
  Plymouth PL4 . . . . 248 E4
Grafton Terr TQ1 . . . . 220 B4
Graham Cl EX16 . . . . 161 D5
Graham Rd TQ3 . . . . 219 A1
Grainger Cl EX2 . . . . 178 C5
Grainge Rd PL6 . . . . 245 A1
Gramercy Fields TQ5 . . . . 230 B2
Grampian Cl EX4 . . . . 173 D2
Grampian Cl TQ4 . . . . 225 D4
Granary La EX9 . . . . 198 C1
Granby Cl TQ1 . . . . 247 E2
Granby Gn PL1 . . . . 247 E2
Granby St PL1 . . . . 247 E2
Granby Way PL1 . . . . 247 E2
Grand Hotel Rd PL1 . . . . . 262 B1
Grandison Ave TQ14 . . . . . 209 A8
Grandisson Ct EX2 . . . . . . 178 A2

Grandisson Dr EX11...... 169 F3
Grand Par PL1 .... 262 B1
Grand View Rd (Cliff Rd)
TQ7 .... 147 B7
Grand Western Canal Ctry Pk
Nature Reserve★ EX16.. 64 F7
Grand Western Canal (Ctry
Pk Nature Reserve)★
EX16 .... 50 F2
Grange Ave
Barnstaple EX31 .... 154 C2
Exmouth EX8 .... 202 B8
Paignton TQ4 .... 226 B2
Grange Bglws EX39 ..... 157 B1
Grange Cl
Bratton Fleming EX32 .... 18 A8
Exmouth EX8 .... 202 B8
Ipplepen TQ12 .... 211 C3
Lympstone EX8 .... 195 F5
Newton Abbot TQ12 .... 207 D1
Wellington TA21........ 160 E5
Grange Cotts EX5 .... 99 C6
Grange Cross EX14...... 84 D7
Grange Ct
4 Barnstaple EX32 .... 155 A6
Teignmouth TQ14...... 210 A5
Grange Dr
1 Barnstaple EX32 .... 155 A6
Teignmouth TQ14...... 210 B6
Grange Heights Cl TQ4.. 226 A1
Grange Hill EX32 .... 18 B8
Grange Hill Ind Est EX31 . 18 B8
Grange Hts TQ4 .... 226 A2
Grange La EX20......... 57 A7
GRANGE PK........... 208 D8
Grange Pk TQ12 .... 212 A6
Grange Rd
Abbotskerswell TQ12.... 212 B6
Bideford EX39 .... 157 B1
Buckfast TQ11 .... 236 B7
Paignton TQ4 .... 226 B2
Plymouth PL7........... 251 A4
Torquay TQ1............ 220 C5
Yelverton PL20.......... 126 F3
Grange The
Braunton EX33.......... 152 E5
Dousland PL20.......... 127 A2
Grange View TQ4 .... 226 A2
Grantham Cl PL7 .... 250 B4
Grantland Hill EX16, EX17 . 63 A4
Grantlands EX15 .... 66 A7
Grantley Gdns PL3 ..... 249 A5
Grant's Hill EX16, TA22... 33 F2
Granville Ave EX32 ..... 154 F6
Granville Pl EX15 ...... 162 C5
Granville Rd EX34 ...... 150 B6
Gras Lawn EX2.......... 177 E4
Grasmere Cl
Plymouth PL6........... 244 E5
Torquay TQ2............ 214 B2
Grasmere Ct EX4....... 176 F5
Grassendale Ave PL2.... 247 F7
Grass La PL2............ 248 C6
Grasslands Dr EX1 ..... 178 F8
Grassmere Way PL12... 242 D4
Grasspark Hill EX32 .... 18 E3
Grass Rd TQ13 .... 131 A3
Grassy La PL8........... 136 C4
Grattan La EX31........ 16 B6
Grattans Way EX17..... 78 C4
GRATTON 54 F5
Gratton Cl TQ6......... 146 B8
Gratton Cross
Shebbear EX22 .... 55 A5
Yelverton PL20.......... 127 A2
Gratton Ct EX31 .... 154 C2
Gratton Dr TQ7 .... 145 A1
Gratton La
Bittadon EX31 .... 9 C5
Chulmleigh EX18 .... 59 D3
Combe Martin EX31...... 3 F2
Lower Tippacott EX35.... 6 A4
Yelverton PL20.......... 127 A2
Gratton Pl PL6.......... 245 A1
Grattons La TQ9........ 216 E2
Gratton Way EX31...... 154 C2
Gravel La EX12.......... 192 B7
Gravel Pit Cross EX36.. 20 A6
Gravel Wlk EX15........ 163 C3
Gravesend Gdns PL11... 247 B3
Gravesend Wlk PL5 .... 243 D4
Graybridge Rd PL20.... 126 F4
Gray Cres PL5.......... 247 C8
Graynfylde Dr EX39 .... 157 B2
Grays Ct TQ13 .... 112 B3
Gray's Hill EX15......... 52 D1
Gray's La EX15.......... 52 D1
Grays Mdw TQ13 .... 111 F5
Great Ambrook Ave
TQ12 .... 217 A7
Great Berry Rd PL6..... 244 F1
Great Bridge TQ13 ..... 133 C6
Great Burrow Rise EX39. 156 F8
Great Churchway PL9 .. 256 A7
Great Cl EX15........... 51 E1
Great Fellingfield PL19.. 117 E6
Great Field Gdns EX33 . 152 C5
Greatfield Rd PL3....... 249 B7
Great Furlong TQ14 .... 208 E8
Great Gate Flats 13 TQ5 . 230 C4
GREAT HAYNE 63 A2
Great Headland Cres
TQ3 .... 219 D1
Great Headland Rd TQ3 . 219 C1
Great Hele La EX36..... 158 D2
Great Hill 3 TQ13...... 123 E6

Great Hill Cross TQ1 .... 213 F5
Great Hill Rd TQ2 ...... 213 F4
Great Hill View EX4 .... 173 E2
Great La TQ7 .... 147 E6
Greatlands Cres PL2 ... 248 A6
Greatlands Pl 5 PL2.... 248 A5
Great Lightleigh La EX18 . 44 F5
Great Links Tor RdEX20. 170 E5
Great Mdw TA22........ 33 D6
Great Mead EX6 .... 112 F7
Great Mis Tor Cl 5 PL20 . 126 F3
Greatoak Cross TQ12 ... 212 C5
Great Oak Cross EX5.... 81 D2
Great Oak Mdw EX22... 164 C5
Great Orchard Cl PL9 ... 255 E5
Great Park Cl 4 PL7 .... 251 C5
Greatpark La TQ1 ...... 225 D6
Great Parks Rd TQ3 .... 225 E5
Great Pitford La EX18 .. 58 D6
Great Rea Rd TQ5...... 230 D5
Great Ringaton La EX36 . 32 B6
Great Tor Cl TQ3........ 218 F1
GREAT TORRINGTON .. 159 C5
Great Torrington Bluecoat
CE Inf Sch EX38......... 159 C5
Great Torrington Com Sch
Sports Coll EX38........ 159 E5
Great Torrington Jun Sch
EX38 .... 159 C5
Great Tree Pk TQ13 .... 96 A1
Greatweek Cross TQ13 . 111 B6
GREAT WEEKE 111 B6
Great Western Cl TA4 .. 226 C4
Great Western Ind Est
EX32 .... 155 B3
Great Western Rd
6 Paignton TQ4 .... 226 B6
Plymouth PL1.......... 262 B1
Great Western Way
EX16..................... 161 D3
Great Woodford Dr PL7. 250 B6
Greatwood Terr EX3 ... 182 F5
Grebe Cl PL7 .... 250 F5
Grecian Way EX2 .... 178 C4
Greebys The TQ3 .... 226 A6
Greenacre EX33.......... 152 C6
Green Acre EX16........ 65 B7
Greenacre Cl
Bradworthy EX22........ 53 E8
North Tawton EX20 ..... 157 A7
North Tawton EX20 ..... 77 C4
Greenacres
Exeter EX4.............. 173 A3
Tiverton EX16........... 161 F6
Torquay TQ1............ 220 E5
Greenacres Cl EX14 .... 84 D1
Greenaway Ho EX22.... 164 C3
Greenaway La TQ12.... 213 B6
Greenaway Rd TQ12.... 213 A6
Greenwell Cl TQ13 ..... 111 D2
Greenbank EX38......... 159 F6
Green Bank EX15....... 163 F7
Green Bank PL10....... 186 E8
Greenbank Ave
Kingsteignton TQ12 .... 207 D8
Plymouth PL4........... 263 B3
Greenbank Cl EX38..... 159 F6
Greenbank Cottages
PL4...................... 263 B4
Greenbank Rd
Barnstaple EX32 .... 155 C4
Brixham TQ5 .... 230 B4
Plymouth PL4........... 263 B4
Greenbanks TQ7........ 145 C3
Green Banks Cl TQ7 ... 145 C3
Greenbank Terr
Plymouth PL4........... 263 B4
Yelverton PL20.......... 127 A3
Green Cl
Cornworthy TQ9........ 227 B4
Exmouth EX8 .... 202 C8
Kingsbridge TQ7 .... 258 D6
Greenclose Ct 3 EX24. 103 A4
Green Close La EX31.... 10 B5
Greenclose Rd EX34.... 150 B6
Greendale Cross EX5... 183 F7
Greendale La
Exeter EX5.............. 99 A1
Woodbury Salterton EX5. 184 A8
Greendale Rd PL2....... 248 A7
Greendown Cross EX20. 74 C2
Green End La EX15...... 83 F5
Greenfield Cl EX39...... 156 E2
Greenfield Dr
Ivybridge PL21 .... 237 D4
5 South Brent TQ10... 134 F2
Greenfield Rd
Paignton TQ4 .... 219 A1
Saltash PL12 .... 242 D2
Greenfield Terr TA20... 88 D8
Greenfinch Cres PL12.. 242 E4
Greenford Villas EX2... 261 A1
Green Gables EX10...... 188 A4
GREEN GATE........... 50 B2
Green Gate EX13........ 50 B2
Green Gdns EX39 ...... 156 E6
GREENHAM............ 51 B7
Greenham Bsns Pk TA21 . 51 C5
Greenhayes ★ TQ12 ... 197 F2
Greenhayes
Charmouth DT6 .... 104 F4
Dartington TQ9 .... 222 E8
Greenhays Foot EX13 .. 88 B6
Greenhead EX15 .... 101 B2
GREENHILL 207 E5
Greenhill
East Allington TQ9...... 144 D7
Kingsteignton TQ12 .... 207 E6

Green Hill
Lamerton PL19.......... 116 E3
Poughill EX16, EX17..... 62 D3
Sampford Courtenay EX20 . 76 F3
Tavistock PL19.......... 171 D5
Greenhill Ave
Exmouth EX8 .... 202 C7
Lympstone EX8 .... 195 C5
Greenhill Cl PL9 .... 255 F5
Greenhill Cross
East Knowstone EX36.... 32 B2
Knowle EX33 .... 8 E1
Poughill EX17........... 62 D3
Sampford Chapple EX20 .. 77 A3
Greenhill Gdns TQ12... 212 F4
Greenhill Ind Units TQ12 207 E6
Greenhill La TQ12 ...... 211 B6
Greenhill Rd
Kingskerswell TQ12 .... 212 F4
Kingsteignton TQ12 .... 207 E6
Plymouth PL9........... 256 A5
Greenhill Terr TQ9 ..... 144 D7
Greenhill Way TQ12.... 207 E6
Greenings Rd EX39..... 40 C7
Green Knap La TA20.... 69 F2
Green La
23 Appledore EX39..... 15 A1
Axmouth EX12, DT7..... 193 B8
1 Barnstaple EX31..... 154 F5
Beaford EX19........... 42 D1
Bittaford TQ10.......... 137 E8
Blackawton TQ9........ 139 B1
Braunton EX33.......... 152 E6
Buckfastleigh TQ11 .... 236 F4
Chard Junction EX13 ... 88 B7
Chardstock EX13 .... 88 B7
Cheriton Bishop EX6.... 97 C2
Churston Ferrers TQ5 .. 229 E5
East Allington TQ9...... 144 D8
Exeter EX4.............. 176 E5
Exton EX3............... 183 B2
Hatherleigh EX20....... 75 D7
Ilsington TQ13 .... 122 C4
Kingsand PL10.......... 253 A2
Merton EX20 .... 57 A7
Molland EX36........... 31 B8
Rackenford EX16........ 47 C5
Raymond's Hill EX13 ... 104 C7
Rewe EX5............... 82 A2
Rousdon DT7........... 193 F8
Sampford Arundel TA21.. 51 F4
Sidbury EX10........... 101 D2
Southleigh EX24........ 102 D3
Spreyton EX17.......... 96 A7
Swimbridge EX32 ...... 28 B8
Tavistock PL19.......... 171 E5
Totnes TQ9............. 223 A4
Yelverton PL20.......... 126 F1
Greenlake Cross EX39 .. 22 D1
Greenland PL10......... 252 F5
Greenland Head Cross
Churchstow TQ7........ 143 E6
Pennymoor EX16........ 62 E6
Greenlands Ave TQ3 ... 225 F6
Greenlands Est PL19 ... 171 D5
Greenlane Cross EX36.. 31 C8
Green Lane End
Blackawton TQ9........ 139 B1
Buckfastleigh TQ11 .... 236 E4
Green Lanes Sh Ctr
EX31.................... 154 F5
Greenlees Dr PL7....... 251 B3
Greenmeadow Dr EX31. 155 A7
Green Mews EX9........ 198 A1
Green Mount EX10...... 188 C6
Greenover Cl TQ5 ...... 230 B3
Greenover Rd TQ5 ..... 230 B3
Green Park Ave PL4.... 248 D4
Green Park Rd PL8 ..... 196 D2
Green Park Rd
Paignton TQ3 .... 218 F1
Plymouth PL9........... 255 E5
Green Park Way TQ7 .. 145 A1
Green Park Wlk TQ3 ... 218 F1
Green Pk TQ10.......... 253 A2
Greenside Cross EX20 .. 77 A3
Greenslade Rd
Blackawton TQ9........ 139 E1
Totnes TQ9............. 145 B8
Witheridge EX16........ 46 E1
Greenslinch La EX5 .... 82 D6
Greensway Rd PL19.... 171 A4
Greens Wood EX36 .... 20 C7
Greenswood La 4 TQ5. 232 B1
Greenswood Rd TQ5... 230 C3
Green The
Ashburton TQ13........ 130 F4
Bridgerule EX22........ 70 F5
Brushford TA22 .... 33 B4
Denbury TQ12 .... 211 A6
Down St Mary EX17..... 78 E7
Exmouth EX8 .... 202 F8
Ide EX2................. 176 D1
Kingsand PL10.......... 253 A2
Meavy PL20............. 127 C8
Newton Abbot TQ12 ... 208 F8
Otterton EX9 .... 198 E7
Plymouth, Ernesettle PL5 . 243 E3
Plymouth, Hooe PL9 .... 255 B6
Saltash PL12 .... 242 C3
Teignmouth TQ14...... 210 A3
Whimple EX5 .... 99 E8
Green Tree La EX5 ..... 175 D6
Greenville Way EX15... 163 C4
Greenway
Crediton EX17.......... 165 B5

Greenway continued
Exeter EX2.............. 176 F3
Greenway★ TQ5 .... 228 E2
Greenway
Halberton EX16........ 65 A8
Lyme Regis DT7........ 260 C3
Seaton EX12 .... 191 F7
Woodbury EX5.......... 184 C3
Greenway Ave PL7 ..... 250 B6
Greenway Cl
3 Horrabridge PL20... 126 F5
Ivybridge PL21 .... 237 D5
Torquay TQ2............ 214 A1
Greenway Gdns
Tiverton EX16........... 161 C4
Torquay TQ2............ 214 A1
Greenway La
Ashcombe EX7.......... 124 F5
Awliscombe EX14...... 85 B5
Beacon EX14 .... 85 D8
Budleigh Salterton EX9 . 198 A2
Sidmouth EX10......... 187 E8
Torquay TQ1............ 220 B8
Greenway Pk TQ5 ...... 229 B4
Greenway Rd
Galmpton TQ5 .... 229 B4
Paignton TQ5 .... 228 E3
Rockwell Green TA21... 160 A5
Torquay, Chelston TQ2 . 219 E4
Torquay, St Marychurch
TQ1..................... 220 B8
Greenways EX34........ 150 A5
Greenwich Pl PL12 ..... 242 F3
Greenwood Cl
Aveton Gifford TQ7 .... 143 C6
Ivybridge PL21 .... 237 C5
Greenwood Dr EX2..... 178 D5
Greenwood Park Cl PL7. 251 B6
Greenwood Park Rd PL7 251 B6
Greenwoods The EX39 .. 22 E3
Gregory Cl
Torquay TQ1............ 78 C4
Tiverton EX16........... 161 F4
Gregory's Ct TQ13 ..... 110 F6
Gregory's Mdw PL15 .. 105 A2
Gregory Terr EX39 ..... 22 E3
Grenadier Rd EX14..... 178 E7
Grenadine Cl TQ2 ...... 213 E3
Grendon Almshouses
EX1..................... 177 E6
Grendon Bldgs 2 EX1.. 261 A2
Grendon Ct TQ14 ...... 210 A5
Grendon La EX16....... 46 E4
Grendon Rd EX1........ 177 E6
Grenfell Ave PL12 ...... 242 D3
Grenfell Gdns PL12..... 242 C3
Grenofen Cross PL19... 126 D6
GRENOFEN 126 D6
Grenofen Cl PL19 ...... 126 D6
Grenville Ave
Exeter EX4.............. 178 D8
Teignmouth TQ14...... 210 D7
Torquay TQ2............ 219 D6
Grenville Cl
Dartmouth TQ6 .... 233 D3
Newton Abbot TQ12.... 207 E3
Stokenham TQ7 .... 145 B2
Grenville Ct PL7........ 251 C6
Grenville Dr PL19 ...... 171 B3
Grenville Estate Cres
EX39.................... 25 E4
Grenville Est The EX39 . 25 E4
Grenville Ho EX31...... 155 A8
Grenville Pk PL20...... 127 A2
Grenville Rd
Exmouth EX8 .... 196 C2
Plymouth PL4........... 263 C3
Salcombe TQ8 .... 259 D4
Grenville Road Lane S
PL4...................... 249 B2
Grenville St 16 EX39... 157 A2
Grenville Terr
4 Bideford EX39 ...... 157 B1
Northam EX39.......... 157 A7
Grenville Way TQ4..... 226 B3
Gresham Cl PL5......... 244 A2
Greycoat La TQ12 ...... 206 F7
Greyfriars Rd EX4...... 177 F8
Greyhill Cross TQ7..... 138 A1
Greysand Cres 31 EX39. 15 A1
Greysholt Cross EX32 .. 28 B8
Greystoke Ave PL6..... 249 D7
Greystone Cross EX6 .. 96 D2
Greystone La TQ12 .... 220 C7
Gribble Cl EX32......... 155 C4
Gribbleford Cross EX20. 75 A4
Gribble La EX5.......... 99 D6
Gribblemead EX24 ..... 103 A4
Grieg Dr EX32........... 155 C4
Griffin Way PL9 .... 256 C6
Griggs Cl
Northam EX39.......... 157 A6
Plymouth PL7........... 251 B4
Griggs Gdn EX14 ...... 193 D5
Grigg's La EX10......... 188 D7
Grimspound★ TQ13 ... 121 A7
Grimspound Cl PL6..... 249 D8
Grimstone Terr PL20... 126 E2
Grinacombe Cross PL16 . 91 B2
Grinacombe Moor cross
PL16.................... 91 B2
Grindhill Cross EX20 ... 92 B8
Grindle Way EX5........ 179 B2
Grizedale Rd PL6....... 249 D7
Gronau Cl EX14 .... 166 C4
Grooms Orch TA20 .... 160 C5

Gropers La
Ipplepen TQ3, TQ12.... 218 C8
North Whilborough TQ12 . 212 B1
Gropy La
Ash Mill EX36........... 31 D1
South Molton EX36..... 46 B8
Grosvenor Ave TQ2 .... 213 C1
Grosvenor Cl TQ2 ...... 213 C1
Grosvenor Cotts 1 PL4 . 248 F4
Grosvenor Ct
3 Barnstaple EX32 .... 155 A5
Ivybridge PL21 .... 237 C5
Grosvenor Pl EX1 ...... 261 C4
Grosvenor Rd
Paignton TQ4 .... 226 B5
Plymouth PL6........... 244 F2
Grosvenor St 2 EX32 .. 155 A5
Grosvenor Terr
4 Barnstaple EX32 .... 155 A5
Paignton TQ4 .... 226 B5
Groundhead Rd 4 EX14. 86 F6
Grove Ave 12 TQ14 .... 210 B5
Grove Cl 3 TQ9........ 223 C5
Grove Cres 6 TQ14 .... 210 B5
Grove Cross EX22...... 39 D3
Grove Ct
Dawlish EX7............ 204 F6
Teignmouth TQ14...... 210 C6
Grove Hill
12 Colyton EX24 .... 103 A4
Topsham EX3........... 182 F5
Grove Ho EX3........... 182 F5
Grove La EX26.......... 32 D6
Grove Mdw EX20........ 94 F5
Grove Mews 10 TQ9 ... 223 C5
Grove Pk
Tavistock PL19.......... 171 D5
Torpoint PL11 .... 246 E3
Grove Prim Sch The 18
TQ9 .... 223 C5
Grove Rd EX5........... 99 F7
Groves The PL21....... 237 C6
Grove Terr 11 TQ14 .... 210 B5
Grove The
5 Bittaford PL21 ...... 137 C8
Blackawton TQ9........ 139 E1
Exeter EX4.............. 174 E2
Paignton TQ4 .... 225 E4
Plymouth, Plymstock PL9 . 255 D8
Plymouth, Stoke PL3 ... 248 A4
Sidmouth EX10......... 188 B4
Totnes TQ9............. 223 C5
Woolacombe EX34...... 7 F6
Gubbin's La EX33 ...... 152 D5
Guernsey Cnr EX24..... 102 F4
Guestland Rd TQ1...... 220 C7
Guildford Cl
Exeter EX4.............. 176 E6
Plymouth PL5........... 244 E3
Guildford St Pl4........ 263 A3
Guildhall Sh Ctr EX4 .. 261 A3
Guildhall Sq TQ1 ...... 262 C2
Guildhall Yd TQ9....... 223 C5
Guinea St EX1.......... 261 A2
Guinevere Way EX4 .... 174 A1
Guinness La EX4 .... 176 E8
Gulland Cross TQ12.... 212 B4
Gullet Cross TQ7....... 148 F6
Gulliford Cotts EX8 .... 195 F6
Gulliver La EX20........ 77 D7
Gullyhole Hill EX36..... 31 F7
Gully La EX14........... 86 C5
Gully Shoot EX24 ...... 103 A3
Gulway Mead TA20..... 88 D8
GULWORTHY........... 125 E8
Gulworthy Cotts PL19 . 125 E8
Gulworthy Cross PL19 . 125 E7
Gulworthy Prim Sch
PL19.................... 125 E7
Gun La EX36............ 19 D4
Gunn Cl TQ12 .... 17 F4
Gunn Cross EX32....... 17 F3
GUNNISLAKE 125 D6
Gunnislake Prim Sch
PL18.................... 125 C6
Gunnislake Rural Workshops
PL18.................... 125 D6
Gunsdown Villas EX36.. 158 D5
Gunstone Cross EX17 .. 79 E2
Gunstone Mill Cross EX17 79 E1
Gunstone La EX17 ..... 158 B5
Gurnard Wlk PL3 ...... 249 C6
Gurney Cl PL11 .... 246 F3
Gurneys The TQ3....... 226 A5
GUSCOTT 26 E2
Guscott La EX38 .... 26 E2
Gussiford La EX8....... 202 B6
Guy Miles Way PL5..... 244 B3
Guys Rd EX4............ 176 F6
Gwel Avon Bsns Pk PL12 242 D4
Gwithian Cl PL11....... 246 F4
Gwyn Rd PL4........... 263 C3
Gwythers EX36.......... 158 D4

H

Hacche La EX36......... 158 C6
Haccombe Cl EX14 .... 196 E5
Haccombe Cross TQ12 . 213 C6
Haccombe Path TQ12 .. 208 A2
Hacker Cl EX10......... 186 F7
Hackney La
Kingsteignton TQ12 .... 207 C6
Newton Abbot TQ12.... 208 B4

Hackney Marshes Nature Reserve ★ TQ12 .... 207 E6
Hackpen Cross Way EX15. 66 E6
Hackworthy Cnr EX4 .... 98 F5
Hackworthy Cross EX6 .. 97 E5
Hackworthy Cross La EX6 97 E5
Hackworthy La
　Nadderwater EX4 .... 98 F5
　Tedburn St Mary EX6. .. 97 D4
HADDACOTT 26 E3
Haddacott Cross EX38. 26 F3
Haddeo Dr EX2 .... 178 D4
Haddington Rd PL2 .... 247 F4
Haddon Cross EX13 .. 103 C8
Haddon Ct **4** TQ3. .. 226 B7
Haddon La TA4 .... 34 C7
Haddon Rd EX3 .... 103 B8
Hadfield Ct **4** TQ13 .. 123 C4
Hadrian Dr EX4 .... 174 B2
Hadrians Way EX8 .. 196 D3
HADWORTHY 65 B8
Halberton Prim Sch EX16 65 A7
Halcyon Ct EX2 .... 248 A6
Halcyon Rd
　Newton Abbot TQ12.. .. 207 B3
　Plymouth PL2 .... 248 A6
Haldane Terr **8** EX32 .. 154 F6
Haldon Ave TQ14 .... 210 C6
Haldon Belvedere ★ EX6. 113 F5
Haldon Cl
　2 Newton Abbot TQ12.... 207 F2
　Topsham EX3. .... 182 E6
　Torquay TQ1. .... 220 E4
Haldon Ct EX8 .... 196 B2
Haldon Dr EX6. .... 114 A4
Haldon La TQ13 .... 124 B4
Haldon Lodge EX6 .... 114 B5
Haldon Pl PL5 .... 244 A3
Haldon Rd
　Exeter EX4 .... 177 A6
　Torquay TQ1. .... 220 D4
Haldon Rise **1** TQ12 .. 207 F2
Haldon Terr **14** EX7 .. 204 D6
Haldon View TQ13 .... 123 F6
Haldon View Terr EX2. .. 177 F5
Haldron's Almshouses EX16. .... 161 C4
Hale La EX14 .... 166 E6
Haley Barton **4** EX38. 248 A5
Haley Cl EX8 .... 196 C2
Halfmoon Ct TQ11 .... 236 A3
HALF MOON VILLAGE .. 172 C7
HALFORD 122 F1
Halford Cross TQ12 .. 122 E1
Halfpenny Cross EX16. .. 49 B7
Halfsbury Cross EX37 .. 43 E4
Halfway House Flats TQ5. .... 230 F6
Hallamore La PL21 .. 133 B2
Hallerton Cl PL21 .... 133 B2
Hallerton Cl PL6 .... 245 E2
Hallett Cl PL12. .... 242 E3
Hallett Ct DT7 .... 260 D4
Halletts Way TQ14 .. 167 E6
Halley Gdns PL5 .... 243 E1
Hall Hill EX5. .... 6 B5
Hall La EX7. .... 210 E8
HALLSANDS 149 E5
Halsdon Cross EX31. .. 10 E4
Halls Cross EX31. .... 10 E4
Hall's La TQ12 .... 212 F4
Hall's Mill La EX31 .. 154 E8
HALLSPILL. 26 A2
Hallswell Ct TQ4 .... 226 B6
Halmpstone Cross EX32 . 28 C7
Halsbury Rd EX16 .... 161 F4
Halscombe La EX2 .... 176 C1
Halscombe Ave EX8. .. 196 A1
Halsdon Cross EX22. .. 54 C1
Halsdon La EX8 .... 196 A2
Halsdon Rd EX8 .... 202 A7
Halsdon Terr EX38 .... 159 C5
Halsdon Wildlife Reserve ★ EX19. .... 57 D6
Halsgate Cross EX20 .. 77 D3
Halse Hill EX9 .... 197 F1
Halse La
　North Tawton EX20 .... 77 D4
　West Worlington EX17.... 61 A6
Halses Ct EX4 .... 176 D8
Halsewood Gate EX15... 64 E2
Halsey Lake Cross EX31 . 10 D1
HALSFORDWOOD. 98 F4
Halsfordwood La EX4 .. 98 F4
Halshanger Cross TQ13 . 130 F8
HALSINGER. 8 E1
Halsteads Rd TQ2 .. 214 A2
Halswell Cross EX36 .. 29 D2
Hal The EX2 .... 177 B1
HALWELL. 139 B4
Halwell Bsns Pk TQ9 . 139 C3
Halwell Cross
　Denbury TQ12 .... 211 A5
　Halwell TQ9. .... 139 C4
Halwill Ho TQ7 .... 148 E7
HALWILL. 73 C2
HALWILL JUNCTION .. 73 E2
Halwill Mdw EX21 .... 73 D3
Halwill Prim Sch EX21.. 73 D3
Halyards EX3 .... 182 E5
HAM
　Axminster 86 F4
　Plymouth 248 A8
　Wellington 52 D8
Hambeer La EX2 .... 176 E3
Hamberhayne Cross EX24. .... 102 D6

Hamble Cl PL3. .... 249 D7
Hamblecombe La TQ13. 124 A4
Hambleton Ho **4** TA4.. 210 C5
Hambleton Way TQ4 .. 226 A2
Ham Butts TQ7 .... 143 F7
Ham Cl PL2 .... 248 B8
Ham Cross EX13 .... 86 F4
Ham Dr PL2 .... 248 B8
Hameldown Cl TQ12 .. 219 B7
Hameldown Rd EX20 .. 170 E5
Hameldown Way TQ12 . 207 D6
Hamelin Way TQ2, TQ3... 219 A8
Ham Gn PL2 .... 248 A7
Ham Green La PL2 .. 248 A7
Ham Green La PL2 .. 248 A7
Ham Hill
　Ashreigney EX18 .... 58 E8
　Street Ash TA20 .... 69 E8
Ham Ho PL2 .... 248 A8
Hamilton Ave EX2 .... 177 F2
Hamilton Cl
　Bideford EX39 .... 25 E4
　14 Sidford EX10 .... 101 B1
Hamilton Ct **4** EX8 .. 202 B6
Hamilton Dr
　Exeter EX2 .... 178 D5
　Newton Abbot TQ12 .... 207 B5
Hamilton Gdns EX8 .. 202 B7
Hamilton Gr EX8 .... 201 B7
Hamilton La EX8 .... 202 C7
Hamilton Rd
　Exmouth EX8 .... 202 D7
　Topsham EX3. .... 182 E6
Hamiltons The TQ14 .. 210 A3
Ham La
　Colyton EX24 .... 103 A4
　Dittisham TQ6 .... 228 C3
　Plymouth PL2. .... 248 A8
　Shaldon TQ14. .... 209 D4
Hamley La TA20. .... 69 E8
Hamlin Gdns EX1 .... 178 A7
Hamlin Ho EX1 .... 178 A7
Hamlin La EX1 .... 178 A7
Hamlintoo La EX17.... 95 E7
Hamlyns Way TQ11.. 236 B5
Hammett Rd EX15. .. 163 B3
Hammetts La
　Barnstaple EX32 .... 155 B1
　Bishop's Tawton EX32 .. 16 E1
Hammond Croft Way EX2 .... 181 B8
Hamoaze Ave PL5 .... 247 D8
Hamoaze Pl PL1 .... 247 D2
Hamoaze Rd PL11 .. 247 B2
Hampden Pl EX1 .... 261 A1
Ham Pl **10** EX14 .... 161 C3
Hampshire Cl EX4 .... 176 E4
Hampson Cross EX17.. 78 A4
Hampson La EX17 .... 78 A4
HAMPTON. 103 C7
Hampton Ave TQ1.... 220 C8
Hampton Bldgs EX4 .. 261 C4
Hampton Cl EX13 .... 103 C6
Hampton La
　Torquay TQ1 .... 220 C8
　Whitford EX13 .... 103 C6
Hampton Rd
　Newton Abbot TQ12.... 207 C3
　Whitford EX13 .... 103 C7
Hampton St PL4 .... 263 A3
Ham Rd
　Dalwood EX13 .... 87 A3
　Wellington TA21. .... 52 D8
Hamslade Cross EX16.. 48 D8
Hamslade Hill EX16 .. 48 D8
Hams The EX2 .... 176 D1
Hamstone Ct TQ8 .... 259 D4
Hamway La TA20 .... 69 F8
Hancock Cl PL6 .... 244 D6
HAND & PEN. 99 E6
Hand & Pen Cotts EX5.. 99 E6
Handy Cross EX39 .... 25 E4
Hanger La EX14 .... 84 F8
Hanging La EX31 .... 5 A3
Hangman Path EX34 .. 2 F6
Hangman's Cross PL21 . 138 A2
Hangman's Hill EX16.. 48 D7
Hangman's Hill Cross EX16 .... 48 E7
Hankford Cross EX22.. 39 E2
Hannaburrow La EX33.. 14 F8
HANNAFORD 28 C8
Hannaford Cross EX32. 28 C8
Hannaford La EX32.. 28 C8
Hannaford Rd
　Lifton PL16. .... 105 E3
　Nass Mayo PL8 .... 140 F5
Hannaton Cross EX32.. 28 D8
Hanover Ct
　7 Brixham TQ5. .... 230 C3
　Exeter EX1. .... 177 F6
　Plymouth PL3. .... 249 B5
Hanover Gdns
　Dulverton TA22 .... 33 D7
　Exeter EX2. .... 181 C8
　15 Sidmouth EX10 .... 101 A1
Hanover Gdns EX15.. 163 C5
Hanover Ho TQ1 .... 220 D3
Hanover Rd
　Exeter EX1. .... 177 F6
　Plymouth PL3. .... 249 C4
Hansard Cross
　Ashreigney EX18 .... 44 A1
　Burrington EX37. .... 44 B2
Hansford Cross EX14.. 166 C5
Hansford Way EX11.. 169 C3

Hanson Pk EX39 .... 157 A4
Happaway Cl TQ2 .... 214 A2
Happaway Rd TQ2 .... 214 A2
HARBERTON. 222 D1
Harberton St TQ4 .... 225 E3
HARBERTONFORD .. 139 C6
Harbour Ave
　Plymouth, Camels Head PL5 .... 247 E8
　Plymouth PL4. .... 263 A2
Harbour Ct
　Exmouth EX8 .... 201 F6
　4 Seaton EX12. .... 192 B4
Harbourne Ave TQ4 .. 225 F3
HARBOURNEFORD .. 135 B5
Harbourneford Cross TQ10 .... 135 B4
Harbour Rd EX12 .... 192 B4
Harbourside **8** EX34.. 150 C6
Harbour Sq TQ8 .... 259 D5
Harbour St PL1 .... 247 F1
Harbour Terr EX2 .... 192 C5
Harbour View
　Plymouth PL9. .... 255 A7
　Saltash PL12 .... 242 E1
Harbour View Cl **1** TQ5 . 230 C5
HARCOMBE
　Chudleigh. 124 A4
　Sidford. 101 D1
HARCOMBE BOTTOM . 104 D6
Harcombe Cross
　Chudleigh TQ13 .... 124 A8
　Raymond's Hill EX13 .. 104 C6
　Sidbury EX10 .... 101 C1
Harcombe Fields EX10 . 188 D8
Harcombe La EX10.. 188 D8
Harcombe Lane E EX10. 188 D8
Harcombe Rd
　Raymond's Hill DT7 .... 104 D6
　Uplyme DT7 .... 260 D8
Hardaway Head **7** EX32 . 155 A5
Harden Ho TQ3 .... 225 E7
Harding Cres EX16 .. 161 E5
Hardings Cl PL12 .... 242 E3
HARDISWORTHY. .. 37 A7
Hardisworthy Cross EX39. 37 B7
Hardwick Farm PL7 .. 250 C3
Hardwick Rd TQ1 .... 220 C2
Hardy Cres PL5 .... 244 E1
Hardy Rd EX2 .... 178 D5
Hardys Cl EX10 .... 186 D4
Harebell Cl PL12 .... 242 D4
Harebell Copse EX4 .. 176 D8
Harebell Dr EX15 .. 162 E5
Haredon Cross PL21 . 137 D6
Harefield Cl EX8 .... 177 A8
Harefield Cotts EX8 .. 195 D5
Harefield Dr
　Lympstone EX8 .... 195 F5
　Stoke Fleming TQ6. .... 146 B7
Harefield Rd EX8 .... 195 F6
Harefoot Cross TQ13.. 121 D3
Hare La EX4 .... 98 D4
Harepath Hill EX12.. 192 A7
Harepathstead Rd EX5.. 83 B1
Harepie Cross EX31 .. 27 C6
Haresdown Cross EX36... 47 A7
Hares Gn EX36. .... 158 C4
Hares La TQ13 .... 130 F4
Hareston Cl PL7 .... 251 B3
Hareston Cross PL8 .. 257 D8
Harestone Cross EX13.. 88 B7
Hare Tor **LG** EX20. .... 170 C5
HAREWOOD 125 E4
Harewood TQ11. .... 236 B5
Harewood Cl PL7 .... 250 E5
Harewood Cres PL5.. 244 B2
Harewood Rd PL18.. 125 D3
HARFORD
　Cornwood. 133 F2
　Tedburn St Mary. 97 F7
Harford Cross EX17 .. 17 C2
Harford Rd
　Ivybridge PL21 .... 237 D6
　Landkey EX32. .... 17 B2
Hargood Terr **6** PL2.. 247 F4
Hargreaves Cl PL5 .. 243 F2
Harker La EX6 .... 114 B2
Harlech Cl PL3. .... 249 A7
Harlequins Sh Ctr EX4 . 261 A3
HARLESTON 145 A4
Harleston Cross TQ7.. 144 F4
Harley Cl PL21 .... 237 D5
Harlington Ct TQ12 .. 207 C4
Harleywood EX39 .... 156 E2
Harman Wlk EX32.. 155 C5
Harmerton Rd PL2 .. 248 D7
Haroldsleigh Ave PL5 .. 244 E2
Harper's Hill
　Northlew EX20. .... 74 E2
　Totnes TQ9. .... 223 A5
HARPFORD 100 C1
Harpins Ct TQ12 .... 213 A6
Harpitt Cl EX15 .... 162 C3
Harp La EX5 .... 99 E3
Harp's Corner Cross EX36 . 46 F6
Harpson Rd EX36. .... 31 F1
Harpson La
　Bishops Nympton EX36.. 31 F1
　South Molton EX36 .... 46 F8
Harracott Cross EX37... 27 E6
Harraton Cross PL21.. 137 D1
Harriers Cl EX12 .... 192 A6
Harrier Way EX2. .... 178 C4
Harriet Gdns PL7 .... 250 B6

Harringcourt Rd EX4 .. 174 E2
Harrington Dr EX4 .... 174 E2
Harrington Gdns EX4.. 174 E1
Harrington La EX4 .... 174 D2
Harris Cl EX4 .... 51 A4
Harris Cotts
　Blackawton TQ9 .... 139 E1
　Ivybridge PL21 .... 237 C5
Harris Cross EX39 .... 38 D8
Harris Ct PL9 .... 255 B6
Harrison St **7** PL2 .. 247 F4
Harrisons Way EX5.. 173 F8
Harris Way PL21 .... 136 B6
HARROWBARROW .. 125 A4
Harrowbarrow Prim Sch PL17 .... 125 A4
Harrowbeer La PL20.. 126 F3
Harrowby Cl EX16.. 161 F4
HARTFORD. 34 C8
HARTLAND. 22 E3
Hartland Abbey & Gdns ★ EX39 .... 22 C2
Hartland Cl PL21 .... 245 A7
Hartland Cross EX17.. 79 C4
Hartland Prim Sch EX39. 22 E3
Hartland Quay Mus ★ EX39 .... 22 C3
Hartland Tor Cl TQ5.. 230 A2
Hartland View Rd EX34.. 8 A1
HARTLEY. 248 E1
Hartley Ave PL3. .... 249 A6
Hartley Park Gdns PL3 . 248 F6
Hartley Rd
　Exmouth EX8 .... 202 A6
　Paignton TQ4 .... 226 A5
　Plymouth PL3. .... 248 E6
Hartleys The EX8 .... 202 A6
HARTLEY VALE. 249 A8
Hart Manor EX13 .... 152 E3
Hartnoll Cross EX16.. 64 E8
Harton Cross EX39 .. 22 E3
Harton Way EX39 .... 22 E3
Harton Way Ind Pk EX39 . 22 E3
Hartop Rd EX8. .... 202 A8
Hartop Rd TQ1 .... 214 B1
Harts Cl
　Exeter EX1. .... 178 E8
　Teignmouth TQ14.. 210 A6
Hart's La EX1 .... 178 D8
Hart St **9** EX39 .... 157 A2
Hartwell Ave PL9 .... 256 D7
Harvest La EX39 .... 156 D2
Harvey Ave EX4 .... 249 B1
Harveys Cl
　11 Chudleigh Knighton TQ13 .... 123 C4
　Sampford Courtenay EX20 . 76 C3
Harvey St PL11. .... 247 B2
Harwell Ct **6** PL1. .. 262 B3
Harwell La PL1 .... 135 A3
Harwell St PL1. .... 262 B3
Harwood Ave PL5 .... 244 C2
Harwood Cl EX8 .... 196 D1
Haskins Cross EX14 .. 84 C5
Hask La EX6 .... 113 A2
Haslam Rd TQ1 .... 220 A7
Haslam Rd TQ1 .... 220 A7
Hastings St PL1 .... 262 B3
Hastings Terr PL1 .. 262 B3
Haswell Cl PL6 .... 249 A8
HATCH 143 E5
Hatcher Cl EX14 .... 166 C5
Hatcher St **10** EX7 .. 204 D6
Hatchland Rd EX4 .. 174 F2
Hatchmoor Common La EX38. .... 159 F6
Hatchmoor Est EX38 . 159 F5
Hatchmoor Ind Est EX38 . 75 B6
Hatchmoor Lane Ind Est EX38. .... 159 F6
Hatchmoor Rd EX38.. 159 F5
Hatfield TQ1. .... 220 B6
Hatfield Rd TQ1. .... 220 B6
Hatherden Hill TQ13.. 123 B6
HATHERLEIGH 75 C6
Hatherleigh Com Prim Sch EX20. .... 75 C7
Hatherleigh La TQ13.. 122 F1
Hatherleigh Rd
　Exeter EX4. .... 177 A2
　Okehampton EX20 .... 93 F7
　Winkleigh EX19 .... 58 E2
Hatherton La EX20.. 76 E2
Hathpool EX10. .... 187 F8
Hatshill Cl PL6. .... 132 A2
Hatshill Farm Cl PL6.. 132 A5
Hatway Hill EX10. .... 101 C3
Hatway Rd TQ6 .... 233 F3
Havelock Rd TQ1 .... 214 B1
Havelock Terr
　Lutton PL21. .... 133 B2
　Plymouth PL2. .... 247 F3
Haven Banks EX2 .... 261 B1
Haven Banks Ret Pk EX2 . 261 A1
Haven Cl EX16 .... 161 E5
Haven Ct **5** EX12 .... 192 B4
Haven Rd EX2 .... 261 A1
Haven The EX8 .... 208 F7
Havenview Rd EX12 .. 192 A5
Have's Hill EX17 .... 61 C8
Hawarden Cotts PL4 . 249 B1
Hawcombe La EX31.. 4 E8
Haweswater Cl PL6 .. 244 E4
HAWKCHURCH. 88 E3
Hawkchurch CE Prim Sch EX13. .... 88 E3
Hawkchurch Cross EX13.. 88 E2

Hawkchurch Rd EX13 .... 88 E3
Hawkerland Rd EX10.. 186 C4
Hawkers Ave PL4 .... 263 A2
Hawkers La PL3. .... 248 E5
Hawkesdown Ct EX12 . 192 D7
Hawking Gdns PL5.. 243 E4
Hawkins Ave TQ2 .... 219 C2
Hawkins Cl PL6 .... 245 A5
Hawkins Dr TQ14 .... 210 B6
Hawkins La EX11. .... 168 E3
Hawkin's La TA4 .... 35 E7
Hawkins Pl EX15. .... 163 C4
Hawkins Rd TQ12 .... 207 F3
Hawkins Way EX17.. 165 E5
Hawkins St EX20 .... 170 D5
Hawkmoor Cotts TQ13 . 122 E7
Hawkmoor Pk TQ13.. 122 F7
Hawkridge. 21 D1
Hawkridge Cross
　Hawkridge TA22. .... 21 D1
　Umberleigh EX37. .... 28 C4
Hawkridge Rd EX31.. 15 E5
Hawksdown View EX12.. 192 A7
Hawks Dr **8** EX16. .. 161 E6
Hawks Pk PL12 .... 242 C2
Hawks Way EX34.. 17 A2
Hawkwell Cross EX16 .. 32 F4
Hawley Cl EX32 .... 155 C5
Hawley Cross EX13.. 86 F3
Hawley Manor EX32.. 155 C5
Hawson Cross PL21.. 130 B3
Hawthorn Ave
　Ilfracombe EX34 .... 150 D5
　Torpoint PL11 .... 246 F3
Hawthorn Cl
　Cullompton EX15 .... 163 B2
　Honiton EX14. .... 166 B5
　Kingsbridge TQ7 .... 258 C4
　Plymouth, Hooe PL9 .... 255 C5
　Plymouth, Woolwell PL6 . 245 D7
Hawthorn Dr
　Sidmouth EX10 .... 187 F8
　Wembury PL9 .... 140 D7
Hawthorne Cl TQ12 .. 212 F8
Hawthorne Rd
　10 Tiverton EX16.. 161 F6
　Wellington TA21. .... 160 F5
Hawthorn Gr
　Exmouth EX8 .... 196 E1
　Plymouth PL2. .... 248 C7
Hawthorn Park Cl TQ2 . 219 D3
Hawthorn Park Rd PL9 . 140 D7
Hawthorn Pk
　Bideford EX39 .... 156 E1
　Lydford EX20 .... 107 F4
Hawthorn Rd
　Barnstaple EX32 .... 155 E4
　Crediton EX17 .... 165 C5
　Exeter EX2. .... 177 F3
　Tavistock PL19 .... 171 C2
Hawthorns PL12 .... 242 D2
Hawthorn Way
　Exeter EX2. .... 181 A8
　Plymouth PL3. .... 249 B7
Haxter Cl PL6 .... 241 B1
Haxton Down La EX31.. 18 B8
Haxton La EX31. .... 18 A8
Haycroft Ho **3** EX39 .. 157 A1
Haycross Hill EX21.. 55 D4
Haydn Cl EX32 .... 155 C5
Haydon Cl EX16 .... 48 C4
Haydon Gr PL5 .... 243 C1
Haydon Rd EX16 .... 161 B5
Haydons Pk EX14 .... 166 C5
Haye Cl DT7 .... 260 C4
Haye Gdns DT7 .... 260 C4
Haye La
　Colyford DT7, EX13 .... 103 C3
　Lyme Regis DT7 .... 260 D4
Haye Rd PL7, PL9 .... 250 C1
Haye Road S PL9 .... 256 C7
Hayes Barton Ct EX4 . 177 A5
Hayes Cl
　Budleigh Salterton EX9 . 198 A3
　Otterton EX9 .... 198 E2
　Totnes TQ9. .... 223 E4
Hayes Copse EX32 .. 17 B2
Hayes Cross EX21.. 55 E3
Hayes Ct
　Lyme Regis DT7 .... 260 D3
　Paignton TQ3. .... 225 F5
Hayes The TQ5. .... 229 E5
Hayeswood La EX9 .. 198 A6
Hayfield Rd EX20.. 76 C5
Hay La TQ7. .... 147 E6
Hayle Ave TQ4 .... 229 B8
Hayley Pk TQ12 .... 212 F3
Hayman's Cl EX15.. 163 B2
Haymans Gdns EX15.. 163 B2
Haymans Orch EX5.. 184 C3
Hayne Barton Cotts EX15. .... 163 E6

Hayne Cl
Exeter EX4 .... 178 A7
Tipton St John EX10 ..... 100 D2
Hayne Cross
Ashill EX15 .... 66 F5
Bishops Nympton EX36 .... 31 A4
Cheriton Fitzpaine EX17 ... 63 A2
Lewtrenchard EX20 ...... 106 B5
Lustleigh TQ13 .... 121 F7
Morebath EX16 .... 34 B4
Plymtree EX15 .... 83 F6
Zeal Monachorum EX17 .... 78 B6
Hayne Ct EX16 .... 161 E7
Hayne Hill EX10 .... 100 D2
Hayne Ho EX16 .... 49 B2
Hayne La
Bolham EX16 .... 49 B2
Butterleigh EX15 .... 64 C2
Honiton EX14 .... 85 C2
Silverton EX5 .... 82 C4
Wilmington EX14 .... 86 D3
Hayne Pk
Barnstaple EX32 .... 155 B4
Tipton St John EX10 ..... 100 D2
Haynes La EX6 .... 176 A2
Hayne Town Cross EX37 .. 44 B8
Hayrish Cross EX20 ...... 95 B7
Haystone Pl PL1 .... 262 B4
Haytor Ave TQ4 .... 225 F3
Haytor Cl
Plymouth PL5 .... 244 B3
Teignmouth TQ14 .... 209 D8
Haytor Ct TQ13 .... 122 A4
Haytor Dr
Exeter EX4 .... 176 E7
Ivybridge PL21 .... 237 D4
Newton Abbot TQ12 ...... 208 A3
Haytor Gr TQ12 .... 208 A3
Haytor Pk TQ12 .... 207 E7
Haytor Rd TQ1 .... 220 B7
Haytor Rocks* TQ13 ...... 121 F3
Haytor Terr 17 TQ12 ..... 207 B3
Haytor Vale TQ13 .... 122 B4
Haytor View Prim Sch
TQ12 .... 207 F3
HAYTOWN 39 E1
Haytown Pottery* EX22 .. 39 E1
Haywain Cl TQ2 .... 213 B1
Haywards Prim Sch 5
EX17 .... 165 D5
Hazel Ave EX33 .... 152 E7
Hazel Cl
Kingsbridge TQ7 .... 258 C4
Newton Abbot TQ12 ...... 208 A1
Newton Poppleford EX10 . 186 F8
Plymouth PL6 .... 245 B6
Seaton EX12 .... 192 A7
Teignmouth TQ14 .... 210 C8
Hazel-Crest TQ13 .... 123 B7
Hazeldene TQ8 .... 259 C3
Hazeldene Cl PL21 .... 136 B6
Hazeldene Gdns EX8 ..... 196 A1
Hazeldown Prim Sch
TQ14 .... 210 B8
Hazeldown Rd TQ14 ...... 210 B7
Hazel Dr PL9 .... 256 C7
Hazel Gr
4 Barnstaple EX31 .... 154 C2
Plymouth PL9 .... 256 C7
Rockbeare EX5 .... 99 C5
Yelverton PL20 .... 127 A3
Hazelmead Rd EX5 .... 179 E2
Hazel Rd
Exeter EX2 .... 177 F2
Tavistock PL19 .... 171 C2
Hazelwood 6 TQ1 .... 220 D5
Hazelwood Cl EX14 ...... 166 C4
Hazelwood Cres PL9 ..... 256 D7
Hazelwood Dr
Dawlish Warren EX7 ..... 201 A2
Plymouth PL6 .... 245 D8
Hazelwood Pk EX7 .... 201 B2
Headborough Rd TQ13 ... 130 F5
Headgate EX36 .... 20 B1
Head Hill EX18, EX37 ..... 44 C5
Headingley Cl EX2 .... 178 C4
Headland Cl EX1 .... 178 C7
Headland Cres EX1 ...... 178 C7
Headland Cross EX17 ..... 96 A6
Headland Ct
8 Brixham TQ5 .... 230 D5
Woolacombe EX34 .... 7 F8
Headland Gr TQ3 .... 219 C1
Headland La EX17 .... 96 A5
Headland Park Rd TQ3 .. 219 C1
Headland Pk PL4 .... 263 A4
Headland Rd TQ2 .... 219 E2
Headlands The TQ2 ...... 219 E2
Headlands View Ave EX34 .. 1 B1
Headless Cross TQ13 .... 112 B6
HEADON 72 C5
Headon Cross EX22 .... 72 C5
Headon Gdns EX2 .... 178 A1
Headson Cross EX20 ...... 91 E1
Headstock Rd TA20 .... 88 E7
Headway Cl TQ14 .... 209 D7
Headway Cross Rd TQ14 209 D8
Headway Rise TQ14 ...... 209 D8
Head Weir Rd EX15 ...... 163 C5
HEALE 4 A3
Heale Down La EX31 .... 4 A3
Heal Park Cres EX31 ..... 153 D5
Heal's Field EX13 .... 167 F7
Healy Ct 9 PL2 .... 247 F4
Healy Pl PL2 .... 247 F4
Heanton Cl EX33 .... 152 E6
Heanton Ct TQ1 .... 220 C4
Heanton Hill EX33 .... 152 F4
Heanton Hill La EX31 ..... 15 E6
Heanton Lea EX31 .... 15 E6
HEANTON PUNCHARDON 15 E6
Heanton St EX33 .... 152 D5
Heanton Terr PL10 ...... 252 E6
Heard Ave EX8 .... 202 E8
Heard Cl EX39 .... 22 E3
Hearl Rd PL12 .... 242 B3
Hearson Cross EX32 ...... 28 B8
Heasley Cross EX36 ...... 19 C3
Heasley La EX36 .... 19 D3
HEASLEY MILL 19 D3
Heasley Mill Cross EX36 .. 19 D3
HEATH 175 D6
Heathayne Cross EX24 ... 102 F5
Heathbrook Mews EX4 .. 174 C2
Heath Cl
Heathfield TQ12 .... 123 B2
15 Honiton EX14 .... 85 C2
Heathcoat Prim Sch
EX16 .... 161 B3
Heathcoat Sq EX16 ...... 161 C4
Heathcoat Way EX16 ..... 161 F5
Heath Comm EX13 .... 87 E6
Heath Cross
Cheriton Fitzpaine EX16 ... 63 A5
Spreyton EX17 .... 96 A8
Tedburn St Mary EX4 ...... 98 C5
Heath Ct
Brixham TQ5 .... 230 E6
1 Totnes TQ9 .... 223 C5
Heather Cl
Exeter EX1 .... 178 B6
9 Honiton EX14 .... 85 C2
Newton Abbot TQ12 ...... 206 F4
Okehampton EX20 .... 170 B5
Seaton EX12 .... 192 B7
Tavistock PL19 .... 171 D4
Teignmouth TQ14 .... 210 B7
8 Tiverton EX16 .... 161 F6
Heatherdale EX8 .... 202 C6
Heatherdene TQ13 .... 180 C7
Heather Est TQ12 .... 180 F3
Heatherfield EX6 .... 98 C4
Heather Grange EX11 .... 168 D4
Heather Pk TQ10 .... 135 A3
Heathers The
Okehampton EX20 .... 170 D6
Plymouth PL6 .... 245 D7
Heather Terr PL20 ...... 128 A8
Heatherton Park Ho TA4 . 52 E8
Heather Way TQ5 .... 230 A4
Heather Wlk PL21 .... 237 D4
HEATHFIELD 180 F2
Heathfield Cl TQ13 ...... 180 C5
Heathfield Cotts TQ12 ... 123 B3
Heathfield Cross
Axmouth DT7 .... 193 D8
Cornwood PL21 .... 133 B3
Heathfield TQ12 .... 123 B2
Modbury PL21 .... 137 E2
Poltimore EX4 .... 174 C7
Woodbury Salterton EX5 . 184 A7
Heathfield Ind Est TQ12 . 180 F3
Heathfieldlake Hill TQ13 123 F7
Heathfield Mdw TQ13 .... 180 D5
Heathfield Pk PL20 ...... 127 A3
Heathfield Rd
Bideford EX39 .... 157 C1
Denbury TQ12 .... 211 A6
Plymouth PL4 .... 249 B3
Heathfield Terr
Bovey Tracey TQ13 ...... 180 C6
Denbury TQ12 .... 211 A6
Heath Hill TQ12 .... 123 B2
Heath La
Cheriton Fitzpaine EX16 ... 63 A6
Hollocombe EX19 .... 58 F5
Tedburn St Mary EX4, EX6 .. 98 C4
Heathlands Ct TQ14 ...... 210 A8
Heathlands Rise TQ14 ... 210 A8
Heathland View EX38 ..... 40 D1
Heathpark Ind Est EX14 . 166 A5
Heathpark Way 13 EX14 .. 85 C2
Heath Pk
Brixham TQ5 .... 230 E5
Newton Abbot TQ12 ...... 208 A1
Heath Rd
Brixham TQ5 .... 230 E5
Dunsford EX6 .... 112 F7
Exeter EX2 .... 178 B5
Spreyton EX17 .... 95 F8
Heath Rise TQ5 .... 230 E5
HEATHSTOCK 87 A6
Heath Terr PL18 .... 125 C5
Heatree Cl TQ14 .... 210 B8
Heatree Cross TQ13 ..... 121 D7
Heaviside Cl TQ2 .... 214 B3
HEAVITREE 178 B6
Heavitree Gallows EX1 .. 178 C5
Heavitree Pk EX1 .... 178 A5
Heavitree Rd
Exeter EX1 .... 177 E6
Kingsand PL10 .... 253 A2
Hectors Cl EX19 .... 57 F7
Heddeswell Cross TQ7 .. 143 E2
HEDDON 29 B7
Heddon Cross
Heddon EX32 .... 29 A7
Milton Damerel EX22 ...... 54 C5
Hederman Cl EX5 .... 82 B5
Hedge Cross EX20 .... 107 C4
Hedgend Rd EX14 .... 86 B5
Hedgerow Cl
Crediton EX17 .... 165 E6
Plymouth PL6 .... 245 E8
Hedgerows The PL12 ..... 242 B3
Hedingham Cl PL7 .... 251 C4
Hedingham Gdns PL6 .... 245 B7
Heggadon Cl EX5 .... 83 A7
Heiffers La EX16 .... 47 A5
Heights The PL19 .... 171 A6
Heirland Cross TQ7 ..... 143 D3
HELE
Bradninch 82 F5
Ilfracombe 150 F6
Torquay 219 F8
Hele Almshouses PL9 ... 140 E8
Hele Barton Cross EX17 .. 61 D6
Helebridge Rd EX23 ...... 70 A6
Hele Cl
Barnstaple EX31 .... 154 A3
Bickleigh PL6 .... 132 A5
Torquay TQ2 .... 213 F1
Hele Corn Mill* EX34 ... 150 E5
Hele Cross
Ashburton TQ13 .... 130 E5
Bradworthy EX22 .... 38 E4
Cornwood PL21 .... 133 D4
King's Nympton EX37 ..... 44 D7
St Giles on t H PL15 ...... 90 B3
Torquay TQ2 .... 213 F1
Hele Gdns PL7 .... 251 A4
Hele Hill EX17 .... 61 C5
Hele La
Barnstaple EX31 .... 154 A3
Frithelstock Stone EX38 ... 40 F5
Roborough PL6 .... 241 F2
Shaugh Prior PL6, PL7 .... 132 A6
Hele Lane Hill EX17 ...... 61 D6
Hele Mill EX34 .... 150 E6
Helena Pl 7 EX8 .... 202 A6
Helens Mead Cl TQ2 ..... 214 A4
Helens Mead Rd TQ2 .... 214 A4
Hele Rd
Bradninch EX5 .... 82 F6
Exeter EX4 .... 261 A4
Kingsteignton TQ12 ...... 123 E1
Torquay TQ2 .... 213 F1
Hele Rise EX31 .... 154 A3
Hele Sq EX5 .... 82 F5
Hele's Sch PL7 .... 250 C6
Hele's Terr PL4 .... 249 B2
Helford Dr TQ4 .... 229 B8
Helford Wlk TQ4 .... 229 B8
Heligan Dr TQ3 .... 225 E8
Hellevoetsluis Way TQ3 . 218 F4
Hellier Cl EX14 .... 166 A4
Hellinghayes La EX16 .... 46 C3
Hellings Gdns EX5 ...... 175 C7
Hellings Parks La EX5 ... 175 E4
Helmdon Rise TQ2 .... 219 B8
Helston Cl TQ3 .... 225 F7
HELTOR 112 D6
Heltor Bsns Pk TQ12 ..... 180 F4
Hembury Cock Hill TQ11 236 A7
Hembury Cotts TQ9 ..... 131 E1
Hembury Cross
Holbeton PL8 .... 141 F8
Stibb Cross EX38 .... 40 C4
Hembury Fort Cross EX14 84 E5
Hembury Pk TQ11 .... 236 B7
HEMERDON 251 D7
Hemerdon Hts PL7 .... 251 A6
Hemerdon La PL7 .... 251 C8
Hemerdon Way PL7 ...... 250 D6
Hems Brook Ct TQ2 ...... 219 B8
HEMSFORD 216 F4
Hems La TQ9 .... 216 D7
Hemsworthy Gate TQ13 . 121 E3
HEMYOCK 67 C8
Hemyock Castle* EX15 ... 67 B8
Hemyock Prim Sch EX15 . 67 B8
Hemyock Rd EX15 .... 66 E8
Henacre Rd TQ7 .... 258 D5
Henacroft Cross EX19 .... 58 B3
Henbury Cl TQ1 .... 220 B6
Henceford Cross EX17 .... 62 A6
Henderbarrow Cross
EX21 .... 73 E1
Henders Cnr 6 PL3 ...... 248 F6
Henderson Pl PL2 .... 247 F6
Hendon Cross EX16 .... 50 B8
Hendwell Cl PL6 .... 244 E6
Heneaton Sq EX2 .... 182 B8
HENFORD 90 C5
Henlake Cl PL21 .... 237 B6
Henley Cl EX13 .... 88 B7
Henley Dr PL5 .... 244 C7
Henley Ho TQ7 .... 143 A1
Henley Rd EX8 .... 202 C7
Hennapyn Rd TQ2 .... 219 E3
HENNOCK 123 B7
Hennock Com Prim Sch
TQ13 .... 123 B7
Hennock Ct EX2 .... 181 D8
Hennock Rd TQ4 .... 225 F2
Hennock Rd Central EX2 177 C1
Hennock Road E EX2 ..... 177 D1
Hennock Road N EX2 ..... 177 C2
Henrietta Pl 7 EX8 ...... 202 A7
Henrietta Rd 8 EX8 ...... 202 A7
Henry Cl PL21 .... 136 B6
Henry Lewis Cl 7 EX5 .... 99 E8
Henry's Way DT7 .... 260 E4
Hensbury La PL20 .... 239 F4
Hensford Mews EX7 ..... 200 C3
Hensford Rd EX7 .... 200 C2
Hensleigh Dr EX2 .... 177 E5
Hensleigh Rd EX16 .... 63 F7
Hensons Dr EX16 .... 51 A3
Hen St EX5 .... 83 A7
Henstill La EX17 .... 79 F7
HENSTRIDGE 3 A1
Henty Ave EX7 .... 204 F7
Henty Cl EX7 .... 204 F8
Heppenstall Rd EX32 .... 155 B6
Heraldry Way EX2 .... 178 D4
Herbert Ho TA22 .... 33 D6
Herbert Pl PL2 .... 247 E4
Herbert Rd
Exeter EX1 .... 177 F7
Salcombe TQ8 .... 259 D4
Torquay TQ2 .... 219 D4
Herbert St PL2 .... 247 E4
Herdicott Cross EX22 ..... 71 F2
Hereford Cl EX8 .... 196 D4
Hereford Rd
Exeter EX4 .... 176 D6
Plymouth PL5 .... 244 B5
Heritage Cl PL12 .... 242 C3
Heritage Ct 15 EX14 ..... 166 C6
Heritage Pk PL19 .... 171 D6
Heritage Way EX10 ...... 188 B8
Hermes Ave EX16 .... 161 E3
Hermitage Ct 1 PL4 ..... 248 E4
Hermitage Rd
Dartmouth TQ6 .... 233 D4
Ilfracombe EX34 .... 150 B6
Plymouth PL3 .... 248 E5
Hermitage The 1 EX34 .. 150 B5
Hermosa Gdns 5 TQ14 .. 210 B5
Hermosa Rd TQ14 .... 210 B5
Hernaford Cross TQ9 .... 139 B6
Hernaford Rd TQ9 .... 139 C6
Hern La PL8 .... 257 F4
Heron Cl PL10 .... 252 F6
Heron Ct
Barnstaple EX32 .... 155 E4
Exmouth EX8 .... 202 C6
Heron Ind Units EX2 .... 178 E5
Heron Rd
Exeter, Middle Moor EX2 . 176 D3
Exeter, Sowton EX2 ...... 178 E5
Honiton EX14 .... 166 B4
Herons Brook EX20 ..... 170 A6
Herons Reach TQ7 ...... 144 C1
Heron Way
Cullompton EX15 .... 163 B2
Torquay TQ2 .... 213 C3
Herschel Gdns PL5 ...... 243 E1
Herschell Rd EX4 .... 177 E8
Hertland Wlk PL2 .... 248 A7
Hescane Pk EX6 .... 97 B4
Hesketh Cres TQ1 .... 220 D3
Hesketh Mews TQ1 ...... 220 D3
Hesketh Rd TQ1 .... 220 D3
Hessary Dr PL6 .... 241 C1
Hessary Terr PL20 ...... 128 A8
Hessary View
Saltash PL12 .... 242 E4
Tavistock PL19 .... 171 B6
Hestow Rd TQ12 .... 123 F1
Hetling Cl PL1 .... 262 B3
Hewer's Row PL4 .... 263 A3
Hewett Cl TQ12 .... 208 A3
Hewitt Cl PL12 .... 242 C1
Hexdown Barns TQ7 .... 142 F3
Hexham Pl PL2 .... 248 A8
Hexton Hill Rd PL9 ..... 255 B6
Hexton Quay PL9 .... 255 C6
HEXWORTHY 129 B7
Hexworthy Ave EX4 ..... 176 E8
Heybrook Ave PL5 .... 243 D1
HEYBROOK BAY 140 B8
Heybrook Dr PL9 .... 140 A7
Heydon's La EX10 .... 188 A4
Heyridge Mdw EX15 ...... 163 B1
Heyswood Ave EX32 ..... 155 C2
Heywood Cl
Hartland EX39 .... 22 E3
Torquay TQ2 .... 219 E7
Heywood Cross EX18 ..... 59 D5
Heywood Dr EX6 .... 201 A8
Heywood Est TQ12 .... 207 D6
Heywood Rd EX39 .... 156 F5
Heywoods Cl 11 TQ14 ... 210 C5
Heywoods Rd TQ14 ...... 210 C5
Hibernia Terr PL5 ...... 247 E8
Hickory Cl EX14 .... 166 E5
Hickory Dr PL7 .... 251 B5
Hick's La PL4 .... 263 A2
Hides Rd EX10 .... 188 C8
Hidewood La EX15 .... 52 F1
Hierns La EX34 .... 150 C6
High Acre Dr PL21 ...... 237 A6
HIGHAMPTON 74 C7
Highampton Com Prim Sch
EX21 .... 74 C7
Highampton Cross EX21 .. 74 C7
Highaton Head Cross
EX36 .... 32 C4
High Bank
Exeter EX4 .... 178 B8
West Hill EX11 .... 168 D3
Highbank Cl PL19 .... 171 A4
Highbarrow Cross EX22 .. 54 A4
HIGH BICKINGTON 43 B7
High Bickington CE Prim Sch
EX37 .... 43 B7
High Bolham EX16 .... 33 C1
HIGH BRAY 18 F5
Highbridge Ct PL7 ...... 250 E5
HIGH BULLEN 42 B7
High Bullen EX5 .... 82 B6
High Bullen Cross EX36 .. 19 E1
High Bullen La EX35 .... 5 B3
Highbury Cres PL7 ...... 250 D7
Highbury Hill EX39 ...... 157 A8
Highbury Pk EX8 .... 196 A1
Highbury Rd
Barnstaple EX32 .... 155 C3
Torquay TQ1 .... 220 B6
High Cl TQ13 .... 180 E7
Highclere Gdns PL6 ..... 245 B8
Highcliff Ct EX7 .... 204 E6
Highcliffe Cl
Lympstone EX8 .... 195 D4
Seaton EX12 .... 191 F6
Highcliffe Cres EX12 .... 191 F6
Highcliffe Ct EX8 .... 195 D4
Highcliffe Mews TQ4 .... 226 C4
Highcliff Rd DT7 .... 260 C3
Highclyffe Ct EX12 ...... 191 F6
High Cott EX36 .... 19 C2
High Creek Cross EX10 .. 188 F8
Highcroft EX4 .... 173 A1
High Cross
Bampton EX16 .... 34 A1
14 Combe Martin EX34 ...... 3 A3
High Cross Ho* TQ9 ..... 216 A1
Highcross Rd EX4 .... 177 C8
Highdown Cross EX39 .... 23 A4
Higher Aboveway EX6 ... 182 B3
Higher Aller La TQ13 ... 122 E6
Higher Alston Farm TQ5 229 D3
Higher Anderton Rd
PL10 .... 252 F5
HIGHER ASHTON 113 D3
Higher Audley Ave TQ2 .. 219 F8
Higher Axmouth Cotts
EX12 .... 192 F6
Higher Barley Mount
EX4 .... 176 E5
HIGHER BATSON 259 C6
Higher Beara Cross
TQ11 .... 236 F4
Higher Bedlands EX9 .... 197 F2
Higher Bibbery TQ13 .... 180 E7
HIGHER BLAGDON 225 A7
Higher Borough TQ7 .... 149 A4
Higher Brand La EX14 ... 166 C4
Higher Brimley Rd TQ14 . 210 C5
HIGHER BRIXHAM 230 B3
Higher Broad Oak Rd
EX11 .... 168 D2
Higher Broad Pk TQ6 ... 233 D3
Higher Brook Mdw 1
EX10 .... 101 B1
Higher Brook Pk PL21 ... 237 A5
Higher Brownston Cross
PL21 .... 138 A4
Higher Buckeridge Rd
TQ14 .... 210 B7
Higher Budleigh Mdw
TQ12 .... 206 F3
Higher Bulkamore Cross
TQ10 .... 135 E5
Higher Bull Ring EX15 ... 163 C3
Higher Bulworthy Cross
EX16 .... 47 E4
Higher Bulworthy La
EX16 .... 47 E4
HIGHER BURROWTON 99 A8
Higher Cadewell La TQ2 . 219 C8
Higher Cheglinch La EX34 .. 8 F6
HIGHER CHERITON 84 E3
Higher Church St 6
EX32 .... 155 A4
Higher Churchway PL9 .. 256 A7
Higher Clevelands EX39 . 156 F6
HIGHER CLOVELLY 23 D2
Higher Collaton Cross
TQ7 .... 147 F6
Higher Colleybrook
TQ13 .... 124 B4
HIGHER COMPTON 249 A6
Higher Compton Barton
TQ3 .... 218 E6
Higher Compton Rd PL3 . 248 F6
Higher Contour Rd TQ6 . 234 B3
Higher Coombe Dr TQ14 210 A7
Higher Coombses TA20 ... 88 D8
Higher Copythorne TQ5 . 230 A4
Higher Cotteylands EX16 161 B3
Higher Cross EX15 .... 51 C1
Higher Cross Rd EX31 ... 154 B4
HIGHER DEAN 135 C7
Higher Dean TQ11 .... 135 C7
Higher Doats Hayne La
EX13 .... 103 D5
Higher Down EX6 .... 194 D3
Higher Downs Rd TQ1 ... 220 C8
Higher Dr EX7 .... 204 F8
Higher East St EX36 ...... 30 D8
Higher Edginswell La
TQ2 .... 219 B8
Higher Efford Rd PL3 ... 249 B5
Higher Elmwood EX31 ... 154 C3
Higher Elstone Cross
EX18 .... 44 D3
Higher Erith Rd TQ1 .... 220 D4
Higher Exeter Rd TQ14 .. 124 E2
Higher Exwick Hill EX4 .. 176 E7
Higher Forches Cross
EX17 .... 60 D4
Higher Fortescue EX10 .. 188 D7
Higher French Pk TQ12 .. 206 F3
Higher Furzeham Rd
TQ5 .... 230 C6
HIGHER GABWELL 214 B7
Higher Gn TQ10 .... 135 A2
Higher Green Cross TQ7 . 145 C4
Higher Greenway La
EX10 .... 187 E7
Higher Gunstone EX39 .. 157 A2

Higher Hendham Barns TQ7 ... 138 E1
Higher Hewish La EX31 ... 9 D4
Higher Hill View EX10 ... 188 A5
Higher Ho EX38 ... 42 B5
Higher Holcombe Cl TQ14 ... 210 C7
Higher Holcombe Dr TQ14 ... 210 C8
Higher Holcombe Rd TQ14 ... 210 C8
Higher Hoopern La EX4 ... 173 C1
Higher Island TQ9 ... 139 E2
HIGHER KEATON ... 237 D1
Higher Kelly PL18 ... 125 D3
Higher King's Ave EX4 ... 177 D8
Higher Kingsdown Rd TQ14 ... 209 D7
Higher Kinsman's Dale TQ13 ... 111 F5
Higher La
 Axmouth EX12 ... 192 E7
 Plymouth PL1 ... 262 C2
Higher Lane Cl EX12 ... 192 D7
Higher Ley EX17 ... 60 B3
Higher Lincombe Rd TQ1 ... 220 E3
Higher Longford Cvn Site PL19 ... 117 F1
Higher Loughborough EX16 ... 161 B5
Higher Manor Rd TQ5 ... 230 C5
Higher Manor Terr ◆ TQ3 ... 226 A5
Higher Marley Rd EX8 ... 196 D4
Higher Maudlin St ◆ EX32 ... 155 A6
Higher Maunders Hill EX9 ... 198 E7
Higher Mdws
 Beer EX12 ... 191 D5
 High Bickington EX37 ... 43 B7
Higher Mead EX15 ... 67 B8
HIGHER METCOMBE ... 168 D1
Higher Mill Flats DT7 ... 260 D4
Higher Millhayes EX15 ... 52 B1
Higher Mill La
 Buckfast TQ11 ... 236 B7
 Cullompton EX15 ... 163 C3
Higher Mogworthy Cross EX16 ... 47 D4
Highermoor Cross EX22 ... 53 B1
Higher Moor Sq ◆ EX16 ... 161 F6
Higher Mowles PL3 ... 249 B6
HIGHER MUDDIFORD ... 9 D1
Higher Newclose La EX31 ... 16 B6
Higher Park Cl PL7 ... 251 B3
Higher Park Rd EX33 ... 152 E5
Higher Penn TQ5 ... 230 D3
Higher Pk TQ7 ... 149 A3
Higher Polsham Rd TQ3 ... 226 B7
Higher Port View PL12 ... 242 F2
HIGHER PRESTACOTT ... 90 F7
Higher Preston Cross TQ12 ... 123 D1
Higher Queens Terr TQ1 ... 220 B5
Higher Rake La TQ7 ... 143 F6
Higher Raleigh Rd EX31 ... 155 A7
Higher Ramshill La TQ3 ... 225 C8
Higher Ranscombe Rd TQ5 ... 230 D4
Higher Rd
 Crediton EX17 ... 165 B6
 Fremington EX31 ... 153 E5
 Woodbury Salterton EX5 ... 184 B7
Higher Redgate EX16 ... 161 D5
Higher Ridgeway EX11 ... 169 E4
Higher Ringmore Rd TQ14 ... 209 D4
Higher Roborough ◆ TQ13 ... 131 A5
HIGHER ROSCOMBE BARTON ... 214 A6
Higher Row PL10 ... 253 A2
Higher Rydons TQ5 ... 230 A4
Higher Sackery TQ12 ... 208 D4
Higher Shapter Cl EX3 ... 182 F4
Higher Shapter St EX3 ... 182 F4
HIGHER SLADE ... 1 E3
Higher Slade Rd EX34 ... 150 A2
Higher Spring Gdns EX11 ... 169 E3
Higher St
 Brixham TQ5 ... 230 C5
 Cullompton EX15 ... 163 C4
 Dartmouth TQ6 ... 233 F3
 Dittisham TQ6 ... 228 B2
 Hatherleigh EX20 ... 75 C7
 Kingswear TQ6 ... 234 A3
Higher Steert Terr PL4 ... 263 C3
Higher Stockley Mead EX20 ... 170 F6
Higher Summerlands EX1 ... 261 C3
HIGHER TALE ... 84 A4
Higher Tamar Terr PL18 ... 125 D7
HIGHER TOWN ... 236 A5
Higher Town
 Malborough TQ7 ... 147 E6
 Sampford Peverell EX16 ... 50 C1
Higher Tuckers Pk EX22 ... 38 E1
Higher Union La TQ2 ... 220 A5
Higher Union Rd TQ7 ... 258 C5
Higher Venn Cross EX32 ... 17 A1
Higher Warberry Rd TQ1 ... 220 D5
Higher Warborough Rd TQ5 ... 229 B6

HIGHER WARCOMBE ... 1 B2
Higher Warcombe Cross TQ7 ... 144 A5
Higher Warren Rd TQ7 ... 258 E3
Higher Way EX10 ... 187 A8
HIGHER WEAR ... 178 A1
Higher Wear Rd EX2 ... 182 C7
Higher Weaver Cross EX15 ... 83 E7
Higher Wellbrook St EX16 ... 161 B4
Higher Westlake Rd
 ◆ Barnstaple EX31 ... 154 A2
 Barnstaple EX31 ... 154 A2
Higher Westonfields TQ9 ... 223 E5
Higher Woodfield Rd TQ1 ... 220 D3
Higher Woodford La PL7 ... 250 C7
Higher Woodway Cl TQ14 ... 210 C7
Higher Woodway Rd TQ14 ... 210 B8
HIGHER WOOLBROOK ... 187 F7
Higher Woolbrook Pk EX10 ... 187 F7
HIGHER YALBERTON ... 225 C3
Higher Yalberton Rd TQ4 ... 225 D3
Higher Yannon Dr TQ14 ... 210 A6
Highfield
 Honiton EX14 ... 166 B5
 Lapford EX17 ... 60 D3
 Northam EX39 ... 156 F6
 Sidmouth EX10 ... 188 A5
 Topsham EX3 ... 182 F7
Highfield Cl
 Barnstaple EX32 ... 155 B4
 Brixham TQ5 ... 230 A4
 High Bickington EX37 ... 43 B7
 Plymouth PL3 ... 249 C5
Highfield Cres TQ3 ... 225 E6
Highfield Ct ◆ EX8 ... 202 B6
Highfield Dr
 Kingsbridge TQ7 ... 258 D4
 ◆ Wembury PL9 ... 140 D8
Highfield Gdns EX34 ... 3 A3
Highfield La EX8 ... 202 B6
Highfield Pk PL12 ... 242 B3
Highfield Rd
 Dunkeswell EX14 ... 67 C1
 Ilfracombe EX34 ... 150 C5
Highfield Terr
 Beer EX12 ... 191 D5
 ◆ Bishop's Tawton EX32 ... 16 E1
 ◆ Bittaford PL21 ... 137 C7
 ◆ Ilfracombe EX34 ... 150 C5
High Gate EX16 ... 62 F6
Highglen Dr PL7 ... 251 B7
Highgrove Pk TQ14 ... 210 C7
High House Cl EX7 ... 204 E7
High House La TQ7 ... 258 D4
Highland Cl TQ2 ... 219 C6
Highland Pk EX15 ... 66 A7
Highland Rd TQ2 ... 219 C5
Highlands
 Ottery St Mary EX11 ... 169 D3
 Wembury PL9 ... 256 B3
 Yealmpton PL8 ... 257 F4
Highlands Pk ◆ TQ13 ... 123 E6
Highland St PL21 ... 237 D5
Highland Terr
 ◆ Tiverton EX16 ... 161 D4
 Uffculme EX15 ... 66 A7
Highland View EX20 ... 170 C3
High Mdw EX10 ... 188 B7
High Mdws EX4 ... 176 E5
High Moorland Visitor Ctr* PL20 ... 128 A8
High Park Cl EX39 ... 25 D4
High Path TA21 ... 160 C7
High Rd PL9 ... 140 C8
Highridge Cross EX37 ... 45 B7
High School for Girls EX4 ... 263 A4
High St
 Bampton EX16 ... 34 B1
 Barnstaple EX31 ... 154 F5
 Bideford EX39 ... 157 A2
 Budleigh Salterton EX9 ... 199 G2
 Chagford TQ13 ... 111 A6
 Clovelly EX39 ... 23 D3
 Combe Martin EX34 ... 3 A3
 Crediton EX17 ... 165 C5
 Cullompton EX15 ... 163 C3
 Dawlish EX7 ... 204 E6
 Dulverton TA22 ... 33 D6
 Exeter EX4 ... 261 B3
 Exmouth EX8 ... 202 A6
 Great Torrington EX38 ... 159 D5
 Halberton EX16 ... 65 A7
 Hatherleigh EX20 ... 75 C7
 Hemyock EX15 ... 67 B8
 High Bickington EX37 ... 43 B7
 ◆ Holsworthy EX22 ... 164 C4
 Honiton EX14 ... 166 C6
 Ide EX2 ... 176 D1
 Ilfracombe EX34 ... 150 B6
 Kentisbeare EX15 ... 66 A3
 Kenton EX6 ... 194 D3
 Newton Poppleford EX10 ... 186 D8
 North Tawton EX20 ... 77 C4
 Okehampton EX20 ... 170 B5
 Plymouth, Stonehouse PL1 ... 248 A2
 Sidford EX10 ... 188 B8

High St continued
 Sidmouth EX10 ... 188 B4
 Silverton EX5 ... 82 B6
 Stoke Canon EX5 ... 173 F8
 Swimbridge EX32 ... 28 E8
 Topsham EX3 ... 182 E6
 Totnes TQ9 ... 223 C5
 Uffculme EX15 ... 66 A7
 Wellington TA21 ... 160 E6
 Winkleigh EX19 ... 58 F3
Highstead Cross EX22 ... 73 C8
High Street Prim Sch PL1 ... 248 A2
High Street & Waterloo Street Flats PL1 ... 248 A1
High Trees EX7 ... 204 E7
High View
 Bideford EX39 ... 156 E1
 Feniton EX14 ... 84 E2
 Sheepwash EX21 ... 56 C1
High View Gdns EX8 ... 202 E7
High View Prim Sch PL3 ... 249 D5
High View Terr EX39 ... 156 C6
High Wall EX31 ... 154 E4
High Way EX16 ... 48 D8
Highweek Com Prim Sch TQ12 ... 207 A3
Highweek Cross EX21 ... 73 E8
Highweek Rd TQ12 ... 207 A4
Highweek St TQ12 ... 207 B3
Highweek Village TQ12 ... 206 F5
Highwell Rd TQ12 ... 207 B3
Highwell Rd EX12 ... 192 A5
Highwood Grange TQ12 ... 207 B2
Highworthy Cross EX21 ... 55 E3
Hilary Cl EX13 ... 167 E6
Hilary Gdns EX13 ... 167 E6
Hill Barton Bsns Pk
 Clyst St Mary EX5 ... 179 F2
 Exeter EX5 ... 99 A1
Hill Barton Cl EX1 ... 178 C7
Hill Barton La EX1 ... 178 C7
Hill Barton Rd EX2 ... 178 C7
Hillbrook Rd TQ9 ... 223 E5
Hillbrook Rise ◆ TQ9 ... 223 E5
Hill Budge Terr ◆ EX17 ... 165 C5
Hill Cl
 Exeter EX4 ... 173 D1
 Plymouth PL7 ... 250 D4
Hillcliffe Terr ◆ EX39 ... 15 A1
Hill Cres EX14 ... 166 D6
Hillcrest
 Ilsington TQ13 ... 122 C3
 Oakford EX16 ... 48 D5
 Ottery St Mary EX11 ... 169 D3
Hill Crest
 Exminster EX6 ... 182 A4
 Kilmington EX13 ... 87 C1
 Plymouth PL3 ... 248 E5
 South Tawton EX20 ... 95 B5
 Tiverton EX16 ... 161 D5
Hillcrest Cl
 Plymouth PL7 ... 251 A5
 ◆ Wembury PL9 ... 140 D8
Hillcrest Dr PL7 ... 251 A4
Hillcrest Pk EX4 ... 173 C2
Hillcrest Rd
 Barnstaple EX32 ... 155 B2
 Bideford EX39 ... 26 A4
 Silverton EX5 ... 82 C6
Hillcroft Terr ◆ EX37 ... 157 A2
Hill Cross
 Cobbaton EX32 ... 28 B5
 Kingsbridge TQ7 ... 144 B5
Hilldale Rd PL9 ... 255 E6
Hilldean Cl PL5 ... 244 C7
Hilldown TQ9 ... 223 E5
Hilldown Cross EX17 ... 78 D2
Hilldown La EX17 ... 78 D2
Hilldown Rd EX17 ... 78 C3
Hill Dr EX8 ... 196 B3
Hilldrop Terr TQ1 ... 220 B5
Hiller La TQ12 ... 208 B2
HILLERTON ... 78 C1
Hillerton Cross EX17 ... 78 B1
Hillesdon Rd TQ1 ... 220 B4
HILLFIELD ... 232 C3
Hillfield
 South Zeal EX20 ... 95 A4
 Stoke Gabriel TQ9 ... 227 F7
Hill Garden Cl ◆ EX39 ... 157 A2
Hill Gdns PL12 ... 242 B3
HILLHEAD ... 234 F8
Hillhead
 Colyton EX24 ... 103 A4
 Halberton EX16 ... 65 A7
 Noss Mayo PL8 ... 140 F6
Hillhead EX37 ... 28 F4
Hillhead Bglws ◆ EX24 ... 103 A4
Hillhead Cross TQ12 ... 137 D7
Hill Head Cross
 Chittlehampton EX37 ... 28 F4
 King's Nympton EX37 ... 44 C5
Hillhead Rd TQ5 ... 234 E8
Hillhead Terr EX11 ... 169 D3
Hillhouse EX14 ... 69 A3
Hilliers EX19 ... 57 F7
Hillingdon Cross TQ7 ... 143 E6
Hill La
 Chipstable TA4 ... 35 C6
 Exeter EX1 ... 178 B7
 Plymouth PL3 ... 248 F7
 Waterrow TA4 ... 35 E5
 Whitestone EX4 ... 98 E4
Hillmans Rd TQ12 ... 207 D2
HILLMOOR ... 66 E8

Hillmoor Cross EX21 ... 73 F7
Hill Park Cl TQ5 ... 230 E4
Hill Park Cres PL4 ... 263 A4
Hill Park Mews PL4 ... 263 B4
Hill Park Rd
 Brixham TQ5 ... 230 E4
 Newton Abbot TQ12 ... 206 F4
 Torquay TQ1 ... 220 A7
Hill Park Terr TQ4 ... 226 C5
Hill Path PL5 ... 243 F5
Hill Pk
 Ashprington TQ9 ... 139 F8
 Kellaton TQ7 ... 149 C6
Hill Rd
 Bondleigh EX20 ... 77 C7
 Lyme Regis DT7 ... 260 D3
 Newton Abbot TQ12 ... 207 B2
Hillrise TQ5 ... 229 B5
Hill Rise EX1 ... 178 C7
Hill Rise Rd DT7 ... 260 D3
Hillsborough
 ◆ Plymouth PL4 ... 248 F4
 Torquay TQ1 ... 220 B4
Hillsborough Ave EX4 ... 261 A4
Hillsborough Cross EX22 ... 71 C7
Hillsborough Nature Reserve* EX34 ... 150 E6
Hillsborough Park Rd EX34 ... 150 E5
Hillsborough Rd EX34 ... 150 D5
Hillsborough Terr ◆ EX34 ... 150 C6
Hillsborough Terr Mews ◆ EX34 ... 150 C6
Hillsdunne Rd PL3 ... 248 E6
HILLSIDE ... 135 A3
Hillside
 Bittaford PL21 ... 137 C8
 Branscombe EX12 ... 190 B5
 ◆ Colyton EX24 ... 103 A4
 George Nympton EX36 ... 30 A2
 Honiton EX14 ... 85 E5
 Newton Poppleford EX10 ... 186 D8
 Northleigh EX24 ... 102 B6
 Payhembury EX14 ... 84 C4
 Rawridge EX14 ... 68 C1
 Sidbury EX10 ... 101 B2
 South Brent TQ10 ... 135 A3
 Talaton EX5 ... 84 B1
Hillside Ave
 Exeter EX4 ... 261 B4
 Plymouth PL4 ... 248 D4
 Saltash PL12 ... 242 F3
Hillside Cl
 Buckland Monachorum PL20 ... 126 C3
 South Brent TQ10 ... 135 A3
 Teignmouth TQ14 ... 124 E1
Hillside Cotts
 Abbotskerswell TQ12 ... 212 A6
 Noss Mayo PL8 ... 140 F6
Hillside Cres PL9 ... 255 F8
Hill Side Cross EX36 ... 45 F5
Hillside Ct TQ11 ... 236 C5
Hillside Dr
 Kingsbridge TQ7 ... 258 D4
 Yealmpton PL8 ... 257 F3
Hillside Ind Units EX32 ... 155 F1
Hillside Pk TQ4 ... 224 F5
Hillside Rd
 Brixham TQ5 ... 230 C4
 Ilfracombe EX34 ... 150 E5
 Paignton TQ3 ... 225 F7
 Saltash PL12 ... 242 E3
 Sidmouth EX10 ... 188 C4
Hillside Terr
 ◆ Bideford EX39 ... 157 A2
 Kingswear TQ6 ... 234 A3
 ◆ Plymouth PL9 ... 226 A6
Hillside Way PL8 ... 136 A2
Hill's La EX14 ... 86 C5
Hill St EX14 ... 263 A3
Hills View
 Barnstaple EX32 ... 155 A5
 Braunton EX33 ... 152 D6
Hill The EX13 ... 87 C1
Hilltop TQ7 ... 142 F6
Hilltop Cotts EX31 ... 153 E5
Hill Top Crest PL5 ... 243 E2
Hilltop Rd EX39 ... 156 E4
Hilltown Cross
 Chittlehampton EX37 ... 29 B2
 Okehampton EX20 ... 93 E5
 Rackenford EX16 ... 47 D2
 Whitnham Hill EX36 ... 31 C5
Hilltown La EX18 ... 59 F5
Hill View
 Buckland Monachorum PL20 ... 126 C3
 Ottery St Mary EX11 ... 169 D3
 Sidmouth EX10 ... 188 B5
Hill View Terr ◆ TQ2 ... 220 A7
Hillway EX10 ... 187 A7
Hillyfield Rd EX1 ... 178 C7
Hilly Gardens Rd TQ1 ... 214 B1
Hilly Head TA21 ... 160 B5
Hillymead EX12 ... 192 B6
Hilton Ave PL5 ... 244 D1
Hilton Cres TQ3 ... 219 C1
Hilton Dr TQ3 ... 219 C1
Hilton Park Homes EX33 ... 152 C5
Hilton Rd
 Marhamchurch EX23 ... 70 A6
 Monkleigh EX39 ... 40 F7
 Newton Abbot TQ12 ... 207 C3

Hinam Cross TA22 ... 33 B7
Hindharton La EX39 ... 22 E3
Hind St
 Bovey Tracey TQ13 ... 180 D8
 Ottery St Mary EX11 ... 169 D3
Hingston Ct PL6 ... 249 A8
Hingston Post TQ9 ... 144 E8
Hingston Rd TQ1 ... 220 C7
Hinton Ct PL6 ... 245 C1
Hirmandale Rd PL5 ... 243 F1
HISCOTT ... 27 C5
HITTISLEIGH ... 96 D5
Hittisleigh Cross EX6 ... 96 D6
Hittisleigh Mill La EX6 ... 96 D5
Hittsford La EX36 ... 32 A1
Hobart St PL1 ... 262 A2
Hobbs Cottage La EX23 ... 70 A6
Hobbs Cres PL12 ... 242 C3
Hobb's Hill EX33 ... 7 E2
Hobbs La EX32 ... 18 E2
Hobbs Way EX17 ... 78 B4
Hobby Dr The EX39 ... 23 E3
Hobby House La EX36 ... 45 F8
Hobbymoor Cross EX17 ... 60 A1
HOCKHOLLER ... 52 E8
HOCKHOLLER GREEN ... 52 E8
Hockmoor Head TQ11 ... 130 C2
Hockmoor Hill TQ11 ... 130 C2
HOCKWORTHY ... 50 D6
Hodder's La DT7 ... 260 C8
Hodders Way PL12 ... 239 A2
Hodge Cl PL12 ... 242 C2
Hodges Wlk EX38 ... 159 E5
Hodson Cl TQ3 ... 225 F7
Hoe App PL1 ... 262 C2
Hoe Ct PL1 ... 262 C2
Hoegate Ct PL1 ... 262 C2
Hoegate Pl PL1 ... 262 C2
Hoegate St PL1 ... 263 A2
Hoe Gdns PL1 ... 262 C2
Hoe Rd PL1 ... 262 C2
Hoe St PL1 ... 262 C2
Hoe The PL1 ... 262 C1
Hofheim Dr EX16 ... 161 A6
Hogarth Cl PL9 ... 256 B6
Hogarth Ho ◆ PL19 ... 171 B6
Hogarth Wlk PL9 ... 256 B6
HOGGS PARK ... 54 A1
Hoile La TQ9 ... 224 E1
Hoker Rd EX2 ... 178 A5
Holbeam Cl TQ12 ... 206 E4
Holbeam La
 Bickington TQ12 ... 131 F6
 Newton Abbot TQ12 ... 206 C7
HOLBETON ... 136 D1
Holberton Prim Sch PL8 ... 136 D1
Holborn Pl PL7 ... 250 E6
Holborn Rd TQ5 ... 230 C6
Holborn St PL4 ... 263 B2
Holbrook Terr TQ7 ... 145 B1
HOLCOMBE
 Lyme Regis ... 104 B4
 Teignmouth ... 204 D3
Holcombe Barton Cnr EX6 ... 98 D2
Holcombe Cross EX7 ... 210 F8
Holcombe Down Cross TQ14 ... 124 F2
Holcombe Down Rd EX7, TQ14 ... 204 A2
Holcombe Dr
 Holcombe EX7 ... 210 F8
 Plymouth PL5 ... 255 F5
Holcombe La
 Ottery St Mary EX11 ... 100 F7
 Uplyme DT7 ... 104 B4
Holcombe Rd EX7, TQ14 ... 210 E8
HOLCOMBE ROGUS ... 50 F5
Holcroft Cl PL12 ... 242 D2
Holden Cross EX6 ... 113 E2
Holditch La EX13 ... 88 D5
Holdstone Way EX34 ... 3 B2
Holdsworth St PL4 ... 262 B4
Hole Ball Cross EX21 ... 92 A8
Holebay Cl PL9 ... 256 A5
Holebrook Cross EX20 ... 76 C4
Holebrook La EX20 ... 76 C5
Hole Cleave Rd EX33 ... 8 A1
Hole Cross
 Halwill EX21 ... 73 F1
 Hittisleigh EX6 ... 96 E4
 Yelverton PL20 ... 239 E7
Hole Ct EX20 ... 75 C7
Hole Hill
 Branscombe EX12 ... 190 C6
 Exbourne EX20 ... 76 C4
 Witheridge EX16 ... 46 F2
Hole La
 Chulmleigh EX18 ... 45 B3
 Combe Martin EX31 ... 10 B6
 Croyde EX33 ... 7 F1
 North Tawton EX20 ... 77 E6
Holemoor Cross EX22 ... 73 C8
Holemore Cross EX14 ... 68 C5
Hole's La
 Broadhempston TQ9 ... 131 D1
 Staverton TQ9 ... 216 B8
HOLEWATER ... 19 A6
Holewater Cross EX32 ... 19 A6
Holewater Hill EX32 ... 19 A6
Holewell La EX6 ... 96 E4
HOLLACOMBE ... 72 D6
Hollacombe Brake PL9 ... 256 C1

Hollacombe Cross
 Holsworthy EX22 . . . . 72 D6
 Yeoford EX17 . . . . 79 D3
HOLLACOMBE HILL 256 A2
Hollacombe La TQ3 . . . . . . 219 D1
Hollam Cross TA22 . . . . 33 E7
Hollam Dr TA22 . . . . 33 D6
Hollam La TA22 . . . . 33 D7
Hollamoor View EX31 . . 154 B3
Hollam Way TQ12 . . . . . . 207 F8
Holland Cl EX31 . . . . 154 A4
Holland Copse EX6 . . . . . . 98 C4
Holland Rd
 Exeter EX2 . . . . 176 F4
 Exmouth EX8 . . . . 196 D1
 Plymouth, Chaddlewood
  PL7 . . . . 251 D5
 Plymouth, Peverell PL3 . 248 E6
 Plymouth, Plymstock PL9 . 255 F4
Holland's La TA4 . . . . 35 E8
Hollands Park Ave EX34 . . 3 A3
Hollands Rd 4 TQ14 . . 210 C4
Holland St 7 EX31 . . . . . 154 F5
Holley Cl EX6 . . . . 182 A4
Holley Pk EX20 . . . . 170 D6
Holleys Cl TQ20 . . . . 88 D8
HOLLICOMBE 219 D1
Hollies The EX31 . . . . 154 B3
Hollingarth Way EX15 . . . 67 B8
Hollington Ho 18 TQ1 . . 220 D4
Hollis Cl EX11 . . . . 169 C4
HOLLOCOMBE 58 F6
Hollocombe Cnr EX18 . . 58 D6
Hollocombe Moor Gate
 EX18 . . . . 58 D7
Hollocombe Moor Head
 EX18 . . . . 58 D7
HOLLOCOMBE TOWN . . . 58 E6
Holloway Gdns PL9 . . . . 256 A5
Holloway St EX2 . . . . 261 B2
Holloway The TA21 . . . . . . 51 E7
Hollowcombe Cross
 PL21 . . . . 136 E3
Hollowcombe Head TQ7 149 D5
Hollow Hayes PL6 . . . . . . 249 B8
Hollow Head Cross EX10 100 F2
Hollow La EX11 . . . . 178 E7
Hollow Pits Ct EX2 . . . . . 181 B8
Hollows The
 Exmouth EX8 . . . . 202 B7
 Plymouth PL9 . . . . 256 B8
Hollow Tree Cross EX18 . . 60 A7
Hollowtree Ct 5 EX32 . . 155 B3
Hollowtree Rd EX32 . . . . 155 B3
Holly Cl
 Broadclyst EX5 . . . . 175 C7
 2 Chudleigh TQ13 . . . . . 123 F6
 Honiton EX14 . . . . 166 C4
 Tiverton EX16 . . . . 161 E5
Hollycombe Cross 95 E4
Hollycombe La TQ9 . . . . 216 F7
Hollycroft Rd PL3 . . . . . . 249 A7
Holly Ct PL6 . . . . 249 E7
Hollyford La EX17 . . . . 62 C2
Hollyhead Cross EX12 . . 191 C7
Hollyhead Rd EX12 . . . . 191 B8
Holly Ho 2 EX34 . . . . 150 B6
Hollymount Cl EX8 . . . . . 196 C3
Holly Park Cl PL5 . . . . . . 244 A5
Holly Park Dr PL5 . . . . . 244 A5
Holly Rd
 Exeter EX2 . . . . 177 F3
 Tiverton EX16 . . . . 161 E5
Holly Villas TQ9 . . . . 139 F8
Hollywater Cl TQ1 . . . . . 220 D6
Holly Water Rd EX17 . . . . 62 E1
Holly Way EX15 . . . . 163 C5
Holly Wlk EX8 . . . . 196 D3
Hollywood Terr 2 PL1 . . 262 A3
HOLMACOTT 26 F2
Holmacott Cross EX39 . . 26 F7
Holman Cl EX7 . . . . 204 F8
Holman Ct PL2 . . . . 248 C8
Holmans Bldgs PL1 . . . . 247 D2
Holmans Mdw PL15 . . . . 105 B1
Holman Way
 Ivybridge PL21 . . . . 237 A6
 Topsham EX3 . . . . 182 F5
Holmbush Way PL8 . . . . 257 A4
Holm Cross EX17 . . . . 59 F2
Holmdale EX10 . . . . 188 B4
Holmead Cross EX16 . . . . 48 B3
Holmes Ave PL3 . . . . 249 B9
Holmes Rd TQ12 . . . . . . 180 F2
Holm Hill EX17 . . . . 59 E2
Holmleigh Rd TQ7 . . . . . 145 D1
Holmsleigh Cross EX14 . . 86 C5
HOLMSLEIGH GREEN . . . 86 C5
Holmwood Ave PL9 . . . . 255 E5
HOLNE 130 A4
Holne Chase PL6 . . . . . . 245 B7
Holne Cross TQ13 . . . . . 130 E5
Holne Ct EX4 . . . . 176 E8
Holne Moor Cl TQ3 . . . . 225 E7
Holne Rd TQ11 . . . . 236 B6
Holne Rise EX2 . . . . 178 B4
Holne Turn
 Ashburton TQ13 . . . . 130 E5
 Holne TQ13 . . . . 130 B5
Holset Cross TQ8 . . . . . . 148 D5
Holsome La TQ9 . . . . 138 D7
Holstock Cross EX20 . . . . 74 D3
HOLSWORTHY 164 D5

HOLSWORTHY BEACON . . . 54 C3
Holsworthy CE Prim Sch
 EX22 . . . . 164 C5
Holsworthy Com Coll
 EX22 . . . . 164 C5
Holsworthy Hospl EX22 . 164 D6
Holsworthy L Ctr EX22 . 164 C5
Holsworthy Mus* EX22 . 164 C4
Holsworthy Rd EX20 . . . . 93 D5
Holt The
 19 Appledore EX39 . . . . . 15 A1
 Honiton EX14 . . . . 166 E7
Holtwood Dr PL21 . . . . . 237 A5
Holtwood Rd PL6 . . . . . . 245 D6
Holway TA20 . . . . 88 D8
Holwell Cl PL9 . . . . 256 A5
Holwell La EX16 . . . . 64 B5
Holwell Rd TQ5 . . . . 230 B4
Holwill Dr EX38 . . . . 159 D5
Holwill Tor Wlk TQ4 . . . 225 F3
HOLY CITY 87 F7
Holy Cross RC Prim Sch
 PL4 . . . . 263 A4
Holyford La EX24 . . . . . . 102 F3
Holyford Woods Nature
 Reserve* EX12 . . . . 102 E3
Holy Moor Cross EX36 . . 32 C1
Holy Moor La EX36 . . . . . 32 C1
Holyoake St TA21 . . . . . 160 C7
Holyrood Pl PL1 . . . . 262 C2
Holyshute Cross EX14 . . 166 D6
Holywell CE Prim Sch
 EX14 . . . . 27 D8
Holywell Cross EX36 . . . . 19 F2
HOLYWELL LAKE 51 E7
Holywell Pk EX31 . . . . 73 D3
Homebaye Ho 3 EX12 . 192 B4
Homebourne Ho TQ4 . . . 226 C5
Home Cl
 Brixham TQ5 . . . . 230 C3
 Chillington TQ7 . . . . 145 A1
Homeclose La EX13, TA20 88 A8
Homeclyst Ho EX2 . . . . . 261 A1
Homecombe Ho TQ1 . . . 220 C8
Homecourt Ho EX4 . . . . 261 A2
Homedown Cross EX37 . . 28 F4
Home Farm EX6 . . . . 114 E1
Home Farm Cl
 Croyde EX33 . . . . 7 E2
 Kingston TQ7 . . . . 142 C6
Home Farm Cross EX15 . . 65 F4
Home Farm Ct TQ12 . . . 209 B2
Home Farm N DT7 . . . . . 193 E6
Home Farm Rd
 Fremington EX31 . . . . . . 153 D5
 Plymouth PL9 . . . . 255 E8
Home Farm S DT7 . . . . . 193 E6
Homefield
 Thurlestone TQ7 . . . . 143 A1
 Wellington TA21 . . . . 160 E4
Homefield Cl EX11 . . . . . 169 E3
Homefield Cotts
 Thurlestone TQ7 . . . . 143 A1
 Torquay TQ1 . . . . 220 D7
Homefield Rd EX1 . . . . . 177 F8
Home Gate EX6 . . . . 98 A3
Home La EX34 . . . . 1 C3
Homelace Ho EX14 . . . . . 166 C7
Homelands PL7 . . . . 258 C6
Homelands Prim Sch
 TQ1 . . . . 220 B8
Homelands Rd TQ7 . . . . 258 C6
Home Mdw TQ9 . . . . 223 C5
Homemeadows Ho EX10. 188 B5
Home Orch EX15 . . . . 50 D1
Homepalms Ho 3 TQ1 . . 219 F6
Home Park Ave PL3 . . . . 248 E6
Home Park (Plymouth Argyle
 FC) PL2 . . . . 248 C5
Home Park Rd PL12 . . . . 243 A3
Home Pk
 Ashburton TQ13 . . . . 130 F5
 Plymouth PL2 . . . . 247 F4
Homer Cl EX31 . . . . 18 A8
Homer Cres EX33 . . . . . . 152 B7
Homer Ct EX33 . . . . 152 B7
Homer Dr EX33 . . . . 152 B7
Homer La EX12 . . . . 191 F8
Homer Park Lane S PL9 . 255 C5
Homer Pk
 Plymouth PL9 . . . . 255 C5
 Saltash PL12 . . . . 242 D3
Homer Rd EX33 . . . . 152 B7
Homer Rise EX7 . . . . 256 B7
Homers Cl TQ12 . . . . 207 D6
Homers Cres TQ12 . . . . 207 D6
Homershill Cross PL21 . . 137 B6
Homesleigh Rd EX14 . . . 86 A5
Homestead Rd TQ1 . . . . 220 A8
Homestead Terr TQ1 . . . 220 A8
Home Sweet Home Terr
 PL4 . . . . 263 C2
Hometeign Ho TQ12 . . . 207 D4
Hometor Ho EX8 . . . . . . 202 A8
Homeyards The TQ14 . . . 210 A3
Homing Down Cross
 EX20 . . . . 75 A1
Honcray PL9 . . . . 255 D8
Hone Cross EX16 . . . . 34 F5
Honest Heart Cross EX16 . 46 A3
Honestone St EX39 . . . . 157 A1
Honeybeetle Cross EX37 . 29 A5
HONEYCHURCH 76 E5
Honeychurch La EX20 . . 76 E5
Honeychurch Moor Cross
 EX20 . . . . 76 F6
Honeycroft Cross EX22 . . 54 A4

Honey Ditches Dr EX12 . . 191 F8
Honey La
 Daccombe TQ1, TQ12 . . . 213 F5
 Exeter EX1 . . . . 174 F2
 Woodbury Salterton EX5 . 184 D7
Honeylands Childrens Ctr
 (Royal Devon & Exeter
 Hospl) EX4 . . . . 178 B7
Honeylands Dr EX4 . . . . 178 A7
Honeylands Way EX4 . . 178 A7
Honey Mdws EX22 . . . . . 164 C4
Honey Park Rd EX9 . . . . 198 B2
Honey St EX39 . . . . 157 A7
Honeysuckle Cl
 2 Barnstaple EX31 . . . . 154 B3
 Paignton TQ3 . . . . 225 E8
 Plymouth PL6 . . . . 245 E7
 Saltash PL12 . . . . 242 D4
 Tiverton EX16 . . . . 161 F6
Honeysuckle Ct EX14 . . 166 B5
Honeysuckle Dr EX14 . . . 85 C2
Honeysuckle Gdns PL15 . 105 A2
Honeywell TQ12 . . . . 207 E6
Honeywell Cl EX32 . . . . 155 B2
Honeywell La TQ13 . . . . 122 C3
Honeywell Rd TQ12 . . . 207 E6
Honeywells Cross EX36 . . 19 C2
HONICKNOWLE 244 B2
Honicknowle La PL5 . . . 244 B2
Honicknowle Gn PL5 . . . 244 B2
Honicknowle Rd PL5 . . . 244 B1
Honicombe Cnr PL17 . . 125 B5
Honicombe Pk PL17 . . . 125 B5
HONITON 166 D4
Honiton Bottom Rd
 EX14 . . . . 166 C4
Honiton Bsns Pk EX14 . 166 B6
Honiton Cl PL5 . . . . 244 B3
Honiton Com Coll EX14 . 166 C6
Honiton Cross EX36 . . . . 29 F3
Honiton Hospl EX14 . . . 166 C5
Honiton La EX36 . . . . 29 E3
Honiton L Ctr EX14 . . . . 166 C7
Honiton Prim Sch EX14 . 166 C6
Honiton Rd
 Blackhorse EX5 . . . . 179 C7
 Cullompton EX15 . . . . . . 163 E3
 Exeter EX1 . . . . 178 C5
 Honiton Sta EX14 . . . . . 166 C5
 Honiton Wlk PL5 . . . . . . 244 B4
Honors Farm EX15 . . . . 173 F8
Hooda Cl EX32 . . . . 171 E1
Hoodown La TQ6 . . . . . . 234 B4
HOOE 255 C5
Hooe Hill PL9 . . . . 255 C5
Hooe La PL9 . . . . 255 D3
Hooe Manor PL9 . . . . . . 255 C5
Hooe Prim Sch PL9 . . . . 255 B5
Hooe Rd PL9 . . . . 255 C5
HOOK 88 B8
Hook Cross EX13 . . . . 87 D7
Hooker Cl EX9 . . . . 197 F2
Hookhill La EX17 . . . . 62 A3
Hookhills Dr TQ4 . . . . . . 226 B2
Hookhills Gdns TQ4 . . . 229 B7
Hookhills Rd TQ4 . . . . . . 226 C1
Hookhills Rd TQ4 . . . . . . 226 B1
Hookmoor Cross PL21 . . 137 E7
Hooksbury Ave PL7 . . . . 251 B3
Hooks Cross TQ12 . . . . . 131 C7
Hookway EX17 . . . . 61 A4
Hookway Cross EX5 . . . . 80 D1
Hookway Hill EX35 . . . . . . 6 F3
Hookway La EX16 . . . . . . 63 B5
HOO MEAVY 132 A8
Hoop Cross EX15 . . . . 83 B4
Hooper Cl EX20 . . . . 75 B7
Hooperhayne Rd EX24 . 102 E5
Hoopern Ave EX4 . . . . . . 173 D1
Hoopern La EX4 . . . . 177 C8
Hoopern St EX4 . . . . 261 B4
Hoopern Terr 4 EX7 . . . 204 D6
Hoopers Cross EX16 . . . . 34 D3
Hoopers La PL18 . . . . . . 125 C6
Hooper St PL11 . . . . 247 C3
Hoopers Way EX38 . . . . 159 F5
Hooperton Cross EX6 . . . 96 E3
Hooperton La EX6 . . . . . . 96 E3
HOOPS 24 D2
Hope By-Pass TQ7 . . . . 147 B7
Hope Cl TQ9 . . . . 223 F5
Hope Rd EX2 . . . . 178 A3
Hope's Cl TQ1 . . . . 210 A6
Hope Wlk TQ9 . . . . 223 F5
Hopkins Ct 3 TQ12 . . . 207 C3
Hopkins La TQ12 . . . . . . 207 C3
Hopperstyle EX31 . . . . . 154 B3
Hopton Cl PL6 . . . . 248 F8
Hopton Dr EX38 . . . . 159 F5
HOPWORTHY 71 C5
Horace Rd TQ2 . . . . 213 F2
Hore Down Gate EX34 . . . 9 B6
Hore's Cross EX21 . . . . . 137 D7
Horestone Cross EX16 . . 47 F4
Hornapark Cl PL16 . . . . 105 E3
Hornbeam Cl
 Honiton EX14 . . . . 166 A4
 Tiverton EX16 . . . . 161 F5
Hornbeam Gdns PL6 . . . . 245 E7
Hornbeam Hollow 1
 SL3 . . . . 154 C2
Hornbrook Gdns PL6 . . 244 D6
Hornby St 8 PL2 . . . . . 247 F4
Hornchurch La PL5 . . . . 243 E4
Hornchurch Rd PL5 . . . . 243 E5
Horn Cross
 Kentisbeare EX15 . . . . . . 65 F2
 Plymouth PL9 . . . . 255 E7

Horn Cross Rd PL9 . . . . . 255 F7
HORNDON 118 A7
Hornebrook Ave 9 EX34 150 B5
Horne Park Ave 14 EX34. 150 B5
Horne Park Rd EX34 . . . . 150 B5
Horne Rd EX34 . . . . 150 B5
Horner Tongue TQ9 . . . 138 F5
Horner Turn Cross TQ9 . 139 A5
Horn Hill TQ6 . . . . 233 F3
Horn La
 Brixton PL8 . . . . 257 A5
 Plymouth PL9 . . . . 255 F7
Horn Lane Flats 4 PL9 . 255 F7
Horn La EX5 . . . . 65 E2
HORNS CROSS 24 E2
Hornshayes Knap Cross
 EX14 . . . . 86 F7
Hornshayne Rd EX24 . . 102 B5
Horns Pk TQ14 . . . . 208 E7
HORRABRIDGE 126 F5
Horrabridge Com Prim Sch
 PL20 . . . . 126 F4
Horridge La EX18 . . . . 59 A8
Horry Mill La EX18 . . . . . 58 F6
Horsdon Rd EX16 . . . . . . 161 F4
Horsdon Terr EX16 . . . . 161 F4
HORSEBRIDGE 116 A1
Horsebrook La TQ9 . . . . 223 A6
Horse Hill EX17 . . . . 60 F7
Horsehill Cross EX17 . . . . 60 F7
Horseman Cl 3 EX32 . . 155 A1
Horse La EX36 . . . . 19 D8
Horsepond Mdw EX36 . . 158 C3
Horsepool St TQ5 . . . . . . 230 B3
Horseshoe Bend TQ4 . . 226 C2
Horseshoe Cl 10 TQ13 . 123 E6
Horseshoe Dr PL7 . . . . . 250 D5
Horsham La
 Plymouth, Honicknowle
  PL5 . . . . 244 C2
 Plymouth, Tamerton Foliot
  PL5 . . . . 244 C7
Horslears EX13 . . . . 167 C4
Horswell Cl PL7 . . . . 251 B5
Horton Cross EX22 . . . . . 38 C3
HORWOOD 26 E6
Horwood Cross EX39 . . . 26 D7
Horwood & Newton Tracey
 Com Prim Sch EX31 . . 27 A6
Horwood Rd 11 EX31 . . 154 F5
Hosegood Way TQ12 . . 207 D7
Hosford Cl PL9 . . . . 256 A4
Hoskings Ct TQ11 . . . . . 236 B5
Hospital Hill EX7 . . . . . . 204 D6
Hospital La
 17 Ashburton TQ13 . . . 131 A5
 Exeter EX1 . . . . 178 C8
Hospital Rd PL4 . . . . 263 B4
Hostle Park Gdns 12
 EX34 . . . . 150 C6
Hostle Park Rd EX34 . . . 150 C6
Hostle Pk EX34 . . . . 150 C6
Hotham Pl PL1 . . . . 262 A4
Hothill La
 Ashprington TQ9 . . . . . . 139 F6
 Cornworthy TQ9 . . . . 139 F6
Hotspur Terr PL1 . . . . . . 262 C4
HOUGHTON 206 C6
Houghton La EX10 . . . . . 187 A5
Houldsworth Rd PL9 . . . 255 C7
Houndbeare La EX5 . . . . 99 E4
Houndhead Cross TQ9 . 216 D8
Houndiscombe Rd PL4 . 248 E4
Houndspool* EX7 . . . . . 200 A2
Hound Tor Cl TQ4 . . . . . 229 B7
Hounster Dr PL10 . . . . . 252 D4
Hounster Hill PL10 . . . . 252 D4
Housman Cl PL5 . . . . . . 244 D3
Hove Villas EX2 . . . . 261 A1
Howard Ave EX32 . . . . . 155 B4
Howard Cl
 Exeter EX4 . . . . 176 F8
 Okehampton EX20 . . . . 170 D6
 Plymouth PL5 . . . . 243 F2
 Saltash PL12 . . . . 242 D3
 Tavistock PL19 . . . . 171 A5
 Teignmouth TQ14 . . . . . 210 A7
Howard Cross EX6 . . . . . 96 D7
Howard Ct TQ14 . . . . . . 210 A7
Howard La
 Hittisleigh EX6 . . . . 96 D7
 Marhamchurch EX23 . . . 70 B8
Howard Rd
 Plymouth PL9 . . . . 255 E8
 Wellington TA21 . . . . 160 D7
Howards Cl EX36 . . . . . . 158 C2
Howards Way
 Ivybridge PL21 . . . . 237 A6
 Newton Abbot TQ12 . . . 207 F4
Howarth Cl EX10 . . . . . . 188 A8
Howden Ind Est EX16 . . 161 B3
Howden La EX16 . . . . . . 161 B3
Howden Rd EX16 . . . . . . 161 C3
Howell Rd EX4 . . . . 261 A4
Howeson Ct 10 PL1 . . . 262 A3
Howeson La PL6 . . . . . . 245 A4
HOWLEY 69 C4
How St PL4 . . . . 263 A2
Howton La TQ12 . . . . . . 206 B5
Howton Rd TQ12 . . . . . . 206 C6
Hoxton Rd TQ1 . . . . 220 B5
Hoyles Cl TA21 . . . . 160 E4
Hoyle's Ct TQ3 . . . . 225 E6
Hoyles Rd TA21 . . . . 160 E4
Hoyle's Rd TQ3 . . . . 225 E8

Hubbastone Rd EX39 . . . 157 C8
HUCCABY 129 C7
Huccaby Cl TQ5 . . . . 229 F2
HUCCOMBE 149 C7
Huckham Barn Cross
 TQ7 . . . . 149 C7
Huckham La EX31 . . . . . . 10 F3
Huckland Cross EX20 . . . 76 E4
HUDDISFORD 38 C6
Huddisford Cross EX39 . . 38 D7
Hudley Mill Hill EX32 . . . 18 D3
Hudson Cross EX22 . . . . . 53 B4
Hue La EX33 . . . . 8 F1
Huggaton Cross EX19 . . . 76 A8
Hughes Ave EX32 . . . . . 155 B6
Hugh Squier Ave EX36 . . 158 D5
HUISH 57 B6
HUISH CHAMPFLOWER . . 35 F8
Huish Cleeve TA4 . . . . . . 35 E7
Huish Cross TQ13 . . . . . 123 C6
Huishlane End EX6 . . . . . 97 F5
Hukeley Head Cross EX16 34 D3
HULHAM 196 B3
Hulham Rd EX8 . . . . 196 B2
Hulham Vale EX8 . . . . . . 196 C2
Hulk La EX5 . . . . 81 F4
HUMBER 124 C2
Humber Cl PL3 . . . . 249 D6
Humber La TQ12, TQ14 . 124 B1
Hume Ave EX35 . . . . 151 A5
Hummingbird Cl EX1 . . 174 E1
Humphrey's Cross TQ13 . 130 C4
Humphreys Rd TA21 . . . 160 E7
Humphries Pk EX8 . . . . 196 D1
Humpy The EX7 . . . . 204 C8
Hungerford Rd PL2 . . . . 248 B5
Hungry Fox Est EX5 . . . . 175 C3
Huniver's La EX17 . . . . . 165 C4
Hunivers Pl EX17 . . . . . . 165 D4
Hunsdon Ct TQ1 . . . . . . 220 C4
Hunsdon Rd
 Ivybridge PL21 . . . . 237 A2
 Lee Mill PL21 . . . . 136 D6
 Torquay TQ1 . . . . 220 C4
Hunstone Cross EX36 . . . 19 B2
Huntacott Way TQ2 . . . 219 B8
Hunter Cl PL6 . . . . 244 F2
Hunter La EX34 . . . . 7 F6
Hunters Cl TQ3 . . . . 224 F7
Hunters Ct TQ13 . . . . . . 224 F7
Hunters Gate EX20 . . . . 170 D6
Hunters Hill PL5 . . . . 51 E1
Hunters Moon TQ2 . . . . 222 F7
Hunter's Oak PL20 . . . . 126 A2
Hunters Tor Dr TQ4 . . . . 229 B7
Hunter's Way PL5 . . . . . . 51 E1
Hunterswell Rd TQ12 . . 207 A3
Hunterswood EX38 . . . . 159 F5
Huntingdon La EX13 . . . 167 B6
Huntingdon Gdns PL7 . . 250 F4
Huntley Cl EX13 . . . . 167 F7
Huntley La EX13 . . . . 88 A8
Huntley Pl PL3 . . . . 249 C4
Hunton Cl EX8 . . . . 195 F5
Hunts Cross PL21 . . . . . 137 B1
HUNTSHAM 50 A7
HUNTSHAW 26 E1
Huntshaw Cross EX31 . . 27 B1
Huntshaw Moor Cross
 EX38 . . . . 26 F2
HUNTSHAW WATER 26 D2
Hurdwick Rd PL19 . . . . . 171 A5
Hurrabrook Cl PL6 . . . . 245 E2
Hurrabrook Gdns PL6 . . 245 E2
Hurrell Cl PL4 . . . . 244 D6
Hurrell Ct
 Kingsbridge TQ7 . . . . . . 258 C5
 Plymouth PL3 . . . . 249 C5
Hurrell Rd TQ7 . . . . 258 C5
Hursley Bsns Pk PL6 . . . 241 D1
Hurst Ave EX2 . . . . 178 B4
Hurst Cl PL9 . . . . 255 F5
Hurstone Nature Reserve*
 TA4 . . . . 35 F3
Hurst's Almshouses EX2 . 261 C2
Husseys Cross EX14 . . . . 86 F6
Hussey's La EX14 . . . . . . 86 F6
Hutcherleigh Cross TQ9 139 B1
Hutcherleigh Turn TQ9 . 139 D1
Hutchings Cl PL6 . . . . . 244 D6
Hutchings Mead PL6 . . . 178 F8
Hutchings Way TQ14 . . 209 D8
Hutgate Rd EX14 . . . . 86 A4
Hutton Rd TQ3 . . . . 219 A1
Huxford La EX37 . . . . 44 F7
HUXHAM 174 B8
Huxham Cl PL6 . . . . 249 A8
Huxham's Cross EX21 . . 215 E3
Huxham's Cross Est TQ9. 215 E3
HUXHILL 26 D2
Huxley Cl PL7 . . . . 250 F7
Huxley Vale TQ12 . . . . . 212 F3
Huxnor Cross TQ12 . . . . 212 F2
Huxnor Rd TQ12 . . . . . . 212 F2
Huxtable Hill TQ2 . . . . . 219 C4
Huxtable La EX32 . . . . . . 18 C2
Huxton Cross TQ7 . . . . . 143 C3
Huxton Fork TQ7 . . . . . . 143 D3
Hyacinth Terr TQ1 . . . . . 220 B6
Hyde Park Jun & Inf Schs 1
 PL3 . . . . 248 E5
Hyde Park Rd PL3 . . . . . 248 E5
Hyde Rd TQ4 . . . . 226 B6
Hyfield Gdns TQ1 . . . . . 220 B4
Hylands Cl EX11 . . . . 168 D3
Hylton Gdns EX4 . . . . . . 176 F6
Hynetown Rd TQ6 . . . . . 145 E5

I

Hyne Town Rd TQ6......145 E5
Hyperion TQ2............219 E2

I

Ian Hay Cl EX39.........157 C1
Ibex Ct EX39.............15 A1
Ice House La EX10......187 F7
Icy Pk TQ7..............143 C6
IDDESLEIGH.............57 F7
Iddesleigh Cross EX19....57 E3
Iddesleigh Rd EX4......177 E8
Iddesleigh Terr 10 EX7...204 E6
IDE....................176 D1
IDEFORD................124 A4
Ide La EX2.............177 A1
Ide Prim Sch EX2.......176 E1
Idestone Brook Cross
  EX2..................113 F7
Idestone Cross EX2.....114 A7
Idewell Rd TQ2.........214 B2
Idston Cross TQ7.......143 D7
Ilbert Cotts PL7.......250 E4
Ilbert Rd
  Kingsbridge TQ7......258 C5
  Thurlestone TQ7......143 A4
Ilbert St PL1..........262 B4
Ilex Cl
  Exeter EX4...........174 E2
  Shillingford St George EX2 114 C6
ILFRACOMBE............150 B6
Ilfracombe Aquarium★
  EX34.................150 D6
Ilfracombe Arts Coll
  EX34.................150 C5
Ilfracombe CE Jun Sch
  EX34.................150 C5
Ilfracombe & District Tyrrell
  Hosp EX34............150 B5
Ilfracombe Inf Sch 16
  EX34.................150 B5
Ilfracombe Mus★ EX34..150 B6
Ilfracombe Rd
  Braunton EX33........152 D7
  West Down EX34.......8 F5
Ilfracombe Swimming Pool
  EX34.................150 D5
Ilkerton Hill EX35.....151 A1
Ilsham CE Prim Sch TQ1..220 E5
Ilsham Cl TQ1..........220 F5
Ilsham Cres TQ1........220 F4
Ilsham Dr TQ1..........220 E5
Ilsham Marine Dr TQ1...221 A4
Ilsham Rd TQ1..........220 F5
ILSINGTON..............122 C3
Ilsington CE Prim Sch
  TQ13.................122 C3
Ilton Cross TQ7........259 A7
Ilton Way TQ7..........258 D5
Immenstadt Dr TA21.....160 D4
Imperial Bldgs TQ12....207 D8
Imperial Ct
  Lynton EX35..........151 C5
  Torquay TQ1..........220 C7
Imperial Mews 12 TQ12...207 F2
Imperial Rd EX8........201 F6
Imperial St EX4........176 F5
Improvement Pl 5 TA21..160 D5
Ince Cl PL11...........246 F4
Inchcoulter EX8........202 C5
Inchkeith Rd PL6.......244 F7
Incledon Rd EX33........3 A3
Indicombe La EX32......18 B2
India Rd TQ13..........180 C6
Ingleside EX13.........167 E6
Ingleside Ct EX9.......198 A1
Ingra Rd PL3...........249 A6
Ingra Tor Cl 1 PL20....126 F3
Ingra Wlk PL3..........245 B8
INLEIGH GREEN..........58 C2
Innerbrook Rd TQ2......219 E5
INNER HOPE.............147 C6
Inner Ting Tong EX9....197 C3
Innes Ho PL1...........262 B3
Instaple Cross EX22....53 D6
INSTOW.................15 B1
Instow Com Prim Sch
  EX39.................15 C2
Instow Ho 4 EX34.......15 B1
Instow Signal Box (Mus)★
  EX39.................15 B1
Instow Wlk PL5.........243 A3
Inswell Ct PL17........171 A6
INSWORKE...............252 F6
Insworke Cl PL10.......253 A6
Insworke Cres PL10.....252 F6
Insworke Pl PL10.......253 A6
International Ho TQ12...180 F7
Inverdene PL3..........248 D5
Invertergn Dr TQ14.....210 A5
Invertegn Prim Sch
  TQ14.................209 D8
INWARDLEIGH............75 E2
Inwardleigh Cross EX20..75 D2
Iolanthe Dr EX4........174 A2
Iona Ave EX8...........196 A2
IPPLEPEN...............211 C2
Ipplepen Bsns Pk TQ12...217 D8
Ipplepen Cross TQ12....211 C6
Ipplepen Prim Sch TQ12..211 D1
Ipplepen Rd TQ3........218 C4
Ipswich Cl PL5.........244 C4
Irene Way EX16.........161 F6
Iris Ave EX2...........261 A1
Irishcombe Gate EX36....46 B5
Irishcombe La EX36......46 C4
Iron Bridge EX4........261 A3

Iron Bridge Cross EX20...77 B3
Iron Letters Cross EX34...2 B1
Iron Mine La PL20......127 B3
Iron Post TA22..........33 B5
Iron Shovel La EX36.....31 A3
Irsha St EX39...........15 A1
Irving Cl EX33.........152 B6
Isaac Cl EX9...........198 C7
Isaac Gr TQ2...........213 F3
Isaacs Rd TQ2..........214 A2
Isabella Rd EX16.......161 D5
Isambard Ct TQ2........214 B3
Isambard Par EX4.......177 A7
ISCA Coll of Media Arts
  EX2..................177 E2
Isca Rd EX2............177 D1
Isigny Rd TQ7..........258 C5
Isis Cl EX14...........166 E7
Island Lodge Camping & Cvn
  Site TQ7.............144 B6
Island Quay TQ8........259 E5
Island St TQ8..........259 E5
Island Terr TQ8........259 E5
Island View TQ7........143 A2
Isleworth Rd EX4.......176 F5
Iter Cnr EX17..........78 C4
Iter Cross EX17........78 C4
Iter Ct EX17...........78 C4
Iter Pk EX17...........78 C4
Itton Cross EX20.......77 D2
Itton Moor La EX17......77 F2
Itton Rd EX17..........77 E2
Ivanhoe Rd PL5.........243 D2
Ivatt Rd TQ6...........233 C3
Iveagh Ct EX4..........176 F8
IVYBRIDGE..............237 C6
Ivybridge Com Coll PL21..237 D6
Ivybridge L Ctr PL21....237 D4
Ivybridge Sta PL21.....237 F6
Ivy Cl
  Exeter EX2...........178 A4
  Sidmouth EX10........188 B7
Ivycombe Hill TQ7......149 B5
Ivy Cotts PL18.........125 C6
Ivy Cross TA21..........51 D7
Ivy Ct 28 EX39..........15 A1
Ivydale EX8............196 D3
Ivydale Rd PL4.........248 F4
Ivydene Rd PL21........237 C5
Ivy Ho TA21............160 C6
Ivyhouse Cross PL16.....91 A4
Ivy La
  Dartmouth TQ6........233 F3
  15 Teignmouth TQ14...210 B4
Ivy Tree Hill TQ12.....209 A2

J

Jack Backs Cross EX17...79 F7
Jack Bears Ho 10 TQ4...226 B6
Jackets Cl EX9.........198 E7
Jackets Cotts EX9......198 E7
JACK-IN-THE-GREEN......99 B6
Jackmans Cl TQ9........222 E6
Jackman's La TQ9.......222 F4
Jackman's Mdw PL10.....253 A3
Jackmoor Cross
  Bramford Speke EX5....81 C1
  Newton St Cyres EX5...81 B1
Jack's La
  St John PL11.........252 B8
  Torquay TQ2..........213 F3
Jackson Cl PL5.........247 F8
Jackson Mdw EX5........195 C6
Jackson Pl PL2.........247 F8
Jackson Way PL12.......242 E3
Jacobs Field EX39......39 E8
Jacob's Ford EX20......170 B5
Jacolind Wlk TQ5.......230 D5
Jago Ave PL11..........247 B8
James Ave TQ3..........218 E1
James Ct EX4...........261 B2
James La EX14..........69 C2
James Lane Cross EX13...69 C2
James Owen Ct EX4......261 C4
James Rd PL19..........171 C2
James St
  Plymouth, Mount Wise
  PL1..................247 E1
  Plymouth PL4.........262 C4
James's Week EX18......59 E8
James's Week La EX18....59 E8
Jane Way's Grave EX17...61 E1
Jardine Pk EX2.........177 C1
Jarmins Pit Cross EX16...46 E4
Jarvis Cl EX8..........202 E7
Jasmine Cl EX16........161 F6
Jasmine Gdns
  Plymouth, Chaddlewood
  PL7..................251 C6
  Plymouth, Glenholt PL6..245 E6
Jasmine Gr TQ3.........218 D8
Jaspers Cotts TQ9......227 B4
Jawbone Hill TQ6.......233 E2
Jaycroft EX15..........162 E4
Jays Cross PL15........149 B6
Jean Cres PL3..........263 A8
Jedburgh Cres PL2......248 A8
Jeffery Cl
  Hartland EX39.........22 E3
  Plymouth PL6.........244 D6

Jefford Ho EX4.........173 A1
Jeffs Way EX13.........167 E6
Jellicoe Rd
  Newton Abbot TQ12....207 F3
  Plymouth PL5.........244 E1
Jellicoe Villas TQ9....223 B5
Jenker's Hill EX33......8 B2
Jenkins Cl PL9.........256 A5
Jennifer Cl EX2........177 E3
Jenns Cross EX22.......53 D7
Jennycliff La PL9......255 A6
Jennys Combe Cl PL9....255 F4
Jenny's Portion EX5....82 A6
Jenwood Rd EX14.........67 B1
Jephson Rd PL4.........249 B3
Jericho DT7............260 D4
Jericho St EX5..........81 E5
Jerrard Cl EX14........166 C5
Jerrard Cres EX14......166 C5
Jesmond Rd EX1.........177 F7
Jessops PL7............250 D7
Jesu St EX11...........169 D3
Jetty Marsh Nature
  Reserve★ TQ12........207 C5
Jetty Marsh Rd TQ12....207 B5
Jewell Cl EX14.........155 C6
JEWEL'S CROSS..........70 E6
J.H.Taylor Dr PL9......157 A7
Jingles La EX32........155 A4
Jinkin Ave PL4.........263 B4
Joan Spry Cl EX16.......46 E1
Jobble's La EX24.......102 E4
Jocelyn Mead EX17......165 B6
Jocelyn Rd EX9.........198 A2
Jockey Hill EX17.......165 C6
Joeys Field EX36........30 F3
John Acres La TQ12.....123 D3
John Gay Cl EX32.......155 C4
John Gay Rd EX32.......155 C4
John Greenway Cl EX16..163 D3
John Grinter Way TA21...160 D6
John Hannam Ho EX1.....261 C3
John Howe Cl EX18......159 D5
John Kitto Com Coll The
  PL5..................244 B1
John La PL4............262 C4
John Levers Way EX4....176 F5
John Nash Dr EX7.......204 C4
John Smale Rd EX31.....154 C4
Johnson Cl 2 PL20......125 E1
Johnson Pk PL18........125 D3
John Sparke Ho 10 PL1..263 A3
John St
  Plymouth PL1.........247 E3
  Tiverton EX16........161 C4
John's Terr 7 EX16.....161 B4
Johnstone Dr EX16......161 B5
Johnstone La EX36.......30 D4
Jones's Hill EX33.......77 D7
Jonida Cl TQ2..........220 A7
JORDAN.................121 A2
Jordan Cl EX32.........155 C3
Jordan Cross TQ13......121 A2
Jordan Dr EX14.........209 D8
Jordan La PL21.........237 C5
Jordan Mdw 18 TQ13.....131 A5
Jordan Orch TQ11.......236 A5
Jordans Brook TQ9......222 E6
Jordan St TQ11.........236 A5
Jose's Cnr EX37........44 F8
Jose's La EX31..........4 B5
Joslin Ct TQ12.........207 D8
Joslin Rd EX14.........166 B5
Joy St EX31............154 F5
Jubilee Cl
  Dartmouth TQ6........233 C3
  Exminster EX6........182 B4
  2 Ilfracombe EX34....150 B5
  Ivybridge PL21.......237 F6
  Okehampton EX20......170 B5
  Saltash PL12.........242 D2
Jubilee Cotts PL12.....242 C1
Jubilee Ct
  Ashwater EX21.........90 C6
  Exeter EX4...........261 A3
  Torquay TQ1..........220 B5
  8 Wellington TA21....160 D5
Jubilee Dr
  Exmouth EX8..........196 C3
  8 Hemyock EX15.......67 B8
Jubilee Gdns
  Cullompton EX15......163 C2
  North Molton EX36.....30 D8
  Sidmouth EX10........188 C8
Jubilee Gr EX8.........195 F5
Jubilee Lodge EX12.....192 B5
Jubilee Pl PL3.........249 C4
Jubilee Rd
  Appledore EX39........14 F1
  Bradninch EX5.........82 F6
  Exeter EX1...........177 E7
  Malborough TQ7.......147 F6
  Newton Abbot TQ12....207 B2
  Plymouth PL5.........243 F3
  Totnes TQ9...........223 E6
  Tiverton TQ7.........143 C6
Jubilee Terr
  1 Bittaford PL21.....137 C7
  Copplestone EX17......79 B5
  Kingswear TQ6........234 B3
  Paignton TQ3.........219 D7
  2 Plymouth PL4.......249 B2
  Julian Cotts PL21....136 D6
  Julian Rd EX11.......237 B5
  Julian St PL4........263 C3
  Julian Wlk PL6.......245 E6
  Jump Cl PL6..........241 C1
  Junction Gdns PL4....263 C3

Junction Rd EX17........78 C4
Juniper Cl
  Exeter EX4...........174 B2
  3 Honiton EX14.......166 A4
  3 Tiverton EX16......161 F6
Juniper Ct EX31........154 C3
Juniper Way PL7........251 B5
Junket Cl EX14..........43 B7
Junket St EX3..........182 B3
Juries La EX38.........159 D6
Jurston Cross TQ13.....110 F4
Jurston La TA21........160 E6
Jury Hill IA22..........33 E6
Jury Pk EX36...........158 B4
Jury Rd TA22............33 E6
Jurys Cnr TQ12.........213 A4
Jurys Corner Cl TQ12...213 A4
Justment Cross EX17.....77 F2

K

Kabale Cl EX16.........161 A6
Kala Fair EX39.........156 E7
Karen Cl EX39..........157 D1
Katherines La EX11.....169 E4
Kathleaven St PL5......243 D1
Kay Cl
  Exmouth EX8..........202 C8
  Plymouth PL7.........250 F7
Keals Croft EX35.......151 A5
Keatings La TQ14.......210 A5
Keaton Barns PL8.......141 E6
Keaton La PL21.........237 D1
Keaton Rd PL21.........237 C4
Keats Cl
  Exmouth EX8..........196 C4
  4 Tiverton EX16......124 E1
Keat St PL2............247 E4
Kedlestone Ave PL5.....244 A3
Keep Cotts TQ4.........224 B7
Keepers Cross EX16......49 A2
Keeper's Ct EX11.......169 B7
Keep Gdns The TQ6......233 C3
Keighley Bglws EX22....164 E1
Keigwin Cl PL5.........233 E4
Keep La TQ6............242 C2
KELLACOTT..............105 F7
Kelland Cl TQ3.........226 A5
Kelland Cnr EX6........98 C1
Kelland Cross EX17.....60 C2
Kelland Hill EX17.......60 C2
Kellands Row TQ7.......258 D5
KELLATON...............149 B6
Kellaton Cross
  East Allington TQ9...144 E7
  Kellaton TQ7.........149 C6
Kellett Cl 7 EX14.....131 A5
Kellock Dr TQ9.........223 B5
KELLY..................115 F8
Kelly Cl
  Plymouth PL5.........247 C7
  Tavistock PL19.......171 D7
Kelly Coll Prep Sch
  PL19.................171 D7
Kelly College TQ12.....122 D8
Kelly La EX16...........62 E8
Kelvin Ave PL4.........263 C4
Kelvin Ct
  Brixham TQ5..........230 D5
  Torquay TQ1..........214 C1
Kelway Rd TA21.........160 E7
KEMACOTT...............4 C4
Kemmings Cl EX14.......225 F1
Kempe Cl PL2...........247 F6
Kempland La EX18........45 B2
Kempley Rd EX20........170 B5
Kemp's La EX12.........192 D7
Kemps Way TA22.........33 D6
Kempton Terr PL11.....247 B2
Kemyell Pl PL2.........247 E4
Kenbury Cres EX6.......181 C8
Kendall Cl EX4.........261 C4
Kendall Ho EX14........166 C5
Kendal Pl PL5..........244 E4
Kendlewood Cl TQ4......225 F3
Kenilworth Rd PL2......243 F4
Kenley Gdns PL5........243 F4
Kenmare Dr PL7.........251 A5
KENN...................114 E4
Kennacott Cross EX22....72 B1
Kennaway Rd EX11.......169 F4
Kenn CE Prim Sch EX6...181 B1
Kenn Cl PL5............244 B3
Kennedy Way
  Dunkeswell EX14.......67 C2
  Tiverton EX16........161 C5
Kennel Bridge Cross EX20 92 E8
Kennel Cl PL7..........250 D4
Kennel Hill Cl PL7.....250 C4
Kennel La
  Georgeham EX33........8 A2
  Ivybridge PL21.......237 B5
Kennels Rd TQ5.........229 C4
Kennels The PL21.......237 B6
Kennerland Cross EX19...8 B8
Kennerleigh EX17........61 F2
Kenner Ct EX4..........178 B8
Kennet Cl PL3..........249 B6
Kenneth St TQ2.........219 C8
KENNFORD...............181 B2
Kennford Rd EX4........177 B3
Kennford Cross EX5.....183 D8

Kenn La
  Exeter EX6...........181 F1
  Exminster EX6........182 A2
Kenn La EX18...........59 B7
Kensall Cross EX36......20 B1
Kensey Cl TQ1..........220 E6
Kensey Valley Mdw
  PL15.................105 A3
Kensham Ave EX5........83 A6
Kensham Cl EX5.........82 F6
Kensington Pl 8 PL4....248 F4
Kensington Rd PL4......263 B4
Kenson Hill EX5........82 B5
Kent Cl EX2............178 A4
KENTISBEARE............66 A3
Kentisbeare CE Prim Sch
  EX15.................66 A3
KENTISBURY.............10 E6
KENTISBURY FORD........10 E5
Kentisbury Prim Sch
  EX31.................10 E6
Kentisknowle TQ1.......220 E5
KENTON.................194 E3
Kenton Brook Ct TQ2....219 B8
Kenton Hill EX6........194 E3
Kenton Mews EX6........194 C3
Kenton Pl EX2..........177 C2
Kenton Prim Sch EX6....194 D3
Kenton Vineyard★ EX6...194 A3
Kent Rd
  Plymouth PL2.........247 F5
  Tatworth TA20.........88 D8
Kent's Bglws TQ10......88 D8
Kents Cavern★ TQ1......220 E5
Kents Cl
  Tatworth TA20.........88 C8
  Uffculme EX15.........66 A7
Kent's Cotts TA20......88 D8
Kents La
  Tatworth TA20.........88 D8
  Torquay TQ1..........220 E5
Kent's Orch TA20.......88 D8
Kents Rd TQ1...........220 E5
Kenwith Dr TQ7.........258 D5
Kenwith Rd EX39........156 F4
Kenwith Terr EX39......156 F3
Kenwith Valley Nature
  Reserve★ EX39........156 F3
Kenwith View EX39......156 D2
Kenwyn Rd TQ1..........220 C6
Kenyon Ct 6X3..........182 F5
Keppel Pl PL2..........247 F4
Keppel St PL2..........247 F4
Keppel Terr 8 PL2......247 F4
KERNBOROUGH...........149 B8
Kernou Rd TQ4..........226 C6
Kernow Cl PL11.........246 E3
Kernow Cl PL11.........246 E3
Kernstone Cross EX39....22 B2
Kerria Cl TQ3..........225 E8
Kerries Ct TQ10........135 A2
Kerries La TQ10........135 A2
Kerries Rd TQ10........135 A2
Ker St 9pe PL1.........247 E2
KERSBROOK.............198 B3
Kersbrook Gdns DT7.....260 D3
Kersbrook La EX9.......198 A3
KERSCOTT...............28 F8
Kerscott EX32..........28 F8
Kerscott Hill EX32.....28 F8
Kerse Cross
  Thurlestone, South Milton
  TQ7.................143 C2
  Thurlestone TQ7......143 B2
Kerse La TQ7...........143 B2
Kerslake's Ct 10 EX14..166 C6
Ker St PL1.............247 E1
KERSWELL...............66 C1
Kerswell Cross TQ13....124 A7
Kerswell La
  Kingskerswell TQ12...213 A5
  Molland EX36.........31 C8
Kerswill Cross TQ9.....135 D1
Kerswill Rd EX4........176 F4
Kestell Rd EX10........188 C4
Kestor Cl EX20.........170 D5
Kestor Dr
  Exeter EX4...........176 E8
  Paignton TQ3.........219 A1
Kestral Bsns Pk EX2....178 F5
Kestral Units PL5......244 A1
Kestrel Cl
  Okehampton EX20......170 B6
  Plymouth PL6.........245 D8
  5 Tiverton EX16......161 E6
Kestrel Ct TQ2.........220 C8
Kestrel Pk PL19........171 D2
Kestrel Way
  Barnstaple EX32......155 E5
  Exeter EX4...........178 E5
Keswick Cres PL6.......245 D2
Kewerel Rd EX8.........196 A1
Kew Ct EX2.............178 C3
Keyberry Cl TQ12.......207 D1
Keyberry Pk TQ12.......207 D1
Keyberry Rd TQ12.......207 D1
Keyes Cl PL1...........247 F2
KEYHAM.................247 E5
Keyham Ct PL2..........247 E6
Keyham Rd PL2..........247 E6
Keyham St PL5..........247 E6
Keyham Sta PL2.........247 E6
Keymelford Cross EX17...79 C2
Keysfield Rd TQ4.......226 C5
Khartoum Pl TQ2........258 C5

Khyber Cl PL11 . . . . 247 A3
Kiddicott EX17 . . . . 165 B5
Kidland La
  Bishops Nympton EX36 . . . 31 E1
  South Molton EX36 . . . . 46 E8
Kidwelly Cl PL7 . . . . 251 C4
Kiel Pl PL3 . . . . 249 D5
Kieran Ct TQ1 . . . . 220 A6
Kigbeare Cross EX20 . . . . 93 B5
Kilbarran Rise EX4 . . . . . 177 A8
Kildere TQ7 . . . . 258 C4
Killatree Cross EX22 . . . . 71 E7
Killerton Cl TQ3 . . . . . . 226 B7
Killerton House★ EX5 . . . 82 D3
Killerton Wlk EX6 . . . . . 181 F5
Killigrew Ave PL12 . . . . . 242 D1
KILLINGTON 4 C1
Killington Cross EX31 . . . 4 D2
KILMINGTON 103 D8
Kilmington Prim Sch
  EX13 . . . . 103 D8
Kilmorie TQ1 . . . . 220 F3
Kilmorie Cl TQ1 . . . . . . 220 F3
Kiln Cl
  Bovey Tracey TQ13 . . . 180 C5
  Cawsand PL10 . . . . . . 253 A1
  Plymouth PL5 . . . . . . 247 C8
Kiln Close La EX39 . . . . 15 B1
Kiln Cross TQ3 . . . . 218 D3
Kilnford Rd TQ12 . . . . . 207 F7
Kiln Ho TQ7 . . . . 258 C4
Kiln La
  Barnstaple EX32 . . . . 155 A4
  Branscombe EX12 . . . . 190 B4
  Combe Martin EX34 . . . 3 B2
  Stokenham TQ7 . . . . . 145 B1
Kiln Orch TQ12 . . . . 206 F3
Kiln Path TQ5 . . . . 230 C4
Kiln Rd
  Bovey Tracey TQ13 . . . 180 C5
  Marldon TQ3 . . . . 218 C3
Kilnwood Pk EX31 . . . . . 154 A3
Kilworthy TQ1 . . . . 220 B8
Kilworthy Hill PL19 . . . . 171 C6
Kilworthy Rd PL19 . . . . . 171 C6
Kimber Cross EX20 . . . . . 74 E2
Kimberlands EX30 . . . . . 74 E2
Kimberley Ct PL21 . . . . . 237 D5
Kimberley Pk EX39 . . . . . 157 A7
Kimberley Rd EX2 . . . . . 261 B2
Kimberley Terr EX39 . . . . 157 A8
Kimberley Villas PL21 . . . 237 C4
Kimberly Dr PL6 . . . . . . 245 B1
Kimbland Cross EX32 . . . 18 C5
Kincraig EX8 . . . . 202 C6
Kinevor Cl EX34 . . . . . . 7 F8
King Alfred Cres EX39 . . . 157 A6
King Alfred Way EX10 . . . 186 E8
King Arthur's Rd EX4 . . . 176 A1
King Charles I Bsns Pk
  TQ12 . . . . 180 C4
King Charles Way EX10 . 188 B8
Kingdom Ave EX36 . . . . . 158 B5
Kingdom Mews EX4 . . . . . 177 A7
Kingdom's Cnr EX16 . . . . 63 C4
Kingdon Ent Pk EX39 . . . 25 D4
King Edward Rd
  Axminster EX13 . . . . . 167 C5
  Saltash PL12 . . . . 242 F2
King Edward St
  Barnstaple EX32 . . . . 154 F6
  Exeter EX4 . . . . 173 A1
King Edward Studios
  EX4 . . . . 173 A1
King Edward VI Com Coll
  (Kennicott Sixth Form)
  TQ9 . . . . 223 B6
King Edward VI Com Coll
  (The Mansion) TQ9 . . 223 C5
Kingfisher Cl
  Plymouth PL4 . . . . . . 245 E6
  Tavistock PL19 . . . . . 171 D2
  Torquay TQ2 . . . . 213 D2
Kingfisher Ct EX4 . . . . . 174 D1
Kingfisher Dr
  Barnstaple EX32 . . . . 155 E4
  Exeter EX4 . . . . 173 D2
  Okehampton/North Tawton
  EX20 . . . . 170 A6
Kingfisher Gdns EX15 . . . 163 B2
Kingfisher Rd EX2 . . . . . 176 D3
Kingfisher Way
  Exeter EX2 . . . . 178 E5
  Plymouth PL9 . . . . . . 255 C7
KINGFORD 43 E6
King Henry's Rd EX2 . . . . 177 E3
Kingsacre EX33 . . . . 152 C6
Kingsacre Prim Sch
  EX33 . . . . 152 C6
King St Bsns Pk EX1 . . . 261 A2
Kingsale Rd TQ8 . . . . . . 259 C4
KINGSAND 253 A1
King's Ash Cross TQ3 . . . 225 E6
King's Ash Prim Sch TQ3 225 E7
King's Ash Rd TQ3 . . . . . 225 E6
Kings Ave
  Ottery St Mary EX11 . . 169 F4
  Paignton TQ3 . . . . . . 226 C7
KINGSBRIDGE 258 E5
Kingsbridge TQ1 . . . . . . 220 B8
Kingsbridge Com Coll
  TQ7 . . . . 258 C4
Kingsbridge Com Prim Sch
  TQ7 . . . . 258 E6

Kingsbridgefork Cross
  TQ9 . . . . 144 E5
Kingsbridge La TQ9 . . 223 C4
Kingsbridge La TQ13 . . 130 F4
Kingsbridge Rd TQ10 . . 137 E8
Kings Cl PL6 . . . . 245 E6
King's Cl EX32 . . . . 155 C2
King's Cnr TA22 . . . . . . 33 D6
Kings Coombe Dr
  TQ12 . . . . 123 F1
KINGSCOTT 42 B5
Kingscott Hill EX38 . . . 42 B4
Kings Cotts
  Newton Abbot TQ12 . . 207 C3
  Salcombe TQ8 . . . . . . 259 E5
King's Cres EX16 . . . . . . 161 E4
King's Cres TQ13 . . . . . 122 E6
Kings Ct
  Honiton EX14 . . . . . . 166 C6
  Kingsbridge TQ7 . . . . 258 D3
  Kingsteignton TQ12 . . 207 E6
  Plymouth PL1 . . . . . . 248 A3
  Seaton EX12 . . . . 192 B4
Kingsdale TQ1 . . . . 220 D4
Kingsdon EX31 . . . . 103 B5
Kingsdon Hill EX24 . . . 103 B5
Kingsdown Cl
  Dawlish EX7 . . . . 204 E7
  Teignmouth TQ14 . . . 209 D7
Kingsdown Cres EX7 . . 204 E7
Kingsdown Rd TQ14 . . 209 D7
Kingsdown Sh TQ5 . . . 230 D4
King's Dr The TQ2 . . . . 219 F4
Kingsdown Workshops Ctr
Kingsgate EX4 . . . . 177 D8
Kingsgate Bsns Ctr
  EX14 . . . . 166 A4
Kingsgate Cl TQ2 . . . . . 214 B4
King's Gdns EX14 . . . . . 166 B3
Kingsholme EX24 . . . . . 103 B3
Kingshurst Dr TQ3 . . . . 226 B8
KINGSKERSWELL 213 B4
Kingskerswell CE Prim Sch
  TQ12 . . . . 213 A5
Kingskerswell Cross
  TQ2 . . . . 213 C3
Kingskerswell Rd
  Newton Abbot TQ12 . . 212 D7
  Torquay TQ2 . . . . 213 D3
Kingsland La EX10 . . . . 188 B3
King's La
  Bishop's Tawton EX32 . 27 F7
  Lynton EX31 . . . . 4 B5
Kingslade La EX10 . . . . 187 B2
Kingslake Ct EX8 . . . . . 202 A8
Kingslake Rise EX8 . . . 202 A8
Kingsland Ct TQ4 . . . . . 225 C4
Kingsland Dr TQ4 . . . . . 225 E4
Kingsland Gardens Cl
  PL3 . . . . 248 E6
Kingsleigh Manor
  TQ1 . . . . 220 C5
Kingsley Ave
  Appledore EX39 . . . . . 15 A1
  Barnstaple EX32 . . . . 154 F6
  Exeter EX4 . . . . 178 B8
  Ilfracombe EX34 . . . . 150 B3
  Torpoint PL11 . . . . . . 247 B2
  Torquay TQ2 . . . . 213 F3
Kingsley Cl PL21 . . . . . 136 D6
Kingsley Ct EX39 . . . . . 156 C6
Kingsley Ho EX31 . . . . . 155 A8
Kingsley Pk EX39 . . . . . 156 E7
Kingsley Rd
  Bideford EX39 . . . . . . 157 A3
  Kingsbridge TQ7 . . . . 258 C4
  Plymouth PL4 . . . . . . 248 E4
  Westward Ho! EX39 . . . 156 C6
Kingsley Sch EX39 . . . . 156 E2
Kingsley St EX39 . . . . . 157 A2
Kingsley Terr
  Bideford EX39 . . . . . . 157 A1
  Combe Martin EX34 . . . 3 A3
Kings Mdw TQ12 . . . . . 212 F4
Kingsmead Dr EX38 . . 159 E6
Kingsmead Ho TQ3 . . . 226 C7
Kings Meadow Dr EX31 . 58 F3
King's Mews EX14 . . . . . 166 C6
Kingsmill Ind Est EX15 . 163 E5
Kingsmill Rd PL12 . . . . 242 C5
King's Mill Rd EX15 . . . 163 E5
Kingsmoor Cross EX21 . 73 F7
KING'S NYMPTON 44 E6
King's Nympton Prim Sch
  EX37 . . . . 44 E5
King's Nympton Sta EX37 44 C3
Kings Orch TQ9 . . . . . . 223 E5
King's Rise EX18 . . . . . . 44 E1
King's Quay TQ6 . . . . . . 233 F4
King's Quay Ho TQ6 . . . 233 F4
Kings Rd
  Barnstaple EX32 . . . . 155 B6
  Paignton TQ3 . . . . . . 226 C7
  Plymouth, Devonport PL1 247 F2
  Plymouth, West Park PL5 . 243 F3
King's Rd
  Exeter EX4 . . . . 177 E8
  Honiton EX14 . . . . . . 166 D6
  Plymouth PL1 . . . . . . 248 A2
King's Sch The EX11 . . 169 B3
King St
  Bideford EX39 . . . . . . 157 A2
  Brixham TQ5 . . . . 230 D5
  Colyton EX24 . . . . 103 A5
  Combe Martin EX34 . . . 3 A3
  Dawlish EX7 . . . . 204 D6

King St continued
  Exeter EX1, EX4 . . . . . 261 A2
  Exmouth EX8 . . . . . . 202 A6
  Gunnislake PL18 . . . . 125 D6
  Honiton EX14 . . . . . . 166 C6
  Millbrook PL10 . . . . . 252 E5
  Newton Abbot TQ12 . . 207 C3
  Plymouth PL1 . . . . . . 262 B3
  Silverton EX5 . . . . . . 82 B6
  South Molton EX36 . . 158 C4
  Tavistock PL19 . . . . . 171 B6
  Tiverton EX16 . . . . . . 161 C3
  Torpoint PL11 . . . . . . 247 C3
KING'S TAMERTON 243 F2
King's Tamerton Rd PL5 . 243 F2
KINGSTEIGNTON 207 C8
Kingsteignton Rd TQ12 . 207 C4
King Stephen Cl EX4 . . . 261 B4
King's Terr EX14 . . . . . . 166 C6
KINGSTON
  Bigbury 142 C6
  Colaton Raleigh 186 A4
  Stoke Climsland 115 C2
Kingston Ave EX34 . . . . 3 A3
Kingston Cl
  Kingskerswell TQ12 . . 213 A5
  Plymouth PL7 . . . . . . 251 A5
Kingston Dr PL7 . . . . . . 251 B5
Kingston Gate Cross
  TQ9 . . . . 216 A6
Kingston La TQ6 . . . . . . 233 E3
Kingston Rd
  Exmouth EX8 . . . . . . 202 C7
  Stoke Climsland PL17 . 115 C1
Kingston Workshops
  TQ9 . . . . 216 A7
Kingswater Ct TQ5 . . . 230 C5
Kingsway
  Exeter EX2 . . . . 177 F5
  Kingsteignton TQ12 . . 253 B2
  Lyme Regis DT7 . . . . 260 E4
  South Molton EX36 . . 158 C3
  Teignmouth TQ14 . . . 209 D7
Kingsway Ave TQ4 . . . 226 A1
Kingsway Cl
  Kingsbridge TQ7 . . . 258 C4
  Paignton TQ4 . . . . . 226 A1
Kingsway Ct TQ4 . . . . 226 A1
Kingsway Dr TQ4 . . . . 226 A1
Kingsway Gdns PL6 . . 244 F3
Kingsway Sq TQ7 . . . . 258 C4
KINGSWEAR 234 B2
Kingswear Cres PL6 . . . 245 B1
Kingswear Prim Sch
  TQ6 . . . . 234 B3
Kingswear Rd TQ5 . . . . 234 E8
Kingswear Sta★ TQ6 . . 234 A3
Kingswood Ct TQ4 . . . 225 E4
Kingswood Ct TQ10 . . 134 F2
Kingswood Park Ave
  PL3 . . . . 248 D6
Kingswood Rd PL18 . . 125 D6
King William Ho EX4 . . 261 B4
King William St EX4 . . . 261 B4
Kinlacey Ct TQ1 . . . . . 220 C4
Kinnard Cres PL6 . . . . 244 F7
Kinnerton Ct EX4 . . . . . 176 B8
Kinnerton Way EX4 . . . 176 E8
Kinross Ave PL4 . . . . . 249 A4
Kinsale Rd PL5 . . . . . . 243 F3
Kinscome Ct TQ1 . . . . . 220 B5
Kinsford Gate Cross TA24 19 D7
Kinsford Hill TA24 . . . . 19 E7
Kinterbury Rd PL5 . . . . 247 B8
Kinterbury St PL1 . . . . 263 A2
Kinterbury Terr PL5 . . . 247 B8
Kintyre Cl TQ2 . . . . . . 213 E2
Kinver Cl PL6 . . . . 245 D4
Kipling Ct EX8 . . . . . . 196 C3
Kipling Ct EX39 . . . . . . 156 C6
Kipling Dr EX2 . . . . . . 177 F4
Kipling Gdns PL5 . . . . . 244 D2
Kipling Ho EX31 . . . . . 155 A8
Kipling Terr EX39 . . . . . 156 C6
Kipscombe Cross EX35 . 6 A6
Kipscombe Hill EX31 . . 11 D2
Kirby Cl EX13 . . . . 167 D5
Kirkby Pl PL4 . . . . 262 C4
Kirkby Terr PL4 . . . . . . 262 C4
Kirkdale Gdns PL2 . . . 248 B7
Kirkella Rd PL20 . . . . . 127 A2
Kirkham Ct TQ3 . . . . . 226 A7
Kirkham House★ TQ3 226 B6
Kirkham St TQ3 . . . . . 226 B7
Kirkland Cl PL6 . . . . . . 245 C7
Kirkstall Cl PL2 . . . . . . 248 A8
Kirkstead Cl TQ2 . . . . . 219 D7
Kirkwall Rd PL5 . . . . . 244 E3
Kirton Dr EX17 . . . . . . 165 D4
Kirton La EX16 . . . . . . 47 E4
Kirton Pl PL3 . . . . 249 B5
Kirtons Rd TQ12 . . . . . 214 B7
Kismeldon Cross EX22 . 39 B3
Kissing Gate Cross EX16 . 48 D5
KITBRIDGE 24 A6
Kitchadon Gate EX18 . . 59 D4
Kitchadon Rd EX18 . . . 59 D3
Kitcott Cross EX36 . . . . 45 F6
Kitcott Hill EX36 . . . . . 45 F6
Kit Hill Cres PL5 . . . . . 247 C8
Kitley View Pl8 . . . . . . 257 B5
Kitley Way PL5 . . . . . . 243 D1
Kitridge La TA24 . . . . . 21 B7
Kits Cl TQ13 . . . . 123 F6
Kitter Dr PL9 . . . . 256 A5

Kitterford Cross PL21 . 137 F7
Kittersley Dr TQ12 . . . 122 F1
Kittiwake Dr TQ2 . . . . 213 C2
Kitts TA21 . . . . 160 D4
Kitts Cross EX10 . . . . . 187 A7
Kitts La EX10 . . . . 187 B6
Kitt's La EX5 . . . . 81 F2
Kitwell St EX15 . . . . . . 66 A3
Klondyke Rd EX20 . . . . 170 C3
Knackershole La EX17 . 61 B2
Knacker's Hole La TA3 . 68 C6
Knap Cross PL21 . . . . . 136 C4
KNAP DOWN 3 B4
Knapp Copse Nature
  Reserve★ EX11 . . . . 101 D6
Knapp Hill EX10 . . . . . 188 A5
Knapp Park Rd TQ4 . . 226 C2
Knapps Cl PL9 . . . . . . 256 C6
Knapp's La EX10 . . . . . 100 D1
Knaves Ash Cross TQ9 . 217 A5
Kneela Hill EX21 . . . . . 74 A8
Kneele Gdns PL3 . . . . . 248 E8
Kneller Cl EX34 . . . . . . 150 C4
Knick Knack La TQ5 . . . 230 C3
Knightacott Cross EX31 . 11 C2
Knighthayes Wlk EX6 . 181 F5
Knightley Rd EX2 . . . . . 177 E3
KNIGHTON 140 D8
Knighton Cross TQ12 . . 131 F8
Knighton Hill Bsns Ctr
  PL9 . . . . 140 E8
Knighton Rd
  Plymouth PL4 . . . . . . 263 C3
  Wembury PL9 . . . . . . 140 D8
Knighton Terr PL20 . . . 126 F5
Knights Cres EX2 . . . . . 178 D3
Knights Field Way EX39 . 157 A8
Knightshayes Court★
  EX16 . . . . 49 C2
Knight's La EX13 . . . . . 88 A4
Knights Mead TQ13 . . 123 C4
Knights Rd TA21 . . . . . 52 D8
Knightstone Down La
  EX17 . . . . 61 C2
Knightstone La
  Ottery St Mary EX11 . 169 F3
  Ottery St Mary, Wiggaton
  EX11 . . . . 169 F1
Knightstone Rd EX11 . . 169 F1
Knightswood EX15 . . . 163 C2
Knill Cross PL10 . . . . . 252 E5
Knill Cross Cotts PL10 . 252 E5
Knockworthy Cross EX38 . 26 F1
Knoll Knap EX13 . . . . . 103 E4
Knoll The PL7 . . . . 250 B6
KNOTTY CORNER 25 B4
Knowland Cl PL1 . . . . . 247 F3
KNOWLE
  Braunton 8 D1
  Budleigh Salterton . . . 197 E2
  Copplestone 79 C4
Knowle Ave PL2 . . . . . 247 E6
Knowle Bsns Units EX2 . 181 D8
Knowle Cl
  Ashburton TQ13 . . . . 130 E4
  Cullompton EX15 . . . . 163 A3
  Honiton EX14 . . . . . . 166 C6
  Landkey EX32 . . . . . . 17 B2
Knowle Cnr EX9 . . . . . 197 D1
Knowle Cross
  Copplestone EX17 . . . 79 C4
  Hennock TQ13 . . . . . 123 C8
  Whimple EX5 . . . . . . 99 E8
Knowle Ct TQ8 . . . . . . 259 D5
Knowle Dr
  Exeter EX4 . . . . 176 F7
  Sidmouth EX10 . . . . . 188 A4
Knowle Fork TQ7 . . . . 148 F4
Knowle Gdns
  Combe Martin EX34 . . 3 A3
  Kingsbridge TQ7 . . . . 258 C6
  Sidmouth EX10 . . . . . 187 F4
Knowle Grange EX10 . . 188 A4
Knowle Hill EX9 . . . . . 197 C2
Knowle House Cl TQ7 . . 258 D6
Knowle Ind Est EX33 . . 8 D1
Knowle La
  Butterleigh EX15 . . . . 64 F1
  Copplestone EX17 . . . 79 C4
  Drewsteignton EX6 . . 96 D1
Knowle Mews EX9 . . . 197 E2
Knowle Rd
  Knowle EX9 . . . . 197 E1
  Lustleigh TQ13 . . . . . 122 C8
  Salcombe TQ8 . . . . . 259 D5
Knowles Cross TQ13 . . 130 E4
Knowles Dr EX24 . . . . 103 A4
Knowles Hill Rd TQ12 . 207 B4
Knowle Terr PL20 . . . . 127 B4
Knowle View EX20 . . . 170 C6
KNOWSTONE 32 A2
Knowstone Cross EX16 . 47 D6
Knowstone Moor Cross
  EX36 . . . . 47 B8
Kyl Cober Parc PL17 . . 115 C1
Kynance Cl PL11 . . . . . 246 F4
Kynock Ind Est EX39 . . 25 F4

L

Labatt Cl PL6 . . . . 245 D3
Labbett's Cross EX18 . . 60 C6
Laboon La EX18 . . . . . . 59 C7
Laburnham Gr TQ9 . . . 223 A7
Laburnum PL19 . . . . . . 171 C6

Laburnum Cl
  Exmouth EX8 . . . . . . 196 D3
  Honiton EX14 . . . . . . 85 C2
Laburnum Cotts TA21 160 D5
Laburnum Ct TQ12 . . . 212 B6
Laburnum Dr
  Barnstaple EX32 . . . . 155 E3
  Wembury PL9 . . . . . . 140 D8
Laburnum Rd
  Exeter EX2 . . . . 177 F3
  Newton Abbot TQ12 . . 207 E1
  Wellington TA21 . . . . 160 E5
Laburnum Row TQ2 . . 219 F6
Laburnum St TQ2 . . . . 219 F5
Laburnum Terr TQ12 . . 212 B7
Laburnum Villas PL19 . 117 E6
Laburnum Way
  East Allington TQ9 . . 144 E7
  Okehampton EX20 . . 170 C5
Lace Wlk EX14 . . . . . . 166 C6
Lackabourgh Ct EX2 . . 181 A8
Lacy Rd TQ3 . . . . 219 A1
Ladford Mill Cross EX21 . 55 C6
Ladies Mile EX31 . . . . . 4 A4
Ladies' Mile EX32 . . . . 155 A3
Ladram Rd EX9 . . . . . . 199 A8
Ladyfern Rd PL6 . . . . . 241 C1
Lady Harriet Acland's Dr
  TA22 . . . . 34 A8
Ladymead EX10 . . . . . . 187 F8
Lady Meadow Terr TQ13 . 121 B2
Lady Modifords CE Prim Sch
  PL20 . . . . 127 B4
Lady Park Rd TQ2 . . . . 219 C7
Lady Seawards CE Prim Sch
  EX3 . . . . 183 C6
Ladysmith Ct PL4 . . . . 263 C4
Ladysmith Inf Sch EX1 . 177 F7
Ladysmith Jun Sch EX1 . 177 F7
Ladysmith Rd
  Exeter EX1 . . . . 177 F7
  Plymouth PL4 . . . . . . 249 B3
Lady St TA22 . . . . 33 D7
Lady Victoria's Dr TA22 . 33 E6
Ladywell EX31 . . . . . . 154 F7
Ladywell Pl PL4 . . . . . 263 B3
Lafrowda Cott EX4 . . . 177 C8
Lagge Hill Cross EX17 . 80 F8
Lag Hill EX17 . . . . 62 F1
Lagoon View EX31 . . . 153 A4
LAIRA 249 C4
Laira Ave PL3 . . . . 249 D4
Laira Bridge Rd PL4 . . 249 B1
Laira Gdns PL3 . . . . . . 249 C4
Laira Green Prim Sch
  PL3 . . . . 249 C4
Laira Park Cres PL4 . . 249 B4
Laira Park Pl PL4 . . . . 249 B4
Laira Park Rd PL4 . . . . 249 B4
Laira Pl PL4 . . . . 263 C2
Laira St PL4 . . . . 263 C3
Laity Wlk PL6 . . . . 244 D6
LAKE
  Barnstaple 154 E2
  Yelverton 127 B3
Lake Ave TQ14 . . . . . . 210 A7
Lake Cl EX14 . . . . 166 D5
Lake Cross TQ9 . . . . . . 131 D2
Lake End Ind Est EX21 . 55 E4
Lake La
  Ashreigney EX18 . . . . 58 F7
  Dousland PL20 . . . . . 127 B3
  Newton St Cyres EX5 . 80 D8
  Northlew EX20 . . . . . 74 D2
  Stockleigh Pomeroy EX17 . 81 A7
Lakeland TQ12 . . . . . . 212 B6
Lakelands Cl EX16 . . . 46 E1
Lakelands Dr EX14 . . . 176 F6
Lake Mews PL10 . . . . . 252 E5
Lakenham Cotts EX39 . 156 F7
Lakenham Hill EX39 . . 156 F7
Lake Rd PL9 . . . . 255 B6
Lakerise EX7 . . . . 201 A2
Lake Rural Workshops
  EX21 . . . . 55 E4
Lakes Cl TQ5 . . . . 230 A5
Lakes Cross EX20 . . . . 57 A8
Lakes Ct EX10 . . . . . . 188 B3
Lakeside
  Salcombe TQ8 . . . . . 259 D5
  Tavistock PL19 . . . . . 171 B6
Lakeside Ave EX2 . . . . 182 B8
Lakeside Cl TQ13 . . . . 180 C4
Lakeside Dr PL5 . . . . . 243 E5
Lakes La EX4 . . . . 98 F4
Lakes Rd TQ5 . . . . 230 A4
Lakeview EX7 . . . . 201 A2
Lakeview Dr PL5 . . . . . 244 B6
Lakewater Cross TQ9 . 131 E1
Lalebrick Rd PL9 . . . . . 255 B5
Lamacraft Cl EX7 . . . . 204 F8
Lamacraft Dr EX4 . . . . 178 A7
Lama Cross EX18 . . . . 59 C4
Lamaton Pk EX36 . . . . 158 D3
Lambert Cl EX17 . . . . . 165 D5
Lambert Ct PL7 . . . . . . 75 A3
Lambert La EX6 . . . . . . 96 F3
Lambert Rd EX4 . . . . . 244 B6
Lambert's La TQ14 . . . 209 D4
Lambhay Hill PL1 . . . . 263 A1
Lambhay St PL1 . . . . . 263 A1
Lamb Park Cl TQ12 . . . 123 F1
Lampark Ct TA3 . . . . . 68 C6

Lamb Pk
Chagford TQ13........111 A6
Drewsteignton EX6......96 D1
Ilfracombe EX34.......150 A4
Lambs Cl TQ7..........143 A2
Lambscombe Cross EX36. 31 A8
Lambscombe Hill EX36... 31 A8
Lamb The TQ9..........223 B5
Lamejohns Field EX17...165 D6
Lamerhooe Cross PL19...116 A1
Lamerhooe Dr PL19......116 A1
LAMERTON..............116 F3
Lamerton CE Prim Sch
PL19...................116 E3
Lamerton Cl PL5.......244 B3
Lamerton Cross EX20....75 F2
Lamerton Cross EX17....78 E5
Lammacott La EX17......78 E6
Lammas La TQ3.........226 A8
Lamorna Pk PL11.......246 E4
Lampard Com Sch The
EX32..................155 C3
Lamplighters EX14.....166 C6
Lamplough Rd EX8......196 A3
LANA
Holsworthy............53 C2
Tetcott................89 F7
Lana Cross EX22.......89 F7
Lana Cross EX22.......55 C1
Lanbridge Cross TQ9...222 F1
Lancaster Cl
Cullompton EX15.......163 C5
Exeter EX2............178 B5
Lancaster Dr TQ4......226 A2
Lancaster Gdns PL5....244 D4
Lancaster Ho TQ4......226 C5
Lancelot Rd EX4.......174 A2
Lancercombe La EX10...100 D3
Lancer Ct TA21........160 D6
Lanchitt Cross EX36....19 B2
Lancock St TA21.......160 A5
Landacre La TA24......21 A7
Landboat Cotts EX17....62 F1
Landboat View EX17....62 F1
Landcroft La EX15......66 F4
LANDCROSS.............26 A2
Lander Rd PL12........242 F3
Landhayes Rd EX4.....176 F5
LANDKEY..............17 B2
LANDKEY NEWLAND.....17 B1
Landkey Prim Sch [3]
EX32..................17 B2
Landkey Rd EX32......155 C2
Landlord's Hill TA21....51 E7
Landmark The TQ7.....259 B4
Landmark Theatre★
EX34..................150 B6
Landpath TQ7.........143 A2
Land Pk [1] EX18.......44 E1
Landrake Cl PL5.......247 C8
Landscore EX17........165 B5
Landscore Cl
Crediton EX17.........165 B5
Teignmouth TQ14......210 B5
Landscore Prim Sch
EX17..................165 A5
Landscore Rd
[3] Exeter EX4........177 A5
Teignmouth TQ14......210 B5
LANDSCOVE............131 B1
Landscove CE Prim Sch
TQ13..................131 B1
Landsend La EX17......78 E3
Lands Pk PL9..........255 F7
Lands Rd
Brixham TQ5..........230 F6
Exeter EX4...........174 D1
LANDULPH.............243 A7
Landulph Cross PL12...238 F1
Landulph Gdns PL5....247 C8
Landulph Sch PL12....238 F1
Landunvez Prl EX5.....82 F6
Lane Cross EX22........53 F7
LANE END..............73 D3
Lane End Cl [1] EX39...15 B1
Lane End Cross
Broadwoodkey La EX4...84 E8
Broadhempston TQ13...131 D3
Halwill EX21...........73 D3
Horsebridge PL19.....116 B2
Ipplepen TQ12.........211 D2
Lane End Rd EX32.....155 D4
Lane End Pool TQ9.....227 B3
Lane End Rd EX39......15 B1
Lane Field Rd EX39....156 D2
Lane Head Cl EX33......7 E2
Lanehead Rd EX12.....191 D5
Lane The
Dittisham TQ6........228 D2
Lutton PL21..........133 B2
Plymouth PL7.........250 D6
LANGFORD.............73 B2
Langaford La EX21.....73 B2
Langage Cross PL7....251 F6
Langage Ind Est EX7...251 D4
Langage Pk PL7.......251 C4
Langage Science Pk
PL7...................251 D5
Langaller Cl TQ13.....180 B5
Langaller Hill TA22.....33 D4
Langaller La TQ13.....180 B4
Langarron Pk EX32....155 B5
Langaton Gdns EX1....174 F1
Langaton La EX1.......175 A1
LANGBROOK...........136 D3
Langbrook Cross PL21. 136 E3
Langdale Cl PL6.......245 D1
Langdale Gdns PL6....245 D1

Langdon Cross PL21....137 F1
Langdon Ct PL9........256 B6
Langdon Down Way
PL11..................246 E3
Langdon Fields TQ5....229 B6
Langdon Hospl EX7....200 E2
Langdon La
Dawlish EX7...........204 C8
Galmpton TQ4, TQ5....229 B6
Langdon Rd
Bradworthy EX22.......38 E1
Dawlish EX7...........204 D8
Paignton TQ3.........219 C1
Langdons Way TA20....88 C8
LANGDOWN.............95 D7
Langerwehe Way EX8...201 F6
Langerwell Cl PL12....242 C3
Langerwell La PL12....242 C3
LANGFORD
Brampford Speke......172 E8
Plymtree..............83 C5
Langford Ave EX14....166 D6
Langford Cres TQ2.....213 F3
Langford Cross EX17....78 C4
Langford Gate PL21...137 F8
Langford Gn EX15......83 D5
Langford Rd
Honiton EX14.........166 D7
Langford EX5..........172 E7
Lang Gdns PL18.......125 D3
Lang Gr
Plymouth PL9.........256 C7
Tavistock PL19.......171 D5
Langham Cross EX19....57 D6
Langham La EX17.......61 F2
Langham Levels PL21..237 B6
Langham Pl PL4........263 C3
Langham Way PL21....237 C5
Langhill Rd PL3.......248 D5
Langland Hill EX17.....61 A4
Langlands Bsns Pk EX15. 65 F6
Langlands Cl EX17.....225 E4
Langlands Cross EX14...87 A6
Langlands Rd EX15....163 A3
LANGLEIGH.............150 A4
Langleigh La EX34.....150 A4
Langleigh Pk EX34.....150 A4
Langleigh Rd EX34.....150 A4
Langley EX18...........44 E1
Langley Ave TQ5......230 C4
Langley Cl
Brixham TQ5..........230 C4
Plymouth PL6.........244 F7
Langley Cres PL6......244 F7
Langley Cross EX37....27 F3
Langley Gdns [2] EX18..44 E1
Langley La EX18.......44 E1
Langman Ct [1] PL20...125 E1
Langmans Cross TQ7...143 A2
Langmead Cl PL6......159 D5
Langmead Cl PL6......249 C8
Langmead Rd PL6......249 C8
Langmoor Cl DT7......260 D3
Langmoor La EX13......88 D2
Langmore Cl PL6......249 A7
Langridge Cross EX37...27 F1
LANGRIDGEFORD........27 F1
Langridge Rd TQ3.....225 E8
Langsfield EX33.........7 D1
Langsford Rd PL19....117 E3
Langs Rd TQ3.........226 C8
Langston Cross
Whiddon Down EX20....142 D7
Langstone Cl
Heathfield TQ12.......180 F2
Torquay TQ1..........220 D6
Langstone Dr EX8.....196 C1
Langstone Hill
Lustleigh TQ13........111 E1
Moretonhampstead TQ13. 111 E1
Langstone Rd PL2.....248 C7
Langstone Terr PL2....248 C7
Langton Rd [8] PL20...126 F3
LANGTREE.............40 F2
LANGTREE COMMON....41 A3
Langtree Com Prim Sch
EX38..................40 F2
Lang Way TQ12........211 E2
Langwells Ct TQ9.....139 E1
Langworthys Barn TQ7. 143 E2
Lanherne EX7.........204 E6
Lanherne Fst Sch [20]
EX7...................204 D6
Lanhydrock Cl TQ3....225 D8
Lanhydrock Rd PL4....249 B2
Lannacombe Gn TQ7...149 C5
Lanscore La EX14.....101 A8
Lansdowne EX2........178 B4
Lansdowne La [2] TQ2. 219 F5
Lansdowne Pk
Northam EX39.........156 F8
Totnes TQ9...........139 F1
Lansdowne Rd
Budleigh Salterton EX9. 197 D1
Plymouth PL6.........244 F2
Torquay TQ2..........219 F5
Lansdowne Terr
Bideford EX39.........156 F1
Exeter EX2............225 B2
Lansdown Terr [2] EX32. 155 A6
Lanteglos Cl [5] PL21..137 C7
LAPFORD..............60 C3
Lapford Com Prim Sch
EX17..................60 D3
LAPFORD CROSS........60 C2
Lapford Cross EX17....60 C2

Lapford Sta EX17.......60 C2
Lapthorn Cl PL9.......255 C7
Lapwing Cl EX15.......163 A3
Larch Cl
Exmouth EX8..........196 D3
Saltash PL12..........242 C3
Seaton EX12..........192 A8
Larch Dr PL6..........245 E7
Larch Rd EX12........132 C1
Larch Rd EX2..........176 F3
Larch Wlk TQ2........219 C8
Larcombe End TQ9....135 F1
LARKBEARE............100 B8
Larkbeare Ave EX5....100 B8
Larkbeare Cross EX5...100 B8
Larkbeare Rd EX2.....261 B1
Lark Cl EX4...........173 D1
Larkey La EX16.........63 D4
Larkhall Rise PL3.....249 B5
Larkham Cl PL7.......250 C6
Larkham La PL7.......250 C6
Lark Hill PL2..........248 A6
Lark Rise
[5] Barnstaple EX31...154 A2
Newton Poppleford EX10. 186 E8
Larks Cl TQ14.........209 D4
Larkshayes Cross EX13. 86 E3
Larkshayes Droveway
EX13..................86 F3
Larkshayes Knap EX13. 86 F3
Larksmead Cl TQ12....207 A1
Larks Rise EX15........55 E6
Larkstone Cres [8] EX34. 150 D5
Larkstone Gdns EX34..150 D5
Larkstone La EX34.....150 D6
Larkstone Terr EX34...150 D6
Larks Way EX32.........17 F4
Lashbrook EX5.........84 B2
Lashingcott Cross EX31. 27 B3
Lashingcott Lane End
EX31..................27 B2
Laskeys Heath [1] TQ12. 122 F1
Laskeys La EX10.......188 C4
Latches Wlk EX15.....167 D6
Latchgate Cross EX36...31 F7
Latchgate Hill EX36...137 B3
Latch La EX38..........40 E2
Latchmount Gdns EX13. 167 D6
Latham Cl PL6........249 A7
Latimer Cl PL7........251 B5
Latimer Rd EX4.......174 B6
Latimer Wlk PL6......244 E7
Lauderdale [2] EX32...155 B4
Lauderdale La EX32...155 B4
Lauder La EX31........154 C1
LAUNCESTON...........105 B2
Launceston Cl PL6....244 D7
Launceston Head EX5...83 C1
Launceston Rd EX20...107 E8
Laundry Cotts EX5......98 F8
Laura Ave TQ3........226 B8
Laura Gr TQ3.........226 A8
Laura Pl [3] TQ3.......226 A6
Laurel Ave EX39.......156 E1
Laurel Bank EX14.......85 B4
Laurel Cl PL2.........248 A7
Laurel Dene PL7......248 A7
Laurel Dr PL6.........245 E5
Laurel La TQ14........209 D5
Laurel Rd
Exeter EX2............177 F3
[1] Honiton EX14.......166 A4
Plymouth PL2.........248 A7
Laurel Rise EX8.......202 D8
Laurels The
Barnstaple EX31......154 B2
Dunkeswell EX14.......67 C3
Gunnislake PL18......125 B5
Sidmouth EX10........188 A5
Torquay TQ1..........220 D8
Laureston Rd TQ12....207 C2
Laurie Ave TQ12......206 F4
Lauriston Cl TQ2......220 A5
Lavender Cl TQ5......230 A4
Lavender Rd EX4......177 E8
Lavington Cl PL7......251 B5
Lavinia Dr PL7........250 C5
LAWHITTON............108 B1
Law Memorial Ho [5]
EX32...................16 E1
Lawn Cl
[2] Plymouth PL7......251 C5
Torquay TQ2..........213 F4
Lawn Dr TQ13.........123 E6
Lawn Gdns [16] TQ13..123 E6
Lawn Hill [3] EX7......204 E6
Lawn Rd EX8..........202 A7
Lawns End TQ14......208 E8
Lawns The
Plymouth PL5.........244 E1
Torpoint PL11.........247 A4
Lawn Terr [25] EX7....204 E6
Lawn The
[3] Budleigh Salterton
EX9...................198 A1
Tavistock PL19.......171 D6
[1] Wellington TA21...160 D6
Lawn Vista EX10......188 B5
Lawrence Ave EX4.....177 A4
Lawrence Cl EX14......84 D7
Lawrence Pl TQ12....220 B4
Lawrence Rd PL6......255 A6
Lawrence Wlk EX6....181 F5
Lawson Gr PL9.........255 C7
Law Wlk PL6.........244 D6
Laxton Ave EX1.......178 C6

Layne Cl EX6..........113 B4
Layne Fields EX6......113 B4
Laywell Cl TQ5.......230 B2
Laywell Rd TQ5.......230 A3
Lazenby Rd EX16......161 F3
Leaches La EX18........60 B7
Leachway La EX2......113 F7
Leachway Lane Cross
EX2...................113 F7
Lea Combe EX13.......167 D5
Leadengate Cl EX33....7 E1
Leadengate Fields EX33. 7 D1
Leader La TQ3........218 D2
Leaholes Ave EX20....170 C5
Lea La EX9............198 F7
Lealands TQ13........180 C6
Lea Mount TQ14......209 A8
Lea Mount Cl EX7.....204 D5
Lea Mount Dr EX7.....204 D5
Lea Mount Rd EX7.....204 E5
Leander Ct [8] TQ14...210 B8
Leander Way PL5.......244 D2
Leanway PL12.........242 E2
Lea Rd
Otterton EX9..........198 E7
Tiverton EX16.........161 F6
Torquay TQ2..........214 A3
Lear Pk EX15..........83 F5
Lears La TQ13.........123 F6
Leary Cross EX32......29 B8
Lease Cotts EX5.......82 C4
Lea Side EX6..........112 E8
Leas Rd EX9..........198 A1
Leas The EX34........150 A3
Lea Ter EX39...........15 A1
Leat Cl PL20..........127 B3
Lea Terr EX39.........15 A1
Leatfield Dr PL6......244 F4
Lea The TQ14.........209 C7
Leatherby [1] PL6.....244 E7
Leather Tor Cl [4] PL20. 126 F3
Leat Mdw
[3] Coldeast TQ12....122 F1
Tiverton EX16.........161 B5
Leat Rd PL16.........105 F3
Leatside
Exeter EX2............261 A2
Roborough PL6........241 C1
Leatside Ho TQ12.....207 A3
Leat St EX16..........161 B5
Leat View PL12.......242 B3
Leatway Gdns EX15...163 B3
Leat Wlk
Plymouth PL3.........248 E6
Roborough PL6........241 A4
Saltash PL12..........242 D4
Lea Vale Rd TQ12.....207 A3
Leaveacre EX17........90 E7
Leaves Yd PL3.........249 B7
Lea View EX15........162 D5
Leaway Cotts EX16....161 E4
Leaze Rd TQ12........207 D8
Lebanon Cl EX4.......173 E1
Leburnick Cross PL15..115 B8
Ledgate La PL7........251 F8
Ledsgrove TQ12.......211 E2
LEDSTONE.............144 B5
Ledstone Cross TQ7...144 B5
LEE....................1 C3
Lee Ball Cross EX31....11 D3
Lee Ball Hill EX31......11 D3
Leechwell La TQ9.....223 C5
Leechwell St TQ9.....223 B5
Lee Cl EX14...........166 B6
Lee Cliff Pk EX7.......201 B1
Lee Cross
Broadhempston TQ9...131 E1
Great Torrington EX37...42 F7
North Molton EX36.....30 B8
Woolacombe EX34......1 C1
Leecross Gate EX17....61 A7
Leecross La EX5.......81 F8
Lee Ct TQ5...........230 E4
LEEFORD...............6 B5
Leeford La EX35........6 B5
Lee La
Bishops Nympton EX36. 31 F6
Dartmouth TQ6.......232 C7
Dunsford EX6.........112 E7
Lee Lane End TQ7.....148 F8
LEE MILL.............136 C2
Lee Mill Ind Est PL21. 136 C6
LEE MOOR.............132 F5
Lee Pk TA21...........52 F7
Lee Pk EX34..........150 C6
Lee Rd EX35..........151 B5
Leeside Ct [7] PL2.....248 A4
Lees Mdw EX5..........84 A2
Lee Terr [2] TQ13.....123 E6
Leeward Ct EX8.......201 E6
Leeward La TQ2.......213 E3
Leeze Park Est EX20...170 B4
Leggetts La DT7.......193 F7
Legion La PL8..........257 A5
Legion Way EX2.......177 B2
Legis Wlk PL6.........245 B8
Leicester Mead EX4...176 E7
LEIGHAM..............249 E8
Leigham Ct
[7] Dawlish EX7.......204 E6
Plymouth PL4.........262 B2
Leigham Manor Dr PL6. 249 F8
Leigham Prim Sch PL6. 245 E1
Leigham St PL1.......262 B1
Leigham Terr TQ7.....258 C5
Leigham Terrace La PL1. 262 B2

Leigham Terrace Lane W
PL1...................262 B2
Leighan Bsns Units EX2. 181 D8
Leigh Cl PL21.........137 C8
Leighcott Cross EX17...62 A2
Leighcott La EX17......62 A2
Leigh Cross
Ashill EX15............66 F6
Bittaford PL21........137 D8
Bridford EX6..........113 B6
Chulmleigh EX18.......59 C8
Hennock TQ13........123 C7
Kingsbridge TQ7......258 A8
Modbury PL21.........137 F3
South Brent TQ10....135 A4
Zeal Monachorum EX17..77 F7
Leigh Ct PL6..........249 A8
Leighdene Cl EX2.....177 E4
Leigh Dene Cl EX2....177 E4
Leigh La
Bittaford PL21........137 C8
Combe Martin EX34.....3 C2
Roborough PL6........241 D2
Leighmoor Cross PL21. 137 F3
Leighon Rd TQ3.......226 C7
Leigh Rd
Bideford EX39.........156 E1
Chulmleigh EX18.......44 D1
Combe Martin EX34.....3 B2
Leighton Rd PL3......248 E6
Leighton Terr EX4....261 B4
Leighty Water EX38....42 A6
Leigh Villas EX18......44 E1
Leland Gr PL21........237 D4
Le Locle Cl EX10......187 F8
Le Marchant Ct EX14...67 B1
Lembury Rd TQ9......225 A1
Le Molay-Litrry Way
TQ13..................180 C2
Lemonford La TQ12....131 D7
Lemonford Mills TQ12. 131 D6
Lemon Pl TQ12........207 C3
Lemon St EX2.........207 C3
Lenards Rd EX39......156 F6
Lenda La TQ12.........122 C2
Lendon Way EX19......58 F2
Lennard Rd [6] EX17..165 C5
Lennon Ct EX16.......188 B4
Lennox Ave EX10......188 B4
Lentney Cl PL9........140 A8
Lenton La EX37........44 C6
Lenwood Ctry Club EX39. 156 E5
Lenwood Pk EX39.....156 E5
Lenwood Rd EX39.....156 E5
Leofric Rd EX16.......161 D6
Leonard Moor Cross EX15. 65 F8
Leonards Cl TQ7......143 A1
Leonards Rd PL21.....237 D5
Lerwell Beech Tree Cross
EX37..................29 A5
Leslie Rd EX8.........202 A8
Lester Cl PL3.........249 B6
Lester Ct EX8.........202 F7
Lethaby Rd EX2.......155 B6
Lethbridge Rd EX2....178 B4
Lethbridge's & Davey's
Almshouses EX1......261 C4
Letheren 's La EX20....77 B5
Lettaford Cross TQ13. 130 A8
LEUSDON..............130 A8
Level The TQ6........228 C2
Lever Cl EX39.........156 F8
Leverlake Cl EX16.....161 F6
Leverlake La EX16.....161 F7
Lewdon Cross EX7......97 A5
LEWDOWN..............106 E5
Lewesdon Ct [2] DT7..260 D3
Lewes Gdns PL5.......244 C4
Lewhaven Cl EX20....106 E5
Lewis Ave EX16.......161 E4
Lewis Cres EX2........178 D3
Lewis Ct [3] EX34.....150 B3
Leworthy Cross
Holsworthy EX22.......71 D4
Woolfardisworthy EX39. 39 B6
Leworthy Hill EX31....11 D1
Leworthy Post EX31....11 C1
Lewsley Cross EX13....87 E4
Lewsley La EX13.......87 E4
Lewthorn Cross TQ13. 122 B3
LEWTRENCHARD.......106 F4
Lew Trenchard Prim Sch
EX20..................106 F5
Lexhayne La EX13.....103 A7
Leyburn Gr TQ4.......226 A4
Ley Cl TQ12...........180 B1
Ley Cres TQ12........180 B1
Ley Cross
Ashreigney EX18......58 F8
Aveton Gifford PL21...143 A8
Ermington PL21........136 D4
Holsworthy Beacon EX22. 54 F3
North Molton EX36.....30 F8
Widecombe in the Moor
TQ13..................121 D6
Leyfield Wlk EX17.....204 E7
Leyford Cl PL9........140 D7
Ley La
Ben Ferrers PL20......239 C6
Kentisbury EX31.......10 D6
Kingsteignton TQ12...207 D8
Ley La Cross TQ12....207 D8
Leyland Cross TQ12....53 E8
Ley Meadow Dr EX31. 154 A3
Leypark Cl EX1........178 C7

Leypark Cres EX1 . . . . . . 178 C7
Leypark Ct PL6 . . . . 245 E2
Leypark Dr PL6 . . . . 245 E2
Leypark Rd EX1 . . . . 178 C7
Leypark Wlk PL6 . . . . . . 245 E2
Ley's Cross EX17 . . . . 62 E2
Ley's La EX31 . . . . 4 C1
Leys Rd TQ2 . . . . 219 D5
Leyton Ct EX15 . . . . 163 C3
Leywood EX14 . . . . 86 D7
Libby Ct PL12 . . . . 242 C5
Liberator Way EX14 . . . . 67 C1
Liberty Rd EX31 . . . . 154 B2
Liberty Stile EX39 . . . . . 22 C2
Liberty Way EX2 . . . . . . 178 E1
Libra Gdns EX4 . . . . 2 F4
Libra Sch The EX36 . . . . . 19 E3
Lichfield Ave TQ2 . . . . . . 214 A1
Lichfield Cl TQ5 . . . . 230 A4
Lichfield Dr TQ5 . . . . . . 230 A4
Lichfield Rd EX4 . . . . . . 176 D6
Lichgate Rd EX1 . . . . . . 181 C8
Lidburn Hill EX6 . . . . 97 E5
LIDDATON 106 F1
Liddle Way PL7 . . . . 251 B6
Lidford Tor Ave TQ4 . . . . 225 F3
Lidyates La DT7, EX13 . . 103 F3
Liffey Rise EX4 . . . . 176 E8
LIFTON 105 E4
LIFTONDOWN 105 C4
Liftondown Cross PL16 . . 105 C4
Lifton La EX19 . . . . 59 B3
Lifton Prim Sch PL16 . . . 105 E4
Lighthouse Cross EX39 . . 23 B3
Light La TQ5 . . . . 229 B4
Lightleigh Cross EX18 . . . 44 F5
Lilac Cl PL9 . . . . 255 C5
Lilac Rd
  Exeter EX2 . . . . 177 F3
  Tiverton EX16 . . . . 161 F5
Lilac Terr 2 EX16 . . . . . . 161 D4
Lilian Cl EX17 . . . . 78 B4
Lillage La EX9 . . . . 198 A6
Lilleborne Cl TA21 . . . . . 166 D8
Lilley Wlk EX14 . . . . 166 D5
Lillicrap Ct EX20 . . . . . . 170 B5
Lillybrook La EX6 . . . . . . 98 A5
Lillycombe La TA3, EX15 . 67 E8
Lily La EX5 . . . . 172 A8
Lilybridge EX39 . . . . 157 A7
Lily Cl EX39 . . . . 157 A7
Lilylake Cross EX24 . . . . 102 F7
Lily Mount EX4 . . . . 176 D8
Lime Ave TQ2 . . . . 219 F5
Lime Cl
  Broadclyst EX5 . . . . . . 175 C6
  Tiverton EX16 . . . . 161 F5
Lime Cres EX15 . . . . 162 C4
Lime Gr
  Bideford EX39 . . . . 156 F2
  Exmouth EX8 . . . . 182 A5
  Exmouth EX8 . . . . 196 C3
  Kingsbridge TQ7 . . . . . 258 C5
Limegrove Rd EX4 . . . . . 176 F5
Limehayes Rd EX20 . . . . 170 C5
Limekiln La EX31 . . . . . . 16 A6
Lime Kiln La
  Exeter EX2 . . . . 178 A1
  Uplyme DT7 . . . . 260 A6
Lime Kiln Rd EX16 . . . . . 161 F3
Lime Rd EX16 . . . . 161 F5
Limerick Pl PL4 . . . . 263 C3
Limers Cross
  Chittlehampton EX37 . . . 29 A4
  Wolverstone EX14 . . . . . 85 C7
Limer's Hill EX38 . . . . . . 159 B5
Limers La
  Merton EX20 . . . . 57 A7
  Northam EX39 . . . . 157 A5
  Wolverstone EX14 . . . . . 85 C7
Limer's La EX36 . . . . 158 B2
Limers Lane Cross EX36 158 B2
Limes Cotts EX6 . . . . . . 182 A4
Limes Ct EX6 . . . . 182 B4
Limes La PL19 . . . . 171 A6
Lime St TQ13 . . . . 111 F5
Limes The PL6 . . . . 244 F2
Lime Tree Cl EX2 . . . . . . 178 C3
Limetree Cross EX6 . . . . . 6 D6
Limetree Gr EX33 . . . . . . 152 C6
Lime Tree Mead 1 EX16 64 D7
Limetree Rd PL3 . . . . . . 248 D7
Lime Tree Wlk TQ1 . . . . 207 E1
Lime Way EX12 . . . . 192 A7
Linacre La TQ12 . . . . . . 213 C6
Linacre Rd TQ2 . . . . 213 F4
Lincoln Ave PL4 . . . . 263 C4
Lincoln Cl
  Exmouth EX8 . . . . 196 E4
  Feniton EX14 . . . . 84 D2
Lincoln Gn TQ2 . . . . 214 A1
Lincoln Rd EX4 . . . . 176 E6
LINCOMBE 1 D3
Lincombe Cross
  Diptford TQ9 . . . . 138 D8
  Salcombe TQ8 . . . . . . 259 D7
Lincombe Dr TQ1 . . . . . 220 E3
Lincombe La EX17 . . . . . 78 B5
Linda Cl EX1 . . . . 178 B5
Linden Cl
  Barnstaple EX31 . . . . . 154 C3
  Braunton EX33 . . . . . . 152 D6
  Exmouth EX8 . . . . 196 B2
  Great Torrington EX38 . 159 C5
Linden Ct 2 TQ5 . . . . . . 230 C5

Linden Gdns EX31 . . . . . 154 C3
Linden Hill TA21 . . . . . . 160 A6
Linden Rd
  Cullompton EX15 . . . . . 163 C4
  Dawlish EX7 . . . . 204 D5
Linden Terr
  Newton Abbot TQ12 . . . 207 A3
  Plymouth PL4 . . . . 263 C3
Lindfield Cl TQ2 . . . . . . 219 F8
Lindisfarne Way TQ2 . . . 213 E2
Lindridge Cl 6 TQ12 . . . 123 E1
Lindridge Hill TQ12 . . . . 123 F1
Lindridge La 6 TQ12 . . . 123 E1
Lindridge Pk TQ14 . . . . 124 B2
Lindridge Rd TQ1 . . . . . 220 C8
Lindsay Rd TQ3 . . . . . . 219 A2
Lindthorpe Way TQ5 . . . 230 B4
Liney Cross TQ11 . . . . . 236 A6
Linfield Gdns EX4 . . . . . 176 F4
Linhay Cl
  Brixham TQ5 . . . . 234 F8
  Honiton EX14 . . . . 166 B3
  Millmoor EX15 . . . . 51 E1
Linhay Dr EX31 . . . . 153 F6
Linhay Pk EX17 . . . . 80 A5
Linhey Cl TQ7 . . . . 258 D4
Linkadells PL7 . . . . 250 D6
Linketty La PL7 . . . . 250 C5
Linketty Lane E PL6 . . . . 245 A1
Linketty Lane W PL6 . . . 248 F8
Linkhay TA20 . . . . 88 D8
Linkhay Cl TA20 . . . . . . 88 D8
Linkhay Ct TA20 . . . . . . 88 D8
Link House Cl EX39 . . . . 156 C7
Link Rd EX20 . . . . 170 C6
Links Cl
  Churston Ferrers TQ5 . . 229 E6
  Exmouth EX8 . . . . 202 C8
Links Ct TQ7 . . . . 143 A1
Links Rd EX9 . . . . 203 E8
Links The
  Northam EX39 . . . . . . 156 E7
  Torquay TQ1 . . . . 214 C1
Linnet Cl EX4 . . . . 173 D2
Linnet Ct PL12 . . . . 242 C2
Linnet Dene EX15 . . . . . 163 A2
Linscott Cres EX31 . . . . 153 A4
Linton Cl PL5 . . . . 244 C8
Linton La EX39 . . . . 37 B5
Linton Rd PL5 . . . . 244 C7
Linton Sq PL5 . . . . 244 C8
Lion Cl TQ12 . . . . 230 C5
Lion Ho EX8 . . . . 202 A5
Lion's Close Hill EX24 . . 103 A5
Lions Mill EX31 . . . . 154 F7
Lion's Rump EX32, EX36 . 18 F1
Lippell Dr PL9 . . . . 255 E6
LIPSON 263 C4
Lipson Ave PL4 . . . . 263 C4
Lipson Com Coll PL4 . . . 249 C2
Lipson Ct PL4 . . . . 263 B3
Lipson Rd PL4 . . . . 263 B4
Lipson Sp Ctr PL4 . . . . . 249 A4
Lipson Terr PL4 . . . . 263 C4
Lipson Vale PL4 . . . . . . 249 A4
Lipstone Cres PL4 . . . . . 263 C4
Lisa Cl EX2 . . . . 178 A4
Lisburne Cres 16 TQ1 . . 220 D4
Lisburne Pl 10 TQ1 . . . . 220 D4
Lisburne Sq TQ1 . . . . . . 220 D4
Liscawn Terr PL11 . . . . . 247 B3
Liscombe Cl PL18 . . . . . 125 D7
Lisham's Drain EX24 . . . 103 A5
Lishaperhill Cross EX22 . 53 B2
Liskeard Rd PL12 . . . . . 242 B3
Lisson Gr PL4 . . . . 248 F4
Lister Cl
  Exeter EX2 . . . . 177 E4
  Plymouth PL7 . . . . 250 F6
Lister Way TQ9 . . . . 144 E7
Litchardon Cross EX31 . . 26 F8
Litchaton Cres PL7 . . . . 250 B7
Litchaton Cross
  East Buckland EX32 . . . 18 F1
  North Molton EX36 . . . 30 A8
Litchaton Hill
  East Buckland EX32 . . . 18 F1
  North Molton EX36 . . . 30 A8
Litchaton Way PL7 . . . . 250 B7
Litchdon La EX32 . . . . . 154 F4
Litchdon St EX32 . . . . . 155 A4
Litchfield Cl PL7 . . . . . . 251 B6
Litelbury Rd EX16 . . . . . 64 D7
Littabourne EX31 . . . . . 154 F7
Little Ash Gdns PL5 . . . . 243 B1
Little Ash Rd PL5 . . . . . 243 B1
Little Barley EX4 . . . . . . 176 F5
Little Barton 2 TQ12 . . . 123 F1
Little Bicton Cl EX8 . . . . 202 A6
Little Bicton Pl EX8 . . . . 202 A6
Littleborough Cross EX17 62 A1
Little Bossell La TQ11 . . 236 B4
Little Bray Cross EX32 . . 18 E6
Littlebray La EX32 . . . . . 18 E6
Little Bridge Bsns Pk
  EX5 . . . . 179 D1
Little Bridge Cross EX22 . 70 F5
Littlebridge Mdw EX22 . . 70 F5
Little Butts PL9 . . . . 255 E6
Little Castle St EX4 . . . . 261 B3
Little Cl
  Kingsteignton TQ12 . . . 207 E8
  Ottery St Mary EX11 . . 169 D3
LITTLE COMFORT 115 A7
Little Cross TQ13 . . . . . 130 A4
Little Dock La PL5 . . . . . 244 B2
Littledown Cl EX8 . . . . . 202 F7

Littledown La EX10 . . . . 186 D7
Little Down La
  East Budleigh EX9 . . . . 198 A5
  Roborough PL6 . . . . . . 241 E3
Little Down Orch EX10 . . 186 D7
Little Esworthy La EX16 . 48 A1
Little Fancy Cl PL6 . . . . 245 C7
Little Field TQ14 . . . . . . 208 E8
Little Field EX39 . . . . . . 156 D2
Littlefield Cl
  Barnstaple EX32 . . . . . 155 D4
  Torquay TQ2 . . . . 213 D1
Littlefields EX12 . . . . . . 192 A7
Littleford Cross EX22 . . . 53 E8
Little Gate TQ7 . . . . 143 F7
Littlegate Rd TQ14 . . . . 226 B6
Little Gorhay La
  Chevithorne EX16 . . . . . 49 D1
  Tiverton EX15 . . . . 64 D8
5 Tiverton EX16 . . . . . . 161 F6
LITTLEHAM
  Bideford 25 D2
  Exmouth 202 F7
Littleham CE Prim Sch
  EX8 . . . . 202 F7
Littleham Cross
  Bideford EX39 . . . . 25 C2
  Exmouth EX8 . . . . 202 D7
Littleham Rd EX8 . . . . . 202 E7
Little Hayes 12 TQ12 . . 123 F1
Little Hayes La EX18 . . . 58 D8
Little Heath Cross EX16 . 63 A6
Little Helstonbench Cross
  TQ13 . . . . 123 B6
LITTLEHEMPSTON 216 F2
Littlehempston Cross
  TQ9 . . . . 216 F2
Littlehill TA20 . . . . 69 C8
Little Hill TQ8 . . . . 259 C5
Little Hill Cl TQ12 . . . . . 123 E1
Little John's Cross Hill
  EX2 . . . . 176 E3
Little John's Wlk TQ13 . . 122 F6
Littlejoy Rd TQ12 . . . . . 206 C4
LITTLE KNOWLE 197 F1
Little Knowle EX9 . . . . . 197 F1
Little Knowle Ct EX9 . . . 197 F1
Little La
  Beer EX12 . . . . 191 D4
  Kingsand PL10 . . . . . . 253 A2
  Staddiscombe PL9 . . . . 255 D3
Little Mdw
  Exmouth EX8 . . . . 196 E3
  Pyworthy EX22 . . . . . . 71 D5
Little Mdws EX18 . . . . . 59 C4
Littlemead La EX8 . . . . . 196 B3
Little Meadow Way EX39 156 C2
Littlemoor Cl PL7 . . . . . 153 A4
Little Normans EX15 . . . 83 F6
Little Park Rd TQ3 . . . . 219 B6
Little Point Cres PL10 . . 252 F5
Little Princes TQ1 . . . . . 220 C3
Little Queen St EX4 . . . 261 B3
Little Rackenford La EX16 47 C5
Little Rack St 4 EX1 . . . 261 A2
Little Raddon Cross EX17 80 F6
Little Roborough TQ13 . 130 F5
LITTLE SILVER 63 D4
Little Silver
  Exeter EX4 . . . . 261 A4
  Tiverton EX16 . . . . 161 D3
Little Silver La
  Exeter EX2 . . . . 181 D5
  Wellington TA21 . . . . . 160 D2
Little Toms EX15 . . . . . . 65 A2
Littleton Pl PL2 . . . . . . 247 F4
LITTLE TORRINGTON . . . 41 D3
Little Torrington EX38 . . 159 B1
LITTLETOWN 166 B4
Littletown Prim Sch
  EX14 . . . . 166 C4
Littletown Rd EX14 . . . . 166 B4
Littletown Villas EX14 . . 166 B4
Littleway EX2 . . . . 176 F3
Little Week Cl PL7 . . . . . 200 F1
Little Week Gdns EX7 . . 200 F1
Little Week La EX7 . . . . 200 F1
Little Week Rd EX7 . . . . 200 F1
Little Wiveliscombe La
  TA4 . . . . 35 D6
Littlewood Cl PL7 . . . . . 251 A4
Livarot Wlk EX36 . . . . . 158 B4
Livaton Cross EX20 . . . . 95 D4
LIVERMEAD 219 E2
Livermead Hill TQ2 . . . . 219 E2
Livermore Rd EX14 . . . . 166 C5
Liverpool Hill EX4 . . . . . 176 E7
LIVERTON 180 A1
Liverton Bsns Pk EX8 . . 196 F1
Liverton Cl EX8 . . . . . . 202 D8
Liverton Ct TQ12 . . . . . 180 A1
Liverton Hill EX8 . . . . . 197 B1
Livery Dole Almshouses
  EX2 . . . . 177 E5
Living Coasts (Zoo)★
  TQ1 . . . . 220 B3
Livingshayes Rd EX5 . . . 82 C6
Livingstone Ave EX8 . . . 141 B8
Livingstone Rd TQ14 . . . 210 C6
Livonia Rd EX16 . . . . . . 188 B6
Lixton Pk PL21 . . . . 137 F1
Lizard Cl PL6 . . . . 244 F7
Lizard Wlk PL6 . . . . 244 F7
Llantillio Dr PL2 . . . . . . 248 B8
Lloyd Ave TQ2 . . . . 219 D7
Lloyd Maunder Rd PL6 . . 162 C5
Lloyds Cres EX1 . . . . . . 178 C8
Lloyds Ct EX1 . . . . 178 C8

Loatmead Cross EX22 . . 38 B3
LOBB 152 A8
Lobbthorn Stile EX33 . . . 8 B1
LOBHILLCROSS 107 A5
Locarno Ave TQ3 . . . . . 219 D1
Locarno Rd EX4 . . . . . . 176 F4
Lock Cl EX10 . . . . 188 A8
Lockeridge Rd PL20 . . . 125 E1
Lockfield Ct EX2 . . . . . . 177 B1
Lockington Ave PL3 . . . 248 F7
Lock La EX31 . . . . 10 E4
Lock Lane Cross EX31 . . 10 F3
Locks Cl
  Braunton EX33 . . . . . . 152 D5
  Torquay TQ1 . . . . 220 A7
Locksey's La EX12 . . . . . 192 B6
Lock's Gate Cross TQ13 129 F8
Locks Hill TQ1 . . . . 220 D7
Locksley Cl
  Exeter EX2 . . . . 182 A8
  Torquay TQ1 . . . . 220 B7
Locksley Grange TQ1 . . 220 A7
Locks Wlk PL1 . . . . 247 E4
Lockyer Ave EX10 . . . . . 188 C8
Lockyer Cres EX16 . . . . 161 A6
Lockyer Ct PL1 . . . . 262 C2
Lockyer Mews PL19 . . . 171 C6
Lockyer Rd PL3 . . . . . . 248 E5
Lockyers Quay PL4 . . . . 263 B2
Lockyer St PL1 . . . . 262 C2
Lockyer Terr PL12 . . . . . 243 A3
Loddiswell
  Dawlish EX7 . . . . 204 D6
  Plymouth PL9 . . . . 255 D8
LODDISWELL 143 F7
Loddiswell Butts TQ7 . . 143 E8
Loddiswell Prim Sch
  TQ7 . . . . 143 F7
Lodge Cl TA21 . . . . 160 D6
Lodge Cnr EX31 . . . . . . 27 D8
Lodge Cross
  Chulmleigh EX18 . . . . . 45 A1
  Longdown EX6 . . . . . . 98 E1
Lodge Gdns PL6 . . . . . . 244 E3
Lodge Hill
  Exeter EX4 . . . . 177 A8
  Okehampton EX20 . . . 170 B5
Lodge La
  Axminster EX13 . . . . . . 88 B2
  Bratton Fleming EX31 . . 18 E8
  Brixton PL8 . . . . 256 F5
  Shute EX13 . . . . 103 A8
  Woodbury EX6 . . . . . . 161 E4
Lodge Rd EX16 . . . . 161 E4
Lodge The
  Crediton EX17 . . . . . . 165 A6
1 Ilfracombe EX34 . . . . 150 D5
  Lodge Trad Est EX5 . . . 175 E3
Lofoten Cl PL1 . . . . 247 E2
Loftus Gdns PL5 . . . . . . 243 C2
Logan Rd TQ3 . . . . 226 C7
Logan Way EX15 . . . . . . 67 B8
Lolesbury Cross PL8 . . . 136 A1
Lollabury Rd PL12 . . . . . 242 E3
Lombard Cl EX39 . . . . . 25 D4
London Ct The PL21 . . . 237 D5
London Inn Sq EX1 . . . . 261 B3
Longacre PL7 . . . . 250 B7
Long Acre PL12 . . . . 242 B4
Long Acres EX2 . . . . . . 261 C2
Long Barton 5 TQ12 . . . 123 E1
LONGBRIDGE 249 F7
Longbridge Cl PL6 . . . . 249 F6
Long Bridge Cross EX13 87 B8
Longbridge Meadow Trad Est
  EX15 . . . . 163 D6
Longbridge Rd
  Plymouth, Laira PL3 . . . 249 C4
  Plymouth, Longbridge PL6 249 E7
Longbridge Wharf 13
  EX39 . . . . 157 A1
Longbrook Barton PL7 . . 250 D5
Longbrook Cl PL21 . . . . 237 B5
Longbrook La EX8 . . . . . 195 F4
Longbrook Rd PL21 . . . 237 B5
Longbrook St
  Exeter EX4 . . . . 261 B4
  Plymouth PL7 . . . . 250 F4
Longbrook Terr EX4 . . . 261 B4
Longcause PL7 . . . . 250 F4
Longcause Cross TQ9 . . 223 A7
Longcause Specl Sch
  PL7 . . . . 250 F4
Longcombe Cross TQ9 . . 224 C5
Long Copp EX9 . . . . . . 198 A2
Longcroft Ave TQ5 . . . . 230 B3
Longcroft Dr TQ5 . . . . . 230 B3
Long Cross
  Dartmouth TQ6 . . . . . . 233 C3
  South Pool TQ7 . . . . . . 148 F7
Longcross Cotts PL19 . . 116 D6
Long Cswy EX8 . . . . . . 202 B6
Longdogs Cl EX11 . . . . 169 E3
Longdogs La EX11 . . . . 169 E3
LONGDOWN 98 E2
Long Down Gdns PL6 . . 245 E3
Longdown Rd EX2, EX6 . 176 B3
Long Dog EX15 . . . . 65 E3
Longdrag Hill EX16 . . . . 161 A4
Long Entry DT7 . . . . . . 260 E3
Longfield
11 Appledore EX39 . . . 15 A1
  Lutton PL21 . . . . 133 B1
Longfield Ave TQ12 . . . 207 F8
Longfield Cl
  Braunton EX33 . . . . . . 152 C5
  Lutton PL21 . . . . 133 B2
Longfield Dr TQ8 . . . . . 259 C5
Longfield Est EX6 . . . . . 201 A8
Longfield Pl PL4 . . . . . . 263 B4

Longfields TQ7 . . . . 258 A4
Longfield Terr 7 EX34 . . 150 C5
Longfield Villas PL9 . . . . 255 D8
Longford Cross TQ12 . . . 207 E8
Longford Down Head
  PL21 . . . . 137 F6
Longford La TQ12 . . . . . 207 E8
Longford Pk TQ12 . . . . . 207 E8
Longforth Rd TA21 . . . . 160 D6
Long-Go La EX14 . . . . . 84 E8
Long Hill EX12 . . . . 191 D5
Long Holcombe Cross
  EX36 . . . . 20 A6
Long La
  Appledore EX39 . . . . . . 14 F1
  Ashford EX31 . . . . 16 B6
  Calverleigh EX16 . . . . . 48 D2
  Combe Martin EX31, EX34 3 D1
  Dawlish EX7 . . . . 200 B1
  Exmouth EX8 . . . . 202 C6
  Georgeham EX33 . . . . . 8 B1
  Newton Abbot TQ12 . . 208 B1
  Northam EX39 . . . . . . 157 A8
  Shaldon TQ14 . . . . . . 209 C4
  Tiverton EX16 . . . . 161 A7
  Wolverstone EX14 . . . . . 85 B8
Longland Cl EX32 . . . . . 17 B5
Longland Cross TQ9 . . . 227 C3
Longland La EX33 . . . . . 8 A2
Longlands EX33 . . . . . . 8 A2
Longlands
  Dawlish EX7 . . . . 204 D6
  Plymouth PL9 . . . . 255 D8
Longlands Cross
  Ashwater EX21 . . . . . . 90 E6
  Corlott Green EX22 . . . 71 F2
Longlands Dr PL9 . . . . . 140 A8
Longlands La PL12 . . . . 242 B1
Long Ley PL3 . . . . 249 B6
Long Mdw
  Plymouth PL7 . . . . 250 D7
  South Brent TQ10 . . . . 134 F2
Longmead
  Hemyock EX15 . . . . . . 67 B8
  Huish Champflower TA4 . 35 E8
  Lynton EX35 . . . . 151 A5
Longmead Cl TA21 . . . . 160 B8
Longmead Cotts TA21 . . 160 B8
Longmead La EX20 . . . . 76 F4
Longmeadow
  Budlake EX5 . . . . 82 E1
  Tiverton EX16 . . . . 161 D5
Long Meadow EX5 . . . . 184 C3
Longmeadow Cl PL7 . . . 250 E7
Long Meadow Dr EX32 155 B6
Longmeadow Rd
  Lympstone EX8 . . . . . . 195 F5
  Saltash PL12 . . . . 242 E3
Longmeadows EX17 . . . 165 D6
Longmeadow Rd TQ3 . . 218 F1
Long Moor
  Cullompton EX15 . . . . . 163 F6
  Willand EX15 . . . . 162 E1
Long Orch PL20 . . . . . . 125 E1
Long Park Cl PL9 . . . . . 255 F5
Long Park Dr PL6 . . . . . 245 D7
Longpark Hill TQ1 . . . . 214 C6
Long Park Rd PL12 . . . . 242 D2
Long Pk
  Ashburton TQ13 . . . . . 131 A5
  Modbury PL21 . . . . . . 137 B3
  Woodbury EX5 . . . . . . 184 C3
Longpot La EX31 . . . . . 17 D8
Long Ragg Ct EX13 . . . . 167 D5
Long Rd
  Paignton TQ4 . . . . 225 D1
  Saltash PL12 . . . . 242 B4
Loo Cross TQ7 . . . . 144 F1
Looe Rd EX4 . . . . 177 A7
Looe St PL4 . . . . 263 A2
Lookout Cotts EX31 . . . 16 B6
Loosebeare Cross PL7 . . 78 B8
Loosebeare La EX17 . . . 78 B8
Loosedon Cross EX19 . . 58 B4
Looseland Cross EX16 . . 47 D1
Looseleigh Cl PL6 . . . . . 245 A4
Looseleigh La PL6 . . . . . 244 F5
Looseleigh Pk PL6 . . . . 244 E5
Lopes Cres EX20 . . . . . 170 C5
Lopes Dr PL6 . . . . 241 C1
Lopes Rd
  Dousland PL20 . . . . . . 127 B3
  Plymouth PL2 . . . . 248 B6
Lopwell Cl PL6 . . . . 244 F8
Lopwell Dam Nature Reserve★
  PL6 . . . . 240 C7
Loram Way EX2 . . . . . . 181 C8
Lord Louis Cres PL9 . . . 254 F6

Lord Mamhead Homes
　EX2 .... 177 E4
Lord Nelson Dr TQ6 .... 233 C3
Lords Meadow La 5
　EX16 .... 34 B1
Lords Meadow L Ctr
　EX17 .... 165 E5
Lords Pl TQ1 .... 220 B6
Lords Way EX2 .... 178 C4
Loretto Gdns EX13 .... 167 C5
Loretto Rd EX13 .... 167 E5
Loring Rd TQ8 .... 259 D4
Lorrie Dr TQ14 .... 210 B6
Lorrimore Ave PL2 .... 247 F5
Lotherton Cl PL7 .... 251 B3
Lotus Cotts TQ9 .... 227 F7
Loughboro Rd PL5 .... 243 C1
Loughborough EX16 .... 161 B5
Loughwood La EX13 .... 87 B2
Louisa Gate TA22 .... 33 F7
Louisa Pl EX8 .... 202 A5
Louisa Terr EX8 .... 202 A5
Louis Terr EX8 .... 159 C5
Louis Way EX14 .... 67 C1
Loup Ct EX13 .... 167 F5
Louvigny Cl EX14 .... 84 E2
Louville Cl TQ4 .... 226 C2
Lovacott Cross EX31 .... 27 A6
Lovacott School Cross
　EX31 .... 27 A6
LOVATON 127 C1
Love La
　Ashburton TQ13 .... 130 F4
　Bickington TQ12 .... 131 D7
　Bideford EX39 .... 156 E4
　Colyton EX24 .... 103 A4
　Marldon TQ3 .... 218 D4
　Saltash PL12 .... 242 E2
Lovelace Cres EX8 .... 202 D8
Lovelace Gdns EX2 .... 181 B8
Loveland Cross EX20 .... 74 C1
Love Lane Cl TQ3 .... 218 D4
Lovell Cl EX8 .... 196 C3
Lovell Rd PL3 .... 248 F6
Loventor Cres TQ3 .... 218 D2
Loventor La TQ3, TQ9 .... 217 F3
Loveridge La TA20 .... 88 D8
Lovering Cl EX14 .... 196 C3
Loverings Ct 8 EX31 .... 154 F5
Low Brook EX5 .... 99 C5
Lower Albert St EX1 .... 261 C3
Lower Aller La TQ13 .... 122 E6
Lower Almshouses 2
　EX31 .... 154 F6
Lower Anderton Rd PL10 ... 252 F5
Lower Argyll Rd EX4 .... 173 A2
LOWER ASHTON 113 C3
Lower Audley Rd TQ2 .... 219 F8
Lower Ave EX1 .... 177 F6
LOWER BATSON 259 D6
Lower Biteford Cross
　EX39 .... 38 B6
Lower Blagdon 225 B6
Lower Blagdon Cross
　TQ3 .... 225 B6
Lower Blagdon La TQ3 .... 225 C6
Lower Brand La EX14 .... 166 C4
LOWER BRIMLEY 180 A5
Lower Brimley Cl 2
　TQ14 .... 210 C5
Lower Brimley Rd TQ14 ..... 210 C5
Lower Broad Oak Rd
　EX11 .... 168 E4
Lower Broad Path TQ9 .... 228 A7
Lower Broad Pk TQ6 .... 233 D3
Lower Brookfield Cotts
　TQ13 .... 122 C4
Lower Brook Mdw 2
　EX10 .... 101 B1
Lower Brook Pk PL21 .... 237 A5
Lower Brook St 13 TQ14 ... 210 C5
Lower Budleigh EX9 .... 198 B5
Lower Budleigh Mdw
　TQ12 .... 206 F3
Lower Bulkamore Cross
　TQ10 .... 135 E5
Lower Bull Ring EX15 .... 163 C3
Lower Bulworthy Cross
　EX16 .... 47 D4
Lower Bulworthy La EX16 ... 47 D4
Lower Burston EX17 .... 78 B5
Lower Burwood Rd EX38 .... 159 E5
Lower Cannon Rd TQ12 ..... 123 E2
LOWER CHERITON 84 E4
Lower Church St
　5 Barnstaple EX32 .... 155 A4
　Colyton EX24 .... 103 A5
Lower Cl EX16 .... 65 A7
Lower Claypark EX34 .... 7 F7
Lower Cleave
　Braunton EX33 .... 152 C7
　Northam EX39 .... 157 B5
Lower Cloister Wlk EX6 ...... 181 F5
Lower Cobbaton EX37 .... 28 D5
Lower Collapark TQ9 .... 223 B6
Lower Collins Rd TQ9 .... 223 B8
LOWER COMPTON 249 A5
Lower Compton Rd PL3 ..... 248 F5
Lower Congella Rd TQ1 ..... 220 D4
Lower Contour Rd TQ6 ...... 234 B3
Lower Cookworthy Cross
　PL16 .... 106 A6
Lower Coombe La EX16 ...... 63 D4
Lower Coombe Rd TQ12 .... 207 F7
Lower Coombe St EX1 .... 261 A2
Lower Coombses TQ13 .... 88 D8
Lower Cotteylands EX16 ... 161 B3
Lower Court Rd PL8 .... 140 F7

Lower Crooked Mdw
　EX20 .... 170 C5
Lower Cross EX16 .... 51 C1
Lower Cross Rd EX31 .... 154 B4
Lowerdale Turn TQ9 .... 144 B8
Lower Dawlish Water Rd
　EX7 .... 204 A7
LOWER DEAN 236 A2
Lower Dean Cross EX31 .... 2 F7
Lowerdown TQ13 .... 122 D5
Lower Dr EX7 .... 204 F8
Lower Duck St EX6 .... 182 B3
Lower East St EX36 .... 30 E8
Lower Ellacombe Church Rd
　TQ1 .... 220 C6
Lower Erith Rd TQ1 .... 220 D4
Lower Fairview Rd TQ6 ...... 233 E3
Lower Farm Rd PL7 .... 251 A4
Lower Farthings EX10 .... 186 F8
Lower Fern Rd TQ12 .... 212 F8
Lower Forches Cross
　EX17 .... 60 D4
Lower Fore St
　8 Exmouth EX8 .... 202 A6
　Saltash PL12 .... 243 A2
Lower Fowden TQ1 .... 229 D6
Lower Foxmoor Rd TA21 ... 160 B5
Lower French Pk TQ12 .... 206 F3
Lower Fyldon Cross EX36 ... 19 D4
LOWER GABWELL 214 B8
Lower Gaydon St 1
　EX32 .... 155 A5
Lower Green Cross TQ7 ..... 145 C4
Lower Greystone EX34 .... 1 C3
Lower Griggs EX10 .... 188 D7
Lower Gunstone EX39 .... 157 A2
Lower Harrington La
　EX4 .... 174 E1
Lower Haske Cross EX17 ... 165 F7
Lower Hill Barton Rd
　EX1 .... 178 C6
LOWER HOLDITCH 88 D5
Lower Hollicombe Cotts
　TQ3 .... 219 D1
LOWER KEATON 237 E1
Lower Kelly PL18 .... 125 D3
Lower King's Ave EX4 .... 177 D8
Lower Kingsdown Rd
　TQ14 .... 209 D7
Lower Kinsman's Dale
　TQ13 ....111 F5
Lower Knowle Rd TQ13.. 122 D7
Lower La
　Chulmleigh EX18 .... 59 C8
　Dalwood EX13 .... 87 B2
　5 Plymouth PL1 .... 262 A3
Lower Ladram La EX9 .... 199 A7
Lower Lodfin EX16 .... 34 B2
LOWER LOVACOTT 27 B7
Lower Lowton La EX16 ...... 112 E6
LOWER LOXHORE 11 C8
Lower Manor Rd TQ5 .... 230 C5
Lower Marlpits Hill
　EX14 .... 166 D4
Lower Meadow Rise
　EX7 .... 204 C6
LOWER MILCOTT 173 A4
Lower Millhayes EX15 .... 67 C8
Lower Mill La EX15 .... 163 C3
Lower Moor EX32 .... 155 D4
Lower Moor Way EX15 .... 64 D8
LOWER NETHERTON 208 C4
Lower Northcote Rd
　EX14 .... 166 E7
Lower North St EX4 .... 261 A3
Lower Park TQ37 .... 28 D2
Lower Park Dr PL9 .... 255 F4
Lower Park Rd EX33 .... 152 C5
Lower Penns Rd TQ3 .... 219 C1
Lower Pk 2 TQ3 .... 226 A7
Lower Polsham Rd TQ3 ..... 226 C7
Lower Port Voller TQ12 ..... 242 F2
Lower Preston TQ12 .... 123 D1
Lower Preston Cross
　TQ9 .... 223 C1
Lower Racklose Cl EX1 ...... 261 A2
Lower Raleigh Rd EX31 ..... 155 A7
Lower Rea EX5 .... 184 B7
Lower Rea Rd TQ5 .... 230 D5
LOWER RIDGE 86 F4
Lower Ridings PL7 .... 251 B6
Lower Row PL10 .... 253 A2
Lower St German's Rd
　EX4 .... 177 C8
Lower Saltram PL9 .... 255 C7
Lower Shapter St EX3 .... 182 F4
Lower Shirburn Rd TQ1 ..... 220 A7
Lower Slade PL2 .... 248 A8
LOWER SLADE 150 B2
Lower St
　Chagford TQ13 ....111 A6
　Dartmouth TQ6 .... 233 F3
　Dittisham TQ6 .... 228 B3
　Plymouth PL4 .... 263 A3
　West Alvington TQ7 .... 258 A4
Lower Summerlands
　EX1 .... 261 C3
LOWER TALE 84 F5
Lower Tamar Terr PL18 ..... 125 D7
Lower Terr EX22 .... 38 E1
Lower Thurlow Rd TQ1 ...... 220 A6
Lower Tidderson Cross
　EX16 .... 47 E4
LOWER TIPPACOTT 6 A4

LOWER TOWN
　Ashburton TQ13 .... 130 A7
　Buckfastleigh 236 C5
　Halberton 65 A7
Lower Town
　Halberton EX16 .... 65 A7
　Malborough TQ7 .... 147 E6
　Sampford Peverell EX16 ... 50 D1
　Stoke Climsland PL17 ...... 115 C1
　Winkleigh EX19 .... 58 F2
　Woolfardisworthy EX39 ..... 38 F7
Lowertown Cotts EX20 ..... 107 A3
Lower Union La TQ2 .... 220 B5
Lower Union Rd TQ7 .... 258 C5
LOWER WADSTRAY 232 B2
Lower Warberry Rd TQ1 .... 220 C4
Lower Warcombe Cross
　TQ7 .... 144 A6
Lower Warren Rd TQ7 .... 258 D3
Lower Way EX10 .... 187 A8
LOWER WEAR 182 B7
Lower Wear Rd EX2 .... 182 B8
LOWER WESTFORD 160 A6
Lower Westlake Rd
　EX31 .... 154 A2
Lower Wheathill EX10 .... 188 B8
Lower Winsham Rd EX33 ..... 8 D1
Lower Woodfield Rd
　TQ1 .... 220 C4
Lower Woodhayes Ct EX5 ... 99 F3
LOWER WOOLBROOK 188 A6
Lower Yalberton Rd TQ4 ... 225 C2
Lowery Cross PL20 .... 127 C4
Loweswater Ho EX4 .... 176 F6
Lowley Brook Ct TQ2 .... 219 B8
Lowman Cross EX16 .... 50 B2
Lowman Units EX16 .... 64 D8
Lowman Way EX15 .... 64 D8
Lowmoor Ind Est TA21 ..... 160 B8
Lownard Cross TQ9 .... 222 E8
Low Rd PL9 .... 140 D8
Lowton Cross EX20 .... 77 C7
Lowton La EX6 .... 112 E6
Lowtrow Cross TA4 .... 35 A8
LOXBEARE 48 C3
Loxbury Rd TQ2 .... 219 D4
Loxbury Rise TQ2 .... 219 D5
Loxdown Rd EX39 .... 41 A7
LOXHORE 10 D1
LOXHORE COTT 10 D1
Loxhore Cross EX31 .... 17 D7
Lucas Ave EX4 .... 177 D8
Lucas La PL7 .... 250 D6
Lucas Terr PL4 .... 249 B2
Lucerne 1 TQ1 .... 220 D4
Lucius St TQ2 .... 219 F5
Luckhams La TQ7 .... 147 E6
Lucky La EX2 .... 261 B2
Lucombe Ct EX4 .... 261 C4
Lucombe Oaks EX5 .... 179 B6
LUDBROOK 137 C5
Ludbrook Gate PL21 .... 137 C5
Ludlow Rd 2 PL3 .... 248 E6
Ludwell La EX2 .... 178 A3
LUFFINCOTT 89 F5
Lugsmoor La EX10 .... 189 E7
Lugworthy Cross PL21 .... 91 B5
Lukesland Gardens *
　PL21 .... 237 E8
Luke St EX16 .... 34 B1
Lulworth Cl TQ4 .... 225 F2
Lulworth Dr PL6 .... 245 B7
Lumley Cl EX6 .... 194 E3
Lummaton Cross TQ2 .... 214 A2
Lummaton Pl TQ2 .... 214 B1
Lundy Cl
　Barnstaple EX32 .... 155 C5
　Plymouth PL6 .... 244 F7
Lundy View EX39 .... 156 E6
LUPPITT 67 E1
Lurley Cross EX16 .... 48 E2
Luscombe Cl
　Ipplepen TQ12 .... 211 D1
　Ivybridge PL21 .... 237 A4
Luscombe Cross TQ3 .... 225 E6
Luscombe Cross TQ9 .... 139 D8
Luscombe Hill
　Dawlish EX7 .... 204 A6
　Teignmouth EX7 .... 204 C3
Luscombe La TQ3 .... 225 D8
Luscombe Rd TQ3 .... 225 D8
Luscombe Terr 12 EX7 ...... 204 C6
LUSON 136 C1
Luson Cross PL8 .... 136 C1
LUSTLEIGH 122 C8
Lustleigh Cl EX2 .... 181 C8
Lusways Ct EX14 .... 188 C4
Lutehouse La EX19 .... 58 E3
LUTON
　Payhembury 84 B5
　Teignmouth 124 C3
LUTSFORD 37 D6
Lutsford Cross EX39 .... 37 D6
Lutterburn St PL21 .... 137 D6
LUTTON
　Cornwood 138 B2
　South Brent 134 C4
Lutyens Dr TQ3 .... 225 D7
Lutyens Fold PL19 .... 116 A6
Luxmoore Way EX20 .... 170 D6
Luxmore Cl PL6 .... 245 E1
LUXTON 68 D6
Luxton Cl EX31 .... 73 E3
Luxton Cross EX15 .... 163 C3
Luxton La EX20 .... 77 B8
Luxton Moor La EX20 .... 59 A1
Luxton Rd TQ12 .... 211 F8
Luxtons Pk EX11 .... 169 C3

Lych Cl PL9 .... 255 A6
Lychgate Pk EX17 .... 79 A5
Lydacott Cross EX31 .... 153 F3
LYDCOTT 18 F7
Lydcot Wlk PL6 .... 245 A1
Lyddicleave EX31 .... 154 A3
Lyddon Cl TA21 .... 160 D4
LYDFORD 107 F4
Lydford Castle & Saxon
　Town * EX20 .... 107 E3
Lydford Cl PL21 .... 237 D4
Lydford Gorge * EX20 ...... 107 E3
Lydford Ho TQ12 .... 207 D4
Lydford Park Rd PL3 .... 248 D5
Lydford Prim Sch EX20 .... 107 F4
Lydgates Rd EX12 .... 192 A6
Lyd Gdns PL19 .... 171 D5
Lydia Cl EX10 .... 186 D8
Lydiate La EX35 .... 5 A5
Lydia Way PL4 .... 263 B4
Lydon La TA4 .... 35 D5
Lydwell Park Rd TQ1 .... 220 E5
Lydwell Rd TQ1 .... 220 D6
Lye La EX14 .... 87 A8
Lym Cl DT7 .... 260 E3
Lyme Bay Ct 3 DT7 .... 260 D3
Lyme Bay Rd TQ14 .... 210 C7
Lymebourne Ave EX10 ...... 188 B6
Lymebourne Ho EX10 .... 188 B6
Lymebourne La EX10 .... 188 B6
Lymebourne Pk EX10 .... 188 B6
Lyme Ct EX13 .... 167 D5
Lyme Mews 10 EX13 .... 192 B4
Lyme Rd
　Axminster EX13 .... 167 C5
　Uplyme DT7 .... 104 B5
LYME REGIS 260 E2
Lyme Regis Ind Est DT7 ... 260 C4
Lyme Regis Mus * DT7 ..... 260 E3
Lyme St EX13 .... 167 D6
Lyme View Cl TQ1 .... 220 D7
Lyme View Rd TQ1 .... 220 D7
Lymington Rd TQ1 .... 220 A6
Lympne Ave PL5 .... 243 F5
LYMPSTONE 195 E5
Lympstone CE Prim Sch
　EX8 .... 195 E5
Lympstone Commando Sta
　EX8 .... 195 C8
Lympstone Village Sta
　EX8 .... 195 D5
Lynbridge Cl 5 PL19 .... 171 B5
Lynbridge Hill EX35 .... 151 B3
Lynbridge Rd EX35 .... 151 C4
Lynbro Rd EX31 .... 154 F7
Lynch Cl
　Axminster EX13 .... 167 D7
　Thorverton EX5 .... 81 E5
Lynch Head EX13 .... 100 C1
Lyncombe Ct EX4 .... 173 E1
Lyncombe Cres TQ1 .... 220 E3
Lyncourt TQ1 .... 220 D3
Lyndale Rd TQ12 .... 207 D8
Lyndhurst Ave TQ12 .... 213 A5
Lyndhurst Cl
　Kingskerswell TQ12 .... 213 A6
　Plymouth PL2 .... 248 C6
Lyndhurst Rd
　Exeter EX1 .... 177 E5
　Exmouth EX8 .... 202 A8
　Plymouth PL2 .... 248 C6
Lyndon Ct PL12 .... 242 D4
Lyndrick Rd PL3 .... 248 E2
LYNEHAM 257 F7
Lyneham Cross TQ13 .... 123 D6
Lyn & Exmoor Mus *
　EX35 .... 151 C5
Lyn Gr TQ12 .... 212 F6
Lyngrove Ct TQ12 .... 212 F6
Lynhayes EX13 .... 87 C1
Lynher Ct PL12 .... 242 F1
Lynher Dr PL12 .... 242 F1
Lynher St PL5 .... 243 D2
Lynher View EX31 .... 153 D3
Lyn La EX35 .... 151 D3
LYNMOUTH 151 D5
Lynmouth Ave TQ4 .... 225 F2
Lynmouth Cl PL7 .... 250 C7
Lynmouth Hill EX35 .... 151 C5
Lynmouth St EX35 .... 151 C5
LYNTON 151 C6
Lynton & Barnstaple Rly *
　EX31 .... 4 D3
Lynton CE Prim Sch
　EX35 .... 151 C5
Lynton Cross EX34 .... 9 B6
Lynton & Lynmouth Cliff
　Rlwy * EX35 .... 151 C5
Lynton Rd EX34 .... 3 B1
Lynway EX35 .... 151 C4
Lynway Ct TQ1 .... 220 B6
Lynwood TQ12 .... 206 F1
Lynwood Ave
　Exeter EX4 .... 177 A5
　Plymouth PL7 .... 250 B6
Lyster Cl 9 PL21 .... 262 A3
Lyte Hill La TQ2 .... 213 F3
Lyte La TQ7 .... 144 C1
Lyte's Rd TQ5 .... 230 D4
Lythe-Land Cross EX16 ...... 63 A6
Lytton Rd TQ4 .... 220 A4

M

Mabel Pl TQ4 .... 226 B5
MacAdam Rd PL4 .... 263 C1
MacAndrew Wlk PL21 .... 237 E6
MacAulay Cres PL5 .... 244 C1
MacAuley Cl EX14 .... 166 E6
McCoys Arcade 10 EX1 ..... 261 A2
McDonald Ct 12 PL11 .... 262 A3
Macey St PL11 .... 262 A3
Macey's Terr EX20 .... 170 B6
Machine Cross TA22 .... 33 F6
McKay Ave TQ1 .... 219 F6
Mackenzie Pl PL5 .... 243 C2
Mackenzie Way EX16 .... 161 F4
MACKHAM 67 D4
Mackrell's Almshouses
　TQ12 .... 207 A2
Maclins Ct EX36 .... 158 C4
Macwood Dr EX12 .... 192 A6
Madagascar Cl EX8 .... 202 E8
Maddacombe Cross
　TQ12 .... 212 C4
Madden Rd PL1 .... 247 F2
Maddock Cl PL7 .... 251 A4
Maddock Dr PL7 .... 251 B4
Maddocks Cross EX22 .... 38 D2
Madeira Ct EX8 .... 202 B5
Madeira Pl TQ2 .... 220 A5
Madeira Rd PL1 .... 263 A1
Madeira Villas
　Exmouth EX8 .... 202 A7
　1 Horrabridge PL20 .... 126 F5
Madeira Wlk EX9 .... 199 H2
MADFORD 67 D6
Madford Cross EX15 .... 67 C6
Madge Ct 3 PL19 .... 171 B6
Madge La PL19 .... 171 B6
Madgeon La TA20 .... 69 B8
Madges Cross
　Aylesbeare EX5 .... 99 E2
　Rockbeare EX5 .... 99 E6
Madicks Orch TQ9 .... 227 F8
Madison Ave EX1 .... 178 A6
Madison Cl EX5 .... 173 F8
Madison Wharf EX8 .... 201 E6
Madrepore Rd TQ1 .... 220 B4
Maer Bay Ct EX8 .... 202 B5
Maer La EX8 .... 202 E5
Maer Nature Reserve The *
　EX8 .... 202 B5
Maer Rd EX8 .... 202 C5
Maer Top Way EX31 .... 155 A7
Maer Vale EX8 .... 202 C6
Magdalen Bridge Ct 8
　EX2 .... 261 B2
Magdalen Court Sch
　EX2 .... 177 E5
Magdalene Ct TQ9 .... 223 C5
Magdalene Lawn 9
　EX32 .... 155 A6
Magdalene Rd TQ1 .... 220 A6
Magdalen Gdns
　Exeter EX2 .... 177 E5
　Plymouth PL7 .... 250 F3
Magdalen Rd EX2 .... 261 C2
Magdalen St EX1, EX2 ..... 261 B2
Magnolia Ave
　Exeter EX2 .... 178 A3
　Exmouth EX8 .... 202 E8
Magnolia Cl
　Barnstaple EX32 .... 155 E4
　Plymouth PL7 .... 251 B5
Magnolia Ct
　5 Exmouth EX8 .... 202 B6
　3 Plymouth PL9 .... 255 F7
Magnolia Ho 10 EX8 .... 202 A6
Magnolia Way EX8 .... 202 E8
Magpie Cres EX2 .... 176 D4
Magpie Hill TQ13 .... 130 C4
Maida Vale Terr PL4 .... 248 F4
MAIDENCOMBE 214 D6
Maidencombe Cross
　TQ1 .... 214 C6
Maidencombe Ho TQ1 ..... 214 C4
MAIDENHAYNE 103 D6
Maidenhayne La EX13 ..... 103 D6
Maidenhead Cross EX16 .... 51 C2
Maiden St 17 EX31 .... 154 F5
Maidenway La TQ3 .... 225 F8
Maidenway Rd TQ3 .... 225 F8
Maidment Rd PL7 .... 250 C5
Maidstone Pl PL5 .... 243 E4
Main Ave TQ1 .... 220 A8
Maine Cl EX39 .... 156 D2
Maine Gdns PL2 .... 247 F7
Main Rd
　Exeter EX4 .... 174 E2
　Salcombe TQ8 .... 259 C4
Mains Down La EX33 .... 8 B4
Main St TQ9 .... 139 E1
MAINSTONE 245 F2
Mainstone Ave PL4 .... 263 C2
Maire Rd EX36 .... 46 E5
Maitland Dr PL3 .... 248 F8
Major Cl PL21 .... 237 B6
Major Cross EX16 .... 64 A2
Majorfield Rd EX3 .... 182 F5
Major's Mdw EX20 .... 170 C5
Major Terr 3 EX12 .... 192 A5
Maker La PL10 .... 253 B4

Maker Rd PL11 .... 247 A2
Maker View PL3 .... 248 B4
MALBOROUGH 147 E6
Malborough Gn TQ7 .. 147 E6
Malborough Pk TQ7 ... 147 F6
Malborough with South
 Huish CE Prim Sch
 TQ7................147 E6
Malden Cl EX10....... 188 B7
Malden La EX10....... 188 B8
Malden Rd EX10 ...... 188 C8
Malderek Ave TQ3 .... 219 C1
Mallands Mdw TQ12 .. 212 A7
Mallard Cl
 Plymouth PL7........ 250 F5
 Torquay TQ2........ 213 D3
Mallard Rd EX2 .... 178 E5
Mallet Rd PL21 .... 237 A6
Malletts La EX12 ...... 155 A5
Mallingbrook Cross EX18. 44 E1
Mallison Cl EX4....... 176 F8
Mallock Rd TQ3 ...... 219 E5
Mallocks Cl EX10 ..... 100 D2
Mallow Cl EX15 .... 162 D5
Malmesbury Cl PL2 ... 248 B8
MALMSMEAD 6 C4
Malory Cl PL5......... 244 D2
Malson La EX16....... 47 B4
Malston Cross TQ7.... 144 D4
Malt Field EX8........ 195 F5
Malthouse The
 Bridgend PL8........ 141 A7
 5 Totnes TQ9 ...... 223 D5
Malting Ct **4** EX7.... 204 E6
Maltings The
 21 Appledore EX39 ... 15 A1
 Black Torrington EX21... 74 A8
 Crediton EX17 .... 165 D5
 Exeter EX2 .... 177 F5
 South Allington TQ7 .. 149 B5
Malt Mill TQ9 .... 223 B6
Malvern Gdns EX2 .... 178 A4
Malvernleigh TQ1 ..... 220 B8
Malvern Rd EX10...... 188 B6
Malvern Way EX39 .... 156 D2
Mambury Cross EX22... 39 D3
Mamhead Bsns Units
 EX2................181 D8
Mamhead Rd
 Exeter EX2 .... 178 C4
 Kenton EX6 .... 194 C2
Mamhead Sensory Trail*
 EX6................124 E7
Mamhead View EX8.... 201 E6
MANADON 244 D1
Manadon Cl PL5....... 244 E1
Manadon Dr PL5....... 244 E1
Manadon Football Ctr
 PL2................244 D2
Manadon Hill PL5, PL6.. 244 E1
Manadon Vale Prim Sch **1**
 PL5................248 E8
MANATON 121 F8
Manaton Cl EX2....... 181 C8
Manaton Dr EX2 ...... 181 C8
Manaton Tor Rd TQ3 .. 218 F1
Manby Gdns PL5....... 243 F5
Manchester Rd EX8 ... 201 F6
Manchester St EX8.... 201 F6
Mandrake Cl EX2 ..... 177 B1
Mandrake Rd EX2 ..... 177 A1
Manifold Gdns PL3.... 249 D5
Manitoba Gdns EX15 .. 163 B3
Manley Cl **1** EX5 ..... 99 E8
Manleys La EX14 ...... 67 B2
Manna Ash Ct EX2 .... 261 C1
Mannacott La EX31 .... 4 C4
Mannacott Lane Head
 EX31...............4 C4
MANNAMEAD 248 F5
Mannamead Ave PL3 .. 248 F5
Mannamead Ct **8** PL3. 248 F6
Mannamead Rd PL3 ... 248 F6
Manning Ave EX15.... 163 A2
Mannings Mdw PL3 ... 180 D7
Mannings Way EX31... 154 F7
Manor Ave
 Lyme Regis DT7...... 260 D4
 Paignton TQ3 .... 226 C8
Manor Bend TQ5 ...... 229 C5
MANOR BOURNE 140 A8
Manor Bourne Rd
 Down Thomas PL9.... 255 C1
 Heybrook Bay PL9 ... 140 A8
Manor Cl
 Newton Abbot TQ12.. 212 A7
 Awliscombe EX14..... 85 C3
 Barnstaple EX31 ..... 154 C3
 Dawlish EX7......... 204 D6
 Fremington EX31..... 153 E6
 Ivybridge PL21 ...... 237 C5
 Kentisbeare EX15 .... 66 A3
 Kingskerswell TQ12 .. 213 A3
 1 Seaton EX12 ..... 192 A5
 Sidmouth EX10 ...... 188 A5
 Tavistock PL19....... 171 A6
 Uffculme EX15....... 66 B8
 Wrafton EX33 .... 152 E4
Manor Cottages
 5 Newton Abbot TQ12.. 207 B3
 Rackenford EX16..... 47 C6
Manor Court Barns TQ7. 147 F8
Manor Cres
 Honiton EX14........ 166 C4
 Paignton TQ3 .... 226 C8

Manor Ct
 Barnstaple EX32 ...... 155 F1
 5 Dawlish EX7...... 204 D6
 Galmpton TQ5 .... 229 A5
 Kingskerswell TQ12 ... 213 A3
 Landkey EX32 .... 17 B2
 2 Paignton TQ3 .... 226 C7
 Seaton EX12 .... 192 A5
 5 South Brent TQ10. 134 F3
 Stoke Fleming TQ6.... 146 B7
 Torquay TQ2......... 219 F6
Manor Dr
 Chagford TQ13....... 110 F6
 Kingskerswell TQ12 ... 213 A3
Manor Est PL20....... 126 E4
Manor Farm TQ12 .... 127 B3
Manor Farm Cl TA20 .. 88 C8
Manor Farm Mews EX5.. 99 E4
Manor Gdn TQ1....... 220 E3
Manor Gdns
 Abbotskerswell TQ12.. 212 B6
 Exbourne EX20 ...... 76 C5
 Halwill Junction EX21.. 73 E2
 Horrabridge PL20 .... 126 E4
 Kingsbridge TQ7 ..... 258 D6
 Kingskerswell TQ12 .. 213 A3
 Millbrook PL10....... 252 F6
 2 Paignton TQ3 .... 226 C8
 Plymouth PL1........ 262 B2
 Seaton EX12 .... 192 A5
Manorglade Ct **1** TQ1. 220 D5
Manor Gn EX14 .... 68 C2
Manor Ho
 Lympstone EX8 ...... 195 D5
 Torquay TQ1......... 220 E3
Manor Ho The TQ9.... 223 C6
Manor House Sch EX14. 166 F5
Manor La PL3......... 249 D5
Manor Mead TQ12 .... 131 D7
Manor Mill Rd EX33 .. 8 D1
Manor Park Cl PL7.... 250 F5
Manor Park Dr PL7.... 251 A4
Manor Pavilion Theatre*
 EX10...............188 A3
Manor Pk
 Ashwater EX21....... 90 E6
 Barnstaple EX31 ..... 154 C3
 Bradworthy EX22..... 53 E8
 Clyst St Mary EX5 .... 179 A3
 Dousland PL20........ 127 B3
 Kingsbridge TQ7 ..... 258 D6
 Saltash PL12 .... 242 D8
 Woolfardisworthy EX39.. 38 F8
Manor Prim Sch PL21.. 237 C5
Manor Rd
 Abbotskerswell TQ12.. 212 B7
 Bishopsteignton TQ14. 208 F8
 Chagford TQ13....... 110 F6
 Exeter EX4 .... 177 A5
 Landkey EX32 .... 17 B2
 Newton Abbot TQ12.. 206 F3
 Paignton TQ3 .... 226 C8
 Plymouth PL9........ 255 E8
 Seaton EX12 .... 192 A5
 Tavistock PL19....... 171 B6
 Torquay TQ1......... 220 C8
Manor St
 Dittisham TQ6 .... 228 D2
 Plymouth PL1........ 262 A3
Manor Terr
 Brixham TQ5 .... 230 C5
 Paignton TQ3 .... 226 A5
Manor Vale Rd TQ5 ... 229 C5
Manor View TQ12 .... 207 A3
Manor Way
 Ivybridge PL21 ...... 237 C5
 Tavistock PL19....... 171 B6
 Totnes TQ9.......... 223 C6
Manot Gdns **22** EX7... 204 E6
Mansands La TQ5 ..... 235 B8
Mansbridge Rd TQ9 ... 223 E5
Manscombe Cl TQ2 ... 219 D3
Manscombe Rd TQ2 .. 219 D3
Mansfield Rd EX4..... 177 B7
Mansfield Terr EX9 ... 198 B2
Mansion Ho EX6 ...... 181 F5
Mansion Ho The PL1... 254 A8
Mansion House St TQ6. 233 F3
Mansion Terr **6** EX34... 3 A3
Mansion The PL21 .... 137 C8
Manston Cl PL5....... 243 F5
Manston Cl TQ1 ...... 220 C2
Manstone Ave EX10... 188 A7
Manstone Cl EX10..... 188 B7
Manstone La EX10 .... 188 B7
Manstone Mead EX10. 188 B8
Manstone Workshops
 EX10...............188 B7
Manston Rd EX1 ...... 177 E7
Manston Terr EX2 .... 177 E5
Manstree Cross EX2 .. 114 A6
Manstree Rd EX2 ..... 114 B6
Manstree Terr EX2.... 114 C6
Manteo Way EX39 .... 157 C2
Mantle Gdns PL5...... 247 D8
Mantle St TA21 ...... 160 C5
Maple Ave
 Bovey Tracey TQ13.... 180 C4
 Torpoint PL11 .... 247 A3
Maple Cl
 Brixham TQ5 .... 230 A2
 10 Chudleigh Knighton
  TQ13.............123 C4
 Honiton EX14........ 85 C2
 Kingsteignton TQ12 .. 207 E6
 Plymouth PL6........ 245 E6

Maple Cl continued
 Seaton EX12 .... 192 A7
 Tavistock PL19....... 171 C3
 Willand EX15......... 162 C4
Maple Ct
 Paignton TQ4........ 226 B2
 2 Plymouth PL6.... 259 F7
Mapledene Cl TQ9 ... 227 F8
Maple Dr EX8......... 196 D3
Maple Gr
 Barnstaple EX31 ..... 154 C3
 Plymouth, Mutley PL4 .. 248 D4
 Plymouth, Plympton PL7. 250 B5
 Tiverton EX16 .... 161 D4
Maple Rd
 Brixham TQ5 .... 230 A2
 Broadclyst EX5 ...... 175 D6
 Exeter EX4 .... 177 A5
Maples Ct **7** EX32 ... 154 F6
Mapleton Cl TQ12..... 206 F4
Maple Way PL6 ...... 245 E7
Maple Wlk TQ2 ...... 219 C8
Marber Cross TQ7 .... 149 A8
Marcent Row TQ5..... 230 D3
Marchant's Cross TQ20. 127 C1
Marchant's Way PL20 . 127 C2
March Ct EX20........ 170 B5
Marchweeke La EX16 .. 61 D6
Marcombe Rd TQ2 ... 219 E5
Marcom Cl EX8 ...... 196 D3
Marcus Rd
 Dunkeswell EX14..... 67 B2
 Exmouth EX8 .... 196 D1
Marder's Bequest DT7. 260 E3
Mardle Way TQ11..... 236 B5
Mardle Way Bsns Pk
 TQ11..............236 B5
Mardon Cl PL6........ 245 D4
Mardon Cross EX6.... 112 E2
Mardon Hill EX4 ..... 173 B1
Mare Hill EX17....... 62 C5
Mare La EX12........ 191 B5
Marepark Cross TQ7 .. 144 D3
Marepark Gate EX20 .. 77 C7
Mareltt Rd PL5 ...... 243 F3
Margaret Cl
 East Ogwell TQ12..... 206 F1
 Kingsteignton TQ12 .. 207 E7
Margaret Ct **7** EX4 .. 178 C8
Margaret Gdns TQ12 .. 207 F2
Margaret Pk PL3...... 248 E8
Margaret Rd
 East Ogwell TQ12..... 206 F1
 Exeter EX1, EX4 ..... 173 E1
 Kingsteignton TQ12 .. 207 E7
Margaret St **4** EX8 .. 202 A6
Margrove Terr **10** EX32. 154 F6
Marguerite Cl TQ12 .. 206 F4
Marguerite Rd EX16... 161 C6
Marguerite Way TQ12. 213 A4
MARHAMCHURCH 70 A6
Marhamchurch CE Prim Sch
 EX23...............70 A6
Maria Montessori Sch
 EX2................261 C2
MARIANSLEIGH 30 D1
Mariansleigh Cross EX36. 30 E1
Marina Cl TQ5 .... 230 E5
Marina Ct
 Brixham TQ5 .... 230 F6
 Exmouth EX8 .... 202 B5
 Paignton TQ4........ 226 C5
 3 Teignmouth TQ14. 210 C4
Marina Dr TQ5 .... 230 E5
Marina Rd
 Brixham TQ5 .... 230 E4
 Plymouth PL5........ 243 F3
Marina Terr **7** EX4... 248 F4
Marina Way **8** EX16 .. 64 D7
Marine Aquarium* DT7. 260 D2
Marine Cres EX12 .... 192 A4
Marine Ct
 Budleigh Salterton EX9. 199 H2
 Instow EX31 .... 15 B1
 Torpoint PL11 .... 247 B2
Marine Dr
 Bigbury-on-S TQ7..... 142 E3
 Heybrook Bay PL9 ... 140 A7
 Paignton TQ3 .... 226 C7
 Teignmouth TQ14 ... 210 B3
Marine Pk TQ3....... 226 C7
Marine Pl
 Ilfracombe EX34 ..... 150 B6
 Seaton EX12 .... 192 A4
Marine Rd PL9 .... 255 B7
Mariners Cl TQ3 ..... 152 D5
Mariners Ct
 7 Brixham TQ5..... 230 D5
 13 Dawlish EX7..... 204 E6
Mariner's Way **8** EX39. 15 A1
Marine Terr **3** TQ14 .. 210 B4
Marine Theatre* DT7.. 260 E3
Marine Way EX8 ..... 196 A8
Marino The EX10...... 187 F3

Marions Way EX8 .... 196 D2
Marion View TQ1 .... 220 C4
Maristow Ave
 Exmouth EX8 .... 196 B2
 Plymouth PL2........ 247 F5
Maristow Cl PL6...... 244 F5
Maristow La PL12..... 242 F3
Maris Way EX2....... 155 C2
Marjery Cross PL21 ... 237 A2
Marjorie Ct PL12...... 242 C4
Marjorie Cl PL8....... 136 B1
Marjorie Kelly Way PL21. 237 D4
Marjory Wlk PL8...... 257 E3
Markadon Cotts EX39. 22 B4
Markers EX15........ 66 A7
Marker's Cottage* EX5. 175 D7
Markers Pk EX14...... 84 C4
Markers Rd EX15..... 66 A7
Marker Way EX14 .... 166 C4
Market Ave PL1 ...... 262 B3
Market Cl
 4 Bampton EX16 ... 34 B1
 Brushford TA22 ...... 33 E4
 Buckfastleigh TQ11 .. 236 B5
 Plymouth PL1........ 248 A1
Market Forum the (Sh Ctr)
 TQ1................220 B5
Market Pl
 Bideford EX39 .... 157 A2
 Burlescombe EX16.... 51 B4
 Colyton EX24 .... 103 A5
 Sidmouth EX10 ...... 188 B3
 Willand EX15......... 162 C5
Market Rd
 Plymouth PL7........ 250 D5
 Tavistock PL19....... 171 C2
Market Sq
 Axminster EX13 ...... 167 D6
 Dartmouth TQ6 ..... 233 F3
 3 Ilfracombe EX34 .. 150 B6
 Plymouth PL1........ 262 C3
Market St
 2 Appledore EX39 .. 15 A1
 4 Barnstaple EX31.. 154 F5
 8 Brixham TQ5..... 230 C5
 Buckfastleigh TQ11 .. 236 B5
 Crediton EX17 .... 165 C5
 Dartmouth TQ6 ..... 233 F3
 Exeter EX1, EX4 ..... 261 A2
 Exmouth EX8 .... 202 A6
 Hatherleigh EX20..... 75 C7
 Ilfracombe EX34 ..... 150 B6
 Kingsand PL10....... 253 A1
 Lynton EX35......... 151 C5
 Newton Abbot TQ12.. 207 B3
 North Tawton EX20 .. 77 C4
 Okehampton EX20 ... 170 B5
 Plymouth PL1........ 248 A1
 Salcombe TQ8 .... 259 E5
 South Molton EX36 .. 158 C4
 Tavistock PL19....... 171 C5
 Torquay TQ1......... 220 B5
Market Terr EX16 .... 161 C4
Market Way
 7 Plymouth TQ13 .. 123 E6
 Plymouth PL1........ 262 C3
Market Wlk **7** TQ12.. 207 B3
Market Wlk EX16 .... 161 D4
Markham Cross EX2.. 114 B8
Markham La
 Exeter EX2 .... 181 B7
 Ide EX2 .... 114 C8
Mark's Cross EX6 .... 176 B2
Mark Twain Ho **4** EX4. 178 C8
Marland Cross PL8.... 136 B1
Marland Terr EX39 ... 156 F1
Marlborough Ave TQ1. 220 D5
Marlborough Cl
 Exmouth EX8 .... 196 E2
 Ilfracombe EX34 ..... 150 B5
 Musbury EX13 .... 103 D5
 Saltash PL12 .... 242 F1
Marlborough Cres EX5. 179 D6
Marlborough Ct
 Bideford EX39 .... 157 A3
 Exeter, Alphington EX2 . 181 C8
 Exeter, Heavitree EX2 . 177 E5
Marlborough Dr **9** EX2. 178 D5
Marlborough Pk **7** EX34. 150 B5
Marlborough Pl TQ12. 207 A4
Marlborough Prim Sch
 PL1................247 E2
Marlborough Rd
 Exeter EX2 .... 261 C2
 Ilfracombe EX34 ..... 150 C5
 Musbury EX13 .... 103 D5
 Plymouth PL4........ 263 A4
Marlborough Row PL1. 247 E2
Marlborough St PL1... 247 E2
Marlborough Terr TQ13. 180 C7
Marlborough Way EX34. 150 C4
Marlcombe Cross EX14. 85 A6
MARLDON 218 C3
Marldon Ave TQ3 .... 226 A6
Marldon CE Prim Sch
 TQ3................218 D3
Marldon Cl PL5....... 244 B3
Marldon Cross TQ3 .. 218 D2
Marldon Cross Hill TQ3. 218 D3
Marldon Gr TQ3 ..... 218 B3
Marldon La TQ3...... 218 B4
Marldon Rd
 Paignton TQ3 .... 225 F8
 Torquay TQ2......... 219 B7
Marldon Way TQ3.... 218 E2

Marlen Ct EX39 ...... 25 F4
Marles Cl EX14 ...... 85 B4
Marles The EX8 ...... 196 C2
Marley Cl EX16 ...... 161 D6
Marley Ct EX8 .... 196 D5
Marley Dr EX8 .... 196 D5
Marley Head TQ10 ... 135 C3
Marley Rd EX8....... 196 C3
Marlow Cres PL16.... 106 D1
Marlow Dr EX39 ..... 156 D7
Marlowe Cl TQ2 ..... 219 D7
Marlpit Cl EX12 ...... 191 F7
Marlpit Cross EX14... 87 A6
Marlpit La EX12 ..... 192 A5
Marlpits La EX14 .... 166 C5
Marl Pk
 Harbertonford TQ9 .. 139 C7
 Holne TQ13.......... 130 A3
Marmora Terr EX12 .. 191 D5
Marnham Rd TQ1 .... 220 B7
Marpool Cres EX8.... 202 C8
Marpool Hill EX8..... 202 B7
Marpool Prim Sch EX8. 202 C8
Marridge Cross PL21.. 137 F5
Marrowbone Slip PL4. 263 B2
Marryat Gdns PL5.... 244 E1
MARSH 69 B5
Marshall Cl
 Tavistock PL19....... 171 D2
 Tiverton EX16 .... 161 F3
Marshall Dr PL21 .... 237 D4
Marshall Rd
 Plymouth PL7........ 250 A5
 Tavistock PL19....... 171 D2
Marsh Barton La EX5. 172 D8
Marsh Barton Rd EX2. 177 B3
Marsh Barton Trad Est
 EX2................177 C2
Marshbridge Cross TA22. 33 C7
Marsh Cl PL6......... 249 F6
Marshclose Hill TA22. 21 E2
Marsh Cotts **14** EX39. 15 B1
Marsh Cross EX15.... 83 E4
Marsh Dro EX13 ..... 87 B2
Marsh End EX17 ..... 165 F5
MARSH GREEN...... 99 E4
Marsh Green La EX5.. 99 E5
Marsh Green Road E
 EX2................177 C2
Marsh Green Road N
 EX2................177 C2
Marsh Green Road W
 EX2................177 C2
Marsh Hill
 Cheriton Fitzpaine EX16. 63 A4
 Dulverton TA22 ..... 33 C8
Mars Hill Way EX35 . 151 C5
Marsh La
 Bow EX17............ 78 B5
 Calstock PL18 .... 125 D3
 Cheriton Fitzpaine EX16. 63 A4
 Chudleigh TQ13 ..... 123 F8
 Clyst St George EX3 . 183 B6
 Crediton EX17 .... 165 E5
 Instow EX39 .... 15 B1
 Newton St Cyres EX5.. 98 F8
 Seaton EX12 .... 192 B7
 South Molton EX36 .. 158 F7
 West Charleton TQ7... 144 C1
Marsh La Cross TQ13. 123 F8
Marsh Mill Ct EX5 ... 172 C2
MARSH MILLS 249 F6
Marsh Mills Pk PL6 .. 249 F6
Marsh Mills Ret Pk Pk. 249 E7
Marsh Mills Sta* PL7. 250 A7
Marsh Rd
 Crediton EX17 .... 165 E5
 Newton Abbot TQ12.. 207 C3
 Seaton EX12 .... 192 B5
Marston Cl EX7 ...... 204 F7
MARTINHOE 4 C5
Martinhoe Cross EX31. 4 E3
Martinique Gr TQ2 .. 213 F3
Martin La PL4........ 263 A2
Martin Rd EX32 ..... 155 B5
Martins Bldgs **4** TA21. 160 D5
Martins Cl
 Great Torrington EX38. 159 F5
 Okehampton/North Tawton
  EX20..............75 C7
 Wellington TA21...... 160 D5
Martins Gate – City Coll
 PL4................263 A2
Martins La EX16 ..... 161 D4
Martin's La EX1, EX4.. 261 B3
Martins Rd EX8 ...... 196 E2
Martin St Pl1........ 262 B2
Martlesham Pl PL5... 243 F4
Mart The EX20........ 170 B5
Marven Ct DT7....... 260 B6
Marwell Cross TQ7... 142 E6
MARWOOD 16 C8
Marwood Cross EX5.. 99 B3
Marwood Ct EX38.... 159 D5
Marwood Hill Gdns*
 EX31...............16 C8
Marwood La EX5 .... 175 A3
Marwood Pl EX14 ... 166 D6
Marwood Prim Sch EX31. 9 D1
Marwood's Cross TQ10. 134 D1
Mary Cross PL21..... 137 C3
Mary Dean Ave PL5.. 244 C7
Mary Dean Cl PL5.... 244 C7

Mary Dean's CE Prim Sch PL5 244 C7
Maryfield Ave EX4 177 D8
Mary La 10 EX16 34 B1
Maryland Gdns PL2 247 F7
Mary Newman's Cottage* PL12 243 A2
Marypole Rd EX4 173 F1
Marypole Wlk EX4 173 F1
Mary Rose Ho
9 Hemyock EX15 67 B8
Torquay TQ1 220 D7
Mary Seacole Rd PL1 262 A3
Mary St TQ13 180 D8
MARYSTOW 106 D1
MARY TAVY 117 E6
Mary Tavy & Brentor Com Prim Sch PL19 117 E6
Marythorne Rd 15 PL20 125 E1
Masefield Ave EX31 154 F7
Masefield Gdns PL5 244 B1
Masefield Rd EX4 178 C8
Masey Rd EX8 202 D8
Mashford Ave TQ6 233 C4
Masons Row PL18 125 C6
Massey Rd EX16 161 E6
Masterman Rd PL2 247 F4
Masterson St EX2 177 F3
Matford Ave EX2 177 E4
Matford La EX2 261 C1
Matford Mews EX2 181 D7
Matford Park Rd EX2 181 D8
Matford Rd EX2 177 E4
Mathew Ho 2 TQ1 219 F6
Mathews Cl EX14 166 B4
Mathill Cl TQ5 230 B3
Mathill Rd TQ5 230 B3
Maton Cl PL21 237 D4
Matthews Cross EX15 66 B1
Matthews Ct EX4 174 D2
Matthew's Ct EX15 163 C3
Matthews Pas TQ7 258 C5
Mattiscombe Cross TQ7 145 B1
Mattys Cross EX14 68 A3
Maudlin Dr TQ14 210 B8
Maudlin Rd TQ9 223 C5
Maudlins La PL19 171 A5
Maunder's Hill EX9 198 E7
MAUNDOWN 35 F7
Maunsell Cl PL2 247 F7
Mavisdale PL2 247 F6
Mawes Ct PL18 125 A5
Maxstoke Ct 4 TQ1 220 D5
Maxwell Rd PL4 255 B8
Maybank Rd PL4 263 C3
Maybrook Dr PL12 242 D2
Mayers Way PL9 255 D6
Mayfair EX16 64 E8
Mayfair Cres PL6 245 B1
Mayfair Ho PL4 263 A3
Mayfair Rd TQ12 211 D2
Mayfield PL21 237 A4
Mayfield Cres TQ12 206 F3
Mayfield Dr EX8 202 D6
Mayfield Rd
Exeter, Pinhoe EX4 174 E1
Exeter, Wonford EX2 178 A5
Mayfield Specl Sch TQ2 214 B3
Mayflower Ave
Exeter EX4 173 D2
Newton Abbot TQ12 207 F2
Mayflower Cl
18 Bere Alston PL20 125 E1
Chittlehampton EX37 28 F4
Dartmouth TQ6 233 D4
Dawlish EX7 204 E6
Plymouth PL9 255 F7
Mayflower Com Sch PL2 248 A7
Mayflower Ct TQ6 233 F4
Mayflower Dr
6 Brixham TQ5 230 C3
Plymouth PL2 248 B5
Mayflower L Ctr PL2 248 C5
Mayflower St PL1 262 C3
Maynarde Cl PL7 251 B5
Maynard Pk PL20 125 E1
Maynard Sch The EX1 261 C3
Mayne Cl EX20 75 B7
Mayor's Ave TQ6 233 F4
May St EX4 261 C4
May Terr
Plymouth PL4 263 B3
Sidmouth EX10 188 B4
Maytree Cl EX21 73 D3
Mazard Tree Hill
Ash Mill EX36 31 C1
South Molton EX36 46 C8
Mazzard Cl 9 EX32 17 B2
MEAD 37 A4
Mead Cl
Cullompton EX15 163 B2
Ivybridge PL21 237 A6
Paignton TQ3 226 C7
Mead Cnr EX39 37 A4
Meadcombe Rd TQ7 143 A1
Mead Cotts EX8 202 F7
Meadcourt TQ3 226 C7
Mead Cross TQ13 131 B6
Mead Dr TQ7 143 A1
Meadfoot TQ7 143 A1
Meadfoot Cl TQ1 220 F4
Meadfoot Ct TQ1 220 C3
Meadfoot Grange TQ1 220 C3
Meadfoot La TQ1 220 C3
Meadfoot Rd TQ1 220 C3
Meadfoot Sea Rd TQ1 220 D3
Meadfoot Terr 2 PL4 248 F5
Meadhurst Ct EX10 188 A3
Mead La
Paignton TQ3 226 C7
Thurlestone TQ7 143 A1
Meadow Ave EX12 192 A6
Meadow Bank EX13 87 D1
Meadow Brook
Barnstaple EX31 154 B2
Tavistock PL19 171 A4
18 Totnes TQ9 223 D5
Meadowbrook Cl EX4 176 E8
Meadow Bsns Pk EX17 165 F5
Meadow Cl
Bratton Fleming EX31 18 A8
Budleigh Salterton EX9 197 F1
Clyst St Mary EX5 179 E3
Harberton TQ9 222 D2
Ilfracombe EX34 150 B4
Kingskerswell TQ12 212 F6
Landkey EX32 17 C1
Lympstone EX8 195 F5
7 Newton Ferrers PL8 141 A7
Ottery St Mary EX11 169 E4
Plymouth PL7 251 D4
Saltash PL12 242 F3
Totnes TQ9 223 F5
Meadow Cotts TQ6 228 C2
Meadow Court Barns TQ7 145 B1
Meadow Cres EX8 203 A6
Meadowcroft Dr TQ12 123 E1
Meadow Dr
Brixton PL8 257 A4
Newton Poppleford EX10 186 F8
Saltash PL12 242 D4
Meadowfield Pl PL7 251 B3
Meadow Gdns EX17 165 D5
Meadow Halt TQ12 207 A1
Meadow La
Croyde EX33 7 E2
Cullompton EX15 163 C2
Instow EX39 15 B1
Meadowlands
Newton St Cyres EX5 98 F8
Plymouth PL6 245 D7
Meadowlands L Pool 7 PL19 171 B5
Meadow Lea EX5 82 B6
Meadow Park Dr EX37 43 F3
Meadow Pk
Barnstaple EX31 154 B2
Bideford EX39 25 D4
Brixham TQ5 230 B5
Dawlish EX7 204 C7
Marldon TQ3 218 D3
Molland EX36 31 E7
Plymouth PL9 255 C5
Shebbear EX21 55 E4
South Molton EX36 158 C3
Willand EX15 162 C4
Meadow Rd
Barnstaple EX31 154 E7
Budleigh Salterton EX9 197 F1
Seaton EX12 192 A5
Torquay TQ2 219 E3
Meadow Rise
Dawlish EX7 204 C7
Plymouth PL7 251 A4
Spreyton EX17 96 A7
Teignmouth TQ14 124 E1
Meadows Cres EX14 166 C5
Meadows Edge EX6 97 B4
Meadowside
Ashford EX31 16 B6
Chillington TQ7 145 A1
Plymouth PL9 255 F7
Rockwell Green TA21 160 B5
Meadow Side TQ12 207 A3
Meadowside Rd EX17 80 B5
Meadow St EX8 202 A7
Meadows The
Beer EX12 191 D5
Kingsteignton TQ12 207 F6
Okehampton/North Tawton EX20 74 E2
St Dominick PL12 125 A2
Torpoint PL11 246 E4
Yeoford EX17 79 C2
Meadowstone Cl EX38 40 F5
Meadowsweet La 3 EX31 154 B3
Meadowsweet Pk PL12 242 C2
Meadow Vale EX20 57 A7
Meadow View
2 Bampton EX16 34 B1
Bishops Nympton EX36 30 F2
East Ogwell TQ12 206 F1
Hartland EX39 22 E3
Holsworthy EX22 164 C6
Lympstone EX8 195 F5
Rackenford EX16 47 D5
Uffculme EX15 66 A7
Meadow View Cl EX10 188 C5
Meadowview Rd EX8 196 E2
Meadow View Rd PL7 250 D5
Meadowville Ct EX39 157 A3
Meadowville Rd EX39 157 A3
Meadow Way
Colaton Raleigh EX10 186 D3
Exeter EX2 177 F5
Gunn EX32 17 F4
Plymouth PL7 250 D7
Mead Park Cl EX31 16 A3
Mead Pk EX31 16 A3
Mead Rd TQ2 219 D2
Mead The
Plymouth PL7 250 D7
Silverton EX5 82 B5
Mead View Rd EX14 166 C5
Meadville TQ1 220 D3
Meadway
Newton Abbot TQ12 212 D8
Saltash PL12 242 E1
Sidmouth EX10 188 B6
Mead Way EX12 192 A6
MEADWELL 116 A8
Meadwood TQ1 220 D3
Mear Top EX31 154 F7
Measbury Moor Cross EX18 45 C5
Meatherel Cl PL21 237 B4
MEAVY 127 C2
Meavy Ave
Plymouth PL5 244 E2
Torquay TQ2 219 B7
Meavy Bourne PL20 127 A2
Meavy CE Prim Sch PL20 127 C2
Meavy La PL20 127 A2
Meavy Villas PL20 127 A2
Meavy Way
Plymouth PL5 244 E2
Tavistock PL19 171 D5
Medard Ho 17 EX32 155 A5
MEDDON 37 F4
Meddon Cross
Edistone EX39 37 F5
Welcombe EX39 37 F4
Meddon Green Nature Reserve* EX39 37 F4
Meddon St EX39 157 A1
Mede The
Exeter EX4 178 B8
Topsham EX3 182 E5
Medland Cres PL6 244 D6
Medland Cross EX6 97 C6
Medland La EX6 97 B6
Medley Ct EX4 176 E8
Medway Pl PL3 249 D6
Medway Rd TQ2 214 B2
Meerhay La DT6 104 F6
Meetford Cross EX6 97 F7
MEETH 57 C3
MEETHE 29 D1
Meethe Gate Cross EX36 29 D2
Meethe Hill EX36 29 D1
Meeting La EX8 195 E6
Meeting St
Appledore EX39 15 A1
Exmouth EX8 202 A7
Melbourne Cotts PL1 262 B3
Melbourne Ct
10 Exeter EX2 261 B2
Torquay TQ1 220 A6
Melbourne Gn 2 PL1 262 B3
Melbourne Pl
Exeter EX2 261 B2
Plymouth PL1 262 B4
Melbourne St
Exeter EX2 261 B2
Plymouth PL1 262 B3
Tiverton EX16 161 B4
Melbury Rd EX39 39 E8
Melcot Cl TQ12 207 E7
MELDON 93 D3
Meldon La EX20 93 E3
Meldon Quarry Sta* EX20 93 E3
Meldon Rd TQ13 111 A6
Meldrum Cl EX7 204 E6
Melhuish Cl EX16 46 E1
Mellons Cl TQ12 206 D4
Mellons Wlk TQ12 206 D4
Mellowmead TQ13 121 F7
Mellows Mdw TQ12 206 F3
Melrose Ave PL2 248 C8
Melville La TQ1 220 B4
Melville Pl 1 PL2 248 A5
Melville Rd PL2 248 A5
Melville St TQ1 220 B4
Melville Terrace La PL2 248 A5
MEMBLAND 141 B7
Membland Ct PL8 141 C6
MEMBURY 87 D6
Membury Cl EX1 178 D6
Membury Com Sch EX13 87 D6
Membury Rd EX13 87 E3
Memory Cross TQ13 215 E8
Memory La PL9 255 E7
Mena Park Cl
Paignton TQ4 225 F2
Plymouth PL9 256 B7
Mena Park Rd PL9 256 B7
MENDENNICK 252 C7
Mendip Rd TQ2 219 D3
Menors Pl EX22 164 C5
Merafield Cl PL7 250 B5
Merafield Dr PL7 250 C4
Merafield Farm Cotts PL7 250 B4
Merafield Rd PL7 250 B4
Merafield Rise PL7 250 C4
Mercer Ct EX2 178 A2
Mercers Dr EX16 161 E6
Merchants Cnr EX17 61 C1
Merchant's Gdn TQ7 143 A1
Merchant's House (Mus)* PL1 262 C2
Meredith Rd PL2 248 C6
Mere La 15 TQ14 210 C5
Meresyke EX8 202 C6
Meriden TQ14 210 C7
Meridian Ho PL4 263 A3
Meridian Pl EX34 150 B6
Merivale PL20 126 F2
Merivale Cl TQ14 210 C7
Merley Rd EX39 156 B7
Merlin Bsns Pk EX5 99 A4
Merlin Cl PL6 245 E8
Merlin Cres EX4 174 A1
Merlin Way TQ2 213 D2
Mermaid Ct 6 EX1 261 A2
Mermaid Yd EX1 261 A2
MERRIFIELD 70 F4
Merrifield Cross
Bridgerule EX22 70 E4
Slapton TQ7 145 C6
Merrifield Rd TQ11 130 C1
Merrion Ave EX8 202 D6
Merritt Flats 5 TQ3 226 A5
Merritt Rd TQ3 226 A5
MERRIVALE 118 C2
Merrivale Cl TQ2 214 B4
Merrivale Rd
Exeter EX4 176 F4
Okehampton EX20 170 E6
Plymouth, Ham PL2 248 B7
Plymouth, Honicknowle PL5 244 B3
Merrivale View Rd PL20 127 B3
Merrow Down Dr EX12 191 F8
Merrydale Cres EX31 27 D6
Merryfield La EX6 95 F2
Merryfield Rd EX39 157 C1
Merryland Cl TQ3 219 B2
Merryland Gdns TQ3 219 B2
Merrylees Dr EX32 155 C3
Merrymeet
Tedburn St Mary EX17 97 F8
Whitestone EX4 98 E4
Merryside Villas EX16 61 E8
Merrythorn Rd EX31 153 D5
Merrywood TQ12 206 F1
Mersey Cl PL3 249 D6
MERTON 57 A7
MESHAW 45 F6
Meshaw Cross Rds EX36 46 A5
Meshaw Moor Cross EX36 46 A5
Meshaw Rectory Cross EX36 46 A5
METCOMBE 100 B2
Metcombe Cross EX31 9 C2
Metcombe La EX31 9 B1
Metcombe Rise EX11 100 C2
Metcombe Vale EX11 100 C2
Meteor Wlk 2 EX32 155 B5
METHERELL 125 A4
Metherell Ave TQ5 230 D3
Metherell Avenue Ind Est TQ5 230 C3
Metherell Cross EX21 91 F8
Metherell Rd EX39 156 F1
Metley Cross TQ12 131 E5
Mettaford Cross EX39 22 F3
Mews Ct 19 EX7 204 E6
Mews Gdns TQ6 233 F3
Mews The
1 Bittaford PL21 137 C8
Dawlish EX7 204 E6
Exmouth EX8 196 F3
Plymouth, Devonport PL1 248 A3
Plymouth, Stonehouse PL1 262 A3
7 Teignmouth TQ14 210 B4
Mewstone Ave PL9 140 D8
Meyrick Rd TQ1 220 C7
Michael Browning Way EX2 261 B1
Michael Rd PL3 249 A5
MICHELCOMBE 129 F4
Michelcombe La TQ13 130 A4
Michigan Way
Exeter EX4 173 C2
Plymouth PL3 249 C6
Mid Churchway PL9 256 A7
Middle Blagdon La TQ3 225 B6
Middleborough La EX33 7 D3
Middle Budleigh Mdw TQ12 206 F3
Middle Combe Dr EX31 154 A3
Middlecombe La PL8 140 F6
MIDDLECOTT 73 B8
Middlecott Cross
Holemoor EX22 73 B8
Virginstow EX21 90 E4
Middlecott Hill EX32 18 D3
Middlecott La EX17 60 F2
Middle Down Cl PL9 256 A5
Middlefield Rd PL6 244 D6
Middlefield Cl PL12 242 B2
MIDDLE GREEN 160 D3
Middle Green Rd TA21 160 E3
Middle Leigh PL8 140 F7
Middle Lincombe Rd TQ1 220 D3
MIDDLE LUXTON 68 C5
MIDDLE MARWOOD 9 B1
Middlemead Rd EX16 161 D5
Middle Mill La EX15 163 C3
MIDDLEMOOR 171 F2
MIDDLE MOOR 178 D4
Middlemoor Cross EX37 43 C3
Middlemoor Police Training Coll EX2 178 D5
Middle Park Terr TQ7 143 B1
Middle Ramshill La TQ3 225 C7
Middle Rd PL9 140 D8
MIDDLE ROCOMBE 213 F7
Middle St
Brixham TQ5 230 C5
East Budleigh EX9 198 B6
Teignmouth TQ14 210 A3
Middleton Rd EX39 156 F3
Middleton Wlk PL5 243 D4
Middletown La EX9 198 B6
MIDDLE WADSTRAY 232 A3
Middle Warberry Rd TQ1 220 D5
Middle Westerland Cross TQ3 218 D1
Middlewood EX6 201 A5
MIDDLE WOOLBROOK 188 A8
Midella Rd PL20 127 A2
Midvale Rd TQ4 226 B5
Midway
Exmouth EX8 202 E8
Kingskerswell TQ12 212 F6
Midway Cl EX2 177 A1
Midway Terr EX2 177 A1
Miers Cl PL5 247 C8
Miers Ct PL5 247 C8
Miglo Ind Est TQ4 225 E3
MILBER 207 F1
Milber La TQ12 213 B6
Milber Trad Est TQ12 208 A1
Milbury Cl EX6 182 B5
Milbury La EX6 182 B4
Milch Pk PL12 242 C2
Mildmay Cl EX4 176 F7
Mildmay St PL4 263 A4
MILE END 206 E5
Mile End Rd TQ12 206 E5
Mile Gdns EX4 173 F2
Milehouse Rd PL2 248 A5
Mile La EX4 174 A1
Miles Mitchell Ave PL6 245 A1
Milestone Cotts EX6 182 B3
Milestone Cross TQ13 123 F8
Milestone La TQ13 123 F8
MILFORD 22 B1
Milford Ave EX10 188 B4
Milford Cl TQ14 210 A5
Milford Cotts EX6 181 B2
Milford Cross EX39 22 B1
Milford La PL5 244 B5
Milford Rd EX10 188 B4
Military Rd
Millbrook PL10 252 C3
Plymouth PL3 249 C6
Rame PL10 140 I2
Milizac Cl PL8 257 E4
Milkaway La EX33 7 E1
Milk Hill EX5 81 D7
Milky Way Adventure Pk* EX39 23 E1
Milland Cross EX20 75 B1
Millards Hill 10 EX39 15 B1
Mill Ave EX17 79 A6
Millbarn Cross EX16 61 F8
MILLBAY 262 B2
Millbay Rd PL1 262 A2
Mill Bottom La TQ12 209 A3
Mill Bridge PL1 262 A3
MILLBROOK
Axminster 167 E6
North Molton 19 F1
Torpoint 252 E5
Millbrook Bsns Ctr PL11 252 C6
Millbrook CE Prim Sch PL10 252 E5
Millbrook Cross EX13 167 E6
Millbrook Dale EX13 167 E6
Millbrook La EX2 177 F2
Millbrook Park Rd TQ2 219 E5
Millbrook Rd 2 TQ3 226 B6
Mill Cl
Lee Mill PL21 136 D6
Newton Abbot TQ12 206 F4
Millcombe Cnr TQ9 139 E1
Millcombe La TQ9 224 C3
Mill Cotts
Okehampton EX20 170 B5
Stoke Canon EX5 173 F7
Mill Cres TQ6 233 D4
Millcroft EX11 169 D3
Mill Cross
Bickington TQ12 131 F7
Halwill EX21 73 C1
Harberton TQ9 222 C2
Rattery TQ10 135 D4
Milldale Cres EX14 166 B5
Mill Dr EX2 177 F1
Mill End 1 TQ12 123 F1
Millen La TQ12 209 C2
Millennium Way
Cullompton EX15 163 C5
Westward Ho! EX39 156 E7
Miller Cl EX2 178 C4
Miller Cres EX32 155 A5
Miller Ct PL1 262 A2
Millers Brook EX33 7 E2
Millers La TQ9 227 E7
Millers Way
Honiton EX14 166 B5
Tedburn St Mary EX6 97 F4
Miller Way
Exminster EX6 181 F5
Plymouth PL6 245 E3
Milletts Cl EX6 182 A4
Millfields Trust Bsns Units 11 PL1 262 A3
Mill Ford Specl Sch PL5 243 F4
Mill Gn DT7 260 E3
Millgreen Ct DT7 260 E3
Millgreen La EX13 87 D1
Millham La TA22 33 D6
MILLHAYES
Hemyock 52 C1
Honiton 86 F6
Millhayes Cross EX14 86 F6
Millhayes Rd EX14 86 F6

Mill Head EX34 150 C6
Millhead Rd EX14 166 B5
MILLHILL 116 F1
Mill Hill
Barnstaple EX31 16 A3
Fremington EX31 153 F5
Stoke Gabriel TQ9 227 F7
Witheridge EX16 61 F7
Mill Hill Cotts PL19 116 F1
Mill Hill Ct TQ9 227 F7
Millhouse Pk PL11 247 A2
Mill La
Alfington EX11 84 F1
Aveton Gifford TQ7 143 C6
Axminster EX13 88 F3
Barnstaple EX31 154 E6
Barton Town EX31 11 E3
Berrynarbor EX34 2 D4
Bow EX17 78 B4
Branscombe EX12 190 D4
Brayford EX32 18 F6
Brixham TQ5 230 A1
Burrington EX37 44 A2
Charmouth DT6 104 F6
Cheriton Fitzpaine EX17 62 E2
Clyst Honiton EX1 175 C1
East Buckland EX32 18 E2
East Ogwell TQ12 206 D1
Exeter, Alphington EX2 177 B1
Exeter, Higher Wear EX2 177 F1
Exton EX3 183 D2
Galmpton TQ5 229 A4
George Nympton EX36 30 A1
Loddiswell TQ7 138 C7
Lower Loxhore EX31 17 F8
Lyme Regis DT7 260 E3
Meshaw EX36 45 F7
Newton Poppleford EX10 186 F6
North Tawton EX20 77 B4
North Whilborough TQ12 212 D2
Offwell EX14 86 B1
4 Paignton TQ3 226 B7
Sandford EX17 80 B5
Stockland EX13 87 B7
Stoke Fleming TQ6 146 A7
Teignmouth TQ14 209 D7
Torpoint PL11 247 A2
Torquay TQ2 219 F5
Totnes TQ9 223 D5
Uplyme DT7 260 C5
Wambrook TA20 69 F2
Woolacombe EX34 7 F6
Wrafton EX33 152 F4
Mill Lane Cotts EX20 77 B4
Mill Leat 14 EX15 67 B8
Mill Leat Cotts EX17 78 B4
Mill-Leat Gdns EX32 17 B2
Millmans Rd TQ3 218 D3
Mill Mdw
Ashburton TQ13 130 F5
10 Combe Martin EX34 3 A3
Ivybridge PL21 237 D5
MILLMOOR 51 E1
Millmoor Cross EX37 44 B2
Millmoor La EX10 186 F8
Millmoor Vale EX10 186 F8
Mill-on-the-Mole Mobile Home Pk EX36 158 E4
Mill Park Ind Est EX5 184 E8
Mill Path TQ13 130 F4
Mill Pk 2 TQ12 123 E1
Millpool Head PL10 252 E4
Millpool Rd PL10 253 A6
Mill Rd
Barnstaple EX31 154 E5
Bradworthy EX22 38 E1
Exeter EX2 177 F1
Fremington EX31 153 E5
High Bickington EX37 43 B7
Landkey EX32 17 B1
Millbrook PL10 253 A5
Okehampton EX20 170 B4
Totnes TQ9 222 E8
Mill Rise EX14 85 F8
Millsome La
Bondleigh EX18 77 C8
North Tawton EX18 59 D1
Mills Rd PL1 247 F2
Mill St
Bideford EX39 157 A2
Chagford TQ13 110 F6
Crediton EX17 165 D5
Great Torrington EX38 159 C4
Honiton EX14 166 B5
Kingsbridge TQ7 258 C5
Ottery St Mary EX11 169 C3
Sidmouth EX10 188 B4
South Molton EX36 158 D4
Uffculme EX15 66 B7
Mill Steep
Molland EX36 31 C8
Twitchen EX36 20 C1
Mill Stile EX33 152 C5
Mill Stream Ct EX11 169 D3
Mill Stream Gdns
Halberton EX16 65 A7
Wellington TA21 160 B7
Millstream Mdw 4 TQ13 123 F6
Mills Way EX31 154 F6
Mill Tail TQ9 223 D5
Mill The EX2 261 C1
MILLTOWN 9 D1
Milltown Hill EX36 45 F7
Milltown La
Northlew EX20 74 E2
Milltown La *continued*
Sidmouth EX10 188 C6
Mill View 13 TQ13 123 F6
Mill View Gdns PL10 252 F5
Mill View Rd PL10 252 F5
Mill Water Specl Sch EX14 166 C4
Millway
Bradninch EX5 82 F6
18 Chudleigh TQ13 123 E6
Wambrook TA20 69 F2
Millway Gdns EX5 82 F6
Millway Pl PL9 255 D8
Millwey Ave EX13 167 F7
Millwey Ct EX13 167 F7
MILLWEY RISE 167 F7
Millwey Rise Ind Est EX13 167 F7
Millwood TQ13 180 C4
Millwood Bsns Pk TQ12 207 E3
Millwood Dr PL6 245 E1
Millwood Terr EX37 28 C2
Milne Pl PL1 247 F3
Milsfords La EX5 81 E5
MILTON ABBOT 116 B6
Milton Abbot Sch PL19 116 B5
Milton Cl
Brixham TQ5 230 B2
Exmouth EX8 196 C4
Plymouth PL5 244 D2
MILTON COMBE 240 F8
Milton Cres
Brixham TQ5 230 B2
Tavistock PL19 171 D5
Milton Ct
2 Newton Abbot TQ12 207 C2
Plymouth, Cattedown PL4 263 C2
Plymouth, Prince Rock PL4 249 B1
MILTON DAMEREL 54 D5
Milton Fields TQ5 230 A2
MILTON GREEN 116 B5
MILTON HILL 124 E5
Milton La TQ6 233 C2
Milton Pk TQ5 230 B2
Milton Pl EX39 156 F1
Milton Rd
Exeter EX2 177 F3
Newton Abbot TQ12 207 B4
Milton St TQ5 230 A2
Miltons Yard EX13 167 D5
Milverton Rd TA21 160 B8
Mimosa Cl 2 EX16 161 F6
Mimosa Ct EX9 198 C1
Minacre La TQ12 212 E1
Mincent Cl TQ2 214 A3
Mincent Hill TQ2 214 A3
Minchin La EX5 99 D2
Minchin Orch EX5 99 E2
Mincinglake Rd EX4 173 F1
Minden Rd 4 TQ14 210 B5
Minehead La TA22 33 F7
Miners Cl 11 TQ13 131 A5
Minerva Cl PL7 251 A6
Minerva Way TQ12 207 E3
Mines Rd EX39 157 C1
Miniature Pony Ctr The★ TQ13 111 B3
Minifie Rd EX14 166 B6
Minniemoor Cross EX31 4 B1
Minniemoor La EX31 4 C1
Minses Cl PL9 256 C7
Minster Rd EX6 182 B5
Mint Park Rd EX33 152 B7
Mint The EX4 261 A3
Mirador Pl PL4 249 C3
Miranda Rd TQ3 225 F8
Mire La EX10 189 B7
Mirey La EX5 184 C3
Misdon Cotts EX20 75 F1
Mission Ct EX1 261 A2
Misterton Cl PL9 256 B8
Mitchell Cl PL9 255 D5
Mitchell Ho EX4 177 D8
Mitchell's Pool TA21 160 E6
Mitchell St TA21 160 C7
Mitre Cl
Bishopsteignton TQ14 208 E8
Tavistock PL19 171 A3
Mitre Ct 14 PL1 263 A2
Mitre La EX4 261 A3
Moat Hill TQ9 223 C4
Moat Pk PL6 245 C1
Mockham Down Gate EX32 18 C7
MODBURY 137 C2
Modbury Cl PL5 244 B3
Modbury Cross PL21 136 E2
Modbury Ct 5 PL21 137 B2
Modbury Prim Sch PL21 137 B2
Model Terr 2 EX39 157 A1
Modred Cl EX4 174 A1
Modyford Wlk PL20 126 C3
MOGWORTHY 47 D4
Mogworthy La EX16 47 D3
Mohun's Cl PL19 171 C4
Mohun's Pk PL19 171 C3
Mole Bridge La EX36 158 E4
Mole Ridge Way EX36 158 C5
Moles Cotts EX6 182 A4
Moles Cross TQ3 218 E7
Moles La
Kingskerswell TQ12 212 E1
Paignton TQ3 218 E8
Molesworth Rd
Plymouth, Plympton PL7 250 C6
Plymouth, Stoke PL1, PL3 248 A3
Molesworth Terr PL10 252 F5
MOLLAND 31 E7
Molland Cross
Brayford EX36 19 B4
Chulmleigh EX18 45 E3
Molland Hill EX32, EX36 19 A5
Mollison Rd PL5 243 E2
Moll Tall's Cross PL7 136 A8
Molyneaux Pl 10 PL1 247 F3
Monastery Rd TQ3 226 A6
Mondeville Way
Northam EX39 156 F6
8 Northam EX39 156 F7
Money Acre Cross EX24 101 E7
Money Acre Rd EX24 101 E7
Money Pit La EX13 69 D1
Monica Wlk PL4 263 B4
Monitor Cl EX2 261 A1
MONKERTON 178 E8
Monkerton Ct EX1 178 E8
Monkerton Dr EX1 178 E8
Monkey La EX10 186 E6
Monkey Puzzle Dr EX20 170 E5
MONKLEIGH 40 F7
Monkleigh Mill La EX39 40 D8
Monkleigh Prim Sch EX39 40 F7
MONKOKEHAMPTON 76 B8
Monkokehampton Cross EX19 76 A8
Monksbridge Rd TQ5 230 B3
Monks Cl
Bideford EX39 26 A4
Crediton EX17 165 B6
Monks Hill PL15 115 A4
Monksmead PL19 171 A4
Monks Orch TQ12 212 A6
Monk's Rd EX4 177 F7
Monkstone Gdns EX13 167 E5
Monkston Point TQ8 259 D4
Monks Way TQ13 180 C6
Monkswell Rd EX4 177 E8
MONKTON 86 A5
Monkton Rd EX14 166 E7
MONKTON WYLD 104 D7
Monkton Wyld Camping Site DT6 104 C7
Monkton Wyld Cross DT6 104 C7
Monkton Wyld La DT6 104 E7
Monmouth Ave EX3 182 F4
Monmouth Beach Chalets DT7 260 C2
Monmouth Gdns PL5 244 C4
Monmouth Hill EX3 182 F4
Monmouth St
Lyme Regis DT7 260 E3
Topsham EX3 182 F4
Monmouth Way EX14 166 D5
Monroe Gdns PL4 262 B4
Monro Mead 7 TQ12 122 F1
Monshall EX19 57 E3
Mons Terr 11 TQ10 134 F3
Montacute Ave PL5 244 B2
Montagu Cl TQ7 258 C6
Montague Gdns EX9 197 E1
Montague Pl EX39 156 F1
Montague Rise EX4 261 B4
Montague Terr PL7 132 F4
Montagu Rd TQ7 258 C5
Monterey TQ4 226 C1
Monterey Cl TQ2 219 E3
Monterey Gdns EX4 173 E1
Monterey Pk TQ12 207 F1
Montery Pl 3 EX32 155 B3
Montesson Cl TQ3 225 D7
Montesson Rd TQ3 225 D7
Montgomery Cl
Ivybridge PL21 237 E5
Saltash PL12 242 D3
Montgomery Comb Sch 11 EX4 177 A5
Montgomery Dr PL19 171 A6
Montgomery Rd 6 EX2 178 D5
Mont Le Grand EX1 177 E6
Montpelier Ct
Exeter EX4 177 A7
Paignton TQ3 219 B1
Montpelier Prim Sch PL2 248 B6
Montpelier Rd
Ilfracombe EX34 150 C6
Plymouth PL2 248 C7
Montpelier Terr 13 EX34 150 C6
Montpellier Ct 1 EX8 202 B6
Montpellier Rd
Exmouth EX8 202 A6
Torquay TQ1 220 B4
Montserrat Rise TQ2 213 E3
Monument Cl TA21 160 E4
Monument Rd TA21 160 E3
Monument St PL1 247 E1
Monument View TA21 52 D8
Moonhayes Cross EX14 68 C4
Moon Hill Cl EX2 181 C8
Moon La 4 PL21 137 B2
Moonridge EX2 182 C7
Moon's Cross EX20 95 B5
Moon St PL4 263 A3
Moorashes 17 TQ9 223 C5
Moor Cl TQ14 210 C7
Moorcourt Cl EX10 187 F3
Moorcox Cross EX13 86 E2
Moor Cres PL20 128 A8
Moorcroft Cl
Okehampton EX20 170 E5
Plymouth PL9 256 A7
Moorcroft Ct EX20 170 E5
MOOR CROSS 133 C1
Moor Cross EX22 71 C3
Moor Ct EX10 187 F3
Moore Cl TQ12 212 F8
Moore Ct EX17 165 C5
Mooredge La EX5 82 E1
Moor Farm Cotts TQ8 148 F4
Moorfield PL16 105 E4
Moorfield Ave 4 PL6 249 C7
Moorfield Cl EX8 202 C8
Moorfield Gdn TA24 21 C6
Moorfield Rd
Exmouth EX8 202 C8
St Giles on t H PL15 90 C1
Moorfields
6 Bittaford PL21 137 C8
19 Colyton EX24 103 A4
Moorfoot Cross TQ12 131 E3
Moor Gate EX20 170 C1
Moorhaven EX9 197 F2
MOORHAVEN VILLAGE 137 C8
MOORHAYES 161 E6
Moorhayes TQ13 180 D7
Moorhayes Bglws EX16 161 E5
Moorhayes Cross EX15 67 B6
Moorhayes Ct EX5 84 A1
Moorhayne Cross EX15 66 A2
Moorhouse La TA4 35 A8
Moorings Reach TQ5 230 D5
Moorings The
Braunton EX33 152 D6
Exmouth EX8 202 C5
Exmouth, The Point EX8 201 E6
Kingsbridge TQ7 258 D3
Paignton TQ4 226 C5
Saltash PL12 242 F1
Moor La
Bittadon EX31 9 C5
Bovey Tracey TQ13 180 C5
Braunton EX33 152 A5
Broadclyst EX5 175 C8
Brushford TA22 33 F4
Budlake EX5 82 E1
Budleigh Salterton EX9 197 F2
Churchinford TA3 68 D7
Croyde EX33 7 D2
Exeter EX2 178 F5
Hatherleigh EX20 75 D7
Molland EX36 31 E7
Plymouth PL5 243 E1
Poltimore EX4 174 F7
Shobrooke EX17 80 E4
Staverton TQ9 216 B5
Torquay TQ2 214 B3
Yarnscombe EX31 27 E2
Zeal Monachorum EX17 78 B8
MOORLAKE 79 F2
Moorland Ave
Denbury TQ12 211 A7
Plymouth PL7 250 F6
Moorland Cl
7 Bittaford PL21 137 C8
Yelverton PL20 241 D8
Moorland Ct PL20 126 F2
Moorland Dr PL7 250 E6
Moorland Gate
Heathfield TQ12 123 B2
Roborough EX19 43 B3
Moorland Gdns PL7 250 F6
Moorland Pk TQ13 180 D5
Moorland Rd PL7 250 E5
Moorland Rise EX36 158 C4
Moorlands
Chagford TQ13 110 F6
Tiverton EX16 161 E6
West Hill EX11 168 D5
Moorlands La PL12 242 C4
Moorlands Rd EX9 197 E1
Moorlands Sch EX14 67 E1
Moorlands Trad Est PL12 242 C4
Moorland Terr EX38 159 B5
Moorland View
Buckfastleigh TQ11 236 A5
Lapford EX17 60 D3
Newton Abbot TQ12 208 A2
Plymouth, Derriford PL6 245 A5
Plymouth, Plymstock PL9 256 B7
Princetown PL20 128 A8
Saltash PL12 242 F4
South Molton EX36 46 D8
Moorland Way
Exeter EX4 176 F8
Gunnislake PL18 125 C5
Moor Lane Cl TQ2 214 A3
Moor Lane Cross N EX36 31 E8
Moor Lea EX33 152 F5
Moormead EX9 197 F1
Moorpark
Bittaford PL21 137 C8
Exmouth EX8 202 C6
Moor Park Cl EX33 7 D2
Moor Park Rd TQ12 212 F6
Moor Pk
Chagford TQ13 111 A6
Honiton EX14 166 B3
Kingskerswell TQ12 212 F6
Moor Rd
Ipplepen TQ12 211 E3
Staverton TQ9 216 B5
Moorsend TQ12 206 E4
Moor's End TQ12 207 D8
Moorshead Cross
Buckfastleigh TQ11 135 B6
Yealmpton PL21 136 D2
Moorside
Malborough TQ7 147 E6
Mary Tavy PL19 117 E6
Moors Pk TQ14 208 F7
Moorstone Leat TQ4 226 C1
MOORTOWN
Great Torrington 41 F7
Tavistock 127 A8
Tetcott 89 F7
Moortown EX18 59 F8
Moortown Cross
Chulmleigh EX18 59 F8
Rackenford EX36 47 B8
Moorview
Broadhempston TQ13 131 B1
Marldon TQ3 218 D2
North Tawton EX20 77 C4
Payhembury EX14 84 D3
Moor View
Bovey Tracey TQ13 180 C5
Chudleigh TQ13 123 E6
Hatherleigh EX20 75 B6
Mary Tavy PL19 117 E6
Northlew EX20 74 E2
Pennymoor EX16 62 E6
Plymouth, Keyham PL2 247 F5
Plymouth, Laira PL3 249 C4
Plymouth PL9 255 D7
Torpoint PL11 247 B3
Moorview Cl EX4 173 D1
Moor View Cl EX10 187 F7
Moorview Ct PL6 245 F5
Moorview Dr TQ14 209 D8
Moor View Dr TQ14 210 A6
Moorview End TQ3 218 D2
Moor View Prim Sch TQ12 123 B3
Moor View Terr
9 Bittaford PL21 137 C8
Plymouth PL4 248 E4
Yelverton PL20 127 A2
Moory Mdw EX34 2 F4
Moothill Cross TQ9 216 A6
MORCHARD BISHOP 61 A2
Morchard Bishop CE Prim Sch EX17 61 B2
MORCHARD ROAD 78 F7
Morchard Road Sta EX17 78 F8
MOREBATH 34 B3
Morecombe Cross EX21 73 A4
MORELEIGH 139 A3
Moreton Ave
Bideford EX39 156 E1
Plymouth PL6 244 F1
Moreton Dr EX39 156 E2
MORETONHAMPSTEAD 111 E4
Moretonhampstead Com Hospl TQ13 111 F5
Moretonhampstead Prim Sch TQ13 111 F5
Moretonhampstead Rd TQ13 122 F6
Moreton Park Rd EX39 156 E1
Moreton Terr EX6 112 F5
Morgan Ave TQ2 220 A5
Morgan Ct EX8 202 A6
Morganhayes Cross EX24 102 D4
Morgans Quay TQ14 210 B3
Morice Sq PL1 247 E2
Morice St PL1 247 E2
Morice Terr EX22 54 A6
MORICE TOWN 247 D3
Morice Town Prim Sch PL2 247 E4
Morin Rd TQ3 226 C8
Morlaix Dr PL6 245 B4
Morleigh Cross TQ9 139 A3
Morleigh Gn TQ9 139 A3
Morleigh Green Cross TQ9 139 A4
Morleigh Rd TQ9 139 C6
MORLEY 206 B3
Morley Cl PL7 250 A5
Morley Ct PL1 262 B3
Morley Dr PL20 126 D2
Morley Rd EX4 177 E8
Morley View Rd PL7 250 C6
Mornacott Cross EX36 31 A4
Mornacott Rd EX36 31 A4
Morningside
Dawlish EX7 204 C4
Torquay TQ1 220 E5
Mornington Pk TA21 160 E5
Morrell's Cross EX16 34 B4
Morrell's La EX16 50 B6
Morris Cl EX20 75 B7
Morrish Pk PL9 255 F6
Morshead Rd PL6 244 F2
Mortain Rd PL12 242 D4
MORTEHOE 7 F8
Mortehoe Her Ctr★ EX34 7 F8
Mortehoe Station Rd EX34 1 B1
Mortimer Ave TQ3 226 B8
Mortimer Ct EX2 178 A2
Mortimer Ho EX1 177 E6
Mortimers Cross EX15 66 B4
Mortimore Cl PL12 242 D2
Morton Cres EX8 201 F6
Morton Crescent Mews EX8 201 F6
Morton Dr EX38 159 D5
Morton Rd EX8 201 F6
Morton Way EX13 167 D4
Morven Dr EX8 196 A2
Morwell Gdns PL2 248 A6
MORWELLHAM 125 E4
Morwellham Quay★ PL19 125 E4
Morwenna Park Rd EX39 156 F7
Morwenna Rd EX23 37 A1
Morwenna Terr 2 EX39 156 F7
MORWENSTOW 36 E2

Moses Cl PL6 . . . . 244 E7
Moses Ct PL6 . . . . 244 E7
Mosshayne La EX1, EX5 . . 175 B2
Mossop Cl EX11 . . . . 169 D3
Mostyn Ave PL4 . . . . 249 A4
Motehole Rd TQ12 . . . . . 211 D2
Mote Pk PL12 . . . . 242 C3
MOTHECOMBE 142 A6
Mothecombe Wlk PL6 . . . 245 E1
Mott's Cross EX15 . . . . . . 84 A7
Motts La EX15 . . . . 84 A7
Moulton Cl PL7 . . . . 251 B5
Moulton Wlk PL7 . . . . 251 B4
Moult Rd TQ8 . . . . 259 B2
Mounson Hill EX6 . . . . 97 C5
Mountain Cl EX8 . . . . 202 F8
Mountain Hill EX8 . . . . . . 197 A1
Mountbatten Cl
  Exmouth EX8 . . . . 196 D2
  Plymouth PL9 . . . . 255 D6
Mount Batten Ctr * PL9 . 258 F7
Mountbatten Rd EX16 . . . 161 C5
Mountbatten Way PL9 . . . 255 E6
Mount Boone Cl TQ6 . . . . 233 F4
Mount Boone Hill TQ6 . . 233 F4
Mount Boone La TQ6 . . . . 233 F4
Mount Boone Way TQ6 . . 233 E4
Mount Dinham EX4 . . . . . 177 A6
Mount Edgcumbe Ho &
  Country Pk * PL10 . . . . 253 E6
Mounter's Hill TA20 . . . . . 69 E2
Mount Ford PL19 . . . . 171 A5
MOUNT GOULD 249 B3
Mount Gould Ave PL4 . . . 249 B2
Mount Gould Cres PL4 . . 249 B3
Mount Gould Hospl PL4 . 249 B3
Mount Gould Rd PL4 . . . . 249 B3
Mount Gould Way PL4 . . . 249 B3
Mount Hermon Rd TQ1 . . 220 B6
Mounthill Cotts TQ12 . . . 122 F1
Mounthill Cross EX24 . . . 103 B5
Mounthill La EX13 . . . . . . 103 E5
Mount House Sch PL19 . . 171 E7
Mounticombe Cross EX18 45 C1
Mounticombe La EX18 . . . 45 C1
MOUNT LANE 90 B6
MOUNT PLEASANT 86 B3
Mount Pleasant
  Bideford, East-t-W EX39 . 157 C3
  Bideford, Littleham EX39 . 25 D2
  3 Bishop's Tawton EX32 . 16 E1
  4 Chudleigh TQ13 . . . . 123 F6
  5 Crediton EX17 . . . . . 165 C5
  Millbrook PL10 . . . . 252 E5
  Moretonhampstead TQ13 . 111 F4
  Plymouth PL5 . . . . 244 B2
Mount Pleasant Ave EX6 196 B3
Mount Pleasant Cl
  Kingsbridge TQ7 . . . . 258 D6
  Kingskerswell TQ12 . . . . 213 A3
Mount Pleasant Ct EX8 . 196 B2
Mount Pleasant La **7**
  TQ14 . . . . 210 A3
Mount Pleasant Mews
  TQ5 . . . . 230 C4
Mount Pleasant Rd
  Brixham TQ5 . . . . 230 C4
  Dawlish Warren EX7 . . . . 201 B1
  Exeter EX4 . . . . 177 E8
  Kingskerswell TQ12 . . . . 213 A3
  Newton Abbot TQ12 . . . . 207 C2
  2 Torquay TQ2 . . . . . . 220 B6
MOUNT RADFORD 261 C2
Mount Radford Cres
  EX2 . . . . 261 C2
Mount Radford Sq EX2 . . 261 C2
Mount Raleigh Ave EX39 . 156 C4
Mount Raleigh Dr EX39 . 156 E3
Mount Rd TQ5 . . . . 230 D5
Mount Ridley Rd TQ6 . . . 234 C3
Mount Rise EX6 . . . . 114 E4
Mount Sandford Rd
  EX32 . . . . 155 D1
Mount St
  Plymouth, Mount Wise
  . . . . 247 E1
  Plymouth, Mutley PL4 . . 263 A4
Mount Stone Rd PL1 . . . . 254 A8
Mount Street Prim Sch
  PL4 . . . . 263 A4
Mount Stuart Hospl (Private)
  TQ1 . . . . 219 F7
Mount Tamar Cl PL5 . . . . 243 E2
Mount Tamar Spec1 Sch
  PL5 . . . . 243 E2
Mount Tavy Rd PL19 . . . . 171 E6
Mount The
  32 Appledore EX39 . . . . 15 A1
  Brixham TQ5 . . . . 230 C6
  Teignmouth TQ14 . . . . . 210 B6
  Torquay TQ2 . . . . 213 F4
  Totnes TQ9 . . . . 223 C4
Mount View
  18 Colyton EX24 . . . . . 103 A4
  Feniton EX14 . . . . 84 B2
  2 Ilfracombe EX34 . . . 150 D5
Mount View Home Pk
  EX32 . . . . 155 E2
Mount View Terr **2** TQ9 252 C5
Mount Wear Sq EX2 . . . . 182 C8
MOUNT WISE 247 F1
Mount Wise Ct PL1 . . . . . 247 F1
Mount Wise Prim Sch
  PL1 . . . . 247 F1
Mourne Villas PL9 . . . . . . 255 F8
Mouseberry Cross EX17 . . 46 A4

Mouseberry La TQ13 . . . . 124 B4
Mousehole Cross EX14 . . . 84 D5
Mouse Hole La EX14 . . . . 84 C4
MOUTH MILL 23 B5
Mowbars Hayes EX13 . . . 87 A3
Mowbray Ave EX4 . . . . . . 261 B4
Mowbray Ct EX2 . . . . 178 A5
Mowbray Dr PL9 . . . . 252 B8
Mowbray Mdw PL11 . . . . 252 B8
Mowhay Rd PL5 . . . . 244 A2
Mowhay The **18** EX22 . . 164 C4
Mowlish La EX6 . . . . 200 B7
Mowstead Pk EX33 . . . . . 152 B7
Mowstead Rd EX33 . . . . . 152 B7
Moxey La EX17 . . . . 62 E1
Moyses La EX20 . . . . 170 B4
Moyses Mdw EX20 . . . . . 170 A4
Mrs Ethelston's CE Prim Sch
  DT7 . . . . 260 A5
Mucky Duck EX20 . . . . . . 107 E2
Mucky La EX19 . . . . 57 D6
Muddiford La EX4 . . . . . . 202 A8
MUDDIFORD 16 A3
Muddix Mews EX39 . . . . . 156 F6
MUDDLEBRIDGE 16 A3
Muddy La EX32 . . . . 18 E2
Mudford Gate EX16 . . . . 62 E7
Mudgate Cross EX36 . . . . 20 D3
Mudge La TQ12 . . . . 217 E6
Mudges Terr PL18 . . . . . . 125 D6
Mudge Way PL7 . . . . 250 E5
Mudhouse Cross EX19 . . . 58 B7
Mudstone La TQ5 . . . . . . 230 E3
Mulberry Cl
  Exeter EX1 . . . . 178 B6
  Paignton TQ3 . . . . 225 E6
  Plymouth PL6 . . . . 245 E7
  Willand EX15 . . . . 162 D4
Mulberry Gr PL19 . . . . . . 171 C2
Mulberry Rd PL12 . . . . . . 242 E1
Mulberry St **3** TQ14 . . . 210 B4
Mulberry Way EX31 . . . . 154 B2
Mulgrave St PL1 . . . . 262 C2
Mullacott Cross EX34 . . . . . 1 E1
Mullacott Cross Ind Est
  EX34 . . . . 1 F1
Mullet Ave PL3 . . . . 249 C4
Mullet Cl PL3 . . . . 249 C4
Mullet Rd PL3 . . . . 249 C4
Mullion Cl PL11 . . . . 246 F4
Muralto Ho PL19 . . . . 171 A4
MURCHINGTON 110 E7
Murchington Cross
  TQ13 . . . . 110 E7
Murdock Rd PL11 . . . . . . 246 F3
Murley Cl EX17 . . . . 165 A6
Murley Cres TQ14 . . . . . . 208 E8
Murley Grange TQ14 . . . 208 E8
MUSBURY 103 D5
Musbury Castle* EX13 . . 103 D5
Musbury Prim Sch EX13 103 D5
Musbury Rd EX13 . . . . . . 167 C4
MUSEHILL 106 F6
Museum Ct TQ7 . . . . 258 C6
Museum Rd TQ1 . . . . 220 C4
Musgrave Ho EX4 . . . . . . 261 B3
Musgrave Row EX4 . . . . . 261 B3
Musgraves TQ12 . . . . 33 E6
Mushroom Rd EX5 . . . . . . 99 A1
Musket Rd TQ12 . . . . 180 F2
Mus of Barnstaple & North
  Devon* EX32 . . . . 154 F4
Mus of Dartmoor Life*
  EX20 . . . . 170 B5
MUTLEY
  . . . . 248 E4
  . . . . 248 F4
Mutley Cl PL4 . . . . 263 A4
Mutley Plain PL4 . . . . 248 E4
Mutley Plain La PL4 . . . . 248 E4
Mutley Rd PL3 . . . . 248 E5
Muttersmoor Rd EX10 . . 187 E5
MUTTERTON 83 D8
Mutton La
  Exeter EX2 . . . . 181 C8
  Torrington EX38 . . . . . . 159 C3
Mylor Cottage La EX32 . . 19 A8
Mylor Cl PL2 . . . . 248 D8
Myra Ct **27** EX39 . . . . . . 15 A1
Myrtle Cl
  Exeter EX2 . . . . 177 B1
  Yelverton PL20 . . . . 127 B8
Myrtle Cottage Rd EX39 . 157 B8
Myrtle Farm View EX33 . . . 7 E2
Myrtle Gdns EX39 . . . . . . 157 A2
Myrtle Gr EX39 . . . . 157 A2
Myrtle Hill TQ14 . . . . 210 C5
Myrtle La TA21 . . . . 51 E7
Myrtle Rd EX4 . . . . 176 E4
Myrtle Row
  28 Exmouth EX8 . . . . . 202 A6
  4 Torquay TQ2 . . . . . . 220 B5
Myrtles Ct PL12 . . . . 242 D4
Myrtle St **17** EX39 . . . . . 15 A1
Myrtleville PL2 . . . . 248 A6

N

Nadder Bottom EX4 . . . . 176 B8
Nadder La
  Barnstaple EX4 . . . . 176 B8
  South Molton EX36 . . . . 158 A4
Nadder Mdw EX36 . . . . . 158 B4
Nadder Park Rd EX4 . . . . 176 D5
NADDERWATER 176 B7
Nadrid Cross EX36 . . . . . . 30 A8

Nadrid East Cross EX36. . . 30 A8
Naida Vale TQ6 . . . . 233 F5
Naish's La EX13 . . . . 87 B3
Nancarrows PL12 . . . . . . 242 C2
Napier St PL1 . . . . 247 F3
Napier Terr
  8 Exeter EX4 . . . . 261 A3
  Plymouth PL4 . . . . 248 E4
Nap La EX18 . . . . 44 C1
Naps La EX10 . . . . 186 C5
Nap View EX14 . . . . 85 B4
NARFORD'S 69 F1
Narfords La TA20 . . . . . . 69 F1
Narracott La
  Hollacombe EX18 . . . . . . 58 E7
  South Molton EX36 . . . . 158 A2
Narratons Rd EX20 . . . . . 93 E6
Narrow La
  Botusfleming PL12 . . . . . 242 C7
  Tiverton EX16 . . . . 161 C2
Narrowmoor Cross TQ7 . 144 D4
Naseby Dr TQ12 . . . . 180 F2
Nash Cl PL7 . . . . 251 A5
Nash Gdns EX7 . . . . 204 D4
Nash La DT6 . . . . 88 H2
Nasmith Cl EX8 . . . . 196 D1
NATCOTT 22 F2
Natcott La EX39 . . . . 22 F2
National Marine Aquarium *
  PL4 . . . . 263 A2
Nats La
  Cornwood PL21 . . . . 133 D1
  Sparkwell PL21 . . . . 136 C8
Natsley La EX32 . . . . 18 F8
Natson Mill La EX17 . . . . 78 B4
Nattadon Rd TQ13 . . . . . 111 A6
Natty Cross EX38. . . . . . . 43 A5
Nautilus EX39 . . . . 156 C7
Neadon La EX6 . . . . 112 F5
Neal Cl PL7 . . . . 251 B4
Neath Rd PL4 . . . . 263 C4
Needlewood Cl EX11 . . . 168 C3
Neet Way EX22 . . . . 164 C6
Neilgate Cnr TQ13 . . . . . 131 A3
Nelson Ave PL1 . . . . 247 F3
Nelson Cl
  Staverton TQ9 . . . . 216 A5
  Teignmouth TQ14 . . . . . 210 A6
  Topsham EX3 . . . . 182 E5
  Torquay TQ2 . . . . 220 D2
Nelson Dr
  Exmouth EX8 . . . . 202 E8
  Westward Ho! EX39 . . . . 156 C7
Nelson Gdns **5** PL1 . . . 247 F3
Nelson Mews EX39 . . . . . 156 C7
Nelson Pl TQ12 . . . . 207 B5
Nelson Rd
  Brixham TQ5 . . . . 230 C5
  Dartmouth TQ6 . . . . 233 C3
  Exeter EX4 . . . . 177 A5
  Westward Ho! EX39 . . . . 156 C7
Nelson St PL4 . . . . 263 A4
Nelson Terr
  Plymouth PL6 . . . . 245 E6
  Westward Ho! EX39 . . . . 156 C7
Nelson Way **1** EX2 . . . . 178 D5
NEOPARDY 79 D1
Neopardy Cross EX17 . . . 79 D1
Nepean St **3** PL2 . . . . . 247 F5
Neptune Ct **8** EX1 . . . . 261 A2
Neptune Pk PL9 . . . . 255 B8
Ness Dr TQ14 . . . . 210 B2
Ness View Rd TQ14 . . . . . 210 C8
Neswick St PL1 . . . . 262 B3
Neswick Street Ope PL1 . 262 A3
NETHERCOTT 8 C2
Nethercott Cross
  Ashwater EX21 . . . . 90 C7
  Oakford EX16 . . . . 48 C8
Nethercott Hill EX16 . . . 48 C7
Nethercott La EX17, EX20 . 95 F6
Nethercott Rd EX33 . . . . . 8 C2
NETHEREXE 81 F2
Netherham Cross EX33 . . . 8 A2
Netherham La EX33 . . . . . 8 A2
Netherleigh Rd TQ1 . . . . 220 B7
Nether Mdw TQ3 . . . . . . 218 D3
NETHERTON 208 C3
Netherton Cross EX16 . . . 3 A4
Netherton Est PL20 . . . . 126 D3
Netherton Hill EX6 . . . . . 96 D1
Netherton La EX34 . . . . . 3 A4
Netley Rd TQ12 . . . . 207 B4
NETTACOTT 81 C2
Nettacott Cross EX5 . . . . 81 B2
Nettleford Hill EX16 . . . . 46 F5
Nettlehayes PL9 . . . . 256 D7
Netton Cl PL9 . . . . 256 B6
Nevada Cl PL3 . . . . 249 D6
Nevada Ct **10** EX12 . . . 192 A5
Neville Rd
  Newton Abbot TQ12 . . . 207 A4
  Okehampton EX20 . . . . 170 C5
Newacott Cross EX22 . . . 70 E5
New Barn Cross EX5 . . . . 172 A7
New Barn Hill PL7 . . . . . . 250 F3
New Barnstaple Rd EX34 150 E3
Newberry Cl EX34 . . . . 2 F4
Newberry Cotts EX33 . . . . 8 A2
Newberry Hill EX34 . . . . . 2 F4
Newberry La EX34 . . . . . . 2 F4
Newberry Rd
  Combe Martin EX34. . . . . 2 F4
  Georgeham EX33 . . . . 8 A2
Newberry's Patch TA3. . . 68 D7
Newbery Cl
  Axminster EX13 . . . . 167 E6
  Colyton EX24 . . . . 103 A4

Newbery Comm Ctr EX5. . 99 A4
New Bldgs
  3 Bampton EX16 . . . . . 34 C1
  8 Barnstaple EX32 . . . 155 A6
  Chittlehampton EX37 . . . 28 F3
  Doddiscombsleigh EX6 . . 113 D5
  Fremington EX31 . . . . . . 153 E5
  Thurlestone TQ7 . . . . . . 143 C2
Newbridge Cl EX39 . . . . . 157 B4
Newbridge Cross
  Bishop's Tawton EX32 . . . 27 F7
  Cowley EX5 . . . . 172 D6
New Bridge Cross EX31 . . 27 E7
Newbridge Cswy EX31,
  EX32 . . . . 27 E7
Newbridge Hill
  Cowley EX5 . . . . 172 E6
  Gunnislake PL18 . . . . . . 125 D6
  Holne TQ13 . . . . 130 A4
  Witheridge EX16 . . . . . . 46 D1
New Bridge St EX4 . . . . . 261 A2
Newbridge Rd
  Newbury Cl PL5 . . . . 244 B4
  Newbury Dr TQ13 . . . . . 180 E7
Newcastle Gdns PL5 . . . . 244 B5
Newcombe Ct EX20 . . . . 170 D5
Newcombes **5** EX17 . . . 165 C5
Newcombes La EX5 . . . . . 178 A6
Newcombe Street Gdns
  EX1 . . . . 178 A6
Newcombe Terr EX1 . . . . 177 F6
Newcomen Rd TQ6. . . . . 233 F3
Newcot Cross EX15 . . . . . 67 D5
NEWCOTT 68 F3
New Cotts EX8 . . . . 202 F7
Newcourt Rd
  Silverton EX5 . . . . 82 B5
  Topsham EX3 . . . . 182 E7
New Cross
  Avonwick TQ10 . . . . 135 C2
  Kingsteignton TQ12 . . . . 123 E1
  Nevcross Pk **10** TQ12 . 123 E1
  New Cswy **10** EX39 . . . 156 F7
New Cut
  Beer EX12 . . . . 191 D5
  Crediton EX17 . . . . 165 B5
New England Hill PL7 . . . 136 B5
New England Rd PL7 . . . 136 B5
New Esplanade Ct TQ4 . . 226 C6
New Est EX5 . . . . 81 A2
New Exeter St TQ13 . . . . 123 E6
Newfoundland Cl EX4 . . . 173 E2
Newfoundland Way **13**
  TQ12 . . . . 207 B3
Newgate Cross TA22 . . . . 33 D7
New George St PL1 . . . . . 262 C3
NEWHAVEN 24 F1
Newhay Cl EX7 . . . . 204 C6
Newhay Cross TQ12 . . . . 211 C1
Newhayes EX12 . . . . 211 C1
Newhayes Cl EX2 . . . . . . 177 A2
Newhouse Hill EX16 . . . . 46 E2
Newhouse La
  Chipstable TA4 . . . . 35 E6
  Hittisleigh EX6 . . . . 96 D5
New Houses TQ7 . . . . . . 149 A5
New Inn Cross EX5 . . . . . 99 E8
New Inn Cr
  Cullompton EX15 . . . . . 163 C3
  6 Holsworthy EX22 . . 164 C4
New La
  Bampton EX16 . . . . 33 F2
  Broadhempston TQ9 . . . 131 E1
  Ottery St Mary EX11 . . . 169 E4
  Staverton TQ9 . . . . 215 F5
  Tatworth TA20 . . . . 88 C8
Newland Cotts EX32 . . . . 17 C1
Newland Cross
  King's Nympton EX37 . . 44 C8
  North Tawton EX20 . . . . 77 B3
  Rackenford EX16 . . . . . . 47 B2
Newlands
  Dawlish EX7 . . . . 204 E7
  Honiton EX14 . . . . 166 C6
Newlands Ave EX8 . . . . . 202 D8
Newlands Cl
  Exeter EX2 . . . . 178 A1
  Landkey EX32 . . . . 17 C2
  Sidmouth EX10 . . . . 188 B8
Newlands Cotts PL21 . . . 237 D3
Newlands Dr TQ13 . . . . . 180 C4
Newlands Pk
  Aylesbeare EX5 . . . . 99 E1
  Seaton EX12 . . . . 192 A6
Newlands Rd EX10 . . . . . 188 B8
Newlane End TQ9 . . . . . . 215 F5
New Launceston Rd
  PL19. . . . . 171 A5
New London PL20 . . . . . . 128 B8
Newman Cres TQ9 . . . . . 222 F8
Newman Ct EX4 . . . . 176 E5
Newman Rd
  Exeter EX4 . . . . 176 F5
  Plymouth PL5 . . . . 243 E2
  Saltash PL12 . . . . 242 F3
New Mdw PL21 . . . . 237 B6
New Mills Ind Est PL21 . . 237 B6
Newnham Cross EX37 . . . 44 B4
Newnham Ind Est PL7 . . 250 F6
Newnham Rd PL7 . . . . . . 250 F7
Newnham Way PL7 . . . . 250 F6
New North Rd
  Exeter EX4 . . . . 261 A4
  Exmouth EX8 . . . . 202 A7

New Orchard **9** TQ10 . . 134 F2
New Park TQ13 . . . . 180 C4
New Park Cl TQ5. . . . . . . 230 D4
New Park Cres TQ12 . . . . 207 D8
New Park Rd
  Kingsteignton TQ12 . . . . 207 D8
  Lee Mill PL7, PL21. . . . . 136 B6
  Paignton TQ3 . . . . 225 F7
  Plymouth PL7. . . . . 251 A4
New Passage Hill PL1 . . . 247 E3
New Path EX1. . . . . 97 C7
New Pk
  Bridford EX6 . . . . 112 F5
  East Anstey EX16 . . . . . . 32 E4
  Horrabridge PL20 . . . . . 126 F4
NEWPORT 155 B3
Newport Comm Sch EX32 155 B3
Newport Rd
  Barnstaple EX32 . . . . . . 155 A3
  Exeter EX2 . . . . 182 C7
Newport St
  Dartmouth TQ6 . . . . 233 F3
  Millbrook PL10. . . . . 252 E5
  Plymouth PL1 . . . . 248 A1
  Tiverton EX16 . . . . 161 D4
Newport Terr
  Barnstaple EX32 . . . . . . 155 A3
  7 Bideford EX39 . . . . . 157 B1
New Quay La TQ5 . . . . . . 230 D5
New Quay St
  Appledore EX39 . . . . 15 A1
  Teignmouth TQ14 . . . . . 210 B4
New Rd
  Allercombe EX5 . . . . 168 B5
  Barnstaple EX32 . . . . . . 155 A4
  Beer EX12 . . . . 191 D6
  Bere Alston PL20 . . . . . . 125 E2
  Bickleigh PL6, PL7 . . . . . 132 A5
  Bideford EX39 . . . . 157 A1
  Bishop's Tawton EX32 . . . 16 B3
  Brixham TQ5 . . . . 230 B4
  Buckfastleigh TQ11 . . . . 236 B5
  Cawsand PL10 . . . . 253 A1
  Chard Junction TA20 . . . 88 F8
  Clyst St Lawrence EX5. . . 83 B3
  Great Torrington EX38 . . 159 D4
  Instow EX39 . . . . 15 C1
  Kingsand PL10 . . . . 253 B2
  Lifton PL16 . . . . 105 F4
  Loddiswell TQ7 . . . . 143 F7
  Lutton PL21 . . . . 133 B2
  Merton EX20 . . . . 57 A6
  Modbury PL21 . . . . 137 B2
  Morchard Bishop EX17. . . 61 B2
  Oare EX35 . . . . 6 C4
  Okehampton EX20 . . . . 170 A3
  Roborough PL6 . . . . 241 D2
  Saltash PL12 . . . . 242 E3
  South Molton EX36 . . . . 158 D4
  Starcross EX6 . . . . 201 A8
  Stoke Fleming TQ6. . . . . 146 B7
  Stoke Gabriel TQ9 . . . . . 227 F7
  Teignmouth TQ14 . . . . . 210 C7
  Totnes TQ9 . . . . 223 D6
  Upottery EX14 . . . . 68 B1
  Waterrow TA21 . . . . 35 F4
  Wilmington EX14 . . . . . . 86 D2
  Yealmpton PL8. . . . . 136 A2
New Road Cl PL10 . . . . . 253 A2
New Road Cross
  Milton Damerel EX22. . . . 54 D3
  Okehampton EX20 . . . . . 93 F5
  South Molton EX36 . . . . 46 D6
  Wilmington EX14 . . . . . . 86 D1
New Road East EX20 . . . 93 F8
New Road Gate EX35. . . . . 6 D5
New Row **8** EX34 . . . . . 157 A2
New Sch Exeter The EX6 182 A5
New Sidmouth Rd EX4 . 102 F4
New St
  6 Appledore EX39 . . . . 15 A1
  5 Bideford EX39 . . . . . 157 A2
  Chagford TQ13 . . . . 111 A6
  14 Chulmleigh EX18 . . 44 E1
  Cullompton EX15 . . . . . 163 B3
  Exmouth EX8. . . . . 202 A7
  Great Torrington EX38. . . 159 C5
  Honiton EX14 . . . . 166 C6
  Millbrook PL10. . . . . 252 E5
  Moretonhampstead TQ13 111 F5
  Ottery St Mary EX11 . . . 169 E4
  Paignton TQ3 . . . . 226 B6
  Plymouth PL1 . . . . 263 A2
  Sidmouth EX10 . . . . 188 B3
NEWTAKE 208 A1
Newtake Rd PL19 . . . . . . 171 E2
Newtake Rise TQ12 . . . . 207 F2
Newte's Hill EX16 . . . . . . 64 D5
New Theatre (Cygnet)* .
  EX1 . . . . 261 B2
NEWTON ABBOT 207 B4
Newton Abbot Coll
  TQ12 . . . . 207 A4
Newton Abbot Hospl
  TQ12 . . . . 207 C3
Newton Abbot L Ctr
  TQ12 . . . . 207 A4
Newton Abbot Racecourse*
  TQ12 . . . . 207 D6
Newton Abbot StaTQ12 207 B3
Newton Abbot Town & GWR
  Mus* TQ12 . . . . 207 C3
Newton Ave PL5 . . . . 243 E2
Newton Cl **3** PL8 . . . . . 141 A7

Newton Cross
Blackawton TQ9 . . . . 145 B7
Denbury TQ12 . . . . 211 B6
Hartland EX39 . . . . 22 C2
Zeal Monachorum EX17. . . 77 F7
Newton Ct
16 Bampton EX16 . . . . 34 B1
Newton Ferrers PL8 . . . . . 140 F7
NEWTON FERRERS 140 F7
Newton Ferrers CE Prim Sch
PL8 . . . . 141 A7
Newton Gdns PL5 . . . . . . 243 F2
Newton Hall TQ12. . . . . . 207 C2
Newton Hill
Daccombe TQ12 . . . . 213 F6
Newton Ferrers PL8 . . . . . 140 F7
Newton Ho EX5. . . . . 80 F1
Newton La EX17 . . . . 77 F7
NEWTON POPPLEFORD . . 186 E7
Newton Poppleford Prim Sch
EX10 . . . . 186 F8
Newton Rd
Bideford EX39 . . . . 157 A3
Bishopsteignton TQ14 . . . 208 D7
Bovey Tracey TQ13. . . . . . 180 C6
Heathfield TQ13. . . . . 180 E3
Kingskerswell TQ12. . . . . 213 A5
Kingsteignton TQ12. . . . . 207 D5
Salcombe TQ8 . . . . 259 D4
Torquay TQ2. . . . . 213 D1
Newton Road Ret Pk
TQ12. . . . . 207 D6
NEWTON ST CYRES. 172 A8
Newton St Cyres Prim Sch
EX5 . . . . 172 A8
Newton St Cyres Sta EX5. 81 A1
NEWTON ST PETROCK . . . 55 B7
Newton St Petrock Cross
EX38. . . . . 40 B1
Newton School EX38. . . . . 55 C7
Newtons Orch EX13 . . . . . . 87 C1
Newton Sq 8 EX16 . . . . . . 34 B1
Newton's Row PL7 . . . . . . 136 A8
NEWTON TRACEY 27 A5
NEWTOWN
Buckland St Mary 69 D7
Exeter 177 E6
South Molton 31 A4
NEW TOWN 188 B4
Newtown
Cornwood PL21 . . . . 133 C2
Sidmouth EX10 . . . . 188 B4
Newtown Cl EX1 . . . . 261 A3
Newtown Cross EX36. . . . 31 A4
Newtown La EX36. . . . . . . 31 A3
Newtown Prim Sch EX1 . 261 C3
New Valley Rd EX4 . . . . . 184 C6
New Village Cross EX17 . 59 F2
New Way EX5 . . . . 184 C6
New Way Est EX14 . . . . . . 67 B2
New Wlk TQ9 . . . . 223 D5
New Wood Cl PL6 . . . . . . 245 E8
New Zealand Ho PL3. . . . 248 B4
Nibbys Cross EX15 . . . . . 66 B5
Nicholas Cl TA22. . . . . 33 E4
Nicholas Mdw EX17 . . . . 125 B4
Nicholas Rd EX1 . . . . 178 A6
Nichols Nymett Cross
EX20. . . . . 77 F4
Nichols Nymett La EX20 . . 77 F5
Nichols Nymett Moors Cross
EX20. . . . . 77 F5
Nicholson Rd
Plymouth PL5. . . . . 244 E2
Torquay TQ2. . . . . 213 D1
Nichols Way 4 EX1 . . . . 177 E7
Nick Reed's La EX15 . . . . 52 D1
Nightingale Cl
Plymouth PL9. . . . . 256 C8
Torquay TQ2. . . . . 213 E2
Nightingale Lawns EX15. 163 A2
Nightingale Wlk EX2 . . . 176 D3
Nilgala Cl EX39 . . . . 156 E4
Nine Ash Cross EX16 . . . . 49 D6
Nine Milestone Cross
PL21. . . . . 137 D7
Nine Oaks
Aylesbeare EX5 . . . . 99 C1
Dousland PL20. . . . . 127 C3
Nirvana PL21 . . . . 237 C5
Nirvana Cl PL21 . . . . 237 C5
Noelle Dr TQ12 . . . . 207 A4
Noland Pk TQ10. . . . . 135 A2
Nomandsland Cross EX16 62 B8
No Mans Chaple EX5 . . . . 81 A3
Nomansland EX17. . . . . . . 80 D5
No Man's Land
Georgeham EX33. . . . . 8 B1
Whiddon EX31 . . . . 9 C1
Nook The PL19. . . . . 171 D6
No Place Hill TQ9 . . . . . . 131 E1
Norah Bellot Ct 2 EX31 154 F7
Norbury Ct 3 PL1. . . . . . 262 A3
Norden La TQ7 . . . . 258 B5
Nordon Cross TQ12 . . . . 131 F3
Norfolk Cl PL3 . . . . 249 C5
Norfolk Rd PL3 . . . . 249 C4
Norfolk Terr 23 EX32. . . 155 A4
Norleigh Cross EX20 . . . . 75 C3
NORLEY. 74 E3
Norley Rd EX33 . . . . 8 D1
Norman Cl
Exmouth EX8 . . . . 196 D2
Newton Abbot TQ12. . . . . 206 E5
Norman Cres EX9 . . . . . . 198 A2

Norman Ct EX2 . . . . 177 C1
Norman Dr EX15 . . . . 163 C5
Normandy Cl EX8 . . . . 196 E1
Normandy Hill PL5. . . . . . 243 B2
Normandy Ho 10 EX32. . 155 A5
Normandy Rd EX1. . . . . . 177 F6
Norman Lockyer
Observatory*
. . . . 188 D5
Norman Mews EX2. . . . . . 178 D4
Norman Pl EX2 . . . . 178 D4
Norman Rd TQ3. . . . . 226 C7
Normans Cleave EX35. . . 151 B5
Norman Terr EX39 . . . . . 157 A7
Norns La TQ6. . . . . 145 F6
NORRIS GREEN. 125 B8
Norsworthy's Grave EX17. 97 E8
NORTHAM. 157 A4
Northam Burrows Ctry Pk*
EX39 . . . . 14 E1
Northam Ho EX39. . . . . . . 156 F6
Northampton Cl PL5 . . . . 244 B5
Northam Rd EX39 . . . . . . 156 F3
Northams Mdw EX20 . . . 170 A4
North Ave
Bideford EX39 . . . . 157 D1
Exeter EX1. . . . . 177 E6
Lyme Regis DT7 . . . . 260 D4
NORTHAY
Axminster 88 G3
Chard. 69 E6
Northay Cross EX13 . . . . . 88 H3
Northay La
Axminster EX13 . . . . 88 G3
Northay TA20 . . . . 69 E6
Northbeer Cross EX17. . . 96 A8
Northbeer La EX17 . . . . . . 95 F8
North Boundary Rd TQ5. 230 B5
NORTH BOVEY. 111 E2
NORTH BRENTOR. 117 C8
North Bridge Pl EX4 . . . . 261 A3
Northbrook Cl EX4 . . . . . 174 A1
Northbrook Swimming Pool
EX4 . . . . 174 B1
NORTH BUCKLAND. 8 C3
North Buckland Hill EX33. . 8 C3
North Castle Mews 8
TQ9 . . . . 223 C6
Northclose Rd EX18. . . . . . 59 D2
North Combe Cross EX16. 48 A3
Northcombe La TA22. . . . . 33 E7
North Combe Rd EX14. . . . 86 C2
North Coombe La EX16. . . 47 A3
Northcote Cross EX37. . . . 43 E4
North Coombe Rd EX14. . 167 F7
Northcote La
Colebrooke EX17. . . . . . . 166 B6
Pennymoor EX16. . . . . 62 F8
Northcote Rd EX14. . . . . . 166 E7
NORTHCOTT. 90 A3
Northcott Gdns EX39 . . . 157 A7
Northcott Terr 8 EX39. . 164 C4
North Courts The 4 PL1 262 A3
North Cross PL1 . . . . 262 C4
Northdene EX39 . . . . 156 F4
North Devon Cottage Rd
EX16. . . . . 161 B5
North Devon District Hospl
EX31. . . . . 155 A8
North Devon Farm Pk*
. . . . 17 D1
North Devon L Ctr EX31. . 154 F4
North Devon Maritime Mus*
EX39. . . . . 15 A1
North Dimson Cotts
PL18. . . . . 125 C6
North Down Cres PL2 . . . 247 F6
North Down Cross EX17 . . 79 B1
Northdown Dr EX39. . . . . 156 F3
North Down Gdns PL2. . . 247 F6
Northdown La EX36 . . . . . 45 F6
Northdown Rd
Bideford EX39 . . . . 156 F2
Cadbury EX5 . . . . 81 F7
North Down Rd
Braunton EX33. . . . . 152 E6
North East St EX39 . . . . . 157 A7
North Emb TQ6 . . . . 233 F4
NORTH END. 51 E3
North End Cl TQ12 . . . . . 207 E2
Northenhay 7 TQ12. . . . . 207 C3
Northenhay Pl EX4 . . . . . 261 B3
Northenhay Sq EX4 . . . . . 261 A3
Northenhay St EX4. . . . . . 261 A3
Northern La
Branscombe EX12. . . . . . . 190 B5
Sidmouth EX10 . . . . 189 E8
Northesk St PL2 . . . . 248 A4
Northfield EX13. . . . . 103 D5
Northfield La EX31. . . . . . 154 F7
Northfield Pk EX31. . . . . . 154 F7
Northfield Rd
Bideford EX39 . . . . 157 C1
Georgeham EX33. . . . . 8 B2
Ilfracombe EX34 . . . . 150 B6
Okehampton EX20 . . . . . . 170 B5
Northfields La
Brixham TQ5 . . . . 230 B4
Brixham TQ5 . . . . 230 B5
Northfield Terr 1 EX34. 150 B6
North Ford Rd TQ6. . . . . . 233 F3
North Furzeham Rd TQ5. 230 C6

North Garron 3 EX32. . . 155 B5
Northgate EX39 . . . . 22 D3
North Gate Ct EX4 . . . . . . 261 A3
Northgate La EX14 . . . . . . 86 A3
North Gn 8 EX22 . . . . 155 B4
North Grange EX2 . . . . . . 178 D3
Northground La EX10 . . . 101 D1
North Hayne Cross EX36. . 31 B4
North Heasley Cross EX36 19 C4
NORTH HEASLEY 19 D4
North Hill Cl TQ5. . . . . . . 230 B5
North Hill La
Morchard Bishop EX17 . . . 61 B3
Stockland EX14 . . . . 86 F8
North Hill Terr PL4. . . . . 263 A4
NORTH HUISH. 138 B7
North Huish Cross TQ10. 138 B8
North Jaycroft EX15. . . . 162 D5
North La
Ashford EX31. . . . . 16 A6
Barnstaple, Bickington
EX31. . . . . 154 A4
Challacombe EX31, TA24. . 12 B4
Middle Marwood EX31. . . . . 9 B3
Whiddon EX31. . . . . 9 C1
Northland Cir EX31. . . . . . 11 D2
Northland Cross EX36 . . . 19 A1
North Lawn Ct EX1 . . . . . 177 F6
Northleat Ave TQ3 . . . . . 225 E5
NORTHLEIGH. 102 B7
Northleigh Cross
Cheltham EX2. . . . . 17 C6
Northleigh EX24. . . . . 102 B7
Northleigh Hill Rd
Honiton EX14 . . . . 166 E3
Offwell EX14 . . . . 86 A1
Northleigh Rd EX24 . . . . 102 D6
NORTHLEW. 74 E1
North Lew PL16 . . . . 91 E4
North Lodge CE EX7 . . . . 204 C5
NORTH MOLTON. 30 D8
North Molton Cross EX36. 30 D8
North Molton Sch EX36. . 30 D8
NORTHMOOR 38 C3
North Moor Cross EX22 . . 38 C3
Northmoor Rd TQ22 . . . . . 33 D7
North Morte Rd EX34. . . . . 7 F8
Northmostown EX7 . . . . . 187 B7
Northmostown Cir EX10 . 187 A7
Northolt Ave PL5 . . . . 243 D4
North Park Almshouses
EX2. . . . . 261 C2
North Park Cnr TQ9 . . . . 139 C6
North Park Rd
Exeter EX4 . . . . 173 B1
Tedburn St Mary EX6. . . . . 97 F4
North Park Villas PL2 . . . 242 C4
NORTH PROSPECT. 248 A6
North Prospect Rd PL2. . 248 A6
NORTH RADWORTHY 19 F5
North Rd
Barnstaple EX31 . . . . 155 A7
Bideford EX39 . . . . 157 A2
Bradworthy EX22. . . . . 38 E1
Hartland EX39 . . . . 22 D3
High Bickington EX37 . . . . 43 B7
Okehampton EX20 . . . . . . 170 C7
Lee Mill PL21. . . . . 136 C7
Lifton PL16. . . . . 105 F4
Okehampton EX20 . . . . . . 170 C7
Saltash PL12 . . . . 242 F3
South Molton EX36 . . . . . 158 C5
Torpoint PL11 . . . . 247 B3
Yelverton PL20. . . . . 126 F3
Northridge Cross EX5 . . . . 98 E7
Northridge La EX5 . . . . . . 98 E7
North Road E PL4 . . . . . . 262 C4
North Road W PL1 . . . . . . 262 B4
North Rocks Rd TQ4 . . . . 229 C7
Northside TA21 . . . . 160 B5
North St
Ashburton TQ13 . . . . 130 F5
Axminster EX13 . . . . 167 D6
Braunton EX33. . . . . 152 D6
Braunton EX33. . . . . 152 D6
Chagford TQ13 . . . . 111 A6
Crediton EX17 . . . . 165 C5
Denbury TQ12 . . . . 211 A7
Dolton EX19 . . . . 57 F7
Exeter EX4. . . . . 261 A3
Exeter, Heavitree EX1 . . . 177 F6
Exmouth EX8 . . . . 202 A7
Hartland EX39 . . . . 22 D3
Ipplepen TQ12 . . . . 211 D2
Ottery St Mary EX11 . . . . 169 D3
North Tawton EX20 . . . . . . 77 C4
Okehampton EX20 . . . . . . 170 B5
Ottery St Mary EX11 . . . . 169 E4
Plymouth PL4. . . . . 263 A3
Sheepwash EX21. . . . . 56 C6
South Molton EX36 . . . . . 158 C5
Tavistock PL19 . . . . 171 C5
Topsham EX3 . . . . 182 F4
2 Totnes TQ9 . . . . 223 C6
Wellington TA21. . . . . 160 D6
Winkleigh EX19 . . . . 58 F2
NORTH STAR. 198 F8
NORTH TAMERTON. 89 C8
NORTH TAWTON. 77 C5
North Tawton Prim Sch
EX20. . . . . 77 C4
North Terr EX31 . . . . 154 A4
North Thorne La EX31 . . . 11 A4
NORTH TOWN 96 E4

Northumberland Pl
TQ14. . . . . 210 B4
Northumberland St PL5 . 247 E8
Northumberland Terr
PL1. . . . . 262 B1
North Upton Barns TQ7 . 143 B3
North View EX21. . . . . 55 E4
North View Ave EX39 . . . 156 F3
North View Hill EX39 . . . 156 F3
Northview Rd EX9. . . . . . 203 F8
North View Rd TQ5. . . . . . 230 D5
North Villas 2 EX20. . . . . 170 B6
Northville Pk TQ7 . . . . . . 258 C6
Northville Rd TQ7 . . . . . . 258 C6
North Walk Hill EX35. . . 151 C6
NORTHWAY. 24 D2
Northways La PL21. . . . . . 137 D7
North Weald Gdns PL5 . . 243 E5
NORTH WHILBOROUGH . . 212 E2
North Wlk
Barnstaple EX31 . . . . 154 F5
Lynton EX35. . . . . 151 B6
Northwood Cross EX17 . . 61 B3
Northwood La
Buckfast TQ11 . . . . 236 C8
Buckland Brewer EX39 . . . 40 C7
Morchard Bishop EX17 . . . 61 B3
Northwoods TQ13. . . . . . . 180 C4
North Wyke Cotts EX20. . 77 B1
NORTON
Dartmouth 233 A2
Hartland. 22 E4
Norton Ave PL4 . . . . 263 C4
Norton Cross TQ6. . . . . . . 233 A3
Norton Pk TQ6 . . . . 233 A3
Norton Pl EX8 . . . . 202 E8
Nortons Cross EX5. . . . . . . 81 A2
Norton View TQ6 . . . . . . 233 C3
Norwich Ave PL5. . . . . . . 244 B5
Norwich Cl EX8 . . . . 196 D4
Norwich Rd EX4 . . . . 176 F6
Norwood Ave EX2 . . . . . . 261 C1
Norwood Ho EX4. . . . . . . 261 B4
Norwood Rd EX16. . . . . . 161 D6
NOSS MAYO. 140 F6
Notre Dame Cl PL6. . . . . 244 F5
Notre Dame Ho PL1. . . . . 262 B3
Notre Dame RC Sch PL6. 244 F5
Notte St PL1 . . . . 262 C2
Nottiston Cross EX31. . . . 16 A1
Novorossisk Rd PL6. . . . . 245 E2
Nower Rd EX3. . . . . 87 C3
Nowers La TA21 . . . . 160 C3
Nuffield Health Plymouth
Hospl PL6. . . . . 245 B4
Nuffield Health Plymouth
Hospl (private) EX2. . . . . 177 E4
Nurseries Cl
Exton EX3. . . . . 183 C1
Topsham EX3 . . . . 182 E6
Nursery Cl
Exmouth EX8 . . . . 202 C8
Paignton TQ3 . . . . 226 A5
Plymouth PL5. . . . . 244 B6
Nursery End EX11. . . . . . 154 F7
Nursery Mews EX8. . . . . . 202 C8
Nursery Rd TQ12. . . . . . . 207 E2
Nursey Cl EX16 . . . . 49 B2
Nutaberry Hill EX39 . . . . 157 B1
Nutaberry Yd EX39 . . . . . 157 B1
Nutbrook EX8 . . . . 196 B1
Nut Bush Cnr TQ2 . . . . . 219 B7
Nut Bush La TQ2 . . . . . . 219 C6
Nutcombe Hill EX34. . . . . . 3 C2
Nuthatch Cl TQ2 . . . . 213 E2
Nuthatch Dr TQ2. . . . . . . 213 E2
Nuttaberry Bglws EX39. . . 24 F4
Nut Tree Ct TQ5 . . . . 230 B2
Nut Tree Orch TQ5. . . . . . 230 B2
Nutwell Rd EX8 . . . . 195 E7
Nymet Ave EX17 . . . . 78 C4
Nymet Bridge Cross EX17 60 B4
NYMET ROWLAND 60 B3
NYMET TRACEY. 78 B3
Nymet Villas EX37. . . . . . . 44 E6
Nymetwood Cross EX6 . . . 96 D8
Nymphayes La EX17. . . . . 78 C8
Nynehead Rd TA21 . . . . . 160 F8

O

Oakapple Cl PL7 . . . . 250 B7
Oak Apple Cl PL12 . . . . . 242 D4
Oakbank TQ13 . . . . 180 C4
Oak Cl
Dulford EX15 . . . . 84 B8
Exeter EX4. . . . . 174 E1
Exminster EX6. . . . . 182 A4
Kingsteignton TQ12 . . . . . 207 F6
Ottery St Mary EX11 . . . . 169 D3
Shillingford Abbot EX2. . . 181 A6
Silverton EX5 . . . . 82 C6
Tavistock PL19 . . . . 161 D5
Oak Cottage Cross EX22 . 7 E4
Oak Cres EX15 . . . . 162 C4
Oakcroft Rd PL2 . . . . 248 B6
Oak Cross
Bondleigh EX18 . . . . 77 D8
Inwardleigh EX20 . . . . 75 C1
Oak Ct
Holsworthy EX22. . . . . . . 164 C5
Lee Mill PL21. . . . . 136 D6
Oakdale Ave EX32. . . . . . . 17 E1
Oakdene Cl EX6 . . . . 114 F1
Oakdene Rise PL9. . . . . . 255 F6
Oak Dr
Cullompton EX15 . . . . 163 C5

Oak Dr continued
Plymouth PL6. . . . . 244 F3
Oak End Ct TQ3. . . . . 218 D2
Oaken Ground TA21. . . . . 160 B5
Oaken Hill
Great Torrington EX31. . . . 42 E8
Yarnscombe EX31 . . . . 27 D1
Oakery Cres PL20 . . . . . . 128 B8
Oakey Orch PL17. . . . . . . 125 A4
Oakfield Cl PL7 . . . . 251 C6
Oakfield Pk TA21 . . . . . . 160 E4
Oakfield Pl PL4 . . . . 249 B1
Oakfield Rd
Exeter EX4. . . . . 177 A5
Hatherleigh EX20. . . . . 75 C7
Plymouth PL7. . . . . 250 C6
Oakfields EX16. . . . . 161 D6
Oakfield St EX1. . . . . 177 F5
Oakfield Terr EX39 . . . . . 157 A7
Oakfield Terrace Rd PL4 249 B1
OAKFORD. 48 C8
Oakford TQ12 . . . . 207 D7
OAKFORDBRIDGE. 48 D8
Oakford Cl EX36 . . . . 30 D8
Oakford Cross
Kingsteignton TQ12 . . . . . 207 D7
North Molton EX36 . . . . . . 30 C8
Oakford Villas EX36. . . . . 30 D8
Oak Gdns PL21. . . . . 237 E5
Oakham Rd PL5. . . . . 244 B5
Oakhayes Rd EX5 . . . . . . 184 B3
Oakhayes Rd EX36. . . . . . 158 D4
Oak Hill
Budleigh Salterton EX9 . . 198 C6
Dawlish EX7. . . . . 204 C5
East Budleigh EX9 . . . . . . 198 B6
Oak Hill Cross Rd
Dawlish EX7. . . . . 204 C4
Teignmouth TQ14. . . . . . . 210 D8
Oak Hill Rd TQ1 . . . . 219 F6
Oakhill Rise 3 EX31 . . . 154 C3
Oak La
East Anstey TA22 . . . . 32 E6
Stockleigh Pomeroy EX17 . 81 A4
Whitstone EX22 . . . . 70 E1
Oakland Ave EX31. . . . . . 154 D4
Oakland Dr EX7. . . . . 204 D5
Oakland Park S EX31. . . 154 B4
Oakland Rd TQ12 . . . . . . 207 F2
Oaklands
Bideford EX39 . . . . 25 D4
Petrockstow EX20 . . . . 56 F4
Tavistock PL19. . . . . 171 D2
Oaklands Cl
Buckfastleigh TQ11 . . . . . 236 A5
Plymouth PL6. . . . . 245 C7
Seaton EX12 . . . . 192 A8
Oaklands Ct EX31 . . . . . . 154 D4
Oaklands Dr
Okehampton EX20. . . . . . 170 B6
Saltash PL12 . . . . 242 C3
Oaklands Gdns EX31 . . . 154 D4
Oaklands Gn PL12. . . . . . 242 D3
Oaklands Park Specl Sch
EX7 . . . . 204 C5
Oaklands Pk
Buckfastleigh TQ11 . . . . . 236 A5
Okehampton EX20 . . . . . . 170 A5
Oaklands Rd TQ11 . . . . . 236 A6
Oakland Wlk EX7 . . . . . . 204 D5
Oak Lawn TQ12 . . . . 207 C2
Oaklawn Ct TQ1 . . . . 219 F7
Oaklawn Terr TQ1. . . . . . 219 F7
Oaklea
Honiton EX14 . . . . 166 B6
Tiverton EX16 . . . . 161 D6
Oaklea Cl TQ7 . . . . 258 C4
Oaklea Cres EX31 . . . . . . 153 D5
Oakleaf Cl EX21. . . . . 73 E2
Oakleaf Way EX32 . . . . . . 17 F4
Oaklea Pk TQ12 . . . . 123 A1
Oakleigh EX15 . . . . 66 F3
Oakleigh Rd
Barnstaple EX32 . . . . 155 A4
Exmouth EX8 . . . . 202 B7
Oakley Cl
Exeter EX1. . . . . 174 E1
Teignmouth TQ14. . . . . . . 210 B2
Oakley Wlk EX5. . . . . 179 E3
Oak Mdw EX36. . . . . 158 B4
Oak Park Rd TQ12 . . . . . 219 D8
Oak Park Cl TQ2 . . . . 219 D8
Oakpark Cross PL21. . . . 137 E6
Oakpark La EX7 . . . . 124 E6
Oak Park Rd TQ12. . . . . . 206 F4
Oak Park Villas EX7. . . . . 204 F4
Oak Pl TQ12 . . . . 207 D3
Oak Rd
Exeter EX4. . . . . 176 F4
Okehampton EX20 . . . . . . 170 C6
Tavistock PL19. . . . . 171 C5
West Hill EX11. . . . . 168 C2
Oakridge TQ1. . . . . 220 C3
Oak Ridge
Exeter EX2. . . . . 181 A8
Lifton PL16. . . . . 105 E4
Oaks The
Bovey Tracey TQ13. . . . . . 180 E7
4 Hemyock EX15. . . . . . . 67 B8
Mary Tavy PL19 . . . . 117 E6
Yeoford EX17. . . . . 79 C1
Oaktree Cl
Broadclyst EX5 . . . . 175 D6
Exmouth EX8 . . . . 196 B3
Ivybridge PL21. . . . . 237 A5
Oak Tree Cl EX14 . . . . 68 C2
Oaktree Ct PL6 . . . . 244 F1

Oak Tree Dr
Barnstaple EX32 . . . . 155 E4
Newton Abbot TQ12 . . . . . . 212 F8
Oaktree Fishery★ EX36. . . 31 F4
Oak Tree Gdns EX34 . . . . 150 B5
Oak Tree Gr 8 TQ14 . . . . 210 A3
Oak Tree La PL19 . . . . . 171 C3
Oak Tree Pk
Plymouth PL6. . . . . 245 D6
Sticklepath EX20 . . . . 95 A5
Oak Tree Pl EX2 . . . . 181 C8
Oak Tree Villas EX10 . . . 186 B8
Oak Units EX17 . . . . 165 F5
Oak View EX14 . . . . 166 A3
Oakwell Cl EX38 . . . . 159 E5
Oakwood Cl
Barnstaple EX31 . . . . 154 C2
Dartmouth TQ6 . . . . 233 C3
Plymouth PL6. . . . . 245 D7
Oakwood Court Coll EX7 **204** E7
Oakwood Cross EX36. . . . 158 D4
Oakwood Dr PL21. . . . . . 137 B3
Oakwood Pk TQ7 . . . . 143 E7
Oakwood Rise PL6 . . . . 245 A6
Oakwood Rise EX8 . . . . . . 196 E3
Oakymead Pk TQ12 . . . . . 207 D6
OARE 6 E4
OAREFORD 6 F3
Oates Rd PL2 . . . . 248 B5
Oatlands Ave EX32 . . . . . 155 A1
Oatlands Dr TQ4 . . . . . . 226 A4
Oberon Rd EX1 . . . . 178 E7
Occombe Cross TQ3 . . . . 218 F3
Occombe Farm & Scadson
Woods Nature Reserve★
TQ3. . . . . 219 A3
Occombe Valley Rd TQ3 . 219 A2
Occombe Valley Woods
Nature Reserve★ TQ3 . . 218 F2
Ocean Pk PL1 . . . . 253 F8
Ocean Pk EX39 . . . . 156 B7
Ocean St PL2 . . . . 247 E6
Ocean View Cres TQ5 . . 230 A1
Ocean View Dr TQ5 . . . . 230 A1
Ochil Cl EX39 . . . . 26 A4
Ockington Cl EX20 . . . . . 170 D5
Ockment Ct EX20 . . . . . . 170 B5
Octagon St PL1 . . . . 262 B3
Octagon The PL1 . . . . 262 B2
Octon Gr TQ12 . . . . 219 E7
Odam Cross EX36. . . . . . . 45 E7
Odam Moor Cross EX36. . 45 E5
Oddicombe Beach Hill
TQ1 . . . . 220 D8
ODHAM 74 B5
Odle Hill TQ12 . . . . 212 A6
Odlehill Gr TQ12 . . . . 212 A6
Odun Pl 34 EX39 . . . . 15 A1
Odun Rd 32 EX39 . . . . 15 A1
Odun Terr 38 EX39 . . . . . 15 A1
OFFWELL 86 B2
Offwell CE Prim Sch EX14 86 B2
Offwell Turn EX14. . . . . . 102 B8
Ogwell Cross TQ12 . . . . . 207 A1
Ogwell End Dr TQ12. . . . 206 F2
Ogwell Mill Rd TQ12 . . . 206 F1
Ogwell Rd EX2 . . . . 179 C2
Oilmill Cross EX5 . . . . . . 179 C2
Oilmill La
Clyst St George EX3 . . . . . 183 D8
Clyst St Mary EX5 . . . . . . 179 C1
Okefield Ave EX17 . . . . . 165 C6
Okefield Rd EX17 . . . . . . 165 C6
Okefield Ridge EX17 . . . 165 C6
OKEHAMPTON 170 A6
Okehampton Bsns Ctr
EX20 . . . . 170 F5
Okehampton Castle★
EX20 . . . . 170 A3
Okehampton Cl PL7 . . . . 251 B4
Okehampton Coll EX20 . . 170 B4
Okehampton Com Hospl
EX20 . . . . 170 C6
Okehampton Pl 8 EX4 . . 177 A5
Okehampton Prim Sch
EX20 . . . . 170 B5
Okehampton Rd EX4 . . . . 177 A5
Okehampton St EX4. . . . . 177 A5
Okehampton Sta EX20 . . . 170 B5
Okehampton Way PL21. . 237 D4
OKEMOOR PARK 170 D7
Oketor Cl EX20 . . . . 170 D5
Oke Tor Cl TQ3 . . . . 219 A2
Okewill Cross EX31 . . . . . 10 A2
Okewood Ct EX8 . . . . 202 B5
Olands Rd TA21 . . . . 160 D6
OLCHARD 123 F3
Olchard La TQ12, TQ13 . . 124 A4
Old Abbey Ct EX2 . . . . . . 177 E2
Oldaway La EX5 . . . . 172 C7
Oldaway Tongue TQ7 . . . 143 E1
Old Bakery Cl EX14. . . . . 176 F7
Old Bakery Cotts PL8. . . 257 F4
Old Bakery The EX8 . . . . 202 B8
Old Barn Cl
Stoke Canon EX5 . . . . 173 F8
Winkleigh EX19 . . . . 58 E2
Old Barnstaple Rd
Bideford, East-t-w EX39 . . 157 C2
Braunton EX31. . . . . 15 F7
Ilfracombe EX34 . . . . 150 D2
Old Beer Rd EX12 . . . . . . 191 E6
Old Bell Hill EX14 . . . . . 103 D8
Oldberry La TA22 . . . . 33 D6
Old Berrynarbor Rd
EX34. . . . . 150 F5

Old Bideford Rd EX31 . . . 154 C2
Old Blundell's★ EX16 . . . 161 D3
OLDBOROUGH 61 B1
Oldborough Cross EX17 . . 61 B1
Oldborough La EX17 . . . . . 61 B1
Old Bridge Rd EX15 . . . . . 83 F6
Old Bridwell EX15 . . . . . . 65 F7
Old Butterleigh Rd EX5. . 82 B6
Old Bystock Dr EX8 . . . . 196 E3
Old Canal Cl EX23 . . . . . . 70 A6
Old Chapel Gdns EX19. . . 58 F3
Old Chapel Way PL10. . . 252 F6
Old Chard Rd EX14. . . . . . 86 C6
Old Cider Press The 3
TQ4 . . . . 226 B5
Old Cider Works La
TQ12 . . . . 212 A7
Old Cider Works The
TQ12 . . . . 212 A7
Old Coach Rd EX5. . . . . . 175 C6
Old Coastguard Cotts
PL9. . . . . 140 C7
Old Coastguard Sta
EX12. . . . . 192 D5
Old Coast Rd EX34 . . . . 2 E4
Old Cooperage The EX2 . 177 F5
Old Dairy The PL3. . . . . . 249 B6
Old Dawlish Rd EX8 . . . . 181 C2
Old Ebford La EX3 . . . . . 183 C4
Old Exeter Rd EX14. . . . . 164 C3
Oldenburg Pk TQ3 . . . . . 226 C7
Old English Ind Est PL20 127 B3
Old Exeter Rd TQ13 . . . . 123 B6
Old Farm Bglws EX10 . . . 188 B7
Old Farm Rd PL5. . . . . . . 247 C8
Old Farm Way EX7 . . . . . 204 D4
Old Ferry Rd PL12. . . . . . 243 A3
Oldfields EX8. . . . . 202 C6
Old Fire Sta The TQ13 . . 110 F6
Old Fore St EX10 . . . . . . 188 B3
Old Foundry The PL19 . . 171 D6
Old Gatehouse Rd EX7 . . 204 F7
Old George St PL1 . . . . . 262 C2
Old Greystone Hill PL15,
PL19. . . . . 115 D6
Oldham Rd EX20 . . . . 75 B7
Old Hayes 3 EX10 . . . . . 188 A4
Old Hazard Cotts TQ9 . . 135 F2
Old Hill
Bickington TQ12. . . . . 131 D7
Cullompton EX15 . . . . 163 D2
Old Home Farm DT7 . . . . 193 E6
Oldhouse La TQ12 . . . . . . 142 E7
Old Ide La EX2 . . . . 176 E2
Old Inn Mews EX38. . . . . 159 D5
Old Jaycroft EX15. . . . . . 162 D4
Old Laira Rd PL3. . . . . . . 249 C4
Oldlands Cl PL6 . . . . 245 B6
Old Launceston Rd PL19. 171 B6
Old Laundry The PL1. . . . 262 A3
Old Liverton Rd TQ12. . . 180 D1
Old Lyme Hill DT6 . . . . . 104 F4
Old Lyme Rd DT6 . . . . . . 104 F4
Old Manor Cl TQ13 . . . . 130 E5
Old Manor Rd 21 EX4 . . 176 F7
Old Manor Gdns EX24 . . 103 B3
Old Market Cl EX2 . . . . . 177 B3
Old Market Rd EX39 . . . . . 38 F8
Old Market Field EX16 . . . 46 E1
Old Market Field Ind Est
EX16. . . . . 46 E1
Old Matford La EX6, EX2 . 181 E6
Old Mill Cl EX2 . . . . 261 C1
Old Mill Ct PL7. . . . . 250 B7
Old Mill Ind Est EX15. . . 173 E7
Old Mill La TQ6 . . . . 233 C4
Old Mill Rd TQ2. . . . . 219 E4
Old Mill The
Culmstock EX15. . . . . 66 E8
Harbertonford TQ9 . . . . . . 139 B8
Old Mine La PL18 . . . . . . 125 B6
Old Mkt The 15 EX16 . . . . 67 B8
Old Newton Rd
Bovey Tracey TQ13. . . . . . 180 E4
Kingskerswell TQ12. . . . . 212 E5
Old Nursery Dr EX4 . . . . 178 B8
Old Orchard TQ13 . . . . . . 180 D7
Old Orchard Cl EX23 . . . . . 70 A6
Old Orchard The EX7 . . . . 74 E2
Old Paignton La TQ2 . . . 219 D2
Old Paignton Rd TQ2 . . . 219 D3
Old Park Rd
Exeter EX4 . . . . 261 B4
Plymouth PL3 . . . . 248 D6
Old Pavilion Cl EX2 . . . . . 177 E6
Old Pinn La EX1 . . . . 174 E1
Old Plymouth Rd PL3. . . 249 E5
Old Post Office Mews 19
EX39. . . . . 157 A2
Old Printworks The TQ1 . 220 B4
Old Priory PL7. . . . . 250 D5
Old Priory Jun Sch PL7 . 250 D5
Old Quarry Rd PL7 . . . . . 126 D3
Old Quay La 8 EX39. . . . . 15 B1
Old Quay St TQ14 . . . . . . 210 B4
Old Rd
Brixton PL8 . . . . 257 A5
Galmpton TQ5 . . . . 229 C7
Harbertonford TQ9 . . . . . 139 C7
Lutton PL21. . . . . 133 B2
Okehampton EX20 . . . . . . 170 A4
Stoke Fleming TQ6 . . . . . 146 B7

Old Rd *continued*
Tiverton EX16 . . . . 161 E4
Old Rectory Cl EX39. . . . . 15 C2
Old Rectory Cross TQ13 . 110 C7
Old Rectory Gdns
Morchard Bishop EX17 . . . 61 B2
Thurlestone TQ7 . . . . 143 A2
Old Rectory La
Ashwater EX21. . . . . 90 E6
Bratton Fleming EX31 . . . . 18 A8
Oldridge Rd EX4 . . . . 98 B6
Oldridge View EX6. . . . . . 97 F5
Old Rydon Cl EX2 . . . . . . 178 E2
Old Rydon La EX2 . . . . . . 178 E2
Old Rydon Ley EX2. . . . . 178 D2
Old Saddlery The 18
EX14. . . . . 166 C6
Old Sawmills Ind Est The
EX10. . . . . 186 C4
Old Sawmills The EX37. . . 28 B1
Old School Cl EX16 . . . . . 161 B4
Old School Ct
6 Hemyock EX15 . . . . . . 67 B8
6 Honiton EX14 . . . . . . 166 C6
Topsham EX3 . . . . 182 F5
Old School Ho The
Cawsand PL10. . . . . 253 A1
North Tawton EX20 . . . . . . 77 C4
Old School La EX31 . . . . 153 E5
Old School Rd
Barnstaple EX32 . . . . 155 C2
Plymouth PL5. . . . . 247 C8
Old School The 21 EX16 . 161 D4
Oldshute La EX22 . . . . 33 C7
Old Sidmouth Rd EX4 . . . 103 A4
Old Smithy Cotts EX39 . . . 37 B4
Old Stables The
14 Bideford EX39 . . . . . 157 A1
Clyst St Mary EX5 . . . . . . 179 A1
Old Station Rd
Barnstaple EX32 . . . . 155 B4
Horrabridge PL20. . . . . . . 126 F4
Old Station The PL20. . . . 126 E4
Old Sticklepath Hill
EX31. . . . . 154 E3
Old Stone Cl EX39 . . . . . . 156 B6
Oldstone Cross TQ9 . . . . 139 F2
Old's View EX4 . . . . 177 A7
Old Tannery Bsns Pk The 4
PL4. . . . . 263 A4
Old Tannery The EX32 . . . 28 D8
Old Teignmouth Rd EX7 . 204 D4
Old Tinhay PL16 . . . . 105 F4
Old Tiverton Rd
Bampton EX16. . . . . 34 C1
Crediton EX17. . . . . 165 E6
Exeter EX4 . . . . 177 D8
Old Torquay Rd TQ3. . . . 226 C8
Old Totnes Rd
Ashburton TQ13 . . . . 130 F4
Buckfastleigh TQ11 . . . . . 236 C5
Newton Abbot TQ12. . . . . 207 A1
Old Town EX39 . . . . 157 A1
Old Town Cl TQ13 . . . .
TQ13 . . . . 122 C2
Old Town Park Nature
Reserve★ EX20 . . . . 170 A3
Old Town St
Dawlish EX7. . . . . 204 D6
Plymouth PL1 . . . . 262 C3
Old Vicarage Cl EX2. . . . 176 D1
Old Vicarage Gdn DT7. . . 260 D3
Old Vicarage Rd EX2 . . . 177 A4
Old Vicarage The
Sidmouth EX10 . . . . 187 F3
Wellington TA21. . . . . 160 E6
Old Walls Hill TQ14 . . . . 124 D1
Old Warleigh La PL5 . . . 244 B7
Oldway TQ13 . . . . 123 E6
Old Way
Chipstable TA4. . . . . 35 D6
Chudleigh TQ13 . . . . 123 E6
Oldway Ho TA21 . . . . 160 F4
Oldway Mansion★ TQ3 . 226 A7
Oldway Pk TA21 . . . . 160 F4
Oldway Prim Sch TQ3 . . 226 B7
Oldway Rd
East Anstey TA22 . . . . 32 F5
Paignton TQ3 . . . . 226 B8
Wellington TA21. . . . . 160 E4
OLDWAYS END. 32 C2
Old Weighbridge The 10
EX8 . . . . 202 A6
Old Wharf The PL9 . . . . . 255 C7
Old Widdicombe Rd TQ3 225 D6
Old Widdicombe La TQ3 . 225 C7
Old Woodlands Rd PL5. . 244 D3
Old Woods Hill TQ2. . . . . 219 E7
Old Woods Trad Est TQ2 219 E8
Olga Terr EX8 . . . . 195 F5
Olive Gdns EX7. . . . . 201 B2
Olive Gr EX7. . . . . 201 A2
Olivia Ct PL4. . . . . 263 B4
Omaha Dr EX2 . . . . 178 D1
Omega Ctr The EX2 . . . . 178 C5
One End St 4 EX39 . . . . . . 15 A1
One Fir EX15. . . . . 83 C4
Onslow Rd
Plymouth PL2 . . . . 248 C7
Salcombe TQ8 . . . . 259 D5
Ora Cl EX33 . . . . 7 E2
Ora La EX33 . . . . 7 E2
Orange Gr TQ2 . . . . 214 A2

Orange Moor Cross EX18. . 44 F3
Orangery The EX6 . . . . . . 181 F5
Ora Stone Pk EX33 . . . . 7 E1
Orbec Ave TQ12. . . . . 207 F7
Orchard Ave PL6 . . . . 249 B7
Orchard Cl
Ashprington TQ9 . . . . 139 E7
Barnstaple EX31 . . . . 154 C3
Beesands TQ7 . . . . 149 D7
Braunton EX33. . . . . 152 C6
8 Brixham TQ5 . . . . 230 C3
10 Chudleigh TQ13 . . . . . 123 F6
Coldridge EX18 . . . . 59 C4
Colyford EX24 . . . . 103 B3
3 Combe Martin EX34. . . . 3 A3
Dawlish EX7. . . . . 204 D6
Denbury TQ12 . . . . 211 A6
East Budleigh EX9 . . . . . . 198 B6
East Ogwell TQ12. . . . . . . 206 D1
Exeter EX1 . . . . 174 F1
Exmouth EX8. . . . . 196 B1
Exmouth, Littleham EX8. . 203 A6
Frogmore TQ7 . . . . 144 E1
Galmpton TQ5 . . . . 229 C5
Kingsteignton, Sandygate
TQ12 . . . . 123 E2
Kingsteignton TQ12 . . . . . 207 F7
Lympstone EX8 . . . . 195 E5
Newton Poppleford EX10 . 186 D8
Okehampton EX20 . . . . . . 170 B4
Ottery St Mary EX11 . . . . 169 E3
3 Plymouth PL7 . . . . . . 251 C5
Rockwell Green TA21. . . . 160 A5
Sandford EX17. . . . . 80 A5
Shaldon TQ14 . . . . 209 D5
Sidford EX10 . . . . 188 C8
Sidmouth EX10 . . . . 187 F3
St Giles on t H PL15 . . . . . 90 C1
Talaton EX5 . . . . 84 A2
Tavistock PL19 . . . . 126 A8
Uffculme EX15 . . . . 66 A7
Upton Pyne EX5 . . . . 173 A7
Whitford EX13 . . . . 103 B6
Wilmington EX14. . . . . 86 C2
Woodbury EX5 . . . . 184 C3
Yealmpton PL8. . . . . 257 F3
Orchard Cotts
Holbeton PL8. . . . . 136 D1
Lamerton PL19 . . . . 116 F3
Newton Tracey EX31 . . . . . 27 A6
Orchard Cres PL9 . . . . . . 255 C7
Orchard Cross EX17 . . . . . 60 D3
Orchard Ct
5 Crediton EX17 . . . . . . 165 C5
Exeter EX1 . . . . 178 E6
Ivybridge PL21 . . . . 237 B5
Lamerton PL19 . . . . 116 E3
22 Newton Abbot TQ12 . . 207 B3
Newton St Cyres EX5. . . . . 81 A3
North Tawton EX20 . . . . . . 77 C4
Wellington TA21. . . . . 160 E6
3 Whimple EX5 . . . . 99 E8
Orchard Dr
Ipplepen TQ12 . . . . 211 D2
Kingskerswell TQ12 . . . . . 212 E5
Tiverton EX16 . . . . 161 E7
Orchard Farm EX14 . . . . . 85 A3
Orchard Gate EX19. . . . . . 57 F7
Orchard Gdns
Bideford EX39 . . . . 157 A4
Broadclyst EX5 . . . . 175 D6
15 Dawlish EX7 . . . . 204 D6
Exeter EX4 . . . . 176 F8
10 Teignmouth TQ14 . . . 210 C4
West Buckland TA21 . . . . . 52 F7
Orchard Gr
Brixham TQ5 . . . . 230 C3
Croyde EX33 . . . . 7 E1
ORCHARD HILL. 157 A4
Orchard Hill
Bideford EX39 . . . . 157 A4
Exeter EX2 . . . . 176 F3
Yealmpton PL8. . . . . 136 B3
Orchard Ho
8 Chudleigh TQ13 . . . . . 123 E6
1 Teignmouth TQ14 . . . 210 C4
Torquay TQ1. . . . . 220 A5
Orchard Ind Est's North &
South TQ7 . . . . 258 C5
Orchard La
Plymouth PL7. . . . . 250 E6
Silverton EX5 . . . . 82 E6
Starcross EX6 . . . . 201 A4
Orchard Leigh EX16 . . . . 161 C3
Orchard Mdw TQ13 . . . . . 111 A6
Orchardon La EX33. . . . . . . 8 B1
Orchard Pk
Dartington TQ9 . . . . 222 F8
Dittisham TQ6 . . . . 228 C3
Ivybridge PL21 . . . . 237 C4
Orchard Pl 3 TQ1 . . . . . . 220 A5
Orchard Rd
Ashburton TQ13 . . . . 130 F4
Barnstaple EX32 . . . . 155 B3
Knowle EX33 . . . . 8 D1
Plymouth PL2. . . . . 248 B7
4 Torquay, Ellacombe
TQ1 . . . . 220 B6
Torquay, Hele TQ2 . . . . . 213 F1
Wrafton EX33 . . . . 152 E3
Orchard Rise EX7 . . . . . . 204 A4
Orchardside EX10 . . . . . . 188 B7
Orchard Side EX10 . . . . . 101 C3
Orchards The
Galmpton TQ5 . . . . 229 B5
Landkey EX32 . . . . 17 B2
Swimbridge EX32. . . . . . . 28 E8

Orchard Terr
Abbotskerswell TQ12. . . . 212 B7
Barnstaple EX32 . . . . 155 B2
3 Bovey Tracey TQ13 . . 180 D8
Buckfastleigh TQ11 . . . . . 236 B5
Chagford TQ13. . . . . 111 A6
Crediton EX17 . . . . 165 B5
Kingskerswell TQ12 . . . . 212 F5
Kingswear TQ6 . . . . 234 B3
Totnes TQ9 . . . . 223 C5
Tuckenhay TQ9 . . . . 139 F6
Orchard The
Abbotskerswell TQ12. . . . 212 B6
Avonwick TQ10 . . . . 135 B1
Barnstaple EX31 . . . . 154 A3
Bishopsteignton TQ14 . . . 208 F8
Dunsford EX6. . . . . 112 F7
Gunnislake PL18 . . . . 125 D6
Holcombe EX7 . . . . 210 E8
Holywell Lake TA21. . . . . . 51 E7
Kilmington EX13 . . . . 87 D1
Modbury PL21 . . . . 137 C2
Seaton EX12 . . . . 192 B7
Tipton St John EX10 . . . . 100 D2
Totnes TQ9 . . . . 223 C5
Whiddon Down EX20 . . . . 95 C1
Yealmpton PL8. . . . . 257 F3
Orchardton Terr 2 PL9 . 255 F5
Orchard Vale Com Sch
EX32. . . . . 155 A4
Orchard View
Frogmore TQ7 . . . . 144 E1
Halberton EX16 . . . . 65 B7
Orchard Way
1 Bovey Tracey TQ13 . . 180 D8
Chillington TQ7 . . . . 145 A1
Cullompton EX15 . . . . 163 B2
Honiton EX14 . . . . 166 D6
Kenton EX6 . . . . 194 D3
Lapford EX17 . . . . 60 D3
Stoke Gabriel TQ9 . . . . . . 227 F8
Tiverton EX16 . . . . 161 B3
Topsham EX3 . . . . 182 E5
Uffculme EX15. . . . . 66 A7
Willand EX15 . . . . 162 D4
Orchard Waye TQ9 . . . . . 223 B5
Orchid Ave
Ivybridge PL21 . . . . 237 A6
Kingsteignton TQ12 . . . . . 207 E7
Orchid Cl 7 EX36 . . . . . . 161 F6
Orchid Ho EX4 . . . . 176 E8
Orchid Vale 14 TQ12 . . . 123 F1
Orcombe Ct EX8 . . . . 202 D8
Ordnance St PL1. . . . . . . 247 E2
Ordulf Rd PL19 . . . . 171 A5
Oregon Way PL3 . . . . 249 D6
ORESTON 255 C7
Oreston Com Prim Sch
PL9. . . . . 255 C7
Oreston Cross TQ2. . . . . 213 D3
Oreston Dr TQ1. . . . . 214 C6
Oreston La TQ2, TQ12. . . 213 C3
Oreston Rd PL9 . . . . 255 C8
Orient Rd TQ3 . . . . 226 D8
Oriole Dr EX4 . . . . 173 D1
Orkney Cl TQ2 . . . . 213 E2
Orkney Mews EX16. . . . . 161 D6
Orleigh Ave TQ12 . . . . . . 207 B5
Orleigh Ct EX39 . . . . 25 C1
Orleigh Pk TQ12 . . . . 207 B5
Orley Rd TQ12 . . . . 211 B2
Ormonde Ct EX36 . . . . . . 158 D4
Orpington Ct PL6. . . . . 65 B7
Orstone Cross EX32 . . . . . 18 E3
Orway Ash Cross EX15 . . . 66 B2
Orway Cross EX15. . . . . . . 66 C1
Orwell Garth EX4 . . . . . . 178 C8
Osborn Rd TQ3 . . . . 219 A2
Osborn Cl TQ12 . . . . 211 D2
Osborne Cl EX39. . . . . . . 156 C2
Osborne Ct PL1. . . . . 262 C2
Osborne La 4 EX39 . . . . 156 C2
Osborne Pl PL1 . . . . 262 C2
Osborne Rd
Ilfracombe EX34 . . . . 150 A5
Plymouth PL3. . . . . 248 A3
Osborne St TQ12 . . . . . . 207 D3
Osborne Villas 2 PL3 . . 248 A3
Osborn Rd TQ3 . . . . 154 F4
Osmond Lodge TQ4 . . . . 226 C5
Osmond's La 12 TQ14 . . 210 B4
Osney Ave TQ4 . . . . 226 B4
Osney Cres TQ4 . . . . 226 B4
Osney Gdns TQ4 . . . . 226 B4
Osprey Dr TQ2. . . . . 213 D3
Osprey Gdns PL9 . . . . . . 256 C7
Osprey Ho TQ1 . . . . 220 D7
Osprey Rd EX2 . . . . 178 F6
OSSABOROUGH. 8 B6
Ossaborough La EX34 . . . . 8 B5
Oswald Browning Way 4
EX31. . . . . 155 A7
Otterbourne Ct EX9 . . . . 198 B1
Otter Cl
Okehampton EX20 . . . . . . 170 D6
Tipton St John EX10 . . . . 100 D3
Torquay TQ2. . . . . 219 C2
West Hill EX11. . . . . 168 D4
Otter Ct
Bickington TQ12 . . . . 131 F8
Budleigh Salterton EX9 . . 198 C1
Exeter EX2 . . . . 181 C8
Otter Estuary Reserve★
EX9 . . . . 198 D1

Otterhead Lake Nature
 Reserve★ TA3 .... 68 E8
Otter Rd TQ2 .... 219 C7
Otter Reach EX10 ...... 186 F8
Otters The EX16 .... 49 B2
OTTERTON 198 F7
Otterton CE Prim Sch
 EX9 .... 198 E7
Otterton Mews EX13 .. 167 F7
Otterton Mill★ EX9 .. 198 D7
Otter Vale CE EX14 .... 68 C1
Ottervale Rd EX9 ...... 198 C1
Otter Valley Pk EX14 . 166 F8
Otter Way EX32 .... 155 D4
OTTERY 116 E2
Ottery Cotts PL19 ..... 116 E2
Ottery La EX10 .... 101 A1
Ottery Moor La EX14 . 166 A6
Ottery Park Ind Est PL19 116 E2
OTTERY ST MARY 169 E3
Ottery St Mary Hospl
 EX11 .... 169 C3
Ottery St Mary L Ctr
 EX11 .... 169 B3
Ottery St Mary Prim Sch
 EX11 .... 169 E3
Ottery St EX9 .... 198 F8
Our Lady & St Patrick's RC
 Prim Sch TQ14 .... 210 A6
Our Lady's RC Prim Sch
 EX32 .... 155 B5
Outer Down PL19 ...... 116 E3
OUTER HOPE 147 C7
Outer Ting Tong EX9 . 197 B3
Outland Rd PL2 .... 248 C7
Oval Gn EX2 .... 178 C3
Overbeck's Mus & Gdn★
 TQ8 .... 259 B1
Overbrook EX7 .... 204 D6
Overcliff Ct EX7 .... 204 E7
Overclose TQ3 .... 225 F8
Overcott La EX36 ...... 46 D8
Overdale Cl TQ2 .... 213 F4
Overdale Rd PL2 .... 248 A7
Overgang TQ5 .... 230 D5
Overgang Rd TQ5 ..... 230 C6
Overland Ct EX4 ...... 174 E2
Overlangs TQ7 .... 142 C6
Overseas Est TQ6 ..... 146 B6
Overton Cl DT7 .... 260 E5
Overton Gdns ⬛ PL3 . 248 F5
Owen Dr PL7 .... 250 C7
Owen St TA21 .... 160 C6
Owlaborough La EX36 . 32 B2
Owlacombe Cross TQ12 . 131 A7
Oxenham Cross EX20 .. 95 C5
Oxenham Gn TQ2 ..... 219 D6
Oxenpark Gate EX6 ... 112 F5
Oxenpark La
 Ilfracombe, Goosewell
  EX34 .... 2 C3
 Ilfracombe, Two Pots EX34 .. 2 C2
 Morchard Bishop EX17 .. 61 C1
 Stockleigh Pomeroy EX17 . 80 F7
Oxford Ave PL3 .... 248 E5
Oxford Cl EX8 .... 196 E4
Oxford Cross EX33 ..... 8 A3
Oxford Ct TQ2 .... 213 F1
Oxford Gdn PL3 .... 248 E5
Oxford Gr EX34 .... 150 B6
Oxford La TQ5 .... 230 A4
Oxford Pk EX34 .... 150 B5
Oxford Pl PL1 .... 262 C3
Oxford Rd EX4 .... 261 C4
Oxford St
 Dartmouth TQ6 .... 233 F3
 Exeter EX2 .... 177 A4
 Plymouth PL1 .... 262 B3
Oxford Terr
 Crediton EX17 .... 165 D5
 ⬛ Plymouth PL1 ..... 262 B3
 Sandford EX17 .... 80 A5
Oxham Cross EX36 .... 45 D8
Ox Hill La EX24 .... 102 F4
Oxlea Cl TQ1 .... 220 E4
Oxlea Rd TQ1 .... 220 E4
Oxman's Cotts EX39 .. 157 E6
Oxmead EX5 .... 99 D3
Oxmon's La EX39 ..... 157 A7
Oxton Ho EX6 .... 114 E1
Oyster Bend TQ4 ..... 226 C2
Oystercatcher Ct ⬛
 TQ14 .... 210 A3
Oyster Ct TQ4 .... 226 C2
Ozone Terr DT7 ...... 260 D2

P

Paccombe Pool La EX10. 189 C7
Pacehayne La
 Dalwood EX13 .... 87 A1
 Shute EX13 .... 103 A8
Packhall La TQ5 ...... 230 A2
Packhorse Cl EX10 ... 188 D8
Packington St PL2 ... 248 A4
Packs Cl TQ9 .... 139 C7
Padacre Rd TQ2 ..... 214 A4
Paddock Cl
 Plymouth PL9 .... 255 E5
 Saltash PL12 .... 242 D4
 Seaton EX12 .... 191 F7
Paddock Dr PL21 .... 237 D4
Paddocks The
 Abbotskerswell TQ12. 212 B7

Paddocks The continued
Dolton EX19 .... 57 F7
Honiton EX14 .... 166 A2
Membury EX13 .... 87 D6
Totnes TQ9 .... 223 D6
Wellington TA21 ...... 160 E5
Whimple EX5 .... 99 E7
Paddock The
Brixham TQ5 .... 230 B4
Dawlish EX7 .... 204 E7
Dulverton TA22 ...... 33 D6
Torquay TQ1 .... 214 B1
Paddons Coombe ⑨
 TQ12 .... 123 F1
Paddons La EX14 .... 210 A7
Paddons Row PL19 .. 171 C6
Pafford Ave TQ2 .... 214 B2
Pafford Cl TQ2 ..... 214 A2
Page Ho TQ4 .... 226 C6
Page's Cross EX16 . 62 F7
Paige Adams' Rd TQ9 . 223 B6
Paiges Farm PL9 ... 255 C1
Paiges La ⑦ EX31 .. 154 F5
PAIGNTON 226 D6
Paignton Com Coll ⑱
 TQ4 .... 226 B6
Paignton Com Coll Lower
 TQ4 .... 225 D4
Paignton Com Coll Upper
 TQ3 .... 225 E5
Paignton Hospl TQ3 .. 226 B6
Paignton Rd TQ9 ... 228 A8
Paignton Sta★ TQ4 . 226 B6
Paignton Sta TQ4 .. 226 B6
Paignton Zoological &
 Botanical Gdns★ TQ4 . 225 F4
Pail Pk EX33 .... 8 D1
Painsford Cross TQ9 . 139 D7
Painter's Cross EX13 . 102 F7
Painters Ct EX2 .... 261 A1
Painton Water EX39 .. 37 D8
Paizen La EX12 .... 191 B6
Palace Ave TQ3 ... 226 B6
Palace Cotts ⑩ EX8.. 202 A7
Palace Ct EB PL1 .. 263 A2
Palace Gate EX1 .. 261 B2
Palace La PL21 .... 137 B7
Palace Mdw TQ13 .. 123 E6
Palace Pl TQ3 ..... 226 B6
Palace St PL1 ..... 263 A2
Pale Gate Cl EX14 . 166 D7
Palegate Cross TQ7 . 258 A8
Palermo ⑫ TQ1 ... 220 D4
Palermo Rd TQ1 .. 220 C7
Palfrey's La EX16 .. 49 C5
Palk Cl TQ14 ...... 209 D5
Palk Gardens TQ12 . 130 C3
Palm Cl EX8 ...... 196 D3
Palm Cross ⓵ PL21 . 137 B2
Palm Ct EX7 ...... 201 A2
Palmer Ct EX9 .... 198 A1
Palmers Ct EX33 .. 152 D5
Palmers Ct EX38 .. 159 E5
Palmer's La EX5 .. 99 E5
Palmerston Dr EX4.. 176 E7
Palmerston Park Wood
 Nature Reserve EX5. 161 B2
Palmerston Pk EX16. 161 B2
Palmerston St PL1 . 262 A4
Palm Ho EX34 .... 176 E8
Palm Rd TQ2 ..... 220 A5
Palms The ⑨ TQ1. 220 D4
Pamela Rd EX1 ... 177 F7
PANCRASWEEK ... 71 B8
Pankhurst Cl EX8 . 202 E7
Panney The EX4 .. 178 A7
Pannier Mkt
 Great Torrington EX38... 159 D5
 Tavistock PL19 ...... 171 C5
Panorama TQ2 .... 219 E2
Panson Cross PL15. 90 B3
Papermakers La PL21 . 237 E6
Parade
Chudleigh TQ13 ... 123 E6
Exmouth EX8 ...... 202 A7
Plymouth PL1 ...... 263 A2
Parade Bsns Pk ⑭ PL19 . 171 B4
Parade Ope PL1 .. 263 A2
Parade Rd PL5 .... 244 A3
Parade The
 Chardstock EX13 ... 88 A7
 Millbrook PL10 ..... 252 E5
 Milton Abbot PL19 .. 116 A6
Paradise Glen TQ14 . 210 B6
Paradise Lawn EX36 . 158 D4
Paradise Pk EX22 .. 70 E1
Paradise Pl
 ⑪ Brixham TQ5 .... 230 D5
 Plymouth PL1 ...... 248 A2
Paradise Rd
 Plymouth PL1 ..... 248 A2
 Teignmouth TQ14 .. 210 C6
Parford Cross TQ9 . 139 A3
Paragon EX34 ..... 150 B6
Paramore Way EX36 . 158 C4
Parehayne La EX24. 102 E7
Parely Hill TQ13 .. 110 F6
Paris Rd TQ3 ...... 226 C8
Paris St EX1 ...... 261 B3
Park Ave
 Barnstaple EX31 ... 154 C4
 Bideford EX39 ..... 157 A3
 Brixham TQ5 ...... 230 B3
 Plymouth, Devonport PL1 . 247 E3
 Westward Ho! EX39. 156 C7
Park Bglws EX16 .. 51 B3

Park Cl
Clyst Hydon EX15 .... 83 D4
Fremington EX31 .... 153 E5
Holsworthy EX22 ... 164 C6
Ivybridge PL21 ..... 237 C5
Plymouth PL7 ...... 250 B7
Sidmouth EX10 ..... 82 C5
Tiverton EX16 ..... 161 D5
Woodbury EX5 .... 184 C2
Park Com Sch The EX32 . 155 A3
Park Cotts
Bigbury TQ7 .... 142 F5
Ugborough PL21 ... 137 D6
Park Cres
 Combe Martin EX34.. 3 A3
 Plymouth PL9 ..... 255 C7
Park Cross EX17 .. 62 C3
Park Ct
 Brixham TQ5 ..... 230 E5
 Chillaton PL16 ... 106 D1
 Honiton EX14 .... 85 C2
 Ilfracombe EX34 . 150 B4
Parkelands TQ13 . 180 C7
Parker Cl
 Plymouth PL7 .... 250 B5
 Tiverton EX16 ... 160 E6
Parker Rd
 Bigbury-on-S TQ7 .. 142 E3
 Plymouth PL2 .... 248 B6
Parkers Cl TQ9 ... 223 D4
Parkers Cross La EX14 . 174 F2
Parker's Gn PL18 . 125 C6
Parkers Hollow EX31 . 154 B3
Parker's Rd EX6 .. 201 A8
Parkers Way TQ9 . 223 D4
Parkesway PL12 .. 242 D2
Parkfield TQ7 .... 143 A2
Parkfield Cl
 Marldon TQ3 ..... 218 D3
 Totnes TQ9 ...... 223 F5
Parkfield Cross TQ13 . 131 A3
Parkfield Dr PL6 . 245 F1
Parkfield Rd
 Topsham EX3 ..... 182 F5
 Torquay TQ1 ..... 219 F7
Park Field Terr EX12 . 190 D4
Parkfield Way EX13 . 182 F5
Parkfield Wlk TQ7 . 143 A2
Park Five Bsns Ctr EX2 . 178 E4
Park Gate EX37 .. 28 D2
Park Gdns EX35 .. 151 B5
Park Hall TQ1 ... 220 B3
PARKHAM 39 E8
PARKHAM ASH ... 39 C7
Parkham Cl EX39.. 24 F1
Parkham Glade TQ5.. 230 C4
Parkham La TQ5 .. 230 C4
Parkham Prim Sch EX39 . 39 E8
Parkham Rd TQ5 . 230 C4
Parkham Terr ⑫ TQ5 . 230 C4
Parkham Twrs ⑥ TQ5 . 230 C4
Parkhayes EX5 ... 184 C7
Park Hill
Teignmouth TQ14.. 210 B5
Tiverton EX16 .... 161 C5
Parkhill Cotts PL21. 136 F4
Parkhill Ho TQ1 .. 211 F3
Parkhill Rd TQ1 .. 220 C3
Park Hill Rd EX34 . 150 B5
Park Hills Ind Units EX34.. 3 A3
Parkhouse Rd EX2 . 176 F2
Parkhurst Rd EX1.. 219 F7
Park La
 Barnstaple EX32 ... 155 A3
 ⑧ Bere Alston PL20.. 125 E1
 Bideford EX39 .... 157 A3
 Blackawton TQ7 .. 139 C1
 Budleigh Salterton EX9 . 197 F1
 Chittlehampton EX37 . 43 F8
 Combe Martin EX34.. 3 A3
 Combe St Nicholas TA20 . 69 F6
 Exeter EX4 .... 174 E2
 Exmouth EX8 .... 202 A8
 Filleigh EX32 ... 29 D7
 Madford EX14 ... 67 C4
 Otterton EX9 ... 198 E6
 Pennymoor EX16 . 62 D6
 Plymouth PL9 ... 255 C7
 Sparkwell PL7 .. 132 C1
 Torquay TQ1 ... 220 B3
 Wellington TA21. 160 C1
 Whitford EX13 .. 103 B6
Parkland Dr EX2 . 178 C3
Parklands
 Barnstaple EX31 . 154 C3
 ⑫ Hemyock EX15.. 67 B8
 Okehampton EX20 . 170 B3
 ⑧ Seaton EX12 .. 192 A7
 South Molton EX36 . 158 B3
 Totnes TQ9 ..... 223 C6
Parklands Cl EX36 . 158 B3
Parklands Rd TQ1. 160 D7
Parklands Way TQ13 . 180 C4
Park Lane Cotts EX32 . 29 D7
Park Lodge EX9 .. 197 F1
Park Mdw TQ13 .. 130 C3
Park Mews TQ5 .. 230 E5
Park Mill Cross EX17 . 59 F3
Park Mill La EX18 . 59 F8
Park Pl
 Exeter, Heavitree EX1.. 177 F6
 Exeter, Mount Radford
  EX2 .... 261 C2
 Winkleigh EX19 .. 58 F3
Park Place La ⑫ PL3.. 248 A4
Park Rd
 Beer EX12 .... 191 C5

Park Rd continued
Crediton EX17 ...... 165 D4
Dartington TQ9 .... 216 B2
Dawlish EX7 .... 204 D6
Exeter EX1 .... 177 E7
Exmouth EX8 ..... 202 A8
Hatherleigh EX20 . 75 C7
Kingskerswell TQ12 . 212 F5
Lapford EX17 .... 60 D3
Lifton PL16 ...... 105 E3
Plymouth PL3 .... 249 A6
Silverton EX5 .... 82 C5
St Dominick PL12 . 125 A2
Tiverton EX16 .... 161 D5
Torquay TQ1 .... 214 B1
Park Rise
Dawlish EX7 ..... 204 D4
Salcombe TQ8 ... 259 C4
Park Row EX20 ... 170 B5
Park School TQ9 . 216 C3
Parks Dr PL9 .... 256 A5
Parkside
Ivybridge PL21 .. 237 E5
Plymouth PL2 ... 247 F5
Salcombe TQ8 .. 259 D5
Parkside Cres EX1 . 174 F3
Parkside Ct EX2 . 261 B2
Parkside Dr EX8 . 196 E3
Parkside Rd
Exeter EX1 ..... 174 F3
Paignton TQ4 ... 226 C6
Parkside Villas TQ1 . 220 C7
Park St
Crediton EX17 .. 165 D5
Ivybridge PL21 . 237 C4
Lynton EX35 ... 151 B5
Plymouth PL3 .. 248 A4
Tiverton EX16 . 161 D5
Parkview EX17.. 80 A5
Park View
 Axminster EX13 .. 88 A3
 Beaford EX19 ... 42 D1
 Kenton EX6 ..... 194 F3
 Lifton PL16 .... 105 E4
 Newton Abbot TQ12 . 212 F8
 Plymouth PL4 ... 263 C3
 Pyworthy EX22 . 71 D5
 Shute EX13 .... 103 A7
Park View Cl EX34.. 3 A3
Park View Cotts EX38 . 42 B6
Park View Rd EX32 . 155 A6
Park View Terr
 Kingston TQ7 .... 142 C6
 Okehampton EX20 . 170 C3
 Westward Ho! EX39 . 156 C7
Park Villas EX32 . 27 E8
Parkway
Exeter EX2 ..... 176 F3
Ilfracombe EX34 . 150 B3
Park Way
Exmouth EX8 ... 202 C8
Woodbury EX5 . 184 C2
Parkway Ct PL6 . 249 E7
Parkway Ind Est The
 PL6 .... 249 E7
Parkway Rd TQ13 . 123 E6
Parkway The PL3, PL5,
 PL6 .... 244 B1
Parkwood Cl PL6 . 241 B2
Parkwood Ct PL19 . 171 D6
Parkwood Rd PL19 . 171 D6
Park Wood Rise PL16 . 105 E4
Parkyns Cross EX19 . 43 B4
Parliament Ct ⑨ EX34 . 150 B6
Parliament St EX17 . 165 C5
PARNACOTT ... 71 D8
Parnell Cl PL6 ... 249 A8
PARRACOMBE .. 4 C2
Parracombe La EX31.. 4 D2
Parracombe Lane Head
 EX31 .... 4 D2
Parracombe Parochial Prim
 Sch EX31 .... 4 C1
Parr Cl EX1 ...... 261 C4
Parricks La EX13 . 88 D3
Parr La PL4 ...... 263 B2
Parrocks La TA20 . 88 C8
Parr's La TQ13 .. 123 E6
Parr St
Exeter EX1 ..... 261 C4
Plymouth PL4 .. 263 B2
Parsonage Cross
Chulmleigh EX18 .. 44 F7
Dartington TQ9 . 215 F2
Germansweek EX21.. 91 D5
Staverton TQ9 . 216 E3
West Putford EX22 . 39 B2
Woodbury EX5 . 184 C3
Parsonage Ct PL16 . 105 E4
Parsonage Hill EX36 . 31 A3
Parsonage La
Awliscombe EX14.. 85 C1
George Nympton EX36 . 29 F2
Hittisleigh EX6 . 96 C6
Honiton EX14 .. 166 D5
Kentisbury EX31 . 10 E5
Morleigh TQ9 .. 139 A3

Parsonage La continued
Silverton EX5 .... 82 B6
South Molton EX36 . 158 C5
Staverton TQ9 ..... 216 E4
Ugborough PL21 .. 137 D6
Parsonage Lane Cross
 EX32 .... 18 B2
Parsonage Lane End
 PL21 .... 137 D6
Parsonage Rd EX13 . 141 A7
Parsonage St EX5 . 83 A7
Parsonage Way
Plymouth PL4 .... 263 B2
Whimple EX5 .... 184 C4
Parson Cl EX8 ... 196 C2
Parsons Cl
 ⑬ Holsworthy EX22 . 164 C4
 Newton Poppleford EX10 . 186 D8
 Plymouth PL9 ... 256 A4
Parson's Cl EX15.. 66 A3
Parson La PL10 .. 252 F6
Parsons La EX5 .. 99 B5
Parson St TQ14 . 210 B5
Parthia Pl EX8 .. 196 E1
Partridge Cross EX16 . 63 A8
Partridge Hill EX36.. 45 D7
Partridge La EX16 . 63 A8
Partridge Rd EX16 . 196 C2
Partwayes PL19 . 116 E3
Pasley St PL2 ... 247 E4
Pasley Street E PL2 . 247 F4
Passage Rd PL8 . 140 F6
Passmore Rd EX5 . 82 F6
Pasture Cross TQ9 . 144 F8
Pastures The EX20 . 92 A2
PATCHACOTT ... 74 B1
Patchacott Cross
 Bratton Clovelly EX21 . 92 A8
 Northlew EX21 .. 74 B1
Patchel Cross EX20 . 56 F7
Patches Rd EX16 . 161 B4
PATCHOLE 10 D5
Paternoster La TQ12 . 211 C2
Paternoster Row
⑧ Barnstaple EX31 . 154 F5
Ottery St Mary EX11 . 169 D4
Pathdown La EX33 . 7 F2
Pathfield EX38 ... 159 F5
Pathfield Cl
Barnstaple EX31 . 154 A3
Totnes TQ9 ..... 223 D5
Path Field Cl EX32 . 18 B2
Pathfield Lawn EX31 . 154 E6
Pathfields
Croyde EX33 .... 7 E2
Totnes TQ9 ..... 223 D5
Uffculme EX15 .. 66 A7
Pathfields Bsns Pk EX36 158 D6
Pathfields Rd EX31 . 154 E6
PATHFINDER VILLAGE . 98 C4
Path The ⑳ EX39.. 15 A1
Pathwhorlands EX10 . 188 A6
Patna Pl PL1 .... 262 B4
Pato Point PL11 .. 247 A5
Patricia Cl EX4 .. 173 C2
Pattard Cross EX39 . 22 D4
Patterdale Cl PL6 . 245 D3
Patterdale Wlk PL6 . 245 D3
Patterson's Cross EX11. 169 D8
Patteson Dr EX11 . 100 F8
Patteson Dr EX11 . 169 F4
Pattinson Cl PL6 . 245 E2
Pattinson Ct PL6 . 245 E2
Pattinson Dr PL6 . 245 E2
Paullet EX16 .... 50 C1
Paul St EX4 ..... 261 A3
Pauntley Gdn EX10 . 187 F3
Paviland Grange ⑥ PL1 . 248 A3
Pavilion Pl EX2 .. 261 A2
Pavilions Cl TQ5 . 230 B5
Pavilion Sh Ctr TQ2 . 220 B3
Pavington Cross EX37 . 43 E3
Pavor Rd TQ2 ... 214 B2
Paws Rd EX37 ... 43 B7
PAYHEMBURY ... 84 C4
Payhembury Prim Sch
 EX14 .... 84 C4
Payne Ct EX4 .... 178 B8
Payne's Cotts EX14.. 85 C3
Paynsford Mews TQ12. 207 B4
Paynsford Rd ⑴ TQ12. 207 B4
Paynter Wlk ⑤ PL7 . 251 B5
PAYTON 51 F7
Payton Rd
Holywell Lake TA21.. 51 F7
Rockwell Green TA21. 160 A5
Peacegate Cross EX20.. 76 E4
Peacehay La TA21.. 51 E4
Peacock Ave PL11.. 247 A3
Peacock Cl PL7 .. 250 F7
Peacock La PL4 .. 263 A2
Peacock Rd EX16 . 201 A8
Peadhill La EX16 . 49 D2
Peak Cnr EX16 .. 62 E7
Peak Cross TQ9 . 222 F3
Peakfield Cross Ways
EX5 .... 82 E6
Peak Hill Llamas★ EX10 187 C2
Peak Hill Rd EX10 . 187 E3
Peak Tor Ave TQ1 . 220 C4
Pear Dr EX15 .... 162 D4
Pear La PL6 ..... 64 D6
Peards Down Cl EX32 . 155 D4
Pearl Assurance Ho ⑵
 TQ12 .... 207 C3
Pearmain Cl EX15 . 162 D4
Pearn Cotts ⑵ PL3 . 248 E6

Pearn Gdns PL3...........249 A7
Pearn Rd PL3..............249 A7
Pearn Ridge PL3...........249 A7
Pearse Cl EX20...............75 B7
Pearson Ave **3** PL4....248 E3
Pearson Cl EX2............164 C5
Pearson Rd PL4............248 F4
Peartree Cross
  Ashburton TQ13...........130 E4
  Denbury TQ12.............211 A7
Pear Tree Way **3** EX32...17 B2
Peaseditch TQ13............230 D3
Peasland Rd TQ2...........214 A4
Peaslands Rd EX10.........188 A5
Peaspark Cross TQ7.......144 D3
Peazen Flats EX12.........191 C6
Pebble Cl PL9..............256 D7
Pebble Cl TQ4..............156 D7
Pebbleridge Rd EX39......156 E8
Pecorama Pleasure Gdns★
  EX12......................191 C5
Pedlerspool La EX17.......165 E7
Pedley La EX17..............61 B6
Peek La TQ12...............137 C8
Peek Mead DT7.............193 F7
Peek Moor Cross EX22......90 B4
Peeks Ave PL9..............255 F7
Peel Row **3** EX4.........178 C3
Peel St PL1.................248 A1
Peep La **4** EX17.........165 D5
Pegasus Ct
  Exeter EX1................177 F6
  Paignton TQ3.............226 B8
Pegwell La TQ4.............209 B3
Pelican Cl EX39............156 B6
Pellew Arc **3** TQ14.....210 B4
Pellew Ho **3** TQ14......210 B4
Pellew Pl PL2...............247 F4
Pellew Way TQ14...........210 A7
Pellinore Rd EX4...........174 A1
Pembrey Wlk PL1...........243 E4
Pembroke La PL1...........247 E1
Pembroke Lodge **15**
  EX34.....................150 B5
Pembroke Pk
  Paignton TQ3.............225 E2
  Torquay TQ1..............220 B5
Pembroke St PL1...........247 E1
Pemros Rd PL5.............243 C1
Pencair Ave PL11...........246 E2
Pencarwick Ho EX8.........202 A5
Pencepool Cotts EX15......83 F6
Pencepool Orch EX15........83 F6
Pencombe Rocks EX31.......4 C1
Pencrose Rd TQ2...........213 D7
Pencreber Rd **3** PL20...126 F4
Pencross View **1** EX15...67 B8
Pendarves TQ2.............222 D2
Pendeen Cl PL6.............244 F6
Pendeen Cres PL6..........245 A6
Pendeen Pk TQ7............145 A1
Pendennis Cl
  Plymouth PL3.............248 F8
  Torpoint PL11............246 F3
Pendennis Rd PL3..........219 F8
Pendilly Ave PL11...........246 F2
Pendragon Rd EX4.........174 A2
Penfield Gdns **1** EX7....204 D6
Pengelly Cl PL11...........246 D6
Pengelly Hill PL11..........247 A5
Pengelly Pk PL11...........246 F5
Pengelly Way TQ3..........213 F3
Pengilly Way EX39...........22 E3
PENHALE....................252 D7
Penhale Dr EX22...........252 D7
Penhayes Cl EX6...........194 E3
Penhayes Rd EX6...........194 E3
PENHILL......................16 A4
Penhill Chalets TQ6........146 B7
Penhill Cross EX6...........113 F5
Penhill La TQ5.............234 E8
Peninsula Medical Sch
  Exeter EX2................177 F5
  Plymouth PL6.............245 C3
Peninsular Pk PL12........242 C4
Penlee Cl EX9...............199 G3
Penlee Cotts PL10..........140 12
Penlee Gdns PL3............248 A4
Penlee Pk PL11.............246 D4
Penlee Pl **3** EX4.........248 F4
Penlee Rd PL3..............248 A4
Penlee Way PL3.............248 B4
Penleonard Cl EX2..........177 E5
PENN......................104 E6
Pennant Ho EX8............201 E6
Pennant Way PL21..........136 D6
Pennball Cross TQ9........217 B3
Penn Court TQ5.............230 D3
Penn Cross DT6.............260 F7
Pennine Dr TQ4.............225 D4
Pennington Cl EX17..........79 A5
Penn Inn Cl TQ12...........207 E2
Penn Ho TQ12..............207 E2
Penn La TQ5................230 D3
Penn Mdws TQ5............230 D3
Penn Meadows Cl TQ5.....230 D3
PENNSYLVANIA..............173 C1
Pennsylvania Cl EX4.......177 C8
Pennsylvania Cres EX4....177 C8
Pennsylvania Pk EX4......173 D1

Pennsylvania Rd
  Exeter EX4................173 C3
  Torquay TQ1..............220 B5
Penn Torr TQ8.............259 D4
Penn View TQ5.............230 D3
Pennyacre Rd TQ14........210 C6
Penny Cl
  Exminster EX6............182 A4
  Wellington TA21..........160 D7
PENNYCOMEQUICK.........262 B4
Pennycomequick Hill
  PL4.......................262 B4
PENNYCROSS...............248 C8
Pennycross Cl PL2..........248 C8
Pennycross Park Rd PL2...248 C7
Pennycross Prim Sch
  PL2.......................248 C8
PENNYMOOR..................62 D6
Penny Plot DT7............260 C4
Penny's Hill TQ1...........219 F7
Penny's La PL7..............258 D6
Penny's Terr EX13.........167 D5
Penny Thorn Cross EX14...88 D7
Pennywell Farm & Wildlife
  Ctr★ TQ11................115 E6
Penpethy Cl TQ5...........230 B4
Penpethy Rd TQ5..........230 B5
PENQUIT....................237 F1
Penrith Cl EX4.............245 D3
Penrith Gdns PL6..........245 D3
Penrith Wlk PL6...........245 D3
Penrose Almshouses **4**
  EX32.....................155 A4
Penrose St PL1.............248 C2
Penroses Terr **9** EX22..164 C4
Penrose Terr **7** EX2.....261 A2
Penrose Villas **5** PL4....248 F4
Penscombe Cross PL15....115 A6
Penshurst Rd TQ12........207 B1
Pensilva Pk TQ5............230 C2
Penson Cross EX20..........59 B1
Penson Rd EX20.............77 B8
PENSTONE....................62 D4
Penstone Barns EX5.........82 E4
Penswell Cross TQ11......135 E4
Pentamar St PL2............247 E4
Pentgrove Ct EX4...........202 D7
Pentice La EX34...............3 A3
Pentillie Cl **20** PL20....125 E1
Pentillie View **21** PL20...125 E1
Pentillie Rd
  Bere Alston PL20.........125 E1
  Plymouth PL4.............248 E4
Pentire Rd PL11............246 F3
Pentland Cl PL6............244 F7
Penton Cl EX17............165 D6
Penton La EX17............165 D5
Penton Rise EX17..........165 D6
Pentridge Ave TQ12.......219 C2
Pentyre Ct PL4.............263 C4
Pentyre Terr PL4...........263 C4
Penwill Way TQ4...........226 A4
Pen-y-dro EX15.............105 D8
Peoples Park Rd EX17.....165 C6
PEPPERCOMBE................24 E2
Pepperdon Hall La PL13...112 B3
Pepper La
  Kingswear TQ6...........234 E4
  Plymouth PL7.............256 D7
Pepper's Cnr EX9..........198 F7
Pepper St PL19.............171 C6
Peppery La TQ14...........209 D5
Pepys Pl PL5...............244 E1
Perceval Rd EX4............174 A2
Perches Cl PL8.............141 B7
Percy Cross EX14...........67 B2
Percy Rd EX7...............177 B3
Percy St PL5...............243 D1
Percy Terr PL4.............249 A4
Peregrine Cl TQ2...........213 D3
Perinville Cl TQ1...........220 E6
Perinville Rd TQ1..........220 D7
Periwinkle Dr
  Barnstaple EX31..........154 B3
  Plymouth PL7.............251 C5
Perkins Cross EX5..........99 C1
PERKIN'S VILLAGE..........99 C2
Perranporth Cl PL5........243 E4
Perriam's Pl EX9...........199 G2
Perridge Cl EX17............92 E6
Perridge Cross EX6.........98 E1
Perriman's Row EX8.......202 A7
Perriton Cross EX5..........99 E8
Perros Rd TQ14............209 D8
Perry Cl PL19..............171 B6
Perry Cross TQ12..........206 D7
Perry Hill EX17...............80 E8
Perry La
  Doddiscombsleigh EX6...113 D5
  Newton Abbot TQ12......206 D6
Perryman Cl PL7...........250 E7
Perryman's Hill EX17.......79 F7
Perry New Rd TA22..........33 F6
Perry Rd EX4...............177 B8
Perrys Gdns EX31..........168 D4
Perry St TA20...............88 D8
PERRY STREET...............88 D8
Perseverance Cotts **1**
  PL7.......................250 E7
Perth Cl EX4...............173 E2
Peryam Cres EX4..........178 A4
Peryn Rd PL19..............171 A5
Peterborough Rd EX4.....176 F2
Peterclose Rd EX16........161 F3

Peter Hopper's Hill PL5...240 C2
Peter's Cl PL9..............256 C7
Peters Cres TQ3...........218 D3
Petersfield Cl PL3..........249 B6
PETER'S FINGER.............105 B7
Peters Park Cl PL5.........243 E1
PETERS MARLAND............56 C8
Peters Park Cl PL5.........243 E1
Peter's St EX5...............82 F7
Peter's Well Hill EX1........61 E5
PETER TAVY..................117 F4
Petherbray Cross PL19....117 C3
Pethertons EX16.............65 A7
Pethick Cl PL6..............248 F6
Pethill Cl PL6..............245 F2
Pethybridge TQ13.........122 B8
Petitor Mews TQ1..........214 B1
Petitor Rd TQ1.............214 C1
Petit Well La TQ1..........214 B1
Petrel Cl TQ2...............213 C3
PETROC
  Barnstaple EX31..........154 E3
  Tiverton EX16............161 C6
Petroc Cl PL18.............125 A6
Petroc Dr TQ12............207 C4
PETROCKSTOW................56 F4
Petticoat La EX16..........167 A6
PETTON......................35 A3
Petton Cross EX16..........35 A3
PEVERELL....................248 D6
Peverell Park Rd PL3.......248 D5
Pew Tor Cl
  Tavistock PL19...........171 E5
  3 Yelverton PL20....126 F3
Phear Ave EX8..............202 B7
PHILHAM.....................22 D1
Philham Cross EX39........22 D1
Philham La EX39............22 D1
Philham Water EX39........22 D1
Philip Ave EX3.............154 D2
Philip Cl PL9...............256 A6
Philip Gdns PL9............255 F6
Philip Ho EX1...............178 E6
Philip Rd EX4...............177 F8
Philips La **2** EX33......153 D5
Phillimore St **3** PL2.....247 F4
Phillipps Ave EX8..........196 B1
Phillips Cl EX13............167 D5
Phillips Sq EX14...........166 B6
Phoenix Bsns Pk PL6......245 F4
Phoenix Ct PL12...........126 F4
Phoenix La EX16............161 D3
Phoenix Pl
  Kingsbridge TQ7..........258 C5
  West Alvington TQ7......258 B4
Phoenix Rd EX13...........161 D3
Phoenix St PL1.............262 A2
Piazza Terracina EX2......262 A2
Picket Head Hill EX7.......210 A2
Pick Pie Dr PL6............245 E8
Picton Pl EX2...............33 D6
Pidgeley Rd EX7...........204 F8
Pidgeon's La EX13.........104 B7
Pidland La EX16.............47 F1
Pidsley Hill EX17............79 F7
Pidsley La EX17.............79 F7
Piece Hill EX6...............97 E4
Piend La EX17...............62 B1
Pier Head EX8..............201 E6
Pier La PL10................253 A1
Piermont Pl EX7............204 E6
Pier St PL1..................262 B1
Piggy La EX39..............156 F7
Pig La EX13.................167 D6
Pigs Leg Cross EX20.......108 A8
Pigspark Cross TQ13......131 A5
Pike Rd PL3.................249 D5
Pikes Hill EX6...............97 E2
Pike's Mead EX20...........170 B4
Pilchers Field PL20.........126 E3
Pilemoor La EX16............48 E3
Pilemore Cross EX16........48 E4
Piley La TA21.................51 D8
Pilgrim Cl PL2..............248 B6
Pilgrim Ct **11** EX20.....125 E1
Pilgrim Dr PL20.............125 E1
Pilgrim Prim Sch PL1.....262 B3
Pilland Way EX31...........154 D6
Pillar Ave TQ5.............230 B5
Pillar Cl TQ5...............230 B5
Pillar Cres TQ5............230 B5
Pillar Ct TQ5...............230 B5
Pillar Flats TQ5............230 B5
Pillar Wlk PL6..............244 E7
Pillavins La EX36..........158 F6
Pill Gdns EX33.............152 D5
Pill Ho EX32................155 A2
Pilliven Cross EX16..........46 F2
Pilliven La EX16.............47 A2
Pill La
  Barnstaple EX31..........155 A2
  Saltash PL12..............242 E4
Pill Lawn EX32..............155 A2
Pillmere Dr PL12...........242 B3
Pillory Hill PL8.............140 F6
Pill Rd EX39................157 A2
Pilmuir Ave TQ2............219 E5
PILTON......................155 A4
Pilton Bluecoat CE Jun Sch
  EX31......................154 F6
Pilton Com Coll EX31......154 E7
Pilton Cswy EX32..........154 F6
Pilton Inf Sch EX31........154 F6
Pilton La EX1...............178 D8
Pilton Lawn EX31..........154 F6

Pilton Quay EX31...........154 F6
Pilton St EX31..............154 F6
Pimlico TQ1................220 B5
Pimm Rd TQ3..............225 E7
Pinaster Cl EX14..........166 E5
Pinbridge Mews EX4......174 D1
Pinbrook Ind Est EX4.....174 D1
Pinbrook Mews EX4........174 C2
Pinbrook Rd EX4...........174 D1
Pinbrook Units EX4........174 D1
Pinces Cotts EX2...........177 A3
Pinces Gdns EX2...........177 A3
Pinces Rd EX2..............177 A3
Pinch Hill EX23..............70 A7
Pincombe Cnr EX36........31 B3
Pinder Cl PL19.............171 B5
Pine Ave EX4...............176 F7
Pine Cl
  Brixham TQ5.............230 B2
  Ilfracombe EX34.........150 E4
  Teignmouth TQ14.......210 D7
  Tiverton EX16............161 C5
Pine Ct TQ1................220 D5
Pinefields Cl EX11..........168 E3
Pine Gdns EX14............166 C6
Pine Gr EX21...............166 D6
Pine Park Rd EX14.........166 C5
Pine Ridge DT7............260 E5
Pineridge Cl EX4...........176 F4
Pines Cl EX39................22 E3
Pines Rd
  Exmouth EX8.............196 D3
  Paignton TQ3.............225 F8
Pines The
  Exeter EX4................176 F7
  Honiton EX14.............166 D5
Pine Tree Cl PL7...........201 B2
Pine Tree PL18.............125 D6
Pine View Ave TQ1.........220 C6
Pine View Cl
  Exmouth EX8.............196 F2
  Halwill Junction EX21....73 E3
Pine View Gdns TQ1.......220 C6
Pine View Rd TQ1..........220 C6
Pine Wlk DT7...............260 D2
Pinewood Cl
  Dawlish EX7..............205 A8
  Plymouth PL7.............250 F6
Pinewood Ct TQ4..........226 C5
Pinewood Dr PL6...........245 E2
Pinewood Rd TQ1..........174 B2
Pinewood Rd TQ12........174 D1
PINHAY.....................104 B2
Pinhay Hollow DT7........104 B2
Pinhey's Cross TQ7........144 F5
PINHOE.....................174 F2
Pinhoe CE Prim Sch EX4..174 E1
Pinhoe Rd EX4.............174 C1
Pinhoe Sta EX1.............174 E1
Pinhoe Trad Est EX4......174 D1
Pinkhams Cotts PL12......242 B6
Pinksmoor La TA21..........51 E2
Pinkworthy Cross EX16....48 C8
Pinkworthy Hill EX16.......48 B7
Pinn La EX1.................263 A2
Pinnacle Quay PL4.........263 B2
Pinnbridge Ct EX1.........178 E8
Pinncourt La EX1...........174 F2
Pinnex Moor Rd EX16.....161 E6
Pinn Hill EX1...............174 F2
Pinn La
  Exeter EX1................178 F8
  Ottery St Mary EX11....187 B2
Pinn Lane Cnr EX10.......187 A1
Pinn Valley Rd EX1.........174 F1
Pinslow Cross PL15........105 B8
Pins Pk EX22...............164 C5
Pinwood La EX4............174 B1
Pinwood Meadow Dr
  EX4.......................174 B2
Pioneer Cotts EX2 **2**...191 D5
Pioneer Terr TQ11.........236 A5
Pipehouse La TQ13.........123 C4
Pipers Cross TQ7..........142 C7
Pipers Pl EX14.............68 C2
Pippin Cl EX13.............178 C6
Pippins EX12...............191 D5
Pippins Field EX15..........66 A7
Pippins The PL21..........237 A5
Piran Cl PL18..............125 A6
Pirates Bay Adventure Golf★
  TQ4......................230 B5
Piscombe La EX9..........198 F7
Pissleton La EX7............61 A1
Pitcairn Cres TQ2.........213 E3
Pitchingstone Cross
  TQ7......................147 C7
Pitcombe La EX34..........35 B5
Pitfield La EX15............162 D3
Pitham La EX15............169 F7
Pitt Hill EX3..................2 D4
Pitland Cnr EX19..........117 B4
Pitland La TQ13...........213 E6
Pitlands La EX15............67 A8
Pitley Cross TQ13.........131 A5
Pitley Rd TQ13.............131 B5
Pitman's La PL21...........133 C2
Pitsham La TA4..............34 F1
Pits La PL10................140 H2
Pitson La EX10.............187 A5
Pitt Ave **12** EX39.........15 A1
Pitt Cross EX39.............22 C4
Pitt Ct
  8 Appledore EX39....15 A1
  Loddiswell TQ7...........143 F7

Pitt Hill
  Appledore EX39..........157 B8
  Crediton EX17.............79 F3
  Kenton EX6...............194 D3
  Shebbear EX21............55 D4
Pitt Hill Rd TQ12..........206 F4
Pitt Ho TQ13...............123 D5
Pitt La
  Bideford EX39.............157 A2
  Bow EX17..................78 B5
  Butterleigh EX16..........64 C4
  Cadbury EX5...............81 C8
  Chevithorne EX16........49 D2
  Huish Champflower TA4...35 E8
  North Molton EX36........30 F8
  Thorverton EX5............81 F7
  Waterrow TA4.............35 F5
Pitton Cross EX6............96 E5
Pitts Cleave Ind Est
  PL19......................117 D3
Pitts Cnr EX2................63 D4
Pitts Ct EX2................261 C1
Pixey Palm EX36............31 B3
Pixie La EX33...............152 B7
Pixie Lane EX33............152 B7
Pixon La PL19..............171 B4
Pixon Trad Ctr **2** PL19..171 B4
Pixton Cross EX19..........58 B2
Pixton Way TA22............33 E6
Place Cross
  Ashburton TQ13..........131 A6
  Okehampton EX20.........93 E5
Place de Brest PL1.........262 C3
Place La TQ13..............131 A5
Plainfield La EX16..........63 C7
PLAINMOOR.................220 B7
Plainmoor Rd **3** TQ1....220 B7
Plainmoor (Torquay United
  FC) TQ1..................220 B7
Plains The TQ9.............223 D5
Plaistow Cl PL5............243 E2
Plaistow Cres PL5.........243 E2
Plaistow Hill Inf Sch PL5..243 E2
Plantagenet Dr EX15......163 C6
Plantagenet Wlk EX2.....178 D4
Plantation Cl PL12.........207 F1
Plantation Terr EX7.......204 E6
Plantation Way
  Torquay TQ2..............213 C2
  Totnes TQ9...............222 F6
Plantings Sch The PL3....248 E6
Plant World (Gdns)★
  TQ12......................213 C3
Plassey Cl EX4.............173 D2
Plaston Gn EX6.............112 D5
Platt Cl TQ8................259 B4
Plat The TQ6..............145 E5
Platway La EX3............209 D5
Play Cross TQ13............130 A4
Playmoor Cotts EX1.......174 E1
Playmoor Dr EX1...........174 F1
PLEAMORE CROSS..........160 A2
Pleasant Terr **1** TQ3....226 A6
Pleasure Hill Cl EX2........63 C8
Plintona View PL7..........250 E7
Ploudal Rd EX15...........163 B2
Plougastel Dr PL12.........242 F3
Plough Gn PL12.............242 C3
Ploughman Way PL8.......136 A2
Plover Rise PL21............237 B5
Plume of Feathers Cl
  EX11......................169 C4
Plumer Rd PL6..............244 F2
Plumper's Cross EX38......41 A7
Plumtree Dr EX2...........178 B4
Plumtree La EX5.............99 E7
Plum Way EX15..............162 D4
Plymbridge Gdns PL7......250 C7
Plymbridge La PL7..........250 B5
Plymbridge Rd
  Plymouth, Eggbuckland
    PL6.....................245 C1
  Plymouth, Estover PL6...245 E5
  Plymouth, Mainstone PL6.245 C2
  Plymouth, Plympton PL7...250 C7
Plym Cl TQ2................219 D2
Plym Cres PL19.............171 D5
PLYMOUTH..................262 C4
Plymouth Arts Ctr★ PL1..262 B2
Plymouth Athenaeum &
  Theatre★ PL1.............262 B2
Plymouth Business Sch
  PL4.......................263 A3
Plymouth City Airport
  PL6.......................245 C5
Plymouth City Mus & Art
  Gal★ PL4................263 A3
Plymouth Coll Inf Sch
  PL3.......................248 E5
Plymouth Coll of Art
  PL4.......................263 A3
Plymouth Coll Prep Sch
  PL1.......................262 A3
Plymouth Coll (Senior Sch)
  PL4.......................248 E4
Plymouth Discovery Ctr★
  PL3.......................249 F6
Plymouth Drake Prim Sch
  PL2.......................247 E6
Plymouth Eggbuckland Com
  Coll PL6..................249 A8
Plymouth Eggbuckland Vale
  Prim Sch PL6............249 A8
Plymouth Gin Distillery★
  PL4.......................263 A2

Plymouth Hill PL20 ... 128 A8
Plymouth Keyham Barton RC Prim Sch PL2 ... 247 E6
Plymouth Knowle Prim Sch PL5 ... 244 A4
Plymouth Lipson Vale Prim Sch PL4 ... 249 A4
Plymouth Medical & Tech Pk PL6 ... 245 A3
Plymouth Pavilions PL1 ... 262 B2
Plymouth Rd
 Buckfastleigh, Lower Dean TQ11 ... 236 A3
 Buckfastleigh TQ11 ... 236 B4
 Kingsbridge TQ7 ... 258 C6
 Plymouth PL7 ... 250 B6
 South Brent TQ10 ... 134 F2
 Tavistock PL19 ... 171 B4
 Totnes TQ9 ... 223 B5
Plymouth Road Ind Est PL19 ... 171 C3
Plymouth St Joseph's RC Prim Sch PL1 ... 247 E2
Plymouth St Paul's RC Prim Sch PL5 ... 243 D1
Plymouth Ski & Snowboard Ctr★ PL6 ... 249 E7
Plymouth Sta PL4 ... 262 C4
Plymouth Thornbury Prim Sch PL6 ... 245 D4
Plymouth Trade Pk PL4 ... 263 C1
Plymouth Whitleigh Prim Sch PL5 ... 244 D4
PLYMPTON ... 250 E5
Plympton Cross TQ7 ... 147 F5
Plympton Hill PL7 ... 250 F3
Plympton Hospl PL7 ... 250 D5
Plympton St Mary CE Inf Sch PL7 ... 250 D5
PLYMPTON ST MAURICE ... 250 E4
Plympton St Maurice Prim Sch PL7 ... 250 F3
Plym St PL4 ... 263 A3
PLYMSTOCK ... 255 E6
Plymstock Rd PL9 ... 255 D7
Plymstock Sch PL9 ... 255 F8
Plymstock Sp Ctr PL9 ... 255 F8
PLYMTREE ... 83 E5
Plymtree CE Prim Sch EX15 ... 83 F5
Plymtree Dr PL7 ... 250 C7
Plym Valley Rly★ PL7 ... 250 A7
Poadmarsh Cross EX36 ... 31 D1
Poadmarsh Hill
 Ash Mill EX36 ... 31 D1
 Bishops Nympton EX36 ... 30 F1
Pocklington Rise PL7 ... 250 E5
Pocombe Hill EX2 ... 176 D3
Pode Dr PL7 ... 251 B4
Pod La EX13 ... 87 F4
Point In View Cotts EX8 ... 196 B3
Point Terr EX8 ... 201 E6
POLEHAYS ... 74 B1
Polehouse La EX2 ... 176 E1
Pole Rue La TA20 ... 69 F6
Poles Hill EX31 ... 154 E7
Poleshill La EX31 ... 154 D7
Polhearne La TQ5 ... 230 B3
Polhearne Way TQ5 ... 230 B3
Pollard Cl
 Plymouth PL9 ... 255 B5
 Saltash PL12 ... 242 B2
Pollard's La TA21 ... 52 F7
Pollards Pl EX39 ... 157 C2
Pollards The EX32 ... 155 C3
Pollards Way PL12 ... 242 E3
Pollyblank Rd [2] TQ12 ... 207 B3
Pollybrook EX5 ... 184 C2
Polmer Mews EX9 ... 199 G2
Polruan Terr PL1 ... 262 A3
Polsham Pk TQ3 ... 226 B7
Polsloe Bridge Sta EX4 ... 178 A7
POLSLOE PARK ... 177 E7
POLSLOE PRIORY ... 177 F8
Polsloe Rd EX1 ... 177 E6
Polson Hill EX17 ... 61 A2
POLTIMORE ... 174 F6
Poltimore Cl EX36 ... 158 D4
Poltimore Cross EX4 ... 174 E6
Poltimore Ct EX4 ... 174 F7
Poltimore House★ EX4 ... 174 F5
Poltimore Lawn EX32 ... 155 B6
Poltimore Rd
 Farway EX24 ... 101 F7
 Offwell EX14, EX24 ... 102 A8
 South Molton EX36 ... 158 D4
Poltimore Sq EX4 ... 261 B4
Polwhele Rd [14] EX16 ... 64 D7
Polywell EX39 ... 14 F1
Polzeath Gdns PL2 ... 248 D8
Pomeroy Ave TQ5 ... 230 A5
Pomeroy Pl [8] TQ12 ... 122 F1
Pomeroy Rd
 Newton Abbot TQ12 ... 207 B3
 Tiverton EX16 ... 64 E8
POMPHLETT ... 255 E8
Pomphlett Cl PL9 ... 255 D8
Pomphlett Farm Ind Est PL9 ... 249 E1
Pomphlett Gdns PL9 ... 255 D8
Pomphlett Prim Sch PL9 ... 255 E8
Pomphlett Rd PL9 ... 255 E8
Pondfield Rd PL12 ... 242 B3
Pond Hill EX16 ... 65 A7
Pond La TA21 ... 51 D3
Ponsford Cross EX15 ... 65 A2
Ponsford La EX15 ... 65 A2
Ponsonby Rd PL3 ... 248 B4
PONSWORTHY ... 130 A8
Pooks La TQ13 ... 130 F5
Pool Anthony Dr EX16 ... 64 E8
Pool Cross EX20 ... 107 F8
POOLE ... 160 F8
Poole Cross TQ12 ... 211 A1
Poole Hill TA22 ... 33 B5
Poole Park Rd PL5 ... 247 C8
Poole's Ct DT7 ... 260 E3
Pooley Cross TQ7 ... 143 E4
Pool Hill
 Ashbrittle TA21 ... 35 E1
 Bridestowe EX20 ... 107 F8
Pool La
 Burrington EX37 ... 44 A4
 Chittlehampton EX37 ... 29 A1
 Woolacombe EX34 ... 1 B1
Poolmill Cross TQ13 ... 112 E1
Pool Pk TQ10 ... 135 A3
Pools Weir TQ12 ... 214 B8
Popes Cl EX17 ... 165 C6
Popes La EX24 ... 103 A3
Pope's La
 Lapford EX17 ... 60 C3
 Rockwell Green TA21 ... 160 B4
POPHAM ... 19 A3
Popham Cl EX16 ... 161 F4
Popham Cross EX36 ... 19 A3
Popham Flats TA21 ... 160 D6
Popham La EX36 ... 19 A3
Pop La EX13, TA20 ... 88 B8
Poplar Cl
 Brixham TQ5 ... 229 F2
 Exeter EX2 ... 177 A3
 Exmouth EX8 ... 196 D3
 Newton Abbot TQ12 ... 213 A8
 Plymouth PL7 ... 251 B5
Poplar Dr TQ7 ... 258 C5
Poplar Mount EX13 ... 167 D6
Poplar Row EX9 ... 199 H2
Poplars Dr TQ3 ... 218 D2
Poplars The
 [7] Chudleigh Knighton TQ13 ... 123 C4
 Exeter EX4 ... 174 E2
Poplars Wlk EX5 ... 179 E2
Poplar Terr
 High Bickington EX37 ... 43 C7
 Ipplepen TQ12 ... 211 D2
Poplar Tree Cnr EX12 ... 192 A8
Poplar Tree Dr EX12 ... 192 A7
Popplestone Pk PL8 ... 256 F5
Poppy Cl EX4 ... 176 D8
Popular EX7 ... 201 A2
Porch EX13 ... 88 A3
Porch Cotts [18] EX10 ... 101 B1
Pork Hill PL19 ... 117 F1
Porlock Way TQ4 ... 225 F2
Porsham Cl PL6 ... 241 B1
Porsham La PL5 ... 244 E8
Porspoder Pl PL10 ... 253 A2
Portal Pl PL21 ... 237 B5
Portbridge Cross TQ9 ... 215 F8
Portchester Hts EX4 ... 261 C4
Port Cross
 Bishops Nympton EX36 ... 31 B4
 Kentisbury EX31 ... 10 F5
Porteous Cl PL1 ... 247 F3
Porter's La EX8 ... 195 E8
Porter Way PL12 ... 242 C3
Portford Cross EX31 ... 27 E3
Portford La TQ10 ... 135 A2
PORTGATE ... 106 C4
Portgate Cross EX36 ... 30 B8
Port Hill EX31 ... 10 F5
PORTINGTON ... 116 C3
Port La
 Bishops Nympton EX36 ... 31 C4
 Bury TA22 ... 34 A5
 Chillington TQ7 ... 145 A1
 Wotter PL7 ... 132 C4
Portland Ave
 Exmouth EX8 ... 202 B6
 Teignmouth TQ14 ... 210 C7
Portland Bldgs [6] EX32 ... 155 A6
Portland Ct
 [19] Barnstaple EX32 ... 155 A4
 Lyme Regis DT7 ... 260 C3
 [9] Plymouth PL1 ... 247 F3
 Torquay TQ1 ... 220 D7
Portland La
 Kilmington EX13 ... 103 C8
 Meavy PL20 ... 127 D2
Portland Pk EX34 ... 150 C6
Portland Rd
 Plymouth PL1 ... 247 F3
 Torquay TQ1 ... 220 D7
Portland Sq PL4 ... 262 C4
Portland Square Lane N PL4 ... 263 A4
Portland St
 Barnstaple EX32 ... 155 B3
 Exeter EX1 ... 177 E6
 Ilfracombe EX34 ... 150 C6
Portland Villas PL4 ... 262 C4
Port Lane Cl TQ7 ... 144 F1
Portledge Pl EX39 ... 25 A3
Portlemore Cl TQ7 ... 147 E6
Portlemore Gdns TQ7 ... 147 E6
Portmarsh La EX32 ... 155 A4
Port Mer Cl EX8 ... 196 E3
Port Rd EX6 ... 200 D4
Portsmouth Arms Cross EX18 ... 60 B7
Portsmouth Arms Sta EX37 ... 43 F6
Portugal Way EX20 ... 170 D5
Portway EX15 ... 66 C7
Portway Cl PL9 ... 256 D7
POSBURY ... 97 F8
Possession Cross EX37 ... 28 E7
Post Box Cross
 Bondleigh EX20 ... 76 F6
 Cheriton Fitzpaine EX17 ... 63 B3
POSTBRIDGE ... 120 A6
Post Cl TA21 ... 160 E4
Post Cross EX15 ... 65 F2
Post Cross Bsns Pk EX15 ... 65 F2
Post Hill EX16 ... 64 E8
Post La
 Malmsmead EX35 ... 6 C4
 Skilgate TA4 ... 34 E7
Post Office La
 Cheriton Fitzpaine EX17 ... 62 F1
 Tatworth TA20 ... 88 C8
Potacre St EX38 ... 159 D5
Potems' Cross EX37 ... 27 F1
Potshop Cross EX17 ... 79 D2
Potters Cl EX11 ... 168 D5
Potter's Cross TA4 ... 35 C7
Potters Hill TQ1 ... 220 B5
Potters Stile EX14 ... 67 B1
Potters Way PL7 ... 250 D5
Potterswell EX31 ... 154 B3
Potters Yd TQ12 ... 180 B1
Pottery Cl
 Bovey Tracey TQ13 ... 180 C5
 Honiton EX14 ... 166 D6
Pottery Ct TQ6 ... 233 D4
Pottery Est PL10 ... 252 E6
Pottery La EX31 ... 153 A4
Pottery Mews TQ3 ... 218 D3
Pottery Rd
 Bovey Tracey TQ13 ... 180 C5
 Kingsteignton TQ12 ... 207 D6
 Plymouth PL1 ... 247 D3
Pottery Units TQ12 ... 207 D4
POTTINGTON ... 154 D6
Pottington Bsns Pk EX31 ... 154 C6
Pottington Dr EX31 ... 154 E6
Pottington Ind Est EX31 ... 154 D5
Pottington Rd EX31 ... 154 E6
Pottles Cl EX6 ... 182 B3
POUGHILL ... 62 D3
Poultney Cl PL7 ... 251 A5
Pouncers Cross EX18 ... 60 E6
Pound Cl
 Burrington EX37 ... 43 F3
 Exmouth EX8 ... 196 C1
 Sidbury EX10 ... 101 B2
 Topsham EX3 ... 182 E6
Pound Cnr
 Clyst Honiton EX5 ... 179 E7
 Whitestone EX4 ... 98 C5
Pound Cross EX5 ... 99 B5
Pound Down Cnr EX4 ... 98 D5
Pound Field TQ9 ... 227 F8
Poundfield Cl EX31 ... 153 F5
Pound Gate EX6 ... 112 F5
Pound Hill
 Axmouth EX12 ... 192 D7
 Holcombe Rogus TA21 ... 51 A5
Poundhouse Cross TQ6 ... 146 B8
Pound La
 Bridford EX6 ... 113 A5
 Buckland St Mary TA20 ... 69 D8
 Colaton Raleigh EX10 ... 186 C5
 [15] Combe Martin EX34 ... 3 A3
 Exmouth EX8 ... 196 C1
 High Bickington EX37 ... 43 C8
 Kingskerswell TQ12 ... 212 F4
 Nadderwater EX4 ... 98 F4
 Raymond's Hill DT6 ... 104 D8
 Shaldon TQ14 ... 209 C5
 Stoke Climsland PL17 ... 115 C1
 [5] Teignmouth TQ14 ... 210 C4
 Topsham EX3 ... 182 E6
 Uplyme DT7 ... 260 B5
 Upottery EX14 ... 68 C1
 Woodbury EX5 ... 184 C3
 Yarcombe EX14 ... 69 B2
Pound Lane End EX37 ... 43 D8
Pound Lane Trad Est EX8 ... 196 C1
Pound Mdw
 Great Torrington EX38 ... 42 B7
 Hatherleigh EX20 ... 75 C7
 Parkham EX39 ... 39 E8
Pound Pk EX20 ... 170 D6
Pound Pl
 Bovey Tracey TQ13 ... 180 D8
 [19] Newton Abbot TQ12 ... 207 B3
Pound Rd
 Axminster EX13 ... 88 F2
 Crapstone PL20 ... 126 E3
 Lyme Regis DT7 ... 260 D3
Poundsclose TA22 ... 33 E4
Pound's Cross PL6 ... 240 E5
POUNDSGATE ... 130 A7
Poundsgate Cl TQ5 ... 230 E4
Pounds Hill EX17 ... 165 D6
Poundshill Cross EX17 ... 165 D6
Poundsland EX5 ... 175 C6
Pounds Park Rd
 [1] Bere Alston PL20 ... 125 E1
 Plymouth PL3 ... 248 D7
Pounds Pk PL12 ... 242 F3
Pound Sq EX15 ... 163 C2
Pound St
 Exmouth EX8 ... 202 A6
 Lyme Regis DT7 ... 260 D3
Pound St *continued*
 Moretonhampstead TQ13 ... 111 F4
 Plymouth PL1 ... 254 A8
Poundstone Ct TQ8 ... 259 D4
Pound Terr [3] TA21 ... 160 D5
Poundwell Ho [8] PL21 ... 137 B2
Poundwell Mdws [7] PL21 ... 137 B2
Poundwell St [9] PL21 ... 137 B2
Powderham Castle★ EX6 ... 194 F4
Powderham Cl
 Newton Abbot TQ12 ... 207 B2
 Topsham EX3 ... 182 E6
Powderham Cres EX4 ... 177 D8
Powderham Ct
 [20] Newton Abbot TQ12 ... 207 B3
 [21] Teignmouth TQ14 ... 210 C4
Powderham Rd
 Exeter EX2 ... 177 A4
 Newton Abbot TQ12 ... 207 B2
 Plymouth PL3 ... 248 F7
 Torquay TQ2 ... 213 F1
Powderham Terr
 Newton Abbot TQ12 ... 207 B2
 Teignmouth TQ14 ... 210 C4
Powderham Wlk EX6 ... 181 F5
Powell Cl EX12 ... 192 A6
Powells Way EX14 ... 67 C1
Powis Gdns PL5 ... 244 B2
Powisland Dr PL6 ... 245 A5
Powlesland La EX17 ... 95 E6
Powlesland Rd EX4 ... 177 B1
Powys Ho EX10 ... 188 A4
Poyers EX33 ... 152 E4
Pratt's La TQ7 ... 143 B7
Precinct The TQ7 ... 258 D6
Premier Pl EX2 ... 261 C2
Prescot Rd EX4 ... 176 E5
PRESCOTT ... 51 C1
Prescott Rd EX15 ... 51 D1
Prestbury Ct EX4 ... 176 D8
Prestbury Pk [4] TQ2 ... 219 F5
PRESTON ... 226 B8
Preston Barns TQ9 ... 222 D1
Prestonbury Cl PL6 ... 245 B7
Preston Cross
 Loddiswell TQ7 ... 138 E3
 West Alvington TQ7 ... 143 E2
Preston Down Ave TQ3 ... 219 B2
Preston Down Rd
 Paignton TQ3 ... 219 B2
 Torquay TQ2 ... 219 C6
Preston Fork TQ9 ... 138 E2
Preston Gate EX31 ... 10 E6
Preston La EX17 ... 80 D7
Preston Prim Sch TQ2 ... 219 D2
Preston St EX1 ... 261 A2
Prestor EX13 ... 167 E5
Pretoria Rd EX1 ... 177 F7
Pretoria Terr EX34 ... 150 A3
Pretty Top
 Little Torrington EX20 ... 41 F1
 Petrockstow EX20 ... 56 F8
Prickly Ball Farm & Hedgehog Hospl★ TQ12 ... 211 F7
Priddis Cl EX8 ... 196 C3
Priddles La TA20 ... 69 F8
Prideaux Cl PL12 ... 242 C5
Prideaux Cres EX16 ... 161 D6
Prideaux Ct [22] PL1 ... 263 A2
Prideaux La TQ6 ... 145 F6
Prideaux Mdw EX38 ... 159 F5
Prideaux Rd PL21 ... 237 E6
Pridham La PL2 ... 248 D7
Pridhams Way EX6 ... 182 A4
PRIESTACOTT ... 55 C1
Priest Hill EX15 ... 66 A3
Priesthood Terr PL10 ... 252 E5
Priestley Ave
 Exeter EX4 ... 178 B8
 Plymouth PL5 ... 243 E2
Prigg Mdw TQ13 ... 130 F4
Primley Cross TQ3 ... 225 F5
Primley Ct TQ3 ... 225 E5
Primley Gdns EX10 ... 188 C7
Primley Mead EX10 ... 188 C7
Primley Paddock EX10 ... 188 B7
Primley Park E TQ3 ... 226 A5
Primley Pk TQ3 ... 225 F5
Primley Rd EX10 ... 188 B7
Primrose Ave EX32 ... 155 E4
Primrose Cl
 Chillington TQ7 ... 144 F1
 Ivybridge PL21 ... 237 D5
 Kingsteignton TQ12 ... 207 E7
 [6] Tiverton EX16 ... 161 F6
 Torpoint PL11 ... 246 E4
Primrose Gdns PL19 ... 171 E4
Primrose La EX39 ... 157 B8
Primrose Lawn EX4 ... 176 D8
Primrose Mdw PL21 ... 237 A6
Primrose Way
 Crediton EX17 ... 165 E6
 Kingskerswell TQ12 ... 212 F6
 Seaton EX12 ... 192 B7
Primrose Wlk PL12 ... 242 D4
Prince Charles Cl EX8 ... 196 E1
Prince Charles Ct TQ2 ... 214 A3
Prince Charles Rd EX4 ... 177 F8
Prince Charles Way EX12 ... 192 A8
Prince Maurice Ct PL4 ... 263 B3
Prince Maurice Rd PL4 ... 248 F4
Prince of Wales Dr
 Dartmouth TQ6 ... 233 F4
 Exmouth EX8 ... 196 E1
Prince of Wales Rd
 Crediton EX17 ... 165 C6
 Exeter EX4 ... 177 B8
 Kingsbridge TQ7 ... 258 C5
PRINCE ROCK ... 249 B1
Prince Rock Prim Sch PL4 ... 249 B2
Prince Rupert Way TQ12 ... 123 B2
Princes Ct [6] TQ1 ... 220 B6
Princes Point TQ1 ... 220 C3
Princes Rd
 Plymouth PL6 ... 245 E6
 Torquay TQ1 ... 220 B5
Princes Road E TQ1 ... 220 C5
Princes Road W TQ1 ... 220 B5
Princess Alexandra Ct [9] EX4 ... 177 A5
Princess Ave
 Ilfracombe EX34 ... 150 C5
 Plymouth, Plymstock PL9 ... 255 E6
 Plymouth, West Park PL5 ... 244 A3
Princess Cotts TQ12 ... 213 C6
Princess Cres PL9 ... 255 E6
Princess Elizabeth Terr EX20 ... 107 F8
Princesshay Sh Ctr EX1 ... 261 B3
Prince's Sq EX2 ... 177 A3
Princess Rd
 Kingskerswell TQ12 ... 213 A4
 Kingsteignton TQ12 ... 207 D8
Princess St
 Barnstaple EX32 ... 155 A6
 Plymouth PL1 ... 262 C2
Princess Street Ope PL1 ... 262 C2
Princes St
 [16] Dawlish EX7 ... 204 D6
 [23] Exmouth EX8 ... 202 A6
 Paignton TQ3 ... 226 B6
 Plymouth PL1 ... 247 E2
 Torquay TQ1 ... 220 D7
Princess Theatre★ TQ2 ... 220 B3
Prince's Street E EX2 ... 177 A3
Prince's Street N EX2 ... 177 A4
Prince's Street S EX2 ... 177 A3
Prince's Street W EX2 ... 177 A4
Princess Way PL1 ... 262 C2
Prince St TQ12 ... 207 C3
PRINCETOWN ... 128 B8
Princetown Prim Sch PL20 ... 128 A8
Prince William Ct [1] TQ5 ... 230 C4
Prince William Quay TQ5 ... 230 D5
Prings Ct [13] TQ5 ... 230 C5
Priorton Hill EX17 ... 80 B7
Priorton La EX17 ... 80 B7
Priory
 Bovey Tracey TQ13 ... 180 C8
 Wellington TA21 ... 160 E6
Priory Ave
 Kingskerswell TQ12 ... 213 A5
 Totnes TQ9 ... 223 C6
Priory Cl
 Barnstaple EX31 ... 154 F7
 East Budleigh EX9 ... 198 B7
 Ivybridge PL21 ... 237 B5
 Tavistock PL19 ... 171 D3
Priory Ct
 [3] Totnes TQ9 ... 223 C6
 Wellington TA21 ... 160 E7
Priory Dr
 Plymouth PL7 ... 250 D5
 Totnes TQ9 ... 223 C6
Priory Gdns
 Barnstaple EX31 ... 154 F7
 [1] Dawlish EX7 ... 204 E6
 Tavistock PL19 ... 171 D3
 Totnes TQ9 ... 223 C6
 Wellington TA21 ... 160 E6
Priory Gn EX4 ... 178 A7
Priory Hill
 [2] Dawlish EX7 ... 204 E6
 Totnes TQ9 ... 223 C6
Priory Lawn Terr PL3 ... 249 A6
Priory Mill PL7 ... 250 D5
Priory Park Rd [13] EX7 ... 204 D6
Priory RC Prim Sch [3] TQ1 ... 220 B8
Priory Rd
 Abbotskerswell TQ12 ... 212 C7
 Barnstaple EX31 ... 154 F7
 Dawlish EX7 ... 204 E6
 Exeter EX4 ... 177 E8
 Plymouth PL3 ... 249 A6
 Tiverton EX16 ... 161 F6
 Torquay TQ1 ... 220 B8
Priory Ridge PL7 ... 250 D5
Priory St TQ6 ... 234 A2
Priory Terr [7] TQ9 ... 223 C6
Priory The
 Abbotskerswell TQ12 ... 212 C7
 [3] Modbury PL21 ... 137 B2
Priory View TQ9 ... 227 B4
Priory Wall Cross EX15 ... 66 B2
Prisam La EX20 ... 75 E2
Prisam Lane Cross EX20 ... 75 F2
Priscott Way TQ12 ... 207 E6
Prispen Dr EX5 ... 82 B6
Prispen Ho EX5 ... 82 B6
Prispen View EX5 ... 82 B6
PRISTACOTT ... 27 C5
PRIXFORD ... 16 C7
Prixford EX31 ... 16 C7
Promenade
 Ilfracombe EX34 ... 150 B6
 Kingsbridge TQ7 ... 258 D5

Promenade continued
Paignton, Goodrington TQ4 . . . 226 C4
Paignton TQ3 . . . 226 D8
Prospect EX7 . . . 204 E6
Prospect Cnr EX31 . . . 27 A7
Prospect Cotts EX35 . . . 151 B5
Prospect Cres EX15 . . . 66 A7
Prospect Gdns 2 EX4 . . . 177 E7
Prospect Hill
Okehampton EX20 . . . 170 B4
Slapton TQ7 . . . 145 C4
Prospect La PL12 . . . 242 C3
Prospect Pk EX4 . . . 177 D8
Prospect Pl
Barnstaple EX32 . . . 155 B3
Exeter EX4 . . . 177 A4
Ottery St Mary EX11 . . . 169 D3
Plymouth PL1 . . . 262 B2
5 Tiverton EX16 . . . 161 B4
Prospect Rd 3 TQ5 . . . 230 C5
Prospect Row PL1 . . . 247 E1
Prospect St PL4 . . . 263 A3
Prospect Terr
Gunnislake PL18 . . . 125 D6
Gunnislake, St Ann's Chapel PL18 . . . 125 B5
Newton Abbot TQ12 . . . 207 C3
Prospect Way EX17 . . . 60 D3
Prospect Wlk PL12 . . . 242 C3
Prouse Cres PL2 . . . 248 C8
Prouse Rise PL12 . . . 242 E2
Providence Pl
Calstock PL18 . . . 125 D3
Plymouth PL1 . . . 248 A3
Providence Row 16 EX39 . . . 157 A2
Providence St PL4 . . . 263 A4
Prowse La
East Village EX17 . . . 80 C8
Lapford EX17 . . . 60 D3
Prowse's La EX16 . . . 67 B8
Prowse's La EX16 . . . 63 E1
Pryn Ct PL1 . . . 262 A3
Prynne Cl PL1 . . . 262 B3
Puckridge Rd EX4 . . . 174 D2
PUDDAVEN . . . 223 A8
Puddavine Terr TQ9 . . . 223 A8
PUDDINGTON . . . 62 B4
PUDDINGTON BOTTOM . . . 62 B4
Pudleylake Rd
Axminster EX13 . . . 167 B1
Musbury EX13 . . . 103 E6
Puffin Ct EX39 . . . 156 C6
Puffin Way EX2 . . . 176 D3
Pugsley Rd 3 EX16 . . . 64 D7
Pulchrass St EX1 . . . 261 A2
Pullen's Row EX16 . . . 46 E1
Pulleys Cl TQ7 . . . 143 C6
Pulling Rd EX4 . . . 174 D2
Pullins Terr 10 TQ13 . . . 123 E6
Pulpit Wlk EX2 . . . 181 C7
Pump La EX39 . . . 156 A2
Pump St
4 Brixham TQ5 . . . 230 D5
Newton St Cyres EX5 . . . 172 A8
Punchards Down TQ9 . . . 222 F6
Purbeck Ave TQ2 . . . 219 D2
Purcell Cl EX2 . . . 178 C5
Purcombe Cross TQ13 . . . 131 D3
Purlbridge Cross EX24 . . . 102 D6
Purzebrook Cl EX13 . . . 167 D5
Purzebrook Cotts EX13 . . . 167 D5
PUSEHILL . . . 156 B5
Pusehill Rd EX39 . . . 156 B5
PUTSBOROUGH . . . 7 F3
Putsborough Cl EX33 . . . 8 A2
Putsborough Rd EX33 . . . 7 F3
Putshole La EX38 . . . 40 E1
Putson Cross EX16 . . . 64 E8
Putts Cnr EX10 . . . 101 C7
Pye Cnr
Brampford Speke EX5 . . . 81 D1
Cullompton EX15 . . . 163 C3
Kennford EX6 . . . 181 B2
Pye La TA20 . . . 88 E8
Pykes Down PL21 . . . 237 F4
Pykes Thorne TA21 . . . 160 F4
Pyne Thorne Cl TA21 . . . 160 E3
Pyne Thorne Rd TA21 . . . 160 E4
Pym St
Plymouth PL1 . . . 247 F3
Tavistock PL19 . . . 171 C6
Pyne Gdns EX5 . . . 173 A7
Pyne Meadow Cross EX18 . . . 44 D3
Pynes Cr
Cheriton Fitzpaine EX17 . . . 62 E1
East Budleigh EX9 . . . 198 B6
Pynes Hill EX2 . . . 178 C2
Pynes Hill Bsns Pk EX2 . . . 178 C3
Pynes Inf Sch EX39 . . . 156 F1
Pynes La EX39 . . . 156 G3
Pynes Wlk EX39 . . . 25 E4
Pynsent Ct 4 TQ13 . . . 123 E6
Pyramids Swimming & Ctr The EX1 . . . 261 C3
Pytte Gdns EX3 . . . 183 C7
Pytte Ho EX3 . . . 183 C7
PYWORTHY . . . 71 D5
Pyworthy CE Prim Sch EX22 . . . 71 D5

Q

Quadrangle The EX4 . . . 177 C8
Quadrant The EX2 . . . 261 C2
Quagmire La EX22 . . . 164 C7
Quantock Rd TA21 . . . 160 D7
Quantocks EX33 . . . 152 B6
Quantocks Rd TQ2 . . . 219 C3
Quant Pk PL19 . . . 171 C6
Quarries La EX37 . . . 43 C7
Quarries The EX4 . . . 176 D4
Quarry Cl
Bideford EX39 . . . 156 E2
Totnes TQ9 . . . 222 F6
Quarry Cotts
Beer EX12 . . . 191 B5
Plymouth, Honicknowle PL5 . . . 244 B2
Plymouth PL1 . . . 262 A3
Quarryfields EX20 . . . 170 C6
Quarry Foot Cross EX17 . . . 79 C4
Quarry Gdns TQ3 . . . 226 A7
Quarry La
Exeter EX4 . . . 191 B5
Down St Mary EX17 . . . 78 F6
Exeter EX4 . . . 178 C4
Gunnislake PL18 . . . 125 C6
Silverton EX5 . . . 82 B5
Thorverton EX5 . . . 81 D4
Quarry Park Ave PL9 . . . 255 D7
Quarry Park Rd
Exeter EX2 . . . 178 C4
Plymouth, Peverell PL3 . . . 248 D5
Plymouth, Plymstock PL9 . . . 255 D7
Quarry Rd EX37 . . . 43 B7
Quarry St PL11 . . . 247 C3
Quarterdeck The PL1 . . . 254 A8
Quarter Mile La EX5 . . . 95 D3
Quartley Hill EX16 . . . 34 E4
Quayfield Rd EX34 . . . 150 C6
Quicks Wlk EX20 . . . 170 A4
Quay House Visitor Ctr* EX2 . . . 261 B2
Quay La
Instow EX39 . . . 15 B1
Lympstone EX8 . . . 195 D4
Quay Rd
Newton Abbot TQ12 . . . 207 D3
Plymouth PL1 . . . 263 A2
Teignmouth TQ14 . . . 210 B4
Quayside 6 PL19 . . . 171 B5
Quayside L Ctr TQ7 . . . 258 D4
Quay Terr TQ12 . . . 207 D3
Quay The
Appledore EX39 . . . 15 A1
Ashprington TQ9 . . . 139 F7
Bideford EX39 . . . 157 A2
Brixham TQ5 . . . 230 D5
Dartmouth TQ6 . . . 233 F3
Dittisham TQ6 . . . 228 D2
Exeter EX2 . . . 261 B2
Ilfracombe EX34 . . . 150 C6
Plymouth PL9 . . . 255 C7
Salcombe TQ8 . . . 259 C6
Queen Annes 14 EX39 . . . 157 A2
Queen Annes Copse TQ12 . . . 206 F1
Queen Anne's Ct 14 EX31 . . . 154 F5
Queen Anne's Mews 13 EX31 . . . 154 F5
Queen Anne's Quay PL4 . . . 263 B2
QUEEN DART . . . 47 C3
Queen Dart Cross EX16 . . . 47 B4
Queen Dart Hill EX16 . . . 47 B3
Queen Elizabeth Ave TQ6 . . . 233 E4
Queen Elizabeth Ct EX39 . . . 156 C6
Queen Elizabeth Dr
Crediton EX17 . . . 165 A6
Crediton EX17 . . . 225 E6
Queen Elizabeth's Com Coll
Crediton EX17 . . . 165 B5
Crediton EX17 . . . 165 B6
Queen La 8 EX7 . . . 204 D6
Queen's Ave EX34 . . . 150 C5
Queens Cl
Kingsteignton TQ12 . . . 207 F8
Plymouth PL6 . . . 245 E6
Queen's Cres
Brixham TQ5 . . . 230 D3
Exeter EX4 . . . 261 B4
Queens Ct 25 EX24 . . . 103 A4
Queen's Ct 17 EX8 . . . 202 A6
Queen's Ct EX5 . . . 202 C5
Queen's Dr The EX4 . . . 177 B8
Queenshays EX17 . . . 95 A5
Queen's Ho 8 EX32 . . . 155 A5
Queensland Dr EX4 . . . 173 E2
Queen's Park Rd TQ4 . . . 226 C6
Queens Pk EX17 . . . 80 D4
Queen's Pk EX22 . . . 55 C1
Queen's Sq EX15 . . . 163 C3
Queens Rd
Brixham TQ5 . . . 230 C6
Budleigh Salterton EX9 . . . 197 F2
Moretonhampstead TQ13 . . . 111 F5
Paignton TQ4 . . . 226 C6

Queen's Rd continued
Plymouth PL4 . . . 263 B4
Queen's Sq
Broadclyst EX5 . . . 175 C7
8 Colyton EX24 . . . 103 A4
Queen St
Barnstaple EX32 . . . 155 A5
Bideford EX39 . . . 157 A2
Budleigh Salterton EX9 . . . 199 G2
9 Colyton EX24 . . . 103 A4
Dawlish EX7 . . . 204 D6
Exeter EX4 . . . 261 A3
11 Exmouth EX8 . . . 202 A6
17 Honiton EX14 . . . 166 C6
Lynton EX35 . . . 151 C5
Newton Abbot TQ12 . . . 207 D3
Northlew EX20 . . . 74 E2
Plymouth PL1 . . . 247 D2
Seaton EX12 . . . 192 A5
South Molton EX36 . . . 158 C4
13 Teignmouth TQ14 . . . 210 B4
Tiverton EX16 . . . 161 C3
Torquay TQ1 . . . 220 B5
Winkleigh EX19 . . . 58 F3
Queen's Terr
Exeter EX4 . . . 261 A4
Great Torrington EX38 . . . 159 B5
Stoke Canon EX5 . . . 81 F1
4 Totnes TQ9 . . . 223 C6
Queensway
Newton Abbot TQ12 . . . 207 E2
Tiverton EX16 . . . 161 F5
Torquay TQ2 . . . 219 D6
Queensway Cl TQ2 . . . 219 E7
Queensway Cres TQ2 . . . 219 E7
Queensway Ho TQ12 . . . 207 E2
Queensway RC Prim Sch TQ2 . . . 219 D7
Queens Wlk DT7 . . . 260 E4
Quentin Ave TQ5 . . . 230 B2
Questant La EX10 . . . 188 C6
Quicks Wlk EX20 . . . 38 A5
Quillets The TQ7 . . . 147 E6
Quince Cross
South Molton EX36 . . . 46 B8
Spreyton EX17 . . . 96 C7
Quince Hill EX36 . . . 31 A1
Quince Honey Farm* EX36 . . . 158 C5
Quinnel Ho 7 TQ14 . . . 210 B5
Quinta Cl TQ1 . . . 220 C6
Quinta Ct TQ1 . . . 220 C7
Quinta Rd TQ1 . . . 220 D6
Quintet Cl EX1 . . . 178 C5
Quirk Hill EX16 . . . 63 D7
QUODITCH . . . 71 B1
Quoditch Cross EX21 . . . 73 B1
Quoitgate Cross EX22 . . . 38 D3

R

Raceworld Karting* EX5 . . . 184 D8
Rackclose La EX4 . . . 261 A2
RACKENFORD . . . 47 D5
Rackenford CE Prim Sch EX16 . . . 47 D5
Rackenford Cross EX16 . . . 47 D5
Rackenford Rd
Tiverton EX16 . . . 161 A6
Witheridge EX16 . . . 46 E1
Rackfield
Rockwell Green TA21 . . . 160 A5
8 Tiverton EX16 . . . 161 C3
Rackfield Cotts EX4 . . . 176 F8
Rackfield Ct EX32 . . . 154 F6
Rackfield Dr EX32 . . . 155 C8
Rackleigh La EX17 . . . 46 A2
Rackmead EX37 . . . 28 F4
Rack Park La EX38 . . . 159 C5
Rack Park Rd TQ7 . . . 258 D5
Rack St EX1 . . . 261 A2
Radcliffe Cl PL6 . . . 244 E6
Radcliffe Ct TQ3 . . . 226 C7
Raddenstile La EX8 . . . 202 B6
Raddenstile La EX8 . . . 202 B6
Raddick La PL20 . . . 127 F5
Raddicombe Cl TQ5 . . . 234 F8
Raddicombe Dr TQ5 . . . 234 F8
Raddicombe Farm TQ5 . . . 234 F8
RADDINGTON . . . 35 B4
Raddon Cross EX17 . . . 81 A5
Raddon Down Cross EX17 . . . 79 F4
Raddon Hill EX17 . . . 81 A6
Raddon Top EX17 . . . 81 A6
Radford Ho PL4 . . . 249 B1
Radford Ho 11 TQ4 . . . 226 B6
Radford La PL10 . . . 252 D4
Radford Park Dr PL9 . . . 255 D6
Radford Park Rd PL9 . . . 255 D6
Radford Rd
Exeter EX2 . . . 261 C2
Plymouth PL1 . . . 262 B1
Radfords Orch TQ9 . . . 131 E1
Radford View TQ9 . . . 255 D6
Radford Way EX20 . . . 170 A4
Radish La EX12 . . . 102 A2
Radley Cross EX34 . . . 30 D2
Radnidge La EX16 . . . 32 D4
Radnor Hall PL4 . . . 263 A3
Radnor Pl
Exeter EX2 . . . 261 C2
Plymouth PL4 . . . 263 A3
Radnor St PL4 . . . 263 A3
Radnor Villa EX2 . . . 261 C2

Radsbury La EX35 . . . 5 B3
Radway EX10 . . . 188 B4
Radway Dr TQ14 . . . 209 A8
Radway Gdns TQ14 . . . 209 A8
Radway Hill TQ14 . . . 209 A8
Radway St TQ14 . . . 209 A8
Ragg La EX9 . . . 199 G2
Rag La
Aylesbeare EX5 . . . 99 D4
Colebrooke EX17 . . . 79 A2
Yarcombe EX14 . . . 68 B2
Raglan Ct PL1 . . . 247 F2
Raglan Gdns PL1 . . . 247 F2
Raglan Rd PL1 . . . 247 F2
Raglans EX2 . . . 181 C8
Railway Cotts
Holsworthy EX22 . . . 164 C3
8 Holsworthy EX22 . . . 164 C4
6 Plymouth, Ford PL2 . . . 247 F5
Plymouth, Plymstock PL9 . . . 255 D7
Tavistock PL19 . . . 171 B6
Railway Terr
8 Bideford EX39 . . . 157 B1
Broadclyst EX5 . . . 175 E3
Rainbow Ct TQ2 . . . 219 E2
Rainbow La TA3 . . . 67 F8
Raisey La TA20 . . . 69 F7
Rake Cnr TQ7 . . . 143 F6
Rakeham Cotts EX38 . . . 41 B6
Rakeham La EX38 . . . 41 B6
Rakelane Cross TQ7 . . . 143 F6
RALEIGH . . . 155 A7
Raleigh Ave TQ2 . . . 219 D6
Raleigh Cl
Dartmouth TQ6 . . . 233 C3
Sidmouth EX10 . . . 188 B7
South Molton EX36 . . . 158 C4
Raleigh Cotts 3 EX31 . . . 155 A7
Raleigh Ct
Budleigh Salterton EX9 . . . 198 B2
Plymouth PL7 . . . 251 B6
Raleigh Dr TQ4 . . . 226 B2
Raleigh Hts EX31 . . . 154 F7
Raleigh Lawn EX31 . . . 154 F7
Raleigh Mdw EX31 . . . 155 A7
Raleigh Mead EX36 . . . 158 C4
Raleigh Pk EX36 . . . 158 C4
Raleigh Rd
Barnstaple EX32 . . . 154 F6
Budleigh Salterton EX9 . . . 198 B2
Dartmouth TQ6 . . . 233 E4
Exeter EX1 . . . 261 C2
Exmouth EX8 . . . 202 A6
Ivybridge PL21 . . . 237 A6
Newton Abbot TQ12 . . . 207 F3
Ottery St Mary EX11 . . . 169 E4
Salcombe TQ8 . . . 259 D4
RALEIGH HILL . . . 156 D5
Raleigh Hill
Bideford, Raleigh Hill EX39 . . . 156 E4
Bideford, Silford EX39 . . . 156 D5
Raleigh Ho
Exeter EX2 . . . 261 C2
Ottery St Mary EX11 . . . 169 B7
Sidmouth EX10 . . . 188 B7
Ralph Cl EX33 . . . 152 B6
Ralph Rd EX33 . . . 152 B6
Ralph's Ct PL19 . . . 171 B5
Ramage Cl PL6 . . . 245 E6
RAME . . . 140 H2
Ramehead Cotts PL10 . . . 140 H1
Ramehead La PL10 . . . 140 H2
Rame La
Cawsand PL10 . . . 140 F1
Rame PL10 . . . 140 H2
Ramillies Ave PL5 . . . 244 A4
Ramsey Gdns PL5 . . . 244 D1
Ramsey La
Runnington TA21 . . . 51 F8
Sampford Courtenay EX20 . . . 76 F3
Ramshill Cross TQ3 . . . 225 E8
Ramshill Rd TQ3 . . . 225 E8
Rance Dr EX8 . . . 196 E3
Randolph Ct TQ12 . . . 207 A4
Randwick Park Rd PL9 . . . 255 D7
Ranelagh Rd EX20 . . . 170 A5
Rangers Cl TQ11 . . . 236 B4
Ranscombe Cl TQ5 . . . 230 E5
Ranscombe Ct 5 TQ5 . . . 230 D5
Ranscombe Rd TQ5 . . . 230 D5
Ransum Way PL19 . . . 171 B4
Raphael Cl PL9 . . . 256 B5
Raphael Dr PL9 . . . 256 A6
Rapscott Cross EX36 . . . 18 F1
Rashleigh Ave
Plymouth PL7 . . . 250 F7
Saltash PL12 . . . 242 D1
Rashleigh La EX12 . . . 59 D7
Ratcliffe Specl Sch EX7 . . . 204 C4
Rathlin TQ1 . . . 220 C2
Rathole La EX16 . . . 33 A8
Rathshole Gate EX24 . . . 102 E5
RATSLOE . . . 174 D8
Ratsloe Cross EX4 . . . 174 D8
Rattenbury Cotts EX12 . . . 191 C6
Rattenbury Cross EX19 . . . 76 A8
RATTERY . . . 135 D4
Rattle St EX13 . . . 113 D1
Ravelin Gdns 5 EX32 . . . 155 B5
Ravelin Manor Rd EX32 . . . 155 B5
Raven Cl EX4 . . . 173 C1

Ravensbourne La TQ6 . . . 146 B7
Ravensbury Dr TQ6 . . . 234 A2
Rawlin Cl PL6 . . . 249 C8
Rawlyn Rd TQ2 . . . 219 E4
Rawnsley La EX34 . . . 7 F6
RAWRIDGE . . . 68 C1
Rayer Rd 8 EX16 . . . 64 D7
RAYMOND'S HILL . . . 104 C7
Raymond Way PL7 . . . 250 D6
Rayners EX6 . . . 181 A1
Raynham Rd PL3 . . . 248 B4
Rea Barn Cl TQ5 . . . 230 D4
Rea Barn Rd TQ5 . . . 230 C4
Read Cl EX8 . . . 196 C1
Reading Wlk PL5 . . . 244 C4
Rea Dr TQ5 . . . 230 D5
Recreation Rd PL2 . . . 248 C7
Recreation Road Ind Est PL2 . . . 248 C7
Recreation Way PL7 . . . 132 F4
Rectory Cl
Filleigh EX32 . . . 29 B6
9 Whimple EX5 . . . 99 E8
Willand EX15 . . . 162 D4
Wrafton EX33 . . . 152 F4
Rectory Close Cross EX33 . . . 152 F3
Rectory Cross TQ10 . . . 138 A7
Rectory Dr EX2 . . . 181 B8
Rectory Hill
Berrynarbor EX34 . . . 2 D3
Cheriton Fitzpaine EX17 . . . 62 E1
Rectory La
Parkham EX39 . . . 39 E8
Stoke Fleming TQ6 . . . 146 B7
Yelland EX39 . . . 15 C2
Rectory Pk EX39 . . . 156 F2
Rectory Rd
Ashbrittle TA21 . . . 50 F8
Bridestowe EX20 . . . 107 F8
Combe Martin EX34 . . . 3 A3
Dolton EX19 . . . 57 F7
East Ogwell TQ12 . . . 211 E8
Morchard Bishop EX17 . . . 61 A2
Plymouth PL8 . . . 257 A8
Rectory Rise EX20 . . . 56 F4
Redavon Rise TQ2 . . . 219 B8
RED BALL . . . 51 C4
Red Brook Cl TQ4 . . . 226 C1
Redburn Cl TQ3 . . . 226 A7
Redburn Rd TQ3 . . . 226 A7
Redcliff Ct EX9 . . . 199 G2
Redcliffe Rd TQ1 . . . 214 C1
Redcliffes The EX20 . . . 106 E5
RED COW VILLAGE . . . 177 A8
Red Cross
Colyton EX24 . . . 102 F6
Raymond's Hill EX13 . . . 104 C7
Silverton EX5 . . . 82 C5
Red Cross Hill EX17 . . . 165 F6
Reddacleave Kiln Cross TQ11 . . . 135 A6
Reddaway Dr EX6 . . . 182 A4
Reddenhill Rd TQ1 . . . 220 C7
Red Devon Ct 8 TQ12 . . . 207 E4
Reddicliff Cl PL9 . . . 255 E5
Reddicliffes The EX20 . . . 106 E5
Reddicliff Rd PL9 . . . 255 D5
Reddington Rd PL3 . . . 249 B7
Redford Cross TQ9 . . . 131 E1
Redford Mdw TQ7 . . . 258 C5
Redford Way TQ7 . . . 258 C5
Red Gate
King's Nympton EX37 . . . 44 E8
Winkleigh EX19 . . . 58 D2
Redgate Cl TQ1 . . . 220 D6
Redgate La EX16 . . . 50 C5
Redhill Cl PL5 . . . 243 E4
Redhill Cotts EX11 . . . 169 F6
REDHILLS . . . 176 E3
Redhills
Budleigh Salterton EX9 . . . 199 G2
Exeter EX4 . . . 176 E3
Redhills Cl EX4 . . . 176 E3
Redhills Com Prim Sch EX4 . . . 176 F5
Red Ho The EX17 . . . 165 B5
Red House Cl 9 TQ13 . . . 123 C4
Red La
Churchinford TA3 . . . 68 C7
Hatherleigh EX20 . . . 56 C7
Hemyock EX15 . . . 52 E3
Raymond's Hill EX13 . . . 104 C6
Redlake TQ9 . . . 222 F8
Redlake Cross TQ9 . . . 222 F8
Redlake Trad Est PL21 . . . 137 B7
Redland Cross EX18 . . . 58 F7
Redland Cross TQ3 . . . 226 C5
Redlands Cl EX4 . . . 176 A8
Redlands Ct TQ3 . . . 225 F7
Redlands The EX10 . . . 188 A3
REDLANE . . . 68 C7
Redlane Cross DT7 . . . 104 C6
Redlap Cl TQ6 . . . 233 E1
Redlap Rd TQ6 . . . 233 E1
Red Lion Ct TA21 . . . 160 E6
Red Lion Hill PL8 . . . 257 B5
Red Lion La EX1, EX4 . . . 261 C4
Red Lion Pl 2 EX7 . . . 204 D6
Red Lion Yard EX20 . . . 170 B5
REDMONSFORD . . . 38 C2
Redmoor Cl PL19 . . . 171 A7
Redoubt Hill TQ6 . . . 234 B3
RED POST . . . 70 E8

Redpost Cross
North Tawton EX20 . . . . 76 F5
Sampford Courtenay EX20 . 76 F5
Red Post Cross
Burrington EX37 . . . . . . 43 F4
Totnes TQ9 . . . . 217 C4
Red Rock EX5 . . . . 81 C2
Red Rock Rd EX5 . . . . . 81 D1
Redruth Cl PL15 . . . . . 244 A5
Redside Terr EX5 . . . . . 172 E5
Redstart Cl TQ12. . . . . 206 F1
Redvers Gr PL7 . . . . . . 250 E4
Redvers Ho 7 EX17 . . . 165 C5
Redvers Rd EX4 . . . . . . 177 A6
Redvers Way 5 EX16 . . 161 E6
Redwalls Mdw TQ6. . . . 233 E4
Redwell La TQ3. . . . . . 225 F8
Redwell Rd TQ3. . . . . . 225 F8
Redwing Dr PL6 . . . . . 245 D8
Redwood Cl
Bovey Tracey TQ13. . . . 180 C4
Exmouth EX8 . . . . 196 D3
10 Hemyock EX15 . . . . 67 B8
4 Honiton EX14 . . . . . 85 C2
Redwood Dr PL7 . . . . . 251 B5
Redwood Rd EX10 . . . . 188 C5
Redwoods TQ13 . . . . . 180 C5
Redworth Terr TQ9 . . . . 223 C6
Redyeates Cross EX17. . . 63 A2
Reed Mdw EX20 . . . . . . 75 C7
Reed's Cross
Ashill EX15. . . . . 66 C6
Bittadon EX31 . . . . 9 E4
Reedsdown Cross EX17. . . 79 F6
Reeds Pl EX15 . . . . . . 163 C3
Reed Vale TQ14. . . . . . 210 A5
REEDY 116 A5
Reedy Hill EX6. . . . . . . 112 F8
Reeveacre Cross TQ9 . . 223 A5
Reeves Cl 3 TQ9 . . . . 223 D5
Reeves Rd The TQ2 . . . 219 D5
Reform St 3 EX31 . . . . 154 F6
Regal Cl PL12. . . . . . . 242 F2
Regency Cl 202 C6
Regency Ct 8 EX34. . . . 150 C8
Regency Gate EX10 . . . 188 C5
Regent Cl
Barnstaple EX31 . . . . . 154 C2
Fremington EX31. . . . . 153 F5
Torquay TQ2. . . . . . . 219 E8
Regent Ct PL4 . . . . . . 263 A3
Regent Pl EX34 . . . . . . 150 B6
Regents Ct TQ4 . . . . . 226 C5
Regents Gate EX8. . . . . 202 B6
Regents Gdns 6 TQ14 . . 210 C4
Regent's Pk EX1. . . . . . 177 E6
Regent Sq EX1. . . . . . . 177 F5
Regent St
Dawlish EX7. . . . . 204 D6
Exeter EX2. . . . . 177 A3
Plymouth PL4. . . . . . . 263 A3
18 Teignmouth TQ14 . . 210 C4
Regis Ct EX10. . . . . . . 188 C4
Reigate Rd PL9 . . . . . . 255 E8
Reme Dr EX14 . . . . 85 C2
Rena Hobson Ct EX16 . . 161 F3
Renaissance Gdns PL2 . . 248 C2
Rendells Mdw TQ13. . . . 180 E7
Rendlesham Gdns PL6 . . 245 E3
Rendle St PL1 . . . . 262 B3
Rennes Dr EX4. . . . . . . 173 C1
Rennes Ho EX1. . . . . . . 178 B7
Renney Rd
Down Thomas PL9. . . . 255 C1
Heybrook Bay PL9. . . . 140 B8
Rennie Ave PL5 . . . . . . 243 C1
Rennie Rd 2 EX16 . . . . 64 D7
Renoir Cl PL9. . . . . 256 A6
Renown St PL2 . . . . . . 247 E6
Rensey La EX17 . . . . . . 60 C4
Renslade Ho EX4 . . . . . 261 A2
Renton La TQ7 . . . . . . 142 E7
Research Way PL6. . . . . 245 C4
Reservoir Cres PL16 . . . 256 E7
Reservoir Cross PL16. . . 91 A4
Reservoir La 1 PL3 . . . 248 F6
Reservoir Rd
Plymouth, Hartley PL3. . 248 F6
Plymouth, Plymstock PL9 . 256 B7
Reservoir Way PL9 . . . . 256 B7
Resolution Ho PL4 . . . . 263 B3
Rest Hill TQ12 . . . . 131 D7
Restland La EX20 . . . . . 94 F7
Restormel Rd PL4 . . . . . 262 C4
Restormel Terr PL4 . . . . 262 C4
Retail Park Cl EX2 . . . . 177 B3
Retreat Cl TQ7 . . . . . . 258 C5
Retreat Dr The EX3 . . . . 182 D6
Retreat Rd EX3 . . . . . . 182 E6
Retreat The
Exmouth EX8 . . . . 202 D7
Paignton TQ3 . . . . . . 226 C8
Plymouth PL3. . . . . . . 249 B7
Tiverton EX16 . . . . . . 161 D4
Topsham EX3. . . . . . . 182 D6
Revell Park Rd PL7 . . . . 250 D6
Revel Rd PL3. . . . . 249 A6
Revelstoke Rd PL8 . . . . 140 F6
Revill Ind Units EX5. . . . 99 A4
REW
Ashburton 130 F6
Malborough 147 F5
Rew Cross
Ashburton TQ13. . . . . 130 F5
Newton St Cyres EX5. . . 81 A2

Rewdown Cross TQ13 . . . 130 F6
REWE. 82 A2
Rewe Barton EX5 . . . . . 82 A2
Rewe Cross EX5 . . . . . . 82 A2
Rewe Ct EX5. . . . . 82 B3
Rewe La EX5. . . . . 99 D6
Rewes Cross EX5 . . . . . 82 F2
Rewlea Cotts TQ13. . . . 130 F5
Rewlea Cross TQ13 . . . . 130 F6
Rew Rd TQ13 . . . . 180 C5
Rew's Cl EX34 . . . . 2 F4
Rews Cross EX36. . . . . . 19 C2
Rews Mdw EX1 . . . . . . 174 F1
Rews Park Dr EX1. . . . . 174 F1
REXON 106 B7
Rexona Cl EX2 . . . . . . 177 A2
Rexon Cross PL16. . . . . 106 B7
Reynell Ave TQ12 . . . . 207 F3
Reynell Rd TQ12 . . . . . 211 F8
Reynolds Cl EX4 . . . . . 174 D1
Reynolds Gr PL5 . . . . . 247 C8
Reynolds Rd PL7. . . . . 250 C6
REZARE. 115 C4
Rheola Gdns PL6. . . . . 245 D3
Rhodanthe Rd TQ3 . . . . 219 B1
Rhode La DT7 . . . . . . 260 C6
Rhodes Cl PL7. . . . . . . 250 E7
Richard Cl
Bideford EX39 . . . . 25 E4
Okehampton/North Tawton
EX20 . . . . 170 D5
Richard Ford Ct EX2 . . . 177 F5
Richards Cl
Dawlish EX7. . . . . 204 D5
Exmouth EX8 . . . . 196 D2
Wellington TA21. . . . . 160 C8
Richardson Dr PL8 . . . . 141 B8
Richards Row PL3 . . . . 248 F7
Richmond Ave EX34 . . . 150 C6
Richmond Cl
Samford Peverell EX16 . . 50 D1
Torquay TQ2. . . . . . . 221 A4
Richmond Ct
14 Dawlish EX7. . . . . 204 E6
Exeter EX1. . . . . 261 A3
Richmond Gn EX39. . . . 14 F1
Richmond Hill TQ12. . . 213 A5
Richmond Pk EX39. . . . 156 F7
Richmond Pl
15 Dawlish EX7. . . . . 204 E6
Ivybridge PL21. . . . . . 136 C7
Richmond Rd
Appledore EX39 . . . . . 15 A1
Exeter EX4. . . . . 261 A3
Exmouth EX8 . . . . 202 D7
Ilfracombe EX34. . . . . 150 A4
Plymouth PL6. . . . . . . 245 A2
Richmond St EX32 . . . . 155 A5
Richmond Terr
9 Appledore EX39 . . . . 15 A1
Buckland Monachorum
PL20 . . . . 126 C3
Kingsbridge TQ7 . . . . 258 D6
Richmond Villas EX34. . 150 A5
Richmond Wlk
10 Barnstaple EX32 . . . 155 A6
Plymouth PL1. . . . . . . 247 F1
RICKARD'S DOWN 156 A3
Rickards Gdn EX39. . . . 156 B2
Rickards Row EX39. . . . 40 B7
Rickham Cross TQ8 . . . 148 D4
Riddell Ave EX32. . . . . 154 F6
Riddistone Cross EX20 . . 77 A8
Riddlestone La EX20 . . . 77 A8
RIDDLECOMBE 58 D8
Ride The
Beaworthy EX21 . . . . . 55 F4
Plymouth PL7, PL9. . . . 249 D2
Ridge Cross
Chillington TQ7. . . . . . 149 B8
Plymouth PL9. . . . . . . 256 A3
Wilmington EX14. . . . . 86 E4
Ridge Hill
Berrynarbor EX34 . . . . 2 E3
Combe Martin EX34. . . . 3 A2
Dartmouth TQ6 . . . . . 233 F4
Ridge Ho PL4. . . . . . . 249 A4
Ridge La
Chudleigh TQ13. . . . . 124 B7
Cornworthy TQ9. . . . . 139 F4
Paignton TQ3 . . . . . . 218 F8
Tiverton EX16. . . . . . . 63 F8
Ridge Lane Cross TQ9 . . 139 E4
Ridgeleigh Ct 11 EX14 . 166 C6
Ridgemark Cl TQ5 . . . . 230 E5
Ridge Park Ave EX4 . . . 248 D4
Ridge Park Rd PL7 . . . . 250 F5
Ridge Pk PL7 . . . . 250 E5
Ridge Rd
Combeinteignhead TQ12 . 208 D2
Maidencombe TQ1, TQ12 . 214 B7
Modbury PL21. . . . . . 137 B4
Plymouth PL7. . . . . . . 250 E3
Stokeinteignhead TQ12 . 209 A1

Ridge Rd *continued*
Ugborough PL21 . . . . . 137 D7
West Anstey TA22 . . . . . 32 D7
Ridges The TQ6. . . . . . 233 D1
Ridgeway
Exeter EX4. . . . . 173 A3
Honiton EX14. . . . . . . 166 B4
Ottery St Mary EX11 . . . 169 E4
Plymouth, Plympton PL7 . 250 D5
Plymouth PL6. . . . . . . 245 C4
Saltash PL12 . . . . 242 D1
Sidbury EX10 . . . . 101 B2
Ridge Way EX6 . . . . . . 194 E2
Ridgeway Ave EX39 . . . 156 E7
Ridgeway Cl
Newton Abbot TQ12. . . 207 F1
Sidbury EX10 . . . . 101 B2
Westward Ho! EX39. . . 156 D7
Ridgeway Ct EX39. . . . 156 D7
Ridgeway Dr EX39 . . . . 156 D7
Ridgeway Gdns EX11. . . 169 E4
Ridgeway Hts 17 TQ1. . 220 D4
Ridgeway La
Awliscombe EX14. . . . . 85 A5
Coffinswell TQ12 . . . . 213 D6
Ridgeway Mead EX10 . . 187 F7
Ridgeway Rd
Newton Abbot TQ12. . . 207 F1
Torquay TQ1. . . . . . . 220 E4
Ridgeway Sch PL7 . . . . 250 E5
Ridgeway's Cross EX17. . 79 E6
Ridgeway Sp Ctr PL7. . . 250 E5
Ridgewood Cross EX15 . . 67 D8
Ridgewood La EX15 . . . 67 D8
Ridgway Cross EX36 . . . 20 E1
Ridgway Ct EX13. . . . . 167 D5
Ridgway La EX24. . . . . 102 F4
Riding Cross EX37. . . . . 29 A4
Ridings The EX3 . . . . . 183 C4
Ridley Hill TQ6. . . . . . 234 A3
Rifford Rd EX2 . . . . . . 178 B4
Rifton La EX16. . . . . . . 48 B4
Riga Terr PL3. . . . . . . 249 C4
Rigdale Cl PL6. . . . . . . 249 A7
Riggles Cross EX14 . . . . 68 A3
Rillage La TQ2. . . . . . 219 F6
Rill Cnr EX5. . . . . 99 D3
Rill La EX9. . . . . 199 H2
Ringdown La EX15 . . . . 52 F2
Ring Hill EX20 . . . . 95 C5
Ringhill Cross EX20 . . . . 95 D5
RINGMORE 142 E3
Bigbury-on-Sea 142 E4
Teignmouth 209 D4
Ringmore Cl TQ14 . . . . 209 D5
Ringmore Dr TQ7 . . . . 142 E3
Ringmore Way PL5. . . . 244 B3
Ringrona TQ8. . . . . . . 259 B2
Ringslade Cl TQ12 . . . . 206 F5
Ringslade Rd TQ12. . . . 206 F5
Ringswell Ave EX1 . . . . 178 C6
Ringswell Cross TQ9 . . . 216 E6
Ringswell Pk 8 EX2 . . . 178 D5
Riphay Cross TA22 . . . . 33 E3
Ripon Cl EX14 . . . . . . 176 E6
Rippon Cl
Brixham TQ5 . . . . 229 F2
17 Tiverton EX16. . . . . 64 D7
Riscombe Hill EX5 . . . . 98 F8
Risdon Ave PL4. . . . . . 249 B1
Rising Sun EX13 . . . . . . 87 A3
Ritson La TQ9. . . . . . . 139 D3
Rivenford La EX5, EX17 . . 81 C3
Riverbank Cotts EX39 . . 157 B4
River Cl
Newton Abbot TQ12. . . 207 F6
Stoke Canon EX5 . . . . 173 F8
River Ct
3 Okehampton EX20 . . 170 B6
Saltash PL12 . . . . 242 D5
Tavistock PL19. . . . . . 171 D6
Riverdale
Harbertonford TQ9 . . . 139 C7
Seaton EX12 . . . . 192 B7
Riverdale Cl EX12. . . . . 192 B7
River Dart Ctry Pk*
TQ13. . . . . 130 D5
River Dr EX15. . . . . . . 163 D3
Riverford Cl PL6. . . . . . 245 D7
River Front EX3 . . . . . . 183 C4
Riveria Ct TQ1. . . . . . . 220 C4
River Mdws EX2 . . . . . 177 C3
Rivermead Cl EX15 . . . . 163 C2
Rivermead Ave EX8 . . . 196 A3
Rivermead Ct EX8. . . . . 196 A3
Rivermead Rd EX2 . . . . 177 D3
River Pk PL21. . . . . . . 137 B4
River Pk 14 PL20 . . . . . 126 F4
Rivers Cl EX16 . . . . . . 237 E5
Riversdale Ave EX34 . . . 150 A6
RIVERSIDE
Plymouth 243 A1
Wellington 160 B6
Riverside
Chillaton PL16 . . . . . . 116 D8
Dawlish Warren EX7 . . . 201 A2
Hemyock EX15. . . . . . . 67 C8
Kingsbridge TQ7 . . . . 258 D4
Totnes TQ9. . . . . 210 A3
Wellington TA21. . . . . 223 B7
Riverside Apartments
EX36. . . . . 158 E4
Riverside Bsns Pk PL1 . . 247 E3

Riverside Cl
Bideford EX39 . . . . . . 157 B4
Honiton EX14. . . . . . . 166 B6
1 Horrabridge PL20. . . 126 F4
Riverside Com Prim Sch
PL5 . . . . 247 C8
Riverside Cott PL12 . . . 242 C1
Riverside Cross EX17. . . 62 A3
Riverside Ct
2 Barnstaple EX31 . . . 154 F5
Bideford EX39 . . . . . . 157 B4
Dartmouth TQ6 . . . . . 233 F3
Exeter EX2. . . . . 261 B2
Newton Abbot TQ12. . . 207 B3
Riverside L Ctr EX4 . . . 261 A1
Riverside Leat PL5 . . . . 243 A3
Riverside Orch EX12 . . . 192 B7
Riverside Pl PL1 . . . . . 247 D2
Riverside Rd
Barnstaple EX31 . . . . . 154 C6
Dittisham TQ6 . . . . . . 228 C3
Lynmouth EX35. . . . . . 151 C6
Sidmouth EX10 . . . . . 188 B3
Topsham EX3. . . . . . . 182 E6
Riverside Road E PL8 . . 140 F6
Riverside Road W PL8. . 140 F6
Riverside Terr TQ9. . . . 223 D5
Riverside Units EX31. . . 154 C6
Riverside Valley Pk*
EX2 . . . . 177 E2
Riverside View EX11 . . . 169 D3
Riverside Way
Newton Abbot TQ13. . . 130 F7
Seaton EX12 . . . . 192 C5
Riverside Wlk
Plymouth PL5. . . . . . . 244 B6
Yealmpton PL8. . . . . . 136 A2
Riverside Workshops
EX12. . . . . 192 C5
Riversmeet EX39. . . . . . 15 A1
Rivers The PL12. . . . . . 242 C1
Rivers Wlk EX2 . . . . . . 182 C7
River Tamar Way EX22 . . 164 C6
Rivervale Cl TQ13 . . . . 110 F6
River Valley Rd 12 TQ13 . 123 C4
Riverview TQ12 . . . . . . 207 F2
River View
Barnstaple EX32 . . . . . 155 C2
Exebridge TA22 . . . . . 33 F3
Gunnislake PL18 . . . . 125 B5
Plymouth PL4. . . . . . . 249 B1
Saltash PL12 . . . . 242 F3
River View Cl
12 Chudleigh Knighton
TQ13 . . . . 123 C4
20 Colyton EX24 . . . . 103 A4
River View Commercial Ctr
EX31. . . . . 154 D6
Riverview Dr EX4 . . . . . 176 F8
River View Dr 8 EX24 . . 103 A4
River View La PL4 . . . . 249 B1
Riverview Pl TQ7 . . . . . 258 C5
River View Terr EX6. . . . 182 B3
Riviera Int Con Ctr*
TQ2. . . . . 219 F4
Riviera Terr
Dawlish EX7. . . . . 204 F7
Exminster EX6. . . . . . 182 B3
Riviera The
Paignton TQ4 . . . . . . 226 B5
Torquay TQ1. . . . . . . 220 B3
Riviera Way TQ2 . . . . . 213 D1
Rixafer Rd TQ13 . . . . . 124 A4
Rixdale Rd TQ13 . . . . . 124 C4
Rixey La EX17 . . . . 61 B2
Rixeypark Cnr TQ13 . . . 123 D3
RIXLADE 25 B5
Roach Hill EX36. . . . . . 31 F7
Roachill Cross EX36. . . . 32 C1
Road Down Cross EX6. . . 96 F7
Road End Cross EX14. . . 87 A8
Roadford Lake Nature
Reserve* EX21 . . . . . . 91 D4
ROAD GREEN 103 A5
Road Pk TQ13 . . . . . . 123 B7
Roadway Cnr EX34 . . . . 8 A5
Robert Way EX10 . . . . . 186 F8
Robin Cl EX15 . . . . . . 163 B2
Robin Dr EX15 . . . . . . 163 B2
Robins Cross EX16 . . . . 63 A6
Robins Field TQ7 . . . . . 144 F1
Robins Rd EX39. . . . . . 156 E4
Robins Way PL9 . . . . . 255 E8
Robin Wlk 9 EX16 . . . . 161 E6
ROBOROUGH
Great Torrington 42 F3
Plymouth 241 D1
Roborough Ave PL6 . . . 245 B5
Roborough Cl PL6 . . . . 245 B5
ROBOROUGH DOWN . . . 126 F3
Roborough Down La PL6 . 241 F5
Roborough Gdns 3
TQ13 . . . . 131 A5
Roborough La
Ashburton TQ13. . . . . 130 F5
Plymouth PL5. . . . . . . 244 D8

Roborough Rd EX31. . . 155 A8
Roborough Terr TQ13 . . 130 F5
Robyns Cl PL7 . . . . . . 251 B5
Roche Gdn EX2 . . . . . . 182 A8
Rochester Rd
3 Plymouth PL4 . . . . . 248 E4
6 Plymouth PL4 . . . . . 263 A4
Rochford Cres PL5. . . . 243 F5
ROCK 87 D5
Rock Ave
Barnstaple EX32 . . . . . 155 A3
Lynton EX35. . . . . . . 151 B5
ROCKBEARE 99 C6
Rockbeare CE Prim Sch
EX5 . . . . 99 B5
Rock Cross EX15 . . . . . 168 A5
Rock Cl TQ4 . . . . 229 C7
Rockcliffe Ct 1 EX34 . . 150 C6
Rock Cotts TQ7 . . . . . 142 C6
Rock Cross EX17 . . . . . 97 B7
Rockdale Rd PL8 . . . . . 136 A2
Rock End Ave TQ1 . . . . 220 C2
Rockerhayne Cross
EX24. . . . . 102 D7
Rockey La EX20. . . . . . 74 E2
Rockfield Ave PL6. . . . . 244 F6
Rockfield Cl TQ14. . . . . 210 D7
Rockfield Cotts TA21. . . 51 F7
Rockfield Ho EX4 . . . . . 261 B4
Rockfield Rd EX34 . . . . 7 F4
ROCKFORD 5 F4
Rock Gdns
Barnstaple EX32 . . . . . 155 A3
Plymouth PL5. . . . . . . 249 D1
Rock Gdns The* TQ13 . . 123 E5
Rock Head EX37 . . . . . 28 C2
Rock Hill
Aveton Gifford TQ7 . . . 143 C6
Berrynarbor EX34 . . . . 2 D3
Braunton EX33. . . . . . 152 D6
Chulmleigh EX18 . . . . 59 E8
Georgeham EX33. . . . . 8 A2
Plymouth PL5. . . . . . . 244 C7
Umberleigh EX37. . . . . 28 C2
West Down EX34 . . . . . 8 F4
Rock House La TQ1 . . . 214 C5
Rockingham Rd PL5. . . 249 A5
Rock La
Cheriton Bishop EX17 . . 97 B7
Chudleigh TQ13 . . . . . 123 F8
16 Combe Martin EX34. . 3 A3
Offwell EX14 . . . . 86 C1
Rocklands TQ13 . . . . . 123 E5
Rock Lodge Pk EX35 . . 151 B5
Rockmount Terr 6
EX39. . . . . 157 A2
Rockpark Cross TQ13 . . 131 A5
Rock Park Terr 24 EX32 . 155 A4
Rock Pk
4 Ashburton TQ13. . . . 131 A5
Dartmouth TQ6 . . . . . 233 D4
Rock Rd
Chudleigh TQ13 . . . . . 123 E5
Torquay TQ2. . . . . . . 220 B4
Rockshead Hill EX32 . . 18 F3
Rockside EX4. . . . . 173 B6
Rocks The EX39 . . . . . 156 B6
Rockstone The EX7 . . . 205 A7
Rock Terr PL7 . . . . 250 D4
Rock The EX31. . . . . . . 154 F7
Rock View EX16. . . . . . 65 B7
Rock Villas PL16 . . . . . 105 F4
Rockville Pk PL9 . . . . . 255 E8
Rock Walk Mts TQ1. . . . 220 A4
Rockwell Gate TA21. . . 160 B5
ROCKWELL GREEN . . . 160 B5
Rockwell Green CE Prim Sch
TA21. . . . . 160 B5
Rockwood Rd PL6. . . . . 245 D8
Rocky Hill PL19 . . . . . . 171 B5
Rocky La
Abbotsham EX39 . . . . 156 A3
Buckfastleigh TQ11 . . . 236 A3
3 Combe Martin EX34. . . 3 A4
Teignmouth TQ14. . . . 210 A6
Rocky Park Ave PL9 . . . 255 E8
Rocky Park Rd PL9 . . . . 255 E8
Rocombe Cl TQ2 . . . . . 219 F7
Rocombe Cross
Daccombe TQ12 . . . . . 213 F6
Raymond's Hill EX13 . . 104 C6
Rocombe Hill TQ12 . . . 213 F7
Rocombe La TQ12 . . . . 214 A6
Roddick Way 8 PL7 . . . 251 C5
Rodgements Cross EX18 . 59 E8
Rodgements Cross EX18 . 59 F8
Rodgemont's La EX18. . . 59 F8
Rodgers Ind Est TQ4 . . 225 D3
Rodney Cl
Dartmouth TQ6 . . . . . 233 D3
Exmouth EX8 . . . . 203 A7
Rodney St PL5 . . . . . . 247 D8
Rods La PL19 . . . . 117 E6
Rodway Cross EX14 . . . 87 A6
Roeselare Ave PL11. . . . 247 A3
Roeselare Cl PL11. . . . . 247 A3
Rogada Ct TQ5 . . . . . . 230 D3
Rogate Dr PL6 . . . . . . 245 D4
Rogate Wlk PL6. . . . . . 245 D4
Rogers Cl EX16 . . . . . . 161 E6
Rogers Cres EX39 . . . . 157 D2
Roger St PL12. . . . . . . 242 D4
Roland Bailey Gdns
PL19. . . . . 171 A6
Rolle Barton EX9. . . . . 198 D7
Rolle Cotts EX9 . . . . . . 197 E2

Rolle Ct EX38 . . . . 159 C5
Rolle Rd
 Budleigh Salterton EX9 . . 199 G2
 Exmouth EX8 . . . . . . 202 A6
 Great Torrington EX38. . . 159 A5
Rolle's Quay EX31. . . . . 154 F5
Rolle St
 Barnstaple EX31 . . . . . 154 F6
 Exmouth EX8 . . . . . . 202 A6
Rolles Terr EX39 . . . . . . 40 C7
Rollestone Cres EX4 . . 173 E2
Rolle The EX9 . . . . 199 G2
Rolle Villas EX8 . . . . . . 202 A6
Rollis Park Cl PL9 . . . . 255 C8
Rollis Park Rd PL9 . . . . 255 C8
Rolston Cl PL6 . . . . . . 244 D6
Romaleyn Gdns TQ4 . . . 226 B4
Roman Rd
 Feniton EX5 . . . . 84 C2
 Kilmington EX13 . . . . . 87 C1
 Lyme Regis DT7. . . . . 260 D4
 Plymouth PL5. . . . . . . 243 E2
ROMANSLEIGH 45 C7
Romansleigh Cross EX36 . 45 C7
Romansleigh Ridge EX18. 45 C5
Roman Way EX16 . . . . 161 F6
Roman Way
 Honiton EX14. . . . . . . 166 E7
 Plymouth PL5. . . . . . . 243 E2
 Seaton EX12 . . . . 192 A6
Romilly Gdns PL7 . . . . 250 B5
Romney Cl PL5 . . . . . . 244 B1
Romsey Dr EX2 . . . . . . 177 E5
Ronald Terr PL2 . . . . . 247 F5
Roncombe Cnr EX24 . . 101 E5
Roncombe Gate EX24 . . 101 E5
Roncombe Hill EX10 . . . 101 E5
Rookbear La PL9 . . . . . 255 D8
Rookbear La EX31. . . . . . 9 E2
Rookery Cvn Pk EX20 . . . 77 F5
Rookery Hill EX16. . . . . 48 C8
Rookery La DT7. . . . . . 260 C8
Rookery Terr EX17. . . . 160 C5
Rook La PL21. . . . . . . 133 C3
Rooklands ■ TQ12. . . . 207 B3
Rooklands Ave TQ2 . . . 219 E6
Rook Lane End PL21 . . . 133 C3
Rooks Cl EX31 . . . . . . 154 B3
Rooks Cross EX31. . . . . 27 D3
Rooks Farm Rd EX31 . . 153 A4
Rooks Nest EX31. . . . . 153 E5
Rooks Way EX16 . . . . . 161 E6
Rookswood La EX5. . . . . 99 C5
Rookwood Cl EX14 . . . 166 B5
Rookwood Ho EX14 . . . 166 B6
Room Hill Rd TA24 . . . . 21 D7
Roope Cl PL5 . . . . 247 C7
Rooty Cross PL19. . . . . . 27 A7
Roper's Cross EX9 . . . . 255 D8
Ropers Ct EX9 . . . . . . 198 E7
Roper's La EX9 . . . . . . 198 E7
Ropery Rd EX34. . . . . . 150 C6
Ropewalk
 Bideford EX39 . . . . . . 157 A2
 Kingsbridge TQ7 . . . . 258 C4
Ropewalk Hill TQ5. . . . 230 C5
Ropewalk Ho EX8 . . . . 201 E6
Rope Wlk
 ■ Teignmouth TQ14 . . . 210 B5
 Wellington TA21. . . . . 160 C4
Rorkes Cl PL5 . . . . . . 243 E2
Roscoff Cl EX38. . . . . . 159 E5
Rosea Bridge La EX34 . . . 3 A4
Rose Acre Terr EX3 . . . 230 D4
Rose And Crown Hill
 EX17. . . . . 80 A5
Rosebank Cres EX4 . . . 173 E1
Rosebarn Ave EX4 . . . . 173 E1
Rosebarn La EX4 . . . . . 173 E1
Rosebery Ave PL4. . . . 263 C4
Rosebery La PL4 . . . . 263 C4
Rosebery Rd
 Exeter EX4 . . . . 177 E8
 Exmouth EX8 . . . . . . 202 A7
 Plymouth PL4. . . . . . 263 C4
Rose Cl EX16 . . . . 161 F6
Roseclave Cl PL7 . . . . 251 C6
Rose Cotts
 Beer EX12 . . . . 191 D5
 ❾ Bishop's Tawton EX32 . 16 E1
 Frogmore TQ7 . . . . . 144 E3
 Plymouth PL6. . . . . . 249 B8
Rosedale Ave PL2. . . . 248 D7
Rose Dene TQ2 . . . . . 213 F2
ROSEDOWN 22 F3
Rosedown Ave PL2. . . 248 A6
Rose Duryard EX4. . . . 173 A1
Rose Gdns PL6. . . . . . 245 E6
Rose Hill
 Kingskerswell TQ12 . . 212 F4
 Wembury PL9 . . . . . . 140 D7
Rosehill Cl TQ1 . . . . . 220 C5
Rose Hill Cl TQ12 . . . 212 F4
Rosehill Gdns TQ12 . . 212 F4
Rosehill Rd TQ1. . . . . 220 C5
Rose Hill Terr PL17 . . 125 D3
Rosehip Cl PL6 . . . . . . 245 E7
Rose Ho TQ1 . . . . 220 D7
Rose La EX32 . . . . . . 155 C3
Roseland Ave EX1. . . . 178 A6
Roseland Cres EX1 . . . 178 A6
Roseland Cres EX24 . . 54 C8
Roseland Dr EX1 . . . . 178 A5
Roselands EX10. . . . . . 188 A5
Roselands Cotts EX24 . 103 A5
Roselands Dr TQ4 . . . 225 F2
Roselands Prim Sch TQ4 225 F2

Roseland Sq TQ12 . . . . 207 E7
Roselands Rd TQ4 . . . . 226 B2
Rosemary Ave TQ12. . . 206 F4
Rosemary Cl PL7. . . . . 132 D4
Rosemary Ct TQ3 . . . . 226 C8
Rosemary Gdns TQ3 . . 225 F8
Rosemary La
 Colyton EX24. . . . . . . 103 A5
 Dulverton TA22 . . . . . . 33 D6
 Holne TQ11 . . . . 130 A3
 Musbury EX13. . . . . . 103 D5
ROSEMARY LANE. 52 D1
Rosemarylane Cross
 EX15. . . . . 52 D1
Rosemary St EX4 . . . . 176 F5
Rosemont ❾ TQ1. . . . . 220 D4
Rosemont Cl EX2. . . . . 177 B1
Rosemoor Rd EX38. . . . 159 E5
Rosemount
 Bideford EX39 . . . . . . 156 E4
 Paignton TQ4 . . . . . . 226 C5
Rosemount Cl EX14. . . 166 B5
Rosemount Ct TQ8 . . . 259 D5
Rosemount La EX14 . . 166 B5
Rosery Rd TQ2. . . . . . 219 E5
Rose Terr PL18 . . . . . . 125 B5
Rosevean Ct ❽ PL3 . . . 248 F6
Rosevean Gdns PL3 . . 248 F6
Rosevean Ho ❼ PL3 . . 248 F6
Roseveare Cl PL9 . . . . 256 A8
Roseville St EX4. . . . . . 177 E8
Roseway EX8 . . . . 202 F8
Rosewell Cl EX14 . . . . 166 D7
Rosewood Cl PL9 . . . . 255 F5
Rosewood Cres EX5. . . 179 E2
Rosewood Gr EX31. . . . 154 C3
Rosewood Terr ❺ EX4 . 177 F8
Rospeath Cres PL2. . . . 248 D8
Rossall Dr TQ3. . . . . . 226 A5
Ross Cl EX1. . . . . 174 F1
Rose Rd EX16 . . . . . . 161 D6
Rosshayne La EX14 . . . 68 F2
Rosslyn Park Rd PL3 . . 248 D5
Rossiter St PL2. . . . . . 247 E4
Rosyl Ave EX7 . . . . . . 204 C3
Rothbury Cl PL6 . . . . . 245 E4
Rothbury Gdns PL6 . . 245 D4
Rotherfold TQ9 . . . . . . 223 B5
Rothesay Gdns PL5. . . 244 D3
Rougemont Ave TQ2 . . 213 D1
Rougemont Ct PL3 . . . 249 B7
Rougemont Ct EX6. . . . 181 F4
Rougemont Terr EX13. . 167 D5
Roundball Cl EX14 . . . 166 C4
Roundball La EX14 . . . 166 B2
Round Berry Dr TQ8. . . 259 C4
Round Cross TQ11. . . . 236 B6
Roundham Ave TQ4 . . . 226 D5
Roundham Cres TQ4 . . 226 D5
Roundham Gdns TQ4. . 226 C5
Roundham Ho TQ4 . . . 226 C5
Roundham Rd TQ4 . . . 226 C5
Roundhead Rd TQ12 . . 180 F3
Roundhill Cl EX14. . . . 161 B3
Roundhill Cl TQ14 . . . 173 A3
Roundhill Rd TQ2 . . . 219 D2
Roundhouse La EX8 . . 196 B2
Roundings The TQ5 . . 229 B5
Roundmoors Cl TQ12. . 213 A3
Roundslays La PL19 . . 117 E6
ROUNDSWELL 154 B2
Roundtable Meet EX4 . 174 B1
Roundway The TQ12 . . 212 F6
Rousdon TQ9 . . . . 193 F7
Rousdown Rd TQ2 . . . 219 E4

Rowland Cl PL9. . . . . . 255 E5
Rowley Cross EX31. . . . . 4 D1
Rowley Gate EX31. . . . . 11 B6
Rowley Rd TQ1 . . . . . . 214 C1
Rowlstone Cl EX8. . . . . 196 C3
Rowse Gdns PL18 . . . . 125 D3
Rowsell's La TQ9 . . . . . 223 D5
Rows La
 Bampton EX16. . . . . . . 34 A1
 ❷ Combe Martin EX34 . . 3 A3
Row The EX36 . . . . 30 A2
Row Tor Cl EX20 . . . . . 170 D5
Rowtry Cross EX20 . . . . 76 F5
Royal Albert Meml Mus & Art
 Gall* EX4 . . . . 261 A3
Royal Ave The EX8 . . . 201 F7
Royal Charter Pk ❼ PL18. 44 E1
Royal Citadel* PL1 . . . 263 A1
Royal Ct EX2. . . . . 181 B7
Royal Clarence Apps ❹
 EX12. . . . . 192 B4
Royal Clarence Apps ❹
 EX34. . . . . 150 B6
Royal Cres TQ1 . . . . . 178 D3
Royal Ct
 Princetown PL20 . . . . 128 A8
 Torquay TQ1 . . . . 220 B6
Royal Devon & Exeter Hospl
 (Heavitree) EX1. . . . . 177 E6
Royal Devon & Exeter Hospl
 (Wonford) EX2. . . . . . 177 F4
Royal Eye Infmy PL4 . . 248 E4
Royal London Ct EX10. . 188 B3
Royal Navy Ave PL2 . . . 247 F6
Royal Oak Cotts EX20 . 107 H8
Royal Oak Cross EX14 . . 86 E6
Royal Par PL1 . . . . 262 C2
Royal Pines TQ1 . . . . . 220 E3
Royal Way EX6. . . . . . . 201 B8
Royal William Rd PL1 . . 254 A8
Royston Cl ❸ EX4 . . . . 178 C8
Royston Rd
 Bideford EX39 . . . . . . 156 F1
 Churchinford PL3. . . . . 68 D7
ROYSTON WATER 68 F8
Royston Rd 220 D3
Rubby Cross EX6. . . . . . 97 E5
Ruckamore Rd TQ2 . . . 219 E5
Ruckham La EX16 . . . . . 62 F6
Rudds Bldgs ❹ EX4 . . 161 B4
Rudolf Steiner Sch TQ9 . 215 C3
Rudyard Way EX39. . . . 156 B6
Rudyerd Wlk PL3. . . . . 249 D6
Rue de Courseulles sur Mer
 TQ6. . . . . 233 F4
Rue St Pierre PL21. . . . 237 E5
Rufford Cl PL21 . . . . . 248 A7
Rugby Rd EX4 . . . . . . 177 A4
Ruggaton La EX34 . . . . . 2 D2
Rull Cross EX23 . . . . . . 37 B2
Rull Cross EX16 . . . . . . 48 C5
Rull Hill
 Oakford EX16. . . . . . . 48 C5
 West Worlington EX17. . 61 B8
Rull La EX15 . . . . 163 B6
Rumbelow Rd EX16 . . . 161 E6
RUMSAM. 155 B1
Rumsam Cl EX32 . . . . 155 B2
Rumsam Gdns EX32. . . 155 C2
Rumsam Rd EX32 . . . . 155 B2
Runaway La PL21 . . . . 137 A2
Rundle Rd TQ12 . . . . . 207 C4
Rundlestone Cl EX20 . . 70 B8
Runnacleave Rd EX34 . 150 B6
RUNNINGTON 51 F8
Runnymede Ct PL6. . . . 245 E2
Rupert Price Way TQ12. 123 B2
Rupertswood EX34 . . . 150 C6
Rus Cotts EX17 . . . . . . 165 A5
Rushcott Cl EX31. . . . . 153 A4
Rushcott Cross EX31 . . 27 B7
RUSHFORD 116 E3
Rushforth Pl EX4 . . . . 176 E8
Rushlade Cl TQ4 . . . . 225 F2
Rush Park Terr PL18 . . 125 C7
Rush Way TQ9 . . . . . . 223 F5
Ruskin Cres PL5 . . . . 244 E2
Rusper Cl EX15 . . . . . . 83 F6
Russel Cl EX32. . . . . . . 17 C1
Russel La EX15 . . . . . . 65 A1
Russell Ave PL3. . . . . . 248 F7
Russell Cl
 East Budleigh EX9 . . . 198 B6
 Gunnislake PL18 . . . . 125 D7
 Plymouth PL9. . . . . . 256 B7
 Saltash PL12 . . . . . . 242 D2
Russell Court Gdns PL19 171 B6
Russell Ct
 Plymouth PL1. . . . . . 262 C2
 Salcombe TQ8 . . . . . 259 E5
 Saltash PL12 . . . . . . 242 C3
 Tavistock PL19 . . . . . 171 B6
Russell Dr EX9 . . . . . . 198 B6
Russell Pl PL1. . . . . . . 262 B4
Russell St
 Exeter EX4 . . . . 261 C3
 Sidmouth EX10 . . . . . 188 B3
 Tavistock PL19 . . . . . 171 C5
Russell Terr EX4 . . . . 261 C3
Russell Way EX2 . . . . 178 D2
Russell Wlk EX2 . . . . 178 C3
Russell's Mead ❹ TQ13. 111 F5
Russet Cl
 Uffculme EX15. . . . . . . 66 A7
 Wellington TA21 . . . . 160 E7
Russets La TQ13 . . . . 236 C5
Russet Wood PL5 . . . . 243 F4
Ruston Hill EX17 . . . . . 61 A6

Rutger Pl PL1. . . . . . . 262 A4
Rutherford St EX2 . . . 178 A4
Ruthven Cl PL6 . . . . . 248 F8
Rutland Rd PL4 . . . . . 248 F4
Rutt's Cross EX14 . . . . 84 E2
Ruxhill La EX31 . . . . . . 10 D5
Ryall's Cnr
 Bamford EX20. . . . . . . 42 A1
 Merton EX20 . . . . 57 A8
Ryalls Ct EX12 . . . . . 192 A5
Rydal Cl PL6 . . . . 245 D2
Rydal Mews EX4 . . . . 176 F5
Ryde Cl TQ2 . . . . 214 A2
Ryder Cl 10 EX16. . . . . 64 D7
Ryder Rd PL2 . . . . . . 247 F4
Rydon Acres
 Kingsteignton TQ12 . . 207 E8
 Stoke Gabriel TQ9 . . . 227 F8
Rydon Ave TQ12 . . . . 207 E8
Rydonball Cross TQ12 . 211 F7
Rydon Cross
 Denbury TQ12 . . . . . 211 D6
 Stoke Gabriel TQ9 . . . 227 F8
Rydon End TQ12. . . . . 207 E8
Rydon Ind Est TQ12. . . 207 D6
Rydon La
 Abbotskerswell TQ12 . 212 C6
 Exeter EX2. . . . . 178 C3
 Exton EX3, EX5 . . . . . 183 E2
 Holsworthy EX22 . . . . 71 E7
Rydon Lane Ret Pk EX2 . 178 C3
Rydon Prim Sch TQ12 . 207 E8
Rydon Rd
 Holsworthy EX22. . . . 164 B5
 Kingsteignton TQ12 . . 207 E8
Rydons TQ5 . . . . 230 A4
Rye Cl PL21 . . . . 242 C2
Rye La TQ7 . . . . 144 B5
Ryeland Cl PL9 . . . . . 140 D8
Ryelands Farm Ind Est
 TA21. . . . . 160 B3
Rye Park Cl EX19. . . . . 42 D1
Rye Pk
 Beaford EX19. . . . . . . 42 D1
 Monkton EX14 . . . . . . 86 C5
Ryll Cl EX8 . . . . 202 B7
Ryll Court Dr EX8 . . . . 202 B7
Ryll Gr EX8 . . . . 202 B7

S

Sabre Cl TQ12 . . . . . . 180 E3
Sabre Wlk ❶ EX32 . . . 155 B5
Sackery TQ12. . . . . . . 208 D4
Sacred Heart RC Prim Sch
 TQ3. . . . . 226 B7
Saddlers Cl EX6. . . . . . 96 F3
Saddlers Way EX20. . . 170 D6
Saddle The TQ4. . . . . . 226 C2
Sadler Cl EX8 . . . . . . 202 E8
Saffron Ct TQ7 . . . . . 258 D5
Saffron Pk TQ7 . . . . . 258 D5
Sage Gr EX16. . . . . . . 161 F4
Sage Park Rd EX33. . . 152 B7
Sages Lea EX5. . . . . . 184 C6
Sailmakers Ct EX8 . . . 201 E6
St Agnes La TQ2 . . . . 219 E3
St Albans Cl EX4 . . . . 176 E6
St Albans La TQ1. . . . 220 C7
St Albans Rd PL20. . . . 127 A2
St Albans Rd TQ1 . . . 220 C7
St Andrew's CE Prim Sch
 Buckland Monachorum
 PL20. . . . . 126 C3
 Chardstock EX13 . . . . 88 A7
 Plymouth PL1. . . . . . 262 B2
St Andrews Ct
 ❸ Tiverton EX16 . . . . 161 E6
 Torquay TQ1 . . . . . . 219 C8
St Andrews Dr EX13 . . 167 F7
St Andrew's Dr EX13 . . 167 F7
St Andrews Ho EX8 . . . 201 F6
St Andrews Mdw DT7 . . 260 D4
St Andrews Orch EX24 . 103 A5
St Andrews Pl PL10. . . 253 A1
St Andrews Prim Sch
 EX15. . . . . 163 B3
St Andrews Rd
 Cullompton EX15 . . . . 163 C3
 Fremington EX31 . . . . 153 D6
 Paignton TQ4 . . . . . . 226 C5
 Tavistock PL19 . . . . . 171 D2
St Andrew's Rd
 Cowley EX4 . . . . 172 F2
 Exmouth EX8 . . . . . . 201 F6
St Andrew's Sq EX24 . . 103 A5
St Andrew's St PL10. . . 253 A1
St Andrew St
 Millbrook PL10. . . . . 252 E5
 Plymouth PL1. . . . . . 262 C2
 Tiverton EX16 . . . . . . 161 C3
ST ANDREW'S WOOD . . 84 A8
St Annes EX6 . . . . . . 194 D3

St Annes Cl EX22. . . . . 70 E1
St Annes Cl TQ12 . . . . 207 B3
St Annes Pl EX5. . . . . . 82 B5
St Anne's Rd
 Exeter EX1. . . . . 177 E7
 Plymouth PL6. . . . . . 245 D6
 Saltash PL12 . . . . . . 242 E3
 Torquay TQ1 . . . . . . 220 D7
St Annes Well Brewery
 EX4. . . . . 261 A3
St Annes Well Mews
 EX4. . . . . 261 A3
ST ANN'S CHAPEL
 Gunnislake 125 B6
 Kingston. 142 F6
St Anthony's Cl EX11. . 169 E4
St Aubyn Ave PL2. . . . 247 F5
St Aubyn Rd PL1. . . . . 247 E3
St Aubyn St PL1. . . . . 247 E3
St Aubyn's Villas EX16. 161 F3
St Aubyn Terr PL7 . . . 132 F4
St Augustines Cl TQ2. . 214 A3
St Austin Cl PL21. . . . 237 B5
St Barnabas Com Hospl
 PL12. . . . . 242 F2
St Barnabas Ct PL1. . . 262 A4
St Barnabas Terr PL1 . 262 A4
St Bartholomew Way
 TQ12. . . . . 206 D1
St Bernard's Cl
 Buckfast TQ11 . . . . . 236 B7
 Exeter EX2. . . . . 261 C1
St Boniface Cl PL2. . . 248 C5
St Boniface Dr PL2. . . 248 C7
St Boniface RC Coll PL5 . 244 E1
St Boniface Rd EX17 . . 165 A5
ST BRANNOCKS 152 C7
St Brannock's Park Rd
 EX34. . . . . 150 B4
St Brannock's Rd EX34 . 150 B4
St Brannock's Well Cl
 EX33. . . . . 152 D7
St Briac Way EX8 . . . . 196 E3
St Bridget Ave PL6 . . . 244 F1
ST BUDEAUX
 . . . . 243 D2
 . . . . 243 D2
St Budeaux Cl EX11. . . 169 E3
St Budeaux Ferry Rd Sta
 PL5. . . . . 247 D8
St Budeaux Foundation Jun
 Sch PL5. . . . . 243 F2
St Budeaux Orch EX11. 169 E3
St Budeaux Victoria Rd Sta
 PL5. . . . . 243 D1
St Catherines CE Prim Sch
 TQ12. . . . . 180 F1
St Catherines Pk ❻ PL8. 141 F4
St Catherine's Rd TQ1. 220 B8
St Chad Cl PL5. . . . . . 244 C4
St Christophers Sch TQ9 216 C5
St Clares Cl EX12 . . . . 192 B5
St Clement's Terr TQ9. 223 D2
St Columba Cl TQ12. . . 207 E8
St Columba Cl TQ12. . . 207 E8
St Cuthbert Mayne Sch
 TQ1. . . . . 214 A1
St Cyres Rd EX14. . . . 166 B6
ST DAVID'S. 177 B8
St Davids ❶ EX9 . . . . 157 A1
St David's CE Prim Sch
 EX4. . . . . 261 A3
St Davids Cl EX13 . . . 167 F7
St David's Dr EX13 . . . 167 F7
St David's Hill EX4 . . . 177 A7
St David's Prim Sch EX4. 261 A4
St David's Rd PL19 . . . 210 C8
St David's Rd PL19 . . . 171 E5
St David's Terr EX4 . . . 261 A3
ST DOMINICK 125 A3
St Dominick CE Prim Sch
St Dominic Pk PL17 . . 125 A4
St Dominic's Cl TQ1. . . 220 B8
St Dunstan's Rd TQ8 . . 259 C4
St Dunstan's Terr PL4. 263 C3
St DYMPNA'S. 192 A8
St Edmunds Rd TQ2 . . 258 C6
St Edmund's Rd TQ1 . . 220 B8
St Edmunds wlk TQ2 . . 258 C6
St Edward Gdns PL6 . . 245 B1
St Edward's CE Prim Sch
 PL6. . . . . 245 C1
St Efride's Rd TQ2 . . . 219 F5
Ste Honorine Du Fay Cl
 EX32. . . . . 28 E8
St Elizabeth Cl EX2 . . 250 F3
St Elmo ❸ EX2 . . . . . 192 A4
St Elmo Ct TQ8 . . . . . 259 C3
St Erth Rd PL2. . . . . . 248 D7
St Eval Pl PL5 . . . . . . 243 E4
St Francis CE Prim
St Gabriel's Ave PL4 . . 248 E4
St Georges Ave EX13 . . 167 F7
St George's Ave PL2 . . 248 C7
St George's CE Inf Sch
 EX39 . . . . 156 F8
St George's CE Prim Sch
 Plymouth PL1. . . . . . 262 A1
St Georges Cres ❶ PL2. 137 B2
St Georges Cres TQ2 . . 220 C7
St Georges Ct ❶ PL2. . 247 F4
St Georges Hill DT7 . . 260 C6

St Georges Rd PL12 . . . . . . 242 D3
St George's Rd
  Barnstaple EX32 . . . . 155 A6
  Saltash PL12 . . . . 242 E3
  Torquay TQ1 . . . . 220 C7
St George's Terr
  🚊 Barnstaple EX32 . . . . . 155 A6
  Plymouth PL2 . . . . 247 F4
  Shillingford St George EX2 114 C6
St George's View EX15 . . 163 B4
St George's Way EX16. . 161 C3
ST GEORGE'S WELL 163 C5
St George's Well Ave
  EX15. . . . . 163 B4
St German's Rd EX4 . . . . 177 C8
ST GILES IN THE WOOD . 42 B6
ST GILES ON THE HEATH . . 90 B1
St Giles on the Heath Prim
  Sch PL15 . . . . 90 C1
St Gregorys Ct EX12 . . . . 192 A6
St Helens EX39 . . . . 156 A2
St Helen's CE Prim Sch
  EX39 . . . . 156 A1
St Helen's Cl EX33 . . . . 7 E2
St Helen's Ct EX10 . . . . . . 187 F3
St Helens Wlk PL5 . . . . . . 244 C5
St Hilary Sch of English 🔢
  TQ4 . . . . 226 B6
St Hilary Terr PL4 . . . . . . 263 C3
SAINT HILL 66 D3
St Hill Cl EX2 . . . . 177 A2
St Ida's Cl EX2 . . . . 176 D1
St Ives Ct 🔢 TQ1 . . . . 220 A6
ST JAMES' 177 D8
St James Cl
  Exeter EX4 . . . . 261 C4
  Landkey EX32 . . . . 17 C1
  Parkham EX39 . . . . 39 E8
St James Ct
  Exeter EX4 . . . . 177 E8
  Plymouth PL1 . . . . 262 B2
  Torpoint PL11 . . . . 247 B3
St James' Ho 🔢 TQ14 . . . . 210 B5
St James Mews
  Plymouth PL1 . . . . 262 B2
  🔢 Teignmouth TQ14 . . . . . 210 B5
St James' Park (Exeter City
  AFC) EX4 . . . . 261 C4
St James' Park Sta EX4 . 261 C4
St James Pl TQ1 . . . . 220 D7
St James' Place E PL1 . . 262 B2
St James' Place W PL1 . . 262 B2
St James' Prec 🔢 TQ14 . 210 B5
St James Rd
  Torquay PL11 . . . . 247 B2
  Torquay TQ1 . . . . 220 A7
St James' Rd EX4 . . . . . . 261 C4
St James Sch EX4 . . . . . . 174 B1
St James' Pl EX34 . . . . . . 150 C6
St James St EX20 . . . . . . 170 B5
St James Terr
  Exeter EX4 . . . . 261 C4
  Plymouth PL1 . . . . 262 B2
St James Way 🔢 EX16 . . 161 E6
St Joesph's RC Prim Sch
  TQ2 . . . . 207 A4
ST JOHN
  . . . . 252 C8
  . . . . 252 C8
St Johns PL19 . . . . 171 C5
St Johns Ave PL19 . . . . . . 171 C5
St John's Bridge Rd PL4. 263 B2
St John's CE Prim Sch
  Totnes TQ9 . . . . 223 E5
  Wellington TA21 . . . . 160 E6
ST JOHN'S CHAPEL 27 B8
St Johns Cl
  🔢 Colyton EX24 . . . . 103 A4
  Plymouth PL6 . . . . 245 D4
  🔢 Tiverton EX16 . . . . 161 E6
  Wellington TA21 . . . . 160 E6
St John's Cl
  Bishopsteignton EX9. . . . . 208 F7
  Bovey Tracey TQ13 . . . . . . 180 C6
  Honiton EX14 . . . . 166 C6
  Ivybridge PL21 . . . . 237 B5
  Millbrook PL10 . . . . 252 E5
  Skilgate TA4 . . . . 34 E6
St John's Cotts TQ13 . . . 180 C6
St Johns Ct
  Bradworthy EX22 . . . . 53 E8
  Tavistock PL19 . . . . 171 C4
St John's Ct 🔢 TQ3 . . . . . 226 B6
St John's Dr
  Bradworthy EX22 . . . . 53 E8
  Plymouth PL9 . . . . 255 B6
St Johns Farm Mews
  EX8 . . . . 196 F3
St Johns La PL11 . . . . 252 B8
St John's La
  Barnstaple EX32 . . . . 155 C3
  Bovey Tracey TQ13 . . . . . . 180 C7
St John's Pl TQ1 . . . . 220 B4
St John's RC Prim Sch
  EX16 . . . . 161 B4
St John's Rd
  Exeter EX4 . . . . 177 E7
  Exmouth EX8 . . . . 196 E2
  Horrabridge PL20 . . . . 126 F4
  Ivybridge PL21 . . . . 237 B5
  Millbrook PL10 . . . . 252 F5
  Plymouth PL4 . . . . 263 B2
  Plymouth, Turnchapel PL9 255 A6
St Johns St TQ12 . . . . 207 D4

St John's St PL4 . . . . 263 B2
St John's Terr TQ9 . . . . . . 223 B6
St John's Villas EX2 . . . . . 177 F5
St John the Baptist RC Prim
  Sch TQ6 . . . . 233 C2
St Joseph's Cl PL6 . . . . . . 244 F1
St Joseph's RC Prim Sch
  EX8 . . . . 202 B7
ST JUDE'S
  . . . . 263 B3
  . . . . 263 B3
St Jude's Rd PL4 . . . . 263 B2
St Julians Cres PL10 . . . . 253 E7
St Katharine's Rd TQ2 . . 219 E6
St Katherine's Cl EX13 . 153 A5
St Katherine's Mews 🔢
  TQ9 . . . . 223 C5
St Katherines Rd EX4 . . 178 A8
St Katherine's Way TQ9 223 C5
St Keverne Pl PL2 . . . . . . 248 D8
St Keyes Cl 🔟 EX32 . . . . . 17 B2
St Kitts Cl TQ2 . . . . 213 F2
St Lawrence Cl 🔢 EX16 . . 64 D7
St Lawrence Cres EX1 . . 178 D6
St Lawrence Dr EX17 . . . 165 B5
St Lawrence La TQ13 . . . 130 F4
St Lawrence Mews PL4 . 263 A2
St Lawrence Rd PL4 . . . . 263 A4
St Lawrence's Gn EX17 . 165 B5
St Leonard's Ave EX22 . 261 B1
St Leonard's CE Prim Sch
  EX2 . . . . 261 C1
St Leonard's Cl 🔟 TQ12 . 207 B3
St Leonard's Pl EX2 . . . . 261 C2
St Leonards Rd EX4 . . . . 166 A5
St Leonard's Rd
  Exeter EX2 . . . . 261 C2
  Newton Abbot TQ12. . . . . 207 B3
  Plymouth PL4 . . . . 263 C2
St Levan Pl PL2 . . . . 247 E4
St Levan Rd PL2 . . . . 247 F5
ST LOYE'S 178 A3
St Loye's Ct EX2 . . . . 178 A4
St Loyes Rd EX2 . . . . 178 A4
St Loye's Terr EX2 . . . . . . 178 A4
Saint Luke's Campus
  EX1 . . . . 177 E6
St Luke's Campus (Univ of
  Exeter) EX1 . . . . 261 C3
St Luke's Cl TQ12 . . . . . . 207 F1
St Lukes Dr TQ14 . . . . . . 210 A6
St Luke's Pk TQ2 . . . . 220 A4
St Luke's Rd
  Kingskerswell TQ12 . . . . . 212 E8
  Torquay TQ2 . . . . 220 A4
St Luke's Road N TQ2 . . 220 B4
St Luke's Road S TQ2 . . 220 A4
St Luke's Science & Sports
  Coll EX1 . . . . 178 D8
St Malo Cl EX8 . . . . 196 E3
St Marco Gdns TQ7 . . . . . 258 C5
St Margaret Clitherow RC
  Prim Sch TQ5 . . . . 230 B3
St Margaret's Ave TQ1 . 220 B7
St Margaret's Cl TQ1 . . . 220 B8
St Margaret's Cl EX15 . . . 67 B8
St Margarets Cl TQ1 . . . . 220 B8
St Margarets Ct EX3 . . . . 182 E5
St Margaret's Ct 🔢 EX39 156 F7
St Margarets Gdn 🔢
  EX31 . . . . 154 F6
St Margarets La TA20 . . . . 88 C8
St Margaret's Prim Sch 🔢
  TQ1 . . . . 220 B8
St Margarets Rd PL7 . . . . 250 B7
St Margaret's Rd TQ1 . . . 220 B8
St Margaret's Sch EX2 . 177 E5
St Margarets Terr EX3 . . 182 E5
St Margaret's View EX4. 203 A7
St Marks 🔢 EX7 . . . . 204 E6
St Marks Ave EX1 . . . . . . 177 F7
St Mark's CE Prim Sch
  EX23 . . . . 37 B2
St Marks Dr TQ1 . . . . 220 D3
St Marks Rd PL6 . . . . 245 D5
St Mark's Rd
  Honiton EX14 . . . . 166 A4
  Plymouth PL6 . . . . 245 D5
St Martin's Ave PL3 . . . . 248 D7
St Martins Cl EX10 . . . . . 188 B6
St Martin's Cl EX17 . . . . . 78 C4
St Martins Ct TQ2 . . . . . . 213 F1
St Martin's La EX17 . . . . . 165 B6
St Martins Mews TQ1 . . 220 C8
St Martins Rd EX23 . . . . . . 70 A8
St Marwenne Cl EX39 . . . . 70 A6
ST MARYCHURCH 214 C1
St Marychurch CE Prim Sch
  TQ1 . . . . 214 B1
St Marychurch Rd
  Newton Abbot TQ12. . . . . 207 F1
  St Marychurch TQ1 . . . . . . 214 C1
  Torquay, Plainmoor TQ1. . 220 B6
St Maryhaye PL19 . . . . . . 171 A5
St Mary Magdalen Cl
  TQ14 . . . . 208 F7
St Mary's CE Prim Sch
  Bideford EX39 . . . . 157 A4
  Brixton PL8 . . . . 257 A4
St Mary's Cl
  Axminster EX13 . . . . 167 E5
  Brixham TQ5 . . . . 230 B2
  Great Torrington EX38. . . . 159 B4

St Mary's Cotts EX7 . . . . 200 F4
St Marys Ct PL7 . . . . 250 D5
St Mary's Ct
  🔢 Newton Abbot TQ12. . 207 B3
  Paignton TQ3 . . . . 226 A6
  Torquay TQ1 . . . . 214 B1
St Mary's Dr TQ5. . . . . . . 230 D3
St Mary's Flats 🔢 EX39 . 157 A1
St Marys Hill TQ5 . . . . . . 230 D3
St Mary's Hill TQ5 . . . . . . 230 D3
St Marys La DT7. . . . . 104 B6
St Mary's Pk EX11 . . . . . . 169 F3
St Mary's Pk TQ4 . . . . 225 C4
St Mary's RC Prim Sch
  Axminster EX13 . . . . 167 E5
  Buckfast TQ11 . . . . 236 C7
St Mary's Rd
  Barnstaple EX32 . . . . 155 A6
  Brixham TQ5 . . . . 230 D2
  Croyde EX33 . . . . 7 E2
  Newton Abbot TQ12. . . . . 207 B2
  Plymouth PL7 . . . . 250 C6
  Teignmouth TQ14 . . . . 210 A7
St Mary St PL1 . . . . 262 A2
St Mary Steps Terr 🔢
  EX1 . . . . 261 A2
St Marys View
  Silverton EX5. . . . . 82 B5
  West Hill EX11 . . . . 168 E5
St Matthews Cl EX1 . . . . 177 E6
St Matthew's Rd TQ2 . . . 219 D4
St Matthews Wlk EX1 . . 261 C3
St Matthias Church Rd
  TQ1 . . . . 220 E5
St Maurice Cl PL7. . . . . . . 250 F4
St Maurice Mews PL7 . . 250 E4
St Maurice Rd PL7 . . . . . . 250 F3
St Maurice View PL7 . . . 250 F3
St Mawes Dr TQ4 . . . . . . 229 B8
St Mawes Terr 🔢 PL2 . . 247 F5
St Michael Ave PL2 . . . . 247 F5
ST MICHAELS 226 A5
St Michaels Cl EX11 . . . . 260 E4
St Michael's TQ2 . . . . 219 E6
St Michael's Bsns Ctr
  DT7. . . . . 260 E3
St Michael's CE Prim Sch
  Exeter EX1. . . . . 177 F6
  Kingsteignton TQ12 . . . . . 207 E7
  Lyme Regis DT7. . . . . 260 E4
St Michaels Cl
  Lawhitton PL15 . . . . 105 B1
  Otterton EX9 . . . . 198 E7
St Michael's Cl
  Clyst Honiton EX5 . . . . 179 D8
  Exeter EX2 . . . . 177 B1
  Plymouth PL1 . . . . 247 E1
  Torquay TQ1 . . . . 219 E6
St Michael's Ct
  Paignton TQ4 . . . . 226 A4
  🔢 Plymouth PL1 . . . . 247 F3
St Michaels Ho 🔟 DT7 . 260 D3
St Michaels Rd
  Kingsteignton TQ12 . . . . . 207 D6
  Teignmouth TQ14 . . . . 210 C7
St Michael's Rd
  Newton Abbot TQ12. . . . . 207 D1
  Paignton TQ4 . . . . 226 B5
  Torquay TQ1 . . . . 219 E7
St Michaels Sch EX13 . . . 27 D8
St Michaels Terr 🔢
  TQ10 . . . . 134 F2
St Michael's Terr
  🔢 Plymouth, Devonport
    PL1 . . . . 247 F3
  🔢 Torquay TQ1 . . . . 220 B5
St Michaels View EX21 . . 55 E4
St Modwen Rd PL6 . . . . . . 249 F7
St Nazaire App PL1 . . . . . 247 F2
St Nazaire Cl PL1 . . . . 247 E2
St Nicholas CE Jun Sch 🔢
  EX10. . . . . 188 A4
St Nicholas Priory* EX4 261 A2
St Nicholas RC Comb Sch
  EX1. . . . . 178 C6
St Olave's Cl EX4 . . . . 261 A3
St Olaves Mews EX4 . . . . 261 A3
St Oswins TQ1 . . . . 220 B8
St Pancras Ave PL2 . . . . 248 D8
St Patrick's Cl TQ14 . . . . 210 A6
St Pauls Cl
  Bovey Tracey TQ13 . . . . . . 180 D7
  Plymouth PL3 . . . . 249 C5
St Paul's Cres TQ1 . . . . . . 220 B7
St Pauls Cl 🔢 TQ12 . . . . . 207 C3
St Pauls Dr EX22 . . . . 164 B5
St Paul's Rd
  Honiton EX14 . . . . 166 A5
  🔢 Newton Abbot TQ12 . . 207 C3
  Paignton TQ3 . . . . 219 D1
  Torquay TQ1 . . . . 220 B7
St Paul's Sq EX16 . . . . . . 161 C3
St Paul St
  Plymouth PL1 . . . . 254 A8
  Tiverton EX16 . . . . 161 C4
St Peter Cl TQ14 . . . . 210 A5
St Peter's CE Prim Sch
  TQ9 . . . . 171 D5
St Peter's CE Prim Sch
  Budleigh Salterton EX9 . . 197 F2
  Plymouth PL1 . . . . 262 B3
  St Peter's CE Sch EX2 . . 178 C5
St Peters Ct
  Shirwell EX31 . . . . 17 B8
  Torquay TQ1 . . . . 219 D6
  West Buckland EX32 . . . . . . 18 B2

St Peter's Cl TQ13 . . . . . . 180 E8
St Peters Ct
  Plymouth PL1 . . . . 262 A3
  Sidmouth EX10 . . . . 188 B3
St Peter's Hill 🔢 TQ5 . . . 230 D5
St Peters Mount EX4 . . . 176 D7
St Peter's Quay TQ9 . . . . 223 D4
St Peter's RC Prim Sch
  PL5 . . . . 244 B5
St Peters Rd
  Fremington EX31 . . . . 153 D5
  Holsworthy EX22 . . . . 164 B5
  Plymouth PL6 . . . . 244 C2
St Peter's Rd EX14 . . . . . 166 A4
St Peter's School EX8 . . 196 A6
St Peter St EX16 . . . . 161 A4
St Peters Terr 🔢 EX34 . . 150 C5
St Peter's Terr 🔢 EX31. . 154 F6
St Peter's Way PL21 . . . . 237 E3
St Peters Well La EX22 . . 53 E8
St Petrock's Cl EX2 . . . . . 261 C2
St Phillips Ct EX4 . . . . . . 176 F4
St Ronans 2 TQ1 . . . . 220 D5
St Rumon's CE Inf Sch
  PL19 . . . . 171 C6
St Saviours Ho 🔟 EX8 . . 202 A6
St Saviours Rd EX11. . . . . 169 D3
St Saviour's Way EX17 . 165 B5
St Scholastica's Abbey
  TQ14 . . . . 210 D7
St Sevan Way EX8. . . . . . 196 E3
St Sidwell's Ave EX4 . . . 261 C4
St Sidwell's CE Prim Sch
  EX4 . . . . 261 C4
St Sidwell's Ct EX4 . . . . . 261 B4
St Simon's La EX4 . . . . . . 249 B3
St Stephen Rd PL7 . . . . . 250 F3
ST STEPHENS. 242 C1
St Stephen's Hill PL12 . . 242 C1
St Stephen's Pl PL7 . . . . 250 E5
St Stephens Prim Sch
  PL12. . . . . 242 E2
St Stephen's Rd PL12 . . . 242 E2
St Swithin's EX17 . . . . 80 A5
St Teresa Ho PL4 . . . . 263 A3
St Teresa's Ct 🔢 EX39. . 156 F7
St Therese's Ct PL1 . . . . 247 F3
ST THOMAS 177 A3
St Thomas Ct
  Bovey Tracey TQ13 . . . . . . 180 E7
  Plymouth PL7 . . . . 250 F3
St Thomas Ct
  Exeter EX4 . . . . 177 A4
  2 Tiverton EX16. . . . . 161 E6
St Thomas Prim Sch
  EX4 . . . . 177 A4
St Thomas Sta Ct EX4 . . 177 A4
St Thomas Sta EX4 . . . . . 177 A4
St Vincent Ho TQ1 . . . . . . 220 C3
St Vincents Cl TQ1 . . . . . 219 F7
St Vincent's Rd TQ1 . . . . 219 F7
St Vincent St PL2 . . . . . . 247 E4
St Werburgh Pl PL9 . . . . 140 D7
St Wilfrid's Sch EX4 . . . . 261 A3
Salamanca St PL11 . . . . . 247 B3
SALCOMBE 259 B4
Salcombe CE Prim Sch
  TQ8 . . . . 259 C5
Salcombe Ct EX10 . . . . . 188 C4
Salcombe Hill Cl EX10 . . 188 C4
Salcombe Hill Rd EX10 . . 188 C4
Salcombe Lawn EX10 . . . 188 B4
Salcombe Maritime & Local
  History Mus* TQ8 . . . . . . 259 C5
Salcombe Rd
  Malborough TQ7, TQ8 . . . 147 F6
  Plymouth PL6 . . . . 263 C4
  Sidmouth EX10 . . . . 188 B4
SALCOMBE REGIS 188 F6
Salcombe The TQ8 . . . . . 259 B4
Salcombe to Kingsbridge
  Nature Reserve* TQ7 . . 148 C7
Salem Almshouses 🔢
  EX32. . . . . 155 A4
Salem Pl EX4 . . . . 261 C4
Salem St 🔢 EX32 . . . . 155 A4
Salisbury Ave
  Fenton EX4 . . . . 84 D2
  Torquay TQ2 . . . . 213 F1
Salisbury Cl EX14 . . . . 84 D2
Salisbury Ope PL3 . . . . . . 248 B5
Salisbury Rd
  Exeter EX4 . . . . 177 E8
  Exmouth EX8 . . . . 202 A7
  Newton Abbot TQ12. . . . . 207 D4
  Plymouth PL4 . . . . 263 C4
Salisbury Road Prim Sch
  PL4 . . . . 263 C3
Salisbury Terr
  Kilmington EX13 . . . . 87 C1
  Torquay TQ1 . . . . 220 B7
Salliscombe Rd EX24 . . . 101 F6
SALMONHUTCH 165 B2
Salmonhutch Cotts EX17 165 B3
Salmon Leap Cl TQ11 . . . 236 C5
Salmonpool La EX2 . . . . . 177 E3
Salston Barton EX11 . . . . 169 C2
Salston Ride EX11 . . . . . . 169 C3
SALTASH 242 B1
Saltash Bsns Pk PL12 . . . 242 C4
Saltash Com Sch PL12 . . 242 E2
Saltash Her Mus* PL12. . 243 A2
Saltash L Ctr PL12 . . . . . . 242 E2
Saltash Parkway Ind Est
  PL12. . . . . 242 B4

Saltash Rd
  Plymouth, Keyham PL2 . . . 247 E6
  Plymouth PL3. . . . . 262 C4
Saltash Sta PL12. . . . . 243 A2
Saltburn Rd PL5 . . . . 243 C1
Salterne Mdws EX9 . . . . . 198 A2
Saltern Rd TQ4 . . . . 226 C1
Salterns Terr EX39 . . . . . 157 B2
Salter's Bldgs 4 EX16. . 161 D4
Salter's Cross EX10 . . . . 187 D6
Salters Ct EX2 . . . . 178 A4
Salter's La EX24 . . . . 103 A4
Salters Mdw EX10 . . . . . . 188 B5
Salter's Rd EX2 . . . . 178 A4
Salterton Ct EX8 . . . . 202 F8
Salterton Rd
  Budleigh Salterton EX8,
    EX9 . . . . 197 B1
  Exmouth EX8 . . . . 202 C7
Salterton Workshops 🔢
  EX9. . . . . 198 A1
Salting Hill EX9 . . . . 199 I2
Saltings The
  Seaton EX12 . . . . 192 B7
  Shaldon TQ14 . . . . 209 D5
Saltmer Cl EX34 . . . . 150 A2
Salt Mill PL12. . . . . 242 F4
Saltmill Cl PL12 . . . . 242 F4
Saltram House* PL7. . . . 250 A4
Saltram Terr
  Lee Moor PL7 . . . . 132 F4
  Plymouth PL7. . . . . 250 E5
SALTRENS. 25 F1
Saltrens EX39. . . . . 40 F8
Saltways La EX10 . . . . . . 100 F1
Salt Wood La EX34 . . . . 2 F3
Salty La TQ14 . . . . 209 D5
Salutary Mount EX1 . . . 177 F5
Salway Cl EX15 . . . . 163 B3
Salway Gdns EX13 . . . . . 167 F5
Samara Bsns Pk TQ12 . . 180 F3
SAMPFORD ARUNDEL . . 51 E5
Sampford Arundel Com Prim
  Sch TA21. . . . . 51 E5
SAMPFORD CHAPPLE . . 76 E3
SAMPFORD COURTENAY . 76 F4
Sampford Courtenay Sta
  EX20. . . . . 77 A2
Sampford Cross EX20. . . . 76 F4
Sampford Gdns PL20. . . . 127 A3
SAMPFORD MOOR. 51 E5
SAMPFORD PEVERELL . . 50 E1
Sampford Peverell CE Prim
  Sch EX16. . . . . 50 C1
SAMPFORD SPINEY 127 B7
Sampford Terr 🔢 PL20 . . 126 F5
Sampson Cross EX37 . . . . 44 E8
Sampson's Hill EX2 . . . . 114 C6
Sampsons La EX1 . . . . . . 177 E7
Sampsons Plantation
  EX31. . . . . 153 C5
Sanctuary Cl EX32 . . . . . 16 E1
Sanctuary La
  Hatherleigh EX20. . . . . 75 C7
  Woodbury Salterton EX5. . 185 B7
Sanctuary Rd EX22 . . . . . 164 C4
Sandaway La EX34 . . . . 2 F4
Sandclose La EX36 . . . . . . 31 D7
Sand Down La EX5 . . . . . 172 A8
Sanders Cl EX5 . . . . 175 D6
Sanders Cross EX22 . . . . 54 C8
Sandersfield EX15 . . . . . . 83 F6
Sanders La 🔢 EX22 . . . . 164 C5
Sanders' La EX22 . . . . . . 164 C5
Sanderspool Cross TQ10 135 A2
Sanders Rd
  Bow EX17. . . . . 78 C4
  Brixham TQ5 . . . . 230 A5
  Exeter EX4 . . . . 174 E1
Sanders Way EX15 . . . . . . 66 C6
SANDFORD 80 A5
Sandford Ash La EX17. . . 79 A7
Sandford Cl EX32 . . . . . . 155 D1
Sandford Cross EX20. . . . . 77 E4
Sandford La EX20 . . . . 77 F3
Sandford Orleigh TQ12. . 207 B5
Sandford Rd PL9 . . . . 255 F8
Sandfords EX6. . . . . 181 B1
Sandfords Gdns EX38 . . 159 B4
Sandford View TQ12 . . . 207 B4
Sandford Wlk EX1 . . . . . . 261 C3
Sandgate La EX11 . . . . . . 100 D4
Sandheap Cross TQ7 . . . 143 C2
Sand Hill PL18 . . . . 125 D6
Sandhill Cross TQ13 . . . . 111 E5
Sand Hill Pk PL18 . . . . . . 125 C6
Sandhills TQ8. . . . . 259 C3
Sandhills Rd TQ8 . . . . . . 259 C3
Sandhill St EX11 . . . . 169 E4
Sandhole Cross EX39 . . . . 37 A8
Sandick Cross EX22 . . . . . 17 F2
Sand La
  Culleech PL18 . . . . 224 A8
  Totnes TQ9 . . . . 224 A8
Sandon Wlk PL6 . . . . 245 A1
Sandown Rd TQ4 . . . . 225 F2
Sandpark La EX11 . . . . . . 10 D5
Sandpark Rd EX18 . . . . . . 59 D2
Sandpark Rd TQ12 . . . . . 59 D2
Sandpiper Ct
  Exeter EX4 . . . . 174 D1
  Woolacombe EX34. . . . . 8 A6
Sandpiper Dr EX3 . . . . . . 183 C2
Sandpiper Gn EX2 . . . . . . 176 D3
Sandpiper Way TQ2 . . . . 213 C2
Sandpit Hill Cross EX24 . 101 E6
Sand Pit Hill La EX24 . . . 101 E6

Sandquay Rd TQ6 . . . . . . 233 F5
Sandringham Dr TQ3 . . . . 219 B2
Sandringham Gdns TQ3 . . 219 C1
Sandringham Rd TQ12 . . 207 E3
Sands Ct
  Paignton TQ4 . . . . 226 B5
  Seaton EX12 . . . . 191 F7
Sands Gate Cross TQ13 . . 95 F1
Sands Rd
  Paignton TQ4 . . . . 226 C5
  Slapton TQ7 . . . . 145 D3
Sands Sch TQ13 . . . . 130 F4
Sanduck Cross TQ13 . . . 112 A2
Sandy Cross EX9 . . . . . . 198 A8
SANDYGATE 123 E1
SANDY GATE 178 F3
Sandygate Bsns Pk TQ12 123 E1
Sandygate Mill TQ12 . . . 123 E1
Sandy La
  Brampford Speke EX5 . . 81 E1
  Braunton EX33 . . . . 15 A6
  Broadclyst EX5 . . . . . . 175 D5
  Chittlehampton EX37 . . 29 A5
  Croyde EX33 . . . . 7 E2
  Ivybridge PL21 . . . . . . 237 D5
  Kingsbridge TQ7, TQ9 . 144 A5
  Staverton TQ9 . . . . 216 A6
  Woolacombe EX34 . . . . . 1 A1
Sandylane Cross EX38 . . 41 A2
Sandy Lane EX34 . . . . 7 F6
Sandy Lane End TQ9 . . . 144 B6
Sandymere Rd EX39 . . . 156 F7
Sandymoor Cross EX21 . . 72 E1
SANDY PARK 111 B8
Sandypark La EX12 . . . . . 18 E3
Sandy Rd PL7 . . . . 251 C4
Sandy's La EX14 . . . . 68 C2
Sandy Way EX33 . . . . 7 E1
Sandyways Cross TQ13 . 111 C7
Sanford Rd TQ2 . . . . 219 E5
Sango Ct PL10 . . . . 252 F6
Sango Rd PL11 . . . . 247 A2
Sannerville Way EX6 . . . 182 B5
San Remo Terr EX7 . . . . 204 F7
San Sebastian Sq PL1 . . 262 C2
Sanson Cl EX5 . . . . 173 F8
Sarah Cl PL20 . . . . 125 E1
Sargent Cl EX1 . . . . 178 C6
Sargents Mdw EX23 . . . . 37 A1
Sarlsdown Rd EX8 . . . . . 202 D7
Sarum Cl PL3 . . . . 248 F7
SATTERLEIGH 29 C1
Satterleigh Cross EX37 . . 29 C1
Saturday's La TQ12 . . . . 212 F1
Saundercroft Rd EX5 . . . . 99 B7
Saunders Way
  Cullompton EX15 . . . . . 163 E4
  West Charleton TQ7 . . . 144 C1
Saunders Wlk PL6 . . . . . 244 D6
SAUNTON 14 F8
Saunton Beach Villas
  EX33 . . . . 14 E8
Saunton Cl EX33 . . . . . . 152 C6
Saunton Rd EX33 . . . . . . 152 B6
Savage Rd PL5 . . . . 247 D7
Savery Cl PL21 . . . . 237 E6
Savery Terr PL4 . . . . 249 A4
Savile Rd EX4 . . . . 176 F5
Savoy Hill EX4 . . . . 174 A2
Sawmill La EX9 . . . . 197 F7
Sawmills Way ❸ EX14 . . 166 C5
Sawpit La TQ9 . . . . 222 F7
Sawrey St PL1 . . . . 262 A2
Sawyer Dr TQ14 . . . . . . 124 E1
SAWYER'S HILL 52 E7
Sawyers Mill EX16 . . . . . 34 E2
Saxe St ❷ TQ14 . . . . . . 210 B5
Saxon Ave EX4 . . . . 174 F2
Saxon Cl EX17 . . . . 165 D4
Saxon Hts ❷ TQ5 . . . . . 230 C4
Saxon Mdw TQ3 . . . . . . 225 C5
Saxon Rd
  Exeter EX1 . . . . 177 F6
  Tavistock PL19 . . . . . . 171 A6
Saxons Croft EX22 . . . . 155 C3
Saxon Way EX15 . . . . . . 163 C6
Scabbacombe La TQ6 . . 235 A6
Scadsbury La EX20 . . . . . 75 A4
Scalders La EX12 . . . . . 137 C2
Scalwell La EX12 . . . . . 192 A7
Scalwell Mead EX12 . . . 192 A7
Scalwell Pk EX12 . . . . . 192 A7
Scarborough Pl TQ2 . . . 219 F5
Scarborough Rd TQ2 . . . 219 F5
Scarhill Cross EX20 . . . . 95 D4
Scarsdale EX8 . . . . 202 C5
Scattor View EX6 . . . . . 112 F5
Scholars Wlk TQ7 . . . . . 258 D6
School Cl
  Bampton EX16 . . . . 34 B1
  Chulmleigh EX18 . . . . . . 60 A7
  Fremington EX31 . . . . . 153 E5
  Plymouth PL7 . . . . 250 D7
  Shobrooke EX17 . . . . . . 80 E4
Plymouth PL9 . . . . 171 D5
School Cnr EX39 . . . . 22 E3
School Cotts TQ12 . . . . 207 A8
School Ct TQ6 . . . . 233 D3
School Dr PL6 . . . . 245 D7
School Hill
  Cockwood EX6 . . . . 201 B6
  ❶ Dawlish EX7 . . . . . . 204 D6
  Lympstone EX8 . . . . . . 195 E5
  Stoke Gabriel TQ9 . . . . 227 F7
School La
  ❼ Bishop's Tawton EX32 . 16 E1
  Blackawton TQ9 . . . . . 139 E1

School La continued
  Broadclyst EX5 . . . . . . 175 C7
  Chilsworthy EX22 . . . . . 53 E1
  ❺ Colyton EX24 . . . . . 103 A4
  Exeter EX2 . . . . 178 A1
  Exmouth EX8 . . . . 196 C1
  Great Torrington EX38 . 159 C6
  Hartland EX39 . . . . 22 E3
  Honiton EX14 . . . . 166 C6
  Newton Poppleford EX10 186 F8
  Plymouth PL7 . . . . 250 E4
  Rousdon DT7 . . . . 193 F7
  Tatworth TA20 . . . . 88 C8
  Tedburn St Mary EX6 . . 97 F4
  ❺ Teignmouth TQ14 . . 210 A3
  Thorverton EX5 . . . . 81 E4
  West Hill EX11 . . . . . . 168 E5
School Rd
  Ermington PL21 . . . . . 136 F4
  Exeter EX2 . . . . 177 A4
  Kingskerswell TQ12 . . 212 F4
  Lydford EX20 . . . . 107 F4
  Newton Abbot TQ12 . . 207 C3
  Silverton EX5 . . . . 82 B5
  Stoke Fleming TQ6 . . . 146 A7
  Tavistock PL19 . . . . . . 171 D2
  Teignrace TQ12 . . . . . 206 F8
School St ❾ EX10 . . . . . 101 B1
School Way EX20 . . . . . 170 B5
Schooners Ct EX8 . . . . . 201 E6
Schumacher Coll TQ9 . . 215 F2
Scobhill Rd EX35 . . . . 5 E3
Scoldens Cl ❶ EX21 . . 137 B2
Sconner Rd PL11 . . . . . 247 A3
Scoresby Cl TQ2 . . . . . 214 B3
Score View EX34 . . . . . 150 C3
SCORRITON 99 D3
Scott Ave
  ❸ Appledore EX39 . . . . 15 A1
  Exeter EX2 . . . . 177 F3
  Plymouth PL5 . . . . 247 C8
Scott Bsns Pk PL2 . . . . 248 A6
Scott Dr EX8 . . . . 196 B2
Scottleigh TQ2 . . . . 219 F3
Scott Rd PL2 . . . . 248 A6
Scotts ❶ EX16 . . . . 49 B8
Scott's Cl TQ7 . . . . 143 E4
Scott's Hill TA4 . . . . 35 E8
Scott's La
  Raymond's Hill EX13 . . 104 C7
  Wellington TA21 . . . . . 160 E6
Scouse Cross EX13 . . . . . 88 E2
Scouse La EX13 . . . . 88 E2
Scrapton La TQ20 . . . . . . 69 F5
Scratchface La
  Bideford EX39 . . . . 25 D4
  Bideford, Littleham EX39 . 25 F2
  Buckland Brewer EX39 . . 40 B6
  Stockleigh Pomeroy EX17 . 81 B6
Scratch Face La EX2 . . . 176 C2
Scratton Path TQ12 . . . 211 E8
Screechers Hill TQ13 . . 130 F5
Scurfield Cl EX33 . . . . . 152 D7
Sea Birds Pk EX33 . . . . . . 7 E1
Seabourne Ct TQ4 . . . . 226 C4
Seabrook Ave EX2 . . . . 182 C7
Seabrook Mews EX2 . . . 182 C7
Seacliff TQ2 . . . . 220 B4
Seacroft Rd PL5 . . . . . . 243 C2
Seafield Ave EX8 . . . . . 196 A2
Seafield La EX10 . . . . . 188 A3
Seafield Rd
  Seaton EX12 . . . . 192 A5
  Sidmouth EX10 . . . . . . 188 A4
Seafields TQ4 . . . . 226 C2
Seaforth Lodge EX12 . . 191 F6
Sea Haven EX12 . . . . . . 192 B4
Sea Hill
  Beer EX12 . . . . 191 E5
  Seaton EX12 . . . . 192 A4
Seale Cl TQ6 . . . . 233 D4
Seapoint ❶❶ TQ14 . . . . 210 B4
Sea Point TQ4 . . . . 226 D5
Searle St EX17 . . . . 165 C5
Searle Terr EX39 . . . . . 157 A7
Seashore Ctr * TQ4 . . . 226 C4
Seaside Hill EX34 . . . . . . 2 F4
Seasons The ❺ EX4 . . . 178 C8
SEATON 192 B5
  Seaton EX12 . . . . 192 B5
Seaton Ave PL4 . . . . . . 248 E4
Seaton Bsns Pk EX12 . . 245 B3
Seaton Burn EX10 . . . . 187 F4
Seaton Cl TQ1 . . . . 220 D7
Seaton Down Cl EX12 . . 191 F8
Seaton Down Hill EX12 . 191 F8
Seaton Down Rd EX12 . . 192 A5
Seaton Hospl EX12 . . . . 192 A6
Seaton La PL4 . . . . 248 E4
Seaton Marshes Nature
  Reserve * EX12 . . . . . 192 C6
Seaton Orch PL7 . . . . . 136 A8
Seaton Pl PL2 . . . . 247 F5
Seaton Prim Sch EX12 . 192 A6
Seaton Rd
  Colyford EX24 . . . . . . 103 A3
  Farway EX10, EX24 . . . 101 E5
  Musbury EX13 . . . . . . 103 D5
  Seaton EX24 . . . . 102 B4
Seaton Tramway * EX12 . 192 C7
Seaton Way PL6 . . . . . . 126 D2
Sea Trout Mews TQ9 . . 216 A5
Seaview TQ7 . . . . 149 A3
Sea Way
  Gunnislake PL18 . . . . . 125 B5
  Ilfracombe EX34 . . . . . 150 D4

Sea View Ave PL4 . . . . . 263 C4
Seaview Cres TQ3 . . . . . 219 C1
Sea View Dr ❼ PL9 . . . 140 D8
Sea View Gdns TQ7 . . . 147 B7
Seaview Rd DT7 . . . . . . 104 B4
Sea View Rd
  Northam EX39 . . . . 156 F7
  Thurlestone TQ7 . . . . . 143 A2
Sea View Terr
  Beer EX12 . . . . 191 D5
  Brixham TQ5 . . . . 230 C6
  Plymouth PL4 . . . . 263 B4
  Sidmouth EX10 . . . . . . 188 A5
  Thurlestone TQ7 . . . . . 143 A2
Seaward Cl EX12 . . . . . 190 E4
Seaway Cl TQ2 . . . . 219 E3
Seaway Cres TQ3 . . . . . 226 D8
Seaway Cres TQ5 . . . . . 230 B4
Seaway Gdns TQ3 . . . . 226 D8
Seaway La
  Tipton St John EX10 . . 100 D2
  Torquay TQ2 . . . . 219 E3
Seaway Rd TQ3 . . . . . . 226 D8
Seckerleigh Cross EX16 . 64 E5
Seckington Cross EX19 . 58 E4
Secmaton La EX7 . . . . . 200 E1
Secmaton Rise EX7 . . . 200 E1
Second Ave
  Axminster EX13 . . . . . 167 F7
  Dawlish EX7 . . . . 204 C5
  Exeter, Countess Wear
    EX2 . . . . 182 D7
  Exeter, Heavitree EX1 . 177 F6
  Plymouth, Billacombe PL9 250 A1
  Plymouth, Devonport PL1 248 A2
  Plymouth, Weston Mill PL2 247 E7
  Teignmouth TQ14 . . . . 210 A5
  Torquay TQ2 . . . . 220 A8
Second Dr TQ14 . . . . . . 210 B5
Second Field La EX33 . . 152 C6
SECTOR 88 B1
Sector Hill EX13 . . . . . . 88 B1
Sector La EX13 . . . . . . 167 F5
Sedemuda Cl EX10 . . . . 188 A8
Sedemuda Rd EX10 . . . 187 F8
Sedge Cl PL21 . . . . 237 D4
Sedgeclaire Cl EX1 . . . 174 F1
Sedgewell Cross EX21 . . 55 F4
Sedley Way PL5 . . . . . . 244 D3
Sefton Ave PL4 . . . . . . 249 B3
Sefton Cl PL4 . . . . 263 C4
Sefton Ct
  ❷❷ Dawlish EX7 . . . . 204 E6
  Torquay TQ2 . . . . 220 D7
Segrave Rd PL2 . . . . . . 248 B6
Selcombe Cross TQ9 . . 144 E4
Selesbro Cl PL21 . . . . . 137 D6
Selkirk Ho PL3 . . . . 255 F7
Selkirk Pl PL5 . . . . 244 E2
Sellbed Cross TA24 . . . . 21 A8
Sellers Cl EX24 . . . . . . 103 B3
Seller's Grave EX24 . . . 103 A4
Seller's Wood Hill EX12 . 190 E6
Sellick Ave TQ5 . . . . . . 230 D3
Selsdon Cl PL9 . . . . . . 256 C6
Senate Ct EX8 . . . . 196 E1
Senate Way EX8 . . . . . 196 E1
Sendall's Way PL6 . . . . 244 F4
Sennen Cl PL11 . . . . . . 246 F4
Sennen Pl PL2 . . . . 247 E5
Sentry Cnr EX39 . . . . . 157 C1
Sentry Cross EX31 . . . . . 18 A8
Sentry La
  Bishop's Tawton EX32 . 16 F1
  Huntsham EX16 . . . . . 49 E6
Sentrys Orch EX6 . . . . 182 B3
Sercombes Gdns EX6 . . 201 B8
Sergei Cl PL9 . . . . 261 A2
Serpell Cl PL6 . . . . 244 E6
Serstone Cross EX7 . . . . 78 C5
Sessland La
  North Tawton EX17 . . . 77 E1
  Spreyton EX17 . . . . . . 95 D8
Sett Cl TQ13 . . . . 180 D7
Seven Acres Cross EX36 . 31 E6
Seven Acre La
  Braunton EX33 . . . . . . 152 E5
  Bridford EX6 . . . . 112 F5
Seven Acres Pk EX33 . . 152 E5
Seven Ash Cross EX34 . . 3 C1
Seven Brethren Ind Est
  EX31 . . . . 154 F3
Seven Crosses EX16 . . . 63 F6
Seven Crosses Rd EX16 . 161 A3
Seven Hills Ho TQ2 . . . 220 A5
Seven Stars La PL5 . . . 244 C6
Seven Stones Cross TQ7 142 E8
Seventh St ❸❶ EX12 . . 154 F6
Seven Trees Ct PL4 . . . 263 B4
Severn Pl PL3 . . . . 249 C5
Severn Rd TQ2 . . . . . . 219 B7
Sewell Ct PL3 . . . . 248 E5
Sexton's Cross EX6 . . . 113 E6
Seymour Ave PL4 . . . . . 263 B4
Seymour Bglws EX34 . . . 1 A1
Seymour Cl
  Exmouth EX8 . . . . 196 B2
  ❾ Totnes TQ9 . . . . . . 223 D5
Seymour Dr
  Dartmouth TQ6 . . . . . 233 C3
  Plymouth PL7 . . . . 248 F5
  Torquay TQ2 . . . . 220 B4
Seymour Mews PL4 . . . 263 C4
Seymour Pk PL3 . . . . . 249 A5
Seymour Pl
  Plymouth PL1 . . . . 262 A4
  Totnes TQ9 . . . . 223 D5

Seymour Rd
  Exmouth EX8 . . . . 196 B2
  Newton Abbot TQ12 . . 207 C4
  Plymouth, Mannamead PL3 248 F5
  Plymouth, Plympton PL7 250 C6
Seymour St
  Plymouth PL4 . . . . 263 A3
  Wellington TA21 . . . . . 160 C6
Seymour Terr EX16 . . . 161 C4
Seymour Villas EX34 . . . 1 A1
Shackel Cross TA3 . . . . . 67 E8
Shackhayes EX34 . . . . . . 3 A4
Shackleton Cl EX8 . . . . 196 B2
Shackleton Ct PL5 . . . . 244 E1
Shadrack Cross TQ9 . . . 217 B3
SHADYCOMBE 259 D5
Shadycombe Ct TQ8 . . . 259 D5
Shadycombe Rd TQ8 . . . 259 D5
Shady La TQ6 . . . . 146 B7
Shady Nook Pk TQ12 . . 207 E7
Shaftesbury Cl ❷❼ PL4 . 204 E6
Shaftesbury Cotts PL4 . 263 A4
Shaftesbury Ct ❸ PL4 . 263 A4
Shaftesbury Rd
  Exeter EX2 . . . . 177 A4
  ❽ Ilfracombe EX34 . . 150 C5
Shaftesbury Theatre *
  EX7 . . . . 204 D6
Shaftsborough La EX34 . . 1 C1
Shaftsbury Pl ❾ TQ9 . . 223 C5
Shakespeare Cl
  Tiverton EX16 . . . . . . 161 D6
  Torquay TQ2 . . . . 219 D6
Shakespeare Prim Sch
  PL5 . . . . 244 B2
Shakespeare Rd
  Exeter EX2 . . . . 177 F3
  Plymouth PL5 . . . . 244 C2
Shakespeare Way EX8 . . 196 C4
SHALDON . . . . 210 AB
Shaldon Cres PL5 . . . . . 244 B3
Shaldon Prim Sch TQ14 210 A3
Shaldon Rd
  Combeteignhead TQ12 . 208 F5
  Newton Abbot TQ12 . . 207 F2
Shaldon Wildlife Trust *
  TQ14 . . . . 210 B2
Shalford Terr EX13 . . . 103 B6
Shallowford Cl PL6 . . . 249 C8
Shallowford Rd PL6 . . . 249 C8
Shamble Way EX35 . . . 151 E2
Shameface La TQ13 . . . 123 B7
Shamel's End EX16 . . . . 64 E7
Shamples Dr EX17 . . . . . 79 A6
Shamrock Cl EX9 . . . . . 156 F7
Shamwickshire Cl EX7 . 157 C1
Shand Pk
  Axminster EX13 . . . . . 167 C5
  Axminster EX13 . . . . . 167 D5
Shapcott La EX36 . . . . . 32 C2
Shapcott Wood Hill EX36 . 31 F2
Shapland Pl EX16 . . . . . 161 C2
Shapleys Gdns PL9 . . . 256 A5
Shapley Ct TQ5 . . . . . . 230 A2
Shapley Way TQ12 . . . . 180 C1
Shapters Rd PL4 . . . . . 263 C2
Shapters Way PL4 . . . . 255 B8
Shaptor View TQ13 . . . 180 B5
Sharkham Ct TQ5 . . . . . 230 D3
Sharkham Point National
  Nature Reserve * TQ5 . 230 F2
Sharland La EX17 . . . . . 78 F8
Sharland's La EX33 . . . 152 C6
Sharlands Rd EX23 . . . . 70 A6
Sharon Way PL6 . . . . . . 245 A5
Sharper La TQ14 . . . . . 209 C3
Sharpham Dr TQ9 . . . . 223 D4
Sharpham Vineyard &
  Cheese Dairy * TQ9 . . 227 B8
Sharpitor Cl TQ3 . . . . . 218 F1
Sharpitor Row PL20 . . . 127 B4
Sharp Rock EX34 . . . . . 150 D5
Sharps Cl TQ12 . . . . . . 123 B2
Sharps Crest TQ12 . . . . 123 B2
Sharps Ct EX8 . . . . 201 F6
Sharrose Rd PL9 . . . . . 255 B5
SHAUGH PRIOR 132 C6
Shaugh Prior Prim Sch
  PL7 . . . . 132 C6
Shaw Way PL9 . . . . 255 D8
Sheafhayne Cross EX14 . 69 B4
Shearman Ct ❶❽ EX2 . . 261 A2
Shearwater Dr TQ2 . . . 213 D3
Shearwood Cl PL7 . . . . 250 C6
SHEBBEAR 55 D4
Shebbear Coll EX21 . . . 55 E4
Shebbear Com Sch EX21 . 55 E4
Shebbear Cross EX38 . . 41 A2
Shedden Hill Rd TQ2 . . 220 A4
SHEDDON 127 E2
Sheepstor Rd PL6 . . . . 245 D1
SHEEPWASH 56 C1
Sheepwash Cross EX36 . 31 C6
Sheepwash La EX36 . . . 31 C6
Sheirs Orch EX9 . . . . . 197 F8
SHELDON 66 F3
Sheldon Cross EX14 . . . 66 F2
Sheldon's La TA22 . . . . 33 A7
Shell Cl PL9 . . . . 245 E1
Shelley Ave
  Tavistock PL19 . . . . . . 171 D5
Shelley Ct ❽ TQ1 . . . . 220 D4
Shelley Way PL5 . . . . . 243 D1
Shell La EX16 . . . . 47 F1
Shells La EX24 . . . . . . 103 A3

Shell's La TA20 . . . . 69 D3
Shelly Ct EX20 . . . . 95 B4
Shelly Rd
  Exmouth EX8 . . . . 201 E6
  South Zeal EX20 . . . . . 95 B4
Shelly Reach EX8 . . . . . 201 F6
Shelston Tor Dr TQ4 . . . 225 F3
Shelton Pl EX1 . . . . . . 177 F6
Shepherd Cl TQ3 . . . . . 225 E5
Shepherd's Hl EX2 . . . . 178 A1
Shepherds La
  Colaton Raleigh EX10 . 186 E4
  Plymouth PL4 . . . . 263 B2
  Teignmouth TQ14 . . . . 124 E1
Shepherd's La EX15 . . . 52 F1
Shepherds Mdw
  Abbotsham EX39 . . . . 156 A2
  Beaford EX19 . . . . 42 D1
Sheplegh Ct TQ9 . . . . . 145 B8
Sheppard Rd EX4 . . . . . 173 D2
Sheppard's Knap EX13 . . 87 A2
Sheppard's Row EX8 . . 202 A7
Sheppaton La EX18, EX19,
  EX7 . . . . 43 B2
SHERBERTON 129 A8
Sherborne Cl PL9 . . . . . 256 C6
Sherborne La DT7 . . . . 260 E3
Sherborne Rd TQ12 . . . 207 B3
Sherbrook Cl EX9 . . . . 203 F8
Sherbrook Hill EX9 . . . 203 F8
Shercroft Cl EX5 . . . . . 175 E2
SHERFORD 144 F3
Sherford Cres
  Plymouth, Elburton PL9 . 256 C7
  Plymouth, West Park PL5 . 244 A3
Sherford Cross TQ7 . . . 145 A3
Sherford Down Cross
  TQ7 . . . . 144 D3
Sherford Down Rd TQ7 . 144 E3
Sherford Rd PL9 . . . . . 256 D7
Sherford Wlk PL9 . . . . 256 C6
Sheridan Rd
  Exeter EX4 . . . . 178 C8
  Plymouth PL5 . . . . 244 C1
Sherman Ho EX11 . . . . 169 E3
Sherracombe Cross EX36 . 19 C6
Sherracombe La EX36 . . 6 A5
Sherratt's Oak EX31 . . . 155 B7
Sherrell Pk PL6 . . . . . . 125 E1
Sherril Cl PL9 . . . . 255 F4
Sherwell La
  Dawlish Warren EX7 . . 201 A2
  Staverton TQ9 . . . . . . 216 A5
Sherwell Ct TQ11 . . . . 236 B5
Sherwell Hill TQ2 . . . . 219 E5
Sherwell La
  Plymouth PL4 . . . . 263 A4
  Torquay TQ2 . . . . 219 E5
Sherwell Park Rd TQ2 . . 219 E5
Sherwell Rise S TQ2 . . 219 D5
Sherwell Valley Prim Sch
  TQ2 . . . . 219 C7
Sherwell Valley Rd TQ2 . 219 C7
Sherwill Cl PL21 . . . . . 237 A6
Sherwill La TQ9 . . . . . . 216 A5
Sherwood DT7 . . . . 260 C4
Sherwood Cl EX2 . . . . . 177 F5
Sherwood Cross EX14 . . 84 D2
Sherwood Dr EX8 . . . . 196 E3
Sherwood Gn EX38 . . . 42 E7
Shetland Cl TQ2 . . . . . 213 E2
Shewte Cross TQ13 . . . 122 D5
Shields The EX34 . . . . . 150 C4
Shieling Rd EX31 . . . . . 16 A3
Shillands EX16 . . . . 161 B5
Shillingate Cl EX7 . . . . 204 C4
SHILLINGFORD 34 E2
SHILLINGFORD ABBOT . . 181 A6
Shillingford La EX6 . . . 181 A3
Shillingford Rd EX2 . . . 181 A7
SHILLINGFORD ST
  GEORGE 114 C7
Shilstone Cross EX32 . . 28 C5
Shilstone La TQ13 . . . . 113 C1
Shilston Gate PL21 . . . 137 D4
Shindle Pk TQ7 . . . . . . 228 C2
Shinners Cotts TQ6 . . . 228 C2
SHIPHAY 219 C7
Shiphay Ave TQ2 . . . . . 219 D7
Shiphay La TQ2 . . . . . . 219 D7
Shiphay Manor Dr TQ2 . 219 D8
Shiphay Park Rd TQ2 . . 219 D8
Shiphay Prim Sch TQ2 . 219 D8
Shipley Cl TQ10 . . . . . . 135 A3
Shipley Cl TQ10 . . . . . . 135 A3
Shipley Rd EX14 . . . . . 166 E6
Shipley Wlk PL6 . . . . . 245 A1
Shipney La TQ13 . . . . . 124 A7
Shirburn Rd
  Plymouth PL6 . . . . 249 B8
  Torquay TQ1 . . . . 220 A7
Shire Cl
  Honiton EX14 . . . . 166 A5
  Paignton TQ4 . . . . 229 B8
Shire Ct EX22 . . . . 70 E1
Shire La DT7 . . . . 104 D4
Shirley Cl EX34 . . . . . . 196 D4
Shirley Cnr EX17 . . . . . 79 B5
Shirley Ct TQ1 . . . . . . 220 D4
Shirley Gdns PL5 . . . . . 244 C1
Shirley Towers TQ1 . . . 220 C3
SHIRWELL 17 B8
Shirwell Com Prim Sch
  EX31 . . . . 17 B8

Shirwell Cross
Barnstaple EX31 . . . . 16 E6
Shirwell EX31 . . . . 17 B8
Shirwell Rd EX31 . . . . 17 A7
Shoalgate Cross EX20 . . . . . 94 F8
Shobbrook Hill TQ12 . . . . . 206 E4
SHOBROOKE 80 E4
Shobrooke Cross EX17 . . . . 80 D4
Shobrook La EX17 . . . . 78 F7
Shoemaker's La PL12 . . . . 242 E2
Shooting La EX14 . . . . 60 B7
Shooting Marsh Stile
EX2 . . . . 261 A1
Shoots Barn Cross EX14 . . 84 D3
Shoot's La EX14 . . . . 67 A3
SHOP
Kilkhampton 37 A1
Milton Damerel 54 F6
Shop Cotts PL7 . . . . 132 F4
SHORE BOTTOM 86 F6
Shore Head EX14 . . . . 86 F5
Shoreland Cross EX18 . . . . 44 F5
Shorelands Rd EX31 . . . . . 154 D3
Shorelands Way EX31 . . . . 154 D3
Shoreland Way EX39 . . . . . 156 E7
Shoresgate Cross EX19 . . . 76 F8
Shoreside EX14 . . . . 210 A3
Shorland Cl EX7 . . . . 204 F8
Shorneywell TQ7 . . . . 145 A1
SHORTACOMBE 108 A5
Shortacombe Cnr EX31 . . . 10 A1
Shortacombe Dr EX33 . . . . 152 B7
Shortcross TQ7 . . . . 143 C2
Short Cl EX39 . . . . 156 D2
Short Cotts PL11 . . . . 247 A3
Short Cross TQ9 . . . . 139 B3
Shorter Cross TQ9 . . . . 135 D2
Short Furlong EX12 . . . . . . 191 D5
Short La
Combe Martin EX34 . . . . 2 F1
Halwell TQ9 . . . . 139 B3
Shaldon TQ14 . . . . 209 C4
Shortlands
Pyworthy EX22 . . . . 71 D5
Yettington EX9 . . . . 197 F8
Shortlands La EX15 . . . . . . 163 B3
Shortlands Rd EX15 . . . . . . 163 B3
SHORT MOOR 86 E7
Shortmoor Cross EX14 . . . . 86 E6
SHORTON 219 A1
Shorton Rd TQ3 . . . . 226 A8
Shorton Valley Rd TQ3 . . . 219 A1
Short Park Rd PL3 . . . . 248 D5
Shortridge Cl
Honiton EX14 . . . . 166 C4
Witheridge EX16 . . . . 46 E1
Shortridge Mead 🏠
EX16 . . . . 161 B4
Shorts Way TQ9 . . . . 222 E6
Shortwood Cl EX9 . . . . 197 F2
Shortwood Cres PL9 . . . . . 256 A7
Shovelpiece La EX32 . . . . . 19 A7
Shrewsbury Ave TQ2 . . . . 214 A1
Shrewsbury Rd PL5 . . . . . 244 C4
Shrinkhill La EX16 . . . . 161 D3
Shrubbery Cl EX22 . . . . . . 155 C3
Shrubbery La EX14 . . . . 86 E6
Shrubbery The
Axminster EX13 . . . . 167 D5
Exbourne EX20 . . . . 76 C5
SHUTE
Kilmington 103 A8
Newton St Cyres 81 A3
Shute TQ7 . . . . 147 E6
Shute Barton * EX13 . . . . . 103 B8
Shute Cross
Newton St Cyres EX17 . . . . 81 B2
South Brent TQ10 . . . . 134 E1
Shute Ct TQ14 . . . . 209 A8
Shute Hill
Bishopsteignton TQ14 . . . . 209 A8
Malborough TQ7 . . . . 147 E6
Teignmouth TQ14 . . . . 210 C5
Shute Hill Cres 🔟 TQ14 . . 210 C5
Shute Hill La EX13 . . . . 103 B7
Shute La
Combe Martin EX34 . . . . 3 A4
Denbury TQ12 . . . . 211 A6
Huish Champflower TA4 . . . 35 C8
Moretonhampstead TQ13 . 111 F5
Winkleigh EX19 . . . . 58 F2
Shuteleigh TA21 . . . . 160 E5
Shute Meadow St 🔟
EX8 . . . . 202 A7
Shute Park Rd PL9 . . . . . . 255 F6
Shute Pk TQ7 . . . . 147 E6
Shute Prim Sch EX13 . . . . 103 B8
Shute Rd
Kilmington EX13 . . . . 87 C1
Shute EX13 . . . . 103 A7
Totnes TQ9 . . . . 223 D5
Shute Row TA21 . . . . 160 E5
Shutes Mead EX11 . . . . . . 169 E4
Shute Wood EX18 . . . . 58 F6
Shutscombe Hill EX32 . . . . 18 E5
Shuttern Cl EX5 . . . . 172 A8
Shutterton Ind Est EX7 . . 200 F1
Shutterton La EX7 . . . . . . 201 A3
Shutter Water Rd
Westwood EX15 . . . . 83 C1
Yarcombe EX15 . . . . 99 C8
Sicklemans Cl TQ7 . . . . . . 144 C1
SID 188 C5
Sidborough Hill EX17 . . . . 61 B1
SIDBURY 101 B2

Sidbury CE Prim Sch
EX10 . . . . 101 C2
Sidcliffe EX10 . . . . 188 C6
Siddalls Gdns EX16 . . . . . 161 E5
Siddals Gdns EX16 . . . . . . 161 E4
Sideling Cl EX2 . . . . 114 A6
Sideling Fields EX16 . . . . 161 F2
Side Wood La EX36 . . . . . . 32 A1
SIDFORD 101 B1
Sidford Cross 🔟 EX10 . . . 101 B1
Sidford Rd EX10 . . . . 188 B7
Sidgard Rd EX10 . . . . 188 C6
Sidholme Cotts EX10 . . . . 188 B5
Siding Cross TQ10 . . . . . . 137 E8
Sidings The
Braunton EX33 . . . . 152 D6
Kingsbridge TQ7 . . . . 258 C5
Sid La EX10 . . . . 188 C5
Sidlands EX10 . . . . 188 A4
Sidleigh EX10 . . . . 188 C5
Sidmount Gdns EX10 . . . . 188 A5
SIDMOUTH 188 C7
Sidmouth Coll EX10 . . . . . 188 C7
Sidmouth Inf Sch 🔟 188 B7
Sidmouth Int Sch 🔟
EX10 . . . . 188 B4
Sidmouth Mus* EX10 . . . . 188 B3
Sidmouth Rd
Bradninch EX5 . . . . 83 B5
Clyst St Mary EX2, EX5 . . 179 A3
Colyton EX24 . . . . 103 A4
Exeter EX2 . . . . 178 D5
Exeter EX5 . . . . 99 A1
Honiton EX14 . . . . 166 A3
Lyme Regis DT7 . . . . 260 C3
Ottery St Mary EX11 . . . . 169 E2
Sidmouth Sp Ctr EX10 . . 188 C7
Sidmouth Victoria Hospl
EX10 . . . . 188 B4
Sidney Ct 🔟 EX7 . . . . 204 D6
Sid Park Rd EX10 . . . . 188 B5
Sid Rd EX10 . . . . 188 C5
Sid Vale Cl 🔟 EX10 . . . . . 101 B1
Sidvale Ct 🔟 EX10 . . . . . . 101 B1
Sidvale Mews 🔟 EX10 . . . 101 B1
Sidwell Ho EX1 . . . . 261 C4
Sidwell St EX4 . . . . 261 C4
SIGFORD 131 B8
Sigford Cross TQ13 . . . . . 122 B2
Sigford Rd EX2 . . . . 181 D8
Signal Ct EX33 . . . . 152 D5
Signals The EX14 . . . . 84 D2
Signal Terr EX31 . . . . 154 F4
Sign of the Owl Cross
TQ10 . . . . 137 E8
Signpost La EX17 . . . . 80 A7
Silbury Terr EX17 . . . . 165 C5
Silcombe Cross EX36 . . . . . 30 F3
Silcombe Hill EX36 . . . . 30 E4
SILFORD 156 D4
Silford Cross EX39 . . . . . . 156 D5
Silford Rd EX39 . . . . 156 E5
Silvan Dr EX33 . . . . 152 E7
Silver Birch Cl
Exeter EX2 . . . . 178 A3
Plymouth PL6 . . . . 245 C7
Silver Birch Ct 🔟 EX31 . . 154 C2
Silver Bridge Cl EX11 . . . 229 C8
Silverdale
Exmouth EX8 . . . . 196 E3
Silverton EX5 . . . . 82 B6
Silverdale Cl TA22 . . . . 33 E4
Silver Head Hill TQ9 . . . . 216 F1
Silverhill Bldgs TQ12 . . . . 212 D8
Silverhills Rd TQ12 . . . . . 212 D8
Silver La
Exeter EX4 . . . . 261 C4
Rockbeare EX5 . . . . 99 C5
Silver Lea EX13 . . . . 87 C1
Silver Pk EX15 . . . . 66 A3
Silver St
🔳 Appledore EX39 . . . . 15 A1
Axminster EX13 . . . . 167 D5
🔟 Bampton EX16 . . . . 34 B1
🖽 Barnstaple EX32 . . . . . . 155 A5
Bere Ferrers PL20 . . . . . . 240 A3
Berrynarbor EX34 . . . . 2 E3
Bideford EX39 . . . . 157 A1
Braunton EX33 . . . . 152 D7
Buckfastleigh TQ11 . . . . . 236 B5
Colyton EX24 . . . . 103 A5
Culmstock EX15 . . . . 66 E6
Honiton EX14 . . . . 166 C6
Ipplepen TQ12 . . . . 211 C1
Kentisbeare EX15 . . . . 66 A3
Kilmington EX13 . . . . 87 C1
Lydford EX20 . . . . 107 F3
Lyme Regis DT7 . . . . 260 D3
Ottery St Mary EX11 . . . . 169 D4
Saltash PL12 . . . . 243 A2
Thorverton EX5 . . . . 81 E4
Tiverton EX16 . . . . 161 D4
West Buckland TA21 . . . . . 52 F7
Willand EX15 . . . . 162 D4
Silvers The EX3 . . . . 178 F2
Silver Stream Way PL8 . . 257 B5
SILVER STREET 52 F8
Silver Terr
Exeter EX4 . . . . 261 A3
Millbrook PL10 . . . . 253 A6
SILVERTON 82 B5
Silverton CE Prim Sch
EX5 . . . . 82 B6
Silverton Rd EX2 . . . . 181 D8
Silverway EX17 . . . . 80 E4

Silverwell Pk PL21 . . . . . . 137 C2
Silverwood Ave TQ12 . . . . 207 E1
Silverwood Hts EX31 . . . . 155 B6
Silworthy Cross EX22 . . . . . 38 F2
Simcoe Pl EX15 . . . . 67 B8
Simcoe Way EX14 . . . . 67 B1
Simey Cl EX4 . . . . 176 F7
Simmonds Pl EX15 . . . . . . 163 E4
Simmons Cl EX20 . . . . 170 C5
Simmons Way EX20 . . . . . 170 C5
Simms Hill TQ12, TQ13 . . 122 C2
Simon Cl PL9 . . . . 255 E6
Simon Ct 🔟 TQ1 . . . . 220 B6
SIMONSBATH 13 B2
SIMONSBURROW 52 C3
Simons Cross EX13 . . . . . . 87 E4
Sims Terr PL18 . . . . 125 D6
Sinai Hill EX35 . . . . 151 C5
Singer Cl TQ3 . . . . 226 A5
Singmore Rd TQ3 . . . . 218 E2
Sing's La EX33 . . . . 152 D5
Sir Alex Wlk EX3 . . . . 182 E5
Sir John Hunt Com Sports
Coll PL5 . . . . 244 D4
Sir Robert's Path EX31 . . . 4 D5
Siskin Chase EX15 . . . . . . 163 A2
Sisna Pk Rd PL6 . . . . 245 F5
SITCOTT 90 C2
Sithney St PL5 . . . . 243 C1
Sivell Mews EX1 . . . . 177 F5
Sivell Pl EX2 . . . . 177 F5
Six Acre Cross EX35 . . . . . . 5 A4
Six Acre La EX35 . . . . 5 A5
Six Acres EX6 . . . . 98 C4
Six Mile Hill
Dunsford EX6 . . . . 113 A8
Tedburn St Mary EX6 . . . . . 98 A5
Skardale Gdns PL6 . . . . . . 249 D8
Skardon Pl PL4 . . . . 263 A4
Skelmersdale Cl TQ7 . . . . 258 D5
Skern Cl EX39 . . . . 156 F8
Skern Way EX39 . . . . 156 F8
Skerries Rd PL6 . . . . 244 F7
SKILGATE 34 E6
Skinnard La PL18 . . . . 125 C5
Skinner Cl 🔳 EX2 . . . . . . 161 B4
Skirhead La EX34 . . . . 3 B3
Skye Cl TQ2 . . . . 213 E2
Skylark Rise
Plymouth PL6 . . . . 245 E8
Tavistock PL19 . . . . 171 D1
Skylark Spinney 🔳 EX31 154 A2
Skyways Bsns Pk EX5 . . . . 99 A4
Slade EX39 . . . . 156 E2
Slade Cl
Ottery St Mary EX11 . . . . 169 F4
Plymouth PL9 . . . . 256 A5
Slade Cross
Kingsbridge TQ7 . . . . 144 B6
Lustleigh TQ13 . . . . 122 D8
North Tawton EX20 . . . . . . 77 D5
Slade La
Abbotskerswell TQ12 . . . . 212 B6
Combe Martin EX31 . . . . . . 3 E1
Galmpton TQ5 . . . . 229 B5
Hawkridge TA22 . . . . 21 D1
Sidmouth EX10 . . . . 189 C7
West Anstey EX36 . . . . 32 B6
Slade Lane Cross EX34 . . . 3 E1
Slade Rd
Ilfracombe EX34 . . . . 150 A4
Ottery St Mary EX11 . . . . 169 F3
Slade Valley Rd EX34 . . . . 150 A3
Sladnor Park Rd TQ1 . . . . 214 C5
Sladnor Pk TQ1 . . . . 214 C5
Slanns Mdw TQ12 . . . . . . 207 D6
Slappers Hill TQ4, TQ5 . . 234 E7
SLAPTON 145 C4
Slapton Ley National Nature
Reserve* TQ7 . . . . 145 D2
Slate La PL1 . . . . 262 A2
Slatelands Cl PL7 . . . . 251 B3
Slattensdale La EX31 . . . . . 4 D5
Sleap Hill EX9 . . . . 198 C7
Sleepy Hollow EX2 . . . . . 182 C7
Sleepy La TQ3 . . . . 219 A1
SLERRA 23 D3
Sletchcott Cross EX37 . . . 44 E8
Slew Hill EX34 . . . . 2 C2
Slewhill Cross EX20 . . . . . . 95 B5
Slewton Cres EX5 . . . . 99 E8
Slipperstone TQ9 . . . . 139 A7
Slipperstone Cross TQ9 . 216 C7
Slipper Stone Dr PL21 . . 237 A6
Slipperstone La TQ9 . . . . 216 C7
Slipway Quay PL12 . . . . . 239 B2
Slittercombe La EX6 . . . . 194 E3
Sloe La 🔳 EX32 . . . . 17 B2
SLONCOMBE 111 E5
Slough La
Bishops Nympton EX36 . . . 30 F3
Uplyme DT7 . . . . 261 C8
Smallack Cl PL6 . . . . 244 F2
Smallack Dr PL6 . . . . 244 F2
Smallcombe Dross
TQ10 . . . . 135 D6
Smallcombe Hill EX16,
EX36 . . . . 32 D4
Smallcombe Rd EX36 . . . . 31 F8
Smallcombe Rd EX16 . . . 161 B4
Smallacott Hill EX6 . . . . . . 97 D3
Smallcombe Cross TQ3 . . 225 E8
Smallcombe Rd TQ3 . . . . 225 E8
Smalldon La TQ1, TQ2 . . 214 B8
Small La
Broadclyst EX5 . . . . 175 D7
Burlescombe EX16 . . . . 51 B2
Rattery TQ10 . . . . 135 D3

Smallpark La TQ13 . . . . . . 131 E1
Smallridge Cl PL9 . . . . . . 255 F5
Smallridge Rd EX13 . . . . . . 87 F4
Small Sch The EX39 . . . . . . 22 E3
Smallwell La
Ashprington TQ9 . . . . 139 E7
Marldon TQ3 . . . . 218 C3
Smardon Ave TQ5 . . . . . . 230 A5
Smardon Cl TQ5 . . . . 230 A5
SMEATHARPE 68 B5
Smeathy La EX15 . . . . 52 F3
Smeaton Sq PL3 . . . . 249 D6
Smeaton's Twr* PL1 . . . . 262 C1
Smedie's Pit La EX13 . . . . 87 A1
SMITHALEIGH 136 A6
Smithay Mdws EX6 . . . . . 113 B4
Smithfield Dr PL12 . . . . . . 242 B3
Smith Field Rd EX2 . . . . . 181 A8
Smithfields TQ9 . . . . 223 A6
Smith Hill TQ14 . . . . 208 F8
SMITHINCOTT 66 A6
Smiths Ct EX2 . . . . 261 A1
Smith's La
Calverleigh EX16 . . . . 48 E4
Hollocombe EX18 . . . . 58 E6
Smith St TQ6 . . . . 233 F3
Smiths Way EX16 . . . . 50 D1
Smockpark La PL9 . . . . . . 140 B8
Smokehouse Cross TQ13 . 122 B3
Smugglers' La EX7 . . . . . 210 F8
Smythen Cross EX34 . . . . . 9 E6
Smythen St EX1, EX4 . . . 261 A2
Smythes Cross EX15 . . . . . 67 F7
Snell Dr PL12 . . . . 242 B3
Snodbrook Cross EX10 . . 101 C1
Snowball Rd TQ1 . . . . 219 F7
Snowdonia Cl TQ4 . . . . . 225 D4
Snowdrop Cl 🔳 EX14 . . . 166 A4
Snowdrop Cres PL15 . . . . 105 A2
Snowdrop Mews EX4 . . . . 176 D8
Snows EX17 . . . . 80 B5
SOAR 147 E4
Solar Cres EX4 . . . . 176 F4
SOLDON CROSS 53 E5
Solland Cross EX20 . . . . . . 76 D4
Solland La EX20 . . . . 76 D4
Soloman Dr EX39 . . . . 157 A1
Solsbro Rd TQ2 . . . . 219 E4
Solways PL7 . . . . 260 C5
Somer Fields PL7 . . . . 260 B3
Somerlea EX15 . . . . 162 D5
Somerset Ave EX4 . . . . . . 176 E4
Somerset Cotts 🔟 PL3 . . 248 E3
Somerset Ct
🖽 Brixham TQ5 . . . . 230 C5
🔟 Torquay TQ2 . . . . 223 D5
Somerset Pl
🖾 Barnstaple EX31 . . . . . 154 F5
Plymouth PL3 . . . . 248 A4
🔟 Teignmouth TQ14 . . . . 210 B4
Torquay TQ2 . . . . 223 D5
Somerset Place La 🔟
PL3 . . . . 248 A4
Somerslea EX21 . . . . 73 E2
Somers Rd DT7 . . . . 260 C3
Something La EX33 . . . . 7 E1
Somerville Cl
Exmouth EX8 . . . . 196 D1
Willand EX15 . . . . 162 C5
Somerville Pk EX15 . . . . . 162 C4
Somerville Rd EX15 . . . . . 162 C5
Sommers' Cres EX34 . . . . 150 C6
Soper Rd TQ4 . . . . 210 A7
Soper's Hill PL5 . . . . 240 E1
Soper Wlk TQ14 . . . . 210 A7
Sophia Way TQ12 . . . . . . 207 A2
Sorley Cl 🔳 EX14 . . . . . . 166 A4
Sorley Green Cross TQ7 . 143 F5
Sorley La TQ7 . . . . 143 F5
Sorrell Ct TQ12 . . . . 207 D7
Sorrento 🔟 TQ1 . . . . 220 C5
SOURTON 93 B1
SOUTH ALLINGTON 149 B5
South Ave
Bideford EX39 . . . . 157 D1
Exeter EX1 . . . . 177 E6
Lyme Regis DT7 . . . . 260 D4
Southay Cross TA20 . . . . . 69 D4
Southay La TA20 . . . . 69 D4
Southbank TQ12 . . . . 207 C4
South Bank Dr EX39 . . . . 156 F2
SOUTH BRENT 134 F3
South Brent Prim Sch
TQ10 . . . . 135 A3
South Brent Rd TQ7 . . . . 143 E8
Southbrook Cl 🔳 TQ13 . . 180 C8
Southbrook La
Bovey Tracey TQ13 . . . . . 180 B8
🔳 Bovey Tracey TQ13 . . 180 C8
Otterton EX10 . . . . 187 B1
Rockbeare EX5 . . . . 99 C7
Southbrook Rd
Bovey Tracey TQ13 . . . . . 180 A8
Exeter EX2 . . . . 178 A2
Southbrook Sch EX2 . . . . 178 A2
South Burrow Rd 🔟
EX34 . . . . 150 B5
SOUTH CHARD 88 C8
South Church La EX20 . . 170 A4
Southcombe Cross
Hittisleigh EX6 . . . . 96 F4
Widecombe in the Moor
TQ13 . . . . 121 B3
Southcombe Hill EX6 . . . . 96 F4
Southcombe St TQ13 . . . 111 A6
SOUTH COMMON 88 A4

South Common La EX13 . . 88 A5
Southcoombe Terr EX12 . 192 E7
Southcote La EX14 . . . . 86 C4
Southcote Orch TQ9 . . . . 223 E5
SOUTHCOTT 157 D4
Southcott Cross
Chawleigh EX18 . . . . 60 A6
Langtree EX38 . . . . 40 F3
Okehampton EX20 . . . . 93 C5
Southcott Rd EX39 . . . . . 156 F4
South Courts The 🔳
PL1 . . . . 262 A3
South Dartmoor Com Coll 🔟
TQ13 . . . . 131 A5
South Dean Cnr EX31 . . . . 4 A5
South Dean La EX31 . . . . . 4 A5
South Devon Coll
🗹 Newton Abbot TQ12 . . 207 C3
Paignton TQ4 . . . . 225 E1
South Devon Rly*
Buckfastleigh TQ11 . . . . . 236 E4
Staverton TQ9 . . . . 215 D4
Totnes TQ9 . . . . 223 C8
SOUTHDOWN 253 B6
SOUTH DOWN 68 C6
Southdown Ave TQ5 . . . . 230 B2
Southdown Cl
Beer EX12 . . . . 191 D5
Brixham TQ5 . . . . 230 B1
Southdown Cotts PL10 . . 253 B6
Southdown Cross
Brixham TQ5 . . . . 230 B1
Burlescombe EX16 . . . . 51 B2
South Molton EX36 . . . . . . 46 A5
South Down Cross EX19 . . 76 C7
South Down Farm TQ7 . . 147 F5
Southdown Hill
Brixham TQ5 . . . . 230 B2
Copplestone EX17 . . . . 79 D7
Meshaw EX36 . . . . 45 F6
Southdown Ho 🔳 TQ13 . 180 D8
Southdown La EX37 . . . . . 43 D3
South Down La EX36 . . . . 31 E6
Southdown Rd
Beer EX12 . . . . 191 D5
Brixham TQ5 . . . . 230 B1
Millbrook PL10 . . . . 253 A6
South Down Rd PL2 . . . . 248 B6
South Down Rd EX7 . . . . 204 D4
Southdown Terr PL10 . . . 253 A6
South Dr EX36 . . . . 159 B5
Southella Rd PL20 . . . . . . 127 A2
South Emb TQ6 . . . . 233 F3
South End Cl 🔟 EX33 . . . 152 D5
SOUTHERLY 108 A7
Southern Cl
Plymouth PL2 . . . . 247 F7
Torquay TQ2 . . . . 214 A4
Southernhay
Newton Abbot TQ12 . . . . 207 C2
Winkleigh EX19 . . . . 58 F2
Southernhay E EX1 . . . . . 261 B3
Southernhay Gdns EX1 . . 261 B2
Southern Rd EX10 . . . . . . 202 A8
Southerns Cross EX13 . . . 103 D5
Southern Terr PL4 . . . . . . 248 F4
Southernway PL9 . . . . 256 A8
Southern Wood EX8 . . . . 196 E2
SOUTHERTON 100 B1
Southey Cres TQ12 . . . . . 213 A3
Southey Dr TQ12 . . . . 213 A3
Southey La
Kingskerswell TQ12 . . . . . 213 A3
Sampford Courtenay EX20 . 76 F3
South Farm Rd EX9 . . . . . 198 C3
Southfield
Saltash PL12 . . . . 242 C3
🔟 Torquay TQ1 . . . . 220 D4
West Alvington TQ7 . . . . . 258 A4
Southfield Ave TQ3 . . . . . 226 A8
Southfield Cl TQ3 . . . . . . 226 A8
Southfield Dr EX17 . . . . . 165 B6
Southfield Rd
Bideford EX39 . . . . 157 C1
Paignton TQ3 . . . . 226 A7
Southfield Rise TQ3 . . . . 226 A8
Southfields
Bridgerule EX22 . . . . 70 F5
Totnes TQ9 . . . . 224 B6
Southfield Way EX16 . . . . 161 B4
Southford La TQ9 . . . . . . 216 A4
South Ford Rd TQ6 . . . . . 233 F3
South Furzeham Rd TQ5 230 C5
Southgate EX2 . . . . 261 B2
Southgate Ave PL9 . . . . . 255 E4
Southgate Cl PL9 . . . . . . 255 E4
Southgate Ct PL9 . . . . . . 261 B2
South Gn 🖽 EX22 . . . . . . 261 B2
South Grange EX2 . . . . . . 178 D3
South Hams Bsns Pk
TQ7 . . . . 143 E4
South Hams Hospl TQ7 . 258 A4
South Hayes Copse EX32 . 17 B2
South Hele Cross EX36 . . 31 B4
South Hill
Plymouth, Hooe PL9 . . . . 255 C5
Plymouth, Stoke PL1 . . . 248 A3
South Hill Cotts EX22 . . . 38 C1
South Hill Rd TQ1 . . . . . . 220 C4
SOUTH HOLE 36 C4
Southholme Terr EX39 . . 157 B2
SOUTH HUISH 147 D7
SOUTH KNIGHTON 131 F7
South La
Braunton EX33 . . . . 15 E8
Challacombe EX31 . . . . . . 11 F3
Hartland EX39 . . . . 22 E2

South La *continued*
Lynton EX35. . . . . .5 F5
Southland Park Cres 8
PL9. . . . . .140 D8
Southland Park Rd PL9. .140 D8
Southlands
 8 Braunton EX33. . . . . . .152 D5
Exeter EX1. . . . . .177 E6
Wrafton EX33. . . . . .152 E4
Southlands Dr EX38. . . . . .40 F2
Southlands Rd TQ2. . . . . .220 A5
South Lawn
Exeter EX2. . . . . .261 C2
Sidmouth EX10. . . . . .188 C8
South Lawn Terr EX1. . . .177 F6
Southlea EX39. . . . . .156 E6
South Lea EX33. . . . . .152 E5
South Lea Cl EX33. . . . . . .152 E5
South Lee Cross EX36. . . .30 B7
SOUTHLEIGH. 102 C4
Southleigh Hill Cross
EX24. . . . . .102 B3
Southleigh Rd EX24. . . . . .102 B3
South Ley Cross EX31. . . .3 D1
Southley Rd EX36. . . . . . .158 C4
Southmead Prim Sch
EX33. . . . . .152 E4
SOUTH MILTON. 143 D1
South Milton St PL4. . . . . .263 C2
SOUTH MOLTON. 158 D3
South Molton Com Coll
EX36. . . . . .158 C3
South Molton & District
Mus* EX36. . . . . .158 C4
South Molton Hospl
EX36. . . . . .158 C4
South Molton Inf Sch
EX36. . . . . .158 C5
South Molton Rd EX16. . .34 B1
South Molton St EX18. . . .44 E1
South Molton United Jun Sch
EX36. . . . . .158 C5
South Moor La EX17. . . . .59 E4
South Par EX9. . . . . .199 H2
South Parks Rd TQ2. . . . .213 F2
SOUTH PILL. 242 E3
South Pk
Barnstaple EX32. . . . . . . .155 B3
Braunton EX33. . . . . .152 F5
Woolfardisworthy EX39. . .38 F7
SOUTH POOL. 148 F7
Southport Ave EX4. . . . . .176 E5
South Quay TQ4. . . . . .226 C5
SOUTH RADWORTHY. 19 F3
South Rd
Barnstaple EX32. . . . . . . .155 B3
Bideford EX39. . . . . .25 E4
Brixham TQ5. . . . . .230 C3
Millbrook PL10. . . . . .252 F5
Speedwell Cres PL6. . . . . .249 B7
Speedwell Units TQ6. . . . .233 C3
Speedwell Wlk PL6. . . . . . .249 B7
Spekes Cross EX18. . . . . .59 C4
Spence Combe Cross
EX17. . . . . .79 C4
South Sands TQ4. . . . . . . .226 C2
Southside EX17. . . . . .59 F2
Southside Ope PL1. . . . . . .263 A2
Southside St PL1. . . . . . . .263 A2
South Sq 10 EX24. . . . . . . .103 A4
South St
Axminster EX13. . . . . .167 D5
Barnstaple EX32. . . . . . . .155 B3
Braunton EX33. . . . . .152 D5
Colyton EX24. . . . . .103 A4
Denbury TQ12. . . . . .211 A6
Dolton EX19. . . . . .57 F7
Exeter EX1. . . . . .261 B2
Exmouth EX8. . . . . .202 A6
Great Torrington EX38. . . .159 C5
Hatherleigh EX20. . . . . . . .75 C7
Holcombe Rogus TA21. . . .50 F5
Sheepwash EX21. . . . . .56 C1
South Molton EX36. . . . . .158 C4
Torquay TQ2. . . . . .219 F6
Totnes TQ9. . . . . .223 C5
Wellington TA21. . . . . . . .168 E5
Winkleigh EX19. . . . . .58 E5
Woolacombe EX34. . . . . . . .7 F6
SOUTH TAWTON. 95 B5
South Tawton Prim Sch
EX20. . . . . .95 B4
Southtown
Dartmouth TQ6. . . . . .233 F2
Kenton EX6. . . . . .194 F3
Southview PL10. . . . . .253 A6
South View
Abbotskerswell TQ12. . . . .212 B6
Barnstaple EX31. . . . . .154 D7
Bideford EX39. . . . . .156 F2
Bovey Tracey TQ13. . . . . .180 D7
Bratton Fleming EX31. . . .18 A8
Braunton EX33. . . . . .152 D4
 5 Hemyock EX15. . . . . . .67 B8
 10 Horrabridge PL20. . . . .126 F4
Ilfracombe EX34. . . . . .1 E3
Lydford EX20. . . . . .107 F4
Mary Tavy PL19. . . . . .117 E6
Plymouth, Crownhill PL5. .244 E2
Plymouth, Elburton PL9. . .256 B6
Prixford EX31. . . . . .16 C7
Tiverton EX16. . . . . .161 D4
Westleigh EX16. . . . . .51 A3
South View Cl
Braunton EX33. . . . . .152 D4
Plymouth PL7. . . . . .250 D7
Willand EX15. . . . . .162 D5
South View Est EX15. . . . .162 D5
South View Pk PL7. . . . . .250 D7
Southview Rd TQ3. . . . . . .226 A7
South View Rd EX15. . . . .162 D5
South View Terr
Exeter EX4. . . . . .177 D8
Exminster EX6. . . . . .182 B4
Plymouth PL4. . . . . .263 C3
Sidmouth EX10. . . . . .188 A5

SOUTHVILLE. 258 E3
Southville Gdns TQ7. . . . .258 D3
SOUTHWAY. 244 F6
Southway
Sidmouth EX10. . . . . .188 C4
Tedburn St Mary EX6. . . . .97 F4
Southway Ave TQ2. . . . . .213 F1
Southway Dr PL6. . . . . . . .244 E6
Southway La
Plymouth, Southway PL6. .245 B6
Plymouth, Tamerton Foliot
PL6. . . . . .244 C6
**Southway Valley Nature
Reserve*** PL6. . . . . .244 F6
Southwell Rd PL6. . . . . . .244 E1
SOUTH WONFORD. 54 E3
Southwood Cross EX5. . . .99 C4
Southwood Ct TQ1. . . . . . .220 C5
Southwood Dr EX39. . . . . .157 A3
Southwood Mdws EX3. . . .40 C7
South Yeo Cross
Northlew EX20. . . . . .74 F2
Poughill EX17. . . . . .62 E3
SOUTH YEO HILL EX17. . .62 E3
SOUTH ZEAL. 95 B3
Sovereign Cl EX8. . . . . . . .196 E1
Sovereign Ct PL7. . . . . . . .250 C5
Sowden La
Barnstaple EX32. . . . . . . .155 B5
Lympstone EX8. . . . . .195 E4
Sowden Pk EX32. . . . . . . .155 C4
SOWTON. 179 B6
Sowton Ind Est EX2. . . . .178 E5
Sowton La EX5. . . . . .179 B6
SOWTONTOWN. 117 F3
Spa Ct TQ1. . . . . .220 C4
Spanishlake Cross EX6. . .113 C6
Spanish Lane End TQ9. . .139 A5
Sparhanger Cross EX35. . .5 B3
Sparhanger La EX35. . . . . .5 B3
Sparkatown La PL20. . . . .127 B3
Sparke Cl PL7. . . . . .251 B4
Sparks Barn Rd TQ4. . . . .226 B4
SPARKWELL. 251 F8
Sparrow La TA24. . . . . . . .21 C7
Sparrow Pk TQ7. . . . . . . .147 F6
Sparrow Rd TQ9. . . . . . . .223 B5
Speakers The PL21. . . . . .237 E5
Speares The PL21. . . . . . .242 B2
Spearfield Cl EX36. . . . . . .158 D4
Spears La TA21. . . . . .35 F4
Speedwell Cl
Barnstaple EX32. . . . . . . .155 E3
Bideford EX39. . . . . .25 E4
Brixham TQ5. . . . . .230 C3
Millbrook PL10. . . . . .252 F5

Springfield
Dunkeswell EX14. . . . . . . .67 C2
 15 Horrabridge PL20. . . . .126 F4
Membury EX13. . . . . .87 D6
Winkleigh EX19. . . . . .58 E3
Spring Field EX39. . . . . . . .22 D3
Springfield Ave
Barnstaple EX32. . . . . . . .155 B3
Plymouth PL9. . . . . .256 B6
Springfield Cl PL9. . . . . . .256 B7
Springfield Cres
Fremington EX31. . . . . . . .153 F6
Northam EX39. . . . . .156 F7
Springfield Dr
Kingsbridge TQ7. . . . . . . .258 C5
Plymouth PL3. . . . . .248 A4
 9 Tiverton EX16. . . . . . . .161 B4
Springfield Gdns EX7. . . .200 F1
Springfield La PL9. . . . . . .256 B7
Springfield Pk
Bridestowe EX20. . . . . . . .107 F8
Bucktastleigh TQ11. . . . . .236 D5
Springfield Rd
Barnstaple EX31. . . . . . . .154 B3
Exeter EX4. . . . . .177 D8
Exmouth EX8. . . . . .196 B1
Honiton EX14. . . . . .166 F5
Ilfracombe EX34. . . . . . . .150 B6
Offwell EX14. . . . . .86 A3
Plymouth PL9. . . . . .256 B6
South Brent TQ10. . . . . . .134 F3
Torquay TQ1. . . . . .220 B7
Springfields EX21. . . . . . .103 A3
Springfield Rise PL9. . . . .256 B7
Springfield Terr
 1 Bideford EX39. . . . . . . .157 B1
 12 Combe Martin EX34. . . . .3 A3
 8 Northam EX39. . . . . . . .156 F7
Tatworth TA20. . . . . .88 D8
Westward Ho! EX39. . . . . .156 C7
Spring Gdns EX11. . . . . . .169 E3
Springhead Cross EX12. .193 A6
Springhead La EX13. . . . . .87 C1
Spring Head Rd DT7. . . . .260 B6
Springhill
Lyme Regis DT7. . . . . .260 D4
Plymouth PL2. . . . . .248 C8
Spring Hill PL19. . . . . .171 B5
Springhill Down Hill EX16. 47 D4
Springhill Gdns DT7. . . . .260 D4
Springhill La PL2. . . . . . . .248 C8
Spring Rd TQ9. . . . . .223 B5
Spring Pk PL6. . . . . .245 E7
Spring Rd PL9. . . . . .140 B8
Springwood Cl
Ivybridge PL21. . . . . .237 E5
Plymouth PL7. . . . . .251 A3
Spruce Cl
Exeter EX4. . . . . .174 B2
Exmouth EX8. . . . . .196 D3
Spruce Gdns PL7. . . . . . . .251 B5
Spruce Way TQ3. . . . . . . .225 E8
Spry La PL16. . . . . .106 A4
Sprys Shop Cross EX22. . .72 D2
SPRYTOWN. 106 B4
Sprytown Cross PL16. . . .106 B4
Sprywood Cross EX21. . . .56 A1
Spur Cross EX39. . . . . .22 E2
Spurfield Cotts EX6. . . . . .182 A4
Spurway Gdns EX14. . . . .167 E4
Spurway Hill EX16. . . . . . .48 A7
Spurway Mill Cross EX16. 48 A8
Spurway Rd EX16. . . . . . .161 F3
Square's Quay TQ7. . . . . .258 C4
Square The
Ashreigney EX18. . . . . . . .58 E8
Beaford TQ3. . . . . .154 F5
Beer EX12. . . . . .191 D5
 16 Bere Alston PL20. . . . .125 E1
 11 Bishop's Tawton EX32. .16 E1
Braunton EX33. . . . . .152 D6
Bridestowe EX20. . . . . . . .107 F8
Cawsand PL10. . . . . .253 A1
Chagford TQ13. . . . . .111 A6
Chittlehampton EX37. . . . .28 F4
 12 Chulmleigh EX18. . . . . .44 E1
Ermington PL21. . . . . .136 F4
Exeter, Exwick EX4. . . . . .176 F8
 3 Exeter, Middle Moor
EX2. . . . . .178 D5
Fremington EX31. . . . . . . .153 E5
Gunnislake PL18. . . . . . . .125 D6
Gunnislake, St Ann's Chapel
PL18. . . . . .125 B5
Hartland EX39. . . . . .22 D3
 5 Holsworthy EX22. . . . . .164 C4
Inner Hope TQ7. . . . . .147 B6
Kingswear TQ6. . . . . .234 A3
Lutton PL21. . . . . .133 B2
Moretonhampstead TQ13. .111 F5
 6 Northam EX39. . . . . . . .156 F7
North Molton EX36. . . . . .30 D8
North Tawton EX20. . . . . .77 C5
Petrockstow EX20. . . . . . .56 F4
Plymouth, Stonehouse PL1. 248 A2
Rockbeare EX5. . . . . .99 C5
Saltash PL12. . . . . .242 C3
Sandford EX17. . . . . .80 A5
 8 Seaton EX12. . . . . .192 A5
Shebbear EX21. . . . . .55 D8
Sheepwash EX21. . . . . .56 C1
South Molton EX36. . . . . .158 C4
Uffculme EX15. . . . . .66 A7
Ugborough PL21. . . . . . . .137 D6
 6 Whimple EX5. . . . . .99 E8

Square The *continued*
Witheridge EX16. . . . . .46 E1
Squires Cl EX32. . . . . .155 B2
Squires La EX21. . . . . .72 F4
Squire's La EX12. . . . . . . .192 C5
Squires' La EX21. . . . . .55 D6
Squirrel Ct TA21. . . . . . . .160 D5
Stabb Dr TQ4. . . . . .226 A1
Stabb Dr TQ4. . . . . .226 A1
Stabdon La EX19, EX20. . . .59 C1
Stable Cotts PL7. . . . . . . .250 F5
Stable Ctyd DT7. . . . . . . .193 E6
Stable La TQ1. . . . . .214 B1
Stables The TQ9. . . . . .223 D6
Stadbury Cross EX14. . . . .86 B5
Stadbury La EX14. . . . . . . .86 C5
Staddens La TA2. . . . . . . .219 C6
STADDISCOMBE. 255 F3
Staddiscombe Rd PL9. . . . .255 F4
STADDON. 72 C6
Staddon Cl
Braunton EX33. . . . . .152 C6
Exeter EX4. . . . . .178 B7
Staddon Court Cotts PL9 140 B8
Staddon Cres PL9. . . . . . .255 E6
Staddon Cross EX22. . . . . .72 C6
Staddon Gate EX20. . . . . . .77 F5
Staddon Gdns TQ2. . . . . .214 B2
Staddon La PL9. . . . . .255 D6
Staddonhill Rd TA24. . . . . .21 F8
Staddon La PL9. . . . . .255 B4
Staddon Moor Cross
EX20. . . . . .77 D5
Staddon Park Rd PL9. . . . .255 E6
Staddon Rd
Appledore EX39. . . . . .15 A1
Holsworthy EX22. . . . . . . .164 F3
Tedburn St Mary EX6. . . . .97 E2
Staddon Terrace La PL7. .262 D4
Stadium Dr TQ12. . . . . . . .213 A2
Stadium Way EX4. . . . . . .261 C4
Staffick Cl EX6. . . . . .194 E3
Stafford Cl EX16. . . . . .161 E5
Stafford Ct 11 TQ9. . . . . .223 E5
Stafford Hill EX14. . . . . . .84 F8
Stafford La EX4. . . . . .176 C8
Stafford Moor Fishery*
EX19. . . . . .58 B6
Stafford Rd
Dolton EX19. . . . . .57 F7
Paignton TQ4. . . . . .226 C5
Stafford Way EX19. . . . . . .57 F7
Stag Cnr EX15. . . . . .162 E1
Staggers La EX33. . . . . . . .152 E3
Stag La
Plymouth, Elburton PL9. . .256 B8
Plymouth, Plympton PL9. .250 B1
Stag Mill Cross EX16. . . . .50 B3
Stag's Head Ct EX2. . . . . .178 D5
Stag's Head EX22. . . . . . . .29 C6
Stags Wood Dr EX21. . . . . .73 E2
Stakes Hill TQ7. . . . . .143 A5
Stallards
Braunton EX33. . . . . .152 C7
Wellington TA21. . . . . . . .160 C3
Stamford Cl PL9. . . . . .255 A6
Stamford Fort Cotts PL9. .255 A6
Stamford La PL9. . . . . .255 A6
Stammery Hill EX13. . . . . .88 C1
Stamps Hill PL8. . . . . .257 A6
Stamps The PL17. . . . . . . .125 A5
Stanborough Cross PL9. . .256 C7
Stanborough Ct TQ9. . . . .139 A3
Stanborough Rd PL9. . . . .256 B7
Stanbridge Pk EX39. . . . . .156 D2
Stanbury Ave PL6. . . . . . . .244 F1
Stanbury Cl PL15. . . . . .90 C1
Stanbury Copse EX34. . . .150 A4
Stanbury Cross
Holsworthy EX22. . . . . . . .164 D6
Morwenstow EX23. . . . . . . .36 F1
Stanbury Ct EX17. . . . . . . .165 C5
Stanbury Rd
Knowle EX33. . . . . .8 D1
Torquay TQ2. . . . . .219 C7
Stanbury's Orch EX6. . . . . .96 F3
Stancombe Cross TQ7. . . .144 E4
Standard Ct PL19. . . . . . . .117 E6
Standarhay Cl PL9. . . . . . .256 C7
Standarhay Villas PL9. . . .256 C7
Stanfield TQ1. . . . . .220 E5
Stanford Rd EX2. . . . . .178 C5
Stang La EX34. . . . . .8 F5
Stangray Ave PL4. . . . . . . .248 D4
Stanhope Cl EX22. . . . . . . .164 C5
Stanhope Dr EX10. . . . . . .188 B6
Stanhope Rd PL5. . . . . . . .243 C1
Stanhope Sq 7 EX22. . . . .164 C5
Stanhope Terr EX31. . . . . .157 A3
Staniforth Dr PL21. . . . . . .237 D4
Stanley Cotts EX24. . . . . .103 A3
Stanley Ct TQ1. . . . . .220 C8
Stanley Gdns TQ3. . . . . . .226 A7
Stanley Mews EX9. . . . . . .198 A1
Stanley Pl PL4. . . . . .249 B2
Stanley Rd TQ1. . . . . .220 C8
Stanley Sq EX33. . . . . .182 F4
Stanley St 10 TQ14. . . . . .210 B4
Stanley Wlk EX33. . . . . . . .196 D4
Stanmore Rise EX7. . . . . . .204 E7
Stanmore Tor TQ3. . . . . . .226 A5
Stannary Bridge Rd
PL19. . . . . .171 D6
Stannary Cl EX17. . . . . . . .237 E5
Stannary Ct EX20. . . . . . . .170 B6
Stannary Pl TQ13. . . . . . . .111 A6
Stansfeld Ave TQ3. . . . . . .226 A6

Stantaway Pk TQ1. . . . . . .219 F7
Stanton Ct TQ7. . . . . .138 A1
Stantor La TQ3. . . . . .218 F5
Stant Way TA20. . . . . .69 F6
Stantyway Cross EX9. . . . .198 F6
Stantyway Ct EX9. . . . . . . .198 E7
Stantyway Rd EX9. . . . . . .198 F5
Stanwell Dr EX33. . . . . . . .156 C6
Stanwell Hill
Bideford EX39. . . . . .25 C4
Westward Ho! EX39. . . . . .156 C6
Stanwey EX1. . . . . .178 A5
Staplake La EX6. . . . . .201 A7
Staplake Rd EX6. . . . . .195 B1
Staplake Rise EX6. . . . . . .195 A1
Stapleback Cross EX19. . .57 E5
Staple Back La EX19. . . . . .57 E5
Staple Cl PL6. . . . . .241 C1
Staple Cross EX19. . . . . . . .57 F5
Stapledon Cotts EX22. . . . .72 E7
Stapledon La TQ13. . . . . . .130 F5
Stapleford Dr TQ14. . . . . .210 B7
Stapleford Gdns PL5. . . . .243 F5
Staplegate EX16. . . . . .50 A3
Staplehill Rd
Coldeast TQ12. . . . . .122 F1
Newton Abbot TQ12. . . . . .206 B8
Staple Orch TQ9. . . . . .222 F8
Staple Row TQ9. . . . . .222 F8
Staples Mdw 4 EX8. . . . . .202 A7
Staples Terr DT7. . . . . .260 E4
Stapleton Cl TQ4. . . . . . . .225 E3
STAPLEY. 68 A8
Star Barton La EX5. . . . . . .172 D4
Starcombe La EX10. . . . . . .101 D4
STARCROSS. 201 A8
Starcross Sta EX13. . . . . . .87 E6
Starcross Prim Sch EX6. .201 A8
Starcross Sta EX6. . . . . . . .201 B8
Starkey Cl 10 EX16. . . . . . .64 D7
Starlings Roost EX15. . . . .163 A2
Starpitten Gr TQ2. . . . . . . .214 B3
Starpitten Lane W TQ2. . . .214 A2
Star Pk PL18. . . . . .125 D6
Starre Cl EX12. . . . . .192 A7
START. 145 B4
Start Ave
Chillington TQ7. . . . . .145 A1
Teignmouth TQ14. . . . . . .210 C7
Start Bay Pk TQ6. . . . . . . .145 F6
Start Cross TQ12. . . . . . . .211 B7
Starved Oak Cross EX5. . .81 D1
Station App TQ10. . . . . . . .134 F3
Station Cl
Braunton EX33. . . . . .152 D5
 7 Holsworthy EX22. . . . . .164 C4
Station Cotts
Bittaford TQ10. . . . . .137 E8
Brandis Corner EX22. . . . . .73 A5
Station Cross
Bittaford TQ10. . . . . .137 E8
Crediton EX17. . . . . .165 E4
Sampford Peverell TA21. . .113 E5
 1 Tavistock PL19. . . . . . .180 C7
Station Fields EX21. . . . . . .73 E2
Station Hill
Barnstaple EX32. . . . . .18 A4
Bideford EX39. . . . . .157 B1
Bratton Fleming EX31. . . . .11 A1
Brixham TQ5. . . . . .230 C5
Great Torrington EX38. . . .159 A4
Lynton EX35. . . . . .151 B4
Swimbridge EX32. . . . . . . .17 E1
Station La
Calstock PL18. . . . . .125 D3
Paignton TQ4. . . . . .226 B5
Station Rd
Bampton EX16. . . . . .34 B1
Barnstaple EX31. . . . . .154 F4
Bere Alston PL20. . . . . . . .125 E2
Bere Ferrers PL20. . . . . . .239 E3
Bovey Tracey TQ13. . . . . .180 C7
Bow EX17. . . . . .78 B3
Bratton Fleming EX31. . . .18 A8
Bridestowe EX20. . . . . . . .107 F7
Broadclyst EX5. . . . . .175 D3
Buckfastleigh TQ11. . . . . .236 C5
Budleigh Salterton EX9. . .198 A1
Burlescombe EX16. . . . . . . .51 B3
Chard Junction EX13. . . . .88 D8
Chulmleigh EX18. . . . . .44 C3
Colyton EX24. . . . . .103 A5
Crediton EX17. . . . . .165 C4
Cullompton EX15. . . . . . . .163 C4
 17 Dawlish EX7. . . . . .204 E6
Exeter, Pinhoe EX1. . . . . . .178 A8
Exeter, St David's EX4. . . .177 A8
Exminster EX6. . . . . .182 D3
Exton EX3. . . . . .183 C1
Feniton EX14. . . . . .84 D2
Gunnislake PL18. . . . . . . .125 C6
Halwill Junction EX21. . . . .73 E2
Hele EX5. . . . . .82 F5
Hemyock EX15. . . . . .67 B8
Holsworthy EX22. . . . . . . .164 C4
Horrabridge PL20. . . . . . . .126 F4
Ide EX2. . . . . .176 D1
Ilfracombe EX34. . . . . . . .150 A4
Ivybridge PL21. . . . . .237 D6
Lifton PL16. . . . . .105 F4
Lydford EX20. . . . . .108 A6
Mary Tavy PL19. . . . . .117 E6
Meeth EX20. . . . . .57 B6
Moretonhampstead TQ13. .111 F4
Newton Abbot TQ12. . . . .207 D3

Station Rd continued
Newton Poppleford EX10 .186 F8
Newton St Cyres EX5.....81 A1
North Brentor PL19.....117 C8
Northlew EX20.....74 E1
Okehampton EX20.....170 B4
Plymouth, Elburton PL9...256 C7
Plymouth, Keyham PL2 ..247 E5
Plymouth, Plympton PL7 .250 E5
Plymouth, Tamerton Foliot
  PL5.....244 A6
Princetown PL20.....128 A8
Saltash PL12.....243 A2
Sidmouth EX10.....188 A4
5 South Brent TQ10.....134 F3
South Molton EX36....158 D5
3 Topsham PL14.....210 C4
Tiverton EX16.....161 D4
Topsham EX3.....182 F5
Totnes TQ9.....223 C6
Wellington TA21.....160 C7
Willand EX15.....162 C5
Woolacombe EX34.....8 A6
Yelverton PL20.....127 A2
Yeoford EX17.....79 C1
Station Road Ind Est EX15 67 B8
Station View PL19.....117 C8
Station Yard Bsns Pk
  TQ14.....210 C5
Station Yard Ind Est
  TQ7.....258 C5
STAVERTON.....216 B5
Staverton Cotts TQ13....130 F4
Staverton Sta ★ TQ9....215 E4
Stawley Prim Sch TA21...51 B8
Steamer Quay Rd TQ9 ..223 D4
Steamer Quay Wharf 11
  TQ9.....223 D5
Steartfield Rd TQ3, TQ4. .226 C7
Steddaford Ct EX20.....95 A5
Stedhams Ct TA21.....160 D7
Steel Cl TQ4.....229 A8
Steel Cl EX14.....166 D6
Steeperton Cl EX20.....170 D5
Steep Head EX36.....19 B1
Steep Hill TQ1.....214 D6
Steep La
  Hartford TA22.....34 C8
  Landkey EX32.....17 D2
Steeple Cl PL9.....255 F4
Steeple Dr EX2.....181 B8
Steer Park Rd PL7.....251 C5
Steer Point Cotts PL8 ..256 F2
Steer Point Rd PL8.....257 A4
Stefan Cl PL9.....255 B5
Stella Maris Ct EX39....157 A2
Stella Rd TQ3.....219 A1
Stenlake Pl PL4.....249 B2
Stenlake Terr PL4.....249 B2
Stentaway Cl PL9.....255 F8
Stentaway Dr PL9.....256 A8
Stentaway La EX33.....7 E2
Stentaway Rd PL9.....255 F8
Stentiford Hill TQ7.....258 D7
Stentiford Hill Rd TQ1. .220 B5
Stentiford La TQ13.....122 D4
Stepcote Hill EX1.....261 A2
Steppes Mdw TQ12.....207 A2
Steppingstone Cross EX33. 8 D1
Stepps Cross EX12.....192 E7
Stepps Rd EX12, DT7....193 B5
Steps Cl EX1.....174 F1
Steps Cross TQ2.....214 B3
Steps La TQ7.....214 B3
Stepstone La EX33.....8 D1
Steven's Cross EX10....188 D8
Steven's Cross Cl EX10 ..188 E8
Stevens La EX10.....188 A7
STEVENSTONE.....42 A6
Stevenstone Ct EX38....42 A6
Stevenstone Rd EX8....202 D7
Stewart Cl EX8.....196 E1
Stewart Ct EX13.....167 F7
Stewart Gdns EX7.....204 E2
Stewart Ho EX7.....204 E2
Stewarts Rd EX22.....70 C1
STIBB CROSS.....40 C1
Stibb La PL1.....136 D7
STICKLEPATH
  Barnstaple.....154 E4
  Okehampton.....95 A5
Stickle Path EX16.....154 E4
Sticklepath Com Sch
  EX31.....154 C3
Sticklepath Ct EX31....154 E3
Sticklepath Hill EX31....154 E4
Sticklepath Terr EX31 ..154 F4
Stidson Cross TQ10.....135 B3
Stidston La TQ10.....135 A3
Stile Ct EX15.....163 B2
Stile Orch TQ7.....143 F7
Stillman Cl 6 PL4.....263 A2
Stillman St PL4.....263 A2
Stiniel Cross TQ13.....111 A4
Stintway La EX10.....187 E5
Stirling Ct PL5.....243 C1
Stirling Rd PL5.....243 C1
Stitchill Rd TQ1.....220 C4
Stitworthy Cross EX39. .23 C1
Stoat Pk EX32.....155 D4
Stoats Cl EX36.....158 C2
Stoats Mews EX20.....77 C4
Stockadon Farm Barns
  PL12.....238 B4
Stockadon La EX17.....63 A1

Stocker Rd EX4.....173 B1
Stockeydown La EX17....79 E2
Stockham Hill TQ2.....33 E8
Stockham La TA20.....88 C7
Stock Hill EX35.....151 A1
Stock La EX12.....192 A5
STOCKLAND.....87 A7
Stockland CE Prim Sch
  EX14.....87 A7
Stockland Cross EX15 ..66 A3
Stockland Head Cross
  EX15.....84 B7
Stockland Hill EX14....86 E6
Stockleigh Cross
  Cheriton Fitzpaine EX17 ..62 C1
  Stockleigh Pomeroy EX17 . 80 F6
STOCKLEIGH ENGLISH ..62 D1
STOCKLEIGH POMEROY ..81 A6
STOCKLEY HAMLET.....94 D6
Stockman La TA20.....88 C7
Stockmeadow Gdns
  TQ14.....209 A7
Stock Rd EX35.....5 B3
Stockstyle La EX13.....88 A8
Stockton Ave EX7.....204 E6
Stockton Hill EX7.....204 D6
Stockton La 4 EX7.....204 D6
Stockton Rd EX7.....204 D6
STOCKWELL.....82 D5
Stockwell Cross EX5....82 D5
Stoford Lane TA21.....52 F7
STOFORD WATER.....66 B3
Stoggy La PL7.....251 A6
STOKE
  Ashburton.....129 F5
  Hartland.....22 B3
  Plymouth.....248 A3
Stoke Canon CE Prim Sch
  EX5.....173 F8
STOKE CLIMSLAND.....115 C1
Stoke Climsland Sch
  PL17.....115 B1
Stoke Cross PL8.....141 B5
Stoke Dameral Bsns Ctr 2
  PL3.....248 A4
Stoke Damerel Com Coll
  PL3.....248 B4
Stoke Damerel Prim Sch
  PL1.....248 A3
STOKE FLEMING.....146 B7
Stoke Fleming Com Prim Sch
  TQ6.....146 A7
STOKE GABRIEL.....227 F7
Stoke Gabriel Prim Sch
  TQ9.....227 F7
Stoke Gabriel Rd TQ5 ..229 A5
STOKE HILL.....173 E1
Stoke Hill
  Exeter EX4.....173 E2
  Stoke Canon EX5.....173 B6
Stoke Hill Cres EX4....173 E1
Stoke Hill Inf Sch EX4 ..173 E1
Stoke Hill Jun Sch EX4 ..173 E1
Stoke Hill La PL20.....126 E2
Stoke House Gdns TQ6 ..146 B7
STOKEINTEIGNHEAD....209 B1
Stokeinteignhead Prim Sch
  TQ12.....209 B1
Stokelake TQ13.....123 B5
Stoke Lyne EX8.....196 C1
Stoke Meadow Cl EX7 ..173 E2
STOKENHAM.....145 B1
Stokenham Area Prim Sch
  TQ7.....145 B1
Stokenham Cross TQ7...145 B1
STOKE POST.....174 A5
Stoke Rd
  Higher Gabwell TQ1,
    TQ12.....214 C7
  Noss Mayo PL8.....141 A6
  Paignton, Higher Yalberton
    TQ4.....225 C2
  Paignton, Waddeton TQ5. .228 F6
  Plymouth PL1.....262 A3
  Stoke Canon EX4, EX5 ..173 D5
STOKE RIVERS.....17 F6
Stokesay Ave PL6.....245 A5
Stokes La PL1.....263 A2
Stokes Mead EX5.....184 D3
Stoke Valley Rd EX4....173 D2
Stokingway Cl PL9.....255 E5
Stoneacre Cl TQ5.....230 C3
Stone Ash La EX17.....61 C3
Stonebarrow La EX13 ..88 F2
Stonebarton Cl PL7....250 C6
Stonebarton Rd PL7....250 C6
Stoneborough Cl EX9. .198 B1
Stoneborough La EX9. .198 B1
Stone Cl EX14.....166 B4
STONECOMBE.....10 C6
Stonecombe Hill EX31. .10 C6
Stone Cross
  Chagford TQ13.....96 A1
  Lifton PL16.....105 E5
  Meeth EX20.....57 C4
  Molland EX36.....31 F7
  North Tawton EX20.....77 E4
  West Buckland EX32 ..18 A4
  Widecombe in the Moor
    TQ13.....121 B1
Stone Ct TQ2.....213 D1
Stonehall Flats PL1.....248 A1
Stonehanger TQ8.....259 D4
Stonehanger Ct TQ8 ..259 D4
Stonehedge Cl PL21.....237 D4

STONEHOUSE.....248 A1
Stonehouse Bridge PL1 .248 A1
Stonehouse St PL1.....262 A2
Stone La
  Cadbury EX5.....81 F7
  Lympstone EX8.....195 E5
Stoneland Cross EX16.. .47 F4
Stoneland La EX16.....47 F5
Stonelands EX6.....96 F3
Stonelands Mews EX7. .204 C6
Stonelands Pk EX7.....204 C6
Stonelands Terr EX7....204 C6
Stone Lane Gdns ★ TQ13. .96 A1
Stone Lane Ret Pk EX2. .177 B3
Stoneleigh
  Sidmouth EX10.....189 C7
  Wellington TA21.....160 B8
Stoneleigh Cl TQ12.....206 F4
Stoneleigh Dr TQ12....219 D3
Stoneman's Hill TQ12 ..212 B7
Stonemans La EX38....159 C5
Stone Moor Cross EX38. .56 B7
Stone Moor Cross EX18. .45 C1
Stoneman La EX36.....31 F7
Stonepark TQ13.....130 F4
Stonepark Cres TQ13. .130 F4
Stone Pk TQ4.....229 D6
Stoneridge La TA4.....35 D5
Stones Cl
  8 Kingsteignton TQ12 ..123 F1
  Modbury PL21.....137 C2
Stone's Hill EX17.....80 A7
Stoneshill Cross EX17 ..80 A7
Stonewall La EX17.....165 C6
Stoneycliffe Pl PL20....128 B8
STONEYCOMBE.....212 D3
STONEYFORD
  Cullompton.....163 E4
  Newton Poppleford.....186 A6
Stoneyford Pk EX9.....198 B1
Stoneyhill TQ12.....212 B3
Stoneyhouse La EX14 ..86 D1
Stoney La
  Axminster EX13.....167 E6
  Bradninch EX5.....82 F7
  Honiton EX14.....166 D2
Stoneylands EX5.....99 C5
Stoney Lane Cross EX16. .50 B3
Stoney Lane Hill EX16. .48 C2
Stoney Park La EX20....170 A4
Stoneywell 3 EX39.....15 B1
Stoning Cross EX20.....72 C2
Stonley Cl 9 PL1.....262 A3
Stonybridge Cross EX36. .30 B8
Stonybridge Hill EX36. .30 B8
Stony Cnr EX34.....3 D3
STONY CROSS.....26 F4
Stony Hill Cross EX36. .31 A3
Stony La
  Gunnislake PL18.....125 D6
  Landkey EX32.....17 B1
  Lympstone EX8.....195 F8
  Parracombe EX31.....4 D1
  Swimbridge EX32.....28 B8
  Woodbury Salterton EX5 ..184 C6
STONYLAND.....27 B8
Stony Lane End EX32....17 B1
STOODLEIGH.....48 E5
Stoodleigh Cross
  Calverleigh EX16.....48 B4
  West Buckland EX32 ..18 B2
Stoodleigh Moor Cross
  EX16.....48 D6
Stoodley Knowle Sch
  TQ1.....220 F5
Stooke Bridge Rd EX15.. .83 C1
Stooks Cl EX5.....173 F6
Stoop EX39.....23 D3
Stoop Cross TQ9.....131 E1
Stooper's Hill TA20.....69 F6
Stopford Pl PL1.....247 F3
STOPGATE.....68 F4
Stopgate Cross
  Yarcombe EX14.....68 F4
  Zeal Monachorum EX17.. .78 C8
STORMSDOWN.....131 B7
Stormsdown Cotts TQ12.131 B7
Storridge La EX13.....88 B6
Storrs Cl TQ13.....180 C8
Storrs La PL3.....249 D5
Stour Cl PL3.....249 D6
STOURSCOMBE.....105 A2
Stourscombe Wood
  PL15.....105 A2
Stout Cross EX14.....68 F5
Stovar Long La EX12....191 D6
Stover Cl TQ12.....123 F1
Stover Ctry Pk ★ TQ12 ..123 B2
Stover Sch TQ12.....123 B1
Stowe Gdns PL5.....244 B2
Stowe La EX20.....76 C4
Stowell La TA20.....88 D8
STOWFORD
  Bradworthy EX22.....53 C8
  Challacombe.....11 B4
  Chittlehampton.....28 E5
  Colaton Raleigh.....186 A3
  Halwill Junction.....91 D8
  Lewdown.....106 D5
  Sidmouth.....187 E8
  South Molton EX36.....19 B2

Stowford Cross continued
  Stowford EX31.....11 C3
  West Putford EX22.....39 E2
Stowford Gate EX10.....187 E8
Stowford Hill EX17.....61 A7
Stowford Mts EX12.....191 F8
Stowford Prim Sch PL21 237 E5
Stowford Rise EX10.....187 F8
Straightway Head EX5. .100 A7
Strand
  Exmouth EX8.....202 A6
  Teignmouth TQ14.....210 A3
  Topsham EX3.....182 F4
  Torquay TQ1.....220 B4
Strand Cl EX31.....16 B6
Strand Ct
  1 Bideford EX39.....157 A2
  Topsham EX3.....182 F4
Strand Hill EX7.....204 E6
Strand La EX31.....16 B6
Strand St PL1.....254 A8
Strand The
  Barnstaple EX32.....154 F5
  Bideford EX39.....157 A2
  3 Brixham TQ5.....230 D5
  Culmstock EX15.....66 D8
  Dawlish EX7.....204 E6
  13 Ilfracombe EX34.....150 C6
  Lympstone EX8.....195 D5
  Shaldon TQ14.....209 C5
  Starcross EX6.....201 B7
  Topsham EX3.....182 F4
  Strand View EX3.....182 F4
Strashleigh View PL21. .136 D6
Stratford Ave EX4.....178 C8
Strathculm Rd EX5.....82 F5
Strathmore Ct EX39.....25 E4
Stratton Wlk PL2.....248 D8
Strawberry Ave EX2....181 C8
Strawberry Fields EX20. .77 C4
Strawberry Hill EX8.....195 F5
Strawberry La EX7.....204 C3
Strawberry Terr TQ12 ..207 E8
Straypark Cnr EX35.....5 E4
Stray Pk PL8.....257 F4
Streamcombe La TA22 ..33 B5
Stream Ct EX2.....261 A1
Streamers Mdws EX14 ..166 C5
Streams La PL8.....9 B2
Streatham Dr EX4.....177 B8
Streatham Rise EX4.....177 A8
STREET.....149 A8
STREET Ash.....69 F8
Street Ash La TA20.....69 F8
Street The
  Kilmington EX13.....87 C1
  Musbury EX13.....103 D5
STRETE.....145 E5
Strete Ralegh EX5.....168 A8
Strode Rd
  Buckfastleigh TQ11.....236 B4
  Plymouth PL7.....250 F6
Stroma Cl PL6.....244 F7
Stroud Hill Cross EX21 ..73 F1
Stroud Park Rd PL2....248 C7
STROXWORTHY.....39 A6
Stroxworthy Cross EX39. .38 F6
Stuart Cres EX15.....163 C6
Stuart Ct EX7.....204 D4
Stuart Rd
  Exeter EX1.....177 F6
  Plymouth, Pennycomequick
    PL3.....262 A4
Stuart Road Prim Sch
  PL1.....262 A4
Stuart Way EX15.....99 A1
Stubbins Cross EX24....102 C5
Stubbing Cross TQ12 ..211 D7
Stubborn Cross EX16 ..62 C7
Stuckeridge Cross EX16. .48 D8
Stucley Rd EX39.....156 E1
Studd Dr EX32.....29 C7
Studhayes Cross EX13 ..87 C1
Studhayes La EX13.....87 B2
Studhayes Rd EX13.....87 B2
Studley Ho 9 EX14....166 C5
Studley Rd TQ1.....220 A7
Stumpy Cross
  Shobrooke EX17.....80 F4
  Silverton EX5.....82 B4
Stumpypost Cross TQ7 ..144 B6
Sturcombe Ave TQ4....225 F3
Sturdee Rd PL2.....248 A5
Sturges Rd EX8.....202 D8
Sturt Cotts EX17.....78 E7
Sturtlebury La TQ7.....143 F5
Style Cl EX32.....155 B2
Suddon's Cross EX14....102 A6
Suddon's La EX24.....102 A6
Sugar Loaf Hill & Saltern
  Cove Nature Reserve ★
  TQ4.....226 C1
Sugar Mill Bsns Pk PL9. 249 C1
Sullivan Rd EX2.....178 C5
Summer Cl
  Exeter EX4.....178 B8
  Exmouth EX8.....202 E8
  13 Hemyock EX15.....67 B8
Summercourt Way TQ5. .230 A2
Summerfield
  Sidmouth EX10.....188 B8
  Woodbury EX5.....184 C4
Summer Field EX19.....58 E4
Summerfield Ave TA21. .52 D8
Summerfield Cl
  Ivybridge PL21.....237 A5
  Paignton TQ4.....226 C5
Summerfield Rd TQ2....219 E8

Summerfields PL12.....242 D1
Summerfield Way TA21.. .52 D8
Summerhayes EX7.....204 D4
Summerhill Cl 5 TQ12. .122 F1
Summerhill Cres 17
  TQ12.....122 F1
Summerhill Cross TQ13. .130 E4
Summerhill Ho DT7.....260 E4
Summerhill Rd
  16 Coldeast TQ12.....122 F1
  Lyme Regis DT7.....260 E4
Summer La
  Alfington EX11.....100 F8
  Bovey Tracey TQ13.....123 C2
  Brixham TQ5.....230 B2
  Exeter EX4.....174 B1
  Exmouth EX8.....196 B4
  Northlew EX20.....74 F2
Summerland EX14.....166 C5
Summerland Ave EX7. .204 D7
Summerland Cl EX7....204 D6
Summerland Cotts
  Alfington EX11.....100 F8
  5 Newton Abbot TQ12 ..207 C3
Summerland Ct 6 TQ12.207 C3
Summerland Pl 8 EX32. .155 A4
Summerlands TQ12.....123 A1
Summerlands Cl
  Brixham TQ5.....230 A2
  Plymouth PL7.....251 C5
Summerlands Ct
  Brixham TQ5.....230 A2
  16 Coldeast TQ12.....122 F1
  Exeter EX1.....261 C3
Summerlands Gdns PL7..251 C5
Summerland St
  Barnstaple EX32.....155 A5
  Exeter EX1, EX4.....261 C4
Summerland Terr 1 EX34. 3 A3
Summermoor La EX37. ..28 E6
Summersby Cl EX12....192 A6
Summers Cl PL6.....249 B7
Summers Moor Cross
  EX19.....58 F1
Summerville Cross EX39 .37 F6
Summerway EX4.....178 C8
Summerwell La EX34....9 A5
Sumner Rd 7 PL21.....137 C7
Sunbury Hill TQ1.....220 A6
Sunbury Rd TQ4.....226 B5
Sunbury Terr 8 TQ1....220 A6
Suncrest Cl TQ2.....213 F3
Sun Ct 9 TQ12.....207 B3
Sunderland Cl PL9.....255 A6
Sunflower Rd EX32.....155 A5
Sunhill Ave EX3.....182 F6
Sunhill La EX3.....182 F6
Sunleigh TQ2.....219 E2
Sunningbrook Rd EX16. .161 E5
Sunningdale EX39.....157 A3
Sunningdale Rd PL12 ..242 C2
Sunnybank
  Kenton EX6.....194 E3
  Newton Abbot TQ12.....207 B5
Sunny Bank EX32.....155 B4
Sunny Cl TQ12.....207 F3
Sunny Ct 1 EX16.....161 D4
Sunnydale
  Beesands TQ7.....149 E8
  9 Bittaford PL21.....137 C8
Sunny Dene PL5.....243 D1
Sunnyfield EX5.....175 C7
Sunny Gdns TQ1.....220 A6
Sunny Hill
  Ottery St Mary EX11.....169 E4
  Torquay TQ1.....220 C5
Sunnyhill Mews TQ1....220 C5
Sunny Hollow TQ12.....211 D8
Sunnylands Cross EX13.. .87 A2
Sunnylands Way EX7. .210 F8
Sunnymead EX17.....79 B5
Sunnymead Terr 8 TQ9.223 C5
Sunnymoor Cl EX1.....174 F2
Sunnyside
  Awliscombe EX14.....85 C4
  9 Bideford EX39.....157 B1
  3 Braunton EX33.....152 D5
  Burlescombe EX16.....51 C2
  Combe Martin EX34.....3 A3
  Cullompton EX15.....163 C2
  St Giles in t W EX38.....42 B5
  Thurlestone TQ7.....143 C1
  Woolfardisworthy EX39... .38 F8
Sunnyside Cotts 18 EX34. .3 A3
Sunnyside La EX5.....4 D1
Sunnyside Rd
  Kingskerswell TQ12.....213 A4
  Plymouth PL4.....249 B2
  Woolacombe EX34.....7 F6
Sunnyside Terr EX35....151 B5
Sunny View EX19.....58 F3
Sun Ray EX34.....2 F4
Sunset Ho 5 EX12.....192 A4
Sunset Hts EX32.....155 A5
Sunshine Terr PL19.....171 D6
Sun Valley Cl TQ5.....230 C5
Sunway Cl PL19.....171 A6
Sunwell La PL1.....252 A8
Sunwine Pl EX8.....202 B6
Surbiton Cres EX4.....176 F4
Sussex Cl
  Exeter EX4.....176 A4
  Torquay TQ2.....214 A3
Sussex Pl PL1.....262 C2
Sussex St PL1.....262 C2
Sussex Terr 5 PL1.....247 F5

Sutcliffe Cl TQ9 . . . . 222 F7
SUTCOMBE 54 A6
Sutcombe Com Prim Sch
EX22 . . . . 54 A6
SUTCOMBEMILL 54 A6
Suter Rd 10 EX16 . . . . 161 E6
Sutherland Cl TQ12 . . . . . 212 F8
Sutherland Dr TQ2 . . . . . . 214 B2
Sutherland Rd
Plymouth PL4 . . . . 263 A4
Torquay TQ1 . . . . 220 C5
SUTTON 143 D1
Sutton Cl
Dawlish EX7 . . . . 204 D7
Torquay TQ2 . . . . 213 F4
Sutton Cross
Moretonhampstead
TQ13 . . . . 111 E5
Thurlestone TQ7 . . . . 143 D1
Sutton Ct PL1 . . . . 247 F1
Sutton Mews 21 PL4 . . . . 263 A2
Sutton Pk PL4 . . . . 263 B2
Sutton Rd PL4 . . . . 263 B2
Suttons Cross EX14 . . . . . . 86 D1
Sutton Wharf PL4 . . . . . . 263 A2
Swaddicott Cross EX21. . . . 56 C2
Swain Cl EX13 . . . . 167 D4
Swaindale Rd 8 PL3. . . . . 248 E6
Swains TA21 . . . . 160 D4
Swains Ct EX3 . . . . 182 E5
Swains La TA21 . . . . 160 D4
Swains Rd EX9 . . . . 198 B1
Swale Cl
Plymouth PL3. . . . . 249 B6
Torquay TQ2 . . . . 214 A3
Swallerton Gate TQ13 . . . 121 D6
Swallow Cl EX32 . . . . 155 E4
Swallow Ct EX4 . . . . 176 F8
Swallow Ct EX16. . . . . 50 F1
Swallow Dr EX2 . . . . 176 D3
Swallow Field EX31 . . . . . 154 A2
Swallowfield Rd EX2 . . . . 178 B2
Swallowfield Rise TQ2 . . . 213 C2
SWALLOWFIELDS 223 C7
Swallowfields TQ9 . . . . . . 223 B7
Swallows Acre EX7. . . . . . 204 E7
Swallows End PL9 . . . . . . 255 E8
Swallowtree Cross EX6. . . . 96 C7
Swallow Units EX2 . . . . . 177 D1
Swallow Way EX15 . . . . . 163 B2
Swanaford Rd EX6 . . . . . . 112 F7
Swan Ave 1 EX16. . . . . . . 161 E6
Swanborough Rd TQ12 . . 208 A2
Swan Ct PL10 . . . . 253 A6
Swan Ct
Dartmouth TQ6 . . . . 233 E3
Exeter EX2 . . . . 261 B1
Swan Gdns PL7 . . . . 250 F5
Swan Hill Rd EX24 . . . . . 103 A3
Swan Maisonettes 10
EX2 . . . . 177 A5
Swannadon La
Crediton EX17 . . . . 79 E8
Morchard Bishop EX17 . . . . 61 A4
Swannaton Rd TQ6. . . . . . 233 F1
Swanwell Hill EX17 . . . . . . 78 F8
Swan Rd EX6 . . . . 201 A8
Swanswood Gdns EX39 . . 156 D7
Swan Units EX2 . . . . 178 E5
Swan Yd
Exeter EX2 . . . . 177 A5
17 Honiton EX14 . . . . 166 C6
Swaynes Mews TQ1 . . . . 220 C6
Swedwell La TQ2 . . . . 214 A4
Swedwell Rd TQ2 . . . . . . 214 A4
Sweetbriar Cl EX7 . . . . . . 204 C3
Sweetbriar La EX7 . . . . . . 204 C3
Sweetbrier La EX1 . . . . . . 178 B6
Swiddacombe La EX36 . . . 32 C7
Swift Gdns PL5 . . . . 244 C2
Swift Ind Est TQ12 . . . . . 207 D6
SWIMBRIDGE 17 D1
Swimbridge CE Prim Sch
EX32 . . . . 17 C2
SWIMBRIDGE NEWLAND . 17 C2
Swinburne Gdns PL5 . . . . 244 C1
Swincombe Dr TQ3 . . . . . 225 F6
Swincombe La EX31. . . . . . 11 F4
Swingate Cross EX22. . . . . 90 B8
Swing Gate EX6. . . . . 194 A4
Swing Gate Cross EX37. . . 29 A2
Swiss Cl EX38 . . . . 196 B3
SYCAMORE 87 F8
Sycamore Ave
Dawlish Warren EX7 . . . . . 201 A4
Plymouth PL6 . . . . 263 C2
Tavistock PL19 . . . . 171 C2
Sycamore Cl
Broadclyst EX5 . . . . 175 D6
Exeter EX1 . . . . 178 B5
Exmouth EX8 . . . . 196 E2
Honiton EX14 . . . . 166 A4
13 Instow EX39 . . . . 15 B1
Paignton TQ4 . . . . 229 D7
Willand EX15 . . . . 162 C4
Sycamore Dr
Plymouth PL6 . . . . 245 C7
Torpoint PL11 . . . . 247 A3
Sycamore Rd
Saltash PL12 . . . . 242 B3
Tiverton EX16 . . . . 161 E5
Sycamore Way
Brixham TQ5 . . . . 230 A2
8 Chudleigh TQ13 . . . . . . 123 F6
Plymouth PL6. . . . . 245 C7
Sydenham TQ1 . . . . 220 D4
Sydenham Cross PL19. . . 116 A2

SYDENHAM DAMEREL . . . 116 B2
Sydenham Ho 6 EX4. . . . 177 E7
Sydenham La EX16. . . . . . 47 E6
Sydney Cl PL7 . . . . 250 E4
Sydney Rd
Exeter EX2 . . . . 177 A4
Torpoint PL11 . . . . 247 B3
Sydney St PL1 . . . . 262 B4
Sylvan Ave EX4 . . . . 173 D1
Sylvan Cl EX4 . . . . 196 A2
Sylvan Ct
Exmouth EX8 . . . . 196 A2
Plymouth PL1. . . . . 248 A3
Sylvania Dr EX4. . . . . 173 E2
Sylvan Rd
Exeter EX4 . . . . 173 D1
Wellington TA21. . . . . . . 160 E5
Symons Rd PL12 . . . . 242 F2
Synagogue Pl EX4 . . . . . . 261 A3
Syncock's Cross EX39. . . 157 F3

T

Tabernacle Ct 9 EX1 . . . . 261 A2
Tackbear Rd EX22, EX23. . 70 D4
Tacket Ct TQ7 . . . . 258 C4
Taddiford Rd EX4 . . . . . . 177 A7
Taddiport EX38 . . . . 159 B4
Taddyforde Court Mans
EX4 . . . . 177 A8
Taddyforde Ct EX4 . . . . . 177 A8
Taddyforde Est EX4 . . . . 177 A8
Tadworthy Rd EX39 . . . . 156 E7
Tal Cnr EX17 . . . . 79 D7
Tailyour Rd PL6. . . . . 244 F2
TALATON. 84 A2
Talbot Gdns PL5 . . . . 247 D7
Talbot Rd DT7 . . . . 260 D5
Tale Common Head Cross
EX14. . . . . 84 B4
TALEFORD 169 C6
Taleford Cl EX11 . . . . 169 C7
Taleford Villas EX11. . . . . 169 C7
Talewater Cross EX5 . . . . 84 C2
Tallow Wood Cl TQ3 . . . . 225 E6
Tamar Ave
Plymouth PL2. . . . . 247 E5
Tavistock PL19. . . . . 171 D5
Torquay TQ2 . . . . 219 B7
Tamar Bridge PL5. . . . . . 243 A2
Tamar Bsns Units EX22. . 164 C6
Tamar Cl PL20 . . . . 125 E1
Tamar Cotts PL19 . . . . . . 116 A1
Tamar Ho PL1 . . . . 247 E1
Tamarind EX15 . . . . 162 C4
Tamarisk Cl EX4 . . . . 174 B2
Tamar Rd EX31 . . . . 15 E5
Tamar Science Pk PL6 . . 245 C4
Tamar's Dr EX15 . . . . . . 162 C4
Tamarside Com Coll PL5 243 E1
Tamarside Sp Complex
PL5 . . . . 243 F2
Tamar St
Plymouth PL1. . . . . 247 E3
Saltash PL12 . . . . 243 A2
Torpoint PL11 . . . . 247 C3
Tamar Terr
Calstock PL17 . . . . 125 D3
Horsebridge PL19 . . . . . . 116 A1
Saltash PL12 . . . . 243 B2
Tamar Valley Donkey Pk*
PL18 . . . . 125 A5
Tamar Valley Sch PL5 . . 243 B1
Tamar View
Milton Abbot PL19 . . . . . 116 A6
St Dominick PL12. . . . . . 125 A2
Tamar View Ind Est
PL12 . . . . 242 D5
Tamar Villas PL9 . . . . . . 255 D7
Tamar Way PL18 . . . . 125 A6
Tamar Wharf PL1. . . . . . . 247 D3
Tamerton Ave PL5 . . . . . 243 D1
Tamerton Cl PL5. . . . . . . 244 A6
TAMERTON FOLIOT 244 B7
Tamerton Foliot Rd PL6 244 D5
Tamerton Rd PL5. . . . . . . 244 B6
Tamworth Ho TQ7 . . . . . 143 A1
Tangmere Ave PL5 . . . . . 243 E5
Tan La EX2 . . . . 177 B3
Tanners Cl EX15 . . . . 163 B2
Tanner's Hill TA4 . . . . 35 E7
Tanners Mews EX15. . . . . 162 E5
Tanners Rd
Landkey EX32 . . . . 17 C2
Paignton TQ4 . . . . 226 C4
Tannery Flats 4 EX17. . 165 C5
Tanpits Cross TQ7 . . . . . 145 A1
Tanpits Mdw TQ7 . . . . . 145 A1
Tanworth Ho TQ7 . . . . . 143 A1
Tanyard La EX12 . . . . 217 F6
Tanyards Ct 7 EX12 . . . . 192 A5
Tape La EX14 . . . . 85 B3
Tapeley Park & Gdns*
EX39 . . . . 157 F7
Tapfield Cross TQ7. . . . . 142 F4
Tapley Gdns TQ14. . . . . . 209 A8
Tappers Cl EX15 . . . . 182 E5
Tappers Knapp DT7 . . . . 260 B5
Tappers Mdw EX20. . . . . 170 D5
Tapp's La PL8 . . . . 257 B5
Taps Cl EX6 . . . . 182 B4
Tapson Dr PL9 . . . . 255 A6
Tarbet Ave EX1 . . . . 177 F7
Tarka Cl EX20. . . . . 170 D6
Tarn Wearfield Flats
EX10. . . . . 188 B3
Tarraway Rd TQ3 . . . . . . 219 D1

Tarr Post TA22. . . . . 21 C1
Tarr's Ave TQ12 . . . . 207 E7
Tarrs End TQ12 . . . . 207 E7
Tarrs La TQ12. . . . . 207 E7
Tarr Steps* TA22 . . . . 21 E3
Tarr Stps Woodland National
Nature Reserve* TA22 . . 21 D3
TATWORTH. 88 C8
Tatworth Prim Sch TA20. . 88 C8
Tatworth St TA20 . . . . 88 C8
Taunton Ave PL5. . . . . . . 244 B5
Taunton Cl EX2 . . . . 177 A3
Taunton Cross EX13. . . . . 87 A1
Taunton Ct 8 TQ9 . . . . . 223 D5
Taunton Dr PL5 . . . . 244 B5
Taunton Rd TA21 . . . . . . 160 E7
Tavern Gdns EX39 . . . . . . 26 B1
Tavern Mews EX38. . . . . . 159 D5
Tavis Rd TQ3 . . . . 225 F8
Tavistock Coll PL19 . . . . 171 E5
Tavistock Com Prim Sch
PL19. . . . . 171 B4
Tavistock Cross PL20. . . 125 F2
Tavistock Hospl PL19. . . 171 B5
Tavistock Mus* PL19 . . . 171 C5
Tavistock Pl
Paignton TQ4 . . . . 229 B8
Plymouth PL4 . . . . 263 A3
Tavistock Rd
Exeter EX4 . . . . 177 A7
Launceston PL15 . . . . 105 A2
Okehampton EX20 . . . . . . 93 E4
Plymouth, Manadon PL5 . 244 E1
Plymouth PL6 . . . . 245 B5
Princetown PL20 . . . . . . 128 A8
Yelverton PL20. . . . . 126 F3
Tavistock Woodland Wlk
Nature Reserve* PL19 . . 171 A5
Tavy Ave TQ2 . . . . 219 B8
Tavy Pl PL4 . . . . 248 F4
Tavy Rd
Saltash PL12 . . . . 243 A3
Tavistock PL19 . . . . 171 D5
Taw Bridge Cross EX20. . . 77 B4
Taw Cl PL3 . . . . 249 D6
Taw Cres EX31 . . . . 15 E5
Taw Ct 14 EX32. . . . . . . 155 A4
Tawgreen Cross EX18 . . . 59 C1
Taw Green Cross EX20 . . 95 F7
Tawgreen Rd EX18. . . . . . 59 C1
Tawgreen Rd EX20 . . . . . 59 C1
Taw Meadow Cres EX31. 153 F6
Taw Mill Bsns Pk EX32 . 155 C4
Taw Mills La EX18. . . . . . 59 C1
Tawmoor Cross EX20. . . . 95 C7
Taw Rd EX31. . . . . 15 E5
TAWSTOCK 27 D8
Tawton La EX20. . . . . 95 B4
Taw Trade Pk EX31. . . . . 154 E6
Taw Vale EX32 . . . . 154 F4
Taw Vale Ave EX20. . . . . . 77 B4
Taw Vale EX20. . . . . 77 B4
Taw View
1 Bishop's Tawton EX32 . 16 E1
Fremington EX31. . . . . . . 153 F6
Umberleigh EX37. . . . . . . 28 D3
Tay Gdns PL3 . . . . 249 D7
Taylor Cl
Dawlish EX7. . . . . 204 D5
Ottery St Mary EX11 . . . 169 B4
Saltash PL12 . . . . 242 C3
Taylor Rd PL12 . . . . 242 C4
Taylors Ct EX16 . . . . 161 E7
Taylors Field EX20 . . . . . . 77 C4
Taylor's Hill EX16, EX17 . . 62 A4
Taylor's La EX37 . . . . 43 D6
Taylors Newtake 2
TQ12 . . . . 122 F1
Taylor Sq TQ9 . . . . 171 B6
TDC Units EX20 . . . . 164 C6
Teachers Cl PL9 . . . . 255 F6
Teal Cl TQ2 . . . . 213 C2
Teats Hill Flats PL4 . . . . 263 B1
Teats Hill Rd PL4 . . . . . . 263 B1
Teazle Ct EX2 . . . . 261 A2
Tedburn Rd EX4 . . . . 176 B5
TEDBURN ST MARY 97 F5
Tedburn St Mary Sch EX6 97 F5
Tedburrow La EX15 . . . . . 67 B8
Tedders Cl 8 EX15. . . . . . 67 B8
Tedstone Ho EX8 . . . . . . 196 A6
Tedstone La EX8. . . . . . . 196 A6
Ted's Way EX20 . . . . 170 B5
Tees Cl PL3. . . . . 249 C7
Teignbridge Bsns Ctr
TQ12 . . . . 180 F3
Teign Cl TQ14 . . . . 208 E8
TEIGNCOMBE 110 A6
Teigncombe Ct EX6 . . . . 113 B4
Teign Cl
Bishopsteignton TQ14 . . 209 A8
Stokeinteignhead TQ12 . . 209 B1
TEIGNGRACE 207 A4
Teignharvey Rd TQ12 . . 209 A3
Teignholt Cross EX6 . . . . 96 D7
Teign La
Chudleigh TQ13 . . . . 123 D7
Trusham TQ13 . . . . 113 D1
TEIGNMOUTH 210 C5
Teignmouth Com Coll
TQ14. . . . . 210 B5
Teignmouth Hill EX7. . . . 204 E5
Teignmouth Hospl TQ14 210 A5

Teignmouth Rd
Bishopsteignton TQ14 . . 209 B7
Holcombe EX7, TQ14 . . . 210 E7
Kingsteignton TQ12, TQ14 . 208 B6
Maidencombe TQ1 . . . . . 214 C6
Shaldon TQ1, TQ14. . . . . 210 A1
Torquay TQ1 . . . . 220 A8
Teignmouth & Shaldon
Mus* TQ14 . . . . 210 C4
Teignmouth Sta TQ14 . . 210 C5
Teign Rd
Newton Abbot TQ12. . . . 207 D4
Teign Sch TQ12 . . . . 207 D8
Teign St TQ14 . . . . 210 B4
Teign Terr EX6 . . . . 113 B5
Teign View TQ13 . . . . . . 123 C4
Teign View Pl 14 TQ14 . 210 B4
Teignview Rd TQ14 . . . . 208 F8
Teign Village TQ13 . . . . . 123 B7
Tekoa Units EX2 . . . . 177 C1
Telegraph Cross PL21 . . . 136 D4
Telegraph Hill EX6. . . . . . 114 D2
Telegraph La EX5, EX11 . 168 B6
Telegraph View TQ12 . . . 180 B1
Telford Cres PL5 . . . . 243 F2
Telford Rd EX4 . . . . 177 A7
Temeraire Rd PL5 . . . . . . 244 B8
Temperance Pl 6 TQ5. . . 230 D5
Temperance St TQ2 . . . . 220 A5
Templar Way TQ12. . . . . 123 C1
Temple Cl EX16 . . . . 161 F4
Temple Gdns EX10 . . . . . 188 B5
Temple Mews EX10 . . . . 188 B5
Temple Rd EX2 . . . . 261 B2
Temple Rd TQ3 . . . . 219 A3
Temple Rd TQ3 . . . . 207 D4
Templer's Way 11 TQ12 . 123 C1
Temple St EX10 . . . . 188 B5
TEMPLETON. 48 A1
Templeton Cross EX16 . . . 48 A1
Templeton La EX16 . . . . . 47 F1
Templetown Ct EX8 . . . . 201 F6
Tencreet Hts EX39 . . . . . . 26 A4
Ten Acre Gate EX13 . . . . . 87 E7
Tenby Rd PL5 . . . . 243 C1
Tencery Orch EX14. . . . . . 67 C2
Tenerife 7 TQ1 . . . . 220 C5
Tennacott La EX39 . . . . . . 26 B4
Tennyson Ave EX2 . . . . . 177 F6
Tennyson Cl TQ1. . . . . . . 220 A8
Tennyson Gdns PL5 . . . . 244 B1
Tennyson Way PL5. . . . . 196 C4
Tern Gdns PL7 . . . . 250 F5
Terrace The
Braunton EX33. . . . . 152 D6
Harrowbarrow PL17. . . . 125 A5
Loddiswell TQ7 . . . . 143 E7
Torquay TQ1. . . . . 220 B4
Terra Nova Gn PL2 . . . . . 248 B5
Terris Cross EX20 . . . . 76 A6
TETCOTT 89 F7
Tewkesbury Cl PL2 . . . . . 248 A8
Tews La
Barnstaple, Bickington
EX31 . . . . 154 A3
Barnstaple, Roundswell
EX31 . . . . 154 A2
Tewsley Cl EX31 . . . . 154 A3
Thackeray Gdns PL5 . . . 244 B1
Thackeray Rd EX4 . . . . . 178 C8
Thames Gdns PL3 . . . . . . 249 D5
Thanckes Cl PL11 . . . . . . 247 A3
Thanckes Dr PL11 . . . . . . 247 A4
Thatcher Ave TQ1 . . . . . 221 A3
Thatcher Dr TQ14 . . . . . 210 C8
Thatcher Hts TQ1 . . . . . 221 A3
Thatcher's La EX5. . . . . . . 81 E6
Thatcher's Lane End EX5. 81 E5
Thatches The PL21. . . . . 137 E2
Theatre La EX4. . . . . 154 F5
Theatre Ope PL1. . . . . . . 247 F1
Theatre Royal Plymouth*
PL1 . . . . 262 C2
Thelbridge Cross EX17 . . . 61 D6
Thelbridge Hill EX17 . . . . 61 E7
Thelma Hulbert Gall*
EX14. . . . . 166 C2
THE MOUNTS 144 C7
THE POINT 201 E7
Therlow Rd PL3 . . . . 249 B6
Thetford Gdns PL6 . . . . . 245 D8
Third Ave
Dawlish EX7. . . . . 204 D5
Exeter, Countess Wear
EX2 . . . . 182 C7
Exeter, Heavitree EX1 . . . 177 F6
Plymouth, Billacombe PL9 250 A1
Plymouth, Camels Head
PL2 . . . . 247 E7
Plymouth, Stoke PL1 . . . 248 A2
Teignmouth TQ14 . . . . . 210 A8
Torquay TQ1 . . . . 220 A8
Third Dr TQ14 . . . . 210 A8
Thirlmere Gdns PL6. . . . 244 F4
Thistle Cl PL6 . . . . 245 D8
Thomas Bassett Dr EX24 103 A3
Thomas Cl EX4 . . . . 196 C4
Thomas La EX4 . . . . 177 A8
Thomas Newcomen Ct
TQ6 . . . . 233 C3
Thomas's Cross EX6 . . . . 112 F8
Thompson Rd EX1 . . . . . 178 A7
THORN. 110 E5
Thornberry Ave EX1. . . . 178 B6
THORNBURY 55 A3

Thornbury Cross
Sampford Courtenay EX20 . 76 E4
Thornbury EX22 . . . . 55 A3
Thornbury Mill EX22 . . . . 55 A3
Thornbury Park Ave PL3 248 D6
Thornbury Rd PL6. . . . . . 245 E4
Thorn Cl
Exeter EX1 . . . . 178 B6
Newton Abbot TQ12. . . . 206 E4
Thorncliff Cl TQ1 . . . . . . 220 E5
Thorn Cnr EX18. . . . . 77 E8
Thorn Cotts
Combeinteignhead TQ12 . 208 E3
Woodbury EX5. . . . . 184 C3
Thorn Cross
Bovey Tracey TQ13 . . . . . 180 C5
Chagford TQ13 . . . . 110 E5
Slapton TQ7 . . . . 145 C6
Thorndale Cts EX4 . . . . . 176 D8
THORNDON CROSS 93 A4
Thorndon Cross EX22 . . . 71 E5
Thorne Cotts EX11 . . . . . 169 B3
Thorne Cross EX6. . . . . . . 96 E4
Thorne Cross Way TQ7 . . 50 D8
Thorne Farm Way EX11 . 169 C3
Thorne La
Bow EX17. . . . . 78 D3
Spreyton EX17 . . . . 96 D8
Thorne Manor & Remains
EX22. . . . . 71 C8
Chapel* EX22 . . . . 71 C8
THORNE MOOR 105 E8
Thorne Moor Cross EX6 . 96 E4
Thornemoor La EX17. . . . 78 D2
Thorne Park Rd TQ2 . . . . 219 F6
Thorne Pk EX14 . . . . 8 F5
THORNE ST MARGARET . 51 D8
Thornes Cross EX16. . . . . 64 E5
Thornes Mdw EX2 . . . . . 114 A6
Thornes Terr EX36 . . . . . 158 C4
Thornes Cross EX21. . . . . 90 E7
Thornfield Cl
Exmouth EX8 . . . . 196 A2
Seaton EX12 . . . . 192 A7
THORNHAM. 237 E1
Thornham Chapel Cross
EX17. . . . . 46 B1
Thornham La EX17. . . . . . 46 B1
Thornhedges Cross EX17 . 80 B5
Thornhedges La EX17 . . . 80 B5
Thorn Hill EX16 . . . . 63 B6
THORNHILLHEAD 40 B3
Thornhill Rd PL3. . . . . . . 248 E6
Thornhill Way PL3 . . . . . 248 E6
Thorning St TQ8 . . . . 259 E5
Thorn La
Membury EX13 . . . . 87 D7
Saltash PL12 . . . . 242 C3
Thornlea Ave EX31. . . . . 153 D5
Thornlea (Univ of Exeter)
EX4 . . . . 261 A4
Thornley Dr TQ14 . . . . . 210 A5
Thorn Moor Cross PL15 . 105 E4
Thorn Orch TQ12 . . . . . . 211 E2
Thornpark Cross EX32. . . 18 C6
Thornpark Rise EX1. . . . . 178 B6
Thorns Cross TQ13. . . . . 111 C4
Thornton Ave PL4 . . . . . 263 B4
Thornton Dr EX39 . . . . . 156 E2
Thornton Hill EX4 . . . . . 261 B4
Thorntree Bsns Units
EX8. . . . . 196 F1
Thorn Villas PL9 . . . . 208 E3
Thornville Terr PL9 . . . . . 255 C7
Thorny Park La EX31 . . . . 10 D3
Thornyville Cl PL9 . . . . . 255 C7
Thornyville Dr PL9 . . . . . 255 D8
Thornyville Villas PL9 . . 255 C8
Thorpe Ave EX8. . . . . 196 B3
THORVERTON. 81 D5
Thorverton CE Prim Sch
EX5. . . . . 81 E4
Three Ash Cross EX14 . . . 87 B5
Three Cnrs TQ12 . . . . . . 207 F8
Three Corner Cross EX36. 45 C5
Three Corner Pl EX2 . . . 181 C8
Three Crossways
4 Chulmleigh EX18 . . . . . 44 E1
Zeal Monachorum EX17. . 78 A4
Three Cross Ways EX19 . . 58 D2
Three Elms Cross EX15 . . 83 D3
Three Firs EX15 . . . . 83 D4
Threefoot Stool EX6 . . . . 98 A3
Three Gate Cross
Cheriton Bishop EX17 . . . 97 B6
Yeoford EX17 . . . . 79 D2
Three Gates Cross
Dulverton TA22 . . . . 33 C6
Hartshaw EX16 . . . . 49 E6
Yarnscombe EX31 . . . . . . 27 D1
Three Gates Hill EX16 . . . 49 E6
Three Hammers Cross
EX17. . . . . 61 A6
THREE HORSE SHOES . . 172 E5
Three Lane End EX22. . . . 38 E1
Three Limbed Oak EX5. . . 81 D3
Three Mariners Cross
EX14. . . . . 86 C6
Three Sycamores Cross
EX24. . . . . 102 F6
Three Tree La TQ14 . . . . 124 C2
Three Ways EX31 . . . . 18 A8

Threshers EX17 . . . . 165 A5
Threwstones CI EX16 . . . 161 E5
Thriverton Cross EX22 . . . 39 B1
Throgmorton Ho **1** TQ9 223 D5
Throwcombe Cross EX16 . 48 A6
Throwcombe La EX16 . . . 48 A6
Thrushel CI TQ5 . . . . 230 A2
THRUSHELTON 106 E6
Thuborough Cross EX22. . 54 A4
Thurlescombe Cross
  EX16 . . . . 64 E6
THURLESTONE 143 A2
Thurlestone, All Saints CE
  Prim Sch TQ7 . . . . 143 A2
Thurlestone Beach Ho
  TQ7 . . . . 143 A1
Thurlestone Gdns TQ6 . . 233 E3
Thurlestone Rock **3** TQ12 207 B4
Thurlestone Rock TQ7 . . 147 B8
Thurlestone Wlk PL6 . . . 249 D8
Thurlow CI EX17 . . . . 64 D7
Thurlow Hill TQ1 . . . . 220 A6
Thurlow Pk TQ1 . . . . 220 A6
Thurlow Rd
  Exeter EX4 . . . . 177 E7
  Torquay TQ1 . . . . 220 A6
Thursby Wlk EX4 . . . . 174 D1
Tichfield Gdns TQ5 . . . . . 225 F7
Tick La EX6 . . . . 113 E5
Ticklemore St TQ9 . . . . . . 223 D5
Tidcombe CI **11** EX16 . . . . 64 D7
Tidcombe La EX16 . . . . 64 D7
Tidcombe Prim Sch EX16 64 D7
Tidcombe Wlk **8** EX16 . . 64 D7
Tidderson Cross EX16 . . . 47 F4
Tidderson La EX16 . . . . . . 47 E3
Tiddy Brook Rd
  Tavistock PL19 . . . . 171 E2
  Whitchurch PL19 . . . . . . 171 E2
Tiddy CI PL3 . . . . 81 B3
Tideford Cross TQ9 . . . . . 227 A1
Tidlake La EX36 . . . . 45 C8
Tidwell Bsns Units EX8 . 196 F11
Tidwell CI EX9 . . . . 198 A2
Tidwell La EX9 . . . . 198 B5
Tidwell Rd EX9 . . . . 198 A2
TIGLEY 135 F3
Tigley Cross TQ9 . . . . 135 F3
Tilery EX14 . . . . 69 A3
Tillard CI PL7 . . . . 251 C5
TILLWORTH 88 D3
Tilly CI PL9 . . . . 255 F4
Timber Hill DT7 . . . . 260 E5
Timbers CI TQ11 . . . . 236 A3
Timbers Rd TQ11 . . . . 236 A3
Timber Terr TQ12 . . . . 212 F4
Times Mews **18** TQ9 . . . . . 223 C5
Timewell Hill EX16 . . . . . . 34 C4
Timridge La EX6 . . . . 113 E6
Tincombe PL12 . . . . 242 C2
TINHAY 105 F4
Tinhay Cross PL16 . . . . . . 105 F4
Tinhay Mill Ind Est PL16. 105 F4
Tinker's Cross EX18 . . . . . 59 A5
Tinkers Wood CI **4** TQ5. 230 C4
Tinkley La TQ13 . . . . 123 C8
Tin La PL4 . . . . 263 A2
Tinpit Hill EX5 . . . . 98 F7
Tinside Lido PL1 . . . . 262 C1
Tintagel CI
  Exeter EX4 . . . . 174 A2
  Torquay TQ1 . . . . 219 F8
Tintagel Cres PL2 . . . . . . 248 C8
Tintern Ave PL4 . . . . 263 C2
Tip Hill EX11 . . . . 169 D3
Tipleyhill Cross TQ12,. . 122 C2
Tipleyhill La TQ12, TQ13. 122 D3
Tippacott La EX35 . . . . 6 A4
Tipple Cross PL15 . . . . . . 105 B6
Tipton Cross EX11 . . . . . . 168 B2
TIPTON ST JOHN 100 D2
Tipton St John CE Prim Sch
  EX10 . . . . 100 C2
Tipton Vale EX11 . . . . 100 C3
TITCHBERRY 22 C6
Titchen's La
  Calverleigh EX16 . . . . . . 48 B1
  Tiverton EX16 . . . . 63 B8
Titching Park La EX34 . . . 9 B5
Titham Hill EX16 . . . . 47 C6
Tithe Barn Cross EX15.. 51 D2
Tithebarn La EX16 . . . . . . 179 A8
Tithe Rd PL7 . . . . 250 B7
TITSON 70 C4
Titterton Cross EX20 . . . 77 D7
TIVERTON 161 D3
Tiverton Bsns Pk EX16 . . 64 D8
Tiverton Castle* EX16 . . . 161 C4
Tiverton CI PL6 . . . . 245 B8
Tiverton & District Hospl
  EX16 . . . . 161 C5
Tiverton High Sch EX16. 161 C5
Tiverton Mus of Mid Devon
  Life* EX16 . . . . 161 C3
Tiverton Parkway Sta
  EX16 . . . . 65 E8
Tiverton Rd
  1 Bampton EX16 . . . . . 34 C1
  Bampton EX16 . . . . 49 B8
  Silverton EX5 . . . . 163 B3
  Silverton EX5 . . . . 163 B3
Tiverton Way EX16 . . . . . 161 F5
Toadpit La EX11 . . . . 168 E6
Tobruk Rd PL12 . . . . 242 E3

Toby Cross PL21 . . . . 137 D6
Toby La EX5 . . . . 184 E5
Tod Moor Cross PL21 . . . 237 A1
Tolchers TQ9 . . . . 222 F8
Tolcis Cross EX13 . . . . 87 D3
Tollards Rd EX2 . . . . 178 B2
Tollbar CI PL21 . . . . 237 F5
Tollbar Cross EX31 . . . . . . 17 B8
Tolit Gdn **12** TQ9 . . . . . . 223 D5
Tolleys EX17 . . . . 165 E5
Tollit Gdn **12** TQ9 . . . . . . 223 D5
Tollox Pl PL3 . . . . 249 B4
Tolman Cres EX12 . . . . . . 192 B6
Tombstone La EX16 . . . . . 63 D8
Tomhead Cross EX4 . . . . 98 B6
Tom Maddock Gdns
  PL21 . . . . 237 E4
Tomouth Cres **14** EX39. . 15 A1
Tomouth Rd EX39 . . . . 15 A1
Tomouth Sq **18** EX39 . . . 15 A1
Tomouth Terr **18** EX39. 15 A1
Tom Sanders CI EX34 . . . 3 A3
Tomsclose La EX18 . . . . . . 59 C2
Tom's Field EX33 . . . . 7 F2
Tom's La EX39 . . . . 25 A3
TONE 160 A8
TONEDALE 160 B7
Tonedale Bsns Pk TA21.. 160 B7
Tonedale Ind Est TA21.. 160 B8
Tone Hill TA21 . . . . 160 B8
Tongue End Cross EX20.. 94 E5
Tongue Gate EX36 . . . . . . 45 E7
Tongue Gate Hill EX36. . 45 E7
Tongue Lake La EX37 . . . 44 E5
Tonyfield Wood Cross
  EX17 . . . . 60 B4
Top Cliff TQ14 . . . . 209 D5
Topcliff Rd TQ14 . . . . 209 D5
Top of the Town Ctyd
  PL12 . . . . 242 F2
TOPSHAM 182 F5
Topsham Mus* EX3 . . . . . 182 F4
Topsham Rd EX2 . . . . 178 B1
Topsham Sch The EX3.. 182 E5
Topsham Sta EX3 . . . . . . 182 F5
TOR 133 D3
Torbay Ct TQ5 . . . . 230 E5
Torbay Hospl TQ2 . . . . . . 219 D8
Torbay Hospl Annexe
  TQ2 . . . . 213 D1
Torbay L Ctr TQ4 . . . . . . 226 B3
Torbay Rd
  Paignton TQ4 . . . . 226 C6
  Torquay TQ2 . . . . 219 F3
  Torquay TQ3 . . . . 226 C7
Torbay Trad Est TQ5 . . . 230 C4
Torbridge CI PL21 . . . . . . 242 D2
Torbridge Rd
  7 Horrabridge PL20 . . 126 F4
  Plymouth PL7 . . . . 250 E6
TORBRYAN 211 A2
Torbryan CI PL6 . . . . 249 E8
Torbryan Hill TQ12 . . . . . 211 A3
Torches Cnr EX19 . . . . . . 42 D1
Tor Church Rd TQ2 . . . . . 220 A5
Tor CI
  Exeter EX4 . . . . 174 A1
  Paignton TQ4 . . . . 229 B7
  Plymouth, Hartley PL3.. 248 E7
Tor Cres PL3 . . . . 248 E7
TORCROSS 145 D1
Tor Dale **3** TQ1 . . . . 220 A6
Tor Down EX20 . . . . 94 D5
Tordown Farm & Nature
  Trail* EX32 . . . . 17 F2
Tordown Gn EX32 . . . . 17 F2
Tor Gdns TQ12 . . . . 206 D1
Tor Haven TQ12 . . . . 220 B4
Tor Hill Rd TQ2 . . . . 220 A5
Tor La PL12 . . . . 242 B1
Torland Rd PL3 . . . . 248 E7
Torlands Ct PL20 . . . . 126 E2
Tor Lane End TQ9 . . . . . . 223 B6
Tor Mare Ct TQ2 . . . . 219 E4
Toronto Ho EX4 . . . . 177 E8
Toronto Rd EX4 . . . . 261 C4
Tor Park Rd
  Paignton TQ4 . . . . 225 D3
  Torquay TQ2 . . . . 219 F6
Torpeek Cross PL21 . . . . 137 C7
TORPOINT 247 C3
Torpoint Com Sch PL11. 247 A4
Torpoint Inf Sch PL11.. 247 B3
TORQUAY 220 B2
Torquay Com Coll TQ2
  TQ2 . . . . 219 D7
Torquay Com Coll TQ2.. 219 F8
Torquay Grammar Sch for
  Girls TQ1 . . . . 219 D7
Torquay Mus* TQ1 . . . . . 220 C4
Torquay Rd
  Kingskerswell TQ12 . . . 213 A3
  Newton Abbot, Milber
  TQ12 . . . . 212 E8
  Newton Abbot TQ12 . . . 207 C3
  Paignton TQ3 . . . . 226 C8
Torquay Sta TQ2 . . . . 219 F4
Torr Bridge Pk PL8 . . . . . 136 A2
Tor Rd PL3 . . . . 248 E7
TORRE 219 F5
Torre Abbey* TQ2 . . . . . . 219 F4
Torre CE Prim Sch **1**
  TQ1 . . . . 219 E7
Torre CI PL21 . . . . 237 F5
Torre Sta TQ2 . . . . 219 E6

Torres Vedras Dr TA21 . . 160 F7
Torr Farm Cotts PL8 . . . 136 A2
Torr Hill PL8 . . . . 257 F4
Torridge Ave TQ2 . . . . . . 219 B7
Torridge CI
  12 Bideford EX39 . . . . . 157 B1
  Plymouth PL7 . . . . 251 A6
Torridge Ho **15** EX39 . . . 157 A1
Torridge Ho **15** EX39 . . . 157 B1
Torridge Mount EX39 . . 157 B1
Torridge PI **13** EX39 . . . 157 B1
Torridge Pool EX39 . . . . 157 A7
Torridge Rd
  Appledore EX39 . . . . 15 A1
  Braunton EX31 . . . . 15 E6
  Plymouth PL7 . . . . 250 F6
Torridge St EX39 . . . . 157 B1
Torridge View EX38 . . . . 159 B5
Torridge View Bglws
  EX38 . . . . 159 B5
Torridge Way
  Holsworthy EX22 . . . . . . 164 C6
  Plymouth PL3 . . . . 249 C5
Torrington Cross EX37 . . . 29 C4
Torrington Heritage Mus*
  EX38 . . . . 159 C5
Torrington Hospl EX38. 159 D5
Torrington La EX39 . . . . . 157 B1
Torrington Pl EX6 . . . . . . 194 D3
Torrington Pool EX38 . . 159 C5
Torrington Rd EX19 . . . 58 E3
Torrington St **10** EX39. . 157 B1
Torr La
  East Allington PL21 . . . . 144 B7
  Plymouth PL3 . . . . 248 E7
  Yealmpton PL8 . . . . 136 A2
Tor Royal La PL20 . . . . . . 128 B8
Torr Quarry Ind Est TQ9 144 B7
Tor Rd PL3 . . . . 248 E7
TORRS PARK 150 A5
Torrs Pk EX34 . . . . 150 A5
Torrs Walk Ave EX34 . . 150 A6
Tor View Ave PL3 . . . . . . 248 D7
Tor Sands **1** TQ4 . . . . . . 226 B5
Tors Pk EX35 . . . . 151 D5
Tor Square Ho **6** TQ2.. 219 F6
Tors Rd
  Lynmouth EX35 . . . . 151 D5
  Okehampton EX20 . . . . 170 B3
Tors The TQ12 . . . . 212 F4
Tors View EX36 . . . . 156 B6
Tor Vale TQ1 . . . . 219 F6
Torver CI PL6 . . . . 245 D2
Tor View
  Buckfastleigh TQ11 . . . 236 A4
  8 Horrabridge PL20. . 126 F4
  Princetown PL20 . . . . . . 119 A1
Tor View Gdns TQ3 . . . . 226 A6
Torville Pk EX39 . . . . 156 D7
Torwood CI TQ1 . . . . 220 C3
Torwood CI TQ1 . . . . 220 D4
Torwood Gables TQ1 . . 220 C4
Torwood Gardens Rd
  TQ1 . . . . 220 C4
Torwood Ho **4** TQ1 . . . . 220 D4
Torwood Mount **6** TQ1. 220 C4
Torwood St TQ1 . . . . 220 C4
Torwood Villas TQ1 . . . . 220 C4
Tory Brook Ave PL7 . . . . 250 E6
Tory Brook Ct PL7 . . . . . . 250 E6
Tory Way PL7 . . . . 250 D6
TOSBERRY 37 E8
Tosberry Cross EX39 . . . . 37 E8
Tothill Ave PL4 . . . . 263 B3
Tothill CI **2** TQ14 . . . . . . 210 A3
Tothill Rd PL4 . . . . 263 B3
TOTNES 223 B6
Totnes Castle* TQ9 . . . . 223 B6
Totnes CI PL7 . . . . 251 B4
Totnes Com Hospl TQ9. 223 C6
Totnes Costume Mus* **20**
  TQ9 . . . . 223 C5
Totnes Cross TQ9 . . . . . . 139 C3
Totnes Down Hill TQ9. . 223 A5
Totnes Elizabethan Ho Mus*
  TQ9 . . . . 223 C5
Totnes Littlehempston Sta*
  TQ9 . . . . 223 C6
Totnes Pavilion TQ9 . . . . 223 C6
Totnes Rd
  Buckfastleigh TQ11 . . . 236 D5
  Ipplepen TQ12 . . . . 211 F5
  Marldon TQ3 . . . . 226 C1
  Paignton TQ3, TQ4 . . . . 225 F5
  South Brent TQ10 . . . . . 134 F3
  Torquay TQ2 . . . . 219 C4
Totnes Sta TQ9 . . . . 223 B7
Tottons Ct EX2 . . . . 181 A8
Touts CI EX36 . . . . 158 D4
Tovey Cres PL5 . . . . 244 D2
Towell La EX17 . . . . 42 D2
Tower Cross EX14 . . . . . . 86 A3
Tower Ct
  Dunchideock EX6 . . . . . 114 A5
  Saltash PL12 . . . . 242 C2
Towerfield Dr PL6 . . . . . . 245 C8
Tower Gdns EX37 . . . . 165 C6
Tower Hill
  Cheriton Fitzpaine EX17. 62 E1
  Holcombe Rogus TA21. . 50 D5
Tower Hill Cross EX17 . . 62 E1
Towerhill La TQ13 . . . . . . 124 B4
Tower Hill Rd PL15 . . . . . 90 D1

Tower House Sch **8**
  TQ4 . . . . 226 B5
Tower La **2** PL21 . . . . . . 137 C8
Tower Moor EX37 . . . . 28 F6
Tower Pk EX36 . . . . 158 C3
Tower Rd
  Honiton EX14 . . . . 166 F4
  Offwell EX14 . . . . 86 A3
  Paignton TQ6 . . . . 226 B6
Towers CI PL6 . . . . 245 F2
Tower St
  8 Bideford EX39 . . . . . . 157 A1
  18 Exmouth EX8 . . . . . 202 A6
  Northam EX39 . . . . 156 F7
Tower View
  Broadclyst EX5 . . . . 175 C5
  Saltash PL12 . . . . 242 D1
Tower Way EX14 . . . . 67 B1
Tower Wlk EX2 . . . . 181 C8
Town CI TQ6 . . . . 233 E3
Town Ct EX13 . . . . 87 A3
Town End EX5 . . . . 175 D7
Town End Cross EX20 . . 76 C5
Town Farm Bglws EX14. . 85 B1
Town Farm CI
  8 Honiton EX14 . . . . . . 166 B6
  6 Horrabridge PL20 . . . 126 F4
Town Farm Cotts TQ9 . . 139 E1
Town Farm Ct
  Braunton EX33 . . . . 152 C6
  Ideford TQ13 . . . . 124 B4
  Shirwell EX31 . . . . 17 B8
Town Farm La TQ13 . . . . 124 B4
Townfield EX6 . . . . 182 A4
Town Hall Pl **4** TQ13.. 180 D8
Town Hill
  Broadclyst EX5 . . . . 175 C7
  Culmstock EX15 . . . . . . 66 E8
  Ermington PL21 . . . . . . 136 F3
Town Living Cross EX20. 76 B5
Town Marsh TA22 . . . . . . 33 D7
Town Mdw
  Ilsington TQ13 . . . . 111 D3
  Little Torrington EX38 . . 41 D3
  Newton Abbot TQ13 . . . 38 E8
Town Mill Gdns PL19 . . . 171 C6
Town Mills EX7 . . . . 204 C6
Town Mill The* DT7 . . . . 260 E3
Town Moor Cross EX17. . 46 B1
Town Moor Hill EX17 . . . 46 B1
Town Pk
  Crediton EX17 . . . . 165 B5
  Great Torrington EX38. 159 C5
  West Alvington TQ7 . . . 258 B4
Town Rd TQ7 . . . . 148 F3
Townsend Ave EX12 . . . . 191 C6
Townsend CI TQ7 . . . . . . 258 A4
Townsend Rd
  Seaton EX12 . . . . 192 A5
  West Alvington TQ7 . . . 258 A4
Townsend Terr TQ7 . . . . 144 E7
Townshend Ave PL2 . . . . 247 E6
Town's La TQ7 . . . . 143 E7
TOWNSTAL 233 D3
Townstal Cres TQ6 . . . . . 233 D4
Townstal Hill TQ6 . . . . . . 233 E3
Townstal Pathfields TQ6 233 D3
Townstal Rd TQ6 . . . . 233 D3
Town Tree Hill **19** EX7.. 204 D6
Town Wlk EX32 . . . . 155 B4
TRACEBRIDGE 51 A8
Tracey Cl PL11 . . . . 262 B3
Tracey Vale TQ13 . . . . . . 180 C6
Tracey View **2** EX14 . . . 166 B6
Trackdownmoor Cross
  TA22 . . . . 33 B3
Trafalgar Arc **20** EX34 . . 3 A3
Trafalgar CI
  Newton Abbot TQ12 . . . 207 B5
  Plymouth PL5 . . . . 247 D8
Trafalgar Ct
  Topsham EX3 . . . . 182 E5
  Uffculme EX15 . . . . 66 A7
Trafalgar Gdns EX32 . . . 155 A3
Trafalgar Lawn EX32 . . . 155 A3
Trafalgar PI
  4 Bideford EX39 . . . . . . 156 F1
  Exeter EX4 . . . . 261 C4
Trafalgar Place La PL1.. 247 F3
Trafalgar Rd EX8 . . . . 195 F6
Trafalgar St PL4 . . . . 263 A3
Trafalgar Terr TQ5 . . . . . 230 C6
Trafalgar Way EX13 . . . . 167 C5
Trafford Mews EX2 . . . . . 178 C3

Trago Mills Sh & L Pk
  TQ12 . . . . 123 A1
Traine Brake PL9 . . . . 256 C1
Traine Rd
  Wembury PL9 . . . . 140 D8
  Wembury PL9 . . . . 256 B1
Traine Terr PL1 . . . . 137 C2
Traine Villas PL21 . . . . . . 137 C3
Tramway Rd PL6 . . . . 245 E7
Tramways TQ1 . . . . 220 B7
Transit Way PL5 . . . . 244 C3
Travellers Rest Cross
  EX37 . . . . 28 D6
Travershes CI EX8 . . . . . 196 B1
Traylane EX37 . . . . 28 B1
Treable La EX6 . . . . 96 B3
Treago Gdns PL6 . . . . 245 C8
Treasbeare La EX5 . . . . . . 99 A5
Trebblepark Rd TQ7 . . . . 258 C6
TREBURLEY 115 A4
Treburley CI PL5 . . . . 115 A4
Treburley Ind Est PL15. 115 A4
Treby Rd PL7 . . . . 250 F4
TRECOMBE 115 D4
Trecott Cross EX20 . . . . 76 F3
Tree Beech Rural Ent Pk
  EX32 . . . . 17 F4
Tree CI EX32 . . . . 17 F4
Treefield EX31 . . . . 18 A8
Treefields TQ5 . . . . 230 B4
Treefield Wlk EX32 . . . . . 155 C4
Trees Ct EX3 . . . . 182 F5
Treesdale CI TQ3 . . . . . . 225 F6
Tree Surfers* PL19 . . . . 125 D7
Treetop CI PL12 . . . . 242 D4
Trefusis Gdns PL3 . . . . . . 249 A4
Trefusis PI EX8 . . . . 202 A5
Trefusis Terr
  Exmouth EX8 . . . . 202 A5
  Merton EX20 . . . . 57 A7
  Millbrook PL10 . . . . 252 E6
Trefusis Way EX9 . . . . . . 198 B6
Tregenna CI PL7 . . . . 251 C4
TREGONHAWKE 252 B4
Tregoning Rd PL11 . . . . . 246 F2
TREHAN 242 A1
Trehill Ho PL6 . . . . 114 D3
Trehill La PL10 . . . . 140 H2
Trehill Rd PL21 . . . . 237 E5
TREKENNER 115 A5
Trekenner Prim Sch
  PL15 . . . . 115 A5
Trelawney Ave PL5 . . . . . 243 D1
Trelawney CI PL11 . . . . . 246 E3
Trelawney Ct EX39 . . . . . 157 A7
Trelawney PI PL5 . . . . . . 243 D1
Trelawney Rd
  Plymouth PL5 . . . . 248 D5
  Saltash PL12 . . . . 242 E2
Trelawney Rise PL11 . . . 246 E3
Trelawney Way PL11 . . . 246 E3
Trelawny Rd
  Plymouth PL5 . . . . 250 C6
  Tavistock PL19 . . . . 171 C6
Trelissick CI TQ3 . . . . . . 225 D7
Trelissick Rd TQ3 . . . . . . 225 D7
Trelivan Ct EX8 . . . . 196 E3
Trelorrin Gdns PL3 . . . . . 248 E5
Treloweth CI PL2 . . . . . . 248 D8
Tremaine CI EX14 . . . . . . 166 C6
Tremarran PL21 . . . . 237 C6
Trematon Ave TQ2 . . . . . 220 A5
Trematon CI PL11 . . . . . . 246 D3
Trematon Dr PL21 . . . . . . 237 E5
Trematon Terr PL4 . . . . . 248 E4
Tremayne Rise PL19 . . . 171 B5
Tremere Ct **22** EX32 . . . 155 A4
Tremlett Gr TQ12 . . . . . . 211 D2
Tremletts CI EX6 . . . . 97 F5
Trenance Dr PL19 . . . . . . 116 E3
Trenchfirs Cnr TQ9 . . . . 139 E2
Trenchford Resr Woodland
  Wlk* TQ13 . . . . 112 A1
Trendlewood Rd PL6 . . . 245 D7
Trengrouse Ave PL11 . . . 246 F3
Treninnow & Wiggle Chalets
  PL10 . . . . 252 C2
Trennaway Cross EX6 . . . 96 C1
Trenode Ave EX34 . . . . . . 2 F4
Trentbridge Sq EX2 . . . . 178 C4
Trent CI
  Bideford EX39 . . . . 26 A4
  Plymouth PL3 . . . . 249 B6
Trentham CI
  Paignton PL6 . . . . 225 E8
  Plymouth PL6 . . . . 245 B6
TRENTISHOE 4 A5
Trentishoe La EX31 . . . . 4 A5
Trentworthy Cross EX22. 38 B2
Trescote Way EX20 . . . . 92 F1
Tresillian Cotts EX3 . . . 182 F3
Tresillian Gdns
  Exeter EX4 . . . . 177 E8
  Topsham EX3 . . . . 182 F4
Tresillian St PL4 . . . . 263 A2
Tresluggan Rd PL5 . . . . . 243 D1
Treston CI EX7 . . . . 204 E7
Trethewey Gdns PL7 . . . 132 D4
Tretower CI PL6 . . . . 244 F5
Trevanna Rd TQ7 . . . . . . 258 C4
Trevannion CI PL6 . . . . . 249 A8
Trevelyan Rd EX12 . . . . . 192 C4
Trevendon PL7 . . . . 115 B1
Treveneague Gdns PL2. 248 D8
Trevenn Dr TQ12 . . . . . . 213 A3
Treveor Gdns PL21 . . . . . 137 B3
Treverbyn CI PL7 . . . . . . 250 D6

Tre–Ven 313

Treverbyn Rd PL7 250 D6
Trevessa Cl PL2 248 D8
Trevethan Pk PL20 239 F4
Trevithick Ave PL11 246 F4
Trevithick Rd PL5 243 E2
Trevol Bsns Pk PL11 246 D3
Trevol Pl PL11 246 E3
Trevol Rd PL11 246 E3
Trevone Gdns PL2 248 D8
Trevorder Cl PL11 246 F2
Trevorder Rd PL11 246 F2
Trevose Way PL3 249 C6
Trewithy Ct PL6 244 F1
Trewithy Dr PL6 244 F1
Trews Weir Ct EX2 261 C1
Trews Weir Reach EX2 261 C1
TREWYN 164 B5
Trewyn Pk EX22 164 B5
Trewyn Rd EX22 164 B6
Triangle Pl 15 TQ14 210 C4
Triangle The 16 TQ14 210 C4
Trickey Cl EX16 161 F5
Trick's Terr EX19 42 D1
Tridley Foot Cross EX17 61 F4
Tridley Foot Hill EX17 61 F3
Trigger's Hill EX19 42 D3
Trill Cross EX13 103 E6
Trill La
Axminster EX13 167 C2
Musbury EX13 103 E6
TRIMSTONE 8 E6
Trimstone Cnr EX34 8 F5
Trimstone Cross EX34 8 E6
Trimstone La
West Down EX34 8 E5
Woolacombe EX34 8 D6
Trinfield Ave EX8 196 B1
TRINITY 82 F8
Trinity Cl
19 Bere Alston PL20 125 E1
1 Teignmouth TQ14 210 B6
Wellington TA21 160 C5
Trinity Cotts EX5 82 F8
Trinity Cross EX5 83 A8
Trinity Ct
Sidmouth EX10 188 B3
Westward Ho! EX39 156 B6
Trinity Gdns EX34 150 A5
Trinity Hill TQ1 220 C3
Trinity Hill Nature Reseve★ EX13 104 A6
Trinity Hill Rd
Axminster EX13 167 F1
Raymond's Hill EX13 104 B7
Uplyme EX13 104 B5
Trinity Mews TQ14 210 B7
Trinity Pl 15 EX32 155 A4
Trinity Rd EX8 201 E6
Trinity Row TA21 160 C5
Trinity Sch TQ14 210 B7
Trinity Sq EX13 167 D6
Trinity St EX32 155 A4
Trinity Way PL19 171 A4
Trinnaman Cl PL21 237 D4
Trinnicks Orch PL21 137 D6
Tristan Cl EX4 174 A2
Tristford Cross TQ9 223 A4
Tristford Rd TQ9 222 D2
Trittencott Cross EX36 46 A8
Triumphal Cres PL7 250 A6
Troarn Way 21 TQ13 123 E6
Trobridge Cross EX17 165 D2
Trojan Ind Pk TQ4 225 E3
Trood La EX2 181 D6
Trough La TQ13 123 A6
Trouville 16 EX32 155 A5
TROW 189 A7
Trowbridge Cl PL5 244 C4
Trowell La TA4 35 E4
Trow Hill EX10 188 D8
Truckham La EX34 3 D2
TRUE STREET 224 A6
Trumans Ct EX4 261 A2
Trumlands Rd TQ1 214 B1
Trumpers Cl PL21 237 A6
Trumps Cross EX16 50 E3
Trumps Ct EX10 188 B3
Trumps Orch EX15 163 A4
Truro Ave TQ2 214 A1
Truro Dr
Exeter EX4 176 F7
Exmouth EX8 196 D4
Plymouth PL5 244 A5
TRUSHAM 113 D1
Trusham Cross TQ13 113 D1
Trusham Rd EX2 177 C2
Tub Cnr EX5 99 C7
TUCKENHAY 139 F7
Tucker Cl PL5 247 F8
Tucker Ct EX14 166 C6
TUCKERMARSH 125 E2
Tuckers Brook 12 PL21 137 B2
Tuckers Cl EX17 165 A5
Tucker's Hill PL21 133 C1
Tucker's Hill Head PL21 133 C2
Tuckers Maltings★ TQ12 207 D4
Tuckers Mdw EX17 165 A5
Tucker's Moor Cross EX16 32 F3
Tuckers Pk
Bradworthy EX22 38 E1
Buckland Brewer EX39 40 B7
Tuckfield Cl EX2 178 A4
Tucking Mill La EX36 158 E3
Tuckmill Cross EX14 84 C4
TUDHAY 88 C3
Tudor Cl
Lifton PL16 105 E4
Tudor Cl *continued*
11 Newton Abbot TQ12 207 B3
Northam EX39 156 F6
Paignton TQ4 226 A2
Plymouth PL9 255 E5
Tudor Ct
Exeter EX4 261 A2
Saltash PL12 243 A2
Tudor Dr EX31 154 D2
Tudor Gr EX15 163 C5
Tudor Rd TQ12 207 B3
Tudor St EX4 261 A2
Tuffery Ct EX4 177 F8
Tugela Terr EX5 179 A3
Tully Gdns EX10 188 B7
Tuly St EX31 154 F5
Tumbles The EX20 76 C5
Tumbling Field La EX16 161 D3
Tumbling Fields EX16 161 D3
Tumbly Hill TQ7 258 D4
Tunnaford Cross TQ13 110 E4
Tunnel La EX14 166 F8
Tuns La EX5 82 B5
Tunworth Ct 1 EX1 261 A2
Tuplins TQ12 207 E8
Turbill Gdns 4 PL7 251 B5
Turbury Cross EX14 85 A8
TURFMOOR 87 D4
Turkey La EX5 99 E5
Turlake Ho EX5 172 F5
Turlake Mews EX5 172 F5
TURNCHAPEL 255 B7
Turner Ave EX8 202 C7
Turner Cl EX10 186 F7
Turners Cres EX39 22 E3
Turner's La DT6 88 H2
Turning Ways EX17 61 A2
Turnpike
Gunnislake/Calstock PL18 125 B5
Halberton EX16 65 C8
Honiton EX14 166 D6
Sampford Peverell EX16 50 C1
Turnpike Cl
Clovelly EX39 23 D3
Whiddon Down EX20 95 F3
Turnpike Cross EX34 8 C6
Turnpike Rd EX20 95 F3
Turnquay PL9 255 C7
Turpins Plot EX20 170 D5
Turret Gr PL4 248 F4
TUTWELL 115 E2
Tuxton Cl PL7 251 C3
Tweed Cl EX14 166 C4
Tweenaway Ct TQ4 225 E4
TWEENAWAYS 225 E4
Tweenaways TQ11 236 A4
Tweenaways Cross TQ4 225 E4
Tween Moor Cross EX17 60 F6
Tweenways TQ12 207 D7
Twelve Acre Post TA22 33 A4
Twelve Milestone Hill EX17 79 D7
Twelve Oaks Cross EX18 58 E6
Twickenham Rd TQ12 208 A1
Twinaway La EX2 114 B8
Twindle Beer TQ13 123 E6
Twiscombe Cnr EX4 98 D5
Twiscombe La EX4 98 C6
Twisted Oak EX6 97 D5
Twistgates La EX14 68 D4
TWITCHEN 20 D1
Twitchen Ball Cnr EX36 20 C3
Twitchen Cross
Great Torrington EX38 26 F2
West Down EX34 8 E6
Twitchen Gate EX31 11 F3
Twitchen La
Arlington EX31 10 F4
Burrington EX37 43 F3
Stowford EX31 11 A3
Two Acre Cl TQ3 225 E6
Twoacre Ct EX2 181 A8
TWO BRIDGES 119 C1
Two Bridges Rd
Princetown PL20 128 B8
Sidford EX10 101 B1
Two Crosses
Dunsford EX6 113 A8
Yealmpton PL8 136 A1
Two Gate Cross EX37 44 A4
Two Gates Cross EX16 47 E5
Two Hills Pk PL12 242 C2
Two Mile Oak Cross TQ12 211 F5
Two Moors Prim Sch EX16 161 E5
Two Post Cross
Pennymoor EX16 62 E7
Taw Green EX17 95 D7
Two Post La EX17 95 D7
TWO POTS 2 B1
Two Rivers Ind Est EX31 154 E6
Two Stone La EX6 114 C5
Two Trees Rd EX31 153 D5
Twyford Pl
Tiverton EX16 161 D4
Wellington TA21 160 D5
Tyes Orch EX15 83 F5
Tylney Cl PL6 245 B6
Tyndale Cl PL5 244 B1
Tyrrell Mead EX10 188 B7
Tyrrell Rd EX16 161 B4
TYTHECOTT 40 B4
Tytheing Cl EX5 172 A8
TYTHERLEIGH 88 C6
Tything Wlk 4 PL3 248 E6

U

UFFCULME 66 A8
Uffculme Ct EX15 66 A7
Uffculme Prim Sch EX15 66 A7
Uffculme Rd
Culmstock EX15 66 D8
Uffculme EX15 66 A7
Willand EX15 162 E6
Uffculme Sch EX15 66 A7
UGBOROUGH 137 E6
Ugborough Prim Sch PL21 137 D6
Ugborough Rd PL21 137 C7
Ugbrooke House & Pk★ TQ13 123 F5
Uggaton Cross EX14 84 D5
ULLCOMBE 68 D4
Ullcombe La EX14 68 C4
Ullswater Cres PL6 244 E4
Ullswater Ct EX4 176 F5
Umber Cl EX34 2 F4
UMBERLEIGH 28 D2
Umberleigh Com Prim Sch EX37 28 D2
Umberleigh Sta EX37 28 C2
Umberside 19 EX34 3 A3
UMBORNE 102 F8
Undercliff TQ6 233 F4
Undercliff Rd PL9 255 B7
Underdown
Clovelly EX39 23 D3
Kennford EX6 114 A4
Underdown La EX20 76 D4
Underfleet The EX12 192 B5
Underhay PL8 257 E4
Underheath 5 TQ1 220 D5
Underhill EX8 195 E5
Underhill Cl EX8 195 E4
Underhill Cres EX8 195 E4
Underhill Rd
Plymouth PL3 248 A4
Torquay TQ2 219 E3
Underhill Terr EX3 182 F5
Underhill Villas 1 PL3 248 A3
Underidge Cl TQ3 225 E6
Underidge Dr TQ3 225 E6
Underidge Rd TQ3 225 E6
Under La
Bovey Tracey TQ13 180 A5
Holsworthy EX22 164 C3
Sidbury EX10 101 C1
Underlane
Boyton PL15 89 D3
Marhamchurch EX23 70 A6
Plymouth, Plympton PL7 250 C5
Plymouth, Plymstock PL9 255 E6
Underleat Cl 3 TQ13 123 F6
Underleys EX12 191 C5
Under Minnow Rd EX31 154 E7
Under Rd
Bridgerule EX22 70 F5
Gunnislake PL18 125 D6
Undertown PL21 137 D6
Under Way TQ12 213 A6
Underways PL20 125 E1
UNDERWOOD 250 C5
Underwood Cl EX7 204 D4
Underwood Cotts EX15 83 C4
Underwood Rd PL7 250 D4
Unicorn Cl PL7 250 B6
Unicorn St EX2 178 D4
Union Cl EX39 156 F1
Union Hill EX17 78 E7
Union La 9 TQ5 230 C5
Union Pl PL1 262 A2
Union Rd
Crediton EX17 165 C5
Exeter EX4 177 D8
Union Sq Sh Ctr TQ1 220 B5
Union St
Dartmouth TQ6 233 F3
Dulverton TA22 33 D6
Exeter EX2 177 A4
5 Exmouth EX8 202 A6
Newton Abbot TQ12 207 C3
Plymouth PL1 262 A2
Salcombe TQ8 259 E5
Torquay TQ1, TQ2 220 A5
Union Terr
Barnstaple, Bickington EX31 154 A4
Barnstaple EX32 155 A4
Crediton EX17 165 C5
Unity Cl PL6 245 D5
Univ of Exeter EX4 177 B8
Univ of Plymouth
Exeter EX2 177 E2
Plymouth PL4 263 A3
UPCOTT
Dolton 57 F4
Holsworthy 72 E7
Upcott Ave EX31 154 C6
Upcott Cross
Cobbaton EX32 28 C5
Halwill EX21 91 D8
Holsworthy EX22 72 D7
Iddesleigh EX19 57 F4
St Giles on t H PL15 90 E1
Welcombe EX39 37 C5
West Buckland EX32 18 C3
Upcott Gate EX18 59 B3
Upcott Hill
Barnstaple EX31 154 D8
Bideford EX39 25 F4
Okehampton EX20 170 A6
Upcott La
Thorverton EX5 81 E6
West Buckland EX32 18 C3
Upcott Mead Rd EX16 161 B4
Upcott Valley EX20 170 A6
UP EXE 82 A5
Upexe La EX5 82 B5
UPHAM 63 A3
Upham Cross EX17 63 A3
Upham La EX5 99 C1
Uphay La EX13 167 B8
UPHEMPSTON 217 A3
Uphill Cl PL21 237 E5
Upland Chase EX14 166 B3
Upland Dr PL6 245 A5
Upland Gdns PL9 140 D8
Uplands
Saltash PL12 242 E1
Tavistock PL19 171 A4
Uplands Dr EX4 174 A1
Uplands Rd TQ3 219 A2
Uplands Terr EX22 164 C3
UPLOWMAN 50 B2
Uplowman CE Prim Sch EX16 50 B2
Uplowman Rd
Chevithorne EX16 49 F1
Tiverton EX16 64 E8
UPLYME 260 B5
Uplyme Rd DT7 260 C4
Uplyme Road Ind Est DT7 260 C4
UPOTTERY 68 C2
Upottery Prim Sch EX14 68 C2
UPPACOTT 27 D7
Uppacott Cnr EX31 27 D8
Uppacott Cross
Meshaw EX36 45 F8
Moretonhampstead TQ13 111 D7
Uppaton La PL21 133 D1
Upper Braddons Hill Rd TQ1 220 C4
Upper Church St 9 EX8 202 A6
Upper Churston Rise EX12 191 E8
Upper Claypark EX34 7 F7
Upper Cloister Wlk EX6 181 F5
Upper Cockington La TQ2 219 C7
Upper Crooked Mdw EX20 170 C5
Upper Headland Park Rd TQ3 219 C1
Upper Hermosa Rd 1 TQ14 210 B5
Upper Highfield EX10 188 A5
Upper Knollys Terrace La PL3 248 C4
Upper Longlands EX7 204 D7
Upper Manor Rd TQ3 226 B8
Upper Morin Rd TQ3 226 C7
Upper Paul St EX4 261 A3
Upper Penns Rd TQ3 219 C1
Upper Ridings PL7 251 B7
Upper Stoneborough La EX9 198 A1
Upperton La PL6 241 F3
Upperton Rd EX6 97 D1
Upper Torrs EX34 1 E4
Upper Westhill Rd DT7 260 C3
Upper West Terr EX9 198 A1
Upper Wood La TQ6 234 B3
UPPINCOTT 81 A5
Uppincott Hill EX5 63 C1
Uppincott La
Bickleigh EX5 63 C1
Cadbury EX5 81 C8
Upright Villas 4 EX33 152 D5
UPTON
Payhembury 84 D5
Skilgate 34 F8
Torquay 220 A6
Upton Cl PL3 249 B7
Upton Cross
Payhembury EX14 84 D5
Thurlestone TQ7 143 D2
Upton Ct 2 TQ1 220 A6
UPTON HELLIONS 80 C6
Upton Hill TQ1 220 A6
Upton Hill Rd TQ5 230 C2
Upton Manor Ct TQ5 230 C2
Upton Manor Pk TQ5 230 C2
Upton Manor Rd TQ5 230 C2
UPTON PYNE 173 A8
Upton Pyne Cross EX5 172 E4
Upton Pyne Hill EX5 172 F6
Upton Rd
11 Bideford EX39 157 B1
Torquay TQ1 219 F6
Upton St James CE Prim Sch 5 TQ1 220 A7
Usticke La EX34 3 B3
UTON 165 B1
Uton Steep Cross EX17 165 B1
Uxbridge Dr PL5 243 E4

V

Vaagso Cl PL1 247 E2
Vachell Cres EX2 178 D5
Vale Cl
Barnstaple EX32 155 A6
Galmpton TQ5 229 B5
Vale Ct 17 EX10 101 B1
VALE DOWN 108 A5
Vale Dr EX2 177 E3
Vale La EX13 167 D6
Valentine Manor TQ11 236 C5
Valentines TA22 33 E6
Vale Rd
Exmouth EX8 202 D7
Kingskerswell TQ12 213 A5
Newton Abbot TQ12 207 D1
Vales Rd EX9 198 B1
Valiant Ave PL5 244 A4
Valiant Soldier Mus The★ TQ11 236 C5
Valletort Flats PL1 248 A2
Valletort Ho PL1 262 C3
Valletort La PL1 248 A3
Valletort Pk TQ5 230 A4
Valletort Pl PL1 248 A2
Valletort Rd PL1, PL3 248 A3
Valletort Terr PL1 262 A4
Valley Cl
Barnstaple EX32 155 B5
Teignmouth TQ14 124 E1
Valley Dr PL9 140 D8
Valley La 7 EX34 3 A3
Valley of Rocks The★ EX35 5 A6
Valley Park Cl EX4 173 D2
Valley Path TQ12 206 E4
Valley Rd
Clyst St Mary EX5 179 E3
Exeter EX4 176 F7
Plymouth PL7 250 B5
Saltash PL12 242 E2
Valleyside TQ7 143 A2
Valley View
Axminster EX13 167 E5
Bideford EX39 156 D2
Chagford TQ13 111 A6
Farway EX24 101 F6
Landkey EX32 17 C1
Millmoor EX15 51 E1
Morebath EX16 34 B3
Plymouth PL6 245 D7
Seaton EX12 192 A6
Shebbear EX21 55 E4
Valley View Cl
Plymouth PL3 249 B6
Seaton EX12 192 B6
Torquay TQ1 219 F7
Valley View Rd PL3 249 B7
Valley Way EX8 196 E3
Valley Wlk PL6 245 E6
Van Buren Pl EX2 178 D3
Vanehill Rd TQ1 220 C3
Vanguard Cl PL5 244 D1
Van Post EX16 49 D6
Vanpost Hill EX16 49 D5
Vansittart Dr EX8 196 C3
Vansittart Rd TQ2 219 F6
Vapron Rd PL3 248 F6
Varco Sq EX2 178 C4
Varian Ct 4 TQ9 223 E5
Varley Ct EX16 161 E6
Vauban Pl PL2 247 F4
Vaughan Cl PL2 248 C7
Vaughan Par TQ2 220 B4
Vaughan Rd
Exeter EX1 178 B6
Torquay TQ2 220 B3
Vaughan Rise EX1 178 B6
Vauxhall Ct 9 PL4 263 A2
Vauxhall Quay PL4 263 A2
Vauxhall St PL4 263 A2
Vauxhall Street Flats 18 PL4 263 A2
Vavasours Slip TQ6 233 F4
Veale Cl EX20 75 B6
Vealenia Terr TQ13 130 F4
Veales Rd TQ7 258 C4
Veasypark PL9 140 D8
Veille La TQ2 219 C8
Veitch Cl EX2 177 E4
Veitch Gdns EX2 181 B8
VELATOR 152 C4
Velator Cl EX33 152 D4
Velator Dr EX33 152 D4
Velator Lane Ave EX33 152 D5
Velator Rd EX33 152 D4
Vellacott La EX34 3 C3
Vellaford Cross EX20 75 E7
Velland Ave TQ2 213 F4
Vellator Way EX33 152 D4
VELLY 23 B3
Velwell Rd EX4 261 A4
Venborough Cl EX12 191 F8
Venbridge Hill EX6 97 B4
Venford Cl TQ4 229 B8
Venford Hill
East Anstey TA22 32 E8
Hawkridge TA22 21 D1
Venford Villas EX36 30 D4
Venhay Cross EX36 46 D6
Venlake DT7 260 A5
Venlake Cl DT7 260 A5
Venlake End DT7 260 A5
Venlake Mdw DT7 260 A5
Venlock Cl EX32 155 D4
Venmore Orch EX5 184 B2
VENN 143 D5
Venn Bridge TQ10 137 E8
Venn Cl
Instow EX39 15 C2
6 Plymouth PL3 248 E6
Stoke Fleming TQ6 146 B7
Venn Cotts EX39 15 C2
Venn Cres PL3 248 E6
Venn Cross
Barnstaple EX32 155 D1

Venn Cross *continued*
Broadhempston TQ12 . . . **131** D4
East Allington TQ9 . . . . . **144** E5
Stoke Fleming TQ6. . . . . **146** B8
Ugborough PL21 . . . . . . **137** E7
Waterrow TA4 . . . . **35** D3
West Putford EX22 . . . . . **39** D3
Venn Ct
Brixton PL8 . . . . **257** A4
Plymouth PL3. . . . . **248** E6
Venn Dr PL8 . . . . **257** A4
Venn Gdns PL3 . . . . **248** E7
Venn Gr PL3 . . . . **248** E6
VENNGREEN **54** D6
Venn Hill
Copplestone EX17 . . . . . **79** B8
Milton Abbot PL19 . . . . **116** A6
Venn La
Cheriton Fitzpaine EX17 . . **63** A1
Dartmouth TQ6 . . . . . . **233** B1
Plymouth PL2, PL3. . . . . **248** C6
Stoke Fleming TQ6. . . . . **146** A8
Venn Lane End EX32 . . . **17** B1
VENN OTTERY **100** B2
Venn Ottery Rd EX10 . . **186** E8
Venn Pk TQ6 . . . . **146** B8
Venn Rd EX32. . . . . **155** C1
Venn Way
Plymouth PL3. . . . . **248** E7
Stoke Fleming TQ6. . . . . **146** B7
Venny Bridge EX4. . . . . **174** D1
VENNY TEDBURN. **98** A8
VENTERDON **115** B2
Ventiford Cotts TQ12 . . **123** C2
VENTION **7** F3
Vention La EX33 . . . . . . **7** E3
Vention Rd EX33 . . . . . . **7** E3
VENTON
Drewsteignton **95** F1
Ivybridge. **136** B7
Venton Cross
Highampton EX21 . . . . . **74** E6
Tigley TQ9 . . . . **135** F3
Venton Ct TQ9 . . . . **144** F5
Venton Dr EX39 . . . . . . **156** D7
Venture Ct TQ12 . . . . . **207** A3
Verbena Terr TQ14. . . . **209** D5
Verden Cl PL2 . . . . **248** E5
Vermont Gdns PL2 . . . . **247** F7
Verna Pl PL5 . . . . **243** D2
Verna Rd PL5 . . . . **243** E2
Verney St EX1. . . . . **261** C4
Vernhill Cross PL7 . . . . . **132** E3
Vernon Cl TQ1 . . . . **220** C2
Vernon Ct TQ1. . . . . **220** A4
Vernon Rd EX8 . . . . **196** D2
Vernons La EX39 . . . . . **15** A1
Verona Ct EX32 . . . . . . **155** A6
Verwill La EX34 . . . . . . **3** D3
Veryan Cl EX7 . . . . **200** E1
Vestry Dr EX2 . . . . **181** B8
Viaduct View EX22 . . . . **164** C4
Vial's Cnr EX16 . . . . . . **48** D5
VICARAGE **190** F4
Vicarage Ball TQ9. . . . . **222** C2
Vicarage Cl
Brixham TQ5 . . . . **230** C5
Hartland EX39 . . . . **22** D3
Stoke Gabriel TQ9 . . . . . **227** F7
Vicarage Gdns
Dawlish EX7. . . . . **204** C6
Milton Abbot PL19 . . . . **116** A6
Plymouth PL5. . . . . **243** B1
Vicarage Gr TQ9 . . . . . . **227** F8
Vicarage Hill
Brixham TQ5 . . . . **230** C5
Cornwood PL21 . . . . . . **133** D3
Dartmouth TQ6 . . . . . . **233** E3
Dulverton TA22 . . . . . . **33** D6
Holbeton PL8 . . . . **136** D1
Kingsteignton TQ12 . . . **207** F7
Marldon TQ3 . . . . **218** E3
Torquay TQ2. . . . . **219** D4
Vicarage St
Barnstaple EX32 . . . . . . **154** F5
Colyton EX24 . . . . **103** A5
Vicary Cl TQ12. . . . . . . **207** F8
Vickers Ground EX39 . . **156** F8
Vickery Cl EX15. . . . . . . **163** B3
Vicks Mdw EX20 . . . . . . **75** C7
Victor Cl EX1. . . . . **178** A5
Victoria Ave PL1 . . . . . **262** A4

Victoria Cl
7 Barnstaple EX32 . . . . . **155** B4
Kenton EX6 . . . . **194** D3
Willand EX15. . . . . **162** D4
Victoria Cotts
2 Holsworthy EX22 . . . . **164** C4
Lee Mill PL21. . . . . **136** D6
North Tawton EX20 . . . . **77** C4
Plymouth PL6. . . . . **249** B8
Victoria Cres EX17 . . . . **165** D6
Victoria Ct
Dartmouth TQ6 . . . . . . **233** D3
4 Totnes TQ9 . . . . **223** C5
Victoria Gdns 1 EX39 . . **157** A1
Victoria Gr EX39 . . . . . . **157** A1
Victoria Hill 1 EX22 . . . **164** C4
Victoria Hts TQ6 . . . . . **233** D3
Victoria La PL12 . . . . . . **242** F2
Victoria Lawn EX32 . . . **155** B4
Victoria Par TQ1. . . . . . **220** B3
Victoria Park Rd
Exeter EX2. . . . . **177** E5
Torquay TQ1. . . . . **220** B7
Victoria Pl
Axminster EX13. . . . . . . **167** D6
Brixham TQ5 . . . . **230** C6
Budleigh Salterton EX9 . . **199** G2
Chardstock EX13. . . . . . **88** A7
Dartmouth TQ6 . . . . . . **233** F3
6 Exmouth EX8 . . . . . . **202** A6
Kingsbridge TQ7 . . . . . . **258** D5
Newton Abbot TQ12. . . . **207** C3
Plymouth, Devonport PL2 . **247** F4
Plymouth PL1. . . . . **262** A2
Salcombe TQ8 . . . . **259** E5
Victoria Rd
Barnstaple EX32 . . . . . . **155** A4
Black Torrington EX21 . . . **74** A8
Brixham TQ5 . . . . **230** F6
Dartmouth TQ6 . . . . . . **233** E3
1 Exeter EX4 . . . . **177** D8
Exmouth EX8 . . . . **201** F6
Hatherleigh EX20. . . . . . **75** C7
Ilfracombe EX34 . . . . . . **150** B5
Plymouth PL5. . . . . **243** D2
Saltash PL12 . . . . **242** F2
Sidmouth EX10 . . . . **188** B4
Topsham EX3. . . . . **182** F5
Torquay TQ1. . . . . **220** B6
Victoria Road Prim Sch 11
PL5 . . . . **243** D1
Victoria Sh Ctr TQ4 . . . **226** C6
Victoria Sq
3 Holsworthy EX22 . . . . **164** C4
Paignton TQ4 . . . . **226** C6
Victoria St
Barnstaple EX32 . . . . . . **155** B4
Exeter EX4. . . . . **177** D8
Holsworthy EX22 . . . . . **164** C4
Okehampton EX20 . . . . **170** C5
Paignton TQ4 . . . . **226** B6
Torpoint PL11 . . . . **247** B3
Totnes TQ9 . . . . **223** C5
Wellington TA21. . . . . . . **160** D6
Victoria Terr
Barnstaple EX32 . . . . . . **155** A4
15 Bideford EX39 . . . . . **157** A1
2 Bovey Tracey TQ13 . . . **180** D8
Cullompton EX15. . . . . . **163** C3
Honiton EX14. . . . . **166** B6
Kingsteignton TQ12 . . . **207** F7
Ottery St Mary EX11 . . . **169** C3
Plymouth PL4. . . . . **262** C4
Victoria Way EX8 . . . . . **201** F6
Victor La EX1. . . . . **178** A5
Victor St EX1 . . . . **178** A5
Victory Cl TQ12 . . . . . . **207** B5
Victory Rd
Dartmouth TQ6 . . . . . . **233** D3
North Tamerton EX22. . . . **89** D8
Victory St PL2 . . . . **247** E6
Victory Way EX38 . . . . . **159** C6
Vieux Cl EX9 . . . . **198** E7
View Rd DT7. . . . . **260** D3
Vigo Bridge Rd PL19 . . **171** C6
Vigo Mews PL19 . . . . . . **171** C6
Villa Capri TQ1 . . . . **220** D2
Villa Cl EX32. . . . . **155** B2
Village Cl EX8 . . . . **202** F7
Village Cross
Coldridge EX17 . . . . **59** F2
Loddiswell TQ7. . . . . . . **143** E7
Morchard Bishop EX17 . . **61** B2
Village Cross Rd TQ7. . . **143** E7
Village Dr PL6 . . . . **241** C1
Village Farm Cl EX23 . . . **70** A6
Village La EX14 . . . . **86** B1
Village Rd
Christow EX6. . . . . **113** B3
Marldon TQ3 . . . . **218** D3
Woodbury Salterton EX5 . . **184** C6
Village St 10 EX20 . . . . **16** E1
Village The PL20 . . . . . . **126** C3
Village Way PL19 . . . . . **117** F4
Villa Pardiso 4 TQ1 . . . **220** C5
Villa Rd EX38 . . . . **159** C5
Villas The TQ12 . . . . . . **123** E1
Villiers Ave TQ12 . . . . . **207** F2
Villiers Cl PL9 . . . . **255** D7
Vincents Rd TQ7. . . . . . **258** D5
Vincent Way PL12 . . . . **242** F2
Vine Cl EX2. . . . . **261** C2
Vine Cres PL2 . . . . **248** B6
Vinegar Hill EX39 . . . . . **157** B2
Vine Gdns PL2 . . . . **248** B6
Vine Passage EX14. . . . **166** C6
Vine Rd TQ2 . . . . **219** F6

Vinery La PL7, PL9 . . . . . **250** E1
Vinery The TQ1 . . . . **220** B4
Vine St EX19. . . . . **58** F2
Vineyard TQ9 . . . . **223** A8
Vineyard Hill TQ9 . . . . . **223** A8
Vineyards The EX22 . . . . **164** C5
Vineyard Terr TQ9 . . . . **144** D7
Vineycroft La EX10. . . . **188** F7
Viney Cross EX14 . . . . . **86** B6
Viney La
Monkton EX14. . . . . **86** C7
Upottery EX14 . . . . **68** C1
Viney Lane Cross EX14 . . **86** B5
Vinivers Cross TQ8. . . . . **148** F4
Vinnicombes Rd EX5 . . . **173** F8
Vinstone Way PL5. . . . . **243** D1
Violet Dr PL6 . . . . **245** E8
Violet La PL12 . . . . **171** E6
Virginia Cl EX39 . . . . . . **157** A1
Virginia Gdns PL2 . . . . . **247** F7
Virginia Lodge 14 TQ1 . . **220** D4
VIRGINSTOW **90** D3
Vision Hill Rd EX9. . . . . . **198** B2
Visitors Hill EX16 . . . . . **63** D4
Vision Cl TQ5 . . . . **230** B5
Vix Ct TQ5. . . . . **230** B5
Vixen Tor Cl
Okehampton EX20 . . . . **170** C5
Yelverton PL20. . . . . **126** F3
Vognacott Cross TQ22. . **53** F3
Voscombe Cross EX31. . . **26** F7
Voulsdon Cross EX20. . . **92** A4
VOXMOOR. **160** F1
Voysey Hill EX17 . . . . . . **62** F1
Vranch House Sch EX4 . . **178** B7
Vuefield Hill EX2. . . . . . **176** E3
Vulcombe Cross EX16 . . **63** A6
Vulscombe La EX16 . . . . **63** B6
Vyvyan Ct EX1 . . . . **178** A5

W

WADBROOK **88** C4
Wadbrook Cross EX13. . . **88** C4
Waddens Cross EX24 . . . **102** D4
Wadderly Hill EX17. . . . . **79** F7
Waddeton Cl TQ4. . . . . **225** F1
Waddeton Ind Est TQ4 . . **225** F1
Waddeton Rd
Paignton TQ4 . . . . **225** F1
Stoke Gabriel TQ5 . . . . . **228** D6
WADDICOMBE **32** E6
Waddington Cross EX36 . **31** A3
Waddington La EX18 . . . **45** A5
Waddles Down Cross EX4 **98** E5
WADDON **124** A6
Waddon Cl PL7. . . . . . . **250** E7
Waddons Cross TQ9. . . . **216** C6
Wade Cl EX8. . . . . **202** E8
Wadham Cross
West Anstey EX36. . . . . . **32** A2
West Anstey EX36. . . . . . **32** A4
Wadham Ho EX4 . . . . . . **173** A1
Wadham Terr 6 PL2 . . . **248** A5
Wadlands Mdw EX20 . . **170** D5
Waggoners Way EX4 . . . **177** A8
Waggon Hill PL7 . . . . . . **251** A4
WAGGS PLOT **88** B4
Waggs Plot EX13. . . . . . **88** B4
Waie Cotts EX17 . . . . . . **78** C6
Waie Cross EX17 . . . . . . **78** B6
Wain La TQ12. . . . . **207** A4
Wain Pk PL7. . . . . **250** F4
Wakefield Ave PL5 . . . . **243** E1
Wakeham Ct EX33 . . . . **152** E4
Wakehams Cl PL21. . . . . **137** C2
Wake St PL4. . . . . **262** B4
Walcot Cl PL6 . . . . **245** E3
Walcott Way EX14 . . . . **67** C1
Walden Rd EX14 . . . . . . **67** C1
Waldon Cl PL7. . . . . **251** B6
Waldon Ct TQ2 . . . . . . **220** B4
Waldon Ho TQ2. . . . . . **220** B4
Waldon Point TQ2 . . . . **220** B4
Waldons Cross EX19 . . . **57** F1
Waldon Way EX22 . . . . **164** C6
Waldron's Cross TA11 . . **35** E1
Walkers Gate TA21. . . . **160** D5
Walker Terr PL1. . . . . . . **262** B1
Walkham Bsns Pk PL5. . . . **244** B1
Walkham La PL19 . . . . . **171** D5
Walkham Mdws PL20. . . **126** F4
WALKHAMPTON **127** A4
Walkhampton Rd PL20 . . **126** F4
Walkhampton Wlk PL6. . . **245** E1
Walkham Rise TQ2. . . . . **219** B8
Walkham Terr 5 PL20 . . **126** F3
Walk La EX36. . . . . **30** F6
Wallace Ave
Dawlish EX7. . . . . **204** E7
Exeter EX4. . . . . **178** B8
Torquay TQ2. . . . . **219** C8
Wallace La EX35 . . . . . . **5** A3
Wallace Rd PL7 . . . . **251** A4
Wallaford Rd TQ11 . . . . **135** C8
Walland Cross EX22 . . . . **18** E3
Wallaton Cross TQ9 . . . **144** E1
Walled Gdn The EX2 . . . **182** C7
Wallfield Rd TQ13 . . . . . **180** B5
Wallingford Rd TQ7 . . . **258** D6
Wallis Gr TQ14 . . . . **209** A8
Wallon Cross TQ13. . . . . **110** F7
Wallpark Cl PL7. . . . . . . **250** F7
Wall Park Cl TQ5 . . . . . . **230** E5
Wall Park Rd TQ5 . . . . . **230** D5

Wall Pk TQ9 . . . . **222** F6
Walls Cl EX8. . . . . **196** D2
Wallsend Ind Est PL4 . . **263** C1
Walls Hill Rd TQ1 . . . . . **220** D7
Walnut Cl
9 Chudleigh TQ13 . . . . . **123** F6
Exminster EX6. . . . . **182 A4
Plymouth PL7. . . . . **251** B5
Totnes TQ9. . . . . **223** B6
Walnut Ct
Brixham TQ5 . . . . **230** D4
Torquay TQ2. . . . . **219** E4
Walnut Dr
Crediton EX17 . . . . **165** D6
Plymouth PL7. . . . . **251** C5
Tiverton EX16 . . . . **161** F5
Walnut Gdns PL7 . . . . . **251** C5
Walnut Gr EX8 . . . . **202** C7
Walnut La TQ2. . . . . . . **219** E4
Walnut Rd
Exeter EX2. . . . . **177** F2
Honiton EX14. . . . . **166** A4
Torquay TQ2. . . . . **219** E4
Walnut Way EX32 . . . . . **155** D4
Walpole Cl EX4. . . . . . . **174** C1
Walreddon Cl PL19 . . . . **171** B4
Walronds The EX16 . . . . **161** C2
Walshams EX14. . . . . . . **87** A7
Walsingham Ct PL7 . . . . **251** B6
Walsingham Pl EX2 . . . . **178** D4
Walsingham Rd EX2 . . . **178** D4
Walson Cross EX17. . . . . **78** D2
Walson La EX19. . . . . . . **76** E7
Walson Rd EX17 . . . . . . **78** D3
Waltacre PL8 . . . . **257** F3
Walter Daw Fst Sch EX2. . **178** B4
Walters Orch EX15. . . . . **163** C3
Walters Rd PL5. . . . . . . **243** C2
Waltham PL2 . . . . **248** A8
Waltham Pl PL2. . . . . . . **248** A8
Waltham Rd TQ12 . . . . . **207** A3
Waltham Way PL21 . . . . **237** E4
Walton Cres PL5 . . . . . . **244** C1
Walton Rd EX2. . . . . . . **178** C5
Walton Way EX22 . . . . . **155** C5
WAMBROOK **69** B3
Wandle Pl PL3. . . . . **249** D5
Wanstead Gr PL5 . . . . . **244** A2
Wantage Gdns PL1 . . . . **262** A3
Warberry CE Prim Sch
TQ1 . . . . **220** C5
Warberry Rd W TQ1. . . . **220** B5
Warberry Vale 5 TQ1 . . **220** B6
Warborough Rd EX6 . . . **201** B8
Warborough Hill EX6. . . **194** E3
Warborough Rd TQ5 . . . **229** C6
Warbrigsleigh Hill EX16 . **48** B7
Warbro Cl 11 TQ1. . . . . **220** B7
Warbro Rd TQ1 . . . . . . **220** C7
Warburton Gdns PL5 . . **243** C1
Warcombe La EX34 . . . . **1** B2
Wardens Cl EX37. . . . . . **43** B7
Ward La EX19. . . . . **59** A2
Wardleworth St TA21 . . **160** C7
Wardleworth Way TA21 . **160** C7
Wardlow Cl PL6. . . . . . . **248** F8
Wardlow Gdns PL6. . . . . **248** F8
Wardour Wlk PL6 . . . . . **245** B7
Ward Pl PL3 . . . . **249** B5
Wardrew Rd EX4. . . . . . **176** F5
Wards Cross EX5 . . . . . . **99** C8
Ware Cl TQ12 . . . . **207** F7
Ware Cliff Chalets DT7. . **260** D2
Warecroft Rd TQ12 . . . . **207** F7
Ware Cross
Kingsteignton TQ12 . . . **207** F7
Ugborough PL21 . . . . . . **137** D6
Warecross Gdns TQ12. . **207** F7
Warefield Rd TQ3 . . . . . **226** C7
Wareham Cross EX13 . . . **88** E1
Wareham Rd EX13 . . . . . **88** E2
Ware La DT7 . . . . **260** B2
Waresfoot Dr EX17. . . . . **165** B6
Warfelton Cres PL12 . . . **242** E2
Warfelton Gdns PL12 . . . **242** E2
Warfelton Terr PL12 . . . . **242** E2
Warfield Villas EX34 . . . **150** C5
WARFLEET. **234** A1
Warfleet Creek Rd TQ6. . **234** A1
Warfleet Rd TQ6 . . . . . . **234** A2
Waring Bowen Ct EX2. . **177** F1
Waring Rd PL6. . . . . **244** E7
Warkidons Way EX35. . . **185** A5
WARKLEIGH **29** A2
Warkleigh Cross EX37. . . **29** B1
Warland TQ9 . . . . **223** C5
Warleigh Ave PL2. . . . . . **247** E5
WARLEIGH BARTON **243** F8
Warleigh Cres PL6 . . . . . **244** F5
Warleigh La PL2 . . . . . . **247** E5
Warleigh Rd PL2 . . . . . . **248** E4
Warm Hill TQ13 . . . . . . **123** B7
Warmwell Rd PL5 . . . . . **243** E4
Warneford Gdns EX8 . . . **196** E2
Warne La PL19. . . . . **117** E6
Warnicombe La EX16. . . **64** D6
Warran La PL19 . . . . . . **171** C3
Warraton Cl PL12 . . . . . **242** D3
Warraton Gn PL12 . . . . **242** D3
Warraton La PL12. . . . . **242** D3
Warraton Rd PL12 . . . . **242** D3
Warren Cl
Great Torrington EX38. . . **159** C5
Wembury PL9 . . . . **140** D7
West Hill EX11. . . . . **168** D4
Warren Cross EX16 . . . . **161** B7
Warren Dr PL9 . . . . **198** B2
Warren Hill TQ2 . . . . . . **220** B4

Warren La
Dartington TQ9 . . . . . . **216** B3
Exeter EX4. . . . . **261** B4
Farway EX24 . . . . **102** A7
Great Torrington EX38. . . **159** C5
Lee Mill PL21. . . . . **136** D6
Plymouth PL5. . . . . **244** A8
Wembury PL9 . . . . **140** E7
Warren Pk
Plymouth PL6. . . . . **245** D7
West Hill EX11. . . . . **168** D4
Warren Rd
Bigbury-on-S TQ7. . . . . . **142** E3
Dawlish EX7. . . . . **205** A8
Kingsbridge TQ7 . . . . . . **258** E3
Mary Tavy PL19 . . . . . . **117** E6
Thurlestone TQ7 . . . . . . **143** A1
Torquay TQ2. . . . . **220** B4
Warrens Mead EX10. . . . **188** D8
Warren St
Plymouth PL2. . . . . **247** E4
Rockwell Green TA21. . . . **160** A4
Warren The TQ12 . . . . . **206** F3
Warren View EX39 . . . . **156** E2
Warspite Gdns PL5. . . . . **244** D2
Warton Cl PL5 . . . . **244** D3
Warwick Ave
Exeter EX1. . . . . **178** C5
Plymouth PL5. . . . . **244** D3
Warwick Cl
Feniton EX14 . . . . **84** E2
Torquay TQ1. . . . . **220** F7
Warwick Orchard Cl PL5 **244** B3
Warwick Rd EX1. . . . . . **178** C6
Warwick Terr 8 EX32. . . **154** F6
Warwick Way EX4. . . . . **178** C8
Wasdale Cl PL6 . . . . **245** D2
Wasdale Gdns PL6 . . . . **245** D2
WASH **215** B7
Washabrook La TQ7. . . . **258** E6
Washabrook Way TQ7 . . **258** E5
WASHBOURNE **139** D5
Washbourne Cl
Brixham TQ5 . . . . **230** E5
Plymouth PL1. . . . . **247** E3
Washbourne Cross TQ9 . **139** D6
Washbrook View EX11 . . **169** E4
Wash Cross TQ11 . . . . . **215** B8
WASHFIELD **48** F2
Washfield La
Calverleigh EX16 . . . . . . **48** F2
Tiverton EX16 . . . . **161** B7
WASHFORD PYNE **61** F6
Washford Pyne Cross
EX17. . . . . **61** E4
Washington Cl TQ3 . . . . **219** B1
Washington Ho 5 EX2. . **192** A4
Wastor Cross PL21 . . . . **142** D7
Wastor Pk TQ12 . . . . . . **142** D7
WATCHCOMBE **102** F8
Watching Place Cross
TQ13 . . . . **111** B3
Watch The TQ7 . . . . . . **143** A2
WATCOMBE **214** B2
Watcombe Heights Rd
TQ1 . . . . **214** C4
Watcombe Prim Sch
TQ2. . . . . **214** B2
WATER **121** F7
Waterbeer St EX4. . . . . **261** A3
Water Bridge Cross EX17 **78** F6
Water Cotts TQ13 . . . . . **121** F7
Waterdale Pk TQ12 . . . . **213** A4
Waterford Cross TQ9 . . **131** E1
Waterford La EX13. . . . . **103** C5
Water Gate EX2. . . . . . . **261** B2
Watergate Cotts PL9 . . **140** D8
Watergate Cross EX20. . **167** F6
Waterhayes La TA20 . . . **68** F8
WATERHEAD. **143** B6
Waterhead Cl TQ6 . . . . **234** B4
Waterhead Terr TQ6 . . . **234** B4
Waterhouse Cross EX17. . **62** E1
Waterhouse Hill EX20 . . **74** F1
Waterleat Ave EX13, EX14 **87** C6
Watering Ct EX9 . . . . . . **198** E7
Water La
Barnstaple EX32 . . . . . . **155** B3
Bow EX17. . . . . **78** C4
Combe Martin EX34. . . . . **3** A3
Cornworthy TQ9 . . . . . . **227** A3
Exeter EX2. . . . . **177** C5
Kingskerswell TQ12 . . . . **213** A4
Sidmouth EX10 . . . . **188** B5
Tiverton EX16 . . . . **161** D4
Torquay TQ2. . . . . **219** C8
Waterlake La EX31 . . . . **16** A7
Waterlake Rd TA20. . . . . **88** C8
Water Lane Cl 2 EX2 . . **155** B3
Water Lane Cotts 4
EX32. . . . . **155** B3
Water Lane End TQ9 . . . **215** B3
Waterleaers Cross TQ7. . **147** D8
Waterleat Ave
Honiton EX14. . . . . **166** D5
Paignton TQ3 . . . . **225** E6
Waterleat Cl TQ3 . . . . . **225** F5
Waterleat Ct TQ3 . . . . . **225** F5
Waterleat Rd TQ3 . . . . . **225** F5
Waterloo Cl PL1 . . . . . . **248** A2
Waterloo Cotts EX15 . . . **163** C2
Waterloo Cross PL15 . . . **65** F8
Waterloo Ct PL1 . . . . . . **248** A2
Waterloo Hill EX14 . . . . **87** B6
Waterloo Rd
Exeter EX1. . . . . **177** A3
Holsworthy EX22. . . . . . **164** D5
Kingsbridge TQ7 . . . . . . **258** D5

Waterloo Rd continued
Torquay TQ1......220 B6
Wellington TA21......160 C6
Waterloo St
Plymouth PL4......263 A4
Plymouth, Stoke PL1......248 A3
Teignmouth TQ14......210 C4
Waterloo Terr EX39......156 F1
Waterloo Yard Flats PL1 248 E2
Water Mdw EX15......163 C2
Watermead TA20......88 D8
Watermill Ct TQ5......230 C4
Watermore Ct EX4......177 E7
Watermouth Castle★ EX34 2 D4
Watermouth Rd EX34......150 E6
Waterpark Ct EX7......187 F4
Water Park Rd EX39......156 D2
Water Path TA21......160 A5
Waterpool Rd TQ6......233 E2
WATERROW......35 F4
Waters Edge PL19......171 D6
Waterside
Exeter EX2......261 A1
Kingsbridge TQ7......258 D4
Newton Abbot TQ13......180 D7
Uplyme DT7......260 B5
Waterside Ho
Ivybridge PL21......237 C4
Totnes TQ9......223 D5
Waterside Mews PL1......247 D3
Waterside Rd TQ4......226 C1
Waterside Dr PL21......237 F4
Waterslake La EX5......179 E8
Watersmeet House★ EX35. 5 E5
Watersmeet Rd EX35......151 E4
Waterstream Sq TQ13 123 F6
Water Terr EX34......3 A3
Water Turn TQ13......130 E5
Waterwell La TQ12......213 C8
Waterworks La TQ14......209 D4
Watery La
Axminster EX13......88 A3
Beara EX31......9 A1
Braunton EX33......152 F5
Budlake EX5......82 E3
Colyton EX13, EX24......103 A6
Combe Martin EX34......3 A3
Croyde EX33......7 E2
Great Torrington EX38......159 B4
Milton Combe PL6......240 D6
Stoke Canon EX5......81 E3
Tiverton EX16......161 E5
Whiddon EX31......9 C1
Woodbury EX5......184 B4
Watkins Way
Bideford EX39......157 C2
Paignton TQ3......225 D7
Watson Gdns PL4......263 B3
Watson Pl
Exeter EX2......177 E4
Plymouth PL4......263 B2
Watts Park Rd PL2......248 C2
Watts Rd PL19......171 B5
Watt Av PL4......263 C3
Waveney Gdns PL5......244 C3
Waverley EX4......261 B4
Waverley Rd
Exmouth EX8......202 A8
Kingsbridge TQ7......258 C4
Newton Abbot TQ2......207 B4
Plymouth PL5......243 D2
Waverley Terr EX35......151 B5
Wavish Pk PL11......246 E3
Waybrook Cotts EX2......181 B7
Waybrook Cres EX2......181 C8
Waybrook La EX2......181 B6
Way Cnr EX16......63 A5
Waycroft Wlk PL6......244 D6
Way Cross EX20......107 D8
Way Down Cross TQ13......110 F8
Waye Cross TQ13......110 F5
Wayfaring EX32......155 D3
Way La EX6......98 B5
Wayland Ave EX2......261 C1
Waylands Cnr EX16......161 D7
Waylands Rd EX16......161 D6
Wayside
Brixham TQ5......230 A4
Ivybridge PL21......237 C4
Wayside Cl TQ5......230 A4
Wayside Cres EX1......178 B7
Way's La EX15......163 C2
WAYTOWN......24 D1
Waytown Cross TQ9......131 D2
WAY VILLAGE......63 A5
Wear Barton Rd EX2......182 B7
Wear Cl EX2......182 C7
WEARDE......242 F2
Wearde Rd PL12......242 E1
WEARE GIFFARD......26 B1
Weatherdon Dr PL21......237 F5
Weatherill Rd EX14......166 C4
Weaver Cross EX15★......83 E6
Weaver Ct TQ12......219 B8
Weavers Cl EX2......83 C7
Weavers Ct EX2......261 A2
Weaver's Reach TA21......160 B7
Weavers Way TQ12......213 A4
Weavers Wlk EX15......163 B2
Webber Cl TQ12......211 F8
Webbers CE Prim Sch
TA21......50 F5
Webbers Cl
Wellington TA21......160 C6
Whimple EX5......99 E8
Webbers Way
Dartington TQ9......222 F8
Tiverton EX16......161 E6

Webbers Way continued
Willand EX15......162 D4
Webbers Yard Est TQ9...222 E8
Webberton Cross EX2...113 F6
Webbery Cross EX39......26 C4
Webber Moor Cross
EX36......31 A3
Webble Green Cross
EX13......87 C8
Webbs Orch EX20......77 C4
Webland La TQ10......135 C3
Webley Rd EX2......176 C7
Weddicott Cross TQ13...111 A4
Wedding Well La EX33......8 F1
Wedgwood Cl TQ14......210 B4
Wedlake Mews EX7......204 D6
Weech Cl EX7......204 C6
Weeches The EX16......48 F2
Weech Rd EX7......204 C6
WEEK
Barnstaple......27 E6
North Tawton......77 B4
Totnes......215 D1
Weekaborough Dr TQ3...218 D2
Weekaborough Oak Cross
TQ12......217 E4
Week Cross
Bishop's Tawton EX31......27 F6
Bradninch EX5......82 F7
Burrington EX37......43 C5
Chulmleigh EX18......45 D3
Moretonhampstead TQ13...111 C4
Puddington EX16......62 D6
South Zeal EX20......95 B3
Zeal Monachorum EX17...78 C7
Weeke Cross PL21......137 D4
Weeke Hill TQ6......146 C8
Weekes Mdw TA21......51 E6
Week La
Dawlish Warren EX7......201 A1
High Bickington EX37......43 D5
Week Lane End EX31......27 F5
Week Park Cross EX37...43 D5
Weeksland Rd TQ2......219 C6
Weeks Row PL18......125 D6
Weekstone Cross......71 B8
Weir EX13......245 F2
Weirfield Ho EX2......261 B1
Weirfield Rd EX2......261 B1
Weirfields TQ9......223 C6
Weirford La EX20......76 F4
Weir Gdns PL6......245 F2
Weir Head Cotts TA22......33 D7
Weir Rd PL6......245 F2
Weirside Pl EX2......261 B1
Weirside Way EX32......155 B6
Weirslck Ave PL4......245 C2
Welch's La EX31......15 C2
WELCOMBE......37 A5
Welcombe Cross EX39......37 E4
Welcombe St EX2......177 A4
Weld Park Ave EX34...150 D5
Welland Gdns PL3......249 C5
Wellands Cl EX15......66 B7
Wellands Cross EX33......87 D4
Wellbrook Gn EX16......161 B4
Wellbrook St EX16......161 C4
Wellbrook Terr
Bideford EX39......157 A1
Tiverton EX16......161 B4
Wellclose Rd EX33......152 D5
Well Cross PL21......137 E6
Welle House Gdns TQ7...258 D6
Weller Ct EX13......167 D4
Wellesley Park Prim Sch
TA21......160 E4
Wellesley Pk TA21......160 D4
Wellesley Rd TA21......160 B6
Wellesley Way TA3......68 D7
Wellfield Cl PL7......215 C3
Wellfield Hill EX13, DT6...88 H2
Well Gdns PL11......262 B3
Wellhay Cl PL9......256 C6
Well Hill TQ7......147 E6
Well Hill Cl EX7......147 E6
Wellings Cl TA20......88 C8
WELLINGTON......160 C6
Wellington Basin Nature
Reserve★ TA21......160 B6
Wellington Cl EX2...178 D5
Wellington Com Hospl
TA21......160 F2
Wellington Hill TA21......160 F2
Wellington Jun Sch
TA21......160 C6
Wellington Mus★ TA21...160 D6
Wellington Pl TQ1...220 B6
Wellington Rd
Exeter EX2......177 A3
Torquay TQ1......220 B6
Wellington Sch TA21......160 E5
Wellington Sports Ctr
TA21......160 C6
Wellington Sq TQ10...134 F3
Wellington St
Plymouth PL4......263 A4
Plymouth, Stoke PL1......248 A3
Teignmouth TQ14......210 C4
Torpoint PL11......247 B3
WELLISFORD......51 D8
Well La EX39......37 B5
Well Mead EX17......87 C1
Well Oak Pk EX2......177 F3
Wellpark Cl EX4......176 F6
Well Park Flats EX39......159 D5
Wellpark Rd PL18......125 C5
Well Park Rd
Great Torrington EX38...159 D4

Well Park Rd continued
Torpoint PL11......247 B3
Well Pk EX22......164 C5
Wells Ave EX14......84 E2
Wellsbourne Pk PL3......249 A6
Wells Cl EX8......196 E4
Wells Ct PL10......252 E4
Well Spring Cl EX39......22 E3
Wellsprings La EX20......76 F3
Wells St EX32......154 F5
Well St
Exeter EX4......261 C4
Great Torrington EX38...159 D5
Paignton TQ3......226 B6
Starcross EX6......201 B8
Wells Terr EX17......62 E1
Well Stones Cl PL21......237 E4
WELLSWOOD......220 D5
Wellswood Ave TQ1......220 E5
Wellswood Gdns
Exeter EX4......176 E5
Torquay TQ1......220 E5
Wellswood Manor
Torquay TQ1......220 D5
Wellswood Path TQ1......220 D5
Wellswood Pk TQ1......220 D5
Well The TA21......160 B5
Welman Rd PL10......252 F6
Welsbere La EX17......62 C3
WELSFORD......37 F8
Welsford Ave PL2......247 F5
Welstor Cross TQ13......130 E7
WEMBURY......256 B1
Wembury Dr TQ2......214 B2
Wembury Marine Ctr★
PL9......140 C7
Wembury Mdw PL9...140 D8
Wembury Park Rd PL9...248 D6
Wembury Prim Sch PL9...140 D8
Wembury Rd
Plymouth PL9......256 A4
Wembury PL9......140 E8
WEMBWORTHY......59 C4
Wembworthy Down La
EX18......59 C4
Wembworthy Learning Ctr
EX18......59 C6
Wendover Way EX2......178 B2
Wenlock Gdns PL2......248 B8
Wensum Cl PL7......251 A4
Wentwood Gdns PL6......245 E3
Wentwood La PL6......245 E3
Wentworth Gdns EX4......176 E4
Wentworth Pl PL4......249 B2
Wentworth Rd TQ12......180 F3
Wesley Ave PL3......248 E5
Wesley Cl
Exeter EX2......177 A3
Tiverton EX16......64 D7
Torquay TQ2......214 A3
Wesley Ct PL11......247 C3
Wesley La TQ12......242 F2
Wesley Mews TQ1......214 A2
Wesley Pl
Harberton TQ9......222 D2
Plymouth, Mutley PL4...248 E5
Plymouth, Stoke PL2...248 A4
Wesley Rd
Holsworthy EX22......164 B5
Saltash PL12......242 F2
Wesley Terr TQ12......211 D2
Wesley View TQ12......211 D2
Wesley Way EX2......181 B8
Wessex Cl EX3......182 D6
Wessex Ho DT7......260 D3
Wessiters EX12......192 A5
Westabrook Ave TQ13...130 F5
Westabrook Cl TQ13......130 F5
Westabrook Dr TQ13......130 F5
Westacombe EX31......27 B8
WESTACOTT......155 F4
Westacott Cross
Inwardleigh EX20......75 C3
Meshaw EX36......45 E8
North Tawton EX20......77 E5
Westacott La
Coldridge EX17......59 E2
East Buckland EX32......18 D2
North Tawton EX20......77 E5
Westacott Mdw EX32...155 E3
West Acres EX12......191 F7
WEST ALVINGTON......258 A4
West Alvington Butts
TQ7......143 E2
West Alvington CE Prim Sch
TQ7......258 A4
WEST ANSTEY......32 A8
West Anstey School Cross
EX36......32 C5
West Ave
Barnstaple EX31......154 D3
Exeter EX4......177 C8
Tavistock PL19......171 B5
Westaway Cl EX15......153 E5
Westaway Hts EX31......155 A8
Westaway Plain EX31......155 A8
Westaway Rd EX24......103 A4
West Ball Hill EX39......22 D3
West Barton La EX20......76 E4
West Beckon Cl EX31......37 A1
Westborne Gr EX34......150 A5
Westbourne Rd
Plymouth PL3......248 D5

Westbourne Rd continued
Torquay TQ1......220 A7
Westbourne Terr
Budleigh Salterton EX9...203 F8
Saltash PL12......242 F3
Westward Ho! EX39......156 C7
Westbourne Villas EX34...150 B6
Westbridge Cl EX20......170 B5
Westbridge Cotts PL19...171 B4
Westbridge Ct EX2......181 D8
Westbridge Ind Est
PL19......171 B4
Westbrook Ave EX4......210 A5
Westbrook Cl EX4......178 B8
Westbrook Pl EX16......161 E4
West Brushford La EX18...59 C2
West Buckeridge TQ14...210 B6
WEST BUCKLAND
Barnstaple......18 B2
Wellington......52 F7
West Buckland Cross
EX32......18 B2
West Buckland Prim Sch
EX32......52 F7
West Buckland Rd TA21...52 D7
West Buckland St EX32...18 C2
West Burridge Cross
EX18......60 E7
West Challacombe La EX34 3 A4
WEST CHARLETON......144 C1
West Charleton Ct TQ7...144 C1
West Cl EX13......167 C5
West Cliff EX7......204 E6
West Cliff Ct EX7......204 D5
West Cliff Park Dr EX7...204 C5
Westcliff Prim Sch EX7...204 C5
Westcliff Rd DT6......104 F4
West Cliff Rd EX7......204 D6
West Cliff Terr EX12...192 A4
Westclyst EX1......175 A3
Westcombe EX1......181 B8
Westcombe Cres PL9......255 D5
Westcombe La EX39......156 F2
Westcombe La EX31......8 B7
Westcots Dr EX19......58 F2
WESTCOTT......83 C7
Westcott Cl PL6......249 A8
Westcott Cross EX14......66 F2
Westcott La
Aylesbeare EX5......99 D4
Witheridge EX16......61 E7
Westcott Rd EX16......64 D7
West Cotts TA21......160 D8
West Cross EX33......152 D6
Westcountry Sch PL9......247 F7
Westcroft Ct EX39...156 F1
West Croft Jun Sch
EX39......156 F1
Westcroft Rd PL5......243 D1
West Croft Rd EX32......164 B4
West Cross EX33......152 D6
Westcroyde EX33......7 D1
WEST CURRY......89 A4
West Devon Bsns Pk
PL19......171 B3
WEST DOWN......8 F5
West Down EX16......65 A6
West Down Hill EX33, EX34...8 F4
West Down La EX8......203 A6
West Down Prim Sch EX34...8 F5
West Down Rd PL2......248 B6
West Down View EX8......203 B6
West & East Putford Prim
Sch EX22......39 C2
Westella Rd PL20......127 A2
West Emlett La EX17......61 E3
West End Cross EX16......48 D5
West End La EX16......48 D5
West End Rd
Bradninch EX5......82 F6
Buckfastleigh TQ11......236 B4
West End Terr
Ashburton TQ13......130 F4
Denbury TQ12......211 A6
South Molton EX36......158 C4
Westentown TQ7......142 C6
Westeria Terr PL2......248 C6
WESTERLAND......218 D1
Westerland TQ6......234 B3
Westerland Gn TQ3......218 D2
Westerland La TQ3......218 D2
Wester-Moor Cl EX31...154 A2
Wester-Moor Dr EX31...154 A2
Wester-Moor Way EX31...154 A2
West App PL1......262 B2
Western Ave
Appledore EX39......15 A1
Exeter EX2......182 D7
Western Bsns Pk TQ4...225 F2
Western By-Pass TQ9...223 B5
Western College Rd PL4...248 F5
WESTERN COMMON......19 D7
Western Cl EX20......107 E1
Western Ct EX10......188 A3
Western Dr
Newton Abbot TQ12......206 F4
Plymouth PL3......249 B6
Starcross EX6......201 B8
Western Field EX10......188 A3
Western Gardens Rd EX34...3 A3
Western Hill EX6......204 E7
Westernlea EX17......165 A5
Western Peice La EX31...9 D1
Western Pl EX24......103 A4
Western Rd
Ashburton TQ13......130 F4

Western Rd continued
Crediton EX17......165 A6
Exeter EX4......177 A5
Holsworthy EX22......164 C4
Ivybridge PL21......237 C4
Newton Abbot TQ12......207 C3
Torquay TQ1......214 B1
Zeal Monachorum EX17...78 B6
Western Rise EX34......8 A6
Western Terr
Barnstaple EX31......154 E5
Ilfracombe EX34......150 A4
Totnes TQ9......223 B6
WESTERN TOWN......188 A3
Western Units TQ13......180 D5
Western Villas
Crediton EX17......165 B5
Totnes TQ9......223 B5
Western Way
Exeter, Barnfield EX1,......261 C3
EX4......261 C3
Exeter, Friars' Green EX1 261 A2
Western Way Ind Est
EX15......163 C4
Western Wood Way PL7 251 D5
West Exe N EX16......161 C4
West Exe S EX16......161 C3
West Exe Tech Coll EX2...177 A2
Westfield
Bradninch EX5......82 F6
Plymouth PL7......251 A6
Westfield Ave
Barnstaple EX31......154 D4
Plymouth PL9......255 C6
Westfield Cl
Brixham TQ5......230 B3
Budleigh Salterton EX9...198 A1
Westfield Rd
Budleigh Salterton EX9...198 A1
Tiverton EX16......161 C3
West Field Rd EX6......182 B3
Westfield Terr EX16...161 C3
WESTFORD......51 F7
Westford Cl TA21......160 A5
Westford La TA21......160 A5
Westford Rd TA21......160 A5
Westford Grange TA21...160 A5
West Garth Ct EX4......172 F2
West Garth Rd EX4......173 A3
Westgate EX17......60 D3
West Grove Rd EX2......261 C2
Westhampett Pl PL5......243 F4
West Hartley TQ9......139 C3
Westhay Cross EX13......88 F3
Westhays Cl PL9......255 F4
Westhead Rd PL6......140 H2
WEST HILL......168 E4
West Hill
Budleigh Salterton EX9...203 F8
Heybrook Bay PL9......140 A7
Westhill Ave TQ1......220 B7
Westhill Avenue Cl TQ1...220 B7
Westhill Cres TQ3......226 B7
West Hill Ct EX9......203 F8
West Hill Gdns EX9......203 F8
West Hill La
Braunton EX33......152 C6
Budleigh Salterton EX9...197 F1
Parracombe EX31......4 B2
West Hill Prim Sch EX11...168 D4
Westhill Rd
Paignton TQ3......226 B7
Torquay TQ1......220 B8
West Hill Rd
Lyme Regis DT7......260 D3
Plymouth PL4......248 F4
West Hill EX11......168 D4
Westhill Terr TQ12......213 A4
West Hoe Rd PL1......262 B1
WEST HOE......262 B1
Westholme TQ1......220 C5
WEST ILKERTON......5 A3
West La
Braunton EX33......152 D6
Challacombe EX31......11 D4
Dolton EX19......57 E6
Knowle EX33......8 C2
Lapford EX17......60 C3
Paignton TQ3......225 A6
WESTLAKE......136 E4
Westlake La PL9......246 F3
Westlake Rise PL9......140 A8
Westland La EX16......62 C6
Westlands
Exmouth EX8......202 C6
Wrafton EX33......152 C6
Westlands La TQ1......220 B7
Westlands Sec Sch TQ1...220 C7
Westleat Ave TQ3......225 F6
WESTLEIGH
Bideford......157 C6
Wellington......51 A4
West Leigh Cross TQ9...135 F1
West Leigh La EX34......3 C2
West Lodge DT7......193 D5
West Lyn Rd EX35......151 C2
West Malling Ave PL5...243 E5
West Manley La EX16......64 E7
Westmead EX13......88 C2
West Meadow Cl EX33...152 B7
West Meadow Rd EX33...152 A7
West Mill Cross TQ11......236 B4

Westminster Cl
Exmouth EX8 . . . . 196 D3
Feniton EX14 . . . . 84 D2
Westminster Rd EX4 . . . . 176 E6
Westminster Villas EX34 150 D5
West Molland La EX36. . . 31 D7
Westmoor Cl PL7 . . . . . . 251 C6
West Moor Cl EX39. . . . . 156 F8
Westmoor Pk PL19. . . . . 171 C4
West Moor Way EX39 . . 156 F8
West Mount TQ12. . . . . . 207 D1
West of England Sch The
EX2 . . . . 178 B1
WEST OGWELL 206 A1
West Ogwell Cross TQ12 211 C8
WESTON 189 D6
Weston Cl
Brixham TQ5 . . . . 230 C3
Broadhembury EX14 . . . 84 D7
Weston Cross
Awliscombe EX14. . . . . . 85 C3
Sidmouth EX10 . . . . . . 189 D8
Westonfields TQ9 . . . . . . 223 E5
Weston La
Awliscombe EX14. . . . . . 85 B4
Totnes TQ9. . . . . 223 E4
WESTON MILL 247 E8
Weston Mill Dr PL5 . . . . 247 E8
Weston Mill Hill PL5 . . . 243 F1
Weston Mill La PL5 . . . . 247 E8
Weston Mill Prim Sch
PL2 . . . . 247 E7
Weston Mill Rd PL3 . . . . 243 E1
Weston Park Rd PL3 . . . 248 D6
Weston Rd TQ9 . . . . 223 D5
Weston Terr EX11. . . . . . 169 E4
WESTON TOWN 188 A3
Westover Cl
Brixham TQ5 . . . . 230 D4
Ivybridge PL21 . . . . 237 E5
Westover Hill DT6 . . . . . 104 F5
Westover Ind Est PL21 . . 237 C4
Westover La PL21. . . . . . 237 B4
Westown Rd EX2. . . . . . 176 C1
West Pafford Ave TQ2 . . 214 B3
WEST PARK 244 A3
West Park Dr PL7 . . . . . 251 C5
West Park Hill PL7 . . . . 251 B7
West Park Rd EX10. . . . 188 A5
Westpark Villas ⑥ PL20. 126 F5
West Pk
Braunton EX33. . . . . . . 152 C6
Outer Hope TQ7. . . . . . 147 B7
South Molton EX36 . . . . 158 B4
Stoke Fleming TQ6. . . . 146 B8
Westpoint (County
Showground) EX5 . . . . 179 C3
West Pugsley Cross EX39 29 A2
WEST PUTFORD 39 C2
West Quay PL10. . . . . . . 252 E5
West Rd
Roborough EX19 . . . . . . 42 F4
Sheepwash EX21. . . . . . 56 C1
Woolacombe EX34. . . . . . 7 F6
Westridge Cross EX16. . . 63 C4
WEST SANDFORD 79 E5
West Spurway La EX16 . . 48 A8
West St
Ashburton TQ13. . . . . . 130 F4
Axminster EX13 . . . . . . 167 D5
Bampton EX16. . . . . 34 B2
Bishops Nympton EX36 . . 30 F2
Bishopsteignton TQ14 . . 208 F8
Denbury TQ12 . . . . 211 A6
Exeter EX1, EX4. . . . . . 261 A2
Hartland EX39 . . . . 22 D3
Millbrook PL10. . . . . . . 252 E5
Okehampton EX20 . . . . 170 B5
South Molton EX36 . . . . 158 C4
Tavistock PL19. . . . . . . 171 B5
Torpoint PL10 . . . . 252 E4
Witheridge EX16. . . . . . . 46 E1
West Terr
Budleigh Salterton EX9 . 198 A1
Churston Ferrers TQ5 . . 229 E4
Exeter EX1. . . . . 177 F6
WEST TOWN
Crediton. 165 B5
Newton St Cyres. 98 F8
Woolfardisworthy 38 E8
West Town Cross EX39 . . 38 E8
West Town Way TQ14 . . 208 E8
West Town Rd EX5. . . . . . 98 F8
West Ugworthy Cross
EX22. . . . . 53 E3
West Underleys EX12. . . 191 C5
West View
Beer EX12 . . . . 191 D5
Colyford EX24 . . . . 103 A3
Holsworthy EX22. . . . . . 164 C5
Tavistock PL19. . . . . . . 171 E2
West View Ave EX39 . . . 157 B2
Westview Cl EX5. . . . . 99 E8
West View Ct TQ12 . . . . 206 F1
West View Ct ① EX32 . . 155 B4
West View Rd
⑤ Bere Alston PL20 . . 125 E1
Marldon TQ3 . . . . 218 D2
Okehampton EX20. . . . 170 C5
West View Terr
Exeter EX4 . . . . 261 A2
⑧ Honiton EX14 . . . . . 166 B6
Lympstone EX8 . . . . . . 195 F5
WESTVILLE 258 B5
Westward Cl TQ9 . . . . . . 223 C5

Westward Dr EX8 . . . . . . 202 B7
WESTWARD HO! 156 D8
Westward View TQ12. . . 208 A2
Westwater Hill EX6. . . . . 97 E5
West Waters La EX34. . . . . 4 D5
Westway PL9 . . . . 255 B5
Westway Cross EX16 . . . . 61 F8
WESTWEEKMOOR 91 A4
WESTWOOD
Cockwood. 201 A6
Crediton. 165 A5
Whimple. 83 C1
Westwood Ave PL6. . . . . 245 C6
Westwood Cl EX17. . . . . 165 A5
Westwood Cleave TQ12 . 211 F8
Westwood Cotts EX6 . . . . 98 E2
Westwood Hill EX6. . . . . 201 A5
Westwood La EX6. . . . . . 176 B4
Westwood Rd
Crediton EX17. . . . . . . 165 A5
East Ogwell TQ12. . . . . 212 A8
Westwoods EX6 . . . . 98 B4
Westbrook Terr TA21. . . . 50 F5
Westwood Units EX2 . . . 177 D1
Westwood Way EX12 . . . 192 B7
WEST WORLINGTON 61 A8
Wethered Cl EX16. . . . . 161 C3
Wet La
Christow EX6. . . . . 113 B4
⑧ Combe Martin EX34 . . 3 A3
WEYCROFT 88 B2
Weycroft Ave EX13. . . . . 167 F7
Weycroft Cl EX11 . . . . . 178 D6
Weymouth Pk TQ7 . . . . . 147 B7
Whalley La DT7 . . . . 260 B4
Wharf Cotts TA21. . . . . . 160 B8
Wharf Rd TQ12 . . . . 207 C4
Wharf Theatre & Gall The★
PL19. . . . . 171 B5
Whatley La TA20. . . . . . . 69 A7
Wheadon Cross EX16. . . . 46 D4
Wheal Betsy★ PL19 . . . 117 F8
Wheal Maria Cotts PL19 116 B1
Wheal Rd PL19. . . . . 117 E6
Wheatclose Cross EX36 . . 20 D2
Wheatcombe Ct TQ2 . . . 214 B3
Wheatfield Cl EX15. . . . . 163 B2
Wheatland La EX16 . . . . . 48 C6
Wheatlands Rd TQ4 . . . . 226 B4
Wheatley Cl EX4 . . . . . . 176 E5
Wheatley Ct ⑤ EX1 . . . . 261 A2
Wheatly Cotts EX17 . . . . . 78 C4
Wheatly La EX31. . . . . 4 B2
Wheat Pk TQ9 . . . . 138 D8
Wheatridge PL7 . . . . 250 B7
Wheatridge La TQ12 . . . 219 E2
Wheatsheaf Way EX2. . . 177 A1
Wheelbarrow La EX15. . . 67 C8
Wheel Cross EX34. . . . . . . 2 F1
Wheeldon Off-road Bike
Ctr★ TQ9. . . . . 138 C5
Wheelers Cross EX22 . . . . 39 B1
Wheel La EX34. . . . . 2 F1
Wheelwright Ct PL20. . . 127 B4
Whelmstone Cross EX17. . 78 E3
Whetcombe Cross PL21 . 137 F6
Whey Cross EX37 . . . . . . 28 D3
Whidborne Ave TQ1. . . . 221 A4
Whidborne Cl TQ1 . . . . . 220 F3
Whidborne Mews TQ14. . 124 D1
WHIDDON
Barnstaple. 155 D2
Marwood. 9 D1
Whiddon Cross
Abbotskerswell TQ12. . . 212 B4
Whiddon EX31. . . . . 9 D1
WHIDDON DOWN. 95 F3
Whiddon Dr EX32 . . . . . 155 D3
Whiddon La
Ide EX2. . . . . 114 A8
Whiddon EX31. . . . . 9 D1
Whiddon Rd TQ12. . . . . 212 B4
Whiddon Valley Ind Est
EX32. . . . . 155 D3
Whidley La EX6. . . . . . . 112 E8
Whilborough Rd TQ12. . . 212 E2
WHIMBLE 54 F4
Whimble Hill EX22 . . . . 164 D3
WHIMPLE 99 E7
Whimple Prim Sch EX5 . . 99 E8
Whimple St PL1. . . . . . . 262 C2
Whimple Sta EX5 . . . . 99 E8
Whin Bank Rd PL5 . . . . 244 E2
WHIPCOTT 51 B5
Whippenscott Hill EX36 . . 46 B8
Whipple's Cross PL21 . . . 136 E4
WHIPTON. 178 C8
Whipton Barton Ho EX1 . 178 B7
Whipton Barton Inf Sch
EX1 . . . . 178 B7
Whipton Barton Jun Sch
EX1 . . . . 178 B7
Whipton Barton Rd EX1. . 178 C7
Whipton Hospl EX1 . . . . 178 C7
Whipton La EX1. . . . . . . 178 A6
Whipton Rd EX4 . . . . . . 178 A8
Whipton Village Rd EX4 . 178 B8
Whistley Down PL20 . . . 126 E2
Whistley Hill TQ13 . . . . 131 A4
Whistley Hill Cross TQ13 131 A4
Whitby Cres PL6. . . . . . 245 A1
Whitby Rd PL6. . . . . 245 A1

WHITCHURCH 171 D3
Whitchurch Ave EX2 . . . 178 B4
Whitchurch Prim Sch
PL19 . . . . 171 D2
Whitchurch Rd
Horrabridge PL20 . . . . 126 F5
Tavistock PL19. . . . . . . 171 C3
Whitcott Hill EX36 . . . . . 31 A8
Whiteabury Cross TQ13 . 111 C7
Whitear Cl TQ14 . . . . . . 124 E1
Whitear's Way TQ12. . . . 207 E7
White Ash La TA20. . . . . 69 D5
WHITE BALL 51 D6
White Cross
Exeter EX4. . . . . 174 B2
Paignton TQ3 . . . . 225 E7
Whitebeam Gr EX14. . . . . 67 B1
Whitebear Cross EX22 . . . 54 F6
Whiteborough La
Chudleigh TQ13 . . . . . 123 D8
Trusham TQ13 . . . . 113 D1
Whitebridges EX14. . . . . 166 B4
Whitebrook Terr TA21. . . 50 F5
Whitechapel La EX36. . . . 30 F6
White Cl TQ3 . . . . 219 B2
Whitecleave Cross EX37. . 43 F2
White Cliff ⑥ EX12. . . . . 192 B4
Whitecross Cross
Aylesbeare EX5. . . . . . . 99 C1
Cheriton Fitzpaine EX17 . 62 F1
Malborough TQ7 . . . . . 147 E6
Ottery St Mary EX11. . . 100 F3
White Cross Ct PL4 . . . . 263 A3
Whitecross Gdns EX12. . 192 B7
White Cross Hill EX17 . . . 62 F1
White Cross Rd EX5. . . . 184 D6
White Ct ⑧ EX7. . . . . . . 204 E6
Whitedown Cross EX15. . . 67 B8
White Down Cross EX16. . 64 C5
White Farm La EX11. . . . 168 D3
Whitefield EX14. . . . . 86 C3
Whitefield Cross EX36. . . 32 D3
Whitefield Hill EX31. . . . . 9 E7
Whitefield La EX32. . . . . . 19 A6
Whitefield Terr PL4 . . . . 263 B4
Whiteford Rd PL3. . . . . . 248 E6
White Friars La PL4 . . . . 263 B3
White Gate EX24 . . . . . . 102 E3
Whitegates EX34 . . . . 2 F4
White Gates Cross TQ13 110 F7
WHITEHALL 52 A1
Whitehall Cl EX36. . . . . . 158 C3
Whitehall Dr
⑧ Bere Alston PL20. . . 125 E1
Plymouth PL9 . . . . 256 B7
Whitehall La EX3. . . . . . 182 F8
Whitehall Manor TQ7 . . . 143 E4
White Hart La TA21 . . . . 160 D6
Whitehaven Way PL6. . . 245 A7
Whiteheads Cross TQ13 . 135 C7
White Heather Terr
TQ13 . . . . 180 D8
Whitehill Cl TQ12 . . . . . 207 B5
Whitehill Cotts TQ12 . . . 206 F5
Whitehill Cross PL15 . . . 105 B6
Whitehill Gdns PL7. . . . . 132 F4
Whitehill La TQ9, TQ9. . . 228 B8
Whitehill Rd TQ12. . . . . 207 A5
Whitehorse La EX39. . . . 157 A8
Whitehouse Cl ② EX39 . . 15 B1
Whitehouse Cross EX39 . 156 B3
Whitehouse La EX18 . . . . 58 D5
White La PL1 . . . . 263 A2
White Ladies TQ6. . . . . . 146 B7
White Lady Rd PL9 . . . . 255 D5
White Lady Waterfall★
EX20. . . . . 107 C2
Whiteland Head EX20 . . . 92 B8
Whiteley Ave TQ9. . . . . . 222 F6
Whiteley Cross PL21 . . . 137 B5
White Lodge EX9. . . . . . 198 B1
Whitemoor Dale PL8 . . . 142 A8
Whitemoor Hill EX32. . . . 16 E1
Whitemoor La EX5, EX17 . 81 C8
Whitexen Cross TQ10 . . . 135 C2
White Pk TQ9 . . . . 139 A3
White Post EX36 . . . . 20 F2
White Rock Prim Sch
TQ4. . . . . 229 A8
Whiterocks Pk PL18. . . . 125 A6
Whites Cotts EX20 . . . . . 95 B4
Whiteside Cl EX2 . . . . . 178 E3
Whites La EX31. . . . . 154 F7
White's La EX35. . . . . . . 159 C5
White St EX3 . . . . 182 F4
Whitestaunton Cross
TA20 . . . . 69 E5
WHITESTONE 98 E4
Whitestone Cross TQ7 . . 145 C5
Whitestone Dr EX16. . . . 161 C6
Whitestone La EX33. . . . . 8 D1
Whitestone Orch ② TQ4 226 D5
White Stones EX8 . . . . . 202 C6
Whitethorn Cl
Honiton EX14. . . . . . . 166 C4
Sidmouth EX10 . . . . . . 187 F8
Whitethorn Pk EX4. . . . . 173 C3
White Tor Rd EX20. . . . . 170 E5
Whitewater Ct PL7 . . . . . 250 E6
Whiteway Cl EX5 . . . . 99 E8
Whiteway Dr EX1 . . . . . . 178 C4
Whiteway La TQ12 . . . . . 214 D8
Whiteway Rd TQ12 . . . . . 207 D7
WHITFORD 103 B6

Whitford Rd EX13 . . . . . 103 C6
Whitham Pk PL19 . . . . . 171 C4
WHITLEIGH. 244 C5
Whitleigh Ave PL5 . . . . . 244 E2
Whitleigh Cotts PL5 . . . 244 E2
Whitleigh Ct PL5. . . . . . 244 D4
Whitleigh Gn PL5 . . . . . 244 C4
Whitleigh Villas PL5 . . . 244 E2
Whitleigh Way PL5. . . . . 244 C4
Whitleigh Wood Nature
Reserve★ PL6 . . . . . . 244 E4
Whitlow Cross TQ7 . . . . 143 C3
Whitley Rd
Farway EX24 . . . . 101 F7
Paignton TQ4 . . . . 226 A4
Whitley Rocks EX36 . . . . 31 C7
Whitlocks Mews TQ14 . . 210 A6
Whitlow Copse EX2 . . . . 178 C4
Whitman Cl EX8 . . . . . . 196 C4
Whitmore La PL21 . . . . . 137 C4
Whitmore Way EX14 . . . 166 A4
WHITNAGE 50 C2
Whitnage Terr EX16. . . . . 50 C2
Whitnole Cross EX16. . . . 48 A5
Whitnole La EX16. . . . . . 48 A4
Whitsam Cross PL20 . . . 125 D1
Whitsley Cross EX19, EX38 42 C4
Whitsone Cotts PL5 . . . . 244 C7
Whitsoncross La PL5. . . 244 C7
WHITSTONE 70 E1
Whitstone Com Prim Sch
EX22. . . . . 70 E1
Whitstone Head Sch EX22 70 E1
Whitstone La
Bovey Tracey TQ13. . . . 180 C8
Meshaw EX36 . . . . 46 B5
Whitstone Rd TQ4 . . . . . 226 B5
Whittington Rd
Ilfracombe EX34 . . . . . 150 C5
Yealmpton PL8. . . . . . . 141 B8
Whittington St PL3. . . . . 262 B4
Whitton Ct EX10 . . . . . . 187 F7
Whitwell La EX24. . . . . . 103 A3
Whitycombe Way EX4 . . 176 D8
Whity Cross PL21 . . . . . 242 A4
Whympston Cross PL21 . 137 D1
Wicaford Cross EX36. . . . 31 A2
Wicaford La EX36. . . . . . 31 A2
Wick Cross EX14. . . . . . . 85 F7
Wicket The EX2 . . . . 178 C3
Wickham Cl EX39 . . . . . 157 C1
Wickington La EX20. . . . . 95 B7
Widdicombe Cross
Marldon TQ3 . . . . 218 F5
Paignton TQ3 . . . . 218 E5
Widdicombe Dr PL21. . . 237 D4
WIDECOMBE IN THE
MOOR 121 B4
Widecombe in the Moor
Prim Sch TQ13. . . . . . 121 B3
Widecombe Way EX4 . . . 173 E1
Widegate Nursery PL9 . . 256 D8
Widepost La EX13. . . . . 167 C5
WIDEWELL 245 B7
Widewell La PL6. . . . . . . 245 C7
Widewell Prim Sch PL6 . 245 B7
Widewell Rd PL6. . . . . . . 245 B7
Widey Court Prim Sch
PL6 . . . . 244 F1
Widey Cross PL6. . . . . . . 244 F1
Widey Ct PL6 . . . . 244 F1
Widey Hill EX36. . . . . . . 141 A7
Widey La PL6 . . . . 244 F1
Widey View PL3 . . . . 248 F6
Widgery Dr EX36. . . . . . 158 C4
Widgery Rd EX4 . . . . . . 178 A8
WIDWORTHY. 86 D2
Widworthy Ct EX14. . . . . 86 C2
Wigford Cross TQ7. . . . . 138 C1
Wigford La TQ7 . . . . 138 D2
WIGGATON 100 E4
Wigley Cross EX16 . . . . . 16 C8
Wilbarn Rd TQ3. . . . . . . 226 C7
Wilburton Cross PL21 . . 136 C3
Wilbury Way EX7 . . . . . . 204 F7
Wilcocks Rd EX4 . . . . . . 174 D1
Wilcombe Cross EX32 . . . 18 E4
Wilcombe Prim Sch
EX16. . . . . 161 F3
Wilcove La PL11. . . . . . . 246 E5
Wilderness La EX14. . . . . 84 D6
Wilderness Rd PL3. . . . . 248 E5
Wilder Pk EX34 . . . . 150 B5
Wilder Rd EX34 . . . . 150 B6
Wilderwerth Cl EX34 . . . 150 B6
Wildmoor La TA21. . . . . . 52 F6
Wildner Top EX35. . . . . . . 4 A4
Wildwoods Cres TQ12 . . 207 F4
Wilford Rd EX2 . . . . 178 B5
Wilkey Cl EX32. . . . . 155 C4
Wilkinson Rd PL5. . . . . . 247 D8
Wilkake Rd TQ12 . . . . . . 213 A5
WILLAND
Taunton. 68 B8
Tiverton. 162 E4
Willand Ind Est EX15. . . 162 D5
WILLAND MOOR. 162 E5
Willand Moor Mews
EX15. . . . . 162 E5
Willand Moor Rd EX15 . . 162 E5
Willand Old Village
EX15. . . . . 162 C3
Willand Rd
Braunton EX33. . . . . . . 152 C6
Cullompton EX15. . . . . 163 D4
Willand EX15. . . . . 162 D4
Willas Rd PL16. . . . . 105 E4

Willcocks Cl ⑥ TA21. . . . 160 D5
Willet St ③ EX39. . . . . . 157 A2
Willeys Ave EX2. . . . . . . 261 A1
Willeys Ct EX2 . . . . 261 A1
Willhayes Cross EX6 . . . 113 E6
Willhayes Hill EX6 . . . . . 113 E6
Willhayes Pk EX13 . . . . 167 D6
Willhay La EX13. . . . . . . 167 D7
Willhays Cl ⑮ TQ12 . . . 123 F1
William Evans Cl PL6. . . 244 D5
William Prance Rd PL6. . 245 A3
Williams Ave
Exeter EX2. . . . . 261 A1
Plymouth PL4. . . . . 249 B1
Williams Cl
Dawlish EX7. . . . . 204 C5
Wrafton EX33 . . . . 152 E4
Williams Ct ① EX1. . . . 154 C2
Williams Ct TQ11. . . . . . 236 B5
Williamson Cl EX33 . . . . . 8 A2
Williamson Ho EX31. . . . 155 A8
Williamson Way EX36 . . 158 C4
WilliAm St ③ EX16. . . . 161 D4
Williamson Rd TQ3 . . . . 226 A5
WILLINGCOTT 8 D6
Willingcott Cross EX34 . . . 8 C6
Willingcott Hill EX34. . . . 8 D4
Willing Cross TQ10. . . . 135 F5
Willing Gate TQ10. . . . . 135 E5
Willis Ct ① TQ1. . . . . . . 220 A7
Willis's Cross TQ12 . . . . 122 D2
Willmott Cl EX8. . . . . . . 196 E1
Willoughby Cl EX8 . . . . 196 B3
Willoughby Ho EX10 . . . 187 E2
Willoughby Rd TQ1 . . . . 220 C6
Willow Ave
Exmouth EX8 . . . . 196 B3
Torquay TQ2. . . . . 214 A3
Willoway Cl EX33 . . . . . 152 C6
Willoway Gr EX33 . . . . . 152 C6
Willoway La EX33 . . . . . 152 C7
Willowbank Prim Sch
EX15. . . . . 163 B3
Willowbrook Ave ⑥ EX4 178 C8
Willowbrook Sch EX4 . . 174 B1
Willowby Gdns PL20 . . . 127 A2
Willowby Pk PL20. . . . . . 127 A2
Willow Cl
Ilfracombe EX34 . . . . . 150 E4
Newton Abbot TQ12. . . 213 A8
Plymouth PL3. . . . . 249 E5
Seaton EX12 . . . . 192 A8
Stoke Canon EX5 . . . . . 173 F8
Willow Cotts PL7 . . . . . . 250 D4
Willow Ct
Exeter EX2. . . . . 178 A4
Plymouth PL6. . . . . 249 E7
Willowdale Cl ① EX14. . 166 B6
Willowfield EX33. . . . . . 152 C7
Willow Gdns EX5. . . . . . 175 C6
Willow Gn PL12 . . . . 242 D2
Willow Gr
Bideford EX39 . . . . 25 D4
Stibb Cross EX38. . . . . . 40 D2
Willow La
Cornworthy TQ9. . . . . . 227 B3
Hemyock EX15. . . . . 52 F2
Willowpark La TQ12. . . . 213 C4
Willow Rd PL19 . . . . 171 C3
Willows Cl TQ7 . . . . 144 E1
Willow St ② TQ14. . . . . 210 B4
Willows The
Chilsworthy EX22. . . . . . 53 E1
Shillingford St George EX2 114 C6
Willows The TQ2 . . . . . . 213 D2
Willow Tree Cl EX20 . . . 170 D2
Willow Tree Rd EX32. . . 155 B2
Willow View Pk EX5. . . . 100 A7
Willow Way
Dawlish Warren EX7 . . . 201 A2
Exeter EX4. . . . . 178 C8
Willow Wlk
Crediton EX17. . . . . . . 165 E6
② Exeter EX4 . . . . 177 D8
Honiton EX14. . . . . 166 A4
Plymouth PL6. . . . . 245 D6
Wills Ave TQ3. . . . . 219 C1
Wills Cl PL6 . . . . 244 E7
Wilshere Rd EX32 . . . . . 155 C4
Willsland Cl EX6 . . . . . . 194 D3
Wills Rd TQ9. . . . . 223 D6
WILMINGTON 86 D3
Wilmington La EX13, EX14. 86 E2
WILMINSTONE 117 D3
Wilminstone Ind Est
PL19 . . . . 171 E7
Wilmot Gdns PL5 . . . . . 244 D3
Wilncote Lodge ⑥ TQ1. . 220 A6
WILSHAM 5 F5
Wilsham Cross EX35 . . . . 6 A5
Wilsham La EX35 . . . . . . 5 F5
Wilson Gdns PL5. . . . . . 248 B5
Wilson La EX17 . . . . 46 B1
Wilton Cl TQ12. . . . . 207 B1
Wilton Rd
Paignton TQ3 . . . . 219 B2
Plymouth PL1. . . . . 248 A3
Wilton St PL1. . . . . 262 A4
Wilton Way
Abbotskerswell TQ12. . . 212 B4
Exeter EX1. . . . . 178 D6
WILTOWN 52 F3
Wiltown La EX15. . . . . . . 52 F3
Wiltshier Cl EX15 . . . . . 175 C7
Wiltshire Cl
Exeter EX4. . . . . 176 E4
Plymouth PL4. . . . . 248 F4

Wilway La TA22 . . . . 33 C6
Wimble Cross EX22 . . . . . . 164 D3
Winchester Ave
  Exeter EX4 . . . . 176 F7
  Torquay TQ2 . . . . 213 F1
Winchester Cl EX14 . . . . . 84 D2
Winchester Dr EX8 . . . . . . 196 D4
Winchester Gdns PL5 . . . 244 A5
Windabout Cross EX39 . . . 39 B7
Windad Terr EX20 . . . . 93 B1
Widball Hill TA22 . . . . 33 B7
Windbow La EX16 . . . . 48 D3
Windeatt Sq [4] TQ9 . . . . 223 D5
Windermere Cl PL4 . . . . . 176 F6
Windermere Cres PL6 . . . 244 F4
Windermere Rd TQ1 . . . . 220 C6
Windford Hill EX31 . . . . . . 10 C4
Windjammer Ct EX8 . . . . . 201 E6
Windmilland Cross EX21 . 74 A6
Windmill Ave TQ3 . . . . . . 219 A1
Windmill Cl TQ5 . . . . 230 D4
Windmill Cross EX31 . . . . 27 A3
Windmill Gdns TQ5 . . . . . 230 C4
Windmill Gdns TQ5 . . . . . 219 A1
Windmill Hill
  Brixham TQ5 . . . . 230 D4
  Saltash PL12 . . . . 242 E2
Windmill La
  Northam EX39 . . . . 157 B7
  North Whilborough TQ12 . 212 D1
  Paignton TQ3 . . . . 218 F1
  West Hill EX11 . . . . 168 D5
Windmill Rd
  Brixham TQ5 . . . . 230 D4
  Holsworthy EX22 . . . . 164 D4
  Paignton TQ3 . . . . 219 A1
Windout La EX6 . . . . 97 E3
Windrush Rise EX11 . . . . . 169 D3
Windsor Ave TQ12 . . . . . . 207 F3
Windsor Cl
  Cullompton EX15 . . . . . . 163 C6
  Exeter EX4 . . . . 177 A7
  Ivybridge PL21 . . . . 237 E4
  Newton Abbot TQ12 . . . . 207 C2
  Torquay TQ1 . . . . 220 B6
Windsor Ct
  Ilfracombe EX34 . . . . 150 B5
  Kingsbridge TQ7 . . . . . . 258 D5
Windsor Dr EX7 . . . . 200 E2
Windsor Ho EX8 . . . . 202 B7
Windsor La PL12 . . . . 242 E2
Windsor Mead EX10 . . . . 101 A1
Windsor Pl PL1 . . . . 262 C2
Windsor Rd
  Barnstaple EX31 . . . . 154 E7
  Dartmouth TQ6 . . . . 233 C3
  Kingsbridge TQ7 . . . . . . 258 D5
  Northam EX39 . . . . 156 F7
  Plymouth PL3 . . . . 249 B7
  Torquay TQ1 . . . . 220 C6
Windsor Sq EX4 . . . . 202 A7
Windsor Terr EX17 . . . . . 260 D4
Windsor Villas PL1 . . . . . 262 C2
Windthorn Cross TQ12 . . 218 A7
Windthorn La TQ3, TQ12 . 218 A7
Windward Ct EX8 . . . . . . 201 E6
Windward La EX7 . . . . . . 210 F8
Windward Rd TQ2 . . . . . . 213 E3
Windway Hill TA4 . . . . 34 D6
Wind Whistle Cross EX5 . 81 C8
Wind Whistle La EX16 . . . 66 C1
Windwhistle La EX16 . . . . 49 B8
Windy Ash Cross EX32 . . 16 F1
Windy Ash Hill EX32 . . . 155 C1
Windy Cnr TQ4 . . . . 229 B6
Windy Cross
  Ashford EX31 . . . . 16 A6
  [5] Chulmleigh EX18 . . . . 44 E1
  Doddiscombsleigh EX6 . 113 E7
  Great Torrington EX38 . . 159 C5
  Holsworthy Beacon EX22 . 54 F2
Windypost Cross EX35 . . 151 C2
Wingate La EX20 . . . . 75 C7
Wingfield TQ7 . . . . 143 A1
Wingfield Cl [3] EX16 . . . 161 C3
Wingfield Mans PL3 . . . . 248 A3
Wingfield Rd PL3 . . . . . . 262 A4
Wingfield Way PL3 . . . . . 262 A4
Winham La EX15 . . . . 83 B6
Winifred Baker Ct [5]
  PL4 . . . . 263 A4
Winifred Cliff Ct [1] EX16 . 34 B1
WINKLEIGH 58 E2
Winkleigh Cl EX17 . . . . . . 62 A1
Winkleigh Moor Cross
  EX19 . . . . 58 C7
Winkleigh Prim Sch EX19 58 F2
Winneford La EX14 . . . . . . 85 C3
Winner Hill Rd TQ3 . . . . . 226 A6
Winner St TQ3 . . . . 226 A6
Winnicott Cl PL6 . . . . 244 E7
Winnings Way TQ1 . . . . . 220 D7
Winnow Cl PL9 . . . . 255 F8
Winsbeer La
  Rockwell Green TA21 . . . 160 A6
  Runnington TA21 . . . . 51 F8
Winsbury Ct PL6 . . . . 245 A1
Winscott Cotts EX5 . . . . . 81 B1
Winscott Cross
  Holsworthy EX22 . . . . 72 A4
  Newton St Cyres EX5 . . . 81 A1
WINSFORD 156 C2
Winsford Rd TQ2 . . . . . . 219 C1
Winsford Walled Gdn★
  EX21 . . . . 73 F4
WINSHAM 8 E1
Winsham Cross EX33 . . . . 8 D1
Winsham Rd EX33 . . . . . . 8 D1

Winslade Cl TQ7 . . . . 144 E1
Winslade Ct TQ7 . . . . 144 E1
WINSLADE PARK 179 B2
Winslade Park Ave EX5 . 179 B2
Winslade Rd EX10 . . . . . . 188 B6
Winslake Mdw EX6 . . . . . . 97 F4
Winsland Ave TQ9 . . . . . 222 E6
Winson Cross EX37 . . . . . 29 A4
Winsor Cross PL8 . . . . . . 136 C4
Winstanley Wlk PL3 . . . . 249 D6
Winstitchen Cross TA24 . 13 C2
Winstitchen La TA24 . . . . 13 C2
WINSTON 257 B4
Winston Ave PL4 . . . . 262 C4
Winston Cl TQ12 . . . . 207 E7
Winston Cross TQ4 . . . . . 210 C6
Winstone Ave TQ2 . . . . . 214 A1
Winstone Cotts PL8 . . . . 257 B4
Winstone La PL8 . . . . 257 B4
Winston Ho EX36 . . . . . . 158 C5
Winston Pk EX36 . . . . . . 158 C5
Winston Rd EX8 . . . . 196 E2
Winswell Water EX38 . . . 56 D7
WINSWELL 56 D8
Winswood EX17 . . . . 165 D4
Winsworthy EX39 . . . . 23 D3
Winterbourne Rd TQ14 . 210 C5
Winter Gdn TQ2 . . . . 220 B4
Winterland La EX22 . . . . 164 D2
Winters Cross TA4 . . . . . . 35 C8
Winter's La EX11 . . . . 169 D3
Winward Rise EX7 . . . . . . 210 F8
Wiriga Way EX16 . . . . 46 E1
Wishings Rd TQ5 . . . . . . 230 D3
Wisteria Dr TQ7 . . . . 258 C5
Wistford Cross EX32 . . . . 18 C4
Wistman's Wood National
  Nature Reserve★ PL20 . 119 D4
Wiston Cross EX36 . . . . . . 32 D2
Witch La EX14 . . . . 86 F8
Witcombe La EX6 . . . . . . 194 D3
WITHACOTT 40 D2
Witham Gdns PL3 . . . . . . 249 C5
Witheby EX10 . . . . 187 F3
Withecombe Cross TQ13 110 F8
Withen Cross EX5 . . . . 99 C1
Withen La EX5 . . . . 99 D2
Witherdon Cross EX21 . . 91 D5
WITHERIDGE 46 F1
Witheridge CE Prim Sch
  EX16 . . . . 46 E1
Witheridge Mill Cross
  EX16 . . . . 46 E2
Witheridge Moor Cross
  (East) EX16 . . . . 47 E1
Witheridge Moor Cross
  (West) EX16 . . . . 47 E1
Witheridge Pl EX34 . . . . 150 E5
Withey The EX5 . . . . 99 E8
WITHLEIGH 63 D7
Withleigh Cross EX16 . . . 63 D7
Withleigh La EX16 . . . . . . 63 D7
WITHNOE 252 A4
Withnoe La PL10 . . . . . . 252 B6
Withy Cl EX16 . . . . 161 F3
WITHYCOMBE RALEIGH . 196 C2
Withycombe Raleigh CE Prim
  Sch EX8 . . . . 196 C1
Withycombe Rd EX8 . . . . 202 A8
Withycombe Village Rd
  EX8 . . . . 202 B8
Withy Cross EX38 . . . . 42 E6
Withygate La EX32 . . . . . . 19 A5
Withy La EX15 . . . . 52 B1
WITHYPOOL 21 C6
Withypool Cross
  Hawkridge TA22 . . . . 21 C2
  Twitchen EX36 . . . . 20 E4
Withywell La EX33 . . . . 7 E1
Withywine La TA22 . . . . . . 34 C5
Wixenford Ct PL9 . . . . . . 255 F8
Wixon Cross EX18 . . . . . . 45 B3
Wixon La EX18 . . . . 45 B3
Woburn Cl TQ3 . . . . 225 D7
Woburn Terr PL9 . . . . 255 C7
WOLBOROUGH 207 B1
Wolborough CE Prim Sch [18]
  TQ12 . . . . 207 C3
Wolborough Cl TQ12 . . . 207 C2
Wolborough Gdns
  Brixham TQ5 . . . . 230 E6
  Newton Abbot TQ12 . . . 207 C2
Wolborough St TQ12 . . . 207 B2
Wolford Cross EX14 . . . . . 85 B8
WOLLATON 257 B6
Wollaton Cross PL8 . . . . 257 A6
Wollaton Gr PL5 . . . . 243 F3
Wollaton Rd PL5 . . . . 251 B5
Wolrige Way PL7 . . . . 251 A5
Wolsdon Pl PL1 . . . . 262 A3
Wolsdon St PL1 . . . . 262 B3
Wolseley Bsns Pk [2]
  PL2 . . . . 248 A5
Wolseley Cl PL2 . . . . 248 A5
Wolseley Rd
  Plymouth, Camels Head
  PL5 . . . . 247 F6
  Plymouth, St Budeaux PL5 243 C1
Wolseley Road Flats PL2 247 F6
Wolston Cl TQ5 . . . . 230 B6
WOLVERSTONE 85 A7
Wolverstone Cross EX14 . 85 A8
Wolverstone Hill EX14 . . . 85 A7

Wolverton Dr TQ12 . . . . . 207 D7
Wolverwood Cl PL7 . . . . 251 C3
Wolverwood La PL7 . . . . 251 B3
Wombwell Cres PL2 . . . . 247 F7
Wonders Cnr EX38 . . . . . . 40 D2
WONFORD 178 A4
Wonford House Hospl
  EX2 . . . . 177 F4
Wonford Rd EX2 . . . . 261 C2
Wonford Sp Ctr EX1 . . . . 178 A3
Wonford St EX2 . . . . 178 A4
Wonnacott's Rd EX20 . . 176 C5
WONSON 110 D8
Wonton Cross TQ9 . . . . . 135 D2
WOODA 157 C8
Wood Acre PL12 . . . . 242 B4
Woodacre Ct PL12 . . . . . 242 B4
Woodah Rd EX4 . . . . 176 F5
Wooda Rd EX39 . . . . 157 C8
Woodbine Cotts PL7 . . . . 250 E4
Woodbine Pl [3] EX12 . . 192 A5
Woodbine Terr EX4 . . . . . 261 A4
Woodbridge La
  Bondleigh EX18 . . . . 77 D8
  Farway EX24 . . . . 102 B6
  North Tawton EX17 . . . . . . 59 E1
Woodbrook Rd TQ9 . . . . 223 E5
Woodburn Cl PL21 . . . . . 237 B5
Woodburn Cross EX16 . . 32 F2
Woodburn Hill EX16 . . . . 32 F2
Woodburn Water Cross
  EX16 . . . . 32 F1
WOODBURY 184 C3
Woodbury Cl EX8 . . . . . . 202 C6
Woodbury Gdns PL5 . . . 244 A3
Woodbury La EX13 . . . . . 167 E3
Woodbury Pk EX13 . . . . . 167 C4
Woodbury Rd EX3, EX5 . 183 E5
WOODBURY
  SALTERTON 184 C6
Woodbury Salterton CE Prim
  Sch EX5 . . . . 184 C7
Woodbury View
  Broadclyst EX5 . . . . 175 D6
  Exeter EX2 . . . . 177 A2
Woodbury Way EX13 . . . 167 D4
Woodbury Wlk EX6 . . . . . 181 F5
Woodchurch PL20 . . . . . 126 E3
Wood Cl
  Christow EX6 . . . . 113 B4
  Saltash PL12 . . . . 242 B3
Wood Cnr EX6 . . . . 97 C2
Woodcock Cl PL10 . . . . . 253 A6
Woodcock Way EX5 . . . . . 83 B7
Woodcote Ct EX5 . . . . . . 184 C3
Wood Cotts TQ12 . . . . . . 180 C1
Woodcroft Cl TQ2 . . . . . 139 C7
Woodcroft Cross EX19 . . 76 D7
Woodcroft La EX19 . . . . . . 76 D8
Woodcroft Mdws TA20 . . 69 B7
Woodcote Cross EX14 . . . 86 C6
Woodend Rd
  Plymouth PL6 . . . . 245 D7
  Torquay TQ1 . . . . 220 D4
Wooder Wharf [12] EX39 . 157 A1
Woodfield Cl EX8 . . . . . . 196 E2
Woodfield Cres PL7 . . . . 237 E4
Woodfield Ct TQ1 . . . . . . 220 D3
Woodfield Prim Sch PL5 244 C5
Woodfields EX12 . . . . . . 192 A7
WOODFORD
  Blackawton 139 D2
  Plymouth 250 C7
  Plymouth 250 C7
Woodford Ave PL7 . . . . . 250 A7
Woodford Cl PL7 . . . . 250 A7
Woodford Cres PL7 . . . . 250 A6
Woodford Gdns EX32 . . 155 C2
Woodford Gn PL7 . . . . . . 250 B6
Woodford Inf Sch PL7 . . 250 B6
Woodford Jun Sch PL7 . 250 B7
Woodford Rd PL6 . . . . . . 245 D6
WOODGATE 51 E2
Woodhaye Cl [5] TQ10 . 134 F2
Woodhaye Gdns EX4 . . . 173 A1
Woodhaye Terr [1] TQ10 . 134 F2
Woodhead Cross
  Branscombe EX12 . . . . . 190 E7
  Totnes TQ9 . . . . 217 D4
  Cheriton Fitzpaine EX16 . 63 A7
  Totnes TQ12 . . . . 217 E4
Woodhey Rd PL2 . . . . . . 248 A7
Woodhill View EX14 . . . . 166 B4
Woodhouse Cl TQ7 . . . . 258 C4
Woodhouse Cross TQ13 122 D3
Woodhouse Fields DT7 . 104 B4
Woodhouse La
  Axminster EX13 . . . . 88 D1
  Uplyme DT7 . . . . 104 B4
Woodhouse Rd EX13 . . . . 88 D1
Woodhuish La TQ5, TQ6 . 235 F7
Wood La
  Abbotskerswell TQ12 . . . 212 A5
  Ashreigney EX18 . . . . 43 D1
  Broadhembury EX14 . . . . 84 E7
  Christow EX6 . . . . 113 B4
  Combe Martin EX34 . . . . . 3 B2
  Exmouth EX8 . . . . 196 D1
  Kingswear TQ6 . . . . 234 D8
  Monkton EX14 . . . . 86 C6
  Morchard Bishop EX17 . . 61 A2
  Stockleigh Pomeroy EX17 . 81 B4

Wood La continued
  West Alvington TQ7 . . . . 258 A4
  West Down EX34 . . . . 8 F4
WOODLAND
  Ashburton 131 D3
  Ivybridge 237 A5
Woodland Ave
  Kingskerswell TQ12 . . . . 212 F5
  Plymouth PL9 . . . . 256 A8
  Teignmouth TQ14 . . . . . . 210 D7
Woodland Bsns Pk TQ2 . 219 E8
Woodland Cl
  Barnstaple EX32 . . . . 155 C4
  Braunton EX33 . . . . 8 D1
  Denbury TQ12 . . . . 131 F3
  Gunnislake PL18 . . . . . . 125 C6
  Ivybridge PL21 . . . . 237 B5
  Staverton TQ9 . . . . 216 A4
  [2] Tiverton EX16 . . . . 49 B8
  Torquay TQ2 . . . . 219 E8
Woodland Cotts EX31 . . 237 A5
Woodland Cross EX31 . . . 27 B4
Woodland Ct
  [10] Barnstaple EX32 . . . 155 A4
  Ivybridge PL21 . . . . 237 A5
  Paignton TQ3 . . . . 226 B7
Woodland Dr
  Brixton PL8 . . . . 257 B5
  Plymouth PL7 . . . . 250 B4
WOODLAND HEAD 97 C7
Woodlandhead Cross
  EX17 . . . . 97 B7
Woodland Hill EX17 . . . . 97 B8
Woodland La TQ9 . . . . . . 227 D4
Woodland Mews
  Broadclyst EX5 . . . . 175 D6
  [1] Paignton TQ3 . . . . . . 226 B7
Woodland Pk
  Northam EX39 . . . . 157 A5
  Paignton TQ3 . . . . 226 B7
Woodland Rd
  Ashburton TQ13 . . . . . . 130 F4
  Broadclyst EX5 . . . . 175 C6
  Denbury TQ12 . . . . 211 A6
  Exeter EX1 . . . . 178 D7
  Harbertonford TQ9 . . . . . 139 C7
  Ivybridge PL21 . . . . 237 B5
  Lee Mill PL21 . . . . 136 D7
  Plymouth PL7 . . . . 250 C6
  Torquay TQ2 . . . . 219 E8
Woodlands
  Budleigh Salterton EX9 . 203 E8
  Churchstow TQ7 . . . . . . 143 E4
  Combe Martin EX34 . . . . . 2 F4
  Dousland PL20 . . . . 127 B3
  Halwill EX21 . . . . 73 D3
  Kingsteignton TQ12 . . . 123 E2
  Newton St Cyres EX5 . . . 98 F8
  Plymouth PL9 . . . . 255 F6
  Wembury PL9 . . . . 255 F8
Woodlands Bsns Pk EX16. 51 C3
Woodlands Cl
  Churchstow TQ7 . . . . . . 143 E4
  Offwell EX14 . . . . 86 B2
  Teignmouth TQ14 . . . . . 210 C5
Woodlands Ct
  Exmouth EX8 . . . . 196 B3
  Plymouth PL5 . . . . 244 A3
Woodlands Dr EX8 . . . . . 196 B3
Woodlands End PL6 . . . . 245 D5
Woodlands Gdns [5]
  TQ12 . . . . 207 F2
Woodlands La PL6 . . . . . 245 F1
Woodlands L Pk★ TQ9 . 139 F3
Woodlands Park Prim Sch
  PL21 . . . . 237 A5
Woodlands Pk EX6 . . . . . 98 B4
Woodlands Rd TQ12 . . . 207 F2
Woodlands Sch PL5 . . . . 244 D4
Woodlands Way EX5 . . . 179 E3
Woodlands Wlk TQ13 . . 180 C4
Woodland Terr
  Ivybridge PL21 . . . . 237 B4
  Kingswear TQ6 . . . . 234 A3
  Plymouth PL4 . . . . 263 B4
Woodland Terr La PL4 . . 263 B4
Woodland View TQ2 . . . 164 C3
Woodland Way
  Gunnislake PL18 . . . . . . 125 D6
  Torpoint PL11 . . . . 246 F3
Woodland Wood Valley
  Nature Reserve★ PL5 . 244 B4
Woodlark La [3] EX31 . . 154 A2
Woodleigh Cl PL7 . . . . . 144 B7
Woodleigh Cross EX4 . . 173 A3
Woodleigh Pk TQ14 . . . 210 B2
Woodleigh Rd TQ12 . . . 206 F3
Woodley Cross EX5 . . . . . 98 F8
Woodleys Dr EX8 . . . . . . 196 D8
Woodleys Mdw TQ2 . . . 219 E2
Woodman's Cnr PL20 . . 127 A3
Woodmans Cres [2]
  EX14 . . . . 166 C5
Woodmans Orch EX5 . . . 84 A2
WOODMANTON 196 C8
Woodmead Halls DT7 . . 260 D3
Woodmead Rd
  Axminster EX13 . . . . 167 C5
  Lyme Regis DT7 . . . . 260 D3
Woodmere Way TQ12 . . 207 E6
Woodpark Cross EX17 . . . 61 A8
Woodpark La
  Molland EX36 . . . . 31 E6
  Paignton TQ3 . . . . 218 E8
Wood Park La EX34 . . . . . 2 D3

Woodpecker Way
  Cheriton Bishop EX6 . . . . 97 B4
  Tavistock PL19 . . . . 171 D2
Wood Pk
  Ivybridge PL21 . . . . 237 D6
  Plymouth PL6 . . . . 132 A2
Woodplace La EX16 . . . . 62 F7
Woodridge Cross EX19 . . 57 D6
Wood Rock EX36 . . . . 32 C5
Woodroffe Mdw DT7 . . . 260 C4
Woodroffe Sch The DT7 . 260 C4
Woods Cross EX36 . . . . . . 31 D6
Wood's Cross EX36 . . . . . 32 C5
Woodside
  Crapstone PL20 . . . . 126 E2
  Plymouth PL4 . . . . 263 B4
Woodside Ave PL9 . . . . . 255 C6
Woodside Cl PL21 . . . . . 237 D4
Woodside Ct
  Lynton EX35 . . . . 151 D5
  Plymouth PL7 . . . . 250 E4
Woodside Dr TQ1 . . . . . . 220 C4
Woodside La PL4 . . . . . . 263 B4
Woodside Wlk EX14 . . . . 166 D6
Woods The TQ2 . . . . 220 E3
Woodstock Gdns PL5 . . 243 D1
Woodstock Rd EX22 . . . 178 A5
WOODTOWN
  East-the-Water 26 D4
  Fairy Cross 25 B2
Woodvale Ct [8] TQ12. . 207 B3
Wood View TQ12 . . . . . . 207 B3
Woodview Pk PL9 . . . . . . 256 A6
Woodview Rd TQ4 . . . . . 225 E1
Wood View Terr PL21 . . 136 F3
Woodville EX31 . . . . 154 C3
Woodville Ave PL20 . . . 128 A8
Woodville Cl
  Barnstaple EX32 . . . . 154 C4
  Plymouth PL2 . . . . 247 F7
Woodville Cross EX23 . . . 36 F1
Woodville Rd
  Exeter EX2 . . . . 177 B3
  Exmouth EX8 . . . . 202 A8
  Morwenstow EX23 . . . . . 36 F1
  Plymouth PL2 . . . . 247 F6
  Torquay TQ1 . . . . 220 C6
Woodward Rd EX16 . . . . 161 B2
Woodwater La EX2 . . . . . 178 B4
Woodway PL9 . . . . 256 A7
Woodway Cl TQ14 . . . . . 210 C6
Woodway Dr TQ14 . . . . . 210 C6
Woodway St TQ13 . . . . . 123 E6
WOODY BAY 4 D6
Woody Bay Sta★ EX31 . . 4 E3
WOOLACOMBE 7 F7
Woolacombe Cross EX32 . 17 B3
Woolacombe Ct EX34 . . . 8 A6
Woolacombe Rd PL20 . . 125 F1
Woolacombe Rise EX34 . . 8 A6
Woolacombe Station Rd
  EX34 . . . . 8 B6
Woolbarn Lawn EX32 . . 155 D4
Woolbrook Cl EX10 . . . . 188 A6
Woolbrook Mdws EX10 . 188 A7
Woolbrook Rd EX10 . . . 187 F7
Woolbrook Pk EX10 . . . . 188 A7
Woolbrook Rd EX10 . . . . 188 A7
Woolbrook Rise EX10 . . 188 A7
Woolcombe La
  Ivybridge PL21 . . . . 237 D4
  Sidmouth EX10 . . . . 188 B5
Woolcott Way EX15 . . . . 163 B2
WOOLFARDISWORTHY . . 62 A3
Woolfardisworthy Cross
  Clovelly EX39 . . . . 23 D2
  Woolfardisworthy EX17 . 62 A3
WOOLFARDISWORTHY OR
  WOOLSERY 38 E7
WOOLHANGER 4 F2
WOOLLATON 56 B7
Woollcombe Ave PL7 . . . 250 A4
Woolleigh Cross EX19 . . 42 B3
WOOLLEY 37 D3
Woolms Mdw PL21 . . . . 237 A4
Woolpit La TA24 . . . . 21 B7
Woolsery Ave EX4 . . . . . 178 B8
Woolsery Cl EX4 . . . . 178 B8
Woolsery Prim Sch EX39 38 F7
Woolster Ct [7] PL4 . . . . 263 A2
WOOLSTON 147 F8
WOOLSTON GREEN 131 B1
Woolway Ave EX4 . . . . . 182 B4
WOOLWELL 245 C8
Woolwell Cres PL6 . . . . . 245 C8
Woolwell Dr PL6 . . . . 245 C7
Woolwell Rd PL6 . . . . 245 D7
Wootton Cross EX13 . . . . 88 F1
Worcester Cres EX15 . . . 162 D4
Worden Cross
  Milton Damerel EX22 . . . 54 E6
  Sutcombe EX22 . . . . 54 C8
Wordland Cross EX17 . . . 80 F8
Wordsworth Ave EX31 . . 154 F7
Wordsworth Cl
  Exmouth EX8 . . . . 196 C4
  Torquay TQ2 . . . . 219 D7
Wordsworth Cres PL5 . . 247 F7
Wordsworth Rd PL2 . . . . 247 F7
Worham's La EX13 . . . . . . 86 F2
Works The EX16 . . . . 161 C4

World of Country Life★
EX8 . . . . **203** B6
WORLINGTON **15** C1
Worlington Cross EX39 . . **15** C1
Worlington Hill EX39 . . . . **15** C1
Wormsworthy Hill EX16 . . **48** D6
WORSTON **136** B3
Worthele Cl PL21 . . . . **237** A4
Worthele Cross PL21 . . . **237** B1
Worth La
Hele EX5 . . . . **82** E5
Withypool TA22, TA24 . . . **21** C4
Worth Rd EX34 . . . . **150** C5
Worthy La EX16 . . . . **47** C6
WOTTER **132** D4
Wotton Cross TQ12 . . . . **131** E4
Wotton La EX8 . . . . **196** B5
Wotton Pound EX8 . . . . . **196** A5
Wotton Way TQ9 . . . . **131** E1
WRAFTON **152** F4
Wrafton Rd EX33 . . . . **152** E4
WRANGATON **137** D8
Wrangaton Rd PL21,
TQ10 . . . . **137** D8
Wrangcombe La TA21 . . . **52** A4
Wrangcombe Rd TA21 . . **52** A4
WRANGWAY **52** A4
Wrangway Rd EX15 . . . . . **52** A3
Wrangworthy Cross EX39 . **39** E4
Wreford's Cl EX4 . . . . **173** A3
Wreford's Dr EX4 . . . . **173** A3
Wreford's La EX4 . . . . **173** A3
Wreford's Link EX4 . . . . . **173** A3
Wren Cl
Honiton EX14 . . . . **166** B4
Northam EX39 . . . . **157** A6
Wren Ct **10** TQ5 . . . . **230** C4
Wren Gdns PL7 . . . . **250** C6
Wren Ret Pk TQ2 . . . . **213** D2
Wrens Gate PL9 . . . . **255** E8
Wrentham Bsns Ctr EX4 **177** D8
Wrentham Est EX4 . . . . . **177** D8
Wrenwell Cross TQ12 . . **131** F3
Wressing View EX15 . . . . . **66** A3
Wrey Ave EX31 . . . . **154** D4
Wright Cl PL1 . . . . **247** E3
Wright Dr EX17 . . . . **79** A5
Wrights La PL8 . . . . **140** F7
Wright's La
Exmouth EX8 . . . . **196** F6
Torquay TQ1 . . . . **220** A7
Wrigwell Cross TQ12 . . . **211** E1
Wrigwell La TQ12 . . . . . . **217** F8
WRINKLEBERRY **23** D3
Wrinkleberry La EX39 . . . **23** D3
Wroxall Grange TQ1 . . . **220** C4
Wulphere Cl EX14 . . . . **67** B1
Wyatts La PL19 . . . . **171** B6
Wychall Orch EX12 . . . . . **192** A6

Wychall Pk EX12 . . . . **192** A7
Wychbury House Sch **7**
TQ2 . . . . **219** F5
Wych Ct EX13 . . . . **88** E3
Wychwood Cl EX7 . . . . . . **204** E7
Wycliffe Rd PL3 . . . . **249** B4
Wye Gdns PL3 . . . . **249** D7
Wyke Cross EX17 . . . . **80** F2
Wyke Gdns PL3 . . . . **167** D1
Wykeham Dr PL2 . . . . **248** A7
Wyke Hill EX17 . . . . **80** F2
Wyke La EX13 . . . . **167** D2
Wyke Moor Cross EX20 . . . **95** C8
Wyke Rd EX13 . . . . **167** D3
Wykes Rd EX1 . . . . **177** F7
Wylie Ho EX2 . . . . **261** A1
Wynards EX2 . . . . **261** B2
Wynards Ct EX9 . . . . **198** B6
Wynards La **2** EX2 . . . . . **261** B2
Wynards Rd EX9 . . . . **198** B6
Wyndham Ave EX1 . . . . . **177** F6
Wyndham La PL1 . . . . **262** A3
Wyndham Mews **1** PL1 . **262** A3
Wyndham Pl PL1 . . . . **262** A3
Wyndham Rd EX5 . . . . **82** B6
Wyndham Sq PL1 . . . . . . **262** A3
Wyndham Street E PL1 . **262** B3
Wyndham Street W PL1 . **262** B3
Wyndthorpe Gdns **17**
EX34 . . . . **150** C6
Wynford Rd EX4 . . . . **173** F1
Wynstream Prim Sch
EX2 . . . . **177** F3
Wyoming Cl PL3 . . . . **249** C6
Wyre Cl TQ4 . . . . **226** A2
Wytch Gn EX13 . . . . **88** E3
Wythburn Gdns PL6 . . . . **245** D3

Yarde Cl EX10 . . . . **188** B7
Yarde Cotts EX38 . . . . **41** D1
Yarde Cross EX32 . . . . **18** A4
Yarde Gate Cross EX36 . . **19** B5
Yarde Hill Orch EX10 . . . **188** B7
Yardelands EX10 . . . . **188** B7
Yardelands Cl EX10 . . . . **188** B7
Yarde Mead EX10 . . . . . . **188** B7
Yarde's Grave Cross TQ9 **222** F7
Yard Hill TQ13 . . . . **111** D2
Yard La EX36 . . . . **46** B8
Yardleigh Cross EX13 . . . **88** D4
Yardley Gdns PL6 . . . . . . **245** E3
Yards La TQ5 . . . . **230** C2
Yardwells Cross EX36 . . . **19** B5
Yarmleigh La EX17 . . . . . . **79** E7
Yarnacott Cnr EX32 . . . . . **17** E1
Yarnapitts Cross TQ13 . . **110** E7
Yarner Wood Nature Trail★
TQ13 . . . . **122** C5
YARNSCOMBE **27** E2
Yarrow Mead PL9 . . . . . . **256** D7
YAWL **104** B5
Yawl Cres DT7 . . . . **104** B5
Yawl Cross DT7 . . . . **104** B6
Yawl Hill DT7 . . . . **104** C6
Yawl Hill La DT7 . . . . **104** B5
YEALMBRIDGE **136** A2
Yealmbury Hill PL8 . . . . . **257** F4
Yealm Gr TQ2 . . . . **219** C7
Yealm Pk PL8 . . . . **257** E4
Yealmpstone Cl PL7 . . . . **251** B4
Yealmpstone Dr PL7 . . . **251** B3
Yealmpstone Farm Sch
PL7 . . . . **251** B3
YEALMPTON **257** E4
Yealmpton Prim Sch
PL8 . . . . **257** E4
Yealm Rd PL8 . . . . **140** F6
Yealm View Rd PL8 . . . . **141** A6
Yearlstone Vineyard★
EX16 . . . . **63** F3
Yearnor Mill La TA24 . . . . **6** F5
Yeats Cl PL5 . . . . **244** C2
Yeatt Cross TQ12 . . . . . . **131** F3
Yellaford Way **1** EX31 . **154** B3
Yelland **153** A4
Yelland Bglws TQ10 . . . **135** E5
Yelland Cross
Challacombe EX31 . . . . . **11** D4
Rattery TQ10 . . . . **135** E5
Yelland EX31 . . . . **153** A5
Yelland Rd EX31 . . . . **153** C5
Yellands Pk TQ7 . . . . **142** C6
Yellaton La EX34 . . . . **3** B1
Yellow Tor Ct PL12 . . . . . **242** C2
Yellow Tor La PL12 . . . . . **242** C2
Yellow Tor Rd PL12 . . . . **242** B2
YELVERTON **127** A3
Yelverton Bsns Pk PL20 . **126** E2
Yelverton Cl PL5 . . . . **243** E4

Yelverton Paperweight Ctr★
PL20 . . . . **126** F2
Yelverton Terr
Tavistock PL19 . . . . **171** D6
Yelverton PL20 . . . . **127** A2
Yendacott La EX17 . . . . . . **81** B3
Yeo Cl PL3 . . . . **249** B5
Yeo Cotts PL21 . . . . **133** D3
Yeo Dr **20** EX39 . . . . **15** A1
YEOFORD **79** C1
Yeoford Com Prim Sch
EX17 . . . . **79** C1
Yeoford Mdws EX17 . . . . . **79** C1
Yeoford Sta EX17 . . . . **79** C1
Yeoford Way EX2 . . . . . . **181** D8
Yeo Gate EX36 . . . . **31** C4
Yeo La
Molland EX36 . . . . **31** C5
North Tawton EX20 . . . . . **77** B5
Yeoland Down
Crapstone PL20 . . . . **126** F1
Yelverton PL20 . . . . **241** E8
Yeoland La
Swimbridge EX32 . . . . . . **17** F1
Yelverton PL20 . . . . **126** F1
Yeolands The TQ9 . . . . . **227** B5
Yeolland La PL21 . . . . **237** D5
Yeolland Pk PL21 . . . . . . **237** E5
Yeomadon Cross EX22 . . **71** D4
Yeomans Way PL7 . . . . . **251** A4
Yeo Mill Cross EX36 . . . . **32** C5
Yeo Pk PL8 . . . . **136** A3
Yeo Rd
Braunton EX31 . . . . **15** E5
Zeal Monachorum EX17 . **78** D7
Yeotown Cross EX37 . . . . **44** C8
Yeo Vale Cross EX17 . . . . **60** C2
Yeo Vale Ho **5** EX32 . . . **154** F6
Yeo Vale Ind Est EX17 . . . **60** C2
Yeo Vale Rd EX32 . . . . . . **154** F6
Yeo Valley Prim Sch
EX32 . . . . **155** A6
Yeo View EX17 . . . . **79** C1
Yerris Rd EX15 . . . . **65** F2
Yetsonais Cross TQ9 . . . **144** D8
YETTINGTON **197** F8
Yettington Rd EX9 . . . . . **198** A2
Yeu Cl
Brixham TQ5 . . . . **229** F2
Honiton EX14 . . . . **169** D4
Yewdale Gdns PL6 . . . . . **245** D2
Yew Tree Cl
Exeter EX4 . . . . **173** E1
Exmouth EX8 . . . . **196** C3
Yew Tree Dr TQ12 . . . . . . **207** E6
Yew Wood Cross EX15 . . . **66** A4
Yolhey La TQ12 . . . . **212** C5
Yonder Cl EX11 . . . . **169** E3
Yonder Cnr EX11 . . . . **169** E3
Yonder Hill Cotts EX13 . . **88** E7
Yonder Mdw TQ9 . . . . . . **227** F8
Yonder Mount EX13 . . . . **103** D5

Yonder St
Ottery St Mary EX11 . . . . **169** E3
Plymouth PL9 . . . . **255** B6
YONDERTOWN **133** B1
Yon St TQ12 . . . . **212** F4
York Cl
Axminster EX13 . . . . **167** E6
Exmouth EX8 . . . . **196** E2
Feniton EX14 . . . . **84** D2
York Cres
Feniton EX14 . . . . **84** D2
Torquay TQ1 . . . . **220** C8
Yorke Rd TQ6 . . . . **233** D3
York Gdns TQ4 . . . . **226** B4
York Mews TQ4 . . . . **226** B5
York Pl
Bideford EX39 . . . . **157** A3
Cullompton EX15 . . . . . . **163** C5
Plymouth PL2 . . . . **247** F4
York Rd
Exeter EX4 . . . . **261** C4
Paignton TQ4 . . . . **226** B4
Plymouth PL5 . . . . **247** E8
Seaton EX12 . . . . **192** A5
Torpoint PL11 . . . . **247** B3
Torquay TQ1 . . . . **220** C8
York St
Plymouth PL1 . . . . **247** E2
Sidmouth EX10 . . . . **188** B4
York Terr
Exeter EX4 . . . . **261** C4
7 Plymouth PL2 . . . . . . **247** F5
Sidmouth EX10 . . . . **188** B3
York Villas TQ1 . . . . **220** C8
Youings Dr EX31 . . . . **155** A7
Youlden La EX20 . . . . **95** C7
Youltree Cross EX39 . . . . **22** E4
Youngaton Rd EX39 . . . . **156** C7
Young's Park La TQ4 . . . **226** C4
Young's Park Rd TQ4 . . **226** C4

Z

Zeal Cross EX6 . . . . **112** F8
Zealley Est TQ12 . . . . **207** E6
ZEAL MONACHORUM . . . **78** C7
Zeal Rd
Dunsford EX6 . . . . **112** F8
Tedburn St Mary EX6 . . . . **97** F1
Zempson Cross TQ10 . . . **135** B5
Zephyr Cres EX32 . . . . . . **155** B5
Zeth Hill La PL21 . . . . **136** D8
Zion Pl
Dartmouth TQ6 . . . . **233** F4
Ivybridge PL21 . . . . **237** C5
Zion Rd **8** TQ2 . . . . **219** F5
Zion St PL1 . . . . **262** C2